ted with sympathy to children around the world whose lives were marred by the
r 11, 2001 and their aftermath, and with gratitude to children who responded to those
passion and charity.

—*L.E.B.*

anada Cataloguing in Publication Data

lopment/Laura E. Berk.—Canadian ed./adapted by Laura E. Berk and Elizabeth A. Levin

ical references and index.

evelopment. I. Berk, Laura E. II. Title.

305.231          C2002-902944-9

Pearson Education Canada Inc., Toronto, Ontario
Edition published by Allyn & Bacon, Inc., a division of Pearson Education, Needham Heights, Massachusetts.
by Allyn & Bacon, Inc.

53-X

ditorial Director: Michael Young
ons Editor: Jessica Mosher
ager: Judith Allen
mental Editor: Lise Dupont
itor: Avivah Wargon
itor: Susan Messer
isa Berland
anager: Wendy Moran
oan M. Wilson
nd Photo Research: Lisa Brant
Mary Opper
gn: Amy Harnden
: Jennifer Federico
: Heidi Wat ("Untitled," by Heidi Wat, 13 years old, Canada, 2001–02 Lions Clubs International Peace Poster Contest
rinted with kind permission of Lions Club International, Oak Brook, Illinois, U.S.A.)

05 04

bound in the United States of America.

anada information is used with the permission of the Minister of Industry, as Minister responsible for Statistics Canada.
n on the availability of the wide range of data from Statistics Canada can be obtained from Statistics Canada's Regional
World Wide Web site at **http://www.statcan.ca** and its toll-free access number, 1-800-263-1136.

# —CHI
# DEVELOP

## CANADIAN EDITION

# LAU

ILL

CANADIAN E

ILL

AND E

LA

This book is dedica
events of Septembe
tragedies with com

National Library of C

Berk, Laura E.
        Child deve

Includes bibliograph
ISBN 0-205-36053-

        1. Child c

HQ767.9.B473 200

Copyright © 2003
Original U.S. Sixth
Copyright © 2003

**This edition is au**

ISBN 0-205-360

Vice President,
Senior Acquisiti
Marketing Man
Senior Develop
Supervising Ed
Substantive Ed
Copy Editor:
Production M
Page Layout:
Permissions a
Art Director:
Interior Des
Cover Desig
Cover Imag
Finalist. Re

3 4 5        0

Printed an

Statistics
Informati
Offices, its

and

# About the Author and Adapter

Laura E. Berk is a distinguished professor of psychology at Illinois State University, where she teaches child development to both undergraduate and graduate students. She received her bachelor's degree in psychology from the University of California, Berkeley, and her master's and doctoral degrees in early childhood development and education from the University of Chicago. She has been a visiting scholar at Cornell University, UCLA, Stanford University, and the University of South Australia. Berk has published widely on the effects of school environments on children's development, the development of private speech, and most recently the role of make-believe play in the development of self-regulation. Her research has been funded by the U.S. Office of Education and the National Institute of Child Health and Human Development. It has appeared in many prominent journals, including *Child Development, Developmental Psychology, Merrill-Palmer Quarterly, Journal of Abnormal Child Psychology, Development and Psychopathology,* and *Early Childhood Research Quarterly.* Her empirical studies have attracted the attention of the general public, leading to contributions to *Psychology Today* and *Scientific American.* Berk has served as a research editor for *Young Children* and consulting editor for *Early Childhood Research Quarterly.* She is author of the chapter on the extracurriculum for the *Handbook of Research on Curriculum* (American Educational Research Association), the chapter on development for *The Many Faces of Psychological Research in the Twenty-First Century* (Society for Teachers of Psychology), and the entry on Vygotsky for the *Encyclopedia of Cognitive Science.* Her books include *Private Speech: From Social Interaction to Self-Regulation, Scaffolding Children's Learning: Vygotsky and Early Childhood Education,* and *Landscapes of Development: An Anthology of Readings.* In addition to *Child Development,* she is author of the best-selling texts *Infants, Children, and Adolescents* and *Development Through the Lifespan,* published by Allyn and Bacon. Her recently published book for parents and teachers is *Awakening Children's Minds: How Parents and Teachers Can Make a Difference.*

## ABOUT THE ADAPTER

Elizabeth A. Levin is the chair of the psychology program and coordinator of the graduate program at Laurentian University. She teaches child development and clinical child psychology to undergraduate students and psychological diagnosis and assessment to graduate students. Levin graduated from McGill University with a Bachelor of Science degree in psychology, and obtained her master's and doctorate in child psychology from the University of Waterloo. She had the opportunity to teach at the Université canadienne en France. Her research interests focus on parenting styles and children's conceptions of parenting. Elizabeth Levin served as the Canadian adapter for *Child Growth and Development,* Annual Editions, and was a contributor to *The Encyclopedia of Parenting Theory and Research.* She speaks frequently to the media and the public on parenting and child development issues. A registered clinical child psychologist, Levin consults for several agencies providing services to children and families.

# Brief Contents

# List of Features

# Contents

# A Personal Note to Students

MY 32 YEARS OF TEACHING child development have brought me in contact with thousands of students like you—students with diverse university majors, future goals, interests, and needs. Some are affiliated with my own department, psychology, but many come from other child-related fields—education, sociology, anthropology, family studies, and biology, to name just a few. Each semester, my students' aspirations have proven to be as varied as their fields of study. Many look toward careers in applied work with children—teaching, caregiving, nursing, counselling, social work, school psychology, and program administration. Some plan to teach child development, and a few want to do research. Most hope someday to have children, whereas others are already parents who come with a desire to better understand and rear their own youngsters. And almost all arrive with a deep curiosity about how they themselves developed from tiny infants into the complex human beings they are today.

My goal in preparing this edition of *Child Development* is to provide a textbook that meets the instructional goals of your course as well as your personal interests and needs. To achieve these objectives, I have grounded this book in a care-fully selected body of classic and current theory and research. In addition, the text highlights the interacting contributions of biology and environment to the developing child, explains how the research process helps solve real-world problems, illustrates commonalities and differences between ethnic groups and cultures, discusses the broader social contexts in which children develop, and pays special attention to policy issues that are crucial for safeguarding children's well-being in today's world. I have also provided a unique pedagogical program that will assist you in mastering information, integrating various aspects of development, critically examining controversial issues, and applying what you have learned.

I hope learning about child development will be as rewarding for you as I have found it over the years. I would like to know what you think about both the field of child development and this book. I welcome your comments; please feel free to send them to me at Department of Psychology, Box 4620, Illinois State University, Normal, IL 61790, or care of the publisher, who will forward them to me.

Laura E. Berk

# Preface for Instructors

MY DECISION TO WRITE *Child Development* was inspired by a wealth of professional and personal experiences. First and foremost were the interests and needs of hundreds of students of child development with whom I have worked in over three decades of university teaching. I aimed for a text that is intellectually stimulating, that provides depth as well as breadth of coverage, that portrays the complexities of child development with clarity and excitement, and that is relevant and useful in building a bridge from theory and research to children's everyday lives. Instructor and student enthusiasm for the book not only has been among my greatest sources of pride and satisfaction, but also has inspired me to rethink and improve each edition.

The 14 years since *Child Development* first appeared have been a period of unprecedented expansion and change in theory and research. For this edition, it has been my pleasure to enrich the text with Canadian research for students everywhere, as well as to write and edit many sections of the Canadian edition. As a result, the book represents Canada's significant contributions to rapidly transforming aspects of the field. I also have included a wealth of additional new content and teaching tools:

- *Increased attention is granted to multiple levels of the environment in which the child develops.* The contemporary move toward viewing the child's thoughts, feelings, and behaviour as an integrated whole, affected by a wide array of influences in biology, social context, and culture, has motivated developmental researchers to strengthen their links with other fields of psychology and other disciplines. Topics and findings included in the text increasingly reflect the contributions of educational psychology, social psychology, health psychology, clinical psychology, neuropsychology, biology, pediatrics, sociology, anthropology, and other fields.

- *Diverse pathways of change are highlighted.* Investigators have reached broad consensus that variations in biological makeup, everyday tasks, and the people who support children in mastery of those tasks lead to wide individual differences in children's skills. This edition pays more attention to variability in development and to recent theories—including ecological, sociocultural, and dynamic systems—that attempt to explain it.

- *The complex, bidirectional relationship between biology and environment is given greater emphasis.* Accumulating evidence on development of the brain, motor skills, cognitive competencies, temperament, and developmental problems underscores how biological influences share power with experience. The interconnection between biology and environment is revisited throughout the text narrative and in a "Biology and Environment" feature with new and updated topics.

- *The link between theory, research, and applications—a theme of this book since its inception—is strengthened.* As researchers intensify their efforts to generate findings that can be applied to real-life situations, I have placed greater weight on social policy issues and sound theory- and research-based applications.

- *Education and health issues are given stronger focus.* The home, school, and community are featured as vital educational contexts in which the child develops, both throughout the text narrative and in *Social Issues: Education* special feature boxes. Treatment of childhood health concerns is deepened, through enhanced and updated discussion of many health issues and interventions, including *Social Issues: Health* special feature boxes.

- *The role of active student learning is made more explicit. Ask Yourself* questions at the end of each major section have been expanded to promote three approaches to engaging actively with the subject matter—*Review, Apply,* and *Connect.* This feature assists students in reflecting on what they have read from multiple vantage points.

## TEXT PHILOSOPHY

The basic approach of this book has been shaped by my own professional and personal history as a teacher, researcher, and parent. It consists of seven philosophical ingredients that I regard as essential for students to emerge from a course with a thorough understanding of child development:

- **1. An understanding of major theories and the strengths and shortcomings of each.** The first chapter begins by emphasizing that only knowledge of multiple theories can do justice to the richness of child development. In each topical domain, I present a variety of theoretical perspectives, indicate how each highlights previously overlooked contributions to development, and discuss research that has been used to evaluate them. If one or two theories have emerged as especially prominent in a particular area, I indicate why, in terms of the theory's broad explanatory power. Consideration of contrasting theories also serves as the context for an evenhanded analysis of many controversial issues throughout the text.

- **2. An appreciation of research strategies for investigating child development.** To evaluate theories, students need a firm grounding in basic research design and methodology. I devote an entire chapter to a description and critique of research strategies. Throughout the book, numerous studies are discussed in sufficient detail for students to use what they have learned to critically assess the findings, conclusions, and implications of research.

- **3. Knowledge of both the sequence of child development and the processes that underlie it.** Students are provided with a discussion of the organized sequence of development, along with processes of change. An understanding of process—how complex combinations of biological and environmental events produce development—has been the focus of most recent research. Accordingly, the text reflects this emphasis. But new information about the timetable of change has also emerged. In many ways, children are more competent than they were believed to be in the past. Current evidence on the timing and sequence of development, along with its implications for process, is presented throughout the book.

- **4. An appreciation of the impact of context and culture on child development.** A wealth of research indicates that children live in rich physical and social contexts that affect all aspects of development. In each chapter, the student travels to distant parts of the world as I review a growing body of cross-cultural evidence. The text narrative also discusses many findings on socioeconomically and ethnically diverse children within Canada and the United States. Besides highlighting the role of immediate settings, such as family, neighbourhood, and school, I underscore the impact of larger social structures—societal values, laws, and government programs—on children's well-being.

- **5. An understanding of the joint contributions of biology and environment to development.** The field recognizes more powerfully than ever before the joint roles of hereditary/constitutional and environmental factors—that these contributions to development combine in complex ways and cannot be separated in a simple manner. Numerous examples of how biological dispositions can be maintained as well as transformed by social contexts are presented throughout the book.

- **6. A sense of the interdependency of all aspects of development—physical, cognitive, emotional, and social.** Every chapter takes an integrated approach to understanding children. I show how physical, cognitive, emotional, and social development are interwoven. Within the text narrative and in a special series of *Ask Yourself* questions at the end of major sections, students are referred to other parts of the book to deepen their grasp of relationships between various aspects of change.

- **7. An appreciation of the interrelatedness of theory, research, and applications.** Throughout this book, I emphasize that theories of child development and the research stimulated by them provide the foundation for sound, effective practices with children. The link between theory, research, and applications is reinforced by an organizational format in which theory and research are presented first, followed by implications for practice. In addition, a current focus in the field—harnessing child development knowledge to shape social policies that support children's needs—is reflected in every chapter. The text addresses the current condition of children in Canada, the United States, and around the world, and shows how theory and research have sparked successful interventions.

## NEW COVERAGE IN THE CANADIAN EDITION

In this edition I continue to represent a rapidly transforming contemporary literature with theory and research from more than 1,300 new citations. To make room for new coverage, I have condensed and reorganized some topics and eliminated others that are no longer crucial in view of new evidence. The following is a sampling of major content changes, organized by chapter:

- **Chapter 1:** New section on evolutionary developmental psychology • Updated consideration of Vygotsky's view of development • Updated section on the dynamic systems perspective • New section discussing the influence of Canadian child and family policies on development • New Social Issues: Education box on Cybermoms, a Canadian computer-mediated program for young mothers.

- **Chapter 2:** Updated discussion of psychophysiological methods • Inclusion of a Canadian microgenetic study • New Social Issues: Education box on immigrant youths, illustrating ethnography.

- **Chapter 3:** New findings on how PKU leads to mental retardation • Updated discussion of teratogens • New Biology and Environment box on what controls the timing of birth • Canadian research on prenatal diagnostic methods, prenatal environmental influences, and approaches to childbirth • Expanded section on understanding birth complications • New section on environmental influences on gene expression, including discussion of epigenesis • New Biology and Environment box on uncoupling genetic–environmental correlations for mental illness and antisocial behaviour • A cross-national perspective on Canadian health care for parents and newborns, including information on health care in Aboriginal communities.

■ **Chapter 4:** New evidence on the functions of REM sleep • New research on maternal characteristics related to sensitivity to infant crying • Updated findings on the impact of NBAS-based interventions on parent–newborn interaction • Enhanced discussion of limitations of habituation research on infant memory • Research on the high incidence of otitis media among Canada's Aboriginal children • New evidence on crawling and coordinating action with depth information • New research on infants' perception of complex, meaningful visual patterns • Expanded consideration of newborn face perception • Revised and updated section on perception of object unity • Expanded discussion of the role of affordances in perceptual development • New evidence on intermodal perception • Revised and updated section on infancy as a sensitive period • Canadian research on adopted Romanian orphans.

■ **Chapter 5:** New evidence on lateralization and handedness, including genetic and environmental contributions • Enhanced coverage of sensitive periods in brain development • Discussion of physical activity rates among Canadian youth • New data on breast-feeding rates in Canada • Updated discussion of childhood obesity, including rates among Canada's youth and Aboriginal communities • New evidence on the contribution of family experiences to pubertal timing • New research on adolescent moodiness • Discussion of factors related to Canada's adolescent pregnancy and parenthood rates • New Biology and Environment box on intergenerational continuity in adolescent parenthood • Discussion of immunization rates among Canadian children.

■ **Chapter 6:** New findings on development and benefits of make-believe play • Revised and updated section on preschoolers' understanding of symbol–real world relations, focusing on mastery of dual representation • New research on development of cognitive maps • New findings on implications of the personal fable for adolescent risk taking • New evidence on development of propositional thought • Revised overall evaluation of Piaget's theory, including Canadian research • New section on the core knowledge perspective • New Biology and Environment box on children's understanding of health and illness • New research on the development of private speech • Enhanced discussion of features of adult–child and peer interaction that promote cognitive development • Expanded section on Vygotsky's view of make-believe play • Expanded section evaluating Vygotsky's theory • New Cultural Influences box on young children's daily life in a Yucatec Mayan village.

■ **Chapter 7:** Revised consideration of the store model of information processing • Enhanced consideration of children's planning • Revised and condensed section on strategies for storing information • New research on

children's reconstructive memory • Revised section on fuzzy-trace theory • Expanded and updated Social Issues: Health box on children's eyewitness memory, including Canadian research • New evidence on development of metacognition • New Social Issues: Education box on balanced teaching of whole language and basic skills in promoting reading progress.

■ **Chapter 8:** Expanded treatment of Gardner's theory of multiple intelligences • New From Research to Practice box on social and emotional intelligence • New From Research to Practice box on the Canadian standardization of the WISC–III • New Biology and Environment box on the Flynn effect • Expanded and updated discussion of dynamic testing • Enhanced consideration of the impact of family beliefs about intellectual success on academic behaviour • New evidence on nonshared environmental influences and IQ, including implications for Canadian Aboriginal children • Discussion of Canada's Aboriginal Head Start program and CANSTART • New research on family and school influences on creativity.

■ **Chapter 9:** Revised and updated section addressing whether animals can acquire language • Updated section on language areas in the brain, including Canadian research • New evidence on infants' capacity to statistically analyze the speech stream, including Canadian research • New findings on the relationship of caregiver–child interaction to early language development • New From Research to Practice box on the impact of parent–child interaction on deaf children's language and cognitive development • Updated discussion of factors contributing to the vocabulary spurt at the end of the second year • New research on the influence of the language environment on children's early vocabularies • Revised and updated consideration of strategies for word learning • New research on development of referential communication • Enhanced discussion of sociolinguistic understanding • Updated section on bilingual development, including Canadian research and French–English bilingualism rates among Canada's young people • New Social Issues: Education box on French immersion schooling in Canada.

■ **Chapter 10:** Expanded discussion of development of self-conscious emotions • Updated sections on development of emotional self-regulation and mastery of emotional display rules • New research on empathy • Expanded discussion of Rothbart's model of temperament • Revised section on measuring temperament • New research on the stability of temperament • Enhanced treatment of cultural influences on development of temperament • New findings on the relationship of disorganized/disoriented attachment to later development • Updated Social Issues: Health box on whether child care in infancy threatens attachment security • New section on attachment, parental employment, and child care in Canada.

- **Chapter 11:** New research on self-development in early infancy • New Cultural Influences box on implications of cultural variations in personal storytelling for early self-concept • New section on infants' and toddlers' developing understanding of mental states • New section on consequences of a belief–desire theory of mind for social development • Expanded discussion of factors contributing to young children's theory of mind • Enhanced consideration of cultural influences on self-esteem • New research on the impact of teachers' messages on achievement-related attributions • Updated discussion of adolescent suicide, including suicide rates in Canada and special attention to youth suicide in the Aboriginal population • Enhanced discussion of social influences on identity development • Revised and updated section on understanding intentions • New evidence on development of prejudice • Revised section on development of perspective taking.

- **Chapter 12:** Expanded and updated coverage of the evolutionary roots of morally relevant behaviours • Enhanced discussion of induction as a disciplinary strategy for fostering conscience development • New evidence on Canadian parents' use of physical punishment • New Social Issues: Health box on the Canadian controversy over whether parents should be permitted to spank their children • Expanded attention to children's grasp of ideal reciprocity as essential for moral-judgment maturity • New evidence on cultural variations in justice and care reasoning • New research on the relation of moral self-relevance to moral behaviour • New Social Issues: Education box on development of civic responsibility • Enhanced consideration of the limitations of Kohlberg's theory • New Canadian research on school-age children's integration of moral and social-conventional domains • Inclusion of Metcalfe and Mischel's hot- and cool-processing account of development of self-control • Updated section on development of stability and aggression, based on Canadian research • Enhanced discussion of antisocial youths' social-cognitive deficits and distortions.

- **Chapter 13:** New research on adults' gender-stereotyped views of children • Canadian evidence on the development of gender stereotypes • Expanded treatment of evolutionary interpretations of gender typing • New Biology and Environment box on a Canadian case study of a boy who was reared as a girl • New research on peer influences on gender-role behaviour • New findings on the influence of older siblings on children's gender-role adoption • Updated evidence on factors contributing to boys' higher rate of overt aggression • Enhanced discussion of issues related to developing non-gender-stereotyped children.

- **Chapter 14:** Updated treatment of child-rearing styles and their impact on children's development • New Biology and Environment box addressing the question, Does parenting really matter? • Expanded treatment of parenting and adolescent autonomy, with special attention to Canadian studies • New findings on ethnic variations in child-rearing styles • New Canadian research on sibling relationships • Updated findings on blended families, with enhanced attention to age differences in children's adjustment • Canadian divorce, parental employment, child care, and child maltreatment rates • New evidence on the consequences of child maltreatment, with special attention to psychophysiological effects and implications for long-term adjustment problems.

- **Chapter 15:** Revised and expanded section on parental influences—both direct and indirect—on children's peer sociability • Expanded treatment of cultural influences on children's peer sociability • Section on friendship moved from Chapter 11 to Chapter 15 • New research on characteristics of children's friendships • Expanded discussion of implications of friendship for adjustment • New evidence on peer acceptance, including consideration of popular-prosocial and popular-antisocial children • Revised section on peer groups, including Canadian research • Canadian statistics on adolescent substance abuse • Canadian statistics on children's television viewing • Updated findings on media violence and aggression • New section on regulation of children's television in Canada • New evidence on implications of violent computer games for social learning • New Social Issues: Education box on school readiness and early retention, reporting Canadian findings • Enhanced discussion of grouping practices in schools, including recent findings on multigrade classrooms • New evidence on academic achievement of Canadian youth in cross-national perspective.

## PEDAGOGICAL FEATURES

Maintaining a highly accessible writing style—one that is lucid and engaging without being simplistic—continues to be one of this text's goals. I frequently converse with students, encouraging them to relate what they read to their own lives. In doing so, I hope to make the study of child development involving and pleasurable.

- **Chapter Introductions and End-of-Chapter Summaries.** To provide a helpful preview, I include an outline and overview of chapter content in each chapter introduction. Especially comprehensive end-of-chapter summaries, organized according to the major divisions of each chapter and highlighting important terms, remind students of key points in the text discussion. Review questions are included in the summaries to encourage active study.

- **Ask Yourself.** Active engagement with the subject matter is also supported by study questions at the end of each major section. Three types of questions prompt students to think about child development in diverse ways: *Review* questions help students recall and comprehend information they have just read; *Apply* questions encourage the application of knowledge to controversial issues and problems faced by parents, teachers, and children; and *Connect* questions help students build an image of the whole child by integrating what they have learned across age periods and domains of development. An icon in the text indicates that each question is answered on the text's companion website. Students may compare their reasoning to a model response.

Three types of thematic boxes accentuate the philosophical themes of this book:

■ **Biology and Environment.** New to this edition, this special feature highlights the growing attention to the complex, bidirectional influence of biology and environment on development. Examples are *Resilient Children, Uncoupling Genetic–Environmental Correlations for Mental Illness and Antisocial Behaviour,* and *Do Parents Really Matter?*

■ **From Research to Practice** integrates theory, research, and applications, on such topics as *Social and Emotional Intelligence, The Canadian Standardization of the WISC–III,* and *Parent–Child Interaction: Impact on Language and Cognitive Development of Deaf Children.*

■ **Cultural Influences** boxes have been expanded and updated to deepen attention to culture threaded throughout the text. They emphasize both multicultural and cross-cultural variations. Topics include *Young Children's Daily Life in a Yucatec Mayan Village, Identity Development Among Ethnic Minority Adolescents,* and *Cultural Variations in Personal Storytelling: Implications for Early Self-Concept.*

Two types of *Social Issues* boxes underscore the influence of social policy on all aspects of development.

■ **Social Issues: Education** boxes focus on home, school, and community influences on children's learning. Topics include *Development of Civic Responsibility, French Immersion Schooling,* and *School Readiness and Early Retention.*

■ **Social Issues: Health** boxes discuss values and practices relevant to children's physical and mental health. Topics include *The Pros and Cons of Reproductive Technologies* and *Adolescent Suicide: Annihilation of the Self.*

- **Milestones Tables.** *Milestones* tables summarize major developments within each topical area, providing a convenient overview of the chronology of development.

- **Additional Tables, Illustrations, and Photographs.** Additional tables are liberally included to help readers grasp essential points in the text discussion, extend information on a topic, and consider applications. The many full-color illustrations throughout the book depict important theories, methods, and research findings. In this edition, the photo program has been carefully selected to portray the text discussion and to represent the diversity of children around the world.

- **Marginal Glossary, End-of-Chapter Term List, and End-of-Book Glossary.** Mastery of terms that make up the central vocabulary of the field is promoted through a marginal glossary, an end-of-chapter term list, and an end-of-book glossary. Important terms and concepts also appear in boldface type in the text narrative and in the end-of-chapter summaries.

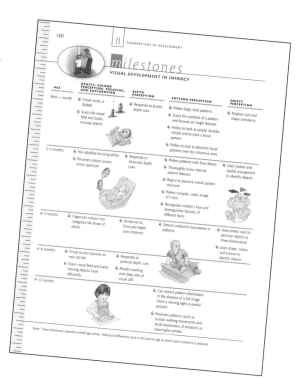

## ACKNOWLEDGMENTS

The dedicated contributions of many individuals helped make this book a reality and contributed to refinements and improvements in each edition. An impressive cast of reviewers provided many helpful suggestions, constructive criticisms, and encouragement and enthusiasm for the organization and content of the book. I am grateful to each one of them.

### REVIEWERS FOR THE U.S. FIRST THROUGH FIFTH EDITIONS

Daniel Ashmead, Vanderbilt University
Margarita Azmitia, University of California, Santa Cruz
Dana W. Birnbaum, University of Maine at Orono
Kathryn N. Black, Purdue University
Cathryn L. Booth, University of Washington
J. Paul Boudreau, University of Prince Edward Island
Sam Boyd, University of Central Arkansas
Celia A. Brownell, University of Pittsburgh
Toni A. Campbell, San Jose State University
Beth Casey, Boston College
John Condry, Cornell University
Rhoda Cummings, University of Nevada, Reno
James L. Dannemiller, University of Wisconsin, Madison
Zoe Ann Davidson, Alabama A&M University
Darlene DeSantis, West Chester University
Rebecca Eder, Bryn Mawr College
Claire Etaugh, Bradley University

Bill Fabricius, Arizona State University
Beverly Fagot, University of Oregon
James Garbarino, Cornell University
John C. Gibbs, Ohio State University
Peter Gordon, University of Pittsburgh
Katherine Green, Millersville University
Kenneth Hill, Saint Mary's University, Halifax
Alice S. Honig, Syracuse University
Elizabeth J. Hrncir, University of Virginia
Janis Jacobs, Pennsylvania State University
Mareile Koenig, George Washington University Hospital
Claire Kopp, Claremont Graduate School
Beth Kurtz-Costes, University of North Carolina, Chapel Hill
Gary W. Ladd, University of Illinois at Urbana–Champaign
Daniel Lapsley, Ball State University
Frank Laycock, Oberlin College
Elise Lehman, George Mason University
Mary D. Leinbach, University of Oregon
Robert S. Marvin, University of Virginia
Tom McBride, Princeton University
Carolyn J. Mebert, University of New Hampshire
Gary B. Melton, University of Nebraska, Lincoln
Mary Evelyn Moore, Illinois State University
Lois Muir, University of Wisconsin, La Crosse
John P. Murray, Kansas State University
Bonnie K. Nastasi, State University of New York at Albany
Larry Nucci, University of Illinois at Chicago
Peter Ornstein, University of North Carolina

Randall Osbourne, Indiana University East
Carol Pandey, Pierce College, Los Angeles
Thomas S. Parish, Kansas State University
B. Kay Pasley, Colorado State University
Ellen F. Potter, University of South Carolina at Columbia
Kimberly K. Powlishta, Northern Illinois University
Kathleen Preston, Humboldt State University
Bud Protinsky, Virginia Polytechnic Institute and
     State University
Daniel Reschly, Iowa State University
Rosemary Rosser, University of Arizona
Alan Russell, Flinders University
Jane Rysberg, California State University, Chico
Phil Schoggen, Cornell University
Maria E. Sera, University of Iowa
Beth Shapiro, Emory University
Robert Siegler, Carnegie Mellon University
Gregory J. Smith, Dickinson College
Robert J. Sternberg, Yale University
Harold Stevenson, University of Michigan
Ross A. Thompson, University of Nebraska, Lincoln
Barbara A. Tinsley, University of Illinois at Urbana–Champaign
Kim F. Townley, University of Kentucky
Janet Valadez, Pan American University
Amye R. Warren, University of Tennessee at Chattanooga

## REVIEWERS FOR THE U.S. SIXTH EDITION

Curt Acredolo, University of California, Davis
Martha W. Alibali, University of Wisconsin, Madison
Catherine L. Bagwell, University of Richmond
Lynne Baker-Ward, North Carolina State University
Carole R. Beal, University of Massachusetts
Rebecca S. Bigler, University of Texas, Austin
James H. Bodle, College of Mount Saint Joseph
M. Michele Burnette, Community College of
     Allegheny County
Robert Cohen, University of Memphis
James L. Dannemiller, University of Wisconsin, Madison
Francine Favretto, University of Maryland
Larry Fenson, San Diego State University
Jane F. Gaultney, University of North Carolina, Charlotte
John C. Gibbs, The Ohio State University
Craig H. Hart, Brigham Young University
Scott Johnson, Cornell University
Katherine Kipp, University of Georgia
Paul Klaczynski, The Pennsylvania State University
Gary Ladd, Arizona State University
Richard Lerner, Tufts University
Larry Nucci, University of Illinois, Chicago
Kathy Pezdek, Claremont Graduate School
Jane Ann Rysberg, California State University, Chico

Linda Siegel, University of British Columbia
Ross A. Thompson, University of Nebraska

In addition, I thank the following individuals for responding to a survey that provided vital feedback for the new U.S. sixth edition:

James Barnard, University of South Florida
Lyn Boulter, Catawba College
Claire Etaugh, Bradley University
Fred Grote, Western Washington University
Marc A. Lindberg, Marshall University
Mary Ann McLaughlin, Clarion University of Pennsylvania
Gary T. Montgomery, University of Texas–Pan American
Tina Moreau, Queens College
Dan Mossler, Hampden-Sydney College
Randall E. Osborne, Indiana University East
Thomas S. Parish, Kansas State University
Nancy Segal, California State University, Fullerton
Roger Van Horn, Central Michigan University

Colleagues and students at Illinois State University aided my research and contributed significantly to the text's supplements. Richard Payne, Department of Politics and Government, Illinois State University, is a kind and devoted friend with whom I have shared many profitable discussions about the writing process, the condition of children and families, and other topics that have significantly influenced my perspective on child development and social policy. Sara Harris joined me in preparing a thoroughly revised Instructor's Resource Manual and Video Observation Guide, bringing to this task enthusiasm, imagination, depth of knowledge, and impressive writing skill. JoDe Paladino's outstanding, dedicated work in helping conduct literature searches and in revising the Study Guide have been invaluable. Denise Shaefer and Lisa Sowa spent countless hours gathering library materials and assisted me with selection of video segments for the new running observational footage video.

The supplement package also benefited from the talents and diligence of several other individuals: Leslie Barnes-Young of Francis Marion University prepared the excellent Lecture Enhancements included in the Instructor's Resource Manual. Gabrielle Principe of Cornell University and Naomi Tyler of Vanderbilt University authored a superb Test Bank and set of Practice Tests.

I have been fortunate to work with an outstanding editorial team at Allyn and Bacon. Tom Pauken became my editor midstream. His careful reading of the manuscript, organizational skills, and many insights and suggestions have greatly enhanced the quality of this edition. I thank Tom for collaborating with me in writing and editing many sections of the companion website, for providing a variety of creative and cutting-edge ideas for revision, and for being a pleasure to work with in all respects.

I would like to express a heartfelt thank you to Joyce Nilsen, Director of Sales Specialists, and Brad Parkins, Executive Marketing Manager, for the outstanding work they have done in marketing my texts. Joyce and Brad have made sure that accurate and clear information about my books and their ancillaries reached Allyn and Bacon's sales force and that the needs of prospective and current adopters were met. Marcie Mealia, Field Marketing Specialist, has also devoted much time and energy to marketing activities, and I greatly appreciate the lovely social occasions she has planned and the kind greetings she sends from time to time.

Susan Messer served as development editor. It is difficult to find words that do justice to her contributions. Susan worked closely with me as I wrote each chapter, making sure that every thought and concept would be precisely expressed and well developed. Her keen writing and editing skills and prompt and patient responses to my concerns and queries made working with her an exceptional learning experience and pleasure.

Liz Napolitano, Senior Production Editor, coordinated the complex production tasks that resulted in an exquisitely beautiful U.S. sixth edition. I am grateful for her exceptional aesthetic sense, attention to detail, flexibility, efficiency, and thoughtfulness, and I look forward to working with her on future editions of my texts. I thank Sarah Evertson for obtaining the exceptional photographs that so aptly illustrate the text narrative. Betty Nylund Barr and Bill Heckman provided outstanding copyediting and proofreading.

A final word of gratitude goes to my family, whose love, patience, and understanding have enabled me to be wife, mother, teacher, researcher, and text author at the same time. My sons, David and Peter, grew up with my child development texts, passing from childhood to adolescence and then to young adulthood as successive editions were written. David has a special connection with the books' subject matter as an elementary school teacher; Peter embarked on a career in law as the book goes to press. Both continue to enrich my understanding through reflections on events and progress in their own lives. My husband, Ken, willingly made room for yet another time-consuming endeavour in our life together and communicated his belief in its importance in a great many unspoken, caring ways.

Laura E. Berk

## ABOUT THE CHAPTER-OPENING ART

I would like to extend grateful acknowledgments to the International Museum of Children's Art, Oslo, Norway, for the exceptional chapter-opening art, which depicts the talents, concerns, and viewpoints of child and adolescent artists from around the world. I was privileged to visit the museum in 2001, just prior to beginning work on the U.S. sixth and Canadian editions of *Child Development*. I was profoundly moved by the endless variety and imaginativeness of the works gracing the museum's walls. They express family, school, and community themes; good times and personal triumphs; profound appreciation for beauty; and great depth of emotion. I am pleased to share this journey into children's creativity, insightfulness, sensitivity, and compassion with readers of *Child Development*.

## A NOTE FROM THE CANADIAN ADAPTER

As a professor of psychology, I have always attempted to teach my students about child development in a relevant Canadian context. Students want and need to know about Canadian statistics, such as those for teen pregnancy and maternal employment. In addition, Canadian laws and government policies in areas such as health and education are quite different from those in the United States. Canadian researchers have made significant contributions to the field of child development. The purpose of this adaptation is to enhance students' understanding of child development by including a Canadian perspective. I hope that learning about these important statistics, policies, and research findings will inspire and encourage Canadian students.

Contributing to this adaptation has been an exciting, rewarding, and challenging task. I am especially grateful to my family and my students, and to my friends and colleagues who supported me in this endeavour. I have been particularly fortunate to work with two outstanding students: Kerry Byrne and Lauren Bonder. These two bright shining stars were enthusiastic and tremendously efficient research assistants. Jennifer Levin Bonder and Claudette Larcher also provided valuable assistance. Special thanks to Paul Johnson of Confederation College of Applied Arts and Technology for his insightful feedback. Tanja Schaefer and Cara Duval provided valued assistance with the supplement that preceded this adaptation.

I would like to extend my gratitude to the following colleagues who wrote reviews of various portions of the Canadian edition manuscript:

Scott A. Adler, York University
Anne Barnfield, University of Western Ontario, Brescia University College
Elizabeth Bowering, Mount St. Vincent University
Christine Chambers, University of British Columbia
Karl H. Hennig, St. Francis Xavier University
Marcia Moshé, Ryerson University
Gillian Wark, Simon Fraser University

Finally, I am grateful to Laura Berk for giving me this wonderful opportunity to participate in preparing the Canadian adaptation and to Jessica Mosher, Senior Acquisitions Editor, at Pearson Education Canada. Thanks also to Lise Dupont, Senior Developmental Editor. In addition, I would like to thank Avivah Wargon, Supervising Editor, Training and Special Projects, and Wendy Moran, Production Manager, for their expertise and management of the production teams.

## SUPPLEMENTARY MATERIALS

**INSTRUCTOR SUPPLEMENTS** A variety of teaching tools are available to assist instructors in organizing lectures, planning demonstrations and examinations, and ensuring student comprehension.

- **Instructor's Resource Manual (IRM)**, ISBN 0-205-38183-9. Prepared by Sara Harris and Laura E. Berk of Illinois State University, and Leslie Barnes-Young of Francis Marion University, this thoroughly revised IRM contains additional material to enrich your class presentations. For each chapter, the IRM provides a Chapter-at-a-Glance grid, Brief Chapter Summary, detailed Lecture Outline, Lecture Enhancements, Learning Activities, *Ask Yourself* questions with answers, Suggested Student Readings, and Media Materials.

- **Test Bank**, ISBN 0-205-38185-5. Prepared by Gabrielle Principe of Cornell University, Naomi Tyler of Vanderbilt University, and Mike Lee of the University of Manitoba, the test bank contains essay questions and over 2000 multiple-choice questions, each of which is page-referenced to chapter content and classified by type (factual, applied, or conceptual).

- **Computerized Test Bank**, ISBN 0-205-38181-2. This computerized version of the test bank, in easy-to-use software, lets you prepare tests for printing as well as for network and online testing. It has full editing capability for Windows and Macintosh.

- **Transparencies 2.0**, ISBN 0-205-34370-8. Two hundred full-colour transparencies taken from Berk's texts and other sources are referenced in the Instructor's Resource Manual for the most appropriate use in your classroom presentations.

- *Child Development in Action* **Observation Program**, ISBN 0-205-37812-9. Laura E. Berk has revised and expanded this real-life videotape, containing hundreds of observation segments that illustrate the many theories, concepts, and milestones of child development. New additions include *Childbirth* and *Adolescent Friendship*, plus a separate videotape of running observational footage. An Observation Guide (ISBN 0-205-37811-0) helps students use the videos in conjunction with the textbook, deepening their understanding and applying what they have learned to everyday life. (The videotapes and Observation Guide are free to instructors who adopt the text and are available to students at a discount when packaged with the text).

- **Films for the Humanities and Sciences: Child and Adolescent Development Videotape 3.0**, ISBN 0-205-37810-2. This revised video complements the text's linkage of theory and research to application.

- **PowerPoint™ CD-ROM**, ISBN 0-205-37819-6. This CD offers electronic slides of lecture outlines and illustrations from the textbook and allows you to customize content.

- **Allyn & Bacon Digital Media Archive for Berk**, ISBN 0-205-36778-X. This collection of media products—including charts, graphs, tables, figures, audio, and video clips—assists you in meeting your classroom goals.

**STUDENT SUPPLEMENTS** Beyond the study aids found in the textbook, Pearson Education Canada offers a number of supplements for students:

- **Study Guide**, ISBN 0-205-37581-2. Prepared by JoDe Paladino and Laura E. Berk of Illinois State University, this helpful guide offers Chapter Summaries, Learning Objectives, Study Questions organized according to major headings in the text, *Ask Yourself* questions that also appear in the text, Crossword Puzzles for mastering important terms, and multiple-choice Self-Tests.

- **Practice Tests**, ISBN 0-205-37329-1. Twenty multiple-choice items per chapter plus an answer key with justifications are drawn from the test bank to assist students in preparing for course exams.

- **Website.** The companion website, *http://www.pearsoned. ca/berk,* offers support for students through practice tests, weblinks, learning objectives, and chapter summaries.

# —CHILD—
## DEVELOPMENT

"Blossoming Trees"
Anna Gruszczynska
15 years, Poland

Reprinted with permission from
The International Museum of
Children's Art, Oslo, Norway

As these children wander down an idyllic village path, captivated by the sights and sounds of a newly blossoming spring, they remind us that development is complex, fascinating, and in many ways mystifying. Chapter 1 opens the door to a multiplicity of ways of thinking about children's development.

# one

## History, Theory, and Applied Directions

NOT LONG AGO, I HAD AN opportunity to return to the city where I spent my childhood. One morning, I visited the neighbourhood where I grew up—a place I had not been to since I was 12 years old.

I stood at the entrance to my old school-yard. Buildings and grounds that had looked large to me as a child now seemed strangely small. I peered through the window of my first-grade classroom. The desks were no longer arranged in rows but grouped in intimate clusters. Computers rested against the far wall, near where I once sat. I walked my old route home from school, the distance shrunk by my longer stride. I stopped in front of my best friend Kathryn's house, where we once drew side-walk pictures, crossed the street to play kickball, and produced plays in the garage. In place of the small shop where I had purchased penny candy stood a child-care centre, filled with the voices and vigorous activity of toddlers and preschoolers.

As I walked, I reflected on early experiences that contributed to who I am and what I am like today—weekends helping my father in his downtown clothing shop, the year my mother studied to become a high school teacher, moments of companionship and rivalry with my sister and brother, Sunday outings to museums and the seashore, and visits to my grandmother's house, where I became someone extra special.

As I passed the homes of my childhood friends, I thought of what I knew about their present lives: Kathryn, star pupil and president of our sixth-grade class—today a successful corporate lawyer and mother of two. Shy, withdrawn Phil, cruelly teased because of his cleft lip—now owner of a thriving chain of hardware stores and member of the city council. Julio, immigrant from Mexico who joined our class in third grade—today director of an elementary school bilingual education program and single parent of an adopted Mexican boy. And finally, my next-door neighbour Rick, who picked fights at recess, struggled with reading, repeated fourth grade, dropped out of high school, and (so I heard) moved from one job to another over the following 10 years.

As you begin this course in child development, perhaps you, too, are wondering about some of the same questions that crossed my mind during that nostalgic neighbourhood walk:

- In what ways are children's home, school, and neighbourhood experiences the same today as they were in generations past, and in what ways are they different?

- How is the infant's and young child's perception of the world the same as the adult's, and how is it different?

- What determines the features that humans have in common and those that make us unique, physically, mentally, and behaviourally?

- How did Julio, transplanted to a foreign culture, master its language and customs and succeed in its society, yet remain strongly identified with his ethnic community?

- How does cultural change—employed mothers, child care, divorce, smaller families, and new technologies—affect children's characteristics and skills?

- Why do some of us, like Kathryn and Rick, retain the same styles of responding that characterized us as children, whereas others, like Phil, change in essential ways?

These are central questions addressed by **child development,** a field devoted to understanding human constancy and change from conception through adolescence. Child development is part of a larger discipline known as **developmental psychology,** or, in its interdisciplinary sense, **human development,** which includes all changes we experience throughout the lifespan. Great diversity characterizes the interests and concerns of investigators who study child development. But all have a common goal: to describe and identify those factors that influence the dramatic changes in young people during the first two decades of life.

# Child Development as a Scientific, Applied, and Interdisciplinary Field

LOOK AGAIN AT THE questions just listed, and you will see that they are not just of scientific interest. Each is of *applied,* or practical, importance as well. In fact, scientific curiosity is just one factor that has led child development to become the exciting field of study it is today. Research about development has also been stimulated by social pressures to better the lives of children. For example, the beginning of public education in the early part of the twentieth century led to a demand for knowledge about what and how to teach children of different ages. Pediatricians' interest in improving children's health required an understanding of physical growth and nutrition. The social service profession's desire to treat children's anxieties and behaviour problems required information about personality and social development. And parents have continually asked for advice about child-rearing practices and experiences that would promote the well-being of their child.

Our large storehouse of information about child development is *interdisciplinary.* It has grown through the efforts of people from many fields. Because of the need for solutions to everyday problems concerning children, researchers from psychology, sociology, anthropology, and biology joined forces with professionals from education, family studies, medicine, public health, and social service, to name just a few. Today, the field of child development is a melting pot of contributions. Its body of knowledge is not just scientifically important but relevant and useful.

**child development**
A field of study devoted to understanding human constancy and change from conception through adolescence.

**developmental psychology**
A branch of psychology devoted to understanding all changes that human beings experience throughout the lifespan.

**human development**
An interdisciplinary field devoted to understanding all changes that human beings experience throughout the lifespan.

## DOMAINS OF DEVELOPMENT

To make the vast, interdisciplinary study of human constancy and change more orderly and convenient, development is often divided into three broad *domains,* or aspects:

- *Physical development*—changes in body size, proportions, appearance, and the functioning of various body systems; brain development; perceptual and motor capacities; and physical health.

- *Cognitive development*—development of a wide variety of thought processes and intellectual abilities, including attention, memory, academic and everyday knowledge, problem solving, imagination, creativity, and the uniquely human capacity to represent the world through language.

- *Emotional and social development*—development of emotional communication, self-understanding, ability to manage one's feelings, knowledge about other people, interpersonal skills, friendships, intimate relationships, and moral reasoning and behaviour.

Child development is so dramatic that researchers divide it into age periods. These brothers and sisters illustrate, counterclockwise from top, toddlerhood (age 1), early childhood (age 4), middle childhood (age 6), and middle childhood (age 7).

In this book, we will largely consider the domains of development in the order just listed. Yet we must keep in mind that they are not really distinct. Instead, they combine in an integrated, holistic fashion to yield the living, growing child. Furthermore, each domain influences and is influenced by the others. For example, in Chapter 4, we will see that new motor capacities, such as reaching, sitting, crawling, and walking (physical), contribute greatly to infants' understanding of their surroundings (cognitive). When babies think and act more competently, adults stimulate them more with games, language, and expressions of delight at the child's new achievements (emotional and social). These enriched experiences, in turn, promote all aspects of development.

You will encounter instances of the interwoven nature of all domains on almost every page. Also, look for the *Ask Yourself* boxes at the end of major sections. In these boxes, you will find *Review* questions, which help you recall and think about information you have just read; *Apply* questions, which encourage you to apply your knowledge to controversial issues and problems faced by parents, teachers, and children; and *Connect* questions, which help you form a coherent, unified picture of child development. The questions are designed to deepen your understanding and inspire new insights.

## PERIODS OF DEVELOPMENT

Besides distinguishing and then reconnecting the three domains, another dilemma arises in discussing development: how to divide the flow of time into sensible, manageable phases. Usually, researchers segment child development into the following five periods. Each brings with it new capacities and social expectations:

1. *The prenatal period: from conception to birth.* This 9-month period is the most rapid phase of change, during which a one-celled organism is transformed into a human baby with remarkable capacities for adjusting to life in the surrounding world.

2. *Infancy and toddlerhood: from birth to 2 years.* Dramatic changes in the body and brain support the emergence of motor, perceptual, and intellectual capacities; language; and first intimate ties to others. Infancy spans the first year; toddlerhood spans the second, during which children take their first independent steps, marking a shift to greater autonomy.

3. *Early childhood: from 2 to 6 years.* The body becomes longer and leaner, motor skills are refined, and children become more self-controlled and self-sufficient. Make-believe play blossoms and supports all aspects of psychological development. Thought and language expand at an astounding pace, a sense of morality becomes evident, and children establish ties with peers.

4. *Middle childhood: from 6 to 11 years.* Children learn about the wider world and master new responsibilities that increasingly resemble those they will perform as adults. Improved athletic abilities, participation in organized games with rules, more logical thought processes, mastery of basic literacy skills, and advances in self-understanding, morality, and friendship are hallmarks of this phase.

5. *Adolescence: from 11 to 20 years.* This period is the bridge between childhood and adulthood. Puberty leads to an adult-size body and sexual maturity. Thought becomes abstract and idealistic, and school achievement becomes more serious as young people prepare for the world of work. Defining personal values and goals and establishing autonomy from the family are major concerns of this phase.

With this introduction in mind, let's turn to some basic issues that have captivated, puzzled, and divided child development theorists. Then we will trace the emergence of the field and survey major theories.

# Basic Issues

BEFORE SCIENTIFIC STUDY of the child, questions about children were answered by turning to common sense, opinion, and belief. Systematic research on children did not begin until the late nineteenth and early twentieth centuries. Gradually it led to the construction of theories, to which professionals and parents could turn for understanding and guidance.

For our purposes, we can define a **theory** as an orderly, integrated set of statements that describes, explains, and predicts behaviour. For example, a good theory of infant–caregiver attachment would (1) *describe* the behaviours of babies around 6 to 8 months of age as they seek the affection and comfort of a familiar adult, (2) *explain* how and why infants develop this strong desire to bond with a caregiver, and (3) *predict* what might happen if babies do not form this close bond.

Theories are vital tools for two reasons. First, they provide organizing frameworks for our observations of children. In other words, they *guide and give meaning to what we see.* Second, theories that are verified by research often serve as a sound basis for practical action. Once a theory helps us *understand* development, we are in a much better position to *know what to do* to improve the welfare and treatment of children.

As we will see later, theories are influenced by cultural values and belief systems of their times. But theories differ in one important way from mere opinion and belief: A theory's continued existence depends on *scientific verification* (Scarr, 1985). This means that the theory must be tested using a fair set of research procedures agreed on by the scientific community. (We will consider research strategies in Chapter 2.)

In the field of child development, there are many theories about what children are like and how they develop. The study of child development provides no ultimate truth because investigators do not always agree on the meaning of what they see. In addition, children are complex beings; they grow physically, cognitively, emotionally, and socially. As yet, no single theory has been able to explain all these aspects. However, the existence of many theories helps advance knowledge, since researchers continually try to support, contradict, and integrate these different points of view.

Although there are many theories, we can easily organize them, since almost all take a stand on three basic issues about child development. To help you remember these controversial issues, they are briefly summarized in Table 1.1. Let's take a close look at each.

## CONTINUOUS OR DISCONTINUOUS DEVELOPMENT?

Recently, the mother of 20-month-old Angelo reported to me with amazement that her young son had pushed a toy car across the living room floor while making a motorlike

**theory**
An orderly, integrated set of statements that describes, explains, and predicts behaviour.

**continuous development**
A view that regards development as a cumulative process of gradually adding more of the same types of skills that were there to begin with.

**TABLE** 1.1

Basic Issues in Child Development

| ISSUE | QUESTIONS RAISED ABOUT DEVELOPMENT |
|---|---|
| Continuous or discontinuous development? | Is child development a matter of cumulative adding on of skills and behaviours, or does it involve qualitative, stagewise changes? Do *both* continuous and discontinuous changes characterize development? |
| One course of development or many? | Does one course of development characterize all children, or are there many possible courses, depending on the contexts—unique combinations of personal and environmental circumstances—that children experience? Does development have *both* universal features and features unique to the individual and his or her context? |
| Nature or nurture as more important? | Are genetic or environmental factors more important determinants of development? If *both* nature and nurture play major roles, how do they work together? To what extent do early experiences establish lifelong patterns of behaviour? Can later experiences overcome early negative effects? |

sound, "Brmmmm, brmmmm," for the first time. When he hit a nearby wall with a bang, Angelo let go of the car, exclaimed, "C'ash," and laughed heartily.

"How come Angelo can pretend, but he couldn't a few months ago?" queried his mother. "And I wonder what 'Brrmmmm, brmmmm' and 'Crash!' mean to Angelo? Is his understanding of motorlike sounds and collision similar to mine?"

Angelo's mother has raised a puzzling issue about development: How can we best describe the differences in capacities and behaviour between small infants, young children, adolescents, and adults? As Figure 1.1 illustrates, major theories recognize two possibilities.

On the one hand, babies and preschoolers may respond to the world in much the same way as adults. The difference between the immature and mature being may simply involve amount or complexity of behaviour. For example, little Angelo's thinking might be just as logical and well organized as our own. Perhaps (as his mother reports) he can sort objects into simple categories, recognize whether there are more of one kind than another, and remember where he left his favourite toy at child care the week before. Angelo's only limitation may be that he cannot perform these skills with as much information and precision as we can. If this is so, then Angelo's development must be **continuous**—a process that consists of gradually adding more of the same types of skills that were there to begin with.

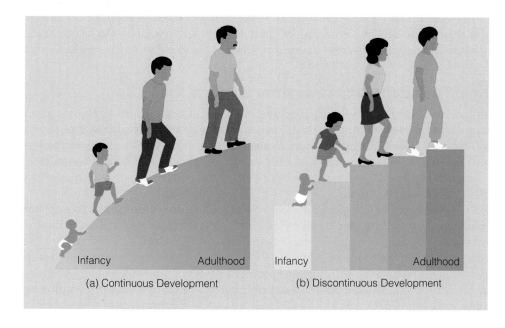

(a) Continuous Development

(b) Discontinuous Development

**FIGURE** 1.1

**Is development continuous or discontinuous?** (a) Some theorists believe that development is a smooth, continuous process. Children gradually add more of the same types of skills. (b) Other theorists think that development takes place in discontinuous stages. Children change rapidly as they step up to a new level of development and then change very little for a while. With each step, the child interprets and responds to the world in a qualitatively different way.

On the other hand, Angelo's thoughts, emotions, and behaviour may be quite different from our own. If so, then development is a **discontinuous** process in which new ways of understanding and responding to the world emerge at specific times. From this perspective, Angelo is not yet able to organize objects or remember and interpret experiences as adults do. Instead, he will move through a series of developmental steps, each of which has unique features, until he reaches the highest level of human functioning.

Theories that accept the discontinuous perspective regard development as taking place in **stages**—qualitative changes in thinking, feeling, and behaving that characterize specific periods of development. In stage theories, development is much like climbing a staircase, with each step corresponding to a more mature, reorganized way of functioning. The stage concept also assumes that children undergo periods of rapid transformation as they step up from one stage to the next, followed by plateaus during which they stand solidly within a stage. In other words, change is fairly sudden rather than gradual and ongoing.

Does development actually take place in a neat, orderly sequence of stages? For now, let's note that this is an ambitious assumption that has not gone unchallenged. We will review some very influential stage theories later in this chapter.

## ONE COURSE OF DEVELOPMENT OR MANY?

Stage theorists assume that children everywhere follow the same sequence of development. For example, in the domain of cognition, a stage theorist might try to identify the common biological and environmental factors that lead children to represent their world through language and make-believe play in early childhood; think more logically and systematically in middle childhood; and reason abstractly in adolescence.

At the same time, the field of child development is becoming increasingly aware that children grow up in distinct **contexts;** that is, each child experiences unique combinations of genetic and environmental circumstances. For example, a shy child who fears social encounters develops in very different contexts from those of a sociable agemate who readily seeks out other people (Rubin & Coplan, 1998). Children in non-Western village societies encounter experiences in their families and communities that differ sharply from those of children in large Western cities. These different circumstances can result in markedly different cognitive capacities, social skills, and feelings about the self and others (Shweder et al., 1998).

As we will see, contemporary theorists regard the contexts that shape development as many-layered and complex. They include immediate settings, such as home, child-care centre, school, and neighbourhood, as well as circumstances more remote from children's everyday lives—community resources, societal values and priorities, and historical period. Finally, a special interest in culture has led child development researchers to be more conscious than ever before of diversity in development.

## NATURE OR NURTURE AS MORE IMPORTANT?

In addition to describing the course of development, each theory takes a stand on a major question about its underlying causes: Are genetic or environmental factors more important? This is the age-old **nature–nurture controversy.** By *nature,* we mean inborn biological givens—the hereditary information children receive from their parents at the moment of conception. By *nurture,* we mean the complex physical and social worlds that influence children before and after birth.

Although all theories grant at least some role to both nature and nurture, they vary in emphasis. For example, consider the following questions: Is the older child's ability to think in more complex ways largely the result of an inborn timetable of growth? Or is it primarily influenced by stimulation from parents and teachers? Do children acquire language because they are genetically predisposed to do so, or because parents teach them from an early age? And what accounts for the vast individual differences among children—in height, weight, physical coordination, intelligence, personality, and social skills? Is nature or nurture more responsible?

**discontinuous development**
A view in which new ways of understanding and responding to the world emerge at specific times.

**stage**
A qualitative change in thinking, feeling, and behaving that characterizes a specific period of development.

**contexts**
Unique combinations of genetic and environmental circumstances that can result in markedly different paths of development.

**nature–nurture controversy**
Disagreement among theorists about whether genetic or environmental factors are more important determinants of development and behaviour.

The stances theories take on nature versus nurture affect their explanations of individual differences. Some theorists emphasize *stability*—that children who are high or low in a characteristic (such as verbal ability, anxiety, or sociability) will remain so at later ages. These theorists typically stress the importance of *heredity*. If they regard environment as important, they generally point to *early experiences* as establishing a lifelong pattern of behaviour. Powerful negative events in the first few years, they argue, cannot be fully overcome by later, more positive ones (Bowlby, 1980; Sroufe, Egeland, & Kreutzer, 1990). Other theorists take a more optimistic view. They believe that *change* is possible and likely if new experiences, or nurture, support it (Masten & Coatsworth, 1998; Sampson & Laub, 1993; Werner & Smith, 1992).

Throughout this chapter and the remainder of this book, we will see that investigators disagree, often sharply, on the question of *stability or change*. The answers they provide are of great applied significance. If you believe that development is largely due to nature, then providing experiences aimed at stimulating change would seem to be of little value. If, on the other hand, you are convinced of the supreme importance of early experience, then you would intervene as soon as possible, offering high-quality stimulation and support to ensure that children develop at their best. Finally, if you think that environment is profoundly influential throughout development, you would provide assistance any time children or adolescents face difficulties, believing that they can recover from early negative events with the help of favourable life circumstances.

© LAURA DWIGHT

Will this 15-month-old's tantrums extend into a lifelong pattern of difficult behaviour? Theorists emphasizing stability—that she will remain difficult to manage—typically stress the importance of heredity. Others regard stability as due to early experiences—the way the mother handles her young child's emotional outbursts. Still others believe that change is possible at later ages if new experiences support it.

## A BALANCED POINT OF VIEW

So far, we have discussed the basic issues of child development in terms of extremes—solutions on one side or the other. As we trace the unfolding of the field in the rest of this chapter, you will see that the positions of many theories have softened. Modern ones, especially, recognize the merits of both sides. Some theorists believe that both continuous and discontinuous changes occur. And some acknowledge that development can have both universal features and features unique to the individual and his or her contexts. Furthermore, an increasing number of investigators regard heredity and environment as inseparably interwoven, each affecting the potential of the other to modify the child's traits and capacities (de Waal, 1999; Wachs, 2000). We will discuss these new ideas about nature and nurture in Chapter 3.

Finally, as we will see in later parts of this book, the relative impact of early and later experiences varies substantially from one domain of development to another and even (as the Biology & Environment box on page 10 indicates) across individuals! Because of the complex network of factors contributing to human change and the challenge of isolating the effects of each, many theoretical points of view have gathered research support. Although debate continues, this circumstance has also sparked more balanced visions of child development.

## ASK YOURSELF

**review** Why are there many theories of child development? Cite three basic issues on which almost all theories take a stand.

**apply** A school counsellor advises a parent, "Don't worry about your teenager's argumentative behaviour. It shows that she understands the world differently than she did as a young child." What stance is the counsellor taking on the issue of continuous or discontinuous development? Explain.

**connect** Cite an aspect of your development that differs from a parent's or a grandparent's when he or she was your age. How might contexts explain this difference?

# biology & environment

## RESILIENT CHILDREN

John and his best friend, Gary, grew up in a run-down, crime-ridden inner-city neighbourhood. By age 10, each had experienced years of family conflict followed by parental divorce. Reared for the rest of childhood and adolescence in mother-headed households, John and Gary rarely saw their fathers. Both dropped out of high school and were in and out of trouble with police.

Then John and Gary's paths diverged. By age 30, John had fathered two children with women he never married, had spent time in prison, was unemployed, and drank alcohol heavily. In contrast, Gary had returned to finish high school, studied auto mechanics at a community college, and become manager of a gas station and repair shop. Married with two children, he was happy, healthy, and well adapted to life.

A wealth of evidence shows that environmental risks—poverty, negative family interactions, and parental divorce, job loss, mental illness, and drug abuse—predispose children to future problems (Masten & Coatsworth, 1998). Why did Gary "beat the odds" and come through unscathed?

New evidence on **resiliency**—the ability to adapt effectively in the face of threats to development—is receiving increasing attention because investigators want to

EYEWIRE

find ways to protect young people from the damaging effects of stressful life conditions (Masten, 2001). This interest has been inspired by several long-term studies on the relationship of life stressors in childhood to competence and adjustment in adolescence and adulthood (Garmezy, 1993; Masten et al., 1995; Werner & Smith, 1992). In each study, some children were shielded from negative outcomes, whereas others had lasting problems. Three broad factors seemed to offer protection from the damaging effects of stressful life events.

### PERSONAL CHARACTERISTICS OF CHILDREN

A child's biologically endowed characteristics can reduce exposure to risk or lead to experiences that compensate for early stressful events. Intellectual ability, for example, is a protective factor. It increases the chances that a child will have rewarding experiences in school that offset the impact of a stressful home life and enhance mental ability further (Masten et al., 1999). Temperament is particularly powerful. Children with easygoing, sociable dispositions have a special capacity to adapt to change and elicit positive responses from others. Children who are emotionally reactive and irritable often strain the patience of people around them (Milgram & Palti, 1993; Smith & Prior, 1995). For example, both John and Gary moved several times during their childhoods. Each time, John became anxious and angry. Gary looked forward to making new friends and exploring a new neighbourhood.

This boy's special relationship with his grandfather provides the social support he needs to cope with stress and solve problems constructively. A warm tie with a person outside the immediate family can promote resilience.

### A WARM PARENTAL RELATIONSHIP

A close relationship with at least one parent who provides affection and assistance and introduces order and organization into the child's life fosters resiliency. But note that this factor (as well as the next one) is not independent of children's personal characteristics. Children who are relaxed, socially responsive, and able to deal with change are easier to rear and more likely to enjoy positive relationships with parents and other people. At the same time, some children may develop more attractive dispositions as a result of parental warmth and attention (Smith & Prior, 1995; Wyman et al., 1999).

### SOCIAL SUPPORT OUTSIDE THE IMMEDIATE FAMILY

A person outside the immediate family—perhaps a grandparent, teacher, or close friend—who forms a special relationship with the child can promote resiliency. Gary received support in adolescence from his grandfather, who listened to Gary's concerns and helped him solve problems. In addition, Gary's grandfather had a stable marriage and work life and handled stressors skilfully. Consequently, he served as a model of effective coping (Zimmerman & Arunkumar, 1994).

Research on resiliency highlights the complex connections between heredity and environment. Armed with positive characteristics, which may stem from innate endowment, favourable rearing experiences, or both, children take action to reduce stressful situations. Nevertheless, when many risks pile up, they are increasingly difficult to overcome (Quyen et al., 1998). Therefore, interventions must reduce risks and enhance relationships at home, in school, and in the community that inoculate children against the negative effects of risk. This means attending to both the person and the environment—building the child's capacity as well as fixing problems.

# Historical Foundations

MODERN THEORIES OF CHILD DEVELOPMENT are the result of centuries of change in Western cultural values, philosophical thinking about children, and scientific progress. To understand the field as it exists today, we must return to its beginnings—to influences that long preceded scientific child study. We will see that many early ideas about children linger as important forces in current theory and research.

## MEDIEVAL TIMES

In medieval Europe (from the sixth through the fifteenth century), little importance was placed on childhood as a separate phase of the life cycle. Once children emerged from infancy, they were regarded as miniature, already-formed adults, a view called **preformationism** (Ariès, 1962). This attitude is reflected in the art, entertainment, and language of the times. Look carefully at medieval paintings, and you will see that children are depicted in dress and expression as immature adults. Before the sixteenth century, toys and games were not designed to amuse children but were for all people. And age, so central to modern personal identity, was unimportant in medieval custom and usage. It was not even recorded in family and civil records until the fifteenth and sixteenth centuries.

Nevertheless, faint glimmerings of the idea that children are unique emerged during medieval times. Some laws recognized that children needed protection from adults who might mistreat them, and medical works provided special instructions for children's care. But even with some awareness of the vulnerability of children, no theories described the uniqueness of childhood or separate developmental periods (Borstelmann, 1983).

In this medieval painting, young children are depicted as miniature adults. Their dress and expressions resemble those of their elders. Through the fifteenth century, little emphasis was placed on childhood as a unique phase of the life cycle.

## THE REFORMATION

In the sixteenth century, a revised image of childhood sprang from the Puritan belief in original sin. According to Puritan doctrine, children were born evil and stubborn and had to be civilized (Shahar, 1990). Harsh, restrictive child-rearing practices were recommended to tame the depraved child. Children were dressed in stiff, uncomfortable clothing that held them in adultlike postures, and disobedient students were routinely beaten by their schoolmasters. Although punitiveness was the prevailing child-rearing philosophy, love and affection for their children prevented many Puritan parents from exercising extremely repressive measures (Moran & Vinovskis, 1986).

As the Puritans immigrated to North America, they brought the belief that child rearing was one of their most important obligations. Although they continued to regard the child's soul as tainted by original sin, they tried to promote reason in their sons and daughters so they could separate right from wrong (Clarke-Stewart, 1998). The Puritans were the first to develop special reading materials for children that instructed them in religious and moral ideals. As they trained their children in self-reliance and self-control, Puritan parents gradually adopted a moderate balance between severity and permissiveness (Pollock, 1987).

## PHILOSOPHIES OF THE ENLIGHTENMENT

The seventeenth-century Enlightenment brought new philosophies of reason and emphasized ideals of human dignity and respect. Conceptions of childhood were more humane than those of centuries past.

**JOHN LOCKE.** John Locke (1632–1704), a leading British philosopher, viewed the child as a **tabula rasa.** Translated from Latin, this means a "blank slate." According to this idea, children are, to begin with, nothing at all, and all kinds of experiences can shape their characters.

**resiliency**
The ability to adapt effectively in the face of threats to development.

**preformationism**
Medieval view of the child as a miniature adult.

**tabula rasa**
Locke's view of the child as a blank slate whose character is shaped by experience.

Locke (1690/1892) described parents as rational tutors who can mould the child in any way they wish, through careful instruction, effective example, and rewards for good behaviour. He was ahead of his time in recommending child-rearing practices that present-day research supports. For example, Locke suggested that parents not reward children with money or sweets but with praise and approval. He also opposed physical punishment: "The child repeatedly beaten in school cannot look upon books and teachers without experiencing fear and anger." Locke's philosophy led to a change from harshness toward children to kindness and compassion.

Look carefully at Locke's ideas, and you will see that he took a firm stand on the basic issues discussed earlier in this chapter. Locke regarded development as *continuous;* adultlike behaviours are gradually built up through the warm, consistent teachings of parents. Furthermore, Locke's view of the child as a tabula rasa led him to champion *nurture*—the power of the environment to shape the child. And his faith in nurture suggests the possibility of *many courses of development* and of *change at later ages* due to new experiences.

Finally, Locke's philosophy characterizes children as passive—as doing little to influence their own destiny, which is written on blank slates by others. This vision has been discarded. All contemporary theories view children as active, purposeful beings who make sense of their world and contribute substantially to their own development.

**JEAN-JACQUES ROUSSEAU.** In the eighteenth century, a new theory of childhood was introduced by French philosopher of the Enlightenment Jean-Jacques Rousseau (1712–1778). Children, Rousseau (1762/1955) thought, are not blank slates and empty containers to be filled by adult instruction. Instead, they are **noble savages,** naturally endowed with a sense of right and wrong and with an innate plan for orderly, healthy growth. Unlike Locke, Rousseau thought children's built-in moral sense and unique ways of thinking and feeling would only be harmed by adult training. His was a child-centred philosophy in which adults should be receptive to the child's needs at each of four stages: infancy, childhood, late childhood, and adolescence.

Rousseau's philosophy includes two influential concepts. The first is the concept of *stage,* which we discussed earlier in this chapter. The second is the concept of **maturation,** which refers to a genetically determined, naturally unfolding course of growth. Unlike Locke, Rousseau saw children as determining their own destinies. And he took a different stand on basic developmental issues. He saw development as a *discontinuous, stagewise* process that follows a *single, unified course* mapped out by *nature.*

## DARWIN: FOREFATHER OF SCIENTIFIC CHILD STUDY

A century after Rousseau, another ancestor of contemporary child study—this time of its scientific foundations—emerged. In the mid-nineteenth century, Charles Darwin (1809–1882), a British naturalist, joined an expedition to distant parts of the world, where he made careful observations of fossils and animal and plant life. Darwin (1859/1936) noticed the infinite variation among species. He also saw that within a species, no two individuals are exactly alike. From these observations, he constructed his famous theory of evolution.

The theory emphasized two related principles: *natural selection* and *survival of the fittest.* Darwin explained that certain species survived in particular parts of the world because they had characteristics that fit with, or were adapted to, their surroundings. Other species died off because their traits were not well suited to their environments. Individuals within a species who best met the survival requirements of the environment lived long enough to reproduce and pass their more favourable characteristics to future generations. Darwin's emphasis on the adaptive value of physical characteristics and behaviour eventually found its way into important twentieth-century theories (Cairns, 1998).

During his explorations, Darwin discovered that the early prenatal growth of many species was strikingly similar. Other scientists concluded from Darwin's observation that the development of the human child, from conception to maturity, followed the same general plan as the evolution of the human species. Although this belief eventually proved inaccurate, efforts to chart parallels between child growth and human evolution prompted

**noble savage**
Rousseau's view of the child as naturally endowed with a sense of right and wrong and with an innate plan for orderly, healthy growth.

**maturation**
A genetically determined, naturally unfolding course of growth.

researchers to make careful observations of all aspects of children's behaviour. Out of these first attempts to document an idea about development, the science of child study was born.

## SCIENTIFIC BEGINNINGS

Scientific child study evolved quickly during the late nineteenth and early twentieth centuries. Rudimentary observations of single children were soon followed by improved methods and theoretical ideas. Each advance contributed to the firm foundation on which the field rests today.

**THE BABY BIOGRAPHIES.** Imagine yourself as a forerunner in the field of child development, confronted with studying children for the first time. How might you go about this challenging task? Scientists of the late nineteenth and early twentieth centuries did what most of us would probably do—they selected a child of their own or of a close relative. Then, beginning in early infancy, they jotted down day-by-day descriptions and impressions of the youngster's behaviour. Dozens of these baby biographies were published by the early twentieth century. In the following excerpt from one, the author reflects on the birth of her young niece:

> Its first act is a cry, not of wrath, . . . nor a shout of joy, . . . but a snuffling, and then a long, thin tearless á—á, with the timbre of a Scotch bagpipe, purely automatic, but of discomfort. With this monotonous and dismal cry, with its red, shriveled, parboiled skin . . . , it is not strange that, if the mother . . . has not come to love her child before birth, there is a brief interval occasionally dangerous to the child before the maternal instinct is fully aroused.
>
> It cannot be denied that this unflattering description is fair enough, and our baby was no handsomer than the rest of her kind . . . Yet she did not lack admirers. I have never noticed that women (even those who are not mothers) mind a few little aesthetic defects, . . . with so many counterbalancing charms in the little warm, soft, living thing. (Shinn, 1900, pp. 20–21)

Can you tell from this passage why baby biographies have sometimes been upheld as examples of how *not* to study children? These first investigators tended to be emotionally invested in the infants they observed, and they seldom began with a clear idea of what they wanted to find out. Not surprisingly, many of their records were eventually discarded as biased.

Nevertheless, the baby biographies were a step in the right direction. In fact, two nineteenth-century theorists, Darwin (1877) and German biologist William Preyer (1882/1888), contributed to these early records of children's behaviour. Preyer, especially, set high standards for making observations, recording what he saw immediately and checking the accuracy of his own notes against those of a second observer (Cairns, 1998). These are the same standards that today's researchers use when observing children. As a result of the biographers' pioneering efforts, the child became a common subject of scientific research.

**THE NORMATIVE PERIOD OF CHILD STUDY.** G. Stanley Hall (1844–1924), one of the most influential U.S. psychologists of the early twentieth century, is generally regarded as the founder of the child study movement (Dixon & Lerner, 1999). Inspired by Darwin's work, Hall and his well-known student Arnold Gesell (1880–1961) developed theories based on evolutionary ideas. These early leaders regarded child development as a genetically determined series of events that unfolds automatically, much like a blooming flower (Gesell, 1933; Hall, 1904).

Hall and Gesell are remembered less for their one-sided theories than for their intensive efforts to collect a sound body of facts on all aspects of child development. This launched the **normative approach** to child study. In a normative investigation, measures of behaviour are taken on large numbers of children. Then age-related averages are computed to represent typical development. Using this approach, Hall constructed elaborate questionnaires asking children of different ages almost everything they could tell about themselves—interests, fears, imaginary playmates, dreams, friendships, favourite toys, and more (White, 1992).

In the same fashion, Gesell collected detailed normative information on the motor achievements, social behaviours, and personality characteristics of infants and children. He

**normative approach**
A child-study approach in which age-related averages are computed to represent typical development.

hoped to relieve parents' anxieties by informing them of what to expect at each age. If, as he believed, the timetable of development is the product of millions of years of evolution, then children are naturally knowledgeable about their needs. His child-rearing advice, in the tradition of Rousseau, recommended sensitivity and responsiveness to children's cues (Thelen & Adolph, 1992). Gesell's books were widely read. Along with Benjamin Spock's famous *Baby and Child Care*, they became a central part of a rapidly expanding child development literature for parents (see the From Research to Practice box on the following page).

**THE MENTAL TESTING MOVEMENT.** While Hall and Gesell were developing their theories and methods in the United States, French psychologist Alfred Binet (1857–1911) was also taking a normative approach to child development, but for a different reason. In the early 1900s, Binet and his colleague Theodore Simon were asked by Paris school officials to find a way to identify children with learning problems who needed to be placed in special classes. The first successful intelligence test, which they constructed for this purpose, grew out of practical educational concerns.

Binet's effort was unique in that he began with a well-developed theory. In contrast to earlier views, which reduced intelligence to simple elements of reaction time and sensitivity to physical stimuli, Binet captured the complexity of children's thinking (Fancher, 1998). He defined intelligence as good judgment, planning, and critical reflection. Then he selected age-graded test items that directly measured these abilities.

In 1916, at Stanford University, Binet's test was translated into English and adapted for use with U.S. children. It became known as the *Stanford-Binet Intelligence Scale.* Besides providing a score that could successfully predict school achievement, the Binet test sparked tremendous interest in individual differences in development. The mental testing movement was in motion. Comparisons of the intelligence test scores of children who vary in sex, ethnicity, family background, and other characteristics became a major focus of research, and intelligence test scores rose quickly to the forefront of the nature–nurture controversy.

**JAMES MARK BALDWIN: EARLY DEVELOPMENTAL THEORIST.** A final important figure, overlooked in the history of child development for decades, is U.S. psychologist James Mark Baldwin (1861–1934). Baldwin was the first psychologist appointed to a faculty in Canada. In 1889 he set up the first experimental psychology laboratory at the University of Toronto (Hoff, 1992). A theorist rather than an observer of children, Baldwin's (1897) rich interpretations of development are experiencing a revival today. He believed that children's understanding of their physical and social worlds develops through a sequence of stages, beginning with the simplest behaviour patterns of the newborn infant and concluding with the adult's capacity to think abstractly and reflectively (Cairns, 1992, 1998).

Yet Baldwin regarded neither the child nor the environment as in control of development. Instead, nature and nurture were granted equal importance. Children, he argued, actively revise their ways of thinking about the world, but they also learn through habit or by copying others' behaviours. As development proceeds, the child and his social surroundings influence each other, forming an inseparable, interwoven network.

Consider these ideas, and you will see why Baldwin (1895) argued that heredity and environment should not be viewed as distinct, opposing forces. Instead, he claimed, most human characteristics are "due to both causes working together" (p. 77). As we turn now to an overview of modern theories of child development, you will find Baldwin's ideas represented in several, especially the more recent ones.

**ASK YOURSELF** www

**review**  Suppose we could arrange a debate between John Locke and Jean-Jacques Rousseau on the nature–nurture controversy. Summarize the argument each historical figure is likely to present.

**review**  Explain how Darwin, Hall and Gesell, and Binet each contributed to the scientific study of children.

# from research to practice

## SOCIAL CHANGE AND THE POPULAR LITERATURE ON PARENTING

almost all parents—especially new ones—feel a need for sound advice on how to rear their children. To meet this need, experts have long been communicating with the general public through a wide variety of popular books and magazines.

Prior to the 1970s, publications emphasized the central role of mothers in healthy child development. In the 1980s, fathers were encouraged to share in the full range of child-rearing responsibilities, since research revealed that their role is unique and important to all aspects of development. Around that time, information about non-parental child care appeared. Experts reassured employed mothers that their babies did not require their continuous presence and offered advice on how to select good child care (Young, 1990).

From the mid-1990s to the present, an increasing number of books express concern over the consequences of social change for parents' and children's well-being. Arlie Hochschild (1997), in *The Time Bind,* reports that the majority of working parents, whether clerical workers or executives, complain about overly demanding lives, with little time for home and child rearing. In *The War Against Parents,* Sylvia Hewlett and Cornel West (1998) extend this theme of parental overload, emphasizing that good parenting is receiving less and less support in contemporary society. Too many parents earn low wages, must work longer hours to make ends meet, and are under siege by the media, which readily blame them for troubled children.

In *Awakening Children's Minds,* Laura Berk (2001a) points out that parents' efforts to rear competent, well-adjusted children are complicated by both societal changes and a contradictory

parenting-advice literature. In the face of these incompatible messages, many parents come to doubt their own importance. Berk argues that in view of the many factors in society that threaten children's development, parenting today not only matters, but matters more than ever.

In a similar vein, James Garbarino and Claire Bedard (2001), in *Parents under Siege,* address youth antagonism and violence, including the recent spate of heinous crimes resulting in family and school maimings and murders. Because multiple factors—including an impulsive, explosive temperament; unfavourable school experiences; and antisocial peer influences—contribute to these tragedies, parents are not to blame for them. But, Garbarino and Bedard emphasize, parents nevertheless bear considerable responsibility. They are often unaware of everyday experiences that lead their youngster down the path to violence.

In terms of solutions, most experts writing for parents affirm the need for greater adult involvement in children's lives. Berk (2001a) cites evidence that contemporary parents—even those with demanding careers—have more time than they are aware of to spend with children. She shows how essential cognitive, moral, and social capacities emerge from parent–child communication, in such seemingly mundane pursuits as a bedtime story, a homework assignment, or a family dinner. Garbarino and Bedard (2001) make a case for "empowered parenting," in which parents try to see the world through the young person's eyes by attending to his or her strengths and limitations while closely monitoring and, when necessary, intervening in the social environment. They also admonish

Parents often turn to books and magazines for expert advice on how to rear their children. The information they find reflects cultural beliefs and social realities of their times.

parents to provide a "moral compass of character" by insisting that children meet standards for personal achievement and caring for others.

Yet, increasingly, popular advice has underscored that parents cannot do the job alone; they need the help of a caring community and society. Hochschild (1997) appeals to employers to require working parents to leave earlier, for the sake of children. Hewlett and West (1998) call for an assault on policies that fail to provide parents with essential resources for rearing children effectively.

As you study child development, read one or more popular books on parenting and evaluate its advice on the basis of what you have learned. An old African proverb states, "It takes a village to rear a child." Is this view consistent with the focus of current theories on *contexts for development,* described later in this chapter?

# Mid-Twentieth-Century Theories

IN THE MID-TWENTIETH CENTURY, the field of child development expanded into a legitimate discipline. As child development attracted increasing interest, a variety of mid-twentieth-century theories emerged, each of which continues to have followers today. In these theories, the European concern with the child's inner thoughts and feelings contrasts sharply with the focus of North American academic psychology on scientific precision and concrete, observable behaviour.

## THE PSYCHOANALYTIC PERSPECTIVE

By the 1930s and 1940s, many parents whose children suffered from serious emotional stress and behaviour problems sought help from psychiatrists and social workers. The earlier normative movement had answered the question, What are children like? But child guidance professionals had to address the question, How and why do children become the way they are? They turned for help to the **psychoanalytic perspective** on personality development.

According to the psychoanalytic approach, children move through a series of stages in which they confront conflicts between biological drives and social expectations. The way these conflicts are resolved determines the individual's ability to learn, to get along with others, and to cope with anxiety. Although many individuals contributed to the psychoanalytic perspective, two have been especially influential: Sigmund Freud, founder of the psychoanalytic movement, and Erik Erikson.

 **FREUD'S THEORY.** Freud (1856–1939), a Viennese physician, saw in his practice patients with a variety of nervous symptoms, such as hallucinations, fears, and paralyses, that appeared to have no physical basis. Seeking a cure for these troubled adults, Freud found that their symptoms could be relieved by having patients talk freely about painful events of their childhood. On the basis of adult remembrances, he examined the unconscious motivations of his patients and constructed his **psychosexual theory**. It emphasized that how parents manage their child's sexual and aggressive drives in the first few years is crucial for healthy personality development.

*Three Parts of the Personality.* In Freud's theory, three parts of the personality—id, ego, and superego—become integrated during five stages (summarized in Table 1.2). The *id*, the largest portion of the mind, is the source of basic biological needs and desires. The *ego*—the conscious, rational part of personality—emerges in early infancy to redirect the id's impulses so they are discharged in acceptable ways. For example, aided by the ego, the hungry baby of a few months of age stops crying when he sees his mother unfasten her clothing for breast-feeding. And the more competent preschooler goes into the kitchen and gets a snack on her own.

Between 3 and 6 years of age, the *superego*, or conscience, develops from interactions with parents, who eventually insist that children conform to the values of society. Now the ego faces the increasingly complex task of reconciling the demands of the id, the external world, and conscience (Freud, 1923/1974). For example, when the ego is tempted to gratify an id impulse by hitting a playmate to get an attractive toy, the superego may warn that such behaviour is wrong. The ego must decide which of the two forces (id or superego) will win this inner struggle or work out a compromise, such as asking for a turn with the toy. According to Freud, the relations established between the id, ego, and superego during the preschool years determine the individual's basic personality.

*Psychosexual Development.* Freud believed that over the course of childhood, sexual impulses shift their focus from the oral to the anal to the genital regions of the body. In each stage, parents walk a fine line between permitting too much or too little gratification of their

**psychoanalytic perspective**
An approach to personality development introduced by Freud that assumes children move through a series of stages in which they confront conflicts between biological drives and social expectations. The way these conflicts are resolved determines psychological adjustment.

**psychosexual theory**
Freud's theory, which emphasizes that how parents manage their child's sexual and aggressive drives during the first few years is crucial for healthy personality development.

**psychosocial theory**
Erikson's theory, which emphasizes that at each Freudian stage, individuals not only develop a unique personality, but also acquire attitudes and skills that help them become active, contributing members of their society. Recognizes the lifespan nature of development and the impact of culture.

**TABLE** 1.2

Freud's Psychosexual Stages

| PSYCHOSEXUAL STAGE | APPROXIMATE AGE | DESCRIPTION |
| --- | --- | --- |
| Oral | Birth–1 year | The new ego directs the baby's sucking activities toward breast or bottle. If oral needs are not met appropriately, the individual may develop such habits as thumb sucking, fingernail biting, and pencil chewing in childhood, and overeating and smoking later in life. |
| Anal | 1–3 years | Young toddlers and preschoolers enjoy holding and releasing urine and feces. Toilet training becomes a major issue between parent and child. If parents insist that children be trained before they are ready or make too few demands, conflicts about anal control may appear in the form of extreme orderliness and cleanliness or messiness and disorder. |
| Phallic | 3–6 years | Id impulses transfer to the genitals, and the child finds pleasure in genital stimulation. Freud's Oedipus conflict for boys and Electra conflict for girls arise, and young children feel a sexual desire for the other-sex parent. To avoid punishment, they give up this desire and, instead, adopt the same-sex parent's characteristics and values. As a result, the superego is formed. The relations between id, ego, and superego established at this time determine the individual's basic personality. |
| Latency | 6–11 years | Sexual instincts die down, and the superego develops further. The child acquires new social values from adults outside the family and from play with same-sex peers. |
| Genital | Adolescence | Puberty causes the sexual impulses of the phallic stage to reappear. If development has been successful during earlier stages, it leads to mature sexuality, marriage, and the birth and rearing of children. |

child's basic needs. If parents strike an appropriate balance, then children grow into well-adjusted adults with the capacity for mature sexual behaviour, investment in family life, and rearing of the next generation.

Freud's psychosexual theory highlighted the importance of family relationships for children's development. It was the first theory to stress the role of early experience. But Freud's perspective was eventually criticized. First, the theory overemphasized the influence of sexual feelings in development. Second, because it was based only on the problems of sexually repressed, well-to-do adults, it did not apply in cultures differing from nineteenth-century Victorian society. Finally, Freud had not studied children directly.

**ERIKSON'S THEORY.** Several of Freud's followers took what was useful from his theory and improved on his vision. The most important of these neo-Freudians for the field of child development is Erik Erikson (1902–1994).

Although Erikson (1950) accepted Freud's basic psychosexual framework, he expanded the picture of development at each stage. In his **psychosocial theory,** Erikson emphasized that the ego does not just mediate between id impulses and superego demands. At each stage, it acquires attitudes and skills that make the individual an active, contributing member of society. A basic psychosocial conflict, which is resolved along a continuum from positive to negative, determines healthy or maladaptive outcomes at each stage. As Table 1.3 on page 18 shows, Erikson's first five stages parallel Freud's stages, but Erikson added three adult stages. He was one of the first to recognize the lifespan nature of development.

Finally, unlike Freud, Erikson pointed out that normal development must be understood in relation to each culture's life situation. For example, among the Yurok Indians on the northwest coast of the United States, babies are deprived of breast-feeding for the first 10 days after birth and instead are fed a thin soup from a small shell. At age 6 months, infants are abruptly weaned—if necessary, by having the mother leave for a few days. These experiences, from our cultural vantage point, might seem cruel. But Erikson explained that the Yurok live in a world in which salmon fill the river just once a year, a circumstance that requires considerable self-restraint for survival. In this way, he showed that child rearing can be understood only by making reference to the competencies valued and needed by the child's society.

Erik Erikson expanded Freud's theory, emphasizing the psychosocial outcomes of development. At each psychosexual stage, a major psychological conflict is resolved. If the outcome is positive, individuals acquire attitudes and skills that permit them to contribute constructively to society.

**TABLE** 1.3

Erikson's Psychosocial Stages, with Corresponding Psychosexual Stages Indicated

| PSYCHOSOCIAL STAGE | PERIOD OF DEVELOPMENT | DESCRIPTION |
| --- | --- | --- |
| Basic trust versus mistrust (Oral) | Birth–1 year | From warm, responsive care, infants gain a sense of trust, or confidence, that the world is good. Mistrust occurs when infants have to wait too long for comfort and are handled harshly. |
| Autonomy versus shame and doubt (Anal) | 1–3 years | Using new mental and motor skills, children want to choose and decide for themselves. Autonomy is fostered when parents permit reasonable free choice and do not force or shame the child. |
| Initiative versus guilt (Phallic) | 3–6 years | Through make-believe play, children experiment with the kind of person they can become. Initiative—a sense of ambition and responsibility—develops when parents support their child's new sense of purpose. The danger is that parents will demand too much self-control, which leads to overcontrol, meaning too much guilt. |
| Industry versus inferiority (Latency) | 6–11 years | At school, children develop the capacity to work and cooperate with others. Inferiority develops when negative experiences at home, at school, or with peers lead to feelings of incompetence. |
| Identity versus identity confusion (Genital) | Adolescence | The adolescent tries to answer the question, Who am I, and what is my place in society? Self-chosen values and vocational goals lead to a lasting personal identity. The negative outcome is confusion about future adult roles. |
| Intimacy versus isolation | Young adulthood | Young people work on establishing intimate ties to others. Because of earlier disappointments, some individuals cannot form close relationships and remain isolated. |
| Generativity versus stagnation | Middle adulthood | Generativity means giving to the next generation through child rearing, caring for other people, or productive work. The person who fails in these ways feels an absence of meaningful accomplishment. |
| Integrity versus despair | Old age | In this final stage, individuals reflect on the kind of person they have been. Integrity results from feeling that life was worth living as it happened. Old people who are dissatisfied with their lives fear death. |

**CONTRIBUTIONS AND LIMITATIONS OF THE PSYCHOANALYTIC PERSPECTIVE.** A special strength of the psychoanalytic perspective is its emphasis on the individual's unique life history as worthy of study and understanding (Emde, 1992). Consistent with this view, psychoanalytic theorists accept the *clinical method,* which synthesizes information from a variety of sources into a detailed picture of the personality of a single child. (We will discuss the clinical method further in Chapter 2.) Psychoanalytic theory has also inspired a wealth of research on many aspects of emotional and social development, including infant–caregiver attachment, aggression, sibling relationships, child-rearing practices, morality, gender roles, and adolescent identity.

Despite its extensive contributions, the psychoanalytic perspective is no longer in the mainstream of child development research (Cairns, 1998). Psychoanalytic theorists may have become isolated from the rest of the field because they were so strongly committed to the clinical approach that they failed to consider other methods. In addition, many psychoanalytic ideas, such as psychosexual stages and ego functioning, are so vague that they are difficult or impossible to test empirically (Thomas, 2000; Westen & Gabbard, 1999).

**BEHAVIOURISM AND SOCIAL LEARNING THEORY**

As psychoanalytic theory gained in prominence, child study was also influenced by a very different perspective: **behaviourism,** a tradition with philosophical roots in Locke's tabula rasa. Behaviourism began with the work of psychologist John Watson (1878–1958) in the

**behaviourism**
An approach that views directly observable events—stimuli and responses—as the appropriate focus of study, and the development of behaviour as taking place through classical and operant conditioning.

early twentieth century. Watson wanted to create an objective science of psychology. Unlike psychoanalytic theorists, he believed in studying directly observable events—stimuli and responses—rather than the unseen workings of the mind.

**TRADITIONAL BEHAVIOURISM.** Watson was inspired by studies of animal learning carried out by famous Russian physiologist Ivan Pavlov. Pavlov knew that dogs release saliva as an innate reflex when they are given food. But he noticed that his dogs were salivating before they tasted any food—when they saw the trainer who usually fed them. The dogs, Pavlov reasoned, must have learned to associate a neutral stimulus (the trainer) with another stimulus (food) that produces a reflexive response (salivation). As a result of this association, the neutral stimulus by itself could bring about a response resembling the reflex. Anxious to test this idea, Pavlov successfully taught dogs to salivate at the sound of a bell by pairing it with the presentation of food. He had discovered *classical conditioning*.

Watson wanted to find out if classical conditioning could be applied to children's behaviour. In a historic experiment, he taught Albert, an 11-month-old infant, to fear a neutral stimulus—a soft white rat—by presenting it several times with a sharp, loud sound, which naturally scared the baby. Little Albert, who at first had reached out eagerly to touch the furry rat, began to cry and turn his head away when he caught sight of it (Watson & Raynor, 1920). In fact, Albert's fear was so intense that researchers eventually questioned the ethics of studies like this one. On the basis of findings like these, Watson concluded that environment is the supreme force in child development. Adults could mould children's behaviour, he thought, by carefully controlling stimulus–response associations. And development consists of a gradual increase with age in the number and strength of these associations.

After Watson, behaviourism developed along several lines. The first was Clark Hull's *drive reduction theory*. According to this view, people continually act to satisfy physiological needs and reduce states of tension. As *primary drives* of hunger, thirst, and sex are met, a wide variety of stimuli associated with them become *secondary,* or *learned, drives*. For example, a Hullian theorist believes that infants prefer the closeness and attention of adults who have given them food and relieved their discomfort. To ensure these adults' affection, children will acquire all sorts of responses that adults desire of them—politeness, honesty, patience, persistence, obedience, and more.

Another form of behaviourism was B. F. Skinner's (1904–1990) *operant conditioning theory*. Skinner rejected Hull's idea that primary drive reduction is the only way to get children to learn. According to Skinner, a child's behaviour can be increased by following it with a wide variety of *reinforcers* besides food and drink, such as praise, a friendly smile, or a new toy. A behaviour can also be decreased through *punishment,* such as withdrawal of privileges, parental disapproval, or being sent to one's room. As a result of Skinner's work, operant conditioning became a broadly applied learning principle in child psychology. We will consider these conditioning principles more fully when we explore the infant's learning capacities in Chapter 4.

**SOCIAL LEARNING THEORY.** Psychologists quickly became interested in whether behaviourism might better explain the development of children's social behaviour than the less precise concepts of psychoanalytic theory. This concern sparked the emergence of **social learning theory.** Social learning theorists accepted and built on the principles of conditioning and reinforcement, offering expanded views of how children and adults acquire new responses. By the 1950s, social learning theory had become a major force in child development research.

Several kinds of social learning theory emerged. The most influential was devised by Albert Bandura and his colleagues. Bandura (1977) demonstrated that *modelling,* otherwise known as *imitation* or *observational learning,* is an important basis for children's behaviour. The baby who claps her hands after her mother does so, the child who angrily hits a playmate in the same way that he has been punished at home, and the teenager who wears the same clothes and hairstyle as her friends at school are all displaying observational learning.

Bandura's work continues to influence much research on children's social development. However, like changes in the field of child development as a whole, today his theory stresses

**social learning theory**
An approach that emphasizes the role of modelling, or observational learning, in the development of behaviour. Its most recent revision stresses the importance of thinking in social learning and is called *social-cognitive theory*.

the importance of *cognition,* or thinking. Bandura has shown that children's ability to listen, remember, and abstract general rules from complex sets of observed behaviour affects their imitation and learning. In fact, in the most recent revision of his theory, Bandura (1986, 1989, 1992) places such strong emphasis on how children think about themselves and other people that he calls it a *social-cognitive* rather than a social learning approach.

According to this view, children gradually become more selective in what they imitate. From watching others engage in self-praise and self-blame and through feedback about the worth of their own actions, children develop *personal standards* for behaviour and a *sense of self-efficacy*—beliefs about their own abilities and characteristics—that guide responses in particular situations (Bandura, 1999). For example, imagine a parent who often remarks, "I'm glad I kept working on that task, even though it was hard," who explains the value of persistence, and who encourages it by saying, "I know you can do a good job on that homework!" Soon the child starts to view himself as hardworking and high achieving and selects people with these characteristics as models.

**CONTRIBUTIONS AND LIMITATIONS OF BEHAVIOURISM AND SOCIAL LEARNING THEORY.** Behaviourism and social learning theory have had a major applied impact. **Behaviour modification** refers to procedures that combine conditioning and modelling to eliminate undesirable behaviours and increase desirable responses. It has been used to relieve a wide range of serious developmental problems, such as persistent aggression, language delays, and extreme fears (Pierce & Epling, 1995; Wolpe & Plaud, 1997). But it is also effective in dealing with common, everyday difficulties, including poor time management; unwanted habits, such as nail biting and smoking; and anxiety over such recurrent events as test taking, public speaking, and medical and dental treatments. In one study, preschoolers' anxious reactions during dental treatment were reduced by reinforcing them with small toys for answering questions about a story read to them while the dentist worked. Because the children could not listen to the story and kick and cry at the same time, their disruptive behaviours subsided (Stark et al., 1989).

Nevertheless, modelling and reinforcement do not provide a complete account of development (Horowitz, 1992). Many theorists believe that behaviourism and social learning theory offer too narrow a view of important environmental influences. These extend beyond immediate reinforcements and modelled behaviours to children's rich physical and social worlds. Finally, behaviourism and social learning theory have been criticized for underestimating children's contributions to their own development. In emphasizing cognition, Bandura is unique among theorists whose work grew out of the behaviourist tradition in granting children an active role in their own learning.

### PIAGET'S COGNITIVE-DEVELOPMENTAL THEORY

If one individual has influenced the contemporary field of child development more than any other, it is Swiss cognitive theorist Jean Piaget (1896–1980). North American investigators had been aware of Piaget's work since 1930. However, they did not grant it much attention until the 1960s, mainly because Piaget's ideas and methods of studying children were very much at odds with behaviourism, which dominated North American psychology during the middle of the twentieth century (Zigler & Gilman, 1998). Piaget did not believe that knowledge could be imposed on a reinforced child. According to his **cognitive-developmental theory,** children actively construct knowledge as they manipulate and explore their world.

**PIAGET'S STAGES.** Piaget's view of development was greatly influenced by his early training in biology. Central to his theory is the biological concept of *adaptation* (Piaget, 1971). Just as the structures of the body are adapted to fit with the environment, so the structures of the mind develop to better fit with, or represent, the external world. In infancy and early childhood, children's understanding is very different from adults'. For example, Piaget believed that young babies do not realize that an object hidden from view—a favourite toy or even the mother—

**behaviour modification**
Procedures that combine conditioning and modelling to eliminate undesirable behaviours and increase desirable responses.

**cognitive-developmental theory**
An approach introduced by Piaget that views children as actively constructing knowledge as they manipulate and explore their world, and cognitive development as taking place in stages.

continues to exist. He also concluded that preschoolers' thinking is full of faulty logic. For example, children younger than age 7 commonly say that the amount of milk or lemonade changes when it is poured into a differently shaped container. According to Piaget, children eventually revise these incorrect ideas in their ongoing efforts to achieve an *equilibrium,* or balance, between internal structures and information they encounter in their everyday worlds.

In Piaget's theory, as the brain develops and children's experiences expand, they move through four broad stages, each characterized by qualitatively distinct ways of thinking. Table 1.4 provides a brief description of Piaget's stages. In the *sensorimotor stage,* cognitive development begins with the baby's use of the senses and movements to explore the world. These action patterns evolve into the symbolic but illogical thinking of the preschooler in the *preoperational stage.* Then cognition is transformed into the more organized reasoning of the school-age child in the *concrete operational stage.* Finally, in the *formal operational stage,* thought becomes the complex, abstract reasoning system of the adolescent and adult.

Through careful observations of and clinical interviews with children, Jean Piaget developed his comprehensive theory of cognitive development. His work has inspired more research on children than any other theory.

■ **PIAGET'S METHODS OF STUDY.** Piaget devised special methods for investigating how children think. In his early career, he carefully observed his three infant children and presented them with everyday problems, such as an attractive object that could be grasped, mouthed, kicked, or searched for. From their reactions, Piaget derived ideas about cognitive changes during the first 2 years. In studying childhood and adolescent thought, Piaget took advantage of children's ability to describe their thinking. He adapted the clinical method of psychoanalysis, conducting open-ended *clinical interviews* in which a child's initial response to a task served as the basis for the next question he would ask. We will look more closely at this technique in Chapter 2.

■ **CONTRIBUTIONS AND LIMITATIONS OF PIAGET'S THEORY.** Piaget's cognitive-developmental perspective convinced the field that children are active learners whose minds consist of rich structures of knowledge. Besides investigating children's understanding of the physical world, Piaget explored their reasoning about the social world. As we will see in Chapters 11 and 12, Piaget's stages have sparked a wealth of research on children's conceptions of themselves, other people, and human relationships. Practically speaking, Piaget's theory encouraged the development of educational philosophies and programs that emphasize discovery learning and direct contact with the environment.

Despite Piaget's overwhelming contributions, in recent years his theory has been challenged. Research indicates that Piaget underestimated the competencies of infants and

**TABLE** 1.4

Piaget's Stages of Cognitive Development

| STAGE | PERIOD OF DEVELOPMENT | DESCRIPTION |
|---|---|---|
| Sensorimotor | Birth–2 years | Infants "think" by acting on the world with their eyes, ears, hands, and mouth. As a result, they invent ways of solving sensorimotor problems, such as pulling a lever to hear the sound of a music box, finding hidden toys, and putting objects in and taking them out of containers. |
| Preoperational | 2–7 years | Preschool children use symbols to represent their earlier sensorimotor discoveries. Development of language and make-believe play takes place. However, thinking lacks the logic of the two remaining stages. |
| Concrete operational | 7–11 years | Children's reasoning becomes logical. School-age children understand that a certain amount of lemonade or play dough remains the same even after its appearance changes. They also organize objects into hierarchies of classes and subclasses. However, thinking falls short of adult intelligence. It is not yet abstract. |
| Formal operational | 11 years and older | The capacity for abstraction permits adolescents to reason with symbols that do not refer to objects in the real world, as in advanced mathematics. They can also think of all possible outcomes in a scientific problem, not just the most obvious ones. |

preschoolers. We will see in Chapter 6 that when young children are given tasks scaled down in difficulty, their understanding appears closer to that of the older child and adult than Piaget believed. This discovery has led many researchers to conclude that the maturity of children's thinking may depend on their familiarity with the task and the kind of knowledge sampled. Furthermore, many studies show that children's performance on Piagetian problems can be improved with training (Caracciolo, Moderato, & Perini, 1988). This finding raises questions about his assumption that discovery learning rather than adult teaching is the best way to foster development. Finally, critics point out that Piaget's stagewise account pays insufficient attention to social and cultural influences—and the resulting wide variation in thinking that exists among same-age children (Rogoff & Chavajay, 1995).

Today, the field of child development is divided over its loyalty to Piaget's ideas. Those who continue to find merit in Piaget's approach accept a modified view of his cognitive stages—one in which changes in the quality of children's thinking take place more gradually than Piaget believed (Bidell & Fischer, 1992; Case, 1992, 1998). Others have turned to an approach that emphasizes continuous rather than stagewise gains in children's cognition: information processing. And still others have been drawn to theories that focus on the role of children's social and cultural contexts. We take up these approaches in the next section.

**ASK YOURSELF** www

*[handwritten annotations: Simil. - 1st 5 stages    diff - Erik. expanded at each stage - 3 more adult stages - Erikson - normal devl in relation to cultures life situation    Freud focused on interaction of id, ego, superego]*

**review**    Cite similarities and differences between Freud's and Erikson's views of development. *[handwritten: sim- 1st 5 stages similar]*

**review**    What aspect of behaviourism made it attractive to critics of psychoanalytic theory? How does Piaget's theory respond to a major limitation of behaviourism? *[handwritten: -behaviourism studied directly observable events (stimuli+response) rather than unseen mind.]*

**review**    Why is the field of child development divided over its loyalty to Piaget's ideas?

**apply**    A 4-year-old becomes frightened of the dark and refuses to go to sleep at night. How would a psychoanalyst and a behaviourist differ in their views of how this problem developed?

**connect**    Although social learning theory focuses on social development and Piaget's theory on cognitive development, they have enhanced our understanding of other domains as well. Mention an additional domain addressed by each theory.

# Recent Theoretical Perspectives

NEW WAYS OF understanding children are constantly emerging—questioning, building on, and enhancing the discoveries of earlier theories. Today, a burst of fresh approaches and research emphases, including information processing, ethology, Vygotsky's sociocultural theory, ecological systems theory, and the dynamic systems perspective, are broadening our understanding of child development.

## INFORMATION PROCESSING

During the 1970s, researchers turned to the field of cognitive psychology for ways to understand the development of children's thinking. Today, a leading perspective is **information processing,** a general approach that emerged with the design of digital computers that use mathematically specified steps to solve problems. These systems suggested to psychologists that the human mind might also be viewed as a symbol-manipulating system through which information flows (Klahr & MacWhinney, 1998). From the time information is presented to the senses at *input* until it emerges as a behavioural response at *output,* information is actively coded, transformed, and organized.

**information processing**
An approach that views the human mind as a symbol-manipulating system through which information flows and that regards cognitive development as a continuous process.

FIGURE 1.2

**Information-processing flow-chart showing the steps that a 5-year-old used to solve a bridge-building problem.** Her task was to use blocks varying in size, shape, and weight, some of which were plank-like, to construct a bridge across a "river" (painted on a floor mat) too wide for any single block to span. The child discovered how to counterweight and balance the bridge, without prior knowledge. The orange arrows reveal that even after building a successful counterweight, she returned to earlier unsuccessful strategies, which seemed to help her understand why the counterweight approach worked. (Adapted from Thornton, 1999.)

Information-processing researchers often use flowcharts to map the precise steps individuals use to solve problems and complete tasks, much like the plans devised by programmers to get computers to perform a series of "mental operations." Let's look at an example to clarify the usefulness of this approach. In a study of children's problem solving, a researcher provided a pile of blocks varying in size, shape, and weight and asked 5- to 9-year-olds to build a bridge across a "river" (painted on a floor mat) that was too wide for any single block to span (Thornton, 1999). Figure 1.2 shows one solution to the problem: two plank-like blocks span the water, each held in place by the counterweight of heavy blocks on the bridge's towers.

Whereas many children age 7 and older built successful bridges, only one 5-year-old did, after initially using unsuccessful strategies—first, trying to find a plank long enough to span the water, then trying to push two planks together. A careful analysis of her efforts revealed that small problem-solving steps (squeezing planks to join them; then pressing down on their ends to hold them in place) triggered novel problem-solving approaches (using blocks as counterweights, creating stable towers) that could not be predicted by the child's original, incorrect strategies. The findings show how a child's actions within a task can facilitate problem solving. This child had no prior understanding of counterweight and balance. Yet she arrived at just as effective a solution as did older children, who came with considerable task-relevant knowledge.

A wide variety of information-processing models exist. Some, like the one just considered, track children's mastery of one or a few tasks. Others describe the human cognitive system as a whole (Atkinson & Shiffrin, 1968; Lockhart & Craik, 1990). These general models are used as guides for asking questions about broad age changes in children's thinking. For example, does a child's ability to search the environment for information needed to solve a problem become more organized and planful with age? What strategies do younger and older children use to remember new information, and how do those strategies affect their recall?

The information-processing approach is also being used to clarify the processing of social information. For example, flowcharts exist that track the steps that children use to solve social problems (such as how to enter an ongoing play group) and acquire gender-linked preferences and behaviours (Crick & Dodge, 1994; Ruble & Martin, 1998). If we can identify how social problem solving and gender stereotyping arise in childhood, then we can design interventions that promote more favourable social development.

Like Piaget's cognitive-developmental theory, the information-processing approach regards children as active, sense-making beings who modify their own thinking in response to environmental demands (Klahr & MacWhinney, 1998). But unlike Piaget's theory, there are no stages of development. Rather, the thought processes studied—perception, attention, memory, planning strategies, categorization of information, and comprehension of written and spoken prose—are regarded as similar at all ages but present to a lesser extent in children. Therefore, the view of development is one of continuous increase.

A great strength of the information-processing approach is its commitment to careful, rigorous research methods. Because it has provided precise accounts of how children of different ages engage in many aspects of thinking, its findings have led to teaching interventions that help children approach tasks in more advanced ways (Geary, 1994; Siegler, 1998). But information processing has fallen short in some respects. Although good at analyzing thinking into its components, it has difficulty putting them back together into a comprehensive theory of development. In addition, aspects of cognition that are not linear and logical, such as imagination and creativity, are all but ignored by this approach (Lutz & Sternberg, 1999). Furthermore, much information-processing research has been conducted in laboratories rather than real-life situations. Recently, investigators have addressed this concern by focusing on more realistic materials and activities. Today, they study children's conversations, stories, memory for everyday events, and strategies for performing academic tasks.

A major advantage of having many theories is that they encourage one another to attend to previously neglected dimensions of children's lives. A unique feature of the final four perspectives we will discuss is a focus on *contexts* for development—the way children's biological makeup combines with environmental circumstances to affect pathways of change. The first of these views emphasizes that the development of many capacities is influenced by our long evolutionary history.

## ETHOLOGY AND EVOLUTIONARY DEVELOPMENTAL PSYCHOLOGY

**Ethology** is concerned with the adaptive, or survival, value of behaviour and its evolutionary history (Dewsbury, 1992; Hinde, 1989). Its roots can be traced to the work of Darwin. Two European zoologists, Konrad Lorenz and Niko Tinbergen, laid its modern foundations. Watching diverse animal species in their natural habitats, Lorenz and Tinbergen observed behaviour patterns that promote survival. The best known of these is *imprinting*, the early following behaviour of certain baby birds that ensures that the young will stay close to the mother and be fed and protected from danger. Imprinting takes place during an early, restricted time period of development. If the mother goose is not present during this time, but an object resembling her in important features is, young goslings may imprint on it instead (Lorenz, 1952).

Observations of imprinting led to a major concept that has been widely applied in child development: the *critical period*. It refers to a limited time span during which the child is biologically prepared to acquire certain adaptive behaviours but needs the support of an appropriately stimulating environment. Many researchers have conducted studies to find out whether complex cognitive and social behaviours must be learned during certain time periods. For example, if children are deprived of adequate food or physical and social stimulation during their early years, will their intelligence be impaired? If language is not mastered during early childhood, is the child's capacity to acquire it reduced?

**ethology**
An approach concerned with the adaptive, or survival, value of behaviour and its evolutionary history.

In later chapters, we will discover that the term *sensitive period* offers a better account of human development than does the strict notion of a critical period (Bornstein, 1989). A **sensitive period** is a time that is optimal for certain capacities to emerge because the individual is especially responsive to environmental influences. However, its boundaries are less well defined than are those of a critical period. Development may occur later, but it is harder to induce.

Inspired by observations of imprinting, British psychoanalyst John Bowlby (1969) applied ethological theory to the understanding of the human infant–caregiver relationship. He argued that attachment behaviours of babies, such as smiling, babbling, grasping, and crying, are built-in social signals that encourage the parent to approach, care for, and interact with the baby. By keeping the mother near, these behaviours help ensure that the infant will be fed, protected from danger, and provided with stimulation and affection necessary for healthy growth.

NINA LEEN/LIFE MAGAZINE © TIME WARNER

Konrad Lorenz was one of the founders of ethology and a keen observer of animal behaviour. He developed the concept of imprinting. Here, young geese who were separated from their mother and placed in the company of Lorenz during an early, critical period show that they have imprinted on him. They follow him about as he swims through the water, a response that promotes survival.

The development of attachment in human infants is a lengthy process that leads the baby to form a deep affectional tie with the caregiver (Main, 1995). As we will see in Chapter 10, it is far more complex than imprinting in baby birds. But for now, note how the ethological view of attachment, which emphasizes the role of innate infant signals, differs sharply from the behaviourist drive-reduction explanation mentioned earlier—that the baby's desire for closeness to the mother is a learned response based on feeding.

Observations by ethologists have shown that many aspects of children's social behaviour, including emotional expressions, aggression, cooperation, and play, resemble those of our primate relatives. Recently, researchers have forged a new arena of theory and research, called **evolutionary developmental psychology.** They seek to understand the adaptive value of species-wide cognitive, emotional, and social competencies as those competencies change over time. Evolutionary developmental psychologists ask such questions as, What role does the newborn's visual preference for facelike stimuli play in survival? Does it support older infants' capacity to distinguish familiar caregivers from unfamiliar (and potentially threatening) people? How do children come to play in sex-segregated groups? What do they learn from such play that might lead to adult gender-typed behaviours, such as male dominance and female investment in caregiving?

As these examples suggest, evolutionary psychologists are not just concerned with the genetic and biological roots of development. They are also interested in how individuals learn because learning lends flexibility and greater adaptiveness to behaviour. They recognize that today's lifestyles differ so radically from those of our evolutionary ancestors that certain evolved behaviours (such as adolescent life-threatening risk taking and male-to-male violence) are no longer adaptive (Geary, 1999). By clarifying the origins and development of such behaviours, evolutionary developmental psychology may help spark more effective interventions.

In sum, the interests of evolutionary psychologists are broad. They want to understand the entire *organism–environment system* (Bjorklund & Pellegrini, 2000). The next contextual perspective we will discuss, Vygotsky's sociocultural theory, serves as an excellent complement to the evolutionary viewpoint, since it highlights the social and cultural dimensions of children's experiences.

## VYGOTSKY'S SOCIOCULTURAL THEORY

The field of child development has recently seen a dramatic increase in studies addressing the cultural context of children's lives. Investigations that make comparisons across cultures, and between ethnic groups within cultures, provide insight into whether developmental pathways apply to all children or are limited to particular environmental conditions. As a result,

**sensitive period**
A time that is optimal for certain capacities to emerge because the individual is especially responsive to environmental influences.

**evolutionary developmental psychology**
An approach that seeks to understand the adaptive value of species-wide cognitive, emotional, and social competencies as those competencies change over time.

According to Lev Vygotsky, many cognitive processes and skills are socially transferred from more knowledgeable members of society to children. Vygotsky's sociocultural theory helps us understand the wide variation in cognitive competencies from culture to culture. Vygotsky is pictured here with his daughter.

This girl of Bali, Indonesia, is learning traditional dance steps through the guidance of an adult expert. According to Vygotsky's theory, social interaction between children and more knowledgeable members of their culture leads to knowledge and skills essential for success in that culture.

cross-cultural and multicultural research helps untangle the contributions of biological and environmental factors to the timing, order of appearance, and diversity of children's behaviours (Greenfield, 1994).

In the past, researchers focused on broad cultural differences in development—for example, whether children in one culture are more advanced in motor development or do better on intellectual tasks than children in another culture. However, this approach can lead us to conclude incorrectly that one culture is superior in enhancing development, whereas another is deficient. In addition, it does not help us understand the precise experiences that contribute to cultural differences in children's behaviour.

Today, more research is examining the relationship of *culturally specific practices* to child development. The contributions of Russian psychologist Lev Vygotsky (1896–1934) have played a major role in this trend. Vygotsky's (1934/1987) perspective is called **sociocultural theory.** It focuses on how *culture*—the values, beliefs, customs, and skills of a social group—is transmitted to the next generation. According to Vygotsky, *social interaction*—in particular, cooperative dialogues between children and more knowledgeable members of society—is necessary for children to acquire the ways of thinking and behaving that make up a community's culture (Wertsch & Tulviste, 1992). Vygotsky believed that as adults and more-expert peers help children master culturally meaningful activities, the communication between them becomes part of children's thinking. As children internalize the essential features of these dialogues, they use the language within them to guide their own thought and actions and acquire new skills (Berk, 2002). The young child instructing herself while working a puzzle or tying her shoes has started to produce the same kind of guiding comments that an adult previously used to help the child master important tasks.

Vygotsky's theory has been especially influential in the study of children's cognition. Vygotsky agreed with Piaget that children are active, constructive beings. But unlike Piaget, who emphasized children's independent efforts to make sense of their world, Vygotsky viewed cognitive development as a *socially mediated process*—as dependent on the support that adults and more mature peers provide as children try new tasks.

In Vygotsky's theory, children undergo certain stagewise transformations. For example, with the acquisition of language, their ability to participate in dialogues with others is greatly enhanced, and mastery of culturally adaptive competencies surges forward. When children enter school, they spend much time discussing language, literacy, and other academic concepts—experiences that encourage them to reflect on their own thinking. As a result, they show dramatic gains in reasoning and problem solving.

At the same time, Vygotsky stressed that dialogues with experts lead to continuous changes in cognition that vary greatly from culture to culture. Consistent with this view, a major finding of cross-cultural research is that cultures select different tasks for children's learning (Rogoff & Chavajay, 1995). For example, among the Zinacanteco Indians of southern Mexico, girls become skilled weavers at an early age through the informal guidance of adult experts (Childs & Greenfield, 1982). In Brazil, child candy sellers with little or no schooling develop sophisticated mathematical abilities as the result of buying candy from wholesalers, pricing it in collaboration with adults and experienced peers, and bargaining with customers on city streets (Saxe, 1988). And as the research reported in the Cultural Influences box on the following page indicates, adults encourage culturally valued skills in children at a very early age.

Vygotsky's theory, and the research stimulated by it, reveals that children in every culture develop unique strengths. At the same time, Vygotsky's emphasis on culture and social experience led him to neglect the biological side of development. Although he recognized the importance of heredity and brain growth, he said little about their role in cognitive change. Furthermore, Vygotsky's focus on social transmission of knowledge meant that he placed less emphasis than did other theorists on children's capacity to shape their own development. Contemporary followers of Vygotsky grant the individual and society more balanced roles (Rogoff, 1998; Wertsch & Tulviste, 1992).

# cultural influences

## !KUNG INFANCY: ACQUIRING CULTURE

*i*nteractions between caregivers and infants take different forms in different cultures. Through those interactions, adults begin to transmit their society's values and skills to the next generation, channelling the course of future development.

Focusing on a culture very different from our own, researchers studied how caregivers respond to infants' play with objects among the !Kung, a hunting-and-gathering society living in the desert regions of Botswana, Africa (Bakeman et al., 1990). Daily foraging missions take small numbers of adults several kilometres from the campground, but most obtain enough food to contribute to group survival by working only 3 out of every 7 days. A mobile way of life also prevents the !Kung from collecting many possessions that require extensive care and maintenance. Adults have many free hours to relax around the campfire, and they spend it in intense social contact with one another and with children (Draper & Cashdan, 1988).

In this culture of intimate social bonds and minimal property, objects are valued as things to be shared, not as personal possessions. This message is conveyed to !Kung children at a very

!Kung children grow up in a hunting-and-gathering society in which possessions are a burden rather than an asset. From an early age, children experience warm social contact with adults and are taught the importance of sharing. ◼

IRVEN DEVORE/ANTHRO-PHOTO

early age. Between 6 and 12 months, grandmothers start to train babies in the importance of exchanging objects by guiding them in handing beads to relatives. The child's first words generally include *i* ("Here, take this") and *na* ("Give it to me").

In !Kung society, no toys are made for infants. Instead, natural objects, such as twigs, grass, stones, and nutshells, are always available, along with cooking implements. However, adults do not encourage babies to play with these objects. In fact, adults are unlikely to interact with infants while they are exploring objects independently. But when a baby offers an object to another person, adults become highly responsive, encouraging and vocalizing much more than at other times. Thus, the !Kung cultural emphasis on the interpersonal rather than physical aspects of existence is reflected in how

adults interact with the very youngest members of their community.

When you next have a chance, observe the conditions under which parents in your own society respond to infants' involvement with objects. How is parental responsiveness linked to cultural values? How does it compare with findings on the !Kung?

---

## ECOLOGICAL SYSTEMS THEORY

Urie Bronfenbrenner, a U.S. psychologist, is responsible for an approach that has risen to the forefront of the field over the past 2 decades because it offers the most differentiated and complete account of contextual influences on children's development. **Ecological systems theory** views the child as developing within a complex *system* of relationships affected by multiple levels of the surrounding environment. Since the child's biological dispositions join with environmental forces to mould development, Bronfenbrenner recently characterized his perspective as a *bioecological model* (Bronfenbrenner & Evans, 2000).

As Figure 1.3 on page 28 shows, Bronfenbrenner envisions the environment as a series of nested structures that includes but extends beyond home, school, and neighbourhood settings in which children spend their everyday lives. Each layer of the environment is viewed as having a powerful impact on children's development.

**sociocultural theory**
Vygotsky's theory, in which children acquire the ways of thinking and behaving that make up a community's culture through cooperative dialogues with more knowledgeable members of society.

**ecological systems theory**
Bronfenbrenner's approach, which views the child as developing within a complex system of relationships affected by multiple levels of the surrounding environment, from immediate settings of family and school to broad cultural values and programs.

FIGURE 1.3

**Structure of the environment in ecological systems theory.** The *microsystem* includes relations between the developing person and the immediate environment; the *mesosystem*, connections between immediate settings; the *exosystem*, social settings that affect but do not contain the child; and the *macrosystem*, the values, laws, customs, and resources of the culture that affect activities and interactions at all inner layers. The *chronosystem* (not pictured) is not a specific context. Instead, it refers to the dynamic, ever-changing nature of the child's environment.

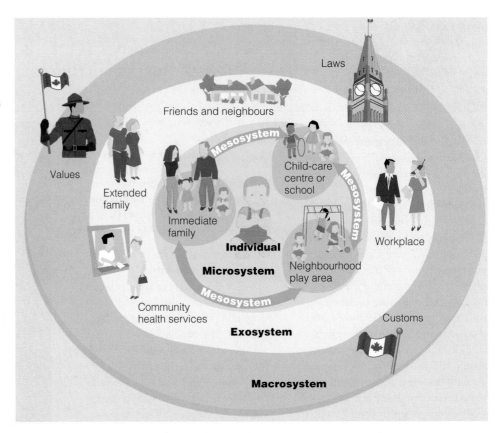

**THE MICROSYSTEM.** The innermost level of the environment is the **microsystem,** which refers to activities and interaction patterns in the child's immediate surroundings. Bronfenbrenner emphasizes that to understand child development at this level, we must keep in mind that all relationships are *bidirectional.* That is, adults affect children's behaviour, but children's characteristics—their physical attributes, personalities, and capacities—also affect the adults' behaviour. For example, a friendly, attentive child is likely to evoke positive and patient reactions from parents, whereas a distractible youngster is more likely to receive restriction and punishment. When these reciprocal interactions occur often over time, they have an enduring impact on development (Bronfenbrenner, 1995; Collins et al., 2000).

Third parties also affect whether parent–child (or other two-person) relationships enhance or undermine development. If other individuals in the setting are supportive, the quality of relationships is enhanced. For example, when parents encourage one another in their child-rearing roles, each engages in more effective parenting (Cowan, Powell, & Cowan, 1998). In contrast, marital conflict is associated with inconsistent discipline and hostile reactions toward children. In response, children typically become hostile, and their adjustment suffers (Hetherington, Bridges, & Insabella, 1998).

**THE MESOSYSTEM.** The second level of Bronfenbrenner's model, the **mesosystem,** encompasses connections between microsystems, such as home, school, neighbourhood, and child-care centre. For example, a child's academic progress depends not just on activities that take place in classrooms. It is also promoted by parental involvement in school life and the extent to which academic learning is carried over into the home (Connors & Epstein, 1996). Similarly, parent–child interaction is likely to be affected by the child's relationships with caregivers at child care, and vice versa. Parent–child and caregiver–child relationships are each likely to support development when links, in the form of visits and exchange of information, are built between home and child-care setting.

**microsystem**
In ecological systems theory, the activities and interaction patterns in the child's immediate surroundings.

**mesosystem**
In ecological systems theory, connections between children's immediate settings.

**THE EXOSYSTEM.** The **exosystem** refers to social settings that do not contain children but nevertheless affect their experiences in immediate settings. These can be formal organizations, such as the parents' workplace or health and welfare services in the community. For example, flexible work schedules, paid maternity and paternity leave, and sick leave for parents whose children are ill are ways that work settings can help parents rear children and, indirectly, enhance development. Exosystem supports can also be informal, such as parents' social networks—friends and extended-family members who provide advice, companionship, and even financial assistance. Research confirms the negative impact of a breakdown in exosystem activities. Families with few personal or community-based ties show increased rates of conflict and child abuse (Emery & Laumann-Billings, 1998).

**THE MACROSYSTEM.** The outermost level of Bronfenbrenner's model, the **macrosystem,** consists of cultural values, laws, customs, and resources. The priority that the macrosystem gives to children's needs affects the support they receive at inner levels of the environment. For example, in countries that require high-quality standards for child care and workplace benefits for employed parents, children are more likely to have favourable experiences in their immediate settings.

**AN EVER-CHANGING SYSTEM.** According to Bronfenbrenner, the environment is not a static force that affects children in a uniform way. Instead, it is ever-changing. Important life events, such as the birth of a sibling, the beginning of school, or parents' divorce, modify existing relationships between children and their environments, producing new conditions that affect development. In addition, the timing of environmental change affects its impact. The arrival of a new sibling has very different consequences for a homebound toddler than for a school-age child with many relationships and activities beyond the family.

Bronfenbrenner refers to the temporal dimension of his model as the **chronosystem** (the prefix *chrono-* means "time"). Changes in life events can be imposed on the child, as in the examples just given. But they can also arise from within the child, since as children get older they select, modify, and create many of their own settings and experiences. How they do so depends on their physical, intellectual, and personality characteristics and their environmental opportunities. Therefore, in ecological systems theory, development is neither controlled by environmental circumstances nor driven by inner dispositions. Instead, children are both products and producers of their environments, in a network of interdependent effects. Notice how our discussion of resilient children on page 10 illustrates this idea. We will see many more examples in this book.

## NEW DIRECTIONS: DEVELOPMENT AS A DYNAMIC SYSTEM

Today, researchers recognize both consistency and variability in child development and want to do a better job of explaining variation. Consequently, a new wave of theorists has adopted a **dynamic systems perspective** on development (Fischer & Bidell, 1998; Thelen & Smith, 1998; Wachs, 2000). According to this view, the child's mind, body, and physical and social worlds form an *integrated system* that guides mastery of new skills. The system is *dynamic,* or constantly in motion. A change in any part of it—from brain growth to physical and social surroundings—disrupts the current organism–environment relationship. When this happens, the child actively reorganizes her behaviour so that the components of the system work together again but in a more complex, effective way.

Researchers adopting a dynamic systems perspective try to find out just how children attain new levels of organization by studying their behaviour while they are in transition. For example, when presented with an attractive toy, how does a 3-month-old baby who shows many, varied movements discover how to reach for it? On hearing a new word, how does a 2-year-old figure out the category of objects or events to which it refers?

Urie Bronfenbrenner is the originator of ecological systems theory. He views the child as developing within a complex system of relationships affected by multiple levels of the surrounding environment, from immediate settings to broad cultural values, laws, and customs.

**exosystem**
In ecological systems theory, social settings that do not contain children but nevertheless affect their experiences in immediate settings. Examples are parents' workplace and health and welfare services in the community, as well as parents' social networks.

**macrosystem**
In ecological systems theory, cultural values, laws, customs, and resources that influence experiences and interactions at inner levels of the environment.

**chronosystem**
In ecological systems theory, temporal changes in children's environments, which produce new conditions that affect development. These changes can be imposed externally or arise from within the child.

**dynamic systems perspective**
A view that regards the child's mind, body, and physical and social worlds as a dynamic, integrated system. A change in any part of the system leads the child to reorganize her behaviour so the components of the system work together again but in a more complex and effective way.

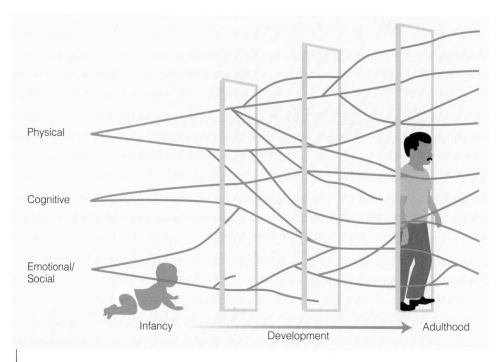

Physical

Cognitive

Emotional/
Social

Infancy

Development

Adulthood

**FIGURE** 1.4

**The dynamic systems view of development.** Rather than envisioning a single line of stagewise or continuous change (refer to Figure 1.1 on page 7), dynamic systems theorists conceive of development as a web of fibres branching out in many directions. Each strand in the web represents a potential area of skill within the major domains of development—physical, cognitive, and emotional/social. The differing directions of the strands signify possible variations in paths and outcomes as the child masters skills necessary to participate in diverse contexts. The interconnections of the strands within the vertical windows portray stagelike changes—periods of major transformation in which various skills work together as a functioning whole. As the web expands, skills become more numerous, complex, and effective. (Adapted from Fischer & Bidell, 1998.)

Dynamic systems theorists acknowledge that a common human genetic heritage and basic regularities in children's physical and social worlds yield certain universal, broad outlines of development. But biological makeup, everyday tasks, and the people who support children in mastery of those tasks vary greatly, leading to wide individual differences in specific skills. Even when children master the same skills, such as walking, talking, or adding and subtracting, they often do so in unique ways. And because children build competencies by engaging in real activities in real contexts, different skills vary in maturity within the same child. From this perspective, development cannot be characterized as a single line of change. As Figure 1.4 shows, it is more like a web of fibres branching out in many directions, each of which represents a different skill area that may undergo continuous and stagewise transformations (Fischer & Bidell, 1998).

Although these children are about the same age, they vary widely in competencies. The dynamic systems perspective aims to explain this variation by examining how the child's mind, body, and physical and social worlds form an integrated system that guides mastery of new skills.

The dynamic systems view has been inspired by other scientific disciplines, especially biology and physics. In addition, it draws on information-processing and contextual theories—evolutionary developmental psychology, sociocultural theory, and ecological systems theory. At present, dynamic systems research is in its early stages. The perspective has largely been applied to children's motor and cognitive skills, but some investigators think that it might explain emotional and social development as well (Fogel, 2000; Lewis, 2000). Today, researchers are analyzing development in all its complexity, in search of an all-encompassing approach to understanding change.

## ASK YOURSELF www

*[handwritten: children's independent efforts to make sense of world.]*

**review** What features of Vygotsky's sociocultural theory distinguish it from Piaget's cognitive-developmental theory?

*[handwritten: - social interaction necessary (co-operative dialogue) — Cognitive devel. as a social mediated process]*

**review** Explain how each recent theoretical perspective regards children as active, purposeful beings who contribute to their own development.

*[handwritten: info processing - thought process studied - perception, memory, planning, strategies + attention]*
*[handwritten: Socioccultural - learning by social interaction]*

**apply** Return to the Biology & Environment box on page 10. How does the story of John and Gary illustrate bidirectional influences within the microsystem, as described in ecological systems theory?

**connect** How does ecological systems theory differ from psychoanalytic theory in its explanation of parents' influence on children's development?

*[handwritten: Ecological System Theory ⤷multiple levels that effect child dev. ⤷bi directional relationships.]*

*[handwritten: Dynamic System ⤷ mind, body + physical/social worlds all guide new skills learning]*

## Comparing Child Development Theories

IN THE PRECEDING sections, we reviewed major theoretical perspectives in child development research. They differ in many respects. First, they focus on different domains of development. Psychoanalytic theory and ethology emphasize children's emotional and social development. Piaget's cognitive-developmental theory, information processing, and Vygotsky's sociocultural theory stress changes in children's thinking. The remaining approaches—behaviourism, social learning theory, evolutionary developmental psychology, ecological systems theory, and the dynamic systems perspective—discuss many aspects of children's functioning.

Second, every theory contains a point of view about development. As we conclude our review of theoretical perspectives, identify the stand each theory takes on the controversial issues presented at the beginning of this chapter. Then check your analysis against Table 1.5 on page 32.

Finally, we have seen that theories have strengths and weaknesses. Perhaps you found that you were attracted to some theories, but you had doubts about others. As you read more about child development in later chapters, you may find it useful to keep a notebook in which you test your theoretical likes and dislikes against the evidence. Don't be surprised if you revise your ideas many times, just as theorists have done throughout this century.

## Applied Directions:
## Child Development and Social Policy

IN RECENT YEARS, the field of child development has become increasingly concerned with applying its vast knowledge base to solving pressing social problems. At the dawn of a new millennium, we know much more than ever before about family, school, and community contexts that foster physically healthy and cognitively and socially competent children. Although many Canadian children fare well, a substantial minority do *not*. Consider the following **childhood social indicators,** or periodic measures of children's health, living conditions, and psychological well-being.

- **Poverty.** Although the poverty rate in Canada in 1998 was the lowest in 7 years, poverty is still a serious problem. Approximately 19 percent of Canadians under age 18—or 1.5 million young people—are affected. This means that close to one in five children lives in poverty, a rate similar to that in the United States. Moreover, between 1993 and 1998

**childhood social indicators**
Periodic measures of children's health, living conditions, and psychological well-being that lend insight into their overall status in a community, region, or nation.

**TABLE** 1.5

Stance of Major Theories on Basic Issues in Child Development

| THEORY | CONTINUOUS OR DISCONTINUOUS DEVELOPMENT? | ONE COURSE OF DEVELOPMENT OR MANY? | NATURE OR NURTURE AS MORE IMPORTANT? |
|---|---|---|---|
| Psychoanalytic perspective | *Discontinuous:* Psychosexual and psychosocial development takes place in stages. | *One course:* Stages are assumed to be universal. | *Both nature and nurture:* Innate impulses are channelled and controlled through child-rearing experiences. *Early experiences* set the course of later development. |
| Behaviourism and social learning theory | *Continuous:* Development involves an increase in learned behaviours. | *Many possible courses:* Behaviours reinforced and modelled may vary from child to child. | *Emphasis on nurture:* Development results from conditioning and modelling. *Both early and later experiences* are important. |
| Piaget's cognitive-developmental theory | *Discontinuous:* Cognitive development takes place in stages. | *One course:* Stages are assumed to be universal. | *Both nature and nurture:* Development occurs as the brain matures and children exercise their innate drive to discover reality in a generally stimulating environment. *Both early and later experiences* are important. |
| Information processing | *Continuous:* Children gradually improve in perception, attention, memory, and problem-solving skills. | *One course:* Changes studied characterize most or all children. | *Both nature and nurture:* Children are active, sense-making beings who modify their thinking as the brain matures and they confront new environmental demands. *Both early and later experiences* are important. |
| Ethology and evolutionary developmental psychology | *Both continuous and discontinuous:* Children gradually develop a wider range of adaptive behaviours. Sensitive periods occur, in which qualitatively distinct capacities emerge fairly suddenly. | *One course:* Adaptive behaviours and sensitive periods apply to all members of a species. | *Both nature and nurture:* Evolution and heredity influence behaviour, and learning lends greater flexibility and adaptiveness to it. In sensitive periods, *early experiences* set the course of later development. |
| Vygotsky's sociocultural theory | *Both continuous and discontinuous:* Language acquisition and schooling lead to stage-wise changes. Dialogues with more expert members of society also lead to continuous changes that vary from culture to culture. | *Many possible courses:* Socially mediated changes in thought and behaviour vary from culture to culture. | *Both nature and nurture:* Heredity, brain growth, and dialogues with more expert members of society jointly contribute to development. *Both early and later experiences* are important. |
| Ecological systems theory | *Not specified.* | *Many possible courses:* Children's characteristics join with environmental forces at multiple levels to mould development in unique ways. | *Both nature and nurture:* Children's characteristics and the reactions of others affect each other in a bidirectional fashion. Layers of the environment influence child-rearing experiences. *Both early and later experiences* are important. |
| Dynamic systems perspective | *Both continuous and discontinuous:* Change in the system is always ongoing. Stagelike transformations occur as children reorganize their behaviour so components of the system join together to work as a functioning whole. | *Many possible courses:* Biological makeup, everyday tasks, and social experiences vary, yielding wide individual differences in specific skills. | *Both nature and nurture:* The child's mind, body, and physical and social surroundings form an integrated system that guides mastery of new skills. *Both early and later experiences* are important. |

children under age 6 were more likely to live in poverty than older children (National Council of Welfare, 2000)—a circumstance that is particularly worrisome because the earlier poverty begins and the longer it lasts, the more devastating its effects (Zigler & Hall, 2000). The poverty rate rises sharply for ethnic minority and female-headed families. Approximately 60 percent of Aboriginal children under age 6 live in poor families. (Aboriginal peoples in Canada include First Nations, Inuit, and Métis.) Furthermore, the poverty rate for single-parent, mother-led families hovers at 53 percent (National Council of Welfare, 2000).

**Health care.** Despite the fact Canada has a publicly funded national health care system, approximately 15 percent of Canadian 2-year-olds are not fully immunized (Rusen & McCourt, 1999). The rate of children not fully immunized rises further for Aboriginal children, making them more at risk for preventable diseases, such as measles (Health Canada, 1997). Furthermore, the Canadian Institute of Child Health estimates that over 20 percent of children between the ages of 4 and 11 suffer from emotional or behavioural disorders (Canadian Institute of Child Health, 2000). While the Canadian health care system funds medical and psychiatric services, it does *not* fund psychological services unless they are hospital based, leaving many of these children without the benefit of treatment.

**Low birth weight and infant death.** In 1999, approximately 5.6 percent of Canadian infants were born underweight (Statistics Canada, Births, 2001). Low birth weight (under 2500 grams) is a powerful predictor of serious health difficulties and early death. Nearly 6 out of every 1000 Canadian babies do not survive their first year, a rate that compares poorly to that of other industrialized nations (Statistics Canada, Health Reports, 2000).

- **Teenage parenthood.** In 1997, 19 723 babies were born to Canadian teenagers (Dryburgh, 2001). Teenagers are neither psychologically nor economically prepared to raise a child (Ventura & Freedman, 2000). Teenage parenthood is strongly linked to poverty and developmental problems for both the adolescent parent and her child. Although the teenage pregnancy rate has been declining in Canada for the past 25 years, it remains a problem.

- **Divorce.** Family breakdown is common in the lives of North American children. In 1998, for example, 69 088 divorces occurred in Canada, up 2.5 percent from the preceding year. Approximately one-third of these divorces involved custody disputes, covering some 37 851 children. This underestimates the number of children affected by divorce, however, because not all divorces with children involve custody disputes. If the divorce rate continues to rise at this rate, 36 percent, or more than one-third, of marriages will dissolve in the next 30 years (Statistics Canada, Divorces, 2000). In Chapter 14, we will see that marital dissolution is linked to temporary—and occasionally long-term—declines in family income, stressful living conditions, and psychological adjustment difficulties for children.

- **Child abuse.** In 1998, approximately 22 child abuse investigations were conducted per 1000 Canadian children (Trocmé et al., 2001).Close to 50 percent of the investigations substantiated the abuse. The true number of abuse cases is likely much greater, since many incidents go unreported. Victims of abuse are at higher risk for a range of behaviour problems, including learning difficulties, emotional troubles, and depression (Statistics Canada, Family Violence, 2001).

ANDREW VAUGHAN/CP PHOTO ARCHIVE

In Canada, close to one in five children lives in poverty, a rate similar to that of the United States. Poverty—a circumstance that threatens all aspects of development—is as high as 60 percent among Aboriginal children under age 6 and as high as 53 percent among single-parent, mother-led families.

■ **Child care.** Seventy percent of Canadian children younger than age 6 have mothers in the workforce. Although close to 1.4 million children are enrolled in child care, only about 500 000 government regulated spots are available in Canada (Canadian Child Care Federation, 2000). Without sufficient, affordable, high-quality child care, children experience less than optimal conditions and their development suffers.

■ **School dropout.** Although the Canadian high school dropout rate fell during the 1990s, it continues to hover at 12 percent (Statistics Canada, Youth in Transition, 2002). The proportion of youth who leave high school without a diploma is of significant concern, especially in the context of growing social and economic demand for higher levels of education. Those who do not finish their education are at risk for unemployment and poverty.

## THE POLICY-MAKING PROCESS

**Social policy** is any planned set of actions directed at solving a social problem or attaining a social goal. Policies can be proposed and implemented by small groups or large formal organizations; by private or public institutions, such as schools, businesses, and social service agencies; and by governing bodies, such as the federal and provincial legislatures, the courts, and city councils.

When widespread social problems arise, nations attempt to solve them by developing a special type of social policy called **public policy**—laws and government programs aimed at improving current conditions. Return to Bronfenbrenner's ecological systems theory on pages 27–29, and notice how the concept of the macrosystem suggests that sound public policies are essential for protecting children's well-being. When governing bodies authorize programs to meet children's health, safety, and educational needs, they serve as broad societal plans for action.

What types of obstacles stand in the way of improving children's conditions? To answer this question, we must understand the complex forces that foster effective public policies. Among the most important are cultural values, special interests, economic decisions, and child development research.

**CULTURAL VALUES.** The political culture of a nation—dominant beliefs about the relationship that should exist between citizen and government—has a major impact on the policy-making process. A widespread opinion in North America is that the care and rearing of young children, and paying for that care, are the duties of parents, and only parents (Rickel & Becker, 1997; Scarr, 1996). This autonomous view of the family has a long history—one in which independence, self-reliance, and the privacy of family life emerged as primary values. It is one reason, among others, that the public has been slow to accept publicly supported benefits for all families, such as high-quality child care. The valuing of an autonomous family has also contributed to the large number of families that remain poverty stricken despite the fact that their members are gainfully employed (Zigler & Hall, 2000).

Consider our discussion so far, and you will see that it reflects a broad dimension on which cultures differ: the extent to which *collectivism versus individualism* is emphasized. In **collectivist societies,** people define themselves as part of a group and stress group over individual goals. In **individualistic societies,** people think of themselves as separate entities and are largely concerned with their own personal needs (Triandis, 1995). Although individualism tends to increase as cultures become more complex, cross-national differences remain. For example, Canada is more collectivistic than the United States in that it has developed

**social policy**
Any planned set of actions directed at solving a social problem or attaining a social goal.

**public policy**
Laws and government programs aimed at improving current conditions.

**collectivist societies**
Societies in which people define themselves as part of a group and stress group over individual goals.

**individualistic societies**
Societies in which people think of themselves as separate entities and are largely concerned with their own personal needs.

more universal programs, such as the Canadian health care plan. Still, it lags behind some European nations in the universality of its social services.

**SPECIAL INTERESTS.** Of course, not all people hold the same political beliefs. In complex societies, distinct *subcultures* exist, based on such factors as geographic region, ethnicity, income, education, and age, that stand alongside a nation's dominant values. The diversity of Canadian society has led special interest groups to play a strong role in policy making. In this jockeying for public influence, the needs of children can remain unrecognized. First, instead of making immediate contributions to the welfare of a nation, children are a costly drain on economic resources. Second, children cannot organize and speak out to protect their concerns, as adults do. Because they must rely on the goodwill of others, children are constantly in danger of becoming a "forgotten constituency."

**ECONOMIC DECISIONS.** Besides dominant values and the demands of special interests, the current state of a nation's economy affects what it does to improve the welfare of children and families. In times of economic difficulty, governments are less likely to initiate new social programs, and they may cut back or even eliminate those that exist. Most Western European nations provide all families with benefits, in the form of child allowances (a standard yearly payment for each child in a family), universal health care, paid parental leave for childbirth and child illness, and free or inexpensive child care (Kamerman, 2000). In the United States, however, support goes primarily to the very poorest children. Canada falls in between the United States and other Western nations: It offers universal health care, an income-dependent tax benefit for parents who have children under 18, and maternity and parental leave benefits through employment insurance, but it does not have universal provisions for child care, or for paid parental leave for child illness.

**CHILD DEVELOPMENT RESEARCH.** For a policy to be most effective in meeting children's needs, research should guide it at every step—during design, implementation, and evaluation of the program. The recent trend toward greater involvement of child development researchers in the policy process was stimulated by events of the 1960s and 1970s, a time of greater receptiveness to government-sponsored social services (Zigler & Finn-Stevenson, 1999).

For example, in 1965, research on the importance of early experiences for children's intellectual development played a major role in the founding of Project Head Start, the largest U.S. preschool educational and family-services intervention program. As we will see in Chapter 8, two decades of research on the long-term benefits of Head Start helped the program survive when its funding was threatened and contributed to recent increased support. In Canada, the Centres of Excellence for Children's Well-Being, whose goals are to provide research-based information on children's physical and mental health needs, are working to increase knowledge of the critical factors for healthy child development. Although it is too early to evaluate the success of the Centres, five currently exist, each dealing with one of these issues: child welfare, communities, early childhood development, special needs, and youth engagement.

As researchers examined the impact of children's services, they saw how settings remote from children's daily lives affected their well-being. As a result, researchers broadened their focus to include wider social contexts, such as school, workplace, community, mass media, and government. They also began to address the impact of societal change on children— poverty, divorce, family violence, teenage parenthood, and child care. All these efforts have, in turn, inspired new policy directions.

*social issues:* **e***ducation*

**CYBERMOMS: A COMPUTER-MEDIATED PROGRAM FOR YOUNG MOTHERS**

Sudbury, Ontario, is home to Cybermoms, a three-year demonstration and research project run by Laurentian University and the Region of Sudbury's Social Planning Council, and supported by a variety of corporate sponsors (Kauppi, 2001). The purpose of the program is to evaluate whether computer technology can be used to support and empower pregnant teenagers during the prenatal period and through the first 18 months of their babies' lives. While the primary goal is to facilitate healthy pregnancy, childbirth, and child development, the secondary goal is to provide participants with computer training and thus improve access to education, decrease social isolation, and provide marketable, computer-related skills.

The project began in 1998 with 45 teens between 15 and 19 years of age. Reflective of the Region of Sudbury, two-thirds of the participants are anglophones and one-third are francophones. Other demographic characteristics of the group are as follows: Most are of European background, but some are of Aboriginal origin. One-third of the teens live with their parents, one-third with their boyfriends, and one-third on their own. The majority of the teens maintain frequent contact with their families and describe their parents as helpful and supportive. The major source of income for the teens is social assistance. All but two live below the

DICK HEMINGWAY

The primary goal of Cybermoms is to facilitate healthy pregnancy, childbirth, and child development. Its secondary goal is to provide participants with computer training and thereby improve access to education, provide social support, and offer marketable, computer-related skills.

### ■ PROGRESS IN MEETING THE NEEDS OF CANADIAN CHILDREN

Public policies aimed at fostering children's development can be justified on two important grounds. The first is that children are the future—the parents, workers, and citizens of tomorrow. Investing in children can yield valuable returns to a nation's quality of life. Failure to invest in children can result in "economic inefficiency, loss of productivity, shortages in needed skills, high health care costs, growing prison costs, and a nation that will be less safe, less caring, and less free" (Hernandez, 1994, p. 20).

Second, child-oriented policies can be justified on humanitarian grounds—children's basic rights as human beings. In 1989, the United Nations' General Assembly drew up the Convention on the Rights of the Child, a legal agreement among nations that commits each cooperating country to work toward guaranteeing environments that foster children's development, protect them from harm, and enhance their community participation and self-determination. Based on research by the Canadian Coalition for the Rights of Children, which represents more than 50 national and provincial non-government organizations concerned with the well-being of children in Canada and abroad, Canada has met most of its obligations under the convention. However, improvement is still needed in some areas. Interestingly, although the United States played a key role in drawing up the convention, the United States and Somalia are the only countries in the world that have still failed to ratify it.

Many government-sponsored child and family programs exist in Canada, such as parental leave benefits and the Canada Child Tax Benefit, a tax-free monthly payment based on family income. In 2001, the government of Canada produced a guide to services for

Statistics Canada poverty line (Kauppi, personal communication, 2002).

Community sponsors provide all 45 teen participants with computers in their homes, Internet access, and computer training. A full-time community worker provides individual support through e-mail and home visits, and makes referrals to community agencies as needed. The teens are also linked with each other via an Internet discussion group and e-mail, with the intent of decreasing the social isolation that new mothers often experience, and connecting them with others who share their parenting concerns. As one 15-year-old commented, her old friends talked about boys, but she now has friends to talk to about raising babies.

In addition to communicating with each other from home, the teen mothers attend informal gatherings and professional workshops on subjects related to child care, such as techniques for positive parenting and discipline.

Although data on the success of the Cybermoms project are just beginning to arrive, preliminary results indicate that it provides young mothers with a high level of social and emotional support and improves their access to a wide range of health and social services (C. Kauppi, personal communication, 2002). Moreover, since participating teens demonstrated more knowledge of child development at the end of the project than at the beginning, their children might benefit over the long

term. Some unexpected findings were that access to computers led to improvements in the teens' writing skills, and many reported that they planned to continue with their schooling. Some participants also secured employment because of the computer skills they acquired through the program.

Cybermoms illustrates how research can be applied to a social problem such as teen parenthood, and it also demonstrates the importance of model programs that can be replicated in other communities. Here and elsewhere, researcher–community partnerships can increase understanding of child development and lead to widespread benefits for children and families.

children and their families, which was distributed nationwide. The guide was designed to inform parents about available services as part of the government's commitment to the future of Canada's children.

Researchers are collaborating with communities in the design, implementation, and evaluation of policy-relevant interventions. In these studies, researchers try to find out what will be feasible, affordable, and lasting in enhancing development in the real world (Jensen, Hoagwood, & Trickett, 1999; Lerner, Fisher, & Weinberg, 2000). While expanding knowledge about contextual influences, the new wave of "outreach research" is also contributing to a better quality of life. Consult the Social Issues: Education box above for an inspiring example.

By forging more effective partnerships with the public, the field of child development can spur the policy process forward. As these efforts continue, attention will increasingly focus on the needs of children and families.

## ASK YOURSELF

**review**    What do the childhood social indicators reveal about the health and well-being of children in Canada?
—many children grow up under conditions that threaten their well-being.

**connect**    How do cultural values, special interests, economic decisions, and child development research affect children's development? What levels of Bronfenbrenner's ecological systems theory contain these influences?

**connect**    How have Canadian cultural values affected government support for children and families?

# summary

## CHILD DEVELOPMENT AS A SCIENTIFIC, APPLIED, AND INTERDISCIPLINARY FIELD

*What is child development, and what factors stimulated expansion of the field?*

- **Child development** is the study of human constancy and change from conception through adolescence. It is part of a larger discipline known as **developmental psychology** or **human development,** which includes the entire lifespan. Research on child development has been stimulated by both scientific curiosity and social pressures to better the lives of children. Our knowledge is interdisciplinary—it has grown through the combined efforts of people from many fields of study.

*How can we divide child development into sensible, manageable domains and periods?*

- To make the vast, interdisciplinary study of human change more orderly and convenient, development is often divided into three domains: (1) physical development, (2) cognitive development, and (3) emotional and social development. These domains are not really distinct; they combine in an integrated, holistic fashion.

- Usually, researchers segment child development into five periods, each of which brings with it new capacities and social expectations that serve as important transitions in major theories: (1) the prenatal period, (2) infancy and toddlerhood, (3) early childhood, (4) middle childhood, and (5) adolescence.

## BASIC ISSUES

*Identify three basic issues on which child development theories take a stand.*

- Child development **theories** take a stand on the following controversial issues: (1) Is development a **continuous** process, or does it follow a series of **discontinuous stages?** (2) Does one general course of development characterize all children, or do many possible courses exist, depending

on the **contexts** in which children grow up? (3) Is development primarily determined by **nature** or **nurture,** and is it stable or open to change?

- Some theories, especially the more recent ones, take an intermediate stand on these issues. Contemporary researchers realize that answers may vary across domains of development and even, as research on **resiliency** illustrates, across individuals.

## HISTORICAL FOUNDATIONS

*Describe major historical influences on theories of child development.*

- Contemporary theories of child development have roots extending far into the past. In medieval times, children were regarded as miniature adults, a view called **preformationism.** By the sixteenth and seventeenth centuries, childhood came to be recognized as a distinct phase of the life cycle. However, the Puritan belief in original sin led to a harsh philosophy of child rearing.

- The Enlightenment brought new ideas favouring more humane treatment of children. Locke's notion of the **tabula rasa** provided the philosophical basis for twentieth-century behaviourism, and Rousseau's idea of the **noble savage** foreshadowed the concepts of stage and **maturation.** A century later, Darwin's theory of evolution stimulated scientific child study.

- Efforts to observe children directly began in the late nineteenth and early twentieth centuries with baby biographies. Soon after, Hall and Gesell introduced the **normative approach,** which produced a large body of descriptive facts about children. Binet and Simon constructed the first successful intelligence test, which initiated the mental testing movement. Baldwin's theory was ahead of its time, granting nature and nurture equal importance and regarding children and their social surroundings as mutually influential.

## MID-TWENTIETH-CENTURY THEORIES

*What theories influenced the study of child development in the mid-twentieth century?*

- In the 1930s and 1940s, child guidance professionals turned to the **psychoanalytic perspective** for help in understanding children with emotional problems. In Freud's **psychosexual theory,** children move through five stages, during which three parts of the personality—id, ego, and superego—become integrated. Erikson's **psychosocial theory** builds on Freud's theory by emphasizing the ego as a positive force in development, the development of culturally relevant attitudes and skills, and the lifespan nature of development.

- Academic psychology also influenced child study. From **behaviourism** and **social learning theory** came the principles of conditioning and modelling and practical procedures of **behaviour modification** with children.

- In contrast to behaviourism, Piaget's **cognitive-developmental theory** emphasizes that children actively construct knowledge as they manipulate and explore their world. According to Piaget, children move through four stages, beginning with the baby's sensorimotor action patterns and ending with the elaborate, abstract reasoning system of the adolescent and adult. Piaget's theory has stimulated a wealth of research on children's thinking and encouraged educational programs that emphasize discovery learning.

## RECENT THEORETICAL PERSPECTIVES

*Describe recent theoretical perspectives on child development.*

- **Information processing** views the mind as a complex, symbol-manipulating system, operating much like a computer. This approach helps researchers achieve a detailed understanding of what children of different ages do when faced with tasks or problems. Information processing has led to teaching interventions that help children approach tasks in more advanced ways.

■ Four perspectives emphasize contexts for development. **Ethology** stresses the evolutionary origins and adaptive value of behaviour and inspired the **sensitive period** concept. In **evolutionary developmental psychology,** researchers have extended this emphasis. They seek to understand the adaptiveness of species-wide cognitive, emotional, and social competencies as those competencies change over time.

■ Vygotsky's **sociocultural theory** has enhanced our understanding of cultural influences, especially in the area of cognitive development. Through cooperative dialogues with more mature members of society, children come to use language to guide their own thought and actions and acquire culturally relevant knowledge and skills.

■ In **ecological systems theory,** nested layers of the environment—**microsystem, mesosystem, exosystem,** and **macrosystem**—are seen as major influences on children's well-being. The **chronosystem** represents the dynamic, ever-changing nature of children and their experiences.

■ Inspired by ideas in other sciences and recent perspectives in child development, a new wave of theorists has adopted a **dynamic systems perspective** to account for wide variation in development. According to this view, the mind, body, and physical and social worlds form an integrated system that guides mastery of new skills. A change in any part of the system prompts the child to reorganize her behaviour so the various components work together again but in a more complex, effective way.

## COMPARING CHILD DEVELOPMENT THEORIES

*Identify the stand taken by each major theory on the basic issues of child development.*

■ Theories that are major forces in child development research vary in their focus on different domains of development, in their view of development, and in their strengths and weaknesses. (For a full summary, see Table 1.5 on page 32.)

## APPLIED DIRECTIONS: CHILD DEVELOPMENT AND SOCIAL POLICY

*Explain the importance of social policies for safeguarding children's well-being, and cite factors that affect the policy-making process, noting the role of child development research.*

■ The field of child development has become increasingly concerned with applying its vast knowledge base to solving pressing social problems. **Childhood social indicators** reveal that many children grow up under conditions that threaten their well-being.

■ A special type of **social policy** called **public policy**—laws and government programs designed to improve current conditions—is essential for protecting children's development. Dominant cultural values, especially **collectivism** versus **individualism;** competing claims of special interest groups; economic decisions; and child development research combine to influence the policy-making process. Policy-relevant research not only helps forge new policy directions but expands our understanding of child development.

■ Although many government-sponsored child and family policies are in effect in Canada, they do not reach all children in need. New policies are under way, and concerned citizens are advocating for children's causes. Furthermore, researchers are collaborating with communities in the design, implementation, and evaluation of policy-relevant interventions. These efforts offer hope of improving the well-being of children and families.

# important terms and concepts

behaviour modification (p. 20)
behaviourism (p. 18)
child development (p. 4)
childhood social indicators (p. 31)
chronosystem (p. 29)
cognitive-developmental theory (p. 20)
collectivist societies (p. 34)
contexts (p. 8)
continuous development (p. 6)
developmental psychology (p. 4)
discontinuous development (p. 8)
dynamic systems perspective (p. 29)
ecological systems theory (p. 27)
ethology (p. 24)

evolutionary developmental psychology (p. 25)
exosystem (p. 29)
human development (p. 4)
individualistic societies (p. 34)
information processing (p. 22)
macrosystem (p. 29)
maturation (p. 12)
mesosystem (p. 28)
microsystem (p. 28)
nature–nurture controversy (p. 8)
noble savage (p. 12)
normative approach (p. 13)
preformationism (p. 11)

psychoanalytic perspective (p. 16)
psychosexual theory (p. 16)
psychosocial theory (p. 16)
public policy (p. 34)
resiliency (p. 11)
sensitive period (p. 25)
social learning theory (p. 19)
social policy (p. 34)
sociocultural theory (p. 27)
stage (p. 8)
tabula rasa (p. 11)
theory (p. 6)

"Beautiful Flowers"
Suwannee Kawsuksi
8 years, Thailand

What does this child hear, see, think, and feel as she spreads her arms to embrace this magnificent garden? Chapter 2 addresses the many strategies researchers use to find out about children's experiences, thoughts, feelings, and behaviours.

Reprinted by permission from The International Museum of Children's Art, Oslo, Norway

# *t*wo

## Research Strategies

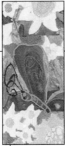

ONE AFTERNOON, MY COLLEAGUE Ron crossed the street between his academic department and our laboratory school, the expression on his face reflecting a deep sense of apprehension. After weeks of planning, Ron was ready to launch his study on the development of children's peer relations. Thinking back to his own school years, he recalled the anguish of several classmates, who were repeatedly taunted and shunned by peers. Ron wanted to help rejected children, many of whom go on to lead troubled lives. In view of the importance of his research, Ron was puzzled by a request from the school's research committee that he appear before them.

At the meeting, Ron met with teachers and administrators charged with evaluating research proposals for their ethical integrity. A third-grade teacher spoke up:

"Ron, I see the value of your work, but frankly, I'm concerned about your asking my pupils whom they like most and least. I've got a couple of kids who are soundly disliked, and I'm doing my best to keep the lid on the situation. There's also an immigrant West Indian child who's new to my classroom, and she's being ostracized because of the way she dresses and speaks. If you come in and start sensitizing my class to whom they like and dislike, the children are going to share these opinions. Unfortunately, I think your study is likely to promote conflict and negative interaction!"

Imagine Ron's dismay at hearing someone suggest that he might have to abandon his research. This chapter takes a close look at the research process—the many challenges investigators face as they plan and implement studies of children. Ron had already travelled a long and arduous path before he arrived at the door of the laboratory school, prepared to collect his data. First, he had spent many weeks developing a researchable idea, based on theory and prior knowledge about children's peer relations. Next, he had selected an appropriate research strategy, which involved two main tasks. First, he had chosen from a variety of *research methods*—the specific activities of participants, such as taking tests, answering questionnaires, responding to interviews, or being observed. Second, he had decided on a *research design*—an overall plan for his study that would permit the best test of his research idea. Finally, Ron had scrutinized his procedures for any possible harm they might cause to participants.

Still, as Ron approached a committee charged with protecting the welfare of young research participants, he faced an ethical dilemma. Research, whether on animals or humans, must meet certain standards that protect participants from stressful treatment. Because of children's immaturity and vulnerability, extra precautions must be taken to ensure that their rights are not violated. In the final section of this chapter, we will see how Ron resolved the committee's earnest challenge to the ethical integrity of his research.

 ## From Theory to Hypothesis

IN CHAPTER 1, WE SAW HOW theories structure the research process by identifying important research concerns and, occasionally, preferred methods for collecting data. We also discussed how theories guide the application of findings to real-life circumstances and practices with children. In fact, research usually begins with a prediction about behaviour drawn directly from a theory, or what we call a **hypothesis.** Think back to the various child development theories presented in Chapter 1. Many hypotheses can be drawn from any one of them that, once tested, would reflect on the accuracy of the theory.

Sometimes research pits a hypothesis taken from one theory against a hypothesis taken from another. For example, a theorist emphasizing the role of maturation in development would predict that adult encouragement will have little effect on the age at which children utter their first words, learn to count, or tie their shoes. A sociocultural theorist, in contrast, would speculate that these skills can be promoted through adult teaching.

At other times, research tests predictions drawn from a single theory. For example, ecological systems theory suggests that providing isolated, divorced mothers with social supports will lead them to be more patient with their children. An ethologist might hypothesize that an infant's cry will stimulate strong physiological arousal in adults who hear it, motivating them to soothe and protect a suffering baby.

Occasionally, little or no theory exists on a topic of interest. In these instances, the investigator may start with a *research question*, such as, Because of recent world events—the attack on the World Trade Center and other terrorist acts—are children today more anxious and fearful than in the past? Hypotheses and research questions offer investigators vital guidance as they settle on research methods and research designs.

At this point, you may be wondering, Why learn about research strategies? Why not leave these matters to research specialists and concentrate on what is already known about the child? There are two reasons. First, each of us must be wise and critical consumers of knowledge, not naive sponges who soak up facts about children. Knowing the strengths and weaknesses of various research strategies becomes important in separating dependable information from misleading results. Second, individuals who work directly with children may sometimes be in a position to test hypotheses or research questions. At other times, they may have to provide information on how well their goals for children are being realized, to justify continued financial support for their programs and activities. Under these circumstances, an understanding of the research process is essential.

**hypothesis**
A prediction about behaviour drawn from a theory.

# Common Methods Used to Study Children

HOW DOES A RESEARCHER choose a basic approach to gathering information about children? Common methods include systematic observation, self-reports, psychophysiological measures, clinical or case studies, and ethnographies of the life circumstances of a specific group of children. As you read about these methods, you may find it helpful to refer to Table 2.1, which summarizes the strengths and limitations of each.

**TABLE** 2.1

Strengths and Limitations of Common Information-Gathering Methods

| METHOD | DESCRIPTION | STRENGTHS | LIMITATIONS |
|---|---|---|---|
| **Systematic Observation** | | | |
| Naturalistic observation | Observation of behaviour in natural contexts | Reflects participants' everyday behaviours. | Cannot control conditions under which participants are observed. Accuracy of observations may be reduced by observer influence and observer bias. |
| Structured observation | Observation of behaviour in a laboratory, where conditions are the same for all participants | Grants each participant an equal opportunity to display the behaviour of interest. Permits study of behaviours rarely seen in everyday life. | May not yield observations typical of participants' behaviour in everyday life. Accuracy of observations may be reduced by observer influence and observer bias. |
| **Self-Reports** | | | |
| Clinical interview | Flexible interviewing procedure in which the investigator obtains a complete account of the participant's thoughts | Comes as close as possible to the way participants think in everyday life. Great breadth and depth of information can be obtained in a short time. | May not result in accurate reporting of information. Flexible procedure makes comparing individuals' responses difficult. |
| Structured interview, questionnaires, and tests | Self-report instruments in which each participant is asked the same questions in the same way | Permits comparisons of participants' responses and efficient data collection and scoring. | Does not yield the same depth of information as a clinical interview. Responses are still subject to inaccurate reporting. |
| **Psychophysiological Methods** | Methods that measure the relationship between physiological processes and behaviour | Reveals which central nervous system structures contribute to development and individual differences in certain competencies. Helps identify the perceptions, thoughts, and emotions of infants and young children, who cannot report them clearly. | Cannot reveal with certainty how an individual processes stimuli. Many factors besides those of interest to the researcher can influence a physiological response. |
| **Clinical Method (Case Study)** | A full picture of a single individual's psychological functioning, obtained by combining interviews, observations, test scores, and sometimes psychophysiological assessments | Provides rich, descriptive insights into processes of development. | May be biased by researchers' theoretical preferences. Findings cannot be applied to individuals other than the participant. |
| **Ethnography** | Participant observation of a culture or distinct social group; by making extensive field notes, the researcher tries to capture the culture's unique values and social processes | Provides a more complete and accurate description than can be derived from a single observational visit, interview, or questionnaire. | May be biased by researchers' values and theoretical preferences. Findings cannot be applied to individuals and settings other than the ones studied. |

## SYSTEMATIC OBSERVATION

Observations of the behaviour of children, and of the adults who are important in their lives, can be made in different ways. One approach is to go into the field, or the natural environment, and record the behaviour of interest, a method called **naturalistic observation.**

MICHAEL NEWMAN/PHOTO EDIT

A study of preschoolers' responses to their peers' distress provides a good example of this technique (Farver & Branstetter, 1994). Observing 3- and 4-year-olds in child-care centres, the researchers recorded each instance of crying and the reactions of nearby children—whether they ignored, watched, or commented on the child's unhappiness; scolded or teased; or shared, helped, or expressed sympathy. Caregiver behaviours, such as explaining why a child was crying, mediating conflict, or offering comfort, were noted to see if adult sensitivity was related to children's caring responses. A strong relationship emerged. The great strength of naturalistic observation is that investigators can see directly the everyday behaviours they hope to explain (Miller, 1998).

Naturalistic observation also has a major limitation: Not all children have the same opportunity to display a particular behaviour in everyday life. In the study just mentioned, some children might have witnessed a child crying more often than others or been exposed to more cues for positive social responses from caregivers. For this reason, they might have displayed more compassion.

| In naturalistic observation, the researcher goes into the field and records the behaviour of interest. This investigator might be observing children's attention, language, emotional expressions, or conflicts. However, a limitation of this method is that some children may have more opportunities than others to display the behaviour in everyday life.

Researchers commonly deal with this difficulty by making **structured observations** in a laboratory. In this approach, the investigator sets up a situation that evokes the behaviour of interest so that every participant has an equal opportunity to display the response. In one study, children's comforting behaviour was observed by playing a tape recording of a baby crying in the next room. Using an intercom, children could either talk to the baby or flip a button so they did not have to listen. Children's facial reactions, the length of time they talked, and the extent to which they spoke in a comforting manner were recorded (Eisenberg et al., 1993).

Structured observation permits greater control over the research situation than does naturalistic observation. In addition, the method is especially useful for studying behaviours—such as parent–child and friendship interactions—that investigators rarely have an opportunity to see in everyday life. For example, one group of researchers wanted to know how teenage boys who frequently engage in antisocial behaviour (such as disobedience in school and delinquent offences) relate to their friends (Dishion, Andrews, & Crosby, 1995). Nearly two hundred 13- and 14-year-old boys brought the friend with whom they spend the most time to a laboratory, where the pairs engaged in the following social tasks: planning an activity they could do together and solving two problems they had experienced—one related to getting along with parents and one related to getting along with peers. Boys who were antisocial engaged in more negative friendship interaction—frequently issuing orders, displaying "noxious" behaviours (physical and verbal aggression and coercive statements, such as "I say we do it this way, or else") and showing poor social skills (expressing impatience, failing to take turns speaking). The researchers concluded that unlike most friendships (which are warm and supportive), antisocial boys' close peer ties provide a context in which they practise hostility and other negative behaviours.

In this study, antisocial boys' laboratory interactions were probably similar to their natural behaviours. The boys acted negatively, even though they knew they would be videotaped. Of course, the great disadvantage of structured observations is that most of the time, we cannot be certain that participants behave in the laboratory as they do in their natural environments.

**COLLECTING SYSTEMATIC OBSERVATIONS.** The procedures used to collect systematic observations vary, depending on the research problem posed. Some investigators choose the **specimen record,** a description of the entire stream of behaviour—everything said and done over a certain time period (Schoggen, 1991). In one of my own studies, I wanted to find

**naturalistic observation**
A method by which the researcher goes into the natural environment to observe the behaviour of interest.

**structured observation**
A method by which the researcher sets up a situation that evokes the behaviour of interest and observes it in a laboratory.

**specimen record**
An observational procedure in which the researcher records a description of the participant's entire stream of behaviour for a specified time period.

out how sensitive, responsive, and verbally stimulating caregivers were when they interacted with children in child-care centres (Berk, 1985). In this case, everything each caregiver said and did—even the amount of time she spent away from the children, taking coffee breaks and talking on the phone—was important.

In other studies, information on only one or a few kinds of behaviour is needed, permitting more efficient procedures. In these instances, a common approach is **event sampling,** in which the observer records all instances of a particular behaviour during a specified time period. In the study of preschoolers' responses to their peers' distress reported earlier, the researchers used event sampling by recording each instance in which a child cried, followed by other children's reactions.

Another way to observe efficiently is **time sampling.** In this procedure, the researcher records whether certain behaviours occur during a sample of short intervals. First, a checklist of the target behaviours is prepared. Then the observation period is divided into a series of brief time segments. For example, a half-hour observation period might be divided into 120 fifteen-second intervals. The observer watches the child for an interval and then checks off behaviours during the next interval, repeating this process until the observation period is complete. One of my students and I used time sampling to compare two preschools in the opportunities they offered for make-believe play. Our observers checked off the type of play each child displayed during eighty 30-second intervals distributed over 4 days, to yield a representative picture of children's play activities (Krafft & Berk, 1998).

**LIMITATIONS OF SYSTEMATIC OBSERVATION.** A major problem in systematic observations is the influence of the observer on the behaviour studied. The presence of a watchful, unfamiliar individual may cause children and adults to react in unnatural ways. For children under age 7 or 8, **observer influence** is generally limited to the first session or two. Young children cannot stop "being themselves" for long, and they quickly get used to the observer's presence. Older children and adults often engage in more socially desirable behaviour when they know that they are being observed. In these instances, researchers can take their responses as an indication of the best behaviour they can display under the circumstances.

Researchers can minimize observer influence. Adaptation periods, in which observers visit the research setting so participants can get used to their presence, are helpful. Another approach is to ask individuals who are part of the child's natural environment to do the observing. For example, in several studies, parents have been trained to record their children's behaviour. Besides reducing the impact of an unfamiliar observer, this method limits the amount of time needed to gather observations, as some information can take a long time to obtain. In one such study, researchers wanted to know how preschool and young school-age children's TV watching affected their other home activities (Huston et al., 1999). To find out, every other month they telephoned parents for a detailed report of children's time use during the previous 24 hours. Results indicated that the more children watched entertainment TV (cartoons and general-audience programs), the less time they spent reading, doing educational activities (such as art, music, and puzzles), and interacting with adults and peers.

In addition to observer influence, **observer bias** is a serious danger. When observers are aware of the purposes of a study, they may see and record what is expected rather than what participants actually do. Therefore, people who have no knowledge of the investigator's hypotheses—or who at least have little personal investment in them—are best suited to collect the observations.

Finally, although systematic observation provides invaluable information on how children and adults behave, it conveys little about the thinking that underlies behaviour. For this kind of information, researchers must turn to self-report techniques.

## SELF-REPORTS: INTERVIEWS AND QUESTIONNAIRES

Self-reports ask research participants to provide information on their perceptions, thoughts, abilities, feelings, attitudes, beliefs, and past experiences. They range from relatively unstructured clinical interviews, the method used by Piaget to study children's thinking, to highly structured interviews, questionnaires, and tests.

**event sampling**
An observational procedure in which the researcher records all instances of a particular behaviour during a specified time period.

**time sampling**
An observational procedure in which the researcher records whether certain behaviours occur during a sample of short time intervals.

**observer influence**
The tendency of participants to react to the presence of an observer and behave in unnatural ways.

**observer bias**
The tendency of observers who are aware of the purposes of a study to see and record what is expected rather than participants' actual behaviours.

**CLINICAL INTERVIEWS.** Let's look at an example of a **clinical interview** in which Piaget questioned a 5-year-old child about his understanding of dreams:

*Where does the dream come from?*—I think you sleep so well that you dream.—*Does it come from us or from outside?*—From outside.—*What do we dream with?*—I don't know.—*With the hands?…With nothing?*—Yes, with nothing.—*When you are in bed and you dream, where is the dream?*—In my bed, under the blanket. I don't really know. If it was in my stomach, the bones would be in the way and I shouldn't see it.—*Is the dream there when you sleep?*—Yes, it is in the bed beside me. (Piaget, 1926/1930, pp. 97–98)

TONY FREEMAN/PHOTOEDIT

Notice how Piaget used a flexible, conversational style to encourage the child to expand his ideas. Although a researcher interviewing more than one child would typically ask the same first question to ensure a common task, individualized prompts are used to obtain a fuller picture of each child's reasoning (Ginsburg, 1997).

The clinical interview has two major strengths. First, it permits people to display their thoughts in terms that are as close as possible to the way they think in everyday life. Second, the clinical interview can provide a large amount of information in a fairly brief period. For example, in an hour-long session, we can obtain a wide range of child-rearing information from a parent—much more than we could capture by observing parent–child interaction for the same amount of time.

Using the clinical interview, this researcher asks a mother to describe her child's development. The method permits large amounts of information to be gathered in a relatively short period. However, a major drawback of this method is that participants do not always report information accurately.

**LIMITATIONS OF CLINICAL INTERVIEWS.** A major limitation of the clinical interview has to do with the accuracy with which people report their thoughts, feelings, and experiences. Some participants, wanting to please the interviewer, may make up answers that do not represent their actual thinking. And because the clinical interview depends on verbal ability and expressiveness, it may underestimate the capacities of individuals who have difficulty putting their thoughts into words. Skilful interviewers minimize these problems by wording questions carefully. They also watch for cues indicating that the participant may not have clearly understood a question or may need extra time to feel comfortable in the situation.

Interviews on certain topics are particularly vulnerable to distortion. In a few instances, researchers have been able to compare parents' and children's descriptions of events with information gathered years earlier, at the same time the events occurred. Reports of psychological states and family processes obtained on the two occasions showed little or no agreement (Henry et al., 1994). Parents often recall their child's development in glowing terms, reporting faster progress, fewer childhood problems, and child-rearing practices more in line with current expert advice than with records of behaviour (Yarrow, Campbell, & Burton, 1970). Interviews that focus on current rather than past information and on specific characteristics rather than global judgments show a better match with observations and other sources of information. Even so, parents are far from perfect in describing their practices and their children's personalities, preferences, and cognitive abilities (Miller & Davis, 1992; Rothbart & Bates, 1998; Waschbusch, Daleiden, & Drabman, 2000).

Finally, as mentioned in Chapter 1, the clinical interview has been criticized because of its flexibility. When questions are phrased differently for each participant, responses may differ due to the manner of interviewing. A second self-report method, the structured interview, reduces this problem.

**STRUCTURED INTERVIEWS, TESTS, AND QUESTIONNAIRES.** In a **structured interview,** each individual is asked the same set of questions in the same way. The approach eliminates the possibility that an interviewer might press and prompt some participants more than others. In addition, compared with clinical interviews, structured interviews are much more efficient. Answers are briefer, and researchers can obtain written responses from an entire class of children or group of parents at the same time. Also, when structured

**clinical interview**
A method in which the researcher uses flexible, open-ended questions to probe for the participant's point of view.

**structured interview**
A method in which the researcher asks each participant the same questions in the same way.

interviews use multiple choice, yes/no, and true/false formats, as is done on many tests and questionnaires, a computer can tabulate the answers. However, these procedures do not yield the same depth of information as a clinical interview. And they can still be affected by the problem of inaccurate reporting.

## PSYCHOPHYSIOLOGICAL METHODS

Researchers' desire to uncover the biological bases of perceptual, cognitive, and emotional responses has led to the use of **psychophysiological methods,** which measure the relationship between physiological processes and behaviour. Investigators who rely on these methods want to find out which central nervous system structures contribute to development and individual differences. Psychophysiological methods also help identify the perceptions, thoughts, and emotions of infants and young children, who cannot report their psychological experiences clearly.

Involuntary activities of the autonomic nervous system[1]—changes in heart rate, blood pressure, respiration, pupil dilation, electrical conductance of the skin, and stress hormone levels—are among the most commonly used physiological measures because of their sensitivity to psychological state. For example, heart rate can be used to infer whether an infant is staring blankly at a stimulus (heart rate is stable), processing information (heart rate slows during concentration), or experiencing distress (heart rate rises) (Izard et al., 1991; Porges, 1991). Heart rate variations are also linked to particular emotional expressions, such as interest, anger, and sadness (Fox & Card, 1998). And as Chapter 10 will reveal, distinct patterns of autonomic activity are related to aspects of temperament, such as shyness and sociability (Kagan & Saudino, 2001).

Autonomic indicators have also been enriched by measures of brain functioning. In an *electroencephalogram (EEG),* researchers tape electrodes to the scalp to record the electrical activity of the brain. EEG waves are linked to different states of arousal, from deep sleep to alert wakefulness, permitting researchers to see how these states change with age. EEG patterns also vary with emotional states—whether children are upbeat and happy or sad and distressed (Jones et al., 1997). At times, investigators study *event-related potentials (ERPs),* or EEG waves that accompany particular events. For example, different wave patterns appear when 3-month-olds from English-speaking homes hear passages in English, Italian, and Dutch, suggesting that the infants can discriminate the intonation patterns of the three languages and indicating the brain regions involved (Shafer, Shucard, & Jaeger, 1999).

*Functional brain-imaging techniques,* which yield three-dimensional pictures of brain activity, provide the most precise information on which brain regions are specialized for certain capacities. *Functional magnetic resonance imaging (fMRI)* is the most promising of these methods, since it does not depend on X-ray photography, which requires injection of radioactive substances. Instead, when a child is shown a stimulus, changes in blood flow within the brain are detected magnetically, producing a computerized image of active areas. Currently, fMRI is being used to study age-related changes in brain organization and the brain functioning of children with serious learning and emotional problems (Gaillard et al., 2000; Georgiewa et al., 1999; Rivkin, 2000).

Despite their virtues, psychophysiological methods have limitations. First, interpreting physiological responses involves a high degree of inference. Even though a stimulus produces a consistent pattern of autonomic or brain activity, investigators cannot be certain that an infant or child has processed it in a particular way. Second, many factors can influence a physiological response. A researcher who takes a change in heart rate, respiration, or brain activity as an indicator of information processing must make sure that it was not due to hunger, boredom, fatigue, or body movements (Fox, Schmidt, & Henderson, 2000). In addition, a

**psychophysiological methods**
Methods that measure the relationship between physiological processes and behaviour. Among the most common are measures of autonomic nervous system activity (such as heart rate, respiration, and stress hormone levels) and measures of brain functioning (such as the electroencephalogram [EEG], event-related potentials [ERPs], and functional magnetic resonance imaging [fMRI]).

[1]The autonomic nervous system regulates involuntary actions of the body. It is divided into two parts: the *sympathetic nervous system,* which mobilizes energy to deal with threatening situations (as when your heart rate rises in response to a fear-arousing event); and the *parasympathetic nervous system,* which acts to conserve energy (as when your heart rate slows as you focus on an interesting stimulus).

B. J. CASEY/UPMC

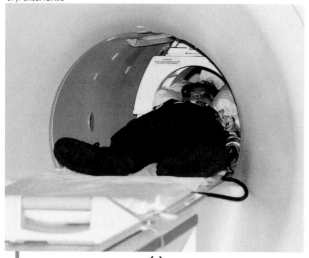

(a)

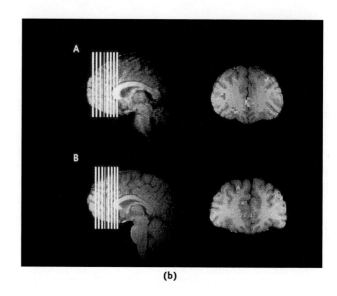

(b)

In functional magnetic resonance imaging (fMRI), the child looks up at a stimulus, and changes in blood flow within brain tissue are detected magnetically (a). The result is a computerized image of activated areas (b), permitting study of age-related changes in brain organization and the brain functioning of children with serious learning and emotional problems.

child's fearful reaction to the equipment affects physiological measures. Preparing children by taking them through a simulated experience greatly reduces their fear (Rosenberg et al., 1997). Without such efforts, detection of correspondences between physiological and psychological reactions is difficult or impossible.

## THE CLINICAL, OR CASE STUDY, METHOD

In Chapter 1, we discussed the **clinical method** (sometimes called the **case study** approach) as an outgrowth of the psychoanalytic perspective, which stresses the importance of understanding the individual. Recall that the clinical method brings together a range of information on a child, including interviews, observations, test scores, and sometimes psychophysiological measures. The aim is to obtain as complete a picture as possible of a child's psychological functioning and the experiences that led up to it.

Although clinical studies are usually carried out on children with developmental problems, they sometimes focus on exceptional, well-adjusted youngsters. For example, the method has been used to find out what contributes to the accomplishments of *prodigies*—extremely gifted children who attain the competence of an adult in a particular field before age 10. Because prodigious children are few in number and vary widely in their special abilities, it is risky to study all of them in the same way. Consequently, the clinical method is well suited to investigating such children. To explore the possibility of common themes in development, researchers can examine other similar cases as they accumulate (Gardner, 1998b). For example, can prodigies realize their abilities without parents who sensitively nurture their talents? For some reflections on this question, refer to the Biology & Environment box on page 49.

The clinical method yields richly detailed case narratives that offer valuable insights into the many factors that affect development. Nevertheless, like other methods, it has drawbacks. Information often is collected unsystematically and subjectively, permitting too much leeway for researchers' theoretical preferences to bias their observations and interpretations. In addition, investigators cannot assume that clinical findings apply to anyone other than the child studied. Even when patterns emerge across several cases, it is wise to confirm them with other research strategies.

**clinical,** or **case study, method**
A method in which the researcher attempts to understand the unique individual child by combining interview data, observations, test scores, and sometimes psychophysiological assessments.

## METHODS FOR STUDYING CULTURE

To study the impact of culture, researchers adjust the methods just considered or tap procedures specially devised for cross-cultural and multicultural research. Which approach investigators choose depends on their research goals (Triandis, 1995, 1998).

# biology & environment

## CASE STUDIES OF PRODIGIES

What factors in the backgrounds of prodigies distinguish them from other children and enable them to realize their extraordinary biological endowment? Case studies suggest that a unique biological disposition to excel in a particular field combines with intense motivation and highly supportive early child rearing to permit full expression of the child's special capacity.

Adam, a linguistically gifted child, could read and write and compose music before he was out of diapers. By age 4, he was immersed in mastering human symbol systems, including French, German, Russian, Sanskrit, Greek, ancient hieroglyphs, music, and mathematics. Adam was more than unusually curious. He made "omnivorous intellectual demands" on his parents (Feldman & Goldsmith, 1991, p. 101). Like other prodigies, Adam figured out a great deal about his domain of interest. But as soon as his parents recognized his gift, it became their highest priority. They were nearly constantly available, offering him rich, varied stimulation; discussing abstract concepts with him; posing interesting questions; and encouraging him to play with ideas. For example, on a walk in the woods, 3-year-old Adam stopped to investigate some decomposing plants. His father helped him speculate about how long the matter had been decaying and what chemical reactions were taking place.

By age 8, as Adam's interests centred on music, he composed a symphony. Immediately, his parents sought teachers who could advance his already astounding level of musical accomplishment. And without being rigid or domineering, they communicated to Adam their expectation that

he work hard and strive to do his very best. He recently graduated from university at age 18 and continues to pursue musical composition (Goldsmith, 2000).

Adam's family background and education resemble those of other prodigies who realize their abilities—for example, Yani, a child who produced extraordinary Chinese brush paintings by age 3; Midori, who by age 11 ranked as a world-class violinist; and Michael Kearney, who performed astounding feats in mathematics by age 3 and graduated from university at age 10. All were blessed with phenomenal biological endowment; a burning desire to achieve; parents who communicated high expectations and were willing to devote all their energies to their child's pursuits; a loving, harmonious family life; outstanding role models and teachers; and a culture that values their field of expertise.

These and other cases suggest that prodigious children are characterized by "a coincidence of factors, all of which converge to yield a level of performance that sometimes seems to border on the unbelievable" (Gardner, 1998b, p. 446). Although each child's development may begin as a sped-up version of the norm, precocious capacity joins with other personal and environmental factors to yield a unique, highly beneficial configuration.

Because prodigies' accomplishments depend on a confluence of crucial factors at a particular time, "failed prodigies" are common (Goldsmith, 2000). Several case studies suggest that quality of early child rearing is vital. When parents are overly demanding and care only about the child's gifts rather than about the child herself, prodigious children can

end up disengaged, depressed, and resentful. And although they need extensive parental involvement in their early years, by adolescence prodigies must develop autonomy with respect to their talent as well as other areas of their lives (Howe, 1999). More research, using a variety of methods, is needed to confirm other necessary conditions—such as the partnership forged between teacher and student at various ages—for prodigies to realize their potential.

*ASSOCIATED PRESS/THE TENNESSEAN*

Nine-year-old Lauren Cooper, a math prodigy, attends a university algebra class in Nashville, Tennessee. Factors that combine to foster her unique ability include phenomenal biological endowment; a burning desire to achieve; parents who do everything they can to nurture her talent; a loving, harmonious family life; outstanding teachers; and a culture that values her expertise.

## social issues: education

### IMMIGRANT YOUTHS: AMAZING ADAPTATION

during the past decade, a rising tide of culturally and ethnically diverse immigrants has come to Canada, fleeing war and persecution in their homelands or otherwise seeking better life chances. Each year about 65 000 immigrant children and youth under the age of 25 arrive in Canada, representing the fastest growing segment of our population. Almost half come from Asia and the Pacific regions and about one-fifth from Africa and the Middle East. Unfortunately, the majority of immigrant youth younger than age 15 are unlikely to know either the English or French language and therefore experience a challenging period, especially during their first year in Canada (Canadian Council on Social Development, 2000a; Statistics Canada, 2001 Census Consultation Guide, 2001).

### ACADEMIC ACHIEVEMENT AND ADJUSTMENT

Although educators and laypeople often assume that the transition to a new country has a negative impact on psychological well-being, recent evidence reveals that children of immigrant parents adapt amazingly well. They usually start school with lower academic performance in reading, writing, and mathematics. But if their parents' mother tongue is either English or French, they catch up to Canadian-born children by age 9 and display above-average performance by the time they complete elementary school. Children whose parents speak neither official language also achieve remarkably well. By age 11, their performance equals their Canadian-born

agemates' (Statistics Canada, School Performance, 2001).

Findings on psychological adjustment resemble those on achievement. Compared with their agemates, youths from immigrant families are less likely to smoke or drink than Canadian-born youth. They are also more likely to participate in religious activities, and the majority of immigrant youth admit that spirituality plays a strong role in their lives (Canadian Council on Social Development, 2000a).

### FAMILY AND COMMUNITY INFLUENCES

Ethnographies reveal that immigrant parents express the belief that education is the surest way to improve life chances. Consequently, they

---

JASON LAURE

Sometimes researchers are interested in characteristics believed to be universal but that vary in degree from one society to the next. These investigators might ask, Do parents demand greater maturity from young children in some societies than in others? How strong are gender stereotypes in different nations? In each instance, several cultural groups will be compared, and all participants must be questioned or observed in the same way. Therefore, researchers draw on the self-report and observational procedures we have already considered, adapting them through translation so they can be understood in each cultural context. For example, to study cultural variation in parenting attitudes, the same questionnaire, asking for ratings on such items as "If my child gets into trouble, I expect him or her to handle the problem mostly by himself or herself," is given to all participants (Chen et al., 1998).

At other times, researchers want to uncover the *cultural meanings* of children's and adults' behaviours by becoming as familiar as possible with their way of life (Shweder et al., 1998). To achieve this goal, researchers rely on a method borrowed from the field of

This Western ethnographer is spending months living in the village of Phuduhuru on the edge of the Kalahari Desert in Botswana, Africa, getting to know members of the !Kung Bakwa clan. The researcher's goal is to uncover the cultural meanings of children's and adults' behaviours by becoming as familiar as possible with their way of life. Here, she asks about various native crafts and their uses.

place a high value on their children's academic achievement (Suarez-Orozco & Suarez-Orozco, 1995; Zhou & Bankston, 1998). Aware of the challenges their children face, immigrant parents underscore the importance of trying hard. They remind their children that educational opportunities were not available in their country of origin and, as a result, they themselves are often limited to menial jobs.

Youth from immigrant families internalize their parents' valuing of education, endorsing it more strongly than agemates with native-born parents (Fuligni, 1997). Because minority ethnicities usually stress allegiance to family and community over individual goals, first- and second-generation young people feel a strong sense of obligation to their parents (Fuligni et al., 1999). They view school success as one of the most important ways they can repay their parents for the hardships they endured in coming to a new land. Both family relationships and school achievement protect these youths from risky behaviours, such as delinquency, early pregnancy, and drug use. Immigrant parents typically develop close ties to an ethnic community. It exerts additional control through a high consensus on values and constant monitoring of young people's activities (Zhou & Bankston, 1998).

This family recently immigrated from Ecuador to North America. Ethnographic research shows that immigrant parents typically place a high value on academic achievement and emphasize family and community goals over individual goals. Their children, who feel a strong sense of obligation to meet their parents' expectations, achieve as well or better than native-born agemates and are less likely to commit antisocial acts.

MICHAEL NEWMAN/PHOTOEDIT

anthropology—**ethnography.** Like the clinical method, ethnographic research is a descriptive, qualitative technique. But instead of aiming to understand a single individual, it is directed at understanding a culture or a distinct social group (Jessor, 1996; Shweder, 1996).

The ethnographic method achieves its goals through *participant observation.* Typically, the researcher lives with the cultural community for a period of months or years, participating in all aspects of its daily life. Extensive field notes are gathered, consisting of a mix of observations, self-reports from members of the culture, and careful interpretations by the investigator. Later, these notes are put together into a description of the community that tries to capture its unique values and social processes.

The ethnographic method assumes that by entering into close contact with a social group, researchers can understand the beliefs and behaviours of its members in a way not possible with an observational visit, interview, or questionnaire. In some ethnographies, investigators focus on many aspects of children's experience, as one team of researchers did in describing what it is like to grow up in a small town (Peshkin, 1978). In other instances, the research is limited to one or a few settings, such as home, school, or neighbourhood life (LeVine et al., 1994; Peshkin, 1997; Valdés, 1998). Researchers interested in cultural comparisons may supplement traditional self-report and observational methods with ethnography if they suspect that unique meanings underlie cultural differences.

**ethnography**
A method by which the researcher attempts to understand the unique values and social processes of a culture or a distinct social group by living with its members and taking field notes for an extended period.

Ethnographers strive to minimize their influence on the culture they are studying by becoming part of it. Nevertheless, at times their presence does alter the situation. And as with clinical research, investigators' cultural values and theoretical commitments sometimes lead them to observe selectively or misinterpret what they see. In addition, the findings of ethnographic studies cannot be assumed to generalize beyond the people and settings in which the research was originally conducted (Hammersley, 1992).

## **ASK** YOURSELF

**review** Why might a researcher prefer to observe children in the laboratory rather than the natural environment? How about the natural environment rather than the lab? Cite factors that can distort the naturalness of systematic observation, regardless of where the information is gathered.

**review** What strengths and limitations do the clinical method and ethnography have in common?

**apply** A researcher wants to study the thoughts and feelings of children who have experienced their parents' divorce. Which method is best suited for investigating this question? Why?

**connect** Why is it better for a researcher to use multiple research methods rather than just one method in testing a hypothesis or answering a research question?

# Reliability and Validity:
# Keys to Scientifically Sound Research

ONCE INVESTIGATORS CHOOSE their research methods, they must ensure that their procedures provide trustworthy information. To be acceptable to the scientific community, self-reports, observations, and physiological measures must be both *reliable* and *valid*—two keys to scientifically sound research.

## RELIABILITY

Suppose you go into a classroom and record the number of times a child behaves in a helpful and cooperative fashion toward others, but your research partner, in simultaneously observing the same child, comes up with very different judgments. Or you ask a group of children some questions about their interests, but a week later when you question them again, their answers are very different. **Reliability** refers to the consistency, or repeatability, of measures of behaviour. To be reliable, observations of people's actions cannot be unique to a single observer. Instead, observers must agree on what they see. And an interview, test, or questionnaire, when given again within a short period of time (before participants can reasonably be expected to change their opinions or develop new responses), must yield similar results on both occasions.

Researchers determine the reliability of data in different ways. In observational research, observers are asked to record the same behaviour sequences, and agreement between them is assessed. Reliability of self-report and psychophysiological data can be demonstrated by comparing children's responses to the same measures on separate occasions. In the case of self-reports, researchers can also compare children's answers on different forms of the same test. If necessary, reliability can be estimated from a single testing session by comparing children's answers on different halves of the test.

Because clinical and ethnographic studies do not yield quantitative scores that can be matched with those of another observer or test form, the reliability of these methods must be assessed with other procedures. After examining the qualitative records, one or more

**reliability**
The consistency, or repeatability, of measures of behaviour.

judges can see if they agree with the researcher that the patterns and themes identified are grounded in evidence and are plausible (Fredericks & Miller, 1997).

## VALIDITY

For research methods to have high **validity,** they must accurately measure characteristics that the researcher set out to measure. Think about this idea, and you will see that reliability is essential for valid research. Methods that are implemented carelessly, unevenly, and inconsistently cannot possibly represent what an investigator originally intended to study.

But researchers must go further to guarantee validity, and they generally do so in several ways. They may carefully examine the content of observations and self-reports to make sure the behaviours of interest are included. For example, a test intended to measure grade 5 children's knowledge of mathematics would not be valid if it contained addition problems but no subtraction, multiplication, or division problems (Miller, 1998). Another approach to validity is to see how effective a method is in predicting behaviour we would reasonably expect it to predict. If scores on a math test are valid, they should be related to how well children do on their math assignments in school or even to how quickly and accurately they can make change in a game of Monopoly.

As we turn now to research designs, you will discover that the concept of validity can also be applied more broadly, to the overall accuracy of research findings and conclusions. If, during any phase of carrying out a study—selecting participants, choosing research settings and tasks, and implementing procedures—the researcher permits factors unrelated to the hypothesis to influence behaviour, then the validity of the results is in doubt, and they cannot be considered a fair test of the investigator's theory.

## ASK YOURSELF

**review** Explain why a research method must be reliable to be valid, yet reliability *does not guarantee* validity.

**connect** Review the limitations of systematic observation on page 45. How do observer influence and observer bias relate to reliability and validity in research?

 # General Research Designs

IN DECIDING ON a research design, investigators choose a way of setting up a study that permits them to test their hypotheses with the greatest certainty possible. Two main types of designs are used in all research on human behaviour: correlational and experimental.

## CORRELATIONAL DESIGN

In a **correlational design,** researchers gather information on already existing groups of individuals, generally in natural life circumstances, and make no effort to alter their experiences. Suppose we want to answer such questions as, Do parents' styles of interacting with their children have any bearing on the children's intelligence? Does attending a child-care centre promote children's friendliness with peers? In these and many other instances, the conditions of interest are very difficult to arrange and control.

The correlational design offers a way of looking at relationships between participants' experiences or characteristics and their behaviour or development. But correlational studies have one major limitation: We cannot infer cause and effect. For example, if we find that par-

**validity**
The extent to which methods in a research study accurately measure what the investigator set out to measure.

**correlational design**
A research design in which the investigator gathers information without altering participants' experiences and examines relationships between variables. Does not permit inferences about cause and effect.

Does attending a child-care centre promote friendliness with peers? A correlational design can be used to examine the relationship between child-care experience and social development, but it does not permit researchers to infer cause and effect.

**correlation coefficient**
A number, ranging from +1.00 to −1.00, that describes the strength and direction of the relationship between two variables.

**experimental design**
A research design in which the investigator randomly assigns participants to two or more treatment conditions and studies the effect that manipulating an independent variable has on a dependent variable. Permits inferences about cause and effect.

**independent variable**
The variable manipulated by the researcher in an experiment.

**dependent variable**
The variable the researcher expects to be influenced by the independent variable in an experiment.

**laboratory experiment**
An experiment conducted in the laboratory, permitting the maximum possible control over treatment conditions.

ents' interaction does correlate with children's intelligence, we would not know whether parents' behaviour actually *causes* intellectual differences among children. In fact, the opposite is certainly possible. The behaviours of highly intelligent children may be so attractive that they cause parents to interact more favourably. Or a third variable, such as the amount of noise and distraction in the home, may cause both parental interaction and children's intelligence to change.

In correlational studies, and in other types of research designs, investigators often examine relationships among variables by using a **correlation coefficient,** a number that describes how two measures, or variables, are associated with one another. Although other statistical approaches to examining relationships are also available, we will encounter the correlation coefficient in discussing research findings throughout this book. So let's look at what it is and how it is interpreted. A correlation coefficient can range in value from +1.00 to −1.00. The *magnitude, or size, of the number* shows the *strength of the relationship.* A zero correlation indicates no relationship; but the closer the value is to +1.00 or −1.00, the stronger the relationship. For instance, a correlation of −.78 is high, −.52 is moderate, and −.18 is low. Note, however, that correlations of +.52 and −.52 are equally strong. The *sign of the number* (+ or −) refers to the *direction of the relationship.* A positive sign (+) means that as one variable *increases,* the other also *increases.* A negative sign (−) indicates that as one variable *increases,* the other *decreases.*

Let's take some examples to illustrate how a correlation coefficient works. In one study, a researcher found that a measure of maternal language stimulation at 13 months was positively correlated with the size of children's vocabularies at 20 months, at +.50 (Tamis-LeMonda & Bornstein, 1994). This is a moderate correlation, indicating that the more mothers spoke to their infants, the more advanced their children tended to be in language development during the second year of life. In another study, a researcher reported that the extent to which mothers ignored their 10-month-olds' bids for attention was negatively correlated with children's willingness to comply with parental demands 1 year later—at −.46 for boys and −.36 for girls (Martin, 1981). These moderate correlations reveal that the more mothers ignored their babies, the less cooperative their children were.

Both investigations found a relationship between maternal behaviour in the first year and children's behaviour in the second. Although the researchers suspected that maternal behaviour affected children's responses, in neither study could they really be sure. However, finding a relationship in a correlational study suggests that tracking down its cause—with a more powerful experimental strategy, if possible—would be worthwhile.

## EXPERIMENTAL DESIGN

Unlike correlational studies, an **experimental design** permits inferences about cause and effect. In an experiment, the events and behaviours of interest are divided into two types: independent and dependent variables. The **independent variable** is the one anticipated by the investigator to cause changes in another variable. The **dependent variable** is the one the investigator expects to be influenced by the independent variable. Inferences about cause-and-effect relationships are possible because the researcher directly *controls* or *manipulates* changes in the independent variable. This is done by exposing participants to two or more treatment conditions and comparing their performance on measures of the dependent variable.

In one **laboratory experiment,** researchers explored the impact of adults' angry interactions on children's adjustment (El-Sheikh, Cummings, & Reiter, 1996). They hypothesized that the way angry encounters end (independent variable) affects children's emotional reactions (dependent variable). Four- and 5-year-olds were brought one at a time to a laboratory, accompanied by their mothers. One group was exposed to an *unresolved-anger treatment,* in which two adult actors entered the room and argued but did not work out their disagreements. The other group witnessed a *resolved-anger treatment,* in which the adults ended their disputes by apologizing and compromising. As Figure 2.1 shows, during a follow-up adult conflict, more children in the resolved-anger treatment showed a decline in distress, as measured by anxious facial expressions, freezing in place, and seeking closeness to their mothers. The experiment revealed that anger resolution can reduce the stressful impact of adult conflict on children.

In experimental studies, investigators must take special precautions to control for characteristics of participants that could reduce the accuracy of the findings. For example, in the study just described, if a greater number of children from homes high in parental conflict ended up in the unresolved-anger treatment, we could not tell whether the independent variable or children's background characteristics produced the results. **Random assignment** of participants to treatment conditions offers protection against this problem. By using an evenhanded procedure, such as drawing numbers out of a hat or flipping a coin, the experimenter increases the chances that children's characteristics will be equally distributed across treatment groups.

Sometimes researchers combine random assignment with another technique called **matching.** In this procedure, participants are measured ahead of time on the factor in question—in our example, parental conflict. Then children from homes high and low in parental conflict are assigned in equal numbers to each treatment condition. In this way, the experimental groups are deliberately matched, or made equivalent, on characteristics likely to distort the results.

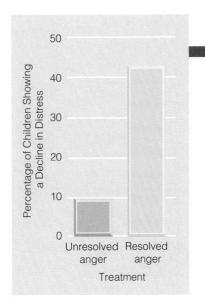

**FIGURE 2.1**

**Does the way adults end their angry encounters affect children's emotional reactions?** A laboratory experiment showed that when adults resolve their disputes by apologizing and compromising, children are more likely to decline in distress when witnessing subsequent adult conflicts than when adults leave their arguments unresolved. Notice in this graph that only 10 percent of children in the unresolved-anger treatment declined in distress (see bar on left), whereas 42 percent of children in the resolved-anger treatment did so (see bar on right). (Adapted from El-Sheikh, Cummings, & Reiter, 1996.)

## MODIFIED EXPERIMENTAL DESIGNS

Most experiments are conducted in laboratories, where researchers can achieve the maximum possible control over treatment conditions. But, as we have already indicated, findings obtained in laboratories may not always apply to everyday situations. The ideal solution to this problem is to do experiments in the field as a complement to laboratory investigations. In **field experiments,** researchers capitalize on rare opportunities to randomly assign people to treatment conditions in natural settings. In the experiment we just considered, we can conclude that the emotional climate established by adults affects children's behaviour in the laboratory. But does it also do so in daily life?

Another study helps answer this question (Yarrow, Scott, & Waxler, 1973). This time, the research was carried out in a child-care centre. A caregiver deliberately interacted differently with two groups of preschoolers. In one condition (the *nurturant treatment*), she modelled many instances of warmth and helpfulness. In the second condition (the *control,* since it involved no treatment), she behaved as usual, with no special emphasis on concern for others. Two weeks later, the researchers created several situations that called for helpfulness. For example, a visiting mother asked each child to watch her baby for a few moments. The baby's toys had fallen out of the playpen, and the investigators recorded whether or not each child returned the toys to the baby. Children exposed to the nurturant treatment behaved in a much more helpful way than did those in the control condition.

Often researchers cannot randomly assign participants and manipulate conditions in the real world, as these investigators were able to do. Sometimes researchers can compromise by conducting **natural experiments.** Treatments that already exist, such as different family environments, schools, child-care centres, and preschool programs, are compared. These studies differ from correlational research only in that groups of people are carefully chosen to ensure that their characteristics are as much alike as possible. Occasionally, the same participants

**random assignment**
An evenhanded procedure for assigning participants to treatment groups, such as drawing numbers out of a hat or flipping a coin. Increases the chances that participants' characteristics will be equally distributed across treatment conditions in an experiment.

**matching**
A procedure in which participants are measured ahead of time on the factor in question, enabling researchers to assign participants with similar characteristics in equal numbers to each treatment condition in an experiment. Ensures that groups will be equivalent on factors likely to distort the results.

**field experiment**
A research design in which participants are randomly assigned to treatment conditions in natural settings.

**natural experiment**
A research design in which the investigator studies already existing treatments in natural settings by carefully selecting groups of participants with similar characteristics.

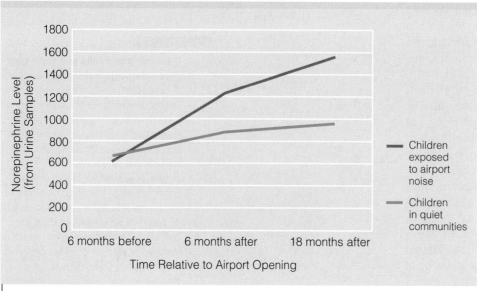

FIGURE 2.2

**Influence of airport noise on stress-hormone level.** In a natural experiment capitalizing on the opening of the new Munich airport, children living in nearby communities showed a dramatic rise in norepinephrine levels (a hormone released into the bloodstream in response to physical or mental stress). The norepinephrine levels of children in quiet communities remained relatively stable. (Adapted from Evans, Bullinger, & Hygge, 1998.)

experience both treatments. In this way, investigators rule out as best they can alternative explanations for treatment effects.

In one such study, the opening of a new international airport in a rural area outside Munich, Germany, created ideal conditions for a natural experiment addressing the effect of chronic environmental noise on children's psychological stress (Evans, Bullinger, & Hygge, 1998). At three time periods—6 months before and 6 and 18 months after the airport opened —researchers invited third and fourth graders residing near the airport to come to a laboratory for blood pressure and stress-hormone level assessments. They also gave the children a questionnaire asking about quality of life. The same data were obtained from comparison children, matched on grade and SES, residing in quiet communities. As Figure 2.2 illustrates, psychophysiological measures of stress rose dramatically for noise-exposed children but remained stable for comparison children. The noise-exposed group also reported a decline in quality of life not evident in the comparison group. Still, natural experiments cannot achieve the precision and rigour of true experimental research. In this investigation, researchers could not untangle the impact of noise from other community changes that coincided with the opening of the airport, such as increased land development and road traffic.

To help you compare the correlational and experimental designs we have discussed, Table 2.2 summarizes their strengths and limitations. Now let's take a close look at designs for studying development.

**TABLE** 2.2

Strengths and Limitations of General Research Designs

| DESIGN | DESCRIPTION | STRENGTHS | LIMITATIONS |
|---|---|---|---|
| Correlational design | The investigator obtains information on already existing groups, without altering participants' experiences. | Permits study of relationships between variables. | Does not permit inferences about cause-and-effect relationships. |
| Laboratory experiment | Under controlled laboratory conditions, the investigator manipulates an independent variable and looks at its effect on a dependent variable; requires random assignment of participants to treatment conditions. | Permits inferences about cause-and-effect relationships. | Findings may not generalize to the real world. |
| Field experiment | The investigator randomly assigns participants to treatment conditions in natural settings. | Permits generalization of experimental findings to the real world. | Control over treatment is generally weaker than in a laboratory experiment. |
| Natural experiment | The investigator compares already existing treatments in the real world, carefully selecting groups of participants to ensure they are alike in characteristics. | Permits study of naturally occurring variables not subject to experimenter manipulation. | Obtained differences may be due to variables other than the treatment. |

# Designs for Studying Development

SCIENTISTS INTERESTED IN child development require information about the way research participants change over time. To answer questions about development, they must extend correlational and experimental approaches to include measurements at different ages. Longitudinal and cross-sectional designs are special *developmental research* strategies. In each, age comparisons form the basis of the research plan.

## THE LONGITUDINAL DESIGN

In a **longitudinal design,** a group of participants is studied repeatedly at different ages, and changes are noted as the participants mature. The time span may be relatively short (a few months to several years) or very long (a decade or even a lifetime). The National Longitudinal Study of Children and Youth (NLSCY) is an unparalleled Canadian study that began in 1994 and continues with data collection every 2 years. A representative sample of almost 23 000 infants and children is being followed as they mature into adulthood. The study is expected to provide unprecedented insights into child development in Canada.

**ADVANTAGES OF THE LONGITUDINAL DESIGN.**   The longitudinal approach has two major strengths. First, since it tracks the performance of each person over time, researchers can identify common patterns as well as individual differences in development. Second, longitudinal studies permit investigators to examine relationships between early and later events and behaviours. Let's illustrate these ideas.

A group of researchers wondered whether children who display extreme personality styles—either angry and explosive or shy and withdrawn—retain the same dispositions when they become adults. In addition, the researchers wanted to know what kinds of experiences promote stability or change in personality and what consequences explosiveness and shyness have for long-term adjustment. To answer these questions, the researchers delved into the archives of the Guidance Study, a well-known longitudinal investigation initiated in 1928 at the University of California, Berkeley, and continued over several decades (Caspi, Elder, & Bem, 1987, 1988).

Results revealed that the two personality styles were only moderately stable. Between ages 8 and 30, a good number of individuals remained the same, whereas others changed substantially. When stability did occur, it appeared to be due to a "snowballing effect," in which children evoked responses from adults and peers that acted to maintain their dispositions (Caspi, 1998). In other words, explosive youngsters were likely to be treated with anger and hostility (to which they reacted with even greater unruliness), whereas shy children were apt to be ignored.

Persistence of extreme personality styles affected many areas of adult adjustment, but these outcomes differed for males and females. For men, the results of early explosiveness were most apparent in their work lives, in the form of conflicts with supervisors, frequent job changes, and unemployment. Since few women in this sample of an earlier generation worked after marriage, their family lives were most affected. Explosive girls grew up to be

**longitudinal design**
A research design in which one group of participants is studied repeatedly at different ages.

hotheaded wives and mothers who were especially prone to divorce. Sex differences in the long-term consequences of shyness were even greater. Men who had been withdrawn in childhood were delayed in marrying, becoming fathers, and developing careers. Because a withdrawn, unassertive style was socially acceptable for females, women who had shy personalities showed no special adjustment problems.

**PROBLEMS IN CONDUCTING LONGITUDINAL RESEARCH.** Despite their strengths, longitudinal investigations have a number of difficulties that can compromise the validity of the findings. **Biased sampling** is a common problem. People who willingly participate in research that requires them to be continually observed and tested over many years are likely to have unique characteristics—at the very least, a special appreciation for the scientific value of research. As a result, we cannot easily generalize from them to the rest of the population. Furthermore, due to **selective attrition,** longitudinal samples generally become more biased as the investigation proceeds. Participants may move away or drop out for other reasons, and the ones who remain are likely to differ in important ways from the ones who do not continue.

The very experience of being repeatedly observed, interviewed, and tested can also interfere with a study's accuracy. Children and adults may gradually be alerted to their own thoughts, feelings, and actions, think about them, and revise them in ways that have little to do with age-related change. In addition, with repeated testing, participants may become "test-wise." Their performance may improve because of **practice effects**—better test-taking skills and increased familiarity with the test—not because of factors commonly associated with development.

The most widely discussed threat to the validity of longitudinal findings is cultural-historical change, or what are commonly called **cohort effects.** Longitudinal studies examine the development of *cohorts*—children developing in the same time period who are influenced by particular cultural and historical conditions. Results based on one cohort may not apply to children growing up at other times. For example, children's intelligence test performance has risen since the middle of the twentieth century and is still rising (Flynn, 1996, 1999). Gains in nutrition, the stimulating quality of schooling and daily life, and parental attitudes toward fostering children's mental development may be involved. And a longitudinal study of child and adolescent social development would probably result in quite different findings if it were carried out in the 1990s, around the time of World War II, or during the Great Depression of the 1930s. (See the Cultural Influences box on page 59.) Cohort effects operate not just as broad, pervasive social changes affecting an entire generation, but also as specific social experiences influencing some children but not others in the same generation—for example, attending a small rather than large secondary school or growing up in a certain region of the country.

Finally, changes occurring within the field of child development may create problems for longitudinal research covering an extended time period. Theories and methods constantly change, and those that first inspired a longitudinal study may become outdated. For this reason, as well as the others just mentioned, many recent longitudinal studies span only a few months or years. Although short-term longitudinal research does not yield the same breadth of information as long-term studies, researchers are spared at least some formidable obstacles.

## THE CROSS-SECTIONAL DESIGN

The length of time it takes for many behaviours to change, even in limited longitudinal studies, has led researchers to a more convenient strategy for studying development. In the **cross-sectional design,** groups of people differing in age are studied at the same point in time.

A study in which children in grades 3, 6, 9, and 12 filled out a questionnaire asking about their sibling relationships provides a good illustration (Buhrmester & Furman, 1990). Findings revealed that sibling interaction was characterized by greater equality and less power assertion with age. Also, feelings of sibling companionship declined during adolescence. The researchers thought that several factors contributed to these age differences. As later-born children become

**biased sampling**
Failure to select participants who are representative of the population of interest in a study.

**selective attrition**
Selective loss of participants during an investigation, resulting in a biased sample.

**practice effects**
Changes in participants' natural responses as a result of repeated testing.

**cohort effects**
The effects of cultural-historical change on the accuracy of findings: Children developing in the same time period who are influenced by particular cultural and historical conditions make up a cohort.

**cross-sectional design**
A research design in which groups of participants of different ages are studied at the same point in time.

# cultural influences

## IMPACT OF HISTORICAL TIMES ON DEVELOPMENT: THE GREAT DEPRESSION AND WORLD WAR II

economic disaster, wars, and periods of rapid social change can profoundly affect people's lives. Yet their impact depends on when they strike during the life course. Glen Elder (1999) capitalized on the economic hardship families experienced during the Great Depression of the 1930s to study its influence on development. He delved into the vast archives of two major longitudinal studies: (1) the Oakland Growth Study, an investigation of individuals born in the early 1920s who were adolescents when the Depression took its toll; and (2) the Guidance Study, whose participants were born in the late 1920s and were young children when their families faced severe economic losses.

In both cohorts, relationships changed when economic deprivation struck. As unemployed fathers lost status, mothers took greater control over family affairs. This reversal of traditional gender roles often sparked conflict. Fathers sometimes became explosive and punitive toward their children. At other times, they withdrew into passivity and depression. Mothers often became frantic with worry over the well-being of their husbands and children, and many entered the labour force to make ends meet (Elder, Liker, & Cross, 1984).

### OUTCOMES FOR ADOLESCENTS

Although unusual burdens were placed on them as family lives changed, the Oakland Growth Study cohort—especially the boys—weathered economic hardship well. As adolescents, they were too old to be wholly dependent on their highly stressed parents. Boys spent less time at home as they searched for part-time jobs, and many turned toward adults and peers

outside the family for emotional support. Girls took over household chores and cared for younger siblings. Their greater involvement in family affairs exposed them to more parental conflict and unhappiness. Consequently, adolescent girls' adjustment in economically deprived homes was somewhat less favourable than adolescent boys' (Elder, Van Nguyen, & Caspi, 1985).

These changes had major consequences for adolescents' future aspirations and adult lives. As girls focused on home and family, they were less likely to think about college and careers and more likely to marry early. Boys learned that economic resources could not be taken for granted, and they tended to make an early commitment to an occupational choice. And the chance to become a parent was especially important to men whose lives had been disrupted by the Depression. Perhaps because they believed that a rewarding career could not be guaranteed, they viewed children as the most enduring benefit of their adult lives.

### OUTCOMES FOR CHILDREN

The Guidance Study participants were young children within the years of intense family dependency when the Depression struck. For young boys (who, as we will see in later chapters, are especially prone to adjustment problems in the face of family stress), the impact of economic strain was severe. They showed emotional difficulties and poor attitudes toward school and work that persisted through the teenage years (Elder & Caspi, 1988).

But as the Guidance Study sample became adolescents, another major historical event occurred: World War II. As a

result, thousands of men left their communities for military bases, leading to dramatic life changes. Some combat veterans came away with symptoms of emotional trauma that persisted for decades. Yet for most young soldiers, war mobilization broadened their range of knowledge and experience. It also granted time out from civilian responsibilities, giving many soldiers a chance to consider where their lives were going. Many expanded their education and acquired new skills after the war. By middle adulthood, the Guidance Study war veterans had reversed the early negative impact of the Great Depression. They were more successful educationally and occupationally than their counterparts who had not entered the service (Elder & Hareven, 1993).

Clearly, cultural-historical change does not have a uniform impact on development. Outcomes can vary considerably, depending on the pattern of historical events and the child's age when the event takes place.

The Great Depression of the 1930s left this farm family without a steady income. The adolescent girl (in the back row on the far right) may have been more negatively affected by economic hardship than her brother (second from left). And overall, younger children probably suffered more than older children.

CULVER PICTURES

more competent and independent, they no longer need and are probably less willing to accept direction from older siblings. In addition, as adolescents move from psychological dependence on the family to greater involvement with peers, they may have less time and emotional need to invest in their siblings. These intriguing ideas about the development of sibling relationships, as we will see in Chapter 14, have been confirmed in subsequent research.

**PROBLEMS IN CONDUCTING CROSS-SECTIONAL RESEARCH.** The cross-sectional design is an efficient strategy for describing age-related trends that is not affected by selective attrition, practice effects, or changes in the field that might make the findings obsolete by the time the study is complete. But evidence about change at the level at which it actually occurs—the individual—is not available (Kraemer et al., 2000). For example, in the cross-sectional study of sibling relationships just discussed, comparisons are limited to age-group averages. We cannot tell if important individual differences exist. Indeed, longitudinal findings reveal that adolescents vary considerably in the changing quality of their sibling relationships, many becoming more distant but some becoming more supportive and intimate (Dunn, Slomkowski, & Beardsall, 1994).

Cross-sectional studies—especially those that cover a wide age span—have another problem. Like longitudinal research, they can be threatened by cohort effects. For example, comparisons of 5-year-old cohorts and 15-year-old cohorts—groups born and reared in different years—may not really represent age-related changes. Instead, they may reflect unique experiences associated with the time period in which each age group grew up.

## IMPROVING DEVELOPMENTAL DESIGNS

Researchers have devised ways of building on the strengths and minimizing the weaknesses of longitudinal and cross-sectional approaches. Several modified developmental designs have resulted.

**COMBINING LONGITUDINAL AND CROSS-SECTIONAL APPROACHES.** Researchers merge longitudinal and cross-sectional strategies in the **longitudinal-sequential design.** It is called sequential because it is composed of a sequence of samples, each of which is followed longitudinally. For example, suppose we select three samples—sixth, seventh, and eighth graders—and follow them for two years. That is, we observe each sample this year and next year, as follows: Sample 1 from grades 6 to 7; Sample 2 from grades 7 to 8; and Sample 3 from grades 8 to 9.

The design has three advantages: (1) We can find out whether cohort effects are operating by comparing children of the same age (or grade in school) who were born in different years. Using our example, we can compare children from different samples at grades 7 and 8. If they do not differ, then we can rule out cohort effects. (2) We can make both longitudinal and cross-sectional comparisons. If outcomes are similar, then we can be especially confident about our findings. (3) The design is efficient. In our example, we can find out about change over a 4-year period by following each cohort for just 2 years.

A study of adolescents' gender-stereotyped beliefs included the longitudinal-sequential features just described (Alfieri, Ruble, & Higgins, 1996). The researchers focused on the development of stereotype flexibility—that is, young people's willingness to say that "masculine" traits (such as *strength)* and "feminine" traits (such as *gentleness)* characterize both males and females. As Figure 2.3 shows, a sharp longitudinal decline in stereotype flexibility occurred for Samples 2 and 3, whose scores were similar when measured at the same grade (grade 8). But Sample 1, on reaching seventh grade, scored much lower than seventh graders in Sample 2!

The reason, the researchers discovered, was that Sample 1 remained in the same school from grade 6 to 7, whereas Samples 2 and 3 had made the transition from elementary to junior high school. Entry into junior high sparked a temporary rise in gender-stereotype flexibility, perhaps because of exposure to a wide range of older peers, some of whom challenged previously held stereotypes. Over time, stereotype flexibility decreases as adolescents experience pressures to conform to traditional gender roles—a topic we will take up in Chapter 13.

Notice how the developmental trend shown in Figure 2.3—high gender-stereotype flexibility at grade 7 that drops off steeply—characterizes only adolescents who enter a self-contained

**longitudinal-sequential design**
A research design with both longitudinal and cross-sectional components in which groups of participants born in different years are followed over time.

**microgenetic design**
A research design in which researchers present children with a novel task and follow their mastery over a series of closely spaced sessions.

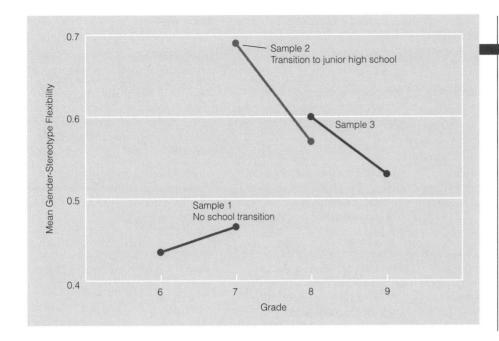

FIGURE 2.3

**A longitudinal-sequential study of the development of gender-stereotyped beliefs during adolescence.** Three samples were followed longitudinally from one school year to the next. To test for cohort effects, the researchers compared Sample 1 with Sample 2 at grade 7 and Sample 2 with Sample 3 at grade 8. The scores of Samples 1 and 2 did not match! The reason, the investigators discovered from additional evidence, was that a cohort effect—transition to junior high school—prompts a temporary rise in gender-stereotype flexibility. Because the scores of Samples 2 and 3 were similar at grade 8, the researchers were confident that gender-stereotype flexibility declines sharply in the years following transition to junior high school. (Adapted from Alfieri, Ruble, & Higgins, 1996.)

junior high school. Researchers have become increasingly interested in identifying such cohort effects because they help explain diversity in development (Magnusson & Stattin, 1998).

**EXAMINING MICROCOSMS OF DEVELOPMENT.** In all the examples of developmental research we have discussed, observations of children are fairly widely spaced. When we observe once a year or every few years, we can describe change, but we have little opportunity to capture the processes that produce it. A modification of the longitudinal approach, called the **microgenetic design,** is becoming more popular because it offers insights into how development takes place. Microgenetic studies present children with a novel task and follow their mastery over a series of closely spaced sessions (Kuhn, 1995; Siegler & Crowley, 1991). Within this "microcosm" of development, researchers see how change occurs.

In one microgenetic study, conducted at Wilfrid Laurier University, researchers watched how parents helped their fifth graders master challenging long-division problems. Children who progressed the fastest had parents who sensitively adjusted the help they offered to the child's moment-by-moment performance. If the child failed to solve a problem, the parent provided more direct guidance on the next try. If the child succeeded, the parent permitted the child to assume greater responsibility for the task (Pratt, Green, & MacVicar, 1992). In this investigation, the researchers focused on parental teaching techniques. In other microgenetic studies, they have examined the strategies children use to solve problems and acquire new knowledge in reading, mathematics, and science (Siegler, 1996; Thornton, 1999).

As these examples illustrate, the microgenetic design is especially useful for studying cognitive development. In Chapter 4, we will see that it has also been used to trace infant mastery of motor skills. Nevertheless, microgenetic studies are difficult to carry out. Researchers must pore over hours of videotaped records, analyzing each participant's behaviour. In addition, the time required for children to change is hard to anticipate. It depends on a careful match between the child's capabilities and the demands of the task (Siegler & Crowley, 1991). Finally, as in other longitudinal research, practice effects can distort the findings. As a check, researchers can compare microgenetic with cross-sectional observations. If new behaviours that emerge microgenetically reflect typical development, they should match the behaviours displayed by more advanced participants in cross-sectional studies, who are observed only once (Kuhn, 1995). In sum, when researchers find ways to surmount the challenges of microgenetic research, they see development as it takes place.

What strategies does this child use to solve puzzles, and how does she become proficient at puzzle solving? In the microgenetic design, researchers track change while it occurs, observing frequently from the time it begins until it stabilizes.

**TABLE** 2.3

Strengths and Limitations of Developmental Research Designs

| DESIGN | DESCRIPTION | STRENGTHS | LIMITATIONS |
|---|---|---|---|
| Longitudinal design | The investigator studies the same group of participants repeatedly at different ages. | Permits study of common patterns and individual differences in development and relationships between early and later events and behaviours. | Age-related changes may be distorted because of biased sampling, selective attrition, practice effects, and cohort effects. Theoretical and methodological changes in the field can make findings obsolete. |
| Cross-sectional design | The investigator studies groups of participants differing in age at the same point in time. | More efficient than the longitudinal design. Not plagued by selective attrition, practice effects, or theoretical and methodological changes in the field. | Does not permit study of individual developmental trends. Age differences may be distorted because of cohort effects. |
| Longitudinal-sequential design | The investigator studies two or more groups of participants born in different years at the same point in time. | Permits both longitudinal and cross-sectional comparisons. Reveals cohort effects. Permits tracking of age-related changes more efficiently than the longitudinal design. | May have the same problems as longitudinal and cross-sectional strategies, but the design itself helps identify difficulties. |
| Microgenetic design | The investigator presents children with a novel task and follows their mastery over a series of closely spaced sessions. | Offers insights into processes of change. | Requires intensive study of participants' moment-by-moment behaviours; the time required for participants to change is difficult to anticipate; practice effects may distort developmental trends. |

**COMBINING EXPERIMENTAL AND DEVELOPMENTAL DESIGNS.** Perhaps you noticed that all the examples of longitudinal and cross-sectional research we have considered permit only correlational, and not causal, inferences. Yet causal information is desirable, both for testing theories and for finding ways to improve children's lives. If a developmental design indicates that children's experiences and behaviour are related, in some instances we can explore the causal link by experimentally manipulating their experiences. If, as a result, development is enhanced, we would have strong evidence for a causal association between experiences and behaviour. Today, research that combines an experimental strategy with either a longitudinal or cross-sectional approach appears with increasing frequency. These designs help investigators move beyond correlated variables to a causal account of development. For a summary of the strengths and limitations of developmental research designs, refer to Table 2.3.

**ASK YOURSELF**

**review**    Explain how cohort effects can distort the findings of both longitudinal and cross-sectional studies. How does the longitudinal-sequential design reveal cohort effects?

**review**    What design is best suited to studying processes of change, and why? When researchers use this design, what factors can threaten the validity of their findings?

**apply**    A researcher wants to find out if children enrolled in child-care centres in the first few years of life do as well in school as those who are not in child care. Which developmental design is appropriate for answering this question? Explain.

**apply**    Suppose a researcher asks you to enrol your baby in a 10-year longitudinal study. What factors would lead you to agree and stay involved? Do your answers shed light on why longitudinal studies often have biased samples? Explain.

# Ethics in Research on Children

RESEARCH INTO HUMAN behaviour creates ethical issues because, unfortunately, the quest for scientific knowledge can sometimes exploit people. When children take part in research, the ethical concerns are especially complex. Children are more vulnerable than adults to physical and psychological harm. In addition, immaturity makes it difficult or impossible for children to evaluate for themselves what participation in research will mean. For these reasons, special ethical guidelines for research on children have been developed by the government, funding agencies, and associations such as the Canadian Psychological Association (2000), the American Psychological Association (1992), and the Society for Research in Child Development (1993). In Canada, psychologists must also adhere to the guidelines set by their provincial regulatory bodies.

Table 2.4 presents a summary of children's basic research rights. Once you have examined them, think back to the ethical controversy faced by my colleague Ron, described at the beginning of this chapter. Then look at the following research situations, each of which poses an additional ethical dilemma. What precautions do you think should be taken to protect the rights of children in each instance? Is either research study so threatening to children's well-being that it should not be carried out?

- To study children's willingness to separate from their caregivers, an investigator decides to ask mothers of 1- and 2-year-olds to leave their child alone briefly in an unfamiliar playroom. The researcher knows that these circumstances will upset some children.

- In a study of moral development, a researcher wants to assess children's ability to resist temptation by videotaping their behaviour without their knowledge. Seven-year-olds are promised a prize for solving difficult puzzles. They are also told not to look at a classmate's correct solutions, which are deliberately placed at the back of the room. Telling children ahead of time that cheating is being studied or that their behaviour is being monitored will destroy the purpose of the study.

TABLE 2.4

Children's Research Rights

| RESEARCH RIGHT | DESCRIPTION |
|---|---|
| Protection from harm | Children have the right to be protected from physical or psychological harm in research. If in doubt about the harmful effects of research, investigators should seek the opinion of others. When harm seems possible, investigators should find other means for obtaining the desired information or abandon the research. |
| Informed consent | All research participants, including children, have the right to have explained to them, in language appropriate to their level of understanding, all aspects of the research that may affect their willingness to participate. When children are participants, informed consent of parents as well as others who act on the child's behalf (such as school officials) should be obtained, preferably in writing. Children, and the adults responsible for them, have the right to discontinue participation in the research at any time. |
| Privacy | Children have the right to concealment of their identity on all information collected in the course of research. They also have this right with respect to written reports and any informal discussions about the research. |
| Knowledge of results | Children have the right to be informed of the results of research in language that is appropriate to their level of understanding. |
| Beneficial treatments | If experimental treatments believed to be beneficial are under investigation, children in control groups have the right to alternative beneficial treatments if they are available. |

*Sources:* American Psychological Association, 1992; Society for Research in Child Development, 1993.

Did you find it difficult to evaluate these examples? Virtually every organization that has devised ethical principles for research has concluded that conflicts like these cannot be resolved with simple right-or-wrong answers. Ultimate responsibility for the ethical integrity of research lies with the investigator.

However, researchers are advised or, for some funded research, required to seek advice from others. Committees, like the one that evaluated Ron's research, exist in universities and other institutions for this purpose. These review boards evaluate proposed studies on the basis of a **risks-versus-benefits ratio.** This involves weighing the costs to participants in terms of inconvenience and possible psychological or physical injury against the study's value for advancing knowledge and improving conditions of life.

Ron's procedures, the school's research committee claimed, might not offer children sufficient **protection from harm.** If there are any risks to the safety and welfare of participants that the research does not justify, then priority should always be given to the research participants. Vulnerability to harm, as the From Research to Practice box on the following page reveals, varies with children's age and characteristics. Occasionally, further inquiry can help resolve perplexing ethical dilemmas. In Ron's case, he provided the research committee with findings showing that asking elementary school children to identify disliked peers does not lead them to interact less frequently or more negatively with those children (Bell-Dolan, Foster, & Sikora, 1989). At the same time, Ron agreed to take special precautions when requesting such information. He promised to ask all the children to keep their comments confidential. Also, he arranged to conduct the study at a time when classmates have limited opportunity to interact with one another—just before a school vacation (Bell-Dolan & Wessler, 1994). With these safeguards in place, the committee approved Ron's research.

The ethical principle of **informed consent** requires special interpretation when the research participants are children. Investigators must take into account the competence of youngsters of different ages to make choices about their own participation. Parental consent is meant to protect the safety of children whose ability to make these decisions is not yet fully mature. Besides obtaining parental consent, researchers should seek agreement of other individuals who act on children's behalf, such as institutional officials when research is conducted in schools, child-care centres, or hospitals. This is especially important when studies include special groups whose parents may not represent their best interests (refer again to the From Research to Practice box).

For children 7 years and older, their own informed consent should be obtained in addition to parental consent. Around age 7, changes in children's thinking permit them to better understand simple scientific principles and the needs of others. Researchers should respect and enhance these new capacities by providing school-age children with a full explanation of research activities in language they can understand (Fisher, 1993).

Finally, young children rely on a basic faith in adults to feel secure in unfamiliar situations. For this reason, some types of research may be particularly disturbing to them. All ethical guidelines advise that special precautions be taken in the use of deception and concealment, as occurs when researchers observe children from behind one-way mirrors, give them false feedback about their performance, or do not tell them the truth regarding what the research is about. When these kinds of procedures are used with adult participants, **debriefing,** in which the experimenter provides a full account and justification of the activities, occurs after the research session is over. Debriefing should also take place with children, but it often does not work as well. Despite explanations, children may leave the research situation with their belief in the honesty of adults undermined. Ethical standards permit deception in research with children if investigators satisfy institutional committees that such practices are necessary. Nevertheless, since deception may have serious emotional consequences for some youngsters, many child development specialists believe that investigators should come up with other research strategies when children are involved.

**risks-versus-benefits ratio**
A comparison of the costs of a research study to participants in terms of inconvenience and possible psychological or physical injury against its value for advancing knowledge and improving conditions of life. Used in assessing the ethics of research.

**protection from harm**
The right of research participants to be protected from physical or psychological harm.

**informed consent**
The right of research participants, including children, to have explained to them, in language they can understand, all aspects of a study that may affect their willingness to participate.

**debriefing**
Providing a full account and justification of research activities to participants in a study in which deception was used.

# from research to practice

### CHILDREN'S RESEARCH RISKS: DEVELOPMENTAL AND INDIVIDUAL DIFFERENCES

researchers interested in children's behaviour face formidable challenges in defining their ethical responsibilities. Compared with adults, children are less capable of benefiting from research experiences. Furthermore, the risks they are likely to encounter are psychological rather than physical (as in medical research) and therefore difficult to anticipate and sometimes even detect (Thompson, 1992). Consider, for example, 7-year-old Henry, who did not want to answer a researcher's questions about how he feels about his younger brother, who has physical disabilities. Since Henry's parents told him they had granted permission for his participation, he did not feel free to say no to the researcher. Or take 11-year-old Isabelle, who tried to solve a problem unsuccessfully. Despite the researcher's assurances that the task was set up to be impossible, Isabelle returned to her classroom concerned about her own competence.

How can we make sure that children are subjected to the least research risk possible? One valuable resource is our expanding knowledge of age-related capacities and individual differences. A close look reveals that research risks vary with development in complex ways. Some risks decrease with age, others increase, and still others occur at many or all ages (Thompson, 1990b). And because of their personal characteristics and life circumstances, some children are more vulnerable to harm than others.

## AGE DIFFERENCES

Research plans for younger children typically receive the most scrutiny, since their limited cognitive competencies restrict their ability to make reasoned decisions and resist violations of their rights. In addition, as Henry's predicament illustrates, young children's limited social power can make it difficult for them to refuse participation. In a study of food metabolism that also examined 5- to 18-year-olds' understanding of

research procedures, no children age 9 or younger comprehended why they were asked to engage in the research activities, and few could identify any potential benefit or harm. And regardless of age, most participants thought withdrawing from the study would lead to negative consequences and felt external pressure to continue (for example, some thought the experimenter would be unhappy if they stopped) (Ondrusek et al., 1998). However, according to Rona Abramovitch of the University of Toronto and others, if a researcher explicitly said that she would not mind if the child stopped, children understood their right much better and were more likely to exercise it (Abramovitch et al., 1995).

Whereas young children have special difficulties understanding the research process, older children are more susceptible to procedures that threaten the way they think of themselves. As children become increasingly sensitive to the evaluations of others, giving false feedback or inducing failure (as happened to Isabelle) is more stressful. In adolescence, however, when views of the self are well established and questioning of authority is common, young people are probably better at sizing up and rejecting researchers' deceptive evaluations (Thompson, 1992).

## CHILDREN'S UNIQUE CHARACTERISTICS

At times, children's backgrounds, prior experiences, and other characteristics introduce special vulnerabilities. For example, parents of maltreated children are not always good advocates for their children. The consent of an additional adult invested in the child's welfare—perhaps a relative, teacher, or therapist—may be necessary to protect the child's rights. And because abuse is associated with deep psychological wounds, such children are at greater risk than their agemates when research proce-

dures induce anxiety or threaten their self-image. In certain cases, such as with adolescent substance abusers or delinquents, parents may be so eager to get their children into contact with professionals that they would agree to any research without much forethought (Drotar et al., 2000).

## CONCLUSION

Finding ways to reconcile the risks–versus-benefits conflicts we have considered is vital, since research on children is of great value to society. As each study is evaluated, participants' age and unique characteristics should be central to the discussion. Because of pressures they sometimes feel, children and adolescents need clear, age-appropriate explanations of benefits and risks and their right to dissent from participation. And their decision should be the final word in most investigations, even though this standard is not mandatory in current guidelines (Thompson, 1992).

WILL FALLER

This investigator is inviting a 6-year-old boy to participate in a research study as his mother looks on. Although the boy seems eager to comply, the researcher must explain that he can end his participation at any time. She must also tell him how he can terminate his involvement if his initial pleasurable response changes. Even after explanation, some children believe that there will be negative consequences, such as parental or researcher disapproval, if they do not continue.

## ASK YOURSELF www

**review**    Why is the use of deception in research more risky with children than with adults?

**review**    Explain why researchers must consider children's age-related capacities to ensure that the children are protected from harm and have freely consented to research.

**apply**    When a researcher engages in naturalistic observation of preschoolers' play, a child says, "Stop watching me!" Using the research rights in Table 2.4, how should the researcher respond, and why?

# summary

## FROM THEORY TO HYPOTHESIS

*Describe the role of theories, hypotheses, and research questions in the research process.*

■ Research usually begins with a **hypothesis,** or prediction about behaviour drawn from a theory. When little or no theory exists on a topic of interest, it starts with a research question. On the basis of the hypothesis or question, the investigator selects research methods (specific activities of participants) and a research design (overall plan for the study).

## COMMON METHODS USED TO STUDY CHILDREN

*Describe research methods commonly used to study children.*

■ **Naturalistic observations,** gathered in children's everyday environments, permit researchers to see directly the everyday behaviours they hope to explain. In contrast, **structured observations** take place in laboratories, where every participant has an equal opportunity to display the behaviours of interest.

■ Depending on the researcher's purpose, observations can preserve participants' entire behaviour stream, as in the **specimen record,** or they can be limited to one or a few behaviours, as in **event sampling** and **time sampling. Observer influence** and **observer bias** can reduce the accuracy of observational findings.

■ Self-report methods can be flexible and open-ended, like the **clinical interview,** which permits participants to express their thoughts in ways similar to their thinking

in everyday life. Alternatively, **structured interviews,** tests, and questionnaires, which permit efficient administration and scoring, can be given. Both approaches depend on people's ability and willingness to engage in accurate reporting.

■ **Psychophysiological methods** measure the relation between physiological processes and behaviour. They help researchers uncover the biological bases of children's perceptual, cognitive, and emotional responses.

■ Investigators rely on the **clinical,** or **case study, method** to obtain an in-depth understanding of a single child. In this approach, interviews, observations, test scores, and sometimes psychophysiological assessments are synthesized into a complete description of the participant's development and unique psychological functioning.

■ A growing interest in the impact of culture has prompted child development researchers to adapt observational and self-report methods to permit direct comparisons of cultures. To uncover the cultural meanings of children's and adults' behaviours, they rely on a method borrowed from the field of anthropology—**ethnography.** It uses participant observation to understand the unique values and social processes of a culture or distinct social group.

## RELIABILITY AND VALIDITY: KEYS TO SCIENTIFICALLY SOUND RESEARCH

*Explain how reliability and validity apply to research methods and to the overall accuracy of research findings and conclusions.*

■ To be acceptable to the scientific community, research methods must be both reliable and valid. **Reliability** refers to the consistency, or repeatability, of observational, self-report, and psychophysiological measures. In the case of clinical and ethnographic research, reliability involves assessing whether the patterns and themes identified by the researcher are grounded in evidence and plausible.

■ A method has high **validity** if, after examining its content and relationships with other measures of behaviour, the researcher finds that it reflects what it was intended to measure. The concept of validity can also be applied more broadly, to the overall accuracy of research findings and conclusions. In designing a study, investigators must take special precautions to make sure that factors unrelated to the hypothesis do not influence participants' behaviour.

## GENERAL RESEARCH DESIGNS

*Distinguish correlational and experimental research designs, noting their strengths and limitations.*

■ Two main types of designs are used in all research on human behaviour. The **correlational design** examines relationships between variables as they happen to occur, without altering people's experiences. The **correlation coefficient** is often used to measure the association between variables. Correlational studies do not permit inferences about cause and effect. However, their use is justified when it is difficult or impossible to control the variables of interest.

- An **experimental design** permits inferences about cause and effect. Researchers manipulate an **independent variable** by exposing groups of participants to two or more treatment conditions. Then they determine what effect this has on a **dependent variable**. **Random assignment** and **matching** ensure that characteristics of participants do not reduce the accuracy of experimental findings.

- **Laboratory experiments** usually achieve high degrees of control, but their findings may not apply to everyday life. To overcome this problem, researchers sometimes conduct **field experiments,** in which they manipulate treatment conditions in the real world. When this is impossible, investigators may compromise and conduct **natural experiments,** in which already existing treatments, involving groups of people whose characteristics are as much alike as possible, are compared. This approach, however, is less precise and rigorous than a true experimental design.

## DESIGNS FOR STUDYING DEVELOPMENT

*Describe designs for studying development, noting their strengths and limitations.*

- Longitudinal and cross-sectional designs are uniquely suited for studying development. The **longitudinal design** permits study of common patterns as well as individual differences in development and the relationship between early and later events and behaviours.

- Researchers face a variety of problems in conducting longitudinal research, including **biased sampling, selective attrition, practice effects,** and changes in accepted theories and methods during long-term studies. But the most widely discussed threat to the validity of longitudinal findings is **cohort effects**—difficulty generalizing to children growing up during different time periods.

- The **cross-sectional design,** in which groups of participants differing in age are studied at the same time, offers an efficient approach to studying development. Although not plagued by such problems as selective attrition, practice effects, or theoretical and methodological changes in the field, it is limited to comparisons of age-group averages. Like longitudinal research, cross-sectional studies can be threatened by cohort effects, especially when they cover a wide age span.

- Modified developmental designs overcome some of the limitations of longitudinal and cross-sectional research. By combining the two approaches in the **longitudinal-sequential design,** researchers can test for cohort effects, make longitudinal and cross-sectional comparisons, and gather information about development efficiently. In the **microgenetic design,** researchers track change as it occurs. In doing so, they obtain insights into the processes of development. Drawbacks of the microgenetic design include extensive analysis of records, the difficulty of anticipating the time required for participants to change, and practice effects. When experimental procedures are combined with developmental designs, researchers can examine causal influences on development.

## ETHICS IN RESEARCH ON CHILDREN

*What special ethical issues arise in doing research on children?*

- Because of their immaturity, children are especially vulnerable to harm and often cannot evaluate the risks and benefits of research. Ethical guidelines and special committees that weigh research in terms of a **risks-versus-benefits ratio** help ensure that children's rights are safeguarded and that they are afforded **protection from harm.** In addition to parental consent and agreement of other individuals who act on children's behalf, researchers should seek the **informed consent** of children age 7 and older for research participation. The use of deception in research with children is especially risky, since **debriefing** can undermine their basic faith in the trustworthiness of adults.

# important terms and concepts

biased sampling (p. 58)
clinical interview (p. 46)
clinical, or case study, method (p. 48)
cohort effects (p. 58)
correlation coefficient (p. 54)
correlational design (p. 53)
cross-sectional design (p. 58)
debriefing (p. 64)
dependent variable (p. 54)
ethnography (p. 51)
event sampling (p. 45)
experimental design (p. 54)
field experiment (p. 55)

hypothesis (p. 42)
independent variable (p. 54)
informed consent (p. 64)
laboratory experiment (p. 54)
longitudinal design (p. 57)
longitudinal-sequential design (p. 60)
matching (p. 55)
microgenetic design (p. 60)
natural experiment (p. 55)
naturalistic observation (p. 44)
observer bias (p. 45)
observer influence (p. 45)

practice effects (p. 58)
protection from harm (p. 64)
psychophysiological methods (p. 47)
random assignment (p. 55)
reliability (p. 52)
risks-versus-benefits ratio (p. 64)
selective attrition (p. 58)
specimen record (p. 44)
structured interview (p. 46)
structured observation (p. 44)
time sampling (p. 45)
validity (p. 53)

"Pregnant Mummy"
Eliska Kocova
5 years, Czech Republic

Reprinted with permission
from The International
Museum of Children's Art,
Oslo, Norway

This portrait of a new developing being, safe within its mother's womb and surrounded by an optimistic world, captures the myriad influences on children's development. Chapter 3 will introduce you to this complex blend of genetic and environmental forces.

# three

## Biological Foundations, Prenatal Development, and Birth

"IT'S A GIRL," ANNOUNCES the doctor, who holds up the squalling little creature, while her new parents gaze with amazement at their miraculous creation. "A girl! We've named her Sarah!" exclaims the proud father to eager relatives waiting by the telephone for word about their new family member. As we join these parents in thinking about how this wondrous being came into existence and imagining her future, we are struck by many questions. How could this baby, equipped with everything necessary for life outside the womb, have developed from the union of two tiny cells? What ensures that Sarah will, in due time, roll over, walk, talk, make friends, imagine, and create—just like every other normal child born before her? Why is she a girl and not a boy, dark-haired rather than blonde, calm and cuddly instead of wiry and energetic? What difference will it make that Sarah lives in one family, community, nation, and culture rather than another?

We begin our discussion of these questions by considering genetic foundations. Because nature has prepared us for survival, all humans have features in common. Yet each human being is also unique. Take a moment to jot down the most obvious similarities in physical characteristics and behaviour for several sets of children and parents you know well. Does one child show combined features of both parents, another resemble just one parent, and still a third favour neither? These directly observable

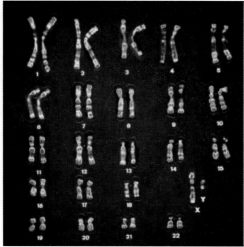 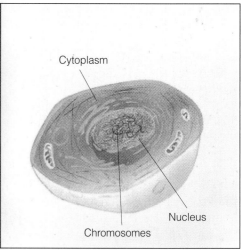

**FIGURE 3.1**

**A karyotype, or photograph, of human chromosomes.** The 46 chromosomes shown on the left were isolated from a human cell, stained, greatly magnified, and arranged in pairs according to decreasing size of the upper "arm" of each chromosome. Note the twenty-third pair, XY. The cell donor is a male. In a female, the twenty-third pair would be XX.

characteristics are called **phenotypes.** They depend in part on the individual's **genotype**—the complex blend of genetic information that determines our species and influences all our unique characteristics. But phenotypes, as our discussion will show, are also affected by a long history of environmental influences—ones that begin even before conception.

Next, we trace development during the most rapid phase of growth, the prenatal period, in which complex transactions between heredity and environment shape the course of development. We consider environmental supports necessary for normal prenatal growth, as well as influences that threaten the child's health and survival. Then we turn to the drama of birth and to developmental risks for infants born underweight or prematurely.

Finally, we take a look ahead. We consider how researchers think about and study the relationship between nature and nurture as they continue to influence the individual's emerging characteristics from infancy through adolescence.

## Genetic Foundations

EACH OF US IS made up of trillions of units called *cells*. When cells are chemically stained and viewed through a powerful microscope, rodlike structures called **chromosomes** are visible in the cell *nucleus*, or control centre. Chromosomes store and transmit genetic information. Their number varies from species to species—48 for chimpanzees, 64 for horses, 40 for mice, and 46 for human beings. Chromosomes come in matching pairs (an exception is the XY pair in males, which we will discuss shortly). Each member of a pair corresponds to the other in size, shape, and the traits it regulates. One is inherited from the mother and one from the father. Therefore, in humans, we speak of *23 pairs* of chromosomes residing in each human cell (see Figure 3.1).

### THE GENETIC CODE

Chromosomes are made up of a chemical substance called **deoxyribonucleic acid,** or **DNA.** As Figure 3.2 shows, DNA is a long, double-stranded molecule that looks like a twisted ladder. Notice that each rung consists of a pair of chemical substances called *bases*. Although the bases always pair up in the same way across the ladder rungs—A with T, and C with G—they can occur in any order. It is this sequence of base pairs that provides genetic instructions. A **gene** is a segment of DNA along the length of the chromosome. Genes can be of different lengths—from about 2 thousand to 2 million ladder rungs long (Genome International Sequencing Consortium, 2001). An estimated 30 000 to 35 000 genes lie along the human chromosomes.

**phenotype**
The individual's physical and behavioural characteristics, which are determined by both genetic and environmental factors.

**genotype**
The genetic makeup of an individual.

**chromosomes**
Rodlike structures in the cell nucleus that store and transmit genetic information.

**deoxyribonucleic acid (DNA)**
Long, double-stranded molecules that make up chromosomes.

**gene**
A segment of a DNA molecule that contains instructions for production of various proteins that contribute to growth and functioning of the body.

Genes accomplish their task by sending instructions for making a rich assortment of proteins to the *cytoplasm,* the area surrounding the nucleus of the cell. Proteins, which trigger chemical reactions throughout the body, are the biological foundation on which our characteristics and capacities are built.

A unique feature of DNA is that it can duplicate itself. This special ability makes it possible for a single cell, formed at conception, to develop into a complex human being composed of a great many cells. The process of cell duplication is called **mitosis.** In mitosis, the DNA ladder splits down the middle, opening somewhat like a zipper (refer again to Figure 3.2). Then, each base pairs up with a new mate from cytoplasm of the cell. This process creates two identical DNA ladders, each containing one new side and one old side. During mitosis, each chromosome copies itself. As a result, each new body cell contains the same number of chromosomes and identical genetic information.

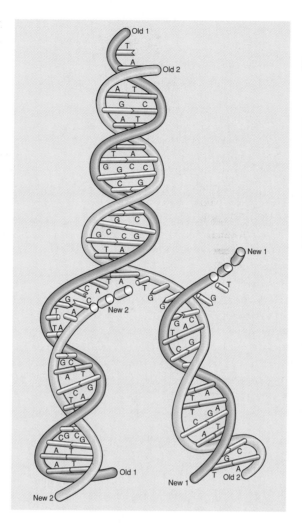

FIGURE 3.2

**DNA's ladderlike structure.**
This figure shows that the pairing of bases across the rungs of the ladder are very specific: adenine (A) always appears with thymine (T), and cytosine (C) always appears with guanine (G). Here, the DNA ladder duplicates by splitting down the middle of its ladder rungs. Each free base picks up a new complementary partner from the area surrounding the cell nucleus.

## THE SEX CELLS

New individuals are created when two special cells called **gametes,** or sex cells—the sperm and ovum—combine. A gamete contains only 23 chromosomes, half as many as a regular body cell. Gametes are formed through a cell division process called **meiosis,** which halves the number of chromosomes normally present in body cells.

Meiosis takes place according to the steps in Figure 3.3 on page 72. First, chromosomes pair up within the original cell, and each one copies itself. Then a special event called **crossing over** occurs. In crossing over, chromosomes next to each other break at one or more points along their length and exchange segments, so that genes from one are replaced by genes from another. This shuffling of genes creates new hereditary combinations. Next, the paired chromosomes separate into different cells, but chance determines which member of each pair will gather with others and end up in the same gamete. Finally, in the last phase of meiosis, each chromosome leaves its duplicate and becomes part of a sex cell containing 23 chromosomes instead of the usual 46.

In the male, four sperm are produced when meiosis is complete. Also, the cells from which sperm arise are produced continuously throughout life. For this reason, a healthy man can father a child at any age after sexual maturity. In the female, meiosis results in just one ovum. In addition, the female is born with all her ova already present in her ovaries, and she can bear children for only three to four decades. Still, there are plenty of ova. About 1 to 2 million are present at birth, 40 000 remain at adolescence, and approximately 350 to 450 will mature during a woman's childbearing years (Moore & Persaud, 1998).

**mitosis**
The process of cell duplication, in which each new cell receives an exact copy of the original chromosomes.

**gametes**
Human sperm and ova, which contain half as many chromosomes as a regular body cell.

**meiosis**
The process of cell division through which gametes are formed and in which the number of chromosomes in each cell is halved.

**crossing over**
Exchange of genes between chromosomes next to each other during meiosis.

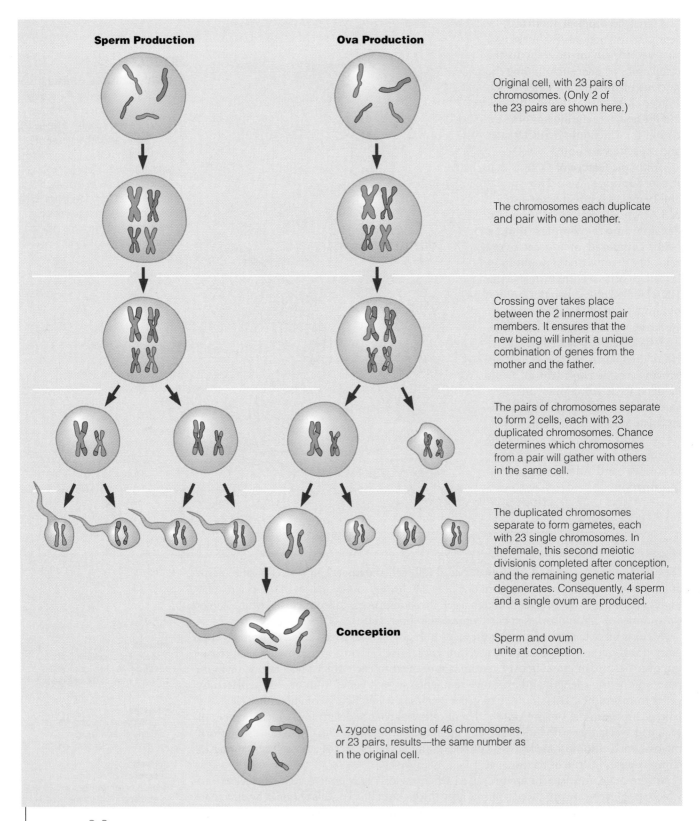

**Sperm Production**

**Ova Production**

Original cell, with 23 pairs of chromosomes. (Only 2 of the 23 pairs are shown here.)

The chromosomes each duplicate and pair with one another.

Crossing over takes place between the 2 innermost pair members. It ensures that the new being will inherit a unique combination of genes from the mother and the father.

The pairs of chromosomes separate to form 2 cells, each with 23 duplicated chromosomes. Chance determines which chromosomes from a pair will gather with others in the same cell.

The duplicated chromosomes separate to form gametes, each with 23 single chromosomes. In thefemale, this second meiotic divisionis completed after conception, and the remaining genetic material degenerates. Consequently, 4 sperm and a single ovum are produced.

**Conception**

Sperm and ovum unite at conception.

A zygote consisting of 46 chromosomes, or 23 pairs, results—the same number as in the original cell.

**FIGURE** 3.3

**The cell division process of meiosis, leading to gamete formation.** (Here, original cells are depicted with 2 rather than the full complement of 23 pairs.) Meiosis creates gametes with only half the usual number of chromosomes. When sperm and ovum unite at conception, the first cell of the new individual (the zygote) has the correct, full number of chromosomes.

The steps of meiosis ensure that a constant quantity of genetic material (46 chromosomes in each cell) is transmitted between generations. When sperm and ovum unite at fertilization, the cell that results, called a **zygote,** will again have 46 chromosomes.

Can you see how meiosis leads to variability among offspring? Crossing over and random sorting of each member of a chromosome pair into separate sex cells mean that the chances of offspring of the same two parents being genetically the same is extremely slim—about 1 in 700 trillion (Gould & Keeton, 1997). Therefore, meiosis helps us understand why siblings differ even though they also have features in common. The genetic variability produced by meiosis is adaptive. It increases the chances that at least some members of a species will cope with ever-changing environments and survive.

## MULTIPLE OFFSPRING

Only under one circumstance do offspring *not* display the genetic variability we have just discussed. Sometimes a zygote that has started to duplicate separates into two clusters of cells that develop into two individuals. These are called **identical,** or **monozygotic, twins** because they have the same genetic makeup. The frequency of identical twins is the same around the world—about 3 out of every 1000 births (Tong, Caddy, & Short, 1997). Animal research has uncovered a variety of environmental influences that prompt this type of twinning, including temperature changes, variation in oxygen levels, and late fertilization of the ovum.

**Fraternal,** or **dizygotic, twins,** the most common type of multiple birth, result when two ova are released from a woman's ovaries at the same time and both are fertilized. The resulting twins are genetically no more alike than ordinary siblings. Older maternal age and fertility drugs are major causes of a dramatic rise in fraternal twinning since the 1970s (Bortolus et al., 1999). As Table 3.1 shows, other genetic and environmental factors are also involved.

## BOY OR GIRL?

Using special microscopic techniques, we can distinguish the 23 pairs of chromosomes in each human cell from one another. Twenty-two of them are matching pairs, called **autosomes.** They are numbered by geneticists from longest (1) to shortest (22) (refer back to Figure 3.1). The twenty-third pair consists of **sex chromosomes.** In females, this

These identical, or monozygotic, twins were created when a duplicating zygote separated into two clusters of cells, and two individuals with the same genetic makeup developed. Identical twins look alike, and as we will see later in this chapter, tend to resemble each other in a variety of psychological characteristics.

**zygote**
The union of sperm and ovum at conception.

**identical, or monozygotic, twins**
Twins that result when a zygote that has started to duplicate separates into two clusters of cells that develop into two individuals with the same genetic makeup.

**fraternal, or dizygotic, twins**
Twins that result from the release and fertilization of two ova. They are genetically no more alike than ordinary siblings.

**autosomes**
The 22 matching chromosome pairs in each human cell.

**sex chromosomes**
The twenty-third pair of chromosomes, which determines the sex of the child. In females, this pair is called XX; in males, it is called XY.

 **TABLE** 3.1

Maternal Factors Linked to Fraternal Twinning

| FACTOR | DESCRIPTION |
|---|---|
| Ethnicity | Occurs in 4 per 1000 births among Asians, 8 per 1000 births among whites, 12 to 16 per 1000 births among blacks[a] |
| Family history of twinning | Occurs more often among women whose mothers and sisters gave birth to fraternal twins |
| Age | Rises with maternal age, peaking between 35 and 39 years, and then rapidly falls |
| Nutrition | Occurs less often among women with poor diets; occurs more often among women who are tall and overweight or of normal weight as opposed to slight body build |
| Number of births | Is more likely with each additional birth |
| Fertility drugs and in vitro fertilization | Is more likely with fertility hormones and in vitro fertilization (see page 82), which also increase the chances of triplets to quintuplets |

[a]Worldwide rates, not including multiple births resulting from use of fertility drugs.
*Sources:* Bortolus et al., 1999; Mange & Mange, 1998.

**TABLE** 3.2

Examples of Dominant and Recessive Characteristics

| DOMINANT | RECESSIVE |
| --- | --- |
| Dark hair | Blond hair |
| Normal hair | Pattern baldness |
| Curly hair | Straight hair |
| Nonred hair | Red hair |
| Facial dimples | No dimples |
| Normal hearing | Some forms of deafness |
| Normal vision | Nearsightedness |
| Farsightedness | Normal vision |
| Normal vision | Congenital eye cataracts |
| Normally pigmented skin | Albinism |
| Double-jointedness | Normal joints |
| Type A blood | Type O blood |
| Type B blood | Type O blood |
| Rh-positive blood | Rh-negative blood |

*Note:* Many normal characteristics that were previously thought to result from dominant–recessive inheritance, such as eye colour, are now regarded as due to multiple genes. For the characteristics listed here, most experts agree that the simple dominant–recessive relationship holds.

*Source:* McKusick, 1998.

**allele**
Each of two or more forms of a gene located at the same place on the chromosomes.

**homozygous**
Having two identical alleles at the same place on a pair of chromosomes.

**heterozygous**
Having two different alleles at the same place on a pair of chromosomes.

**dominant–recessive inheritance**
A pattern of inheritance in which, under heterozygous conditions, the influence of only one allele is apparent.

**carrier**
A heterozygous individual who can pass a recessive trait to his or her offspring.

pair is called XX; in males, it is called XY. The X is a relatively large chromosome, whereas the Y is short and carries less genetic material. When gametes form in males, the X and Y chromosomes separate into different sperm cells. In females, all gametes carry an X chromosome. The sex of the new organism is determined by whether an X-bearing or a Y-bearing sperm fertilizes the ovum. In fact, scientists have isolated a gene on the Y chromosome that triggers male sexual development by switching on the production of male sex hormones. When that gene is absent, the fetus that develops is female (Goodfellow & Lovell, 1993).

### PATTERNS OF GENETIC INHERITANCE

Two or more forms of each gene occur at the same place on the chromosomes, one inherited from the mother and one from the father. Each form is called an **allele.** If the alleles from both parents are alike, the child is said to be **homozygous** and will display the inherited trait. If the alleles differ, then the child is **heterozygous,** and relationships between the alleles determine the trait that will appear.

**DOMINANT–RECESSIVE RELATIONSHIPS.** In many heterozygous pairings, only one allele affects the child's characteristics. It is called *dominant;* the second allele, which has no effect, is called *recessive.* Hair colour is an example of **dominant–recessive inheritance.** The allele for dark hair is dominant (we can represent it with a capital *D*), whereas the one for blond hair is recessive (symbolized by a lowercase *b*). Children who inherit either a homozygous pair of dominant alleles (*DD*) or a heterozygous pair (*Db*) will be dark-haired, even though their genetic makeup differs. Blond hair can result only from having two recessive alleles (*bb*). Still, heterozygous individuals with just one recessive allele (*Db*) can pass that trait to their children. Therefore, they are called **carriers** of the trait.

Some human characteristics and disorders that follow the rules of dominant–recessive inheritance are listed in Table 3.2 above, and Table 3.3 on pages 76–77. As you can see, many disabilities and diseases are the product of recessive alleles. One of the most frequently occurring recessive disorders is *phenylketonuria,* or *PKU.* It affects the way the body breaks down proteins contained in many foods, such as cow's milk, bread, eggs, and fish. Infants born with two recessive alleles lack an enzyme that converts one of the basic amino acids that make up proteins (phenylalanine) into a byproduct essential for body functioning (tyrosine). Phenylalanine disrupts the chemical transmission of neural messages and inhibits the formation of myelin, the fatty sheath coating neural fibres that improves message transfer (Dyer, 1999). Around 3 to 5 months, infants with untreated PKU start to lose interest in their surroundings. By 1 year, they are permanently retarded.

Despite its potentially damaging effects, PKU provides an excellent illustration of the fact that inheriting unfavourable genes does not always lead to an untreatable condition. All Canadian provinces and U.S. states require that each newborn be given a blood test for PKU. If the disease is found, doctors place the baby on a diet low in phenylalanine. Children who receive this treatment show delayed development of higher-order cognitive skills, such as planning and problem solving, in infancy and childhood because even small amounts of phenylalanine interfere with brain functioning. But as long as dietary treatment begins early and continues, children with PKU usually attain an average level of intelligence and have a normal lifespan (Pietz et al., 1998; Smith, Klim, & Hanley, 2000).

In dominant–recessive inheritance, if we know the genetic makeup of the parents, we can predict the percentage of children in a family who are likely to display or carry a trait. Figure 3.4 illustrates this for PKU. Notice that for a child to inherit the condition, each parent must have a recessive allele (*p*). As the figure also shows, a single gene can affect more than one trait. Due to their inability to convert phenylalanine into tyrosine (which is responsible for pigmentation), children with PKU usually have light hair and blue eyes. Furthermore, children vary in the degree to which phenylalanine accumulates in their tissues and in the extent to which they respond to treatment. This is due to the action of **modifier genes,** which can enhance or dilute the effects of other genes.

Only rarely are serious diseases due to dominant alleles. Think about why this is so. Children who inherit the dominant allele would always develop the disorder. They would seldom live long enough to reproduce, and the harmful allele would be eliminated from the family's heredity in a single generation. Some dominant disorders, however, do persist. One is *Huntington disease,* a condition in which the central nervous system degenerates. Why has this disease endured? Its symptoms usually do not appear until age 35 or later, after the person has passed the dominant gene to his or her children.

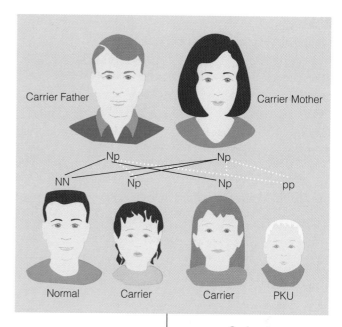

**FIGURE** 3.4

**Dominant–recessive mode of inheritance as illustrated by PKU.** When both parents are heterozygous carriers of the recessive allele, we can predict that 25 percent of their offspring will be normal, 50 percent will be carriers, and 25 percent will inherit the disorder. Notice that the PKU-affected child, in contrast to his siblings, has light hair. The recessive gene for PKU is *pleiotropic* (affects more than one trait). It also leads to fair colouring.

**CODOMINANCE.** In some heterozygous circumstances, the dominant–recessive relationship does not hold completely. Instead, we see **codominance,** a pattern of inheritance in which both alleles influence the person's characteristics.

The *sickle cell trait,* a heterozygous condition present in many black Africans, provides an example. *Sickle cell anemia* (refer to Table 3.3 on page 76) occurs in full form when a child inherits two recessive alleles. They cause the usually round red blood cells to become sickle (or crescent-moon) shaped, a response that is especially great under low-oxygen conditions—for example, at high altitudes or after intense physical exertion. The sickled cells clog the blood vessels and block the flow of blood, causing intense pain, swelling, and tissue damage. About 50 percent of affected people survive to age 40, only 1 percent to age 60 (Ashley-Koch, Yang, & Olney, 2000). Heterozygous individuals are protected from the disease under most circumstances. However, when they experience oxygen deprivation, the single recessive allele asserts itself, and a temporary, mild form of the illness occurs.

The sickle cell allele is prevalent among black Africans for a special reason. Carriers of it are more resistant to malaria than are individuals with two alleles for normal red blood cells. In Africa, where malaria is common, these carriers survived and reproduced more frequently than others, leading the gene to be maintained in the black population. In regions of the world where the risk of malaria is low, the frequency of the gene is steadily declining. For example, only 8 percent of African Americans carry it, compared with 20 percent of black Africans (Mange & Mange, 1998).

**X-LINKED INHERITANCE.** Males and females have an equal chance of inheriting recessive disorders carried on the autosomes, such as PKU and sickle cell anemia. But when a harmful allele is carried on the X chromosome, **X-linked inheritance** applies. Males are more likely to be affected because their sex chromosomes do not match. In females, any recessive allele on one X chromosome has a good chance of being suppressed by a dominant allele on the other X. But the Y chromosome is only about one-third as long and therefore lacks many corresponding alleles to override those on the X.

**modifier genes**
Genes that can enhance or dilute the effects of alleles controlling particular traits.

**codominance**
A pattern of inheritance in which both alleles, in a heterozygous combination, are expressed.

**X-linked inheritance**
A pattern of inheritance in which a recessive gene is carried on the X chromosome. Males are more likely to be affected.

**TABLE** 3.3

Examples of Dominant and Recessive Diseases

| DISEASE | DESCRIPTION | MODE OF INHERITANCE | INCIDENCE | TREATMENT | PRENATAL DIAGNOSIS | CARRIER IDENTIFICATION[a] |
|---|---|---|---|---|---|---|
| **Autosomal Diseases** | | | | | | |
| Cooley's anemia | Pale appearance, retarded physical growth, and lethargic behaviour begin in infancy. | Recessive | 1 in 500 births to parents of Mediterranean descent | Frequent blood transfusions; death from complications usually occurs by adolescence. | Yes | Yes |
| Cystic fibrosis | Lungs, liver, and pancreas secrete large amounts of thick mucus, leading to breathing and digestive difficulties. | Recessive | 1 in 2000 to 2500 Caucasian births | Bronchial drainage, prompt treatment of respiratory infections, dietary management. Advances in medical care allow survival into adulthood with good life quality. | Yes | Yes |
| Phenylketonuria (PKU) | Inability to metabolize the amino acid phenylalanine, contained in many proteins, causes severe central nervous system damage in the first year of life. | Recessive | 1 in 8000 births | Placing the child on a special diet results in average intelligence and normal lifespan. Subtle difficulties with planning and problem solving are often present. | Yes | Yes |
| Sickle cell anemia | Sickling of red blood cells causes oxygen deprivation, pain, swelling, and tissue damage. Anemia and susceptibility to infections, especially pneumonia, occur. | Recessive | 1 in 500 births to North Americans of African descent | Blood transfusions, painkillers, prompt treatment of infections. No known cure; 50 percent die by age 20. | Yes | Yes |
| Tay-Sachs disease | Central nervous system degeneration, with onset at about 6 months, leads to poor muscle tone, blindness, deafness, and convulsions. | Recessive | 1 in 3600 births to Jews of European descent and French Canadians. | None. Death by 3 to 4 years of age. | Yes | Yes |

*Red–green colour blindness* (a condition in which individuals cannot tell the difference between shades of red and green) is one example of an X-linked recessive trait. It affects males twice as often as females (Mange & Mange, 1998). Another example is *hemophilia*, a disorder in which the blood fails to clot normally. Figure 3.5 on page 78 shows its greater likelihood of inheritance by male children whose mothers carry the abnormal allele.

Besides X-linked disorders, many sex differences reveal the male to be at a disadvantage. Rates of miscarriage, infant and childhood deaths, birth defects, behaviour disorders, learning disabilities, and mental retardation are greater for boys (Halpern, 1997). It is possible that these sex differences can be traced to the genetic code. The female, with two X chromosomes, benefits from a greater variety of genes. Nature, however, seems to have adjusted for the male's disadvantage. Worldwide, about 106 boys are born for every 100 girls, and judging from miscarriage and abortion statistics, an even greater number of males are conceived (Pyeritz, 1998).

Nevertheless, in recent decades, the proportion of male births has declined in many industrialized countries (Davis, Gottlieb, & Stampnitzky, 1998). Some researchers blame increased occupational and community exposure to pesticides for a reduction in sperm counts overall, especially Y-bearing sperm.

**TABLE** 3.3
(continued)

| DISEASE | DESCRIPTION | MODE OF INHERITANCE | INCIDENCE | TREATMENT | PRENATAL DIAGNOSIS | CARRIER IDENTIFICATION[a] |
|---------|-------------|---------------------|-----------|-----------|---------------------|----------------------------|
| Huntington disease | Central nervous system degeneration leads to muscle coordination difficulties, mental deterioration, and personality changes. Symptoms usually do not appear until age 35 or later. | Dominant | 1 in 18 000 to 25 000 births | None. Death occurs 10 to 20 years after symptom onset. | Yes | Not applicable |
| Marfan syndrome | Tall, slender build; thin, elongated arms and legs. Heart defects and eye abnormalities, especially of the lens. Excessive lengthening of the body results in a variety of skeletal defects. | Dominant | 1 in 20 000 births | Correction of heart and eye defects sometimes possible. Death from heart failure in young adulthood common. | Yes | Not applicable |
| **X-Linked Diseases** | | | | | | |
| Duchenne muscular dystrophy | Degenerative muscle disease. Abnormal gait, loss of ability to walk between 7 and 13 years of age. | Recessive | 1 in 3000 to 5000 male births | None. Death from respiratory infection or weakening of the heart muscle usually occurs in adolescence. | Yes | Yes |
| Hemophilia | Blood fails to clot normally. Can lead to severe internal bleeding and tissue damage. | Recessive | 1 in 4000 to 7000 male births | Blood transfusions. Safety precautions to prevent injury. | Yes | Yes |
| Diabetes insipidus | Insufficient production of the hormone vasopressin results in excessive thirst and urination. Dehydration can cause central nervous system damage. | Recessive | 1 in 2500 male births | Hormone replacement. | Yes | Yes |

[a]Carrier status detectable in prospective parents through blood tests or genetic analyses.

*Sources:* Behrman, Kliegman, & Arvin, 1996; Chodirker et al., 2001; Gott, 1998; Grody, 1999; Knoers et al., 1993; McKusick, 1998; Schulman & Black, 1997.

**GENETIC IMPRINTING.** More than 1000 human characteristics follow the rules of dominant–recessive and codominant inheritance (McKusick, 1998). In these cases, whichever parent contributes a gene to the new individual, the gene responds in the same way. Geneticists, however, have identified some exceptions. In **genetic imprinting,** alleles are *imprinted,* or chemically *marked,* so that one pair member (either the mother's or the father's) is activated, regardless of its makeup. The imprint is often temporary; it may be erased in the next generation, and it may not occur in all individuals (Everman & Cassidy, 2000).

Imprinting helps us understand certain puzzling genetic patterns. For example, children are more likely to develop diabetes if their father, rather than their mother, suffers from it. And people with asthma or hay fever tend to have mothers, not fathers, with the illness. Imprinting is involved in several childhood cancers and in *Praeder-Willi syndrome,* a disorder with symptoms of mental retardation and severe obesity (Couper & Couper, 2000). It may also explain why Huntington disease, when inherited from the father, tends to emerge at an earlier age and progress more rapidly (Navarrete, Martinez, & Salamanca, 1994).

**genetic imprinting**
A pattern of inheritance in which alleles are imprinted, or chemically marked, in such a way that one pair member is activated, regardless of its makeup.

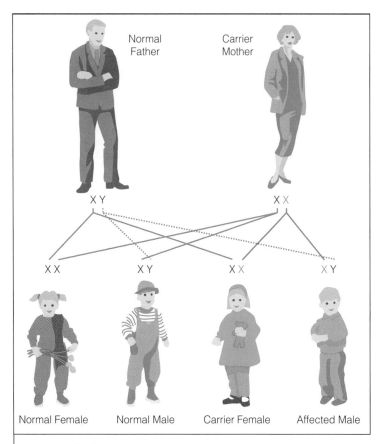

Normal
Father

Carrier
Mother

X Y

X X

X X    X Y    X X    X Y

Normal Female    Normal Male    Carrier Female    Affected Male

FIGURE 3.5

**X-linked inheritance.** In the example shown here, the allele on the father's X chromosome is normal. The mother has one normal and one abnormal recessive allele on her X chromosomes. By looking at the possible combinations of the parents' alleles, we can predict that 50 percent of male children will have the disorder and 50 percent of female children will be carriers of it.

Genetic imprinting can also operate on the sex chromosomes, as *fragile X syndrome* reveals. In this disorder, an abnormal repetition of a sequence of DNA bases occurs on the X chromosome, damaging a particular gene. Fragile X syndrome is the most common inherited cause of mild to moderate mental retardation. It has also been linked to 2 to 3 percent of cases of autism, a serious emotional disorder of early childhood involving bizarre, self-stimulating behaviour and delayed or absent language and communication (Mazzocco, 2000). Research reveals that the defective gene at the fragile site is expressed only when it is passed from mother to child (Ashley-Koch et al., 1998).

**MUTATION.** How are harmful genes created in the first place? The answer is **mutation,** a sudden but permanent change in a segment of DNA. A mutation may affect only one or two genes, or it may involve many genes, as in the chromosomal disorders we will discuss shortly. Some mutations occur spontaneously, simply by chance. Others are caused by hazardous environmental agents.

Although non-ionizing forms of radiation—electromagnetic waves and microwaves—have no demonstrated impact on DNA, ionizing (high-energy) radiation is an established cause of mutation. Women who receive repeated doses before conception are more likely to miscarry or give birth to children with hereditary defects. Genetic abnormalities, such as physical malformations and childhood cancer, are also higher when fathers are exposed to radiation in their occupations (Brent, 1999). However, infrequent and mild exposure to radiation does not cause genetic damage. Instead, high doses over a long period impair DNA.

Although only 3 percent of pregnancies result in the birth of a baby with a hereditary abnormality, these children account for about 40 percent of childhood deaths and 5 to 10 percent of childhood hospital admissions (Shiloh, 1996). Progress in preventing and treating genetic diseases still lags far behind that for nongenetic diseases, although (as we will see shortly) great strides are being made.

**POLYGENIC INHERITANCE.** So far, we have discussed patterns of inheritance in which people either display a trait or do not. These cut-and-dried individual differences are much easier to trace to their genetic origins than are characteristics that vary continuously among people. Many traits of interest to child development specialists, such as height, weight, intelligence, and personality, are of this second type. People are not just tall or short, bright or dull, outgoing or shy. Instead, they show gradations between these extremes. Continuous traits like these are due to **polygenic inheritance,** in which many genes determine the characteristic in question. Polygenic inheritance is complex, and much about it is still unknown. In the final section of this chapter, we will pay special attention to this form of genetic transmission by examining ways that researchers infer the influence of heredity on human attributes when they do not know the precise patterns of inheritance.

**mutation**
A sudden but permanent change in a segment of DNA.

**polygenic inheritance**
A pattern of inheritance involving many genes that applies to characteristics that vary continuously among people.

## CHROMOSOMAL ABNORMALITIES

Besides harmful recessive alleles, abnormalities of the chromosomes are a major cause of serious developmental problems. Most chromosomal defects result from mistakes during meiosis, when the ovum and sperm are formed. A chromosome pair does not separate properly, or part of a chromosome breaks off. Since these errors involve far more DNA than problems due to single genes, they usually produce many physical and mental symptoms.

**DOWN SYNDROME.** The most common chromosomal abnormality, occurring in 1 out of every 800 live births, is *Down syndrome*. In 95 percent of cases, it results from a failure of the twenty-first pair of chromosomes to separate during meiosis, so the new individual inherits three of these chromosomes rather than the normal two. For this reason, Down syndrome is sometimes called *trisomy 21*. In other, less frequent forms, an extra broken piece of a twenty-first chromosome is present. Or an error occurs during the early stages of mitosis, causing some but not all body cells to have the defective chromosomal makeup (called a *mosaic* pattern). In these instances, since less genetic material is involved, symptoms of the disorder are less extreme (Hodapp, 1996).

The consequences of Down syndrome include mental retardation, memory and speech problems, limited vocabulary, and slow motor development (Chapman & Hesketh, 2000). Affected individuals also have distinct physical features—a short, stocky build, a flattened face, a protruding tongue, almond-shaped eyes, and an unusual crease running across the palm of the hand. In addition, they are often born with eye cataracts and heart and intestinal defects. Three decades ago, most died by early adulthood. Today, because of medical advances, many survive into their sixties and beyond (Selikowitz, 1997).

Infants with Down syndrome are more difficult to care for than normal infants. Their facial deformities often lead to breathing and feeding difficulties. Also, they smile less readily, show poor eye-to-eye contact, and explore objects less persistently. When parents take extra steps to encourage them to become engaged in their surroundings, Down syndrome children develop more favourably (Sigman, 1999). They also benefit from infant and preschool intervention programs, although emotional, social, and motor skills improve more than intellectual performance (Hines & Bennett, 1996). Thus, even though Down syndrome is a genetic disorder, environmental factors affect how well these children fare.

As Table 3.4 shows, the risk of a Down syndrome baby rises dramatically with maternal age. Why is this so? Geneticists believe that the ova, present in the woman's body since her own prenatal period, weaken over time. As a result, chromosomes do not separate properly as they complete the process of meiosis at conception. In about 5 to 10 percent of cases, the extra genetic material originates with the father. But Down syndrome and other chromosomal abnormalities are not related to advanced paternal age (Muller et al., 2000; Savage et al., 1998). In these instances, the mutation occurs for other, unknown reasons.

**ABNORMALITIES OF THE SEX CHROMOSOMES.** Disorders of the autosomes other than Down syndrome usually disrupt development so severely that miscarriage occurs. When such babies are born, they rarely survive beyond early childhood. In contrast, abnormalities of the sex chromosomes usually lead to fewer problems. In fact, sex chromosome disorders often are not recognized until adolescence when, in some of the deviations, puberty is delayed. The most common problems involve the presence of an extra X or Y chromosome, or the absence of one X in females (see Table 3.5 on page 80).

A variety of myths exist about individuals with sex chromosome disorders. For example, as Table 3.5 reveals, males with *XYY syndrome* are not necessarily more aggressive and antisocial than are XY males. And most children with sex chromosome disorders do not suffer from mental retardation. Instead, their intellectual problems are usually very specific. Verbal difficulties—for example, with reading and vocabulary—are common among girls with *triple X syndrome* and boys with *Klinefelter syndrome,* both of whom inherit an extra X chromosome. In contrast, Turner syndrome girls, who are missing an X, have trouble with spatial relationships—for example, drawing pictures, telling right from left, following travel directions, and noticing changes in facial expressions (Geschwind et al., 2000; Money, 1993; Ross, Zinn, & McCauley, 2000). These findings tell us that adding to or subtracting from the usual number of X chromosomes results in particular intellectual deficits. At present, geneticists do not know the reason why.

The facial features of the 9-year-old boy on the left are typical of Down syndrome. Although his intellectual development is impaired, this child is doing well because he is growing up in a stimulating home where his special needs are met and he is loved and accepted. Here he collaborates with his normally developing 4-year-old brother in making won ton dumplings.

**TABLE** 3.4

Risk of Giving Birth to a Down Syndrome Child by Maternal Age

| MATERNAL AGE | RISK |
| --- | --- |
| 20 | 1 in 1900 births |
| 25 | 1 in 1200 |
| 30 | 1 in 900 |
| 33 | 1 in 600 |
| 36 | 1 in 280 |
| 39 | 1 in 130 |
| 42 | 1 in 65 |
| 45 | 1 in 30 |
| 48 | 1 in 15 |

*Note:* The risk of giving birth to a Down syndrome baby after age 35 has increased slightly over the past 20 years, due to improved medical interventions during pregnancy and consequent greater likelihood of a Down syndrome fetus surviving to be liveborn.

*Sources:* Adapted from Halliday et al., 1995; Meyers et al., 1997.

**TABLE** 3.5

Sex Chromosomal Disorders

| DISORDER | DESCRIPTION | INCIDENCE | TREATMENT |
|---|---|---|---|
| XYY syndrome | Extra Y chromosome. Above-average height, large teeth, and sometimes severe acne. Intelligence, male sexual development, and fertility are normal. | 1 in 1000 male births | No special treatment necessary. |
| Triple X syndrome (XXX) | Extra X chromosome. Tallness and impaired verbal intelligence. Female sexual development and fertility are normal. | 1 in 500 to 1250 female births | Special education to treat verbal ability problems. |
| Klinefelter syndrome (XXY) | Extra X chromosome. Tallness, body fat distribution resembling females, incomplete development of sex characteristics at puberty, sterility, and impaired verbal intelligence. | 1 in 900 male births | Hormone therapy at puberty to stimulate development of sex characteristics; special education to treat verbal ability problems. |
| Turner syndrome (XO) | Missing X chromosome. Short stature, webbed neck, incomplete development of sex characteristics at puberty, sterility, and impaired spatial intelligence. | 1 in 2500 to 8000 female births | Hormone therapy in childhood to stimulate physical growth and at puberty to promote development of sex characteristics; special education to treat spatial ability problems. |

*Sources:* Money, 1993; Moore & Persaud, 1993; Netley, 1986; Pennington et al., 1982; Ratcliffe, Pan, & McKie, 1992; Rovet et al., 1996; Schiavi et al., 1984.

## ASK YOURSELF

**review**     Explain the genetic origins of PKU and Down syndrome. Cite evidence indicating that both heredity and environment contribute to the development of children with these disorders.

**review**     Using your knowledge of X-linked inheritance, explain why male infants are more vulnerable to miscarriage, infant death, and genetic disorders.

**apply**     Gilbert's genetic makeup is homozygous for dark hair. Jan's is homozygous for blonde hair. What proportion of their children are likely to be dark-haired? Explain.

**connect**     Referring to ecological systems theory (Chapter 1, pages 27–29), explain why parents of children with genetic disorders often experience increased stress. What factors, within and beyond the family, can help these parents support their children's development?

# Reproductive Choices

IN THE PAST, many couples with genetic disorders in their families chose not to have children rather than risk the birth of an abnormal baby. Today, genetic counselling and prenatal diagnosis help people make informed decisions about conceiving or carrying a pregnancy to term.

**genetic counselling**
A communication process designed to help couples assess their chances of giving birth to a baby with a hereditary disorder and choose the best course of action in view of risks and family goals.

**prenatal diagnostic methods**
Medical procedures that permit detection of developmental problems before birth.

### GENETIC COUNSELLING

**Genetic counselling** is a communication process designed to help couples assess their chances of giving birth to a baby with a hereditary disorder and choose the best course of action in view of risks and family goals (Shiloh, 1996). Individuals likely to seek counselling are those who have had difficulties bearing children, such as repeated miscarriages, or who know that genetic problems exist in their families. In addition, women who delay childbearing past age 35 are candidates for genetic counselling. After this time, the overall rate of chromosomal abnormalities rises sharply, from 1 in every 190 to as many as 1 in every 10 pregnancies at age 48 (Meyers et al., 1997).

If a family history of mental retardation, physical defects, or inherited diseases exists, the genetic counsellor interviews the couple and prepares a *pedigree*, a picture of the family tree in which affected relatives are identified. The pedigree is used to estimate the likelihood that parents will have an abnormal child, using the same genetic principles discussed earlier in this chapter. In the case of many disorders, blood tests or genetic analyses can reveal whether the parent is a carrier of the harmful gene. Carrier detection is possible for all the recessive diseases listed in Table 3.3, as well as others, and for fragile X syndrome.

When all the relevant information is in, the genetic counsellor helps people consider appropriate options. These include "taking a chance" and conceiving, adopting a child, or choosing from among a variety of reproductive technologies. The Social Issues: Health box on the next page describes these medical interventions into conception along with the host of legal and ethical dilemmas that have arisen in their application.

## PRENATAL DIAGNOSIS AND FETAL MEDICINE

Several **prenatal diagnostic methods**—medical procedures that permit detection of problems before birth—are available to pregnant women (see Table 3.6). Women of advanced maternal age are prime candidates for *amniocentesis* or *chorionic villus sampling* (see Figure 3.6 on page 84). Maternal blood analysis (serum screening) is non-invasive,

**TABLE** 3.6

Prenatal Diagnostic Methods

| METHOD | DESCRIPTION |
| --- | --- |
| Amniocentesis | The most widely used technique. A hollow needle is inserted through the abdominal wall to obtain a sample of fluid in the uterus. Cells are examined for genetic defects. Can be performed by 11 to 14 weeks after conception but is safest after 15 weeks; 1 to 2 more weeks are required for test results. Entails small risk of miscarriage. |
| Chorionic villus sampling | A procedure that can be used if results are desired or needed very early in pregnancy. A thin tube is inserted into the uterus through the vagina or a hollow needle is inserted through the abdominal wall. A small plug of tissue is removed from the end of one or more chorionic villi, the hairlike projections on the membrane surrounding the developing organism. Cells are examined for genetic defects. Can be performed at 6 to 8 weeks after conception, and results are available within 24 hours. Entails a slightly greater risk of miscarriage than does amniocentesis. Also associated with a small risk of limb deformities, which increases the earlier the procedure is performed. |
| Fetoscopy | A small tube with a light source at one end is inserted into the uterus to inspect the fetus for defects of the limbs and face. Also allows a sample of fetal blood to be obtained, permitting diagnosis of such disorders as hemophilia and sickle cell anemia, as well as neural defects (see below). Usually performed between 15 and 18 weeks after conception, although can be done as early as 5 weeks. Entails some risk of miscarriage. |
| Ultrasound | High-frequency sound waves are beamed at the uterus; their reflection is translated into a picture on a videoscreen that reveals the size, shape, and placement of the fetus. By itself, permits assessment of fetal age, detection of multiple pregnancies, and identification of gross physical defects. Also used to guide amniocentesis, chorionic villus sampling, and fetoscopy. When used five or more times, may increase the chances of low birth weight. |
| Maternal blood analysis | By the second month of pregnancy, some of the developing organism's cells enter the maternal bloodstream. An elevated level of alpha-fetoprotein may indicate kidney disease, abnormal closure of the esophagus, or neural tube defects, such as anencephaly (absence of most of the brain) and spina bifida (bulging of the spinal cord from the spinal column). Markers can be examined for risk of genetic defects, such as Down syndrome. |
| Preimplantation genetic diagnosis | After in vitro fertilization and duplication of the zygote into a cluster of about eight cells, one cell is removed and examined for hereditary defects. Only if that cell is free of detectable genetic disorders is the fertilized ovum implanted in the woman's uterus. |

*Sources:* Eiben et al., 1997; Lissens & Sermon, 1997; Moore & Persaud, 1998; Newnham et al., 1993; Quintero, Puder, & Cotton, 1993; Wapner, 1997; Willner, 1998.

## THE PROS AND CONS OF REPRODUCTIVE TECHNOLOGIES

Some couples decide not to risk pregnancy because of a history of genetic disease. And many others—in fact, one-sixth of all couples who try to conceive—discover that they are sterile. Today, increasing numbers of individuals turn to alternative methods of conception—technologies that, although fulfilling the wish of parenthood, have become the subject of heated debate.

### DONOR INSEMINATION AND IN VITRO FERTILIZATION

For several decades, *donor insemination*—injection of sperm from an anonymous man into a woman—has been used to overcome male reproductive difficulties. In recent years, it has also permitted women without a heterosexual partner to bear children. In the United States, 30 000 children are conceived through donor insemination each year (Nachtigall et al., 1997), while in Canada estimates range from 1500 to 6000 children per year (CBC, 2000).

*In vitro fertilization* is another reproductive technology that has become increasingly common. Since the first "test tube" baby was born in England in 1978, many thousands of infants have been created this way. With in vitro fertilization, hormones are given to a woman, stimulating ripening of several ova. These are removed surgically and placed in a dish of nutrients, to which sperm are added. A recently developed technique permits a single sperm to be injected directly into an ovum, thereby overcoming most male fertility problems (Wood, 2001). Once an ovum is fertilized and begins to duplicate into several cells, it is injected into the mother's uterus.

In vitro fertilization is successful for 20 percent of those who try it. By mixing and matching gametes, pregnancies can be brought about when either or both partners have a reproductive problem. Fertilized ova and sperm can even be frozen and stored in embryo banks for use at some future time, thereby guaranteeing healthy zygotes should age or illness lead to fertility problems.

Children conceived through these methods may be genetically unrelated to one or both of their parents. In addition, most parents who have used in vitro fertilization do not tell their children about their origins, although health professionals now encourage them to do so. Does lack of genetic ties or secrecy surrounding these techniques interfere with parent–child relationships? Perhaps because of a strong desire for parenthood, caregiving is actually somewhat warmer for young children conceived through in vitro fertilization or donor insemination. And in vitro infants are as securely attached to their parents, and children and adolescents as well adjusted, as their counterparts who were naturally conceived (Chan, Raboy, & Patterson, 1998; Gibson et al., 2000; Golombok, MacCallum, & Goodman, 2001).

Although donor insemination and in vitro fertilization have many benefits, serious questions have arisen about their use. For example, donors are not always screened for genetic or sexually transmitted diseases and doctors may not keep records of donor characteristics. Yet the resulting children may someday need to know their genetic backgrounds for medical history. In Canada, most provinces have not yet clarified whether donors have legal obligations to their children. Newfoundland and the Yukon, however, have declared that the donor has no legal responsibility.

### SURROGATE MOTHERHOOD

A more controversial form of medically assisted conception is *surrogate motherhood*. Typically in this procedure, sperm from a man whose wife is infertile are used to inseminate a woman, who is paid a fee for her childbearing services. In return, the surrogate agrees to turn the baby over to the man (who is the natural father). The child is then adopted by his wife.

Although most of these arrangements proceed smoothly, those that end up in court highlight serious risks for all concerned. In one case, both parties rejected the infant with severe disabilities that resulted from the pregnancy. In others, the surrogate mother wanted to keep the baby or the couple changed their mind during the pregnancy. These children came into the world in the midst of conflict that threatened to last for years.

Since surrogacy favours the wealthy as contractors for infants and the less economically advantaged as surrogates, it may promote exploitation of financially needy women (Sureau, 1997). In addition, most surrogates

can detect a range of possible problems, and therefore should be made widely available. In Canada, at present, only Manitoba and Ontario fund serum screening programs (Johnson & Summers, 1999). In support of prenatal screening, the Society of Obstetricians and Gynaecologists of Canada now recommends that women be offered one routine second-trimester ultrasound for uncomplicated pregnancies (Demianczuk, 1999). This recommendation is based on ethical, legal, and psychosocial considerations, as well as evidence on pregnancy outcomes.

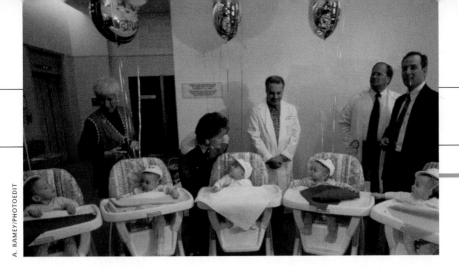

A. RAMEY/PHOTOEDIT

In Canada, 1500 to 6000 children per year, like the ones shown here, are conceived through donor insemination. If a woman requires multiple attempts, the cost of the procedures may become very high.

already have children of their own, who may be deeply affected by the pregnancy. Knowledge that their mother would give away a baby for profit may cause these youngsters to worry about the security of their own family circumstances.

## NEW REPRODUCTIVE FRONTIERS

Reproductive technologies are evolving faster than societies can weigh the ethics of these procedures. Doctors have used donor ova from younger women in combination with in vitro fertilization to help postmenopausal women become pregnant. While most recipients are in their forties, several women in their sixties have given birth this way. Even though candidates for postmenopausal-assisted childbirth are selected on the basis of good health, serious questions arise about bringing children into the world whose parents may not live to see them reach adulthood.

Currently, experts are debating other reproductive options. In one instance, a woman with a busy stage career, who could have become pregnant naturally, chose to combine in vitro fertilization (using her own ova and her husband's sperm) and surrogate motherhood. This permitted the woman to continue her career while the surrogate carried her biological child (Wood, 2001). At donor banks, customers can select ova or sperm on the basis of physical characteristics and even IQ. Some worry that this practice is a dangerous step toward selective breeding through "designer babies"—controlling offspring characteristics by manipulating the genetic makeup of fertilized ova.

Finally, scientists have successfully cloned (made multiple copies of) fertilized ova in sheep, cattle, and monkeys, and they are working on effective ways to do so in humans. By providing extra ova for injection, cloning might improve the success rate of in vitro fertilization. But it also opens the possibility of mass producing genetically identical people. Therefore, it is widely condemned (Fasouliotis & Schenker, 2000).

Although new reproductive technologies permit many barren couples to rear healthy newborn babies, laws are needed to regulate such practices. In Australia, New Zealand, and Sweden, individuals conceived with donated gametes have a right to information about their genetic origins (Hunter, Salter-Ling, & Glover, 2000).

In the case of surrogate motherhood, Australia, Canada, many European nations, and some U.S. states have banned or restricted it, arguing that the status of a baby should not be a matter of commercial arrangement and that a part of the body should not be rented or sold (McGee, 1997). England, France, and Italy have prohibited in vitro fertilization for women past menopause (Andrews & Elster, 2000). At present, nothing is known about the psychological consequences of being a product of these procedures. Research on how such children grow up, including what they know and how they feel about their origins, is important for weighing the pros and cons of these techniques.

In Canada, the Royal Commission on New Reproductive Technologies has examined the social, medical, legal, ethical, economic, and research implications of the new technologies. Nine procedures, including sex selection for non-medical reasons, were banned in 1995 as an interim measure. Development of a final policy is ongoing and focuses on recognizing the differences between reproductive technologies, including in vitro fertilization, that aid conception, and genetic technologies, such as cloning, that manipulate genetic materials (Health Canada, 1999d).

Prenatal diagnosis has led to advances in fetal medicine. For example, by inserting a needle into the uterus, doctors can administer drugs to the fetus. Surgery has been performed to repair such problems as heart and lung malformations, urinary tract obstructions, and neural defects. These techniques frequently result in complications, the most common being premature labour and miscarriage (James, 1998). Yet when parents are told that their unborn child has a serious defect, they may be willing to try almost any option. Currently, the medical profession is struggling with how to help parents make informed decisions about fetal surgery.

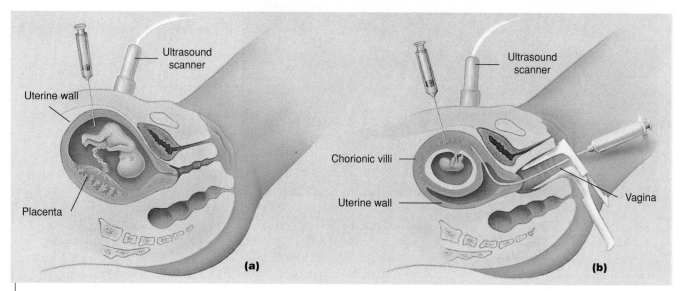

**Amniocentesis and chorionic villus sampling.** Today, more than 250 defects and diseases can be detected before birth using these two procedures. (a) In amniocentesis, a hollow needle is inserted through the abdominal wall into the uterus from 11 to 14 weeks after conception. Fluid is withdrawn and fetal cells are cultured, a process that takes about 2 weeks. (b) Chorionic villus sampling can be performed much earlier in pregnancy, at 6 to 8 weeks after conception, and results are available within 24 hours. Two approaches to obtaining a sample of chorionic villi are shown: inserting a thin tube through the vagina into the uterus and inserting a needle through the abdominal wall. In both amniocentesis and chorionic villus sampling, an ultrasound scanner is used for guidance. (From K. L. Moore & T. V. N. Persaud, 1998, *Before We Are Born,* 5th ed., Philadelphia: Saunders, p. 115. Adapted by permission of the publisher and author.)

Advances in *genetic engineering* also offer new hope for correcting hereditary defects. As part of the Human Genome Project—an ambitious, international research program aimed at deciphering the chemical makeup of human genetic material (genome)—researchers have mapped the sequence of all human DNA base pairs. Using that information, they have begun to "annotate" the genome—identifying all its genes and their functions. A major goal is to understand the estimated 4000 human disorders—those due to single genes and those resulting from a complex interplay of multiple genes and environmental factors. Already, thousands of genes have been identified, including those involved in hundreds of diseases, such as cystic fibrosis, Huntington disease, Duchenne muscular dystrophy, Marfan syndrome, and some forms of cancer. As a result, new treatments are being explored, such as *gene splicing*—delivering DNA carrying a functional gene to the cells, thereby correcting a genetic abnormality.

When prenatal diagnosis reveals an as yet untreatable condition, parents face the painful decision of whether to terminate the pregnancy. If they choose abortion, they experience the grief that comes with losing a wanted child, worries about future pregnancies, and possible guilt about the abortion itself. Fortunately, 95 percent of fetuses examined through prenatal diagnosis are normal (Jones, 1997). Because of such tests, many individuals whose family history would have caused them to avoid pregnancy are having healthy children.

**ASK YOURSELF** www

**review**  Why is genetic counselling called a *communication process?* Who should seek it?

**apply**  A woman over age 35, who has just learned she is pregnant, wants to find out as soon as possible whether her embryo has a genetic defect. She also wants to minimize injury to the developing organism. Which prenatal diagnostic method is she likely to choose?

# Prenatal Development

THE SPERM AND ovum that unite to form the new individual are uniquely suited for the task of reproduction. The ovum is a tiny sphere, measuring 1/70 of a centimetre (1/175 of an inch) in diameter, that is barely visible to the naked eye as a dot the size of the period at the end of this sentence. But in its microscopic world, it is a giant—the largest cell in the human body. The ovum's size makes it a perfect target for the much smaller sperm, which measure only 1/195 of a centimetre (1/500 of an inch).

## CONCEPTION

About once every 28 days, in the middle of a woman's menstrual cycle, an ovum bursts from one of her *ovaries,* two walnut-sized organs deep inside her abdomen (see Figure 3.7). Surrounded by thousands of nurse cells to feed and protect it along its path, the ovum is drawn into one of two *fallopian tubes*—long, thin structures that lead to the hollow, soft-lined uterus. While the ovum travels, the spot on the ovary from which it was released, now called the *corpus luteum,* secretes hormones that prepare the lining of the uterus to receive a fertilized ovum. If pregnancy does not occur, the corpus luteum shrinks, and the uterine lining is discarded 2 weeks later with menstruation.

The male produces sperm in vast numbers—an average of 300 million a day. In the final process of maturation, each sperm develops a tail that permits it to swim long distances, upstream in the female reproductive tract and into the fallopian tube, where fertilization usually takes place. The journey is difficult, and many sperm die. Only 300 to 500 reach the ovum, if one happens to be present. Sperm live for up to 6 days and can lie in wait for the ovum, which

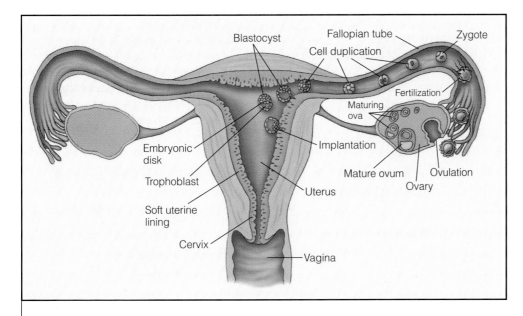

**FIGURE** 3.7

**Journey of the ovum to the uterus.** Once every 28 days, an ovum matures, is released from one of the woman's ovaries, and is drawn into the fallopian tube. After fertilization, it begins to duplicate, at first slowly and then more rapidly. By the fourth day, it forms a hollow, fluid-filled ball called a blastocyst. The inner cells, or embryonic disk, will become the new organism; the outer cells, or trophoblast, will provide protective covering. At the end of the first week, the blastocyst begins to implant in the uterine lining. (Adapted from K. L. Moore & T. V. N. Persaud, 1998, *Before We Are Born,* 5th ed., Philadelphia: Saunders, p. 44. Reprinted by permission of the publisher and author.)

# milestones
## PRENATAL DEVELOPMENT

| TRIMESTER | PERIOD | WEEKS | LENGTH AND WEIGHT | MAJOR EVENTS |
|---|---|---|---|---|
| First | Zygote | 1 | | The one-celled zygote multiplies and forms a blastocyst. |
| | | 2 | | The blastocyst burrows into the uterine lining. Structures that feed and protect the developing organism begin to form—amnion, chorion, yolk sac, placenta, and umbilical cord. |
| | Embryo | 3–4 | 6 mm (¼ inch) | A primitive brain and spinal cord appear. Heart, muscles, backbone, ribs, and digestive tract begin to develop. |
| | | 5–8 | 2.5 cm (1 inch); 4 grams (⅐ ounce) | Many external body structures (face, arms, legs, toes, fingers) and internal organs form. The sense of touch begins to develop, and the embryo can move. |
| | Fetus | 9–12 | 7.6 cm (3 inches); less than 28 grams (less than 1 ounce) | Rapid increase in size begins. Nervous system, organs, and muscles become organized and connected, and new behavioural capacities (kicking, thumb sucking, mouth opening, and rehearsal of breathing) appear. External genitals are well formed, and the fetus's sex is evident. |
| Second | | 13–24 | 30 cm (12 inches); 820 grams (1.8 pounds) | The fetus continues to enlarge rapidly. In the middle of this period, fetal movements can be felt by the mother. Vernix and lanugo keep the fetus's skin from chapping in the amniotic fluid. All the neurons that will ever be produced in the brain are present by 24 weeks. Eyes are sensitive to light, and the fetus reacts to sound. |
| Third | | 25–38 | 50 cm (20 inches); 3400 grams (7.5 pounds) | The fetus has a chance of survival if born during this time. Size increases. Lungs mature. Rapid brain development causes sensory and behavioural capacities to expand. In the middle of this period, a layer of fat is added under the skin. Antibodies are transmitted from mother to fetus to protect against disease. Most fetuses rotate into an upside-down position in preparation for birth. |

*Sources:* Moore & Persaud, 1998; Nilsson & Hamberger, 1990.

survives for only 1 day after being released into the fallopian tube. However, most conceptions result from intercourse during a 3-day period—on the day of or during the 2 days preceding ovulation (Wilcox, Weinberg, & Baird, 1995).

With conception, the story of prenatal development begins to unfold. The vast changes that take place during the 38 weeks of pregnancy are usually divided into three periods: (1) the zygote, (2) the embryo, and (3) the fetus. As we look at what happens in each, you may find it useful to refer to the Milestones table above.

JACK BURNS/ACE/PHOTOTAKE

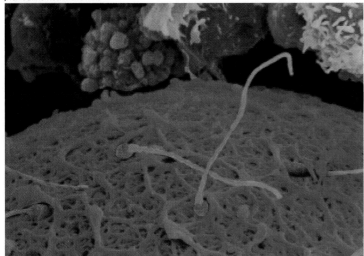

© LENNART NILSSON, *A CHILD IS BORN*/BONNIERS

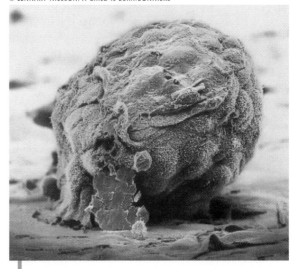

In this photo taken with the aid of a powerful microscope, sperm have completed their journey up the female reproductive tract and are beginning to penetrate the surface of the enormous-looking ovum, the largest cell in the human body. When one of the sperm is successful at fertilizing the ovum, the resulting zygote will begin to duplicate.

**Period of the zygote: seventh to ninth day.** The fertilized ovum duplicates at an increasingly rapid rate, forming a hollow ball of cells, or blastocyst, by the fourth day after fertilization. Here the blastocyst, magnified thousands of times, burrows into the uterine lining between the seventh and ninth day.

## THE PERIOD OF THE ZYGOTE

The period of the zygote lasts about 2 weeks, from fertilization until the tiny mass of cells drifts down and out of the fallopian tube and attaches itself to the wall of the uterus. The zygote's first cell duplication is long and drawn out; it is not complete until about 30 hours after conception. Gradually, new cells are added at a faster rate. By the fourth day, 60 to 70 cells exist that form a hollow, fluid-filled ball called a *blastocyst* (refer again to Figure 3.7). The cells on the inside, called the *embryonic disk,* will become the new organism; the outer ring of cells, termed the *trophoblast,* will provide protective covering and nourishment.

**IMPLANTATION.** Sometime between the seventh and ninth day, implantation occurs: the blastocyst burrows deep into the uterine lining. Surrounded by the woman's nourishing blood, it starts to grow in earnest. At first, the trophoblast (protective outer layer) multiplies fastest. It forms a membrane, called the **amnion,** that encloses the developing organism in *amniotic fluid.* The amnion helps keep the temperature of the prenatal world constant and provides a cushion against any jolts caused by the woman's movement. A *yolk sac* also appears. It produces blood cells until the developing liver, spleen, and bone marrow are mature enough to take over this function (Moore & Persaud, 1998).

The events of these first 2 weeks are delicate and uncertain. As many as 30 percent of zygotes do not make it through this phase. In some, the sperm and ovum do not join properly. In others, for some unknown reason, cell duplication never begins. By preventing implantation in these cases, nature eliminates most prenatal abnormalities (Sadler, 2000).

**THE PLACENTA AND UMBILICAL CORD.** By the end of the second week, cells of the trophoblast form another protective membrane—the **chorion,** which surrounds the amnion. From the chorion, tiny hairlike *villi,* or blood vessels, emerge.[1] As these villi burrow into the uterine wall, a special organ called the **placenta** starts to develop. By bringing the embryo's and mother's blood close together, the placenta will permit food and oxygen to reach the organism

**amnion**
The inner membrane that forms a protective covering around the prenatal organism and encloses it in amniotic fluid, which helps keep temperature constant and provides a cushion against jolts caused by the mother's movement.

**chorion**
The outer membrane that forms a protective covering around the prenatal organism. It sends out tiny hairlike villi, from which the placenta begins to emerge.

**placenta**
The organ that separates the mother's bloodstream from the embryo's or fetus's bloodstream but permits exchange of nutrients and waste products.

[1]Recall from Table 3.6 on page 81 that *chorionic villus sampling* is the prenatal diagnostic method that can be performed earliest, by 6 to 8 weeks after conception.

and waste products to be carried away. A membrane forms that allows these substances to be exchanged but prevents the mother's and embryo's blood from mixing directly.

The placenta is connected to the developing organism by the **umbilical cord.** In the period of the zygote, it appears as a primitive body stalk, but during the course of pregnancy, it grows to a length of 30 to 90 centimetres (1 to 3 feet). The umbilical cord contains one large vein that delivers blood loaded with nutrients and two arteries that remove waste products. The force of blood flowing through the cord keeps it firm, much like a garden hose, so it seldom tangles while the embryo, like a space-walking astronaut, floats freely in its fluid-filled chamber (Moore & Persaud, 1998).

By the end of the period of the zygote, the developing organism has found food and shelter in the uterus. Already, it is a complex being. These dramatic beginnings take place before most mothers know they are pregnant.

### THE PERIOD OF THE EMBRYO

The period of the **embryo** lasts from implantation through the eighth week of pregnancy. During these brief 6 weeks, the most rapid prenatal changes take place. Because the groundwork for all body structures and internal organs is laid down, the embryo is especially vulnerable to interference with healthy development. But a short time span of embryonic growth helps limit opportunities for serious harm.

**LAST HALF OF THE FIRST MONTH.** In the first week of this period, the embryonic disk forms three layers of cells: (1) the *ectoderm*, which will become the nervous system and skin; (2) the *mesoderm*, from which will develop the muscles, skeleton, circulatory system, and other internal organs; and (3) the *endoderm*, which will become the digestive system, lungs, urinary tract, and glands. These three layers give rise to all parts of the body.

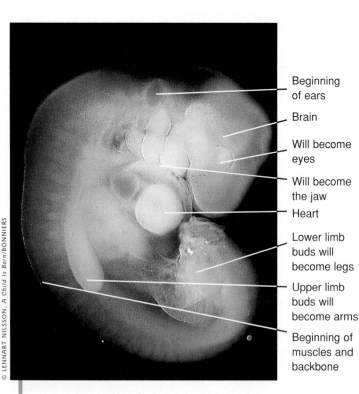

Beginning of ears

Brain

Will become eyes

Will become the jaw

Heart

Lower limb buds will become legs

Upper limb buds will become arms

Beginning of muscles and backbone

© LENNART NILSSON, *A Child Is Born*/BONNIERS

**Period of the embryo: fourth week.** In actual size, this 4-week-old embryo is only 0.6 centimetre (¼ inch) long, but many body structures have begun to form.

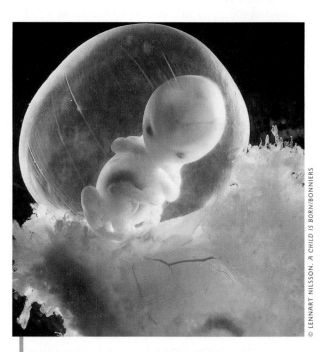

© LENNART NILSSON, *A Child Is Born*/BONNIERS

**Period of the embryo: seventh week.** The embryo's posture is more upright. Body structures—eyes, nose, arms, legs, and internal organs—are more distinct. An embryo of this age responds to touch. It also can move, although at less than 2.5 centimetres (1 inch) long and 4 grams (¹⁄₇ of an ounce) in weight, it is still too tiny to be felt by the mother.

At first, the nervous system develops fastest. The ectoderm folds to form a *neural tube,* or primitive spinal cord. At 3½ weeks, the top swells to form a brain. Production of *neurons* (nerve cells that store and transmit information) begins deep inside the neural tube. Once formed, neurons travel along tiny threads to their permanent locations, where they will form the major parts of the brain (Nelson & Bosquet, 2000).

While the nervous system is developing, the heart begins to pump blood, and muscles, backbone, ribs, and digestive tract appear. At the end of the first month, the curled embryo—only 0.6 centimetre (one-quarter inch) long—consists of millions of organized groups of cells with specific functions.

**THE SECOND MONTH.** In the second month, growth continues rapidly. The eyes, ears, nose, jaw, and neck form. Tiny buds become arms, legs, fingers, and toes. Internal organs are more distinct: the intestines grow, the heart develops separate chambers, and the liver and spleen take over production of blood cells so the yolk sac is no longer needed. Changing body proportions cause the embryo's posture to become more upright. Now 2.5 centimetres (1 inch) long and 4 grams (one-seventh of an ounce) in weight, the embryo can sense its world. It responds to touch, particularly in the mouth area and on the soles of the feet. And it can move, although its tiny flutters are still too light to be felt by the mother (Nilsson & Hamberger, 1990).

## THE PERIOD OF THE FETUS

Lasting from the ninth week until the end of pregnancy, the period of the **fetus** is the "growth and finishing" phase. During this longest prenatal period, the organism increases rapidly in size, especially from the ninth to the twentieth week (Moore & Persaud, 1998).

**THE THIRD MONTH.** In the third month, the organs, muscles, and nervous system start to become organized and connected. The brain signals, and in response, the fetus kicks, bends its arms, forms a fist, curls its toes, opens its mouth, and even sucks its thumb. The tiny lungs begin to expand and contract in an early rehearsal of breathing movements. By the twelfth week, the external genitals are well formed, and the sex of the fetus can be detected with ultrasound. Other finishing touches appear, such as fingernails, toenails, tooth buds, and eyelids that open and close. The heartbeat is now stronger and can be heard through a stethoscope.

Prenatal development is often divided into *trimesters,* or three equal time periods. At the end of the third month, the first trimester is complete.

**THE SECOND TRIMESTER.** By the middle of the second trimester, between 17 and 20 weeks, the new being has grown large enough that the mother can feel its movements. If we could look inside the uterus at this time, we would find the fetus completely covered with a white, cheeselike substance called **vernix.** It protects the skin from chapping during the long months spent in the amniotic fluid. A white, downy hair covering called **lanugo** also appears over the entire body, helping the vernix stick to the skin.

At the end of the second trimester, many organs are quite well developed. And a major milestone is reached in brain development, in that most neurons are in place; few will be produced after this time. However, *glial cells,* which support and feed the neurons, continue to increase at a rapid rate throughout the remaining months of pregnancy, as well as after birth (Nowakowski, 1987).

Brain growth means new behavioural capacities. The 20-week-old fetus can be stimulated as well as irritated by sounds. And if a doctor has reason to look inside the uterus with fetoscopy (refer to Table 3.6), fetuses try to shield their eyes from the light with their hands,

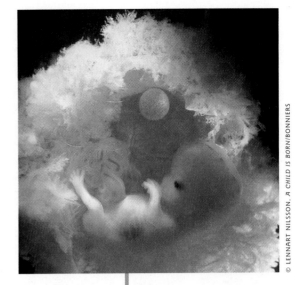

**Period of the fetus: eleventh week.** The organism increases rapidly in size, and body structures are completed. At 11 weeks, the brain and muscles are better connected. The fetus can kick, bend its arms, open and close its hands and mouth, and suck its thumb. Notice the yolk sac, which shrinks as pregnancy advances. The internal organs have taken over its function of producing blood cells.

**umbilical cord**
The long cord connecting the prenatal organism to the placenta that delivers nutrients and removes waste products.

**embryo**
The prenatal organism from 2 to 8 weeks after conception, during which time the foundations of all body structures and internal organs are laid down.

**fetus**
The prenatal organism from the beginning of the third month to the end of pregnancy, during which time completion of body structures and dramatic growth in size take place.

**vernix**
A white, cheeselike substance covering the fetus and preventing the skin from chapping due to constant exposure to the amniotic fluid.

**lanugo**
A white, downy hair that covers the entire body of the fetus, helping the vernix stick to the skin.

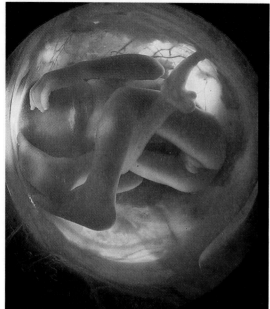

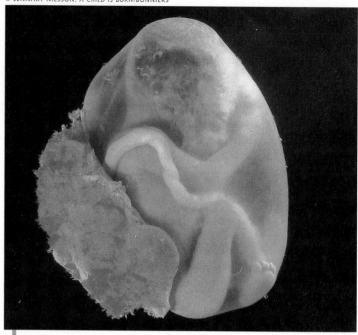

**Period of the fetus: twenty-second week.** This fetus is almost 30 centimetres (1 foot) long and weighs slightly more than 450 grams (a pound). Its movements can be felt easily by the mother and other family members who place a hand on her abdomen. The fetus has reached the age of viability; if born, it has a slim chance of surviving.

**Period of the fetus: thirty-sixth week.** This fetus fills the uterus. To support its need for nourishment, the umbilical cord and placenta have grown large. Notice the vernix (cheeselike substance) on the skin, which protects it from chapping. The fetus has accumulated a layer of fat to assist with temperature regulation after birth. In 2 more weeks, it would be full term.

indicating that sight has begun to emerge (Nilsson & Hamberger, 1990). Still, a fetus born at this time cannot survive. Its lungs are too immature, and the brain cannot yet control breathing and body temperature.

**THE THIRD TRIMESTER.** During the final trimester, a fetus born early has a chance for survival. The point at which the baby can first survive is called the **age of viability.** It occurs sometime between 22 and 26 weeks (Moore & Persaud, 1998). If born between the seventh and eighth months, a baby would still have trouble breathing, and oxygen assistance would be necessary. Although the respiratory centre of the brain is now mature, tiny air sacs in the lungs are not yet ready to inflate and exchange carbon dioxide for oxygen.

The brain continues to make great strides during the last 3 months. The *cerebral cortex,* the seat of human intelligence, enlarges. As neurological organization improves, the fetus spends more time awake. At 20 weeks, heart rate variability reveals no periods of alertness. But by 28 weeks, fetuses are awake about 11 percent of the time, a figure that rises to 16 percent just before birth (DiPietro et al., 1996a).

The fetus also takes on the beginnings of a personality. In a study that tracked fetal responses, pattern of fetal activity just before birth predicted infant temperament, as judged by mothers, at 3 and 6 months of age. Fetuses who cycled between quiet and active periods tended to become calm babies with predictable sleep–waking schedules. In contrast, fetuses who were highly active for long stretches were more likely to become difficult babies—fussy, upset by new experiences, irregular in eating and sleeping, and highly active (DiPietro et al., 1996b). Although these relationships are only modest, they suggest that parents with highly active fetuses can prepare for extra challenges! As we will see in Chapter 10, sensitive care can modify a difficult baby's temperament.

The third trimester brings greater responsiveness to external stimulation. Around 24 weeks, fetuses can first feel pain, so after this time painkillers should be used in any surgical procedures (Royal College of Obstetricians and Gynecologists, 1997). By 25 weeks,

**age of viability**
The age at which the fetus can first survive if born early. Occurs sometime between 22 and 26 weeks.

fetuses react to nearby sounds with body movements (DiPietro et al., 1996a; Kisilevsky & Low, 1998). And in the last weeks of pregnancy, they learn to prefer the tone and rhythm of their mother's voice. In one clever study, mothers read aloud Dr. Seuss's lively book *The Cat in the Hat* to their unborn babies for the last 6 weeks of pregnancy. After birth, their infants were given a chance to suck on nipples that turned on recordings of the mother reading this book or different rhyming stories. The infants sucked hardest to hear *The Cat in the Hat,* the sound they had come to know while still in the womb (DeCasper & Spence, 1986).

During the final 3 months, the fetus gains more than 2300 grams (5 pounds) and grows 18 centimetres (7 inches). As it fills the uterus, it gradually moves less often. In addition, brain development, which permits the organism to inhibit behaviour, may contribute to a decline in physical activity (DiPietro et al., 1996a).

In the eighth month, a layer of fat is added under the skin to assist with temperature regulation. The fetus also receives antibodies from the mother's blood to protect against illnesses, since the newborn's own immune system will not work well until several months after birth. In the last weeks, most fetuses assume an upside-down position, partly because of the shape of the uterus and because of gravity: the head is heavier than the feet. Growth slows, and birth is about to take place.

 **ASK YOURSELF**

**review**   Why is the period of the embryo regarded as the most dramatic prenatal phase? Why is the period of the fetus called the "growth and finishing" phase?

**apply**   Amy, 2 months pregnant, wonders how the developing organism is being fed. "I don't look pregnant yet, so does that mean not much development has occurred?" she asks. How would you respond to Amy?

**connect**   How does brain development relate to fetal behaviour?

# Prenatal Environmental Influences

ALTHOUGH THE PRENATAL environment is far more constant than the world outside the womb, many factors can affect the embryo and fetus. In the following sections, we will see that there is much that parents—and society as a whole—can do to create a safe environment for development before birth.

## TERATOGENS

The term **teratogen** refers to any environmental agent that causes damage during the prenatal period. It comes from the Greek word *teras,* meaning "malformation" or "monstrosity." This label was selected because scientists first learned about harmful prenatal influences from babies who had been profoundly damaged. Yet the harm done by teratogens is not always simple and straightforward. It depends on the following factors:

- *Dose.* We will see as we discuss particular teratogens that larger doses over longer time periods usually have more negative effects.

- *Heredity.* The genetic makeup of the mother and the developing organism play an important role. Some individuals are better able to withstand harmful environments.

- *Other negative influences.* The presence of several negative factors at once, such as poor nutrition, lack of medical care, and additional teratogens, can worsen the impact of a single harmful agent.

- *Age.* The effects of teratogens vary with the age of the organism at time of exposure.

**teratogen**
Any environmental agent that causes damage during the prenatal period.

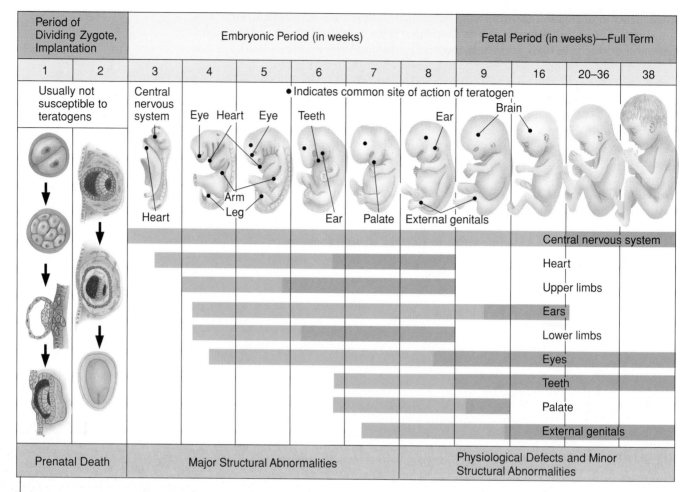

| Period of Dividing Zygote, Implantation | | Embryonic Period (in weeks) | | | | | | | Fetal Period (in weeks)—Full Term | | | |
|---|---|---|---|---|---|---|---|---|---|---|---|---|
| 1 | 2 | 3 | 4 | 5 | 6 | 7 | 8 | 9 | 16 | 20–36 | 38 |

**FIGURE** 3.8

**Sensitive periods in prenatal development.** Each organ or structure has a sensitive period, during which its development may be disturbed. Blue horizontal bars indicate highly sensitive periods. Green horizontal bars indicate periods that are somewhat less sensitive to teratogens, although damage can occur. (From K. L. Moore & T. V. N. Persaud, 1998, *Before We Are Born*, 5th ed., Philadelphia: Saunders, p. 166. Reprinted by permission of the publisher and the author.)

We can best understand this last idea if we think of the *sensitive period* concept introduced in Chapter 1. A sensitive period is a limited time span in which a part of the body or a behaviour is biologically prepared to develop rapidly. During that time, it is especially vulnerable to its surroundings. If the environment is harmful, then damage occurs, and recovery is difficult and sometimes impossible.

Figure 3.8 summarizes prenatal sensitive periods. Look carefully at it, and you will see that some parts of the body, such as the brain and eye, have long sensitive periods. Other sensitive periods, such as those for the limbs and palate, are much shorter. Figure 3.8 also indicates some general statements about the timing of harmful influences. During the period of the zygote, before implantation, teratogens rarely have any impact. If they do, the tiny mass of cells is usually so damaged that it dies. The embryonic period is the time when serious defects are most likely to occur, since the foundations for all body parts are being laid down. During the fetal period, teratogenic damage is usually minor. However, organs such as the brain, eye, and genitals can still be strongly affected.

The effects of teratogens are not limited to immediate physical damage. Some health effects are subtle and delayed. For example, when teratogens disrupt the flow of nutrients across the placenta, they can affect the individual's health decades later. Large-scale studies reveal a consistent link between low birth weight and heart disease, stroke, and diabetes in adulthood, even after other health risks are controlled. A poorly nourished fetus seems to experience physical changes that heighten the chances of these illnesses (Fall et al., 1998; Forsén et al., 2000; Rich-Edwards et al., 1999). Furthermore, psychological consequences may occur indirectly, as a result of physical damage. For example, a defect resulting from drugs the mother took during pregnancy can change reactions of others to the child as well as the child's ability to explore the environment. Over time, parent–child interaction, peer relations, and cognitive and social development may suffer.

Notice how an important idea about development discussed in Chapter 1 is at work here—that of *bidirectional* influences between child and environment. Now let's look at what scientists have discovered about a variety of teratogens.

**PRESCRIPTION AND NONPRESCRIPTION DRUGS.** In the early 1960s, the world learned a tragic lesson about drugs and prenatal development. At that time, a sedative called *thalidomide* was prescribed in Canada, Europe, and South America to help with symptoms associated with morning sickness. When taken by mothers between the fourth and sixth week after conception, thalidomide produced gross deformities of the embryo's developing arms and legs and, less frequently, damage to the ears, heart, kidneys, and genitals. About 7000 infants worldwide were affected (Moore & Persaud, 1998); approximately 125 such children were born in Canada (Thalidomide Victims Association of Canada, 2000). As children exposed to thalidomide grew older, many scored below average in intelligence. Perhaps the drug damaged the central nervous system directly. Or the child-rearing conditions of these severely deformed youngsters may have impaired their intellectual development.

Another medication, a synthetic hormone called diethylstilbestrol (DES), was widely prescribed between 1941 and 1971 to prevent miscarriages. As daughters of these mothers reached adolescence and young adulthood, they showed unusually high rates of cancer of the vagina and malformations of the uterus. When they tried to have children, their pregnancies more often resulted in prematurity, low birth weight, and miscarriage than those of non-DES-exposed women. Young men showed an increased risk of genital abnormalities and cancer of the testes (Giusti, Iwamoto, & Hatch, 1995; Palmlund, 1996).

Any drug taken by the mother that has a molecule small enough to penetrate the placental barrier can enter the embryonic or fetal bloodstream. Despite the bitter lesson of thalidomide, many pregnant women continue to take over-the-counter drugs without consulting their doctors. Aspirin is one of the most common. Several studies suggest that regular use of aspirin is linked to low birth weight, infant death around the time of birth, poorer motor development, and lower intelligence test scores in early childhood (Barr et al., 1990; Streissguth et al., 1987). Other research, however, has failed to confirm these findings (see, for example, Hauth et al., 1995).

Coffee, tea, cola, and cocoa contain another frequently consumed drug, caffeine. Heavy caffeine intake (more than three cups of coffee per day) is associated with low birth weight, miscarriage, and newborn withdrawal symptoms, such as irritability and vomiting (Eskenazi, 1993; Fernandes et al., 1998). Some researchers report *dose-related* effects: the more caffeine consumed, the greater the likelihood of negative outcomes (Eskenazi et al., 1999; Fortier, Marcoux, & Beaulac-Baillargeon, 1993).

Because children's lives are involved, we must take findings like these seriously. At the same time, we cannot yet be sure that these drugs actually cause the problems mentioned. Often mothers take more than one drug. If the prenatal organism is injured, it is hard to tell which might be responsible or if other factors correlated with drug taking are really at fault. Until we have more information, the safest course of action for pregnant women is to cut down on or avoid these drugs entirely.

**ILLEGAL DRUGS.** The use of highly addictive mood-altering drugs, such as cocaine and heroin, has become more widespread, especially in poverty-stricken inner-city areas, where these drugs provide a temporary escape from a daily life of hopelessness. Approximately 5.5 percent of Canadians between 18 and 29 years of age report using cocaine recreationally (Forman, Klein, & Koren, 1994). Babies born to users of cocaine, heroin, or methadone (a less addictive drug used to wean people away from heroin) are at risk for a wide variety of problems,

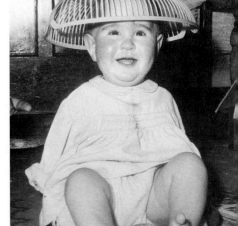

BETTMAN/CORBIS/MAGMA

In the early 1960s, a sedative called thalidomide was prescribed in Canada, Europe, and South America to alleviate morning sickness. Unfortunately, the drug caused limb deformities. This baby uses her feet to play with a basket of fruit because she has no arms.

including prematurity, low birth weight, physical defects, breathing difficulties, and death around the time of birth (Datta-Bhutada, Johnson, & Rosen, 1998; Walker, Rosenberg, & Balaban-Gil, 1999). In addition, these infants arrive drug addicted. They are often feverish and irritable and have trouble sleeping (Delaney-Black et al., 1996; Friedman, 1996; Martin et al., 1996). When mothers with many problems of their own must take care of these babies, who are difficult to calm down, cuddle, and feed, behaviour problems are likely to persist.

Throughout the first year, heroin- and methadone-exposed infants are less attentive to the environment, and their motor development is slow. After infancy, some children get better, whereas others remain jittery and inattentive. The kind of parenting these youngsters receive may explain why problems last for some but not for others (Cosden, Peerson, & Elliott, 1997).

Growing evidence on cocaine suggests that many prenatally exposed babies have lasting difficulties. Cocaine constricts the blood vessels, causing oxygen delivered to the developing organism to fall dramatically for 15 minutes following a high dose. It also alters the production and functioning of neurons and the chemical balance in the fetus's brain. These effects may contribute to a specific set of cocaine-linked physical defects, including eye, bone, genital, urinary tract, kidney, and heart deformities, as well as brain hemorrhages and seizures (Espy, Kaufmann, & Glisky, 1999; Mayes, 1999; Plessinger & Woods, 1998). Motor, visual, attention, memory, and language problems appear in infancy and persist into the preschool years (Mayes et al., 1996). Babies born to mothers who smoke crack (a cheap form of cocaine that delivers high doses quickly through the lungs) seem to be worst off in terms of low birth weight and damage to the central nervous system (Bender et al., 1995; Richardson et al., 1996).

Still, it is difficult to isolate the precise damage caused by cocaine, since users often take several drugs, display other high-risk behaviours, and engage in insensitive caregiving (Addis et al., 2001; Lester, 2000). The joint impact of these factors worsens outcomes for children (Alessandri, Bendersky, & Lewis, 1998; Carta et al., 2001). And because cocaine-exposed babies have not been followed beyond early childhood, long-term consequences are unknown.

Another illegal drug, marijuana, is used more widely than cocaine and heroin. Studies examining its relationship to low birth weight and prematurity reveal mixed findings (Fried, 1993). Several researchers have linked prenatal marijuana exposure to smaller head size (a measure of brain growth), newborn startle reactions, disturbed sleep, and inattention in infancy and childhood (Dahl et al., 1995; Fried, Watkinson, & Gray, 1999; Lester & Dreher, 1989). As with cocaine, however, long-term effects have not been established.

**TOBACCO.** Although smoking has declined in Western nations, an estimated 24 percent of Canadian mothers smoke at some point during their pregnancy (Connor & McIntyre, 1998). And although 25 to 40 percent of pregnant smokers quit for at least some time once they become pregnant, the majority later resume smoking (Moner, 1994).

The most well-known effect of smoking during pregnancy is low birth weight. But the likelihood of other serious consequences, such as miscarriage, prematurity, impaired heart rate and breathing during sleep, infant death, and cancer later in childhood, is also increased (Franco et al., 2000; Walker, Rosenberg, & Balaban-Gil, 1999). And the more cigarettes a mother smokes, the greater the chances that her baby will be affected. If a pregnant woman stops smoking at any time, even during the last trimester, she reduces the likelihood that her infant will be born underweight and suffer from future problems (Ahlsten, Cnattingius, & Lindmark, 1993; Groff et al., 1997).

Even when a baby of a smoking mother appears to be born in good physical condition, slight behavioural abnormalities may threaten the child's development. Newborns of smoking mothers are less attentive to sounds and display more muscle tension (Fried & Makin, 1987). An unresponsive, restless baby may not evoke the kind of interaction from adults that promotes healthy psychological development. Some studies report that prenatally exposed youngsters have shorter attention spans, poorer memories, lower mental test scores, and more behaviour problems in childhood and adolescence, even after many other factors have

**fetal alcohol syndrome (FAS)**
A set of defects that results when pregnant women consume large amounts of alcohol during most or all of pregnancy. Includes mental retardation; impaired motor coordination, attention, memory, language, planning, and problem solving; overactivity; slow physical growth; and facial abnormalities.

**fetal alcohol effects (FAE)**
The condition of children who display some but not all the defects of fetal alcohol syndrome. Usually their mothers drank alcohol in smaller quantities or less often during pregnancy.

been controlled (Cornelius et al., 2001; Trasti et al., 1999; Wasserman et al., 2001). But other researchers have not confirmed these findings (Barr et al., 1990; Streissguth et al., 1989).

Exactly how can smoking harm the fetus? Nicotine, the addictive substance in tobacco, constricts blood vessels, lessens blood flow to the uterus, and causes the placenta to grow abnormally. This reduces the transfer of nutrients, so the fetus gains weight poorly. Also, nicotine raises the concentration of carbon monoxide in the bloodstreams of both mother and fetus. Carbon monoxide displaces oxygen from red blood cells. It damages the central nervous system and reduces birth weight in the fetuses of laboratory animals. Similar effects may occur in humans (Friedman, 1996).

Finally, one-third to one-half of nonsmoking pregnant women are "passive smokers" because their husbands, relatives, or co-workers use cigarettes. Passive smoking is also related to low birth weight, infant death, and possible long-term impairments in attention and learning (Dejin-Karlsson et al., 1998; Makin, Fried, & Watkinson, 1991). Clearly, expectant mothers should do what they can to avoid smoke-filled environments.

**ALCOHOL.** **Fetal alcohol syndrome (FAS)** is the name for a constellation of symptoms that include mental retardation, overactivity, and impairments in motor coordination, attention, memory, language, planning, and problem solving (see, for example, Connor et al., 2001; Schonfeld et al., 2001). Accompanying physical symptoms include slow physical growth and a particular pattern of facial abnormalities: widely spaced eyes; short eyelid openings; a small, upturned nose; a thin upper lip; and a small head, indicating that the brain has not developed fully. Other defects—of the eyes, ears, nose, throat, heart, genitals, urinary tract, or immune system—may also be present.

In all babies with FAS, the mother drank heavily through most or all of her pregnancy. Sometimes children display only some of the physical abnormalities associated with FAS. In these cases, the child is said to suffer from **fetal alcohol effects (FAE).** Usually, their mothers drank alcohol in smaller quantities or less often. The particular defects of FAE children vary with timing and length of alcohol exposure during pregnancy (Goodlet & Johnson, 1999; Mattson et al., 1998).

According to the National Population Health Survey, approximately 25 percent of Canadian women reported drinking at some point during their last pregnancy (Health Canada, 1998b). Of every 1000 live births in Canada, approximately 1 to 3 babies, or at least 1 child each day, are diagnosed with FAS. Moreover, the proportion of children with FAS is significantly higher in some Aboriginal communities. Yet FAS and the milder FAE rank among the leading causes of preventable birth defects and developmental delays for Canadian children (Health Canada, 2000b).

Even when provided with enriched diets, FAS babies fail to catch up in physical size during infancy or childhood. Mental impairment is also permanent. The more alcohol consumed by a woman during pregnancy, the poorer her child's motor coordination, information processing, reasoning, and intelligence and achievement test scores during the preschool and school years (Aronson, Hagberg, & Gillberg, 1997; Hunt et al., 1995; Streissguth et al., 1994). In adolescence, prenatal alcohol exposure is associated with poor school performance, trouble with the law, inappropriate sexual behaviour, alcohol and drug abuse, and lasting mental health problems (Streissguth et al., 1999). Like heroin and cocaine use, alcohol abuse is higher in poverty-stricken sectors of the population (Streissguth, 1997). Unfortunately, when girls with FAS and FAE later become pregnant, the poor judgment caused by the syndrome often prevents them from understanding why they should avoid alcohol themselves. Thus, the tragic cycle is likely to be repeated in the next generation.

How does alcohol produce its devastating effects? First, it interferes with cell duplication and migration in the primitive neural tube. Psychophysiological measures, including fMRI and EEGs, reveal structural damage, arrested brain growth, and abnormalities in brain functioning, including electrical and chemical activity involved in transferring messages from one part of the brain to another (Guerri, 1998; Roebuck, Mattson, & Riley, 1999). Second, the body uses large quantities of oxygen to metabolize alcohol. A pregnant woman's heavy drinking draws away oxygen that the developing organism needs for cell growth.

GEORGE STEINMETZ

The mother of the severely retarded boy above drank heavily during pregnancy. His widely spaced eyes, thin upper lip, and short eyelid openings are typical of fetal alcohol syndrome. The adolescent girl below also has these physical symptoms. The brain damage caused by alcohol before she was born is permanent. It has made learning in school and adapting to everyday challenges extremely difficult.

How much alcohol is safe during pregnancy? One study linked as little as 60 millilitres (2 ounces) a day, taken very early in pregnancy, with FAS-like facial features (Astley et al., 1992). But recall that other factors—both genetic and environmental—can make some fetuses more vulnerable to teratogens. Therefore, a precise dividing line between safe and dangerous drinking levels cannot be established, and it is best for pregnant women to avoid alcohol entirely.

**RADIATION.** Earlier we saw that ionizing radiation can cause mutation, damaging the DNA in ova and sperm. When mothers are exposed to radiation during pregnancy, additional harm can come to the embryo or fetus. Defects due to radiation were tragically apparent in the children born to pregnant Japanese women who survived the atomic bombing of Hiroshima and Nagasaki during World War II. Similar abnormalities surfaced in the 9 months following the 1986 Chernobyl, Ukraine, nuclear power plant accident. After each disaster, the incidence of miscarriage, small head size (indicating an underdeveloped brain), physical deformities, and slow physical growth rose dramatically (Schull & Otake, 1999; Terestchenko, Lyaginskaya, & Burtzeva, 1991).

**ENVIRONMENTAL POLLUTION.** An astounding number of potentially dangerous chemicals are released into the environment in industrialized nations. Over 100 000 are in common use, and many new ones are introduced each year.

*Mercury* is an established teratogen. In the 1950s, an industrial plant released waste containing high levels of mercury into a bay providing food and water for the town of Minimata, Japan. Many children born at the time were mentally retarded and showed other serious symptoms, including abnormal speech, difficulty in chewing and swallowing, and uncoordinated movements. Autopsies of those who died revealed widespread brain damage (Dietrich, 1999).

Another teratogen, *lead,* is present in old paint and in certain industrial materials. High levels of lead exposure are consistently related to prematurity, low birth weight, brain damage, and a wide variety of physical defects (Dye-White, 1986). Even low levels of prenatal lead exposure seem to be dangerous. Affected babies show slightly poorer mental and motor development (Dietrich, Berger, & Succop, 1993; Wasserman et al., 1994).

For many years, *polychlorinated biphenyls (PCBs)* were used to insulate electrical equipment, until research showed that (like mercury) they found their way into waterways and entered the food supply. In Taiwan, prenatal exposure to very high levels of PCBs in rice oil resulted in low birth weight, discoloured skin, deformities of the gums and nails, brain-wave abnormalities, and delayed cognitive development (Chen & Hsu, 1994; Chen et al., 1994).

Steady, low-level PCB exposure is also harmful. Women who frequently ate PCB-contaminated Great Lakes fish (compared with those who ate little or no fish) had infants with slightly lower than average birth weights, smaller heads, more intense physiological reactions to stress, and less interest in their surroundings (Jacobson et al., 1984; Stewart et al., 2000). Follow-ups later in the first year and in early childhood revealed persisting memory difficulties and lower verbal intelligence (Jacobson, 1998; Jacobson et al., 1992).

**MATERNAL DISEASE.** Five percent of women catch an infectious disease while pregnant. Most of these illnesses, such as the common cold, seem to have no impact on the embryo or fetus. However, as Table 3.7 indicates, a few diseases can cause extensive damage.

*Viruses.* Rubella (3-day German measles) is a well-known teratogen. In the mid-1960s, a worldwide epidemic of rubella led to the birth of many thousands of babies with serious defects. Consistent with the sensitive period concept, the greatest damage occurs when rubella strikes during the embryonic period. More than 50 percent of infants whose mothers become ill during that time show heart defects; eye cataracts; deafness; genital, urinary, and

This child's mother was just a few weeks pregnant during the Chernobyl nuclear power plant disaster. Radiation exposure probably is responsible for his limb deformities. He also is at risk for low intelligence and language and emotional disorders.

intestinal abnormalities; and mental retardation. Infection during the fetal period is less harmful, but low birth weight, hearing loss, and bone defects may still occur (Eberhart-Phillips, Frederick, & Baron, 1993). Since the rubella vaccine became available in Canada in 1969, the incidence of rubella has declined markedly, although a large outbreak occurred in Manitoba in 1996 and 1997 (Ford-Jones & Tam, 1999). Even though vaccination in infancy and childhood is routine, about 10 to 20 percent of women in North America and Western Europe lack the rubella antibody, so new disease outbreaks are still possible (Lee et al., 1992; Pebody et al., 2000).

The *human immunodeficiency virus (HIV),* which leads to *acquired immune deficiency syndrome (AIDS),* a disease that destroys the immune system, has infected increasing numbers of women over the past decade. Among AIDS victims, 8 percent in Canada, 13 percent in the United States, and more than 50 percent in Africa are women. When they become pregnant, about 20 to 30 percent of the time they pass the deadly virus to the developing organism (Nourse & Butler, 1998). HIV infection rates are increasing among Canadian women, who now account for 24 percent of new HIV cases (Health Canada, 2001a).

AIDS progresses rapidly in infants. By 6 months, weight loss, diarrhea, and repeated respiratory illnesses are common. The virus also causes brain damage. Most prenatal AIDS babies survive for only 5 to 8 months after the appearance of symptoms (Parks, 1996). The antiviral drug zidovudine (ZDV) reduces prenatal AIDS transmission by as much as 95 percent, with no harmful consequences of drug treatment for children (Culnane et al., 1999). It has led to a dramatic decline in prenatally acquired AIDS in Western nations.

**TABLE** 3.7

Effects of Some Infectious Diseases during Pregnancy

| DISEASE | MISCARRIAGE | PHYSICAL MALFORMATIONS | MENTAL RETARDATION | LOW BIRTH WEIGHT AND PREMATURITY |
|---|---|---|---|---|
| **Viral** | | | | |
| Acquired immune deficiency syndrome (AIDS) | o | ? | + | ? |
| Chicken pox | o | + | + | + |
| Cytomegalovirus | + | + | + | + |
| Herpes simplex 2 (genital herpes) | + | + | + | + |
| Mumps | + | ? | o | o |
| Rubella (German measles) | + | + | + | + |
| **Bacterial** | | | | |
| Syphilis | + | + | + | ? |
| Tuberculosis | + | ? | + | + |
| **Parasitic** | | | | |
| Malaria | + | o | o | + |
| Toxoplasmosis | + | + | + | + |

+ = established finding. o = no present evidence. ? = possible effect that is not clearly established.

*Sources:* Behrman, Kliegman, & Jenson, 2000; Chatkupt et al., 1989; Cohen, 1993; Peckham & Logan, 1993; Qazi et al., 1988; Samson, 1988; Sever, 1983; Vorhees, 1986.

As Table 3.7 reveals, the developing organism is especially sensitive to the family of herpes viruses, for which there is no vaccine or treatment. Among these, *cytomegalovirus* (the most frequent prenatal infection, transmitted through respiratory or sexual contact) and *herpes simplex 2* (which is sexually transmitted) are especially dangerous. In both, the virus invades the mother's genital tract. Babies can be infected either during pregnancy or at birth.

***Bacterial and Parasitic Diseases.***   Table 3.7 also includes several bacterial and parasitic diseases. Among the most common is *toxoplasmosis,* caused by a parasite found in many animals. Pregnant women may become infected from eating raw or undercooked meat or from contact with the feces of infected cats. About 40 percent of women who have the disease transmit it to the developing organism. If it strikes during the first trimester, it is likely to cause eye and brain damage. Later infection is linked to mild visual and cognitive impairments (Jones et al., 2001). Expectant mothers can avoid toxoplasmosis by making sure that the meat they eat is well cooked, having pet cats checked for the disease, and turning over the care of litter boxes to other family members.

## OTHER MATERNAL FACTORS

Besides teratogens, maternal exercise, nutrition, and emotional well-being affect the embryo and fetus. In addition, many expectant parents wonder about the impact of a woman's age on the course of pregnancy. We examine each of these influences in the following sections.

**EXERCISE.**   In healthy, physically fit women, regular moderate exercise, such as walking, swimming, biking, and aerobics, is related to increased birth weight (Hatch et al., 1993). However, very frequent, vigorous exercise (working up a sweat four or more times a week) predicts the opposite outcome—lower birth weight than in healthy, non-exercising controls (Pivarnik, 1998). Pregnant women with health problems, such as circulatory difficulties or a history of miscarriage, should consult their doctors before beginning or continuing a physical fitness routine.

During the last trimester, when the abdomen grows very large, mothers often must cut back on exercise. In most cases, a mother who has remained fit during the earlier months is likely to experience fewer physical discomforts, such as back pain, upward pressure on the chest, and difficulty breathing.

**NUTRITION.**   Children grow more rapidly during the prenatal period than at any other phase, and depend totally on the mother for nutrients. Women who gain either too little or too much weight during pregnancy put their babies at risk. Previous Canadian guidelines recommended a weight gain of 10 to 14 kilograms (22 to 30 pounds), but current guidelines suggest that weight gain be based on pre-pregnancy body mass index (BMI) (Health Canada, 2001b). A woman with a lower BMI should gain more weight than a woman with a higher BMI.

This government-sponsored class in a village in India prevents prenatal malnutrition by promoting a proper diet for pregnant women. Mothers also learn how breast-feeding can protect their newborn baby's healthy growth (see Chapter 5, page 187).

©RICHARD LORD/PHOTOEDIT

***Consequences of Prenatal Malnutrition.***   During World War II, a severe famine occurred in the Netherlands, giving scientists a rare opportunity to study the impact of nutrition on prenatal development. Findings revealed that the sensitive period concept operates with nutrition, just as it does with teratogens. Women affected by the famine during the first trimester were more likely to have miscarriages or to give birth to babies with physical defects. When women were past the first trimester, fetuses usually survived, but many were born underweight and had small heads (Stein et al., 1975).

We now know that prenatal malnutrition can cause serious damage to the central nervous system. The poorer the mother's diet, the greater the loss in brain weight, especially if malnutrition occurred during the last trimester. During that time, the brain is increasing rapidly in size, and a maternal diet high in all the basic nutrients is necessary for it to reach its full potential (Morgane et al., 1993). An inadequate diet during pregnancy can also distort the structure of other organs, resulting in lifelong health problems (Barker, 1994).

Because poor nutrition suppresses development of the immune system, prenatally malnourished babies frequently catch respiratory illnesses (Chandra, 1991). They often are irritable and unresponsive to stimulation. The behavioural effects of poor nutrition quickly combine with an impoverished, stressful home life. With age, low intelligence test scores and serious learning problems become more apparent (Pollitt, 1996).

***Prevention and Treatment.*** Many studies show that providing pregnant women with adequate food has a substantial impact on the health of their babies. Yet the growth demands of the prenatal period require more than just increased quantity of food. Vitamin–mineral enrichment is also crucial.

For example, folic acid can prevent abnormalities of the neural tube, such as anencephaly and spina bifida (see Table 3.6 on page 81). In a study of nearly 2000 women in seven countries who had previously given birth to a baby with a neural tube defect, half were randomly selected to receive a folic acid supplement around the time of conception and half a mixture of other vitamins or no supplement. As Figure 3.9 reveals, the folic acid group showed 72 percent fewer neural tube defects (MCR Vitamin Study Research Group, 1991). In addition, adequate folate intake during the last 10 weeks of pregnancy cuts in half the risk of premature delivery and low birth weight (Scholl, Heidiger, & Belsky, 1996). Canadian guidelines recommend that women contemplating pregnancy take 0.4 mg of folate daily (Health Canada, 1999a). Women should take supplements before they conceive because neural tube defects form early on, and they should continue to take them throughout the pregnancy as well (Motherisk, 2001). Since folic acid is minimal in most diets, bread, flour, rice, pasta, and other grain products are currently being fortified with folic acid.

Other vitamins and minerals also have established benefits. Enriching women's diets with calcium helps prevent maternal high blood pressure and premature births (Repke, 1992). Adequate magnesium and zinc reduce the risk of many prenatal and birth complications (Facchinetti et al., 1992; Jameson, 1993; Spätling & Spätling, 1988). Fortifying table salt with iodine virtually eradicates cretinism—a common cause of mental retardation and stunted growth in many parts of the world (Mathews, Yudkin, & Neil, 1999). And taking a multivitamin supplement beginning in the first few weeks of pregnancy protects against cleft lip and palate (Tolarova, 1986). Nevertheless, a supplement program should complement, not replace, efforts to improve maternal diets during pregnancy. For women who do not get enough food or an adequate variety of foods, multivitamin tablets are a necessary, but not sufficient, intervention.

When poor nutrition is allowed to continue through most or all of pregnancy, infants usually require more than dietary improvement. Their tired, restless behaviour leads mothers to be less sensitive and stimulating. In response, babies become even more passive and withdrawn. Successful interventions must break this cycle of apathetic mother–baby interaction. Some do so by teaching parents how to interact effectively with their infants, whereas others focus on stimulating infants to promote active engagement with their physical and social surroundings (Grantham-McGregor et al., 1994; Zeskind & Ramey, 1978, 1981).

Although prenatal malnutrition is highest in developing countries, poverty and the related problems of malnutrition exist in even the wealthiest nations. The Canada Prenatal Nutrition program sponsors community-based groups that support pregnant women with food, nutrition counselling, social support, access to health care, and shelter. The program is designed for pregnant women at risk for poor birth outcomes (such as those in danger of giving birth to babies with developmental problems), especially adolescents and adults with limited resources and those who live in geographical isolation.

**EMOTIONAL STRESS.** When women experience severe emotional stress during pregnancy, their babies are at risk for a wide variety of difficulties. Intense anxiety is associated with a higher rate of miscarriage, prematurity, low birth weight, and newborn irritability, respiratory illness,

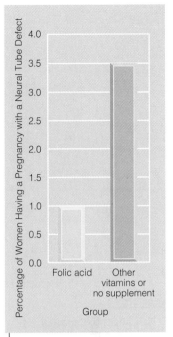

**FIGURE 3.9**

**Percentage of pregnancies with a neural tube defect in folic-acid-supplemented women versus others.** Folic acid taken around the time of conception dramatically reduced the incidence of neural tube defects—a finding confirmed by other large-scale studies. Note, however, that folic acid did not eliminate all neural tube defects. These abnormalities, like many others, have multiple origins in the embryo's genetic disposition and factors in the environment. (Adapted from MCR Vitamin Study Research Group, 1991.)

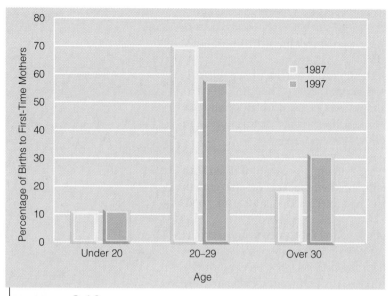

**FIGURE** 3.10

**First births to Canadian women of different ages in 1987 and 1997.** The birth rate decreased during this period for women in their twenties, whereas it increased for women over 30 and remained stable for women under 20. The average age of new mothers is now 29 years. (Adapted from Statistics Canada, Births, 1999: "The Daily," Catalogue no. 11-001, June 16, 1999.)

and digestive disturbances. It is also related to certain physical defects, such as cleft lip and palate and pyloric stenosis (tightening of the infant's stomach outlet, which must be treated surgically) (Carmichael & Shaw, 2000; Hoffman & Hatch, 1996).

When we experience fear and anxiety, stimulant hormones released into our bloodstream cause us to be "poised for action." Large amounts of blood are sent to parts of the body involved in the defensive response—the brain, the heart, and muscles in the arms, legs, and trunk. Blood flow to other organs, including the uterus, is reduced. As a result, the fetus is deprived of a full supply of oxygen and nutrients. Stress hormones also cross the placenta, leading the fetus's heart rate and activity level to rise dramatically. In addition, stress weakens the immune system, making pregnant women more susceptible to infectious disease (Cohen & Williamson, 1991; Monk et al., 2000). Finally, women who experience long-term anxiety are more likely to smoke, drink, eat poorly, and engage in other behaviours that harm the embryo or fetus.

But stress-related prenatal complications are greatly reduced when mothers have husbands, other family members, and friends who offer support (McLean et al., 1993; Nuckolls, Cassel, & Kaplan, 1972). The link between social support and positive pregnancy outcomes is particularly strong for women of low socioeconomic status (Hoffman & Hatch, 1996).

**MATERNAL AGE AND PREVIOUS BIRTHS.** First births to women in their thirties have increased greatly over the past quarter-century in industrialized nations (see Figure 3.10). Many more couples are putting off childbearing until their careers are well established and they know they can support a child. As indicated earlier, women who delay having children face a greater risk of giving birth to babies with chromosomal defects. Are other pregnancy complications more common among older mothers? For many years, scientists thought so. But healthy women in their forties have no more prenatal difficulties than do women in their twenties (Bianco et al., 1996; Dildy et al., 1996; Prysak, Lorenz, & Kisly, 1995).

In the case of teenage mothers, does physical immaturity cause pregnancy complications? Again, research shows that it does not. A teenager's body is large enough and strong enough to support pregnancy. In fact, as we will see in Chapter 5, nature tries to ensure that once a girl can conceive, she is physically ready to carry and give birth to a baby. Infants of teenagers are born with a higher rate of problems for quite different reasons. Many pregnant adolescents do not have access to medical care or are afraid to seek it. In addition, most pregnant

## ASK YOURSELF ⚡www

**review** What is a sensitive period? How is it relevant to understanding the impact of teratogens?

**review** Why is it difficult to determine the effects of many environmental agents, such as drugs and pollution, on the embryo and fetus?

**apply** Nora, pregnant for the first time, has heard about the teratogenic impact of alcohol and tobacco. Nevertheless, she believes that a few cigarettes and a glass of wine a day won't be harmful. Provide Nora with research-based reasons for not smoking or drinking.

**connect** List teratogens and other maternal factors that affect brain development during the prenatal period. Why is the central nervous system often affected when the prenatal environment is compromised?

teenagers come from low-income backgrounds, where stress, poor nutrition, and health problems are common (Coley & Chase-Lansdale, 1998).

# Childbirth

IT IS NOT SURPRISING THAT CHILDBIRTH is often referred to as *labour.* It is the hardest physical work a woman may ever do. As the Biology & Environment box on pages 102–103 explains, a complex series of hormonal changes initiates the process, which naturally divides into three stages (see Figure 3.11):

1. *Dilation and effacement of the cervix.* This is the longest stage of labour, lasting, on the average, 12 to 14 hours in a first birth and 4 to 6 hours in later births. Contractions of the uterus gradually become more frequent and powerful, causing the cervix, or uterine opening, to widen and thin to nothing. As a result, a clear channel from the uterus into the vagina, or birth canal, is formed.

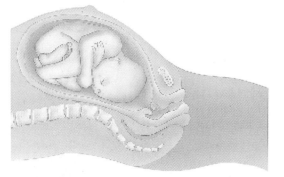
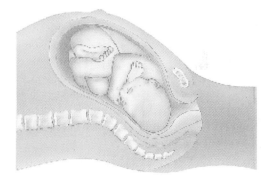

(a) Dilation and Effacement of the Cervix

(b) Transition

(c) Pushing

(d) Birth of the Baby

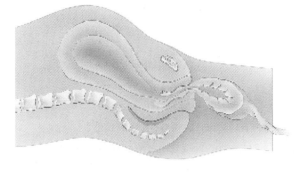

(e) Delivery of the Placenta

**FIGURE** 3.11

**The three stages of labour.** Stage 1: (a) Contractions of the uterus cause the cervix to open and thin. (b) Transition is reached when the frequency and strength of the contractions are at their peak and the cervix opens completely. Stage 2: (c) The mother pushes with each contraction, forcing the baby down the birth canal, and the head appears. (d) Near the end of Stage 2, the shoulders emerge and are followed quickly by the rest of the baby's body. Stage 3: (e) With a few final pushes, the placenta is delivered.

# biology & environment

## WHAT CONTROLS THE TIMING OF BIRTH?

Only in the past decade has animal and human research begun to uncover the precise biological changes that control the timing of birth. Through most of pregnancy, the placenta secretes high levels of the hormone *progesterone,* which keeps the uterus relaxed and the cervix firm and inflexible, so it remains tightly closed and capable of supporting the growing fetus. But the placenta also secretes *estrogen,* which rises during pregnancy and counters the effects of progesterone in three ways:

- by producing a protein called *connexin,* which links uterine muscle cells to one another so they contract in a coordinated fashion;

- by making the uterine muscle sensitive to *oxytocin,* a hormone released from the brain that induces contractions;

- by stimulating the placenta to release *prostaglandins,* hormones that soften the cervix so it will dilate during labour.

What switches on the production of estrogen and leads it to overwhelm progesterone? Researchers began to suspect that another placental hormone called *corticotropin-releasing hormone (CRH)* is involved when they found that mothers who go into premature labour have higher blood levels of CRH than do other women in the same week of pregnancy (see Figure 3.12) (McLean et al., 1995). In fact, CRH levels measured as early as the 16th to 20th week are good predictors of whether a woman will give birth early, on time, or past her due date.

How does CRH work? When it reaches a high enough level, it leads the fetal adrenal glands (located on top of each kidney) to produce *cortisol,* a stress hormone that clears the infants' lungs of fluid so they are ready to breathe air. Cortisol, in turn, further stimulates CRH production, which triggers estrogen secretion in the placenta, resulting in the rapid estrogen rise required for labour (Emanuel et al., 1994; Smith, 1999).

AP/WIDE WORLD PHOTOS

These Muslim women of Indonesia pray in a mosque during the month of Ramadan, a time of daily fasting from dawn to sunset. Pregnant women may postpone the fast to a later time—an exception that recognizes food deprivation as a threat to the mother's and baby's health. Fasting may precipitate early birth by causing the fetus to produce an excess of cortisol, a stress hormone. Cortisol initiates a rise in corticotropin-releasing hormone (CRH), which, in turn, triggers increased estrogen production, required for labour.

2. *Delivery of the baby.* Once the cervix is fully open, the baby is ready to be born. This second stage is much shorter than the first, lasting about 50 minutes in a first birth and 20 minutes in later births. Strong contractions of the uterus continue, but the mother also feels a natural urge to squeeze and push with her abdominal muscles. As she does so with each contraction, she forces the baby down and out.

3. *Birth of the placenta.* Labour comes to an end with a few final contractions and pushes. These cause the placenta to separate from the wall of the uterus and be delivered, in about 5 to 10 minutes.

## THE BABY'S ADAPTATION TO LABOUR AND DELIVERY

At first glance, labour and delivery seem like a dangerous ordeal for the baby. The strong contractions expose the head to a great deal of pressure, and they squeeze the placenta and umbilical cord repeatedly. Each time, the baby's supply of oxygen is temporarily reduced.

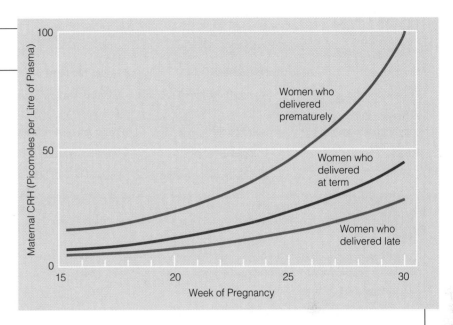

Notice how the "CRH–cortisol circuit" helps ensure that labour will occur only when the fetus is ready to survive outside the womb.

What causes the placenta to make CRH, and what affects how much is produced? Researchers are still trying to answer this question. The genetic makeup of CRH-producing cells may lead CRH to rise too early in some women, resulting in prematurity. Another potential influence is maternal nutrition. Food deprivation precipitates early birth in some mammals; the same effect may operate in humans. In support of this possibility, an Israeli study reported that pregnant Jewish women observing the day-long fast of Yom Kippur showed a sharp rise in delivery rates during the last 6 hours of the fast and the day after. This increase was not observed in other women living in the same region or in Jewish women observing the harvest holiday of Succot, celebrated with a special meal (Wiser et al., 1997). Perhaps even brief periods of inadequate nutrition can activate the fetal stress system, which prompts excess production of CRH.

In sum, a complex hormonal system, initiated by CRH and involving both mother and fetus, controls the timing of birth. New knowledge about birth timing is leading to more effective prevention of prematurity—a major cause of infant death and disability. Already, studies show that CRH production can be chemically inhibited and, in turn, delay birth in sheep (Smith, 1999). If tests of CRH inhibitors in nonhuman primates prove safe and effective, then trials in human mothers are not far off.

Fortunately, healthy babies are well equipped to withstand these traumas. The force of the contractions causes the infant to produce high levels of stress hormones, and this is adaptive. It helps the baby withstand oxygen deprivation by sending a rich supply of blood to the brain and heart. In addition, it prepares the baby to breathe by causing the lungs to absorb any remaining fluid and by expanding the bronchial tubes (passages leading to the lungs). Finally, stress hormones arouse infants into alertness so they are born wide awake, ready to interact with their world (Emory & Toomey, 1988; Lagercrantz & Slotkin, 1986).

## THE NEWBORN BABY'S APPEARANCE

Parents are often surprised at the odd-looking newborn, who is a far cry from the storybook image many created in their minds before birth. The average newborn is 50 centimetres (20 inches) long and 3400 grams (7½ pounds); boys tend to be slightly longer and heavier than girls. The head is very large in relation to the trunk and legs, which are short and

**TABLE** 3.8

The Apgar Scale

| SIGN[a] | SCORE | | |
|---------|---------|---------|---------|
| | 0 | 1 | 2 |
| Heart rate | No heartbeat | Under 100 beats per minute | 100 to 140 beats per minute |
| Respiratory effort | No breathing for 60 seconds | Irregular, shallow breathing | Strong breathing and crying |
| Reflex irritability (sneezing, coughing, and grimacing) | No response | Weak reflexive response | Strong reflexive response |
| Muscle tone | Completely limp | Weak movements of arms and legs | Strong movements of arms and legs |
| Colour[b] | Blue body, arms, and legs | Body pink with blue arms and legs | Body, arms, and legs completely pink |

[a]To remember these signs, you may find it helpful to use a technique in which the original labels are reordered and renamed as follows: colour = **A**ppearance, heart rate = **P**ulse, reflex irritability = **G**rimace, muscle tone = **A**ctivity, and respiratory effort = **R**espiration. Together, the first letters of the new labels spell **Apgar**.

[b]Colour is the least dependable of the Apgar ratings. The skin tone of nonwhite babies makes it difficult to apply the "pink" criterion. However, all newborns can be rated for a rosy glow that results from the flow of oxygen through body tissues, since skin tone is usually lighter at birth than the baby's inherited pigmentation.

*Source:* Apgar, 1953.

bowed. The combination of a big head (with its well-developed brain) and a small body means that human infants learn quickly in the first few months of life. But unlike most mammals, they cannot get around on their own until much later. Still, their round faces, chubby cheeks, large foreheads, and big eyes make adults feel like picking them up and cuddling them (Berman, 1980; Lorenz, 1943). These characteristics, as we will see in later chapters, are among the many ways nature helps get the parent–infant relationship off to a good start.

### ASSESSING THE NEWBORN'S PHYSICAL CONDITION: THE APGAR SCALE

Infants who have difficulty making the transition to life outside the uterus require special help at once. To quickly assess the baby's physical condition, doctors and nurses use the **Apgar Scale.** As Table 3.8 shows, a rating of 0, 1, or 2 on each of five characteristics is made at 1 and 5 minutes after birth. An Apgar score of 7 or better indicates that the infant is in good physical condition. If the score is between 4 and 6, the baby requires special help in establishing breathing and other vital signs. If the score is 3 or below, the infant is in serious danger, and emergency medical attention is needed. Two Apgar ratings are given because some babies have trouble adjusting at first but are doing well after a few minutes (Apgar, 1953).

## Approaches to Childbirth

CHILDBIRTH PRACTICES, like other aspects of family life, are moulded by the society of which mother and baby are a part. In many village and tribal cultures, expectant mothers are well acquainted with the childbirth process. For example, the Jarara of South America and the Pukapukans of the Pacific Islands treat birth as a vital part of daily life. The Jarara mother gives birth in full view of the entire community. The Pukapukan girl is so familiar with the events of labour and delivery that she can frequently be seen playing at it. Using a coconut to represent the baby, she stuffs it inside her dress, imitates the mother's pushing, and lets the nut fall at the proper moment. In most nonindustrialized cultures, women are assisted during the birth process. Among the Mayans of the Yucatán, the mother leans against a woman called the "head helper," who supports her weight and breathes with her during each contraction (Jordan, 1993; Mead & Newton, 1967).

**Apgar Scale**
A rating system used to assess the newborn baby's physical condition immediately after birth.

**natural, or prepared, childbirth**
An approach designed to reduce pain and medical intervention and to make childbirth a rewarding experience for parents.

In large Western nations, childbirth customs have changed dramatically. Before the late 1800s, birth usually took place at home and was a family-centred event. The industrial revolution brought greater crowding to cities, along with new health problems. As a result, childbirth moved from home to hospital, where the health of mothers and babies could be protected. Once doctors assumed responsibility for childbirth, women's knowledge about it declined, and relatives and friends no longer participated (Borst, 1995).

By the 1960s, women started to question the medical procedures that came to be used routinely during labour and delivery. Many felt that frequent use of strong drugs and delivery instruments had robbed them of a precious experience and were often not necessary or safe for the baby. Gradually, a natural childbirth movement arose in Europe and spread to North America. Its purpose was to make hospital birth as comfortable and rewarding for mothers as possible. Today, many hospitals offer birth centres that are family centred and homelike. Freestanding birth centres, which operate independently of hospitals and offer less in the way of backup medical care, also exist. And a small but growing number of women choose to have their babies at home.

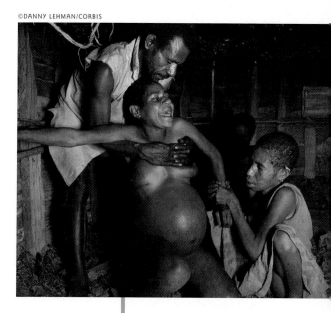

©DANNY LEHMAN/CORBIS

In this village society in Papua New Guinea, a woman gives birth in an upright squatting position. Her husband supports her body while an elderly woman helper soothes and encourages.

### NATURAL, OR PREPARED, CHILDBIRTH

**Natural,** or **prepared, childbirth** tries to overcome the idea that birth is a painful ordeal that requires extensive medical intervention. Although many natural childbirth programs exist, most draw on methods developed by Grantly Dick-Read (1959) in England and Ferdinand Lamaze (1958) in France. These physicians emphasized that cultural attitudes had taught women to fear the birth experience. An anxious, frightened woman in labour tenses muscles throughout her body, turning the mild pain that sometimes accompanies strong contractions into a great deal of pain.

A typical natural childbirth program consists of three ingredients:

1. *Information about labour and delivery.* Expectant mothers and fathers attend classes in which they learn about the anatomy and physiology of labour and delivery. Knowledge about the birth process reduces a mother's fear.

2. *Relaxation and breathing techniques.* Expectant mothers are taught relaxation and breathing exercises aimed at counteracting any pain they might feel during uterine contractions.

3. *Labour coach.* The father or another supportive companion learns how to help during childbirth—by reminding the mother to relax and breathe, massaging her back, supporting her body during labour and delivery, and offering encouragement and affection.

**SOCIAL SUPPORT AND NATURAL CHILDBIRTH.** Social support is an important part of the success of natural childbirth techniques. In one study comparing Guatemalan and U.S. hospitals that routinely isolated patients during childbirth, some mothers were randomly assigned a companion who stayed with them throughout labour and delivery, talking to them, holding their hands, and rubbing their backs to promote relaxation. Supported mothers had fewer birth complications and shorter labours than nonsupported women. Guatemalan mothers who received support also interacted more positively with their babies during the first half-hour after delivery, talking, smiling, and gently stroking (Kennell et al., 1991; Sosa et al., 1980).

The continuous rather than intermittent support of a trained companion during labour and delivery strengthens these outcomes. It is particularly helpful during a first childbirth, when mothers are more anxious (DiMatteo & Kahn, 1997; Scott, Berkowitz, & Klaus, 1999).

This newborn baby is held by his mother's birthing coach (on the left) and midwife (on the right) just after delivery. The umbilical cord has not yet been cut. Notice how the infant's head is moulded from being squeezed through the birth canal for many hours. It is also very large in relation to his body. As the infant takes his first few breaths, his body turns from blue to pink. He is wide awake and ready to get to know his surroundings.

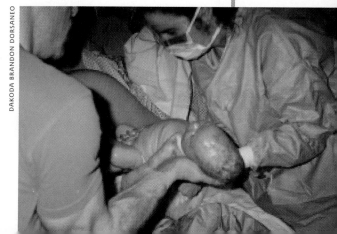

DAKODA BRANDON DORSANEO

**FIGURE** 3.13

**Sitting position often used for delivery in a birth centre or at home.** It facilitates pushing during the second stage of labour; increases blood flow to the placenta, which grants the baby a richer supply of oxygen; and permits the mother to see the delivery, enabling her to track the effectiveness of each contraction.

About to give birth at home, this mother discusses the progress of her labour with the midwife while her husband and their older child look on. Mothers who choose home birth want to make the experience an important part of family life, avoid unnecessary medical procedures, and exercise greater control over their own care and that of their babies.

Finally, this aspect of natural childbirth makes Western hospital birth customs more acceptable to women from parts of the world where assistance from family and community members is the norm (Granot et al., 1996).

**POSITIONS FOR DELIVERY.** With natural childbirth, mothers often give birth in the upright, sitting position shown in Figure 3.13 rather than lying flat on their backs with their feet in stirrups (the traditional hospital delivery room practice). When mothers are upright, labour is shortened because pushing is easier and more effective. The baby benefits from a richer supply of oxygen because blood flow to the placenta is increased (Davidson et al., 1993). And since the mother can see the delivery, she can track the effectiveness of each contraction in pushing the baby out of the birth canal (Kelly, Terry, & Naglieri, 1999). This helps her work with the doctor or midwife to ensure that the baby's head and shoulders emerge slowly, which reduces the chances of tearing the vaginal opening.

### HOME DELIVERY

Home birth has always been popular in certain industrialized nations, such as England, the Netherlands, and Sweden. A small but growing number of Canadian women are choosing to have their babies at home. These mothers want birth to be an important part of family life. In addition, most want to avoid unnecessary medical procedures. They also want greater control over their own care and that of their babies than hospitals permit (Wickham, 1999). Some home births are attended by doctors, but many more are handled by midwives. Although midwives have practised in Canada for many years, only since the 1990s has midwifery come under provincial regulation, and the rules vary by province. Midwifery was typically taught in conjunction with nursing, but recently three universities, McMaster, Ryerson, and Laurentian, joined forces to offer a degree in a program rated a world leader in midwifery education (Shroff, 1997).

Is it just as safe to give birth at home as in a hospital? For healthy women who are assisted by a well-trained doctor or midwife, it seems so, since complications rarely occur (Olsen, 1997). However, if attendants are not carefully trained and prepared to handle emergencies, the rate of infant death is high (Mehlmadrona & Madrona, 1997). Mothers at risk for complications are not suited for home births.

### LABOUR AND DELIVERY MEDICATION

Although natural childbirth techniques lessen or eliminate the need for pain-relieving drugs, some form of medication is used in 80 to 95 percent of births (Glosten, 1998).

*Analgesics* are drugs used to relieve pain. When given during labour, the dose is usually mild and intended to help a mother relax. *Anaesthetics* are a stronger type of painkiller that blocks sensation. During childbirth, they are generally injected into the spinal column to numb the lower half of the body.

Although pain-relieving drugs enable doctors to perform essential life-saving medical interventions, they can cause problems when used routinely. Anaesthetics weaken uterine contractions during the first stage of labour and interfere with the mother's ability to feel contractions and push during the second stage. As a result, labour is prolonged (Alexander et al., 1998). In addition, the chances are greater that the baby will have to be pulled from the birth canal with *forceps* (a metal device placed around the infant's head) or a *vacuum extractor* (a plastic suction cup that fits over the top of the head). Both instruments involve some risk of injury to the infant (King, 1997). Because anaesthesia increases the likelihood that labour will not progress normally, it is linked to *Caesarean section,* a surgical delivery in which the doctor makes an incision in the mother's abdomen and lifts the baby out of the uterus (Young, 1997).

Labour and delivery medication rapidly crosses the placenta. As a result, the newborn baby may be sleepy and withdrawn, suck poorly during feedings, and be irritable when awake (Emory, Schlackman, & Fiano, 1996). Does the use of medication during childbirth have a lasting impact on the infant? Some researchers claim so (Brackbill, McManus, & Woodward, 1985), but their findings have been challenged (Golub, 1996). Still, the negative impact of these drugs on the newborn's adjustment supports the current trend to limit their use.

## ASK YOURSELF

**review**   Name and briefly describe the three stages of labour.

**review**   Describe the ingredients and benefits of natural childbirth. What aspect contributes greatly to favourable outcomes, and why?

**apply**   Jenny is thinking about having her baby at home. What should she consider in making her decision?

**connect**   How do findings on the timing of birth illustrate bidirectional influences between mother and fetus? How do they illustrate the roles of both nature and nurture?

# Birth Complications

WE HAVE SEEN THAT some babies—in particular, those whose mothers are in poor health, do not receive good medical care, or have a history of pregnancy problems—are especially likely to experience birth complications. Inadequate oxygen, a pregnancy that ends too early, and a baby who is born underweight are serious difficulties that we have touched on many times. Let's look more closely at the impact of each complication on development.

## OXYGEN DEPRIVATION

A small number of infants experience *anoxia,* or inadequate oxygen supply, during the birth process. Sometimes the problem results from a failure to start breathing within a few minutes. Healthy newborns can survive periods of little or no oxygen longer than adults can; they reduce their metabolic rate, thereby conserving the limited oxygen available. Nevertheless, brain damage is likely if regular breathing is delayed more than 10 minutes (Parer, 1998).

At other times, anoxia occurs during labour. Squeezing of the umbilical cord is a common cause, a condition that is especially likely when infants are in **breech position**—turned in such a way that the buttocks or feet would emerge first. Because of this danger, breech babies are often delivered by Caesarean section. Another cause of oxygen deprivation is *placenta abruptio,* or premature separation of the placenta, a life-threatening event that requires immediate delivery (Ananth et al., 1999). Although the reasons for placenta abruptio are not well understood, teratogens that cause abnormal development of the placenta, such as cigarette smoking, are strongly related to it.

Incompatibility between mother and baby in a blood protein called the **Rh factor** can also lead to anoxia. This condition occurs if the mother is Rh negative (lacks the protein), the father is Rh positive (has the protein), and the baby inherits the father's Rh-positive blood type. During the third trimester and at the time of birth, some maternal and fetal blood cells usually cross the placenta in small enough amounts to be quite safe. But if even a little of the

**breech position**
A position of the baby in the uterus that would cause the buttocks or feet to be delivered first.

**Rh factor**
A protein that, when present in the fetus's blood but not in the mother's, can cause the mother to build up antibodies if the fetus's blood enters the mother's bloodstream. If these antibodies return to the fetus's system, they destroy red blood cells, reducing the oxygen supply to organs and tissues.

baby's Rh-positive blood passes into the mother's Rh-negative bloodstream, she begins to form antibodies to the foreign Rh protein. If these enter the baby's system, they destroy red blood cells, reducing the supply of oxygen. Mental retardation, damage to the heart muscle, and infant death can occur. Since it takes time for the mother to produce antibodies, first-born children are rarely affected. The danger increases with each pregnancy. Fortunately, most problems of Rh incompatibility can be prevented by giving Rh-negative mothers a vaccine to prevent the buildup of antibodies.

Although anoxic newborns are often behind their agemates in intellectual and motor progress in early childhood, by elementary school most catch up (Corah et al., 1965; Raz, Shah, & Sander, 1996). When serious problems emerge and persist—for example, learning disabilities, epilepsy, or *cerebral palsy* (a general term for motor and mental impairments that result from brain damage before, during, or just after birth)—the anoxia was probably extreme. Perhaps it was caused by prenatal insult to the baby's respiratory system. Or it may have happened because the infant's lungs were not yet mature enough to breathe.

For example, babies born more than 6 weeks early commonly have a disorder called *respiratory distress syndrome* (otherwise known as *hyaline membrane disease*). Their tiny lungs are so poorly developed that the air sacs collapse, causing serious breathing difficulties. Today, mechanical ventilators keep many such infants alive. In spite of these measures, some babies suffer permanent brain damage from lack of oxygen, and in other cases their delicate lungs are harmed by the treatment itself. Respiratory distress syndrome is only one of many risks for babies born too soon, as we will see in the following section.

## PRETERM AND LOW-BIRTH-WEIGHT INFANTS

Babies born 3 weeks or more before the end of a full 38-week pregnancy or who weigh less than 2500 grams (5½ pounds) have, for many years, been referred to as "premature." A wealth of research indicates that premature babies are at risk for many problems. Birth weight is the best available predictor of infant survival and healthy development. Many newborns who weigh less than 1500 grams (3½ pounds) experience difficulties that are not overcome, an effect that becomes stronger as birth weight decreases (Minde, 2000; Palta et al., 2000). Frequent illness, inattention, overactivity, language delays, low intelligence test scores, deficits in motor coordination and school learning, and poor emotional adjustment are some of the difficulties that extend into childhood (Hack et al., 1994, 1995; Mayes & Bornstein, 1997).

About 1 in 18 infants in Canada is born underweight, compared to 1 in 14 in the United States. Although the problem can strike unexpectedly, it is highest among poverty-stricken women, especially ethnic minorities (Statistics Canada, Births, 2001). These mothers, as indicated earlier, are more likely to be undernourished and to be exposed to harmful environmental influences. In addition, they often do not receive adequate prenatal care.

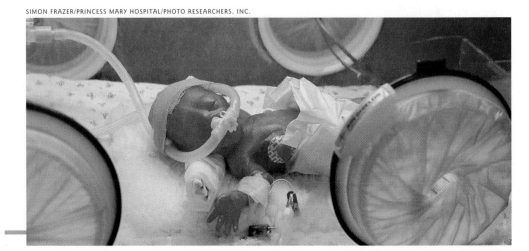

This baby was born 13 weeks before her due date and weighs little more than 900 grams (2 pounds). Since her lungs are too immature to function independently, she breathes with the aid of a respirator. Her survival and development are seriously at risk.

Prematurity is also common when mothers are carrying twins. Twins are usually born about 3 weeks early, and because of restricted space inside the uterus, they gain less weight after the twentieth week of pregnancy than do singletons.

**PRETERM VERSUS SMALL FOR DATE.** Although low-birth-weight infants face many obstacles to healthy development, most go on to lead normal lives; half of those who weighed only a couple of pounds at birth have no disability (see Figure 3.14). To better understand why some babies do better than others, researchers have divided them into two groups. The first is called **preterm.** These infants are born several weeks or more before their due date. Although small in size, their weight may still be appropriate given the time they spent in the uterus. The second group is called **small for date.** These newborns are below their expected weight considering length of the pregnancy. Some small-for-date infants are actually full term. Others are preterm infants who are especially underweight. Small-for-date infants probably experienced inadequate nutrition before birth. Perhaps their mothers did not eat properly, the placenta did not function normally, or the babies themselves had defects that prevented them from growing normally.

Of the two types of babies, small-for-date infants usually have more serious problems. During the first year, they are more likely to die, catch infections, and show evidence of brain damage. By middle childhood, they have lower intelligence test scores, are less attentive, achieve more poorly in school, and are socially immature (Minde, 2000; Schothorst & van Engeland, 1996).

**CONSEQUENCES FOR CAREGIVING.** Imagine a scrawny, thin-skinned infant whose body is only a little larger than the size of your hand. You try to play with the baby by stroking and talking softly, but he is sleepy and unresponsive. When you feed him, he sucks poorly. He is usually irritable during the short, unpredictable periods when he is awake.

The appearance and behaviour of preterm babies can lead parents to be less sensitive and responsive in caring for them. Compared with full-term infants, preterm babies—especially those who are very ill at birth—are less often held close, touched, and talked to gently. At times, mothers of these infants are overly intrusive, engaging in interfering pokes and verbal commands in an effort to obtain a higher level of response from the baby (Barratt, Roach, & Leavitt, 1996). This may explain why preterm babies as a group are at risk for child abuse. When they are born to isolated, poverty-stricken mothers who cannot provide good nutrition, health care, and parenting, the likelihood of unfavourable outcomes is increased (Bacharach & Baumeister, 1998). In contrast, parents with stable life circumstances and social supports usually can overcome the stresses of caring for a preterm infant. In these cases, even sick preterm babies have a good chance of catching up in development by middle childhood (Liaw & Brooks-Gunn, 1993).

These findings suggest that how well preterm infants develop has a great deal to do with the parent–child relationship. Consequently, interventions directed at supporting both sides of this emotional tie have a better chance of helping these infants recover.

**INTERVENTIONS FOR PRETERM INFANTS.** A preterm baby is cared for in a special Plexiglas-enclosed bed called an isolette. Temperature is carefully controlled, since these infants cannot yet regulate their own body temperature effectively. Air is filtered before it enters the isolette to help protect the baby from infection. When a preterm infant is fed through a stomach tube, breathes with the aid of a respirator, and receives medication through an intravenous needle, the isolette can be very isolating indeed! Physical needs that otherwise would lead to close contact and other forms of stimulation from an adult are met mechanically.

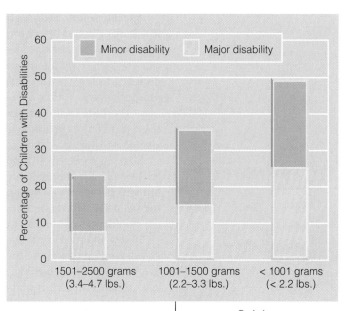

**FIGURE** 3.14

**Incidence of major and minor disabilities by birth weight, obtained from studies of low-birth-weight children at school age.** *Major disabilities* include cerebral palsy, mental retardation, and vision and hearing impairments. *Minor disabilities* include intelligence slightly below average, learning disabilities (usually in reading, spelling, and math), mild difficulties in motor control, and behaviour problems (including poor attention and impulse control, aggressiveness, noncompliance, depression, passivity, anxiety, and difficulty separating from parents at school age). (Adapted from D'Agostino & Clifford, 1998.)

**preterm**
Infants born several weeks or more before their due date.

**small for date**
Infants whose birth weight is below normal when length of pregnancy is taken into account. May be full term or preterm.

*Special Infant Stimulation.*    At one time, doctors believed that stimulating such a fragile baby could be harmful. Now we know that certain kinds of stimulation in proper doses can help preterm infants develop. In some intensive care nurseries, preterm infants can be seen rocking in suspended hammocks or lying on waterbeds—interventions designed to replace the gentle motion they would have received while being carried in the mother's uterus. Other forms of stimulation have also been used: an attractive mobile or a tape recording of a heartbeat, soft music, or the mother's voice. Many studies show that these experiences promote faster weight gain, more predictable sleep patterns, and greater alertness (Marshall-Baker, Lickliter, & Cooper, 1998; Standley, 1998).

Touch is an especially important form of stimulation. In baby animals, touching the skin releases certain brain chemicals that support physical growth—effects believed to occur in humans as well. When preterm infants were massaged several times each day in the hospital, they gained weight faster and, at the end of the first year, were advanced in mental and motor development over preterm infants not given this stimulation (Field, 2001; Field et al., 1986).

In developing countries where hospitalization is not always possible, skin-to-skin "kangaroo care," in which the preterm infant is tucked between the mother's breasts and peers over the top of her clothing, is encouraged. The technique is used often in Western nations as a supplement to hospital intensive care. It fosters oxygenation of the baby's body, temperature regulation, improved sleep and feeding, and infant survival. In addition, mothers practising kangaroo care feel more confident about handling and meeting the needs of their preterm infants (Gale & VandenBerg, 1998).

Some very small or sick babies are too weak for much stimulation. The noise, bright lights, and constant medical monitoring of the intensive care nursery are already quite overwhelming. And like full-term infants, preterm infants differ in how excited and irritable they get (Korner, 1996). Doctors and nurses must carefully adjust the amount and kind of stimulation to fit the baby's needs.

*Training Parents in Infant Caregiving Skills.*    When effective stimulation helps preterm infants develop, parents are likely to feel good about their infant's growth and interact with the baby more effectively. Interventions that support the parenting side of this relationship generally teach parents about the infant's characteristics and promote caregiving skills.

For parents with the economic and personal resources to care for a preterm infant, just a few sessions of coaching in recognizing and responding to the baby's needs is linked to steady gains in mental test performance that, after several years, equal those of full-term youngsters (Achenbach et al., 1990). Warm parenting that helps preterm infants sustain attention (for example, gently commenting on and showing the baby interesting features of a toy) predicts favourable early cognitive and language development (Landry et al., 1996; Smith et al., 1996).

When preterm infants live in stressed, low-income households, long-term, intensive intervention is required to reduce developmental problems. In the Infant Health and Development Project, preterm babies born into poverty received a comprehensive intervention that combined medical follow-up, weekly parent training sessions, and enrolment in cognitively stimulating child care from 1 to 3 years of age. As Figure 3.15 shows, compared with controls receiving only medical follow-up, more than four times as many intervention children were within normal range in intelligence, psychological adjustment, and physical growth (Bradley et al., 1994). In addition, mothers in the intervention group were more affectionate and more often encouraged play and cognitive mastery in their children—a reason their 3-year-olds may have been developing so favourably (McCarton, 1998).

Yet by age 5, the intervention children had lost ground. And by age 8, the development of intervention and control children no longer differed (Brooks-Gunn et al., 1994; McCarton et al., 1997). These very vulnerable children need high-quality intervention well beyond age 3—even into the school years. And special strategies, such as extra adult–child interaction, may be necessary to achieve lasting changes in children with the lowest birth weights (Berlin et al., 1998).

The birthrate of underweight babies in Canada has been declining steadily, remaining below 6 percent since 1979, and is even lower if multiple-birth infants are excluded (Statistics Canada, Births, 2001). However, the rate could be reduced further by improving health and social conditions, as described in the Cultural Influences box on pages 112–113. Fortunately,

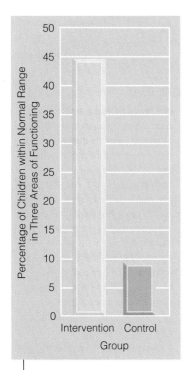

**FIGURE** 3.15

**Percentage of preterm infants born into poverty and assigned to either an intensive intervention or a control group who were developing normally at age 3.** Children who experienced the intervention, consisting of medical follow-up, parent training, and cognitively stimulating child care, were more than four times more likely than medical-follow-up-only controls to be within normal range in intelligence, psychological adjustment, and physical growth. Without continued intervention, however, these gains are not sustained. (Adapted from Bradley et al., 1994.)

today we can save many preterm infants, but an even better course of action would be to prevent this serious threat to infant survival and development before it happens.

## UNDERSTANDING BIRTH COMPLICATIONS

In the preceding sections, we considered a variety of birth complications. Now let's try to put the evidence together. Can any general principles help us understand how infants who survive a traumatic birth are likely to develop? A landmark study carried out in Hawaii provides answers to this question.

In 1955, Emmy Werner and Ruth Smith began to follow nearly 700 infants on the island of Kauai who had experienced mild, moderate, or severe birth complications. Each was matched, on the basis of SES and ethnicity, with a healthy newborn (Werner & Smith, 1982). Findings revealed that the likelihood of long-term difficulties increased if birth trauma was severe. But among mildly to moderately stressed children, the best predictor of how well they did in later years was the quality of their home environments. Children growing up in stable families did almost as well on measures of intelligence and psychological adjustment as those with no birth problems. Those exposed to poverty, family disorganization, and mentally ill parents often developed serious learning difficulties, behaviour problems, and emotional disturbance.

The Kauai study tells us that as long as birth injuries are not overwhelming, a supportive home environment can restore children's growth. But the most intriguing cases in this study were the handful of exceptions. A few children with fairly serious birth complications and troubled families grew into competent adults who fared as well as controls in career attainment and psychological adjustment. Werner and Smith found that these children relied on factors outside the family and within themselves to overcome stress. Some had attractive personalities that caused them to receive positive responses from relatives, neighbours, and peers. In other instances, a grandparent, aunt, uncle, or baby-sitter provided the needed emotional support (Werner, 1989, 1993; Werner & Smith, 1992).

Do these outcomes remind you of the characteristics of resilient children, discussed in Chapter 1? The Kauai study reveals that the impact of early mild to moderate biological risks often wanes as children's personal characteristics and social experiences increasingly contribute to their functioning—an outcome consistent with other similar investigations. For example, when researchers matched birth and school-kindergarten records for more than 300 000 children, a birth weight of less than 1500 grams (3½ pounds) was the strongest predictor of placement in special education. When birth weight exceeded 1500 grams, family factors—having a mother who was poverty stricken, who had not gotten prenatal care, who had less than a high school education, or who was single—were five times more effective in predicting special educational placement than was birth weight (Resnick et al., 1999).

In sum, when the overall balance of life events tips toward the favourable side, children with serious birth problems can develop successfully. When negative factors outweigh positive ones, even a sturdy newborn can become a lifelong casualty.

## ASK YOURSELF www

**review** Cite five possible causes of anoxia during childbirth. How do anoxic newborns fare in development?

**review** Sensitive care can help preterm infants recover, but they are less likely to receive such care than are full-term newborns. Explain why.

**apply** Cecilia and Adena each gave birth to a 1360-gram (3-pound) baby 7 weeks preterm. Cecilia is single and on welfare. Adena and her husband are happily married and earn a good income. Plan an intervention for helping each baby develop.

**connect** List factors discussed in this chapter that increase the chances that an infant will be born underweight. How many of these factors could be prevented by better health care for expectant mothers?

# *cultural influences*

## A CROSS-NATIONAL PERSPECTIVE ON HEALTH CARE AND OTHER POLICIES FOR PARENTS AND NEWBORN BABIES

**infant mortality** is an index used around the world to assess the overall health of a nation's children. It refers to the number of deaths in the first year of life per 1000 live births. Infant mortality has been declining in almost all countries due to advances in sanitation, nutrition, and health care. In Canada, the infant mortality rate stands at fewer than 6 per 1000 live births. In 1901, about one in seven Canadian infants died before their first birthday; now the rate has been lowered to 1 in 182 (Statistics Canada, Health Reports, 2000).

Some Canadian populations are more closely linked with high infant mortality rates than others. For example, although the health of Aboriginal people in Canada has improved over the past 20 years, as of 1994, infant mortality rates among First Nations

peoples were still twice as high as those of the Canadian population as a whole (Wen et al., 2000).

*Neonatal mortality,* the rate of death within the first month of life, accounts for 68 percent of the infant death rate in Canada and is about the same in the United States (Health Canada, 1998a). Two factors are largely responsible for neonatal mortality. The first is serious physical defects, most of which cannot be prevented. The percentage of babies born with congenital defects is about the same in all ethnic and income groups. The second leading cause of neonatal mortality is low birth weight, which is largely preventable. High-quality prenatal care beginning early in pregnancy is consistently related to healthy birth weight and infant survival. Unfortunately, expectant women who wait to see a doctor usually lead highly stressful lives and engage in harmful behaviours, such as smoking and drug abuse (Maloni et al., 1996). These women, who have no medical attention for most or all of their pregnancies, are among those who need it most!

Countries in Figure 3.16 that provide their citizens with government-

sponsored health care benefits have lower infant mortality rates. These countries take extra steps to make sure that pregnant mothers and babies have access to good nutrition, high-quality medical care, and social and economic supports that promote effective parenting.

For example, all Western European nations guarantee women a certain number of prenatal visits at very low or no cost. After a baby is born, a health professional routinely visits the home to provide counselling about infant care and to arrange continuing medical services. Home assistance is especially extensive in the Netherlands. For a token fee, each mother is granted a trained maternity helper, who assists with infant care, shopping, housekeeping, meal preparation, and the care of other children during the days after delivery (Kamerman, 1993).

Paid, job-protected employment leave is another vital societal intervention for new parents. Since 2001, Canadian mothers or fathers have been eligible for maternity and/or parental leave of up to one year, based on qualifying hours of employment. Paid leave is widely available in other

A doctor and nurse use an ultrasound scanner to check the growth of the fetus. In support of prenatal screening, the Society of Obstetricians and Gynaecologists of Canada now recommends that women be offered one routine second-trimester ultrasound for uncomplicated pregnancies.

## Heredity, Environment, and Behaviour: A Look Ahead

THROUGHOUT THIS CHAPTER, we have discussed a wide variety of genetic and early environmental influences, each of which has the power to alter the course of development. When we consider them together, it may seem surprising that any newborn babies arrive intact. Yet the vast majority—over 90 percent in Canada and the United

**infant mortality**
The number of deaths in the first year of life per 1000 live births.

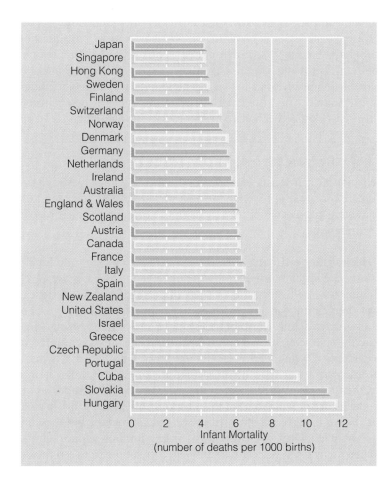

**FIGURE** 3.16

**Infant mortality in 28 nations.** Canada ranks sixteenth in the world, with a death rate of fewer than 6 infants per 1000 births. (Adapted from March of Dimes, 2001; Health Canada, 1998a. Reprinted by permission of Health Canada and Government Works, 2002 and Statistics Canada, "Selected infant mortality and related statistics, Canada 1921–1990," Catalogue no. 82-549, March 1993 and "Births and deaths," Catalogue no. 84-210, 1995.)

When a family is stressed by a baby's arrival, short employment leaves of 6 weeks or less are linked to maternal anxiety and depression and negative interactions with the baby. Longer leaves of 12 weeks or more predict favourable maternal mental health and sensitive, responsive caregiving (Clark et al., 1997; Hyde et al., 1995). Single women and their babies are most hurt by the absence of a paid leave policy. These mothers are usually the sole source of support for their families and can least afford to take time from their jobs.

In countries with low infant mortality rates, expectant mothers need not wonder how they will get health care and other resources to support their baby's development. The powerful impact of universal, high-quality medical and social services on maternal and infant well-being provides strong justification for implementation of such programs.

industrialized nations as well, where it typically ranges from 2 to 12 months. In Sweden, parents have the right to a short, paid birth leave of a few days for the father plus 15 months of paid leave to share between them. Even less-developed nations offer paid employment leave. In the People's Republic of China, a new mother is granted 3 months' leave at full pay.

Furthermore, many countries supplement basic paid leave. In Germany, for example, after a fully paid 3-month leave, a parent can take 2 more years at a modest flat rate and a third year at no pay (Hyde, 1995; Kamerman, 2000). Yet in the United States, the federal government mandates *only 12 weeks of unpaid leave* for employees in businesses with at least 50 workers.

States—do. Born healthy and vigorous, these developing members of the human species vary greatly in traits and abilities. Some are outgoing and sociable; others are shy and reserved. By school age, one child loves to read, another is attracted to mathematics, while a third excels at music. **Behavioural genetics** is a field devoted to uncovering the contributions of nature and nurture to this diversity. We have already seen that researchers are only beginning to understand the genetic and environmental events preceding birth that affect the child's potential. How, then, do they unravel the roots of the many characteristics that emerge later?

**behavioural genetics**
A field of study devoted to uncovering the hereditary and environmental origins of individual differences in human traits and abilities.

T. K. WANSTALL/THE IMAGE WORKS

Identical twins Bob and Bob were separated by adoption shortly after birth and not reunited until adulthood. The two Bobs discovered they were alike in many ways. Both hold bachelor's degrees in engineering, are married to teachers named Brenda, wear glasses, have moustaches, smoke pipes, and are volunteer firemen. The study of identical twins reared apart reveals that heredity contributes to many psychological characteristics. Nevertheless, not all separated twins match up as well as this pair, and generalizing from twin evidence to the population is controversial.

**heritability estimate**
A statistic that measures the extent to which individual differences in complex traits in a specific population are due to genetic factors.

**kinship studies**
Studies comparing the characteristics of family members to determine the importance of heredity in complex human characteristics.

**concordance rate**
The percentage of instances in which both twins show a trait when it is present in one twin.

All behavioural geneticists agree that both heredity and environment are involved in every aspect of development. But for polygenic traits (due to many genes) such as intelligence and personality, scientists are a long way from knowing the precise hereditary influences involved. They must study the impact of genes on these characteristics indirectly.

Some believe that it is useful and possible to answer the question of *how much* heredity versus environment contributes to differences among children. A growing consensus, however, regards that question as unanswerable. These investigators view genetic and environmental influences as inseparable. The important question, they state, is *how* nature and nurture work together. Let's consider each position in turn.

## THE QUESTION, "HOW MUCH?"

Behavioural geneticists use two methods—heritability estimates and concordance rates—to infer the role of heredity in complex human characteristics. Let's look closely at the information these procedures yield, along with their limitations.

**HERITABILITY.** **Heritability estimates** measure the extent to which individual differences in complex traits in a specific population are due to genetic factors. Researchers have obtained heritabilities for intelligence and a variety of personality characteristics. We will take a brief look at their findings here, returning to them in later chapters when we consider these topics in greater detail. Heritability estimates are obtained from **kinship studies,** which compare the characteristics of family members. The most common type of kinship study compares identical twins, who share all their genes, with fraternal twins, who share only some. If people who are genetically more alike are also more similar in intelligence and personality, then the researcher assumes that heredity plays an important role.

Kinship studies of intelligence provide some of the most controversial findings in the field of child development. Some experts claim a strong genetic influence, whereas others believe that heredity is barely involved. Currently, most kinship findings support a moderate role for heredity. When many twin studies are examined, correlations between the scores of identical twins are consistently higher than those of fraternal twins. In a summary of more than 13 000 twin pairs, the correlation for intelligence was .86 for identical twins and .55 for fraternal twins (Scarr, 1997).

Researchers use a complex statistical procedure to compare these correlations, arriving at a heritability estimate ranging from 0 to 1.00. The value for intelligence is about .50 for child and adolescent samples in Western industrialized nations. This indicates that differences in genetic makeup can explain half the variation in intelligence (Plomin, 1994c). The intelligence of adopted children is more strongly related to the scores of their biological parents than to those of their adoptive parents, offering further support for the role of heredity (Horn, 1983; Scarr & Weinberg, 1983).

Heritability research also reveals that genetic factors are important in personality. In fact, for personality traits that have been studied a great deal, such as sociability, emotional expressiveness, and activity level, heritability estimates are at about the same moderate level as that reported for intelligence (Braungart et al., 1992; Loehlin, 1992).

**CONCORDANCE.** A second measure used to infer the contribution of heredity to complex characteristics is the **concordance rate.** It refers to the percentage of instances in which both twins show a trait when it is present in one twin. Researchers typically use concordance to study emotional and behaviour disorders, which can be judged as either present or absent.

A concordance rate ranges from 0 to 100 percent. A score of 0 indicates that if one twin has the trait, the other twin never has it. A score of 100 means that if one twin has the trait, the other one always has it. When a concordance rate is much higher for identical twins than for fraternal twins, heredity is believed to play a major role. As Figure 3.17 reveals, twin studies of schizophrenia (a disorder involving delusions and hallucinations, difficulty distinguishing fantasy from reality, and irrational and inappropriate behaviours) and severe depression show this pattern. Look carefully at the figure, and you will see that the influence of heredity on antisocial behaviour and criminality, although apparent, is less strong. In that case, the difference between the concordance rates for identical and fraternal twins is smaller (Plomin, 1994a). Once again, adoption studies support these results. Biological relatives of schizophrenic and depressed adoptees are more likely to share the disorder than are adoptive relatives (Bock & Goode, 1996; Loehlin, Willerman, & Horn, 1988).

Taken together, concordance and adoption research suggests that the tendency for schizophrenia and depression to run in families is partly due to genetic factors. However, we also know that environment is involved, since the concordance rate for identical twins would have to be 100 percent for heredity to be the only influence.

LIMITATIONS OF HERITABILITY AND CONCORDANCE.
Serious questions have been raised about the accuracy of heritability estimates and concordance rates. First, each value refers only to the particular population studied and its unique range of genetic and environmental influences. For example, imagine a country in which children's home, school, and neighbourhood experiences are very similar. Under these conditions, individual differences in behaviour would be largely genetic, and heritability estimates would be close to 1.00. Conversely, the more environments vary, the greater their opportunity to account for individual differences, and the lower heritability estimates are likely to be (Plomin, 1994c).

Second, the accuracy of heritability estimates and concordance rates depends on the extent to which the twin pairs used reflect genetic and environmental variation in the population. Yet most twins studied are reared together under highly similar conditions. Even when separated twins are available, social service agencies often place them in advantaged homes that are alike in many ways (Eisenberg, 1998). Because the environments of most twin pairs are less diverse than those of the general population, heritability estimates are likely to exaggerate the role of heredity.

Heritability estimates are controversial because they can easily be misapplied. For example, high heritabilities have been used to suggest that ethnic differences in intelligence, such as the poorer performance of black children in relation to white children, have a genetic basis (Jensen, 1969, 1985, 1998). Yet this line of reasoning is widely regarded as incorrect. Heritabilities computed on mostly white twin samples do not tell us what is responsible for test score differences between ethnic groups. We have already seen that large economic and cultural differences are involved. In Chapter 8, we will discuss research indicating that when black children are adopted into economically advantaged homes at an early age, their scores are well above average and substantially higher than those of children growing up in impoverished families.

Perhaps the most serious criticism of heritability estimates and concordance rates has to do with their usefulness. Although they are interesting statistics, they give us no precise information on how intelligence and personality develop or how children might respond when exposed to experiences aimed at helping them develop as far as possible (Bronfenbrenner & Ceci, 1994; Wachs, 1999). Indeed, the heritability of intelligence is higher in advantaged homes and communities, which permit children to actualize their genetic endowment. In disadvantaged environments, children are prevented from realizing their potential. Consequently, enhancing their experiences through interventions (such as parent education and high-quality preschool or child care) has a greater impact on development (Bronfenbrenner & Morris, 1998).

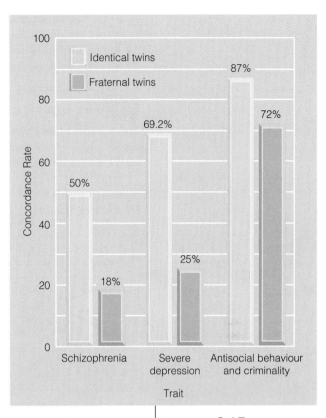

**FIGURE** 3.17

**Concordance rates for schizophrenia, severe depression, and antisocial behaviour and criminality.** Heredity plays some role in schizophrenia and is even more influential in severe depression, since the concordance rate is much higher for identical than for fraternal twins. Heredity contributes less to antisocial behaviour and criminality, since the difference in concordance rates for identical and fraternal twins is smaller. (From Gottesman, 1991; Gottesman, Carey, & Hanson, 1983; McGuffin & Sargeant, 1991.)

According to one group of experts, heritability estimates have too many problems to yield any firm conclusions about the relative strength of nature and nurture (Collins et al., 2000). Although these statistics verify that heredity contributes to complex human characteristics, they do not tell us how environment can modify genetic influences.

## THE QUESTION, "HOW?"

Today, most researchers view development as the result of a dynamic interplay between heredity and environment. How do nature and nurture work together? Several concepts shed light on this question.

**REACTION RANGE.** The first of these ideas is **range of reaction** (Gottesman, 1963). It emphasizes that each person responds to the environment in a unique way because of his or her genetic makeup. Let's explore this idea in Figure 3.18. Reaction range can apply to any characteristic; here it is illustrated for intelligence. Notice that when environments vary from extremely unstimulating to highly enriched, Ben's intelligence increases steadily, Linda's rises sharply and then falls off, and Ron's begins to increase only after the environment becomes modestly stimulating.

Reaction range highlights two important points. First, it shows that because each of us has a unique genetic makeup, we respond differently to the same environment. Notice in Figure 3.18 how a poor environment results in similarly low scores for all three children. But Linda is by far the best-performing child when environments provide an intermediate level of stimulation. And when environments are highly enriched, Ben does best, followed by Ron, both of whom now exceed Linda. Second, sometimes different genetic–environmental combinations can make two children look the same! For example, if Linda is reared in a minimally stimulating environment, her score will be about 100—average for children in general. Ben and Ron can also obtain this score, but to do so they must grow up in a fairly enriched home. In sum, range of reaction reveals that unique blends of heredity and environment lead to both similarities and differences in children's behaviour (Wahlsten, 1994).

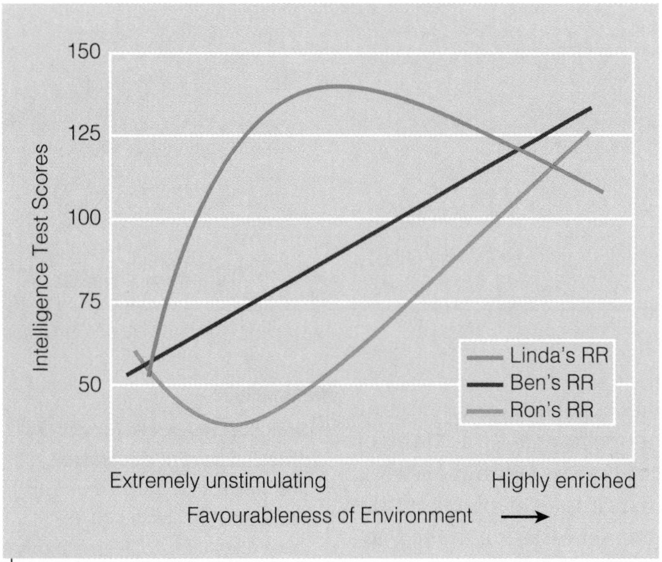

**FIGURE** 3.18

**Intellectual ranges of reaction (RR) for three children in environments that vary from extremely unstimulating to highly enriched.** Each child, due to his or her genetic makeup, responds differently as quality of the environment changes. Ben's intelligence increases steadily, Linda's rises sharply and then falls off, and Ron's begins to increase only after the environment becomes modestly stimulating. (Adapted from Wahlsten, 1994.)

**CANALIZATION.** The concept of canalization provides another way of understanding how heredity and environment combine. **Canalization** is the tendency of heredity to restrict the development of some characteristics to just one or a few outcomes. A behaviour that is strongly canalized follows a genetic growth plan, and only strong environmental forces can change it (Waddington, 1957). For example, infant perceptual and motor development seems to be strongly canalized, since all normal human babies eventually roll over, sit up, crawl, and walk. It takes extreme conditions to modify these behaviours. In contrast, intelligence and personality are less strongly canalized, since they vary much more with changes in the environment.

When we look at the behaviours constrained by heredity, we can see that canalization is highly adaptive. Through it, nature ensures that children will develop certain species-typical skills under a wide range of rearing conditions, thereby promoting survival.

**GENETIC–ENVIRONMENTAL CORRELATION.** Nature and nurture work together in still another way. Several investigators point out that a major problem in trying to separate heredity and environment is that they are often correlated (Plomin, 1994b; Scarr & McCartney, 1983). According to the concept of **genetic–environmental correlation,** our genes influence the environments to which we are exposed. The way this happens changes with development.

*Passive and Evocative Correlation.*    At younger ages, two types of genetic–environmental correlation are common. The first is called *passive* correlation because the child has no control over it. Early on, parents provide environments influenced by their own heredity. For example, parents who are good athletes emphasize outdoor activities and enrol their children in swimming and gymnastics. Besides getting exposed to an "athletic environment," the children may have inherited their parents' athletic ability. As a result, they are likely to become good athletes for both genetic and environmental reasons.

The second type of genetic–environmental correlation is *evocative.* Children evoke responses that are influenced by the child's heredity, and these responses strengthen the child's original style. For example, an active, friendly baby is likely to receive more social stimulation than is a passive, quiet infant. And a cooperative, attentive preschooler probably receives more patient and sensitive interactions from parents than does an inattentive, distractible child.

*Active Correlation.*    At older ages, *active* genetic–environmental correlation becomes common. As children extend their experiences beyond the immediate family and are given the freedom to make more choices, they actively seek environments that fit with their genetic tendencies. The well-coordinated, muscular child spends more time at after-school sports, the musically talented youngster joins the school orchestra and practises his violin, and the intellectually curious child is a familiar patron at her local library.

This tendency to actively choose environments that complement our heredity is called **niche-picking** (Scarr & McCartney, 1983). Infants and young children cannot do much niche-picking, since adults select environments for them. In contrast, older children and adolescents are much more in charge of their environments. The niche-picking idea explains why identical twins reared apart during childhood and later reunited may find, to their great surprise, that they have similar hobbies, food preferences, and vocations—a trend that is especially marked when twins' environmental opportunities are similar (Bouchard et al., 1990; Plomin, 1994b). Niche-picking also helps us understand why identical twins become somewhat more alike and fraternal twins less alike in intelligence from infancy to adolescence (Loehlin, Horn, & Willerman, 1997). The influence of heredity and environment is not constant but changes over time. With age, genetic factors may become more important in influencing the environments we experience and choose for ourselves.

*Environmental Influences on Gene Expression.*    Notice how, in the concepts we have just considered, heredity is granted priority. In range of reaction, it *limits* responsiveness to varying environments; in canalization, it *restricts* the development of certain behaviours. Similarly, some theorists regard genetic–environmental correlation as entirely driven by genetics (Harris, 1998; Rowe, 1994). They believe that children's genetic makeup causes them to receive, evoke, or seek experiences that actualize their inborn tendencies. Others object to this simplistic analysis, arguing that heredity does not dictate children's experiences or development in a rigid way. For example, as the Biology & Environment box on page 118 illustrates, parents and other caring adults can *uncouple* adverse genetic- environmental correlations. They often provide children with experiences that modify the expression of heredity, yielding favourable outcomes.

Accumulating evidence reveals that the relationship between heredity and environment is not a one-way street, from genes to environment to behaviour. Rather, like other system influences considered in this and the previous chapter, it is *bidirectional:* Genes affect children's behaviour and experiences, but their experiences and behaviour also affect gene expression (Gottlieb, 2000). Stimulation—both *internal* to the child (activity within the cytoplasm of the cell, hormones released into the bloodstream) and *external* to the child (home, neighbourhood, school, and community)—triggers gene activity.

Researchers call this view of the relationship between heredity and environment the *epigenetic framework* (Gottlieb, 1992, 1998). It is depicted in Figure 3.20 (on page 119). **Epigenesis** means development resulting from ongoing, bidirectional exchanges between heredity and all levels of the environment. To illustrate, granting a baby a healthy diet

This mother is an accomplished skier who exposes her children to skiing. In addition, the children may have inherited their mother's athletic talent. When heredity and environment are correlated, they jointly foster the same capacities, and the influence of one cannot be separated from the influence of the other.

**range of reaction**
Each person's unique, genetically determined response to a range of environmental conditions.

**canalization**
The tendency of heredity to restrict the development of some characteristics to just one or a few outcomes.

**genetic–environmental correlation**
The idea that heredity influences the environments to which individuals are exposed.

**niche-picking**
A type of genetic–environmental correlation in which individuals actively choose environments that complement their heredity.

**epigenesis**
Development resulting from ongoing bidirectional exchanges between heredity and all levels of the environment.

# *biology & environment*

## UNCOUPLING GENETIC–ENVIRONMENTAL CORRELATIONS FOR MENTAL ILLNESS AND ANTISOCIAL BEHAVIOUR

diagnosed with schizophrenia, Lars's and Sven's biological mothers had such difficulty functioning in everyday life that each gave up her infant son for adoption. Lars had the misfortune of being placed with adoptive parents who, like his biological mother, were mentally ill. His home life was chaotic, and his parents were punitive and neglectful. Sven's adoptive parents, in contrast, were psychologically healthy and reared him with love, patience, and consistency.

Lars displays a commonly observed genetic–environmental correlation: a predisposition for schizophrenia coupled with maladaptive parenting. Will he be more likely than Sven, whose adoption *uncoupled* this adverse genotype-environment link, to develop mental illness? In a large Finnish adoption study, nearly 200 adopted children of schizophrenic mothers were followed up in adulthood (Tienari et al., 1994). Those (like Sven) who were reared by healthy adoptive parents showed little mental illness—no more than did a control group with healthy biological and adoptive parents. In contrast, psychological impairments piled up in adoptees (like Lars) with both disturbed biological and adoptive parents. These children were considerably more likely to develop mental illness than were controls

whose biological parents were healthy but who were being reared by severely disturbed adoptive parents.

Similar findings emerged in several U.S. and Swedish adoption studies addressing genetic and environmental contributions to antisocial behaviour (Bohman, 1996; Yates, Cadoret, & Troughton, 1999). As Figure 3.19 shows, adopted infants whose biological mothers were imprisoned criminal offenders displayed a high rate of antisocial behaviour in adolescence only when reared in adverse homes, as indicated by adoptive parents or siblings with severe adjustment problems. In families free of psychological disturbance, adoptees with a predisposition to criminality did not differ from adoptees without this genetic background.

In sum, the chances that genes for psychological disorder will be expressed are far greater when child rearing is maladaptive. Healthily functioning families seem to promote healthy development in children, despite a genetic risk associated with mental illness or criminality in a biological parent.

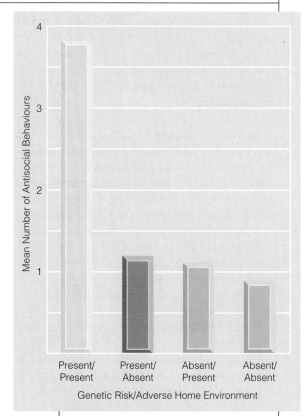

**FIGURE** 3.19

**Mean number of antisocial behaviours of adoptees varying in genetic and home environment risk for criminality.** Adolescent adoptees at genetic risk for criminality displayed a high rate of antisocial behaviour only when reared in adverse home environments. When reared in favourable homes, they did not differ from adoptees at no genetic risk. (Adapted from Cadoret, Cain, & Crowe, 1983.)

increases brain growth, which translates into new connections and faster message transfer between nerve cells and, in turn, transformed gene expression. This series of interactions opens the door to new gene–environment exchanges—for example, advanced exploration of objects and interaction with caregivers, which further enhance brain growth and gene expression. These ongoing, bidirectional influences foster cognitive and social development. In contrast, harmful environments can dampen gene expression, at times so profoundly that later experiences can do little to change characteristics (such as intelligence) that were flexible to begin with. We have seen that this is so for babies prenatally exposed to high levels of alcohol or radiation. And later in this book, we will find that it is also true for children reared in extremely deprived homes and institutions (Gottlieb, 1996).

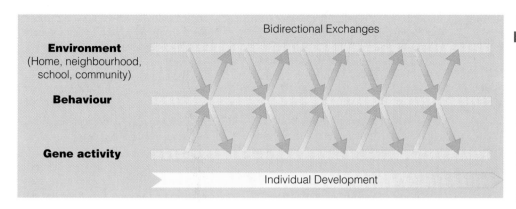

Bidirectional Exchanges

**Environment**
(Home, neighbourhood,
school, community)

**Behaviour**

**Gene activity**

Individual Development

**FIGURE** 3.20

**The epigenetic framework.**
Development takes place through
ongoing, bidirectional exchanges
between heredity and all levels of
the environment. Genes affect
children's behaviour and experiences; their experiences and
behaviour also affect gene expression. (Adapted from Gottlieb,
2000.)

A major reason child development researchers are interested in the nature–nurture issue is that they want to improve environments so that children can develop as far as possible. The concept of epigenesis reminds us that development is best understood as a series of complex exchanges between nature and nurture. Although children cannot be changed in any way we might desire, environments can modify genetic influences. The success of any attempt to improve development depends on the characteristics we want to change, the genetic makeup of the child, and the type and timing of our intervention.

## ASK YOURSELF

**review** Why did one group of experts conclude that heritability estimates cannot yield firm conclusions about the relative strength of hereditary and environmental influences?

**review** What is epigenesis, and how does it differ from range of reaction and genetic–environmental correlation? Provide an example of epigenesis.

**apply** Bianca's parents are accomplished musicians. At age 4, Bianca began taking piano lessons. By age 10, she was accompanying the school choir. At age 14, she asked if she could attend a special music high school. Explain how genetic–environmental correlation promoted Bianca's talent.

**connect** How do the findings shown in Figure 3.19 in the Biology & Environment box, opposite, illustrate the idea that unique blends of heredity and environment lead to both similarities and differences in behaviour?

# summary

## GENETIC FOUNDATIONS

*What are genes, and how are they transmitted from one generation to the next?*

- Each individual's **phenotype,** or directly observable characteristics, is a product of both **genotype** and environment. **Chromosomes,** rodlike structures within the cell nucleus, contain our hereditary endowment. Along their length are **genes,** segments of **DNA** that make us distinctly human and influence our development and characteristics.

- **Gametes,** or sex cells, are produced through the process of cell division known

as **meiosis. Crossing over** and indepen-dent assortment of chromosomes ensure that each gamete receives a unique set of genes from each parent. Once sperm and ovum unite, the resulting **zygote** starts to develop into a complex human being through cell duplication, or **mitosis.**

- **Identical,** or **monozygotic, twins** develop when a zygote divides in two during the early stages of cell duplication. **Fraternal, or dizygotic, twins** result when two ova are released from the mother's ovaries and both are fertilized. If the fertilizing sperm carries an X chromosome, the child will be a girl; if it contains a Y chromosome, a boy will be born.

*Describe various patterns of genetic inheritance.*

- **Dominant–recessive** and **codominant** relationships are patterns of inheritance that apply to traits controlled by single genes. In dominant–recessive inheritance, **heterozygous** individuals with one reces-sive **allele** are **carriers** of the recessive trait. **Modifier genes** enhance or dilute the effects of other genes.

- When recessive disorders are **X-linked** (carried on the X chromosome), males are more likely to be affected. **Genetic imprinting** is a pattern of inheritance in which one parent's allele is activated, regardless of its makeup.

■ Unfavourable genes arise from **mutations,** which can occur spontaneously or be induced by hazardous environmental agents.

■ Human traits that vary continuously, such as intelligence and personality, are **polygenic,** or influenced by many genes. Since the genetic principles involved are unknown, scientists must study the influence of heredity on these characteristics indirectly.

*Describe major chromosomal abnormalities, and explain how they occur.*

■ Most chromosomal abnormalities are due to errors in meiosis. The most common chromosomal disorder is Down syndrome, which results in physical defects and mental retardation. Disorders of the **sex chromosomes**—XYY, triple X, Klinefelter, and Turner syndromes—are generally milder than defects of the **autosomes.**

## REPRODUCTIVE CHOICES

*What procedures are available to assist prospective parents in having healthy children?*

■ **Genetic counselling** helps couples at risk for giving birth to children with hereditary defects decide whether or not to conceive. **Prenatal diagnostic methods** make early detection of abnormalities possible. Although reproductive technologies, such as donor insemination, in vitro fertilization, surrogate motherhood, and postmenopausal-assisted childbirth, permit many barren couples to become parents, they raise serious legal and ethical concerns.

## PRENATAL DEVELOPMENT

*List the three phases of prenatal development, and describe the major milestones of each.*

■ The first prenatal phase, the period of the zygote, lasts about 2 weeks, from fertilization until the blastocyst becomes deeply implanted in the uterine lining. During this time, structures that will support prenatal growth begin to form. The embryonic disk is surrounded by the trophoblast, which forms structures that protect and nourish the organism. The **amnion** fills with amniotic fluid to regulate tempera-

ture and cushion against the mother's movements. From the **chorion,** villi emerge that burrow into the uterine wall, and the **placenta** starts to develop. The developing organism is connected to the placenta by the **umbilical cord.**

■ The period of the **embryo** lasts from implantation through the eighth week of pregnancy, during which the foundations for all body structures are laid down. In the first week of this period, the neural tube forms, and the nervous system starts to develop. Other organs follow and grow rapidly. At the end of this phase, the embryo responds to touch and can move.

■ The period of the **fetus,** lasting until the end of pregnancy, involves a dramatic increase in body size and completion of physical structures. By the middle of the second trimester, the mother can feel movement. The fetus becomes covered with **vernix,** which protects the skin from chapping. White, downy hair called **lanugo** helps the vernix stick to the skin. At the end of the second trimester, most neurons in the brain are in place.

■ The **age of viability** occurs at the beginning of the final trimester, sometime between 22 and 26 weeks. The brain continues to develop rapidly, and new sensory and behavioural capacities emerge. Gradually, the lungs mature, the fetus fills the uterus, and birth is near.

## PRENATAL ENVIRONMENTAL INFLUENCES

*Cite factors that influence the impact of teratogens on the developing organism, noting agents that are known or suspected teratogens.*

■ **Teratogens** are environmental agents that cause damage during the prenatal period. Their effects conform to the sensitive period concept. The organism is especially vulnerable during the embryonic period, when body structures emerge rapidly.

■ The impact of teratogens varies, due to amount and length of exposure, the genetic makeup of mother and fetus, the presence or absence of other harmful agents, and the age of the organism at time of exposure. The effects of teratogens are not limited to immediate physical damage.

Serious health and psychological consequences may appear later in development. Drugs, tobacco, alcohol, radiation, environmental pollution, and certain infectious diseases are teratogens that can endanger the developing organism.

*Describe the impact of additional maternal factors on prenatal development.*

■ In healthy, physically fit women, regular moderate exercise is related to increased birth weight. However, very frequent, vigorous exercise results in lower birth weight. When the mother's diet is inadequate, low birth weight and damage to the brain and other organs are major concerns. Vitamin–mineral supplementation beginning early in pregnancy can improve maternal health and prevent certain prenatal and birth complications. Severe emotional stress is associated with many pregnancy complications, although its impact can be reduced by providing mothers with social support.

■ Aside from the risk of chromosomal abnormalities, older women in good health do not experience more prenatal problems than do younger women. Poor health and environmental risks associated with poverty are the strongest predictors of pregnancy complications in teenagers and older women.

## CHILDBIRTH

*Describe the three stages of childbirth, the baby's adaptation to labour and delivery, and the newborn baby's appearance.*

■ In the first stage of childbirth, contractions widen and thin the cervix. In the second stage, the mother feels an urge to push the baby through the birth canal. In the final stage, the placenta is delivered. During labour, infants produce high levels of stress hormones, which help them withstand oxygen deprivation, clear the lungs for breathing, and arouse them into alertness at birth.

■ Newborn babies have large heads, small bodies, and facial features that make adults feel like picking them up and cuddling them. The **Apgar Scale** is used to assess the newborn baby's physical condition at birth.

## APPROACHES TO CHILDBIRTH

*Describe natural childbirth and home delivery, and explain the benefits and risks of using pain-relieving drugs during labour and delivery.*

■ **Natural,** or **prepared, childbirth** involves classes in which expectant mothers and their partners learn about labour and delivery, relaxation and breathing techniques to counteract pain, and coaching during childbirth. Social support, a vital part of natural childbirth, reduces the length of labour and the incidence of birth complications.

■ As long as mothers are healthy and assisted by a well-trained doctor or midwife, giving birth at home is just as safe as giving birth at a hospital.

■ Analgesics and anesthetics are necessary in complicated deliveries. When given in large doses, these pain-relieving drugs produce a depressed state in the newborn that affects the newborn baby's adjustment. They also increase the likelihood of an instrument or surgical (Caesarean) delivery.

## BIRTH COMPLICATIONS

*What risks are associated with oxygen deprivation and preterm and low birth weight, and what factors can help infants who survive a traumatic birth develop?*

■ Anoxia can result when breathing fails to start immediately after delivery, the umbilical cord is squeezed because the baby is in **breech position,** or **Rh** incompatibility leads to destruction of the baby's red blood cells. Oxygen deprivation is a serious birth complication that can damage the brain and other organs. As long as anoxia is not extreme, most affected children catch up in development by the school years.

■ The incidence of premature births is high among low-income pregnant women and mothers of twins. Compared with **preterm** babies whose weight is appropriate for time spent in the uterus, **small-for-date** infants usually have longer-lasting difficulties. Some interventions provide special stimulation in the intensive care nursery. Others teach parents how to care for and interact with their babies. When preterm infants live in stressed, low-income households, long-term, intensive intervention is necessary. A major cause of **infant mortality** is low birth weight.

■ When infants experience birth trauma, favourable characteristics, a supportive family environment, or relationships with other caring adults can help restore their growth. Even infants with serious birth complications can recover with the help of positive life events.

## HEREDITY, ENVIRONMENT, AND BEHAVIOUR: A LOOK AHEAD

*Explain the various ways heredity and environment may combine to influence complex traits.*

■ **Behavioural genetics** is a field devoted to discovering the contributions of nature and nurture to complex traits. Some researchers believe it is useful and possible to determine "how much" each factor contributes to differences among children. These investigators compute **heritability estimates** and **concordance rates** from **kinship studies.** Although these measures show that genetic factors contribute to such traits as intelligence and personality, their accuracy and usefulness has been challenged.

■ Most researchers view development as the result of a dynamic interplay between nature and nurture and ask "how" heredity and environment work together. The concepts of **range of reaction, canalization, genetic–environmental correlation,** and **epigenesis** remind us that development is best understood as a series of complex exchanges between nature and nurture.

# *important terms and concepts*

age of viability (p. 90)
allele (p. 74)
amnion (p. 87)
Apgar Scale (p. 104)
autosomes (p. 73)
behavioural genetics (p. 113)
breech position (p. 107)
canalization (p. 117)
carrier (p. 74)
chorion (p. 87)
chromosomes (p. 70)
codominance (p. 75)
concordance rate (p. 114)
crossing over (p. 71)
deoxyribonucleic acid (DNA) (p. 70)
dominant–recessive inheritance (p. 74)
embryo (p. 89)
epigenesis (p. 117)
fetal alcohol effects (FAE) (p. 94)

fetal alcohol syndrome (FAS) (p. 94)
fetus (p. 89)
fraternal, or dizygotic, twins (p. 73)
gametes (p. 71)
gene (p. 70)
genetic counselling (p. 80)
genetic–environmental correlation (p. 117)
genetic imprinting (p. 77)
genotype (p. 70)
heritability estimate (p. 114)
heterozygous (p. 74)
homozygous (p. 74)
identical, or monozygotic, twins (p. 73)
infant mortality (p. 112)
kinship studies (p. 114)
lanugo (p. 89)
meiosis (p. 71)
mitosis (p. 71)

modifier genes (p. 75)
mutation (p. 78)
natural, or prepared, childbirth (p. 104)
niche-picking (p. 117)
phenotype (p. 70)
placenta (p. 87)
polygenic inheritance (78)
prenatal diagnostic methods (p. 80)
preterm (p. 109)
range of reaction (p. 117)
Rh factor (p. 107)
sex chromosomes (p. 73)
small for date (p. 109)
teratogen (p. 91)
umbilical cord (p. 89)
vernix (p. 89)
X-linked inheritance (p. 75)
zygote (p. 73)

This baby's captivated expression suggests a strong drive to understand and gain control of her surroundings. How does she make sense of constantly changing sounds, shapes, patterns, and surfaces? Chapter 4 traces these remarkable achievements.

# *f*our

## Infancy: Early Learning, Motor Skills, and Perceptual Capacities

OUR VIEW OF INFANCY—THE period of development that spans the first year of life—has changed drastically over the past century. At one time, the newborn baby, or *neonate,* was considered a passive, incompetent being whose world was, in the words of turn-of-the-century psychologist William James, "a blooming, buzzing confusion." Recently developed methods and equipment permitting researchers to test young babies' capacities have shown this image to be wrong. Consider the following diary notes by a modern child development researcher about her own baby:

At 3.5 weeks, you lift your head when I put you on your tummy, showing off your strength with shaky half-push-ups. In your crib, you stare at your mobile, your face serious and still, utterly absorbed. When you are bored, I carry you to a new place, sing to you. At the sound of my voice, your face perks up, and you turn toward me with rapt attention. When you are unhappy, I hold you close to my heart so you can feel its rhythmic sound. Your cry has become a language I can understand. Your tiny hand grasps whatever comes near—the folds of my clothing, my fingers in your palm—and you hold on tightly. I marvel at your determination to master your world!

These observations clearly reflect the now widely accepted view that infants, from the outset, are skilled, capable beings who display many complex abilities.

Infant development proceeds at an astonishing pace. Excited relatives who visit just after the birth and return a few months later often remark that the baby does not seem like the same individual! Although researchers agree that infants are competent beings, fervent debates continue over questions like these: Which capacities are present from the very beginning? Which mature with the passage of time? And which are acquired through constant interaction with the physical and social worlds? In this chapter, we explore the infant's remarkable capabilities—early reflexes, ability to learn, motor skills, and perceptual capacities—and the debates that surround them.

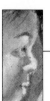

# The Organized Newborn

THE NEWBORN BABY, AS WE SAW IN Chapter 3, is a homely looking creature. The head, misshapen from being squeezed through the narrow birth canal, is overly large in relation to the potbellied trunk and bowlegged lower body. In addition, the baby's skin is usually wrinkled and "parboiled" in appearance. Many parents assume that this odd little being can do nothing but eat and sleep. Yet a few hours spent in the company of a neonate reveals a wide variety of capacities that are crucial for survival and that evoke care and attention from adults. In relating to the physical world and building their first social relationships, babies are active from the very start.

In the Moro reflex, loss of support or a sudden loud sound causes this baby to arch her back, extend her arms outward, and then bring them in toward her body.

MIMI FORSYTH/MONKMEYER PRESS

## NEWBORN REFLEXES

A **reflex** is an inborn, automatic response to a particular form of stimulation. Reflexes are the neonate's most obvious organized patterns of behaviour. Infants come into the world with dozens of them. A father, changing his newborn baby's diaper, accidentally bumps the side of the table. The infant flings her arms wide and brings them back toward her body. A mother softly strokes her infant's cheek, and the baby turns his head in her direction. Table 4.1 lists the major newborn reflexes. See if you can identify the ones described here and in the diary excerpt at the beginning of this chapter. Then let's consider the meaning and purpose of these curious behaviours.

**ADAPTIVE VALUE OF REFLEXES.** Some newborn reflexes have survival value. The rooting reflex helps a breast-fed baby find the mother's nipple. And if sucking were not automatic, our species would be unlikely to survive for a single generation! The swimming reflex helps a baby who is accidentally dropped into water stay afloat, increasing the chances of retrieval by the caregiver.

Other reflexes probably helped babies survive during our evolutionary past. For example, the Moro or "embracing" reflex is believed to have helped infants cling to their mothers when babies were carried about all day. If the baby happened to lose support, the reflex caused the infant to embrace and, along with the powerful grasp reflex (so strong during the first week that it can support the baby's entire weight), regain its hold on the mother's body (Kessen, 1967; Prechtl, 1958).

Finally, several reflexes help parents and infants establish gratifying interaction. A baby who searches for and successfully finds the nipple, sucks easily during feedings, and grasps when her hand is touched, encourages parents to respond lovingly and feel competent as caregivers. Reflexes can also help parents comfort the baby because they permit infants to control distress and amount of stimulation. As any new mother who remembers to bring a pacifier on an outing with her young baby knows, sucking helps quiet a fussy neonate.

**reflex**
An inborn, automatic response to a particular form of stimulation.

**TABLE** 4.1

Some Newborn Reflexes

| REFLEX | STIMULATION | RESPONSE | AGE OF DISAPPEARANCE | FUNCTION |
|---|---|---|---|---|
| Eye blink | Shine bright light at eyes or clap hands near head | Infant quickly closes eyelids | Permanent reflex | Protects infant from strong stimulation |
| Rooting | Stroke cheek near corner of mouth | Head turns toward source of stimulation | 3 weeks (becomes voluntary head turning at this time) | Helps infant find the nipple |
| Sucking | Place finger in infant's mouth | Infant sucks finger rhythmically | Permanent reflex | Permits feeding |
| Swimming | Place infant face down in pool of water[1] | Baby paddles and kicks in swimming motion | 4–6 months | Helps infant survive if dropped into body of water |
| Moro | Hold infant horizontally on back and let head drop slightly, or produce a sudden loud sound against surface supporting infant | Infant makes an "embracing" motion by arching back, extending legs, throwing arms outward and then in toward the body | 6 months | In human evolutionary past, may have helped infant cling to mother |
| Palmar grasp | Place finger in infant's hand and press against palm | Spontaneous grasp of adult's finger | 3–4 months | Prepares infant for voluntary grasping |
| Tonic neck | Turn baby's head to one side while lying awake on back | Infant lies in a "fencing position." One arm is extended in front of eyes on side to which head is turned, other arm is flexed | 4 months | May prepare infant for voluntary reaching |
| Stepping | Hold infant under arms and permit bare feet to touch a flat surface | Infant lifts one foot after another in stepping response | 2 months | Prepares infant for voluntary walking |
| Babinski | Stroke sole of foot from toe toward heel | Toes fan out and curl as foot twists in | 8–12 months | Unknown |

[1]Placing infants face down in water is dangerous. See discussion on page 126.
*Sources:* Knobloch & Pasamanick, 1974; Prechtl & Beintema, 1965.

**ADAPTIVE VALVE OF REFLEXES.** A few reflexes form the basis for complex motor skills that will develop later. For example, the tonic neck reflex may prepare the baby for voluntary reaching. When babies lie on their backs in this "fencing position," they naturally gaze at the hand in front of their eyes. The reflex may encourage them to combine vision with arm movements and, eventually, reach for objects (Knobloch & Pasamanick, 1974).

Certain reflexes—such as the palmar grasp, swimming, and stepping—drop out early, but the motor functions involved seem to be renewed later. The stepping reflex, for example, looks like a primitive walking response. In infants who gain weight quickly in the weeks after birth, the stepping reflex drops out because thigh and calf muscles are not strong enough to lift the baby's increasingly chubby legs. However, if the lower part of the infant's body is dipped in water, the reflex reappears, since the buoyancy of the water lightens the load on the baby's muscles (Thelen, Fisher, & Ridley-Johnson, 1984). When the stepping reflex is exercised regularly, babies display more spontaneous stepping movements and are likely to walk several weeks earlier than if it is not practised (Zelazo, 1983; Zelazo et al., 1993). According to Esther Thelen, stepping exercise permits infants to build leg strength, in the same way that exercise causes athletes to gain muscle power. Stronger leg muscles, in turn, enable babies to retain the reflex and walk earlier. However, there is no special need to get infants to use the stepping reflex, since all normal babies walk in due time.

The palmar grasp reflex is so strong during the first week after birth that many infants can use it to support their entire weight.

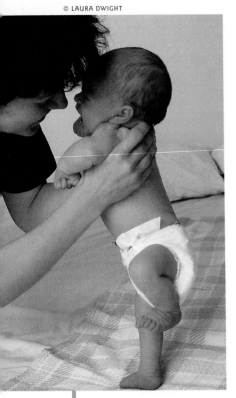

When held upright under the arms, newborn babies show reflexive stepping movements.

**states of arousal**
Different degrees of sleep and wakefulness.

In the case of the swimming reflex, it is risky to try to build on it. Although young babies placed in a swimming pool will paddle and kick, they open their mouths and swallow large amounts of water. Consuming too much water lowers the concentration of salt in the baby's blood, which can cause swelling of the brain and seizures (Micheli, 1985). Despite the presence of this remarkable reflex, swimming lessons are best postponed until at least 3 years of age.

**THE IMPORTANCE OF ASSESSING NEWBORN REFLEXES.** Look at Table 4.1 on page 125 again, and you will see that most newborn reflexes disappear during the first 6 months. Researchers believe that this is due to a gradual increase in voluntary control over behaviour as the cerebral cortex develops.

Pediatricians test infant reflexes carefully, especially if a newborn has experienced birth trauma, since reflexes can reveal the health of the baby's nervous system. In brain-damaged infants, reflexes may be weak or absent or, in some cases, exaggerated and overly rigid (Zafeiriou, 2000). Brain damage may also be indicated when reflexes persist past the point in development when they should normally disappear. However, individual differences in reflexive responses exist that are not cause for concern. Newborn reflexes must be observed along with other characteristics to accurately distinguish normal from abnormal central nervous system functioning (Touwen, 1984).

## NEWBORN STATES

Throughout the day and night, newborn infants move in and out of six **states of arousal,** or degrees of sleep and wakefulness, described in Table 4.2, on page 128. During the first month, these states alternate frequently. Quiet alertness is the most fleeting; it moves relatively quickly toward fussing and crying. Much to the relief of their fatigued parents, newborns spend the greatest amount of time asleep—about 16 to 18 hours a day.

Between birth and 2 years, the organization of sleep and wakefulness changes substantially. The decline in total sleep time is not great; the average 2-year-old still needs 12 to 13 hours. The greatest change is that short periods of sleep and wakefulness are gradually put together. Although at birth babies sleep more at night than during the day, their sleep–wake cycles are regulated more by fullness–hunger than by darkness–light (Goodlin-Jones, Burnham, & Anders, 2000). With age, infants remain awake for longer daytime periods and need fewer naps—by the second year, only one or two (Blum & Carey, 1996).

Although these changing arousal patterns are due to brain development, they are affected by the social environment. In most Western nations, parents usually succeed in getting their babies to sleep through the night around 4 months of age by offering an evening feeding before putting them down in a separate, quiet room. In this way, they push young infants to the limits of their neurological capacities. Not until the middle of the first year is the secretion of *melatonin,* a hormone within the brain that promotes drowsiness, much greater at night than during the day (Sadeh, 1997).

As the Cultural Influences box on the following page reveals, the practice of isolating infants to promote sleep is rare elsewhere in the world. When babies sleep with their parents, their average sleep period remains constant at 3 hours, from 1 to 8 months of age. Only at the end of the first year, as REM sleep (the state that usually prompts waking) declines, do infants move in the direction of an adultlike sleep–waking schedule (Ficca et al., 1999).

Even after infants sleep through the night, they continue to wake at night occasionally. In surveys of parents carried out in Australia, Great Britain, Israel, and the United States, about 30 percent of children between ages 1 and 4 awoke during the night at least once a week (Armstrong, Quinn, & Dadds, 1994; Scher et al., 1995). Night wakings peaked between 18 months and 2 years and then declined. As Chapters 10 and 11 will reveal, the psychological challenges of this period—ability to range farther from the familiar caregiver and awareness of the self as separate from others—often prompt anxiety, evident in disturbed sleep and clinginess. When parents offer comfort and support, these behaviours subside.

# cultural influences

## CULTURAL VARIATION IN INFANT SLEEPING ARRANGEMENTS

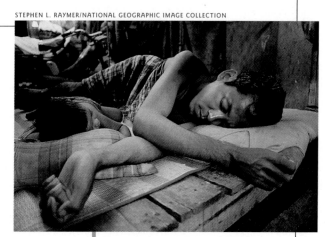

STEPHEN L. RAYMER/NATIONAL GEOGRAPHIC IMAGE COLLECTION

While awaiting the birth of a new baby, North American middle-class parents typically furnish a room as the infant's sleeping quarters. Throughout the twentieth century, child-rearing advice from experts strongly encouraged this nighttime separation of baby from parent. For example, the most recent edition of Dr. Spock's *Baby and Child Care* recommends that babies be moved out of their parents' room early in the first year, explaining, "Otherwise, there is a chance that they may become dependent on this arrangement" (Spock & Parker, 1998, p. 102). Similar advice is provided by British psychologist Penelope Leach (1997), who advocates having the baby sleep with an older sibling if one is available.

Yet parent–infant "cosleeping" is common around the globe. Japanese children usually lie next to their mothers throughout infancy and early childhood and continue to sleep with a parent or other family member until adolescence (Takahashi, 1990). Cosleeping is also frequent in some North American subcultures. African-American children frequently fall asleep with parents and remain with them for part or all of the night (Lozoff et al., 1995). Appalachian children of eastern Kentucky typically sleep with their parents for the first 2 years (Abbott, 1992). Among the Maya of rural Guatemala, mother–infant cosleeping is interrupted only by the birth of a new baby, at which time the older child is moved beside the father or to another bed in the same room (Morelli et al., 1992).

Available household space plays a minor role in infant sleeping arrangements. Instead, cultural values—specifically, collectivism versus individualism (see Chapter 1, page 35)—are

much more important. In one study, researchers interviewed U.S. middle-class mothers and Guatemalan Mayan mothers about their sleeping practices. U.S. mothers conveyed an individualistic perspective, mentioning the importance of establishing early independence, preventing bad habits, and protecting their own privacy. In contrast, Mayan mothers stressed a collectivist perspective, explaining that cosleeping helps build a close parent–child bond, which is necessary for children to learn the ways of people around them. When told that U.S. infants sleep by themselves, Mayan mothers reacted with shock and disbelief, stating that it would be painful for them to leave their babies alone at night (Morelli et al., 1992).

Infant sleeping practices affect other aspects of family life. Sleep problems are not an issue for Mayan parents. Babies doze off in the midst of ongoing social activities and are carried to bed by their mothers. In North America, getting young children ready for bed often requires an elaborate ritual that takes a good part of the evening. Perhaps bedtime struggles, so common in Western homes but rare elsewhere in the world, are related to the stress young children feel when they are required to fall asleep without assistance (Latz, Wolf, & Lozoff, 1999). Still, those parents who permit cosleeping tend to feel uncomfortable about the practice (Lozoff, Askew, & Wolf, 1996).

Infant sleeping arrangements, like other parenting practices, are meant to foster culturally valued characteristics in the young. North American middle-

This Cambodian father and child sleep together—a practice common in their culture and around the globe. When children fall asleep with their parents, sleep problems are rare during the early years. And many parents who practise cosleeping believe that it helps build a close parent–child bond.

class parents view babies as dependent beings who must be urged toward independence, and so they usually require them to sleep alone. In contrast, Japanese, Mayan, and Appalachian parents regard young infants as separate beings who need to establish an interdependent relationship with the community to survive.

Perhaps because cosleeping is rare in North America, those parents who practise it sometimes fail to take appropriate safety precautions. Suffocation due to entrapment in soft covers, wedging between the mattress and other parts of the bed, and overlying by an adult are responsible for about 500 deaths of children under age 2 annually (Nakamura, Wind, & Danello, 1999). In countries where cosleeping is widespread, parents and infants often sleep on hard surfaces, such as floor mats and wooden planks, which minimize these dangers (Nelson, Schiefenhoevel, & Haimerl, 2000).

**TABLE** 4.2

Infant States of Arousal

| STATE | DESCRIPTION | DAILY DURATION IN NEWBORNS |
|---|---|---|
| Regular sleep | The infant is at full rest and shows little or no body activity. The eyelids are closed, no eye movements occur, the face is relaxed, and breathing is slow and regular. | 8–9 hours |
| Irregular sleep | Gentle limb movements, occasional stirring, and facial grimacing occur. Although the eyelids are closed, occasional rapid eye movements can be seen beneath them. Breathing is irregular. | 8–9 hours |
| Drowsiness | The infant is either falling asleep or waking up. The body is less active than in irregular sleep but more active than in regular sleep. Eyes open and close; when open, they have a glazed look. Breathing is even but somewhat faster than in regular sleep. | Varies |
| Quiet alertness | The infant's body is relatively inactive. The eyes are open and attentive. Breathing is even. | 2–3 hours |
| Waking activity | The infant shows frequent bursts of uncoordinated motor activity. Breathing is very irregular. The face may be relaxed or tense and wrinkled. | 2–3 hours |
| Crying | Waking activity sometimes evolves into crying, which is accompanied by diffuse, vigorous motor activity. | 1–2 hours |

*Source:* Wolff, 1966.

Although arousal states become more patterned with age, individual differences in daily rhythms affect parents' attitudes toward and interactions with the baby (Thoman & Whitney, 1990). A few infants sleep for long periods at an early age, increasing the rest their parents get and the energy they have for sensitive, responsive care. Other babies cry a great deal, and their parents must exert great effort to soothe them. If they do not succeed, parents may feel less competent and positive toward their infant. Babies who spend more time alert are likely to receive more social stimulation. And since this state provides opportunities to explore the environment, infants who favour it may have a slight advantage in cognitive development (Moss et al., 1988).

Of the states listed in Table 4.2, the two extremes—sleep and crying—have been of greatest interest to researchers. Each tells us something about normal and abnormal early development.

**SLEEP.**    Sleep is made up of at least two states. The expression "sleeping like a baby" was probably not meant to describe irregular, or **rapid-eye-movement (REM) sleep**! During REM sleep, electrical brain-wave activity, measured with an EEG, is remarkably similar to that of the waking state. The eyes dart beneath the lids; heart rate, blood pressure, and breathing are uneven; and slight body movements occur. In contrast, during regular, or **non-rapid-eye-movement (NREM) sleep,** the body is almost motionless, and heart rate, breathing, and brain-wave activity are slow and regular.

Like children and adults, newborns alternate between REM and NREM sleep. However, as Figure 4.1 on page 129 shows, they spend far more time in the REM state than they ever will again. REM sleep accounts for 50 percent of the newborn baby's sleep time. By 3 to 5 years, it has declined to an adultlike level of 20 percent (Louis et al., 1997).

Why do young infants spend so much time in REM sleep? In older children and adults, the REM state is associated with dreaming. Babies probably do not dream, at least not in the same way we do. But young infants are believed to have a special need for the EEG activity of REM sleep because they spend little time in an alert state, when they can get input from the environment. REM sleep seems to be a way in which the brain stimulates itself (Roffwarg, Muzio, & Dement, 1966). Sleep researchers believe this stimulation is vital for growth of the central nervous system. In support of this idea, the percentage of REM sleep is especially

**rapid-eye-movement (REM) sleep**
An "irregular" sleep state in which brain-wave activity is similar to that of the waking state; eyes dart beneath the lids; heart rate, blood pressure, and breathing are uneven; and slight body movements occur.

**non-rapid-eye-movement (NREM) sleep**
A "regular" sleep state in which the body is almost motionless and heart rate, breathing, and brain-wave activity are slow and regular.

great in the fetus and in preterm babies, who are even less able to take advantage of external stimulation than are full-term newborns (DiPietro et al., 1996a; Sahni et al., 1995).

Rapid eye movements also protect the health of the eye. During the waking state, eye movements cause the vitreous (gelatin-like substance within the eye) to circulate, thereby delivering oxygen to parts of the eye that do not have their own blood supply. During sleep, when the eye and the vitreous are still, visual structures are at risk for anoxia. As the brain cycles through REM-sleep periods, rapid eye movements stir up the vitreous, ensuring that the eye is fully oxygenated (Blumberg & Lucas, 1996).

Because the normal sleep behaviour of the newborn baby is organized and patterned, observations of sleep states can help identify central nervous system abnormalities. In infants who are brain damaged or who have experienced birth trauma, disturbed sleep cycles are often present, generally in the form of disorganized transitions between REM and NREM sleep that cannot be identified as a specific state. Babies with poor sleep organization are likely to be behaviourally disorganized and, therefore, to have difficulty learning and eliciting caregiver interactions that enhance their development (Groome et al., 1997; Halpern, MacLean, & Baumeister, 1995). And the brain-functioning problems that underlie newborn sleep irregularities may culminate in sudden infant death syndrome, a major cause of infant mortality (see the Social Issues: Health box on page 130).

**CRYING.** Crying is the first way babies communicate, letting parents know they need food, comfort, and stimulation. Most of the time, the nature of the cry, combined with the experiences that led up to it, helps guide parents toward its cause. The baby's cry is a complex auditory stimulus that varies in intensity, from a whimper to a message of all-out distress (Gustafson, Wood, & Green, 2000). As early as the first few weeks of life, individual infants can be identified by the unique vocal "signature" of their cries, which helps parents locate the baby from a distance (Gustafson, Green, & Cleland, 1994).

Young infants usually cry because of physical needs. Hunger is the most common cause, but babies may also cry in response to temperature change when undressed, a sudden noise, or a painful stimulus. An infant's state often makes a difference in whether the baby will cry in response to a sight or sound. Infants who, when quietly alert, regard a colourful object or the sound of a toy horn with interest may react with a burst of tears when in a state of mild discomfort. And newborns (as well as older babies) often cry at the sound of another crying baby (Dondi, Simion, & Caltran, 1999). Some researchers believe that this response reflects an inborn capacity to react to the suffering of others.

*Adult Responsiveness to Infant Cries.* The next time you hear a baby cry, notice your own reaction. The sound stimulates strong feelings of arousal and discomfort in just about anyone—men and women, parents and nonparents (Boukydis & Burgess, 1982; Murray, 1985). This powerful response is probably innately programmed in all humans to make sure that babies receive the care and protection they need to survive.

Although parents do not always interpret the baby's cry correctly, experience improves their accuracy. As babies get older, parents react to more subtle cues in the cry—not just intensity but whimpering and calling sounds (Thompson & Leger, 1999). They combine these cues with the context of the cry to figure out what is wrong. If the baby has not eaten

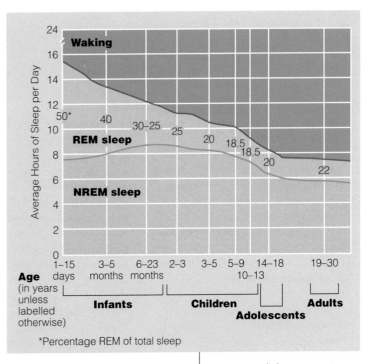

**FIGURE 4.1**

**Changes in REM sleep, NREM sleep, and the waking state from birth to adulthood.** REM sleep declines steadily over the first few years of life. Between 3 and 5 years, it consumes about the same percentage of sleep time as it does in adulthood. In contrast, NREM sleep changes very little over infancy and childhood. (Adapted from H. P. Roffwarg, J. N. Muzio, & W. C. Dement, 1966, "Ontogenetic Development of the Human Sleep–Dream Cycle," *Science, 152,* p. 608. Copyright © 1966 by the AAAS. Revised from original publication by the authors in 1969 on the basis of additional data. Reprinted by permission.)

# social issues: health

## THE MYSTERIOUS TRAGEDY OF SUDDEN INFANT DEATH SYNDROME

illie awoke with a start and looked at the clock. It was 7:30, and Sasha had missed her night waking and early morning feeding. Millie and her husband Stuart tiptoed into the nursery where Sasha lay still, curled up under her blanket. She had died silently during her sleep.

Sasha was a victim of **sudden infant death syndrome (SIDS),** the unexpected death, usually during the night, of an infant under 1 year of age that remains unexplained after thorough investigation. In industrialized nations, SIDS is the leading cause of infant mortality between 1 month and 12 months of age. (Canadian Foundation for the Study of Infant Deaths, 2001).

Although the precise cause of SIDS is not known, its victims usually show physical problems from the very beginning. Early medical records of SIDS babies reveal higher rates of prematurity and low birth weight, poor Apgar scores, and limp muscle tone. Abnormal heart rate and respiration and disturbances in sleep–wake activity are also involved (Leach et al., 1999; Malloy & Hoffman, 1995). At the time of death, many SIDS babies have a mild respiratory infection (Kohlendorfer, Kiechl, & Sperl, 1998). This seems to increase the chances of respiratory failure in an already vulnerable baby.

One hypothesis about the cause of SIDS is that problems in brain functioning prevent these infants from learning how to respond when their survival is threatened—for example,

when respiration is suddenly interrupted (Horne et al., 2000; Panigrahy et al., 1997). Between 1 and 4 months, when SIDS is most likely, reflexes decline and are replaced by voluntary, learned responses. Respiratory and muscular weaknesses may stop SIDS babies from acquiring behaviours that replace defensive reflexes. As a result, when breathing difficulties occur during sleep, infants do not wake up, shift their position, or cry out for help. Instead, they simply give in to oxygen deprivation and death.

In an effort to reduce the occurrence of SIDS, researchers are studying environmental factors related to it. Maternal cigarette smoking, both during and after pregnancy, as well as smoking by other caregivers strongly predicts the disorder. Babies exposed to cigarette smoke have more respiratory infections and are two to three times more likely to die of SIDS than are nonexposed infants (Dwyer, Ponsonby, & Couper, 1999; Dybing & Sanner, 1999). Prenatal abuse of drugs that depress central nervous system functioning (opiates and barbiturates) increases the risk of SIDS tenfold (Kandall et al., 1993).

SIDS babies are also more likely to sleep on their stomachs or sides than their backs and often are wrapped very warmly in clothing and blankets (Kleeman et al., 1999). Researchers suspect that smoke, depressant drugs, sleeping on the stomach, and excessive body warmth lead to physiological stress, which disrupts the normal

sleep pattern. When sleep-deprived babies experience a sleep "rebound," they sleep more deeply, which results in loss of vital muscle tone in the airway passages. In at-risk babies, the airway may collapse, and the infant may fail to arouse sufficiently to reestablish breathing (Simpson, 2001). In other cases, healthy babies sleeping face down in soft bedding may die from continually breathing their own exhaled breath.

In 1999 Health Canada and partners released a "Joint Statement: Reducing the Risk of SIDS in Canada" (Health Canada, 1999b), which recommends that infants be placed to sleep on their backs on flat, firm bedding; that they be reared both before and after birth in a smoke- and drug-free environment; that they be breast-fed; and that they not be overheated. Some sources estimate that 30 percent of SIDS could be prevented if women refrained from smoking while pregnant. Public education campaigns to encourage back sleeping have led to dramatic reductions in SIDS in many industrialized countries (American Academy of Pediatrics, 2000; Schlaud et al., 1999).

When SIDS does occur, surviving family members require a great deal of help to overcome their grief. Parent support groups exist in many communities. As Millie commented 6 months after Sasha's death, "It's the worst crisis we've ever been through. What's helped us most are the comforting words of others who've experienced the same tragedy."

---

**sudden infant death syndrome (SIDS)**
The unexpected death, usually during the night, of an infant younger than 1 year of age that remains unexplained after thorough investigation.

for several hours, she is likely to be hungry. If a period of wakefulness and stimulation preceded the cry, the infant may be tired. A sharp, piercing, sustained cry usually means the baby is in pain. When caregivers hear this sound, they rush to the infant. Very intense cries are rated as more unpleasant and produce greater physiological arousal in adults, as measured by heart rate and skin conductance (Crowe & Zeskind, 1992). These adaptive reactions help ensure that an infant in danger will quickly get help.

**TABLE** 4.3

Ways to Soothe a Crying Newborn

| METHOD | EXPLANATION |
|---|---|
| Lift the baby to the shoulder and rock or walk. | This provides a combination of physical contact, upright posture, and motion. It is the most effective soothing technique. |
| Swaddle the baby. | Restricting movement and increasing warmth often soothe a young infant. |
| Offer a pacifier. | Sucking helps babies control their own level of arousal. Sucking a sweetened pacifier relieves pain and quiets a crying infant. |
| Talk softly or play rhythmic sounds. | Continuous, monotonous, rhythmic sounds, such as a clock ticking, a fan whirring, or peaceful music, are more effective than intermittent sounds. |
| Take the baby for a short car ride or walk in a baby carriage; swing the baby in a cradle. | Gentle, rhythmic motion of any kind helps lull the baby to sleep. |
| Massage the baby's body. | Stroke the baby's torso and limbs with continuous, gentle motions. This technique is used in some non-Western cultures to relax the baby's muscles. |
| Combine several methods just listed. | Stimulating several of the baby's senses at once is often more effective than stimulating only one. |
| If these methods do not work, permit the baby to cry for a short period. | Occasionally, a baby responds well to just being put down and will, after a few minutes, fall asleep. |

*Sources:* Blass, 1999; Campos, 1989; Field, 1998; Lester, 1985; Reisman, 1987.

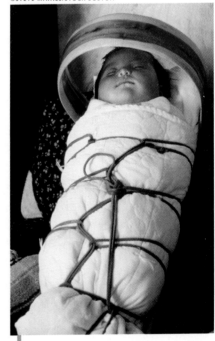

©STEVE MAINES/STOCK BOSTON

***Soothing a Crying Infant.*** Even when parents are fairly certain about the cause of the cry, the baby may not always calm down. Fortunately, as Table 4.3 indicates, there are many ways to soothe a crying baby when feeding and diaper changing do not work. The technique that Western parents usually try first, lifting the infant to the shoulder and rocking or walking, is also the one that works the best.

Another common soothing method is swaddling—wrapping the baby snugly in a blanket. Among the Quechua, who live in the cold, high-altitude desert regions of Peru, young babies are dressed in layers of clothing and blankets. Then a cloth belt is tightly wound around the body, over which are placed additional blankets that cover the head and face and serve as a carrying cloth. The result—a nearly sealed, warm pouch placed on the mother's back that moves rhythmically as she walks—reduces crying and promotes sleep, so that the baby conserves energy for early growth in the harsh Peruvian highlands (Tronick, Thomas, & Daltabuit, 1994).

***How Quickly to Respond to a Crying Baby.*** Will reacting promptly and consistently to infant cries give babies a sense of confidence that their needs will be met and, over time, reduce fussing and complaining? Or will it strengthen crying behaviour and produce a miniature tyrant? Answers are contradictory.

According to *ethological theory*, parental responsiveness is adaptive in that it ensures the infant's basic needs will be met (see Chapter 1, pages 24–25). At the same time, it brings the baby into close contact with the caregiver, who encourages the infant to communicate through means other than crying. In support of this view, two studies showed that mothers who delayed or failed to respond to their young baby's cries had infants who cried more at the end of the first year (Bell & Ainsworth, 1972; Hubbard & van IJzendoorn, 1991).

But not all research indicates that early parental responsiveness reduces infant crying (Van IJzendoorn & Hubbard, 2000). *Behaviourists* have challenged the ethological view, arguing that consistently responding to a crying infant reinforces the crying response and results in a whiny, demanding child (Gewirtz & Boyd, 1977). An Israeli study provides support for this position. Infants of Bedouin (nomadic) tribespeople, who believe that babies should never be left to fuss and cry, were compared with home-reared babies as well as with infants

Some cultures routinely swaddle young infants, restricting movement and increasing warmth by wrapping blankets tightly around the body. This Aboriginal baby rests on a traditional cradle board that can be strapped to the mother's back. Swaddling reduces crying and promotes sleep.

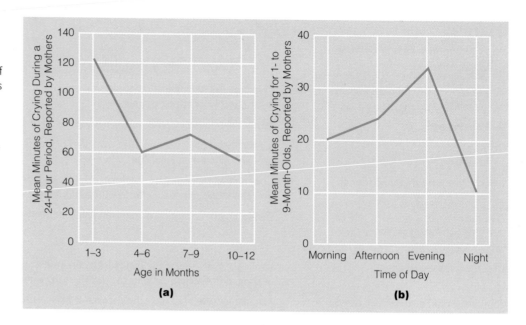

FIGURE 4.2

**Crying patterns during the first year of life.** A sample of 400 mothers answered questions about how much time their infants spent crying. (a) Crying was greatest during the first 3 months but declined with age. The largest drop occurred after 3 months. (b) During the first 9 months, crying peaked in the evening. (Adapted from St. James-Roberts & Halil, 1991.)

reared on Israeli kibbutzim.[1] Bedouin babies (whose mothers rush to them at the first whimper) fussed and cried the most during the first year, followed by infants living in homes, where adults are better able to respond promptly to a crying baby than on a kibbutz, where infants are cared for in groups (Landau, 1982).

In sum, no easy formula exists for how parents should respond to their infant's cries. The conditions that prompt crying are complex, and parents must make reasoned choices about what to do on the basis of culturally accepted practices, the suspected reason for the cry, and the context in which it occurs—for example, in the privacy of the parents' own home or while having dinner at a restaurant. In addition, maternal characteristics influence responsiveness to infant crying. Mothers who, in a laboratory situation, reported that they had a great deal of control over the crying of an artificial baby (whose quieting was unrelated to the mother's behaviour) had difficulty detecting subtle changes in cry sounds, engaged in less sensitive infant care, and had babies who developed into uncooperative toddlers (Donovan, Leavitt, & Walsh, 1997, 2000). The internal state of these mothers—who reacted defensively when they couldn't calm the artificial baby—seemed to interfere with their ability to cope effectively with infant crying.

As Figure 4.2 shows, infant crying is greatest during the first 3 months, and through most of the first year it peaks in the evenings. Because these trends appear in many cultures with vastly different infant care practices, researchers believe that babies' normal difficulties in readjusting the sleep–waking cycle as the central nervous system develops, not parents' attention, are responsible (Barr et al., 1991, 1996). Fortunately, with age, crying declines and occurs more often for psychological (demands for attention, expressions of frustration) than physical reasons. Both ethological and behaviourist investigators would agree that parents can lessen older babies' need to cry by encouraging more mature ways of expressing their desires, such as gestures and vocalizations.

*Abnormal Crying.* Like reflexes and sleep patterns, the infant's cry offers a clue to central nervous system distress. The cries of brain-damaged babies and those who have experienced prenatal and birth complications are often shrill, piercing, and shorter in duration than those of healthy infants (Boukydis & Lester, 1998; Green, Irwin, & Gustafson, 2000).

---

[1]A *kibbutz* (plural: *kibbutzim*) is an Israeli cooperative agricultural settlement in which children are reared communally, freeing both parents for full participation in the economic life of the society.

Even neonates with a fairly common problem—colic, or persistent crying—tend to have high-pitched, harsh, and turbulent-sounding cries (Zeskind & Barr, 1997). Although the cause of colic is unknown, some researchers believe it is due to disturbed brain regulation of sleep–wake cycles (Papousek & Papousek, 1996). Others think it is a temporary difficulty in calming down after becoming upset, which subsides between 3 and 6 months of age (Barr & Gunnar, 2000).

The abnormal cries of at-risk infants prompt a rise in parental heart rate—a physiological response to threat (Bryan & Newman, 1988). Most parents try to respond with extra care and sensitivity, but sometimes the cry is so unpleasant and the infant so difficult to soothe that parents become frustrated, resentful, and angry. Preterm and ill babies are more likely to be abused by their parents, who frequently mention a high-pitched, grating cry as one factor that caused them to lose control and harm the baby (Frodi, 1985).

## NEONATAL BEHAVIOURAL ASSESSMENT

A variety of instruments permit doctors, nurses, and researchers to assess the behaviour of newborn babies. The most widely used of these tests, T. Berry Brazelton's **Neonatal Behavioural Assessment Scale (NBAS),** looks at the baby's reflexes, state changes, responsiveness to physical and social stimuli, and other reactions (Brazelton & Nugent, 1995). A major goal is to evaluate the infant's ability to initiate caregiver support and to adjust his or her behaviour to avoid being overwhelmed by stimulation.

The NBAS has been given to many infants around the world. As a result, researchers have learned a great deal about individual and cultural differences in newborn behaviour and how child-rearing practices can maintain or change a baby's reactions. For example, NBAS scores of Asian and Native-American babies reveal that they are less irritable than Caucasian infants. Mothers in these cultures often encourage their babies' calm dispositions through swaddling, close physical contact, and nursing at the first signs of discomfort (Chisholm, 1989; Freedman & Freedman, 1969; Murett-Wagstaff & Moore, 1989). In contrast, the poor NBAS scores of undernourished infants in Zambia, Africa, are quickly changed by the way their mothers care for them. The Zambian mother carries her baby about on her hip all day, providing a rich variety of sensory stimulation. As a result, by 1 week, a once unresponsive newborn has been transformed into an alert, contented baby (Brazelton, Koslowski, & Tronick, 1976).

Can you tell from these examples why a single NBAS score is not a good predictor of later development? Since newborn behaviour and parenting styles combine to influence development, *changes in NBAS scores* over the first week or two of life (rather than a single score) provide the best estimate of the baby's ability to recover from the stress of birth. NBAS "recovery curves" predict intelligence with moderate success well into the preschool years (Brazelton, Nugent, & Lester, 1987).

Similar to women in the Zambian culture, this Inuit mother of Nunavut carries her baby about all day, providing close physical contact and a rich variety of stimulation.

The NBAS has also been used to help parents get to know their infants. In some hospitals, health professionals discuss with or demonstrate to parents the newborn capacities assessed by the NBAS. Parents of both preterm and full-term newborns who participate in these programs interact more confidently and sensitively with their babies (Eiden & Reifman, 1996). In one study, Brazilian mothers who experienced a 50-minute NBAS-based discussion a few days after delivery were more likely than controls receiving only health care information to establish eye contact, smile, vocalize, and soothe in response to infant signals a month later (Wendland-Carro, Piccinini, & Millar, 1999). Although lasting effects on development have not been demonstrated, NBAS-based interventions are useful in helping the parent–infant relationship get off to a good start.

**Neonatal Behavioural Assessment Scale (NBAS)**
A test developed to assess the behavioural status of the newborn.

## LEARNING CAPACITIES

*Learning* refers to changes in behaviour as the result of experience. Babies come into the world with built-in learning capacities that permit them to profit from experience immediately. Infants are capable of two basic forms of learning, which were introduced in Chapter 1: classical and operant conditioning. In addition, they learn through their natural preference for novel stimulation. Finally, shortly after birth, babies learn by observing others; they can imitate the facial expressions and gestures of adults.

**CLASSICAL CONDITIONING.** Newborn reflexes make **classical conditioning** possible in the young infant. In this form of learning, a new stimulus is paired with a stimulus that leads to a reflexive response. Once the baby's nervous system makes the connection between the two stimuli, the new stimulus produces the behaviour by itself.

Recall from Chapter 1 that Russian physiologist Ivan Pavlov first demonstrated classical conditioning in his famous research with dogs (see page 19). Classical conditioning is of great value to human infants, as well as other animals, because it helps them recognize which events usually occur together in the everyday world. As a result, they can anticipate what is about to happen next, and the environment becomes more orderly and predictable (Rovee-Collier, 1987). Let's take a closer look at the steps of classical conditioning.

Imagine a mother who gently strokes her infant's forehead each time she settles down to nurse the baby. Soon the mother notices that each time the baby's forehead is stroked, he makes active sucking movements. The infant has been classically conditioned. Here is how it happened (see Figure 4.3):

1. Before learning takes place, an **unconditioned stimulus (UCS)** must consistently produce a reflexive, or **unconditioned, response (UCR).** In our example, the stimulus of sweet breast milk (UCS) resulted in sucking (UCR).

2. To produce learning, a *neutral stimulus* that does not lead to the reflex is presented at about the same time as the UCS. Ideally, the neutral stimulus should occur just before the UCS. The mother stroked the baby's forehead as each nursing period began. Therefore, the stroking (neutral stimulus) was paired with the taste of milk (UCS).

3. If learning has occurred, the neutral stimulus by itself produces a response similar to the reflexive response. The neutral stimulus is then called a **conditioned stimulus (CS),** and the response it elicits is called a **conditioned response (CR).** We know that the baby has been classically conditioned because stroking his forehead outside the feeding situation (CS) results in sucking (CR).

If the CS is presented alone enough times, without being paired with the UCS, the CR will no longer occur. In other words, if the mother strokes the infant's forehead again and again without feeding him, the baby will gradually stop sucking in response to stroking. This is referred to as **extinction.**

Young infants can be classically conditioned most easily when the association between two stimuli has survival value. They learn quickly in the feeding situation, since learning which stimuli regularly accompany feeding improves the infant's ability to get food and survive (Blass, Ganchrow, & Steiner, 1984). In contrast, some responses are very difficult to classically condition in young babies. Fear is one of them. Until infants have the motor skills to escape unpleasant events, they do not have a biological need to form these associations. But after 6 months of age, fear is easy to condition, as seen in the famous example of little Albert, conditioned by John Watson to withdraw and cry at the sight of a furry white rat. Return to Chapter 1, page 19, to review this well-known study. Then test your knowledge of classical conditioning by identifying the UCS, UCR, CS, and CR in Watson's study. In Chapter 10, we will discuss the development of fear, as well as other emotional reactions, in detail.

**classical conditioning**
A form of learning that involves associating a neutral stimulus with a stimulus that leads to a reflexive response.

**unconditioned stimulus (UCS)**
In classical conditioning, a stimulus that leads to a reflexive response.

**unconditioned response (UCR)**
In classical conditioning, a reflexive response that is produced by an unconditioned stimulus (UCS).

**conditioned stimulus (CS)**
In classical conditioning, a neutral stimulus that through pairing with an unconditioned stimulus (UCS) leads to a new, conditioned response (CR).

**conditioned response (CR)**
In classical conditioning, a new response produced by a conditioned stimulus (CS) that resembles the unconditioned response (UCR).

**extinction**
In classical conditioning, decline of the conditioned response (CR), as a result of presenting the conditioned stimulus (CS) enough times without the unconditioned stimulus (UCS).

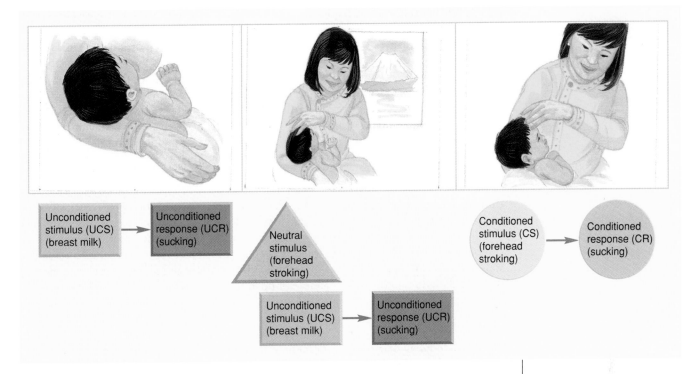

FIGURE 4.3

**The steps of classical conditioning.** The example here shows how a mother classically conditioned her baby to make sucking movements by stroking his forehead at the beginning of feedings.

**OPERANT CONDITIONING.** In classical conditioning, babies build expectations about stimulus events in the environment, but their behaviour does not influence the stimuli that occur. In **operant conditioning,** infants act (or operate) on the environment, and stimuli that follow their behaviour change the probability that the behaviour will occur again. A stimulus that increases the occurrence of a response is called a **reinforcer.** Removing a desirable stimulus or presenting an unpleasant one to decrease the occurrence of a response is called **punishment.**

Because the young infant can control only a few behaviours, successful operant conditioning in the early weeks of life is limited to head-turning and sucking responses. However, many stimuli besides food can serve as reinforcers. For example, researchers have created special laboratory conditions in which the baby's rate of sucking on a nipple produces a variety of interesting sights and sounds. Newborns will suck faster to see visual designs or to hear music and human voices (Floccia, Christophe, & Bertoncini, 1997).

Even preterm babies seek reinforcing stimulation. In one study, they increased their contact with a soft teddy bear that "breathed" quietly at a rate reflecting the infant's respiration, whereas they decreased their contact with a nonbreathing bear (Thoman & Ingersoll, 1993). The infants seemed biologically motivated to snuggle against the breathing bear because of its soothing, rhythmic movements, which induced restful sleep. As these findings suggest, operant conditioning has become a powerful tool for finding out what stimuli babies can perceive and which ones they prefer.

As infants get older, operant conditioning includes a wider range of responses and stimuli. For example, researchers have hung mobiles over the cribs of 2- to 6-month-olds. When the baby's foot is attached to the mobile with a long cord, the infant can, by kicking, make the mobile turn. Under these conditions, it takes only a few minutes for the infant to start kicking vigorously (Rovee-Collier, 1999; Shields & Rovee-Collier, 1992). As we will see shortly, this technique has yielded important information about infant memory. And as Chapter 6 will reveal, it has also been used to study babies' ability to group similar stimuli into categories.

Operant conditioning soon modifies parents' and infants' reactions to each other. As the baby gazes into the adult's eyes, the adult looks and smiles back, and then the infant looks and smiles again. The behaviour of each partner reinforces the other, and both continue their

**operant conditioning**
A form of learning in which a spontaneous behaviour is followed by a stimulus that changes the probability that the behaviour will occur again.

**reinforcer**
In operant conditioning, a stimulus that increases the occurrence of a response.

**punishment**
In operant conditioning, removing a desirable stimulus or presenting an unpleasant one to decrease the occurrence of a response.

pleasurable interaction. In Chapter 10, we will see that this contingent responsiveness plays a role in the development of infant–caregiver attachment.

Recall from Chapter 1 that classical and operant conditioning originated with behaviourism, an approach that views the child as a relatively passive responder to environmental stimuli. If you look carefully at the findings just described, you will see that young babies are active learners; they use any means they can to explore and control their surroundings, in an effort to meet their needs for rest, nutrition, stimulation, and social contact (Rovee-Collier, 1996). In fact, when infants' environments are so disorganized that their behaviour does not lead to predictable, satisfying outcomes, serious difficulties ranging from intellectual retardation to apathy and depression can result (Cicchetti & Aber, 1986; Seligman, 1975).

**HABITUATION.** At birth, the human brain is set up to be attracted to novelty. **Habituation** refers to a gradual reduction in the strength of a response due to repetitive stimulation. Looking, heart rate, and respiration rate may all decline, indicating a loss of interest. Once this has occurred, a new stimulus—some kind of change in the environment—causes responsiveness to return to a high level, an increase called **recovery**. For example, when you walk through a familiar space, you notice things that are new and different, such as a recently purchased picture on the wall or a piece of furniture that has been moved. Habituation and recovery enable us to focus our attention on those aspects of the environment we know least about. As a result, learning is more efficient.

*Clues to Early Attention and Memory.* By studying infants' habituation and recovery, researchers can explore their understanding of the world. For example, a baby who first habituates to a visual pattern (a photo of a baby) and then recovers to a new one (a photo of a bald man) appears to remember the first stimulus and perceive the second one as new and different from it. This method, illustrated in Figure 4.4, provides a marvellous window into infant attention, perception, and memory. It can be used with newborn babies, even those who are preterm. It has even been used to study the fetus's sensitivity to external stimuli—for example, by measuring changes in fetal heart rate when various repeated sounds are presented (Hepper, 1997).

Habituation research reveals that young babies discriminate and remember a wide variety of sights, sounds, and smells. However, preterm and newborn babies require a long time to habituate and recover to novel visual stimuli—about 3 or 4 minutes. By 4 or 5 months, infants process information more efficiently, requiring as little as 5 to 10 seconds to take in a complex visual stimulus and recognize it as different from a previous one. Yet a fascinating exception to this trend exists. Two-month-olds actually take longer to habituate to novel visual forms than do newborns and older infants (Slater et al., 1996). Later we will see that 2 months is also

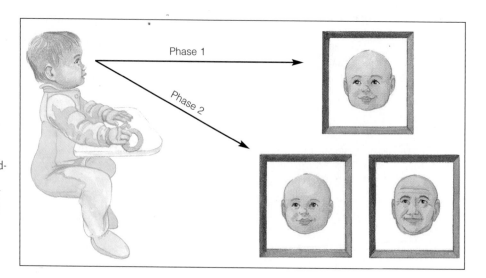

**FIGURE** 4.4

**Example of how the habituation–recovery sequence can be used to study infant perception and memory.** In Phase 1, infants are shown (habituated to) a photo of a baby. In Phase 2, infants are again shown the baby photo, but this time it appears alongside a photo of a bald-headed man. Infants dishabituated to (spent more time looking at) the photo of the man, indicating that they remembered the baby and perceived the man's face as different from it. (Adapted from Fagan & Singer, 1979.)

Phase 1

Phase 2

a time of dramatic gains in visual perception. Perhaps when young babies are first able to perceive certain information, they require more time to take it in (Johnson, 1996).

An important contributor to the long habituation times of young babies is their difficulty disengaging attention from very bright, patterned stimuli, even when they try to do so (Posner et al., 1997). Just as important as attending to a stimulus is the ability to shift attention from one stimulus to another. By 4 months, infants' attention becomes more flexible—a change believed to be due to development of brain structures controlling eye movements (Hood et al., 1996).

### *Limitations of Habituation Research.*

Habituation research reveals that infants gradually make finer distinctions among visual stimuli and remember them longer—at 3 months, for about 24 hours; by the end of the first year, for several days and, in the case of some stimuli (such as a photo of the human face), even weeks (Fagan, 1973; Pascalis, de Haan, & Nelson, 1998). Yet findings of habituation studies are not clear-cut. When looking, sucking, or heart rate declines and recovers, exactly what babies know about the stimuli to which they responded is not always clear. Some researchers argue that infants' understanding is best revealed through their more active efforts to master their environment (Rovee-Collier, 2001). Consistent with this view, when compared with studies that rely on active exploration of objects, habituation research greatly underestimates infants' memory.

Recall the operant conditioning research in which infants learned to make a mobile move by kicking. In a series of studies, Carolyn Rovee-Collier found that 2- to 3-month-olds remember how to activate the mobile 1 week after training, and with a prompt (the experimenter briefly rotates the mobile for the baby), as long as 4 weeks. By 6 months of age, retention increases to 2 weeks and, with prompting, to 6 weeks (Rovee-Collier, 1999; Rovee-Collier & Bhatt, 1993). Around the middle of the first year, operant conditioning tasks in which babies control stimulation by manipulating buttons, switches, or levers work well for studying memory. When infants and toddlers were shown how to press a lever to make a toy train move around a track, duration of memory continued to increase with age; 13 weeks after training, 18-month-olds remembered how to press the lever (Hartshorn et al., 1998b).

These findings also highlight a curious feature of infant memory, not revealed in habituation research. During the first 6 months, memory is highly *context dependent*. If 2- to 6-month-olds are not tested in the same situation in which they were trained—with the same mobile and crib bumper and in the same room—they remember poorly (Hayne & Rovee-Collier, 1995). After 12 months, the importance of context declines. Toddlers remember how to make the toy train move, even when its features are altered and testing takes place in a different room (Hartshorn et al., 1998a; Hayne, Boniface, & Barr, 2000). As babies move on their own and experience frequent changes in context, their memory becomes increasingly context-free. They can apply learned responses more flexibly, generalizing them to relevant new situations.

### *Habituation/Recovery and Later Mental Development.*

Although habituation and recovery to visual stimuli offer a limited view of early memory, they are among the best available infant predictors of intelligence in childhood and adolescence. Correlations between the speed of these responses and the IQs of 3- to 18-year-olds consistently range from the .30s to the .60s (McCall & Carriger, 1993; Sigman, Cohen, & Beckwith, 1997). Habituation and recovery seem to be an especially effective early index of intelligence because they assess quickness of thinking, a characteristic of bright individuals. They also tap basic cognitive processes—attention, memory, and response to novelty—that underlie intelligent behaviour at all ages (Colombo, 1995; Rose & Feldman, 1997).

So far, we have considered only one type of memory—*recognition*. It is the simplest form of memory because all babies have to do is indicate (by looking, kicking, or pressing a lever) whether a new stimulus is identical or similar to a previous one. *Recall* is a second, more challenging form of memory, since it involves remembering something not present. Can infants engage in recall? By the end of the first year, they can, since they find hidden objects and imitate the actions of others hours or days after they first observed the behaviour. We will take up recall in Chapter 7.

**habituation**
A gradual reduction in the strength of a response due to repetitive stimulation.

**recovery**
Following habituation, increase in responsiveness to a new stimulus.

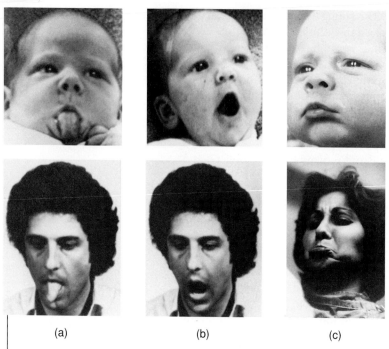

(a)       (b)       (c)

**FIGURE 4.5**

**Photographs from two of the first studies of newborn imitation.** Those on the left show 2- to 3-week-old infants imitating tongue protrusion (a), and mouth opening (b). The one on the right shows a 2-day-old infant imitating a sad (c) adult facial expression. (From A. N. Meltzoff & M. K. Moore, 1977, "Imitation of Facial and Manual Gestures by Human Neonates," *Science, 198,* p. 75; and T. M. Field et al., 1982, "Discrimination and Imitation of Facial Expressions by Neonates," *Science, 218,* p. 180. Copyright 1977 and 1982, respectively, by the AAAS. Reprinted by permission.)

**NEWBORN IMITATION.** Newborn babies come into the world with a primitive ability to learn through **imitation**—by copying the behaviour of another person. For example, Figure 4.5 shows infants from 2 days to several weeks old imitating adult facial expressions (Field et al., 1982; Meltzoff & Moore, 1977). The newborn's capacity to imitate extends to certain gestures, such as head movements, and has been demonstrated in many ethnic groups and cultures (Meltzoff & Kuhl, 1994).

But a few studies have failed to reproduce these findings (see, for example, Anisfeld et al., 2001). And imitation is more difficult to induce in babies 2 to 3 months old than just after birth. Therefore, some investigators regard the capacity as little more than an automatic response that declines with age, much like a reflex. Others claim that newborns imitate diverse facial expressions and head movements with apparent effort and determination, even after short delays—when the adult is no longer demonstrating the behaviour (Butterworth, 1999). Furthermore, these investigators argue that imitation does not decline, as reflexes do. Babies several months old often do not imitate an adult's behaviour right away because they instead try to play social games they are used to in face-to-face interaction—smiling, cooing, and waving their arms. When an adult models a gesture repeatedly, however, older babies soon get down to business and imitate (Meltzoff & Moore, 1992).

According to Andrew Meltzoff and Keith Moore (1999), newborns imitate in much the same way we do—by actively trying to match body movements they "see" with ones they "feel" themselves make. Later in this chapter, we will encounter evidence that young infants are surprisingly good at coordinating information across sensory systems. Still, Meltzoff and Moore's view of newborn imitation as a flexible, voluntary capacity is highly controversial.

As we will see in Chapter 6, a baby's ability to imitate improves greatly over the first 2 years. But however limited it is at birth, imitation is a powerful means of learning. Using imitation, young infants explore their social world, getting to know people by matching behavioural states with them. In the process, babies notice similarities between their own actions and those of others, and they start to find out about themselves. Furthermore, by tapping into infants' ability to imitate, adults can get infants to express desirable behaviours, and once they do, adults can encourage these further. Finally, caregivers take great pleasure in a baby who imitates their facial gestures and actions. Newborn imitation clearly seems to be another capacity that helps get the infant's relationship with parents off to a good start.

## ASK YOURSELF

**review**   What functions does REM sleep serve in young infants? When newborns awaken, about how much time do they spend crying? Can sleep and crying tell us about the health of the baby's central nervous system? Explain.

**review**   Provide an example of classical conditioning, operant conditioning, and habituation/recovery in young infants. Why is each type of learning useful? Cite differences between habituation and operant conditioning research on infant memory, and explain them.

**apply**   After a difficult birth, 2-day-old Kelly scored poorly on the NBAS. How would you address her mother's concerns that Kelly might not develop normally?

**connect**   Provide several examples of how the diverse capacities of newborns contribute to their first social relationships.

# Motor Development in Infancy

VIRTUALLY ALL PARENTS EAGERLY AWAIT mastery of new motor skills, recording with pride when their infants hold up their heads, reach for objects, sit by themselves, and walk alone. Parents' enthusiasm for these achievements makes perfect sense. They are, indeed, milestones of development. With each new motor skill, babies master their bodies and the environment in a new way. For example, sitting alone grants infants an entirely different perspective on the world. Voluntary reaching permits babies to find out about objects by acting on them. And when infants can move on their own, their opportunities for exploration multiply.

Babies' motor achievements have a powerful impact on their social relationships. For example, once infants can crawl, parents start to restrict their activities by saying "no" and expressing mild anger and impatience. Walking often brings first "testing of wills" (Biringen et al., 1995). Despite her parents' warnings, one newly walking 12-month-old continued to pull items from shelves that were "off limits." "I said not to do that!" her mother remarked as she repeatedly took the infant by the hand and redirected her activities.

At the same time, parents increase their expressions of affection and playful activities as their independently moving baby seeks them out for greetings, hugs, and a gleeful game of hide-and-seek (Campos, Kermoian, & Zumbahlen, 1992). Certain motor skills, such as reaching and pointing, permit infants to communicate more effectively. Finally, babies' delight—laughing, smiling, and babbling—as they work on new motor competencies triggers pleasurable reactions in others, which encourage infants' efforts further (Mayes & Zigler, 1992). Motor skills, emotional and social competencies, cognition, and language develop together and support one another.

## THE SEQUENCE OF MOTOR DEVELOPMENT

*Gross motor development* refers to control over actions that help infants get around in the environment, such as crawling, standing, and walking. In contrast, *fine motor development* has to do with smaller movements, such as reaching and grasping. The Milestones table on page 140 shows the average ages at which a variety of motor skills are achieved.

Notice that the table also presents the age ranges during which the majority of infants accomplish each skill. Although the *sequence* of motor development is fairly uniform, large individual differences exist in rate of development. Also, a baby who is a late reacher is not necessarily going to be a late crawler or walker. We would be concerned about a child's development only if many motor skills were seriously delayed.

Look at the table once more, and you will see organization and direction in infants' motor achievements. First, motor control of the head comes before control of the arms and trunk, which comes before control of the legs. This head-to-tail sequence is called the **cephalocaudal trend.** Second, motor development proceeds from the centre of the body outward, in that head, trunk, and arm control is advanced over coordination of the hands and fingers. This is the **proximodistal trend.** Physical growth follows these same trends during the prenatal period, infancy, and childhood (see Chapter 5). These similarities between physical and motor development suggest a genetic contribution to motor progress.

But we must be careful not to think of motor skills as isolated, unrelated accomplishments that follow a fixed, maturational timetable. Instead, each motor skill is a product of earlier motor attainments and a contributor to new ones. Furthermore, children acquire motor skills in highly individual ways. For example, most babies crawl before they pull to a stand and walk. Yet one infant I know, who disliked being placed on her tummy but enjoyed sitting and being held upright, pulled to a stand and walked before she crawled!

Many influences—both internal and external to the child—support the vast transformations in infants' motor competencies. The dynamic systems perspective, introduced in Chapter 1 (see page 29), helps us understand how motor development takes place.

**imitation**
Learning by copying the behaviour of another person. Also called *modelling* or *observational learning*.

**cephalocaudal trend**
An organized pattern of physical growth and motor control that proceeds from head to tail.

**proximodistal trend**
An organized pattern of physical growth and motor control that proceeds from the centre of the body outward.

# milestones

## GROSS AND FINE MOTOR DEVELOPMENT IN THE FIRST 2 YEARS

| MOTOR SKILL | AVERAGE AGE ACHIEVED | AGE RANGE IN WHICH 90 PERCENT OF INFANTS ACHIEVE THE SKILL |
|---|---|---|
| When held upright, holds head erect and steady | 6 weeks | 3 weeks–4 months |
| When prone, lifts self by arms | 2 months | 3 weeks–4 months |
| Rolls from side to back | 2 months | 3 weeks–5 months |
| Grasps cube | 3 months, 3 weeks | 2–7 months |
| Rolls from back to side | 4 1/2 months | 2–7 months |
| Sits alone | 7 months | 5–9 months |
| Crawls | 7 months | 5–11 months |
| Pulls to stand | 8 months | 5–12 months |
| Plays pat-a-cake | 9 months, 3 weeks | 7–15 months |
| Stands alone | 11 months | 9–16 months |
| Walks alone | 11 months, 3 weeks | 9–17 months |
| Builds tower of two cubes | 13 months, 3 weeks | 10–19 months |
| Scribbles vigorously | 14 months | 10–21 months |
| Walks up stairs with help | 16 months | 12–23 months |
| Jumps in place | 23 months, 2 weeks | 17–30 months |
| Walks on tiptoe | 25 months | 16–30 months |

*Note:* These milestones represent overall age trends. Individual differences exist in the precise age at which each milestone is attained.

*Sources:* Bayley, 1969, 1993.

## MOTOR SKILLS AS DYNAMIC SYSTEMS

According to **dynamic systems theory of motor development,** mastery of motor skills involves acquiring increasingly complex *systems of action.* When motor skills work as a *system,* separate abilities blend together, each cooperating with others to produce more effective ways of exploring and controlling the environment. For example, control of the head and upper chest are combined into sitting with support. Kicking, rocking on all fours, and reaching are gradually put together into crawling. Then crawling, standing, and stepping are united into walking alone (Thelen, 1989).

Each new skill is a joint product of the following factors: (1) central nervous system development; (2) movement possibilities of the body; (3) goals the child has in mind; and (4) environmental supports for the skill. Change in any element makes the system less stable, and the child starts to explore and select new, more effective motor patterns.

The factors that induce change vary with age. In the early weeks of life, brain and body growth are especially important as infants achieve control over the head, shoulders, and upper torso. Later, the baby's goals (getting a toy or crossing the room) and environmental supports (parental encouragement, objects in the infants' everyday setting) play a greater

**dynamic systems theory of motor development**
A theory that views new motor skills as reorganizations of previously mastered skills that lead to more effective ways of exploring and controlling the environment. Each new skill is a product of central nervous system development, movement possibilities of the body, the goal the child has in mind, and environmental supports for the skill.

role. The broader physical world also has a profound impact on motor skills. For example, if children were reared in the moon's reduced gravity, they would prefer jumping to walking or running!

When a skill is first acquired, it is tentative and unstable. Infants must refine it so it becomes smooth and accurate. For example, one baby just starting to crawl often collapsed on her tummy and ended up moving backward instead of forward. Gradually, she figured out how to propel herself along by alternately pulling with her arms and pushing with her feet. As she experimented with muscle patterns and observed the consequences of her movements, she perfected the crawling motion (Adolph, Vereijken, & Denny, 1998). Her efforts fostered the growth of new synaptic connections in the brain that govern motor activity.

Look carefully at dynamic systems theory, and you will see why motor development cannot be a genetically predetermined process. Since exploration and the desire to master new tasks motivate it, heredity can map it out only at a very general level. Instead of behaviours being *hardwired* into the nervous system, they are *softly assembled* (Hopkins & Butterworth, 1997; Thelen & Smith, 1998). This means that each skill is acquired by revising and combining earlier accomplishments into a more complex system that permits the child to reach a desired goal. Consequently, different paths to the same motor skill exist.

**DYNAMIC MOTOR SYSTEMS IN ACTION.** To study infants' mastery of motor milestones, researchers have conducted *microgenetic studies* (see Chapter 2, page 61), following babies from their first attempts at a skill until it becomes smooth and effortless. Using this research strategy, Esther Thelen (1994) illustrated how infants acquire motor skills by modifying and reorganizing what the body can already do to fit a new task. She placed 3-month-old babies under a mobile attached to the baby's foot with a long cord. To produce the dazzling sight of the dancing mobile, infants quickly learned to kick with one foot or two feet in alternation.

Then Thelen changed the movement environment; she linked the babies' legs with a soft piece of elastic attached to ankle cuffs (see Figure 4.6). Although this permitted single- or alternate-leg kicking, it made kicking both legs in unison much more effective for activating the mobile. When the elastic was in place, infants gradually discovered the new motion. They began with a few tentative simultaneous kicks and, seeing the effects, replaced earlier movements with this new form. When the elastic was removed, infants quickly gave up the simultaneous pattern in favour of their previous behaviour. They readily experimented, revising their motor behaviour appropriately to fit changing conditions of the task.

As Thelen (1995) sums up, the desire to accomplish a task motivates change in motor behaviour. Then the new behaviour permits the child to reach new goals, and change occurs again. In sum, motor development results from infants' active problem-solving efforts.

**CULTURAL VARIATIONS IN MOTOR DEVELOPMENT.** Cross-cultural research demonstrates how early movement opportunities and a stimulating environment contribute to motor development. Several decades ago, Wayne Dennis (1960) observed infants in Iranian orphanages who were deprived of the tantalizing surroundings that motivate infants in most homes to acquire motor skills. The Iranian babies spent their days lying on their backs in cribs, without toys to play with. As a result, most did not move about on their own until after 2 years of age. When they finally did move, the constant experience of lying on their backs led them to scoot in a sitting position rather than crawl on their hands and knees. Because babies who scoot come

This baby pushes up with arms and legs in unison and then lifts one foot. Now he must combine these accomplishments with other motor skills into a more complex system that permits forward motion. To do so, he will experiment with muscle patterns, observe the consequences of his movements, and revise them, perfecting the crawling motion in his own individual way. A strong desire to explore and control the environment motivates his efforts.

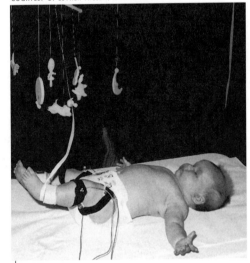

**FIGURE 4.6**

**A 3-month-old infant in the mobile study, with legs linked together by an elastic ankle cuff.** Consistent with dynamic systems theory, the baby revised previously learned motor acts into a more effective motor system for activating the mobile. In response to the cuff, he replaced single- and alternate-leg kicking with simultaneous kicks. (Courtesy of Esther Thelen, Indiana University.)

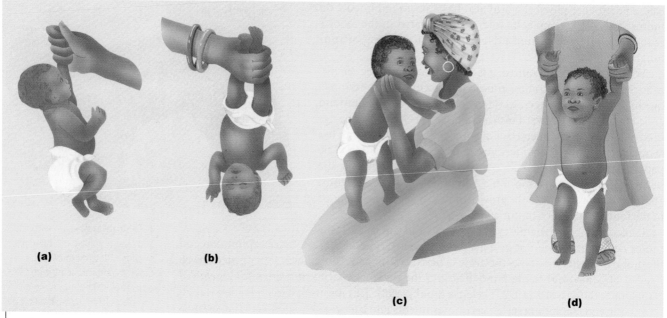

(a)     (b)                          (c)                    (d)

**FIGURE** 4.7

**West Indians of Jamaica use a formal handling routine with their babies.**   Exercises practised in the first few months include (a) stretching each arm while suspending the baby and (b) holding the infant upside-down by the ankles. Later in the first year, the baby is (c) "walked" up the mother's body and (d) encouraged to take steps on the floor while supported. (Adapted from B. Hopkins & T. Westra, 1988, "Maternal Handling and Motor Development: An Intracultural Study," *Genetic, Social and General Psychology Monographs, 14,* pp. 385, 388, 389. Reprinted with permission of the Helen Dwight Reid Educational Foundation. Published by Heldref Publications, 1319 Eighteenth Street, N.W., Washington, DC 20036-1802.)

up against objects such as furniture with their feet, not their hands, they are far less likely to pull themselves to a standing position in preparation for walking. Indeed, only 15 percent of the Iranian orphans walked by 3 to 4 years of age.

Cultural variations in infant-rearing practices also affect motor development. Take a quick survey of parents you know, asking this question: Should sitting, crawling, and walking be deliberately encouraged? Answers vary widely from culture to culture. Japanese mothers, for example, believe such efforts are unnecessary. Among the Zinacanteco Indians of southern Mexico, rapid motor progress is actively discouraged. Babies who walk before they know enough to keep away from cooking fires and weaving looms are viewed as dangerous to themselves and disruptive to others (Greenfield, 1992).

In contrast, among the Kipsigis of Kenya and the West Indians of Jamaica, babies hold their heads up, sit alone, and walk considerably earlier than do North American infants. Kipsigi parents deliberately teach these motor skills. In the first few months, babies are seated in holes dug in the ground, and rolled blankets are used to keep them upright. Walking is promoted by frequently bouncing babies on their feet (Super, 1981). The West Indians of Jamaica do not train their infants in specific skills. Instead, as Figure 4.7 shows, they use a highly stimulating, formal handling routine, explaining that exercise helps infants grow up strong, healthy, and physically attractive (Hopkins & Westra, 1988).

Putting together the evidence we have discussed so far, we must conclude that early motor development is due to complex transactions between nature and nurture. As dynamic systems theory suggests, heredity establishes the broad outlines of change. But the precise sequence and rate of change result from an ongoing dialogue between the brain, the body, and the physical and social environment.

## FINE MOTOR DEVELOPMENT: REACHING AND GRASPING

Of all motor skills, voluntary reaching may play the greatest role in infant cognitive development, since it opens up a whole new way of exploring the environment (Bushnell & Boudreau, 1993). By grasping things, turning them over, and seeing what happens when they are released, infants learn a great deal about the sights, sounds, and feel of objects.

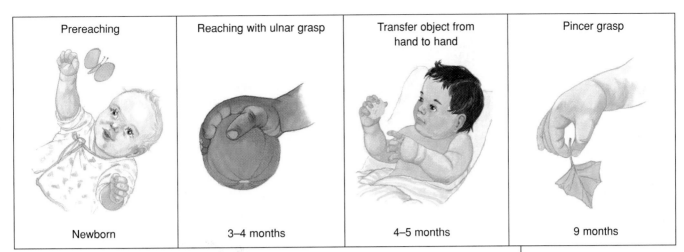

| Prereaching | Reaching with ulnar grasp | Transfer object from hand to hand | Pincer grasp |
|---|---|---|---|
| Newborn | 3–4 months | 4–5 months | 9 months |

**FIGURE** 4.8

**Some milestones of reaching and grasping.** The average age at which each skill is attained is given. (Ages from Bayley, 1969; Rochat & Goubet, 1995.)

The development of reaching and grasping provides an excellent example of how motor skills start out as gross, diffuse activity and move toward mastery of fine movements (refer to the milestones in Figure 4.8). Newborns try hard to bring their hand into the visual field (van der Meer, van der Weel, & Lee, 1995). And they make well-aimed but poorly coordinated swipes or swings, called **prereaching,** toward an object dangled in front of them. Because they cannot control their arms and hands, they rarely contact the object (Hofsten, 1982). Like newborn reflexes, prereaching drops out—around 7 weeks of age. Yet these early behaviours suggest that babies are biologically prepared to coordinate hand with eye in the act of reaching (Thelen, 2001).

**DEVELOPMENT OF REACHING AND GRASPING.** At about 3 months, as infants develop the necessary eye-gaze and head and shoulder postural control, reaching appears and gradually improves in accuracy (Bertenthal & Hofsten, 1998; Spencer et al., 2000). By 5 to 6 months, infants can reach for and grasp an object that has been darkened during the reach, by switching off either the room lights or the illumination within the object. By 9 months, infants can reach for a darkened object just as quickly and accurately as an object that remains visible (Clifton et al., 1994; McCarty & Ashmead, 1999). This indicates that reaching does not require visual guidance of the arms and hands. Instead, it is largely controlled by *proprioception,* our sense of movement and location in space, arising from stimuli within the body. Early on, vision is freed from the basic act of reaching so it can focus on more complex adjustments, such as fine-tuning actions to fit the distance and shape of objects.

Reaching improves as the baby gains greater control of body posture and of arm and hand movements. Around 5 months, babies reduce their efforts when an object is moved beyond their reach (Robin, Berthier, & Clifton, 1996; Yonas & Hartman, 1993). By 7 months, the arms become more independent; infants reach for objects with one arm, rather than extending both (Fagard & Pezé, 1997). Over the next few months, infants make better anticipatory arm and hand adjustments when trying to obtain moving objects—ones that spin, change direction, or move closer or farther away (Ashmead et al., 1993; Wentworth, Benson, & Haith, 2000).

Individual differences in movement styles affect how reaching is perfected (Thelen, Corbetta, & Spencer, 1996). Babies with large, forceful arm movements must make them less vigorous to reach for a toy successfully. Those with quiet, gentle actions must use more muscle power to lift and extend their arms (Thelen et al., 1993). Each infant builds the act of reaching uniquely by exploring the match between current movements and those demanded by the task (Thelen & Smith, 1998).

**prereaching**
The well-aimed but poorly coordinated primitive reaching movements of newborn babies.

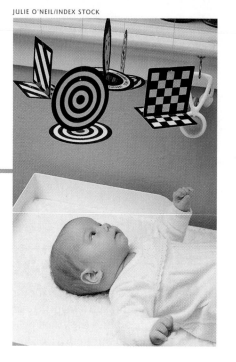

This 3-month-old baby looks at patterns hung over his crib that match his level of visual development. Research shows that a moderate amount of stimulation, tailored to the young baby's needs, results in earlier development of reaching. Either very little or excessive stimulation yields slower motor progress.

Once infants can reach, they start to modify their grasp. When the grasp reflex of the newborn period weakens at 3 to 4 months, it is replaced by the **ulnar grasp,** a clumsy motion in which the fingers close against the palm. Still, even 3-month-olds readily adjust their grasp to the size and shape of objects—a capacity that improves over the first year (Case-Smith, Bigsby, & Clutter, 1998; Newman, Atkinson, & Braddick, 2001). Around 4 to 5 months, when infants begin to master sitting, they no longer need their arms to maintain body balance. This frees both hands to explore objects. Babies of this age can hold an object in one hand while the other scans it with the tips of the fingers, and they frequently transfer objects from hand to hand (Rochat, 1992; Rochat & Goubet, 1995). By the latter part of the first year, infants use the thumb and index finger opposably in a well-coordinated **pincer grasp.** Then the ability to manipulate objects greatly expands. The 1-year-old can pick up raisins and blades of grass, turn knobs, and open and close small boxes.

Between 8 and 12 months, reaching and grasping are well practised. As a result, attention is released from coordinating the motor skill itself to events that occur before and after obtaining the object. As we will see in Chapter 6, around this time infants can first solve simple problems involving reaching, such as searching for and finding a hidden toy.

**EARLY EXPERIENCE AND REACHING.** As with other motor milestones, early experience affects voluntary reaching. In a well-known study, Burton White and Richard Held (1966) found that institutionalized babies provided with a moderate amount of visual stimulation—at first, simple designs and later, a mobile hung over their crib—reached for objects 6 weeks earlier than did infants given nothing to look at. A third group of babies provided with massive stimulation—patterned crib bumpers and mobiles at an early age—also reached sooner than unstimulated babies. But this heavy dose of enrichment took its toll. These infants looked away and cried a great deal, and they were not as advanced in reaching as the moderately stimulated group. White and Held's findings remind us that more stimulation is not necessarily better. Trying to push infants beyond their current readiness to handle stimulation can undermine the development of important motor skills.

**ulnar grasp**
The clumsy grasp of the young infant, in which the fingers close against the palm.

**pincer grasp**
The well-coordinated grasp emerging at the end of the first year, in which thumb and forefinger are used opposably.

## ASK YOURSELF

**review**    Cite evidence indicating that motor development is not hardwired into the brain but rather is a joint product of biological, psychological, and environmental factors.

**review**    Using an example, explain how infants acquire new motor skills by modifying and reorganizing what the body can already do to fit a new task.

**apply**    Roseanne hung mobiles and pictures above her newborn baby's crib and surrounded it with a brightly coloured, patterned bumper, hoping this would stimulate her infant's motor development. Is Roseanne doing the right thing? Why or why not?

**connect**    Provide several examples of how motor development influences infants' social experiences. How do social experiences, in turn, influence motor development?

# Perceptual Development in Infancy

THINK BACK TO WHITE AND HELD'S STUDY, described at the end of the previous section. It illustrates the close link between perception and action in discovering new skills. To reach for objects, maintain balance, or move across various surfaces, infants must continually coordinate their motor behaviour with perceptual information (Bertenthal, 1996). Acting and perceiving are not separate aspects of experience. Instead, motor activity provides infants with a vital means for exploring and learning about the world, and improved perception brings about more effective motor activity. The union of perceptual and motor information is basic to our nervous systems, and each domain supports development of the other (Bertenthal & Clifton, 1998).

What can young infants perceive with their senses, and how does perception change with age? Researchers have sought answers to these questions for two reasons:

■ *Infant perception is relevant to the age-old nature–nurture controversy.* Are infants born with an adultlike perception of the world, or must they acquire it through experience? As we will see shortly, newborns have an impressive array of perceptual capacities. Nevertheless, since improvements occur as the result of both maturation and experience, an appropriate resolution to the nature–nurture debate seems, once again, to lie somewhere between the two extremes.

■ *Infant perception sheds light on other areas of development.* For example, because touch, vision, and hearing permit us to interact with others, they are a basic part of emotional and social development. Through hearing, language is learned. And perception provides the foundation for cognitive development, since knowledge about the world is first gathered through the senses.

Studying infant perception is especially challenging because babies cannot describe their experiences. Fortunately, investigators can make use of a variety of nonverbal responses that vary with stimulation, such as looking, sucking, head turning, facial expressions, and reaching. Psychophysiological measures, such as changes in respiration and heart rate, are also used. And as we noted earlier, researchers sometimes take advantage of operant conditioning and the habituation/recovery sequence to find out whether infants can make certain discriminations. We will see many examples of these methods as we explore the baby's sensitivity to touch, taste, smell, sound, and visual stimulation.

## TOUCH

Touch is a fundamental means of interaction between parents and young babies. Within the first few days of life, mothers can recognize their own newborn by stroking the infant's cheek or hand, and fathers can do the same by stroking the infant's hand (Kaitz et al., 1993a, 1993b). Touch helps stimulate early physical growth (see Chapter 3), and it is vital for emotional development as well. Therefore it is not surprising that sensitivity to touch is well developed at birth. The reflexes listed in Table 4.1 on page 125 reveal that the newborn baby responds to touch, especially around the mouth, palms, and on the soles of the feet. During the prenatal period, these areas, along with the genitals, are the first to become sensitive to touch (Humphrey, 1978).

At birth, infants are quite sensitive to pain. If male newborns are circumcised, anaesthesia is sometimes not used because of the risk of giving pain-relieving drugs to a very young infant. Babies often respond with a high-pitched, stressful cry and a dramatic rise in heart rate, blood pressure, palm sweating, pupil dilation, and muscle tension (Jorgensen, 1999). Recent research establishing the safety of certain local anaesthetics for newborns promises to ease the pain of these procedures. Offering a nipple that delivers

Touch is a major means through which infants investigate their world. This 5-month-old explores her toes by running her lips and tongue over the surface. Then she is likely to remove her toes and take a good look at them. In the next few months, mouthing will give way to increasingly elaborate touching of objects with the hands.

© MICHAEL NEWMAN/PHOTOEDIT

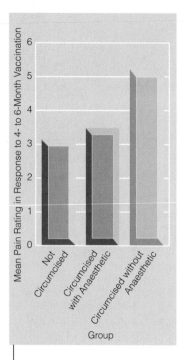

**FIGURE** 4.9

**Pain response to a 4- to 6-month routine vaccination of newborns not circumcised, circumcised with a local anaesthetic, and circumcised without anaesthetic (but given a placebo, or substance with no medication).** Pain ratings were made by an observer who had no knowledge of the infants' circumcision or medication status. Infants who had been circumcised without anaesthetic were rated as having a more intense pain response. (Adapted from Taddio et al., 1997.)

a sugar solution is also helpful; it quickly reduces crying and discomfort in young babies, preterm and full-term alike. And combining the sweet liquid with gentle holding by the parent lessens pain even more (Gormally et al., 2001; Overgaard & Knudsen, 1999). Allowing a newborn to endure severe pain can affect later behaviour. In one study, newborns not given a local anaesthetic during circumcision reacted more intensely to routine vaccination at 4 to 6 months of age than did their anaesthetized counterparts (see Figure 4.9) (Taddio et al., 1997). The Canadian Paediatric Society does not recommend routine circumcision, as the overall evidence for and against the procedure is evenly balanced, but it does endorse appropriate pain relief if a baby is circumcised (Canadian Paediatric Society, 1996).

When touching is pleasurable rather than painful, it enhances babies' responsiveness to the environment. In one study, an adult's soft caresses led babies to smile and become increasingly attentive to the adult's face (Stack & Muir, 1992). And even newborns use touch to investigate their world. They habituate to an object placed in their palms (by reducing their holding) and show recovery to a novel object, indicating that they can use touch to distinguish object shapes (Streri, Lhote, & Dutilleul, 2000). As reaching develops, babies frequently mouth novel objects, running their lips and tongue over the surface, after which they remove the object to take a good look at it. Exploratory mouthing peaks in the middle of the first year as hand–mouth contact becomes more accurate (Lew & Butterworth, 1997). Then it declines in favour of more elaborate touching with the hands, in which infants turn, poke, and feel the surface of things while looking at them intently (Ruff et al., 1992). In Chapter 6, we will see that Piaget regarded this hands-on manipulation of objects as essential for early cognitive development.

## TASTE AND SMELL

All infants come into the world with the ability to communicate their taste preferences to caregivers. Facial expressions reveal that newborns can distinguish several basic tastes. Much like adults, they relax their facial muscles in response to sweetness, purse their lips when the taste is sour, and show a distinct archlike mouth opening when it is bitter (Rosenstein & Oster, 1988; Steiner, 1979). These reactions are important for survival, since (as we will see in Chapter 5) the food that best supports the infant's early growth is the sweet-tasting milk of the mother's breast.

Salty taste develops differently from sweet, sour, or bitter. At birth, infants are either indifferent to or reject salty water (Mennella & Beauchamp, 1998). But by 4 months, they prefer the salty taste to plain water, a change that may prepare them to accept solid foods (Beauchamp et al., 1994). Furthermore, newborns can readily learn to like a taste that at first evoked either a neutral or negative response. For example, babies allergic to cow's-milk formula who are given a soy or other vegetable-based substitute (typically very strong and bitter-tasting) soon prefer it to regular formula. A taste previously disliked can come to be preferred when it is paired with relief of hunger (Harris, 1997).

Like taste, certain odour preferences are innate. For example, the smell of bananas or chocolate causes a relaxed, pleasant facial expression, whereas the odour of rotten eggs makes the infant frown (Steiner, 1979). Newborns can also identify the location of an odour and, if it is unpleasant, defend themselves by turning their heads in the other direction (Reiser, Yonas, & Wikner, 1976).

In many mammals, the sense of smell plays an important role in eating and in protecting the young from predators by helping mothers and babies identify each other. Although smell is less well developed in humans, traces of its survival value remain. Newborns given a choice between the smell of their own mother's amniotic fluid and that of another mother spend more time oriented toward the familiar fluid (Marlier, Schaal, & Soussignan, 1998). The smell of the mother's amniotic fluid is comforting; babies exposed to it cry less than do babies who are not (Varendi et al., 1998).

Immediately after birth, babies placed face down between their mother's breasts spontaneously latch on to a nipple and begin sucking within an hour. If one breast is washed to remove its natural scent, most newborns grasp the unwashed breast, indicating that they are guided by smell (Porter & Winberg, 1999). At 4 days of age, breast-fed babies prefer the smell

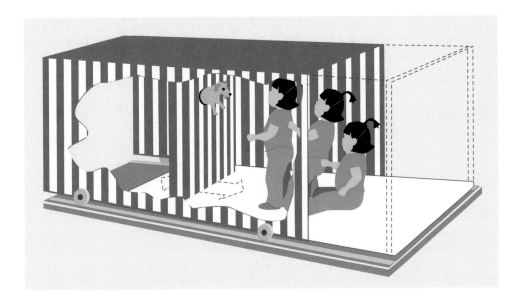

**FIGURE** 4.10

**The "moving room" used to test infants' sensitivity to balance and self-movement.** The front and side walls are mounted on wheels that roll on a track. This permits systematic variation of *optical flow* by moving the walls back and forth at different speeds. To make sure the infant faces forward, a box containing a mechanical dog who "comes alive" is located on the front wall. The figure shows a child falling backward as the front and side walls move toward her. This postural compensation occurs if the child perceives the optical flow as a forward sway of her body. To test 5- to 13-month-olds, a seat with pressure-sensitive receptors is used that measures backward and forward body sway. (From B. I. Bertenthal, J. L. Rose, & D. L. Bai, 1997, "Perception–Action Coupling in the Development of Visual Control of Posture," *Journal of Experimental Psychology: Human Perception and Performance,* 23, p. 1632. Copyright © 1997 by the American Psychological Association. Reprinted by permission.)

of their own mother's breast to that of an unfamiliar lactating mother (Cernoch & Porter, 1985). Bottle-fed babies orient to the smell of any lactating woman over the smells of formula or a nonlactating woman (Marlier & Schaal, 1997; Porter et al., 1992). Newborns' dual attraction to the odours of their mother and of the lactating breast helps them locate an appropriate food source and, in the process, begin to distinguish their caregiver from other people.

In sum, young babies are quite adept at making taste and odour discriminations. Unfortunately, little is known about how these two senses develop as the result of further brain maturation and experience.

## BALANCE AND SELF-MOVEMENT

To take in and make sense of their surroundings, infants must be able to balance the body, adjusting their movements so they remain in a steady position relative to the surface on which they are sitting or standing. Making these postural changes is so important that three sources of sensory information signal a need to adapt body position: (1) *proprioceptive stimulation,* arising from sensations in the skin, joints, and muscles; (2) *vestibular stimulation,* arising from the semicircular canals of the inner ear; and (3) *optical flow stimulation,* arising from movements in the visual field.

Research largely focuses on **optical flow,** since it can be manipulated easily. Consider how you use optical flow information. You sense that you are in motion when the entire visual field moves, and you make postural adjustments in accord with its direction and speed. For example, imagine yourself standing on a train pulling out of the station. Scenery flowing past you signals that you are moving. Your perceived direction (forward) is opposite the direction of optical flow, so you compensate by swaying backward to remain upright.

To examine infants' sense of balance and self-movement, researchers create conditions in the laboratory like those just described. Their findings reveal that even neonates adapt their head movements to optical flow (Jouen & Lepecq, 1989). As motor control improves, postural adjustments become more precise. In a series of studies, researchers placed 5- to 13-month-olds in a seat with pressure-sensitive receptors in the "moving room" shown in Figure 4.10. When the front and side walls of the room oscillated forward and backward, all infants displayed appropriate body movements. Between 5 and 9 months, as infants perfected sitting without support, their back-and-forth sway became more finely tuned to the optical-flow changes produced by oscillating walls of the moving room (Bertenthal, Rose, & Bai, 1997; Rose & Bertenthal, 1995).

Clearly, newborn babies have a built-in sense of balance that is refined with experience and motor control. Like adults', infants' postural adjustments to self-movement take place

**optical flow**
Movements in the visual field signalling that the body is in motion, leading to postural adjustments so the body remains upright.

unconsciously. This frees babies' attention for other pursuits, including motor skills and the auditory and visual attainments we are about to consider (Bertenthal, 1996; Bertenthal & Clifton, 1998). Balance is probably an innate capacity because it is fundamental to everything babies learn through exploration.

## HEARING

Newborn infants can hear a wide variety of sounds, but they are more responsive to some than to others. For example, they prefer complex sounds, such as noises and voices, to pure tones (Bench et al., 1976). In the first few days, infants can already tell the difference between a few sound patterns—a series of tones arranged in ascending and descending order; utterances with two versus three syllables; the stress patterns of words, such as *ma*-ma versus ma-*ma;* and happy-sounding speech as opposed to speech with angry, sad, or neutral emotional qualities (Bijeljac-Babic, Bertoncini, & Mehler, 1993; Mastropieri & Turkewitz, 1999; Sansavini, Bertoncini, & Giovanelli, 1997).

Over the first year, infants organize sounds into increasingly elaborate patterns. For example, between 4 and 7 months, they have a sense of musical and speech phrasing. They prefer Mozart minuets and sentences with pauses between natural phrases to those with awkward breaks (Hirsh-Pasek et al., 1987; Krumhansl & Jusczyk, 1990). And around 12 months, if two melodies differing only slightly are played, infants can tell that they are not the same (Morrongiello, 1986).

Responsiveness to sound provides support for the young baby's visual and tactile exploration of the environment. Infants as young as 3 days old turn their eyes and head in the general direction of a sound. By 4 months, they can reach fairly accurately toward a sounding object in the dark (Clifton et al., 1994). The ability to identify the precise location of a sound improves greatly over the first 6 months and shows further gains into the second year (Litovsky & Ashmead, 1997).

Neonates are particularly sensitive to the sounds of human speech, and they come into the world prepared to respond to the sounds of any human language. Young infants can make fine-grained distinctions among a wide variety of speech sounds—"ba" and "ga," "ma" and "na," and the short vowel sounds "a" and "i," to name just a few. For example, when given a nipple that turns on the "ba" sound, babies suck vigorously and then habituate. When the sound switches to "ga," sucking picks up, indicating that infants detect this subtle difference. Using this method, researchers have found only a few speech sounds that newborns cannot discriminate (Jusczyk, 1995). Their ability to perceive sounds not found in their own language is more precise than adults'.

As we will see in Chapter 9, babies are impressive *statistical analyzers* of the speech stream. They listen carefully to others' speech for frequently occurring sounds and relationships between sounds. By the middle of the first year, they start to "screen out" sounds not used in their own language (Kuhl et al., 1992; Polka & Werker, 1994). Soon after, they detect meaningful speech units, such as word and clause boundaries (Saffran, Aslin, & Newport, 1996). This sensitivity to language structure reveals that the baby is marvellously prepared for the awesome task of acquiring language.

Listen carefully to yourself the next time you talk to a young baby. You will probably speak in a high-pitched, expressive voice and use a rising tone at the ends of phrases and sentences. Adults probably communicate this way because they notice that infants are more attentive when they do so. Indeed, newborns prefer human speech with these characteristics (Aslin, Jusczyk, & Pisoni, 1998). They will also suck more on a nipple to hear a recording of their mother's voice than that of an unfamiliar woman, and to hear their native language as opposed to a foreign language (Moon, Cooper, & Fifer, 1993; Spence & DeCasper, 1987). These preferences may have developed from hearing the muffled sounds of the mother's voice before birth.

Infants' special responsiveness to speech probably encourages parents to talk to the baby. As they do so, both readiness for language and the emotional bond between caregiver and child are strengthened. By 3 months of age, infants pick up information about others' emotions through hearing. They can distinguish happy- from sad-sounding adult voices (Walker-Andrews & Grolnick, 1983).

# from research to practice

## IMPACT OF EARLY HEARING LOSS ON DEVELOPMENT: THE CASE OF OTITIS MEDIA

during his first year in child care, 18-month-old Alex caught five colds, had the flu on two occasions, and experienced repeated *otitis media* (middle ear infection). Alex is not unusual. By age 3, most Canadian children will have had at least one bout of otitis media according to the Canadian Paediatric Society (1996). Although antibiotics eliminate the bacteria responsible for otitis media, they do not reduce fluid buildup in the middle ear, which causes mild to moderate hearing loss that can last for weeks or months.

The incidence of otitis media is greatest between 6 months and 3 years, when children are first acquiring language. Frequent and prolonged infections predict delayed language progress, reduced task persistence, social isolation in early childhood, and poorer academic performance after school entry (Roberts et al., 2000; Rvachew et al., 1999; Vernon-Feagans, Manlove, & Volling, 1996).

How might otitis media disrupt language and academic progress? Difficulties in hearing speech sounds, particularly in noisy settings, may be responsible. Children with many bouts are less attentive to the speech of others and less persistent at tasks (Petinou et al., 2001; Roberts, Burchinal, & Campbell, 1994). Their distractibility may be due to repeated instances in which they could not make out what people around them were saying. When children have trouble paying attention, they may reduce the quality of others' interactions with them. In one study, mothers of preschoolers with frequent illnesses were less effective in teaching their child a task (Chase et al., 1995).

Current evidence strongly favours early prevention of otitis media, especially since the illness is so widespread. Crowded living conditions and exposure to cigarette smoke and other pollutants are linked to the disease—factors that probably account for its high incidence among low-income children. These factors may also account for the finding that Aboriginal children have more frequent and more severe bouts of otitis media than the rest of the Canadian child population (MacMillan et al., 2002). In addition, placement of infants and young children in child care creates opportunities for close contact, greatly increasing otitis media episodes.

Negative developmental outcomes of early otitis media can be prevented in the following ways:

■ *Preventive doses of xylitol, a sweetener derived from birch bark.* A Finnish study revealed that children in child-care centres given a daily dose of xylitol in gum or syrup form show a 30- to 40-percent drop in otitis media compared with controls receiving gum or syrup without the sweetener. Xylitol appears to have natural, bacteria-fighting ingredients (Uhari, Kontiokari, & Niemelä, 1998). However, dosage must be carefully monitored, since too much xylitol can cause abdominal pain and diarrhea.

■ *Frequent screening for the disease, followed by prompt medical intervention.* Plastic tubes that drain the inner ear are often used to treat chronic otitis media, although their effectiveness remains controversial.

■ *Child-care settings that control infection.* Because infants and young children often put toys in their mouths, these objects should be rinsed frequently with a disinfectant. Spacious, well-ventilated rooms and small group sizes also limit the spread of disease.

■ *Verbally stimulating adult–child interaction.* Developmental problems associated with otitis media are reduced or eliminated in responsive home environments and high-quality child-care centres. When caregivers are verbally stimulating and keep noise to a minimum, children have more opportunities to hear spoken language (Roberts, Burchinal, & Campbell, 1994; Roberts et al., 1998).

© BOB MAHONEY/THE IMAGE WORKS

High-quality child care reduces or eliminates language delays, social isolation, and later academic difficulties associated with frequent bouts of otitis media. These children profit from a verbally stimulating caregiver and a small group size, which ensures a relatively quiet environment where spoken language can be heard easily.

Because infants' acute sensitivity to sound supports many competencies, even mild hearing impairments that go untreated can endanger development. To find out more about this topic, read the From Research to Practice box, above. Before we turn to vision, consult the Milestones table on page 150 for a summary of the perceptual capacities we have just considered.

# milestones

## DEVELOPMENT OF TOUCH, TASTE, SMELL, BALANCE/SELF-MOVEMENT, AND HEARING

| AGE | TOUCH | TASTE AND SMELL | BALANCE/SELF-MOVEMENT | HEARING |
|---|---|---|---|---|
| Birth | • Is responsive to touch and pain<br><br>• Can distinguish objects placed in palm<br><br> | • Can distinguish sweet, sour, and bitter tastes; prefers sweetness<br><br>• Distinguishes odours; prefers those of sweet-tasting foods<br><br>• Prefers smell of own mother's amniotic fluid and the lactating breast | • Adapts head movements to optical flow<br><br> | • Prefers complex sounds to pure tones<br><br>• Can distinguish some sound patterns<br><br>• Recognizes differences between almost all speech sounds<br><br>• Turns in the general direction of a sound |
| 1–6 months |  | • Prefers salt solution to plain water<br><br>• Taste preferences can be easily changed through experience<br><br> | • As motor control improves, postural adjustments to optical flow become more precise<br><br> | • Organizes sounds into more complex patterns, such as musical phrases<br><br>• Can identify the location of a sound more precisely<br><br>• By the end of this period, begins to "screen out" speech sounds not used in own language |

*Note:* These milestones represent overall age trends. Individual differences exist in the precise age at which each milestone is attained.

## ■ VISION

Humans depend on vision more than any other sense for active exploration of the environment. Yet vision is the least mature of the newborn baby's senses. Visual structures in both the eye and the brain continue to develop after birth. For example, muscles of the *lens,* the part of the eye that permits us to adjust our focus to varying distances, are weak. Also, cells in the *retina,* the membrane lining the inside of the eye that captures light and transforms it into messages that are sent to the brain, are not as mature or densely packed as they will be in several months (Banks & Bennett, 1988). Furthermore, the optic nerve and other pathways that relay these messages, along with cells in the visual cortex that receive them, will not be adultlike for several years (Hickey & Peduzzi, 1987).

 **ACUITY AND COLOUR PERCEPTION.** Because visual structures are immature, newborn babies cannot focus their eyes very well. In addition, their **visual acuity,** or fineness of discrimination, is limited. At birth, infants perceive objects at a distance of 6 metres (20 feet) about as clearly as adults do at 122 metres (400 feet) (Gwiazda & Birch, 2001). Furthermore, unlike adults (who see nearby objects most clearly), newborn babies see *equally unclearly*

**visual acuity**
Fineness of visual discrimination.

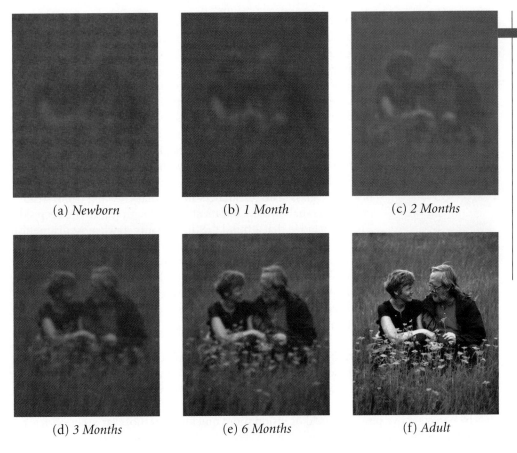

(a) *Newborn*  (b) *1 Month*  (c) *2 Months*

(d) *3 Months*  (e) *6 Months*  (f) *Adult*

**FIGURE 4.11**

**Young infants' view of a distant image from birth to 6 months of age.** To newborns, this image of two adults in a meadow appears as a grey blur. Vision improves steadily, reaching a near-adult level at 6 months. As you read about visual development, list all changes that contribute to the dramatic gain shown here. (From D. Y. Teller, 1997, "First Glances: The Vision of Infants," *Investigative Opthalmology and Visual Science, 38,* pp. 2198–2199. Reprinted by permission.)

across a wide range of distances (Banks, 1980). Distant images look much like the blur shown in Figure 4.11. And close-up people and objects are not much more distinct.

Although newborn infants cannot yet see well, they actively explore their environment by scanning it for interesting sights and tracking moving objects. However, their eye movements are slow and inaccurate. The visual system matures rapidly over the first few months. By 3 months, infants can focus on objects just as well as adults can. Visual acuity improves steadily throughout infancy. By 6 months, it reaches a near-adult level of about 20/20 (Gwiazda & Birch, 2001). Scanning and tracking also undergo rapid gains as eye movements increasingly come under voluntary control (Hofsten & Rosander, 1998; Johnson, 1995).

Colour perception is also refined in the early months. Although newborn babies prefer to look at coloured rather than grey stimuli, they are not yet good at discriminating colours. But pathways in the brain that process colour information mature rapidly, since 2-month-olds can discriminate colours across the entire spectrum (Adams & Courage, 1998; Teller, 1998). Russell Adams and Mary Courage (1998) of Memorial University of Newfoundland have found that infants' limited colour vision is due to generalized immaturities rather than specific immaturities in visual and neural functioning. By 4 to 5 months, they regard a particular colour as the same, even under very different lighting conditions (Dannemiller, 1989). Once colour sensitivity is well established, habituation research reveals that babies organize different hues into categories—red, blue, yellow, and green—just as adults do. Four-month-olds, for example, perceive two blues as more alike than a blue and a green (Catherwood, Crassini, & Freiberg, 1989). This grouping of colours is probably an innate property of the visual system, since young infants could not have learned through language that a certain range of hues is called by the same name.

As babies see more clearly and explore the visual field more adeptly, they figure out the characteristics of objects and how they are arranged in space. We can best understand how they do so by examining the development of three aspects of vision: depth, pattern, and object perception.

SCIENTIFIC AMERICAN

**FIGURE** 4.12

**The visual cliff.** Plexiglas covers the deep and shallow sides. By refusing to cross the deep side and showing a preference for the shallow surface, this infant demonstrates the ability to perceive depth. (*Scientific American*)

**visual cliff**
An apparatus used to study depth perception in infants. Consists of a Plexiglas-covered table and a central platform, from which babies are encouraged to crawl. Checkerboard patterns placed beneath the Plexiglas create the appearance of a shallow and deep side.

**kinetic depth cues**
Depth cues created by movements of the body or of objects in the environment.

**binocular depth cues**
Depth cues that rely on each eye receiving a slightly different view of the visual field; the brain blends the two images, creating three-dimensionality.

**pictorial depth cues**
Depth cues such as those that artists use to make a painting look three-dimensional, including receding lines, texture changes, and overlapping objects.

**DEPTH PERCEPTION.** Depth perception is the ability to judge the distance of objects from one another and from ourselves. It is important for understanding the layout of the environment and for guiding motor activity. To reach for objects, babies must have some sense of depth. Later, when infants crawl, depth perception helps prevent them from bumping into furniture and falling down staircases.

Figure 4.12 shows the well-known **visual cliff,** designed by Eleanor Gibson and Richard Walk (1960) and used in the earliest studies of depth perception. It consists of a Plexiglas-covered table with a platform at the centre, a "shallow" side with a checkerboard pattern just under the glass, and a "deep" side with a checkerboard several feet below the glass. The researchers found that crawling babies readily crossed the shallow side, but most reacted with fear to the deep side. They concluded that around the time infants crawl, most distinguish deep from shallow surfaces and avoid drop-offs that look dangerous.

Gibson and Walk's research shows that crawling and avoidance of drop-offs are linked, but it does not tell us how they are related or when depth perception first appears. To better understand the development of depth perception, investigators have turned to babies' ability to detect particular depth cues, using methods that do not require that they crawl.

*Development of Sensitivity to Depth Cues.* How do we know when an object is near rather than far away? Try these exercises to find out. Pick up a small object (such as your cup) and move it toward and away from your face. Did its image grow larger as it approached and smaller as it receded? When you next take a bike or car ride, notice that nearby objects move past your field of vision more quickly than those far away.

Motion provides a great deal of information about depth, and **kinetic depth cues** are the first to which infants are sensitive. Babies 3 to 4 weeks of age blink their eyes defensively when an object moves toward their face as if it is going to hit (Nánez, 1987; Nánez & Yonas, 1994). As they are carried about and as people and things turn and move before their eyes, infants learn more about depth. For example, by the time they are 3 to 4 months old, motion has helped them figure out that objects are not flat but three-dimensional (Arterberry, Craton, & Yonas, 1993).

**Binocular** (meaning two eyes) **depth cues** arise because our eyes have slightly different views of the visual field. The brain blends these two images but also registers the difference between them. To find out if infants are sensitive to binocular cues, researchers project two overlapping images before the baby, who wears special goggles to ensure that each eye receives one of the images. If babies use binocular cues, they perceive and visually track an organized, 3-dimensional form rather than see random dots. Results reveal that binocular sensitivity emerges between 2 and 3 months and improves rapidly over the first year (Birch, 1993). Infants soon make use of binocular cues in their reaching, adjusting arm and hand movements to match the distance of objects.

Last to develop are **pictorial depth cues**—the ones artists use to make a painting look three-dimensional. Examples are receding lines that create the illusion of perspective, changes in texture (nearby textures are more detailed than faraway ones), and overlapping objects (an object partially hidden by another object is perceived to be more distant). Studies in which researchers observe whether babies reach toward the closer-appearing parts of images containing pictorial cues reveal that 7-month-olds are sensitive to these cues, but 5-month-olds are not (Sen, Yonas, & Knill, 2001; Yonas et al., 1986).

*Explaining Sensitivity to Depth Cues.* Why does perception of depth cues emerge in the order just described? Researchers believe that kinetic sensitivity develops first (and may even be present at birth) because it provides the most dependable information about the location of objects and events (Kellman, 1993). Using motion-carried information, even neonates can protect themselves from harmful situations. For example, their capacity to

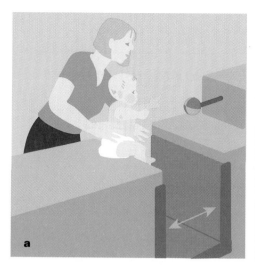 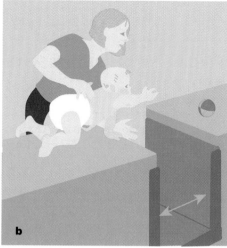

FIGURE 4.13

**Adjustable, shallow drop-off used to test 9-month-olds' detection of danger of falling.** The drop-off could be adjusted to see if infants would avoid leaning out at wide distances that would result in a fall. (a) In the sitting position, the parent (not shown) stood at the far side and coaxed the infant to reach for a toy attached to a rod. (b) In the crawling position, the parent coaxed the infant to reach for a toy on the far landing. In each case, an adult followed closely alongside to ensure the baby's safety. The infants, who were experienced sitters but novice crawlers, resisted leaning out at risky distances when in the sitting position. However, they readily headed over the edge in the crawling position. Babies must learn for each body position to use depth cues to detect threats to falling. (From K. E. Adolph, 2000, "Specificity of Learning: Why Infants Fall Over a Veritable Cliff," *Psychological Science, 11*, p. 292. Reprinted by permission.)

avoid approaching stimuli is adaptive. Their world is full of moving objects—blankets, toys, and their own hands—that could damage the delicate eye.

Motor development may also contribute to depth-cue sensitivity. For example, control of the head during the early weeks of life may help babies notice kinetic and binocular cues. And around 5 to 6 months, the ability to turn, poke, and feel the surface of objects may promote perception of pictorial cues as infants pick up information about size, texture, and shape (Bushnell & Boudreau, 1993). Indeed, as we will see next, research shows that one aspect of motor progress—the baby's ability to move about independently—plays a vital role in his everyday use of depth information.

**CRAWLING AND DEPTH PERCEPTION.** A mother I know described her newly crawling 9-month-old baby as a "fearless daredevil." "If I put April down in the middle of our bed, she crawls right over the edge," the mother exclaimed. "The same thing's happened by the stairs."

Will April become more wary of the side of the bed and the staircase as she becomes a more experienced crawler? Research suggests that she will. Infants with more crawling experience (regardless of when they start to crawl) are far more likely to refuse to cross the deep side of the visual cliff (Bertenthal, Campos, & Barrett, 1984).

What do infants learn from crawling that facilitates this coordination of action with depth information? According to Karen Adolph, from extensive everyday experience, babies gradually figure out how to use depth cues to detect danger of falling. But because the loss of postural control that leads to falling differs greatly for each body position, babies must undergo this learning separately for each posture. In one study, Adolph (2000) placed 9-month-olds, who were experienced "sitters" but novice "crawlers," on the edge of a shallow drop-off that could be widened (see Figure 4.13). While in the familiar sitting position, infants used depth information adaptively; they avoided leaning out for an attractive toy at distances likely to result in falling. But in the unaccustomed crawling posture, they headed over the edge, even when the distance was extremely wide! As infants discover how to avoid falling in diverse postures and situations, their understanding of depth expands.

Crawling experience promotes other aspects of three-dimensional understanding. For example, seasoned crawlers are better than their inexperienced agemates at remembering object locations and finding hidden objects (Bai & Bertenthal, 1992; Campos et al., 2000). Why does crawling make such a difference? Compare your experience of the environment when you are driven from one place to another as opposed to when you walk or drive yourself. When you move on your own, you are much more aware of landmarks and routes of travel, and you take more careful note of what things look like from different points of view. The same is true for infants.

Crawling promotes three-dimensional understanding, such as wariness of drop-offs and memory for object locations. As this baby crawls about, he takes note of how to get from place to place. Eventually, he will be able to remember where objects are in relation to himself and to other objects, and what they look like from different points of view.

# biology & environment

## DEVELOPMENT OF INFANTS WITH SEVERE VISUAL IMPAIRMENTS

esearch on infants who can see little or nothing at all dramatically
illustrates the interdependence of
vision, motor exploration, social interaction, and understanding of the
world. In a longitudinal study, infants
with a visual acuity of 20/800 or worse
(they had only dim light perception or
were blind) were followed through the
preschool years. Compared with agemates who had less severe visual
impairments, they showed serious
delays in all aspects of development—
motor, cognitive, language, and per-
sonal/social. Their motor and cognitive
functioning suffered the most; with
age, performance in both domains
became increasingly distant from that
of other children (Hatton et al., 1997).

What explains these profound
developmental delays? Minimal or
absent vision seems to alter the child's
experiences in at least two crucial,
interrelated ways:

### IMPACT ON MOTOR EXPLORATION AND SPATIAL UNDERSTANDING

Infants with severe visual impairments attain gross and fine motor

milestones many months later than do
their sighted counterparts (Levtzion-
Korach et al., 2000). For example, on
average, blind infants do not reach for
and engage in extensive manipulation
of objects until 12 months, crawl until
13 months, and walk until 19 months
(compare these averages with the
norms given in the Milestones table on
page 140). Why is this so?

Infants with severe visual impairments must rely entirely on sound to
identify the whereabouts of objects.
But sound does not function as a precise clue to object location until much
later than vision—around the middle
of the first year (see page 148). And
because infants who cannot see have
difficulty engaging their caregivers,
adults may not provide them with rich,
early exposure to sounding objects. As
a result, the baby comes to understand relatively late that there is a
world of tantalizing objects to explore.

Until "reaching on sound" is
achieved, infants with severe visual
impairments are not motivated to
move on their own. Even after they do
move, their coordination is poor due
to many months of inactivity and lack

of access to visual cues that assist
with balance (Prechtl et al., 2001;
Tröster & Brambring, 1993). Because
of their own uncertainty and parents'
protection and restraint to prevent
injury, blind infants are typically tentative in their movements. These factors delay motor development further.

Motor and cognitive development
are inextricably linked for infants with
little or no vision, even more than for
their sighted counterparts. These
babies build an understanding of the
location and arrangement of objects
in space only after reaching and crawling (Bigelow, 1992). Inability to imitate the motor actions of others
presents additional challenges as these
children get older, contributing to
declines in motor and cognitive
progress relative to peers with better
vision (Hatton et al., 1997).

### IMPACT ON THE CAREGIVER– INFANT RELATIONSHIP

Infants who see very poorly have
great difficulty evoking stimulating
caregiver interaction. They cannot
make eye contact, imitate, or pick up
nonverbal social cues. Their emotional

---

In fact, crawling promotes a new level of brain organization. While babies master crawling, EEG brain-wave activity in the cerebral cortex becomes more organized. Crawling may
strengthen certain neural connections, especially those involved in vision, motor planning,
and understanding of space (Bell & Fox, 1996). As the Biology & Environment box above
reveals, the link between independent movement and spatial knowledge is evident in a population with very different perceptual experience: infants with severe visual impairments.

**PATTERN PERCEPTION.**  Are young babies sensitive to the pattern, or form, of things
they see, and do they prefer some patterns? Early research revealed that even newborns prefer to look at patterned rather than plain stimuli—for example, a drawing of the human face
or one with scrambled facial features to a black-and-white oval (Fantz, 1961). As infants get
older, they prefer more complex patterns. For example, Canadian research demonstrates that
when shown black-and-white checkerboards, 3-week-old infants look longest at ones with
a few large squares, whereas 8- and 14-week-olds prefer those with many squares (Brennan,
Ames, & Moore, 1966). Infant preferences for many other patterned stimuli have been

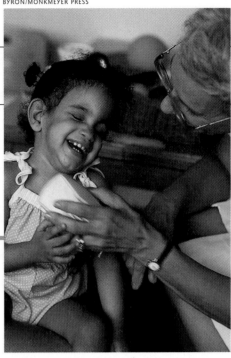

This 20-month-old, who has no vision, reacts with glee as her father guides her exploration of a novel object through touch and sound. Adults who encourage and reinforce children's efforts to make contact with their physical and social surroundings prevent developmental delays typically associated with severely impaired vision.

expressions are muted; for example, their smile is fleeting and unpredictable. Consequently, these infants may receive little adult attention, play, and other stimulation vital for all aspects of development (Tröster & Brambring, 1992).

When a visually impaired child does not learn how to participate in social interaction during infancy, communication is compromised in early childhood. In an observational study of blind children enrolled in preschools with sighted agemates, the blind children seldom initiated contact with peers and teachers. When they did interact, they had trouble interpreting the meaning of others' reactions and responding appropriately (Preisler, 1991, 1993).

### INTERVENTIONS

Although many infants and preschoolers with severe visual impairments are substantially delayed in development, considerable variation exists. Once language emerges and the child can rely on it for learning, some children with limited or no vision show impressive rebounds, eventually acquiring a unique capacity for abstract

thinking and social and practical skills that permit them to lead productive, independent lives (Warren, 1994).

Parents, teachers, and professional caregivers can help infants with minimal vision overcome early developmental delays. Especially important is stimulating, responsive interaction. Until a close emotional bond with an adult is forged, visually impaired babies cannot establish vital links with their environments.

Techniques that help infants focus attention and become aware of their physical and social surroundings include heightened sensory input through combining sound and touch (holding, touching, or bringing the baby's hands to the adult's face while talking or singing), engaging in many

repetitions, and consistently reinforcing the infant's efforts to make contact. Manipulative play with objects that make sounds is also vital (Fraiberg, 1977). These experiences facilitate "reaching on sound," which motivates independent movement. Finally, rich, descriptive language stimulation can compensate for visual loss (Conti-Ramsden & Pérez-Pereira, 1999). It grants young children a ready means of finding out about objects, events, and behaviours they cannot see.

---

tested—curved versus straight lines, connected versus disconnected elements, and whether the pattern is organized around a central focus (as in a bull's eye), to name just a few.

***Contrast Sensitivity.*** A general principle, called ***contrast sensitivity,*** explains these early pattern preferences (Banks & Ginsburg, 1985). Contrast refers to the difference in the amount of light between adjacent regions in a pattern. If babies are sensitive to (can detect) the contrast in two or more patterns, they prefer the one with more contrast.

To understand this idea, look at the two checkerboards in the top row of Figure 4.14 on page 156. To us, the one with many small squares has more contrasting elements. Now look at the bottom row, which shows how these checkerboards appear to infants in the first few weeks of life. Because of their poor vision, very young babies cannot resolve the small features in more complex patterns, so they prefer to look at the large, bold checkerboard. By 2 months of age, when detection of fine-grained detail has improved considerably, infants become sensitive to the greater contrast in complex patterns and spend more time looking at them. Contrast sensitivity continues to improve during infancy and childhood (Gwiazda & Birch, 2001; Teller, 1997).

**contrast sensitivity**
Ability to detect contrast, or differences in the amount of light between adjacent regions in a pattern.

**FIGURE** 4.14

**The way two checkerboards differing in complexity look to infants in the first few weeks of life.** Because of their poor vision, very young infants cannot resolve the fine detail in the more complex checkerboard. It appears blurred, like a grey field. The large, bold checkerboard appears to have more contrast, so babies prefer to look at it. (Adapted from M. S. Banks & P. Salapatek, 1983, "Infant Visual Perception," in M. M. Haith & J. J. Campos [Eds.], *Handbook of Child Psychology: Vol. 2. Infancy and Developmental Psychobiology* [4th ed.], New York: Wiley, p. 504. Copyright © 1983 by John Wiley & Sons. Reprinted by permission.)

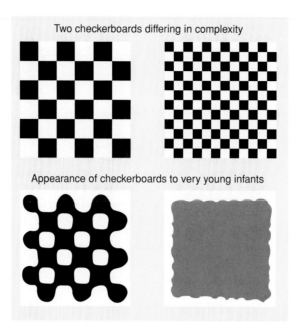

*Combining Pattern Elements.* In the early weeks of life, infants respond to the separate parts of a pattern. For example, when shown drawings of human faces, 1-month-olds limit their visual exploration to the border of the stimulus and stare at single, high-contrast features, such as the hairline or chin (see Figure 4.15). At about 2 months, when scanning ability and contrast sensitivity improve, infants thoroughly explore a pattern's internal features, pausing briefly to look at each salient part (Bronson, 1991).

Once babies can take in all aspects of a pattern, at 2 to 3 months they integrate them into a unified whole. By 4 months, they are so good at detecting pattern organization that they even perceive subjective boundaries that are not really present. For example, they perceive a square in the centre of Figure 4.16a, just as you do (Ghim, 1990). Older infants carry this responsiveness to subjective form even further. For example, 9-month-olds show a special preference for an organized series of moving lights that resembles a human being walking, in that they look much longer at this display than they do at upside-down or scrambled versions (Bertenthal, 1993). Although 3- to 5-month-olds can tell the difference between these patterns, they do not show a preference for one with both an upright orientation and a humanlike movement pattern (Bertenthal et al., 1985; Bertenthal et al., 1987).

By the end of the first year, infants extract meaningful patterns from very little information. For example, 12-month-olds can figure out an object's shape from a succession of partial views as it passes behind a small opening (Arterberry, 1993). They can also recognize a shape by watching a moving light trace its outline (Skouteris, McKenzie, & Day, 1992). Finally, 12-month-olds can detect objects represented by incomplete figures, even when as much as two-thirds is missing (see Figure 4.16b) (Rose, Jankowski, & Senior, 1997). A suggestive image is all older infants need to recognize a familiar form.

**FIGURE** 4.15

**Visual scanning of the pattern of the human face by 1- and 2-month-old infants.** One-month-olds limit their scanning to single features on the border of the stimulus, whereas 2-month-olds explore internal features. (From P. Salapatek, 1975, "Pattern Perception in Early Infancy," in L. B. Cohen & P. Salapatek [Eds.], *Infant Perception: From Sensation to Cognition,* New York: Academic Press, p. 201. Reprinted by permission.)

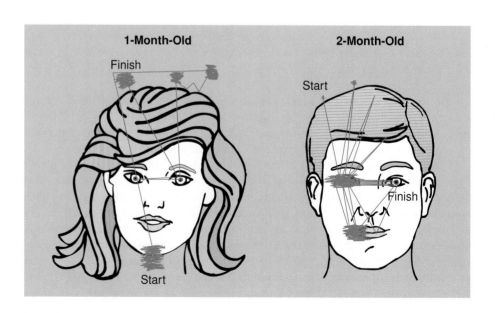

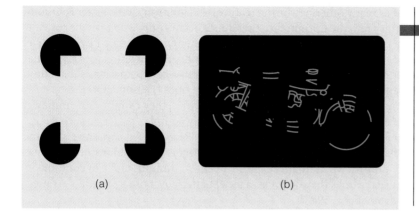

FIGURE 4.16

**Subjective boundaries in visual patterns.** (a) Do you perceive a square in the middle of the figure on the left? By 4 months of age, infants do, too. (b) What does the image on the right, missing two-thirds of its outline, look like to you? By 12 months, infants detect the image of a bicycle. After habituation to the incomplete bicycle image, they were shown an intact bicycle figure paired with a novel form. Twelve-month-olds recovered to (looked longer at) the novel figure, indicating that they recognized the bicycle pattern at right on the basis of very little visual information. (Adapted from Ghim, 1990; Rose, Jankowski, & Senior, 1997.)

*Explaining Changes in Pattern Perception.* Researchers believe that maturation of the visual system combined with exposure to a wide variety of stimuli underlie younger infants' increasing ability to detect more fine-grained pattern elements and integrated forms. As we saw earlier, visual acuity, scanning, and contrast sensitivity improve greatly during the first few months, supporting exploration of complex stimuli. Also, psychophysiological research on animals and humans reveals that brain cells respond to specific pattern stimuli, such as vertical, horizontal, and curved lines. The sensitivity and organization of these receptors improve from 6 weeks on as babies search for regularities in their rich, patterned external world (Gwiazda & Birch, 2001).

Besides gains in basic sensory processes, infants' expanding knowledge of their surroundings affects perception of complex patterns. As we will see in Chapter 6, 3-month-olds begin to categorize their world, extracting common properties of similar stimuli. Consider, for example, older infants' preference for a pattern of moving lights that corresponds to a person walking. From many occasions of observing people move, they build an image of the human gait as distinct from other stimuli (Pinto & Davis, 1991).

In sum, over time, infants' knowledge of familiar actions, objects, and events increasingly governs pattern sensitivity (Bertenthal, 1993). As we turn now to perception of the human face, we will see additional examples of this idea.

**FACE PERCEPTION.** Do babies have an innate tendency to orient toward human faces? Some researchers think so, on the basis of evidence indicating that newborns prefer to look at simple facelike stimuli with features arranged naturally (upright) rather than unnaturally (upside down or sideways) (see Figure 4.17a) (Mondloch et al., 1999; Valenza et al., 1996). Newborns also track a facial pattern moving across their visual field farther than they track other stimuli (Easterbrook et al., 1999; Johnson, 1999). And amazingly, they look longer at facial configurations judged by adults as attractive, compared with less attractive ones. This built-in preference may be the early origins of the widespread social bias favouring physically attractive people (Slater et al., 2000).

Some researchers claim that these behaviours reflect a built-in, adaptive capacity to orient toward members of

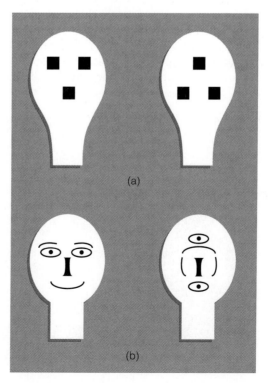

FIGURE 4.17

**Early face perception.**
(a) Newborns prefer to look at the simple pattern resembling a face on the left over the upside-down version on the right. This preference for a crude, facelike stimulus disappears by age 6 weeks. Researchers believe that it is innate, orients newborns toward people, and is supplanted by more complex perceptual learning as the cerebral cortex develops and visual capacities improve.
(b) When the complex face pattern on the left, and the equally complex, scrambled version on the right are moved across newborns' field of vision, they follow the face longer—another finding that suggests a built-in capacity to orient toward people. But present the two stimuli in a static display, and infants show no preference for the face until 2 to 3 months of age. (From Johnson, 1999; Mondloch et al., 1999.)

one's own species, just as many other newborn creatures do (Johnson, 2001; Slater & Quinn, 2001). In support of this view, the upright face preference occurs only when newborns view stimuli in the periphery of their visual field—an area of the retina governed by primitive, prewired brain centres (Cassia, Simion, & Umiltá, 2001). Still, other investigators argue that newborns are exposed to faces more often than other stimuli—early experience that could quickly "wire" the brain to detect faces and prefer attractive ones (Nelson, 2001).

Although newborns respond to a general, facelike structure, they cannot discriminate a complex, static image of the human face from other equally complex patterns, such as one with scrambled facial features (see Figure 4.17b on page 157). As noted earlier, very young infants' visual acuity is poor, and they do not carefully inspect the internal features of a static stimulus. At 2 to 3 months, when infants explore an entire stimulus and can combine its elements into an organized whole, they do prefer a facial pattern over other stimulus arrangements (Dannemiller & Stephens, 1988).

The baby's tendency to search for structure in a patterned stimulus is quickly applied to face perception. Between 1 and 2 months, babies recognize aspects of their mothers' facial features; they look longer at her face than at an unfamiliar woman's face (Bartrip, Morton, & de Schonen, 2001). By 3 months, infants make fine distinctions among the features of different faces. For example, they can tell the difference between the photos of two strangers, even when the faces are moderately similar (Morton, 1993). And between 7 and 10 months, infants start to perceive emotional expressions as meaningful wholes. They treat positive faces (happy and surprised) as different from negative ones (sad and fearful), even when these expressions are demonstrated in slightly varying ways by different models (Ludemann, 1991).

Extensive face-to-face interaction between infants and their caregivers undoubtedly contributes to the refinement of face perception. As we will see in Chapter 10, babies' developing sensitivity to the human face supports their earliest social relationships and helps regulate exploration of the environment in adaptive ways.

**OBJECT PERCEPTION.** Research on pattern perception involves only two-dimensional stimuli, but our environment is made up of stable, three-dimensional objects. Do young infants perceive a world of independently existing objects—knowledge essential for distinguishing the self, other people, and things?

*Size and Shape Constancy.* As we move around the environment, the images objects cast on our retina constantly change in size and shape. To perceive objects as stable and unchanging, we must translate these varying retinal images into a single representation.

**Size constancy**—perception of an object's size as stable, despite changes in the size of its retinal image—is evident in the first week of life. To test for it, researchers capitalized on the habituation response, using the procedure described and illustrated in Figure 4.18. Perception

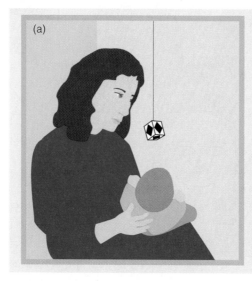
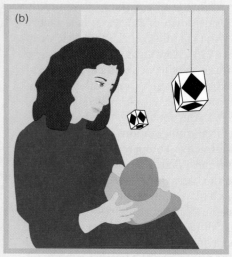

**FIGURE** 4.18

**Testing newborns for size constancy.** (a) First, infants were habituated to a small black-and-white cube at varying distances from the eye. In this way, the researchers hoped to desensitize babies to changes in the cube's retinal image size and direct their attention to its actual size. (b) Next, the small cube and a new, large cube were presented together, but at different distances so they cast the same size retinal image. All babies recovered to (looked much longer at) the novel large cube, indicating that they distinguish objects on the basis of actual size, not retinal image size. (Adapted from Slater, Mattock, & Brown, 1990.)

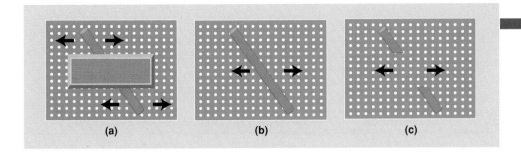

**FIGURE** 4.19

**Display used to test infants' ability to perceive object unity.** (a) Infants are habituated to a rod moving back and forth behind a box against a textured background. Next, they are shown (b) a complete rod or (c) a broken rod with a gap corresponding to the location of the box. Each of these stimuli is moved back and forth against a textured background, in the same way as the habituation stimulus. Infants 2 months of age and older typically recover to (look longer at) the broken rod than the complete rod. This suggests that they perceive the rod behind the box in the first display as a single unit. (Adapted from Johnson, 1997.)

of an object's shape as stable, despite changes in the shape projected on the retina, is called **shape constancy.** Habituation research reveals that it, too, is present within the first week of life, long before babies can actively rotate objects with their hands and view them from different angles (Slater & Johnson, 1999).

In sum, both shape and size constancy appear to be innate capacities that assist babies in detecting a coherent world of objects. Yet they provide only a partial picture of young infants' object perception.

*Perception of Object Unity.* As adults, we distinguish an object from its surroundings by looking for a regular shape and uniform texture and colour. Very young infants, however, are not sensitive to these indicators of an object's boundaries. At first, they rely heavily on motion and spatial arrangement to identify objects (Jusczyk et al., 1999; Kellman, 1996; Spelke & Hermer, 1996). When two objects are touching and either move in unison or stand still, babies younger than 4 months cannot distinguish them. Infants, of course, are fascinated by moving objects; they almost always prefer a moving stimulus to an identical stationary one. As they track a moving object, they pick up additional information about the object's boundaries, such as shape, colour, and texture.

For example, as Figure 4.19 reveals, after 2 months of age, babies realize that a moving rod whose centre is hidden behind a box is a complete rod rather than two rod pieces. Motion, a textured background, alignment of the top and bottom of the rod, and a small box (so most of the rod is visible) are necessary for 2- to 4-month-olds to infer object unity; they cannot do so without all these cues to heighten the distinction between objects in the display (Johnson & Aslin, 1996). As infants become familiar with many objects and can integrate each object's diverse features into a unified whole, they rely more on shape, colour, and texture and less on motion (Cohen & Cashon, 2001; Johnson, 1997). Babies as young as 4½ months can distinguish two touching objects on the basis of their features in very simple, easy-to-process situations (Needham, 1998, 2001). In the second half of the first year, this capacity extends to more complex displays of objects.

The Milestones table on page 160 provides an overview of the vast changes that take place in visual perception during the first year. Up to this point, we have considered the sensory systems one by one. Now let's examine their coordination.

## INTERMODAL PERCEPTION

When we take in information from the environment, we often use **intermodal perception.** That is, we combine information from more than one *modality,* or sensory system. For example, we know that the shape of an object is the same whether we see it or touch it, that lip movements are closely coordinated with the sound of a voice, and that dropping a rigid object on a hard surface will cause a sharp, banging sound. Research reveals that from the start, babies perceive the world in an intermodal fashion (Meltzoff, 1990; Spelke, 1987).

Recall that newborns turn in the general direction of a sound, and they reach for objects in a primitive way. These behaviours suggest that infants expect sight, sound, and touch to go together. Experiencing the integration of sensory modalities in these ways prepares young babies for detecting the wealth of intermodal associations that pervade their everyday worlds (Slater et al., 1999).

**size constancy**
Perception of an object's size as stable, despite changes in the size of its retinal image caused by changes in distance.

**shape constancy**
Perception of an object's shape as stable, despite changes in the shape of its retinal image when seen from different vantage points.

**intermodal perception**
Perception that combines information from more than one modality, or sensory system.

# milestones

## VISUAL DEVELOPMENT IN INFANCY

| AGE | ACUITY, COLOUR PERCEPTION, FOCUSING, AND EXPLORATION | DEPTH PERCEPTION | PATTERN PERCEPTION | OBJECT PERCEPTION |
|---|---|---|---|---|
| Birth–1 month | ♪ Visual acuity is 20/600<br><br>♪ Scans the visual field and tracks moving objects | ♪ Responds to kinetic depth cues | ♪ Prefers large, bold patterns<br><br>♪ Scans the outskirts of a pattern and focuses on single features<br><br>♪ Prefers to look at simple, facelike stimuli and to track a facial pattern<br><br>♪ Prefers to look at attractive facial patterns over less attractive ones | ♪ Displays size and shape constancy |
| 2–3 months | ♪ Has adultlike focusing ability<br><br>♪ Perceives colours across entire spectrum | ♪ Responds to binocular depth cues | ♪ Prefers patterns with finer details<br><br>♪ Thoroughly scans internal pattern features<br><br>♪ Begins to perceive overall pattern structure<br><br>♪ Prefers complex, static image of a face<br><br>♪ Recognizes mother's face and distinguishes features of different faces | ♪ Uses motion and spatial arrangement to identify objects |
| 4–5 months | ♪ Organizes colours into categories like those of adults | ♪ Sensitivity to binocular depth cues improves | ♪ Detects subjective boundaries in patterns | ♪ Uses kinetic cues to perceive objects as three-dimensional<br><br>♪ Uses shape, colour, and texture to identify objects |
| 6–8 months | ♪ Visual acuity improves to near 20/100<br><br>♪ Scans visual field and tracks moving objects more efficiently | ♪ Responds to pictorial depth cues<br><br>♪ Avoids crawling over deep side of visual cliff | | |
| 9–12 months | | | ♪ Can extract pattern information in the absence of a full image (from a moving light or partial picture)<br><br>♪ Perceives patterns (such as human walking movements and facial expressions of emotion) as meaningful wholes | |

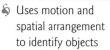

Note: These milestones represent overall age trends. Individual differences exist in the precise age at which each milestone is attained.

Within a few months infants make impressive intermodal matches. Lorraine Bahrick (1983) showed 3- and 4-month-olds two films side by side, one with two blocks banging and the other with two sponges being squashed together. At the same time, the soundtrack for only one of the films (either a sharp banging noise or a soft squashing sound) could be heard. Infants looked at the film that went with the soundtrack, indicating that they detected commonalities in what they saw and heard. In similar research, 4-month-olds related the shape and tempo of a child's or an adult's moving lips to the corresponding sounds in speech (Bahrick, Netto, & Hernandez-Reif, 1998). And 7-month-olds united emotional expressions across modalities, matching a happy- or angry-sounding voice with the appropriate face of a speaking person (Soken & Pick, 1992).

Of course, many intermodal associations, such as the way a train sounds or a teddy bear feels, must be based on direct exposure. Yet even newborns acquire these relationships remarkably quickly, often after just one contact with a new situation (Morrongiello, Fenwick, & Chance, 1998). In addition, when researchers try to teach intermodal matches by pairing sights and sounds that do not naturally go together, babies will not learn them (Bahrick, 1988, 1992).

How does intermodal perception begin so early and develop so quickly? Young infants seem biologically primed to focus on intermodal information. They better detect changes in stimulation that occur simultaneously in two modalities (sight and sound) than those that occur in only one (Lewkowicz, 1996). Furthermore, detection of *amodal relations*—for example, the synchrony and common tempo and rhythm in the sight and sound of clapping hands—precedes and may provide a basis for detecting other intermodal matches (Bahrick, 2001). Finally, early parent–infant interaction presents the baby with a rich context—consisting of many concurrent sights, sounds, touches, and smells—for expanding her intermodal knowledge (Lickliter & Bahrick, 2000). Intermodal perception is yet another capacity that illustrates infants' active efforts to build an organized, predictable world.

## UNDERSTANDING PERCEPTUAL DEVELOPMENT

Now that we have reviewed the development of infant perceptual capacities, how can we put together this diverse array of amazing achievements? Eleanor and James Gibson's **differentiation theory** provides widely accepted answers.

According to the Gibsons, infants actively search for **invariant features** of the environment—those that remain stable—in a constantly changing perceptual world. For example, in pattern perception, at first babies are confronted with a confusing mass of stimulation. But very quickly, they search for features that stand out along the border of a stimulus and orient toward images that crudely represent a face. Soon they explore internal features, noticing stable relationships between those features. As a result, they detect patterns, such as squares and complex faces. The development of intermodal perception also reflects this principle. For example, babies seek out invariant relationships—at first a common tempo and rhythm in concurrent sights and sounds, later more detailed associations—that unite information across different modalities.

The Gibsons use the word *differentiation* (meaning analyze or break down) to describe their theory because over time, the baby detects finer and finer invariant features among stimuli. In addition to pattern perception and intermodal perception, differentiation applies to depth and object perception. Recall how in each, sensitivity to motion precedes awareness of detailed stationary cues. So one way of understanding perceptual development is to think of it as a built-in tendency to search for order and stability in the surrounding world, a capacity that becomes increasingly fine-tuned with age (Gibson, 1970; Gibson, 1979).

Acting on the environment is vital in perceptual differentiation. According to the Gibsons, perception is guided by discovery of **affordances**—the action possibilities a situation offers an organism with certain motor capabilities (Gibson, 2000). As adults, we know when an object can be squeezed, bounced, or rolled and when a surface is appropriate for sitting or walking. Sensitivity to these affordances makes our actions future oriented and largely successful rather than reactive and blundering. Consequently, we spend far less time correcting ineffective actions than we otherwise would.

**differentiation theory**
The view that perceptual development involves the detection of increasingly fine-grained, invariant features in the environment.

**invariant features**
Features that remain stable in a constantly changing perceptual world.

**affordances**
The action possibilities a situation offers an organism with certain motor capabilities. Discovery of affordances plays a major role in perceptual differentiation.

**FIGURE** 4.20

**Acting on the environment plays a major role in perceptual differentiation.** Crawling and walking change the way babies perceive a steeply sloping surface. The newly crawling infant on the left plunges headlong down a steeply sloping surface. He has not yet learned that it affords the possibility of falling. The toddler on the right, who has been walking for more than a month, approaches the slope cautiously. Experience in trying to remain upright but frequently tumbling over has made him more aware of the consequences of his movements. He perceives the incline differently than he did at a younger age.

Infants discover affordances as they act on their world. To illustrate, let's consider how infants' changing capabilities for independent movement affect their perception. When babies start to crawl and again when they begin to walk, they gradually realize that a steeply sloping surface *affords the possibility* of falling (see Figure 4.20). With added weeks of practising each skill, they hesitate to crawl or walk down a risky incline. Experience in trying to keep their balance on various surfaces seems to make crawlers and walkers more aware of the consequences of their movements. Crawlers come to detect when surface slant places so much body weight on their arms that they will fall forward, walkers when an incline shifts body weight so their legs and feet can no longer hold them upright (Adolph, 1997; Adolph & Eppler, 1998, 1999). Each skill leads infants to perceive surfaces in new ways that guide their current means of moving about the environment. As a result, infants act more competently. Can you think of other links between motor milestones and perceptual development described in this chapter?

At this point, it is only fair to note that some researchers believe babies do more than make sense of experience by searching for invariant features and discovering affordances. They also *impose meaning* on what they perceive, constructing categories of objects and events in the surrounding environment. We have seen the glimmerings of this cognitive point of view in this chapter. For example, older babies *interpret* a familiar face as a source of pleasure and affection and a pattern of blinking lights as a moving human being. We will save our discussion of infant cognition for later chapters, acknowledging for now that the cognitive perspective also has merit in understanding the achievements of infancy. In fact, many researchers combine these two positions, regarding infant development as proceeding from a perceptual to a cognitive emphasis over the first year of life (Haith & Benson, 1998; Mandler, 1998).

## ASK YOURSELF

**review**   According to differentiation theory, perceptual development reflects infants' active search for invariant features. Provide examples from research on hearing, pattern perception, and intermodal perception.

**review**   Using research on crawling, show how motor and perceptual development support one another.

**review**   Do changes in pattern perception illustrate how infant development proceeds from a perceptual to a cognitive emphasis? Explain.

**apply**   After several weeks of crawling, Benji learned to avoid going head-first down a steep incline. Now he has started to walk. Can his mother trust him not to try walking down the steep surface? Explain, using the concept of affordances.

**connect**   Illustrate how operant conditioning and habituation/recovery permit researchers to find out about infants' sensitivity to touch, taste, smell, sound, and visual stimulation. Cite examples for each sense.

# Early Deprivation and Enrichment: Is Infancy a Sensitive Period of Development?

THROUGHOUT THIS CHAPTER, we have discussed how a variety of early experiences affect the development of perceptual and motor skills. In view of the findings already reported, it is not surprising that many investigations have found that stimulating physical surroundings and warm caregiving that is responsive to infants' self-initiated efforts promote active exploration of the environment and earlier achievement of developmental milestones (see, for example, Bendersky & Lewis, 1994; Bradley et al., 1989).

The powerful effect of early experience is dramatically apparent in the development of infants who lack the rich, varied stimulation of normal homes. Babies reared in severely deprived family situations or institutions remain substantially below average in physical and psychological development and display behaviour and emotional problems throughout childhood (Fujinaga et al., 1990; Johnson, 2000). These findings indicate that early experience has a profound impact, but they do not tell us that infancy is a *sensitive period*. That is, if babies do not experience appropriate stimulation of their senses in the first year or two of life, can they ever fully recover? This question is highly controversial. Recall from Chapter 1 that some theorists argue that early experience leaves a lasting imprint on the child's competence. Others believe that most developmental delays, and the events that led up to them, can be overcome.

For ethical reasons, we cannot deliberately deprive some infants of normal rearing experiences and wait to observe the long-term consequences. However, natural experiments, in which children are victims of deprived early environments but are later exposed to stimulating, sensitive care, provide the best available test of whether infancy is a sensitive period. If the sensitive period hypothesis is correct, then the effects of deprivation during infancy should persist, even when children are moved into enriched settings.

Research on Eastern European orphanage children consistently shows that the earlier infants are removed from deprived conditions, the greater their catch-up in development. Elinor Ames and Lucy LeMare of Simon Fraser University and others followed the progress of children transferred between birth and 5 years from Romanian orphanages to adoptive families in British Columbia. On arrival, most of the children displayed delays in fine and gross motor skills, as well as social and linguistic development (Fisher, Ames et al., 1997). Within 10 years of being adopted, the developmental catch-up for the children was impressive, although it was not as great as for those adopted after 4 months of age. These children scored lower in IQ than did Romanian children adopted in the first 4 months of life. That Romanian children adopted before age 4 months were similar in IQ to a control group of Canadian-born children suggests that they completely recovered from severe early deprivation (LeMare et al., 2001). Michael Rutter and his colleagues (1998) in Great Britain conducted similar research comparing the IQs of Romanian children adopted at various ages with British children adopted before age 6 months (see Figure 4.21 on page 164). The research in Canada and Great Britain suggests full recovery from severe deprivation is possible with early intervention.

When infants spend the first 2 years or more in deprived institutional care, all domains of development usually remain greatly delayed (Johnson, 2000). Furthermore, abnormal development in one domain often impedes progress in others. For example, parents of adopted orphanage children often report visual impairments. A frequent problem is *strabismus* (commonly known as *crossed eyes*)—a condition in which the eyes, because of muscle weakness in one or both, do not

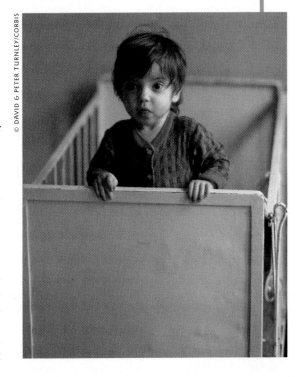

This boy has spent his first 2 years in a Romanian orphanage, with little adult contact and stimulation. The longer he remains in a barren environment, the more he will withdraw and wither and display permanent impairments in all domains of development.

© DAVID & PETER TURNLEY/CORBIS

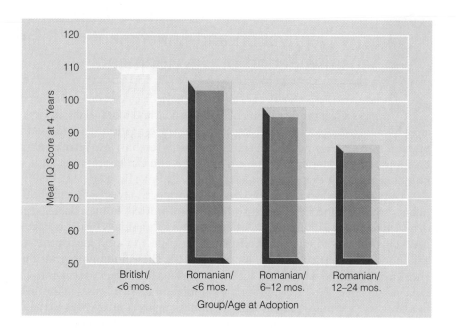

FIGURE 4.21

**IQs of Romanian 4-year-olds who varied in age of entry into British adoptive families, compared with British 4-year-olds adopted before age 6 months.** Romanian children adopted in the first 6 months of life scored nearly as well as their British counterparts, suggesting that they had fully recovered from extreme early deprivation. Romanian children adopted after 6 months of age did not score as well. The older they were, the lower their scores. (Adapted from Rutter et al., 1998.)

converge on the same point in space (Johnson et al., 1996). Untreated infants, for whom strabismus persists longer than a few months, show abnormalities in the brain's visual structures and permanent deficits in visual acuity, depth perception, tracking of moving objects, and perception of the spatial layout of the environment (Tychsen, 2001). Also, the bland, colourless rooms where orphanage infants spend their lonely days, rarely touched or spoken to, lead to deficits in intermodal perception (Cermak & Daunhauer, 1997). Children who have trouble integrating information across modalities tend to be overwhelmed by stimulation, reacting to it with disorganized behaviour or withdrawal. As a result, motor, cognitive, and social development suffers.

Unfortunately, many infants reared in underprivileged environments—whether homes or institutions—continue to be affected by disadvantaged conditions during their childhood years. As we will see in later chapters, interventions that try to break this pattern by training caregivers to engage in warm, stimulating interaction and by providing infants with environmental enrichment have lasting cognitive and social benefits. One of the most important outcomes is that withdrawn, apathetic babies become active, alert beings with the capacity to evoke positive interactions from caregivers and initiate stimulating play and exploration for themselves.

Finally, besides impoverished environments, ones that overwhelm children with expectations beyond their current capacities also undermine development. In recent years, expensive early learning centres have sprung up, in which infants are trained with letter and number flash cards, and slightly older toddlers are given a full curriculum of reading, math, science, art, gym, and more. There is no evidence that these programs yield smarter, better "superbabies." Instead, trying to prime infants with stimulation for which they are not ready can cause them to withdraw, threatening their spontaneous interest and pleasure in learning and creating conditions much like stimulus deprivation! In addition, when such programs promise but do not produce young geniuses, they can lead to disappointed parents who view their children as failures at a very tender age. Thus, they rob infants of a psychologically healthy start, and they deprive parents of relaxed, pleasurable participation in their children's early growth.

## ASK YOURSELF

**review**  Explain why either too much stimulation or too little stimulation for an extended time has adverse effects on infant development.

**connect**  What do research findings on the development of Eastern European orphanage children tell us about the issue of stability versus change in children's development (see Chapter 1, page 9)?

# summary

## THE ORGANIZED NEWBORN

*Explain the functions of newborn reflexes, and describe changing states of arousal during infancy, emphasizing sleep and crying.*

- Infants begin life with remarkable skills for relating to their physical and social worlds. **Reflexes** are the newborn baby's most obvious organized patterns of behaviour. Some have survival value, others help parents and infants establish gratifying interaction, and still others provide the foundation for voluntary motor skills.

- Although newborns alternate frequently between various **states of arousal,** they spend most of their time asleep. Sleep consists of at least two states: **rapid-eye-movement (REM)** and **non-rapid-eye-movement (NREM) sleep.** REM sleep time is greater during the prenatal and newborn periods than at any later age. It provides young infants with stimulation essential for central nervous system development. Rapid eye movements ensure that structures of the eye remain oxygenated during sleep. Individual and cultural differences in sleep–wake patterns are evident in early infancy. Disturbed REM–NREM cycles are a sign of central nervous system abnormalities, which may contribute to **sudden infant death syndrome (SIDS).**

- A crying baby stimulates strong feelings of discomfort in nearby adults. The intensity of the cry and the events that lead up to it help parents figure out what is wrong. Once feeding and diaper changing have been tried, lifting the baby to the shoulder and rocking or walking is the most effective soothing technique. Ethological and behaviourist theories disagree on how promptly caregivers should respond to infant cries. A shrill, piercing cry is an indicator of central nervous system distress.

*Why is neonatal behavioural assessment useful?*

- The most widely used instrument for assessing the organized functioning of newborn infants is Brazelton's **Neonatal Behavioural Assessment Scale (NBAS).** It has helped researchers understand individual and cultural differences in newborn behaviour. Sometimes it is used to teach parents about their baby's capacities, which can help parents interact more confidently and sensitively.

*Describe infant learning capacities, the conditions under which they occur, and the unique value of each.*

- **Classical conditioning** enables infants to recognize which events usually occur together in the everyday world. In this form of learning, a neutral stimulus is paired with an **unconditioned stimulus (UCS)** that produces a reflexive, or **unconditioned, response (UCR).** Once learning has occurred, the neutral stimulus, now called the **conditioned stimulus (CS),** elicits a response similar to the reflexive response, which is called the **conditioned response (CR). Extinction** occurs when the conditional stimulus is presented enough times without the unconditioned stimulus, resulting in a decline of the conditioned response. Young infants can be classically conditioned when the pairing of a UCS with a CS has survival value.

- **Operant conditioning** helps infants explore and control their surroundings. In addition to food, interesting sights and sounds serve as effective **reinforcers,** increasing the occurrence of a preceding behaviour. **Punishment** involves removing a desirable stimulus or presenting an unpleasant one to decrease the occurrence of a response. With age, operant conditioning expands to include a wider range of stimuli and responses.

- **Habituation** and **recovery** reveal that at birth, babies are attracted to novelty. Their ability to discriminate and remember a wide variety of stimuli improves over the first year. Older infants also show more rapid habituation and recovery. However, habituation studies greatly underestimate how long infants can remember events they can actively control, and overlook the context-dependent nature of young infants' memories. Nevertheless, habituation and recovery to visual stimuli are among the best available infant predictors of later mental development.

- Newborn infants have a primitive ability to **imitate** the facial expressions and gestures of adults. Some researchers regard newborn imitation as little more than an automatic response to specific stimuli. Others believe it is a flexible, voluntary capacity that contributes to self- and social awareness and the early parent–infant relationship.

## MOTOR DEVELOPMENT IN INFANCY

*Describe the course of gross and fine motor development during the first 2 years, along with factors that influence it.*

- Like physical development, motor development follows the **cephalocaudal** and **proximodistal trends.** According to **dynamic systems theory of motor development,** new motor skills are a matter of combining existing skills into increasingly complex systems of action. Each new skill is a joint product of central nervous system development, movement possibilities of the body, the goal the child has in mind, and environmental supports for the skill.

- A stimulating environment profoundly affects motor development, as shown by research on infants raised in deprived institutions. Cultural values and child-rearing customs also contribute to the emergence and refinement of motor skills.

- During the first year, infants gradually perfect their reaching and grasping. The poorly coordinated **prereaching** of the newborn period eventually drops out. As control of arm and hand movements improves, voluntary reaching becomes more flexible and accurate, and the clumsy **ulnar grasp** is transformed into a refined **pincer grasp.**

## PERCEPTUAL DEVELOPMENT IN INFANCY

*Describe the newborn baby's senses of touch, taste, smell, and hearing, noting changes during infancy.*

- Newborns are highly sensitive to touch and pain. They have an innate preference for a sweet taste and certain odours; a liking for the salty taste emerges later and probably supports acceptance of solid foods. The taste preferences of young infants can be easily modified. Newborns orient toward the odour of their own mother's amniotic fluid and the lactating breast—responses that help them locate appropriate food and identify their caregiver.

■ As responsiveness to **optical flow** reveals, newborn babies have a built-in sense of balance and self-movement that is fundamental to everything they learn through exploration. Postural adjustments take place automatically and improve with experience and motor control.

■ Over the first year, babies organize sounds into more complex patterns. Newborns are especially responsive to high-pitched expressive voices, their own mother's voice, and speech in their native language as opposed to a foreign language. They can distinguish almost all speech sounds. By the middle of the first year, they become more sensitive to the sounds and meaningful units, such as word and clause boundaries, of their own language.

*Describe the development of vision in infancy, placing special emphasis on depth, pattern, and object perception.*

■ Vision is the least mature of the newborn baby's senses. As the eye and visual centres in the brain develop during the first few months, focusing ability, **visual acuity,** scanning, tracking, and colour perception improve rapidly.

■ Research on depth perception reveals that responsiveness to **kinetic depth cues** appears by the end of the first month, followed by sensitivity to **binocular depth cues** between 2 and 3 months. Perception of **pictorial depth cues** emerges last, around 7 months of age.

■ Experience in crawling facilitates coordination of action with depth information, although babies must learn to avoid drop-offs, such as the deep side of the **visual cliff**, for each body posture. Crawling promotes other aspects of three-dimensional understanding and results in a new level of brain organization.

■ **Contrast sensitivity** accounts for infants' early pattern preferences. At first, babies look at the border of a stimulus and at single features. Around 2 months, they explore the internal features of a pattern and combine pattern elements into a unified whole. In the second half of the first year, they discriminate increasingly complex, meaningful patterns. By 12 months, they extract meaningful patterns from very little information, such as an incomplete figure with as much as two-thirds missing.

■ Newborns prefer to look at and track simple, facelike stimuli, suggesting an innate tendency to orient toward human faces. At 2 to 3 months, with the capacity to combine pattern elements into organized wholes, they prefer a complex, static image of the human face to other equally complex patterns. Face perception follows the same sequence of development as sensitivity to other patterned stimuli. Between 1 and 2 months, babies look longer at their mother's face than a strange woman's face. By 3 months, they make fine distinctions between the features of different faces. Between 7 and 10 months, they react to emotional expressions as organized, meaningful wholes.

■ At birth, **size** and **shape constancy** assist infants in building a coherent world of three-dimensional objects. Initially, infants depend on motion and spatial arrangement to identify objects. After 4 months, they rely increasingly on other features, such as distinct colour, shape, and texture.

*Describe infants' capacity for intermodal perception, and explain the differentiation theory of perceptual development.*

■ Infants have a remarkable, built-in capacity to engage in **intermodal perception.** Although many intermodal associations are learned, babies acquire them quickly, often after just one exposure to a new situation. Detection of amodal relations (such as common tempo and rhythm in sights and sounds) precedes and may provide a basis for detecting other intermodal matches.

■ **Differentiation theory** is the most widely accepted account of perceptual development. Over time, infants detect increasingly fine-grained, **invariant features** in a constantly changing perceptual world. Perception is guided by discovery of **affordances**—the action possibilities a situation offers the individual.

## EARLY DEPRIVATION AND ENRICHMENT: IS INFANCY A SENSITIVE PERIOD OF DEVELOPMENT?

*Explain how research on early deprivation and enrichment sheds light on the question of whether infancy is a sensitive period of development.*

■ Theorists disagree on whether experiences during infancy leave a lasting imprint on the child's competence. Research on Eastern European orphanage children supports the view that infancy is a sensitive period. The later children are removed from deprived rearing conditions, the less favourably they develop. When infants spend the first 2 years or more in unstimulating institutions, they usually remain greatly delayed in all domains. Environments that overwhelm infants with stimulation beyond their current capacities also undermine development.

# important terms and concepts

affordances (p. 161)
binocular depth cues (p. 152)
cephalocaudal trend (p. 139)
classical conditioning (p. 134)
conditioned response (CR) (p. 134)
conditioned stimulus (CS) (p. 134)
contrast sensitivity (p. 155)
differentiation theory (p. 161)
dynamic systems theory (p. 140)
extinction (p. 134)
habituation (p. 137)
imitation (p. 139)
intermodal perception (p. 159)
invariant features (p. 161)

kinetic depth cues (p. 152)
Neonatal Behavioural Assessment Scale
    (NBAS) (p. 133)
non-rapid-eye-movement (NREM)
    sleep (p. 128)
operant conditioning (p. 135)
optical flow (p. 147)
pictorial depth cues (p. 152)
pincer grasp (p. 144)
prereaching (p. 143)
proximodistal trend (p. 139)
punishment (p. 135)
rapid-eye-movement (REM) sleep
    (p. 128)

recovery (p. 137)
reflex (p. 124)
reinforcer (p. 135)
shape constancy (p. 159)
size constancy (p. 159)
states of arousal (p. 126)
sudden infant death syndrome (SIDS)
    (p. 130)
ulnar grasp (p. 144)
unconditioned response (UCR)
    (p. 134)
unconditioned stimulus (UCS) (p. 134)
visual acuity (p. 150)
visual cliff (p. 152)

"Weighing Myself"
Yukimi Yoshida
6 years, Japan

The International Museum of
Children's Art, Oslo, Norway

A transforming body and explosion of new motor skills contribute to children's expanding sense of competence. Chapter 5 highlights the close link between physical growth and other aspects of development.

# f ive

## Physical Growth

ON HER ELEVENTH BIRTHDAY, Sabrina's friend Joyce gave her a surprise party, but Sabrina seemed sombre during the celebration. Although Sabrina and Joyce had been close friends since grade 3, their relationship was faltering. Sabrina was a head taller and some 9 kilograms (20 pounds) heavier than most girls in her grade 6 class. Her breasts were well developed, her hips and thighs had broadened, and she had begun to menstruate. In contrast, Joyce still had the short, lean, flat-chested body of a school-age child. Ducking into the bathroom while the other girls put candles on the cake, Sabrina looked herself over in the mirror and whispered, "Gosh, I feel so big and heavy." At church youth group on Sundays, Sabrina broke away from Joyce and spent time with the grade 8 girls, around whom she didn't feel so large and awkward.

Once a month, parents gathered at Sabrina and Joyce's school for discussions about child-rearing concerns. Sabrina's parents, Franca and Antonio, attended whenever they could. "How you know they are becoming teenagers is this," volunteered Antonio. "The bedroom door is closed, and they want to be alone. Also, they contradict and disagree. I say something to Sabrina, and the next moment she is arguing with me."

"All our four children were early developers," Franca added. "The three boys, too, were tall by age 12 or 13, but it was easier for them. They felt big and important. Sabrina is moody, doesn't want to be with her old friends, and thinks about boys instead of her studies. She was skinny as a little girl,

169

but now she says she is too fat and wants to diet. I try to be patient with her," reflected Franca sympathetically.

During the first 2 decades of life, the human body changes continuously and dramatically. The average individual's height multiplies more than threefold, and weight increases as much as fifteen- to twentyfold. The top-heavy, chubby infant, whose head represents a quarter of the body's total length, gradually becomes the better proportioned child and eventually the taller, broader, more muscular teenager. This chapter traces the course of human growth, along with biological and environmental factors that regulate and control it.

As Sabrina's behaviour indicates, physical and psychological development are closely linked. But just how the child's transforming body is related to cognitive, emotional, and social changes has puzzled philosophers and scientists for centuries. And in particular, they have pondered this question with respect to *puberty*. Ask several parents of young children what they expect their sons and daughters to be like as teenagers. Most will likely say, "rebellious and reckless," or "full of rages and tempers" (Buchanan & Holmbeck, 1998).

This widespread view dates back to eighteenth-century philosopher Jean-Jacques Rousseau, to whom you were introduced in Chapter 1. He believed that a natural outgrowth of the biological upheaval of puberty was heightened emotionality, conflict, and defiance against adults. In the twentieth century, major theorists picked up this perspective. The most influential was G. Stanley Hall, who described adolescence as a cascade of instinctual passions, a phase of growth so turbulent that it resembled the period in which human beings evolved from savages into civilized beings.

Were Rousseau and Hall correct in this image of adolescence as a biologically determined period of storm and stress? Or do social and cultural factors combine with biology to influence psychological development? In our discussion, we will see what contemporary research says about this issue.

## The Course of Physical Growth

COMPARED WITH OTHER animals, primates (including humans) experience a prolonged period of physical growth. For example, among mice and rats, only a few weeks—about 2 percent of the lifespan—intervene between birth and puberty. In chimpanzees, who are closest to humans in the evolutionary hierarchy, growth is extended to about 7 years, or 16 percent of the lifespan. Physical immaturity is even more exaggerated in humans, who devote about 20 percent of their total years to growing. Evolutionary reasons for this long period of physical growth are not hard to find. Because physical immaturity ensures that children remain dependent on adults, it provides added time for them to acquire the knowledge and skills necessary for life in a complex social world.

### CHANGES IN BODY SIZE

To parents, the most obvious signs of physical growth are changes in the overall size of the child's body. During infancy, these changes are rapid—faster than they will be at any other time after birth. By the end of the first year, a typical infant's height is 50 percent greater than it was at birth; by 2 years, it is 75 percent greater. Weight shows similar dramatic gains. By 5 months, birth weight has doubled, at 1 year it has tripled, and at 2 years it has quadrupled. If children kept growing at the rate they do during the early months of life, by age 10 they would be over 3 metres (10 feet) tall and weigh over 90 kilograms (200 pounds)! Fortunately, growth slows in early and middle childhood. Children add about 5 to 7.5 centimetres (2 to 3 inches) in height and 2.5 kilograms (5 pounds) in weight each year. Then, puberty brings a sharp acceleration. On average, adolescents gain nearly 25 centimetres (10 inches) in height and about 18 kilograms (40 pounds) in weight.

Body proportions and muscle–fat makeup change dramatically between 1 and 5 years. The top-heavy, chubby infant gradually becomes the longer-legged, slender young child.

© BILL KEEFREY/INDEX STOCK

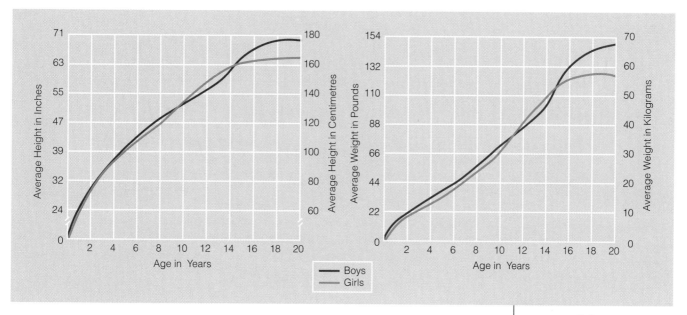

**FIGURE** 5.1

**Height and weight distance curves for North American boys and girls,** drawn from longitudinal measurements of approximately 175 individuals. (From R. M. Malina, 1975, *Growth and Development: The First Twenty Years in Man,* p. 19. Minneapolis: Burgess Publishing Company. Copyright © 1975 by Burgess Publishing Company. Adapted by permission.)

Two types of growth curves are used to track height and weight changes. The first, shown in Figure 5.1, is a **distance curve,** which plots the average height and weight of a sample of children at each age. It is called a distance curve because it indicates typical yearly progress toward mature body size. The group averages are referred to as *growth norms* and serve as useful standards to which individual children can be compared. Notice how during infancy and childhood the two sexes are similar, with the typical girl just slightly shorter and lighter than the typical boy. Around age 10 to 11, the girl becomes taller and heavier for a time because her pubertal growth spurt takes place 2 years earlier than the boy's. But this advantage is short-lived. At age 14, she is surpassed by the typical boy, whose growth spurt has started, whereas hers is almost finished. Growth in height is complete for most North American and European girls by age 16, for boys by age 17½ (Tanner, 1990).

A second type of growth curve is the **velocity curve,** depicted in Figure 5.2 on page 172. It plots the average amount of growth at each yearly interval. As a result, it reveals the exact timing of growth spurts. Note the rapid but decelerating growth in infancy; a slower, constant rate during early and middle childhood; and a sharp increase in early adolescence, followed by a swift decrease as the body approaches its adult size.

## CHANGES IN BODY PROPORTIONS

As the child's overall size increases, parts of the body grow at different rates. Recall from Chapter 3 that during the prenatal period, the head develops first from the primitive embryonic disk, followed by the lower part of the body. After birth, the head and chest continue to have a growth advantage, but the trunk and legs gradually pick up speed. Do you recognize the familiar *cephalocaudal trend* we discussed in Chapter 4? You can see it depicted in Figure 5.3 on page 172. Physical growth during infancy and childhood also follows the *proximodistal trend,* from the centre of the body outward. The head, chest, and trunk grow first, followed by the arms and legs, and finally the hands and feet.

Exceptions to these basic growth trends occur during puberty, when growth proceeds in the reverse direction. At first, the hands, legs, and feet accelerate, and then the torso, which accounts for most of the adolescent height gain (Sheehy et al., 1999). This pattern of development helps explain why young adolescents often appear awkward and out of proportion—long legged with giant feet and hands.

Although girls' and boys' body proportions are similar in infancy and childhood, large differences appear during adolescence, caused by the action of sex hormones on the skeleton. Boys' shoulders broaden relative to the hips, whereas girls' hips broaden relative to the waist.

**distance curve**
A growth curve that plots the average height and weight of a sample of children at each age. Shows typical yearly progress toward mature body size.

**velocity curve**
A growth curve that plots the average amount of growth at each yearly interval for a sample of children. Reveals the timing of growth spurts.

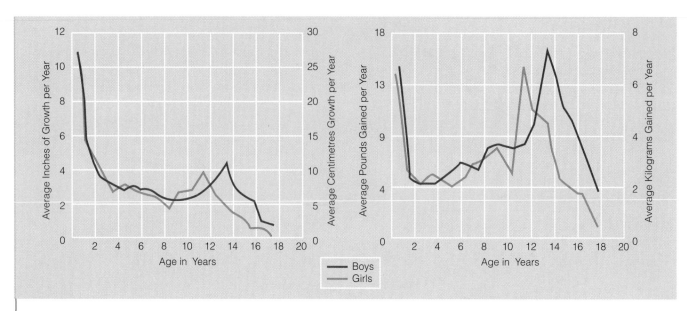

**FIGURE** 5.2

**Height and weight velocity curves for North American boys and girls,** drawn from longitudinal measurements on approximately 175 individuals. (From R. M. Malina, 1975, *Growth and Development: The First Twenty Years in Man,* p. 20. Minneapolis: Burgess Publishing Company. Copyright © 1975 by Burgess Publishing Company. Adapted by permission.)

Of course, boys also end up larger than girls, and their legs are longer in relation to the rest of the body. The major reason is that boys have 2 extra years of preadolescent growth, when the legs are growing the fastest (Graber, Petersen, & Brooks-Gunn, 1996).

### CHANGES IN MUSCLE–FAT MAKEUP

Major changes in the body's muscle–fat makeup take place with age. Body fat (most of which lies just beneath the skin) increases in the last few weeks of prenatal life and continues to do so after birth, reaching a peak at about 9 months of age. This early rise in "baby fat" helps the small infant keep a constant body temperature. Then, during the second year, most children slim down, a trend that continues into middle childhood. At birth, girls have slightly more body fat than boys, a difference that becomes greater over the course of childhood. Around age 8, girls start to add more fat than do boys on their arms, legs, and trunk, and they do so throughout puberty. In contrast, the arm and leg fat of adolescent boys decreases (Siervogel et al., 2000).

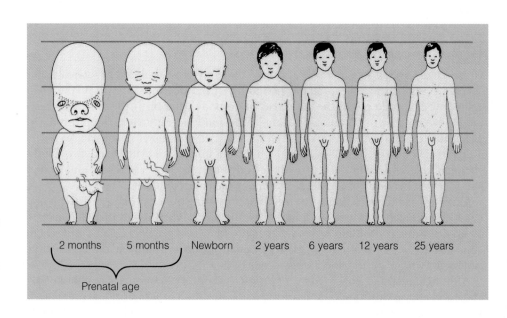

**FIGURE** 5.3

**Changes in body proportions from the early prenatal period to adulthood.** This figure illustrates the cephalocaudal trend of physical growth. The head gradually becomes smaller, and the legs longer, in proportion to the rest of the body.

Muscle accumulates slowly throughout infancy and childhood, then rises dramatically at adolescence. Although both sexes gain muscle at puberty, the increase is much greater for boys, who develop larger skeletal muscles, hearts, and lung capacity. Also, the number of red blood cells, and therefore the ability to carry oxygen from the lungs to the muscles, increases in boys but not in girls. Altogether, boys gain far more muscle strength than do girls, which contributes to sex differences in motor development during the teenage years (Ramos et al., 1998).

### CHANGES IN GROSS MOTOR SKILLS

Changes in size, proportions, and muscle strength support an explosion of new gross motor skills. As the body becomes more streamlined and less top-heavy, the centre of gravity shifts downward, toward the trunk. As a result, balance improves greatly, paving the way for new motor skills involving large muscles. By age 2, preschoolers' gaits become smooth and rhythmic—secure enough that soon they leave the ground, at first by running and jumping and then, between 3 and 6 years, by hopping, galloping, and skipping. Eventually, upper and lower body skills combine into more effective actions (Getchell & Roberton, 1989). For example, at ages 2 and 3, children throw a ball rigidly, using only the arms. By ages 4 and 5, they involve the shoulders, torso, trunk, and legs in a smooth, flexible motion that makes the ball travel faster and farther.

During the school years, improved balance, strength, agility, and flexibility support refinements in running, jumping, hopping, and ball skills. Children sprint across the playground, engage in intricate patterns of hopscotch, kick and dribble soccer balls, and swing bats at balls pitched by their classmates. Increased body size and muscle at adolescence bring continued motor gains. The Milestones table on page 174 summarizes gross motor achievements in early and middle childhood.

The same principle that governs motor development during the first 2 years continues to operate in childhood and adolescence. Children integrate previously acquired skills into more complex, *dynamic systems of action.* (Return to Chapter 4, page 140, to review this concept.) Then they revise each skill as their bodies become larger and stronger, their central nervous systems become better developed, their interests and goals become clearer, and their environments present new challenges. Sex differences in motor skills, present as early as the preschool years, illustrate these multiple influences. Although size and strength contribute to boys' superior athletic performance in adolescence, physical growth cannot fully account for boys' childhood advantage. As the From Research to Practice box on page 176 reveals, the social environment plays a prominent role.

### SKELETAL GROWTH

Children of the same age differ in *rate* of physical growth. As a result, researchers have devised methods for measuring progress toward physical maturity. These techniques are useful for studying the causes and consequences of individual differences in physical growth. They also provide rough estimates of children's chronological age in areas of the world where birth dates are not recorded.

**SKELETAL AGE.** The best way of estimating a child's physical maturity is to use **skeletal age,** a measure of development of the bones of the body. The embryonic skeleton is first formed out of soft, pliable tissue called *cartilage.* In the sixth week of pregnancy, cartilage cells begin to harden into bone, a gradual process that continues throughout childhood and adolescence (Tanner, Healy, & Cameron, 2001).

Once bones have taken on their basic shape, special growth centres called **epiphyses** appear just before birth and increase throughout childhood. In the long bones of the body, epiphyses emerge at the two extreme ends of each bone (see Figure 5.4). As growth continues, the epiphyses get thinner and disappear. When this occurs, no more growth in bone length is

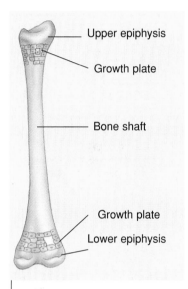

Upper epiphysis

Growth plate

Bone shaft

Growth plate

Lower epiphysis

**FIGURE 5.4**

**Diagram of a long bone showing upper and lower epiphyses.** Cartilage cells are produced at the growth plates of the epiphyses and gradually harden into bone. (From J. M. Tanner, *Foetus into Man* [2nd ed.], Cambridge, MA: Harvard University Press, p. 32. Copyright © 1990 by J. M. Tanner. All rights reserved. Reprinted by permission of the publisher and author.)

**skeletal age**
An estimate of physical maturity based on development of the bones of the body.

**epiphyses**
Growth centres in the bones where new cartilage cells are produced and gradually harden.

# milestones

## GROSS MOTOR DEVELOPMENT IN EARLY AND MIDDLE CHILDHOOD

| AGE | | GROSS MOTOR SKILLS |
|---|---|---|

**2–3 years**

- Walks more rhythmically; hurried walk changes to run.
- Jumps, hops, throws, and catches with rigid upper body.
- Pushes riding toy with feet; little steering.

**3–4 years**

- Walks up stairs, alternating feet, and downstairs, leading with one foot.
- Jumps and hops, flexing upper body.
- Throws and catches with slight involvement of upper body; still catches by trapping ball against chest.
- Pedals and steers tricycle.

**4–5 years**

- Walks downstairs, alternating feet; runs more smoothly.
- Gallops and skips with one foot.
- Throws ball with increased body rotation and transfer of weight on feet; catches ball with hands.
- Rides tricycle rapidly, steers smoothly.

**5–6 years**

- Increases running speed to more than 3½ metres (12 feet) per second.
- Gallops more smoothly; engages in true skipping and sideways stepping.
- Displays mature, whole-body throwing and catching pattern; increases throwing speed.
- Rides bicycle with training wheels.

**7–12 years**

- Increases running speed to 5½ metres (18 feet) per second.
- Displays continuous, fluid skipping and sideways stepping.
- Increases vertical jump from 10 to 30 centimetres (4 to 12 inches) and broad jump from 1 to 1½ metres (3 to over 5 feet); accurately jumps and hops from square to square.
- Increases throwing and kicking accuracy, distance, and speed.
- Involves the whole body in batting a ball; batting increases in speed and accuracy.
- Dribbling changes from awkward slapping of the ball to continuous, relaxed, even stroking.

*Note:* These milestones represent overall age trends. Individual differences exist in the precise age at which each milestone is attained.
*Sources:* Cratty, 1986; Malina & Bouchard, 1991; Newborg, Stock, & Wnek, 1984; Roberton, 1984.

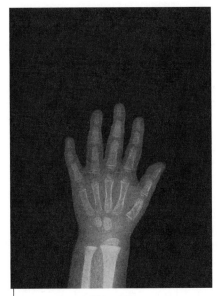
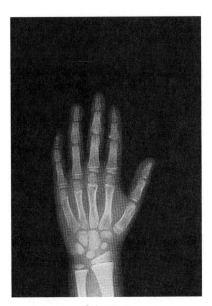
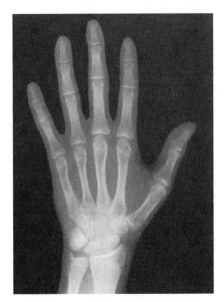

2½ years      6½ years      14½ years

**FIGURE** 5.5

**X-rays of a girl's hand, showing skeletal maturity at three ages.** Notice how, at age 2½, wide gaps exist between the wrist bones and at the ends of the finger and arm bones. By age 6½, these have filled in considerably. At age 14½ (when this girl reached her adult size), the wrist and long bones are completely fused. (From J. M. Tanner, M. J. R. Healy, & N. Cameron, 2001, *Assessment of Skeletal Maturity and Prediction of Adult Height [TW3 Method]*, 3rd ed., Philadelphia: Saunders, p. 86. Reprinted by permission.)

possible. As Figure 5.5 shows, skeletal age can be estimated by X-raying the bones and seeing how many epiphyses there are and the extent to which they are fused.

When skeletal ages are examined, African-American children tend to be slightly ahead of Caucasian-American children. In addition, girls are considerably ahead of boys. At birth, the difference between the sexes amounts to about 4 to 6 weeks, a gap that widens over infancy and childhood (Humphrey, 1998). Girls are advanced in development of other organs as well. Their physical maturity may contribute to their greater resistance to harmful environmental influences. Recall from Chapter 3 that girls experience fewer developmental problems than do boys, and infant and childhood mortality for girls is also lower.

**GROWTH OF THE SKULL.** Pediatricians routinely measure children's head size between birth and 2 years of age. Skull growth is especially rapid during the first 2 years because of large increases in brain size. At birth, the bones of the skull are separated by six gaps, or "soft spots," called **fontanels** (see Figure 5.6). The gaps permit the bones to overlap as the large head of the baby passes through the mother's narrow birth canal. The anterior fontanel, at the top of a baby's skull, is slightly more than 2.5 centimetres (1 inch) across. It gradually shrinks and is filled in during the second year. The other fontanels are smaller and close more quickly. As the skull bones come in contact with one another, they form *sutures,* or seams. These permit the skull to expand easily as the brain grows. The sutures disappear completely after puberty, when skull growth is complete.

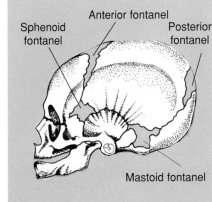

**FIGURE** 5.6

**The skull at birth, showing the fontanels and sutures.** The fontanels gradually close during the first 2 years, forming sutures that permit the skull to expand easily as the brain grows.

### HORMONAL INFLUENCES ON PHYSICAL GROWTH

The endocrine glands control the vast physical changes of childhood and adolescence. They manufacture *hormones,* chemical substances secreted by specialized cells in one part of the body that pass to and influence cells in another.

**fontanels**
Six soft spots that separate the bones of the skull at birth.

## *from research to practice*

### SEX DIFFERENCES IN GROSS MOTOR DEVELOPMENT

Sex differences in gross motor development are present as early as the preschool years, increase during middle childhood, and are large at adolescence. What underlies this expanding gender gap, and how can we ensure that both boys and girls are granted opportunities that optimize skill and enjoyment of athletics?

#### EARLY AND MIDDLE CHILDHOOD

In early childhood, boys are slightly advanced over girls in abilities that emphasize force and power. By age 5, they can broad jump slightly farther, run slightly faster, and throw a ball much farther (about 1.5 metres [5 feet] beyond the distance covered by girls). During middle childhood, these differences intensify. For example, a ball thrown by a 12-year-old boy travels, on average, 13 metres (43 feet) farther than one thrown by a 12-year-old girl. Boys are also more adept at batting, kicking, dribbling, and catching (Cratty, 1986; Fischman, Moore, & Steele, 1992).

Girls' overall greater physical maturity seems to give them an edge in gross motor capacities that require a combination of good balance and foot movement, such as hopping and skipping. Boys' slightly greater muscle mass and (in the case of throwing) longer forearms probably contribute to their skill advantages. But differences in physical growth during childhood are not large enough to explain boys' superiority in so many gross motor capacities. Instead, adult encouragement and example are powerfully influential. From an early age, footballs, baseballs, and bats are purchased for boys; jump ropes, hula hoops, and skates for girls. And most players in public sports events continue to be men (Coakley, 1990; Greendorfer, Lewko, & Rosengren, 1996).

A study of more than 800 elementary school pupils found that parents hold higher expectations for boys' athletic performance, and children absorb these social messages at an early age. Kindergartners through third graders viewed sports in a gender-stereotyped fashion—as much more important for boys. Girls saw themselves as having less talent at sports, and by grade 6 they devoted less time to athletics than did their male classmates (Eccles & Harold, 1991; Eccles, Jacobs, & Harold, 1990). At the same time, girls and older school-age children regard boys' advantage in sports as unjust. They indicate, for example, that coaches should spend equal time with children of each sex and that female sports should command just as much public attention as male sports (Solomon & Bredemeier, 1999).

Parental encouragement of girls' athletic skills and belief in their ability to excel promotes self-confidence, effort, and involvement in sports activities. As this 8-year-old becomes accomplished at basketball, she will also learn much about competition, assertiveness, problem solving, and teamwork.

© JIM CUMMINGS/FPG INTERNATIONAL/GETTY IMAGES

**pituitary gland**
A gland located near the base of the brain that releases hormones affecting physical growth.

**hypothalamus**
A structure located at the base of the brain that initiates and regulates pituitary secretions.

The most important hormones for human growth are released by the **pituitary gland,** located at the base of the brain near the **hypothalamus,** a structure that initiates and regulates pituitary secretions (see Figure 5.8 on page 178). Once pituitary hormones enter the bloodstream, they act directly on body tissues to induce growth, or they stimulate the release of other hormones from endocrine glands located elsewhere in the body. The hypothalamus contains special receptors that detect hormone levels in the bloodstream. Through a highly sensitive feedback loop, it instructs the pituitary gland to increase or decrease the amount of

## ADOLESCENCE

Not until puberty do sharp sex-related differences in physical size and muscle strength account for large differences in athletic ability. During adolescence, girls' gains in gross motor performance are modest, levelling off by age 14. In contrast, boys show a dramatic spurt in strength, speed, and endurance that continues through the teenage years. Consequently, the gender gap widens. By midadolescence, very few girls perform as well as the average boy in running speed, broad jump, and throwing distance. And practically no boys score as low as the average girl (Malina & Bouchard, 1991).

Sex differences also characterize physical activity rates of Canadian youth. As Figure 5.7 shows, more boys than girls engage in regular physical exercise. Nevertheless, most Canadian children and adolescents do not engage in sufficient exercise to yield optimal health benefits. Furthermore, the percentage of young people exercising regularly declines with age. During adolescence, only 40 percent of boys and 30 percent of girls are physically active (Canadian Fitness and Lifestyle Research Institute, 2001).

## INTERVENTIONS

Sports do not just improve motor performance. They influence cognitive and social development as well. Interschool and intramural athletics provide important lessons in competition, assertiveness, problem solving, and teamwork—experiences less available to girls (Newcombe & Boyle, 1995). Perhaps because of the emphasis placed on health and fitness in school and community-based sports programs, young people who participate tend to display certain healthier behaviours—more often eating fruits and vegetables and less often using alcohol, cigarettes, and illegal drugs and engaging in sexual activity (Pate et al., 2000).

Clearly, steps need to be taken to raise girls' confidence that they can do well at athletics. Educating parents about the minimal differences in school-age boys' and girls' physical capacities and sensitizing them to unfair biases against girls' athletic ability may prove helpful. In addition, greater emphasis on skill training, along with increased attention to the athletic achievements of girls, is likely to improve their participation and performance. Finally,

daily physical education in school, emphasizing enjoyable games and individual exercise rather than competition, is particularly motivating for girls (Weinberg et al., 2000). Many have not developed other routes to regular exercise and sports involvement.

**FIGURE 5.7**

**Physical activity of boys compared with girls.** In both age groups studied, a greater percentage of boys than girls was considered to be sufficiently active (Canadian Fitness and Lifestyle Research Institute [2001]. Reprinted by permission of the Canadian Fitness and Lifestyle Research Institute.)

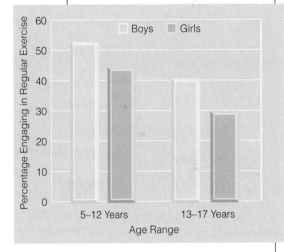

each hormone. In this way, growth is carefully controlled. You may find it useful to refer to Figure 5.9 on page 179 as we review major hormonal influences.

**Growth hormone (GH)** is the only pituitary secretion produced continuously throughout life. It affects the development of all body tissues except the central nervous system and the genitals. GH acts directly on body tissues but also accomplishes its task with the help of an intermediary. It stimulates the liver and epiphyses of the skeleton to release another hormone called *somatomedin*, which triggers cell duplication in the bones. Although GH does not seem to affect

**growth hormone (GH)**
A pituitary hormone that affects the development of all body tissues except the central nervous system and the genitals.

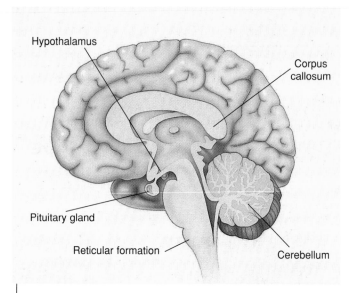

**FIGURE** 5.8

**Cross-section of the human brain, showing the location of the hypothalamus and pituitary gland.** Also shown are three additional structures—the cerebellum, the reticular formation, and the corpus callosum—that we will discuss in a later section.

prenatal growth, it is necessary for physical development from birth on. Children who lack it reach an average mature height of only 132 centimetres (4 feet, 4 inches). When treated early with injections of GH, such children show catch-up growth and then grow at a normal rate, reaching a height much greater than they would have without treatment (Pasquino et al., 2001).

Together, the hypothalamus and pituitary gland prompt the thyroid gland (in the neck) to release **thyroxine,** which is necessary for brain development and for GH to have its full impact on body size. Infants born with a deficiency of thyroxine must receive it at once, or they will be mentally retarded. At later ages, children with too little thyroxine grow at a below-average rate. However, the central nervous system is no longer affected, since the most rapid period of brain development is complete. With prompt treatment, such children eventually reach normal size (Salerno et al., 2001).

Sexual maturation is controlled by pituitary secretions that stimulate the release of sex hormones. Although **estrogens** are thought of as female hormones and **androgens** as male hormones, both types are present in each sex but in different amounts. The boy's testes release large quantities of the androgen *testosterone,* which leads to muscle growth, body and facial hair, and other male sex characteristics. Androgens (especially testosterone for boys) contribute to gains in body size. The testes secrete small amounts of estrogen as well—the reason that 50 percent of boys experience temporary breast enlargement (Larson, 1996).

Like androgens, estrogens contribute to the pubertal growth spurt in both sexes (Juul, 2001). And in girls, estrogens released by the ovaries cause the breasts, uterus, and vagina to mature and the body to take on feminine proportions. In addition, they contribute to regulation of the menstrual cycle. Girls' changing bodies are also affected by the release of androgens from the adrenal glands, located on top of each kidney, which stimulate growth of underarm and pubic hair. Adrenal androgens have little impact on boys, whose physical characteristics are influenced mainly by androgen and estrogen secretions from the testes.

## WORLDWIDE VARIATIONS IN BODY SIZE

Observe a group of same-age children, and you will see that they differ greatly in physical growth. Diversity in physical size is especially apparent when we travel to different nations. Measurements of 8-year-olds living in many parts of the world reveal a 23-centimetre (9-inch) gap between the smallest and largest youngsters. The shortest children tend to be found in South America, Asia, the Pacific Islands, and parts of Africa and include such ethnic groups as Colombian, Burmese, Thai, Vietnamese, Ethiopian, and Bantu. The tallest children reside in Australia, northern and central Europe, Canada, and the United States and consist of Czech, Dutch, Latvian, Norwegian, Swiss, and North American black and white children (Meredith, 1978).

Ethnic variations in rate of growth are also common. For example, African-American and Asian children tend to

Body size is sometimes the result of evolutionary adaptations to a particular climate. These boys of the Sudan, who live on the hot African plains, have long, lean physiques, which permit the body to cool easily.

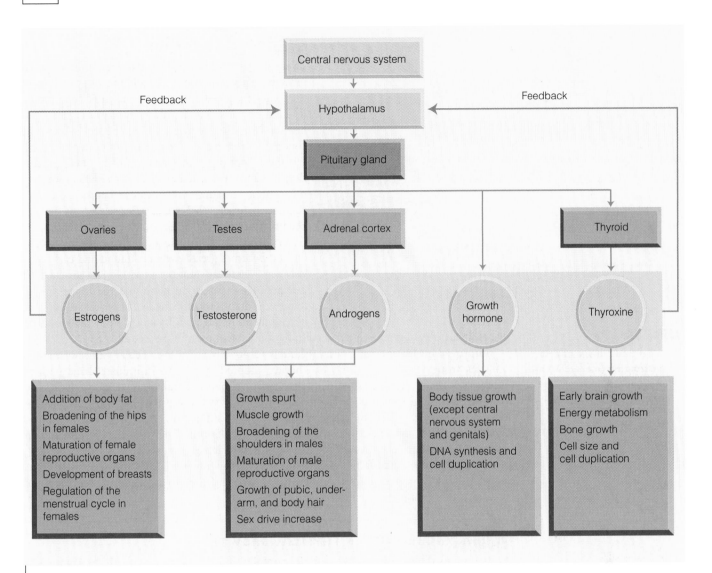

**FIGURE** 5.9

**Hormonal influences on postnatal growth.** The hypothalamus stimulates the pituitary gland to release hormones that either induce growth directly or stimulate other endocrine glands to release growth-inducing hormones (red lines). A highly sensitive feedback loop exists in which the hypothalamus detects hormone levels in the bloodstream and instructs the pituitary gland to increase or decrease the amount of each hormone accordingly (blue lines).

**thyroxine**
A hormone released by the thyroid gland that is necessary for central nervous system development and body growth.

**estrogens**
Hormones produced chiefly by the ovaries that cause the breasts, uterus, and vagina to mature and the body to take on feminine proportions, and that influence the pubertal growth spurt.

**androgens**
Hormones produced chiefly by the testes, and in smaller quantities by the adrenal glands, that influence the pubertal growth spurt, the appearance of body hair, and male sex characteristics.

mature faster than North American Caucasian children, who are slightly advanced over European children (Berkey et al., 1994; Eveleth & Tanner, 1990). These findings remind us that growth norms must be interpreted cautiously, especially in countries where many ethnic groups are represented.

What accounts for these differences? As we will soon see in greater detail, both heredity and environment are involved. Body size is sometimes the result of evolutionary adaptations to a particular climate. For example, long, lean physiques are typical in hot, tropical regions and short, stocky ones in cold, arctic areas. Also, children who grow tallest usually reside in developed countries, where food is plentiful and infectious diseases are largely controlled. In contrast, small children tend to live in regions where poverty, hunger, and disease are common (Tanner, 1990).

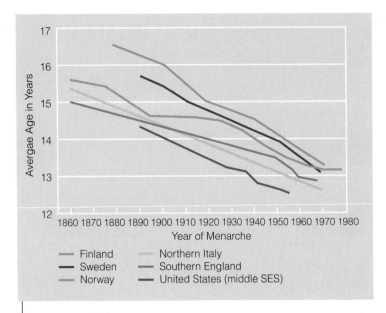

FIGURE 5.10

**Secular trend in age of first menstruation (menarche) in industrialized nations.**
(Reprinted by permission of the publisher from J. M. Tanner, 1990, *Foetus into Man* [2nd ed., p. 160], Cambridge, MA: Harvard University Press. Copyright © 1990 by J. M. Tanner. All rights reserved.)

## SECULAR TRENDS

Over the past 150 years, **secular trends in physical growth**—changes in body size and rate of growth from one generation to the next—have taken place in industrialized nations. Most children today are taller and heavier than their parents and grandparents were as children. These trends have been found in nearly all European nations, Australia, Canada, Japan, New Zealand, and the United States. For example, measurements of more than 24 000 Bogalusa, Louisiana, schoolchildren between 1973 and 1992 revealed an average height gain of nearly 0.8 centimetre (⅓ inch) per decade (Freedman et al., 2000). The secular gain appears early in life and becomes greater over childhood and early adolescence. Then, as mature body size is reached, it declines. This pattern suggests that the larger size of today's children is mostly due to a faster rate of physical development. As Figure 5.10 shows, from 1860 to 1970, age of first menstruation declined steadily, by about 3 to 4 months per decade.

Improved health and nutrition are largely responsible for these secular gains. Orphaned children from developing countries who are adopted by parents in industrialized nations often show faster physical growth and reach greater mature height and weight than do children remaining in the land of origin. Also, secular trends are not as large for low-income children, who have poorer diets and are more likely to suffer from growth-stunting illnesses. And in regions of the world with widespread poverty, famine, and disease, either no secular change or a secular decrease has occurred (Barnes-Josiah & Augustin, 1995; Cole, 2000).

Although the secular gain in height has slowed, weight gain is continuing at a high rate. As we will see later, overweight and obesity have contributed to a continuing secular trend toward earlier first menstruation.

## ASYNCHRONIES IN PHYSICAL GROWTH

Body systems differ in their own unique, carefully timed patterns of growth. As Figure 5.11 shows, physical growth is *asynchronous*. Body size (as measured by height and weight) and a variety of internal organs follow the **general growth curve.** It involves rapid growth during infancy, slower gains in early and middle childhood, and rapid growth again during adolescence. The genitals develop slowly from birth to age 4, change little throughout middle childhood, and then grow rapidly during adolescence. In contrast, the lymph tissue (small clusters of glands found throughout the body) grows at an astounding pace in infancy and childhood, but its growth declines in adolescence. The lymph system fights infection and assists in the absorption of nutrients, thereby supporting children's health and survival (Malina & Bouchard, 1991).

Figure 5.11 illustrates another growth trend. As

FIGURE 5.11

**Growth of three different organ systems and tissues contrasted with the body's general growth.** Growth is plotted in terms of percentage of change from birth to 20 years. Notice how growth of lymph tissue rises to nearly twice its adult level by the end of childhood. Then it declines. (Reprinted by permission of the publisher from J. M. Tanner, 1990, *Foetus into Man* [2nd ed., p. 16]. Cambridge, MA: Harvard University Press. Copyright © 1990 by J. M. Tanner. All rights reserved.)

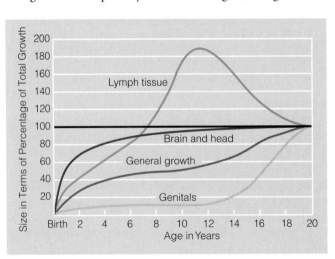

we will see in greater detail in the next section, during the first few years the brain grows faster than any other body structure.

## ASK YOURSELF

**review**   Explain why sex differences in physical growth play little role in boys' childhood advantage over girls in athletic skills.

**review**   Describe the role of the pituitary gland in body growth, brain development, and sexual maturation.

**apply**   At birth, Joey's anterior fontanel had started to close prematurely. At age 3 months, Joey had surgery to open it. Considering the function of the fontanels, why was early surgery necessary?

**connect**   What do secular trends in physical growth and cohort effects, discussed on page 58 of Chapter 2, have in common? Why should a researcher engaged in a longitudinal or cross-sectional study of physical growth be concerned about cohort effects?

# Development of the Brain

THE HUMAN BRAIN IS the most elaborate and effective living structure on earth today. Despite its complexity, it reaches its adult size earlier than any other organ. We can best understand brain growth by looking at it from two vantage points: (1) the microscopic level of individual brain cells, and (2) the larger level of the cerebral cortex, the most complex brain structure and the one responsible for the highly developed intelligence of our species.

## DEVELOPMENT OF NEURONS

The human brain has 100 to 200 billion **neurons,** or nerve cells, that store and transmit information, many of which have thousands of direct connections with other neurons. Neurons differ from other body cells in that they are not tightly packed together. They have tiny gaps, or **synapses,** between them where fibres from different neurons come close together but do not touch. Neurons release chemicals that cross the synapse, thereby sending messages to one another.

The basic story of brain growth concerns how neurons develop and form this elaborate communication system. Recall from Chapter 3 that neurons are produced in the primitive neural tube of the embryo. From there, they migrate to form the major parts of the brain, travelling along threads produced by a network of guiding cells. By the end of the second trimester of pregnancy, production of neurons is largely complete.

Once neurons are in place, they differentiate, establishing their unique functions by extending their fibres to form synaptic connections with neighbouring cells. As Figure 5.12 on page 182 shows, during the first two years, growth of neural fibres and synapses increases at an astounding pace (Huttenlocher, 1994; Moore & Persaud, 1998). Because developing neurons require space for these connective structures, a surprising aspect of brain growth is that many surrounding neurons die when synapses are formed. Consequently, the peak period of development in any brain area is also marked by the greatest rate of **programmed cell death** (Diamond & Hopson, 1999). Fortunately, during embryonic growth, the neural tube produces far more neurons than the brain will ever need.

As neurons form connections, *stimulation* becomes important in their survival. Neurons that are stimulated by input from the surrounding environment continue to establish synapses, forming increasingly elaborate systems of communication that lead to more complex cortical functions. Neurons seldom stimulated soon lose their synapses, a process called **synaptic pruning.** At first, stimulation leads to an overabundance of synapses, many of which

**secular trends in physical growth**
Changes in body size and rate of growth from one generation to the next.

**general growth curve**
Curve that represents changes in overall body size—rapid growth during infancy, slower gains in early and middle childhood, and rapid growth again during adolescence.

**neurons**
Nerve cells that store and transmit information in the brain.

**synapse**
The gap between neurons, across which chemical messages are sent.

**programmed cell death**
Death of many surrounding neurons during the peak period of development in any brain area, to make room for growth of neural fibres that form synaptic connections.

**synaptic pruning**
Loss of connective fibres by seldom-stimulated neurons, thereby returning them to an uncommitted state so they can support the development of future skills.

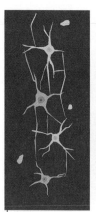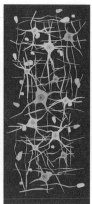

Birth            6 months            2 years

**FIGURE** 5.12

**Development of neurons.**
Growth of neural fibres takes place rapidly from birth to 2 years. During this time, new synapses form at an astounding pace, supporting the emergence of many new capacities. Stimulation is vitally important for maintaining and increasing this complex communication network. (Reprinted by permission of the publisher from *The Postnatal Development of the Human Cerebral Cortex,* Vol. I–III, by Jesse LeRoy Conel, Cambridge, Mass.: Harvard University Press. Copyright ©1939, 1975 by the President and Fellows of Harvard College.)

**glial cells**
Cells responsible for myelinization of neural fibres.

**myelinization**
A process in which neural fibres are coated with an insulating fatty sheath (called myelin) that improves the efficiency of message transfer.

**cerebral cortex**
The largest structure of the human brain; accounts for the highly developed intelligence of the human species.

**lateralization**
Specialization of functions of the two hemispheres of the cerebral cortex.

**brain plasticity**
The ability of other parts of the brain to take over functions of damaged regions.

serve identical functions, thereby ensuring that the child will acquire the motor, cognitive, and social skills that members of our species need to survive. Synaptic pruning returns neurons not needed at the moment to an uncommitted state so they can support the development of future skills (Johnson, 1998). Notice how, for this process to go forward, appropriate stimulation of the child's brain is vital during periods in which the formation of synapses is at its peak (Eisenberg, 1999; Greenough et al., 1993).

Perhaps you are wondering, if few new neurons are produced after the prenatal period, what causes the dramatic increase in skull size mentioned earlier in this chapter? About half the brain's volume is made up of **glial cells,** whose most important function is **myelinization,** the coating of neural fibres with an insulating fatty sheath (called *myelin*) that improves the efficiency of message transfer. Glial cells multiply at a dramatic pace from the fourth month of pregnancy through the second year of life, after which their production slows (Casaer, 1993). Dramatic increase in neural fibres and myelinization are responsible for the rapid gain in overall size of the brain. At birth, the brain is nearly 30 percent of its adult weight; by age 2, it is 70 percent, and at 6 years, 90 percent (Thatcher et al., 1996).

### DEVELOPMENT OF THE CEREBRAL CORTEX

The **cerebral cortex** surrounds the brain, looking much like a half-shelled walnut. It is the largest, most complex brain structure—accounting for 85 percent of the brain's weight, containing the greatest number of neurons and synapses, and responsible for the unique intelligence of our species. The cerebral cortex is the last brain structure to stop growing. For this reason, it is believed to be sensitive to environmental influences for a longer period than any other part of the brain.

**REGIONS OF THE CEREBRAL CORTEX.** As Figure 5.13 shows, regions of the cerebral cortex have specific functions, such as receiving information from the senses, instructing the body to move, and thinking. The order in which cortical regions develop corresponds to the order in which various capacities emerge during infancy and childhood. For example, a burst of synaptic growth in the auditory and visual cortexes (refer to Figure 5.13) occurs from 3 to 4 months until the end of the first year—a period of dramatic gains in auditory and visual perception (Johnson, 1998). Language areas of the cortex develop quickly from late infancy into the preschool years, when young children acquire language (Thatcher, 1991).

Among the last regions of the cortex to form synaptic connections and myelinate are the *frontal lobes,* which are responsible for thought—in particular, consciousness, inhibition of impulses, and regulation of behaviour through planning. From age 2 months on, this area functions more effectively, and it continues its growth for years, well into the second and third decades of life (Huttenlocher & Dabholkar, 1997; Thompson et al., 2000).

**LATERALIZATION OF THE CEREBRAL CORTEX.** The cerebral cortex has two *hemispheres*—left and right—that differ in their functions. Some tasks are done mostly by one hemisphere and some by the other. For example, each hemisphere receives sensory information from and controls only one side of the body—the one opposite to it.[1] For most of us, the left hemisphere is largely responsible for verbal abilities (such as spoken and written language) and positive emotion (for example, joy). The right hemisphere handles spatial abilities (judging distances, reading maps, and recognizing geometric shapes) and negative

---

[1]The eyes are an exception. Messages from the right half of each retina go to the left hemisphere; messages from the left half of each retina go to the right hemisphere. Thus, visual information from *both* eyes is received by *both* hemispheres.

emotion (such as distress) (Banish & Heller, 1998; Nelson & Bosquet, 2000). This pattern may be reversed in left-handed people, but more often, the cortex of left-handers is less clearly specialized than that of right-handers.

Specialization of the two hemispheres is called **lateralization.** Why are behaviours and abilities lateralized? According to one view, the left hemisphere is better at processing information in a sequential, analytic (piece-by-piece) way, which is a good approach for dealing with communicative information—both verbal (language) and emotional (a joyful smile). In contrast, the right hemisphere is specialized for processing information in a holistic, integrative manner, ideal for making sense of spatial information and regulating negative emotion (Banish, 1998). A lateralized brain is certainly adaptive. It permits a wider array of functions to be carried out effectively than if both sides processed information exactly the same way.

*Brain Plasticity.* Researchers are interested in when brain lateralization occurs because they want to know more about **brain plasticity.** In a highly *plastic* cortex, many areas are not yet committed to specific functions. If a part of the brain is damaged, other parts can take over tasks it would have handled. But once the hemispheres lateralize, damage to a particular region means that the abilities controlled by it will be lost forever.

At birth, the hemispheres have already begun to specialize. For example, the majority of neonates favour the right side of the body in their reflexive responses (Grattan et al., 1992; Rönnqvist & Hopkins, 1998). Most also show greater EEG brain-wave activity in the left hemisphere while listening to speech sounds and displaying positive emotion. In contrast, the right hemisphere reacts more strongly to nonspeech sounds as well as stimuli (such as a sour-tasting fluid) that cause infants to display negative emotion (Davidson, 1994; Fox & Davidson, 1986).

Nevertheless, dramatic evidence for early brain plasticity comes from research on brain-damaged children. In a large sample of preschoolers with a wide variety of brain injuries sustained in the first year of life, deficits in language and spatial abilities were milder than those observed in brain-injured adults. And by age 5, cognitive impairments had largely disappeared (Stiles, 1998, 2000). As the children gained perceptual, cognitive, and motor experiences, other stimulated cortical structures compensated for the damaged areas, regardless of the site of injury.

Additional findings indicate mild deficits in general intelligence in children with early brain injuries—the price they seem to pay for massive brain reorganization. But their mental functioning is near normal, and verbal and spatial abilities are intact (Bates et al., 1998). In contrast, older children and adults have only a limited capacity to recover functions following brain injury (Johnson, 1998).

Another illustration of how early experience moulds brain organization comes from studies of deaf adults who, as infants and children, learned to communicate through sign language. EEG brain-wave recordings reveal that compared with hearing adults, these individuals depended more on the right hemisphere for language processing (Neville & Bruer, 2001). Also, toddlers advanced in language development show greater left-hemispheric specialization than do their more slowly developing agemates. Apparently, the very process of acquiring language promotes lateralization (Bates, 1999; Mills, Coffey-Corina, & Neville, 1997).

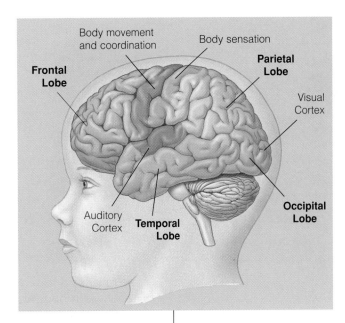

Body movement and coordination

Body sensation

Frontal Lobe

Parietal Lobe

Visual Cortex

Auditory Cortex

Temporal Lobe

Occipital Lobe

**FIGURE** 5.13

**The left side of the human brain, showing the cerebral cortex.** The cortex is divided into different lobes, each of which contains a variety of regions with specific functions. Some major ones are labelled here.

Early experience moulds brain organization. In most people, the left hemisphere of the cerebral cortex is specialized for language. But deaf individuals who as young children learned to communicate through sign language depend more on the right hemisphere for language processing.

© ASSOCIATED PRESS. FORT COLLINS COLORADOAN

LAURA DWIGHT

Twins typically lie in the uterus in opposite orientations during the prenatal period, which may explain why they are more often opposite-handed than are ordinary siblings. Although left-handedness is associated with developmental problems, the large majority of left-handed children are completely normal.

During the early years, the cerebral cortex is more plastic than at any later time of life. Its flexibility protects young children's ability to learn, which is fundamental to survival (Nelson, 2000). And although the cortex is programmed from the start for hemispheric specialization, experience greatly influences the rate and success of this genetic program.

***Lateralization and Handedness.*** A growing literature on handedness also provides insights into the joint contributions of nature and nurture to brain lateralization. Cheryl McCormick of Bates College and Daphne Maurer of McMaster University (1988) found that 6-month-olds tended to use one hand more often than the other when reaching for objects. Hand preference is evident in 10 percent of 11-month-olds and strengthens during early childhood. Ninety percent of 5-year-olds clearly prefer one hand over another (Öztürk et al., 1999).

A strong hand preference reflects the greater capacity of one side of the brain—often referred to as the individual's **dominant cerebral hemisphere**—to carry out skilled motor action. Other important abilities may be located on the dominant side as well. In support of this idea, for right-handed people, who make up 90 percent of the population in Western nations, language is housed with hand control in the left hemisphere. For the remaining left-handed 10 percent, language is often shared between the hemispheres (Knecht et al., 2000). This indicates that the brains of left-handers tend to be less strongly lateralized than those of right-handers. Consistent with this idea, many left-handed individuals are also ambidextrous. That is, although they prefer their left hand, they sometimes use their right hand skilfully as well (McManus et al., 1988).

Is handedness hereditary? Researchers disagree on this issue. Left-handed parents show only a weak tendency to have left-handed children. One genetic theory proposes that most children inherit a gene that *biases* them for right-handedness and left-hemispheric localization of language. However, that bias is not strong enough to overcome experiences that sway them toward a left-hand preference. Left-handed mothers are more likely to have left-handed children than are left-handed fathers. Therefore, male left-handers are believed to carry the right-hand bias gene more often than do female left-handers (Annett, 1994, 1999).

The genetic right-hand bias theory acknowledges that experience can profoundly affect handedness. In support of that view, twins—whether identical or fraternal—are more likely than ordinary siblings to display opposite-handedness. The hand preference of each twin is related to body position in the uterus; twins usually lie in opposite orientations (Derom et al., 1996). This suggests that prenatal events can affect lateralization. Most singleton fetuses orient toward the left, which may promote greater postural control by the right side of the body (Previc, 1991).

Another possibility is that practice heavily affects hand preference. Handedness is strongest for complex skills requiring considerable training, such as eating with utensils, writing, and engaging in athletic skills. Also, wide cultural differences in the percentage of left-handers exist. For example, in Tanzania, Africa, children are physically restrained and punished for favouring the left hand. Less than 1 percent of the Tanzanian population is left-handed (Provins, 1997).

Perhaps you have heard that left-handedness is more frequent among severely retarded and mentally ill people than it is in the general population. Although this is true, recall that when two variables are correlated, this does not mean that one causes the other. Atypical lateralization is probably not responsible for the problems of these individuals. Instead, they may have suffered early brain damage to the left hemisphere, which caused their disabilities and also led to a shift in handedness. In support of this idea, left-handedness is associated with prenatal and birth difficulties that can result in brain damage, including prolonged labour, prematurity, Rh incompatibility, and breech delivery (O'Callaghan et al., 1993; Powls et al., 1996).

**dominant cerebral hemisphere**
The hemisphere of the brain responsible for skilled motor action. The left hemisphere is dominant in right-handed individuals. In left-handed individuals, the right hemisphere may be dominant, or motor and language skills may be shared between the hemispheres.

Keep in mind, however, that only a small number of left-handers show developmental problems. In fact, unusual lateralization may have certain advantages. Left- and mixed-handed youngsters are more likely than their right-handed agemates to develop outstanding verbal and mathematical talents (Flannery & Liederman, 1995). More even distribution of cognitive functions across both hemispheres may be responsible.

## OTHER ADVANCES IN BRAIN DEVELOPMENT

Besides the cerbral cortex, several other areas of the brain make strides during infancy and childhood. As we look at these changes, you will see that they all involve establishing links between parts of the brain, increasing the coordinated functioning of the central nervous system. (To see where the structures we are about to discuss are located, turn back to Figure 5.8 on page 178.)

At the rear and base of the brain is the **cerebellum,** a structure that aids in balance and control of body movement. Fibres linking the cerebellum to the cerebral cortex begin to myelinate after birth, but they do not complete this process until about age 4 (Tanner, 1990). This change undoubtedly contributes to dramatic gains in motor control, so that by the end of the preschool years, children can play hopscotch, pump a playground swing, and throw a ball with a well-organized set of movements.

The **reticular formation,** a structure in the brain stem that maintains alertness and consciousness, myelinates throughout early childhood, continuing its growth into adolescence. Neurons in the reticular formation send out fibres to other areas of the brain. Many go to the frontal lobes of the cerebral cortex, contributing to improvements in sustained, controlled attention (McGuinness & Pribram, 1980).

A final brain structure that undergoes major changes during early childhood is the **corpus callosum.** It is a large bundle of fibres that connects the two hemispheres so that they can communicate directly. Myelinization of the corpus callosum does not begin until the end of the first year of life. Between 3 and 6 years, it grows rapidly and then enlarges at a slower pace into adolescence (Giedd et al., 1999; Thompson et al., 2000). The corpus callosum supports the integration of many aspects of thinking, including perception, attention, memory, language, and problem solving. The more complex the task, the more crucial communication between the hemispheres becomes.

## BRAIN GROWTH SPURTS AND SENSITIVE PERIODS OF DEVELOPMENT

Recall that stimulation of the brain is vital during periods in which it is growing most rapidly—when formation of synapses is at a peak. The existence of sensitive periods in development of the cerebral cortex has been amply demonstrated in studies of animals exposed to extreme forms of sensory deprivation. For example, there seems to be a time when rich and varied visual experiences must occur for the visual centres of the brain to develop normally. If a month-old kitten is deprived of light for as brief a time as 3 or 4 days, these brain areas degenerate. If the kitten is kept in the dark for as long as 2 months, the damage is permanent. Enriched versus deprived early environments also affect overall brain growth. When animals reared as pets are compared with animals reared in isolation, the brains of the pets are heavier and thicker (Greenough & Black, 1992).

Because we cannot ethically expose children to such experiments, researchers interested in sensitive periods for human brain development must rely on less direct evidence. They have identified intermittent brain growth spurts, based on gains in brain weight and skull size as well as changes in neural activity, as measured by the EEG and fMRI. For example, several surges in frontal-lobe activity, which gradually spread to other cortical regions, occur during the first 2 years of life: at 3 to 4 months, when infants typically reach for objects; around 8 months, when they begin to crawl and search for hidden objects; around 12 months, when they walk and display more advanced object-search behaviours; and between $1\frac{1}{2}$ and 2 years, when language flourishes (Bell & Fox, 1994, 1998; Fischer & Bidell, 1998). Between ages 3 and 6 years, frontal-lobe areas devoted to planning and organizing actions show a dramatic

**cerebellum**
A brain structure that aids in balance and control of body movements.

**reticular formation**
A structure in the brain stem that maintains alertness and consciousness.

**corpus callosum**
The large bundle of fibres that connects the two hemispheres of the brain.

increase in activity—a period when children become better at using language to guide their behaviour (Thompson & Nelson, 2001). Later frontal-lobe activity spurts, at ages 9, 12, 15, and 18 to 20, may reflect the emergence and refinement of abstract thought (Fischer & Rose, 1995).

Massive production of synapses may underlie brain growth spurts in the first 2 years. Development of more complex and efficient neural networks, due to synaptic pruning, myelinization, and longer-distance connections between the frontal lobes and other cortical regions, may account for the later ones. Researchers are convinced that what "wires" a child's brain during each of these periods is experience. But they still have many questions to answer about just how brain and behavioural development might best be supported during each growth spurt.

The evidence they do have confirms that the brain is particularly spongelike during the first few years. Recall from Chapter 4 that understimulating infants by depriving them of rich and varied experiences available in caring family environments impairs their development. And overstimulation is harmful as well. The tremendous production of synapses during infancy and toddlerhood does not mean that teaching culturally specific knowledge and skills should begin at this time. To the contrary, no sensitive periods for this kind of learning have been identified (Bruer & Greenough, 2001). Academic, artistic, and athletic mastery occur easily only later—during childhood, adolescence, and adulthood—as the brain gradually undergoes synaptic pruning.

## ASK YOURSELF

**review**    How does stimulation affect early brain development? Cite evidence at the level of neurons and at the level of the cerebral cortex.

**review**    Explain why overproduction of synapses and synaptic pruning are adaptive processes that foster brain development.

**apply**    Lucia had a mild brain hemorrhage shortly after birth. Using what you know about brain plasticity, explain why her doctors believe her mental development will be normal, or near normal.

**connect**    On the basis of findings on sensitive periods in this chapter and in Chapter 4, which infant enrichment program would you choose: one that emphasizes gentle talking and touching, exposure to sights and sounds, and simple social games, or one that includes word and number drills and classical music lessons? Explain.

# Factors Affecting Physical Growth

PHYSICAL GROWTH, LIKE other aspects of development, results from the continuous and complex interplay between heredity and environment. In the following sections, we take a closer look at this familiar theme.

## HEREDITY

Since identical twins are much more alike in body size than are fraternal twins, we know that heredity is an important factor in physical growth. When diet and health are adequate, height and rate of physical growth (as measured by skeletal age and timing of first menstruation) are largely determined by heredity. In fact, as long as negative environmental influences such as poor nutrition or illness are not severe, children typically show **catch-up growth**—a return to a genetically determined growth path—once conditions improve. Physical growth is a strongly canalized process (see Chapter 3, page 116).

**catch-up growth**
Physical growth that returns to its genetically determined path after being delayed by environmental factors.

Genes influence growth by controlling the body's production of and sensitivity to hormones. Sometimes mutations disrupt this process, leading to deviations in physical size. Occasionally, a mutation becomes widespread in a population. Consider the Efe of Zaire, an African people who normally grow to an adult height of less than 1.5 metres (5 feet). During early childhood, the growth of Efe children tapers off. By age 5, the average Efe child is shorter than over 97 percent of 5-year-olds in North America. For genetic reasons, growth hormone (GH) has less effect on Efe youngsters than on other children (Bailey, 1990).

Genetic makeup also affects body weight, since the weights of adopted children correlate more strongly with those of their biological than adoptive parents (Stunkard et al., 1986). However, as far as weight is concerned, environment—in particular, nutrition—plays an especially important role.

## NUTRITION

Nutrition is important at any time of development, but it is especially crucial during the first 2 years because the brain and body are growing so rapidly. An infant's energy needs are twice those of an adult. Twenty-five percent of the total caloric intake is devoted to growth, and infants need extra kilojoules (calories) to keep rapidly developing organs of the body functioning properly (Pipes, 1996).

**BREAST- VERSUS BOTTLE-FEEDING.** Babies not only need enough food, they need the right kind of food. In early infancy, breast-feeding is especially suited to their needs, and bottled formulas try to imitate it. Table 5.1 summarizes the major nutritional and health advantages of breast milk.

Because of these benefits, breast-fed babies in poverty-stricken regions of the world are much less likely to be malnourished and 6 to 14 times more likely to survive the first year of life. Breast-feeding exclusively for the first 6 months would save the lives of one million infants annually. And breast-feeding for just a few weeks would offer some protection against

**TABLE** 5.1

Nutritional and Health Advantages of Breast-Feeding

| ADVANTAGE | DESCRIPTION |
| --- | --- |
| Correct balance of fat and protein | Compared to the milk of other mammals, human milk is higher in fat and lower in protein. This balance, as well as the unique proteins and fats contained in human milk, is ideal for a rapidly myelinating nervous system. |
| Nutritional completeness | A mother who breast-feeds need not add other foods to her infant's diet until the baby is 6 months old. The milks of all mammals are low in iron, but the iron contained in breast milk is much more easily absorbed by the baby's system. Consequently, bottle-fed infants need iron-fortified formula. |
| Protection against disease | Through breast-feeding, antibodies and other infection-fighting agents are transferred from mother to child. As a result, breast-fed babies have far fewer respiratory and intestinal illnesses and allergic reactions than do bottle-fed infants. Components of human milk that protect against disease can be added to formula, but breast-feeding provides superior immunity. |
| Protection against faulty jaw development and tooth decay | Breast-feeding helps avoid malocclusion, a condition in which the upper and lower jaws do not meet properly. It also protects against tooth decay due to sweet liquid remaining in the mouths of infants who fall asleep while sucking on a bottle. |
| Digestibility | Since breast-fed babies have a different kind of bacteria growing in their intestines than do bottle-fed infants, they rarely become constipated or have diarrhea. |
| Smoother transition to solid foods | Breast-fed infants accept new solid foods more easily than do bottle-fed infants, perhaps because of their greater experience with a variety of flavours, which pass from the maternal diet into the mother's milk. |

Sources: Dewey, 2001; Pickering et al., 1998; Raisler, 1999.

Breast-feeding is especially important in developing countries, where infants are at risk for malnutrition and early death due to widespread poverty. This baby of Rajasthan, India, is likely to grow normally during the first year because his mother decided to breast-feed.

respiratory and intestinal infections that are devastating to young children in developing countries. Furthermore, because a mother is less likely to get pregnant while she is nursing, breast-feeding helps increase spacing between siblings, a major factor in reducing infant and childhood deaths in developing countries (Darnton-Hill & Coyne, 1998). (Note, however, that breast-feeding is not a reliable method of birth control.)

Yet many mothers in the developing world do not know about the benefits of breast-feeding. Consequently, they give their babies low-grade nutrients, such as rice water, highly diluted cow's and goat's milk, or commercial formula. These foods often lead to illness because they are contaminated due to poor sanitation. The United Nations has encouraged all hospitals and maternity units in developing countries to promote breast-feeding as long as mothers do not have viral or bacterial infections (such as HIV and turberculosis) that can be transmitted to the baby. Today, most developing countries have banned the practice of giving free or subsidized formula to any new mother who desires it.

Partly as a result of the natural childbirth movement, over the past two decades, breast-feeding has become more common in industrialized nations, especially among well-educated women. Today, nearly 80 percent of Canadian infants under the age of 2 are breast-fed, with 55 percent breast-fed for longer than 3 months (Statistics Canada, Health Indicators, 2001). Not surprisingly, mothers who return to work sooner wean their babies from the breast earlier (Arora et al., 2000). However, a mother who cannot be with her baby all the time can pump her milk into a bottle or combine breast-feeding with bottle-feeding.

In industrialized nations, most women who choose breast-feeding find it emotionally satisfying, but it is not for everyone. Some mothers simply do not like it or are embarrassed by it. A few others, for physiological reasons, do not produce enough milk. Occasionally, medical reasons—such as illness or treatment with certain drugs—prevent a mother from nursing (Kuhn & Stein, 1997).

Some women who cannot breast-feed worry that they are depriving their baby of an experience essential for healthy psychological development. Yet breast- and bottle-fed children in industrialized nations do not differ in emotional adjustment (Fergusson & Woodward, 1999). At the same time, many studies reveal a slight but consistent advantage for breast-fed children and adolescents in mental test performance after many factors are controlled (Anderson, Johnstone, & Remley, 1999). Notice in Table 5.1 that breast milk provides nutrients ideally suited for early rapid brain development.

**NUTRITION IN CHILDHOOD AND ADOLESCENCE.** By 6 months of age, infants require the nutritional diversity of solid foods, and around 1 year, their diets should include all the basic food groups. Early childhood often brings a dramatic change in the quantity and variety of foods children will eat. Around age 2, many become picky eaters. This decline in appetite is normal. It occurs because growth has slowed. And preschoolers' wariness of new foods may be adaptive. By sticking to familiar foods, young children are less likely to swallow dangerous substances when adults are not around to protect them (Birch & Fisher, 1995). Parents need not worry about variations in amount eaten from meal to meal. Over the course of a day, preschoolers' food intake is fairly constant. They compensate for a meal in which they ate little with a later one in which they eat more (Hursti, 1999).

The social environment has a powerful impact on young children's food preferences. Children tend to imitate the food choices of people they admire—peers as well as adults. For example, in Mexico, children often see family members delighting in the taste of peppery foods. Consequently, Mexican preschoolers enthusiastically eat chili peppers, whereas other North American children reject them (Birch, Zimmerman, & Hind, 1980).

A pleasant mealtime climate also encourages healthy eating. Repeated exposure to a new food (without any direct pressure to eat it) increases children's acceptance (Sullivan & Birch, 1990). Sometimes parents bribe their children, saying, "Finish your vegetables, and you can have an extra cookie." This practice causes children to like the healthy food less and the treat more. Too much parental control over children's eating limits their opportunities to develop self-control (Birch, 1998).

Once puberty arrives, rapid body growth leads to a dramatic rise in food intake. This increase in nutritional requirements comes at a time when eating habits are the poorest. Of all age groups, adolescents are the most likely to consume empty kilojoules (calories). In a longitudinal study of Minnesota students from elementary to junior high school, consumption of breakfast, fruits, vegetables, and milk declined, whereas consumption of soft drinks and fast foods increased sharply (Lytle et al., 2000).

The most common nutritional problem of adolescence is iron deficiency. A tired, listless youngster may be suffering from anemia rather than unhappiness and should have a medical checkup. Most teenagers do not get enough calcium, and they are also deficient in folic acid (which supports functioning of the central nervous system) and riboflavin and magnesium (both of which support metabolism) (Cavadini, Siega-Riz, & Popkin, 2000). The eating habits of teenagers are particularly harmful if they extend a lifelong pattern of poor nutrition, less serious if they are just a temporary response to peer influences and a busy schedule.

**MALNUTRITION.** In developing countries where food resources are limited, malnutrition is widespread. Recent evidence indicates that 40 to 60 percent of the world's children do not get enough to eat (Bellamy, 1998). The 4 to 7 percent who are severely affected suffer from two dietary diseases.

**Marasmus** is a wasted condition of the body caused by a diet low in all essential nutrients. It usually appears in the first year of life when a baby's mother is too malnourished to produce enough breast milk and bottle feeding is also inadequate. The starving baby becomes painfully thin and is in danger of dying.

**Kwashiorkor** is caused by an unbalanced diet very low in protein. It usually strikes after weaning, between 1 and 3 years of age. It is common in areas of the world where children get just enough kilojoules (calories) from starchy foods, but protein resources are scarce. The child's body responds by breaking down its own protein reserves. Soon the child's belly enlarges, the feet swell, the hair falls out, and a rash appears on the skin. A once bright-eyed, curious youngster becomes irritable and listless.

Children who survive these extreme forms of malnutrition are growth stunted—much smaller than average in all body dimensions (Galler, Ramsey, & Solimano, 1985a). And when their diets improve, they are at risk for excessive weight gain. Nationwide surveys in Russia, China, and South Africa revealed that growth-stunted children are far more likely to be overweight than their nonstunted agemates (Popkin, Richards, & Montiero, 1996). To protect itself, a malnourished body establishes a low basal metabolism rate, which may endure after nutrition improves. Also, malnutrition may disrupt the functioning of appetite control centres in the brain, causing the child to overeat when food becomes plentiful.

Learning and behaviour are also seriously affected. One long-term study of marasmic children revealed that an improved diet did not result in catch-up in head size (Stoch et al., 1982). The malnutrition probably interfered with myelinization, causing a permanent loss in brain weight. These children score low on intelligence tests, show poor fine motor coordination, and have difficulty paying attention (Galler et al., 1984, 1990; Galler, Ramsey, & Solimano, 1985b).

These negative outcomes extend into middle childhood. Compared with adequately nourished agemates, growth-stunted school-age children respond to fear-arousing situations with a greater rise in blood pressure and stress hormones (Fernald & Grantham-McGregor, 1998). Perhaps the gnawing pain of hunger permanently alters their stress response. Second, animal evidence reveals that a deficient diet alters the production of neurotransmitters in the brain—an effect that can disrupt all aspects of psychological functioning (Levitsky & Strupp, 1995).

Recall from our discussion of prenatal malnutrition in Chapter 3 that the passivity and irritability of malnourished children reduce the child's capacity to evoke sensitive caregiving from parents, whose lives are already disrupted by poverty and stressful living conditions (Lozoff et al., 1998; Sigman & Whaley, 1998). For this reason, interventions for malnourished children must improve the family situation as well as the child's nutrition.

Even better are efforts at prevention—providing food and medical care before the effects of malnutrition run their course. In Guatemala, where dietary deficiencies are common, children

The swollen abdomen and listless behaviour of this Honduran child are classic symptoms of kwashiorkor, a nutritional illness that results from a diet very low in protein.

**marasmus**
A disease usually appearing in the first year of life that is caused by a diet low in all essential nutrients. Leads to a wasted condition of the body.

**kwashiorkor**
A disease usually appearing between 1 and 3 years of age that is caused by a diet low in protein. Symptoms include an enlarged belly, swollen feet, hair loss, skin rash, and irritable, listless behaviour.

receiving food supplements prenatally and during the first 2 years scored higher on mental tests in adolescence than did children given supplements only after their second birthday (Pollitt et al., 1993). Other longitudinal findings reveal that quality of food (higher protein, vitamin, and mineral content) is far more important than quantity in contributing to the favourable cognitive outcomes just described (Watkins & Pollitt, 1998).

Malnutrition is not confined to developing countries. Some Canadian children go to bed and to school hungry, and although few have marasmus or kwashiorkor, their physical growth and ability to learn are still affected.

**OBESITY.** Approximately 15 percent of Canadian children suffer from **obesity,** a greater-than-20-percent increase over average body weight, based on the child's age, sex, and physical build. From 1981 to 1996, the prevalence of overweight children increased by 92 percent for boys and by 56 percent for girls (Tremblay & Willms, 2000). During the past several decades, large increases in overweight and obesity also have been reported for Denmark, Finland, Great Britain, New Zealand, and the United States. Obesity rates are increasing rapidly in developing countries as well, as urbanization shifts the population toward sedentary lifestyles and diets high in meats and refined foods (Troiana & Flegal, 1998).

Over 80 percent of affected youngsters become overweight adults. Besides serious emotional and social difficulties, obese children are at risk for lifelong health problems. High blood pressure and cholesterol levels, along with respiratory abnormalities, appear in the early school years, symptoms that are powerful predictors of heart disease, adult-onset diabetes, gallbladder disease, certain forms of cancer, and early death (Oken & Lightdale, 2000).

STEPHEN TRIMBLE

This Pima Indian medicine man of Arizona is very obese. By the time his two daughters reach adolescence, they are likely to follow in his footsteps. Because of a high-fat diet, the Pima residing in the Southwestern United States have one of the highest rates of obesity in the world. In contrast, the Pima living in the remote Sierra Madre region of Mexico are average weight.

*Causes of Obesity.* Not all children are equally at risk for becoming overweight. Fat children tend to have fat parents, and concordance for obesity is greater in identical than fraternal twins. But similarity among family members is not strong enough for genetics to account for more than a tendency to gain weight (Bouchard, 1994).

One indication that environment is powerfully important is the consistent relation between low SES and obesity (Stunkard & Sørenson, 1993). Among the factors responsible are lack of knowledge about healthy diet; a tendency to buy high-fat, low-cost foods; and family stress, which prompts overeating in some individuals.

Parental feeding practices contribute to childhood obesity as well. Fatter children are more likely to prefer and eat larger quantities of high-fat foods, perhaps because these foods are prominent in the diets offered by their parents, who also tend to be overweight (Fisher & Birch, 1995). Some parents anxiously overfeed their infants and young children, interpreting almost all their discomforts as a desire for food. Others are overly controlling, constantly monitoring what their children eat. In either case, they fail to help children learn to regulate their own food intake. Furthermore, parents of obese children often use food to reinforce other behaviours—a practice that leads children to attach great value to the treat (Birch & Fisher, 1995).

Because of these feeding experiences, obese children soon develop maladaptive eating habits (Johnson & Birch, 1994). They are more responsive to external stimuli associated with food—taste, sight, smell, and time of day—and less responsive to internal hunger cues than are normal-weight individuals (Ballard et al., 1980). They also eat faster and chew their food less thoroughly, a behaviour pattern that appears as early as 18 months of age (Drabman et al., 1979).

Furthermore, fat children are less physically active than their normal-weight peers. This inactivity is both cause and consequence of their overweight condition. Research indicates that the rise in childhood obesity in North America is, in part, due to television viewing. In a study that tracked children's TV viewing over a 4-year period, children who watched more than 5 hours per day were more than 8 times likelier to become obese than were children who watched 2 hours or less per day (see Figure 5.14) (Gortmaker et al., 1996). Television greatly reduces time devoted to physical exercise, and TV ads encourage children to eat fattening, unhealthy snacks. When researchers gave third and fourth graders 2 months of twice-weekly lessons in reducing TV viewing and video game use, the children not only watched less but lost weight (Robinson, 1999).

Finally, the broader food environment affects the incidence of obesity. The Pima Indians of Arizona, who recently changed from a traditional diet of plant foods to an affluent, high-fat diet, have one of the highest rates of obesity in the world. Compared with descendants of their ancestors living in the remote Sierra Madre region of Mexico, the Arizona Pima have body weights 50 percent higher. Half the population has diabetes (8 times the national average), with many disabled by the disease in their twenties and thirties—blind, in wheelchairs, and on kidney dialysis (Gladwell, 1998; Ravussin et al., 1994). Although the Pima have a genetic susceptibility to overweight, it emerges only under Western dietary conditions. Similarly, the diabetes rate in Canadian Aboriginal communities is 3 to 5 times higher than the national average. The major causal factor is obesity. In one Aboriginal community in northern Canada, 50 percent of the children suffer from obesity (Canadian Health Network, 2001).

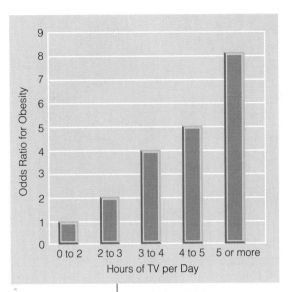

**FIGURE** 5.14

**Relationship between television viewing and development of childhood obesity.** Researchers tracked 10- to 15-year-olds' television viewing over a 4-year period. The more hours young people spent in front of the TV, the greater the likelihood that they became obese by the end of the study. (Adapted from Gortmaker et al., 1996.)

***Consequences of Obesity.*** Unfortunately, physical attractiveness is a powerful predictor of social acceptance in Western societies. Both children and adults rate obese youngsters as unlikable, stereotyping them as lazy, sloppy, ugly, stupid, self-doubting, and deceitful (Kilpatrick & Sanders, 1978; Tiggemann & Anesbury, 2000). By middle childhood, obese children report feeling more depressed and display more behaviour problems than do their normal-weight agemates. Unhappiness and overeating contribute to one another, and the child remains overweight (Braet, Mervielde, & Vandereycken, 1997).

The psychological consequences of obesity combine with continuing discrimination to result in reduced life chances. By young adulthood, overweight individuals have completed fewer years of schooling, have lower incomes, and are less likely to marry than are individuals with other chronic health problems. These outcomes are particularly strong for females (Gortmaker et al., 1993).

***Treating Obesity.*** Childhood obesity is difficult to treat because it is a family disorder. The most effective interventions are family based and focus on changing behaviours. In one study, both parent and child revised eating patterns, exercised daily, and reinforced each other with praise and points for progress, which they exchanged for special activities and times together. Follow-ups after 5 and 10 years showed that children maintained their weight loss more effectively than did adults—a finding that underscores the importance of intervening at an early age. Furthermore, weight loss was greater when treatments focused on both dietary and lifestyle changes, including regular, vigorous exercise (Epstein, 1995).

Schools can help reduce obesity by ensuring regular physical activity and serving healthier meals. Unfortunately, many Canadian schools have been reducing their physical activity programs and do not meet recommended Canadian Medical Association guidelines of 30 minutes per day of physical education (Andersen, 2000). In addition, the high-fat content of school lunches and snacks can greatly affect body weight, since children consume one-third of their daily energy intake at school. In Singapore, school interventions consisting of nutrition education, low-fat food choices, and daily physical activity led child and adolescent obesity to decline from 14 to 11 percent (Schmitz & Jeffery, 2000).

## INFECTIOUS DISEASE

Among well-nourished youngsters, ordinary childhood illnesses have no effect on physical growth. But when children are poorly fed, disease interacts with malnutrition in a vicious spiral, and the consequences can be severe.

**obesity**
A greater-than-20-percent increase over average body weight, based on the child's age, sex, and physical build.

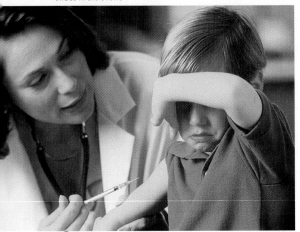

BRUCE AYERS/STONE

Canada's health care system covers the cost of childhood immunizations. Because they dramatically reduce the incidence of childhood diseases, immunizations are widely regarded as a cost-effective means of supporting healthy growth. Although this boy finds a routine inoculation painful, it will offer him lifelong protection.

**INFECTIOUS DISEASE AND MALNUTRITION.** In developing nations where a large proportion of the population lives in poverty, illnesses such as measles and chicken pox (which typically do not appear until after age 3 in industrialized nations) occur in infancy and take the form of severe illnesses. This is because poor diet depresses the body's immune system, making children far more susceptible to disease. Of the 10 million annual worldwide deaths in children under age 5, 99 percent occur in developing countries and 70 percent are due to infectious diseases (World Health Organization, 2000).

Disease, in turn, is a major cause of malnutrition and, through it, affects physical growth. Illness reduces appetite, and it limits the body's ability to absorb foods. These outcomes are especially severe among children with intestinal infections. In developing countries, diarrhea is widespread and increases in early childhood due to unsafe water and contaminated foods, leading to several million childhood deaths each year (Shann & Steinhoff, 1999). Research in poverty-stricken Guatemalan villages showed that 7-year-olds who had been relatively free of diarrhea since birth were significantly heavier than their frequently ill peers (Martorell, 1980).

Most growth retardation and deaths due to diarrhea can be prevented with nearly cost-free **oral rehydration therapy (ORT),** in which sick children are given a glucose, salt, and water solution that quickly replaces fluids the body loses. Since 1990, public health workers have taught nearly half of families in the developing world how to administer ORT. As a result, the lives of millions of children are being saved annually (Victora et al., 2000).

**IMMUNIZATION.** In industrialized nations, childhood diseases have declined dramatically during the past half-century, largely due to widespread immunization of infants and young children. By age 2, 85 percent of Canadian children have full vaccination coverage (Health Canada, 2000). Vaccination rates of Canadian preschoolers exceed 90 percent—a rate comparable to Denmark, Norway, the Netherlands, and Sweden (Bellamy, 2000; Health Canada, 2000c). In the United States, where state law requires that children be immunized by the time they enter school, the immunization rate for preschoolers is 76 percent, but rises to 98 percent for school-age children. Polio has been eliminated in Canada due to widespread vaccination, and Canada is striving to eliminate measles by 2005.

Free childhood vaccinations are included in Canada's health care coverage. Nevertheless, parents sometimes delay taking their child for a vaccination because they believe the child might have an adverse reaction. Misconceptions also contribute—for example, that vaccines do not work or that they weaken the immune system (Gellin, Maibach, & Marcuse, 2000). Consequently, public education programs directed at increasing parental knowledge about the importance and safety of timely immunizations are needed.

### EMOTIONAL WELL-BEING

We are not used to thinking of love and stimulation as necessary for healthy physical growth, but they are just as vital as food. Two serious growth disorders result from lack of affection and attention.

**Nonorganic failure to thrive** is usually present by 18 months of age. Infants who have it show all the signs of marasmus, described earlier in this chapter. However, no organic (or biological) cause for the baby's wasted appearance can be found. The baby is offered enough food and does not have a serious illness. The behaviour of babies with failure to thrive provides a strong clue to its diagnosis. In addition to apathy and withdrawal, these infants keep their eyes on nearby adults, anxiously watching their every move. They rarely smile when the mother comes near or cuddle when picked up (Steward, 2001).

Family circumstances surrounding failure to thrive help explain these typical reactions. During feeding, diaper changing, and play, mothers of these infants seem cold and distant, at other times controlling, impatient, and hostile (Hagekull, Bohlin, & Rydell, 1997). In

**oral rehydration therapy (ORT)**
A treatment for diarrhea, in which sick children are given a glucose, salt, and water solution that quickly replaces fluids the body loses.

**nonorganic failure to thrive**
A growth disorder usually present by 18 months of age that is caused by lack of affection and stimulation.

response, babies try to protect themselves by keeping track of the threatening adult's where-abouts and, when she approaches, avoiding her gaze. Often an unhappy marriage and parental psychological disturbance contribute to these serious caregiving problems (Drotar, Pallotta, & Eckerle, 1994; Duniz et al., 1996). Sometimes the baby is irritable and displays abnormal feeding behaviours, such as poor sucking or vomiting—circumstances that stress the parent–child relationship further (Wooster, 1999). When treated early, by helping parents or placing the baby in a caring foster home, failure-to-thrive infants show quick catch-up growth. But if the disorder is not corrected in infancy, most children remain small and show lasting cognitive and emotional difficulties (Wooster, 2000).

**Psychosocial dwarfism** usually appears between 2 and 15 years of age. Its most striking features are substantially below-average stature, decreased GH secretion, immature skeletal age, and serious adjustment problems, which helps distinguish psychosocial dwarfism from normal shortness (Voss, Mulligan, & Betts, 1998). Children with the disorder do not look malnourished; their weight is usually appropriate for their height. Researchers believe that profound emotional deprivation affects communication between the hypothalamus and pituitary gland, resulting in stunted growth. When such children are removed from their emotionally inadequate environments, their GH levels quickly return to normal, and they grow rapidly. But if treatment is delayed, the dwarfism can be permanent.

## ASK YOURSELF

**review** Explain why breast-feeding offers babies protection against disease and early death in poverty-stricken regions of the world.

**review** How does disease prevention, through immunization and ORT, play a role in preventing malnutrition?

**apply** Ten-month-old Shaun is below average in height and painfully thin. He has one of two serious growth disorders. Name them, and indicate what clues you would look for to tell which one Shaun has.

**connect** Use ecological systems theory (Chapter 1, page 28) to show how bidirectional influences between caregiver and child combine with factors in the surrounding environment to put children at risk for obesity.

## Puberty: The Physical Transition to Adulthood

DURING **puberty,** young people become physically mature and capable of producing offspring. Accompanying rapid changes in body size and proportions are changes in physical features related to sexual functioning. Some, called **primary sexual characteristics,** involve the reproductive organs (ovaries, uterus, and vagina in females; penis, scrotum, and testes in males). Others, called **secondary sexual characteristics,** are visible on the outside of the body and serve as additional signs of sexual maturity (for example, breast development in females, appearance of underarm and pubic hair in both sexes).

Clearly, puberty is the period of greatest sexual differentiation since prenatal life. As we will see in the following sections, its impact on psychological development and social relationships is pervasive. Let's begin with physical changes. As you can see in the Milestones table on page 194, these develop in a fairly standard sequence, although the age at which each begins and is completed varies greatly.

**psychosocial dwarfism**
A growth disorder observed between 2 and 15 years of age. Characterized by substantially below-average stature, weight that is usually appropriate for height, immature skeletal age, and decreased GH secretion. Caused by severe emotional deprivation.

**puberty**
Biological changes during adolescence that lead to an adult-sized body and sexual maturity.

**primary sexual characteristics**
Physical features that involve the reproductive organs (ovaries, uterus, and vagina in females; penis, scrotum, and testes in males).

**secondary sexual characteristics**
Features visible on the outside of the body that serve as signs of sexual maturity but do not involve the reproductive organs (for example, breast development in females, appearance of underarm and pubic hair in both sexes).

# milestones

## PUBERTAL DEVELOPMENT IN NORTH AMERICAN BOYS AND GIRLS

| GIRLS | AVERAGE AGE ATTAINED | AGE RANGE | BOYS | AVERAGE AGE ATTAINED | AGE RANGE |
|---|---|---|---|---|---|
| Breasts begin to "bud." | 10 | (8–13) | Testes begin to enlarge. | 11.5 | (9.5–13.5) |
| Height spurt begins. | 10 | (8–13) | Pubic hair appears. | 12 | (10–15) |
| Pubic hair appears. | 10.5 | (8–14) | Penis begins to enlarge. | 12 | (10.5–14.5) |
| Peak of strength spurt. | 11.6 | (9.5–14) | Height spurt begins. | 12.5 | (10.5–16) |
| Peak of height spurt. | 11.7 | (10–13.5) | Spermarche (first ejaculation) occurs. | 13 | (12–16) |
| Menarche (first menstruation) occurs. | 12.8 | (10.5–15.5) | Peak of height spurt. | 14 | (12.5–15.5) |
| Adult stature reached; underarm hair appears. | 13 | (10–16) | Facial and body hair begin to grow. | 14 | (12.5–15.5) |
| Breast growth completed. | 14 | (10–16) | Voice begins to deepen. | 14 | (12.5–15.5) |
| Pubic hair growth completed. | 14.5 | (14–15) | Penis growth completed. | 14.5 | (12.5–16) |
| | | | Peak of strength spurt. | 15.3 | (13–17) |
| | | | Adult stature reached. | 15.5 | (13.5–17.5) |
| | | | Pubic hair growth completed. | 15.5 | (14–17) |

*Note:* These milestones represent overall age trends. Individual differences exist in the precise age at which each milestone is attained.
*Sources:* Malina & Bouchard, 1991; Tanner, 1990.

## SEXUAL MATURATION IN GIRLS

**Menarche** (from the Greek word *arche,* meaning "beginning") is the scientific name for first menstruation. Because most people view it as the major sign that puberty has arrived in girls, you may be surprised to learn that menarche actually occurs late in the sequence of pubertal events. Female puberty usually begins with the budding of the breasts and the growth spurt. (For about 15 percent of girls, pubic hair is present before breast development.) Menarche typically happens around 12½ years for North American girls, 13 for Europeans. But the age range is wide. Following menarche, pubic hair and breast development are completed, and underarm hair appears. Most girls take about 3 to 4 years to complete this sequence, although this, too, can vary greatly, from 1½ to 5 years (Tanner, 1990; Wheeler, 1991).

**menarche**
First menstruation.

All girls experience menarche after the peak of the height spurt, a sequence that is adaptive. Nature delays menstruation until the girl's body is large enough for successful childbearing. As an extra measure of security, for 12 to 18 months following menarche, the menstrual cycle often takes place without an ovum being released from the ovaries. However, this temporary period of sterility does not apply to all girls, and it cannot be counted on for protection against pregnancy (Tanner, 1990).

## SEXUAL MATURATION IN BOYS

The first sign of puberty in boys is the enlargement of the testes (glands that manufacture sperm), accompanied by changes in the texture and colour of the scrotum. Pubic hair emerges a short time later, about the same time the penis begins to enlarge (Graber, Petersen, & Brooks-Gunn, 1996).

Refer again to the Milestones table on page 194, and you will see that the growth spurt occurs much later in the sequence of pubertal events for boys than for girls. Also, boys' height gain is more intense and longer lasting (Sheehy et al., 1999). When it reaches its peak (at about age 14), enlargement of the testes and penis is nearly complete, and underarm hair appears soon after. Facial and body hair also emerge just after the peak in body growth and gradually increase for several years. Another landmark of male physical maturity is the deepening of the voice as the larynx enlarges and the vocal cords lengthen. (Girls' voices also deepen slightly.) Voice change usually occurs at the peak of the male growth spurt and is often not complete until puberty is over.

While the penis is growing, the prostate gland and seminal vesicles (which together produce semen, the fluid in which sperm are bathed) enlarge. Then, around age 13, **spermarche**, or first ejaculation, occurs (Jorgensen & Keiding, 1991). For a while, the semen contains few living sperm. So, like girls, many boys have an initial period of reduced fertility.

## INDIVIDUAL AND GROUP DIFFERENCES IN PUBERTAL GROWTH

Heredity contributes substantially to the timing of puberty, since identical twins generally reach menarche within a month or two of each other, whereas fraternal twins differ by about 12 months (Kaprio et al., 1995). Nutrition and exercise also make a difference. In females, a sharp rise in body weight and fat may trigger sexual maturation. Fat cells stimulate the ovaries and adrenal glands to produce sex hormones—the likely reason that breast and pubic hair growth and menarche occur earlier for heavier and, especially, obese girls. Indeed, the soaring obesity rate in industrialized nations has contributed to a continuing secular trend toward earlier menarche (Wattigney et al., 1999). In contrast, girls who begin rigorous athletic training at young ages or who eat very little (both of which reduce the percentage of body fat) often are delayed in sexual development (Rees, 1993).

Variations in pubertal growth also exist between regions of the world and social-class and ethnic groups. Heredity seems to play little role, since adolescents with very different genetic origins living under similarly advantaged conditions—for example, in Australia, Canada, Chile, Greece, Israel, Japan, and the United States—reach menarche at about the same average age (Morabia et al., 1998). Instead, physical health is largely responsible. In poverty-stricken regions where malnutrition and infectious disease are widespread, menarche is greatly delayed. In many parts of Africa, it does not occur until age 14 to 17. Within countries, girls from higher-income families consistently reach menarche 6 to 18 months earlier than do those living in economically disadvantaged homes. And African-American girls are ahead of Caucasian-American girls by 6 months in average age of menarche—a difference believed mostly to be due to black girls' heavier body builds (Biro et al., 2001).

Early family experiences also seem to contribute to the timing of puberty. One theory suggests that humans have evolved to be sensitive to the emotional quality of their childhood environments. When children's safety and security are at risk, it is adaptive for them to reproduce early. Consequently, strife-ridden families should promote earlier puberty. In support of this

**spermarche**
First ejaculation of seminal fluid.

Sex-related differences in pubertal growth are obvious among these seventh graders. Although all the children are 12 or 13 years old, some girls are taller and more mature looking.

view, several studies indicate that girls exposed to family conflict tend to reach menarche early, whereas those with highly affectionate family ties reach menarche relatively late (Ellis & Garber, 2000; Ellis et al., 1999; Moffitt et al., 1992).

Notice how, in the research we have considered, threats to physical health delay puberty, whereas threats to emotional health accelerate it. In a study carried out in Poland that distinguished physical stress (poverty) from emotional stress (father absence, parental illness, and parental alcohol abuse), opposite relationships with age at menarche were, indeed, found (Hulanicka, 1999).

## The Psychological Impact of Pubertal Events

THINK BACK TO YOUR late elementary school and junior high days. Were you early, late, or about on time in physical maturation with respect to your peers? How did your feelings about yourself and your relationships with others change? Were your reactions similar to those predicted by Rousseau and Hall, described at the beginning of this chapter?

### IS PUBERTY AN INEVITABLE PERIOD OF STORM AND STRESS?

Recent research suggests that the notion of adolescence as a biologically determined period of storm and stress is greatly exaggerated. A number of problems, such as eating disorders, depression, suicide (see Chapter 11), and lawbreaking (see Chapter 12), occur more often in adolescence than earlier. But the overall rate of serious psychological disturbance rises only slightly from childhood to adolescence, when it is the same as in the adult population—about 20 percent (Costello & Angold, 1995). Although some teenagers encounter serious difficulties, emotional turbulence is not a routine feature of this phase of development.

The first researcher to point out the wide variability in adolescent adjustment was anthropologist Margaret Mead (1928). She travelled to the Pacific islands of Samoa and returned with a startling conclusion: Because of the culture's relaxed social relationships and openness toward sexuality, adolescence "is perhaps the pleasantest time the Samoan girl (or boy) will ever know" (p. 308).

Mead offered an alternative view in which the social environment is entirely responsible for the range of teenage experiences, from erratic and agitated to calm and stress free. Yet this conclusion is just as extreme as the biological perspective it was supposed to replace! Later researchers found that adolescence was not as smooth and untroubled as Mead had assumed (Freeman, 1983).

Still, Mead's work had an enormous impact. Today we know that the experience of adolescence is a product of biological and social forces. In line with Mead's observations, simpler societies have a shorter and smoother transition to adulthood. But adolescence is not absent (Weisfeld, 1997). A study of 186 tribal and village cultures revealed that almost all had an intervening phase, however brief, between childhood and full assumption of adult roles (Schlegel & Barry, 1991).

In industrialized nations, successful participation in economic life requires many years of education. Young people face extra years of dependence on parents and postponement of sexual gratification. As a result, adolescence is greatly extended, and teenagers confront a wider array of psychological challenges. In the following sections, we will see many examples of how biological and social forces combine to affect teenagers' adjustment.

### REACTIONS TO PUBERTAL CHANGES

How do girls and boys react to the massive physical changes of puberty? Most research aimed at answering this question has focused on girls' feelings about menarche.

**GIRLS' REACTIONS TO MENARCHE.** A generation or two ago, menarche was often traumatic. Today, girls commonly react with surprise, undoubtedly due to the sudden nature of the event. Otherwise, they typically report a mixture of positive and negative emotions (Brooks-Gunn, 1988b). Yet wide individual differences exist that depend on prior knowledge and support from family members. Both are influenced by cultural attitudes toward puberty and sexuality.

For girls who have no advance information about sexuality, menarche can be shocking and disturbing. In the 1950s, up to 50 percent were given no prior warning (Shainess, 1961). Today, few are uninformed. This shift is probably due to contemporary parents' greater willingness to discuss sexual matters and more widespread health education classes (Beausang & Razor, 2000; Brooks-Gunn, 1988b). Almost all girls get some information from their mothers and at school. And girls whose fathers know about their daughters' pubertal changes adjust especially well. Perhaps a father's involvement reflects a family atmosphere that is highly understanding and accepting of physical and sexual matters (Brooks-Gunn & Ruble, 1980, 1983).

**BOYS' REACTIONS TO SPERMARCHE.** Boys' reactions to spermarche also reflect mixed feelings. Virtually all boys know about ejaculation ahead of time, but few get any information from parents. Usually they obtain it from reading material (Gaddis & Brooks-Gunn, 1985). Despite advance information, many boys say that their first ejaculation occurred earlier than they expected and that they were unprepared for it. As with girls, the better prepared boys feel, the more positively they react (Stein & Reiser, 1994).

In addition, whereas almost all girls tell a friend that they are menstruating, far fewer boys tell anyone about spermarche (Downs & Fuller, 1991). Overall, boys seem to get less social support for the physical changes of puberty than do girls. This suggests that boys might benefit, especially, from opportunities to ask questions and discuss feelings with a sympathetic parent or health professional.

**CULTURAL INFLUENCES.** The experience of puberty is affected by the larger cultural context. Many tribal and village societies celebrate puberty with a *rite of passage*—a communitywide initiation ceremony that marks an important change in privilege and responsibility. Consequently, young people know that pubertal changes are honoured and valued in their culture (see the Cultural Influences box on page 198). In contrast, Western societies grant little formal recognition to movement from childhood to adolescence or from adolescence to adulthood. Certain religious ceremonies, such as confirmation and the Jewish bar or bat mitzvah, do resemble a rite of passage. But they usually do not lead to any meaningful change in social status.

Instead, Western adolescents are confronted with many ages at which they are granted partial adult status—for example, an age for starting employment, for driving, for leaving high school, for voting, and for drinking. In some contexts (on the highway and at work), they may be treated like adults. In others (at school and at home), they may still be regarded as children. The absence of a widely accepted marker of physical and social maturity makes the process of becoming an adult especially confusing.

## PUBERTAL CHANGE, EMOTION, AND SOCIAL BEHAVIOUR

In the preceding sections, we considered adolescents' reactions to their sexually maturing bodies. Puberty can also affect the young person's emotional state and social behaviour. A common belief is that pubertal change has something to do with adolescent moodiness and the desire for greater physical and psychological separation from parents.

**ADOLESCENT MOODINESS.** Recently, researchers have explored the role of sex hormones in adolescents' emotional reactions. Indeed, higher hormone levels are related to greater moodiness, in the form of anger and irritability for males and anger and depression

# cultural influences

## ADOLESCENT INITIATION CEREMONIES

*a*n **adolescent initiation ceremony** is a ritualized announcement to the community that a young person is ready to make the transition from childhood into adolescence or full adulthood. These special rites of passage reach their fullest expression in small tribal and village societies. Besides celebration, they often include separation from parents and members of the other sex; instruction in cultural customs and work roles; and fertility rituals that incorporate the young person into the sexual and child-bearing world of adults. According to anthropologists, each of these ceremonial features is a cultural expression of the adaptive value of puberty.

### SEPARATION

The beginning of an initiation ceremony is usually marked by separation from parents and members of the other sex, and sometimes by seclusion from the entire settlement. Among the !Kung hunters and gatherers of Botswana, Africa, a girl menstruating for the first time is carried to a special shelter by an old woman, who cares for her until the menstrual flow stops. The Tiwi, an Aboriginal group of northern Australia, greet male puberty by arranging to have a group of unfamiliar men take boys to a special campsite in the bush. Initiates are expected to shed their childish ways abruptly in favour of adultlike reverence and self-restraint (Spindler, 1970). A same-sex nonparent usually oversees the initiation, since puberty is accompanied by psychological distancing between parent and child (see page 200), which reduces parents' power to teach the adolescent (Eibl-Eibesfeldt, 1989).

Boys are typically initiated in large peer groups. When agemates undergo challenging and painful experiences together, they bond, which enhances cooperation in hunting, defending the group, and other adult tasks (Schlegel & Barry, 1991). Girls, in contrast, are generally initiated singly. In adulthood, they will spend more time with their family and in small groups. Consequently, large-group unity is deemed less important (Schlegel, 1995).

### INSTRUCTION

During initiation, elders teach adolescents about ceremonial matters, courtship, sexual techniques, duties to one's spouse and in-laws, and subsistence skills. Elders often convey tribal secrets. Among the Mano of Liberia, older men take boys into the forest, where they learn secret folklore along with farming and other skills they will need to earn a living. They return with a new name, signifying their adult identity, and an even stronger allegiance to their culture. !Kung women teach the newly menstruating girl not to shame her husband or touch his hunting gear and about birth and infant care (Fried & Fried, 1980).

### ENTRY INTO ADULT SOCIETY

The training period culminates in a formal celebration, which usually grants young people permission to engage in sex and to marry. Most of

**adolescent initiation ceremony**
A ritual, or rite of passage, announcing to the community that a young person is ready to make the transition from childhood into adolescence or full adulthood.

for females (Buchanan, Eccles, & Becker, 1992; Nottelmann et al., 1990; Paikoff, Brooks-Gunn, & Warren, 1991). But the link is not strong, and we cannot really be sure that a rise in pubertal hormones causes adolescent moodiness.

What else might contribute to the common observation that adolescents are moody? In several studies, the mood fluctuations of children, adolescents, and adults were tracked over a week by having them carry electronic pagers. At random intervals, they were beeped and asked to write down what they were doing, whom they were with, and how they felt.

As expected, adolescents reported less favourable moods than did school-age children and adults (Csikszentmihalyi & Larson, 1984; Larson & Lampman-Petraitis, 1989). But negative moods were often linked to a greater number of negative life events, such as difficulties getting along with parents, disciplinary actions at school, and breaking up with a boyfriend or girlfriend. Number of negative events increased steadily from childhood to adolescence, and teenagers seemed to react to them with greater emotion than did children (Larson & Ham, 1993).

Furthermore, compared with the moods of adults, adolescents' feelings were less stable. They often varied from cheerful to sad and back again. But teenagers also moved from one situation to another more often, and their mood swings were strongly related to these

© MICHAEL DWYER/STOCK BOSTON

This Ubi girl of Zaire, Africa, studied traditional dance and customs for a year before she was deemed ready for the adolescent initiation ceremony that will grant her adult status among her people.

the time, the appearance of initiates is changed so that all members of the community can identify them and treat them differently. Sometimes these markers involve temporary body decorations, such as painting and jewellery. At other times, the changes are permanent, consisting of new types of clothing or scars engraved on some

part of the body—the face, back, chest, or penis.

Many ceremonies include an ordeal, typically more severe for males than for females. A boy might need to kill game or endure cold and hunger, a girl might grind grain or remain secluded for several days. These rites stress responsibility and bravery (Weisfield, 1997).

Male genital operations (usually circumcision) occur in about one-third of cultures with puberty rites and are typically followed by sexual activity. Female surgery (removal of part or all of the clitoris and sometimes the labia) takes place in only 8 percent of initiation ceremonies, for the purpose of ensuring the girl's continued virginity and therefore her value as a bride (Weisfield, 1990).[1]

## CULTURAL VARIATIONS

In the simplest societies, adolescent initiation ceremonies for girls are more common than those for boys. In small bands of hunters and gatherers, females are in short supply. The loss of any woman of childbearing age can threaten the survival of the group. As cultures move from simple foraging to farming communities, rituals recognize young people of both sexes for their reproductive and economic roles (Schlegel & Barry, 1980). In more complex cultures, adolescent initiation ceremonies recede in importance and disappear.

[1]*Female genital mutilation,* widespread in Africa, Indonesia, Malaysia, and the Middle East, as a means of guaranteeing chastity and therefore a good marriage partner, is usually inflicted on girls in infancy or early childhood, before they know enough to resist (Weisfield, 1997). Although illegal in many countries, the practice is difficult for governments to control. Today, there are millions of genitally mutilated girls and women in the developing world. International organizations are working within each culture's belief system to bring an end to this violation of human rights.

changes. High points of their days were times spent with friends and in self-chosen leisure activities. Low points tended to occur in adult-structured settings—class, job, school halls, school library, and religious services.

Not surprisingly, adolescents' emotional high points are Friday and Saturday evenings, especially at older ages (see Figure 5.15 on page 200). As teenagers move from junior high to high school, frequency of going out with friends and romantic partners—to movies, sports events, and parties or just to cruise around town—increases dramatically, so much so that it becomes a "cultural script" for what is *supposed* to happen. This means that teenagers who fall short of the script—who spend weekend evenings at home—often experience profound loneliness (Larson & Richards, 1998).

Yet another contributor to adolescent moodiness are changes in sleep schedules. Teenagers need almost as much sleep as they did in middle childhood (about 9 hours). Yet they go to bed much later than they did as children. Biological changes may underlie this bedtime delay, as it strengthens with pubertal maturation (Carskadon, Viera, & Acebo, 1993). But evening activities and part-time jobs also contribute. Sleep-deprived teenagers often suffer from depressed mood and achieve less well in school (Link & Ancoli-Israel, 1995). Although later school start times ease sleep loss, they do not eliminate it (Kowalski & Allen, 1995).

FIGURE 5.15

**Younger and older adolescents' emotional experiences across the week.**
Adolescents' reports revealed that emotional high points are on Fridays and Saturdays, especially among ninth to twelfth graders. Mood drops on Sunday, before returning to school, and during the week, as students spend much time in adult-structured settings in school. (From R. Larson & M. Richards, 1998, "Waiting for the Weekend: Friday and Saturday Night as the Emotional Climax of the Week." In A. C. Crouter & R. Larson [Eds.], *Temporal Rhythms in Adolescence: Clocks, Calendars, and the Coordination of Daily Life.* San Francisco: Jossey-Bass, p. 41. Reprinted by permission.)

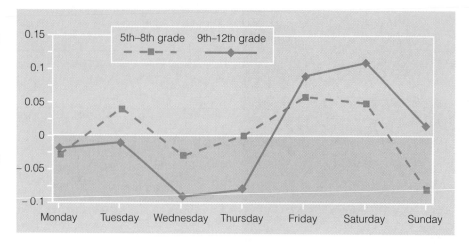

Taken together, these findings suggest that situational factors act in concert with hormonal influences to affect teenagers' moodiness. This explanation is consistent with the balanced view of biological and social forces, described earlier in this chapter.

**PARENT–CHILD RELATIONSHIPS.** Recall the observations of Sabrina's father in the introduction to this chapter—that as children enter adolescence, they often resist spending time with the family and become more argumentative. Many studies show that puberty is related to a rise in parent–child conflict. Although rate of conflict declines with age as parents and adolescents spend less time together, its emotional intensity rises into midadolescence. During this time, both parents and teenagers report feeling less close to one another (Laursen, Coy, & Collins, 1998; Steinberg & Morris, 2001). Frequency of conflict is surprisingly similar across North American subcultures. It occurs about as often in families of European descent as it does in immigrant Chinese, Filipino, and Mexican families, whose traditions respect parental authority and downplay adolescent individuality (Fuligni, 1998).

Why should a youngster's more adultlike appearance trigger these disputes? The association may have some adaptive value. Among nonhuman primates, the young typically leave the family around the time of puberty. The same is true in many nonindustrialized cultures (Caine, 1986; Schlegel & Barry, 1991). Departure of young people from the family discourages sexual relations between close blood relatives. But because children in industrialized societies remain economically dependent on parents long after they reach puberty, they cannot leave the family. Consequently, a modern substitute for physical departure seems to have emerged—psychological distancing (Steinberg, 1990).

In later chapters, we will see that adolescents' new powers of reasoning may also contribute to a rise in family tensions. In addition, friction rises because children have become physically mature and demand to be treated in adultlike ways. Parent–adolescent disagreements largely focus on mundane, day-to-day matters, such as driving, dating partners, and curfews (Adams & Laursen, 2001). But beneath these disputes are serious concerns—parental efforts to protect their teenagers from substance use, auto accidents, and early sex. The larger the gap between parents' and adolescents' views of teenagers' readiness to take on developmental tasks, the more quarrelling (Deković, Noom, & Meeus, 1997).

The conflict that does take place is generally mild. Only a small minority of families experience a serious break in parent–child relationships. In reality, parents and adolescents display both conflict and affection throughout adolescence, and usually they agree on important values, such as honesty and the value of education (Arnett, 1999; Holmbeck, 1996). This also makes sense from an evolutionary perspective. Although separation from parents is adaptive, both generations benefit from warm, protective family bonds that last for many years to come.

DAVID YOUNG-WOLFF/STONE

Compared with children and adults, adolescents often seem moody. But young people whose moods are often negative experience more negative life events. This dispirited boy may have had an argument with his parents, received a detention at school, or broken up with his girlfriend. Events like these increase in adolescence.

## EARLY VERSUS LATE MATURATION

In addition to dramatic physical change, the timing of puberty has a major impact on psychological adjustment. As we will see in the following sections, having physical characteristics that help gain social acceptance can be very comforting to adolescent boys and girls.

**EFFECTS OF PUBERTAL TIMING.** Findings of several studies indicate that both adults and peers viewed early maturing boys as relaxed, independent, self-confident, and physically attractive. Popular with agemates, they held many leadership positions in school and tended to be athletic stars. In contrast, late maturing boys were not well liked. Peers and adults viewed them as anxious, overly talkative, and attention seeking (Brooks-Gunn, 1988a; Clausen, 1975; Jones, 1965). However, early maturing boys (despite being viewed as well adjusted) report slightly more psychological stress than do their later maturing agemates (Ge, Conger, & Elder, 2001).

In contrast, early maturing girls were below average in popularity, withdrawn, lacking in self-confidence, psychologically stressed, and held few leadership positions (Ge, Conger, & Elder, 1996; Graber et al., 1997; Jones & Mussen, 1958). In addition, they were more involved in deviant behaviour (getting drunk, participating in early sexual activity) and achieved less well in school (Caspi et al., 1993; Dick et al., 2000). In contrast, their late maturing counterparts were well adjusted—regarded as physically attractive, lively, sociable, and leaders at school.

Two factors largely account for these trends: (1) how closely the adolescent's body matches cultural ideals of physical attractiveness, and (2) how well the young person "fits in" physically with agemates.

**THE ROLE OF PHYSICAL ATTRACTIVENESS.** Flip through the pages of your favourite popular magazine. You will see evidence for our society's view of an attractive female as thin and long legged and a good-looking male as tall, broad shouldered, and muscular. The female image is a girlish shape that favours the late developer. The male image is consistent with that of the early maturing boy.

As their bodies change, adolescents become preoccupied with their physical selves. Girls, especially, are likely to analyze all their body features (Wertheim et al., 1997). In addition, teenagers get a great deal of feedback from others—both directly, through remarks about their appearance, and indirectly, through the tendency of children and adults to treat physically attractive people more positively. The conclusions young people draw about their appearance strongly affect their self-esteem and psychological well-being (Mendelson, White, & Mendelson, 1996; Usmiani & Daniluk, 1997).

In several studies, early maturing girls reported a less positive **body image**—conception of and attitude toward their physical appearance—than did their on-time and late maturing agemates. Among boys, the opposite occurred: Early maturation was linked to a positive body image, whereas late maturation predicted dissatisfaction with the physical self (Alsaker, 1995). The difference between early and late maturing boys was short-lived; it disappeared as the late maturers reached puberty. Early maturing girls' less favourable body image not only persisted but became more extreme. In sum, the adoption of society's "beauty is best" stereotype seems to be a factor in pubertal timing effects, particularly for girls.

**THE IMPORTANCE OF FITTING IN WITH PEERS.** Physical status in relation to peers also explains differences in adjustment between early and late maturers. From this perspective, early maturing girls and late maturing boys have difficulty because they fall at the extremes in physical development. Recall that Sabrina felt "out of place" when with her agemates. Not surprisingly, adolescents feel most comfortable with peers who match their own level of biological maturity (Brooks-Gunn et al., 1986; Stattin & Magnusson, 1990).

Because few agemates of the same pubertal status are available, early maturing adolescents of both sexes seek out older companions—a tendency that can have some unfavourable consequences. Older peers often encourage early maturing youngsters into activities they are not yet

**body image**
Conception of and attitude toward one's physical appearance.

ready to handle emotionally, including sexual activity, drug and alcohol use, and minor delinquent acts. Perhaps because of involvements like these, early maturers of both sexes are psychologically stressed and show declines in academic performance (Stattin & Magnusson, 1990).

Interestingly, school contexts can modify these maturational timing effects. In one study, early maturing sixth-grade girls felt better about themselves when they attended kindergarten through grade 6 (K–6) rather than kindergarten through grade 8 (K–8) schools, where they could mix with older adolescents. In the K–6 settings, they were relieved of pressures to adopt behaviours for which they were not ready (Blyth, Simmons, & Zakin, 1985). Similarly, a New Zealand study found that delinquency among early maturing girls was greatly reduced in all-girl schools, which limit opportunities to associate with norm-violating peers (most of whom are older boys) (Caspi et al., 1993).

**LONG-TERM CONSEQUENCES.** Do the effects of early and late maturation persist into adulthood? Long-term follow-ups reveal some striking turnabouts. Many early maturing boys and late maturing girls, who had been so admired in adolescence, became rigid, inflexible, conforming, and somewhat discontented adults. In contrast, late maturing boys and early maturing girls, who were stress-ridden as teenagers, often developed into adults who were independent, flexible, cognitively competent, and satisfied with the direction of their lives (Livson & Peshkin, 1980; Macfarlane, 1971). Perhaps the confidence-inducing adolescence of early maturing boys and late maturing girls does not promote the coping skills needed to solve life's later problems. In contrast, the painful experiences associated with off-time pubertal growth may, in time, contribute to sharpened awareness, clarified goals, and greater stability.

Nevertheless, these long-term outcomes may not hold completely. In a Swedish study, achievement difficulties of early maturing girls persisted into young adulthood, in the form of lower educational attainment than their on-time and later maturing counterparts (Stattin & Magnusson, 1990). In countries with highly selective university entrance systems, perhaps it is harder for early maturers to recover from declines in school performance. Clearly, the effects of maturational timing involve a complex blend of biological, immediate social setting, and cultural factors.

## ASK YOURSELF www

**review**    Many people believe that the rising sexual passions of puberty cause rebelliousness in adolescents. Where did this belief originate? Explain why it is incorrect.

**review**    List factors that contribute to pubertal timing. Then summarize the consequences of early versus late maturation for adolescent development.

**apply**    Regina wonders why her 14-year-old daughter Cloe spends hours alone in her room and no longer wants to join in weekend family activities. Explain why Cloe's behaviour is adaptive.

**connect**    How might adolescent moodiness contribute to psychological distancing between parents and adolescents? (Hint: Think about bidirectional influences in parent–child relationships.)

# Puberty and Adolescent Health

THE ARRIVAL OF PUBERTY IS accompanied by new health concerns. Eating disturbances appear in many young people who worry about falling short of their idealized image of attractiveness and fitness. Homosexual teenagers face formidable challenges in forging an open, positive sexual identity. And sexual activity brings with it the risk of sexually transmitted disease and early pregnancy.

As adolescents are granted greater autonomy, their personal decision making becomes important, in health as in other areas (Bearison, 1998). Yet none of the health concerns we are about to discuss can be traced to a single cause. Instead, biological, psychological, family, and cultural factors jointly contribute.

## EATING DISORDERS

Girls who are early maturers, who are very dissatisfied with their body image, and who grow up in homes where concern with weight and thinness is high are at risk for eating problems. Sabrina's mother worried about Sabrina's desire to lose weight when she reached puberty. Severe dieting is the strongest predictor of eating disorders in adolescence (Patton et al., 1999). The two most serious are anorexia nervosa and bulimia.

**ANOREXIA NERVOSA.** **Anorexia nervosa** is a tragic eating disturbance in which young people starve themselves because of a compulsive fear of getting fat. About 1 percent of teenagers in Canada and the United States are affected, a rate that has increased sharply during the past 50 years, due to cultural admiration of female thinness. Occasionally, boys are diagnosed with the disorder; about half are homosexual or bisexual (Brown & Mehler, 2000). Asian-American, Caucasian-American, and Hispanic girls are at greater risk than are African-American girls, who are more satisfied with their size and shape (Halpern et al., 1999; Rhea, 1999; Wildes, Emery, & Simons, 2001). Anorexia nervosa occurs equally often among economically advantaged and disadvantaged teenagers.

Anorexics have an extremely distorted body image. Even after they have become severely underweight, they believe they are fat. Most lose weight by going on a self-imposed diet so strict that they struggle to avoid eating in response to hunger. To enhance weight loss, they exercise strenuously.

In their attempt to reach "perfect" slimness, anorexics lose between 25 and 50 percent of their body weight. Because a normal menstrual cycle requires about 15 percent body fat, either menarche does not occur or menstrual periods stop. Malnutrition causes pale skin; brittle, discoloured nails; fine dark hairs all over the body; and extreme sensitivity to cold. If allowed to continue, the heart muscle can shrink, the kidneys can fail, and irreversible brain damage and loss of bone mass can occur. About 6 percent die of the disorder, as a result of either physical complications or suicide (Schmidt, 2000).

Forces within the person, the family, and the larger culture give rise to anorexia nervosa. We have already seen that the societal image of "thin is beautiful" contributes to the poorer body image of early maturing girls, who are at greatest risk for anorexia (Tyrka, Graber, & Brooks-Gunn, 2000). Many anorexics also have extremely high standards for their own behaviour and performance. Furthermore, they tend to be emotionally inhibited and to avoid intimate ties outside the family. Consequently, these girls are excellent students who are responsible and well behaved—ideal daughters in many respects.

Concordance for anorexia nervosa is higher in identical than fraternal twins, indicating a genetic influence (Klump, Kaye, & Strober, 2001). In addition, parent–child interactions reveal problems related to adolescent autonomy. Often mothers of these girls have high expectations for physical appearance (including body weight), achievement, and social acceptance and are overprotective and controlling; fathers tend to be emotionally distant. Instead of rebelling openly, anorexic girls seem to do so covertly—by fiercely pursuing perfection in achievement, respectable behaviour, and thinness (Bruch, 2001). Nevertheless, whether maladaptive parent–child relationships precede the disorder, emerge as a response to it, or both is not yet clear.

Because anorexic girls typically deny that any problem exists, treating the disorder is difficult. Hospitalization is often necessary to prevent life-threatening malnutrition. Family therapy, aimed at changing parent–child interaction and expectations, is the most successful treatment (Gelbaugh et al., 2001). As a supplementary approach, behaviour modification—in which hospitalized anorexics are rewarded with praise, social contact, and opportunities

©KANSAS CITY STAR/THE LIAISON AGENCY

Cultural admiration of female thinness has contributed to a dramatic increase in anorexia nervosa. This girl died from the disorder. Her strict, self-imposed diet and obsession with strenuous physical exercise led her to become painfully thin. Even so, her body image was so distorted that she regarded herself as fat and continued her destructive behaviour.

**anorexia nervosa**
An eating disorder in which individuals (usually females) starve themselves because of a compulsive fear of getting fat.

for exercise when they eat and gain weight—is helpful (Robin, Gilroy, & Dennis, 1998). Still, only 50 percent of anorexics fully recover. For many others, eating problems continue in less extreme form. Ten percent show signs of a less severe disorder—bulimia nervosa—that is still physically and psychologically damaging (Fichter & Quadflieg, 1999).

**BULIMIA NERVOSA.** In **bulimia nervosa,** young people (again, mainly girls, but gay adolescent boys are also vulnerable) engage in strict dieting and excessive exercise accompanied by binge eating, often followed by deliberate vomiting and purging with laxatives. Bulimia is more common than anorexia nervosa. About 2 to 3 percent of teenage girls are affected; only 5 percent have previously been anorexic.

Twin studies show that bulimia, like anorexia, is influenced by heredity (Klump, Kaye, & Strober, 2001). Although bulimics share with anorexics a pathological fear of getting fat, they may have experienced their parents as disengaged and emotionally unavailable rather than controlling (Fairburn et al., 1997). One conjecture is that bulimics turn to food to compensate for feelings of emptiness resulting from lack of parental involvement (Attie & Brooks-Gunn, 1996).

Some bulimics, like anorexics, are perfectionists. Others lack self-control not just in eating but in other areas of their lives, engaging in petty shoplifting and alcohol abuse (Garner & Garfinkel, 1997). Bulimics differ from anorexics in that they are aware of their abnormal eating habits, feel depressed and guilty about them, and usually are desperate for help. As a result, bulimia is usually easier to treat than anorexia, using therapy focused on support groups, nutrition education, and revising eating habits and thoughts about food (Kaye et al., 2000).

## SEXUALITY

With the arrival of puberty, hormonal changes—in particular, the production of androgens in young people of both sexes—lead to an increase in sex drive (Halpern, Udry, & Suchindran, 1997; Udry, 1990). In response, adolescents become very concerned about how to manage sexuality in social relationships, and new cognitive capacities affect their efforts to do so. Yet, like the eating behaviours we have just discussed, adolescent sexuality is heavily influenced by the young person's social context.

**THE IMPACT OF CULTURE.** Think, for a moment, about when you first learned the "facts of life" and how you found out about them. In your family, was sex discussed openly or treated with secrecy? Exposure to sex, education about it, and efforts to restrict the sexual curiosity of children and adolescents vary widely around the world. At one extreme are a number of Middle Eastern peoples, who are known to kill girls who lose their virginity before marriage. At the other extreme are several Asian and Pacific Island groups with very permissive sexual attitudes and practices. For example, among the Trobriand Islanders of Melanesia, older companions provide children with explicit instruction in sexual practices, and adolescents are expected to engage in sexual experimentation with a variety of partners (Benedict, 1934; Ford & Beach, 1951).

Despite the publicity granted to the image of a sexually free adolescent, sexual attitudes in North America are relatively restrictive. Typically parents give children little information about sex, discourage sex play, and rarely talk about sex in their presence. When young people become interested in sex, they seek information from friends, books, magazines, movies, and television. On prime-time television shows, which adolescents watch the most, sex between partners with little commitment to each other occurs often. Characters are rarely shown taking steps to avoid pregnancy or sexually transmitted disease (Ward, 1995).

Consider the contradictory messages delivered by these sources. On the one hand, adults emphasize that sex at a young age and outside marriage is wrong. On the other hand, the broader social environment extols the excitement and romanticism of sex. Teenagers are left bewildered, poorly informed about sexual facts, and with little sound advice on how to conduct their sex lives responsibly.

**bulimia nervosa**
An eating disorder in which individuals (mainly females) engage in strict dieting and excessive exercise accompanied by binge eating; often followed by deliberate vomiting and purging with laxatives.

**ADOLESCENT SEXUAL ATTITUDES AND BEHAVIOUR.** Although differences between subcultural groups exist, the sexual attitudes of both adolescents and adults have become more liberal over the past 40 years. Compared with a generation ago, more people believe that sexual intercourse before marriage is all right, as long as two people are emotionally committed to each other (Michael et al., 1994). Recently, a slight swing back in the direction of conservative sexual beliefs has occurred, largely due to the risk of sexually transmitted disease, especially AIDS (Glassman, 1996).

Trends in the sexual activity of adolescents are quite consistent with their attitudes. The rate of premarital sex among young people rose over several decades but recently declined (Dryburgh, 2001). Nevertheless, as Table 5.2 reveals, a substantial minority of boys and girls are sexually active quite early, by age 15 (Health Canada, 2001). In addition, contrary to popular opinion, males do not tend to have their first intercourse earlier than do females. Instead, recent trends suggest that girls may be having first intercourse earlier than boys.

Yet timing of first intercourse provides only a limited picture of adolescent sexual behaviour. Most teenagers engage in relatively low levels of sexual activity. The typical sexually active 15- to 19-year-old has relations with only one partner at a time and spends much of the year with no partner (Sonenstein, Pleck, & Ku, 1991; U.S. Department of Health and Human Services, 2000). In Canada, 22 percent of females and 29 percent of males in this age category reported having more than one sex partner in the previous 12 months (Health Canada, 2001). Overall, a runaway sexual revolution does not characterize adolescents, and the rate of teenage sexual activity in North America is about the same as in Western European nations (Creatsas et al., 1995).

**CHARACTERISTICS OF SEXUALLY ACTIVE ADOLESCENTS.** Early and frequent sexual activity is linked to personal, family, peer, and educational variables. These include early physical maturation, parental divorce, single-parent and stepfamily homes, large family size, little or no religious involvement, weak parental monitoring, disrupted parent–child communication, sexually active friends and older siblings, poor school performance, lower educational aspirations, and tendency to engage in norm-violating acts, including alcohol and drug use and delinquency (Kotchick et al., 2001).

Since many of these factors are associated with growing up in a low-SES family, it is not surprising that early sexual activity is more common among young people from economically disadvantaged homes. Living in a hazardous neighbourhood—one high in physical deterioration, crime, and violence—also increases the likelihood that teenagers will be sexually active (Upchurch et al., 1999). In such neighbourhoods, social ties are weak, and adults exert little oversight and control over adolescents' activities.

EBSIN-ANDERSON/FIRSTLIGHT.CA

Adolescence is an especially important time for the development of sexuality. Unfortunately, teenagers receive contradictory and confusing messages from the social environment about the appropriateness of sex. Nevertheless, although the rate of premarital sex has risen among adolescents, most engage in low levels of sexual activity and have only a single partner.

**TABLE 5.2**

Age of First Intercourse for Canadian Youth

| MEDIAN AGE AT FIRST INTERCOURSE | | | | PERCENTAGE WHO HAVE HAD INTERCOURSE BY AGE 15 | | | |
|---|---|---|---|---|---|---|---|
| Born 1942–46 | | Born 1972–76 | | Born 1972–76 | | Born 1977–81 | |
| Male | Female | Male | Female | Male | Female | Male | Female |
| 18 | 20 | 17 | 17 | 21.8 | 21.8 | 19.5 | 25.6 |

*Source:* Adapted from Health Canada (2001a). HIV/AIDS epi update: HIV and AIDS among youth in Canada. Reprinted by permission of Health Canada and Government Works, 2002.

**CONTRACEPTIVE USE.** Although adolescent contraceptive use has increased in recent years, only 60 percent of 15- to 17-year-old sexually active Canadian teenagers reported always using contraception during the previous 6 months (Fisher, Boroditsky, & Bridges, 1999). Many teenagers risk unplanned pregnancy because they do not use contraception at all or delay using it after they have become sexually active (Everett et al., 2000). Why do so many teenagers fail to take precautions? As we will see in Chapter 6, adolescents can consider many more possibilities than school-age children when faced with a problem. But they often fail to apply this reasoning to everyday situations. When asked to explain why they did not use contraception, they often give answers like these: "I was waiting until I had a steady boyfriend." "I wasn't planning to have sex."

One reason for responses like these is that advances in perspective taking—the capacity to imagine what others may be thinking and feeling (see Chapters 6 and 11)—lead teenagers, for a time, to be extremely concerned about others' opinions of them. Another reason for lack of planning before sex is that intense self-reflection leads many adolescents to believe they are unique and invulnerable to danger. In the midst of everyday social pressures, they often seem to overlook the consequences of engaging in risky behaviours (Beyth-Marom & Fischhoff, 1997).

Although adolescent cognition has something to do with teenagers' reluctance to use contraception, the social environment also contributes to it. Among girls, feeling depressed and "like a failure" is linked to unprotected intercourse; among boys, feeling "in control" is associated with it (Kowaleski-Jones & Mott, 1998). Teenagers who do not have the rewards of meaningful education and work are especially likely to engage in irresponsible sex, sometimes within relationships characterized by exploitation and victimization. In Canada, 1 in 3 girls and 1 in 6 boys experience some form of unwanted sexual contact before the age of 18 (Society of Obstetricians and Gynaecologists of Canada, 2002).

In contrast, teenagers who report good relationships with parents and who talk openly with them about sex and contraception are more likely to use birth control (Whitaker & Miller, 2000). Unfortunately, many adolescents say they are too scared or embarrassed to ask parents questions. And too many leave sex education classes with incomplete or factually incorrect knowledge. Some do not know where to get birth control counselling and devices. When they do, they often worry that a doctor or family planning clinic might not keep their visits confidential (American Academy of Pediatrics, 1999). In response to the perceived need for sexuality education and information, the Society of Obstetricians and Gynaecologists of Canada has set up a website for adolescents, parents, and professionals at *www.sexualityandu.ca*.

**SEXUAL ORIENTATION.** Up to this point, our discussion has focused only on heterosexual behaviour. About 3 to 6 percent of young people discover that they are lesbian or gay (see the Biology & Environment box on the following page). An as-yet-unknown but significant number are bisexual (Michael et al., 1994; Patterson, 1995). Adolescence is an equally crucial time for the sexual development of these individuals, and societal attitudes, once again, loom large in how well they fare.

Recent evidence indicates that heredity makes an important contribution to homosexuality. Identical twins of both sexes are much more likely than fraternal twins to share a homosexual orientation; the same is true for biological as opposed to adoptive relatives (Bailey & Pillard, 1991; Bailey et al., 1993). Furthermore, male homosexuality tends to be more common on the maternal than paternal side of families. This suggests that it might be X-linked (see Chapter 3). Indeed, one gene-mapping study found that among 40 pairs of homosexual brothers, 33 (82 percent) had an identical segment of DNA on the X chromosome. One or several genes in that region might predispose males to become homosexual (Hamer et al., 1993).

How might heredity lead to homosexuality? According to some researchers, certain genes affect the level or impact of prenatal sex hormones, which modify brain structures in ways that induce homosexual feelings and behaviour (Bailey et al., 1995; LeVay, 1993). Keep in mind, however, that both genetic and environmental factors can alter prenatal hormones. Girls exposed prenatally to very high levels of androgens or estrogens—because of either a genetic defect or drugs given to the mother to prevent miscarriage—are more likely to become homosexual or bisexual (Meyer-Bahlburg et al., 1995). Furthermore, homosexual

# biology & environment

## HOMOSEXUALITY: COMING OUT TO ONESELF AND OTHERS

Cultures vary as much in their acceptance of homosexuality as they do in their approval of pre-marital sex. In Canada and the United States, homosexuals are stigmatized, as shown by the degrading language often used to describe them. This makes forming a sexual identity a much greater challenge for gay and lesbian youths than for their heterosexual counterparts, who appreciate from an early age that people like themselves fall in love with members of the other sex.

Wide variations in sexual identity formation exist, depending on personal, family, and community factors. Yet interviews with homosexual adolescents and adults reveal that many (but not all) move through a three-phase sequence in coming out to themselves and others:

### FEELING DIFFERENT

Many gay men and lesbians say that they felt different from other children when they were young (Savin-Williams, 1998). Typically, this first sense of their biologically determined sexual orientation appears between ages 6 and 12 and results from play interests more like those of the other gender (Mondimore, 1996). Boys may find that they are less interested in sports, drawn to quieter activities, and more emotionally sensitive than other boys; girls that they are more athletic and active than other girls.

### CONFUSION

With the arrival of puberty, feeling different begins to include feeling sexually different. In research on ethnically diverse gay, lesbian, and bisexual youths, awareness of a same-sex attraction occurred, on the average, between ages 11 and 12 for boys and 14 and 15 for girls, perhaps because social pressures toward heterosexuality are particularly intense for girls (Diamond, 1998;

Herdt & Boxer, 1993). Realizing that homosexuality has personal relevance generally sparks confusion because most young people had assumed they were heterosexual like everyone else.

A few adolescents resolve their discomfort by crystallizing a gay, lesbian, or bisexual identity quickly, with a flash of insight into their sense of being different. But many experience an inner struggle, intensified by lack of role models and social support. Some throw themselves into activities they have come to associate with heterosexuality. Boys may go out for athletic teams; girls may drop softball and basketball in favour of dance. And homosexual youths typically try heterosexual dating, sometimes to hide their sexual orientation and at other times to develop intimacy skills that they later apply to same-sex relationships (Dubé, Savin-Williams, & Diamond, 2001). Those who are extremely troubled and guilt-ridden may escape into alcohol, drugs, and suicidal thinking.

### ACCEPTANCE

The majority of gay and lesbian teenagers reach a point of accepting their homosexuality. Then they face another crossroad: whether to tell others. The most difficult disclosure is to parents, but many fear rejection by peers as well (Cohen & Savin-Williams, 1996). Powerful stigmas against their sexual orientation lead some to decide that no disclosure is possible. As a result, they self-define but otherwise "pass" as heterosexual. In one study of gay adolescents, 85 percent said they tried concealment for a time (Newman & Muzzonigro, 1993).

Many young people eventually acknowledge their sexual orientation publicly, usually by telling trusted friends first, then family members and acquaintances. When people react positively, coming out strengthens the

young person's view of homosexuality as a valid, meaningful, and fulfilling identity. Contact with other gays and lesbians is important for reaching this phase, and changes in society permit many adolescents in urban areas to attain it earlier than they did a decade or two ago (Diamond, Savin-Williams, & Dubé, 1999). Gay and lesbian communities exist in large cities, along with specialized interest groups, social clubs, religious groups, newspapers, and periodicals. Small towns and rural areas remain difficult places to meet other homosexuals and to find a supportive environment. Teenagers in these locales have a special need for caring adults and peers who can help them find self and social acceptance.

Gay and lesbian youths who succeed in coming out to themselves and others integrate their sexual orientation into a broader sense of identity, a process we will address in Chapter 11. They no longer need to focus so heavily on their homosexual self, and energy is freed for other aspects of psychological growth. In sum, coming out can foster many aspects of adolescent development, including self-esteem, psychological well-being, and relationships with family, friends, and co-workers.

This gay couple enjoys an evening at a high school prom. As long as friends and family members react with acceptance, coming out strengthens the young person's view of homosexuality as a valid, meaningful, and fulfilling identity.

DONNA BINDER/IMPACT VISUALS

men tend to have a later birth order and a higher-than-average number of older brothers (Blanchard et al., 1995; Blanchard & Bogaert, 1996). One controversial speculation is that mothers with several male children sometimes produce antibodies to androgens, which reduce the prenatal impact of male sex hormones on the brains of later-born boys.

Family factors are also linked to homosexuality. Looking back on their childhoods, both male and female homosexuals tend to view their same-sex parent as cold, rejecting, or distant (Bell, Weinberg, & Hammersmith, 1981; McConaghy & Silove, 1992). This does not mean that parents cause their youngsters to become homosexual. Rather, for some children, an early biological bias away from traditional gender-role behaviour may prompt negative reactions from same-sex parents and peers. A strong desire for affection from people of their own sex may join with biology to strengthen their homosexual orientation (Green, 1987).

However, homosexuality does not always develop in this way, since some homosexuals are very comfortable with their gender role and have warm relationships with their parents. Homosexuality probably results from a variety of biological and environmental combinations that are not well understood (Huwiler & Remafedi, 1998).

## SEXUALLY TRANSMITTED DISEASE

Sexually active adolescents, both homosexual and heterosexual, are at risk for sexually transmitted disease (STD). Adolescents have the highest incidence of STD of any age group. If left untreated, sterility and life-threatening complications can result. Teenagers in greatest danger of STD are the same ones who tend to engage in irresponsible sexual behaviour—poverty-stricken young people who feel a sense of hopelessness about their lives (Crosby, Leichliter, & Brackbill, 2000).

By far the most serious STD is AIDS. To date, 3.4 percent of AIDS cases in Canada have been diagnosed in youth between 10 and 24 years (Health Canada, 2001a). However, nearly all the cases affecting adults in their early twenties originate in adolescence, since AIDS symptoms typically take 8 to 10 years to emerge in a person infected with HIV. Drug-abusing and homosexual teenagers account for most cases, but heterosexual spread of the disease has increased, especially among females. It is at least twice as easy for a male to infect a female with any STD, including AIDS, as it is for a female to infect a male (U.S. Centers for Disease Control, 2001).

As the result of school courses and media campaigns, over 90 percent of high school students are aware of basic facts about AIDS. But some hold false beliefs that put them at risk—for example, that birth control pills provide some protection or that people cannot get AIDS through oral sex (Montoya, 2001).

**FIGURE** 5.16

**Teenage pregnancy rate in eight industrialized nations.** (Adapted from Singh & Darroch, 2000.)

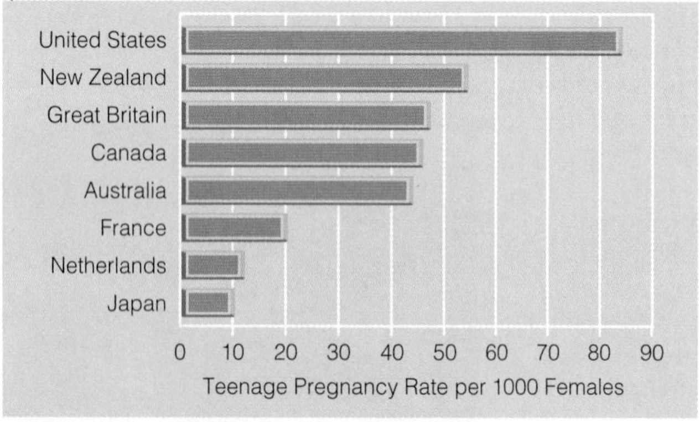

Teenage Pregnancy Rate per 1000 Females

## ADOLESCENT PREGNANCY AND PARENTHOOD

Each year in Canada, thousands of babies are born to teenage mothers. In 1998, 41 588 pregnancies were recorded in Canada to girls between the ages of 15 and 19 (Statistics Canada, Teen Pregnancy, 2002). About 50 percent of Canadian teenage pregnancies end in abortion and 2 percent in miscarriage (Dryburgh, 2001). Still, despite the high number of teenage pregnancies in Canada, the rate is dropping. The Canadian rate is about half the U.S. rate, but more than double the rate of France and more than quadruple that of Japan (see Figure 5.16).

Despite the decrease in adolescent pregnancies teenage parenthood is a much greater problem today, because adolescents are far less likely to marry before childbirth. In 1960, only 15 percent of teenage births were to unmarried females, whereas now, 75 percent are (Coley & Chase-Lansdale, 1998). Increased social acceptance of single motherhood, along with the belief of many teenage girls that a baby might fill a void in their lives, has meant that only a small number give up their infants for adoption.

### CORRELATES AND CONSEQUENCES OF ADOLESCENT PARENTHOOD.

Becoming a parent is challenging and stressful for any person, but it is especially difficult for adolescents. Teenage parents have not yet established a clear sense of direction for their own lives. They have both life conditions and personal attributes that interfere with their ability to parent effectively (Jaffee et al., 2001; Levine, Pollack, & Comfort, 2001).

As we have seen, adolescent sexual activity is linked to economic disadvantage. Teenage parents are many times more likely to be poor than are agemates who postpone childbearing. Their experiences often include low parental warmth and involvement; poor school performance; alcohol and drug use; adult models of unmarried parenthood, limited education and unemployment; and residence in neighbourhoods where other adolescents also display these risks (Scaramella et al., 1998; Woodward & Fergusson, 1999a; Dryburgh, 2001). Many of these young people seem to turn to early parenthood as a way to move into adulthood when educational and career avenues are unavailable (Fagot et al., 1998).

© RAMEY/STOCK BOSTON

Adolescent parenthood imposes lasting hardships on two generations. Early childbearing reduces the chances that teenage mothers will finish high school, marry, and enter a satisfying, well-paid vocation. Because of stressful life conditions, children of teenagers are at risk for poor parenting.

The lives of pregnant teenagers are often troubled in many ways, and after the baby is born, their circumstances tend to worsen in at least three respects:

- *Educational attainment.* Giving birth before age 18 reduces the likelihood of finishing high school. Only 50 percent of adolescent mothers graduate with either a diploma or general equivalency diploma (GED) in the U.S., compared with 96 percent of girls who wait to become parents (Hotz, McElroy, & Sanders, 1997).

- *Marital patterns.* Teenage motherhood reduces the chances of marriage. When these mothers do marry, they are more likely to divorce than are their peers who delay childbearing (Moore et al., 1993). Consequently, teenage mothers spend more of their parenting years as single parents.

- *Economic circumstances.* Because of low educational attainment, marital instability, and poverty, many teenage mothers are on welfare. If they are employed, their limited education restricts them to unsatisfying, low-paid jobs (Moore et al., 1993). Adolescent fathers work more hours than their nonparent agemates in the years following their child's birth. Perhaps for this reason, they obtain less education and are also economically disadvantaged (Brien & Willis, 1997).

Because many pregnant teenage girls have inadequate diets, smoke and use alcohol and other drugs, and do not receive early prenatal care, their babies often experience pregnancy and birth complications—especially low birth weight (Dell, 2001). And compared with adult mothers, adolescent mothers more often have psychological disorders, interact more negatively with the child's father, know less about child development, have unrealistically high expectations of infants, perceive their babies as more difficult, and interact less effectively with them (Brooks-Gunn & Chase-Lansdale, 1995; Moore & Florsheim, 2001). Their children tend to score low on intelligence tests, achieve poorly in school, and engage in disruptive social behaviour. As the Social Issues: Health box on page 210 reveals, too often the cycle of adolescent parenthood is repeated in the next generation (Jaffee et al., 2001; Moore, Morrison, & Greene, 1997).

*social issues: health*

### LIKE MOTHER, LIKE CHILD: INTERGENERATIONAL CONTINUITY IN ADOLESCENT PARENTHOOD

oes adolescent parenthood increase the chances of teenage childbearing in the next generation? To find out, Janet Hardy and her collaborators (1998) conducted a 30-year follow-up of over 1700 inner-city mothers (first generation) and their children (second generation). The first generation became parents between 1960 and 1964—about 28 percent as teenagers. As young people in the second generation grew up, they too became parents between the mid-1970s and early 1990s—25 percent as teenagers.

The researchers capitalized on extensive childhood data that had been gathered on the second generation, including IQ and achievement scores and information about family conditions. In addition, they interviewed both generations between 1992 and 1994, when the second generation reached 27 to 33 years of age, asking for recollections of the second generation's adolescent and early-adult life course.

First-generation mothers' age at first birth was strongly associated with the age at which second-generation young people became parents (see Figure 5.17). Yet becoming a second-generation teenage parent was not just a matter of having been born to an adolescent mother. Rather, adolescent parenthood was linked to a wide array of unfavourable rearing conditions, which predicted intergenerational continuity in teenage childbearing. For example, compared with second-generation daughters who postponed parenthood, daughters who became teenage mothers were more likely to have grown up in a single-parent household, had four or more siblings (reducing parental attention and resources available to each), scored lower in IQ and reading skill, repeated one or more grades, and (in adolescence) had a higher frequency of police arrests for delinquency. Similar trends were found for second-generation sons who became teenage parents. And as these early child bearers moved into

adulthood, they fared less well in education, physical and mental health, and financial security than did their age-mates who waited to become parents.

Finally, even when children born to teenage mothers did not repeat the pattern of early childbearing, their development was compromised. Although they were better off than their counterparts who became adolescent parents, they scored lower than other second-generation members in virtually all child and adult indicators of well-being. In sum, the likelihood of graduating from high school, achieving financial independence, enjoying good health, and avoiding adolescent parenthood with all its costly future consequences is much greater for children born to older mothers than for those born to teenagers.

---

### FIGURE 5.17

**Intergenerational continuity in adolescent parenthood in a 30-year study of more than 1700 inner-city parents and their children.** The graph shows the percentage of second-generation daughters and sons who became adolescent parents for each of three groups of first-generation parents: those who had a first child as a teenager, between ages 20 and 24, or at age 25 or older. First-generation adolescent parents were more likely to have children who were adolescent parents, a tendency that was stronger for second-generation girls than for boys. Fewer boys in this study reported adolescent parenthood. They might not always have known about the birth of a child. And in some cases, they might have chosen not to disclose it. (Adapted from Hardy et al., 1998.)

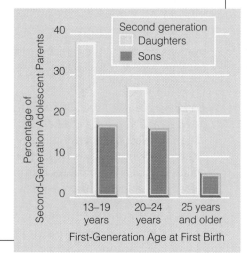

Still, how well adolescent parents and their children fare varies a great deal. If the adolescent finishes high school, avoids additional births, and finds a stable marriage partner, long-term disruptions in her own and her child's development are less severe. The small minority of young mothers who fail in all three of these ways face a life of continuing misfortune (Furstenberg, Brooks-Gunn, & Morgan, 1987).

**PREVENTION STRATEGIES.** Preventing teenage pregnancy means addressing the many factors underlying early sexual activity and lack of contraceptive use. Too often, sex education courses are given late in high school (after sexual activity has begun), last only a few sessions, and are limited to a catalogue of facts about anatomy and reproduction. Sex education that goes beyond this minimum does not encourage early sex, as some opponents claim. It does improve awareness of sexual facts—knowledge that is necessary for responsible sexual behaviour (Katchadourian, 1990).

Knowledge, however, is not sufficient to influence teenagers' behaviour. Sex education must help them build a bridge between what they know and what they do. Today, more effective sex education programs have emerged with the following key elements:

- using creative discussion and role-playing to teach skills for handling everyday sexual situations,

- promoting the value of abstinence to teenagers not yet sexually active, and

- providing information about and ready access to contraceptives.

The combined results of many studies reveal that sex education with these components can delay the initiation of sexual activity, increase contraceptive use, and reduce pregnancy rates (Aarons et al., 2000; Franklin et al., 1997).

The most controversial aspect of adolescent pregnancy prevention is increasing the availability of contraceptives. Many argue that placing birth control pills or condoms in the hands of teenagers is equivalent to saying that early sex is okay. Yet in Western Europe, where many school-based clinics offer contraceptives, teenage sexual activity does not rise and pregnancy, childbirth, and abortion rates remain low (Zabin & Hayward, 1993). Research confirms that knowledge and distribution of contraceptives are the most effective aspect of sex education for preventing adolescent pregnancy (Franklin & Corcoran, 2000).

Efforts to prevent adolescent pregnancy and parenthood must go beyond improving sex education to build social competence. In one study, researchers randomly assigned at-risk high school students to either a year-long community service class, called Teen Outreach, or to regular classroom experiences in health or social studies. In Teen Outreach, adolescents participated in at least 20 hours per week of volunteer work tailored to their interests. They returned to school for discussions that focused on enhancing their community service skills and ability to cope with everyday challenges. At the end of the school year, pregnancy, school failure, and school suspension were substantially lower in the group enrolled in Teen Outreach, which fostered social skills, connectedness to the community, and self-respect (Allen et al., 1997).

Finally, teenagers who look forward to a promising future are far less likely to engage in early and irresponsible sex. Society can provide young people with good reasons to postpone early childbearing by expanding their educational, vocational, and employment opportunities. We will take up these issues in Chapter 15.

**INTERVENING WITH ADOLESCENT PARENTS.** The most difficult and costly way to deal with adolescent parenthood is to wait until after it has happened. Young single mothers need health care for themselves and their children, encouragement to stay in school, job training, instruction in parenting and life-management skills, and high-quality, affordable child care. School programs that provide these services reduce the incidence of low-birth-weight babies, increase mothers' educational success, and decrease their likelihood of rapid additional childbearing (Seitz & Apfel, 1993, 1994; Seitz, Apfel, & Rosenbaum, 1991).

DICK HEMINGWAY

Programs that build competence through community service are associated with lower pregnancy and school failure rates among at-risk high school students.

Adolescent mothers also benefit from family relationships that are sensitive to their developmental needs. Very young mothers who continue to live in the same household as their own mother (the child's grandmother) engage in more positive parent–child interaction. Older teenage mothers, however, benefit from establishing their own residence with the help of relatives—an arrangement that grants the adolescent a balance of autonomy and support. Independent living combined with high levels of grandparent assistance is associated with more effective parenting, warmer family ties, and children who develop more favourably (East & Felice, 1996).

Programs focusing on fathers are attempting to increase their emotional and financial commitment to the baby (Coley & Chase-Lansdale, 1998). Although almost half of young fathers visit their children during the first few years after birth, contact usually diminishes. But new laws that enforce child support payments may increase paternal responsibility and interaction. Teenage mothers who receive financial and child-care assistance from the child's father are less distressed and interact more favourably with their infants (Caldwell & Antonucci, 1997). And the fewer stressful life events teenage mothers experience, the more likely fathers are to stay involved and the better children's long-term adjustment (Cutrona et al., 1998; Furstenberg & Harris, 1993).

## A CONCLUDING NOTE

Because puberty prompts some of the most rapid and complex physical and psychological changes, teenagers are vulnerable to certain problems. Yet the unhealthy behaviours of the adolescent years are not an irrational response to inner turmoil, as theorists once believed. Instead, every level of the ecological system contributes to teenagers' behaviour.

Furthermore, adolescent risks are interconnected; teenagers with one problem frequently display others. This co-occurrence will become even clearer when we take up delinquency, depression, suicide, substance abuse, and school underachievement and failure. In designing more powerful interventions, researchers must deal with simultaneous risks and the multiple contexts in which each is embedded. Think back to the successful intervention efforts discussed in the preceding sections, and notice how they employ several strategies, target multiple behaviours, and involve several contexts.

Finally, adolescence is not just a time of risk; it is also a time of tremendous opportunity. Teenagers gain a better understanding of how the world works, greater control over their own social contexts, broader access to social support, and increased ability to avoid or alter risky behaviours. Yet families, schools, communities, and nations must create conditions that permit adolescents to exercise their expanding capacity for positive health practices (Maggs, Schulenberg, & Hurrelmann, 1997). This is a theme we will revisit when we address other aspects of adolescent development in later chapters.

## ASK YOURSELF

**review**    Compare risk factors for anorexia nervosa and bulimia nervosa. How do treatments and outcomes differ for the two disorders?

**review**    Describe the unfavourable life experiences associated with early and frequent sexual activity.

**apply**    Sixteen-year-old Jamal knows he is homosexual but wonders what has made him this way. What could you tell Jamal about research findings on genetic and environmental links to homosexuality?

**connect**    How do various correlates and consequences of adolescent parenthood promote intergenerational continuity in teenage births?

# summary

## THE COURSE OF PHYSICAL GROWTH

*Describe the course of physical growth, including changes in body size, proportions, and composition and their relation to gains in gross motor skills during childhood and adolescence.*

- Compared with other animal species, humans experience a prolonged period of physical growth. **Distance** and **velocity curves** show the overall pattern of change: Gains in height and weight are rapid during infancy, slower during early and middle childhood, and rapid again during puberty.

- In childhood, physical growth follows cephalocaudal and proximodistal trends. During puberty, growth proceeds in the reverse direction, and sex differences in body proportions appear. Body fat is laid down quickly during the first 9 months, then rapidly again at adolescence for girls. In contrast, muscle development is slow and gradual until puberty, when it rises dramatically, especially for boys.

- In early childhood, body growth causes the child's centre of gravity to shift toward the trunk, and balance improves, paving the way for an explosion of gross motor milestones. During the school years, improved balance, strength, agility, and flexibility support refinements in running, jumping, hopping, and ball skills. Increased body size and muscle strength lead to continued motor gains in adolescence. Children continue to integrate previously acquired motor skills into more complex, dynamic systems of action.

*Describe skeletal growth and hormonal influences on physical growth.*

- **Skeletal age,** a measure based on the number of **epiphyses** and the extent to which they are fused, is the best way to estimate the child's overall physical maturity. Girls are advanced over boys, a gap that widens over infancy and childhood. At birth, infants have six **fontanels,** which permit skull bones to expand as the brain grows rapidly in the first few years.

- Physical growth is controlled by hormones released by the **pituitary gland,** located at the base of the brain near the **hypothalamus,** which initiates and regulates pituitary secretions. **Growth hormone (GH)** affects the development of almost all body tissues. **Thyroxine,** released by the thyroid gland, influences brain growth and body size. Sexual maturation is controlled by the sex hormones—**estrogens** and **androgens.**

*Discuss factors that contribute to worldwide variations, secular trends, and asynchronies in physical growth.*

- Worldwide variations in body size are the combined result of heredity and environment. **Secular trends in physical growth** have occurred in industrialized nations. Because of improved health and nutrition, many children are growing larger and reaching physical maturity earlier than did their ancestors.

- Physical growth is an asynchronous process. The **general growth curve** refers to change in overall body size. Other systems of the body, such as the genitals, the lymph tissue, and the brain, have their own unique timetables.

## DEVELOPMENT OF THE BRAIN

*Cite major milestones in brain development, at the level of individual brain cells and at the level of the cerebral cortex.*

- During the first few years, the human brain grows faster than any other organ. Once **neurons** are in place, they form **synapses** at a rapid rate. During the peak period of development in any brain area, **programmed cell death** makes room for growth of neural fibres that form synaptic connections. Stimulation determines which neurons will continue to establish new synapses and which will lose their connective fibres through **synaptic pruning. Glial cells,** which are responsible for **myelinization,** multiply dramatically through the second year and result in large gains in brain weight.

- **Lateralization** refers to specialization of the hemispheres of the **cerebral cortex.** Although some specialization exists at birth, in the first few years of life there is high **brain plasticity.** Both heredity and early experience contribute to brain organization.

- Hand preference reflects the individual's **dominant cerebral hemisphere.** It first appears in infancy and gradually increases, indicating that lateralization strengthens during early childhood. According to one theory, most children inherit a gene that biases them for right-handedness, but experience can sway children toward a left-hand preference. Body position during the prenatal period and practice can affect handedness.

*Describe changes in other brain structures, and discuss evidence on brain growth spurts as sensitive periods of development.*

- During infancy and early childhood, connections are established between brain structures. Fibres linking the **cerebellum** to the cerebral cortex myelinate, enhancing children's balance and motor control. The **reticular formation,** responsible for alertness and consciousness, and the **corpus callosum,** which connects the two cerebral hemispheres, also develop rapidly.

- Gains in brain weight and skull size along with changes in neural activity indicate that brain growth spurts occur intermittently from infancy through adolescence. These coincide with major cognitive changes and may be sensitive periods in which appropriate stimulation is necessary for full development.

## FACTORS AFFECTING PHYSICAL GROWTH

*How do heredity, nutrition, infectious disease, and affection and stimulation contribute to physical growth?*

■ Twin and adoption studies reveal that heredity contributes to children's height, weight, and rate of physical growth. As long as negative factors are not severe, children and adolescents who lag behind in body size show **catch-up growth** under improved environmental conditions.

■ Good nutrition is crucial for children to reach their full growth potential. Breast-feeding is especially suited to infants' growth needs and is crucial for protecting their health in the developing world. As growth slows in early childhood, appetite declines. It rises sharply during puberty.

■ The importance of nutrition is tragically evident in the dietary diseases of **marasmus** and **kwashiorkor,** which affect large numbers of children in developing countries. Obesity is a growing problem in both industrialized and developing nations. Although heredity contributes to obesity, parental feeding practices, maladaptive eating habits, lack of exercise, and Western high-fat diets also play important roles.

■ Infectious disease can combine with poor nutrition to undermine healthy physical development. In developing countries, diarrhea is widespread and claims millions of young lives. Teaching families how to administer **oral rehydration therapy (ORT)** can prevent most of these deaths.

■ **Nonorganic failure to thrive** and **psychosocial dwarfism** illustrate the importance of affection and stimulation for normal human growth.

## PUBERTY: THE PHYSICAL TRANSITION TO ADULTHOOD

*Describe sexual maturation in girls and boys, noting genetic and environmental influences on pubertal timing.*

■ Accompanying rapid changes in body size and proportions at **puberty** are changes in **primary** and **secondary sexual characteristics. Menarche** occurs relatively late in the girl's sequence of pubertal events, after the growth spurt. In the following year, growth of the breasts and pubic hair are completed, and underarm hair appears. As the boy's body and sex organs enlarge and pubic and underarm hair emerges, **spermarche** and deepening of the voice take place, followed by growth of facial and body hair.

■ Besides genetic influences evident in twin comparisons, nutrition and overall physical health contribute to the timing of puberty. Menarche is delayed in poverty-stricken regions of the world and among girls from economically disadvantaged homes. In contrast, girls exposed to family conflict tend to reach menarche early.

## THE PSYCHOLOGICAL IMPACT OF PUBERTAL EVENTS

*What factors influence adolescents' reactions to the physical changes of puberty?*

■ Puberty is not a biologically determined, inevitable period of storm and stress. Adjustment varies widely and is a product of both biological and social forces.

■ Girls generally react to menarche with surprise and mixed emotions, but whether their feelings are more positive or negative depends on advance information and support from family members. Similarly, boys respond to spermarche with mixed feelings. They receive less social support for the physical changes of puberty than do girls.

■ Tribal and village societies often celebrate puberty with an **adolescent initiation ceremony.** The absence of a widely accepted marker for physical and social maturity in contemporary society makes the process of becoming an adult especially confusing.

■ Besides higher hormone levels, negative life events, adult-structured situations, and sleep loss are associated with adolescent moodiness. Puberty is accompanied by an increase in mild conflict and psychological distancing between parent and child.

*Describe the impact of pubertal timing on adolescent adjustment, noting sex-related differences.*

■ Timing of puberty influences psychological adjustment. Early maturing boys and late maturing girls, whose appearance closely matches cultural standards of physical attractiveness, have a more positive **body image,** are judged more self-confident, and hold more positions of leadership. In contrast, early maturing girls and late maturing boys, who fit in least well physically with peers, experience emotional and social difficulties.

## PUBERTY AND ADOLESCENT HEALTH

*What factors contribute to eating disorders at adolescence?*

■ Girls who reach puberty early, who are dissatisfied with their body images, and who grow up in homes in which thinness is important are at risk for eating disorders. Twin studies reveal a genetic contribution to **anorexia nervosa.** The disorder tends to affect girls who have perfectionist, emotionally inhibited personalities, overprotective and controlling mothers, and emotionally distant fathers. The compulsive eating and purging of **bulimia** are also partly genetic. The condition is associated with disengaged parenting. Some bulimics are perfectionists; others lack self-control in eating and other areas of their lives.

*Discuss individual, social, and cultural influences on adolescent sexual attitudes and behaviour.*

■ The hormonal changes of puberty lead to an increase in sex drive, but social factors affect how teenagers manage their sexuality. Compared with most cultures, North America is fairly restrictive in its attitude toward adolescent sex. Sexual attitudes of adolescents and adults have become more liberal, with a slight swing back in recent years, largely due to the risk of sexually transmitted disease.

■ About 40 percent of sexually active Canadian teenagers do not practise contraception regularly. Adolescent cognitive processes, a sense of hopelessness, and a lack of social support for responsible sexual behaviour underlie this trend.

*Discuss factors involved in the development of homosexuality.*

■ About 3 to 6 percent of young people discover they are lesbian or gay; an unknown number are bisexual. Although heredity makes an important contribution, homosexuality probably results from a variety of biological and environmental combinations that are not yet well understood. Lesbian and gay teenagers face special challenges in establishing a positive sexual identity.

*Discuss factors related to sexually transmitted disease and teenage pregnancy and parenthood, noting prevention and intervention strategies.*

■ Sexually active teenagers are at risk for contracting sexually transmitted diseases (STDs). The most serious is AIDS. Drug-abusing and homosexual young people account for most cases, but heterosexual spread is increasing, especially among females.

■ Although the adolescent pregnancy rate is decreasing in Canada, it remains a problem. Thousands of babies are born to teenage mothers each year. Adolescent parenthood is often associated with high school dropout, reduced chances of marriage, greater likelihood of divorce, and poverty—circumstances that risk the well-being of both adolescent and newborn child.

■ Improved sex education, access to contraceptives, programs that build social competence, and expanded educational, vocational, and employment opportunities help prevent early pregnancy. Adolescent mothers benefit from job training, instruction in parenting and life-management skills, affordable high-quality child care, and extended-family support that is sensitive to their developmental needs. When teenage fathers stay involved, their children develop more favourably.

# important terms and concepts

adolescent initiation ceremony (p. 198)
androgens (p. 179)
anorexia nervosa (p. 203)
body image (p. 201)
brain plasticity (p. 182)
bulimia nervosa (p. 204)
catch-up growth (p. 186)
cerebellum (p. 185)
cerebral cortex (p. 182)
corpus callosum (p. 185)
distance curve (p. 171)
dominant cerebral hemisphere (p. 184)
epiphyses (p. 173)
estrogens (p. 179)
fontanels (p. 175)

general growth curve (p. 181)
glial cells (p. 182)
growth hormone (GH) (p. 177)
hypothalamus (p. 176)
kwashiorkor (p. 189)
lateralization (p. 182)
marasmus (p. 189)
menarche (p. 194)
myelinization (p. 182)
neurons (p. 181)
nonorganic failure to thrive (p. 192)
obesity (p. 191)
oral rehydration therapy (ORT) (p. 192)
pituitary gland (p. 176)

primary sexual characteristics (p. 193)
programmed cell death (p. 181)
psychosocial dwarfism (p. 193)
puberty (p. 193)
reticular formation (p. 185)
secondary sexual characteristics (p. 193)
secular trends in physical growth (p. 181)
skeletal age (p. 173)
spermarche (p. 195)
synapses (p. 181)
synaptic pruning (p. 181)
thyroxine (p. 179)
velocity curve (p. 171)

"Sketch for Father"
Bai Meng
9 years, China

Reprinted with permission from
The International Museum of
Children's Art, Oslo, Norway

This image of an energetic, observant young painter illustrates the most striking cognitive achievement of childhood. As Chapter 6 reveals, all theories of cognitive development address tremendous advances in mental representation.

# six

## Cognitive Development: Piagetian, Core Knowledge, and Vygotskian Perspectives

LESLIE, A PRESCHOOL TEACHER, paused to look around her class of busy 3- and 4-year-olds and said to a visiting parent, "Their minds are such a curious blend of logic, fantasy, and faulty reasoning. Every day, I'm startled by the maturity and originality of many things they say and do. At other times, though, I'm struck by how limited and inflexible their thinking seems."

Leslie's reflections sum up the puzzling contradictions of young children's thought. Earlier, after hearing a loud thunderclap outside, 3-year-old Sammy exclaimed, "A magic man turned on the thunder!" Leslie patiently responded that people can't turn thunder on or off; lightning causes thunder. But Sammy persisted. "Then a magic lady did it," he stated with certainty.

In other respects, Sammy's thinking was surprisingly advanced. His favourite picture books were about dinosaurs, and he could name, categorize, and point out similarities and differences between dozens of them. "Anatosaurus and tyrannosaurus walk on their back legs," he told the class during group time. "Then they can use their front legs to pick up food!" Later, however, at the snack table, Gina poured her milk from a short, wide carton into a tall, thin glass. Sammy looked at his carton, identical to hers. "How come you got lots of milk, and I only got a little?" he asked, failing to realize that he had just as much as Gina; although his carton was shorter than her glass, it was also wider.

217

Cognition refers to the inner processes and products of the mind that lead to "knowing." It includes all mental activity—attending, remembering, symbolizing, categorizing, planning, reasoning, problem solving, creating, and fantasizing. Indeed, we could easily expand this list, since mental processes make their way into virtually everything human beings do. Our cognitive powers are crucial for survival. To adapt to changing environmental conditions, other species are granted camouflage, feathers and fur, and remarkable speed. Humans, in contrast, rely on thinking, through which they not only adapt to their environments but transform them. Among all earthly creatures, we stand out in our extraordinary mental capacities.

This chapter, and the two that follow, address cognitive development—the intellectual capacities that human infants start with and how they change into the capacities of the adult. Researchers concerned with cognitive development address three main issues. First, they chart its *typical course,* identifying infant beginnings and the changes occurring for many children on the way to adult capacities. As part of this endeavour, researchers ask, Do all aspects of cognition develop uniformly, or do some develop at faster rates than others? Second, researchers identify *individual differences,* because at every age, some children think more or less maturely, and differently, than others. Chapters 6 and 7 are largely devoted to the course of development. Chapter 8 delves into individual differences, although we will encounter both concerns in all chapters.

Researchers' third focus is *mechanisms* of cognitive development—how genetic and environmental factors combine to yield a particular pattern of change. In this chapter, we address three perspectives on cognitive development, each differing in its ideas about cognitive change: (1) *Piaget's cognitive-development theory;* (2) *the core knowledge perspective*—an emerging alternative to Piaget's approach; and (3) *Vygotsky's sociocultural theory,* which—in contrast to the biological emphasis of the first two theories—stresses social and cultural contributions to children's thinking.

As we turn now to each of these views, we will see repeatedly that children move from simpler to more complex cognitive skills, becoming more effective thinkers with age. But we must be careful not to view children's immature capacities as just incomplete, less effective versions of adults'. Instead, children's focus on a limited amount of information might be adaptive (Bjorklund, 1997). For example, noticing only a few features of an intricate pattern probably protects young babies from overstimulation during a period in which their nervous systems cannot yet handle much complexity. And comparing the amount of milk in a short, wide carton and a tall, thin glass by attending only to height (not width) may grant preschoolers a thorough grasp of height, in preparation for effectively integrating height with other dimensions.

The adaptiveness of cognitive immaturity has important implications for education. It suggests that hurrying children to higher levels may undermine their progress. Indeed, Piaget was among the first theorists to stress the importance of *readiness* to learn—presenting children with appropriately challenging tasks while avoiding overly complex types and amounts of stimulation that confuse and overwhelm them. Let's begin with Piaget's theory.

# Piaget's Cognitive-Developmental Theory

SWISS COGNITIVE THEORIST Jean Piaget received his academic education in zoology; consequently, his theory has a distinct biological flavour. According to Piaget, human infants do not start out as cognitive beings. Instead, out of their perceptual and motor activities, they build and refine psychological structures—organized ways of making sense of experience that permit children to adapt more effectively to their external world. In the development of these structures, children are intensely active. They select and interpret experiences using their current structures, and they modify those structures so that they take into account more subtle aspects of reality. Because Piaget viewed children as discovering, or *constructing,* virtually all knowledge about their world through their own activity, his theory is often referred to as a **constructivist approach** to cognitive development.

**constructivist approach**
An approach to cognitive development in which children discover virtually all knowledge about their world through their own activity. Consistent with Piaget's theory.

© 2000 LAURA DWIGHT

## BASIC CHARACTERISTICS OF PIAGET'S STAGES

Piaget believed that children move through four stages of development—sensorimotor, preoperational, concrete operational, and formal operational—during which the exploratory behaviours of infancy transform into the abstract, logical intelligence of adolescence and adulthood. Piaget's stage sequence has three important characteristics. First, it is a *general theory;* it assumes that all aspects of cognition develop in an integrated fashion, undergoing a similar course of change. Second, the stages are *invariant,* meaning that they always follow a fixed order, and no stage can be skipped. Third, the stages are *universal;* they are assumed to describe the cognitive development of children everywhere (Piaget, Inhelder, & Szeminska, 1948/1960).

Piaget regarded the order of development as rooted in the biology of our species—the result of the human brain becoming increasingly adept at analyzing and interpreting experiences common to most children throughout the world. But he emphasized that individual differences in genetic and environmental factors affect the speed with which children move through the stages (Piaget, 1926/1928). To appreciate Piaget's view of how development occurs, we must examine a set of important concepts.

According to Piaget's theory, at first schemes are motor action patterns. As this 1-year-old takes apart, bangs, and drops these containers, he discovers that his movements have predictable effects on objects and that objects influence one another in regular ways.

## PIAGET'S IDEAS ABOUT COGNITIVE CHANGE

According to Piaget, specific psychological structures—organized ways of making sense of experience called **schemes**—change with age. At first, schemes are sensorimotor action patterns. For example, watch a 6-month-old baby catch sight of, grasp, and release objects, and you will see that the "dropping scheme" is fairly rigid; the infant simply lets go of a rattle or teething ring in her hand. By 18 months, the "dropping scheme" becomes much more deliberate and creative. Given an opportunity, a baby of this age is likely to toss all sorts of objects down the basement stairs, throwing some up in the air, bouncing others off walls, releasing some gently and others forcefully.

Soon, instead of just acting on objects, the toddler shows evidence of thinking before she acts. For Piaget, this change marks the transition from a sensorimotor to a cognitive approach to the world—one based on **mental representations,** or internal depictions of information that the mind can manipulate. Our most powerful mental representations are of two kinds: (1) *images,* or mental pictures of objects, people, and spaces; and (2) *concepts,* or categories that group together similar objects or events. Using a mental image, we can retrace our steps when we've misplaced our keys. Or we can imitate another's behaviour long after we've observed it. And by thinking in concepts and labelling them (for example, *ball* for all rounded, movable objects used in play), we become more efficient thinkers, organizing our diverse experiences into meaningful, manageable, and memorable units.

In Piaget's theory, two processes account for this change from sensorimotor to representational schemes and for the transformation of representational schemes that follow: *adaptation* and *organization.*

**ADAPTATION.** The next time you have a chance, notice how infants and children tirelessly repeat actions that lead to interesting effects, and you'll see a demonstration of an important Piagetian concept. **Adaptation** involves building schemes through direct interaction with the environment. It consists of two complementary activities: *assimilation* and *accommodation.* During **assimilation,** we use our current schemes to interpret the external world. For example, the infant who repeatedly drops objects is assimilating them to his sensorimotor dropping scheme. And the preschooler who sees her first camel at the zoo and calls out, "Horse!" has sifted through her conceptual schemes until she finds one that resembles the strange-looking creature. In **accommodation,** we create new schemes or adjust old ones after noticing that our current thinking does not capture the environment completely. The baby who drops objects in different ways is modifying his dropping scheme to take account of the varied properties of objects. And the preschooler who calls a camel a "lumpy horse" has noticed that certain characteristics of camels are not like horses and has revised her scheme accordingly.

**scheme**
In Piaget's theory, a specific structure, or organized way of making sense of experience, that changes with age.

**mental representation**
Internal depiction of information that the mind can manipulate. The most powerful mental representations are images and concepts.

**adaptation**
In Piaget's theory, the process of building schemes through direct interaction with the environment. Consists of two complementary activities: *assimilation* and *accommodation.*

**assimilation**
In Piaget's theory, that part of adaptation in which an individual uses current schemes to interpret the external world.

**accommodation**
In Piaget's theory, that part of adaptation in which an individual adjusts old schemes and creates new ones to produce a better fit with the environment.

According to Piaget, the balance between assimilation and accommodation varies over time. When children are not changing much, they assimilate more than they accommodate. Piaget called this a state of cognitive *equilibrium,* implying a steady, comfortable condition. During times of rapid cognitive change, however, children are in a state of *disequilibrium,* or cognitive discomfort. They realize that new information does not match their current schemes, so they shift away from assimilation toward accommodation. Once they modify their schemes, they move back toward assimilation, exercising their newly changed structures until they are ready to be modified again.

Piaget used the term **equilibration** to sum up this back-and-forth movement between equilibrium and disequilibrium. Each time equilibration occurs, more effective schemes are produced. Because the times of greatest accommodation are the earliest ones, the sensorimotor stage is Piaget's most complex period of development.

**ORGANIZATION.** Schemes also change through **organization,** a process that takes place internally, apart from direct contact with the environment. Once children form new schemes, they rearrange them, linking them with other schemes to create a strongly inter-connected cognitive system. For example, eventually the baby will relate "dropping" to "throwing" and to his developing understanding of "nearness" and "farness." According to Piaget, schemes reach a true state of equilibrium when they become part of a broad network of structures that can be jointly applied to the surrounding world (Piaget, 1936/1952b).

In the following sections we will first describe development as Piaget saw it, noting research that supports his observations. Then, for each stage, we consider more recent evidence, some inspired by Piaget's theory and some that challenges Piaget's ideas.

# The Sensorimotor Stage (Birth to 2 Years)

THE DIFFERENCE BETWEEN the newborn baby and the 2-year-old child is so vast that the **sensorimotor stage** is divided into six substages (see Table 6.1 for a summary). Piaget's observations of his own three children served as the basis for this sequence of development. Although this is a very small sample, Piaget watched carefully and also presented his son and two daughters with everyday problems (such as hidden objects) that helped reveal their understanding of the world.

According to Piaget, at birth infants know so little about their world that they cannot purposefully explore their surroundings. The **circular reaction** provides them with a special means of adapting their first schemes. It involves stumbling onto a new experience caused by the baby's own motor activity. The reaction is "circular" because the infant tries to repeat the event again and again. As a result, a sensorimotor response that first occurred by chance becomes strengthened into a new scheme. For example, imagine a 2-month-old who accidentally makes a smacking noise when finishing a feeding. The baby finds the sound intriguing, so she tries to repeat it until, after a few days, she becomes quite expert at smacking her lips.

During the first 2 years, the circular reaction changes in several ways. At first, it centres on the infant's own body. Later, it turns outward, toward manipulation of objects. Finally, it becomes experimental and creative, aimed at producing novel effects in the environment. Young children's difficulty inhibiting new and interesting behaviours may underlie the circular reaction. But this immaturity in inhibition seems to be adaptive! It helps ensure that new skills will not be interrupted before they consolidate (Carey & Markman, 1999). Piaget considered revisions in the circular reaction so important for early development that he named the sensorimotor substages after them (refer again to Table 6.1).

## SENSORIMOTOR DEVELOPMENT

Piaget regarded newborn reflexes as the building blocks of sensorimotor intelligence. At first, babies suck, grasp, and look in much the same way, no matter what experiences they encounter. In one amusing example, a mother reported that her 2-week-old daughter lay

**equilibration**
In Piaget's theory, back-and-forth movement between cognitive equilibrium and disequilibrium that leads to more effective schemes.

**organization**
In Piaget's theory, the internal rearrangement and linking together of schemes so they form a strongly interconnected cognitive system.

**sensorimotor stage**
Piaget's first stage, during which infants and toddlers build schemes through sensorimotor action patterns.

**circular reaction**
In Piaget's theory, a means of building schemes in which infants try to repeat a chance event caused by their own motor activity.

**TABLE** 6.1

**Summary of Piaget's Sensorimotor Substages**

| SENSORIMOTOR SUBSTAGE | ADAPTIVE BEHAVIOURS |
|---|---|
| 1. Reflexive schemes (birth to 1 month) | Newborn reflexes (see Chapter 4, page 125) |
| 2. Primary circular reactions (1–4 months) | Simple motor habits centred around the infant's own body; limited anticipation of events; first efforts at imitation |
| 3. Secondary circular reactions (4–8 months) | Actions aimed at repeating interesting effects in the surrounding world; imitation of familiar behaviours |
| 4. Coordination of secondary circular reactions (8–12 months) | Intentional, or goal-directed, behaviour; ability to find a hidden object in the first location in which it is hidden (object permanence); improved anticipation of events; imitation of behaviours slightly different from those the infant usually performs |
| 5. Tertiary circular reactions (12–18 months) | Exploration of the properties of objects by acting on them in novel ways; imitation of unfamiliar behaviours; ability to search in several locations for a hidden object (accurate AB search) |
| 6. Mental representation (18 months–2 years) | Internal depictions of objects and events, as indicated by sudden solutions to problems; ability to find an object that has been moved while out of sight (invisible displacement); deferred imitation; and make-believe play |

on the bed next to her sleeping father. Suddenly, he awoke with a start. The baby had latched on and begun to suck on his back!

**REPEATING CHANCE BEHAVIOURS.** Around 1 month, as babies enter Substage 2, they start to gain voluntary control over their actions through the *primary circular reaction,* by repeating chance behaviours largely motivated by basic needs. Consequently, they develop some simple motor habits, such as sucking their fists or thumbs. Babies of this substage also begin to vary their behaviour in response to environmental demands. For example, they open their mouths differently for a nipple than for a spoon. Young infants also begin to anticipate events. A hungry 3-month-old is likely to stop crying as soon as his mother enters the room—an event signalling that feeding time is near. Piaget also believed that between 1 and 4 months, first efforts at imitation appear, but they are limited to copying someone else's imitation of the baby's own actions.

During Substage 3, lasting from 4 to 8 months, infants sit up, reaching for, and manipulating objects (see Chapter 4). These motor achievements play a major role in turning their attention outward toward the environment. Using the secondary circular reaction, they try to repeat interesting effects in the surrounding world that are caused by their own actions. For example, Piaget (1936/1952b) tried dangling several dolls in front of his 4-month-old son, Laurent. After accidentally knocking them and producing a fascinating swinging motion, Laurent gradually built the sensorimotor scheme of "hitting." Improved control over their own behaviour also permits infants to imitate others' behaviour more effectively. However, they cannot adapt flexibly and quickly enough to imitate novel behaviours (Kaye & Marcus, 1981). Therefore, although 4- to 8-month-olds enjoy watching an adult demonstrate a game of pat-a-cake or peekaboo, they are not yet able to participate.

**INTENTIONAL BEHAVIOUR.** In Substage 4, 8- to 12-month-olds combine schemes into new, more complex action sequences. As a result, they can engage in **intentional, or goal-directed, behaviour.** Before this substage, actions that led to new schemes had a random, hit-or-miss quality—*accidentally* bringing the thumb to the mouth or *happening* to hit the doll. Now infants coordinate schemes deliberately to solve simple problems. The clearest example is provided by Piaget's simple object-hiding task, in which he shows the baby an attractive toy and then hides it behind his hand or under a cover. Infants of this substage can find the object. In doing so, they coordinate two schemes: "pushing" aside the obstacle and "grasping" the toy. Piaget regarded these *means–end action sequences* as the foundation for all later problem solving.

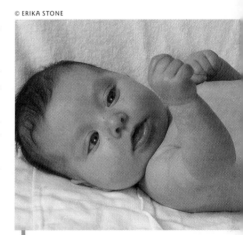

During Piaget's Substage 2, infants' adaptations are oriented toward their own bodies. This young baby carefully watches the movements of her hands, a primary circular reaction that helps her gain voluntary control over her behaviour.

**intentional, or goal-directed, behaviour**
A sequence of actions in which schemes are deliberately combined to solve a problem.

Retrieving hidden objects indicates that infants have begun to master **object permanence,** the understanding that objects continue to exist when they are out of sight. But awareness of object permanence is not yet complete. If the baby reaches several times for an object at a first hiding place (A) and sees it moved to a second (B), she will still search for it in the first hiding place (A). Because 8- to 12-month-olds make this **A-not-B search error,** Piaget concluded that they do not have a clear image of the object as persisting when hidden from view.

Substage 4 brings additional advances. First, infants can better anticipate events, so they sometimes use their capacity for intentional behaviour to try to change those events. For example, a baby of this age might crawl after his mother when she puts on her coat, whimpering to keep her from leaving. Second, babies can imitate behaviours slightly different from those they usually perform. After watching someone else, they try to stir with a spoon, push a toy car, or drop raisins in a cup. Once again, they draw on intentional behaviour, purposefully modifying schemes to fit an observed action (Piaget, 1945/1951).

In Substage 5, lasting from 12 to 18 months, the *tertiary circular reaction* emerges. Toddlers repeat behaviours with variation, provoking new outcomes. Recall the example on page 219 of the child dropping objects down the basement steps, trying this, then that, and then another action. Because they approach the world in this deliberately exploratory way, toddlers become better problem solvers. For example, they can figure out how to fit a shape through a hole in a container by turning and twisting it until it falls through, and they can use a stick to obtain a toy that is out of reach. According to Piaget, this capacity to experiment leads to a more advanced understanding of object permanence. Toddlers look in not just one but several locations to find a hidden toy, displaying an accurate AB search. Their more flexible action patterns also permit them to imitate many more behaviours, such as stacking blocks, scribbling on paper, and making funny faces.

**MENTAL REPRESENTATION.** In Substage 6, sensorimotor development culminates with mental representation. One sign of this capacity is that children arrive at solutions to problems suddenly, suggesting that they experiment with actions inside their heads. Faced with her doll carriage stuck against the wall, Piaget's daughter Lucienne paused for a moment, as if to "think," and then immediately turned the toy in a new direction. Representation results in several other capacities. First, it leads to the capacity to solve advanced object-permanence problems involving *invisible displacement*—finding a toy moved while out of sight, such as into a small box while under a cover. Second, it permits **deferred imitation**—the ability to remember and copy the behaviour of models who are not present. Finally, it makes possible **make-believe play,** in which children act out everyday and imaginary activities. As the sensorimotor period draws to a close, mental symbols are major instruments of thinking.

## FOLLOW-UP RESEARCH ON INFANT COGNITIVE DEVELOPMENT

Many studies suggest that infants display a variety of understandings earlier than Piaget believed. For example, recall the operant conditioning research reviewed in Chapter 4, in which newborns sucked vigorously on a nipple to gain access to a variety of interesting sights and sounds. This use of operant conditioning to study babies' interest in the surrounding world, which closely resembles Piaget's secondary circular reaction, indicates that infants explore and control their external world before 4 to 8 months. In fact, they do so as soon as they are born.

A major method used to find out what infants know about hidden objects and other aspects of physical reality capitalizes on habituation/recovery, discussed in Chapter 4. In the **violation-of-expectation method,** researchers habituate babies to a physical event and then determine whether they recover (look longer at) a possible event (a variation of the first event that follows physical laws) or an impossible event (a variation that violates physical laws). Recovery to the impossible event suggests surprise at a deviation from physical reality and, therefore, awareness of that aspect of the physical world.

**object permanence**
The understanding that objects continue to exist when they are out of sight.

**A-not-B search error**
The error made by 8- to 12-month-olds after an object is moved from hiding place A to hiding place B. Infants in Piaget's Substage 4 search for it in only the first hiding place (A).

**deferred imitation**
The ability to remember and copy the behaviour of models who are not present.

**make-believe play**
A type of play in which children pretend, acting out everyday and imaginary activities.

**violation-of-expectation method**
A method for finding out about infants' understanding of physical experience, in which researchers habituate babies to a physical event and then determine whether they recover to (look longer at) a possible event (a variation of the first event that conforms to physical laws) or an impossible event (a variation that violates physical laws). Recovery to the impossible event suggests surprise at a deviation from reality and, therefore, an understanding of that aspect of the physical world.

**Habituation Events**

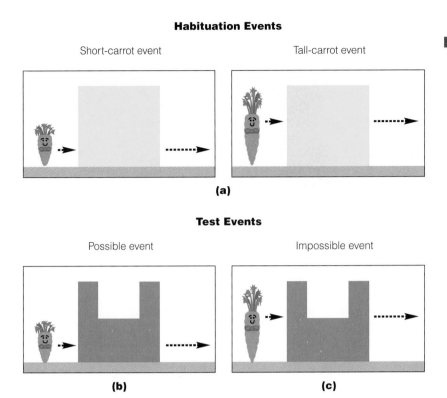

(a)

**Test Events**

(b)                    (c)

**FIGURE 6.1**

**Testing infants for understanding of object permanence using the violation-of-expectation method.** (a) First, infants were habituated to two events: a short carrot and a tall carrot moving behind a yellow screen, on alternative trials. Next the researchers presented two test events. The colour of the screen was changed to help infants notice its window. (b) In the possible event, the carrot shorter than the window's lower edge moved behind the blue screen and reappeared on the other side. (c) In the impossible event, the carrot taller than the window's lower edge moved behind the screen, did not appear in the window, but then emerged intact on the other side. Infants as young as 3½ months recovered to (looked longer at) the impossible event, suggesting that they had some understanding of object permanence. (Adapted from R. Baillargeon & J. DeVos, 1991, "Object Permanence in Young Infants: Further Evidence," *Child Development, 62,* p. 1230. © The Society for Research in Child Development. Reprinted by permission.)

But as we will see, the violation-of-expectation method is controversial. Some critics believe that it indicates only limited awareness of physical events, not the full-blown understandings that Piaget detected when he observed infants acting on their surroundings, such as searching for hidden objects (Bremner, 1998). Other critics are convinced that the violation-of-expectation method is flawed—that it reveals only babies' perceptual preference for novelty, not their understanding of experience (Haith, 1999). Let's examine this debate in light of recent research on object permanence.

**OBJECT PERMANENCE.** In a series of studies using the violation-of-expectation method, Renée Baillargeon and her collaborators claimed they found evidence for object permanence in the first few months of life. In one of Baillargeon's studies, described in Figure 6.1, 3½-month-olds indicated by their looking behaviour that they expected an object moved behind a screen to continue to exist (Baillargeon & DeVos, 1991). After habituating to a short and a tall carrot moving behind a screen, babies were given two test events: (1) a possible event in which the short carrot moved behind a screen, could not be seen in its window, and reappeared on the other side; and (2) an impossible event in which the tall carrot moved behind a screen, could not be seen in its window (although it was taller than the window's lower edge), and reappeared. Infants looked longer at the impossible event, suggesting that they expected an object moved behind a screen to continue to exist (Baillargeon & DeVos, 1991). Indeed, if the screens behind which the objects move are simplified, 2½-month-olds react similarly (Aguiar & Baillargeon, 1999). Consequently, Baillargeon concluded, very young infants appreciate object permanence.

Baillargeon has conducted additional violation-of-expectation studies and reported similar results. But some researchers, using similar (but not identical) procedures, failed to verify some of her findings (Bogartz, Shinskey, & Schilling, 2000; Cashon & Cohen, 2000; Rivera, Wakeley, & Langer, 1999). Baillargeon and others answer that these opposing studies did not include crucial controls. And they emphasize that infants look longer at a variety of impossible events that make it look as if an object covered by a screen no longer exists

As this 15-month-old masters the nuances of object permanence, she delights in hiding-and-finding games, such as peekaboo. Her flexible imitative abilities permit her to participate more actively in the game than she could at a younger age.

(Aslin, 2000; Baillargeon, 2000; Munakata, 2000). For example, the results depicted in Figure 6.1 have not been challenged. Still, critics question what babies' looking preference for impossible physical events actually tells us about their understanding.

If 2- to 3-month-olds do have some notion of object permanence, then what explains Piaget's finding that much older infants (who are quite capable of voluntary reaching) do not try to search for hidden objects? One possibility is that, just as Piaget's theory suggests, they cannot yet coordinate the separate means–end schemes—pushing aside the obstacle and grasping the object—necessary to retrieve a hidden toy. But this account is not the whole story, since 5- to 8-month-olds will retrieve an object from behind a transparent screen but not an opaque screen (Shinskey, Bogartz, & Poirier, 2000).

Instead, searching for hidden objects seems to represent a true advance in object-permanence understanding because infants solve some simple object-hiding tasks before others. For example, 10-month-olds search for an object placed on a table and covered by a cloth before they search for an object that a hand deposits under a cloth (Moore & Meltzoff, 1999). In the second task, infants seem to expect the object to reappear in the hand because that is where the object initially disappeared. When the hand emerges without the object, they may conclude that there is no other place the object could be. Not until age 14 months can most infants infer that the hand deposited the object under the cloth (see Figure 6.2).

**SEARCHING FOR OBJECTS HIDDEN IN MORE THAN ONE LOCATION.** For some years, researchers thought that babies made the A-not-B search error because they had trouble remembering an object's new location after it was hidden in more than one place. But recent findings reveal that poor memory cannot fully account for infants' unsuccessful performance. In violation-of-expectation procedures, in which an experimenter hides a toy at A, moves it to B, and then retrieves it either from B (possible event) or from A (impossible event), 8- to 12-month-olds look longer at the impossible event. This indicates that they remember where the object was last seen (at B) and expect it to reappear there (Ahmed & Ruffman, 1998).

Perhaps infants search at A (where they last found the object) instead of B (its most recent location) because they have trouble inhibiting a previously rewarded reaching response (Diamond, Cruttenden, & Neiderman, 1994). In support of this view, the more prior reaches to A, the greater the likelihood that the infant will reach again toward A when the object is hidden at B. A more comprehensive explanation is that a complex, dynamic system of factors—having built a habit of reaching toward A, continuing to look at A, having the hiding place at B look similar to the one at A, and maintaining a constant body posture—increases the chances that the baby will make the A-not-B search error. In a series of studies, disrupting any one of these factors increased 10-month-olds' searching at B (Smith et al., 1999).

In sum, before 12 months, infants seem to have difficulty translating what they know about an object moving from one hiding place to another into a successful search strategy.

The ability to integrate an AB path of object movement with behaviour coincides with rapid development of the frontal lobes of the cerebral cortex at the end of the first year (Bell, 1998; Diamond, 1991). Also crucial are a wide variety of experiences perceiving, acting on, and remembering objects.

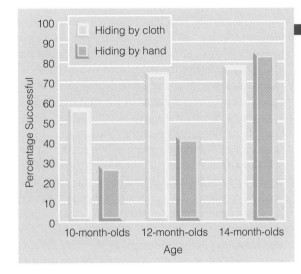

### MENTAL REPRESENTATION.

In Piaget's theory, infants lead purely sensorimotor lives; they cannot mentally represent experience until about 18 months of age. Yet 8-month-olds' ability to recall the location of a hidden object, even

**FIGURE** 6.2

**Performance of 10- to 14-month-olds on two types of object-hiding tasks.** (a) In the hiding-by-cloth task, a hand deposited the object on the table, next to a folded cloth. Then the cloth was unfolded over the object. (b) In the hiding-by-hand task, a hand carried the object toward and under the cloth, deposited the object under the cloth on the table, and emerged empty. Ten-month-olds searched for the object hidden by the cloth before they searched for the object hidden by the hand—a task most toddlers performed successfully only at 14 months. Improved object-search behaviour signifies gains in object-permanence understanding. (Adapted from Moore & Meltzoff, 1999.)

after delays of more than a minute, indicates that they construct mental representations of objects and their whereabouts (McDonough, 1999). And new studies of deferred imitation, categorization, and problem solving reveal that representational thought is evident even earlier.

*Deferred Imitation.* Piaget studied imitation by noting when his children demonstrated it in their everyday behaviour. Under these conditions, a great deal must be known about the infant's daily life to be sure that deferred imitation (which requires infants to mentally represent a model's past behaviour) has occurred. Therefore, Piaget might have missed many instances of deferred imitation, including ones occurring in the first year.

Laboratory studies reveal that deferred imitation is present at 6 weeks of age! Infants who watched an unfamiliar facial expression imitated it when exposed to the same adult 24 hours later (Meltzoff & Moore, 1994). Perhaps young babies use this imitation to identify and communicate with people they have seen before. As motor capacities improve, infants start to copy adults' actions on objects. In one study, 6- and 9-month-olds were shown an "activity" board with twelve novel objects secured to it—for example, a frog whose legs jump when a cord is pulled and an owl whose eyes flash when its belly is pushed. An adult modelled the actions of six objects. When tested 24 hours later, babies of both ages were far more likely to produce the actions they had seen than actions associated with objects that had not been demonstrated (Collie & Hayne, 1999). The babies retained and enacted not just one but, on average, three modelled behaviours.

Between 12 and 18 months, toddlers use deferred imitation skilfully to enrich their range of schemes. They retain modelled behaviours from one to several months, copy the actions of peers as well as adults, and imitate across a change in context—for example, enact in a laboratory a behaviour learned at home and generalize actions to similar objects varying in size and colour (Barr & Hayne, 1999; Hayne, Boniface, & Barr, 2000; Klein & Meltzoff, 1999).

Around 18 months, toddlers imitate not only an adult's behaviour but the actions he or she *tries* to produce, even if these actions are not fully realized (Meltzoff, 1995). On one occasion, a mother attempted to pour some raisins into a small bag but missed, spilling them onto the counter. A moment later, her 18-month-old son climbed on a stool and began dropping the raisins into the bag, indicating that he had begun to infer others' intentions and perspectives. By age 2, children mimic entire social roles—such as mommy, daddy, or baby—during make-believe play.

*Beginnings of Categorization.* Young babies' ability to categorize objects and events is also incompatible with a strictly sensorimotor approach to experience in which mental representation is absent. Recall the operant conditioning research in which infants kicked

This 3-month-old infant discovered that by kicking, she could shake a mobile made of small blocks with the letter *A* on them. After a delay, the baby continued to kick vigorously only if the mobile she saw was labelled with the same form (the letter *A*). She did not kick when given a mobile with a different form (the number 2). The infant's behaviour shows that she groups similar stimuli into categories and can distinguish the category "*A*" from the category "2."

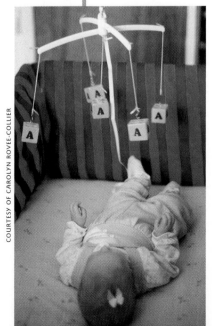

COURTESY OF CAROLYN ROVEE-COLLIER

FIGURE 6.3

**Categorical distinction made by 9- to 11-month-olds.** After infants were given an opportunity to examine (by looking at or touching) the objects in one category, they were shown a new object from each of the categories. They recovered to (spent more time looking at or touching) the object from the contrasting category, indicating that they distinguished the birds from the airplanes, despite their perceptual similarity. (Adapted from Mandler & McDonough, 1993.)

to move a mobile attached to their foot by a long cord (see Chapter 4, page 135). Some creative variations of this task have been used to find out about infant categorization.

In one series of studies, 3-month-olds kicked a mobile made of a uniform set of stimuli—small blocks, all with the letter *A* on them. After a delay, kicking returned to a high level only if the babies were given a mobile whose elements were labelled with the same form (the letter *A*). If the form was changed (from *A*'s to *2*'s), infants no longer kicked vigorously. While learning to make the mobile move, the babies had mentally grouped together its features, associating the kicking response with the category "*A*" and, at later testing, distinguishing it from the category "*2*" (Bhatt, Rovee-Collier, & Weiner, 1994; Hayne, Rovee-Collier, & Perris, 1987).

Habituation/recovery has also been used to study infant categorization. Researchers show babies a series of pictures belonging to one category and then see whether they recover to (look longer at) a picture that is not a member of the category. Findings reveal that 7- to 12-month-olds structure objects into an impressive array of meaningful categories—food items, furniture, birds, animals, vehicles, kitchen utensils, plants, spatial location ("above" and "below"), and more (Mandler & McDonough, 1993, 1996, 1998; Oakes, Coppage, & Dingel, 1997; Quinn & Eimas, 1996; Younger, 1985, 1993). Besides organizing the physical world, infants of this age also categorize their emotional and social worlds. Their looking responses reveal that they sort people and their voices by gender and age (Bahrick, Netto, & Hernandez-Reif, 1998; Poulin-DuBois et al., 1994), have begun to distinguish emotional expressions, and can separate the natural movements of people from other motions (see Chapter 4, pages 156 and 158).

The earliest categories are *perceptual*—based on similar overall appearance or prominent object part, such as legs for animals and wheels for vehicles (Rakison & Butterworth, 1998). But by the end of the first year, more categories are *conceptual*—based on common function and behaviour. In fact, older infants can make categorical distinctions when the perceptual contrast between two categories—animals and vehicles—is made as minimal as possible (for an illustration, see Figure 6.3).

In the second year, toddlers become active categorizers. Around 12 months, they touch objects that go together, without grouping them. Sixteen-month-olds can group objects into a single category. For example, when given four balls and four boxes, they put all the balls together but not the boxes. Around 18 months, toddlers sort objects into two classes (Gopnik & Meltzoff, 1987a). Compared with habituation/recovery, touching, sorting, and other play behaviours better reveal the meanings that children attach to categories because they are applying those meanings in their everyday behaviour. For example, after having watched an experimenter give a toy dog a drink from a cup, 14-month-olds shown a rabbit and a motorcycle usually offer the drink only to the rabbit (Mandler & McDonough, 1998). Their behaviour reveals that they understand that particular actions are appropriate for some categories of items (animals) and not others (vehicles).

How does the perceptual-to-conceptual change in categorization take place? Although researchers disagree on whether this shift requires a new approach to analyzing experience, most acknowledge that exploration of objects and expanding knowledge of the world contribute to older infants' capacity to move beyond physical features and group objects by their functions and behaviours (Mandler, 2000; Quinn et al., 2000).

***Problem Solving.*** As Piaget indicated, infants develop intentional, means–end action sequences around 7 to 8 months, using them to solve simple problems, such as obtaining a toy resting on the far end of a cloth by pulling on the cloth (Willatts, 1999). Soon after, infants' representational skills permit more effective problem solving than Piaget's theory suggests.

By 10 to 12 months, infants can engage in **analogical problem solving**—taking a solution strategy from one problem and applying it to other relevant problems. In one study, babies were given three similar problems, each requiring them to overcome a barrier, grasp a string, and pull it to get an attractive toy. The problems differed in all aspects of their specific features (see Figure 6.4). On the first problem, the parent demonstrated the solution and encouraged the child to imitate. Babies obtained the toy more readily on each additional problem, suggesting that they had formed a flexible mental representation of behaviours that access an out-of-reach object (Chen, Sanchez, & Campbell, 1997).

**analogical problem solving**
Taking a solution strategy from one problem and applying it to other relevant problems.

(a)                              (b)                              (c)

**FIGURE** 6.4

**Analogical problem solving by 10- to 12-month-olds.** After the parent demonstrated the solution to problem (a), infants solved (b) and (c) with increasing efficiency, even though those problems differed in all aspects of their superficial features. (From Z. Chen, R. P. Sanchez, & T. Campbell, 1997, "From Beyond to Within Their Grasp: The Rudiments of Analogical Problem Solving in 10- to 13-month-olds." *Developmental Psychology, 33,* p. 792. Copyright © 1997 by the American Psychological Association. Reprinted by permission of the publisher and author.)

With age, children become better at reasoning by analogy, generalizing across increasingly dissimilar situations (Goswami, 1996). But even in the first year, infants have some ability to move beyond trial-and-error experimentation, to mentally represent a problem solution, and to use it in new contexts.

When we combine the capacities just considered with milestones we will discuss in later chapters—for example, that events taking place before 10 to 11 months can be recalled up to a year and a half later (see Chapter 7) and that at the end of the first year, infants communicate with symbolic gestures (see Chapter 9)—it is clear that mental representation is not the culmination of sensorimotor development. Instead, sensorimotor and representational schemes develop concurrently during the first 2 years.

## EVALUATION OF THE SENSORIMOTOR STAGE

The Milestones table on page 228 summarizes the remarkable cognitive attainments we have just considered, along with related milestones discussed in Chapter 4. Compare this table with the description of Piaget's sensorimotor substages on page 221. You will see that infants anticipate events, actively search for hidden objects, master AB object search, flexibly vary their sensorimotor schemes, and engage in make-believe play within Piaget's time frame. Yet many other capacities—including secondary circular reactions, the glimmering of object permanence, deferred imitation, categorization, and analogical problem solving—seem to emerge earlier than Piaget expected.

Notice, also, that the cognitive attainments of infancy do not develop in the neat, stepwise fashion predicted by Piaget's substages. For example, deferred imitation and the beginnings of analogical problem solving are present long before toddlers can solve Piaget's most advanced object-hiding task. To obtain an object that has been moved while out of sight, infants must go beyond *recall of a past event* to a more complex form of representation; they must *imagine an event they have not seen* (Rast & Meltzoff, 1995). Yet Piaget assumed that all representational capacities develop at the same time, at the end of the sensorimotor stage.

# milestones

## SOME COGNITIVE ATTAINMENTS OF INFANCY

| APPROXIMATE AGE | EXPLORATION/ PROBLEM SOLVING | OBJECT CONCEPT | IMITATION | CATEGORIZATION |
|---|---|---|---|---|
| Birth–1 month | ♪ Newborn reflexes<br><br>♪ Exploration with limited motor skills, such as head turning and sucking | ♪ Awareness of size and shape constancy (see Chapter 4) | ♪ Imitation of adults' facial expressions and gestures (see Chapter 4) | |
| 1–4 months | ♪ Exploration with better coordinated motor skills, such as kicking, reaching, and grasping<br><br>♪ Limited anticipation of events | ♪ Use of motion and spatial arrangement to identify objects (see Chapter 4)<br><br>♪ Some awareness of object permanence | ♪ Deferred imitation of adults' facial expressions after 24 hours | ♪ Categorization of perceptually similar stimuli |
| 4–8 months | ♪ Exploration using well-coordinated reaching, grasping, swiping, banging, and other manual behaviours | ♪ Use of shape, texture, and colour to identify objects (see Chapter 4) | ♪ Deferred imitation of adults' actions on objects after 24 hours | ♪ Beginning categorization of objects by function and behaviour |
| 8–12 months | ♪ Intentional, or goal-directed, behaviour<br><br>♪ Improved anticipation of events<br><br>♪ Problem solving by analogy to other similar problems | ♪ Ability to retrieve an object from the first location in which it is hidden | | ♪ Categorization of many objects by function and behaviour<br><br>♪ Categorization of social stimuli (for example, emotional expressions, human versus nonhuman movement patterns) |
| 12–18 months | ♪ Exploration of objects by acting on them in novel ways<br><br>♪ Experimenting with actions when solving problems | ♪ Ability to search in several locations for a hidden object (AB search) | ♪ Deferred imitation across changes in context and after one to several months | ♪ Active object sorting into a single category |
| 18 months–2 years | ♪ Sudden solutions to problems, without overt experimentation with actions | ♪ Ability to find an object moved while out of sight (invisible displacement) | ♪ Imitation of actions an adult tries to produce, even if these are not fully realized<br><br>♪ Deferred imitation of everyday behaviours in make-believe play | ♪ Active object sorting into two categories |

*Note:* These milestones represent overall age trends. Individual differences exist in the precise age at which each milestone is attained.

These findings, and others like them, are among an accumulating body of evidence that questions Piaget's stages.

Discrepancies between Piaget's observations and those of recent research also raise controversial questions about how infant development takes place. Consistent with Piaget's ideas, sensorimotor action facilitates the construction of some forms of knowledge. For example, in Chapter 4, we indicated that crawling experiences bring enhanced sensitivity to depth cues, memory for object locations, and ability to find hidden objects. Yet we have also seen that infants comprehend a great deal before they are capable of the motor behaviours Piaget assumed led to those understandings. How can we account for babies' amazing cognitive accomplishments?

Most researchers believe that young babies have more built-in cognitive equipment for making sense of experience than granted by Piaget, who thought that they constructed all mental representations out of sensorimotor activity. But intense disagreement exists over how much initial understanding infants have. As we have seen, much evidence on infant cognition rests on habituation/recovery research, especially the violation-of-expectation method. Researchers who lack confidence in these findings argue that babies' cognitive starting point is limited. For example, some believe that newborns begin life with a set of biases, or learning procedures—such as powerful techniques for analyzing complex, perceptual information—that grant the baby a means for constructing and flexibly adapting schemes (Elman et al., 1996; Haith & Benson, 1998; Karmiloff-Smith, 1992). Others, impressed with violation-of-expectation findings, are convinced that infants begin life with considerable innate knowledge, which gets their cognitive development off the ground quickly. We will discuss the strengths and limitations of this *core knowledge perspective,* which has gained ground in the past decade, after considering Piaget's stages of childhood and adolescence.

© REFLECTIONS PHOTOLIBRARY/CORBIS

Did these toddlers acquire the necessary physical knowledge to build a block tower through many opportunities to act on objects, as Piaget assumed? Or did the toddlers begin life with considerable innate knowledge, which enabled them to understand objects and their relationships quickly, with little hands-on exploration?

## ASK YOURSELF

**review**    Explain how cognition changes in Piaget's theory, giving examples of assimilation, accommodation, and organization.

**review**    Using the text discussion on pages 223–227, construct your own table providing an overview of infant and toddler cognitive development. Which entries in the table are consistent with Piaget's sensorimotor stage? Which ones develop earlier than Piaget anticipated?

**apply**    Ten-month-old Mimi's father holds up her favourite teething biscuit, deposits it under a napkin, and shows Mimi his empty hand. Mimi looks puzzled and fails to search for the biscuit. Explain why Mimi finds this object-hiding task difficult.

**connect**    Review research in Chapter 4 indicating that if infants are not tested in the same situation in which they were trained, they remember poorly (see page 137). After 12 months of age, memory becomes more flexible. Do similar changes in the flexibility of object-search behaviours, deferred imitation, and problem solving occur around this time? Explain.

# The Preoperational Stage (2 to 7 Years)

AS CHILDREN MOVE FROM the sensorimotor to the **preoperational stage,** the most obvious change is an extraordinary increase in mental representation. We have seen that infants have some capacity to represent their world. Between ages 2 and 7, this capacity blossoms.

**preoperational stage**
Piaget's second stage, in which rapid development of representation takes place. However, thought is not yet logical. Spans the years from 2 to 7.

## ADVANCES IN MENTAL REPRESENTATION

A visit to a preschool classroom reveals signs of mental representation everywhere—in children's re-creations of experiences in make-believe play, in drawings and paintings that cover the walls, and in their delight at story time. Especially impressive are tremendous strides in language.

**LANGUAGE AND THOUGHT.** Piaget acknowledged that language is our most flexible means of mental representation. By detaching thought from action, it permits far more adept thinking than was possible earlier. When we think with words, we overcome the limits of our momentary experiences. We can deal with the past, present, and future at once and combine concepts in unique ways, as when we think about a hungry caterpillar eating bananas or monsters flying through the forest at night.

Despite the power of language, Piaget did not believe that it plays a major role in children's cognitive development. Instead, he believed that sensorimotor activity leads to internal images of experience, which children then label with words (Piaget, 1936/1952b). Some evidence is consistent with this idea. For example, children's first words have a strong sensorimotor basis. They usually refer to objects that move or can be acted on or to familiar actions (see Chapter 9). Also, certain early words are linked to nonverbal cognitive achievements. For example, disappearance terms, such as "all gone," emerge at about the same time as mastery of advanced object-permanence problems. And success and failure expressions—"There!" and "Uh-oh"—appear when toddlers solve problems suddenly (Gopnik & Meltzoff, 1987b). Finally, toddlers' gains in categorization, as indicated by advanced object-sorting behaviour, coincide with a spurt in vocabulary between 18 months and 2 years (Fenson et al., 1994).

Still, Piaget misjudged the power of language to spur children's cognition forward. For example, we will see later that children's conversations with adults and expanding vocabularies greatly enhance conceptual skills. Research inspired by Vygotsky's theory (which we take up later) confirms that language is a powerful source of cognitive development, not just an indicator of it.

**MAKE-BELIEVE PLAY.** Make-believe play provides another excellent example of the development of representation during the preoperational stage. Piaget believed that through pretending, children practise and strengthen newly acquired representational schemes. Drawing on Piaget's ideas, several investigators have traced changes in make-believe play during the preschool years.

*Development of Make-Believe Play.* Compare an 18-month-old's pretending with that of a 2- to 3-year-old. You are likely to see three important advances. Each reflects the preschool child's growing symbolic mastery:

- *Over time, play increasingly detaches from the real-life conditions associated with it.* In early pretending, toddlers use only realistic objects—for example, a toy telephone to talk into or a cup to drink from. Most of these first pretend acts imitate adults' actions and are not yet flexible. Children younger than age 2, for example, will pretend to drink from a cup but refuse to pretend a cup is a hat (Tomasello, Striano, & Rochat, 1999).

  After age 2, children pretend with less realistic toys, such as a block for a telephone receiver. And during the third year, they can flexibly imagine objects and events, without any support from the real world. Now a play symbol no longer has to resemble the object for which it stands (Corrigan, 1987; O'Reilly, 1995).

- *Play becomes less self-centred with age.* When make-believe first appears, it is directed toward the self—that is, children pretend to feed or wash only themselves. A short time later, children direct pretend actions toward other objects, as when the child feeds a doll. And early in the third year, they become detached participants who make a doll feed itself or a parent doll feed a baby doll. Make-believe gradually becomes less self-centred, as children realize that agents and recipients of pretend actions can be independent of themselves (McCune, 1993).

■ *Play gradually includes more complex scheme combinations.* For example, an 18-month-old can pretend to drink from a cup but does not yet combine pouring and drinking. Later, children combine pretend schemes with those of peers in **sociodramatic play,** the make-believe with other children that is under way by age 2½ and increases rapidly during the next few years (Haight & Miller, 1993). By age 4 to 5, children build on one another's play themes, create and coordinate several roles, and have a sophisticated understanding of story lines (Göncü, 1993).

© LAURA DWIGHT

This 4-year-old involves her dolls and stuffed animals in an elaborate tea party. Her enjoyment of make-believe play strengthens a variety of mental abilities.

The appearance of complex sociodramatic play signals a major change in representation. Children do not just represent their world; they display *awareness* that make-believe is a representational activity, an understanding that increases steadily from 4 to 8 years of age (Lillard, 1998, 2001). Listen closely to preschoolers as they jointly create an imaginary scene. You will hear them assign roles and negotiate make-believe plans: "*You pretend to be* the astronaut, *I'll act like* I'm operating the control tower!" "Wait, *I gotta set up* the spaceship." In communicating about pretend, children think about and manipulate their own and others' fanciful representations. This indicates that they have begun to reason about people's mental activities.

***Benefits of Make-Believe Play.*** Piaget captured an important aspect of make-believe when he underscored its role in exercising representational schemes. He also noted its emotionally integrative function, a feature emphasized in psychoanalytic theory. Young children often revisit anxiety-provoking events, such as a trip to the doctor's office or discipline by a parent, but with roles reversed so the child is in command and compensates for the unpleasant experience (Piaget, 1945/1951).

Nevertheless, today Piaget's view of make-believe as mere practice of representational schemes is regarded as too limited. Play not only reflects but contributes to children's cognitive and social skills. Sociodramatic play has been studied most thoroughly. In contrast to social nonpretend activities (such as jointly drawing a picture or putting a puzzle together), during social pretend, preschoolers' interactions last longer, show more involvement, draw larger numbers of children into the activity, and are more cooperative (Creasey, Jarvis, & Berk, 1998).

When we consider these findings, it is not surprising that John Connolly of Dalhousie University and Anna-Beth Doyle of Concordia University (1984) found that preschoolers who spend more time at sociodramatic play are seen as more socially competent by their teachers. And many studies reveal that make-believe strengthens a wide variety of mental abilities, including sustained attention, memory, logical reasoning, language and literacy, imagination, creativity, and the ability to reflect on one's own thinking and take another's perspective (Bergen & Mauer, 2000; Dias & Harris, 1990; Kavanaugh & Engel, 1998; Newman, 1990; Ruff et al., 1990).

Some children spend much time in solitary make-believe, creating *imaginary companions*—special fantasized friends endowed with humanlike qualities. In the past, imaginary companions were viewed as a sign of maladjustment, but recent research challenges this assumption. Between 25 and 45 percent of 3- to 7-year-olds have them, and those who do display more complex pretend play, are advanced in mental representation, and are often more (not less) sociable with peers (Taylor, 1999; Taylor & Carlson, 1997).

These findings offer strong justification for play as a central part of early childhood education programs and the daily life of the young child. Later we will return to the origins and consequences of make-believe from an alternative perspective—Vygotsky's.

**sociodramatic play**
The make-believe play with other children that is under way by age 2½.

**FIGURE 6.5**

**Examples of young children's drawings.** The universal tadpole-like form that children use to draw their first picture of a person is shown on the left. The tadpole soon becomes an anchor for greater detail as arms, fingers, toes, and facial features sprout from the basic shape. By the end of the preschool years, children produce more complex, differentiated pictures like the one on the right, drawn by a 6-year-old child. Notice the beginning representation of perspective in the converging lines of the railroad tracks. (Tadpole drawings from H. Gardner, 1980, *Artful Scribbles: The Significance of Children's Drawings*, New York: Basic Books, p. 64. Reprinted by permission of Basic Books, a division of HarperCollins Publishers, Inc. Six-year-old's picture from E. Winner, August 1986, "Where Pelicans Kiss Seals," *Psychology Today*, 20[8], p. 35. Reprinted by permission of the author.)

**dual representation**
Viewing a symbolic object as both an object in its own right and a symbol.

**DRAWINGS.** Cognitive advances and cultural emphasis on artistic expression influence the development of children's artful representations. Typically, drawing progresses through the following sequence:

1. *Scribbles.* Western children begin to draw during the second year. At first, gestures rather than the resulting scribbles contain the intended representation. For example, one 18-month-old took her crayon and hopped it around the page, explaining as she made a series of dots, "Rabbit goes hop-hop" (Winner, 1986).

2. *First representational shapes and forms.* By age 3, children's scribbles start to become pictures. Often this happens after they make a gesture with the crayon, notice that they have drawn a recognizable shape, and then decide to label it. In one case, a 2-year-old made some random marks on a page and then, realizing the resemblance between his scribbles and noodles, named the creation "chicken pie and noodles" (Winner, 1986).

   A major milestone in drawing occurs when children use lines to represent the boundaries of objects. This permits them to draw their first picture of a person by age 3 or 4. Look at the tadpole image—a circular shape with lines attached—on the left in Figure 6.5. It is a universal one in which fine motor and cognitive limitations lead the preschooler to reduce the figure to the simplest form that still looks like a human being. Gradually, preschoolers add features, such as eyes, nose, mouth, hair, fingers, and feet.

3. *More realistic drawings.* Young children do not demand that a drawing be realistic. But as cognitive and fine motor skills improve, they learn to desire greater realism. As a result, they create more complex drawings, like the one on the right in Figure 6.5, made by a 6-year-old child. These drawings contain more conventional figures, in which the head and body are differentiated and arms and legs appear. (Look closely at the human and animal figures in the 6-year-old's drawing.) Over time, children improve the proportions of the head, trunk, and extremities and add more details.

   Still, children of this age are not very particular about mirroring reality. Their drawings contain perceptual distortions, since they have just begun to represent depth (Braine et al., 1993). Use of depth cues, such as overlapping objects, smaller distant than near objects, diagonal placement, and converging lines, increase during the elementary school years (Cox & Littleton, 1995; Nicholls & Kennedy, 1992). And instead of depicting objects separately (as in the drawing in Figure 6.5), older school-age children relate them to one another in an organized spatial arrangement (Case & Okamoto, 1996).

In cultures that emphasize artistic expression, children's drawings reflect the conventions of their culture and are more elaborate. In cultures with little interest in art, even older children and adolescents produce simple forms. The Jimi Valley is a remote region of Papua New Guinea with no indigenous pictorial art. Many children do not go to school and therefore have little opportunity to develop drawing skills. When a Western researcher asked nonschooled Jimi 10- to 15-year-olds to draw a human figure for the first time, most produced nonrepresentational scribbles and shapes or simple "stick" or "contour" images (see Figure 6.6) (Martlew & Connolly, 1996). These forms resemble preschoolers' and seem to be a universal beginning in drawing. Once children realize that lines on the page must evoke human features, they find solutions to figure drawing that vary somewhat from culture to culture but, overall, follow the sequence of development described earlier.

**SYMBOL–REAL WORLD RELATIONS.** To make believe and draw—and to understand other forms of representation, such as photographs, models, and maps—preschoolers must realize that each symbol corresponds to a specific state of affairs in everyday life. When do children comprehend symbol–real world relations?

In one study, 2½- and 3-year-olds watched as an adult hid a small toy (Little Snoopy) in a scale model of a room; then children were asked to retrieve it. Next, they had to find a larger toy (Big Snoopy) hidden in the room that the model represented. Not until age 3 could most children use the model as a guide to finding Big Snoopy in the real room (DeLoache, 1987). The younger preschoolers seemed to have trouble with **dual representation**—viewing a symbolic object as both an object in its own right and a symbol. That is, they did not realize that the model could be both *a toy room and a symbol of another room*. In support of this interpretation, when researchers decreased the salience of the model room as an object, by placing it behind a window and preventing children from touching it, more 2½-year-olds succeeded at the search task (see Figure 6.7 on page 234). Nevertheless, about half still could not treat the model as a symbol (DeLoache, 2000).

Recall a similar limitation in early pretending—that 1½- to 2-year-olds cannot use an object with an obvious use (cup) to stand for another object (hat). Likewise, Tara Callaghan (1999) of St. Francis Xavier University found that 2-year-olds do not understand that a drawing (an object in its own right) represents real-world objects. When an adult held up a drawing indicating which of two objects preschoolers should drop down a chute, 3-year-olds used the drawing as a symbol to guide their behaviour, but 2-year-olds did not. Because of their difficulty with dual representation, children rarely make representational drawings before age 3.

How do children grasp the dual representation of models, drawings, and other symbols? Insight into one type of symbol–real world relation helps preschoolers understand others. For example, children understand photos as symbols very early, around age 2, since a photo's

© LAURA BERK

When young children experiment with crayons and paint, they not only develop fine motor skills but acquire the artistic traditions of their culture. This Australian Aboriginal 4-year-old creates a dot painting. To Westerners, it looks abstract. To the child, it expresses a "dreamtime" story about the life and land of his ancestors. If asked about the painting, he might respond, "Here are the boulders on the creek line, the hills with kangaroos and emus, and the campsites."

(a)　　　(b)　　　(c)

**FIGURE 6.6**

**Drawings produced by nonschooled 10- to 15-year-old children of the Jimi Valley of Papua New Guinea when asked to draw a human figure for the first time.** Many produced nonrepresentational scribbles and shapes (a), "stick" figures (b), or "contour" figures (c). Compared with the Western tadpole form, the Jimi "stick" and "contour" figures emphasize the hands and feet. Otherwise, the drawings of these older children, who had little opportunity to develop drawing skills, resemble those of young preschoolers. (Adapted from Martlew & Connolly, 1996.)

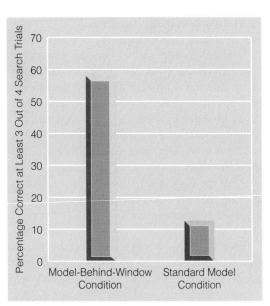

**FIGURE 6.7**

**Use of a model room as a symbol of a real room by 2½-year-olds.** Researchers decreased the salience of the model room as an object, by placing it behind a window and preventing children from touching it. An adult is shown pointing to a miniature pillow on the chair in the model to indicate to the child where Big Snoopy can be found in the real room. More 2½-year-olds used the model to find Big Snoopy under these conditions than in the standard condition, in which children were allowed to explore the model. When the model is made less like an object and more like a symbol, 2½-year-olds perform more successfully. But nearly half still cannot use the model as a symbol. (Adapted from DeLoache, 2000.)

primary purpose is to stand for something; it is not an interesting object in its own right (DeLoache, 1991). And 3-year-olds who pass the model task readily transfer their understanding to a simple map (Marzolf & DeLoache, 1994).

Granting young children many opportunities to learn the functions of diverse symbols—picture books, photographs, models, drawings, make-believe, and maps—helps them appreciate that one object can stand for another. Over time, children come to understand a wide range of symbols that do not bear a strong physical similarity to what they represent (DeLoache, Perralta de Mendoza, & Anderson, 1999; Liben, 1999). As a result, doors open to vast realms of knowledge.

Is this preschooler aware that the doll house is not just an interesting object in its own right, but can stand for a real house—that is, serve as a symbol of the real world? Not until age 3 do most young children grasp the *dual representation* of models.

### LIMITATIONS OF PREOPERATIONAL THOUGHT

Aside from the development of representation, Piaget described preschool children in terms of what they *cannot,* rather than *can,* understand (Beilin, 1992). He compared them to older, more capable children in the concrete operational stage, as the term "preoperational" suggests. According to Piaget, young children are not capable of **operations**—mental representations of actions that obey logical rules. Instead, their thinking is rigid, limited to one aspect of a situation at a time, and strongly influenced by the way things appear at the moment.

**EGOCENTRIC AND ANIMISTIC THINKING.** For Piaget, the most serious deficiency of preoperational thinking, the one that underlies all others, is **egocentrism.** He believed that when children first mentally represent the world, they tend to focus on their own viewpoint and ignore others' perspectives. Hence, they often assume that others perceive, think, and feel the same way they do.

Piaget's most convincing demonstration of egocentrism involves his *three-mountains problem,* described in Figure 6.8. Egocentrism, he pointed out, is responsible for preoperational children's **animistic thinking**—the belief that inanimate objects have lifelike qualities, such as thoughts, wishes, feelings, and intentions, just like themselves (Piaget, 1926/1930). The 3-year-old who charmingly explains that the sun is angry at the clouds and has chased them away is demonstrating this kind of reasoning. According to Piaget, because young children egocentrically assign human purposes to physical events, magical thinking is common during the preschool years.

Piaget argued that preschoolers' egocentric bias prevents them from *accommodating,* or revising their faulty reasoning, in response to their physical and social worlds. But to appreciate their cognitive shortcomings fully, let's consider some additional tasks that Piaget gave children.

**INABILITY TO CONSERVE.** Piaget's famous conservation tasks reveal a variety of deficiencies of preoperational thinking. **Conservation** refers to the idea that certain physical characteristics of objects remain the same, even when their outward appearance changes. A typical example is the conservation-of-liquid problem. The child is shown two identical tall glasses of water and asked if they contain equal amounts. Once the child agrees, the water in one glass is poured into a short, wide container, changing the appearance of the water but not its amount. Then the child is asked whether the amount of water is the same or has changed. Preoperational children think the quantity has changed. They explain, "There is less now because the water is way down here" (that is, its level is so low) or "There is more because the water is all spread out." In Figure 6.9 on page 236, you will find other conservation tasks that you can try with children.

Preoperational children's inability to conserve highlights several related aspects of their thinking. First, their understanding is characterized by **centration.** In other words, they focus on one aspect of a situation to the neglect of other important features. With conservation of liquid, the child *centres* on the height of the water in the two containers, failing to realize that all changes in height are compensated by changes in width. Second, they are easily distracted by superficial perceptual appearances. It *looks like* the short, wide container has less water, so it *must have* less water. Third, children treat the initial and final states of the water as unrelated events, ignoring the *dynamic transformation* (pouring of water) between them.

The most important illogical feature of preoperational thought is *irreversibility.* Children of this stage cannot mentally go through a series of steps and then reverse direction, returning to the starting point. **Reversibility** is part of every logical operation. In the case of conservation of liquid, the preoperational child fails to see how the same amount is ensured by imagining it being poured back into its original container.

**LACK OF HIERARCHICAL CLASSIFICATION.** Lack of logical operations leads preschoolers to have difficulty with **hierarchical classification.** That is, they cannot organize objects into classes and subclasses on the basis of similarities and differences. Piaget's famous *class inclusion problem,* illustrated in Figure 6.10 on page 236, demonstrates this limitation. Preoperational children centre on the overriding perceptual feature of yellow instead of thinking reversibly by moving from the whole class (flowers) to the parts (yellow and blue) and back again.

## FOLLOW-UP RESEARCH ON PREOPERATIONAL THOUGHT

Over the past two decades, Piaget's account of a cognitively deficient preschooler has been challenged. If researchers give his tasks in just the way he designed them, preschoolers do perform poorly. But many Piagetian problems contain unfamiliar elements or too many pieces of information for young children to handle at once. As a result, preschoolers' responses often do not reflect their true abilities. Piaget also missed many naturally occurring instances of preschoolers' effective reasoning. Let's look at some examples.

**EGOCENTRISM.** Do young children egocentrically believe that a person standing in a different location in a room sees the same thing they see? When researchers change the nature of Piaget's three-mountains problem to include familiar objects and use methods other than picture selection (which is difficult even for 10-year-olds), 4-year-olds show clear awareness of others' vantage points (Borke, 1975; Newcombe & Huttenlocher, 1992).

**FIGURE** 6.8

**Piaget's three-mountains problem.** A child is permitted to walk around a display of three mountains. Each is distinguished by its colour and by its summit. One has a red cross, another a small house, and the third a snow-capped peak. Then the child stands on one side, and a doll is placed at various locations around the display. The child must choose a photograph that shows what the display looks like from the doll's perspective. Before age 6 or 7, most children select the photo that shows the mountains from their own point of view.

**operations**
In Piaget's theory, mental representations of actions that obey logical rules.

**egocentrism**
The tendency to focus on one's own viewpoint and ignore others' perspectives.

**animistic thinking**
The belief that inanimate objects have lifelike qualities, such as thoughts, wishes, feelings, and intentions.

**conservation**
The understanding that certain physical characteristics of objects remain the same, even when their outward appearance changes.

**centration**
The tendency to focus on one aspect of a situation to the neglect of other important features.

**reversibility**
The ability to mentally go through a series of steps and then reverse direction, returning to the starting point. In Piaget's theory, part of every logical operation.

**hierarchical classification**
The organization of objects into classes and subclasses on the basis of similarities and differences.

**FIGURE** 6.9

**Some Piagetian conservation tasks.** Children at the preoperational stage cannot yet conserve. These tasks are mastered gradually over the concrete operational stage. Children in Western nations typically acquire conservation of number, length, mass, and liquid sometime between 6 and 7 years and weight between 8 and 10 years.

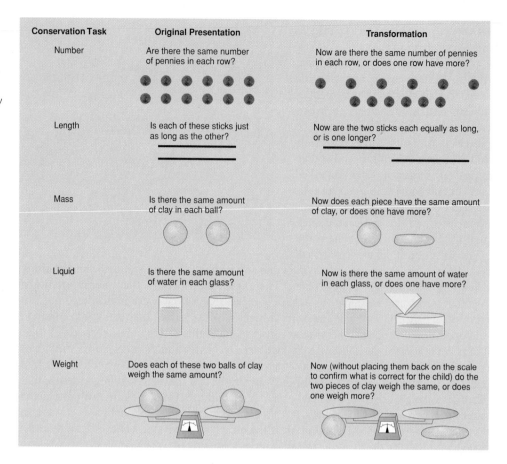

| Conservation Task | Original Presentation | Transformation |
|---|---|---|
| Number | Are there the same number of pennies in each row? | Now are there the same number of pennies in each row, or does one row have more? |
| Length | Is each of these sticks just as long as the other? | Now are the two sticks each equally as long, or is one longer? |
| Mass | Is there the same amount of clay in each ball? | Now does each piece have the same amount of clay, or does one have more? |
| Liquid | Is there the same amount of water in each glass? | Now is there the same amount of water in each glass, or does one have more? |
| Weight | Does each of these two balls of clay weigh the same amount? | Now (without placing them back on the scale to confirm what is correct for the child) do the two pieces of clay weigh the same, or does one weigh more? |

**FIGURE** 6.10

**A Piagetian class inclusion problem.** Children are shown 16 flowers, 4 of which are blue and 12 of which are yellow. Asked "Are there more yellow flowers or more flowers?" the preoperational child responds, "More yellow flowers," failing to realize that both yellow and blue flowers are included in the category "flowers."

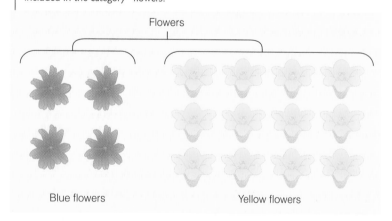

Flowers

Blue flowers                Yellow flowers

Nonegocentric responses also appear in young children's conversations. For example, preschoolers adapt their speech to fit the needs of their listeners. Four-year-olds use shorter, simpler expressions when talking to 2-year-olds than to agemates or adults (Gelman & Shatz, 1978). Also, in describing objects, children do not use such words as "big" and "little" in a rigid, egocentric fashion. Instead, they *adjust* their descriptions, taking account of context. By age 3, children judge a 5-centimetre shoe as small when seen by itself (because it is much smaller than most shoes) but as big for a tiny, 13-centimetre doll (Ebeling & Gelman, 1994).

In later chapters, we will encounter evidence indicating that young children have a much greater appreciation of other people's mental states than is implied by Piaget's notion of egocentrism. At the same time, preschoolers' understanding of others' viewpoints is far from complete. But in fairness, in his later writings Piaget (1945/1951) described preschoolers' egocentrism as a tendency rather than an inability. As we revisit the topic of perspective taking, we will see that it develops gradually throughout childhood and adolescence.

**ANIMISTIC AND MAGICAL THINKING.** Piaget overestimated preschoolers' animistic beliefs because he asked children about objects with which they have little direct experience, such as the clouds, sun, and moon. Three-year-olds do make errors when questioned about certain vehicles, such as trains and airplanes. But these objects *appear* to be self-moving, a characteristic of almost all living things. And they also have some lifelike features—for example, headlights that look like eyes and animate-like movement patterns (Poulin-Dubois & Héroux, 1994; Richards & Siegler, 1986). Children's responses result from incomplete knowledge about objects, not from a belief that inanimate objects are alive.

The same is true for other fantastic beliefs of the preschool years. Most 3- and 4-year-olds believe in the supernatural powers of fairies, goblins, and other enchanted creatures. But they deny that magic can alter their everyday experiences— for example, turn a picture into a real object or a living being (Subbotsky, 1994). Instead, they think that magic accounts for events that violate their expectations or that they cannot otherwise explain (as in 3-year-old Sammy's magical explanation of thunder in the opening to this chapter) (Rosengren & Hickling, 2000).

© J. SOHM/THE IMAGE WORKS

Between 4 and 8 years, as familiarity with physical events increases and as adults provide more scientific explanations, magical beliefs decline. Children figure out who is really behind the activities of Santa Claus and the Tooth Fairy! They also realize that the antics of magicians are due to trickery, not special powers (Phelps & Woolley, 1994; Woolley et al., 1999). How quickly children give up certain fantastic ideas varies with religion and culture. For example, Jewish preschool and school-age children express greater disbelief in Santa Claus and the Tooth Fairy than do their Christian agemates. Having been taught at home about the unreality of Santa, they seem to generalize this attitude to other mythical figures (Woolley, 1997).

Which of the children in this audience realize that a magician's powers depend on trickery? The younger children look surprised and bewildered. The older children think the magician's antics are funny. Between 4 and 8 years, as familiarity with physical events and principles increases, children's magical beliefs decline.

**ILLOGICAL CHARACTERISTICS OF THOUGHT.** Many studies have re-examined the illogical characteristics that Piaget saw in the preoperational stage. Results show that when preschoolers are given tasks that are simplified and made relevant to their everyday lives, they do better than Piaget might have expected.

For example, when a conservation-of-number task is scaled down to include only three items instead of six or seven, 3-year-olds perform well (Gelman, 1972). And when preschoolers are asked carefully worded questions about what happens to familiar substances (such as sugar) after they are dissolved in water, they give very accurate explanations. Most 3- to 5-year-olds know that the substance is conserved—that it continues to exist, can be tasted, and makes the liquid heavier, even though it is invisible in the water (Au, Sidle, & Rollins, 1993; Rosen & Rozin, 1993).

Preschoolers' ability to reason about transformations is evident on other problems. For example, they can engage in impressive *reasoning by analogy* about physical changes. Presented with the problem, *playdough is to cut-up playdough as apple is to?*, even 3-year-olds choose the correct answer from a set of alternatives, several of which share physical features with the right choice (see Figure 6.11 on page 238) (Goswami & Brown, 1989). These findings indicate that preschoolers can overcome appearances and think logically about cause and effect in familiar contexts.

Finally, 3- and 4-year-olds use logical, causal expressions, such as *if–then* and *because*, with the same degree of accuracy as adults do (McCabe & Peterson, 1988). Illogical reasoning seems to occur only when they grapple with unfamiliar topics, too much information, or contradictory facts, which they have trouble reconciling (Ruffman, 1999).

**CATEGORIZATION.** Although preschoolers have difficulty with Piagetian class inclusion tasks, their everyday knowledge is organized into nested categories at an early age. Recall that by the second half of the first year, children have formed a variety of global categories, such as furniture, animals, vehicles, and plants.

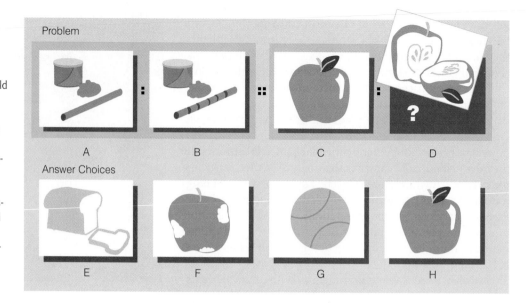

**FIGURE 6.11**

**Analogical problem about physical transformations.**

Preschoolers were told they would be playing a picture-matching game. Then the researchers showed each child the first three pictures of a four-picture sequence—in this example, playdough, cut-up playdough, and apple—and asked the child to complete the sequence by choosing from five alternatives. Several wrong answers shared features with the right choice—for example, correct physical change but wrong object (E), correct object but wrong physical change (F). Children as young as 3 years of age could combine the correct physical change with the correct object and solve the problem. (Adapted from Goswami & Brown, 1989.)

Notice that each of these categories includes objects that differ widely in perceptual features, challenging Piaget's assumption that preschoolers' thinking is governed by the way things appear. Indeed, 2- to 5-year-olds readily draw inferences about non-observable characteristics that category members share (Keil & Lockhart, 1999). For example, after being told that a bird has warm blood and a stegosaurus (dinosaur) has cold blood, preschoolers infer that a pterodactyl (labelled a dinosaur) has cold blood, even though it closely resembles a bird.

Over the early preschool years, children's global categories differentiate. They form many *basic-level categories*—ones at an intermediate level of generality, such as "chairs," "tables," "dressers," and "beds." Performance on object-sorting tasks indicates that by the third year, preschoolers easily move back and forth between basic-level and *superordinate categories,* such as "furniture" (Blewitt, 1994). Soon after, they break down basic-level categories into *subcategories,* such as "rocking chairs" and "desk chairs."

Preschoolers' rapidly growing vocabularies and expanding general knowledge support their impressive categorizing skill. As they learn more about their world, they devise ideas about underlying characteristics that category members share. For example, they realize that animals have an inborn potential for certain physical features and behaviours that determine their identity (Gelman & Wellman, 1991; Hirshfeld, 1995). In one study, researchers made up two categories of animals: One had horns, armour, and a spiky tail; the other had wings, large ears, long toes, and a monkey-like tail (see Figure 6.12). Four-year-olds who were given an explanation for the coexistence of the animals' features—animals in the first category "like to fight," those in the second category "like to hide in trees"—easily classified new examples of animals. Four-year-olds for whom animal features were merely pointed out or who were given a separate function for each feature could not remember the categories (Krascum & Andrews, 1998).

Finally, adults label and explain categories to young children, and picture-book reading is an especially rich context for doing so. While looking at books with their preschoolers, parents make such categorical statements as "Penguins live at the South Pole, swim, and catch fish" and "Fish breathe by taking water into their mouths" (Gelman et al., 1998). The information they provide helps guide children's inferences about the structure of categories.

In sum, young children's category systems are not yet very complex. But the capacity to classify hierarchically is present in early childhood.

**APPEARANCE VERSUS REALITY.** So far, we have seen that preschoolers show remarkably advanced reasoning when presented with familiar situations and simplified problems. Yet in certain situations, young children are easily tricked by the outward appearance of things.

John Flavell and his colleagues presented children with objects that were disguised in various ways and asked what the items were, "really and truly." Preschoolers had difficulty with problems involving sights and sounds. When asked whether a white piece of paper placed behind a blue filter is "really and truly blue" or whether a can that sounds like a baby crying when turned over is "really and truly a baby," preschoolers often respond "Yes!" Not until age 6 to 7 do children do well on these problems (Flavell, 1993; Flavell, Green, & Flavell, 1987). Younger children's poor performance, however, is not the result of a general difficulty in distinguishing appearance from reality, as Piaget suggested. Instead, these problems require a challenging form of *dual representation*—the ability to represent the true identity of an object in the face of a second, contradictory representation.

How do children master appearance–reality distinctions? Make-believe play may be important. Children can tell the difference between pretend play and real experiences long before they answer appearance–reality tasks correctly (Golomb & Galasso, 1995). The more children engage in make-believe in their preschool classrooms, the better they are at distinguishing the real and apparent identities of objects (for example, a candle that looks like an apple) (Schwebel, Rosen, & Singer, 1999). Experiencing the contrast between everyday and playful circumstances seems to help young children realize that objects do not change their identity when their appearance changes.

### EVALUATION OF THE PREOPERATIONAL STAGE

The Milestones table on page 240 provides an overview of the cognitive attainments of early childhood we have just considered. Take a moment to compare them with Piaget's description of the preoperational child on pages 234–235. How can we make sense of the contradictions between Piaget's conclusions and the findings of follow-up research?

The evidence as a whole indicates that Piaget was partly wrong and partly right about young children's cognitive capacities. When given simplified tasks based on familiar experiences, preschoolers show the beginnings of logical operations long before the concrete operational stage. But their reasoning is not as well developed as that of school-age children, since they fail Piaget's three-mountains, conservation, and class inclusion problems and have difficulty with appearance–reality tasks.

That preschoolers have some logical understanding suggests that they attain logical operations gradually. Over time, children rely on increasingly effective mental as opposed to perceptual approaches to solving problems. For example, research shows that children who cannot use counting to compare two sets of items do not conserve number (Sophian, 1995). Once preschoolers can count, they apply this skill to conservation-of-number tasks with only a few items. As counting improves, they extend the strategy to problems with more items. By age 6, they have formed a mental understanding that number remains the same after a transformation as long as nothing is added or taken away. Consequently, they no longer need to use counting to verify their answer (Klahr & MacWhinney, 1998; Siegler & Robinson, 1982). This sequence indicates that children pass through several phases of understanding, although (as Piaget indicated) they do not fully grasp conservation until the school years.

That logical operations develop gradually poses yet another challenge to Piaget's stage concept, which assumes abrupt change toward logical reasoning around 6 or 7 years of age. Although the minds of young children still have a great deal of developing to do, research shows that they are considerably more logical than Piaget thought.

**Categories of Animals**

"Likes to fight"

"Likes to hide in trees"

**New Instances**

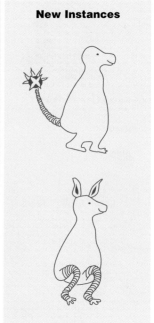

**FIGURE** 6.12

**Categories of imaginary animals shown to preschoolers.** When given a theory about the coexistence of the animals' features—"likes to fight" and "likes to hide in trees"—4-year-olds easily classified new examples of animals with only one or two features. Without the theory, preschoolers could not remember the categories. Theories about underlying characteristics support the formation of many new categories in early childhood. (From R. M. Krascum & S. Andrews, 1998, "The Effects of Theories on Children's Acquisition of Family-Resemblance Categories," *Child Development, 69,* p. 336. © The Society for Research in Child Development, Inc. Reprinted by permission.)

# milestones

## SOME COGNITIVE ATTAINMENTS OF EARLY CHILDHOOD

| APPROXIMATE AGE | COGNITIVE ATTAINMENTS |
| --- | --- |
| 2–4 years  | § Shows a dramatic increase in representational activity, as reflected in the development of language, make-believe play, drawing, and understanding of dual representation |
| | § Takes the perspective of others in simplified, familiar situations and in everyday, face-to-face communication |
| | § Distinguishes animate beings from inanimate objects; denies that magic can alter everyday experiences |
| | § Grasps conservation, notices transformations (reasons by analogy about physical changes), and gives logical, causal explanations in simplified, familiar contexts |
| | § Sorts familiar objects into hierarchically organized categories |
| | § Devises ideas about underlying characteristics (not just perceptual features) that category members share |
| 4–7 years  | § Becomes increasingly aware that make-believe (and other thought processes) are representational activities |
| | § Replaces magical beliefs about fairies, goblins, and events that violate expectations with plausible explanations |
| | § Improves in performance on appearance–reality problems, indicating further gains in dual representation |

*Note:* These milestones represent overall age trends. Individual differences exist in the precise age at which each milestone is attained.

## ASK YOURSELF

**review**  Select two of the following features of Piaget's preoperational stage: egocentrism, a focus on superficial perceptual appearances, difficulty reasoning about transformations, and lack of hierarchical classification. Cite findings that led Piaget to conclude that preschoolers are deficient in those ways. Then present evidence indicating that preschoolers are more capable thinkers than Piaget assumed.

**review**  Summarize evidence indicating that young preschoolers have difficulty with dual representation. Why is mastery of dual representation important?

**apply**  Brett's preschool teacher creates many opportunities for sociodramatic play in his classroom. Brett's mother wonders whether Brett is learning anything from so much pretending. Using research findings, respond to her concern.

**apply**  At home, 4-year-old Will understands that his tricycle isn't alive and can't move by itself. Yet when Will went fishing with his family and his father asked, "Why do you think the river is flowing along?" Will responded, "Because it's alive and wants to." What explains this contradiction in Will's reasoning?

# The Concrete Operational Stage (7 to 11 Years)

PIAGET VIEWED THE **concrete operational stage,** which spans the years from 7 to 11, as a major turning point in cognitive development. When children attain it, their thought more closely resembles that of adults than that of the sensorimotor and preoperational child (Piaget & Inhelder, 1967/1969). According to Piaget, concrete operational reasoning is far more logical, flexible, and organized than cognition was during the preschool years.

## CONCRETE OPERATIONAL THOUGHT

Concrete operations are evident in the school-age child's performance on a wide variety of Piagetian tasks. Let's look closely at these diverse accomplishments.

**CONSERVATION.** The ability to pass *conservation tasks* provides clear evidence of *operations.* In conservation of liquid, for example, children state that the amount of liquid has not changed, and they are likely to explain in ways like this: "The water's shorter but it's also wider. Pour it back; you'll see it's the same amount." Notice how in this response, the child coordinates several aspects of the task rather than centring on only one. The older child engages in *decentration,* recognizing that a change in one aspect of the water (its height) is compensated for by a change in another aspect (its width). This explanation also illustrates *reversibility*—the capacity to imagine the water being returned to the original container as proof of conservation.

**HIERARCHICAL CLASSIFICATION.** Between ages 7 and 10, children pass Piaget's class inclusion problem. This indicates that they are more aware of classification hierarchies and can focus on relations between a general and two specific categories at the same time—that is, three relations at once (Hodges & French, 1988; Ni, 1998). You can see this in children's play activities. Collections—stamps, coins, baseball cards, rocks, bottle caps, and more—become common in middle childhood. At age 10, one boy spent hours sorting and resorting his large box of baseball cards. At times he grouped them by league and team membership, at other times by playing position and batting average. He could separate the players into a variety of classes and subclasses and flexibly rearrange them.

**SERIATION.** The ability to order items along a quantitative dimension, such as length or weight, is called **seriation.** To test for it, Piaget asked children to arrange sticks of different lengths from shortest to longest. Older preschoolers can create the series, but they do so haphazardly. They put the sticks in a row but make many errors. In contrast, 6- to 7-year-olds are guided by an orderly plan. They create the series efficiently by beginning with the smallest stick, then moving to the next largest, and so on, until the ordering is complete.

The concrete operational child can also seriate mentally, an ability called **transitive inference.** In a well-known transitive inference problem, Piaget (1967) showed children pairings of differently coloured sticks. From observing that stick A is longer than stick B and stick B is longer than stick C, children must make the mental inference that A is longer than C. Notice how this task, like Piaget's class inclusion task, requires children to integrate three relations at once—in this instance, A–B, B–C, A–C. About half of 6-year-olds perform well on such problems—performance that improves considerably around age 8 (Andrews & Halford, 1998; Markovits, Dumas, & Malfait, 1995). Furthermore, when an adult encourages 3- and 4-year-olds to use their powers of analogical reasoning, they sometimes succeed at transitive inference. By relating the three sticks to the familiar concepts of *large* (A), *medium* (B), and *small* (C), preschoolers can more easily mentally compare them (Goswami, 1995).

In Piaget's concrete operational stage, school-age children think in an organized and logical fashion about concrete objects. This 8-year-old boy understands that the hamster on one side of the balance scale is just as heavy as the metal weights on the other, even though the two types of objects look and feel quite different from each other.

**concrete operational stage**
Piaget's third stage, during which thought is logical, flexible, and organized in its application to concrete information. However, the capacity for abstract thinking is not yet present. Spans the years from 7 to 11.

**seriation**
The ability to arrange items along a quantitative dimension, such as length or weight.

**transitive inference**
The ability to seriate—or arrange items along a quantitative dimension—mentally.

An improved ability to categorize underlies children's interest in collecting objects during middle childhood. These older school-age children sort baseball cards into an elaborate structure of classes and subclasses.

**SPATIAL REASONING.** Piaget found that school-age children have a more accurate understanding of space than do preschoolers. Let's take three examples—understanding of distance, directions, and maps.

*Distance.* Comprehension of distance improves during middle childhood, as a special conservation task reveals. To give this problem, make two small trees out of modelling clay and place them apart on a table at which the child is seated. Next, put a block or thick piece of cardboard between the trees. Then ask the child whether the trees are nearer together, farther apart, or still the same distance apart.

Preschoolers say the distance has become smaller. They do not understand that a filled space has the same value as an empty space (Piaget, Inhelder, & Szeminska, 1948/1960). By the early school years, children grasp this idea easily. Four-year-olds can conserve distance when questioned about a very familiar scene or when a path is marked between two objects, which helps them represent the distance. However, their understanding is not as solid as that of the school-age child (Fabricius & Wellman, 1993; Miller & Baillargeon, 1990).

*Directions.* School-age children's more advanced understanding of space can also be seen in their ability to give directions. Stand facing a 5- or 6-year-old, and ask the child to name an object on your left and one on your right. Children of this age answer incorrectly; they apply their own frame of reference. Between 7 and 8 years, children start to perform *mental rotations,* in which they align the self's frame to match that of a person in a different orientation. As a result, they can identify left and right for positions they do not occupy (Roberts & Aman, 1993).

Around 8 to 10 years, children can give clear, well-organized directions for how to get from one place to another. Aided by their capacity for operational thinking, they use a "mental walk" strategy in which they imagine another person's movements along a route (Gauvain & Rogoff, 1989). Six-year-olds give more organized directions after they walk the route themselves or are specially prompted. Otherwise, they focus on the end point without describing exactly how to get there (Plumert et al., 1994).

*Cognitive Maps.* Children's drawings of familiar large-scale spaces, such as their neighbourhood or school, also change from early to middle childhood (Piaget & Inhelder, 1948/1956). These **cognitive maps** require considerable perspective-taking skill, since the entire space cannot be seen at once. Instead, children must infer its overall layout by relating its separate parts.

Preschoolers display *landmarks* on the maps they draw, but their placement is fragmented. When asked to place stickers showing the location of desks and people on a map of their classroom, they perform better. But if the map is rotated relative to the orientation of the classroom, preschoolers and young school-age children have difficulty placing the stickers accurately (Liben & Downs, 1993). Their use of a rotated map to find objects hidden in a room improves when the locations form a meaningful pattern, such as the outline of a dog (see Figure 6.13). Showing children the pattern on the map helps them *reason by analogy* from the rotated map to corresponding locations in the room (Uttal et al., 2001).

In the early school grades, children's maps become more organized. They draw landmarks along an *organized route of travel,* such as the path they walk from home to school—an attainment that resembles their improved direction giving. By the end of middle childhood, children form an *overall configuration of a large-scale space* in which landmarks and routes are interrelated (Newcombe, 1982). And they readily draw and read maps when the orientation of the map and space it represents do not match. Clearly, "map literacy" improves greatly during middle childhood (Liben, 1999).

**cognitive maps**
Mental representations of large-scale spaces.

**horizontal décalage**
Development within a Piagetian stage. Gradual mastery of logical concepts during the concrete operational stage is an example.

## LIMITATIONS OF CONCRETE OPERATIONAL THOUGHT

Although school-age children are far more capable problem solvers than they were during the preschool years, concrete operational thinking suffers from one important limitation. Children think in an organized, logical fashion only when dealing with concrete information they can perceive directly. Their mental operations work poorly with abstract ideas—ones not apparent in the real world.

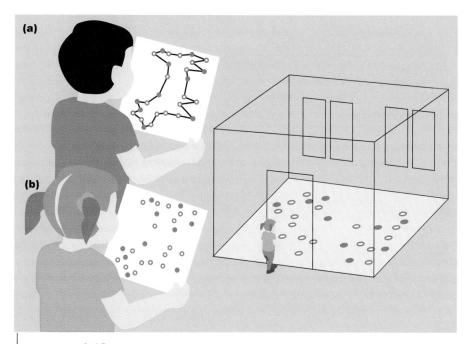

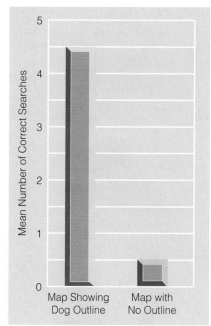

**FIGURE** 6.13

**Five-year-olds' use of a rotated map to find objects hidden in a room.** In one condition (a), locations on the map were connected to form a meaningful pattern—outline of a dog. In a second condition (b), the locations on the map were not connected. The map showing the dog outline resulted in more correct searches than did the map with no outline. The meaningful pattern seemed to help children reason by analogy from the rotated map to locations in the room. (Adapted from Uttal et al., 2001.)

Children's solutions to transitive inference problems provide a good illustration. When shown pairs of sticks of unequal length, 8-year-olds readily figure out that if stick A is longer than stick B and stick B is longer than stick C, then stick A is longer than stick C. But they have great difficulty with a hypothetical version of this task, such as "Susan is taller than Sally and Sally is taller than Mary. Who is the tallest?" Not until age 11 or 12 can children solve this problem easily.

That logical thought is at first tied to immediate situations helps account for a special feature of concrete operational reasoning. Perhaps you have already noticed that school-age children master Piaget's concrete operational tasks step by step, not all at once. For example, they usually grasp the conservation problems in a certain order: first number, followed by length, liquid, and mass, followed by weight. Piaget used the term **horizontal décalage** (meaning development within a stage) to describe this gradual mastery of logical concepts.

The horizontal décalage is another indication of the concrete operational child's difficulty with abstractions. School-age children do not come up with general logical principles and then apply them to all relevant situations. Instead, they seem to work out the logic of each problem separately.

In tribal and village societies, conservation is often delayed. These Vietnamese sisters gather firewood for their family. Although they have many opportunities to handle quantities, compared with their agemates in Western nations they may seldom see two identical quantities arranged in different ways.

### FOLLOW-UP RESEARCH ON CONCRETE OPERATIONAL THOUGHT

According to Piaget, brain development combined with experience in a rich and varied external world should lead children everywhere to reach the concrete operational stage. Yet research indicates that specific experiences have much to do with Piagetian task performance (Rogoff & Chavajay, 1995).

In tribal and village societies, conservation is often delayed. For example, among the Hausa of Nigeria, who live in small agricultural settlements and rarely send their children to school, even the most basic conservation tasks—number, length, and liquid—are not understood until age 11 or later (Fahrmeier, 1978). This suggests that taking part in relevant everyday

# milestones

## SOME COGNITIVE ATTAINMENTS OF MIDDLE CHILDHOOD AND ADOLESCENCE

| APPROXIMATE AGE | COGNITIVE ATTAINMENTS |
|---|---|
| Middle childhood 7–11 years  | ⸎ Thinks in a more organized, logical fashion about concrete information, as indicated by gradual mastery of Piagetian conservation, class inclusion, and seriation problems, including transitive inference<br><br>⸎ Displays more effective spatial reasoning, as indicated by conservation of distance ability to give clear directions and formulate well-organized cognitive maps |
| Adolescence 11–20 years  | ⸎ Reasons abstractly in situations that offer many opportunities for hypothetico-deductive reasoning and propositional thought<br><br>⸎ Grasps the logical necessity of propositional thought, permitting reasoning about premises that contradict reality<br><br>⸎ Displays imaginary audience and personal fable, which gradually decline |

*Note:* These milestones represent overall age trends. Individual differences exist in the precise age at which each milestone is attained.

activities helps children master conservation and other Piagetian problems (Light & Perrett-Clermont, 1989). Many children in Western nations, for example, have learned to think of fairness in terms of equal distribution—a value emphasized by their culture. They have many opportunities to divide materials, such as crayons, Halloween treats, and lemonade, equally among their friends. Because they often see the same quantity arranged in different ways, they grasp conservation early.

The very experience of going to school seems to promote mastery of Piagetian tasks. When children of the same age are tested, those who have been in school longer do better on transitive inference problems (Artman & Cahan, 1993). The opportunities schooling affords for seriating objects, learning about order relations, and remembering the parts of a complex problem are probably responsible.

Yet certain nonschool, informal experiences can also foster operational thought. In one study, Brazilian 6- to 9-year-old street vendors, who seldom attend school, were given two class inclusion problems: (1) the traditional Piagetian task, and (2) an informal version in which the researcher became a customer. After setting aside four units of mint and two units of strawberry chewing gum, the researcher asked, "For you to get more money, is it better to sell me the mint chewing gum or [all] the chewing gum? Why?" As Figure 6.14 shows, street-vendor children did much better on the informal problem, which captured their interest and motivation. Brazilian schoolchildren from economically advantaged homes were more successful on the Piagetian task than on a version in which they were asked to role-play street vendors—an activity unfamiliar to them (Ceci & Roazzi, 1994).

On the basis of findings like these, some investigators have concluded that the forms of logic required by Piagetian tasks do not emerge spontaneously in children. Instead, they appear to be heavily influenced by training, context, and cultural conditions. The Milestones table above summarizes the cognitive attainments of middle childhood discussed in the preceding sections, along with those that will follow in adolescence.

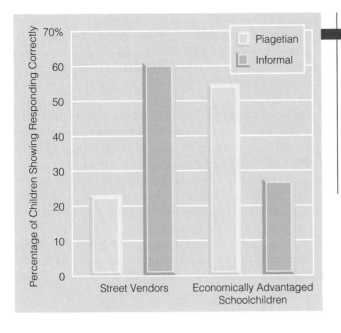

**FIGURE** 6.14

**Comparison of Brazilian street vendors with Brazilian economically advantaged children on the traditional Piagetian class inclusion task and an informal, street-vending version.** For the informal task, the researcher asked the child for the price of two different kinds of chewing gum (mint and strawberry). After setting aside four units of mint and two units of strawberry, the investigator continued, "For you to get more money, is it better to sell me the mint chewing gum or [all] the chewing gum? Why?" Street vendors performed better on the informal version, whereas middle-class children did better on the Piagetian task. (Adapted from Ceci & Roazzi, 1994.)

## ASK YOURSELF

**review**   Mastery of conservation provides one illustration of Piaget's horizontal décalage. Review the preceding sections. Then list additional examples showing that operational reasoning develops gradually during middle childhood.

**review**   Cite evidence indicating that specific experiences influence children's performance on Piagetian concrete-operational tasks.

**connect**   Explain how advances in perspective taking contribute to school-age children's improved capacity to give directions and construct cognitive maps.

## The Formal Operational Stage (11 Years and Older)

ACCORDING TO PIAGET, the capacity for abstract thinking begins around age 11. At the **formal operational stage,** the adolescent reasons much like a scientist searching for solutions in the laboratory. Concrete operational children can only "operate on reality," but formal operational adolescents can "operate on operations." In other words, concrete things and events are no longer required as objects of thought (Inhelder & Piaget, 1955/1958). Instead, adolescents can come up with new, more general logical rules through internal reflection.

### HYPOTHETICO-DEDUCTIVE REASONING

At adolescence, young people become capable of **hypothetico-deductive reasoning.** When faced with a problem, they start with a *general theory* of all possible factors that might affect an outcome and *deduce* from it specific *hypotheses* (or predictions) about what might happen. Then they test these hypotheses in an orderly fashion to see which ones work in the real world. Notice how this form of problem solving begins with possibility and proceeds to reality. In contrast, concrete operational children start with reality—with the most obvious predictions about a situation. When these are not confirmed, they cannot think of alternatives and fail to solve the problem.

**formal operational stage**
Piaget's highest stage, in which adolescents develop the capacity for abstract, scientific thinking. Begins around age 11.

**hypothetico-deductive reasoning**
A formal operational problem-solving strategy in which adolescents begin with a general theory of all possible factors that could affect an outcome in a problem, and deduce specific hypotheses, which they test in an orderly fashion.

**The pendulum problem.**
Adolescents who engage in
hypothetico-deductive reasoning
think of all possibilities. Then
they vary one factor at a time
while holding all others constant.
Soon they discover that the
weight of the object, the height
from which it is released, and
how forcefully it is pushed have
no effect on the speed with
which the pendulum swings
through its arc. Only string length
makes a difference.

Adolescents' performance on Piaget's famous *pendulum problem* illustrates this new hypothetico-deductive approach. Suppose we present several school-age children and adolescents with strings of different lengths, objects of different weights to attach to the strings, and a bar from which to hang the strings (see Figure 6.15). Then we ask each of them to figure out what influences the speed with which a pendulum swings through its arc.

Formal operational adolescents come up with four hypotheses: (1) the length of the string, (2) the weight of the object hung on it, (3) how high the object is raised before it is released, and (4) how forcefully the object is pushed. Then, by varying one factor at a time while holding all others constant, they try out each possibility. Eventually they discover that only string length makes a difference.

In contrast, concrete operational children's experimentation is unsystematic. They cannot separate the effects of each variable. For example, they may test for the effect of string length without holding weight constant by comparing a short, light pendulum with a long, heavy one. Also, school-age children fail to notice variables that are not immediately suggested by the concrete materials of the task—the height, and the forcefulness with which the pendulum is released.

## PROPOSITIONAL THOUGHT

A second important characteristic of the formal operational stage is **propositional thought.** Adolescents can evaluate the logic of propositions (verbal statements) without referring to real-world circumstances. In contrast, children can evaluate the logic of statements only by considering them against concrete evidence in the real world.

In a study of propositional reasoning, a researcher showed children and adolescents a pile of poker chips and indicated that some statements would be made about them. Participants were asked to tell whether each statement was true, false, or uncertain. In one condition, the experimenter hid a chip in her hand and then asked the young person to evaluate the following propositions:

"*Either* the chip in my hand is green *or* it is not green."

"The chip in my hand is green *and* it is not green."

In another condition, the researcher held either a red or a green chip in full view and made the same statements.

School-age children focused on the concrete properties of the poker chips rather than on the logic of the statements. As a result, they were uncertain about both statements when the chip was hidden from view. When it was visible, they judged both statements to be true if the chip was green and false if it was red. In contrast, adolescents analyzed the logic of the statements as propositions. They understood that the "either–or" statement is always true and the "and" statement is always false, regardless of the poker chip's colour (Osherson & Markman, 1975).

Although Piaget did not view language as playing a central role in children's cognitive development, he acknowledged that it is more important during adolescence. Abstract thought requires language-based systems of representation that do not stand for real things, such as those that exist in higher mathematics. Secondary school students use these systems in algebra and geometry. Formal operational thought also involves verbal reasoning about abstract concepts. Adolescents demonstrate their capacity to think in this way when they ponder the relations between time, space, and matter in physics and wonder about justice and freedom in philosophy and social studies.

**propositional thought**
A type of formal operational reasoning in which adolescents evaluate the logic of verbal statements without referring to real-world circumstances.

## CONSEQUENCES OF ABSTRACT THOUGHT

Adolescents' capacity to think abstractly, combined with their physical changes, means that they start to think more about themselves. Piaget believed that a new form of egocentrism accompanies this stage: the inability to distinguish the abstract perspectives of self and others

(Inhelder & Piaget, 1955/1958). As teenagers imagine what others must be thinking, two distorted images of the relation between self and others appear.

The first is called the **imaginary audience.** Young teenagers regard themselves as always on stage. They are convinced that they are the focus of everyone else's attention and concern (Elkind & Bowen, 1979). As a result, they become extremely self-conscious, often going to great lengths to avoid embarrassment. The imaginary audience helps us understand the long hours adolescents spend inspecting every detail of their appearance. It also accounts for their sensitivity to public criticism. To teenagers, who believe that everyone around them is monitoring their performance, a critical remark from a parent or teacher can be mortifying.

A second cognitive distortion is the **personal fable.** Because teenagers are so sure that others are observing and thinking about them, they develop an inflated opinion of their own importance. They start to feel that they are special and unique. Many adolescents view themselves as reaching great heights of glory as well as sinking to unusual depths of despair—experiences that others could not possibly understand (Elkind, 1994). As one teenager wrote in her diary, "My parents' lives are so ordinary, so stuck in a rut. Mine will be different. I'll realize my hopes and ambitions." When combined with a sensation-seeking personality, the personal fable seems to contribute to adolescent risk taking by convincing teenagers of their invulnerability. In one study, young people with both high personal-fable and sensation-seeking scores took more sexual risks, more often used drugs, and committed more delinquent acts than did their agemates (Greene et al., 2000).

The imaginary audience and personal fable are strongest during the transition from concrete to formal operations. They gradually decline as abstract thinking becomes better established (Enright, Lapsley, & Shukla, 1979; Lapsley et al., 1988). Yet these distorted visions of the self probably are not due to egocentrism, as Piaget suggested. Instead, they seem to be an outgrowth of advances in perspective taking, which cause young teenagers to be very concerned with what others think (Lapsley et al., 1986).

Recent evidence indicates that the capacity to "step in another person's shoes" and look back at the self, a perspective-taking milestone of late childhood and early adolescence, contributes to the imaginary audience and personal fable (Vartanian & Powlishta, 1996). Adolescents also may have emotional reasons for clinging to the idea that others are preoccupied with their appearance and behaviour. Doing so assures them that they are important to others as they struggle to separate from parents and establish an independent sense of self (Lapsley, 1993; Vartanian, 1997).

In Piaget's formal operational stage, adolescents can think logically and abstractly. These high school students solve a complex scientific problem by thinking of all possible outcomes, not just the most obvious. Abstract thought also leads to a more intense focus on the self as adolescents imagine what others must be thinking.

### FOLLOW-UP RESEARCH ON FORMAL OPERATIONAL THOUGHT

Research on formal operational thought poses questions similar to those we discussed with respect to Piaget's earlier stages: Does abstract reasoning appear earlier than Piaget expected? And do all individuals reach formal operations during their teenage years?

**ARE YOUNG CHILDREN CAPABLE OF ABSTRACT THINKING?** School-age children show the glimmerings of hypothetico-deductive reasoning, but they are not as competent as adolescents and adults. For example, in simplified situations—ones involving no more than two possible causal variables—6-year-olds understand that hypotheses must be confirmed by appropriate evidence. They also realize that once supported, a hypothesis shapes predictions about what might happen in the future (Ruffman et al., 1993). But unlike adolescents, children cannot sort out evidence that bears on three or more variables at once.

School-age children's capacity for propositional thought is also limited. For example, they have great difficulty reasoning from premises that contradict reality or their own beliefs. Consider the following set of statements: "If dogs are bigger than elephants and elephants are bigger than mice, then dogs are bigger than mice." Children younger than 10 judge this reasoning to be false, since all the relations specified do not occur in real life (Moshman &

---

**imaginary audience**
Adolescents' belief that they are the focus of everyone else's attention and concern.

**personal fable**
Adolescents' belief that they are special and unique. Leads them to conclude that others cannot possibly understand their thoughts and feelings. By convincing teenagers of their invulnerability, may contribute to adolescent risk taking.

**logical necessity**
A basic property of propositional thought, which specifies that the accuracy of conclusions drawn from premises rests on the rules of logic, not on real-world confirmation. A grasp of logical necessity permits individuals to reason from premises that contradict reality or their own beliefs.

Franks, 1986). They fail to grasp the **logical necessity** of propositional reasoning—that the accuracy of conclusions drawn from premises rests on the rules of logic, not on real-world confirmation.

Furthermore, according to Henry Markovits of the Université du Québec à Montréal, Michael Schleifer of Queen's University, and others, in reasoning with propositions, school-age children do not think carefully about the major premise and, therefore, violate the most basic rules of logic (Markovits, Schleifer, & Fortier, 1989). For example, when given the following problem, they almost always draw an incorrect conclusion:

*Major Premise:* If Susan hits a tambourine, then she will make a noise.

*Second Premise:* Suppose that Susan does not hit a tambourine.

*Question:* Did Susan make a noise?

*Wrong Conclusion:* No, Susan did not make a noise.

Notice that the major premise did not state that Susan can make a noise *if, and only if,* she hits a tambourine. Adolescents generally detect that Susan could make noise in other ways, partly because they are better than school-age children at searching their knowledge for examples that contradict wrong conclusions (Klaczynski & Narasimham, 1998b; Markovitz et al., 1998).

As Piaget's theory indicates, around age 11, young people in Western nations begin to analyze the logic of propositions irrespective of their content. Propositional thought improves over the adolescent years (Markovits & Bouffard-Bouchard, 1992; Markovits & Vachon, 1989, 1990).

**DO ALL INDIVIDUALS REACH THE FORMAL OPERATIONAL STAGE?** Try giving the tambourine problem to some of your friends and see how well they do. You are likely to find that some well-educated adults have difficulty! According to Dan Keating (1979) of the Ontario Institute for Studies in Education about 40 to 60 percent of university students fail Piaget's formal operational problems.

If asked, these nonliterate Mongolian nomads would probably refuse to engage in propositional thought, explaining that an event must be seen to discern its logical implications. Because of lack of opportunity to solve hypothetical problems, formal operational reasoning is not evident in all societies.

Why is it that so many university students, and adults in general, are not fully formal operational? The reason is that people are most likely to think abstractly in situations in which they have had extensive experience. This is supported by evidence that taking university courses leads to improvements in formal reasoning related to course content. For example, math and science prompt gains in propositional thought; social science in methodological and statistical reasoning (Lehman & Nisbett, 1990). Consider these findings carefully, and you will see that formal operational thought, like the concrete reasoning that preceded it, is often specific to situation and task (Keating, 1990).

Furthermore, in many tribal and village societies, formal operational tasks are not mastered at all (Cole, 1990). For example, when asked to engage in propositional thought, people in nonliterate societies often refuse. Take this hypothetical proposition: "In the far North, where there is snow, all bears are white. Novaya Zemlya is in the far North and there is always snow there. What colour are the bears there?" In response, a Central Asian peasant explains that he must see the event to discern its logical implications. The peasant insists on firsthand knowledge, whereas the interviewer states that truth can be based on ideas alone. Yet the peasant uses propositions to defend his point of view: "*If* a man . . . had seen a white bear and had told about it, [*then*] he could be believed, *but* I've never seen one and *hence* I can't say" (Luria, 1976, pp. 108–109). Although he rarely displays it in everyday life, clearly the peasant is capable of formal operational thought!

Piaget acknowledged that without the opportunity to solve hypothetical problems, people in some societies might not display formal operations. Still, researchers ask, Is Piaget's highest stage really an outgrowth of children's independent efforts to make sense of their world, as he claimed? Or is it a culturally transmitted way of thinking that is specific to literate societies and taught in school? At present, this question remains unresolved.

## ASK YOURSELF

**review**   Using the concepts of hypothetico-deductive reasoning and propositional thought, illustrate the difference between school-age children's and adolescents' cognition.

**review**   Why do many university students have difficulty with Piaget's formal operational tasks?

**apply**   Thirteen-year-old Rosie had a crush on a boy who failed to return her affections. As she lay on the sofa feeling depressed, her mother assured her that there would be other boys. "Mom," Rosie snapped, "you don't know what it's like to be in love!" Which cognitive distortion—the imaginary audience or the personal fable—does Rosie's thinking illustrate? Explain.

**connect**   How are questions raised about Piaget's formal operational stage similar to those raised about the concrete operational stage?

# Piaget and Education

PIAGET HAS HAD A MAJOR impact on education, especially at the preschool and early elementary school levels. Three educational principles derived from his theory continue to have a widespread influence on teacher training and classroom practices.

- *Discovery learning.* In a Piagetian classroom, children are encouraged to discover for themselves through spontaneous interaction with the environment. Instead of presenting ready-made knowledge verbally, teachers provide a rich variety of activities designed to promote exploration—arts and crafts materials, puzzles, table games, dress-up clothing, building blocks, books, measuring tools, musical instruments, and more.

- *Sensitivity to children's readiness to learn.* A Piagetian classroom does not try to speed up development. Instead, Piaget believed that appropriate learning experiences build on children's current level of thinking. Teachers watch and listen to their students, introducing experiences that permit them to practise newly discovered schemes and that are likely to challenge their incorrect ways of viewing the world. But teachers do not impose new skills before children indicate that they are interested or ready, since this leads to superficial acceptance of adult formulas rather than true understanding.

- *Acceptance of individual differences.* Piaget's theory assumes that all children go through the same sequence of development, but at different rates. Therefore, teachers must plan activities for individuals and small groups rather than just for the total class (Ginsburg & Opper, 1988). In addition, teachers evaluate educational progress by comparing each child to his own previous development. They are less interested in how children measure up to normative standards, or the average performance of same-age peers.

Educational applications of Piaget's theory, like his stages, have met with criticism. Perhaps the greatest challenge has to do with his emphasis on hands-on exploration as the major mode of learning to the neglect of other important avenues, such as verbal communication. Nevertheless, Piaget's influence on education has been powerful (Vergnaud, 1996). He gave teachers new ways to observe, understand, and enhance young children's development and offered strong theoretical justification for child-oriented approaches to classroom teaching and learning.

# Overall Evaluation of Piaget's Theory

PIAGET'S CONTRIBUTIONS TO the field of child development are gigantic—greater than those of any other theorist. He awakened psychologists and educators to a view of children as curious knowledge seekers who contribute actively to their own development. Furthermore, Piaget was among the first theorists not just to describe, but also to *explain* development. His pioneering efforts inspired the contemporary focus on *mechanisms of cognitive change*—precise accounts of what biological, psychological, and environmental factors lead to changes in children's thinking, which we will encounter in Chapter 7 (McClelland & Siegler, 2001). Finally, Piaget's theory offers a useful "road map" of cognitive development—one that is accurate in many respects, despite being wrong in others. His milestones of preoperational, concrete operational, and formal operational thought remain powerful aids to understanding emotional, social, and moral development, and we will return to them many times in later chapters.

Nevertheless, the wealth of research Piaget's theory inspired has uncovered weaknesses in his theory. Let's consider two major challenges posed by his critics.

##  IS PIAGET'S ACCOUNT OF COGNITIVE CHANGE CLEAR AND ACCURATE?

Think, for a moment, about Piaget's explanation of cognitive change—in particular, equilibration and its attendant processes of adaptation and organization. Because Piaget focused on broad transformations in thinking, exactly what the child does to equilibrate is vague (Miller, 1993; Siegler & Ellis, 1996). As an example of this problem, recall our description of organization—that the structures of each stage form a coherent whole. Piaget is not very explicit about how the diverse achievements of each stage are bound together by a single, underlying form of thought. Indeed, efforts to confirm this coherence have not succeeded. On a variety of tasks, infants and young children appear more competent and adolescents and adults less competent than Piaget assumed. Today, researchers agree that the child's efforts to assimilate, accommodate, and reorganize structures cannot adequately explain these patterns of change.

Furthermore, Piaget's belief that infants and young children must act on the environment to revise their thinking is too narrow a notion of how learning takes place. We have seen that cognitive development is not always self-generating. Left to their own devices, children may not notice aspects of a situation that are needed for an improved understanding. Because Piaget's account of change places so much emphasis on the child's initiative to the neglect of specific experiential influences, his theory has been of limited practical usefulness in devising teaching strategies that foster children's optimum learning.

##  DOES COGNITIVE DEVELOPMENT TAKE PLACE IN STAGES?

Throughout this chapter, we have seen that many cognitive changes proceed slowly and gradually. Few abilities are absent during one period and then suddenly present in another. Also, there seem to be few periods of cognitive equilibrium. Instead, children constantly modify structures and acquire new skills. Today, virtually all experts agree that children's cognition is not as broadly stagelike as Piaget believed (Bjorklund, 2000; Flavell, Miller, & Miller, 2002). At the same time, contemporary researchers disagree on how general or specific cognitive development actually is.

Some theorists agree with Piaget that development is a *general process*—that it follows a similar course across diverse cognitive domains, such as physical, numerical, and social knowledge. But they reject the existence of stages. Instead, they believe that thought processes are alike at all ages—just present to a greater or lesser extent—and that uneven performance across domains can largely be accounted for by variations in children's knowledge and experience. These assumptions form the basis of the *information-processing* perspective, discussed in Chapter 7.

Other researchers think that the stage notion is still valid but that it must be modified. They point to strong evidence for certain stagelike changes, such as the flourishing of representation around age 2 and the move toward abstraction in adolescence. Yet they recognize many smaller developments that lead up to these dramatic transformations. In Chapter 7, we will consider the late Canadian psychologist Robbie Case's *neo-Piagetian perspective,* which combines Piaget's stage approach with information-processing ideas (Case, 1992, 1996, 1998). According to this view, Piaget's strict definition of stage needs to be modified into a less tightly knit concept, one in which related competencies develop over an extended period, depending on both brain development and experience.

Still others deny not only Piaget's stages but his belief that the human mind is made up of general reasoning abilities that can be applied to any cognitive task. These theorists grapple with the remarkable competencies of infants and young children. They argue that such early attainments indicate that cognitive development begins with far more than sensorimotor reflexes; instead, infants come into the world with several basic, built-in types of knowledge, each of which gets vital aspects of cognition off the ground quickly. We will take up this *core knowledge perspective* in the next section.

## PIAGET'S LEGACY

Although Piaget's description of development is no longer fully accepted, researchers are a long way from consensus on how to modify or replace it. Some have begun to search for points of contact among the alternative perspectives just mentioned. Others are blending Piaget's emphasis on the child as an active agent with a stronger role for context—the objects, events, and people in the child's life (Fischer & Bidell, 1998; Fischer & Hencke, 1996). For example, followers of Vygotsky's theory are intensively studying social and cultural influences on children's thinking, largely neglected by Piaget.

Diverse theories and lines of investigation leave research into children's thinking far more fragmented today than several decades ago, when Piaget's theory held sway. But despite intense disagreement on how to characterize cognitive development, researchers continue to draw inspiration from Piaget's lifelong quest to understand how children acquire new capacities. His findings have served as the starting point for virtually every major contemporary perspective. And as John Flavell (1985) points out, "Perhaps what the field needs is another genius like Piaget to show us how, and to what extent, all those cognitive developmental strands within the growing child are really knotted together" (p. 297).

### ASK YOURSELF

**review** Cite examples of findings that have led contemporary researchers to question Piaget's account of (1) cognitive change and (2) development as taking place in stages.

**connect** How are educational principles derived from Piaget's theory consistent with his emphasis on an active child who takes responsibility for her own learning?

# The Core Knowledge Perspective

ACCORDING TO THE **core knowledge perspective,** infants begin life with innate, special-purpose knowledge systems, referred to as *core domains of thought.* Each of these "prewired" understandings permits a ready grasp of new, related information and therefore supports early, rapid development of certain aspects of cognition. Core knowledge theorists claim that infants could not make sense of the multifaceted stimulation around them without being genetically "set up" to comprehend crucial aspects of it. Each core domain has a long evolutionary history and is essential for survival (Carey & Markman, 1999;

**core knowledge perspective**
A view that assumes that infants begin life with innate special-purpose knowledge systems, or core domains of thought, each of which permits a ready grasp of new, related information and therefore supports early, rapid development of certain aspects of cognition.

Pinker, 1997; Spelke & Newport, 1998). Two domains have been studied extensively in infants. The first is *physical knowledge*—in particular, understanding of objects and their effects on one another. The second is *numerical knowledge*—the capacity to keep track of multiple objects and add and subtract small quantities. Physical and numerical knowledge permitted our ancestors to secure food and other resources from the environment.

The core knowledge perspective asserts that an inherited foundation makes possible remarkably advanced knowledge systems in early childhood. In Chapter 9, we will consider a nativist (or inborn) view of preschoolers' amazing language skill that regards *linguistic knowledge* as etched into the structure of the human brain. Furthermore, infants' early orientation toward people (see Chapter 4) provides the foundation for rapid development of *psychological knowledge*—in particular, understanding of mental states (such as emotions, desires, beliefs, and perspectives), which is vital for surviving in human groups. And children demonstrate impressive *biological knowledge,* including ideas about bodily processes, such as birth, growth, illness, and death.

The core knowledge perspective assumes that each core domain develops independently. Consequently, core knowledge theorists do not regard development as a general process; rather, they see it as *domain specific* and uneven. And although initial knowledge is regarded as innate, it becomes more elaborate as children explore, play, and interact with others (Geary & Bjorklund, 2000). Children are viewed as *naive theorists,* building on core knowledge concepts to explain their everyday experiences in the physical, psychological, and biological realms. Let's examine a sampling of findings taken as support for the existence of core domains of thought.

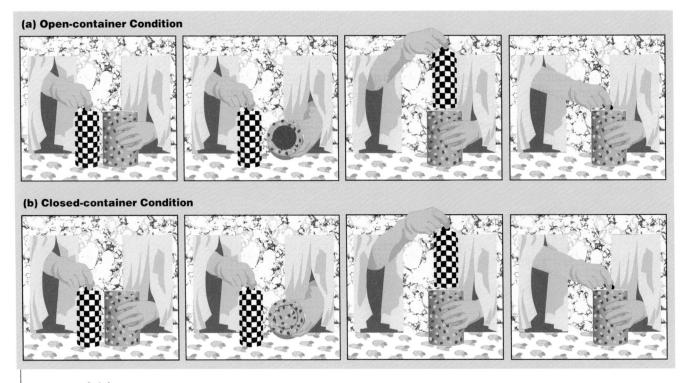

**(a) Open-container Condition**

**(b) Closed-container Condition**

**FIGURE** 6.16

**Testing infants for understanding of object solidity.** Infants in the open-container (possible) condition (a) were shown a tall object and a tall container standing a short distance apart. An adult's right hand grasped a knob attached to the top of the object while her left hand rotated the container forward so infants could see its opening. After a few seconds, the container was returned to its original position. Then the right hand lifted the object and lowered it into the container. Finally, the hand lifted the object out of the container and set it down. Infants in the closed-container (impossible) condition saw the same event, with one exception (b): the container's top was closed so it should have been impossible for the object to be lowered into the container. (In actuality, the container had a false, magnetic top that adhered to the bottom of the object, which could be lowered into it.) Five-month-olds looked longer at the impossible, closed-container event, suggesting awareness of object solidity. (From S. J. Hespos & R. Baillargeon, 2001, "Reasoning About Containment Events in Very Young Infants," *Cognition, 78,* p. 213. Reprinted by permission.)

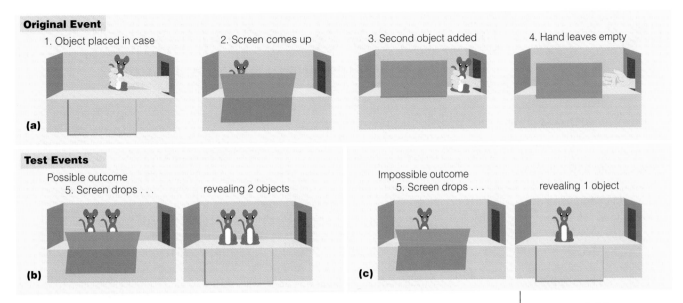

**Original Event**

1. Object placed in case
2. Screen comes up
3. Second object added
4. Hand leaves empty

(a)

**Test Events**

Possible outcome
5. Screen drops . . .
revealing 2 objects

(b)

Impossible outcome
5. Screen drops . . .
revealing 1 object

(c)

**FIGURE 6.17**

**Testing infants for basic number concepts.** (a) First, infants saw a screen raised in front of a toy animal. Then an identical toy was added behind the screen. Next, the researchers presented two outcomes. (b) In the *possible outcome*, the screen dropped to reveal two toy animals. (c) In the *impossible outcome*, the screen dropped to reveal one toy animal. Five-month-olds shown the impossible outcome looked longer than did 5-month-olds shown the possible outcome. The researchers concluded that infants can discriminate the quantities "one" and "two" and use that knowledge to perform simple addition: 1 + 1 = 2. A variation of this procedure suggested that 5-month-olds could also do simple subtraction: 2 − 1 = 1. (From K. Wynn, "Addition and Subtraction by Human Infants," *Nature, 358,* p. 749. Reprinted by permission.)

## INFANCY: PHYSICAL AND NUMERICAL KNOWLEDGE

Do infants display impressive physical and numerical understandings so early that some knowledge must be innate? Once again, the violation-of-expectation method has been used to answer this question. Besides research on early awareness of object permanence (see page 223), core-knowledge theorists point to evidence indicating that young infants are aware of basic object properties and quickly build on this knowledge.

For example, 2½-month-olds seem to recognize that one solid object cannot move through another solid object. In one study, some infants saw an object lowered inside a container with an opening, whereas others saw an object lowered inside a container with no opening (see Figure 6.16 on the previous page). Babies in the closed-container condition looked longer, suggesting that this impossible event violated their notions of physical reality (Hespos & Baillargeon, 2001). Within the next few months, infants extend this understanding. By 5 to 6 months, they look longer when an object much larger than an opening appears to pass through that opening than they do at an appropriately sized object that passes through (Sitskoorn & Smitsman, 1995).

Furthermore, in the first half-year, infants are sensitive to the effects of gravity. They stare intently when a moving object stops in midair without support (Spelke et al., 1992). This understanding advances quickly. Six- and 7-month-olds have some notion of object support. They look intently when an object is placed on top of another object yet most of its bottom surface does not contact the lower object. Under these conditions, infants appear to realize it should fall (Baillargeon, 1994).

Research also suggests that young infants have basic number concepts (Spelke, 2000). In the best known of these studies, 5-month-olds saw a screen raised to hide a single toy animal. Then the infants saw a hand placing a second identical toy behind the screen. Finally, the screen was removed to reveal either one or two toys. If infants kept track of and represented the two objects (which required them to add one object to another), then they should look longer at the impossible, one-toy display—which is what they did (see Figure 6.17). In additional experiments, 5-month-olds given this task looked longer at three objects than two. Overall, these results, and those of similar studies, suggest that infants discriminate quantities up to three and use that knowledge to perform simple arithmetic—addition as well as subtraction (in which two objects are covered by a screen and one object is removed) (Wynn, 1992, 1998).

Nevertheless, these findings—like other violation-of-expectation results—are controversial. Some researchers report that 5-month-olds cannot add and subtract. In experiments similar (but not identical) to those just described, looking preferences were inconsistent (Wakeley, Rivera, & Langer, 2000). These investigators note that claims for number concepts in young infants are surprising, given other research indicating that before 14 to 16 months, toddlers

# biology & environment

## CHILDREN'S UNDERSTANDING OF HEALTH AND ILLNESS

ive-year-old Lizzie lay on the living room sofa with a stuffy nose and sore throat, disappointed that she was missing a birthday party. "How'd I get this dumb cold anyhow?" she wondered aloud to her 9-year-old brother Joey. "I probably got it by playing outside when it was freezing cold."

"No, no," Joey contradicted. "Viruses get into your blood and attack, just like an army."

"Gross. I didn't eat any viruses," responded Lizzie.

"You don't eat them, silly, you breathe them in. Somebody probably sneezed them all over you at school. That's how you got sick!"

Lizzie and Joey are at different developmental levels in their understanding of health and illness, due to cognitive development and exposure to biological knowledge. Researchers have asked preschool through high school stu-

dents questions about the causes of health and certain illnesses, such as colds, AIDS, and cancer.

During the preschool and early school years, children do not have much biological knowledge to bring to bear on their understanding of health and illness. For example, 3- to 8-year-olds know little about their internal organs and how they work. As a result, they fall back on explanations of people's behaviour to account for health and illness (Carey, 1995, 1999; Simons & Keil, 1995). Children of this age regard health as a matter of engaging in specific practices (eating the right foods, getting enough sleep and exercise, and wearing warm clothing on cold days) and illness as a matter of failing to follow these rules or coming too close to a sick person.

By age 9 or 10, children can name many internal organs and view them

as interconnected, working as a system. Around this time, children almost always explain health and illness biologically (Carey, 1999). Joey understands that illness can be caused by contagion—breathing in a harmful substance (a virus), which affects the operation of the body in some way. He likely also realizes that we eat not just because food tastes good or to stay alive (younger children's explanations) but to build new muscle and bone (Inagaki & Hatano, 1993).

By early adolescence, explanations become more elaborate and precise. Eleven- to 14-year-olds recognize health as a long-term condition that depends on the interaction of body, mind, and environment (Hergenrather & Rabinowitz, 1991). And adolescents' notions of illness involve clearly stated ideas about interference in normal biological processes: "You get a

---

have difficulty with less-than and greater-than relationships between small sets. And in Chapter 7, we will see that not until the preschool years do children add and subtract small numbers of objects correctly.

Overall, then, studies on early knowledge provide mixed results. In some, infants display amazing knowledge; in others not. Perhaps young infants' knowledge is evident only under certain conditions. If such knowledge is innate, however, older children should reason in the same way as infants about events that tap this knowledge, yet they do not always do so. Core knowledge theorists respond that infant looking behaviours may be a more reliable indicator of understanding than older children's verbal and motor behaviours, which do not always display their true competence (Hood, Carey, & Prasada, 2000). Critics argue that rather than being built in, physical and numerical knowledge must be constructed over an extended time period (Haith & Benson, 1998).

**theory theory**
A theory that assumes that children build on innate concepts to form naive theories, or explanations of everyday events, in each core domain of thought. Then they test their theory against experience, revising it when it cannot adequately account for new information. Preschoolers have naive physical and biological theories and a psychological theory, or theory of mind.

## CHILDREN AS NAIVE THEORISTS

Do children form naive theories, or explanations of events, that differ between core domains? A growing number of researchers believe they do. According to this **theory theory** (meaning *theory* of *children as theorists*), after observing an event, children explain, or theorize about, its cause by drawing on innate concepts. Then they test their naive theory against experience, revising it when it cannot adequately account for new information (Wellman & Gelman, 1998). These revisions often lead to stagelike changes—dramatic, qualitative shifts in the complexity of concepts and explanations. Notice that this account of cognitive change is similar to Piaget's. But theory theorists claim that because children start with

© SPENCER GRANT/INDEX STOCK

cold when your sinuses fill with mucus. Sometimes your lungs do, too, and you get a cough. Colds come from viruses. They get into the bloodstream and make your platelet count go down" (Bibace & Walsh, 1980).

Young children can grasp basic biological ideas relevant to understanding disease. But whether or not they do so depends on information in their environments. When supplied with relevant facts and biological concepts, such as "gene," "germ," or "virus," 5- and 6-year-olds can use the concepts to organize those facts, and their understanding advances (Solomon & Johnson, 2000).

Without such knowledge, children readily generalize their knowledge of familiar diseases to less familiar ones. As a result, they often conclude that risk factors for colds (sharing a Coke or sneezing on someone) can cause

This child comforts her grandmother, who is dying of cancer. Helping school-age children understand that cancer is not communicable can prevent them from developing negative attitudes toward its victims.

AIDS. And lacking much understanding of cancer, they assume that it (like colds) is communicable through casual contact. These incorrect ideas can lead to unnecessary anxiety about getting a serious disease. In surveys of school-age children, about half incorrectly believed that everyone is at risk for AIDS. And more than half said they worry about getting AIDS and cancer (Chin et al., 1998; Holcomb, 1990). In sum, a basic capacity to reason biologically about health and illness is present by the time children start school.

But this reasoning flourishes only when children are exposed to relevant biological information. Education about the causes of illness leads to an increasingly accurate appreciation of disease transmission and prevention in middle childhood and adolescence.

innate knowledge, their reasoning advances quickly, with sophisticated cause-and-effect explanations evident much earlier than Piaget proposed.

The most extensively investigated naive theory is children's *theory of mind*—psychological knowledge of self and others that forms rapidly during the preschool years, which we will consider in Chapters 7 and 11. Preschoolers also have naive physical and biological theories. In one study, researchers asked 3- and 4-year-olds to explain events that had either a psychological, a physical, or a biological cause. Children reasoned about each event in ways consistent with its core domain. For example, a child who pours orange juice instead of milk on his cereal received mostly psychological explanations ("he *thought* it was milk"), a boy who tries to float in the air by jumping off a stool but falls received mostly physical explanations ("he's too *heavy* to float"), and a girl who tries to hang from a tree branch forever but lets go tended to receive biological explanations ("her arms got *hurting*"). Also, 70 percent of preschoolers' explanations in everyday conversation are psychological, physical, or biological—additional evidence that these are core modes of reasoning (Wellman, Hickling, & Schult, 1997).

Although preschoolers are impressive theorists, their explanations in different domains develop at different rates. Physical and psychological explanations are present at age 2, probably because these understandings originate in infancy. Biological explanations increase between ages 3 and 6. But grasping biological processes is difficult, so young preschoolers frequently explain biological events with psychological concepts (Carey, 1995, 1999; Hantano & Inagaki, 1996). For example, when asked whether they can tell a pain to go away or a heartbeat to stop, many 3-year-olds say yes! In contrast, 4-year-olds know that they cannot control biological processes (Inagaki, 1997). Still, psychological accounts of biological events persist into the early school years, as research on children's understanding of health and illness reveals (see the Biology & Environment box above).

### ■ EVALUATION OF THE CORE KNOWLEDGE PERSPECTIVE

Core knowledge theorists offer a fascinating evolutionary account of why certain cognitive skills emerge early and develop rapidly. And more seriously than other perspectives, they have addressed the question, What allows learning to get off the ground? As a result, this perspective has enriched our understanding of infants' and young children's thinking.

Nevertheless, critics take issue with the core knowledge assumption that infants are endowed with *knowledge*. As we have already noted, infant looking in violation-of-expectation studies may indicate only a perceptual preference, not the existence of concepts or reasoning. And some skeptics claim that human evolution may not have equipped infants with ready-made knowledge, which might limit their ability to adapt to environmental changes (Haith, 1999; Meltzoff & Moore, 1998). At present, just what babies start out with—domain-specific understandings or as yet unspecified general learning strategies that permit them to discover various types of knowledge rapidly—continues to be hotly debated.

Although the core knowledge perspective emphasizes native endowment, it acknowledges that experience is essential for children to elaborate this initial knowledge. But it has not offered greater clarity than Piaget's theory on how biology and environment jointly produce cognitive change. For example, it does not tell us just what children do to revise their innate structures. And it says little about which experiences are most important in each domain and how those experiences advance children's thinking. Finally, the core knowledge perspective shares with Piaget's theory a view of children as independently building more adequate structures. It pays little attention to children's learning in interaction with others—the unique strength of Vygotsky's theory, which we take up next. Despite these limitations, the ingenious studies and provocative findings of core knowledge research have sharpened the field's focus on specifying the starting point for human cognition and carefully tracking the changes that build on it.

### ASK YOURSELF 〰

**review**    What are core domains of thought? Cite an example of infants' innate knowledge in the physical domain and the numerical domain. Why do some researchers question whether infants actually have such knowledge?

**review**    Why do core knowledge researchers characterize young children as naive theorists? Cite findings that support the theory theory.

**connect**    Describe similarities and differences between Piaget's theory and the core knowledge perspective.

## Vygotsky's Sociocultural Theory

PIAGET'S THEORY AND THE core knowledge perspective emphasize the biological side of cognitive development. In both, the most important source of cognition is the child himself—a busy, self-motivated explorer who forms ideas and tests them against the world. Lev Vygotsky also believed that children are active seekers of knowledge, but he did not view them as solitary agents. In his theory, rich social and cultural contexts profoundly affect children's cognition.

Early events in Vygotsky's life contributed to his vision of human cognition as inherently social and language based. As a university student, his primary interest was a verbal field—literature. After graduating, he was first a teacher; only later did he turn to psychology (Kozulin, 1990). Vygotsky died of tuberculosis when he was 37 years old. Consequently, his theory is not as complete as Piaget's. Nevertheless, the field of child development is experiencing a burst of interest in Vygotsky's sociocultural perspective. The major reason for his appeal lies in his rejection of an individualistic view of the developing child in favour of a socially formed mind (Rogoff, 1998; Wertsch & Tulviste, 1992).

**private speech**
Self-directed speech that children use to guide their thinking and behaviour.

According to Vygotsky, infants are endowed with basic perceptual, attentional, and memory capacities that they share with other animals. These develop during the first 2 years through direct contact with the environment. Then rapid growth of language leads to a profound change in thinking. It broadens preschoolers' participation in social dialogues with more knowledgeable individuals, who encourage them to master culturally important tasks. Soon young children start to communicate with themselves in much the same way they conversed with others. As a result, basic mental capacities are transformed into uniquely human, higher cognitive processes. Let's see how this happens.

© LAURA DWIGHT

This 3-year-old makes a sculpture from playdough and plastic sticks with the aid of private speech. During the preschool years, children frequently talk to themselves as they play and tackle other challenging tasks. Research supports Vygotsky's theory that children use private speech to guide their own thinking and behaviour.

### CHILDREN'S PRIVATE SPEECH

Watch preschoolers as they go about their daily activities, and you will see that they frequently talk out loud to themselves as they play and explore the environment. For example, as a 5-year-old worked a puzzle at preschool one day, he said, "Where's the red piece? I need the red one. Now a blue one. No, it doesn't fit. Try it here."

**PIAGET'S VIEW.** Piaget (1923/1926) called these utterances *egocentric speech,* a term expressing his belief that they reflect the preoperational child's inability to imagine the perspectives of others. For this reason, Piaget said, young children's talk is often "talk for self" in which they run off thoughts in whatever form they happen to occur, regardless of whether they are understandable to a listener.

Piaget believed that cognitive maturity and certain social experiences—namely, disagreements with peers—eventually bring an end to egocentric speech. Through arguments with agemates, children repeatedly see that others hold viewpoints different from their own. As a result, egocentric speech gradually declines and is replaced by social speech, in which children adapt what they say to their listeners.

**VYGOTSKY'S VIEW.** Vygotsky (1934/1986) voiced a powerful objection to Piaget's conclusions. He reasoned that children speak to themselves for self-guidance. Because language helps children think about their mental activities and behaviour and select courses of action, Vygotsky regarded it as the foundation for all higher cognitive processes, including controlled attention, deliberate memorization and recall, categorization, planning, problem solving, abstract reasoning, and self-reflection. As children get older and find tasks easier, their self-directed speech declines and is internalized as silent, inner speech—the verbal dialogues we carry on with ourselves while thinking and acting in everyday situations.

Over the past three decades, researchers have carried out many studies to determine which of these two views—Piaget's or Vygotsky's—is correct. Almost all the findings have sided with Vygotsky (Berk, 2002). As a result, children's "speech to self" is now called **private speech** instead of egocentric speech. Research shows that children use more of it when tasks are difficult, after they make errors, or when they are confused about how to proceed. For example, Figure 6.18 shows how 4- and 5-year-olds' private speech increased as researchers made a colour-sequencing task more difficult. Also, just as Vygotsky predicted, Canadian and U.S. research shows that private speech goes underground with age, changing into whispers and silent lip movements (Duncan & Pratt, 1997; Patrick & Abravanel, 2000). Furthermore, children who freely use private speech during a challenging activity are more attentive and involved and show greater improvement in performance (Berk & Spuhl, 1995; Bivens & Berk, 1990; Winsler, Diaz, & Montero, 1997).

Finally, compared with their normally achieving agemates, children with learning problems engage in higher rates of private speech over a longer period of development (Berk &

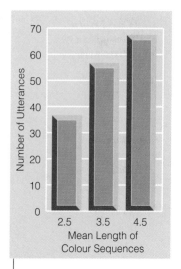

**FIGURE** 6.18

**Relationship of private speech to task difficulty among 4- and 5-year-olds.** Researchers increased the difficulty of a colour-sequencing task, in which children listened to a list of colours and then placed coloured stickers on a page to match the list. The longer the colour list, the more private speech children used. (From E. Patrick and E. Abravanel, 2000, "The Self-Regulatory Nature of Preschool Children's Private Speech in a Naturalistic Setting," *Applied Psycholinguistics, 21,* p. 55. Reprinted by permission.)

Landau, 1993; Winsler et al., 1999). They seem to call on private speech to help compensate for the impairments in cognitive processing and attention that make academic tasks more difficult for them. In one study, inattentive, overactive boys who often used private speech while working math problems scored considerably better than their counterparts who less often talked to themselves (Berk, 2001b).

Where does private speech come from? Vygotsky's answer to this question highlights the social origins of cognition.

## SOCIAL ORIGINS OF COGNITIVE DEVELOPMENT

Vygotsky (1930–1935/1978) believed that all higher cognitive processes develop out of social interaction. Through joint activities with more mature members of society, children come to master activities and think in ways that have meaning in their culture. A special concept, the **zone of proximal** (or potential) **development,** explains how this happens. It refers to a range of tasks that the child cannot yet handle alone but can accomplish with the help of adults and more skilled peers.

Consider the joint activity of 3-year-old Sammy and his mother, who assists him in putting together a difficult puzzle:

> Sammy: "I can't get this one in." [Tries to insert a piece in the wrong place]
>
> Mother: "Which piece might go down here?" [Points to the bottom of the puzzle]
>
> Sammy: "His shoes." [Looks for a piece resembling the clown's shoes but tries the wrong one]
>
> Mother: "Well, what piece looks like this shape?" [Pointing again to the bottom of the puzzle]
>
> Sammy: "The brown one." [Tries it, and it fits; then attempts another piece and looks at his mother]
>
> Mother: "Try turning it just a little." [Gestures to show him]
>
> Sammy: "There!" [Puts in several more pieces. His mother watches.]

Sammy's mother keeps the puzzle within his zone of proximal development—at a manageable level of difficulty—by questioning, prompting, and suggesting strategies. Within the zone, interaction constantly adjusts to fit Sammy's changing competencies and his mother's insights into what will best help him learn. Eventually, children take the language of these dialogues, make it part of their private speech, and use this speech to organize their own thinking and behaviour.

**EFFECTIVE SOCIAL INTERACTION.** To promote cognitive development, social interaction must have certain features. The first is **intersubjectivity,** the process whereby two participants who begin a task with different understandings arrive at a shared understanding (Newson & Newson, 1975). Intersubjectivity creates a common ground for communication, as each partner adjusts to the perspective of the other. Adults try to promote it when they translate their own insights in ways that are within the child's grasp. As the child stretches to understand the interpretation, she is drawn into a more mature approach to the situation (Rogoff, 1998).

The capacity for intersubjectivity is present early, in parent–infant mutual gaze, exchange of emotional signals, and imitation. Later, language facilitates it. As conversational skills improve, preschoolers increasingly seek others' help and direct that assistance to ensure that it is beneficial (Whitington & Ward, 1999). Between ages 3 and 5, children increasingly strive for intersubjectivity in dialogues with peers, as when they affirm a playmate's message, add new ideas, and contribute to ongoing play to sustain it. They can also be heard saying, "I think [this way]. What do you think?"—evidence for a willingness to share viewpoints (Berk, 2001). In these ways, children begin to create zones of proximal development for one another.

Another feature of social interaction that fosters development is **scaffolding** (Bruner, 1983; Wood, 1989). It refers to a changing quality of support over the course of a teaching

**zone of proximal development**
In Vygotsky's theory, a range of tasks that the child cannot yet handle alone but can do with the help of more skilled partners.

**intersubjectivity**
A process whereby two participants who begin a task with different understandings arrive at a shared understanding.

**scaffolding**
A changing quality of support over a teaching session, in which adults adjust the assistance they provide to fit the child's current level of performance. Direct instruction is offered when a task is new; less help is provided as competence increases.

session. Adults who offer an effective scaffold adjust the assistance they provide to fit the child's current level of performance. When the child has little notion of how to proceed, the adult uses direct instruction, breaking the task down into manageable units. As the child's competence increases, effective scaffolders—such as Sammy's mother—gradually and sensitively withdraw support, turning over responsibility to the child.

Michael Pratt of Wilfrid Laurier University and others (1992) studied the effects of parental scaffolding on fifth-graders' ability to learn mathematical skills. When parents used scaffolding during teaching sessions, the children's long-division problem solving improved. In a second study, fourth and fifth graders receiving more effective scaffolding were more likely to sustain gains in problem solving over time and to generalize their new skills to similar but more challenging problems (Pratt & Savoy-Levine, 1998). Furthermore, Tara Callaghan, whose work on graphic symbol representation was discussed earlier in this chapter, found that scaffolding helped children as young 2 and 3 years of age produce better drawings (Callaghan & Rankin, 2002).

Scaffolding captures the form of teaching interaction that occurs as children work on school or school-like tasks, such as puzzles, model building, picture matching, and later, academic assignments. It may not apply to other contexts that are just as vital for cognitive development—for example, play or everyday activities, during which adults usually support children's efforts without deliberately instructing. To account for children's diverse opportunities to learn through involvement with others, Barbara Rogoff (1990, 1994) suggests the term **guided participation,** a broader concept than scaffolding. It calls attention to both adult and child contributions to a cooperative dialogue, without specifying the precise features of communication. Consequently, it allows for variations across situations and cultures.

**RESEARCH ON SOCIAL INTERACTION AND COGNITIVE DEVELOPMENT.** What evidence supports Vygotsky's ideas on the role of social interaction in cognitive development? In infancy and toddlerhood, intersubjectivity, in the form of finely tuned emotional communication and joint gazing at objects, is related to advanced play, language, perspective taking, and problem-solving skills during the preschool years (Bornstein et al., 1992b; Charman et al., 2001; Frankel & Bates, 1990; Morales et al., 2000).

Furthermore, parents who are effective scaffolders in teaching their young child to solve challenging problems have children who use more private speech and are more successful when asked to do a similar task by themselves (Berk & Spuhl, 1995; Conner, Knight, & Cross, 1997; Winsler, Diaz, & Montero, 1997). And many studies support the social origins of private speech. For example, social and private utterances are positively correlated during the preschool years, suggesting that they have common roots. And socially rich contexts seem to foster private speech, since children who have access to social partners—either peers or adults—talk to themselves more (Berk, 1992).

## VYGOTSKY'S VIEW OF MAKE-BELIEVE PLAY

In accord with his emphasis on social experience and language as vital forces in cognitive development, Vygotsky (1933/1978) regarded make-believe as a unique, broadly influential zone of proximal development in which *children advance themselves* as they try out a wide variety of challenging skills. How does make-believe lead development forward? According to Vygotsky, it does so in two ways. First, as children create imaginary situations, they learn to act in accordance with internal ideas, not just in response to external stimuli. Children's object substitutions are crucial in this process. While pretending, children continually use one object to stand for another. By making a stick represent a horse or a folded blanket represent a sleeping baby, they change an object's usual meaning. Gradually they realize that thinking (or the meaning of words) is separate from actions and objects and that ideas can be used to guide behaviour.

GARY CONNER/MAXX IMAGES INC.

This father assists his toddler in building a tower of blocks through gestures and simple words. By presenting a task within the child's zone of proximal development and fine-tuning his support to the child's needs, the father promotes his son's cognitive development.

**guided participation**
A concept that accounts for cultural variations in children's opportunities to learn through involvement with others. Calls attention to both adult and child contributions to a cooperative dialogue, without specifying the precise features of communication.

## *from research to practice*

### SOCIAL ORIGINS OF MAKE-BELIEVE PLAY

One of my husband, Ken's, activities with our two sons when they were young was to bake pineapple upside-down cake, a favourite treat. One Sunday afternoon, when a cake was in the making, 21-month-old Peter stood on a chair at the kitchen sink, busily pouring water from one cup to another.

"He's in the way, Dad!" complained 4-year-old David, trying to pull Peter away from the sink.

"Maybe if we let him help, he'll give us some room," Ken suggested. As David stirred the batter, Ken poured some into a small bowl for Peter, moved his chair to the side of the sink, and handed him a spoon.

"Here's how you do it, Peter," instructed David, with an air of superiority. Peter watched as David stirred, then tried to copy his motion. When it was time to pour the batter, Ken helped Peter hold and tip the small bowl.

"Time to bake it," said Ken.

"Bake it, bake it," repeated Peter, as he watched Ken slip the pan into the oven.

Several hours later, we observed one of Peter's earliest instances of make-believe play. He got his pail from the sandbox and, after filling it with a handful of sand, carried it into the kitchen and put it down on the floor in front of the oven. "Bake it, bake it," Peter called to Ken. Together, father and son lifted the pretend cake inside the oven.

Until recently, most researchers studied make-believe play apart from the social environment in which it occurs, while children played alone. Probably for this reason, Piaget and his followers concluded that toddlers discover make-believe independently, as soon as they are capable of representational schemes. Vygotsky's theory has challenged this view. He believed that society provides children with opportunities to represent culturally meaningful activities in play. Make-believe, like other

mental functions, is initially learned under the guidance of experts. In the example just described, Peter's capacity to represent daily events was extended when Ken drew him into the baking task and helped him act it out in play.

Current evidence supports the idea that early make-believe is the combined result of children's readiness to engage in it and social experiences that promote it. In one observational study of middle-class toddlers, 75 to 80 percent of make-believe involved mother–child interaction (Haight & Miller, 1993). At 12 months, make-believe was fairly one-sided; almost all play episodes were initiated by mothers. By the end of the second year, mothers and children displayed mutual interest in getting make-believe started; each initiated half of pretend episodes.

When adults participate, toddlers' make-believe is more elaborate (O'Reilly & Bornstein, 1993). For example, play themes are more varied.

A second feature of make-believe—its rule-based nature—also strengthens children's capacity to think before they act. Pretend play, Vygotsky pointed out, constantly demands that children act against their impulses because they must subject themselves to the rules of the play scene. For example, a child pretending to go to sleep follows the rules of bedtime behaviour. Another child imagining himself to be a father and a doll to be a child conforms to the rules of parental behaviour. As children enact rules in make-believe, they come to better understand social norms and expectations and strive to follow them.

Was Vygotsky correct that make-believe serves as a zone of proximal development, supporting the emergence and refinement of a wide variety of competencies? Much evidence fits with Vygotsky's conclusion. Turn back to page 231 to review evidence that make-believe enhances a diverse array of cognitive and social skills. Pretend play is also rich in private speech—a finding that supports its role in helping children bring action under the control of thought (Krafft & Berk, 1998). And in a recent study, preschoolers who engaged in more complex sociodramatic play showed greater gains in following classroom rules over a 4-month period (Elias & Berk, 2002).

Finally, Vygotsky took issue with Piaget's view that make-believe arises spontaneously in the second year of life. Instead, Vygotsky argued that the elaborate pretending of the preschool years, like other higher cognitive processes, has social origins. Research reviewed in the From Research to Practice box above supports the view that children initially learn to pretend under the supportive guidance of experts.

When adults participate, toddlers' make-believe is more elaborate and their play themes are more varied. The more parents pretend with their toddlers, the more time their children devote to make-believe play, which extends cognitive development.

And toddlers are more likely to combine schemes into complex sequences, as Peter did when he put the sand in the bucket ("making the batter"), carried it into the kitchen, and (with Ken's help) put it in the oven ("baking the cake"). The more parents pretend with their toddlers, the more time their children devote to make-believe. And in certain collectivist societies, such as Argentina and Japan, mother–toddler other-directed pretending, as in feeding or putting a doll to sleep, is particularly rich in maternal expressions of affection and praise (Bornstein et al., 1999).

In some cultures, older siblings are toddlers' first play partners. For example, in Indonesia and Mexico, where extended-family households and sibling caregiving are common, make-believe is more frequent and complex with older siblings than with mothers. As early as 3 to 4 years of age, children provide rich, challenging stimulation to their younger brothers and sisters. The fantasy play of these toddlers is just as well developed as that of their middle-class counterparts (Farver, 1993; Farver & Wimbarti, 1995a).

Make-believe is a major means through which children extend their cognitive skills and learn about important activities in their culture. Vygotsky's theory, and the findings that support it, tell us that providing a stimulating environment is not enough to promote early cognitive development. Toddlers must be invited and encouraged by more skilled members of their culture to participate actively in the social world around them. Parents and teachers can enhance development of make-believe by

- providing a rich variety of play materials that inspire make-believe (see Bronson, 1995);

- ensuring that children have many real-world experiences, in which they participate in activities with adults and observe adult roles, to inspire positive fantasy play;

- playing often with young children, responding, guiding, and elaborating on their make-believe themes; and

- restricting aggressive toys and viewing of TV programs with violent content, thereby limiting the degree to which aggressive behaviour becomes part of children's play (see Chapter 15, page 625).

# Vygotsky and Education

VYGOTSKY'S THEORY OFFERS new visions of teaching and learning—ones that emphasize the importance of social context and collaboration. Today, educators are eager to use his ideas.

Piagetian and Vygotskian classrooms clearly have features in common, such as opportunities for active participation and acceptance of individual differences. However, a Vygotskian classroom goes beyond independent discovery; it promotes *assisted discovery*. Teachers guide children's learning, tailoring their interventions to each child's zone of proximal development. Assisted discovery is also fostered by *peer collaboration*. Classmates with varying abilities work in groups, teaching and helping one another.

Vygotsky's major educational message for the preschool years was to provide many socially rich, meaningful activities in children's zones of proximal development, and a wealth of opportunities for make-believe play—the ultimate means of fostering the self-discipline required for later academic learning. Once formal schooling begins, Vygotsky emphasized literacy activities (Berk, 2001; John-Steiner & Mahn, 1996). As children talk about reading and writing in literature, mathematics, science, and social studies, they reflect on their own thought processes. As a result, they shift to a higher level of cognitive activity in which they

Reciprocal teaching is a Vygotsky-inspired educational innovation in which a teacher and two to four students form a cooperative learning group and engage in dialogue about a text passage. Elementary and junior high school students who participate in reciprocal teaching show impressive gains in reading comprehension.

think about how to symbolize ideas in socially useful ways. Gradually they become proficient in manipulating and controlling the symbol systems of their culture.

Let's look at two Vygotsky-based educational innovations, each of which incorporates assisted discovery and peer collaboration.

### RECIPROCAL TEACHING

Originally designed to improve reading comprehension in pupils achieving poorly, **reciprocal teaching** has been adapted to other subjects and is a useful model for all school-age children (Palincsar & Herrenkohl, 1999). A teacher and two to four students form a collaborative group and take turns leading dialogues on the content of a text passage. Within the dialogues, group members apply four cognitive strategies: questioning, summarizing, clarifying, and predicting.

The dialogue leader (at first the teacher, later a pupil) begins by *asking questions* about the content of the text passage. Pupils offer answers, raise additional questions, and in case of disagreement, reread the original text. Next, the leader *summarizes* the passage, and children discuss the summary and *clarify* ideas that are unfamiliar to any group members. Finally, the leader encourages pupils to *predict* upcoming content based on prior knowledge and clues in the passage (Palincsar & Klenk, 1992).

Elementary and junior high school students exposed to reciprocal teaching show impressive gains in reading comprehension compared with controls taught in other ways (King & Johnson, 1999; Lederer, 2000; Rosenshine & Meister, 1994). Notice how reciprocal teaching creates a zone of proximal development in which children gradually assume more responsibility for comprehending complex text passages. Also, by collaborating with others, children forge group norms for good thinking and acquire skills vital for learning and success in everyday life.

### COOPERATIVE LEARNING

Although reciprocal teaching uses peer collaboration, a teacher is present to guide it, helping to ensure its success. According to Vygotsky, more expert peers can also spur children's development, as long as they adjust the help they provide to fit the less mature child's zone of proximal development. Recall that Piaget, too, thought that peer interaction could contribute to cognitive change. In fact, he regarded discussion with agemates as more valuable than discussion with adults, since a child might superficially accept an adult's perspective without critically examining it because of the adult's authority. Piaget also asserted that clashing viewpoints—arguments jarring the young child into noticing a peer's point of view—were necessary for peer interaction to foster logical thought (Tudge & Winterhoff, 1993).

Today, peer collaboration is used in many classrooms, but evidence is mounting that it fosters development only under certain conditions. A crucial factor is **cooperative learning**—working toward common goals. Conflict and disagreement seem less important than the extent to which peers achieve intersubjectivity—by resolving differences of opinion, sharing responsibility, and considering one another's ideas (Kobayashi, 1994; Tudge, 1992). And in line with Vygotsky's theory, children's planning and problem solving improve most when their peer partner is an "expert"—especially capable at the task (Azmitia, 1988; Radziszewska & Rogoff, 1988).

Cultural values and practices influence students' ability to learn cooperatively. Working in groups comes more easily to children reared in collectivist than individualistic cultures. For example, Navajo children do so more readily than do Caucasian-American children (Ellis & Gauvain, 1992). Japanese classroom practices, in which children solve problems by building on one another's ideas, are situated in a larger culture that values interdependence (Hatano, 1994). In contrast, cultural-majority children in the United States typically consider competition and independent work to be natural—a perspective that interferes with their ability to attain intersubjectivity in groups (Forman & McPhail, 1993).

**reciprocal teaching**
A method of teaching based on Vygotsky's theory in which a teacher and two to four pupils form a collaborative learning group. Dialogues occur that create a zone of proximal development in which reading comprehension improves.

**cooperative learning**
A learning environment in which groups of peers work toward common goals.

Consequently, for cooperative learning to succeed, Western children usually require extensive guidance in how to work together. In several studies, groups of three to four elementary school students trained in collaborative processes displayed more cooperative behaviour and gave higher-level explanations than did untrained groups (Gillies, 2000; Terwel et al., 2001). And in other research, the quality of children's collaborative discussions predicted gains in diverse cognitive skills that persisted for weeks beyond the cooperative learning experience (Fleming & Alexander, 2001; Manion & Alexander, 1997). Teaching through cooperative learning broadens Vygotsky's concept of the zone of proximal development, from a single child in collaboration with an expert partner (adult or peer) to multiple partners with diverse forms of expertise stimulating and encouraging one another.

# Evaluation of Vygotsky's Theory

IN GRANTING SOCIAL experience a fundamental role in cognitive development, Vygotsky's theory helps us understand the wide cultural variation in cognitive skills. Unlike Piaget, who emphasized universal cognitive change, Vygotsky's theory leads us to expect highly diverse paths of development.

For example, the reading, writing, and mathematical activities of children who go to school in literate societies generate cognitive capacities that differ from those in tribal and village cultures, where children receive little formal schooling. But the elaborate spatial skills of Australian Aborigines, whose food-gathering missions require that they find their way through barren desert regions, or the proportional reasoning of Brazilian fishermen, promoted by their navigational experiences, are just as advanced (Carraher, Schliemann, & Carraher, 1988; Kearins, 1981). Each is a unique form of symbolic thinking required by activities that make up that culture's way of life.

At the same time, Vygotsky's theory underscores the vital role of teaching in cognitive development. Optimum learning does not result from the child's independent efforts. Instead, teaching in the zone of proximal development leads children's development forward. According to Vygotsky (1934/1986), from communicating with more expert partners, children engage in "verbalized self-observation"; they start to reflect on, revise, and control their own thought processes. In this way, parents' and teachers' engagement with children prompts profound advances in the complexity of children's thinking.

Vygotsky's theory, however, has not gone unchallenged. Although he acknowledged the role of diverse symbol systems (such as pictures, maps, and mathematical expressions) in the development of higher cognitive processes, he elevated language to highest importance. But verbal dialogues are not the only means, or even the most important means, through which children learn in some cultures. When Western parents are asked to help their young child with challenging tasks, they assume much responsibility for children's motivation by frequently giving verbal instructions and conversing with the child. Their communication resembles the teaching that takes place in school, where their children will spend years preparing for an adult life. But in cultures that place less emphasis on schooling and literacy, parents often expect children to take greater responsibility for acquiring new skills through keen observation (Rogoff et al., 1993). Turn to the Cultural Influences box on page 264 for research on Mayan preschoolers of Yucatán, Mexico, which illustrates this difference.

Finally, in focusing on social and cultural influences, Vygotsky said little about biological contributions to children's cognition. Consequently, we cannot tell from Vygotsky's theory exactly how basic cognitive processes combine with social experiences and are transformed into higher forms of thinking. For example, Vygotsky's theory does not address the way children's developing motor, perceptual, and cognitive capacities spark changes in their social world, from which more advanced skills spring. And it does not tell us just how children internalize social experiences to advance their mental functioning (Berk & Winsler, 1995; Moll, 1994). Consequently, like the other perspectives addressed in this chapter, Vygotsky's theory is vague in its explanation of cognitive change. It is intriguing to speculate about the broader theory that might exist today had Piaget and Vygotsky—the two twentieth-century giants of cognitive development—had a chance to meet and weave together their extraordinary accomplishments.

# cultural influences

## YOUNG CHILDREN'S DAILY LIFE IN A YUCATEC MAYAN VILLAGE

Conducting ethnographic research in a remote Mayan village of Yucatán, Mexico, Suzanne Gaskins (1999) found that child-rearing values, daily activities, and, consequently, 2- to 5-year-olds' competencies differed sharply from those of Western preschoolers. Yucatec Mayan adults are subsistence farmers. Men spend their days tending cornfields, aided by sons age 8 and older. Women oversee the household and yard, engaging in time-consuming meal preparation, clothes washing, and care of livestock and garden, assisted by daughters as well as sons not yet old enough to work in the fields.

In Yucatec Mayan culture, life is structured around adult work and religious and social events. Children join in these activities from the second year on. Adults make no effort to provide special experiences designed to satisfy children's interests or stimulate their development. When not participating with adults, children are expected to be independent. Even young children make many nonwork decisions for themselves—how much to sleep and eat, what to wear, when to bathe (as long as they do so every afternoon), and even when to start school.

As a result, Mayan preschoolers spend much time at self-care and are highly competent at it. In contrast, their make-believe play is limited; when it occurs, it involves brief imitations of adult work or more common scenes from adult life, organized and directed by older siblings. When not engaged in self-care or play, Mayan children watch others—for hours each day. By age 3, they can report the whereabouts and activities of all family members. At any moment, they may be called on to do a chore—fetch things from the house, run an errand, deliver a message, tend to livestock, or take care of toddler-age siblings. They are constantly "on call," to support adult work.

Mayan parents rarely converse with children or scaffold their learning. Rather, when children imitate adult tasks, parents conclude they are ready for more responsibility. Then they assign chores, selecting ones the child can do with little help, so adult work is not disturbed. If a child cannot do a task, the adult takes over and the child observes, re-engaging when able to contribute. This give-and-take occurs smoothly, with parent and child focused on the primary goal of getting the job done.

Cultural priorities and daily activities lead Mayan preschoolers' skills and behaviour to differ sharply from those of their Western agemates. Expected to be independent and helpful, Mayan children seldom display attention-getting behaviours or ask others for something interesting to do. From an early age, they can sit quietly for long periods with little fussing—through a lengthy religious service or dance, even a 3-hour truck ride into town. And when an adult interrupts their activity and directs them to a chore, Mayan children respond eagerly to a command that Western children frequently avoid or resent. By age 5, Mayan children spontaneously take responsibility for tasks beyond those assigned.

© SUZANNE MURPHY LAURADO/D. DONNE BRYANT STOCK PHOTO

In Yucatec Mayan culture, adults rarely converse with children or scaffold their learning. Instead, children join in work and religious and social events from an early age, spending many hours observing the behaviour of adults. These Mayan preschoolers watch intently as adults of their village celebrate the Yucatán Patron Festival, which honours the region's patron saint.

## ASK YOURSELF

**review**  Describe characteristics of social interaction that support children's cognitive development. How does such interaction create a zone of proximal development?

**review**  Explain how make-believe play strengthens children's capacity to think before they act and follow social rules.

**apply**  Tara sees her 5-year-old son, Toby, talking aloud to himself while he plays. She wonders whether she should discourage this behaviour. Using Vygotsky's theory and related research, explain why Toby's private speech is probably beneficial.

**connect**  Explain how Piaget's and Vygotsky's theories complement one another, in the way each views cognitive development. How would classroom practices inspired by each theory be similar in some ways and different in others?

# summary

## PIAGET'S COGNITIVE-DEVELOPMENTAL THEORY

*According to Piaget, how does cognition develop?*

■ Influenced by his background in biology, Piaget viewed cognitive development as an adaptive process in which thinking gradually achieves a better fit with external reality. Piaget's **constructivist approach** to cognitive development assumes that by acting on the environment, children move through four invariant and universal stages, in which all aspects of cognition undergo similar changes. According to Piaget, infants begin life with little in the way of built-in structures; only at the end of the second year are they capable of a cognitive approach to the world through **mental representations.**

■ In Piaget's theory, psychological structures, or **schemes,** change in two ways. The first is through **adaptation,** which consists of two complementary activities: **assimilation** and **accommodation.** The second is through **organization,** the internal rearrangement of schemes to form a strongly interconnected cognitive system. **Equilibration** sums up the changing balance of assimilation and accommodation that gradually leads to more effective schemes.

## THE SENSORIMOTOR STAGE (BIRTH TO 2 YEARS)

*Describe the major cognitive achievements of the sensorimotor stage.*

■ Piaget's **sensorimotor stage** is divided into six substages. Through the **circular reaction,** the newborn baby's reflexes are gradually transformed into the more flexible action patterns of the older infant. During Substage 4, infants develop **intentional,** or **goal-directed, behaviour** and begin to understand **object permanence.** Substage 5 brings a more flexible, exploratory approach, and infants no longer make the **A-not-B search error.** By Substage 6, they become capable of **mental representation,** as shown by sudden solutions to sensorimotor problems, mastery of object permanence problems involving invisible displacement, **deferred imitation,** and **make-believe play.**

*What does recent research say about the accuracy of Piaget's sensorimotor stage?*

■ Many studies suggest that infants display a variety of understandings earlier than Piaget believed. Some awareness of object permanence, as revealed by the **violation-of-expectation method,** may be evident in the first few months. In addition, young infants display deferred imitation, categorization, and **analogical problem solving,** suggesting that mental representation develops concurrently with sensorimotor schemes during the first 2 years.

■ Today, investigators believe that newborns have more built-in equipment for making sense of their world than Piaget assumed, although they disagree on how much initial understanding infants have. Furthermore, the cognitive attainments of infancy do not develop in the neat, stepwise fashion predicted by Piaget's substages.

## THE PREOPERATIONAL STAGE (2 TO 7 YEARS)

*Describe advances in mental representation and limitations of thinking during the preoperational stage.*

■ Rapid advances in mental representation, including language, make-believe play, and drawing, mark the beginning of the **preoperational stage.** With age, make-believe becomes increasingly complex, evolving into **sociodramatic play.** Preschoolers' make-believe not only reflects but contributes to cognitive and social development. During the preschool years, drawings progress from scribbles to increasingly detailed representational forms.

■ **Dual representation** improves rapidly during the third year of life. Children realize that photographs, drawings, models, and simple maps correspond to circumstances in the real world. Insight into one type of symbol–real-world relation helps preschoolers understand others.

■ According to Piaget, preschoolers are not yet capable of **operations** because they are **egocentric**—focused on their own viewpoint and unable to distinguish it from others' perspectives. Because egocentrism

prevents children from accommodating, it contributes to **animistic thinking, centration,** a focus on superficial perceptual appearances, and irreversibility. As a result, preschoolers fail **conservation** and **hierarchical classification** (class inclusion) tasks.

*Discuss research on preoperational thought and its implications for the accuracy of Piaget's preoperational stage.*

■ When children are given simplified problems relevant to their everyday lives, their performance appears more mature than Piaget assumed. They recognize differing perspectives, distinguish animate from inanimate objects, and reason by analogy about physical transformations. Furthermore, their language reflects accurate causal reasoning and hierarchical classification, and they form many categories based on nonobvious features. However, not until age 6 or 7 do children do well on appearance–reality problems, which require a challenging form of dual representation.

■ These findings indicate that rather than being absent, logical thinking develops gradually over the preschool years. This poses yet another challenge to Piaget's stage concept.

## THE CONCRETE OPERATIONAL STAGE (7 TO 11 YEARS)

*What are the major characteristics of the concrete operational stage?*

■ During the **concrete operational stage,** thought is far more logical and organized than it was during the preschool years. The ability to conserve indicates that children can decentre and reverse their thinking. In addition, they are better at hierarchical classification and **seriation,** including **transitive inference.**

■ School-age children have an improved understanding of distance and can give clear directions. **Cognitive maps** become more organized and accurate during middle childhood.

■ Concrete operational thought is limited in that children can reason logically only about concrete information they can perceive directly; they have difficulty with abstractions. Piaget used the term **horizontal décalage** to describe the school-age child's gradual mastery of logical concepts, such as conservation.

*Discuss research on concrete operational thought and its implications for the accuracy of Piaget's concrete operational stage.*

■ Recent evidence indicates that cultural practices and schooling have a profound effect on Piagetian task performance. Concrete operations may not emerge universally in middle childhood, and they seem to be greatly affected by training, context, and cultural conditions.

## THE FORMAL OPERATIONAL STAGE (11 YEARS AND OLDER)

*Describe major characteristics of the formal operational stage and the consequences of abstract reasoning powers for thinking about the relation between self and other.*

■ In Piaget's **formal operational stage,** abstract thinking appears. Adolescents engage in **hypothetico-deductive reasoning.** When faced with a problem, they think of all possibilities, including ones that are not obvious, and test them systematically against reality. **Propositional thought** also develops. Young people can evaluate the logic of verbal statements without considering them against real-world circumstances.

■ Early in this stage, two distorted images of the relation between self and other appear: the **imaginary audience** and the **personal fable.** Research suggests that these visions of the self result from advances in perspective taking rather than a return to egocentrism.

*Discuss recent research on formal operational thought and its implications for the accuracy of Piaget's formal operational stage.*

■ Recent evidence reveals that school-age children display the beginnings of abstraction, but they are not as competent as adolescents and adults. School-age children

cannot sort out evidence that bears on three or more variables at once. Also, they do not grasp the **logical necessity** of propositional reasoning. And because they do not think carefully about the major premise, they violate the most basic rules of logic.

■ Many university students think abstractly only in situations in which they have had extensive experience, and formal operational tasks are not mastered in many tribal and village societies. These findings indicate that Piaget's highest stage is reached gradually and is affected by specific learning opportunities.

## PIAGET AND EDUCATION

*Describe educational implications of Piaget's theory.*

■ Piaget's theory has had a major impact on educational programs for young children. A Piagetian classroom promotes discovery learning, sensitivity to children's readiness to learn, and acceptance of individual differences.

## OVERALL EVALUATION OF PIAGET'S THEORY

*Summarize contributions and shortcomings of Piaget's theory.*

■ Piaget awakened psychologists and educators to children's active contributions to their own development and inspired the contemporary focus on mechanisms of cognitive change. His stages offer a useful "roadmap" of cognitive development that is accurate in many respects.

■ At the same time, Piaget's notions of adaptation, organization, and equilibration offer only a vague account of how children's cognition develops. Also, children's cognitive attainments are less coherent and more gradual than Piaget's stages indicate.

■ Consequently, some researchers reject Piaget's stages but retain his view of cognitive development as an active, constructive process. Others support a less tightly knit

stage concept. Still others deny both Piaget's stages and his belief that the human mind is made up of general reasoning abilities.

## THE CORE KNOWLEDGE PERSPECTIVE

*Explain the core knowledge perspective on cognitive development, noting research that supports its assumptions.*

■ According to the **core knowledge perspective,** infants begin life with innate, core domains of thought that support early, rapid cognitive development. Each core domain has a long evolutionary history, is essential for survival, and develops independently, resulting in uneven, domain-specific changes. Some violation-of-expectation research suggests that young infants have impressive physical and numerical knowledge. Overall, however, findings on early, ready-made knowledge are mixed.

■ The **theory theory** regards children as naive theorists who draw on innate concepts to explain their everyday experiences, often in remarkably advanced ways. Then children test their naive theory against experience, revising it when it cannot adequately account for new information. In support of this view, children reason about everyday events in ways consistent with the event's core domain. Physical and psychological explanations emerge before biological explanations. Because biological processes are more difficult to understand, young children often use psychological concepts to theorize about biological events.

*Summarize the strengths and limitations of the core knowledge perspective.*

■ Core knowledge researchers have enriched our understanding of children's thinking by testing intriguing ideas about why certain cognitive skills emerge early and develop rapidly. However, critics believe that results of violation-of-expectation studies are not strong enough to show that infants are endowed with knowledge. So far, the core knowledge perspective has not offered greater clarity than Piaget's theory on how cognition changes.

## VYGOTSKY'S SOCIOCULTURAL THEORY

*Explain Vygotsky's view of cognitive development, noting the importance of social experience and language.*

■ In Vygotsky's sociocultural theory, language development broadens preschoolers' participation in dialogues with more knowledgeable individuals, who encourage them to master culturally important tasks. These social experiences transform basic mental capacities into uniquely human, higher cognitive processes. According to Vygotsky, as experts assist children in mastering tasks within their **zone of proximal development,** children integrate the language of these dialogues into their **private speech** and use it to organize their independent efforts. As children get older and find tasks easier, they internalize private speech as silent, inner speech, which they call on for self-guidance and self-direction.

*Describe features of social interaction that promote transfer of culturally adaptive ways of thinking to children, and discuss Vygotsky's view of the role of make-believe play in development.*

■ **Intersubjectivity,** which creates a common ground for communication, and **scaffolding,** involving adult assistance that adjusts to the child's current level of performance, promote cognitive development. The term **guided participation** recognizes cultural and situational variations in the way adults support children's efforts.

■ According to Vygotsky, make-believe play is a unique, broadly influential zone of proximal development. As children create imaginary situations and follow the rules of the make-believe scene, they learn to act in accord with internal ideas rather than on impulse. In Vygotsky's theory, make-believe play, like other higher cognitive processes, is the product of social collaboration.

## VYGOTSKY AND EDUCATION

*Describe educational implications of Vygotsky's theory.*

■ A Vygotskian classroom emphasizes assisted discovery through teachers' guidance and peer collaboration. When formal schooling begins, literacy activities prompt children to shift to a higher level of cognitive activity, in which they proficiently manipulate and control the symbol systems of their culture. Educational practices inspired by Vygotsky's theory include **reciprocal teaching** and **cooperative learning,** in which peers resolve differences of opinion and work toward common goals. Western children usually require extensive training in how to work together for cooperative learning to succeed.

## EVALUATION OF VYGOTSKY'S THEORY

*Cite strengths and limitations of Vygotsky's theory.*

■ Vygotsky's theory helps us understand wide cultural variation in cognitive skills and underscores the vital role of teaching in cognitive development. However, verbal dialogues are not the only means, or even the most important means, through which children learn in some cultures. Furthermore, in focusing on social and cultural influences, Vygotsky said little about biological contributions to children's cognition. It is unclear just how children internalize social experiences to advance their thinking. A broader theory might exist today had Piaget and Vygotsky had the chance to meet and weave together their extraordinary contributions.

# important terms and concepts

A-not-B search error (p. 222)
accommodation (p. 219)
adaptation (p. 219)
analogical problem solving (p. 226)
animistic thinking (p. 235)
assimilation (p. 219)
centration (p. 235)
circular reaction (p. 220)
cognitive maps (p. 242)
concrete operational stage (p. 241)
conservation (p. 235)
constructivist approach (p. 218)
cooperative learning (p. 262)
core knowledge perspective (p. 251)
deferred imitation (p. 222)
dual representation (p. 232)

egocentrism (p. 235)
equilibration (p. 220)
formal operational stage (p. 245)
guided participation (p. 259)
hierarchical classification (p. 235)
horizontal décalage (p. 242)
hypothetico-deductive reasoning (p. 245)
imaginary audience (p. 247)
intentional, or goal-directed, behaviour (p. 221)
intersubjectivity (p. 258)
logical necessity (p. 247)
make-believe play (p. 222)
mental representation (p. 219)
object permanence (p. 222)
operations (p. 235)

organization (p. 220)
personal fable (p. 247)
preoperational stage (p. 229)
private speech (p. 256)
propositional thought (p. 246)
reciprocal teaching (p. 262)
reversibility (p. 235)
scaffolding (p. 258)
scheme (p. 219)
sensorimotor stage (p. 220)
seriation (p. 241)
sociodramatic play (p. 231)
theory theory (p. 254)
transitive inference (p. 241)
violation-of-expectation method (p. 222)
zone of proximal development (p. 258)

How does this spirited kite flyer attend to, remember, transform, store, retrieve, and use the complex information she encounters in her environment? Chapter 7 takes up these diverse aspects of information processing.

# seven

## Cognitive Development: An Information-Processing Perspective

ON FRIDAYS IN MR. SHARP'S grade 4 class, the children often played memory games. One day, Mr. Sharp explained, "I'll put 20 words on the board and leave them up for 1 minute. Let's see how many you can recall. 'Milk, foot, jug, soup, hand, plate, foot, cake, gloves, sock, head, bowl . . . ,'" Mr. Sharp wrote quickly. A few moments later he erased the words.

Victor's hand shot up. "I've got 'em!" he exclaimed, reciting the words perfectly.

"Let's find out how Victor did that," Mr. Sharp continued.

"I put all the food together, the kitchen stuff together, and the clothes together. Then I repeated the words in each group over and over," Victor explained.

Now consider a different scene—a researcher interviewing Kpelle farmers of Liberia about how they would sort 20 familiar objects to remember them (Glick, 1975). Adults in this nonliterate culture arranged the objects in pairs, by function. For example, they placed a knife with an orange and a hoe with a potato rather than putting all the tools in one pile and the food items in another. Puzzled that Kpelle adults failed to use the more effective memorizing techniques typical of Western school-age children (such as Victor), the researcher asked for an explanation. Many Kpelle replied that a wise person would learn the Kpelle way. In exasperation, the researcher blurted out, "How would a fool do it?" Right away, he got the kinds of object groupings he had first expected!

Rather than a unified theory of cognitive development, information processing is an approach followed by researchers who engage in thorough study of one or a few aspects of cognition. A central goal is uncovering *mechanisms of change*—finding out how children and adults operate on different kinds of information, detecting, transforming, storing, accessing, and modifying it further as it makes its way through the cognitive system.

This chapter provides an overview of the information-processing perspective. First, we review models of the human cognitive system that are major forces in child development research. Next, we turn to two basic processes that enter into all human thinking: attention and memory. We also consider how children's growing knowledge of the world and awareness of their own mental activities affect these processes.

As we examine these topics, we will return to a familiar theme: the role of task demands and cultural contexts in children's thinking. A comparison of Victor's memorizing techniques with those of the Kpelle suggests that culture can greatly influence information processing. In this chapter, we pay special attention to how schooling, with its emphasis on literacy, mathematics, scientific reasoning, and retention of discrete pieces of information, channels cognitive development in culturally specific ways. Although information-processing theorists are especially interested in internal, self-generated cognitive changes, they also want to find out how external influences—design of learning environments and tasks, teaching techniques, and cultural values and practices—affect children's thinking. Our discussion concludes with an evaluation of information processing as a framework for understanding cognitive development.

## The Information-Processing Approach

MOST INFORMATION-PROCESSING theorists view the mind as a complex symbol-manipulating system through which information flows, much like a computer. Information from the environment is *encoded,* or taken in by the system and retained in symbolic form. Then a variety of internal processes operate on it, *recoding* it, or revising its symbolic structure into a more effective representation, and then *decoding* it, or interpreting its meaning by comparing and combining it with other information in the system. When these cognitive operations are complete, individuals use the information to make sense of their experiences and to solve problems.

Notice how the computer analogy of human mental functioning offers clarity and precision. Using computerlike diagrams and flowcharts, researchers can map the exact series of steps children and adults go through when faced with a task or problem. Some do so in such detail that the same mental operations can be programmed into a computer. Then the researcher conducts *simulations* to see if the computer responds as children and adults do on certain tasks. Other investigators intensively study children's and adults' thinking by tracking eye movements, analyzing error patterns, and examining self-reports of mental activity. But all share a strong commitment to explicit models of cognitive functioning and thorough testing of each component.

## General Models of Information Processing

MOST INFORMATION-PROCESSING researchers adopt—either directly or indirectly—a computerlike view of the cognitive system that emerged in the late 1960s and early 1970s called the *store model,* which focuses on general units of cognitive functioning, such as sensation and memory. Another influential model, *connectionism,* depicts the mental system at its most basic level: the interconnected workings of neurons in the brain (Klahr & MacWhinney, 1998).

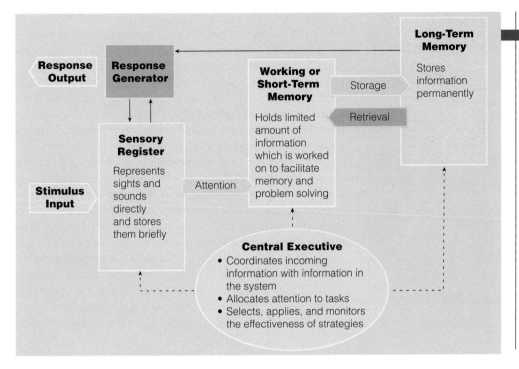

FIGURE 7.1

**Store model of the human information-processing system.** Information flows through three parts of the mental system: the *sensory register; working,* or *short-term, memory;* and *long-term memory.* In each, mental strategies can be used to manipulate information, increasing the efficiency of thinking and the chances that information will be retained. Strategies also permit us to think flexibly, adapting information to changing circumstances. The *central executive* is the conscious, reflective part of working memory. It coordinates incoming information already in the system, allocates attention to cognitive tasks, and oversees the use of strategies.

### THE STORE MODEL

The **store model** of the information-processing system assumes that we hold, or store, information in three parts of the mental system for processing: the *sensory register; working,* or *short-term, memory;* and *long-term memory* (see Figure 7.1). Each is limited in the *speed* with which it can process information. In addition, the sensory register and working memory are limited in *capacity.* They can hold onto only a certain amount of information for a brief time until it fades entirely.

As information flows through each store, we can operate on and transform it using **mental strategies,** as Victor and the Kpelle did in the opening story, increasing the efficiency of thinking and the chances that we will retain the information for later use. These strategies also permit us to think flexibly, adapting information to changing circumstances. To understand this more clearly, let's look at each component of the mental system.

**COMPONENTS OF THE STORE MODEL.** First, information enters the **sensory register.** Here, sights and sounds are represented directly and stored briefly. Look around you, and then close your eyes. An image of what you saw persists for a few seconds, but then it *decays* or disappears, unless you use mental strategies to preserve it. For example, you can *attend to* some information more carefully than others, increasing the chances that it will transfer to the next step of the information-processing system.

The second part of the mind is **working,** or **short-term, memory,** where we actively "work" on a limited amount of information, applying mental strategies. For example, if you are studying this book effectively, you are taking notes, repeating information to yourself, or grouping pieces of information together. Think, for a moment, about why you apply strategies to retain information in working memory. The sensory register, although limited, can take in a wide panorama of information. But when input reaches working memory, a bottleneck occurs; the capacity of working memory is more restricted. By meaningfully connecting pieces of information into a single representation, we reduce the number of pieces we must attend to, thereby making room for more. Also, the more thoroughly we learn information, the more *automatically* we use it. Automatic cognitive processing expands working memory by permitting us to focus on other information simultaneously.

**store model**
A model of mental functioning that views information as being held in three parts of the mental system for processing: the sensory register; working, or short-term, memory; and long-term memory.

**mental strategies**
Learned procedures that operate on and transform information, thereby increasing the efficiency and flexibility of thinking and the chances that information will be retained.

**sensory register**
The first part of the mental system, where sights and sounds are represented directly but held only briefly.

**working,** or **short-term, memory**
The conscious part of the mental system, where we actively "work" on a limited amount of information to ensure that it will be retained.

In reading a complex passage, this third grader seems to be applying her central executive—a special part of working memory that coordinates incoming information with information already in the system, allocates attention, and oversees the use of strategies.

To manage its complex activities, a special part of working memory—called the **central executive**—directs the flow of information. It coordinates incoming information with information already in the system; allocates attention to cognitive tasks; and selects, applies, and monitors the effectiveness of strategies (Baddeley, 1993, 2000). The central executive is the conscious, reflective part of our mental system. As we will see later, it is sometimes referred to as *metacognition,* which means awareness and understanding of thought.

The longer we hold information in working memory, the greater the likelihood that it will transfer to the third, and largest, storage area—**long-term memory,** our permanent knowledge base, which is limitless. In fact, we store so much in long-term memory that we sometimes have problems with *retrieval,* or getting information back from the system. To aid retrieval, we apply strategies, just as we do in working memory. Information in long-term memory is *categorized* according to a master plan based on contents, much like a library shelving system. As a result, we can retrieve it easily by following the same network of associations used to store it in the first place.

**IMPLICATIONS FOR DEVELOPMENT.** When applied to development, the store model suggests that two broad aspects of the cognitive system increase with age: (1) the *basic capacity* of its stores, especially working memory; and (2) the extent and effectiveness of *strategy use* (Guttentag, 1997). Research we will consider throughout this chapter indicates that with age, children gradually acquire more effective strategies for retaining information. Does basic capacity—the amount of information that can be held in mind *without* applying strategies—also expand?

In a study aimed at answering this question, researchers presented first and fourth graders and adults with successive lists of spoken digits to remember. Such lists are often used to assess **memory span**—the longest sequence of items a person can recall, a measure of working-memory capacity. On one set of lists (the *attended-to lists*), no distracters were introduced to prevent participants from using strategies; they listened and, when cued by a display on a computer screen, typed as many digits as they could remember, in the order they had heard them. On another set of lists (the *unattended-to lists*), participants played a picture-matching game on the computer while they listened, which by distracting them prevented them from using strategies. Then, when cued by the computer, they typed in as many digits as they remembered from the last-presented list. As Figure 7.2 shows, memory span increased with age on both sets of lists (Cowan et al., 1999). These findings indicate that development involves expansion of basic working-memory capacity and that more effective strategy use enhances working memory even more.

Research on speed of information processing also supports an age-related gain in basic capacity. Robert Kail (1991, 1993, 1997) gave 7- to 22-year-olds a variety of cognitive tasks in which they had to respond as quickly as possible. For example, in a visual search task, participants were shown a single digit and asked to signal if it was among a set of digits that appeared on a screen. And in a mental addition task, participants were presented with addition problems and answers, and they had to indicate whether the solutions were correct. Findings indicated that processing time decreased with age on all tasks. But even more important, rate of change—a fairly rapid decline in processing time that trailed off around age 12—was the same across many activities (see Figure 7.3). This pattern was also evident when participants performed perceptual–motor tasks, such

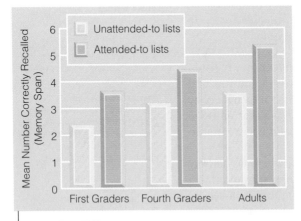

**FIGURE** 7.2

**Digits recalled from attended-to lists and unattended-to lists by first and fourth graders and adults.** Memory span increased with age under both conditions, indicating that development involves expansion of basic capacity (unattended-to list performance) and more effective strategy use (attended-to list performance). (Adapted from Cowan et al., 1999.)

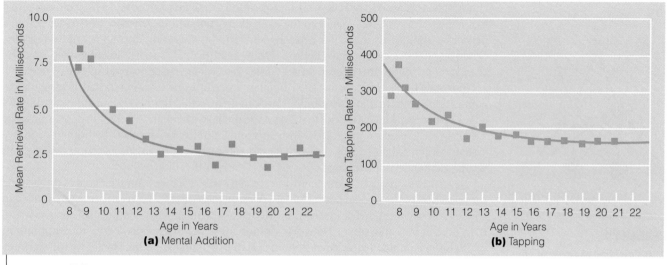

**FIGURE** 7.3

**Decline in processing time from childhood to adolescence, illustrated for mental addition (a) and tapping (b).** The rate of change is the same across many tasks—even perceptual–motor activities, such as tapping as fast as possible, that do not rely on mental strategies. This common trend implies an age-related gain in basic processing capacity. (Part (a) from R. Kail, 1988, "Developmental Functions for Speeds of Cognitive Processes," *Journal of Experimental Child Psychology, 45,* p. 361. Copyright © 1988 by Academic Press. Reprinted by permission of the publisher and author. Part (b) from R. Kail, 1991, "Processing Time Declines Exponentially During Childhood and Adolescence," *Developmental Psychology, 27,* p. 265. Copyright © 1991 by the American Psychological Association. Adapted by permission of the publisher and author.)

as releasing a button or tapping as fast as possible—activities that do not rely on strategies (Kail, 1991).

The changes in processing speed shown in Figure 7.3 have been found in Canada, Korea, and the United States (Fry & Hale, 1996; Kail & Park, 1992). Similarity in development across a diverse array of tasks in several cultures implies increased capacity, perhaps due to myelinization or synaptic pruning in the brain (see Chapter 5) (Kail & Salthouse, 1994; Miller & Vernon, 1997). As a result, older children and adults can hold more information in their cognitive systems at once, scan it more quickly, and generate faster responses in a wide range of situations.

### CONNECTIONISM

**Connectionist,** or **artificial neural network, models** focus on the most basic information-processing units and their connections, using computer simulations to imitate the workings of neurons in the brain. An artificial neural network consists of thousands of simple processing units organized into layers, much like the brain's neurological structure. A typical network includes an *input layer,* which encodes the task; one or more *hidden layers,* which represent information to perform the task; and an *output layer,* which generates a response (see Figure 7.4 on page 274). Like neurons, units send signals when the stimulation they receive from other units reaches a certain strength. Because information is distributed throughout the system—over all the units, acting in parallel (simultaneously)—artificial neural networks are sometimes called *parallel distributed processing systems.*

The connections between units are programmed to change with experience, which grants the network an impressive capacity to learn. After being given a task, the network receives feedback about the accuracy of its responses. If a response is correct, the connections that produced it strengthen; if a response is incorrect, the connections weaken. Researchers compare the network's responses with those of people, including children of different ages. If the two are alike, the researchers conclude that the network is a good model of human learning.

Connectionists, such as Tom Shultz of McGill University, have succeeded in depicting changes in children's performance on a variety of tasks. These include object permanence, early vocabulary growth, mastery of certain grammatical forms, formation of certain concepts, and problem solving

**central executive**
The part of working memory that directs the flow of information by coordinating information coming from the environment with information already in the system, allocating attention to cognitive tasks, and selecting, applying, and monitoring the effectiveness of strategies.

**long-term memory**
The part of the mental system that contains our permanent knowledge base.

**memory span**
The longest sequence of items a person can recall, a measure of working-memory capacity.

**connectionist,** or **artificial neural network, models**
Models of mental functioning that focus on the most basic information-processing units and their connections, using computer simulations to imitate the workings of neurons in the brain. If the network's responses resemble those of people, then researchers conclude that it is a good model of human learning.

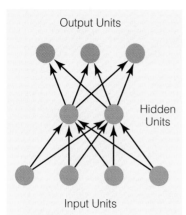

Output Units

Hidden Units

Input Units

FIGURE 7.4

**A simplified example of an artificial neural network.**
Processing units are organized into layers, much like the brain's neurological structure. Stimulation turns on *input units,* which encode the task. *Hidden units* represent information, and *output units* generate a response. Researchers program connections between units to change with experience, granting the network the capacity to learn. Connections that lead to correct responses strengthen; those that lead to incorrect responses weaken.

(Buckingham & Shultz, 2000; Jones, Ritter, & Wood, 2000; Plunkett et al., 1997). Findings reveal that a great deal of inner change in the strength of connections generally takes place before a network—and therefore a child behaving similarly—consistently displays a correct response (Plunkett, 1998). Consequently, networks show that gradual, internal learning often precedes changes in behaviour that appear abrupt, or stagelike, when viewed from outside the system.

In connectionist models, just a few built-in procedures get learning started. Consequently, connectionists claim that their findings present a powerful argument against the core knowledge perspective, which assumes that infants begin life with innate, special-purpose knowledge systems (see Chapter 6, page 253). Instead, connectionists believe that the human cognitive system is a general processing device that gradually attains domain-specific competencies as it is exposed to relevant learning opportunities (Karmiloff-Smith, 1999).

Nevertheless, artificial neural networks remain some distance from their goal of duplicating the operation of the human brain. Perhaps because their internal representations are limited to connection strengths, networks learn slowly, usually requiring many more exposures to a task than do children and adults. Networks do not construct plans, hypotheses, or propositions, which foster complex, highly efficient human learning (Plunkett, 1998). Finally, we will see when we address a developmental theory, strategy choice, that children are great experimenters. To arrive at the most efficient means of solving a problem, they change their strategies not just after they make errors (as artificial neural networks do) but even after they succeed!

Still, connectionist models remind us that a full understanding of cognitive development must take into account the operation of its most basic units. Currently, connectionists are trying to devise more realistic models of brain functioning and the contexts in which children learn (Elman et al., 1996).

# Developmental Theories of Information Processing

ALTHOUGH STORE AND connectionist models have implications for development, neither was devised to explain how children's thinking changes with age. However, several *developmental* approaches have attracted widespread attention. We will take up two of these views. The first is Case's *neo-Piagetian perspective.* To create an overall vision of development, this approach uses Piaget's theory as a starting point, reinterpreting it within an information-processing framework. The second approach is Siegler's *model of strategy choice,* which draws on evolutionary concepts of variation and selection to explain the diversity and ever-changing nature of children's cognition.

###  CASE'S NEO-PIAGETIAN THEORY

Robbie Case's (1992, 1998) **neo-Piagetian theory** accepts Piaget's stages but views change within each, as well as movement from one stage to the next, as due to increases in information-processing capacity. Each major stage involves a distinct type of cognitive structure—in infancy, sensory input and physical actions; in early childhood, internal representations of events and actions; in middle childhood, simple transformations of representations; and in adolescence, complex transformations of representations. As children become more efficient cognitive processors, the amount of information they can hold and combine in working memory expands, making this sequence possible.

Three factors are responsible for gains in working-memory capacity:

- *Brain development.* Recall our discussion of brain growth spurts in Chapter 5—changes in EEG activity of the cerebral cortex that coincide with major gains in cognitive competence (see page 185). According to Case, synaptic growth, synaptic pruning, and myelinization, which underlie these growth spurts, improve the efficiency of thought, leading to readiness for each stage. In this way, biology imposes a system-wide ceiling on cognitive development. At any given time, the child cannot exceed a certain upper limit of processing capacity.

**neo-Piagetian theory**
A theory that reinterprets Piaget's stages within an information-processing framework.

■ *Practice with schemes and automatization.* In Case's theory, Piagetian schemes are the child's mental strategies. As the child repeatedly uses schemes, they become more automatic. This frees working memory for combining existing schemes and generating new ones. Notice how these mechanisms of change offer a clarified view of Piaget's concepts of assimilation and accommodation. *Practising schemes* (assimilation) leads to *automatization,* which *releases working memory* for other activities, permitting *scheme combination and construction* (accommodation).

■ *Formation of central conceptual structures.* Once the schemes of a Piagetian stage become sufficiently automatic, enough working-memory capacity is available to consolidate them into an improved representational form. As a result, children acquire **central conceptual structures,** networks of concepts and relations that permit them to think about a wide range of situations in more advanced ways. Consequently, processing capacity expands further (Case, 1996, 1998). When children form new central conceptual structures, they move to the next stage of development.

Case's neo-Piagetian theory explains children's mastery of conservation in information-processing terms. As these children pour water from one container to another, their understanding of what happens to the height and width of the liquid becomes better coordinated, and conservation of liquid is achieved. Once this logical idea becomes automatic, enough working-memory capacity is available to form a central conceptual structure—a general representation of conservation that can be applied to a wide range of situations.

Let's take a familiar set of tasks—conservation—to illustrate Case's ideas. Imagine a 5-year-old who cannot yet conserve liquid but who has some isolated schemes, such as (1) after water is poured from a tall into a short glass, the height of the water level is reduced; and (2) after water is poured from a thin into a wide glass, the width of the water increases. As the child gains experience transferring liquids from one container to another, these schemes become automatic, and she combines them into a conserving response, recognizing that the amount of water remains the same despite the shape of the container. A similar sequence occurs in other conservation situations, such as length, mass, and weight. Eventually the child coordinates several task-specific conserving responses into a new, broadly applicable principle—a central conceptual structure. When this happens, cognition moves from simple to complex transformations of representations, or from concrete to formal operational thought.

Case and his colleagues have applied his theory to many tasks, including solving arithmetic word problems, understanding stories, drawing pictures, sight-reading music, handling money, and interpreting social situations (Case, 1992, 1998; Case & Okamoto, 1996). In each, preschoolers' central conceptual structures focus on one dimension. In understanding stories, for example, they grasp only a single story line. By the early school years, central conceptual structures coordinate two dimensions. Children combine two story lines into a single plot. Around 9 to 11 years, central conceptual structures integrate multiple dimensions. Children tell coherent stories with a main plot and several subplots. Figure 7.5 on page 276 shows similar changes in children's drawings.

Case's theory offers an information-processing account of the horizontal décalage—that many understandings appear in specific situations at different times rather than being mastered all at once. First, different forms of the same logical insight, such as conservation of liquid and weight, may vary in the processing demands they make of the child. As a result, each successive task requires more working-memory capacity for mastery. Second, children's task-specific experiences vary widely. A child who often listens to and tells stories but rarely draws pictures would display more advanced central conceptual structures in the story domain than in the drawing domain.

Compared with Piaget, Case acknowledges greater domain-specific change, attributing it to the complexity of tasks and children's experiences. Consequently, Case's theory is better able to account for unevenness in cognitive development. Although it must be tested with many more tasks, Case's theory is unique in offering an integrated picture of how basic capacity, practice with strategies, and children's constructive efforts to reorganize their thinking interact to produce development. Unfortunately, Robbie Case died suddenly in May 2000, leaving his work unfinished. At the time, he was the director of the Institute of Child Study at the University of Toronto.

**central conceptual structures**
In Case's neo-Piagetian theory, networks of concepts and relations that permit children to think about a wide range of situations in more advanced ways. Formation of new central conceptual structures marks the transition to a new Piagetian stage.

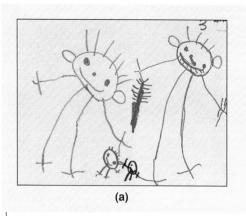
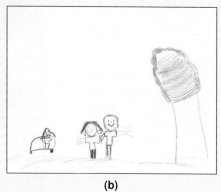

(a)          (b)          (c)

**FIGURE** 7.5

**Development of central conceptual structures in Case's neo-Piagetian theory.** Case identified the same general sequence in children's per-formance on many tasks. Here, it is shown for drawings. Children were asked to "draw a picture of a mother and a father holding hands in a park, with their little baby on the grass in front of them, and a tree far off behind." (a) Preschoolers focused on one dimension. They depicted objects sep-arately, ignoring their spatial arrangement. (b) During the early school years, children coordinated two dimensions. Their drawings showed both the features of objects and their relationship to one another. (c) Nine- to 11-year-olds integrated multiple dimensions. They used perspective to repre-sent several points of reference, such as near, midway, and far. (From R. Case & Y. Okamoto, 1996, "The Role of Central Conceptual Structures in the Development of Children's Thought," *Monographs of the Society for Research in Child Development, 61*[246, 1–2], p. 106. © The Society for Research in Child Development, Inc. Adapted by permission. Courtesy of Robbie Case.)

### SIEGLER'S MODEL OF STRATEGY CHOICE

Robert Siegler's (1996) **model of strategy choice** is one of several current efforts to apply an evolutionary perspective to children's cognition. When given challenging problems, children generate a *variety* of strategies for solving them. With experience, some strategies are *selected;* they become more frequent and "survive." Others become less frequent and "die off." As with physical characteristics, *variation* and *selection* characterize children's mental strategies, yielding adaptive problem-solving techniques.

To study children's strategy use, Siegler used the microgenetic research design (see Chapter 2, page 61), presenting children with many problems over an extended time. He found that children experiment with diverse strategies on many types of problems, includ-ing conservation, memory for lists of items, reading first words, telling time, spelling, basic math facts, and even tic-tac-toe (Siegler, 1996). Let's illustrate with 5-year-olds' learning of basic addition. When given a problem like 2 + 4, children use the following strategies: guess, without applying a strategy; count from 1 on their fingers (1, 2, 3, 4, 5, 6); hold up 4 fingers on one hand, 2 on the other, and recognize 6 as the total; start with the lower digit, 2, and "count on" (2, 3, 4, 5, 6); start with the higher digit, 4, and "count on" (4, 5, 6), a strategy called *min* because it minimizes the work involved; or automatically retrieve the answer from memory.

Siegler found that strategy use for basic math facts—and other types of problems—fol-lows an *overlapping-waves pattern* (see Figure 7.6). Even 2-year-olds solving simple problems, such as how to use a tool to obtain an out-of-reach toy, display it (Chen & Siegler, 2000). While trying strategies, children observe which work best, which work less well, and which are ineffective. Gradually they select strategies on the basis of two adaptive criteria: *accuracy* and *speed*—in the case of basic addition, the *min* strategy. As children "home in" on more successful strategies, they learn more about the problems at hand. As a result, correct solu-tions become more strongly associated with problems, and children display the most efficient strategy—automatic retrieval of the answer.

How do children move from less to more efficient strategies? Often they discover a faster pro-cedure as a result of success with a more time-consuming technique. For example, children fre-quently count on fingers to solve addition problems. Eventually they recognize the number of fingers held up without counting. Soon after, they move to the *min* strategy (Siegler &

**model of strategy choice**
Siegler's evolutionary theory of cognitive development, which states that variation and selec-tion characterize children's men-tal strategies, yielding adaptive problem-solving techniques and an overlapping-waves pattern of cognitive development.

Jenkins, 1989). Also, certain problems dramatize the need for a better strategy. Children who have used *min* at least once recognize its usefulness on problems like 22 + 3, where counting is tedious. Reasoning about number concepts also helps (Canobi, Reeve, & Pattison, 1998). First graders more often use *min* after they realize that regardless of the order in which two sets are combined, they yield the same results (2 + 4 = 6 and 4 + 2 = 6). Finally, when children are taught an effective strategy, they usually adopt it and abandon less successful techniques (Alibali, 1999).

Even when they are aware of a more adaptive strategy, children may not take advantage of it. As we will see in later sections, using a new strategy requires considerable effort, taxing the capacity of working memory. Furthermore, children resist giving up a well-established strategy for a new one, perhaps because gains in speed of thinking are small at first. Clearly, strategy development is gradual on many types of tasks.

Siegler's model reveals that no child thinks in just one way, even on the same task. A child given the same problem on two occasions often uses different approaches. Even on a single item, children may generate varying procedures, as indicated by occasions in which their words and gestures differ (see the From Research to Practice box on page 278 to find out about the significance of these mismatches). Strategy variability is vital for devising new, more adaptive ways of thinking, which "evolve" through extensive experience solving problems.

At present, we more clearly understand the mechanisms that lead children to choose among strategies than we do those that produce strategy variation. Nevertheless, the model of strategy choice offers a powerful image of development that overcomes deficiencies of the stage approach in accounting for both diversity and constant change in children's thinking. In this view, each new way of thinking is seen "as a wave approaching a seashore, with several waves (ways of thinking) overlapping at any given time, with the height of each wave (frequency of use of the ways of thinking) continuously changing, with different waves being most prominent at different times, and with some waves never being the most prominent but still influencing other waves and contributing to the tide" (Siegler, 1996, pp. 237–238).

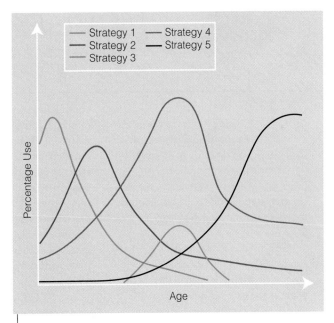

**FIGURE** 7.6

**Overlapping-waves pattern of strategy use.** When given challenging problems, children generate a variety of strategies, each represented by a wave. Several strategies may overlap at any given time. Use of each strategy, depicted by the height of the wave, is constantly changing. Gradually, the strategy that results in the most rapid, accurate solution wins out. (From *Emerging Minds: The Process of Change in Children's Thinking,* by Robert S. Siegler, copyright © 1996 by Oxford University Press, Inc. Used by permission of Oxford University Press, Inc.)

## ASK YOURSELF www

**review**    Summarize evidence indicating that both the basic capacity of the information-processing system and the effectiveness of strategy use increase with age.

**review**    What is a connectionist, or artificial neural network, model? Why do connectionists claim that children's development is continuous rather than stagelike? What evidence leads connectionists to view the information-processing system as a general processing device that attains domain-specific competence through relevant experiences?

**apply**    Five-year-old Kayla used several strategies when solving conservation-of-number problems involving rows of pennies. On the first one, she said, "The rows aren't the same." On the second one, she said, "The rows have the same number because you didn't add any." On the third one, she said, "I counted the pennies. The rows have the same number." Why is it beneficial for Kayla to experiment with strategies? Which strategy is she likely to select over time, and why?

**connect**    Explain how Case's neo-Piagetian theory offers a more precise account of mechanisms of cognitive development than does Piaget's theory.

# from research to practice

## SPEECH–GESTURE MISMATCHES: USING THE HAND TO READ THE MIND

© RICHARD T. NOWITZ/CORBIS

**m**r. Beal introduced his grade 4 class to the concept of equivalence—that the quantity on one side of an equal sign is the same as the quantity on the other side. Then he watched as several children stepped up to the blackboard to work the following problem:
5 + 3 + 4 = ___ + 4.

Carrie tried first. "I added 5 + 3 + 4 + 4 equals 16," she said, pointing at each number as she mentioned it, then at the blank as she gave her answer. Carrie's speech and gestures were consistent; both revealed an incorrect strategy.

Rachel went next. She gave the same incorrect explanation as Carrie did, but her gestures sent a different message. While she spoke, she pointed to each number on the left, next touched the equal sign, then moved to the 4 on the right, and finally rested her finger on the blank. Rachel showed a speech–gesture mismatch. Her hand movements suggested she knew more than she could say. Over the next few weeks, Rachel mastered equivalence problems more rapidly than did Carrie. How can we account for Rachel's faster progress?

According to Susan Goldin-Meadow and her colleagues, children who produce speech–gesture mismatches are in a transitional state. Their behaviour indicates that they are considering two contradictory strategies at once, a sign of readiness to learn. In a microgenetic study, the researchers identified two groups of children who did not have a full understanding of addition-based

equivalence problems: speech–gesture matched and speech–gesture mismatched. Then, as the children worked more problems, some in each group received feedback on the accuracy of their answers along with instruction that explained the equivalence principle, whereas others received no intervention. Finally, children's learning was assessed as they worked problems on their own (Alibali & Goldin-Meadow, 1993).

Speech–gesture mismatch children who received instruction were more likely than others to move out of that state to correct an answer, based on a speech–gesture match. They also more often generalized their new knowledge to multiplication-based equivalence problems ($5 \times 3 \times 4 = 5 \times$ ___). Interestingly, the few speech–gesture match children who improved with instruction generalized what they learned only if they first passed through a speech–gesture mismatch phase. Correct strategies first appeared in gesture, only later in speech.

Children on the verge of learning appear to have a variety of strategies accessible to gesture but not to speech (Church, 1999). Perhaps expressing a strategy in gesture that differs from one in speech facilitates awareness of conflicting ideas, encouraging the child to resolve the discrepancy in favour of the more effective strategy. Children in this state are particularly open to teaching, which seems to help them make explicit in speech what they already know implicitly in gesture.

As this fourth grader works a math problem at the blackboard, do his hand gestures suggest that he knows more than he can say? Speech–gesture mismatches indicate that children are considering two contradictory strategies and are highly receptive to teaching.

Goldin-Meadow's findings reveal that at times, gesture captures children's progress better than speech does. Although children are rarely aware of their hand movements, gestures may promote cognitive change in ways that do not require awareness. Perhaps speech–gesture mismatches indicate that the neural pathways of interest to connectionists are growing stronger and about to reach a critical juncture. Parents and teachers who are attuned to children's gestures can use that information to adjust their interaction, providing development-enhancing instruction at the most opportune moment (Goldin-Meadow, 2001).

# Attention

THE CENTRAL SECTIONS OF this chapter address a wealth of evidence on children's processing in the major parts of the cognitive system. In the following sections, we consider how children of different ages encode information, operate on it in working memory so it will transfer to long-term memory, and retrieve it so they can think and solve problems.

We begin with research on the development of attention. Attention is fundamental to human thinking, since it determines the information that will be considered in any task. Parents and teachers are quick to notice that young children spend only short times involved in tasks, have difficulty focusing on details, and are easily distracted. Attention improves greatly during early and middle childhood, becoming more selective, adaptable, and planful.

## SELECTIVITY AND ADAPTABILITY

During the first year, infants attend to novel and eye-catching events, orienting to them more quickly and tracking their movements more effectively (Richards & Holley, 1999). In the second year, toddlers become increasingly capable of intentional, or goal-directed, behaviour (see Chapter 6, page 221). Consequently, attraction to novelty declines (but does not disappear) and *sustained attention* improves, especially when children play with toys. When a toddler engages in goal-directed behaviour even in a limited way, such as stacking blocks or putting them in a container, attention must be maintained to reach the goal. As goals become more complex, so does the duration of attention (Ruff & Lawson, 1990).

As sustained attention increases, children become better at deliberately focusing on just those aspects of a situation that are relevant to their goals, ignoring other information. One approach to studying this increasing selectivity of attention requires children to respond selectively to certain information in a stream of largely irrelevant information. For example, researchers might present a stream of numbers on a computer screen and ask children to press a button whenever a particular sequence of two digits ("1" and then "9") appears. Findings with this task, and others, show that selective attention improves sharply between 6 and 9 years of age (Aslin & Smith, 1988; Lin, Hsiao, & Chen, 1999; Smith et al., 1998).

Older children are also more adaptable, flexibly adjusting their attention to task requirements. For example, in judging whether pairs of stimuli are the same or different, sixth graders (but not second graders) quickly shift their basis of judgment (from size to shape to colour) when asked to do so (Pick & Frankel, 1974). Furthermore, with age, children adapt their attention to changes in their own learning. When given lists of items to learn and allowed to select half for further study, first graders do not choose systematically. But by grade 3, children select those they had previously missed (Masur, McIntyre, & Flavell, 1973). In studying more complex information, such as prose passages, the ability to allocate attention based on previous performance continues to improve into the university years (Brown, Smiley, & Lawton, 1978).

How do children acquire and perfect strategies that focus on relevant information and adapt to task requirements? Gains in two factors—cognitive inhibition and attentional strategies—are important.

**COGNITIVE INHIBITION.** Selective attention depends on **cognitive inhibition**—the ability to control internal and external distracting stimuli. Individuals who are skilled at cognitive inhibition can prevent the mind from straying to alternative attractive thoughts. They can also keep stimuli that are unrelated to a current goal from capturing their attention (Dempster & Corkill, 1999). By ensuring that working memory will not be cluttered with irrelevant stimuli, cognitive inhibition fosters performance on a wide variety of tasks. Besides helping children remember, reason, and solve problems, it can assist them in controlling behaviour in social situations (Bjorklund & Harnishfeger, 1995; Dempster, 1995). In later chapters, we will see that to get along with others, children must learn to restrain impulses, keep negative emotions in check, and resist temptation.

The ability to inhibit thoughts and behaviour increases with age. Recall from Chapter 4 that very young infants have difficulty disengaging from a visual stimulus and redirecting their attention. And in Chapter 6, we saw that 8- to 12-month-old infants may make the A-not-B search error because they have difficulty inhibiting a previously rewarded response. Overcoming this error coincides with rapid development of the frontal lobes of the cerebral cortex at the end of the first year (see page 224).

Gains in cognitive inhibition are particularly marked from early to middle childhood; further improvements occur in adolescence. Researchers believe that the frontal lobes, among the last

The capacity to engage in complex play supports sustained attention, which increases during the preschool years. This 2-year-old is so focused on her phone call that she is oblivious to the noisy exchange between her child-care centre classmates, taking place in the background.

**cognitive inhibition**
The ability to control internal and external distracting stimuli, preventing them from capturing attention and cluttering working memory with irrelevant information.

brain regions to reach full maturity, are largely responsible. EEG recordings reveal that brain waves in the frontal lobes involved in evaluating stimuli and preparing responses become more pronounced from 5 to 12 years of age (Ridderinkhof & Molen, 1997). When the frontal lobes are damaged, children and adults find it very hard to ignore irrelevant information (Dempster, 1995).

In sum, by clearing unnecessary stimuli from working memory, cognitive inhibition enhances processing capacity. As we will see next, greater capacity opens the door to effective strategy use, which increases capacity further.

**EFFECTIVENESS OF ATTENTIONAL STRATEGIES.** Patricia Miller and her colleagues found that development of a selective attentional strategy follows a predictable sequence. They showed 3- to 9-year-olds a large box with rows of doors that could be opened. Half the doors had pictures of cages on them, indicating that behind each was an animal. The other half had pictures of houses, indicating that they contained household objects. Children were told to remember the location of each object in one group and that, during a study period, they could open any doors they wished. Memory was tested by showing children pictures of each relevant object, one at a time, and asking them to point to where that object was located (DeMarie-Dreblow & Miller, 1988; Miller et al., 1986; Woody-Ramsey & Miller, 1988). Notice that the most efficient attentional strategy is to open only doors with relevant pictures on them. The researchers recorded which doors children opened and found that the emergence and refinement of this strategy tended to occur in the following four phases:

1. **Production deficiency.** Preschoolers fail to use a strategy in situations in which it could be helpful. On the task just described, the youngest children simply opened all the doors, regardless of the pictures on them.

2. **Control deficiency.** Early elementary school children sometimes produce a helpful strategy, but not consistently. They fail to *control*, or execute, strategies effectively. For example, 5-year-olds began to apply a selective attentional strategy, opening only relevant doors. But they did not always use it; at times, they reverted to opening irrelevant doors.

3. **Utilization deficiency.** Slightly later, children apply a strategy consistently, but their performance improves little or not at all. For many 6- and 7-year-olds, opening just the relevant doors did not lead to improved memory for locations of objects after the pictures were removed from the doors.

4. **Effective strategy use.** Finally, children use a strategy consistently, and performance improves.

The phases just described apply to strategies on many types of tasks (Miller, 2000). For example, we will encounter this trend again when we take up memory. Recall from our discussion of Siegler's model of strategy choice that initially, applying a strategy takes so much of children's attentional resources that they do not have enough to both execute the strategy and perform the task well (Miller et al., 1991; Miller, Woody-Ramsey, & Aloise, 1991). In support of this interpretation, reducing the demands of the task by having an adult perform the strategy for the child (by opening relevant doors) led to substantial gains in memory for object locations (DeMarie-Dreblow & Miller, 1988).

Yet another reason a new strategy may not lead to performance gains is that young children are not good at monitoring their task performance (Schneider & Bjorklund, 1998). Because they fail to keep track of how well a strategy is working, they do not apply it consistently or refine it in other ways.

## PLANNING

With age, another change in children's attention is apparent: It becomes more planful. **Planning** involves thinking out a sequence of acts ahead of time and allocating attention accordingly to reach a goal (Scholnick, 1995). The seeds of effective planning are present in infancy. When researchers showed 2- and 3-month-olds a series of pictures that alternated in a predictable left–right sequence, they quickly learned to shift their focus to the location

**production deficiency**
The failure to produce a mental strategy when it could be helpful.

**control deficiency**
The failure to execute a mental strategy effectively.

**utilization deficiency**
Consistent use of a mental strategy, with little or no improvement in performance.

**effective strategy use**
Consistent use of a mental strategy that leads to improvement in performance.

**planning**
Thinking out a sequence of acts ahead of time and allocating attention accordingly to reach a goal.

of the next stimulus before it appeared—a response not apparent when picture locations were random (Wentworth & Haith, 1992, 1998). Even the attention of very young babies seems to be "future oriented," as indicated by their ability to anticipate routine events (Haith, 1997).

As long as tasks are familiar and not too complex, preschoolers sometimes generate and follow a plan. For example, by age 4, they search for a lost object in a play yard systematically, looking only in locations between where they last saw the object and where they discovered it missing (Wellman, Somerville, & Haake, 1979).

Nevertheless, planful attentional strategies have a long way to go. When school-age children are asked to compare detailed pictures, their scanning is more thorough (Vurpillot, 1968). And on complex tasks that require coordinating many acts, they make decisions about what to do first and what to do next in a more orderly fashion. In one study, 5- to 9-year-olds were given lists of items to obtain from a doll-sized grocery store. Older children took more time to scan the store before shopping. They also paused more often to look for each item before moving to get it (see Figure 7.7). Consequently, they followed shorter routes through the aisles (Gauvain & Rogoff, 1989; Szepkouski, Gauvain, & Carberry, 1994).

The development of planning illustrates how attention becomes coordinated with other cognitive processes. To solve problems involving multiple steps, children must postpone action in favour of weighing alternatives, organizing task materials (such as items on a grocery list), and remembering the steps of their plan so they can attend to each one in sequence. Along the way, they must monitor how well the plan is working and revise it if necessary. Clearly, planning places heavy demands on working-memory capacity. Not surprisingly, even when young children do plan, they often forget to implement important steps.

Children learn much about planning effectively by collaborating on tasks with more expert planners. With age, children take on more responsibility in these joint endeavours, such as organizing task materials and suggesting planning strategies. The demands of school tasks—and teachers' explanations for how to plan—also contribute to gains in planning. And parents can foster planning by encouraging it in everyday activities and routines, from completing homework assignments to loading dishes into the dishwasher. In a longitudinal study of family interactions at ages 4, 9, and 15, parent–child discussions involving planning predicted adolescents' initiations of planning interactions with other family members (Gauvain & Huard, 1999). Many opportunities to practise planning help children understand its components and increase the likelihood that they will use this knowledge to guide future activities.

The selective, adaptable, and planful attentional strategies we have just considered are crucial for success in school. Unfortunately, some school-age children have great difficulty paying attention. See the Biology & Environment box on page 282 for a discussion of the serious learning and behaviour problems of children with attention-deficit hyperactivity disorder.

**FIGURE** 7.7

**Play grocery store used to investigate children's planning.** Five- to 9-year-olds were given "shopping lists," consisting of five cards with a picture of a food item on each. Along the walls and on the shelves of the doll-sized store were pictures of food items that could be picked up by moving a figurine called the "shopper" down the aisles. Researchers recorded children's scanning of the store before starting on a shopping trip and along the way. The length of the route used to gather the items served as the measure of planning effectiveness. (Adapted from Szepkouski, Gauvain, & Carberry, 1994.)

## ASK YOURSELF www

**review**  What aspect of brain development supports gains in cognitive inhibition? How does cognitive inhibition increase processing capacity?

**review**  Cite advances in information processing that contribute to improved planning in middle childhood. What can adults do to promote children's planning skills?

**apply**  Seven-year-old Jonah played his piano pieces from beginning to end instead of granting extra practice to the hard sections. Around age 8, he devoted more time to sections he knew least well, but his performance did not improve for several months. What explains Jonah's gradual strategy development and improvement in performance?

# biology & environment

## CHILDREN WITH ATTENTION-DEFICIT HYPERACTIVITY DISORDER

While the other fifth graders worked quietly at their desks, Calvin squirmed in his seat, dropped his pencil, looked out the window, fiddled with his shoelaces, and talked out. "Hey Joey," he yelled over the top of several desks, "wanna play ball after school?"

Joey and the other children weren't eager to play with Calvin. Out on the playground, Calvin was a poor listener and failed to follow the rules of the game. When his team was up at bat, he had trouble taking turns. In the outfield, he tossed his mitt in the air and looked elsewhere when the ball came his way. Calvin's desk at school and his room at home were a chaotic mess. He often lost pencils, books, and other materials necessary for completing assignments. And very often, he had difficulty remembering his assignments and when they were due.

### SYMPTOMS OF ADHD

Calvin is one of 3 to 5 percent of school-age children with **attention-deficit hyperactivity disorder (ADHD)** (American Psychiatric Association, 1994; Canadian Psychological Associ-

ation, 2001). Boys are diagnosed three to nine times more often than girls. However, many girls with ADHD may be overlooked because their symptoms are usually not as flagrant (Gaub & Carlson, 1997).

Children with ADHD cannot stay focused on a task that requires mental effort for more than a few minutes. In addition, they often act impulsively, ignoring social rules and lashing out with hostility when frustrated. Many (but not all) are *hyperactive*. They charge through their days with excessive motor activity, exhausting parents and teachers and so irritating other children that they are quickly rejected by their classmates. For a child to be diagnosed with ADHD, these symptoms must have appeared before age 7 as an early and persistent problem. They must also be pervasive—evident in at least two settings—and have led to academic and social difficulties. According to one view that has amassed substantial research support, a common theme unifies ADHD symptoms: an impairment in inhibition, which makes it hard to delay action in favour of thought (Barkley, 1997, 1999).

The intelligence of ADHD children is normal, and they show no signs of serious emotional disturbance. Instead, because they have trouble thinking before they act, they do poorly on laboratory tasks requiring sustained attention and find it hard to ignore irrelevant information. Their distractibility results in forgetfulness and difficulties with planning, reasoning, and problem solving in academic and social situations (Barkley, 1997; Denckla, 1996). And Canadian research shows that although some children catch up in development, most continue to have problems concentrating and finding friends into adolescence and adulthood (Claude & Firestone, 1995).

### ORIGINS OF ADHD

Heredity plays a major role in ADHD, since the disorder runs in families, and identical twins share it more often than do fraternal twins. Also, an adopted child who is inattentive and hyperactive is likely to have a biological parent (but not an adoptive parent) with similar symptoms (Rhee et al., 1999; Sherman, Iacono, & McGue, 1997). Recent psychophysiological research,

**attention-deficit hyperactivity disorder**
A childhood disorder involving inattention, impulsivity, and excessive motor activity. Often leads to academic failure and social problems.

# Memory

AS ATTENTION IMPROVES, so do memory strategies, deliberate mental activities we use to increase the likelihood of holding information in working memory and transferring it to our long-term knowledge base. Although memory strategies emerge during the preschool years, at first they are not very successful. In middle childhood, these techniques take a giant leap forward (Schneider & Pressley, 1997).

## STRATEGIES FOR STORING INFORMATION

Researchers have studied the development of three strategies that enhance memory for new information: rehearsal, organization, and elaboration.

including EEG and fMRI studies, reveals that ADHD children have reduced electrical and blood-flow activity in the frontal lobes of the cerebral cortex and in other areas responsible for attention and inhibition of behaviour (Giedd et al., 2001; Rapport & Chung, 2000). Several genes that affect neurotransmitter and hormone levels have been implicated in the disorder (Biederman & Spencer, 2000; Faraone et al., 1999).

At the same time, ADHD is associated with a variety of environmental factors. These children are somewhat more likely to come from homes in which marriages are unhappy and family stress is high (Bernier & Siegel, 1994). But researchers agree that a stressful home life rarely causes ADHD. Instead, the behaviours of these children can contribute to family problems, which (in turn) are likely to intensify the child's pre-existing difficulties. Furthermore, prenatal teratogens (particularly those involving long-term exposure, such as illegal drugs, alcohol, and cigarettes) are linked to inattention and hyperactivity (Milberger et al., 1997).

## TREATING ADHD

Calvin's doctor eventually prescribed stimulant medication, the most common treatment for ADHD. As long as dosage is carefully regulated, stimulant drugs reduce activity level and improve attention, academic performance, and peer relations for 70 to 75 percent of children who take them (Greenhill, Halperin, & Abikoff, 1999). Stimulant medication seems to increase brain-wave activity in the frontal lobes, thereby improving the child's capacity to sustain attention and to inhibit off-task and self-stimulating behaviour.

Although stimulant medication is relatively safe, its impact is only short term. Drugs cannot teach children how to compensate for inattention and impulsivity. Combining medication with interventions that model and reinforce appropriate academic and social behaviour seems to be the most effective approach to treatment (Pelham, Wheeler, & Chronis, 1998). Teachers can also create conditions in classrooms that support these students' special learning needs. Short work

The boy on the right frequently engages in disruptive behaviour, disturbing his classmates while they try to work. Children with ADHD have great difficulty staying on task and often act impulsively, ignoring social rules.

periods followed by a chance to get up and move around help them concentrate.

Finally, family intervention is particularly important. Inattentive, overactive children strain the patience of parents, who are likely to react punitively and inconsistently in return—a child-rearing style that strengthens inappropriate behaviour. Breaking this cycle is as important for ADHD children as it is for the defiant, aggressive youngsters we will discuss in Chapter 12. In fact, at least 35 percent of the time, these two sets of behaviour problems occur together (Lahey & Loeber, 1997).

**REHEARSAL AND ORGANIZATION.** The next time you have a list of things to learn, such as major cities in your province or country or items to buy at the grocery store, take note of your behaviour. You are likely to repeat the information to yourself, a memory strategy called **rehearsal.** And you will probably group related items (for example, all the cities in the same part of the country), a strategy called **organization.**

Preschoolers show the beginnings of rehearsal. When asked to remember a set of familiar toys, they name, look at, and manipulate them more and play with them less than when not instructed to remember them. However, they do not name the toys consistently, and their rehearsal efforts have little impact on memory until about age 6 (Baker-Ward, Ornstein, & Holden, 1984).

Similarly, the glimmerings of organization can be seen in young children. For example, when circumstances permit, they use spatial organization to aid their memories. In one study, an adult placed either a piece of candy or a wooden peg in each of 12 identical containers and

**rehearsal**
The memory strategy of repeating information.

**organization**
The memory strategy of grouping together related information.

handed them one by one to preschoolers, asking them to remember where the candy was hidden. By age 4, children put the candy containers in one place and the peg containers in another, a strategy that almost always led to perfect recall (DeLoache & Todd, 1988). But preschoolers do not use *semantic* organization—grouping objects or words into *meaningful* categories. With intensive instruction they sometimes do so, but training usually does not improve performance (Lange & Pierce, 1992).

Why are young children not very adept at rehearsal and organization? Memory strategies take time and effort to perfect. Look closely at the findings so far, and you will see that both *production* and *control deficiencies* are evident. And even when school-age children more often use these strategies—around age 7 for rehearsal and age 8 for organization—they show both *control* and *utilization deficiencies* (Bjorklund & Coyle, 1995).

For example, they often rehearse in a piecemeal fashion. After being given the word "cat" in a list of items, 8-year-olds say, "Cat, cat, cat." In contrast, older children combine previous words with each new item, saying "Desk, man, yard, cat, cat," an approach that results in much better memory (Kunzinger, 1985). Similarly, younger children usually organize items by function, as in "hat–head," "shoes–feet," and "carrot–rabbit"—associations they often see in everyday life. Older children group such items into clothing, body parts, food, and animals. This permits them to organize more efficiently—by placing a great number of items in a few categories. Consequently, recall improves dramatically. Experience with materials that form clear categories helps children organize more effectively and apply the strategy to less clearly related materials (Bjorklund et al., 1994).

Once rehearsal and organization are in place, children often combine them—for example, repeating items and stating the category name of a group of items as they study them. With age, children use more memory strategies simultaneously, and the more they use, the better they remember (Coyle & Bjorklund, 1997). Although younger children's use of multiple strategies has little impact on performance (a *utilization deficiency*), their tendency to experiment is adaptive. By generating a variety of memory strategies, they discover which ones work best on different tasks and how to combine strategies effectively. For example, second to fourth graders know that organizing the items first, rehearsing category names second, and then rehearsing individual items is a good way to study lists (Hock, Park, & Bjorklund, 1998). Recall from Siegler's model of strategy choice that children experiment with strategies when faced with cognitive challenges, and memory is no exception.

**ELABORATION.** Children start to use a third memory strategy, **elaboration,** by the end of middle childhood. It involves creating a relationship, or shared meaning, between two or more pieces of information that are not members of the same category. For example, suppose "fish" and "pipe" are among a list of words you must learn. If, in trying to remember them, you generated a mental image of a fish smoking a pipe, you are using elaboration. Once children discover this memory technique, they find it so effective that it tends to replace other strategies. The very reason elaboration is so successful explains why it is late to develop. To use elaboration, we must translate items into images and think of a relationship between them. Children's working memories must expand before they can carry out these activities at the same time (Schneider & Pressley, 1997). Elaboration becomes more common during adolescence.

**CULTURE, SCHOOLING, AND MEMORY STRATEGIES.** Think about the situations in which the strategies of rehearsal, organization, and elaboration are useful. People usually employ these techniques when they need to remember information for its own sake. On many other occasions, they participate in daily activities that yield excellent memory as a natural by-product of the activity itself (Rogoff & Chavajay, 1995). In a study illustrating this idea, 4- and 5-year-olds were told either to play with a set of toys or to remember them. The play condition produced far better recall. Rather than just naming or touching objects, children engaged in many spontaneous organizations that helped them recall. These included functional use of objects (pretending to eat a banana or putting a shoe on a doll) and narrating their activities, as in "I'm squeezing this lemon" or "Fly away in this helicopter, doggie" (Newman, 1990).

**elaboration**
The memory strategy of creating a relationship between two or more pieces of information that are not members of the same category.

These findings help explain why the Kpelle farmers, described at the beginning of this chapter, viewed functional grouping as "the wise way" to organize familiar objects. Much like young children, people in non-Western cultures who have no formal schooling rarely use or benefit from instruction in memory strategies (Rogoff & Mistry, 1985). They may seldom use these memorizing techniques because they see little reason to remember information without a practical reason to do so.

In contrast, tasks that require children to remember isolated bits of information are common in classrooms, and they provide a great deal of motivation to use memory strategies. In fact, schooled children get so much practice with this type of learning that they apply memory strategies inappropriately when trying to recall information in meaningful contexts (Mistry, 1997). For example, Guatemalan Mayan 9-year-olds do slightly better than their U.S. agemates when told to remember the placement of 40 familiar objects in a play scene. U.S. children often rehearse object names when it is more effective to keep track of spatial relations (Rogoff & Waddell, 1982).

In sum, the development of memory strategies is not just a matter of a more competent information-processing system. It is also a product of task demands and cultural circumstances.

© LAWRENCE MIGDALE/STOCK BOSTON

As this Aleut girl assists her grandmother in the intricate art of weaving a fish net, she demonstrates keen memory for information embedded in meaningful contexts. Yet on a list-memory task of the kind often given in school, her performance may appear less sharp.

## RETRIEVING INFORMATION

Once information enters our long-term knowledge base, it must be *retrieved*, or recovered, to be used again. Information can be retrieved from memory in three ways: through recognition, recall, and reconstruction. As we discuss the development of these approaches to remembering, we also consider how children's expanding long-term knowledge base affects memory performance. And we address an intriguing, universal memory problem: our inability to recollect experiences that occurred during the first few years of our lives.

**RECOGNITION AND RECALL.** Try showing a young child a set of 10 pictures or toys. Then mix them up with some unfamiliar items and ask the child to point to the ones in the original set. Noticing that a stimulus is identical or similar to one previously experienced is called **recognition.** It is the simplest form of retrieval, since the material to be remembered is fully present during testing to serve as its own retrieval cue.

As habituation/recovery research discussed in Chapters 4 and 6 shows, even young infants are capable of recognition. The ability to recognize a larger number of stimuli over longer delays improves steadily with age, reaching a near-adult level during the preschool years. For example, after viewing a series of 80 pictures, 4-year-olds correctly discriminated 90 percent from pictures not in the original set (Brown & Campione, 1972). Because recognition appears early and develops rapidly, it is probably a fairly automatic process that does not depend on a deliberate search of long-term memory. Nevertheless, the ability of older children to apply strategies during storage, such as rehearsal and organization, increases the number of items recognized later (Mandler & Robinson, 1978).

Now give the child a more challenging task. While keeping the 10 items out of view, ask the child to name the ones she saw. This requires **recall**—that the child generate a mental representation of an absent stimulus. The beginnings of recall appear before 1 year of age as long as memories are strongly cued. Think back to our discussion of deferred imitation in Chapter 6. Its presence in infancy is good evidence for recall. Researchers have also asked parents to keep diary accounts of their infants' memories. Many examples of recall for people, places, and objects appear in the records. The following diary entry of a 7-month-old's memory of his father is an example:

> My husband called from work and I let him talk to Rob. (Rob) looked puzzled for a
> while and then he turned and looked at the door. Rob thought of the only time he
> hears his dad's voice when he knows Dad isn't home is when his Dad just got home. He

**recognition**
A type of memory that involves noticing whether a stimulus is identical or similar to one previously experienced.

**recall**
A type of memory that involves generating a mental representation of an absent stimulus.

heard his dad's voice and based on past experiences, he reasoned that his dad must be home, so he looked at the door. (Ashmead & Perlmutter, 1980, p. 4)

In other studies, children between 1½ and 4 years recalled events many months and (in the case of preschoolers) even years earlier, from a time before they had learned to talk (Bauer, 1996, 1997). However, what young children recall about an event that happened long ago is only part of what could be remembered. In one longitudinal study, sixth graders were asked to tell what happened when they went to an archaeological museum in kindergarten. They said much less about the experience than when they were asked the same question 6 weeks after the museum trip occurred. But in response to specific retrieval cues, including photos of the event, sixth graders remembered a great deal. And in some respects, their recall was more accurate. For example, they inferred that adults had hidden artifacts in a sandbox for them to find, whereas in kindergarten they simply recalled digging for relics (Hudson & Fivush, 1991).

Compared with recognition, recall shows much greater improvement with age because older children make use of a wider range of effective retrieval cues. With age, semantic organization of the knowledge base increases. Children develop more consistent and stable categories, which they arrange into elaborate hierarchies (Schneider & Bjorklund, 1998). When representations of experiences are interconnected in long-term memory, then many internal retrieval cues can be used to recall them later.

**RECONSTRUCTION.**  Read the following passage about George, an escaped convict. Then close your book and try to write the story down or tell it to a friend:

> George was alone. He knew they would soon be here. They were not far behind him when he left the village, hungry and cold. He dared not stop for food or shelter for fear of falling into the hands of his pursuers. There were many of them; they were strong and he was weak. George could hear the noise as the uniformed band beat its way through the trees not far behind him. The sense of their presence was everywhere. His spine tingled with fear. Eagerly he awaited the darkness. In darkness he would find safety. (Brown et al., 1977, p. 1456)

Now compare your version with the original. Is it a faithful reproduction?

When people are given complex, meaningful material to remember, condensations, additions, and distortions appear. This suggests that we do not always copy material into the system at storage and faithfully reproduce it at retrieval. Instead, we select and interpret much information we encounter in our daily lives, such as spoken and written language, in terms of our existing knowledge. And once the material is transformed, we often have difficulty distinguishing it from the original (Bartlett, 1932). Notice how this *constructivist* approach to information processing is consistent with Piaget's theory, especially his notions of assimilating new information to existing schemes (Schneider & Bjorklund, 1998).

Constructive processing can take place during any phase of information processing. It can occur during storage. In fact, the memory strategies of organization and elaboration are within the province of constructive memory, since both involve generating relationships between stimuli. Constructive processing can also involve **reconstruction** of information while it is in the system or being retrieved. Do children reconstruct stored information? The answer is clearly yes.

Children's reconstructive processing has been studied by asking them to recall stories. Like adults, when children retell a story, they condense, integrate, and add information. By age 5 or 6, children recall the important features of a story and forget the unimportant ones, combine information into more tightly knit units, and reorder the sequence of events to make it more logical (Bischofshausen, 1985; Mandler, 1984). And they often report information that fits with the meaning of a passage but that was not originally presented. For example, after elementary school students listened to the story of George, the escaped convict, the following statements appeared in their reconstructions: "All the prison guards were chasing him." "He was running so the police would be so far away that their dogs would not catch his trail" (Brown et al., 1977, p. 1459).

**reconstruction**
A type of memory in which complex, meaningful material is reinterpreted in terms of existing knowledge.

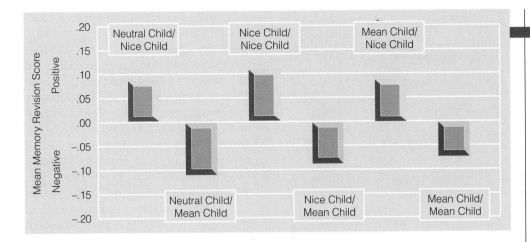

**FIGURE** 7.8

**Memory revision scores after kindergartners received new information related to a main character in a story they had previously recalled.** In some conditions, the information was consistent with previous information; in other conditions, it was inconsistent with previous information. The bars in the graph show how much children's recall of the main character's behaviour changed, in a positive or negative direction. Children reconstructed their recall to match the new information. For example, children first given negative information ("mean child") and later given positive information ("nice child") recalled the character's behaviours more positively than before; children first given positive information ("nice child") and later given negative information ("mean child") recalled the character's behaviour more negatively than before. (Adapted from A. F. Greenhoot, 2000, "Remembering and Understanding: The Effects of Changes in Underlying Knowledge on Children's Recollections," *Child Development, 71*, p. 1321. © The Society for Research in Child Development, Inc. Reprinted by permission.)

Furthermore, when children are given new information related to a story they previously recalled, they reconstruct it further. In one study, before telling each of three stories, an adult gave kindergartners information about a main character that was positive (a "nice child"), negative ("not a nice child"), or neutral. Children reconstructed the main character's behaviours to fit with prior information (Greenhoot, 2000). Those in the positive condition offered a more positive account and those in the negative condition a more negative account than did those in the neutral condition. Seven to 10 days later, a fourth story provided children with additional information about the main character. In some conditions, the new information was consistent with the original information. In others, the new information conflicted with the original information; for example, the "nice child" was described as a "mean child." Children reconstructed again, revising the main character's behaviour to match the new information (see Figure 7.8). And in a further recall session, the children's reconstructions were even more biased in that direction.

In revising information in meaningful ways, children provide themselves with a wealth of helpful retrieval cues that they can use during recall. Over time, as originally provided information decays, children make more inferences about actors and actions, adding events and interpretations that help make sense of a story. This process increases the coherence of reconstructed information and, therefore, its memorableness. At the same time, research on reconstruction shows that much information children and adults recall can be inaccurate.

**ANOTHER VIEW OF RECONSTRUCTION: FUZZY-TRACE THEORY.** So far, we have emphasized deliberate reconstruction of meaningful material, using new information and the long-term knowledge base to interpret it. According to C. J. Brainerd and Valerie Reyna's (1993, 2001) **fuzzy-trace theory,** when we first encode information, we reconstruct it automatically, creating a vague, fuzzy version called a **gist,** which preserves essential content without details and is especially useful for reasoning. Although we can retain a literal, verbatim version as well, we have a bias toward gist because it requires less working-memory capacity, freeing attention for the steps involved in thinking. For example, consider a person choosing among several recipes to prepare a dish for dinner. To decide, he relies on gist representations, noting which recipes are easier and have low-cost ingredients. But once he has selected a recipe, he needs verbatim information to prepare it. Because he is unlikely to have remembered those details, he consults the cookbook.

Fuzzy-trace theorists take issue with the assumption that all reconstructions are transformations of verbatim memory. Instead, they believe that both verbatim and gist memories are present and are stored separately so they can be used for different purposes. In support of this idea, shortly after being read a brief story, children can discriminate sentences they actually heard from ones they did not hear but that are consistent with the story's gist. Only over time, as the complete, verbatim memory decays more quickly than the efficiently represented gist, do children begin to say that statements consistent with but not in the story were ones they heard (Reyna & Kiernan, 1994). Fuzzy-trace theory also helps us understand

**fuzzy-trace theory**
A theory that proposes two types of encoding, one that automatically reconstructs information into a fuzzy version called a *gist,* which is especially useful for reasoning; and a second, verbatim version that is adapted for answering questions about specifics.

**gist**
A fuzzy representation of information that preserves essential content without details, is less likely to be forgotten than a verbatim version, and requires less working-memory capacity to use.

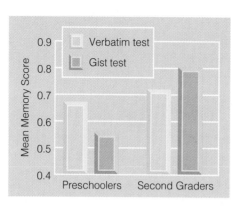

**FIGURE 7.9**

**Preschoolers' and second graders' performance on verbatim and gist memory questions.** Preschoolers did better on the verbatim- than the gist-memory test, whereas the reverse was true for second graders. (Adapted from Brainerd & Gordon, 1994.)

why children (and adults) often reason effectively without recalling specifics.

With age, children rely less on verbatim memory and more on fuzzy, reconstructed gists. In a recent study, researchers presented children with the following problem: "Farmer Brown owns many animals. He has 3 dogs, 5 sheep, 7 chickens, 9 horses, and 11 cows." Then the researchers asked two types of questions: (1) questions requiring verbatim knowledge, as in "How many cows does Farmer Brown own, 11 or 9?" and (2) questions requiring only gist information, such as "Which of Farmer Brown's animals are the most, cows or horses?" As Figure 7.9 shows, preschoolers were better at answering verbatim- than gist-dependent questions, whereas the reverse was true for second graders (Brainerd & Gordon, 1994).

Fuzzy-trace theory adds to our understanding of reconstruction by pointing out that it can occur immediately, as soon as information is encoded, without distorting verbatim memories. The extent to which gist and verbatim representations undergo further reconstruction depends on the type of task (telling an entire story versus answering a single question) and the passage of time. Fuzzy-trace research reveals that although memory is vital for reasoning, getting bogged down in details (as young children tend to do) can interfere with effective problem solving. And since fuzzy traces are less likely than verbatim memories to be forgotten, gists can serve as enduring retrieval cues, contributing to improved recall with age (Brainerd & Reyna, 1995).

## THE KNOWLEDGE BASE AND MEMORY PERFORMANCE

At several points in our discussion, we suggested that children's expanding knowledge may promote improved memory. Many researchers believe that cognitive development is largely a matter of acquiring more knowledge, which makes new, related information more meaningful so that it is easier to store and retrieve.

To test this idea, Michelene Chi (1978) looked at how well chess experts in grade 3 through grade 8 could remember complex chessboard arrangements. The children recalled the configurations considerably better than did adults who knew how to play chess but were not especially knowledgeable. These findings cannot be explained by the selection of very bright youngsters with exceptional memories. When the same participants recalled a list of numbers, the adults did better (see Figure 7.10).

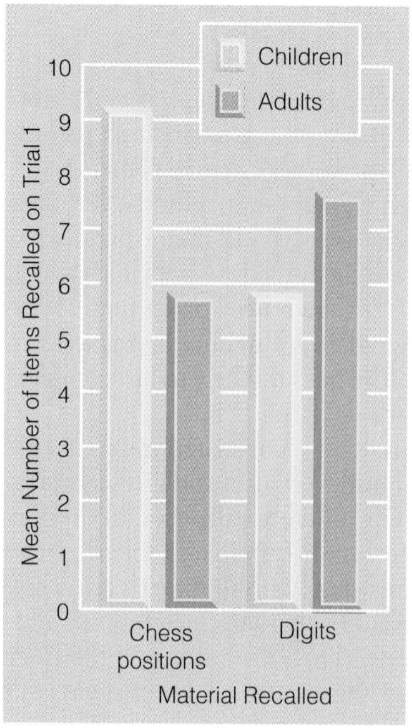

In Chi's study of chess-playing children, better memory was credited to a larger knowledge base. Experts also have more elaborately structured knowledge. In another study, researchers classified elementary school children as experts or novices in knowledge of soccer. Then they gave both groups lists of soccer and nonsoccer items to learn. As in Chi's study, experts remembered far more items on the soccer list (but not on the nonsoccer list) than did nonexperts (Schneider & Bjorklund, 1992). In observing how fourth graders studied soccer items, the researchers found that both groups used organizational strategies. But experts were more likely to apply these strategies during retrieval, as indicated by clustering of items during recall.

Greater organization at retrieval rather than storage suggests that very knowledgeable children apply

**FIGURE 7.10**

**Performance of skilled child chess players and adults on two tasks: memory for complex chessboard arrangements and memory for numerical digits.** The child chess experts recalled more on the chess task, the adults on the digit task. These findings show that size of the knowledge base contributes to memory performance. (Adapted from Chi, 1978.)

memory strategies in their area of expertise with little or no effort. Their recall has become *automatized,* through rapid associations of new items with the large number they already know. Consequently, experts can devote more working-memory capacity to using recalled information to reason and solve problems (Bjorklund & Douglas, 1997).

However, knowledge is not the only factor involved in strategic memory processing. Children who are expert in a particular area, whether it be chess, math, sports, or spelling, are usually highly motivated. Faced with new information, they say to themselves, "What can I do to learn this more effectively?" As a result, they not only acquire knowledge more quickly but actively use what they know to add more. In contrast, academically unsuccessful children fail to ask how previously stored information can clarify new material. This, in turn, interferes with the development of a broad knowledge base (Schneider & Bjorklund, 1998). In sum, extensive knowledge and use of memory strategies are intimately related and support one another.

## SCRIPTS: BASIC BUILDING BLOCKS OF STRUCTURED KNOWLEDGE

Think back to research on categorization in Chapter 6. It shows that a structured long-term knowledge base begins to form in infancy. How do children build a coherent network of knowledge, and in what ways does it change with age?

Our vast, intricately organized general knowledge system, often called **semantic memory,** must grow out of the young child's **episodic memory,** or memory for many personally experienced events. How semantic memory emerges from specific, real-world experiences is one of the most puzzling questions about memory development.

Like adults, preschoolers remember familiar events—what you do when you get up in the morning, go to child care, or get ready for bed—in terms of **scripts,** general representations of what occurs and when it occurs in a particular situation. For very young children, scripts begin as a structure of main acts. For example, when asked to tell what happens at a restaurant, a 3-year-old might say, "You go in, get the food, eat, and then pay." Although children's first scripts contain only a few acts, they are almost always recalled in correct sequence (Fivush, Kuebli, & Clubb, 1992). This is true even for 1- and 2-year-olds, who cannot yet verbally describe events but who act them out with toys (Bauer, 1997). With age, children's scripts become more elaborate, as in the following restaurant account given by a 5-year-old child: "You go in. You can sit in the booths or at a table. Then you tell the waitress what you want. You eat. If you want dessert, you can have some. Then you pay and go home" (Farrar & Goodman, 1992; Hudson, Fivush, & Kuebli, 1992).

Scripts are a special form of reconstructive memory. When we experience repeated events, we fuse them into the same script representation. Then any specific instance of a scripted experience becomes hard to recall. For example, unless it was out of the ordinary, you probably cannot remember exactly what you had for dinner two days ago. The same is true for young children. In this way, scripts prevent long-term memory from being cluttered with unimportant information.

Once held in long-term memory, a script can be used to predict what will happen on similar occasions in the future. In this way, scripts serve as a basic means through which children (and adults) organize and interpret everyday experiences. For example, young children rely on scripts in make-believe play and when listening to and telling stories. Scripts also support children's earliest efforts at planning by helping them represent sequences of actions that lead to desired goals (Hudson, Sosa, & Shapiro, 1997).

Scripts may be the developmental link between early episodic memory and a semantically organized long-term memory store (Lucariello, 1998). In several studies, preschoolers remembered script-related items (such as peanut butter, bologna, cheese—foods often eaten at lunchtime) in clustered form and recalled them more easily than a list of items belonging to the same semantic category (toast, cheese, ice cream—foods) (Lucariello, Kyratzis, & Nelson, 1992; Yu & Nelson, 1993). When children develop an array of script sequences, objects that share the same function but occur in different scripts (eating toast for breakfast, peanut butter sandwiches for lunch) are merged into a typical semantic category (food).

As this dinosaur enthusiast expands his knowledge about various species and connects them into stable, well-formed hierarchies, he will be able to commit new dinosaur information to memory with little or no effort. Extensive, well-structured knowledge makes recall automatic, through rapid associations of new items with the large number already known.

**semantic memory**
The vast, intricately organized knowledge system in long-term memory.

**episodic memory**
Memory for personally experienced events.

**scripts**
General representations of what occurs and when it occurs in a particular situation. A basic means through which children organize and interpret familiar everyday experiences.

© JEFF GREENBERG/PHOTOEDIT

Over time, this 5-year-old is unlikely to remember the details of this particular visit to a restaurant. Instead, she will fuse the event with other similar events and recall it in script form—in terms of what typically occurs when you go to a restaurant. Scripts help us predict what will happen on similar occasions in the future.

## AUTOBIOGRAPHICAL MEMORY

Another type of episodic memory is **autobiographical memory,** representations of one-time events that are long lasting and particularly meaningful in terms of the life story each of us creates. For example, perhaps you recall the day a sibling was born, the first time you took an airplane, a hospitalization, or a move to a new house. Memory for autobiographical events begins in early childhood. But practically none of us can retrieve experiences that happened to us before age 3—a phenomenon called **infantile amnesia.** Why can't we remember? And how does autobiographical memory develop and persist for a lifetime?

**THE MYSTERY OF INFANTILE AMNESIA.** Some researchers speculate that brain development brings an end to the period of infantile amnesia. Perhaps growth of the frontal lobes of the cortex along with other structures is necessary before experiences can be stored in ways that permit them to be retrieved many years later (Boyer & Diamond, 1992).

Several psychological accounts of infantile amnesia are consistent with this explanation. For example, one hypothesis is that two levels of memory exist, one that operates *implicitly,* without conscious awareness, and another that is *explicit,* or conscious and intentional. Infants' memories may be largely implicit, children's and adults' memories explicit; but the second system cannot access events stored by the first. Yet the idea of vastly different approaches to remembering in younger and older individuals has been questioned, since even infants and toddlers can retain memories for extensive periods (Bauer, 1997; Rovee-Collier, 1999). Another conjecture is based on fuzzy-trace theory. Recall that young children tend to encode information verbatim (precisely); older children rely more on gist. Verbatim memories are easily forgotten, whereas gist memories tend to endure (Leichtman & Ceci, 1993).

Other researchers believe that two additional milestones lead to the offset of infantile amnesia. Mark Howe of Lakehead University and Mary Courage of Memorial University of Newfoundland (1993, 1997) believe that for episodic memories to become autobiographical, the child must have a well-developed image of the self so memories can become personally relevant. In Chapter 11, we will see that the "psychological self" has only begun to emerge by age 3. In the first few years of life, it is not mature enough to serve as an anchor for one-time events. In addition autobiographical memory requires that children organize personal experiences into a meaningful, time-organized life story. Recent evidence indicates that preschoolers learn to structure memories in narrative form by talking about them with others (Nelson, 1996).

**FORMING AN AUTOBIOGRAPHICAL NARRATIVE: TALKING ABOUT THE PAST.** As early as 1½ to 2 years, children begin to talk about the past, guided by adults who expand on their fragmented recollections. For example, here is a short excerpt of a mother talking with her nearly 3-year-old daughter about a recent Halloween celebration:

*Child:* Once on Halloween the kids was over and I had a princess dress on me.

*Mother:* You had a princess dress on? Did you get any candy? Did you go door to door? What happened?

*Child:* We went treating.

*Mother:* You went treating! And who took you?

*Child:* Andrea's mother took us . . . and we brought a pumpkin too.

*Mother:* What did you do with the pumpkin?

*Child:* We lighted it.

**autobiographical memory**
Representations of special, one-time events that are long lasting and particularly meaningful in terms of the life story each of us creates.

**infantile amnesia**
The inability of older children and adults to remember experiences that happened before age 3.

*Mother:* What did it look like? Was it scary?

*Child:* Uh-huh. Dad made cuts in it with a razor. He made a face too. That was funny. (Fivush & Hamond, 1990, p. 223)

As children participate in these dialogues, they gradually adopt the narrative thinking that the dialogues generate. Notice how this process is consistent with Vygotsky's theory: Social interaction with more expert partners leads to advances in thinking (see Chapter 6).

Adults use two styles for eliciting children's autobiographical narratives. In the *elaborative style,* they ask many, varied questions; add information to children's statements; and volunteer their own recollections and evaluations of events—as the mother did in the conversation just given. In contrast, parents who use the *repetitive style* provide little information and ask the same short-answer questions over and over, as in, "Do you remember the zoo?" "What did we do at the zoo?" "What did we do there?" Preschoolers who experience the elaborative style produce more coherent and detailed personal stories when followed up 1 to 2 years later (Farrant & Reese, 2000; Reese, Haden, & Fivush, 1993).

Parents' conversations about the past become more complex as preschoolers' language skills expand. Between 2 and 6 years, children adopt parents' narrative style. Their descriptions of special, one-time occurrences become better organized, elaborate, and evaluative (and therefore imbued with personal meaning). Older children also add more background information, placing events in the larger context of their lives (Fivush, Haden, & Adam, 1995; Haden, Haine, & Fivush, 1997).

Girls are more advanced than boys in this sequence. And Western children produce narratives with more talk about thoughts, emotions, and preferences than do Asian children. These differences fit with variations in parent–child conversations. Parents talk about the past in more detail with daughters (Bruce, Dolan, & Phillips-Grant, 2000; Reese, Haden, & Fivush, 1996). And collectivist cultural values lead Asian parents to discourage their children from talking about themselves (Han, Leichtman, & Wang, 1998). Perhaps because women's early experiences were integrated into more coherent narratives, they report an earlier age of first memory and more vivid early memories than do men. Similarly, first memories of Caucasian-American adults are, on the average, 6 months earlier than those of Asians (Mullen, 1994).

The accuracy and completeness of children's autobiographical memories are crucial when they must testify in court cases in which outcomes seriously affect their own and others' welfare. How reliable are children's memories under these conditions? See the Social Issues: Health box on page 292 for a discussion of this topic.

© JEFF GREENBERG/INDEX STOCK PHOTOGRAPHY

Parents who talk about the past help their children build an autobiographical narrative of personally meaningful experiences. As this boy discusses photos in the family album with his father, he recalls significant events and integrates them into his life story.

## ASK YOURSELF www

**review**    What factors contribute to the offset of infantile amnesia after age 3? How can parents foster a rich, detailed autobiographical memory in young children?

**review**    According to fuzzy-trace theory, why do we encode information in gist form? Describe the development of gist and verbatim representations, and explain how gist representations contribute to improved reasoning and recall with age.

**apply**    When asked what happens at kindergarten, 5-year-old Ali replies, "First, you have circle time and centre time. Sometimes you listen to a story. Next is snack time and outdoor play." But Ali can't remember what she did during centre time two days ago. Explain Ali's memory performance. Why is this type of reconstructive memory useful?

**connect**    Using what you have learned about development of gist and autobiographical memory, explain why preschoolers' eyewitness testimony is usually less accurate than that of older children. What situational factors combine with reconstructive processing to heighten children's suggestibility?

## CHILDREN'S EYEWITNESS MEMORY

enata, a physically abused and neglected 8-year-old, was taken from her parents and placed in foster care. There, she was seen engaging in sexually aggressive behaviour toward other children, including grabbing their sex organs and using obscene language. Renata's foster mother suspected that sexual abuse had taken place in her natural home. She informed the child protective service worker, who met with Renata to gather information. But Renata did not want to answer any questions.

Increasingly, children are being called on to testify in court cases involving child abuse and neglect, child custody, and other matters. Having to provide information on such topics can be difficult and traumatic. Almost always, children must report on highly stressful events, and they may have to speak against a parent or other relative toward whom they feel affection and loyalty. In some family disputes, they may fear punishment for telling the truth. In addition, child witnesses are faced with an unfamiliar situation—at the very least, an interview in the judge's chambers, and at most, an open courtroom with judge, jury, spectators, and the possibility of unsympathetic cross-examination. Not surprisingly, these conditions can compromise the accuracy of children's recall.

### AGE DIFFERENCES

Until recently, children younger than age 5 were rarely asked to testify, whereas those age 6 and older often did so. Children between ages 10 and 14 have historically been assumed competent to testify. Yet, as a result of societal reactions to rising rates of child abuse and difficulties in prosecuting perpetrators (see Chapter 14), legal requirements for child testimony have relaxed in Canada and the United States. Children as young as 3 frequently serve as witnesses, according to Stephen Ceci of Cornell University and Maggie Bruck of McGill University (1998), who have done extensive research in the area.

Compared with preschoolers, school-age children are better at giving accurate, detailed descriptions of past experiences and making correct inferences about others' motives and intentions. Older children are also more resistant to misleading questions of the sort asked by attorneys when they probe for more information or, in cross-examination, try to influence the content of the child's response (Bjorklund et al., 2000; Roebers & Schneider, 2001). And compared with preschoolers, older children are more likely to give up misguided memories when an adult shows them that those events never happened (Ceci et al., 1994).

What makes younger children more prone to memory errors? First, responding to interview questions is challenging for children whose language competence is not well developed. They often are unaware when they do not understand, and they answer the question anyway (Carter, Bottoms, & Levine, 1996). Second, when an adult asks specific questions ("Was he holding a screwdriver?"), younger children are more likely to acquiesce, perhaps out of a desire to please. Third, preschoolers are especially poor at *source-monitoring*—identifying where they got their knowledge, even minutes after they acquired it. Consequently, they often confuse what they hear with what actually occurred (Gopnik & Graf, 1988; Poole & Lindsay, 2001). Fourth, preschoolers' bias toward verbatim representations (encoding specifics) leads them to forget more easily than older children, whose gist memories persist over time and serve as retrieval cues for details (Brainerd, Reyna, & Poole, 2000). Finally, younger children are less competent at using narrative structure to report their autobiographical memories systematically and completely. This causes them to omit information that they actually remember (Gordon, Baker-Ward, & Ornstein, 2001).

Nevertheless, when properly questioned, even 3-year-olds can recall past events accurately—including highly stressful ones. Carole Peterson and Regina Rideout (1998) of Memorial University of Newfoundland conducted a longitudinal study of 2- to 13-year-olds who sustained accidental injuries, such as broken bones or cuts requiring stitches. Children at least 26 months old at the time of an accidental injury and visit to the emergency room reported these experiences accurately 2 years later.

### SUGGESTIBILITY

Yet court cases often involve repeated interviews. Parents may induce distorted or false memories even before interviewing by legal representatives begins. When adults lead children by suggesting incorrect facts ("He touched you there, didn't he?"), they increase the likelihood of inaccurate reporting among preschool and school-age children alike. Events that children fabricate in response to leading questions can be quite fantastic. In one study, after a visit to a doctor's office, children said yes to questions about events that not only never occurred but that implied abuse—"Did the doctor lick your knee?" "Did the nurse sit on top of you?" (Ornstein et al., 1997).

By the time children come to court, it is weeks, months, or even years after the target events occurred. When a long delay is combined with suggestions about what happened and stereotyping of the accused ("He's in jail because he's been bad"), children can easily be misled into giving false information (Ceci, Leichtman, & Bruck, 1994; Leichtman & Ceci, 1995). A frightening legal setting further compromises children's ability to report past events completely and accurately (Saywitz & Nathanson, 1993). Also, as specifics of what actually happened fade, children may substitute a script of what usually happens. As a result, they may report features consistent with the original situation (for example, checking the stomach in a physical exam) that were not really part of it—and do so in considerable detail (Ornstein et al., 1998). The more *distinctive*—different from its background context—an event is, the more likely children will recall it accurately after passage of time. For example, Peterson (1999) found that 2 years after being injured, children recall more details about the injury itself than about medical treatment, which tends to be similar across many injuries.

To ease the task of providing testimony, special interviewing methods have been devised for children. In many child sexual abuse cases, anatomically correct dolls are used to prompt children's recall. Although this method helps older children provide more detail about experienced events, it increases the suggestibility of preschoolers, who report physical and sexual contact that never happened (Ceci & Bruck, 1998; Goodman et al., 1999).

### INTERVENTIONS

Adults must prepare child witnesses so they understand the courtroom process and know what to expect. In some places, "court schools" exist in which children are taken through the setting and given an opportunity to role-play court activities. As part of this process, children can be encouraged to admit not knowing an answer rather than guessing or going along with what an adult expects. At the same time, legal professionals must lessen the risk of suggestibility—by limiting the number of times children are interviewed and by asking questions in nonleading ways. And a warm, supportive interview tone fosters accurate recall, perhaps by decreasing children's fear. As a result, they feel freer to counter the interviewer's false suggestions (Ceci, Bruck, & Battin, 2000).

If children are likely to experience emotional trauma or later punishment (in a family dispute), then courtroom procedures can be adapted to protect them. For example, a child advocate can be present to offer emotional support. Renata testified over closed circuit TV so she did not have to face her abusive father. When it is not wise for

© ROB CRANDALL/THE IMAGE WORKS

An attorney prepares this school-age girl for court testimony. The accuracy of her testimony will depend on the way she is questioned, how long ago the events occurred, whether adults in her life have tried to influence her response, and her understanding of and comfort with the courtroom process.

a child to participate directly, expert witnesses can provide testimony that reports on the child's psychological condition and includes important elements of the child's story. But for such testimony to be worthwhile, witnesses must be impartial and trained in how to question children to minimize false reporting (Bruck, Ceci, & Hembrooke, 1998).

# Metacognition

THROUGHOUT THIS CHAPTER, we have mentioned many ways in which cognitive processing becomes more reflective and deliberate with age. These trends suggest that another form of knowledge may influence how well children remember and solve problems. The term **metacognition** refers to awareness and understanding of various aspects of thought.

During early and middle childhood, metacognition expands greatly as children construct a naive **theory of mind,** a coherent understanding of people as mental beings, which children revise as they encounter new evidence. Most investigations into theory of mind address children's "mind reading"—the ability to detect their own and other people's perceptions, feelings, desires, and beliefs. We will take up this aspect when we consider emotional and social understanding in Chapters 10 and 11. A second facet of metacognitive research concerns children's knowledge of mental activity, or *what it means to think.* To work most effectively, the information-processing system must be aware of itself. It must arrive at such realizations as "I'd better write that phone number down or I'll forget it" and "This paragraph is complicated; I'll have to read it again to grasp the author's point."

For metacognitive knowledge to be helpful, children must apply it on a moment-by-moment basis. They must monitor what they do, calling on what they know about thinking to overcome difficulties. In the following sections, we consider these higher-level, "executive" aspects of information processing.

## METACOGNITIVE KNOWLEDGE

With age, knowledge of mental activities expands in three ways. Children become increasingly conscious of cognitive capacities, strategies for processing information, and task variables that aid or impede performance.

**KNOWLEDGE OF COGNITIVE CAPACITIES.** Listen closely to young children's conversations, and you will find early awareness of mental activities. Such words as "think," "remember," and "pretend" are among the first verbs in children's vocabularies. After age 2½, they use these words appropriately to refer to internal states, as when they say, "I thought the socks were in the drawer, 'cept they weren't" (Wellman, 1990). By age 3, children realize that thinking takes place inside their heads and that a person can think about something without seeing it, talking about it, or touching it (Flavell, Green, & Flavell, 1995; Woolley & Wellman, 1992).

But preschoolers' view of the workings of the mind is still limited. Without strong situational cues (a challenging task and a thoughtful expression), 3- and 4-year-olds deny that a person is thinking. They indicate that the minds of people waiting, looking at pictures, listening to stories, or reading books, are "empty of thoughts and ideas." And when told to try to have no thoughts at all and to indicate whether they had some thoughts anyway, most 8-year-olds said they had, but only a few 5-year-olds said they had (see Figure 7.11) (Flavell, Green, & Flavell, 1993, 1995, 2000).

Furthermore, young children pay little attention to the *process* of thinking but, instead, focus on outcomes. For example, 3-year-olds use the word "know" to refer to acting successfully (finding a hidden toy) and the word "forget" to refer to acting unsuccessfully (not finding the toy), even when a person is guessing at the toy's location (Lyon & Flavell, 1994; Perner, 1991). And children younger than age 6 often claim they have always known information they just learned (Taylor, Esbensen, & Bennett, 1994). Finally, according to Jeremy Carpendale and Michael Chandler (1996) of the University of British Columbia, preschoolers believe that all events must be observed directly to be known. They do not understand that *mental inferences* can be a source of knowledge.

School-age children have a more complete grasp of cognitive processes. For example, they realize that doing well on a task depends on focusing attention—concentrating and exerting

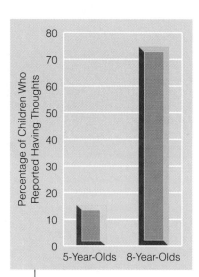

**FIGURE** 7.11

**Children ages 5 and 8 told to have no thoughts or ideas but who responded that they had some anyway.** Many more 5-year-olds than 8-year-olds denied that they had any thoughts. Preschoolers greatly underestimate the amount of mental activity people experience. If people look as if they are not thinking, preschoolers seem to believe they are not thinking. (Adapted from Flavell, Green, & Flavell, 2000.)

effort (Miller & Bigi, 1979). And by late elementary school, they recognize distinct types of attention—that the mind being captured by a stimulus (such as the ring of a telephone) is different from deploying attention to perform a task (for example, deciding if two pictures are the same) (Parault & Schwanenflugel, 2000). School-age children also distinguish mental activities on the basis of the certainty of their knowledge. They realize that if you "remember," "know," or "understand," then you are more certain than if you "guessed," "estimated," or "compared." And they grasp the relationship between certain mental activities—for example, that remembering is crucial for understanding and that understanding strengthens memory (Schwanenflugel, Fabricius, & Noyes, 1996; Schwanenflugel, Henderson, & Fabricius, 1998).

© 1999 LAURA DWIGHT

School-age children have an improved ability to reflect on their own mental life. This child is aware that external aids to memory are often necessary to ensure that information will be retained.

How, then, should we describe the difference between the young child's understanding of cognitive capacities and that of the older child? Preschoolers know that people have an internal mental life, but they seem to view the mind as a passive container of information. Consequently, they greatly underestimate the amount of mental activity that goes on in people and are poor at inferring what people know or are thinking about. In view of their limited awareness of how knowledge is acquired, it is not surprising that preschoolers rarely engage in planning or use memory strategies. In contrast, older children regard the mind as an active, constructive agent that selects and transforms information (Chandler & Carpendale, 1998; Flavell, 2000).

What promotes this more reflective, process-oriented view of the mind? Perhaps children become aware of mental activities through quiet-time observation of their own thinking and through exposure to talk about the mind, as when they hear people say, "I was thinking a lot" or "My mind wandered" (Wellman & Hickling, 1994). Schooling may contribute as well. Instructing children to keep their minds on what they are doing and remember mental steps calls attention to the workings of the mind. And as children engage in reading, writing, and math, they often use private speech, at first speaking aloud and later silently to themselves. As they "hear themselves think," they probably detect many aspects of mental life (Astington, 1995).

**KNOWLEDGE OF STRATEGIES AND TASK VARIABLES.** Consistent with their more active view of the mind, school-age children are far more conscious of mental strategies than are preschoolers. For example, they know quite a bit about effective memory techniques. When shown video clips depicting two children using different recall strategies and asked which one is likely to produce better memory, kindergarten and young elementary school children recognize large gaps in strategy effectiveness—that rehearsing or categorizing is better than looking or naming. Older children are aware of more subtle differences—that organizing is better than rehearsing (Justice, 1986; Schneider, 1986). By grade 3, children realize that in studying material for later recall, it is helpful to devote most effort to items they know least well (Kreutzer, Leonard, & Flavell, 1975).

Older children also have a more complete understanding of task variables that affect performance. Kindergartners are aware of a few factors that make a memory task easy or hard—the number of items, their familiarity, how much study time is available, and whether they must recognize or recall them (Speer & Flavell, 1979). But by the mid-elementary school years, children know much more—for example, that dividing attention between two tasks is harder than focusing on only one, that a list of unrelated items is harder to recall than a list of semantically related items, and that recalling prose material word for word is harder than paraphrasing it (Dossett & Burns, 2000; Kreutzer, Leonard, & Flavell, 1975).

Once children become conscious of the many factors that influence mental activity, they combine them into an integrated understanding. At the end of middle childhood, children take account of interactions among variables—how age and motivation of the learner, effective use

**metacognition**
Awareness and understanding of various aspects of thought.

**theory of mind**
A coherent understanding of people as mental beings, which children revise as they encounter new evidence. Includes knowledge of mental activity and awareness that people can have different perceptions, feelings, desires, and beliefs.

of strategies, and nature and difficulty of the task work together to affect cognitive performance (Wellman, 1990). In this way, metacognition truly becomes a comprehensive theory.

## COGNITIVE SELF-REGULATION

Although metacognitive knowledge expands, school-age children often have difficulty putting what they know about thinking into action. They are not yet good at **cognitive self-regulation,** the process of continuously monitoring progress toward a goal, checking outcomes, and redirecting unsuccessful efforts.

To study cognitive self-regulation, researchers sometimes look at the impact children's awareness of memory strategies has on how well they remember. By grade 2, the more children know about memory strategies, the more they recall—a relationship that strengthens over the elementary school years (Pierce & Lange, 2000; Schneider & Pressley, 1997). Furthermore, children who can explain why a memory strategy works seem to use it more effectively; they show better memory performance (Justice et al., 1997).

Children's difficulties with self-regulation on complex tasks are evident in their *comprehension monitoring*—sensitivity to how well they understand a spoken or written message. Compared with younger students, 12- and 13-year-olds more often notice when a passage does not make sense. Rather than just moving ahead, they slow down and look back to see if they missed some important information (Garner, 1990). Their greater sensitivity to text errors means that they are more likely to revise their written work (Beal, 1990).

Why does cognitive self-regulation develop gradually? Monitoring learning outcomes is cognitively demanding, requiring constant evaluation of effort and progress. By adolescence, cognitive self-regulation is a strong predictor of academic success (Joyner & Kurtz-Costes, 1997). Students who do well in school know when their learning is going well and when it is not. If they run up against obstacles, such as poor study conditions, a confusing text passage, or an unclear class presentation, they take steps to organize the learning environment, review the material, or seek other sources of support. This active, purposeful approach contrasts sharply with the passive orientation of students who achieve poorly (Zimmerman & Risemberg, 1997).

Parents and teachers can foster self-regulation by pointing out the special demands of tasks, suggesting effective strategies, and emphasizing the value of self-correction—practices that have a substantial impact on children's learning. As adults help children monitor their cognitive activity in situations where they are likely to encounter difficulties, children internalize these procedures. In addition, explaining why strategies are effective encourages children to use them in new situations (Pressley, 1995; Schunk & Zimmerman, 1994). When adults tell children not just what to do but why to do it, they provide a rationale for future action. Then children learn not just how to get a task done but what to do when faced with new problems.

Notice how these suggestions for fostering cognitive self-regulation resemble Vygotsky's theory of the social origins of higher cognitive processes. Children who acquire effective self-regulatory skills succeed at challenging tasks. As a result, they develop a sense of *academic self-efficacy*—confidence in their own ability, which supports the use of self-regulation in the future (Schunk & Ertmer, 2000; Zimmerman, 2002). As we turn now to development within academic skill areas, the importance of cognitive self-regulation will be ever-present. But before continuing, turn to the Milestones table on page 297, which summarizes the diverse changes in information processing we have considered.

© ELIZABETH CREWS

This boy's cognitive self-regulatory capacities are evident as he practises the piano. When he makes a mistake, does he ignore it, or does he isolate that passage for further study and practice? The boy's parents and piano teacher can foster his self-regulatory skills by pointing out the special demands of the piece he is learning, showing him how to use strategies to master it, and encouraging him to monitor his progress.

**cognitive self-regulation**
The process of continuously monitoring progress toward a goal, checking outcomes, and redirecting unsuccessful efforts.

## ASK YOURSELF

**review**    What evidence indicates that preschoolers view the mind as a passive container of information, whereas school-age children view it as an active, constructive agent?

**review**    Explain why cognitive self-regulation develops gradually in childhood and adolescence.

**apply**    While doing her homework, 9-year-old Melody makes many careless mistakes. Although her parents constantly tell her to look over her work, her performance hasn't improved. What can they do to help Melody?

# milestones

## DEVELOPMENT OF INFORMATION PROCESSING

| AGE | BASIC CAPACITIES | STRATEGIES | KNOWLEDGE | METACOGNITION |
|-----|------------------|------------|-----------|---------------|
| 2–5 years | ⚲ Many basic processing skills are evident, including attention, recognition, recall, and reconstruction.<br><br>⚲ Overall capacity of the system increases. | ⚲ Attention becomes more focused and sustained.<br><br>⚲ Beginnings of memory strategies are present, but they are seldom used spontaneously and have little impact on performance.<br><br>⚲ Variability and adaptive selection among strategies are evident. | ⚲ Knowledge expands and becomes better organized.<br><br>⚲ Familiar events are remembered as scripts, which become more elaborate.<br><br>⚲ Autobiographical memory emerges, takes on narrative organization, and becomes more detailed. | ⚲ Awareness of mental activities is present, but preschoolers view the mind as a passive container of information. |
| 6–10 years | ⚲ Overall capacity of the system continues to increase. | ⚲ Attention becomes more selective, adaptable, and planful.<br><br>⚲ Cognitive inhibition improves.<br><br>⚲ Memory strategies of rehearsal and semantic organization are used spontaneously and more effectively.<br><br>⚲ Ability to combine strategies increases.<br><br>⚲ Ability to draw inferences in reconstructive processing improves.<br><br>⚲ Reliance on gist memory for reasoning increases. | ⚲ Knowledge continues to expand and become better organized. | ⚲ View of the mind as an active, constructive agent develops.<br><br>⚲ Knowledge of different cognitive processes and their relationships increases.<br><br>⚲ Knowledge of the impact of strategies and task variables on performance increases.<br><br>⚲ Knowledge of interaction between cognitive processes, strategies, and task variables increases.<br><br>⚲ Cognitive self-regulation improves gradually. |
| 11 years–adulthood | ⚲ Overall capacity of the system continues to increase, but at a slower pace. | ⚲ Memory strategy of elaboration improves. | ⚲ Knowledge expands further and becomes more intricately organized. | ⚲ Metacognitive knowledge and cognitive self-regulation continue to improve. |

# Applications of Information Processing to Academic Learning

OVER THE PAST 2 DECADES, fundamental discoveries about the development of information processing have been applied to children's mastery of academic skills. Because paths to competence vary across subject matter areas, each has been studied separately. Nevertheless, the research has features in common. Researchers identify the cognitive capacities and strategies necessary for skilled performance, trace their development, and distinguish good from poor learners by pinpointing differences in cognitive skills. Then, using this information, they design and test teaching methods to improve children's learning. In the following sections, we discuss a sampling of these efforts in reading, mathematics, and scientific reasoning.

## READING

While reading, we use a large number of skills at once, taxing all aspects of our information-processing systems. We must perceive single letters and letter combinations, translate them into speech sounds, learn to recognize the visual appearance of many common words, hold chunks of text in working memory while interpreting their meaning, and combine the meanings of various parts of a text passage into an understandable whole. In fact, reading is so demanding that most or all of these skills must be done automatically. If one or more are poorly developed, they will compete for space in our limited working memories, and reading performance will decline (Perfetti, 1988). Becoming a proficient reader is a complex process that begins in the preschool years.

 **EARLY CHILDHOOD.** Preschoolers understand a great deal about written language long before they begin to read and write in conventional ways. This is not surprising when we consider that children in industrialized nations live in a world filled with written symbols. Each day, they observe and participate in activities involving storybooks, calendars, lists, and signs. As part of these experiences, children try to figure out how written symbols convey meaning. Their active efforts to construct literacy knowledge through informal experiences are called **emergent literacy.**

Young preschoolers search for units of written language as they "read" memorized versions of stories and recognize familiar signs, such as "PIZZA" at their favourite fast food counter. But their early ideas about written language differ from ours. For example, many preschoolers think that a single letter stands for a whole word or that each letter in a person's signature represents a separate name. Gradually, children revise these ideas as their perceptual and cognitive capacities improve, as they encounter writing in many contexts, and as adults help them with written communication.

Soon, preschoolers become aware of general characteristics of written language and create their own printlike symbols, as in the "story" and "grocery list" written by a 4-year-old in Figure 7.12. Eventually children figure out that letters are parts of words and are linked to sounds in systematic ways, as you can see in the invented spellings that are typical between ages 5 and 7. At first, children rely on sounds in the names of letters: "ADE LAFWTS KRMD NTU A LAVATR" ("eighty elephants crammed into a[n] elevator"). Over time, they grasp more subtle sound–letter correspondences. They also learn that some letters have more than one common sound and that context affects their use ("a" is pronounced differently in "cat" than in "table") (McGee & Richgels, 2000; Treiman et al., 1998).

The more informal literacy-related experiences young children have, the better prepared they are to tackle the complex tasks involved in reading and writing after they enter school.

**emergent literacy**
Young children's active efforts to construct literacy knowledge through informal experiences.

Storybook reading, in which adults engage preschoolers in discussion and interpretation of story content, is related to preschoolers' language and reading readiness scores, which predict later academic success (Whitehurst & Lonigan, 1998). Furthermore, in a 5-year longitudinal study, Monique Sénéchal and Jo-Anne LeFevre (1998, 2002) of Carleton University found that the frequency with which parents taught their 4- and 5-year-olds to read and print words was related to enhanced emergent-literacy skills in grade 1, such as knowledge of letter names and sounds. And grade 1 literacy skills predicted more fluent reading in the early school years.

Preschoolers from economically disadvantaged homes generally have far less access to storybooks and reading and writing activities than do their higher-SES agemates (High et al., 1999). In a program that "flooded" child-care centres with high-quality children's books and provided training to caregivers on how to get 3- and 4-year-olds to interact with the books frequently and productively, children showed much greater gains in emergent reading and writing knowledge than did a control group not experiencing the intervention. These differences were still evident after the children entered kindergarten (Neuman, 1999).

**MIDDLE CHILDHOOD.** Look again at the literacy attainments of early childhood. Do they remind you of Siegler's *strategy-choice model*? Children seem to experiment with and choose adaptively among strategies in learning to decode written symbols. In support of this idea, Siegler (1988, 1996) found that each time children encounter a combination of letters they cannot read, they resort to diverse strategies, such as sounding out the word, looking up the spelling of a possible word in the dictionary, or asking for help. With practice, each written word becomes more strongly associated with its meaning in long-term memory. When this happens, children gradually give up capacity-consuming strategies for automatic retrieval.

Psychologists and educators are engaged in a "great debate" about how to teach beginning reading. On one side are those who take a **whole-language approach.** They argue that reading should be taught in a way that parallels natural language learning. From the very beginning, children should be exposed to text in its complete form—stories, poems, letters, posters, and lists—so they can appreciate the communicative function of written language. According to these experts, as long as reading is kept whole and meaningful, children will be motivated to discover the specific skills they need (Watson, 1989). On the other side of the debate are those who advocate a **basic-skills approach.** According to this view, children should be given simplified reading materials. At first, they should be coached on *phonics*—the basic rules for translating written symbols into sounds. Only later, after they have mastered these skills, should they get complex reading material (Rayner & Pollatsek, 1989).

Currently, most experts believe that children learn best when they receive a balanced mixture of both approaches (Pressley, 1994; Stahl, McKenna, & Pagnucco, 1994). Kindergartners benefit from an emphasis on whole language, with gradual introduction of phonics (Jeynes & Littell, 2000; Sacks & Mergendoller, 1997). In grade 1, teaching that includes phonics boosts reading achievement scores, especially for children from economically disadvantaged backgrounds at risk for reading difficulties (Rayner et al., 2001). And, as the Social Issues: Education box on page 300 shows, when teachers integrate real reading and writing with explicit teaching of basic skills and engage in other excellent teaching practices, first graders show far greater literacy progress than do their agemates in classrooms without this blend of teaching ingredients.

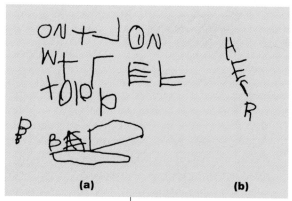

(a)    (b)

**FIGURE** 7.12

**A story (a) and a grocery list (b) written by a 4-year-old child.** This child's writing has many features of real print. It also reveals an awareness of different kinds of written expression. (From L. M. McGee & D. J. Richgels, 2000, *Literacy's Beginnings* [3rd ed.], Boston: Allyn and Bacon, p. 69. Reprinted by permission.)

**whole-language approach**
An approach to beginning reading instruction that parallels children's natural language learning and keeps reading materials whole and meaningful.

**basic-skills approach**
An approach to beginning reading instruction that emphasizes training in phonics—the basic rules for translating written symbols into sounds—and simplified reading materials.

*social issues: education*

## TEACHING FIRST GRADERS TO READ: INSTRUCTION THAT WORKS

debate over how to teach children to read remains contentious because of opposing educational philosophies that have persisted since the early twentieth century. Educators who champion child-centred methods that foster discovery, exploration, and excitement about learning favour the *whole-language approach.* Educators who believe that all children should be taught decoding rules essential for proficient reading advocate the *basic-skills approach.*

In a recent study, Michael Pressley and his collaborators (2001) showed that effective reading instruction involves a complex mix of elements. The researchers asked school administrators to identify two types of grade 1 teachers: "highly effective" and "typical" in promoting reading achievement. Then the researchers intensively observed and interviewed the 30 identified teachers. On the basis of children's classroom engagement in literacy activities and reading and writing competence, the researchers identified most-effective and least-effective teachers to be observed and interviewed intensively.

In the most-effective teachers' classrooms, the majority of students were immersed in reading and writing activities more than 90 percent of the time. By the end of the year, most read books with at least several sentences per page and wrote compositions two to three pages long, with good coherence, capitalization, punctuation, and spelling. In contrast, students in least-effective teachers' classrooms were far less engaged in literacy activities. As the school year concluded, most were still reading books with only a few words per page and wrote compositions with a handful of short sentences containing many errors.

Using ethnographic procedures, the researchers compiled detailed descriptions of how the teachers taught. The most-effective teachers shared the following practices, which distinguished them from the least-effective teachers:

- *Excellent classroom management.* Highly effective classrooms were busy, orderly places with well-planned lessons and activities. Teachers closely monitored all students and insisted that they complete assignments.

- *A positive, encouraging environment.* The most-effective teachers created exceptionally positive learning environments. Children were often praised and prompted to tackle challenges. In contrast, the least-effective teachers frequently criticized children—a teaching style that reflected their difficulties with classroom management and stimulating students' engagement in learning.

- *Balancing basic-skills and whole-language teaching.* The most-effective teachers engaged in much explicit teaching of phonics. But they embedded that teaching in students' exposure to excellent children's literature and writing tasks and consistently stressed comprehension as well.

- *Matching teaching to student progress and encouraging self-regulation.* The most-effective teachers *scaffolded* children's reading (see Chapter 6, page 258). They made sure that students read books that were slightly challenging for them. And they provided enough support to foster reading progress but stopped short

© SYRACUSE NEWSPAPERS/THE IMAGE WORKS

Effective reading instruction involves a complex mix of elements—among them, balancing basic-skills and whole-language teaching. This first-grade teacher works with a small group on identifying, pronouncing, and writing words that begin with "fr." Teaching of phonics is embedded in exposure to interesting stories and challenging writing tasks.

of doing tasks for children. Instead, they suggested many strategies that students could use on their own to decode unfamiliar words.

- *Strong connections across subject areas.* Highly effective teachers integrated reading and writing into all school subjects—an undertaking that demonstrated their strong commitment to making reading meaningful.

In sum, effective teaching of reading cannot be reduced to either a basic-skills or a whole-language philosophy; none of the most-effective teachers preferred one approach over the other. Instead, they combined the two approaches with other successful teaching practices. And they varied their momentary emphasis on phonics and meaningful reading to suit individual students' needs.

Why might combining phonics with whole language work best? Learning the basics—relations between letters and sounds—enables children to decode words they have never seen before. As this process becomes more automatic, it releases working memory for the higher-level activities involved in comprehending the text's meaning (Adams, Treiman, & Pressley, 1998). Children who receive phonics instruction also display more accurate spelling by grade 3 than children experiencing only whole language (Bruck et al., 1998).

Yet if practice in basic skills is overemphasized, children may lose sight of the goal of reading: understanding. Children who read aloud fluently but register little meaning lack metacognitive knowledge of effective reading strategies—for example, that they must read more carefully if they will be tested on a passage than if they are reading for pleasure. And they do not monitor their reading comprehension. Providing instruction aimed at increasing children's knowledge and use of reading comprehension strategies readily enhances reading performance of children from grade 3 on (Cross & Paris, 1988; Dickson et al., 1998).

Around ages 7 to 8, a major shift occurs from "learning to read" to "reading to learn" (Ely, 1997). As decoding and comprehension skills reach a high level of efficiency, adolescent readers can become actively engaged with the text. They adjust the way they read to fit their current purpose—at times seeking new facts and ideas, at other times questioning, agreeing, or disagreeing with the writer's viewpoint.

## MATHEMATICS

Mathematical reasoning, like reading, builds on informally acquired knowledge. Recall from Chapter 6 that some evidence suggests that by 5 months, infants track the number of items, up to three, that a hand hides behind a screen; they look longer at quantities inconsistent with the hand's behaviour (see page 253). Between 14 and 16 months, toddlers display a beginning grasp of **ordinality,** or order relationships between quantities, such as three is more than two and two is more than one—an attainment that serves as the basis for more complex understandings (Starkey, 1992).

**EARLY CHILDHOOD.** In the early preschool years, children start to attach verbal labels (such as "lots," "little," "big," and "small") to different amounts and sizes. And between ages 2 and 3, many begin to count. However, at first, counting is little more than a memorized routine, as in "Onetwothreefourfivesix!" Or children repeat a few number words while vaguely pointing toward objects they have seen others count (Fuson, 1992).

Soon, however, counting becomes more precise. Most 3- to 4-year-olds have established an accurate one-to-one correspondence between a short sequence of number words and the items they represent (Geary, 1995). Three-year-olds may not have memorized the correct number labels. For example, one child counted three items by saying, "1, 6, 10." But her pointing gestures show a one-to-one correspondence, which indicates that she is about to master correct counting (Graham, 1999).

Sometime between ages 4 and 5, children grasp the vital principle of **cardinality.** They understand that the last word in a counting sequence indicates the quantity of items in a set (Bermejo, 1996). Mastery of cardinality increases the efficiency of children's counting. By age 4, children use counting to solve arithmetic problems. At first, their strategies are tied to the order of numbers as presented; when given 2 + 4, they "count on" from 2 (Ginsburg, Klein, & Starkey, 1998). Soon they experiment with various strategies (refer back to our discussion of Siegler's model of strategy choice, page 276) in both addition and subtraction, and they acquire fast, accurate procedures.

Jeff Bisanz, of the University of Alberta, and Joanne LeFevre of Carleton University collaborated on research on the development of children's mathematical skills (1992). They argued that preschoolers' less developed arithmetic performance in comparison to that of older children may partially be explained by too heavy demands being placed on their information-

**ordinality**
A principle specifying order (more-than and less-than) relationships between quantities.

**cardinality**
A principle specifying that the last number in a counting sequence indicates the quantity of items in a set.

Counting on fingers is an early, spontaneous approach that children use to experiment with strategies for solving arithmetic problems. As they try out various routes to solution and select those that are efficient and accurate, answers become more strongly associated with problems. Soon children give up counting on fingers in favour of retrieving the right answer.

processing capacities. Young children's accuracy on arithmetic problems decreases when their working memory is not sufficient. However, when the arithmetic problems are nonverbal in nature, such as when asked to make a group of tokens equal to a demonstrated amount, even some preschoolers can develop spontaneous conceptual solutions.

The basic arithmetic knowledge just described emerges universally around the world, although ways of representing numbers vary. As Figure 7.13 shows, among the Oksapmin, an agricultural society of Papua New Guinea, counting is mapped onto 27 body parts, which serve as number terms. Using this system, Oksapmin children keep track of quantities, measure, and play number games. Instead of counting on fingers, they point to body parts as they expand their calculation skills (Saxe, 1985).

In homes and preschools where adults provide many occasions and requests for counting, comparing quantities, and basic arithmetic in meaningful situations, children construct basic numerical concepts sooner (Geary, 1995). Then these concepts are solidly available as supports for the wide variety of mathematical skills children will be taught in school.

**MIDDLE CHILDHOOD.** Mathematics teaching in elementary school builds on and greatly enriches children's informal knowledge. Written notation systems and formal computational techniques enhance children's ability to represent numbers and compute. Over the early elementary school years, children acquire basic math facts through a combination of frequent practice and reasoning about number concepts. (Return to page 277 for research supporting the importance of both extended practice and a grasp of concepts.) Eventually children retrieve answers automatically and apply this knowledge to more complex problems.

Arguments about how to teach mathematics resemble those in reading. Extensive speeded practice is pitted against "number sense," or understanding. Yet once again, a blend of these two approaches is most beneficial. In learning basic math, poorly performing students move too quickly toward trying to retrieve answers automatically. Their responses are often wrong because the children have not used strategies long enough to test which ones result in rapid, accurate solutions. And when asked to explain math concepts, their performance is weak (Canobi, Reeve, & Pattison, 1998). This suggests that encouraging students to apply strategies and making sure they understand why certain ones work well are vital for solid mastery of basic math.

A similar picture emerges for more complex skills, such as carrying in addition, borrowing in subtraction, and operating with decimals and fractions. Children's mistakes indicate that they draw on their experience with easier problems and invent strategies, which do not always work. Or they try to use a procedure they have been taught but do not fully understand. For example, look at the following subtraction errors:

**FIGURE** 7.13

**Sequence of body parts used for counting by the Oksapmin of Papua New Guinea.** In the Oksapmin language, there are no terms for numbers aside from the body part names themselves (for example, "nose" represents "fourteen"). Children begin to use this system in the preschool years. Instead of counting on fingers, they can often be seen pointing to body parts. With age, they adapt the technique to handle more complex computation. (From G. B. Saxe, 1985, "Effects of Schooling on Arithmetical Understanding: Studies with Oksapmin Children in Papua New Guinea," *Journal of Educational Psychology, 77,* p. 505. Copyright © 1985 by the American Psychological Association. Reprinted by permission of the publisher and author.)

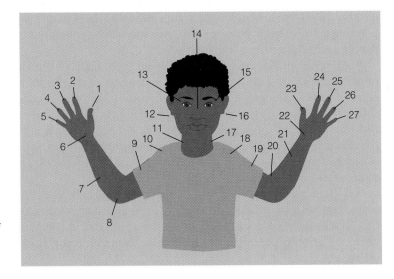

$$\begin{array}{r} 427 \\ -138 \\ \hline 311 \end{array}$$
$$\begin{array}{r} {}^{6}\cancel{7},{}^{1}002 \\ 5,445 \\ \hline 1,447 \end{array}$$

In the first problem, the child consistently subtracts a smaller from a larger digit, regardless of which is on top. In the second, columns with zeros are skipped in a borrowing operation, and the bottom digit is written as the answer. Researchers believe that drill-oriented math instruction that provides children with little opportunity to experiment with problem solving, to grasp the reasons behind strategies, and to evaluate solution techniques and answers is at the heart of these difficulties (Carpenter et al., 1999; Fuson, 1990).

Cross-cultural evidence suggests that North American math instruction may have gone too far in emphasizing computational drill. We will see in Chapter 15 that children in Asian nations are ahead of North American students in mathematical development. As the Cultural Influences box on page 304 illustrates, Asian children receive a variety of supports for acquiring mathematical knowledge. The result is deeper processing—formation of secure numerical concepts that provide a firm foundation for mastery of new skills.

## SCIENTIFIC REASONING

During a free moment in physical education class, 13-year-old Heidi wondered why more of her tennis serves and returns seemed to pass the net and drop in her opponent's court when she used a particular brand of balls. "Maybe it's something about their colour or size? Hmm, possibly it's their surface texture, which might affect their bounce," she thought to herself as she carefully inspected several balls.

The heart of scientific reasoning is coordinating theories with evidence. A scientist can clearly describe the theory he or she favours, knows what evidence is needed to support it and what would refute it, and can explain how pitting evidence against available theories led to the acceptance of one theory as opposed to others.

Deanna Kuhn has conducted extensive research into the development of scientific reasoning, using problems that resemble tasks used by Piaget, in that several variables might affect an outcome. In one series of studies, third, sixth, and ninth graders; adults of mixed educational backgrounds; and professional scientists were provided with evidence, sometimes consistent and sometimes conflicting with theories. Then they were asked questions about the accuracy of each theory.

For example, participants were given a problem much like the one Heidi posed. They were asked to theorize about which of several features of sports balls—size (large or small), colour (light or dark), surface texture (rough or smooth), or presence or absence of ridges—influences the quality of a player's serve. Next, they were told about the theory of Mr. (or Ms.) S, who believes that the ball's size is important, and the theory of Mr. (or Ms.) C, who thinks that colour makes a difference. Finally, the interviewer presented evidence by placing balls with certain characteristics in two baskets, labelled "good serve" and "bad serve" (see Figure 7.14).

**AGE-RELATED CHANGE.** Kuhn and her collaborators (1988) found that the capacity to reason like a scientist improved with age. The youngest participants often ignored conflicting evidence or distorted it in ways consistent with their theory. When one third grader, who judged that size was causal (with large balls producing good serves and small balls, bad serves), was shown incomplete evidence (a single, large, light-coloured ball in the good-serve basket and no balls in the bad-serve basket), he insisted on the accuracy of Mr. S's theory (which was also his own). Asked to explain, he stated flatly, "Because this ball is big...the colour doesn't really matter" (Kuhn, 1989, p. 677).

**FIGURE 7.14**

**Which features of these sports balls—size, colour, surface texture, or presence or absence of ridges—influence the quality of a player's serve?** This set of evidence suggests that colour might be important, since light-coloured balls are largely in the good-serve basket and dark-coloured balls in the bad-serve basket. But the same is true for texture! The good-serve basket has mostly smooth balls; the bad-serve basket, rough balls. Since all light-coloured balls are smooth and all dark-coloured balls are rough, we cannot tell whether colour or texture makes a difference. But we can conclude that size and presence or absence of ridges are not important, since these features are equally represented in the good-serve and bad-serve baskets. (Adapted from Kuhn, Amsel, & O'Loughlin, 1988.)

Good Serve

Bad Serve

# cultural influences

## ASIAN CHILDREN'S UNDERSTANDING OF MULTIDIGIT ADDITION AND SUBTRACTION

*e*lementary school students in Canada find multidigit addition and subtraction problems requiring trades between columns very difficult. Many try to solve these problems by rote, without grasping crucial aspects of the procedure. They seem to have a single-digit conception of multidigit numbers. For example, they tend to view the 3 in 5386 as just 3 rather than 300. As a result, when they carry to or borrow from this column, they are likely to compute the value incorrectly.

Chinese, Japanese, and Korean children, by contrast, are highly accurate at multidigit addition and subtraction. What accounts for their superior performance? To find out, Karen Fuson and Youngshim Kwon (1992) observed Korean second and third graders solving two- and three-digit problems and asked questions about their knowledge. The children's performance was excellent, even when they had not yet had formal instruction on the topic.

Quantitative understanding of multidigit numbers was clearly responsible. Almost all Korean children identified the tens' and hundreds' columns correctly as they described how to solve problems. And no Korean child viewed a "1" mark signalling trading to the tens column as "one," as Canadian children often do. Instead, they clearly identified it as "ten" if it came from the ones' column (addition) and "one hundred" if it came from the hundreds' column (subtraction). Especially remarkable were third graders' clear explanations of how to perform complex, multistep trading operations that stump their North American agemates. In fact, most Korean third graders no longer wrote extra marks when solving these

problems. They handled intricate trading procedures mentally.

Several cultural and language-based factors contribute to the sharp skill advantage of Asian students. First, use of the metric system, which presents one, ten, hundred, and thousand values in all areas of measurement, helps children think in ways that are consistent with place value. Second, English words for two-digit numbers (such as twelve and thirteen) are irregular and do not convey the idea of tens and ones. Asian-language number words ("ten two," "ten three") make this composition obvious. Chinese-speaking 5-year-olds understand that numbers in the "teens" are composed of a tens-value and a ones-value, whereas their North American agemates show no evidence of this knowledge (Ho & Fuson, 1998). Asian number words are also shorter and more quickly pronounced. This facilitates counting strategies and increases the speed with which children can retrieve math facts from long-term memory (Geary et al., 1996; Jensen & Whang, 1994). Finally, Asian children learn to use the abacus in school, which strengthens place-value understanding and computation skill. Using a "mental image" of the abacus, expert children and adults engage in rapid mental calculation with multidigit numbers (Stigler, 1984).

Asian teaching practices support rapid mastery of multidigit problems as well. For example, teachers use phrases that explicitly describe the trading operation. Instead of carrying, they say "raise up," and instead of borrowing, they say "bring down" (Fuson, 1992). Finally, multidigit problems are introduced earlier in Asian schools, and teachers more

© FUJI FOTO/THE IMAGE WORKS

Cultural and language-based factors contribute to Asian children's skill at manipulating multidigit numbers. The abacus supports these Japanese pupils' understanding of place value. Ones, tens, hundreds, and thousands are each represented by a different column of beads, and calculations are performed by moving the beads to different positions. As children become skilled at using the abacus, they generate mental images that assist them in solving complex arithmetic problems.

often provide useful explanations— how to use procedures and when they should be used (Perry, 2000).

In sum, what appears at first glance to be the same cognitive task is actually quite different in different cultures. These findings highlight several ways that teachers and parents might ease children's mastery of numerical concepts.

These findings, and others like them, reveal that instead of viewing evidence as separate from and bearing on a theory, children often blend the two into a single representation of "the way things are." The ability to distinguish theory from evidence and use logical rules to examine their relationship in complex, multi-variable situations improves from childhood into adolescence and adulthood (Foltz, Overton, & Ricco, 1995; Kuhn et al., 1995; Schauble, 1996).

**HOW SCIENTIFIC REASONING DEVELOPS.** What factors support skill at coordinating theory with evidence? Greater processing capacity, permitting a theory and the effects of several variables to be compared at once, is vital. In addition, adolescents benefit from exposure to increasingly complex problems and instruction that highlights critical features of tasks and effective strategies. Consequently, scientific reasoning is strongly influenced by years of schooling, whether individuals grapple with traditional scientific tasks (like the sports ball problem) or engage in informal reasoning—for example, justify a theory about what causes children to fail in school (Kuhn, 1993).

Many researchers believe that sophisticated *metacognitive knowledge* is at the heart of scientific reasoning (Kuhn, 1999; Moshman, 1999). When children receive continuous opportunities to pit theory against evidence, eventually they *reflect* on their current strategies, revise them, and become aware of the nature of logic. Then they apply their abstract appreciation of logic to a wide variety of situations. The ability to *think about* theories, *deliberately isolate* variables, and *actively seek* disconfirming evidence is rarely present before adolescence (Moshman, 1998).

Although much better at scientific reasoning than children, adolescents and adults continue to show a self-serving bias in their thinking. They apply logic more effectively to ideas they doubt than to ones they favour (Klaczynski, 1997; Klaczynski & Narasimham, 1998a). Reasoning scientifically, however, requires the metacognitive capacity to evaluate one's objectivity—a disposition to be fair-minded rather than self-serving (Moshman, 1999). As we will see in Chapter 11, this flexible, open-minded approach is not just a cognitive attainment but a personality trait—one that assists teenagers greatly in forming an identity and developing morally.

Return to page 274, and review Robbie Case's information-processing view of Piaget's stages. Does Case's concept of central conceptual structures remind you of the metacognitive advances just described? Piaget also underscored the role of metacognition in formal operational thought when he spoke of "operating on operations" (see Chapter 6, page 245). However, information-processing findings reveal that scientific reasoning does not result from an abrupt, stagewise change, as Piaget believed. Instead, it develops gradually out of many specific experiences that require children and adolescents to match theory against evidence and reflect on their thinking.

# Evaluation of the Information-Processing Approach

A MAJOR STRENGTH OF THE information-processing approach is its explicitness and precision in breaking down complex cognitive performance into its components. Information processing has provided a wealth of detailed evidence on how younger versus older and more-skilled versus less-skilled individuals attend, remember, reason, and solve problems. It also offers precise mechanisms of cognitive development; Table 7.1 on page 306 summarizes the most important ones. As you review them, think back to theories and evidence discussed throughout this chapter that illustrate the role of each. Finally, because of its precision, information-processing research has contributed greatly to the design of teaching techniques that advance many aspects of children's thinking.

Nevertheless, the information-processing perspective has several limitations. The first, ironically, stems from its central strength: By analyzing cognition into its components, information processing has had difficulty putting them back together into a broad, comprehensive theory of development. In fact, we have seen that the neo-Piagetian perspective is a major effort to build a general theory by retaining Piaget's stages while drawing on information-processing mechanisms to explain cognitive change.

**TABLE** 7.1

Mechanisms of Cognitive Development from the Information-Processing Perspective

| MECHANISM | DESCRIPTION |
|---|---|
| Basic processing capacity | Capacity of the mental system increases as a result of brain development. |
| Processing efficiency | Speed of basic operations increases, freeing up working memory for other mental activities. |
| Encoding of information | Encoding, in the form of attention, becomes more thorough and better adapted to task demands. |
| Cognitive inhibition | Ability to prevent internal and external distracting stimuli from capturing attention improves, freeing up working memory for remembering, reasoning, and solving problems. |
| Strategy execution | Strategies become more effective, improving storage and retrieval of information. |
| Knowledge | Amount and structure of the knowledge base increase, making new, related information more meaningful so it is easier to store and retrieve. |
| Metacognition | Awareness and understanding of cognitive processes expand and self-regulation improves, leading strategies to be applied more effectively in a wider range of situations. |

Furthermore, the computer metaphor, although bringing precision to research on the human mind, has drawbacks. Computer models of cognitive processing, although complex in their own right, do not reflect the richness of real-life learning experiences. For example, they overlook aspects of cognition that are not linear and logical, such as imagination and creativity. In addition, computers do not have desires, interests, and intentions. And they cannot engage in interaction with others as children do when learning from parents, teachers, and peers. Perhaps because of the narrowness of the computer metaphor, information processing has not yet told us much about the links between cognition and other areas of development. Researchers have applied information-processing assumptions to children's thinking about certain aspects of their social world, and we will see some examples in later chapters. But it is still true that extensions of Piaget's theory prevail when it comes to research on children's social and moral understanding.

Finally, information-processing research has been slow to respond to the growing interest in the biological bases of cognitive development. Connectionist theories have begun to fill this gap by creating computer simulations that model human information processing at a neural level. Evolutionary ideas, as well, have started to appear in information-processing theories, as Siegler's model of strategy choice illustrates. And studies of the psychophysiological bases of certain cognitive changes, such as gains in cognitive inhibition, are enlarging our appreciation of the central role of brain development in children's processing capacity.

Despite its shortcomings, the information-processing approach holds great promise. New breakthroughs in understanding neurological changes that underlie various mental activities, mechanisms of cognitive development, and teaching techniques that support children's learning are likely to take place in the years to come.

## ASK YOURSELF

**review**    Cite evidence indicating that reading and mathematics achievement in elementary school build on a rich foundation of informally acquired knowledge during the preschool years.

**review**    Why are gains in processing capacity and metacognition especially important for development of scientific reasoning? What can teachers do to promote the development of scientific reasoning?

**apply**    Review Heidi's reasoning about the impact of several variables on the bounce of tennis balls on page 303. What features of her thinking suggest that she is beginning to reason scientifically?

**connect**    Using mechanisms of cognitive development discussed in this chapter, explain why teaching both basic skills and understanding of concepts and strategies is vital for children's solid mastery of reading and mathematics in middle childhood.

# summary

## THE INFORMATION-PROCESSING APPROACH

*What unique features characterize the information-processing approach to cognitive development?*

- The information-processing approach views the mind as a complex, symbol-manipulating system through which information flows, much like a computer. The computer analogy helps researchers analyze thought into components, each of which can be studied thoroughly to yield a detailed understanding of what children and adults do when faced with a task or problem.

## GENERAL MODELS OF INFORMATION PROCESSING

*Describe the store and connectionist models, noting implications for cognitive development.*

- The **store model** assumes that we hold, or store, information in three parts of the system, where **mental strategies** operate on it so that it can be retained and used efficiently. The **sensory register** and **working,** or **short-term, memory** are limited in capacity. **Long-term memory,** our permanent knowledge base, is limitless. The store model suggests that two broad aspects of the cognitive system increase with age: (1) the capacity of its stores, especially working memory, and (2) the extent and effectiveness of strategy use. Research on **memory span** supports both of these trends.

- **Connectionist,** or **artificial neural network, models** use computer simulations to model the workings of neurons in the brain. Thousands of simple processing units, organized into layers, are programmed to change with experience, granting the network the capacity to learn. Researchers compare the network's responses with those of children and adults. Findings reveal that gradual, internal learning often precedes changes in behaviour that appear stagelike when viewed from outside the system. Because just a few built-in procedures get learning started, connectionists claim that the human cognitive system is a general pro-

cessing device. However, artificial neural networks learn more slowly than do children and adults.

## DEVELOPMENTAL THEORIES OF INFORMATION PROCESSING

*Describe and evaluate Case's neo-Piagetian theory and Siegler's model of strategy choice.*

- According to Case's **neo-Piagetian theory,** cognitive development results from gains in working-memory capacity. Brain development and automatization of strategies due to practice release working memory for combining old schemes and generating new ones. When schemes consolidate into **central conceptual structures,** working memory expands further, and the child moves up to a new Piagetian stage. Case's theory accounts for domain-specific change through variations in the complexity of tasks and children's experiences. His powerful ideas must be tested with many more tasks.

- Siegler's **model of strategy choice** applies an evolutionary perspective to children's cognition. Strategy development follows an overlapping-wave pattern. Faced with challenging problems, children try a variety of strategies, gradually selecting from them on the basis of accuracy and speed. Siegler's findings reveal that no child thinks in just one way, even on the same task. So far, mechanisms that lead children to choose among strategies are clearer than those that produce strategy variation.

## ATTENTION

*Describe the development of attention in terms of selective, adaptable, and planful strategies, noting the role of gains in processing capacity.*

- Attention becomes more sustained and selective with age; children become better at focusing on just those aspects of a situation that are relevant to their goals. Older children are also better at adapting attention to task requirements. Gains in **cognitive inhibition,** believed to be due to development of the frontal lobes of the

cerebral cortex, are particularly marked in middle childhood. They lead to expansion of processing capacity and underlie children's greater selectivity of attention.

- Development of attentional (and memory) strategies tends to occur in the following four phases: (1) **production deficiency** (failure to use the strategy); (2) **control deficiency** (failure to execute the strategy consistently); (3) **utilization deficiency** (consistent use of the strategy, but little or no improvement in performance); and (4) **effective strategy use.**

- During middle childhood, children become better at **planning.** On tasks that require systematic visual search or the coordination of many acts, school-age children are more likely than preschoolers to decide how to proceed in an orderly fashion. Children learn much about planning through adult encouragement and many opportunities to practise planning. The serious attentional and impulse-control difficulties of children with **attention-deficit hyperactivity disorder (ADHD),** which may be due to an impairment in inhibition, lead to both academic and social problems.

## MEMORY

*Describe the development of memory strategies of rehearsal, organization, and elaboration, noting the influence of task demands and culture.*

- Although the beginnings of memory strategies can be seen during the preschool years, young children seldom engage in **rehearsal** or **organization.** As use of these strategies improves, children combine them; the more strategies children use simultaneously, the better they remember. Because it taxes working memory, **elaboration** is a late-developing strategy that appears at the end of middle childhood and becomes more common during adolescence.

- Like young children, people in non-Western cultures who have no formal schooling rarely use, or benefit from instruction in, memory strategies. Tasks requiring children to memorize isolated bits of information in school promote deliberate memorization in middle childhood.

*Describe the development of three approaches to memory retrieval: recognition, recall, and reconstruction.*

■ **Recognition,** the simplest form of retrieval, is a fairly automatic process that is highly accurate by the preschool years. In contrast, **recall,** or generating a mental representation of an absent stimulus, is more difficult and shows much greater improvement with age, as older children make use of a wider range of retrieval cues.

■ Even young children engage in **reconstruction** when remembering complex, meaningful material. Over time, as originally provided information decays and new information is presented, children make more inferences about actors and actions. This increases the coherence of reconstructed information and, therefore, its memorableness. However, reconstruction shows that much recalled information can be inaccurate.

■ According to **fuzzy-trace theory,** information is reconstructed automatically at encoding into a vague, fuzzy version called a **gist,** which is stored separately from the verbatim version and is especially useful for reasoning. With age, children rely less on verbatim and more on gist memory, which contributes to improved reasoning and recall.

*How do gains in knowledge enhance memory performance?*

■ Gains in the quantity and structure of the knowledge base enhance memory performance by making new, related information easier to store and retrieve. More knowledgeable children show greater organization at retrieval, which suggests that they apply memory strategies in their area of expertise with little or no effort. Children differ not only in what they know but in how motivated they are to use their knowledge to acquire new information. Extensive knowledge and use of memory strategies support one another.

*Describe the development and function of scripts and autobiographical memory.*

■ Like adults, young children remember familiar experiences in terms of **scripts**—general representations of what occurs and when it occurs in a particular situation. Scripts become more elaborate with age and permit children to predict what might happen on future similar occasions. They may be the developmental link in the transition from **episodic** to **semantic memory.**

■ Some researchers speculate that brain development, especially growth of the frontal lobes of the cerebral cortex, leads to gains in conscious, explicit memory and the offset of **infantile amnesia** after 3 years of age. Others think that strengthening of gist memory is involved. And still others believe that infantile amnesia subsides as children form a psychological self and talk about past events with adults. Gradually, children adopt the narrative thinking generated in these dialogues, forming an **autobiographical memory.** Parents who use an elaborative rather than repetitive conversational style have children who produce more coherent and detailed personal stories.

## METACOGNITION

*Describe the development of metacognitive knowledge and cognitive self-regulation, and explain why cognitive self-regulation is vital for success on complex tasks.*

■ **Metacognition** expands greatly as children construct a naive **theory of mind,** a coherent understanding of people as mental beings. From early to middle childhood, children's awareness of cognitive capacities, strategies, and task variables becomes more accurate and complete. In addition, their view of the mind changes from a passive to an active, process-oriented approach to mental functioning. Once children become conscious of the many factors that influence mental activity, they take account of interactions between variables, and metacognition becomes a comprehensive theory.

■ **Cognitive self-regulation**—continuously monitoring progress toward a goal, checking outcomes, and redirecting unsuccessful efforts—develops slowly. The relationship between knowledge of memory strategies and recall strengthens over the elementary school years. Gains in com-

prehension monitoring also reflect improved cognitive self-regulation. By adolescence, cognitive self-regulation is a strong predictor of academic success. Parents and teachers who suggest self-regulatory strategies and explain why they are effective help children internalize those procedures and generalize them to new situations.

## APPLICATIONS OF INFORMATION PROCESSING TO ACADEMIC LEARNING

*Discuss development in reading, mathematics, and scientific reasoning, noting the implications of research findings for teaching in each academic domain.*

■ Reading requires executing many cognitive skills simultaneously, taxing all aspects of the information-processing system. **Emergent literacy** reveals that young children understand a great deal about written language before they read and write in conventional ways. Preschoolers gradually revise incorrect ideas about the meaning of written symbols as their perceptual and cognitive capacities improve, as they encounter writing in many contexts, and as adults help them with written communication. The more informal literacy-related experiences young children have, the better prepared they are to learn to read and write after entering school.

■ School-age children experiment and choose adaptively among strategies in learning to decode written symbols. Experts disagree on whether a **whole-language approach** or **basic-skills approach** should be used to teach beginning reading. Research suggests that a balanced mixture of both is most effective.

■ Like reading, mathematical reasoning builds on informally acquired knowledge. Toddlers display a beginning grasp of **ordinality,** which serves as the basis for more complex understandings. As preschoolers experiment with counting strategies, they grasp **cardinality,** which increases the efficiency of counting.

■ During the early school years, children apply diverse strategies adaptively to learn basic math facts. Children's mistakes in solving more complex problems reveal that they sometimes apply strategies incorrectly because they do not understand the basis for them. Mathematics instruction that combines practice in basic skills with conceptual understanding is best.

■ The heart of scientific reasoning is coordinating theories with evidence. Children (and to a lesser degree, adolescents and adults) often blend the two instead of viewing evidence as separate from and bearing on a theory. Greater processing capacity, permitting a theory and the effects of several variables to be compared at once, contributes to development of scientific reasoning. Also, tasks that offer repeated practice in pitting theories against evidence promote the metacognitive knowledge necessary for reasoning scientifically—thinking about theories, isolating variables, and seeking disconfirming evidence.

## EVALUATION OF THE INFORMATION-PROCESSING APPROACH

*Summarize the strengths and limitations of the information-processing approach.*

■ A major strength of the information-processing approach is its precision in breaking down cognition into separate elements so each can be studied thoroughly. As a result, information processing has uncovered a variety of explicit mechanisms of cognitive change and has contributed greatly to the design of teaching techniques that advance children's thinking.

■ Nevertheless, information processing has not yet led to a comprehensive theory nor told us much about the links between cognition and other areas of development. Although information-processing researchers have been slow to address the growing interest in biological bases of cognitive development, they are making strides in this area.

# important terms and concepts

attention-deficit hyperactivity disorder (ADHD) (p. 282)
autobiographical memory (p. 290)
basic-skills approach (p. 299)
cardinality (p. 301)
central conceptual structures (p. 275)
central executive (p. 273)
cognitive inhibition (p. 279)
cognitive self-regulation (p. 296)
connectionist, or artificial neural network, models (p. 273)
control deficiency (p. 280)
effective strategy use (p. 280)
elaboration (p. 284)

emergent literacy (p. 298)
episodic memory (p. 289)
fuzzy-trace theory (p. 287)
gist (p. 287)
infantile amnesia (p. 290)
long-term memory (p. 273)
memory span (p. 273)
mental strategies (p. 271)
metacognition (p. 295)
model of strategy choice (p. 276)
neo-Piagetian theory (p. 274)
ordinality (p. 301)
organization (p. 283)
planning (p. 280)

production deficiency (p. 280)
recall (p. 285)
recognition (p. 285)
reconstruction (p. 286)
rehearsal (p. 283)
scripts (p. 289)
semantic memory (p. 289)
sensory register (p. 271)
store model (p. 271)
theory of mind (p. 295)
utilization deficiency (p. 280)
whole-language approach (p. 299)
working, or short-term, memory (p. 271)

"Untitled"
Myhriha P.
13 years, Switzerland

Intelligence extends far beyond the items included on intelligence tests. For example, it also encompasses innovative interpretations of reality—a type of thinking involved in creativity. Chapter 8 considers the wide variation of children's intelligence, along with genetic, experiential, and cultural factors that underlie that variation.

Reprinted by permission from The International Museum of Children's Art, Oslo, Norway

# *eight*

## Intelligence

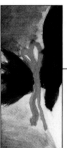

FIVE-YEAR-OLD HASSAN SAT IN A small, unfamiliar testing room while Nora, an adult he had met only moments ago, prepared to give him an intelligence test. Eager to come when Nora had arrived at his kindergarten classroom, Hassan became confused once the testing session began.

Starting with some word definitions, Nora asked, "Hassan, how are wood and coal alike? How are they the same?"

Hassan's eyebrows wrinkled in puzzlement. He shrugged his shoulders and said, "Well, they're both hard."

Nora continued, "And an apple and a peach?"

"They taste good," responded Hassan, looking up at Nora's face for any sign that he was doing all right.

Nora looked back pleasantly but moved along. "A ship and an automobile?"

Hassan paused, unsure of what Nora meant. "They're hard," he finally replied, returning to his first response.

"Iron and silver?"

"They're hard," Hassan repeated, still trying to figure out what Nora's questions were all about. (Adapted from Miller-Jones, 1989, p. 362)

The **psychometric approach** to cognitive development is the basis for the wide variety of intelligence tests available for assessing children's mental abilities. As Nora's testing of Hassan illustrates, the psychometric perspective differs from Piagetian, Vygotskian, and information-processing views in being far more product oriented than process oriented. For the most part, it focuses on outcomes and results—how many and what

**psychometric approach**
A product-oriented approach to cognitive development that focuses on the construction of tests to assess mental abilities.

kinds of questions children of different ages answer correctly. Psychometric researchers ask such questions as these: What factors, or dimensions, make up intelligence, and how do they change with age? How can intelligence be measured so scores predict future academic achievement, career attainment, and other aspects of intellectual success? To what extent do children of the same age differ in intelligence, and what explains those differences?

As we examine these questions, we will quickly become immersed in the IQ nature–nurture debate, along with the controversy over whether intelligence tests are biased and do not accurately measure low-income and ethnic minority children's abilities. As our discussion proceeds, we will see that the cognitive perspectives considered in previous chapters, as well as research on contextual influences, have added much to our understanding of children's test performance.

Our discussion concludes with the development of creativity and special talents. Although these are among the most highly valued human characteristics, they are not represented on current intelligence tests for children.

# Definitions of Intelligence

WHAT FAMOUS PERSON would you name as an example of exceptional intelligence? For almost 20 years, University of British Columbia students have given the most votes to Albert Einstein. The top-voted Canadian has been Pierre Trudeau (Paulhus & Landolt, 2000). Now jot down a list of behaviours that you regard as typical of highly intelligent people. Did you come up with just one or two characteristics or a great many? When Robert Sternberg asked nearly 500 laypeople and 24 experts to complete a similar exercise, he found that both groups viewed intelligence as a complex construct that included verbal ability, practical problem solving, and social competence (Sternberg & Detterman, 1986). But respondents differed in their descriptions of these attributes. And answers of contemporary experts showed less consensus than those gathered in a similar study conducted 50 years earlier! Clearly, most people think of intelligence as made up of a variety of attributes.

Defining children's intelligence is especially challenging, since behaviours that reflect intelligent behaviour change with age. To illustrate, list five traits of intelligent 6-month-olds, 2-year-olds, 10-year-olds, and adults. The responses of students in an introductory psychology course are shown in Table 8.1. Notice how sensorimotor responsiveness becomes less important, whereas verbal ability, problem solving, and reasoning become more important with age (Siegler & Richards, 1980).

The researchers also asked university students to estimate correlations between various abilities. Students thought there would be some close connections, but they predicted considerable distinctiveness as well. This tension between intelligence as a single, overarching ability versus a collection of loosely related skills is also evident in the theories on which mental tests are based.

Behaviours that reflect intelligent behaviour change with age. These children, ages 6 months and 3 years, demonstrate their intelligence in very different ways. After infancy, sensorimotor responsiveness becomes less important and problem solving and reasoning become more important.

## ALFRED BINET: A HOLISTIC VIEW

The social and educational climate of the late nineteenth and early twentieth centuries sparked the intelligence testing movement. The most important influence was the beginning of universal public education in Europe and North America. Once schools opened their doors to all children—not just society's privileged—educators called for methods to help identify students who could not profit from regular classroom instruction. The first successful intelligence test, constructed by French psychologist Alfred Binet and his colleague Theodore Simon in 1905, responded to this need.

The French Ministry of Instruction asked Binet to devise an objective method for assigning pupils to special classes—one based on mental ability, not classroom disruptiveness. Other researchers had tried to assess intelligence using simple measures of sensory responsiveness and reaction time (Cattell, 1890; Galton, 1883). In contrast, Binet believed that test items should assess complex

© SPENCER GRANT/STOCK BOSTON

**TABLE** 8.1

Five Traits Most Often Mentioned by University Students as Characterizing Intelligence at Different Ages

| 6-MONTH-OLDS | 2-YEAR-OLDS | 10-YEAR-OLDS | ADULTS |
|---|---|---|---|
| 1. Recognition of people and objects | 1. Verbal ability | 1. Verbal ability | 1. Reasoning |
| 2. Motor coordination | 2. Learning ability | 2, 3, 4. Learning ability; problem solving; reasoning (all three tied) | 2. Verbal ability |
| 3. Alertness | 3. Awareness of people and environment | | 3. Problem solving |
| 4. Awareness of environment | 4. Motor coordination | 5. Creativity | 4. Learning ability |
| 5. Verbalization | 5. Curiosity | | 5. Creativity |

*Source:* R. S. Siegler & D. D. Richards, 1980. "College Students' Prototypes of Children's Intelligence." Paper presented at the annual meeting of the American Psychological Association, New York. Adapted by permission of the author.

functions involved in intelligent behaviour, such as memory, good judgment, and abstraction. Consequently, Binet and Simon devised a test of "general mental ability" that included a variety of verbal and nonverbal reasoning tasks. Their test was also the first *developmental* approach to test construction. Items varied in difficulty, and each was classified according to the age at which a typical child could first pass it (Brody, 2000).

The Binet test was so successful in predicting school performance that it became the basis for new intelligence tests developed in other countries. For example, in 1916, Lewis Terman at Stanford University in California adapted it, and since then, the test has been known as the Stanford-Binet Intelligence Scale. As we will see later, the Stanford-Binet has changed greatly; it no longer provides just a single, holistic measure of intelligence.

## THE FACTOR ANALYSTS: A MULTIFACETED VIEW

To determine whether intelligence is a holistic trait or an assortment of abilities, researchers used a special statistical procedure. As Figure 8.1 on page 314 shows, a variety of items typically appear on intelligence tests for children. In **factor analysis,** scores on many separate items are combined into a few factors. Then the researcher gives each factor a name, based on common characteristics of items that are closely correlated with the factor. For example, if vocabulary, verbal comprehension, and verbal analogy items all correlate highly with one another, the factor that describes them all might be labelled "verbal ability." Using this method, many researchers tried to identify the underlying mental abilities that contribute to successful intelligence test performance.

**EARLY FACTOR ANALYSTS.** The first influential factor analyst was British psychologist Charles Spearman (1927), who found that all test items he examined correlated with one another. Therefore, Spearman proposed a common underlying **general factor,** called "**g**." At the same time, he noticed that test items were not perfectly correlated. In other words, they varied in the extent to which they tapped "g." Consequently, he suggested that each item or set of similar items also measured a **specific factor,** called "**s**," that was unique to the task. Spearman's identification of "g" and "s" led his view to be called the *two-factor theory of intelligence.*

Spearman viewed "g" as central and supreme, and he was especially interested in its psychological characteristics. With further study, he concluded that "g" represented some kind of abstract reasoning power. Test items that required individuals to form relationships and apply general principles were the strongest correlates of "g." They also were the best predictors of cognitive performance outside the testing situation.

Louis Thurstone (1938), a contemporary of Spearman, soon took issue with the existence of "g." Instead, Thurstone argued, separate, unrelated intellectual abilities exist. Thurstone gave more than 50 intelligence tests to a large sample of university students; their scores produced seven clear factors. As a result, he concluded that intelligence consists of seven distinct **primary mental abilities:** verbal meaning, perceptual speed, reasoning, number, rote memory, word fluency, and spatial visualization.

**factor analysis**
A statistical procedure that combines scores from many separate test items into a few factors, which substitute for the separate scores. Used to identify mental abilities that contribute to successful performance on intelligence tests.

**general factor,** or "**g**"
In Spearman's theory of intelligence, a common factor representing abstract reasoning power that underlies a wide variety of test items.

**specific factor,** or "**s**"
In Spearman's theory of intelligence, a mental ability factor that is unique to a task.

**primary mental abilities**
In Thurstone's theory of intelligence, seven distinct mental abilities identified through factor analysis: verbal meaning, perceptual speed, reasoning, number, rote memory, word fluency, and spatial visualization.

FIGURE 8.1

**Test items like those on common intelligence tests for children.** In contrast to verbal items, nonverbal items do not require reading or direct use of language. Performance items are also nonverbal, but they require the child to draw or construct something rather than merely give a correct answer. As a result, they appear only on individually administered intelligence tests. (Logical reasoning, picture oddities, and spatial visualization examples are adapted with permission of The Free Press, a Division of Simon & Schuster, Inc., from *Bias in Mental Testing* by Arthur R. Jensen. Copyright © 1980 by Arthur R. Jensen.)

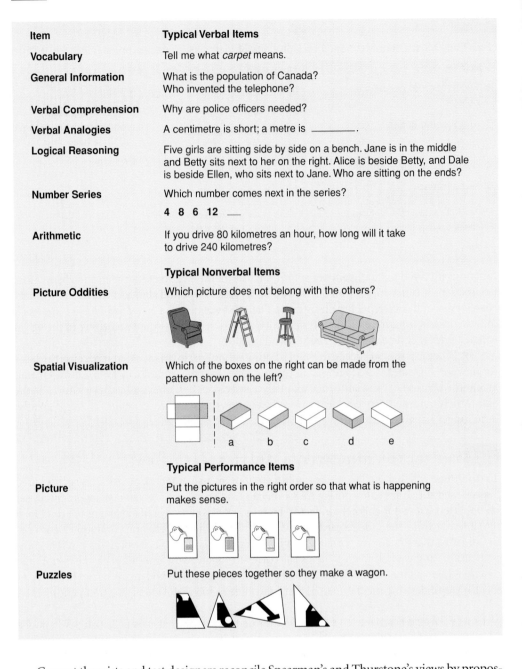

| Item | Typical Verbal Items |
|---|---|
| Vocabulary | Tell me what *carpet* means. |
| General Information | What is the population of Canada? Who invented the telephone? |
| Verbal Comprehension | Why are police officers needed? |
| Verbal Analogies | A centimetre is short; a metre is _____. |
| Logical Reasoning | Five girls are sitting side by side on a bench. Jane is in the middle and Betty sits next to her on the right. Alice is beside Betty, and Dale is beside Ellen, who sits next to Jane. Who are sitting on the ends? |
| Number Series | Which number comes next in the series? 4 8 6 12 __ |
| Arithmetic | If you drive 80 kilometres an hour, how long will it take to drive 240 kilometres? |

**Typical Nonverbal Items**

**Picture Oddities** — Which picture does not belong with the others?

**Spatial Visualization** — Which of the boxes on the right can be made from the pattern shown on the left?

a  b  c  d  e

**Typical Performance Items**

**Picture** — Put the pictures in the right order so that what is happening makes sense.

**Puzzles** — Put these pieces together so they make a wagon.

Current theorists and test designers reconcile Spearman's and Thurstone's views by proposing *hierarchical models* of mental abilities. At the highest level is "g," assumed to be present to a greater or lesser degree in all specialized factors. These factors, in turn, are measured by subtests, or groups of related items. Subtest scores provide information about a child's strengths and weaknesses. They also can be combined into an overall index of general intelligence.

**CONTEMPORARY FACTOR ANALYSTS.** Several contemporary theorists have extended factor-analytic research. The two most influential are R. B. Cattell and John Carroll. Each offers a unique, multifaceted perspective on intelligence.

*Crystallized versus Fluid Intelligence.* According to Raymond B. Cattell (1971, 1987), in addition to "g," intelligence consists of two factors. **Crystallized intelligence** consists of accumulated knowledge and skills; tasks highly correlated with it include vocabulary, general information, and arithmetic problems. In contrast, **fluid intelligence** involves the ability to see relationships among stimuli, as in the number series and spatial visualization

**crystallized intelligence**
In Cattell's theory, a form of intelligence that consists of accumulated knowledge and skills and that depends on culture and learning opportunities.

**fluid intelligence**
In Cattell's theory, a form of intelligence that involves the ability to see relationships among stimuli. Believed to depend largely on conditions in the brain.

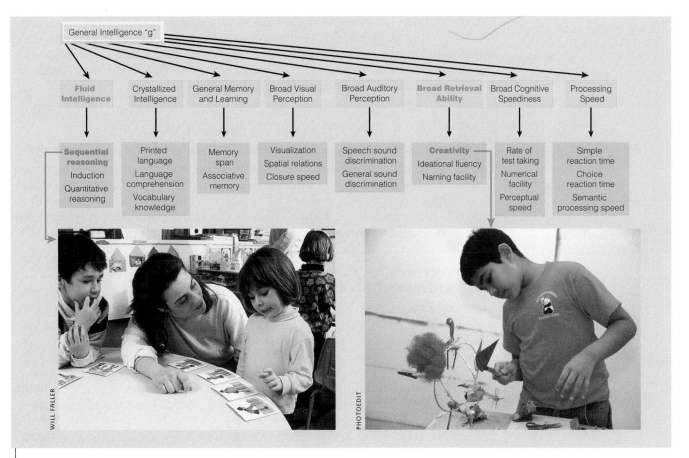

WILL FALLER

PHOTOEDIT

**FIGURE** 8.2

**Carroll's three-stratum theory of intelligence.** Second-stratum abilities are arranged from left to right in terms of their decreasing strength of relationship with "g." The photos depict specific manifestations of second-stratum factors, listed at the lowest stratum. The child on the left completes a sequential reasoning task in which she arranges pictures to tell a story—a type of fluid intelligence. The child on the right uses art materials creatively to build a snowman, applying his broad retrieval ability. (From J. B. Carroll, 1993, *Human Cognitive Abilities: A Survey of Factor-Analytic Studies*, New York: Cambridge University Press, p. 626. Adapted by permission.)

items in Figure 8.1. Although crystallized and fluid intelligence work together, crystallized intelligence depends on culture and learning opportunities, whereas fluid intelligence is believed to depend largely on conditions in the brain.

Among children who are similar in cultural and educational background, crystallized and fluid intelligence are highly correlated and difficult to distinguish, probably because children high in fluid intelligence acquire information more easily. But when children differ greatly in cultural and educational experiences, the two abilities show little relationship; children with the same fluid capacity may perform quite differently on crystallized tasks. As these findings suggest, Cattell's theory has important implications for the issue of cultural bias in intelligence testing (Horn, 1994). Tests aimed at reducing culturally specific content usually emphasize fluid over crystallized items.

***The Three-Stratum Theory of Intelligence.*** Using improved factor-analytic techniques, John Carroll (1993, 1997) reanalyzed hundreds of studies of relationships between mental abilities. His findings yielded a **three-stratum theory of intelligence** that elaborates the models proposed by Spearman, Thurstone, Cattell, and others. As Figure 8.2 shows, Carroll represents the structure of intelligence as a pyramid, with "g" at the top and eight broad abilities in the second stratum, arranged from left to right in terms of decreasing relationship with "g." Each broad ability is believed to be a basic, biological characteristic. At the lowest stratum are narrow abilities—specific manifestations of second-stratum factors that result from experience with particular tasks.

**three-stratum theory of intelligence**
Carroll's theory, which represents the structure of intelligence as a pyramid, with "g" at the top; eight broad, biologically based abilities at the second stratum; and narrower manifestations of these abilities at the lowest stratum that result from experience with particular tasks. The most comprehensive classification of mental abilities to be confirmed by factor-analytic research.

Carroll's model is the most comprehensive factor-analytic classification of mental abilities. As we will see in the next section, it provides a useful framework for researchers seeking to understand mental test performance in cognitive processing terms. The three-stratum theory highlights the multiplicity of intellectual factors sampled by current mental tests. Currently, no test measures all of Carroll's factors (Kranzler, 1997).

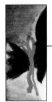

# Recent Advances in Defining Intelligence

MANY RESEARCHERS BELIEVE that factors on intelligence tests have limited use unless we can identify the cognitive processes responsible for those factors. Once we discover exactly what separates individuals who can solve certain mental test items from those who cannot, we will know more about why a particular child does well or poorly and what skills must be worked on to improve performance.

## COMBINING PSYCHOMETRIC AND INFORMATION-PROCESSING APPROACHES

To overcome the limitations of factor analysis, some investigators combine psychometric and information-processing approaches. They conduct **componential analyses** of children's test scores. This means that they look for relationships between aspects (or components) of information processing and children's intelligence test performance.

Which information-processing components have turned out to predict intelligence? Many studies reveal that speed of processing, measured in terms of reaction time on diverse cognitive tasks, is moderately related to general intelligence and to gains in mental test performance over time (Deary & Stough, 1996; Fry & Hale, 1996; Neubauer & Bucik, 1996). In fact, as early as 3 months of age, reaction time to visual stimuli predicts preschool intelligence (Dougherty & Haith, 1997).

These findings suggest that individuals whose nervous systems function more efficiently have an edge in intellectual skills. Because they can take in and manipulate information more quickly, they can grant more attention to solving problems. In support of this interpretation, Philip Vernon (1993) of the University of Western Ontario and others found that fast, strong EEG waves in response to stimulation (called event-related potentials, or ERPs) predict rapid cognitive processing and higher mental test scores (Rijsdijk & Boomsma, 1997). In addition, brain-imaging research reveals that the metabolic rate of the cortex when solving complex tasks is lower for more intelligent people, suggesting that they need to expend less mental effort (Vernon et al., 2001).

But rapid responding is not the only processing correlate of mental test performance. Strategy use also makes a difference, and it explains some of the association between response speed and intelligence (Miller & Vernon, 1992). Children who apply strategies effectively acquire more knowledge and can retrieve that knowledge rapidly—advantages that seem to carry over to performance on intelligence test items.

Componential research has also highlighted cognitive processes that are unrelated to test scores but that greatly aid children's thinking in everyday life. Certain aspects of metacognition—awareness of problem-solving strategies and organizational and planning skills—are not good predictors of general intelligence (Alexander & Schwanenflugel, 1996). In one study, fourth and fifth graders who were average in mental ability but high in metacognitive knowledge about problem solving did far better on Piagetian formal operational tasks (such as the pendulum problem) than did classmates with high test scores who knew little about effective problem-solving techniques (Swanson, 1990).

These first graders solve math problems with a special set of small blocks and help from each other. Children who apply strategies effectively acquire more knowledge and can retrieve it rapidly. As a result, they score higher on intelligence tests.

© RICHARD HUTCHINGS/PHOTOEDIT

As these findings illustrate, componential analyses isolate specific cognitive skills on which training might be especially helpful to some children. Nevertheless, the componential approach has one major shortcoming. It regards intelligence as entirely due to causes within the child. Yet in previous chapters, we have seen that cultural and situational factors profoundly affect children's thinking. Robert Sternberg has expanded the componential approach into a comprehensive theory that views intelligence as a product of inner and outer forces.

## STERNBERG'S TRIARCHIC THEORY

Sternberg's (1985, 1997, 1999a) **triarchic theory of intelligence** is made up of three interacting subtheories (see Figure 8.3). The first, the *componential subtheory,* spells out the information-processing skills that underlie intelligent behaviour. You are already familiar with its main elements—strategy application, knowledge acquisition, metacognition, and self-regulation—from reading Chapter 7.

According to Sternberg, children's use of these components is not just a matter of internal capacity. It is also a function of the conditions under which intelligence is assessed. The *experiential subtheory* states that highly intelligent individuals, compared with less intelligent ones, process information more skilfully in novel situations. When given a relatively new task, the bright person learns rapidly, making strategies automatic so working memory is freed for more complex aspects of the situation.

Think, for a moment, about the implications of this idea for measuring children's intelligence. To accurately compare children in *brightness*—in ability to deal with novelty and learn efficiently—all children would have to be presented with equally unfamiliar test items. Otherwise, some children will appear more intelligent than others simply because of their past experiences. Such children start with the unfair advantage of prior practice on the tasks.

This point brings us to the third part of Sternberg's model, the *contextual subtheory.* It proposes that intelligent people skilfully *adapt* their information-processing skills to fit with their personal desires and the demands of their everyday worlds. When they cannot adapt to a situation, they try to *shape,* or change, it to meet their needs. If they cannot shape it, they *select* new contexts that are consistent with their goals. The contextual subtheory emphasizes that intelligent behaviour is never culture free. Because of their backgrounds, some children come to value behaviours required for success on intelligence tests, and they easily adapt to the tasks and testing conditions. Others with different life histories misinterpret the testing context or reject it entirely because it does not suit their needs. Yet such children may display very sophisticated abilities in daily life—for example, telling stories, engaging in elaborate artistic activities, accomplishing athletic feats, or interacting skilfully with other people (Sternberg, 1996b).

Sternberg's theory emphasizes the complexity of human mental skills and the limitations of current tests in assessing that complexity. Children often use different abilities in academic tasks than in nonacademic, everyday situations. Yet out-of-school, practical forms of intelligence are vital for life success, and they help explain why cultures vary widely in the behaviours they regard as intelligent (Sternberg et al., 2000). When ethnically diverse parents were asked for their view of an intelligent first grader, Caucasian Americans valued cognitive traits over noncognitive ones. In contrast, ethnic minorities (Cambodian, Filipino, Vietnamese, and Mexican immigrants) saw noncognitive capacities—motivation, self-management, and social skills—as particularly important. Mexican parents, especially, highly valued the social

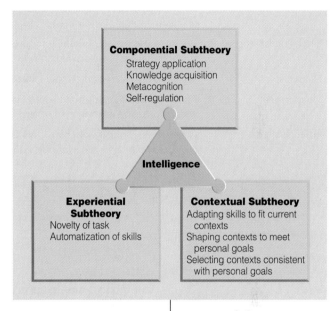

**FIGURE** 8.3

**Sternberg's triarchic theory of intelligence.**

**componential analysis**
A research procedure in which researchers look for relationships between aspects (or components) of information processing and children's intelligence test performance. Aims to clarify the cognitive processes responsible for test scores.

**triarchic theory of intelligence**
Sternberg's theory, which states that information-processing skills, prior experience with tasks, and contextual (or cultural) factors combine to influence intelligent behaviour.

**TABLE** 8.2

Gardner's Multiple Intelligences[a]

| INTELLIGENCE | PROCESSING OPERATIONS | END-STATE PERFORMANCE POSSIBILITIES |
|---|---|---|
| Linguistic | Sensitivity to the sounds, rhythms, and meaning of words and the functions of language | Poet, journalist |
| Logico-mathematical | Sensitivity to, and capacity to detect, logical or numerical patterns; ability to handle long chains of logical reasoning | Mathematician |
| Musical | Ability to produce and appreciate pitch, rhythm (or melody), and aesthetic quality of the forms of musical expressiveness | Instrumentalist, composer |
| Spatial | Ability to perceive the visual-spatial world accurately, to perform transformations on those perceptions, and to re-create aspects of visual experience in the absence of relevant stimuli | Sculptor, navigator |
| Bodily-kinesthetic | Ability to use the body skilfully for expressive as well as goal-directed purposes; ability to handle objects skilfully | Dancer, athlete |
| Naturalist | Ability to recognize and classify all varieties of animals, minerals, and plants | Biologist |
| Interpersonal | Ability to detect and respond appropriately to the moods, temperaments, motivations, and intentions of others | Therapist, salesperson |
| Intrapersonal | Ability to discriminate complex inner feelings and to use them to guide one's own behaviour; knowledge of one's own strengths, weaknesses, desires, and intelligences | Person with detailed, accurate self-knowledge |

[a]Gardner (1998b) also has proposed a possible spiritual intelligence (gift for religion, mysticism, or the transcendent), existential intelligence (concern with "ultimate" issues, such as the significance of life and death), and moral intelligence (capacity to recognize and reason about moral issues). However, these potential intelligences are less well defined and more controversial than the eight intelligences listed above.

*Sources:* Gardner, 1983, 1993, 1998b.

component of intelligence (Okagaki & Sternberg, 1993). As you can see, Sternberg believes that mental tests can easily underestimate, and even overlook, the intellectual strengths of some children, especially ethnic minorities.

### GARDNER'S THEORY OF MULTIPLE INTELLIGENCES

Howard Gardner's (1983, 1993, 1998a) **theory of multiple intelligences** provides yet another view of how information-processing skills underlie intelligent behaviour. But unlike the componential approach, it does not begin with existing mental tests and try to isolate the processing elements required to succeed on them. Instead, Gardner defines intelligence in terms of distinct sets of processing operations that permit individuals to solve problems, create products, and discover new knowledge in a wide range of culturally valued activities. Therefore, Gardner dismisses the idea of a single, overarching mental ability, or "g," and proposes at least eight independent intelligences, described in Table 8.2.

Gardner acknowledges that if tests were available to assess all these abilities, factor analysis should yield low correlations between them. But he regards neurological support for their separateness as more persuasive. Research indicating that damage to a certain part of the adult brain influences only one ability (such as linguistic or spatial) while sparing others suggests that the affected ability is independent. The existence of prodigies, who show precocious development in only one area, such as language, mathematics, music, or visual arts, also fits with Gardner's belief in distinct abilities. (See Chapter 2, page 49, to review findings on the development of prodigies.)

Gardner argues that each intelligence has a unique biological basis, a distinct course of development, and different expert, or "end-state," performances. At the same time, he

**theory of multiple intelligences**
Gardner's theory, which identifies eight intelligences on the basis of distinct sets of processing operations applied in culturally valued activities (linguistic, logico-mathematical, musical, spatial, bodily-kinesthetic, naturalist, interpersonal, intrapersonal).

emphasizes that a lengthy process of education is required to transform any raw potential into a mature social role (Gardner, 1998a; Torff & Gardner, 1999). This means that cultural values and learning opportunities have a great deal to do with the extent to which a child's strengths are realized and the ways they are expressed.

Does Gardner's view remind you of the *core knowledge* view of the mind, discussed in Chapter 6? Indeed, he accepts the existence of innately specified, core cognitive processes, present at birth or emerging early in life. Then, as children respond to the demands of their culture, they transform and combine the intelligences to fit the activities they are called on to perform. Advanced performance in virtually any field requires a blend of intelligences. For example, besides relying on musical intelligence, a pianist calls on logico-mathematical intelligence to interpret the score, linguistic intelligence to respond to teaching, spatial intelligence to orient to the keyboard, interpersonal intelligence to react to the audience, and intrapersonal intelligence to play expressively. Gardner's work has been especially helpful in efforts to understand and nurture children's special talents, a topic we will take up at the end of this chapter.

At the same time, reservations have been raised about his theory. Neurological evidence for the independence of his intelligences is weak. Logico-mathematical ability, in particular, seems to be governed by many brain regions, not just one, and to be linked to spatial intelligence (Casey, Nuttall, & Pezaris, 1997; Casey et al., 1995). Furthermore, some exceptionally gifted individuals have abilities that are broad rather than limited to a particular domain (Goldsmith, 2000). Finally, current mental tests do tap several of Gardner's intelligences (linguistic, logico-mathematical, and spatial), and evidence for "g" suggests that they have some common features.

Nevertheless, Gardner's theory highlights several mental abilities not measured by intelligence tests. For example, his interpersonal and intrapersonal intelligences include a set of capacities for dealing with people and understanding oneself. Currently, researchers are attempting to define and measure social and emotional abilities. See the From Research to Practice box on page 320 for more information on this challenging endeavour.

In sum, Gardner's list of abilities has yet to be firmly grounded in research. Nevertheless, his ideas have been powerful enough to reawaken the debate over a unitary versus multifaceted human intelligence.

DAVID YOUNG-WOLFF/PHOTOEDIT

According to Gardner, children are capable of at least eight distinct intelligences. As these children classify wildflowers during a walk through a meadow, they enrich their naturalist intelligence.

## ASK YOURSELF

**review** Citing the work of the factor analysts, explain why a single IQ score might not adequately represent human mental functioning.

**review** Using Sternberg's triarchic theory and Gardner's theory of multiple intelligences, discuss the limitations of current mental tests in assessing the complexity of human intelligence.

**apply** Eight-year-old Regina, an immigrant from Haiti, couldn't answer test items asking for word definitions and general information. But she figured out which number comes next in a complex series and solved puzzles easily. How does Regina score in crystallized and fluid intelligence, and what might explain the difference?

**connect** Cite similarities between Gardner's theory of multiple intelligences and the core knowledge view of the mind (see Chapter 6, pages 250–251). What questions raised about this view also apply to Gardner's theory?

# *from research to practice*

## SOCIAL AND EMOTIONAL INTELLIGENCE

during recess, Muriel handed a birthday party invitation to each of the grade 5 girls except Claire, who retreated to a bench and watched forlornly as her classmates talked excitedly about the party. Jessica, one of Muriel's friends, caught up with her and exclaimed, "Why'd you do that? You hurt Claire's feelings and embarrassed her! If you bring invitations to school, you've got to give everybody one!" After school, Jessica offered comforting words to Claire. "If you aren't invited, I'm not going, either!"

Jessica's IQ is only slightly above average, but she excels in the ability to act wisely in social situations. Although early theorists of mental abilities recognized the existence of *social intelligence,* they gave scant attention to it. By the

1960s, researchers constructed the first tests of social aptitude (Hendricks, Guilford, & Hoepfner, 1969; O'Sullivan, Guilford, & deMille, 1965). Items assessed adolescents' and adults' capacity to detect others' thoughts and feelings and to come up with effective solutions to social problems. Although studies reported positive correlations between social scores and IQ, these were modest. And factor analyses revealed that social intelligence, like nonsocial intelligence, is made up of diverse abilities (Kihlstrom & Cantor, 2000). Jessica, for example, takes Claire's perspective, communicates sensitively, displays mature morality, and expresses herself confidently.

Today, abilities formerly called social intelligence are labelled *emotional intelligence*—a term that has captured public attention because of popular books suggesting that it is an overlooked set of skills that can greatly improve life success (Goleman, 1995, 1998). Defined in

diverse ways, **emotional intelligence** includes accurately perceiving emotions, expressing emotion appropriately, understanding the causes and consequences of emotions, and managing one's own and others' feelings to facilitate thinking and social interaction.

In one test of emotional intelligence, researchers devised items that tap diverse emotional skills. For example, they asked people to rate the strength of emotion being expressed in photos of faces; to identify how a change in emotion might bring about a change in judgment of another person; and to rate responses for their effectiveness in controlling a negative emotion (see Table 8.3). Factor analyses of hundreds of adolescents' and young adults' scores identified several emotional abilities (perceiving, understanding, and managing emotion) and a higher-order general factor (Mayer, Caruso, & Salovey, 1999). Like social intelligence, emotional intelligence—especially understanding emotion—is modestly related to IQ. And it is positively associated with self-esteem, sociability, and current life satisfaction and

The child on the left displays high emotional intelligence as he establishes eye contact, reads his friend's sadness accurately, and offers comfort. Researchers hope to devise tests of emotional intelligence that can identify children who might profit from interventions aimed at fostering social and emotional skills.

© DON SMETZER/PHOTOEDIT

**emotional intelligence**
A set of abilities that includes accurately perceiving emotions, expressing emotion appropriately, understanding the causes and consequences of emotions, and managing one's own and others' feelings to facilitate thinking and social interaction.

# Representative Intelligence Tests for Children

ALTHOUGH NOT YET responsive to the advances in theory just considered, a variety of tests are currently available to assess children's intelligence. Psychologists and educators often give mental tests to school-age children because the scores, as we will see shortly, are modest to good predictors of life outcomes—in school, on the job, and in other aspects of life. The tests that students take every so often in classrooms are *group-administered tests.* They permit large numbers of students to be tested at once and

**TABLE** 8.3

Sample Items from the MultiFactor Emotional Intelligence Scale

| FACTOR | TEST ITEM |
|---|---|
| Perceiving emotions | Eight photos of faces are shown, each followed by six emotion labels: happiness, anger, fear, sadness, disgust, and surprise. The test-taker answers on a 5-point scale whether a given emotion is "definitely not present" (1) or "definitely present" (5). |
| Assimilating emotions into cognitive processes | "Imagine that Jonathan is one of your relatives. He is a tall, muscular person. Jonathan said something to you that made you feel both guilty and afraid. Feeling both guilty and afraid about Jonathan, how does he seem?" Ability to assimilate present mood into judgments is assessed by having the test-taker rate the following emotions on a 5-point scale, from "definitely does not describe" (1) to "definitely does describe" (5): sad, trusting, tense, cynical, aggressive, controlling, and hasty. |
| Understanding emotion | "Optimism most closely combines which of two emotions? (a) pleasure and anticipation, (b) acceptance and joy, (c) surprise and joy, (d) pleasure and joy." |
| Managing (regulating) emotion | "You have been dating the same person for several months and feel very comfortable. Lately, you are thinking that this relationship may be the one. . . . The last thing you expected was the phone call you received saying that the relationship is over. . . ." The test-taker rates emotion-management responses from "extremely ineffective" (1) to "extremely effective" (5). One such response is "block it out and . . . throw yourself into your work." |

*Source:* J. D. Mayer, D. R. Caruso, & P. Salovey, 1999, "Emotional Intelligence Meets Traditional Standards for an Intelligence," *Intelligence, 27,* 267–298. Adapted by permission.

negatively related to aggressive behaviour (Mayer, Salovey, & Caruso, 2000).

At present, few tests of emotional intelligence are available for young children. But as more and better measures are devised, they may help identify children with weak social and emotional skills who could profit from intervention. Some researchers worry that emotional ability scores will lead psychologists and educators to make overly simplistic comparisons between children and to lose sight of the fact that the adaptiveness of emotional and social behaviour often varies across situations (Saarni, 2000). And as yet, no evidence exists to support a major goal of these measures—prediction of future life success beyond the influence of IQ.

Although much work on test construction remains, the concepts of social and emotional intelligence have increased teachers' awareness that providing experiences that meet students' social and emotional needs can improve their adjustment (Graczyk et al., 2000). Lessons that teach respect and caring for others, communication skills, cooperation, and resistance to unfavourable peer pressure—using active learning techniques that provide skills practice in and out of the classroom—are becoming more common.

require very little training of the teachers who give them. The Canadian Cognitive Abilities Test is an example. Group tests are useful for instructional planning and identifying students who require more extensive evaluation with *individually administered tests.* Unlike group tests, individually administered ones demand considerable training and experience to give well. The examiner not only considers the child's answers but carefully observes the child's behaviour, noting such reactions as attention to and interest in the tasks and wariness of the adult. These observations provide insights into whether the test score is accurate or underestimates the child's ability.

Two individual tests—the Stanford-Binet and the Wechsler—are most often used to identify highly intelligent children and diagnose those with learning problems.

### THE STANFORD-BINET INTELLIGENCE SCALE

The modern descendant of Alfred Binet's first successful intelligence test is the **Stanford-Binet Intelligence Scale,** for individuals between 2 years of age and adulthood. Its latest version measures general intelligence and four intellectual factors: verbal reasoning, quantitative reasoning, abstract/visual (spatial) reasoning, and short-term memory (Thorndike, Hagen, & Sattler, 1986). Within these factors are 15 subtests that permit a detailed analysis of each child's mental abilities. The verbal and quantitative factors emphasize crystallized intelligence (culturally loaded, fact-oriented information), such as vocabulary and sentence comprehension. In contrast, the abstract/visual reasoning factor taps fluid intelligence and, therefore, is believed to be less culturally biased.

Because its items for preschoolers are not adequately adjusted in difficulty for each age group, the Stanford-Binet provides a less accurate measure of intelligence in early childhood than in middle childhood and adolescence (Bradley-Johnson, 2001). Hence, the test is not useful for diagnosing intellectual difficulties of preschoolers. Also, scores on the test tend to be slightly lower than those obtained on other measures.

### THE WECHSLER INTELLIGENCE SCALE FOR CHILDREN

The **Wechsler Intelligence Scale for Children–III (WISC–III)** is the third edition of a widely used test for 6- through 16-year-olds. A downward extension of it, the *Wechsler Preschool and Primary Scale of Intelligence–Revised (WPPSI–R),* is appropriate for children ages 3 through 7 years 3 months (Wechsler, 1989, 1991). The Wechsler tests offered both a measure of general intelligence and a variety of factor scores long before the Stanford-Binet. As a result, over the past two decades, many psychologists and educators have come to prefer the WISC and the WPPSI for individual assessment of children.

Both the WISC–III and the WPPSI–R measure two broad intellectual factors: verbal and performance. On each test, 6 verbal and 5 performance subtests yield 11 separate scores in all. Performance items (look back at Figure 8.1 on page 314 for examples) require the child to arrange materials rather than talk to the examiner. Consequently, these tests provided one of the first means through which non-English-speaking children and children with speech and language disorders could demonstrate their intellectual strengths.

The Wechsler tests were the first to be standardized on children representing the total population of the United States, including ethnic minorities. For many years, Canadian children were evaluated according to these U.S. norms. In 1996, however, Canadian norms became available through the Canadian Standardization of the WISC–III (see the From Research to Practice box on the following page). Canadian norms are not yet available for the WPPSI, which, like the Stanford-Binet, is a less sensitive measure of intelligence at the youngest ages (Kaufman, 2000). And some critics complain that too many items on the Wechsler tests emphasize response speed—even items for young children, who do not understand the importance of working quickly.

### INFANT INTELLIGENCE TESTS

Accurately measuring the intelligence of infants is especially challenging because babies cannot answer questions or follow directions. All we can do is present them with stimuli, coax them to respond, and observe their behaviour. In addition, infants are not necessarily cooperative. They are likely to become distracted, fatigued, or bored during testing. Some tests depend heavily on information supplied by parents to compensate for the uncertain behaviours of these young test-takers.

Most infant measures consist largely of perceptual and motor responses. For example, the *Bayley Scales of Infant Development,* a commonly used test for children between 1 month and

**Stanford-Binet Intelligence Scale**
An individually administered intelligence test that is the modern descendant of Alfred Binet's first successful test for children. Measures general intelligence and four factors: verbal reasoning, quantitative reasoning, abstract/visual (spatial) reasoning, and short-term memory.

**Wechsler Intelligence Scale for Children–III (WISC–III)**
An individually administered intelligence test that includes a measure of general intelligence and a variety of verbal and performance scores.

## *from research to practice*

### THE CANADIAN STANDARDIZATION OF THE WISC–III

Standardization of a test refers to the process of establishing norms for the test by administering it to a large and representative sample of the population for which the test is intended. The norms estimate typical performance for that population, and any individual's performance can be compared with them. However, for a test score to be valid, characteristics of the person being tested—such as age, sex, social class, educational background, and ethnicity—must be represented in the standardization sample in the same proportion as they occur in the population. Herein lies one of the problems

for Canadians in using a test standardized in the United States. If Canadians are not part of the standardization sample, will an assessment by those norms be valid?

Psychologists, educators, and members of the Canadian Psychological Association lobbied for many years for Canadian norms to be established for the WISC. In 1996, a large-scale study was undertaken to determine if Canadian children's scores were comparable to U.S. children's scores, or if the WISC–III required Canadian norms. The study included 1100 English-speaking Canadian schoolchildren

representing diverse social classes and ethnicities.

Results revealed that Canadian children perform slightly better than U.S. children overall, and on most subtest scores (Wechsler, 1996). More research is needed to explain these cross-national differences. However, as a result of the Canadian standardization, Canadian WISC–III norms are now available (Hildebrand & Saklofske, 1996; Roid & Worrall, 1997). A French-Canadian adaptation of the WISC–III recently became available, and indications are that the English-Canadian norms are suitable for use with the translation (Sarrazin et al., 1999).

---

3½ years, was inspired by the early normative work of Arnold Gesell (see Chapter 1, page 13). The test consists of two parts: (1) the Mental Scale, which includes such items as turning to a sound, looking for a fallen object, building a tower of cubes, and naming pictures; and (2) the Motor Scale, which assesses fine and gross motor skills, such as grasping, sitting, drinking from a cup, and jumping (Bayley, 1993).

Despite careful construction, infant tests emphasizing these types of items are poor predictors of intelligence during childhood because infant perceptual and motor behaviours do not represent the same aspects of intelligence assessed at older ages. To increase its predictive validity, the most recent version of the Bayley test includes a few items that emphasize infant memory, problem solving, categorization, and other complex cognitive skills, which are more likely to correlate with later mental test scores. Nevertheless, traditional infant tests are somewhat better at making long-term predictions for very low-scoring babies. As a result, they are largely used for *screening*—helping to identify for further observation and intervention infants who are likely to have developmental problems (Kopp, 1994).

Recall from Chapter 4 that speed of habituation/recovery to visual stimuli is among the best infant correlates of childhood intelligence. The habituation/recovery response seems to tap important aspects of cognitive processing (speed of thinking and attention, memory, and response to novelty). Consequently, a test made up entirely of habituation/recovery items, the *Fagan Test of Infant Intelligence,* has been constructed. To take it, the infant sits on the parent's lap and views a series of pictures. After exposure to each one, the examiner records looking time toward a novel picture that is paired with the familiar one. Besides predicting childhood IQ, the Fagan test is highly effective in identifying babies who (without intervention) will soon show serious delays in mental development (Fagan & Detterman, 1992).

A trained examiner tests this baby with the Bayley Scales of Infant Development while his father holds him and looks on. The perceptual and motor items on most infant tests are different from the tasks given to older children, which emphasize verbal, conceptual, and problem-solving skills. Among normally developing children, infant tests are poor predictors of later intelligence.

© LAURA DWIGHT/PHOTOEDIT

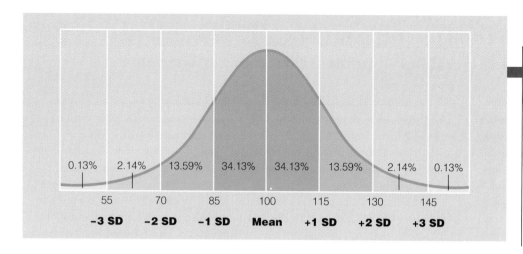

0.13%  2.14%  13.59%  34.13%  34.13%  13.59%  2.14%  0.13%

55    70    85    100    115    130    145

−3 SD   −2 SD   −1 SD   Mean   +1 SD   +2 SD   +3 SD

**FIGURE** 8.4

**The normal curve, with the baseline scaled in both IQ and standard deviation (SD) units.** Areas under the curve are given in percentages. By summing the percentages to the left of an individual's IQ, we can obtain a percentile rank, which refers to the proportion of people of the same age that scored lower than the individual did on the test.

## The Computation and Distribution of IQ Scores

SCORES ON INTELLIGENCE tests for infants, children, and adults are arrived at in the same way—by computing an **intelligence quotient (IQ),** which indicates the extent to which the raw score (number of items passed) deviates from the typical performance of same-age individuals. When a test is constructed, it is given to a large, representative sample of individuals. Performances at each age level form a *normal,* or *bell-shaped, curve* in which most people fall near the centre and progressively fewer out toward the extremes. Two important features of the normal curve are its *mean,* or the average score, and its *standard deviation,* which provides a measure of the average variability, or "spread-outness," of the scores from the mean.

Most intelligence tests convert their raw scores so that the mean is set at 100 and the standard deviation at 15. As Figure 8.4 shows, knowing the mean and standard deviation, we can determine the percentage of individuals at each age who fall above or below a certain score. Then, when we speak of a specific IQ, we know exactly what it means. For example, as Table 8.4 makes clear, a child with an IQ of 100 does better on intelligence tests than 50 percent of same-age children. A child with an IQ of 85 does better than only 16 percent of her agemates, whereas a child with an IQ of 130 outperforms 98 percent of them. Look at Figure 8.4 once more, and notice how most scores cluster near the mean. The IQs of the great majority of people (96 percent) fall between 70 and 130; only a few achieve higher or lower scores.

**TABLE** 8.4

Meaning of Various IQ Scores

| SCORE | PERCENTILE RANK— CHILD DOES BETTER THAN ... PERCENT OF SAME-AGE CHILDREN | |
|---|---|---|
| 70 | 2 | |
| 85 | 16 | |
| 100 (average IQ) | 50 | |
| 115 | 84 | |
| 130 | 98 | |

## What and How Well Do Intelligence Tests Predict?

PSYCHOLOGISTS AND EDUCATORS who use test scores to make decisions about the educational placement of children assume that they are good indicators of future intelligence and scholastic performance. How well does IQ actually fare as a predictive measure?

**intelligence quotient (IQ)**
A score that indicates the extent to which an individual's raw score (number of items passed) on an intelligence test deviates from the typical performance of same-age individuals.

### STABILITY OF IQ SCORES

*Stability* refers to how effectively IQ predicts itself from one age to the next. Do children who obtain a particular IQ at 3 or 4 years perform about the same during elementary school and again when tested in high school? To answer this question, researchers rely on longitudinal studies in which the same children have been tested repeatedly over many ages.

**CORRELATIONAL STABILITY.** One way of examining the stability of IQ is to correlate scores obtained from repeated testings. This tells us whether children who score low or high in comparison to their agemates at one age continue to do so later. Examining these correlations, researchers have identified two generalizations about the stability of IQ:

1. *The older the child at time of first testing, the better the prediction of later IQ.* Preschool IQs do not predict school-age scores well; correlations are typically no higher than in the .30s. But after age 6, there is good stability, with many correlations in the .70s and .80s. Relationships between two testings obtained in adolescence are as high as the .80s and .90s (Hayslip, 1994; Humphreys, 1989).

2. *The closer in time two testings are, the stronger the relationship between the scores.* For example, 4-year-old IQ correlates with 5-year-old IQ at .72, but prediction drops by age 6 to .62. By age 18, it has declined to .42 (Honzik, Macfarlane, & Allen, 1948).

Why do preschool scores predict less well than later scores? One frequently cited reason is differences in the nature of test items. Concrete knowledge tends to be tested at younger ages, abstract problem solving later. Success on the first may require different skills than success on the second. Another explanation is that during early periods of rapid development, one child may spurt ahead of another and reach a plateau, whereas a second child, moving along slowly and steadily, may catch up and eventually overtake the first. Because children frequently change places in a distribution during periods of rapid change, all measures of developmental progress, including height and weight, are less stable and predictable at these times. IQ is no exception. Finally, mental test scores may better predict future IQ after age 6 because once children enter school, greater similarity exists between their daily learning activities and test items. Individual differences in the quality of school experiences and children's mastery of those experiences may help sustain individual differences in IQ.

**STABILITY OF ABSOLUTE SCORES.** So far, we have looked at IQ stability in terms of how well children maintain their relative standing among agemates over time. We can also view stability in absolute terms—by examining each child's profile of IQ scores from repeated testings. Longitudinal research reveals that the majority of children show substantial IQ fluctuations over childhood and adolescence—in most cases, 10 to 20 points, and sometimes much more (McCall, 1993).

Children who change the most tend to have orderly profiles in which scores either increase or decrease with age. A close look at their characteristics and life experiences highlights factors that may be responsible for these varying IQ trends. Gainers were more independent and competitive about doing well in school. In addition, their parents applied greater pressure to succeed and used rational, democratic discipline. In contrast, decliners tended to have parents who made little effort to stimulate them and used either very severe or very lax discipline (Honzik, Macfarlane, & Allen, 1948; McCall, Appelbaum, & Hogarty, 1973; Sontag, Baker, & Nelson, 1958).

When ethnic minority children and other youngsters who live in poverty are selected for special study, many show IQ declines. According to the **environmental cumulative deficit hypothesis,** the effects of underprivileged rearing conditions worsen the longer children remain in them. As a result, early cognitive deficits lead to more deficits that become harder to overcome (Klineberg, 1963). This idea has served as the basis for many early intervention programs, which are intensive efforts to offset these declines.

What evidence exists to support the environmental cumulative deficit? In a study of African-American children growing up under severely depressed conditions in the rural South in the United States, older siblings consistently obtained lower IQs than their younger brothers and sisters. But no such relation appeared for less economically disadvantaged African-American children living in California (Jensen, 1974). This finding is consistent with the environmental cumulative deficit rather than a genetically determined IQ profile.

**environmental cumulative deficit hypothesis**
A view that attributes the age-related decline in IQ among ethnic minority and other children who live in poverty to the cumulative effects of underprivileged rearing conditions.

A wealth of research indicates that IQ predicts academic achievement. However, the correlation is far from perfect. Other factors, such as motivation and personality characteristics, are just as important as IQ in accounting for children's learning in school.

To fit with a genetic explanation, both the rural South- and California-reared groups should have displayed age-related IQ declines.

In sum, many children show substantial changes in the absolute value of IQ that are the combined result of personal characteristics, child-rearing practices, and living conditions. Nevertheless, once IQ becomes reasonably stable in a correlational sense, it predicts a variety of outcomes, as we will see in the following sections.

## IQ AS A PREDICTOR OF ACADEMIC ACHIEVEMENT

Thousands of studies reveal that intelligence tests have accomplished their goal of predicting academic achievement. Correlations between IQ and achievement test scores range from .40 to .70 and are typically around .50 (Brody, 1997). Children with higher IQs also get better grades and stay in school longer. As early as age 7, IQ is moderately correlated with adult educational attainment (McCall, 1977).

Why does IQ predict scholastic performance? Researchers differ in how they answer this question. Some believe that both IQ and achievement depend on the same abstract reasoning processes that underlie Spearman's "g." A child well endowed with "g" can better acquire knowledge and skills taught in school. That IQ correlates best with achievement in the more abstract school subjects, such as English, mathematics, and science, is consistent with this interpretation (Jensen, 1998).

Other researchers argue that both IQ and achievement sample from the same pool of culturally specific information. From this point of view, an intelligence test is partly an achievement test, and a child's past experiences affect performance on both measures. Support for this view comes from evidence that crystallized intelligence (which reflects acquired knowledge) is a much better predictor of academic achievement than is its fluid counterpart (Kaufman, Kamphaus, & Kaufman, 1985).

As you can probably imagine, researchers who believe heredity plays a crucial role in individual differences in IQ prefer the first of these explanations. Those who favour the power of environment prefer the second. Since the IQ–achievement correlation is stronger among identical than fraternal twins, heredity does seem important (Thompson, Detterman, & Plomin, 1991). But children's experiences also contribute. For example, findings reviewed in the Cultural Influences box on page 327 indicate that IQ not only predicts future achievement but is itself increased by years of schooling!

Finally, although IQ predicts achievement better than any other tested measure, the correlation is far from perfect. Other factors, such as motivation and personality characteristics that lead some children to try hard and want to do well in school, are just as important as IQ in accounting for individual differences in scholastic performance (Neisser et al., 1996).

## IQ AS A PREDICTOR OF OCCUPATIONAL ATTAINMENT

Psychologists and educators would probably be less concerned with IQ scores if they were unrelated to long-term life success. But research indicates that childhood IQ predicts adult occupational attainment just about as well as it correlates with academic achievement. By grade 2, children with the highest IQs are more likely when they grow up to enter prestigious professions, such as medicine, science, law, and engineering (McCall, 1977).

Once again, however, the relationship between IQ and occupational attainment is far from perfect. Factors related to family background, such as parental encouragement, modelling of career success, and connections in the world of work, also predict occupational choice and attainment (Bell et al., 1996). Furthermore, one reason that IQ is linked to occupational status is that test scores affect access to higher education. And educational

## *cultural influences*

### DOES SCHOOLING INFLUENCE IQ?

© AFP/CORBIS

It is widely accepted that intelligence affects achievement in school, but how important is schooling in the development of intelligence? Stephen Ceci (1991, 1999) reviewed hundreds of studies addressing this question. Taken together, they suggest that classroom events have a profound effect on mental test performance.

Consider, first, the small but consistent drop in IQ that occurs over the summer, especially among low-income children, whose summer activities least resemble school tasks. For economically advantaged children, whose vacation pursuits often are like those of school, the summer decline does not occur (Heyns, 1978).

Research dating back to the early part of the twentieth century reveals that irregular school attendance has an even greater impact on IQ. In one study, test scores of children growing up in "hollows" of the Blue Ridge Mountains were compared. All were descendants of Scottish-Irish and English immigrants, whose families had lived in the hollows for generations. One hollow was located at the foot of the mountains and had schools in session nine months of the year. In the other, more isolated hollows, schooling was irregular. Children's IQs varied substantially with amount of schooling available. Those who received the most had a 10- to 30-point advantage (Sherman & Key, 1932).

Delayed entry into school is similarly related to test scores. In the Netherlands during World War II, many schools were closed as a result of the Nazi occupation. The IQs of children who started school several years late dropped about 7 points

(DeGroot, 1951). Similarly, children of Indian settlers in South Africa, whose schooling was postponed up to 4 years because their villages did not have teachers, lost 5 IQ points per year compared with Indian children in nearby villages who attended school (Ramphal, 1962).

Dropping out of school also has a detrimental effect on IQ. In a Swedish study, a large random sample of 13-year-old boys took intelligence tests. At age 18, they were retested as part of the country's national military registration. The impact of dropping out was determined by comparing children who were similar at age 13 in IQ, school grades, and parent education and income. Each year of high school not completed amounted to a loss of nearly 2 IQ points, up to 8 points for all 4 years of high school (Härnqvist, 1968).

Yet another illustration of the impact of schooling on IQ is the contrast between children born at different times during the year. Because most provinces have birth-date cutoffs for school entry, some children enter school a year earlier than others. And their IQ is higher—a difference entirely explained by their having attended school 1 year longer (Heckman, 1995). Various Canadian studies yield similar findings for crucial academic skills. Children who were in school gained more in math and literacy than did children of the same age who were

After 5 years of being denied education under Taliban rule, these girls recently returned to school in Afghanistan. Were they to take intelligence tests during this return period, their IQ scores would probably rise. Research indicates that schooling contributes to IQ.

not in school (Bisanz, Morrison, & Dunn, 1995; Varnhagen, Morrison, & Everall, 1994).

Ceci (1999) believes that schooling influences IQ in at least three ways: (1) by teaching children factual knowledge relevant to test questions; (2) by promoting information-processing skills, such as memory strategies and categorization, that are tapped by test items; and (3) by encouraging attitudes and values that foster successful test-taking, such as listening carefully to an adult's questions, answering under time pressure, and trying hard.

attainment is a stronger predictor of occupational success and income than is IQ (Ceci & Williams, 1997).

Personality also figures prominently into occupational achievement. In 1923, Lewis Terman initiated a longitudinal study of over 1500 children with IQs above 135, who were followed well into mature adulthood. By middle age, more than 86 percent of men in the

Practical intelligence is unrelated to IQ. Yet in the adult work world, practical intelligence predicts job performance at least as well or better than IQ. As she fixes her bicycle, this girl demonstrates considerable practical know-how.

sample had entered high-status professional and business occupations (Terman & Oden, 1959).[1] But not all were professionally successful. Looking closely at those who fared best compared to those who fared worst, Terman found that their IQs were similar, averaging around 150. But the highly successful group appeared to have "a special drive to succeed, a need to achieve" from elementary school onward (Goleman, 1980, p. 31).

Finally, once a person enters an occupation, **practical intelligence**—mental abilities apparent in the real world but not in testing situations—predict on-the-job performance at least as well as or better than IQ. Yet mental test scores and practical intelligence differ greatly. Whereas test items are formulated by others, are complete in the information they provide, and have only one solution, practical problems are weakly formulated, of personal interest, missing much information necessary for solution, and generally have several appropriate solutions, each with strengths and limitations (Sternberg et al., 2000). Practical intelligence can be seen in the assembly-line worker who discovers the fewest moves needed to complete a product or the business manager who increases productivity by making her subordinates feel valued. Unlike IQ, practical intelligence does not vary with ethnicity. And growing evidence reveals that the two types of intelligence are unrelated and make independent contributions to job success (Wagner, 1997, 2000).

In sum, occupational outcomes are a complex function of traditionally measured intelligence, education, motivation, family influences, special opportunity, and practical know-how. Current evidence indicates that IQ is not more important than these other factors.

## IQ AS A PREDICTOR OF PSYCHOLOGICAL ADJUSTMENT

Is IQ so influential that it predicts life success beyond school and the workplace, such as emotional and social adjustment? School-age children with higher IQs tend to be better liked by their agemates (Hartup, 1983). But the reasons for this association are not clear. A child's social competence is also related to child-rearing practices, health, physical appearance, and personality, all of which are correlated with IQ.

Another way of exploring the IQ–adjustment relationship is to look at the mental test performance of children who are poorly adjusted, such as highly aggressive children who engage in norm-violating acts. Chronic delinquents have IQs that are, on the average, about 8 points lower than those of nondelinquents (Coie & Dodge, 1998). A lower IQ increases the risk of school failure, which is associated with delinquency. But a more likely direction of influence is that a history of aggressive behaviour prevents children from taking advantage of classroom and other experiences that promote academic learning. In support of this view, research in Canada, China, and the United States reveals that early aggression predicts later academic difficulties. But the reverse is not always true; early academic difficulties do not predict later aggression (Chen, Rubin, & Li, 1997; Masten et al., 1995; Tremblay et al., 1992; Vitaro et al., 2001). However, early intervention can help troubled children. Richard Tremblay of the Université de Montréal and others (1995) found that when a 2-year intervention program was provided at home and at school for disruptive kindergarten boys at risk for later antisocial behaviour, boys in the treatment group were more likely to remain in age-appropriate elementary school classrooms and to report fewer delinquent adolescent behaviours than disruptive boys in a no-treatment control group.

**practical intelligence**
Mental abilities apparent in the real world but not in testing situations.

[1]Born a century ago during an era quite different from our own, nearly half the women in Terman's sample became housewives. However, of those who had professional careers, there were examples of outstanding accomplishments. Among them were scientists (one of whom contributed to the development of the polio vaccine), several novelists and journalists, and highly successful businesswomen (Terman & Oden, 1959).

Finally, many adjustment disorders, such as high anxiety, social withdrawal, and depression, are unrelated to mental test scores. When we look at the evidence as a whole, we must conclude that a high IQ offers little guarantee of happiness and life satisfaction. And its imperfect prediction of other indicators of success, such as academic achievement and occupational attainment, provides strong justification for never relying on IQ alone to forecast a child's future or make important educational placement decisions.

# Ethnic and Socioeconomic Variations in IQ

PEOPLE IN INDUSTRIALIZED nations are stratified on the basis of what they do at work and how much they earn for doing it—factors that determine their social position and economic well-being. Researchers assess a family's standing on this continuum through an index called **socioeconomic status (SES)**. It combines three interrelated, but not completely overlapping, variables: (1) years of education and (2) the prestige of and skill required by one's job, both of which measure social status; and (3) income, which measures economic status.

In searching for the roots of socioeconomic disparities in the population, researchers have compared the IQ scores of SES and ethnic groups, since certain ethnicities are heavily represented at lower SES levels and others at middle and upper SES levels. These findings are responsible for the IQ nature–nurture debate. If group differences in IQ exist, then either heredity varies with SES and ethnicity, or certain groups must have fewer opportunities to acquire the skills needed for successful test performance.

In the 1970s, the IQ nature–nurture controversy escalated, after psychologist Arthur Jensen (1969) published an article in the *Harvard Educational Review,* entitled "How Much Can We Boost IQ and Scholastic Achievement?" Jensen's answer to this question was "not much." He argued that heredity is largely responsible for individual, ethnic, and SES differences in IQ, a position he maintains (Jensen, 1998, 2001).

Jensen's work received widespread public attention. It was followed by an outpouring of responses and research studies. In addition, scientists posed ethical challenges because they were deeply concerned that his conclusions would fuel social prejudices. The controversy was rekindled in Richard Herrnstein and Charles Murray's (1994) *The Bell Curve.* Like Jensen, these authors concluded that heredity contributes substantially to individual and SES differences in IQ. At the same time, they stated that the relative role of heredity and environment in the black–white IQ gap (the main focus of investigations into ethnicity) is unresolved.

Herrnstein and Murray's book, like Jensen's 1969 article, prompted heated debate. Some researchers praised it, such as Phillipe Rushton (1997) of the University of Western Ontario; others, such as the University of Alberta's Douglas Wahlsten (1997), deplored it, underscoring its damaging social consequences. Indeed, a special issue of the *Alberta Journal of Educational Research* (1995) critiqued the work. But before we consider relevant research, let's look at group differences in IQ scores, since they are at the heart of the controversy.

## DIFFERENCES IN GENERAL INTELLIGENCE

In the United States, black children score, on the average, 15 points below white children on measures of general intelligence, although the difference has been shrinking (Hedges & Nowell, 1998; Loehlin, 2000). Hispanic-American children fall midway between black and white children. Asian Americans score slightly higher than their white counterparts—about 3 points (Ceci, Rosenblum, & Kumpf, 1998).

SES differences in IQ also exist. In one large-scale study, low-SES children scored 9 points below children in the middle of the SES distribution (Jensen & Figueroa, 1975). Since 42 percent of African-American children live in poverty compared to 22 percent of all U.S. children, a reasonable question is whether economic status fully accounts for the black–white IQ

**socioeconomic status (SES)** A measure of a family's social position and economic well-being that combines three interrelated, but not completely overlapping, variables: (1) years of education and (2) the prestige of and skill required by one's job, both of which measure social status; and (3) income, which measures economic status.

**IQ score distributions for black and for white children.** The means represent approximate values obtained in studies of children reared by their biological parents.

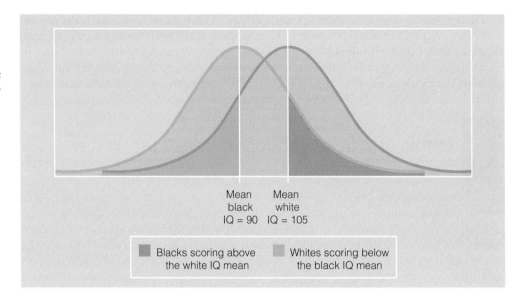

Mean black IQ = 90    Mean white IQ = 105

■ Blacks scoring above the white IQ mean    ■ Whites scoring below the black IQ mean

difference. It accounts for some but not all of it. When black and white children are matched on family income, the black–white IQ gap is reduced by about a third (Jencks, 1972; Jensen & Reynolds, 1982). Similar findings have been reported for Aboriginal children (Dolan, 1999), who do not perform as well on IQ measures as white children and who typically live in poor socioeconomic conditions (Hull, 1988).

No ethnic differences exist on infant measures of habituation/recovery to visual stimuli, which are good predictors of later IQ (Fagan & Singer, 1983). But before age 3, African-American children lag behind their white peers on other mental tests, a difference that persists into adulthood (Peoples, Fagan, & Drotar, 1995). Still, IQ varies greatly *within* each ethnic and SES group. For example, as Figure 8.5 shows, the IQ distributions of blacks and whites overlap substantially. About 16 percent of blacks score above the white mean, and the same percentage of whites score below the black mean. In fact, ethnicity and SES account for only about one-fourth of the total variation in IQ. Nevertheless, these group differences are large enough and of serious enough consequence that they cannot be ignored.

## DIFFERENCES IN SPECIFIC MENTAL ABILITIES

Are ethnic and SES differences limited to certain kinds of mental abilities? Arthur Jensen believes so. In his **Level I–Level II theory,** Jensen distinguishes two types of intelligence. Level I refers to items emphasizing short-term and rote memory, such as digit span and recall of basic arithmetic facts. In contrast, Level II involves abstract reasoning and problem solving—items strongly correlated with Spearman's "g," such as vocabulary, verbal comprehension, and spatial visualization. (Turn back to Figure 8.1 on page 314 to review examples of these items.)

According to Jensen, black–white and (to a lesser extent) SES differences in IQ are due to Level II abilities; the groups are about the same in Level I intelligence (Jensen, 1998). Furthermore, Jensen indicated that among Level II abilities, black children do worst on the least culturally loaded, fluid-type items (such as figure matrices) and best on crystallized tasks (such as vocabulary). Therefore, he argued, black–white IQ differences cannot be caused by cultural bias in the tests. Jensen's conclusion—that blacks are less well endowed than whites with higher-order, abstract forms of intelligence—intensified public outcry over the racist implications of his work.

**Level I–Level II theory**
Jensen's controversial theory, which states that ethnic and SES differences in IQ are due to genetic differences in abstract reasoning and problem-solving abilities (Level II) rather than basic memory skills (Level I).

Is there support for Jensen's Level I–Level II theory? In a series of studies, Jensen (2001) found that specific mental abilities strongly correlated with "g" show large black–white gaps, whereas abilities weakly correlated with "g" show little or no black–white difference. But others report less consistency. For example, Nathan Brody (1997) found that test items strongly correlated with "g" did not always produce the largest disparities between blacks and whites. And one group of researchers reported that both Level I and Level II scores declined similarly with SES (Stankov, Horn, & Roy, 1980).

These findings suggest that "g" contributes to ethnic and SES differences in IQ, but it is not the only basis for them. At present, the evidence on specific mental abilities is not clear enough to favour either a genetic or cultural-bias explanation. For explanations of individual and group differences in IQ, we must turn to a very different set of findings.

## ASK YOURSELF

**review**   Explain how infant intelligence tests differ from childhood intelligence tests in content and correlational stability.

**review**   Discuss factors that might lead a child's IQ to show large gains or declines during childhood and adolescence.

**apply**   Seven-year-old Scott's parents are concerned about Scott's average IQ because they want him to go to university and enter a high-status occupation. What factors besides IQ are likely to contribute to Scott's life success?

**connect**   Describe the bidirectional relationship between IQ and schooling.

# Explaining Individual and Group Differences in IQ

OVER THE PAST TWO decades, researchers have conducted hundreds of studies aimed at uncovering the origins of individual, ethnic, and SES differences in mental abilities. The research falls into three broad classes: (1) investigations addressing the importance of heredity; (2) those that look at whether IQ scores are biased measures of low-SES and minority children's true abilities; and (3) those that examine the quality of children's home environments as a major influence on their mental test performance.

### GENETIC INFLUENCES

Recall from Chapter 3 that behavioural geneticists examine the relative contributions of heredity and environment to complex human characteristics by conducting *kinship studies,* in which they compare individuals of differing degrees of genetic relationship to one another. Let's look closely at what they have discovered about genetic influences on IQ.

**HERITABILITY OF INTELLIGENCE.** In Chapter 3, we introduced the most common method for studying the role of heredity in IQ—the *heritability estimate.* To briefly review, first researchers correlate the IQs of pairs of family members who vary in the extent to which they share genes. Then, using a complicated statistical procedure, the correlations are compared to arrive at an index of heritability, ranging from 0 to 1, that indicates the proportion of variation among individuals in a specific population due to genetic factors.

Let's look closely at the correlations on which heritability estimates are based. Table 8.5 on page 332 summarizes worldwide findings on IQ correlations between kinship pairs. Notice that the greater the genetic similarity between family members, the more they

TABLE 8.5

Worldwide Summary of IQ Correlations between Kinship Pairs

| KINSHIP PAIR | AVERAGE CORRELATION | TOTAL NUMBER OF KINSHIP PAIRS INCLUDED |
|---|---|---|
| Identical twins reared together | .86 | 4 672 |
| Identical twins reared apart | .76 | 158 |
| Fraternal twins reared together | .55 | 8 600 |
| Fraternal twins reared apart | .35 | 112 |
| Siblings reared together | .47 | 26 473 |
| Siblings reared apart | .24 | 203 |
| Parent–biological child living together | .42 | 8 433 |
| Parent–biological child living apart | .22[a] | 814 |
| Nonbiological siblings (adopted–natural pairings) | .29 | 345 |
| Nonbiological siblings (adopted–adopted pairings) | .34 | 369 |
| Parent–adopted child | .19 | 1 397 |

[a]This correlation, reported by Bouchard and McGue (1981), is lower than the values obtained in three subsequent adoption studies, which reported correlations of .31, .37, and .43 (Horn, 1983; Phillips & Fulker, 1989; Scarr & Weinberg, 1983).

*Sources:* Bouchard & McGue, 1981; Scarr, 1997.

resemble one another in IQ. In fact, two of the correlations reveal that heredity is, without question, partially responsible for individual differences in mental test performance. The correlation for identical twins reared apart (.76) is much higher than for fraternal twins reared together (.55).

When researchers look at how these kinship correlations change with age, they find additional support for the importance of heredity. Greater IQ similarity for identical than fraternal twins is evident by 2 years of age (Petrill et al., 1998). And as Figure 8.6 shows, correlations for identical twins increase modestly into adulthood, whereas those for fraternal twins drop sharply at adolescence. Do these trends remind you of the *niche-picking* idea discussed in Chapter 3? Common rearing experiences support the similarity of fraternal twins during childhood. But as they get older and are released from the influence of their families, each fraternal twin follows a course of development, or finds a niche, that fits with

FIGURE 8.6

**Cross-sectional age-related changes in IQ correlations for identical and fraternal twins.** Correlations for identical twins increase modestly into adulthood, whereas those for fraternal twins drop sharply at adolescence. Similar trends appear when twins are followed longitudinally. The findings are derived from studies including thousands of twin pairs. (From M. McGue, T. J. Bouchard, Jr., W. G. Iacono, & D. T. Lykken, 1993, "Behavioural Genetics of Cognitive Ability: A Life-Span Perspective," in R. Plomin & G. E. McClearn, Eds., *Nature, Nurture, and Psychology,* p. 63. Washington, DC: American Psychological Association. Copyright © 1993 by the American Psychological Association. Adapted by permission.)

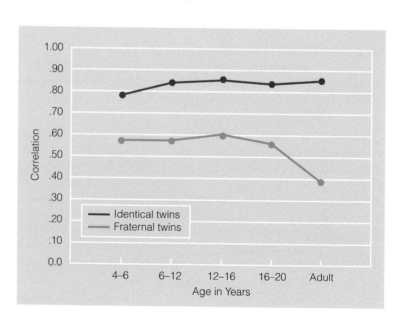

his or her unique genetic makeup. As a result, their IQ scores diverge. In contrast, the genetic likeness of identical twins leads them to seek out similar niches in adolescence and adulthood. Consequently, their IQ resemblance is even greater than it was during childhood. Other studies confirm that the contribution of heredity to IQ strengthens with development (Loehlin, Horn, & Willerman, 1997; McGue et al., 1993).

Although kinship research underscores the importance of heredity, the correlations in Table 8.5 reveal that environment is clearly involved. Correlations for twin and sibling pairs reared together are stronger than for those reared apart. Similarly, for parents and biological children, the correlation for "living together" is stronger than that for "living apart." Finally, parents and adopted children, as well as unrelated siblings, show low positive correlations, again providing support for the effects of common rearing conditions.

As indicated in Chapter 3, heritability estimates usually are computed using correlations for identical and fraternal twins. The typical value in recent research in Western industrialized nations is about .50, which means that half the variation in IQ is due to individual differences in heredity. But the values vary greatly from study to study, usually ranging from the .30s to the .70s (Grigorenko, 2000).

Furthermore, recall from Chapter 3 that this moderate heritability estimate might be too high, since twins reared together often experience very similar overall environments. And even when they are reared apart, they are often placed in foster and adoptive homes that are advantaged and alike in many ways. When the range of environments to which twins are exposed is restricted, heritabilities underestimate the role of environment and overestimate the role of heredity.

In sum, although heritability research offers convincing evidence that genetic factors contribute to IQ, disagreement persists over how large the role of heredity really is (Waldman, 1997). A growing number of researchers regard the heritability approach, which sorts individual differences in IQ into neatly packaged genetic and environmental boxes, as too simplistic a model. They point out that heritability estimates, regardless of their precision, do not bring us closer to understanding the complex processes through which genes and experiences influence intelligence as children develop (Grigorenko, 2000).

## DO HERITABILITY ESTIMATES EXPLAIN ETHNIC AND SES DIFFERENCES IN IQ?

Despite the limitations of the heritability estimate, Jensen (1969, 1998) relied on it to support the argument that ethnic and SES differences in IQ have a strong genetic basis, a view also espoused by Rushton (2000). This line of reasoning is widely regarded as inappropriate. Although heritability estimates computed *within* black and white populations are similar, they provide no direct evidence on what is responsible for between-group differences (Plomin et al., 1997; Suzuki & Valencia, 1997). And recall from Chapter 3 that the heritability of IQ is *higher* under advantaged (higher-SES) than disadvantaged (lower-SES) rearing conditions (Bronfenbrenner & Morris, 1998). Factors associated with low income and poverty, including weak or absent prenatal care, family stress, low-quality schools, and lack of community supports for effective child rearing, prevent children from attaining their genetic potential.

In a well-known example, Richard Lewontin (1976) showed that using within-group heritabilities to explain between-group differences is like comparing different seeds in different soil. Suppose we take a group of corn seeds (which vary in genetic makeup) and plant them in the same pot with a rich supply of fertilizer designed to promote plant growth. Then we take another group of seeds and grow them under quite different conditions, in a pot with half as much fertilizer. We find that although the plants in each group vary in height, the first group, on the average, grows taller than the second group. Within each group, individual differences in plant height are largely due to heredity, since growth environments of all plants were much the same. But the between-group difference is probably environmental, since the second group got far less fertilizer.

To be sure of this conclusion, we could design a second study in which we expose the second group of seeds to a full supply of fertilizer and see if they reach an average height that equals that of the first group. If they do, then we would have more powerful evidence that

FIGURE 8.7

**IQs of adopted children as a function of biological mothers' IQ in the Texas Adoption Project.** In this study, selective placement was not great enough to account for the large difference between the two groups. (Adapted from Loehlin, Horn, & Willerman, 1997.)

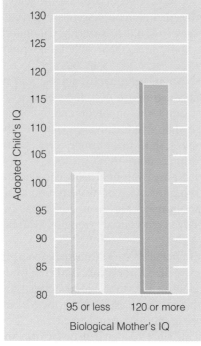

These boys are brothers who are growing up in the same stimulating, advantaged home. Transracial adoption research supports the view that rearing environment is responsible for the black–white IQ gap. African-American children placed in economically well-off white homes early in life score high on intelligence tests because they are "reared in the culture of the tests and schools."

©KEN CHERNUS/FPG INTERNATIONAL/GETTY IMAGES

environment is responsible for the previous group difference. In the next section, we will see that researchers have conducted natural experiments of this kind by studying the IQs of children adopted into homes very different from their family of origin.

**ADOPTION RESEARCH.** Adoption studies provide a wider range of information than the evidence on heritability considered so far. Correlations of children with their biological and adoptive family members can be examined for insight into genetic and environmental influences. Even more important, researchers can gain insight into how malleable IQ is by looking at changes in the absolute value of test scores as the result of growing up in an advantaged family.

In an investigation of this kind called the Texas Adoption Project, children of two extreme groups of mothers—those with IQs below 95 and those with IQs above 120—were chosen for special study. All the children were adopted at birth by parents well above average in income and education. As Figure 8.7 shows, during the school years, children of the low-IQ biological mothers scored above-average in IQ, indicating that test performance can be greatly improved by an advantaged home life! At the same time, they did not do as well as children of high-IQ biological mothers placed in similar adoptive families. Furthermore, when correlations were examined, adopted children increasingly resembled their biological mothers as they grew older and decreasingly resembled their adoptive parents (Loehlin, Horn, & Willerman, 1997). Adoption research confirms that both environment and heredity contribute significantly to IQ.

When mothers low in IQ, education, and income give up their babies for adoption in the first 6 months of life, the children consistently score above average in IQ. This suggests that environment plays a substantial role in SES variations in intelligence. But concluding that SES differences are entirely environmental may be too extreme. Although children of low-SES biological mothers adopted into higher-SES families attain above-average IQs, they score somewhat lower than their adoptive parents' natural children. This difference could be due to heredity, to environmental influences prior to adoption (such as prenatal conditions), to parents' tendency to treat their natural and adopted children differently, or to a combination of these factors (Devlin et al., 1995). In addition, adoption studies repeatedly reveal stronger correlations between the IQ scores of biological than adoptive relatives (Horn, 1983; Plomin & DeFries, 1983; Scarr & Weinberg, 1983). Consequently, some researchers believe that the SES–IQ relationship is partly genetic (Bouchard, 1997; Scarr, 1997).

What about the black–white IQ difference? Research reveals no conclusive genetic influence, so the lower average scores of black children cannot be assigned to racially linked, inferior genes. Indeed, African-American children placed in economically well-off white homes during the first year of life score high on intelligence tests. In two such studies, adopted black children attained mean IQs of 110 and 117 by middle childhood, well above average and 20 to 30 points higher than the typical scores of children growing up in low-income black communities (Moore, 1986; Scarr & Weinberg, 1983).

However, a follow-up in one investigation revealed that adoptees' IQs declined in adolescence. Some researchers claim that adoptive rearing environments influence IQ only temporarily, in childhood. However, the IQ drop may have resulted from giving different tests at the two ages. Or it might have been due to the challenges black adolescents face in establishing an ethnic identity that blends their birth and adoptive backgrounds. When this process is fraught with emotional turmoil, it can affect motivation and performance on intelligence tests (DeBerry, Scarr, & Weinberg, 1996; Waldman, Weinberg, & Scarr, 1994).

Adoption findings do not completely resolve questions about ethnic differences in IQ. Nevertheless, the IQ gains of black children "reared in the culture of the tests and schools" are consistent with a wealth of evidence indicating that poverty severely depresses the intelligence of large numbers of ethnic minority youngsters (Nisbett, 1998; Sternberg, 1996a). Furthermore, dramatic generational gains in IQ support the notion that, with new experiences and opportunities, oppressed groups can move substantially beyond their mean IQs. See the Biology & Environment box on page 336 to find out about the **Flynn effect.**

## ETHNICITY: GENETIC OR CULTURAL GROUPINGS?

DNA analyses reveal wide genetic variation *within* races (distinguished by physical features, such as skin colour) and minimal genetic variation *between* them (Cavalli-Sforza, Menozzi, & Piazza, 1994). Members of ethnic groups that have been the focus of the IQ nature–nurture controversy are far more similar in cultural values, experiences, and opportunities than they are in genetic makeup.

Nevertheless, many people assume that genetic, racial differences determine ethnic-group differences in psychological traits. A close look, however, reveals that commonly used racial labels—assumed to have genetic meaning—are often arbitrary! For example, "black" designates people with dark skin in North America but refers to hair texture, eye colour, and stature in Brazil and Peru, where many African Americans would be called "white." Asians and the !Kung of Botswana, Africa, could be regarded as one race, since they have similarly shaped eyes. Alternatively, Asians, Native Americans, and Swedes could be grouped together because of their similarly shaped teeth (Begley, 1995; Renzetti & Curran, 1998).

In research on race, people self-identify, expressing their cultural heritage and sense of group belonging. Ethnic mixing is extensive in culturally diverse countries. Consider this Hawaiian native's description of his ethnicity: "I'm Asian on my birth certificate and on the Census form, but I'm really multiracial. My mother's parents were Japanese, my father's mother was Filipino, and my father's father was Irish."

As one scholar of race relations recently summed up, "Classification of human beings into races is in the end a futile exercise" (Payne, 1998, p. 32). An ever-present danger of perpetuating the belief that some ethnic groups are genetically inferior in IQ is continued unfair allocation of resources, making an unfounded assumption seem true.

## TEST BIAS

Reread Hassan's responses to Nora's mental-test questions at the beginning of this chapter. Can we conclude that he has a weak grasp of similarities between objects? Or are the test items ill-suited to revealing his abilities? A controversial question raised about ethnic differences in IQ has to do with whether they result from *test bias*. If a test samples culturally specific knowledge and skills that not all groups of children have had equal opportunity to learn, then it is a biased, or unfair, measure.

Some experts reject the idea that intelligence tests are biased, claiming that they were intended to represent success in the common culture. According to this perspective, since IQ predicts academic achievement equally well for majority and minority children, then IQ tests are fair to both groups (Brown, Reynolds, & Whitaker, 1999; Jensen, 1980). Others take a

**Flynn effect**
The large gains in IQ that have occurred over successive generations, from 1930 to the present.

# biology & environment

## THE FLYNN EFFECT: MASSIVE GENERATIONAL GAINS IN IQ

Obtaining IQ scores from every industrialized nation that had either military mental testing or frequent testing of other large, representative samples, James Flynn (1994, 1999) reported a finding so consistent and intriguing that it has become known as the *Flynn effect*. From 1930 to the present, IQs have increased steadily. And the largest gains occurred on fluid-ability tests of abstract reasoning—tasks often assumed to be largely biologically based! Figure 8.8 shows these increases for a nonverbal test of spatial reasoning, administered to military samples consisting of almost all young men in Belgium, Israel, the Netherlands, and Norway. IQ rose, on the average, 18 points per generation (30 years).

Consistent with this *secular trend* (see page 180 to review this concept), when updated versions of intelligence tests are created, the new standardization sample almost always performs better than the previous one. When Flynn (1987) located every study in which the same individuals had taken two or more Stanford-Binet or Wechsler tests (a total of 73 samples, with more than 7500 participants), the average gain in IQ between 1932 and 1978 was 14 IQ points. And when subtest scores were examined, once again gains were largest for fluid-ability tasks. They were minimal for crystallized-ability items, which resemble subjects taught in school.

The Flynn effect is environmental; improved nutrition and education,

technological innovations (including TV and computers), a more stimulating world, and greater test-taking motivation may contribute to the better reasoning ability of each successive generation (Williams, 1998). Notice that the generational gain in fluid intelligence (18 points) is larger than the black–white gap in IQ (about 15 points). Therefore, environmental explanations for ethnic differences in IQ (including fluid-ability differences) are highly plausible. Flynn argues that large, environmentally induced IQ gains between generations present a major challenge to Jensen's assumption that black–white and other ethnic variations in IQ are largely genetic (Dickens & Flynn, 2001).

Other researchers call for more precise information on factors that contribute to the Flynn effect before drawing any implications for ethnicity and IQ (Rodgers, 1999). And once we identify the experiences that created this impressive rise in test scores, we might be able to promote it further and extend it to other mental abilities besides abstract reasoning.

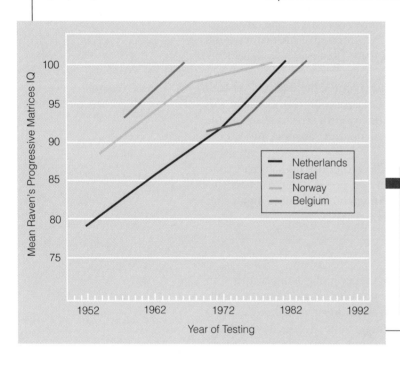

**FIGURE** 8.8

**Generational gain in performance on a nonverbal test of spatial reasoning (Raven's Progressive Matrices) in four nations.** Findings are based on cross-sectional military samples, including nearly all young adults in each country. Average gain is about 18 points per generation (30 years). (From J. R. Flynn, 1999, "Searching for Justice: The Discovery of IQ Gains over Time," *American Psychologist, 54,* p. 7. Copyright © by the American Psychological Association. Adapted by permission.)

broader view of test bias. They believe that lack of specific learning experiences, including exposure to certain language customs and knowledge, leads test scores to underestimate the abilities of certain ethnic minority groups and low-SES children (Ceci & Williams, 1997; Sternberg, 1997). To evaluate this position, let's look at each of these factors.

■ **LANGUAGE CUSTOMS.** Ethnic minority families often foster unique language skills that do not match the expectations of most classrooms and testing situations. Shirley Brice Heath (1982, 1989), an anthropologist who spent many hours observing in low-SES black homes in a southeastern U.S. city, found that black adults asked their children very different kinds of questions than are typical in white middle-SES families. From an early age, white parents ask knowledge-training questions, such as "What colour is it?" and "What's this story about?" that resemble the questioning style of tests and classrooms. In contrast, the black parents asked only "real" questions—ones they themselves could not answer. Often these were analogy questions ("What's that like?") or story-starter questions ("Didja hear Miss Sally this morning?") that called for elaborate responses about personal experiences and no single right answer.

Heath and other researchers report that these experiences lead low-SES black children to develop complex verbal skills at home, such as storytelling and exchanging quick-witted remarks. But their language differs from that of white middle-SES children in emphasizing emotional and social topics rather than facts about the world (Blake, 1994). Not surprisingly, black children may be confused by the "objective" questions they encounter on tests and in classrooms and many withdraw into silence.

The impact of culture on language style is apparent in children's narratives. Most school-age children's narratives increasingly follow a *topic-focused formula;* they build toward a high point, describe a critical event, and then resolve it. African-American children, however, often tell *topic-associating stories,* which blend several similar experiences. One 9-year-old, for example, related having a tooth pulled, then described seeing her sister's tooth pulled, next told how she removed one of her baby teeth before a test at school, and concluded with her offer to take out her cousin's baby tooth: "So I told him, 'I'm a pullin' teeth expert.... if you need somebody to do it, call me, and I'll be over'" (McCabe, 1997, p. 164). Yet many teachers criticize this approach as "disorganized" (McCabe, 1998). And it is not assessed in verbal items on intelligence tests.

Other minority youngsters also develop distinct language customs. For example, children of Hispanic immigrants are taught to respect adult authority rather than express their own knowledge and opinions. Yet teachers, who value self-assertive speaking, typically equate the silence of Hispanic children with having a negative attitude toward learning (Greenfield & Suzuki, 1998). As the child listens politely but does not answer out of deference to the adult, a culturally valued style of communicating quickly leads to unfair, negative evaluations in school and on mental tests. Similar explanations have been offered for why Aboriginal children tend to score below average in verbal ability but average to above average in nonverbal ability (Common & Frost, 1988).

■ **TEST CONTENT.** Many researchers argue that IQ scores are affected by specific information acquired as part of majority-culture upbringing. Unfortunately, attempts to change tests, either by basing them on more familiar content or by eliminating verbal, fact-oriented (crystallized) items and relying only on spatial and performance (fluid) tasks, have not raised the scores of ethnic minority children very much (Reynolds & Kaiser, 1990).

Nevertheless, even fluid test items depend on learning opportunities. In one study, children's performance on the spatial reasoning subscale of the WISC was related to the extent to which they had played a popular but expensive game that (like the test items) required them to arrange blocks to duplicate a design as quickly as possible (Dirks, 1982). Playing video games that require fast responding and mental rotation of visual images also fosters success on spatial test items (Subrahmanyam & Greenfield, 1996). Low-income minority children, who often grow up in more "people-oriented" than "object-oriented" homes, may lack opportunities to use games and objects that promote certain intellectual skills.

ROBERT FINKEN/MAXx IMAGES INC.

How does this Aboriginal girl tell a story to her classmates? Ethnic minority children often use distinct narrative styles derived from listening to and telling stories at home. Their approach to storytelling may not match the topic-focused formula valued in school.

**TESTING CONDITIONS.** When faced with the strangeness of the testing situation, the minority child may look to the examiner for cues about how to respond. Some evidence suggests that minority children are more concerned with pleasing teachers than are white children (Ferguson, 1998). Yet on most intelligence tests, tasks can be presented in only one way, and those taking the test cannot get feedback. When an examiner refuses to reveal whether the child is on the right track, minority children may react with "disruptive apprehension"—giving any answer that comes to mind, rejecting the testing situation as important to personal goals, and not revealing what they know. Notice how, in the chapter introduction, Hassan repeated his first answer, perhaps because he could not figure out the task's meaning. Had Nora prompted him to look at the questions in a different way, his performance might have been better.

When testing conditions grant minority children a chance to get to know the examiner, frequent praise, and easier items after incorrect responses to minimize the emotional consequences of failure, IQs of young children improve. But over time, many low-SES minority children suffer from deep-seated motivational difficulties. As they experience repeated academic failure, they develop a self-defeating style marked by withdrawal and reduced effort. Research indicates a growing discrepancy over the school years between high- and low-achieving children in the desire to do well on standardized tests (Paris et al., 1991). As a result, IQ may become an especially inaccurate indicator of these youngsters' learning potential at older ages.

## REDUCING TEST BIAS

Although not all experts agree, many acknowledge that IQ scores can underestimate the intelligence of culturally different children. A special concern exists about incorrectly labelling minority children as slow learners and assigning them to remedial classes, which are far less stimulating than regular school experiences and linked to negative educational outcomes. Because of this danger, test scores need to be combined with assessments of children's adaptive behaviour—their ability to cope with the demands of their everyday environments. The child who does poorly on an IQ test yet displays considerable practical intelligence—by playing a complex game on the playground, figuring out how to rewire a broken TV, or caring for younger siblings responsibly—is unlikely to be mentally deficient.

In addition, test designers are becoming more aware that minority children often are capable of the cognitive operations called for by test items. But because they are used to thinking in other ways in daily life, they may not access the required operation (Greenfield, 1997). **Dynamic testing,** an innovation consistent with Vygotsky's concept of the *zone of proximal development,* tries to narrow the gap between actual and potential performance. Instead of emphasizing previously acquired knowledge, it introduces purposeful teaching into the testing situation to find out what the child can attain with social support. Three factors distinguish dynamic testing from traditional, static approaches:

- a focus on the *processes* involved in learning and development (rather than on intellectual *products*);

- provision of *feedback* after each task (rather than no feedback); and

- an *examiner–child relationship* based on teaching and helping that is individualized for each child (rather than a neutral relationship that is identical for all children). (Grigorenko & Sternberg, 1998)

Most dynamic-testing models use a pretest–intervene–retest procedure with intelligence test items (Lidz, 1991, 1997).

Dynamic testing introduces purposeful teaching into the situation to find out what the child can attain with social support. This teacher assists a second grader in writing the alphabet. Many ethnic minority children perform more competently after adult assistance. And the approach helps identify the teaching style to which the child is most responsive.

© WILL HART/PHOTOEDIT

The best known is Reuben Feuerstein's (1979, 1980) *Learning Potential Assessment Device.* Using traditional intelligence test items, the adult tries to find the teaching style best suited to the child and communicates principles and strategies that the child can generalize to new situations.

Evidence on the effectiveness of dynamic testing reveals that the IQs of ethnic minority children underestimate their ability to perform intellectual tasks after adult assistance. Children's receptivity to teaching and their capacity to transfer what they have learned to novel problems add substantially to the prediction of future performance (Lidz, 2001; Tzuriel, 2000). In one study of dynamic testing, Ethiopian 6- and 7-year-olds who had recently immigrated to Israel performed substantially below their Israeli-born agemates on fluid-ability reasoning tests. The Israeli children often practised in everyday life the mental operations required to do well on these tests, whereas the Ethiopian children had little experience with this type of thinking. After several intensive teaching sessions, the Ethiopian children's scores increased substantially, approaching their Israeli-born agemates' performance. The Ethiopian children also transferred their learning to new test items (see Figure 8.9) (Tzuriel & Kaufman, 1999).

As yet, dynamic testing is not more effective in predicting academic achievement than are traditional tests. But better correspondence may emerge in classrooms where teaching interactions resemble the dynamic testing approach—namely, individualized assistance on tasks carefully selected to help the child move beyond her current level of development (Grigorenko & Sternberg, 1998).

Dynamic testing is time consuming and requires extensive knowledge of cultural values and practices to work well with minority children. Until we have the resources to implement these procedures broadly, should we suspend the use of intelligence testing in schools? Most experts regard this solution as unacceptable, since important educational decisions would be based only on subjective impressions—a policy that could increase the discriminatory placement of minority children. Intelligence tests are useful as long as they are interpreted carefully by examiners who are sensitive to cultural influences on test performance. And despite their limitations, IQ scores continue to be valid measures of school learning potential for the majority of Western children.

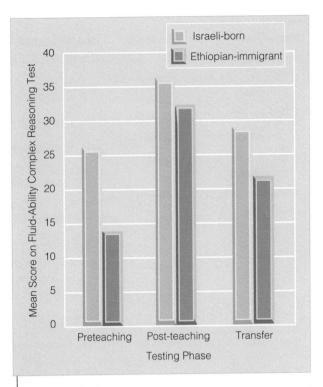

**FIGURE** 8.9

**Consequences of dynamic testing for Ethiopian-immigrant and Israeli-born 6- and 7-year-olds' scores on fluid-ability, complex reasoning tasks.** Each child completed test items during a preteaching phase, a post-teaching phase, and a transfer phase. Transfer items differed considerably from the others; children had to generalize their learning to new problems. Although Ethiopian-immigrant children's pretest scores were well below those of Israeli-born children, after intensive teaching they closed the gap and sustained a level of performance on transfer tasks that was considerably higher than their pretest performance. Dynamic testing revealed that a conventionally administered test (the preteaching phase) underestimated Ethiopian children's learning potential. (Adapted from Tzuriel & Kaufman, 1999.)

## HOME ENVIRONMENT AND IQ

As indicated earlier, children of the *same* ethnic and SES background vary greatly in IQ. Many studies support the conclusion that home environmental factors contribute to these differences.

Researchers divide home influences into two broad types. The first, called **shared environmental influences,** are factors that pervade the general atmosphere of the home and, therefore, similarly affect all children living in it. The availability of stimulating toys and books and parental modelling of intellectual activities are examples. The second type, **nonshared environmental influences,** are factors that make siblings different from one another. Examples include unique treatment by parents, birth order and spacing, as well as special events, such as moving to a new neighbourhood, that affect one sibling more than the other. Let's see what research says about each of these classes of environmental events.

**dynamic testing**
An approach to testing consistent with Vygotsky's concept of the zone of proximal development, in which purposeful teaching is introduced into the testing situation to find out what the child can attain with social support.

**shared environmental influences**
Environmental influences that pervade the general atmosphere of the home and, therefore, similarly affect all children living in it.

**nonshared environmental influences**
Environmental influences that make siblings living in the same home different from one another.

**TABLE** 8.6

Home Observation for Measurement of the Environment (HOME) Subscales

| INFANCY VERSION | PRESCHOOL VERSION | MIDDLE CHILDHOOD VERSION |
|---|---|---|
| 1. Emotional and verbal responsiveness of the parent | 1. Parental pride, affection, and warmth | 1. Emotional and verbal responsiveness of the parent |
| 2. Parental acceptance of the child | 2. Avoidance of physical punishment | 2. Emotional climate of the parent–child relationship |
| 3. Parental involvement with the child | 3. Language stimulation | 3. Parental encouragement of social maturity |
| 4. Organization of the physical environment | 4. Stimulation of academic behaviour | 4. Provision for active stimulation |
| 5. Provision of appropriate play materials | 5. Stimulation through toys, games, and reading material | 5. Growth-fostering materials and experiences |
| 6. Variety in daily stimulation | 6. Parental modelling and encouragement of social maturity | 6. Family participation in developmentally stimulating experiences |
| | 7. Variety in daily stimulation | 7. Parental involvement in child rearing |
| | 8. Physical environment: safe, clean, and conducive to development | 8. Physical environment: safe, clean, and conducive to development |

*Sources:* Bradley & Caldwell, 1979; Bradley et al., 1988; Elardo, Bradley, & Caldwell, 1975.

**SHARED ENVIRONMENTAL INFLUENCES.** Two types of research shed light on the role of shared environmental influences: (1) studies in which researchers observe home environmental qualities and relate them to IQ scores; and (2) research examining the impact of family beliefs about intellectual success on student performance.

***Observations of Home Environmental Qualities.*** Bettye Caldwell and Robert Bradley developed the **Home Observation for Measurement of the Environment (HOME),** a checklist for gathering information about the quality of children's home lives through observation and parental interviews (Caldwell & Bradley, 1994). Table 8.6 shows the subscales measured by the infancy, preschool, and middle childhood versions.

Evidence on HOME confirms the findings of many years of research—that stimulation provided by parents is moderately linked to mental development. Regardless of the SES and ethnicity, an organized, stimulating physical setting and parental encouragement, involvement, and affection repeatedly predict better language and IQ scores in toddlerhood and early childhood (Espy, Molfese, & DiLalla, 2001; Klebanov et al., 1998; Roberts, Burchinal, & Durham, 1999). Furthermore, high HOME scores are associated with IQ gains between 1 and 3 years of age, whereas low HOME scores predict large declines (Bradley et al., 1989). The extent to which parents talk to infants and toddlers is particularly important. It contributes strongly to early language progress. Language progress, in turn, predicts intelligence and academic achievement in elementary school (Hart & Risley, 1995).

The HOME–IQ relationship declines in middle childhood, perhaps because older children spend more time in other settings, such as school (Luster & Dubow, 1992). Nevertheless, two middle-childhood HOME scales are especially strong predictors of academic achievement: provision for active stimulation (for example, encouraging hobbies and organizational memberships) and family participation in developmentally stimulating experiences (visiting friends, attending theatre performances) (Bradley, Caldwell, & Rock, 1988).

Yet we must be cautious about interpreting these correlational findings. In all the studies, children were reared by their biological parents, with whom they share not just a common environment but also a common heredity. Parents who are genetically more intelligent might provide better experiences as well as give birth to genetically brighter children. In addition, brighter children may evoke more parental stimulation. Note that these hypotheses refer to genetic–environmental correlation (see Chapter 3, page 116).

**Home Observation for Measurement of the Environment (HOME)**
A checklist for gathering information about the quality of children's home lives through observation and parental interviews. Infancy, preschool, and middle childhood versions exist.

The HOME–IQ correlation is not as strong for adopted children as it is for biological children (Braungart, Fulker, & Plomin, 1992; Cherny, 1994). This suggests that parent–child genetic similarity elevates the relationship (Coon et al., 1990; Scarr, 1997). But heredity does not account for all the association between home environment and mental test scores. In several studies, family living conditions—HOME scores and affluence of the surrounding neighbourhood—continued to predict children's IQ beyond the effect of maternal intelligence and education. These findings highlight the importance of environment (Chase-Lansdale et al., 1997; Klebanov et al., 1998; Sameroff et al., 1993).

***Family Beliefs About Intellectual Success.*** Support for achievement is greater in high-SES families in which both parent and child IQs are higher, making it difficult to isolate the impact of family beliefs on children's performance. But SES and IQ alone cannot explain the high valuing of educational endeavours among families who have recently immigrated to North America. Regardless of SES, newly arrived parents from Asian and Latin American countries tend to emphasize the importance of intellectual success, and their children do remarkably well in school. (Return to the Social Issues: Education box in Chapter 2, page 50, to review these findings.)

Is IQ responsible for immigrant adolescents' superior academic performance? Probably not, since recent arrivals are unlikely to be more intelligent than individuals who came a decade or two earlier. Rather, immigrant parents' belief that education is the surest way to improve life chances seems to play a profound role (Kao, 2000).

Parental beliefs are also linked to academic success among non-immigrant children. For example, in a study of low-SES African-American families, parents' expectations for their children's educational attainment were positively correlated with 8- to 10-year-olds' reading and math achievement (Halle, Kurtz-Costes, & Mahoney, 1997). Similarly, an investigation of Asian-American, Hispanic, and Caucasian-American families revealed that within each group, the more schooling parents expected their children in grades 4 and 5 to attain, the higher the children's marks in school (Okagaki & Frensch, 1998). Parents' expectations were not simply a response to their child's prior achievements. Regardless of children's marks the previous year, parents' expectations were associated with school performance. Child-rearing practices (warmth plus maturity demands) may be the means by which parents' high expectations are transmitted to children (Okagaki, 2001). We will consider parenting and achievement further in Chapters 11 and 14.

**NONSHARED ENVIRONMENTAL INFLUENCES.** Although children growing up in the same family are affected by common environments, their experiences also differ. Parents may favour one child over another, for example. Each child also experiences sibling relationships differently. And children may be assigned special roles—for example, one expected to achieve, a second to get along well with others.

Kinship research suggests that nonshared environmental factors are more powerful than shared influences. Turn back to Table 8.5 on page 332. Notice the relatively low correlations between nonbiological siblings—a direct estimate of the effect of shared environment on IQ. Recall, also, that in adolescence the IQ resemblance between fraternal twins drops (see page 332). This trend also characterizes nontwin siblings. And it is particularly marked for nonbiological siblings, whose IQs at adolescence are no longer correlated. These findings have led researchers to conclude that the impact of the shared environment on IQ is greatest in childhood (Finkel & Pedersen, 2001; Loehlin, Horn, & Willerman, 1997). Thereafter, it gives way to nonshared influences, as young people spend more time away from home, encounter experiences unlike those of their siblings, and seek environmental niches consistent with their genetic makeup.

Nevertheless, very few studies have examined nonshared environmental influences on IQ. The most extensively studied factors are birth order and spacing between siblings. For years, researchers thought that earlier birth order and wider spacing might grant children more

PETER BECK/CORBIS STOCK MARKET/MAGMA

When parents place a high value on educational endeavours, their children are more successful in school—a relationship that cannot be explained only by SES or IQ. Here, a mother takes an interest in her son's science project.

parental attention and stimulation and, therefore, result in higher IQs. But studies reporting these outcomes were flawed. New evidence indicates that birth order and spacing are unrelated to IQ (Rodgers, 2001; Rodgers et al., 2000). Why is this so? Parents' differential treatment of siblings appears to be far more responsive to siblings' personalities, interests, and behaviours than it is to these family-structure variables.

Finally, some researchers believe that the most potent nonshared environmental influences are unpredictable one-time events. A particularly inspiring English teacher, a summer at a special camp, or a period of intense rivalry with a sibling are examples (McCall, 1993). To understand the role of these nonshared factors in mental development, we need more intensive case studies of children growing up in the same family than have been accomplished to date.

## ASK YOURSELF

**review**    Summarize ethnic differences in IQ. Why can't heritability estimates explain these differences? According to research, what environmental factors contribute to ethnic variations in test scores?

**review**    IQ correlations for fraternal twins and siblings decline from childhood to adolescence. What does this suggest about the impact of shared and nonshared environmental influences on IQ?

**apply**    Desiree, an Aboriginal child, was quiet and withdrawn while taking an intelligence test. Later she remarked, "I can't understand why that lady asked me all those questions, like what a ball and stove are for. She must *know* what a ball and stove are for!" Explain Desiree's reaction. Why is her IQ score likely to underestimate her intelligence?

**connect**    Explain how dynamic testing is consistent with Vygotsky's concepts of the zone of proximal development and scaffolding. (See Chapter 6, page 258.)

# Early Intervention and Intellectual Development

**PROJECT HEAD START** is an early intervention program for economically disadvantaged preschoolers in the United States, begun in 1965. It is based on the assumption that learning problems are best treated early, before formal schooling begins, as well as on the hope that early enrichment will offset the declines in IQ and achievement common among low-SES children of ethnic minority and other backgrounds. A typical Head Start program provides children with a year or two of preschool education, along with nutritional and medical services. Parent involvement is central to the Head Start philosophy. Parents serve on policy councils and contribute to program planning. They also work directly with children in classrooms, attend special programs on parenting and child development, and receive services directed at their own social, emotional, and vocational needs (Head Start Bureau, 2001).

The Canadian Psychological Association, in conjunction with the Canadian Association of School Psychologists, recently launched a program called **CANSTART**. Unlike children in Head Start in the United States, however, Canadian children need not be economically disadvantaged to participate. Instead, the principal goal is to provide teachers, who work with 4- to 6-year-old children from all walks of life, with information on research-based procedures known to be effective in reducing the risk of early school failure. To accomplish this goal, the two sponsoring organizations are issuing a series of brief publications in English and French. These publications contain descriptions of practical procedures to help teachers identify, and then assist, children who lack appropriate language, problem-solving, and/or reading and writing readiness skills (Simner, 1995, 1998, 2002).

Canada also has the **Aboriginal Head Start** program, begun in 1998. The program aims to provide Aboriginal children under the age of 6 who live in urban centres and large northern communities with a positive sense of themselves and a desire for learning. Operated by locally

**Project Head Start**
A U.S. federal program that provides low-income children with a year or two of preschool education, along with nutritional and medical services, and that encourages parent involvement in children's development.

**CANSTART**
A Canadian program with the principal goal of providing teachers with information on research-based procedures to help identify, and then assist, children at risk for early school failure.

**Aboriginal Head Start**
A Canadian Head Start program designed for Aboriginal children under age 6 operated by local nonprofit Aboriginal organizations.

managed Aboriginal non-profit organizations, the program focuses on meeting the developmental needs of young Aboriginal children, while empowering parents to bring forth their children's unique abilities. A preschool program is offered with links to other health and educational services. Currently, Aboriginal Head Start has 99 sites in eight provinces and all territories, with plans to expand to on-reserve sites (Health Canada, 2000a). At present, it is too early to evaluate these two Canadian initiatives. So let's look at the benefits of U.S. early intervention, which has served as a model.

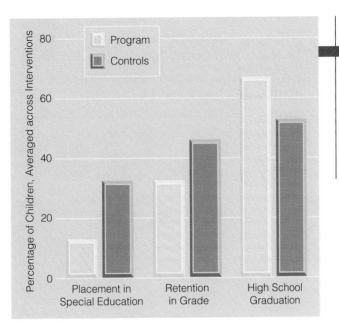

FIGURE 8.10

**Benefits of preschool intervention programs.** Low-income children who received intervention fared better than controls on real-life indicators of school adjustment. (Adapted from Royce, Darlington, & Murray, 1983.)

### BENEFITS OF EARLY INTERVENTION

Over two decades of research establishing the long-term benefits of early intervention helped Head Start survive. The most important of these studies was coordinated by the Consortium for Longitudinal Studies, which combined data from seven university-based interventions. Results showed that children who attended programs scored higher in IQ and achievement than did controls during the first 2 to 3 years of elementary school. After that time, differences in test scores declined (Lazar & Darlington, 1982).

Nevertheless, children who received intervention remained ahead into adolescence on measures of real-life school adjustment. As Figure 8.10 shows, they were less likely to be placed in special education classes or retained in grade, and a greater number graduated from high school. They also showed lasting benefits in attitudes and motivation. Children who attended programs were more likely to give achievement-related reasons (such as school or job accomplishments) for being proud of themselves. A separate report on one program—the High/Scope Perry Preschool Project—revealed benefits lasting into young adulthood. It was associated with a reduction in delinquency and teenage pregnancy, a greater likelihood of employment, and greater educational attainment, earnings, and marital stability at age 27 (Weikart, 1998).

Does the impact of outstanding university-based programs on school adjustment generalize to Head Start programs? Outcomes are similar, although not as strong. Head Start preschoolers are more economically disadvantaged than are children in university-based programs, leading to more severe learning problems. And because Head Start is community based, quality of services is more variable across programs (Barnett, 1998; Ramey, 1999).

A consistent finding is that almost all Head Start children experience an eventual **washout effect;** improvements in IQ and achievement scores do not last for more than a few years. One reason is that children graduating from Head Start and other interventions typically enter underfunded, inferior public schools in poverty-stricken neighbourhoods (Currie & Thomas, 1997; Schnur & Belanger, 2000). The benefits of Head Start are easily undermined when children do not have continuing access to high-quality educational supports. In a program that began at age 4 and continued through grade 3, achievement score gains were still evident in junior high school (Reynolds & Temple, 1998). And when intensive intervention begins in infancy and persists through early childhood, IQ gains endure into adolescence (see the Social Issues: Education box on page 344).

**washout effect**
The loss of IQ and achievement gains resulting from early intervention within a few years after the program ends.

*social issues: education*

## THE CAROLINA ABECEDARIAN PROJECT: A MODEL OF EARLY INTERVENTION

In the 1970s, an experiment was begun to find out if educational enrichment starting at a very early age could prevent the declines in mental development that affect children born into extreme poverty. The Carolina Abecedarian Project identified more than 100 African-American infants at serious risk for school failure, based on parent education and income, poor school achievement among older siblings, and other family problems. Shortly after birth, the babies were randomly assigned to either a treatment or a control group.

Between 3 weeks and 3 months of age, infants in the treatment group were enrolled in a full-time, year-round child-care program, where they remained until they entered school. There they received stimulation aimed at promoting motor, cognitive, language, and social skills and, after age 3, prereading and math concepts. At all ages, special emphasis was placed on rich, responsive adult–child communication. All children received nutrition and health services; the primary difference between treatment and controls was the child-care experience.

As Figure 8.11 shows, by 12 months of age, the IQs of the two groups diverge. Treatment children scored higher than controls throughout the preschool years. Although the high-risk backgrounds of both groups led their IQs to decline during middle childhood, treatment children retained their IQ advantage into adolescence. In addition, at 12 and 15 years of age, treatment youths were achieving considerably better, espe-

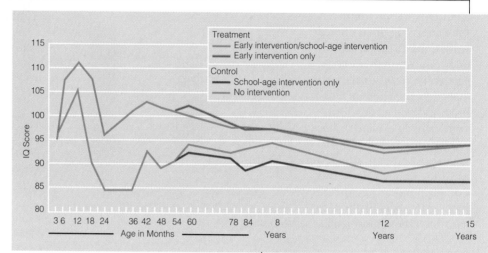

cially in reading and math. And at age 18, high-school graduation rate was higher for the treatment than the control group (Campbell & Ramey, 1994, 1995; Ramey & Ramey, 1999).

While the children were in elementary school, the researchers conducted a second experiment to compare the impact of early and later intervention. From kindergarten through grade 2, half the treatment and half the control group were provided with a resource teacher, who introduced educational activities into the home that addressed the child's specific learning needs. School-age intervention had little impact on IQ (refer again to Figure 8.11). And although it enhanced children's academic achievement, the effects were weaker than the impact of very early intervention.

The Carolina Abecedarian Project shows that providing children with continuous, high-quality enrichment from infancy through the preschool years is an effective way to reduce the devastating impact of poverty on children's mental development. The Better

**FIGURE** 8.11

**IQ scores of treatment and control children from 6 months to 15 years in the Carolina Abecedarian Project.** To compare the impact of early and later intervention, half the treatment and half the control group were provided with supplementary educational activities suited to their learning needs from kindergarten through grade 2. School-age intervention had little impact on age-related changes in IQ; the effects of early intervention were powerful. (From F. A. Campbell & C. T. Ramey, 1995, "Cognitive and School Outcomes for High-Risk African-American Students at Middle Adolescence: Positive Effects of Early Intervention," *American Educational Research Journal, 32,* p. 757. Reprinted by permission of the American Educational Research Association.)

Beginnings, Better Futures Prevention Project, with centres in eight communities in Ontario, is Canada's first long-term project of this kind. Ray Peters (1994) of Queen's University is studying the effectiveness of this early intervention.

Despite Head Start children's declining test scores, their ability to meet school requirements is a remarkable intervention outcome. It may be due to program effects on parents, who create better rearing environments for their children. The more parents are involved in Head Start, the better their child-rearing practices and the more stimulating their home learning environments. These factors are positively related to preschoolers' year-end school readiness scores, which tap academic, language, and social skills as well as independence and task persistence in the classroom (Marcon, 1999; Parker et al., 1999).

### THE FUTURE OF EARLY INTERVENTION

A typical parent component of early intervention teaches parenting skills and encourages parents to act as supplementary intervenors for their children. By emphasizing developmental goals for parents *and* children, program benefits might be extended (Smith, 1995). A parent helped to move out of poverty with education, vocational training, and other social services is likely to gain in psychological well-being, planning for the future, and beliefs and behaviours that foster children's motivation in school. When combined with child-centred intervention, these gains should translate into exceptionally strong benefits for children—not just on IQ tests and report cards but in future life success (Ramey & Ramey, 1998; Zigler & Styfco, 2001).

At present, this *two-generation approach* is too new to have yielded much research on long-term benefits (McLoyd, 1998). But one pioneering effort, the New Chance Demonstration Program, is cause for optimism. In it, teenage mothers who had dropped out of school received services for themselves and their babies, including education, employment, family planning, life management, parent training, and child health care. A follow-up when children were 5 years old revealed that parent participants were more likely to have earned a high school diploma, were less likely to be on welfare, and had higher family earnings than did controls receiving less intensive intervention. In addition, program children experienced warmer and more stimulating home environments, were more likely to have enrolled in Head Start, and had higher verbal IQs (Granger & Cytron, 1999; Quint, Box, & Polit, 1997).

Head Start programs serve only about one-third of eligible children in the United States, yet they are highly cost effective. Program expenses are far less than the funds required to provide special education, treat delinquency, and support welfare dependency. Because of its demonstrated returns to society, a move is under way to expand Head Start by starting intervention earlier, sustaining it longer, and intensifying services directed at parents and children.

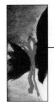

## Development of Creativity

THROUGHOUT THIS CHAPTER, we have seen that intelligence is much more than mental abilities that predict success in school. Today, educators recognize that gifted children—those who display exceptional intellectual strengths—have diverse characteristics. Some are high-IQ youngsters with scores above 130—the standard definition of giftedness based on intelligence test performance (Gardner, 1998b). High-IQ children, as we have seen, are particularly quick at academic work. They have keen memories and an exceptional capacity to solve challenging problems rapidly and accurately. Yet recognition that intelligence tests do not sample the entire range of human mental skills has led to an expanded conception of giftedness, which includes creativity.

**Creativity** is the ability to produce work that is *original* yet *appropriate*—something that others have not thought of but that is useful in some way (Ochse, 1990; Sternberg & Lubart, 1999). Besides the product's quality, the process of arriving at it affects judgments of creativity. Rather than following established rules, a creative work pulls together previously disparate ideas. And it typically involves hard work and overcoming obstacles on the way to the final product (Weisberg, 1993).

**creativity**
The ability to produce work that is original (that others have not thought of before) and that is appropriate (sensible or useful in some way).

**FIGURE** 8.12

**Responses of an 8-year-old who scored high on a figural measure of divergent thinking.** This child was asked to make as many pictures as she could from the circles on the page. The titles she gave her drawings, from left to right, are as follows: "Dracula," "one-eyed monster," "pumpkin," "Hula-Hoop," "poster," "wheelchair," "earth," "moon," "planet," "movie camera," "sad face," "picture," "stoplight," "beach ball," "the letter O," "car," "glasses." Tests of divergent thinking tap only one of the complex cognitive contributions to creativity. (Reprinted by permission of Laura Berk.)

**divergent thinking**
The generation of multiple and unusual possibilities when faced with a task or problem; associated with creativity.

**convergent thinking**
The generation of a single correct answer to a problem; the type of cognition emphasized on intelligence tests.

**investment theory of creativity**
Sternberg and Lubart's theory, in which investing in novel projects depends on diverse cognitive, personality, motivational, and environmental resources, each of which must be present to catalyze creativity.

**talent**
Outstanding performance in a specific field.

Creativity is of great value to individuals on the job and in daily life. In addition, it is vital for societal progress. Without it, there would be no new inventions, scientific findings, movements in art, or social programs. Therefore, understanding its ingredients and nurturing them from childhood are of paramount importance. As we will see in the following sections, ideas about creativity have changed radically during the past two decades.

### THE PSYCHOMETRIC VIEW

Until recently, a purely cognitive perspective dominated research on creativity. Commonly used tests tapped **divergent thinking**—the generation of multiple and unusual possibilities when faced with a task or problem. Divergent thinking contrasts sharply with **convergent thinking,** which involves arriving at a single correct answer and is emphasized on intelligence tests (Guilford, 1985).

Recognizing that highly creative children (like high-IQ children) are often better at some types of tasks than others, researchers devised a variety of tests of divergent thinking (Runco, 1992a, 1993; Torrance, 1988). A verbal measure might ask children to name uses for common objects (such as a newspaper). A figural measure might ask them to come up with drawings based on a circular motif (see Figure 8.12). A "real-world problem" measure either gives children everyday problems or requires them to think of such problems and then suggest solutions. Responses to all these tests can be scored for the number of ideas generated and their originality. For example, on a verbal test, saying that a newspaper can be used "as handgrips for a bicycle" would be more unusual than saying it can be used "to clean things."

Because tests of divergent thinking permit comparisons between people on a standard "creativity" scale, they are referred to as the *psychometric approach to creativity* (Lubart, 1994). Yet critics of these measures point out that they are poor predictors of creative accomplishment in everyday life because they tap only one of the complex cognitive contributions to creativity. And they say nothing about personality traits, motivation, and environmental circumstances that foster creative potential. Still, divergent-thinking tests do tap relevant skills, have been the major focus of research on creativity in children, and (as we will see shortly) have enhanced our understanding of the development of creativity.

### A MULTIFACETED VIEW

Recent theories agree that many elements must converge for creativity to occur (Csikszentmihalyi, 1999; Simonton, 1988; Weisberg, 1993). One influential multifaceted approach is Robert Sternberg and Todd Lubart's (1991, 1996) **investment theory of creativity.** According to Sternberg and Lubart, pursuing novel projects (ones not being tackled by others) increases the chances of arriving at a creative, highly valued product. But whether a person invests in novelty—initiates an original project and brings it to fruition—depends on the cognitive, personality, motivational, and environmental resources summarized in Table 8.7. Each must be present to catalyze creativity, although strength in one (such as

**TABLE** 8.7

Resources Necessary for Creativity

| COGNITIVE | PERSONALITY | MOTIVATIONAL | ENVIRONMENTAL |
|---|---|---|---|
| Problem finding | Innovative style of thinking | Task focused rather than goal focused | Availability of stimulating activities |
| Problem definition | Tolerance of ambiguity | | Emphasis on intellectual curiosity |
| Divergent thinking | Perseverance | | Acceptance of child's individual characteristics |
| Convergent thinking | Willingness to take intellectual risks | | Provision of systematic instruction relevant to child's talent |
| Insight processes | | | |
| Evaluation of competing ideas | Courage of one's convictions | | Availability of time to reflect on ideas |
| | | | Encouragement of original use of knowledge |
| Knowledge | | | Provision of challenging, extended projects that promote tolerance of ambiguity, perseverance, and intellectual risk taking |
| | | | Emphasis on task-focused motivators |

*Sources:* Sternberg & Lubart, 1991b, 1996.

perseverance) can compensate for weakness in another (an environment that is lukewarm toward novel ideas).

Contrary to popular belief, creativity is neither determined at birth nor the prized possession of an elite few. Instead, many people can develop it to varying degrees, and it is likely to reach greater heights when fostered from an early age. Let's look closely at the components of creativity and how we can strengthen them in children.

**COGNITIVE RESOURCES.** Creative work brings together a variety of high-level cognitive skills. It requires *problem finding*—detecting a gap in current knowledge, a need for a new product, or a deficiency with existing procedures. Once a problem is found, *the ability to define it*—to move it from a vague to a clearly specified state—becomes important. In both children and adults, the more effort devoted to defining the problem, the more original the final product (Getzels & Csikszentmihalyi, 1976; Runco & Okuda, 1988).

Divergent thinking is essential for generating novel solutions to problems. But the successful creator must also set aside fruitless options in favour of the best responses. Therefore, creativity involves *alternating between divergent and convergent thinking*. In narrowing the range of possibilities, creative individuals rely on *insight processes*—combining and restructuring elements in sudden but useful ways. For example, using analogies and metaphors to identify unique connections is common among people who have made outstanding creative contributions (Barron, 1988). At an early age, children engage in this kind of thinking (see Chapter 6, page 237, and Chapter 9, page 373). Furthermore, *evaluating competing ideas* to select the most promising is vital. School-age children's evaluative ability can be enhanced by instructions to critically assess the originality of ideas (Runco, 1992b).

Finally, extensive *knowledge* is necessary to make a creative contribution to any field. Without it, people cannot recognize or understand new ideas. Consider this cognitive ingredient, and you will see why high creativity is usually manifested as **talent;** individuals usually demonstrate it in only one or a few related fields. Case studies support the *10-year rule* in development of master-level creativity—that is, a decade between initial exposure to a field and the individual's first significant creative product (Feldman, 1999). Furthermore, only a modest correlation exists between IQ and creativity, typically around .20 to .40 (Sternberg & O'Hara, 1999). Beyond an above-average general intelligence, the presence of other variables determines creative giftedness.

© DAVID YOUNG-WOLFF/STONE/GETTY IMAGES

How can we nurture creativity? Learning environments that encourage children to come up with original ideas and to implement them are crucial. These junior high school students figure out how to grow cultures of mould, speculate on factors that influence their growth, and test their predictions. They also study the creative work of great scientists, such as Louis Pasteur, who formulated the germ theory of disease and developed vaccines for anthrax and rabies, and Sir Alexander Fleming, who isolated the antibiotic penicillin from a mould.

**PERSONALITY RESOURCES.** Personality characteristics foster the cognitive components of creativity, ensuring that they will be applied and reach fruition (Sternberg & Lubart, 1996). The following traits are crucial:

- *Innovative style of thinking.* Creative individuals not only see things in new ways but like to do so. They prefer loosely structured activities that permit innovative problem finding rather than already defined tasks.

- *Perseverance and tolerance of ambiguity.* Creative goals bring periods when pieces of the problem do not fit together. During those times, children and adults may give up or pursue the first (but not the best) solution. Creativity requires patience and persistence in the face of obstacles.

- *Willingness to take risks.* Creativity requires a willingness to "deviate from the crowd," to undertake challenge when outcomes are uncertain.

- *The courage of one's convictions.* Because their ideas are novel, creators may at times doubt them, especially when skeptical teachers or peers criticize them. Independence of judgment and high self-esteem are necessary for creative endeavours.

**MOTIVATIONAL RESOURCES.** Motivation for creativity must be *task focused* rather than *goal focused.* Task-focusing motivators, such as the desire to meet a high standard, energize work and keep attention on the problem. Goal-focusing motivators, often extrinsic rewards such as grades and prizes, divert attention from the task to other goals, thereby impairing performance. In one study, 7- to 11-year-old girls worked on collages, some competing for prizes and others expecting that the prizes would be raffled off. The products of those in the first group were much less creative (Amabile, 1982).

Extrinsic rewards are not always detrimental to creativity. Teaching children how to engage in divergent thinking on a task and rewarding them for original responses increases the frequency of those responses (Collins & Amabile, 1999). And an occasional reward for a creative product can underscore the social value of creativity and encourage children to embark on innovative projects. But when rewards are overemphasized, children see only "the carrot at the end of the stick," and creativity suffers.

**ENVIRONMENTAL RESOURCES.** Studies of the backgrounds of talented children and highly accomplished adults often reveal a family life focused on the child's needs—parents who are warm and sensitive, who provide a stimulating home life, and who are devoted to developing their child's abilities (Albert, 1994; Winner, 2000). These parents are not driving and overly ambitious but, instead, are reasonably demanding. They arrange for caring teachers while the child is young and for more rigorous master teachers as the child's talent develops (Winner, 1996).

Extreme giftedness often results in social isolation. The highly driven, nonconforming, and independent styles of many gifted children and adolescents lead them to spend more time alone, partly because of their rich inner lives and partly because solitude is necessary to develop their talents. Still, gifted children desire gratifying peer relationships, and some—more often girls than boys—try to hide their abilities to become better liked. Compared with their ordinary agemates, gifted youths, especially girls, report more emotional and social difficulties, including low self-esteem and depression.

Classrooms in which gifted youths can interact with like-minded peers, choose topics for extended projects, take intellectual risks, and reflect on ideas without being rushed to the next assignment foster creativity. Unfortunately, in many classrooms, knowledge acquisition is usually stressed over using knowledge originally, leading children's thinking to become *entrenched,* or limited to commonplace associations that produce correct answers. When talented students are not sufficiently challenged, they sometimes lose their drive to excel. And when parents and teachers push them too hard, by adolescence they are likely to ask, "Who am I doing this for?" If the answer is not "myself," they may decide not to pursue their gift anymore (Winner, 1997, 2000, p. 166).

Although programs for the gifted exist in many schools, debate about their effectiveness typically focuses on factors irrelevant to creativity—whether to provide enrichment in regular classrooms, to pull children out for special instruction (the most common practice), or to advance brighter pupils to a higher grade. Children of all ages fare well academically and socially within each of these models (Moon & Feldhusen, 1994). Yet the extent to which programs foster creativity depends on opportunities to acquire skills relevant to their talents.

Gardner's theory of multiple intelligences has inspired several school programs that provide enrichment to all students. A wide variety of meaningful activities, each tapping a specific intelligence or set of intelligences, serve as contexts for assessing strengths and weaknesses and, on that basis, teaching new knowledge and original thinking. For example, linguistic intelligence might be fostered through storytelling or playwriting; spatial intelligence through drawing, sculpting, or taking apart and reassembling objects; and kinesthetic intelligence through dance or pantomime (Gardner, 1993).

Evidence is still needed on how effectively these programs nurture children's talents. But so far, they have succeeded in one way—by highlighting the strengths of some students who previously had been considered unexceptional or even at risk for school failure. Consequently, they may be especially useful in identifying talented low-SES, ethnic minority children, who are underrepresented in school programs for the gifted (Suzuki & Valencia, 1997). How best to maximize the creative resources of the coming generation—the future poet and scientist as well as the everyday citizen—is a challenge for future research.

## ASK YOURSELF

**review** Summarize the benefits of early intervention programs, such as Head Start, for poverty-stricken children. What program characteristics might contribute to those benefits?

**review** How do psychometric measures of creativity differ from psychometric measures of intelligence? Why are psychometric measures poor predictors of creative accomplishment?

**apply** What can parents and schools do to foster the cognitive, personality, motivational, and environmental resources that contribute to creativity?

**connect** Using what you learned about brain development in Chapter 5 (see pages 181–186), explain why intensive intervention for poverty-stricken children starting in infancy and continuing through early childhood has a greater impact on IQ than does intervention starting later.

# summary

## DEFINITIONS OF INTELLIGENCE

*Describe changing definitions of intelligence, from Binet's to those of the modern factor analysts.*

■ The **psychometric approach** to cognitive development is the basis for the variety of intelligence tests used to assess individual differences in children's mental abilities. In the early 1900s, Alfred Binet developed the first successful test, which provided a single, holistic measure of intelligence.

■ **Factor analysis** emerged as a major means for determining whether intelligence is a single trait or a collection of many abilities. The research of Spearman and Thurstone led to two schools of thought. The first, supporting Spearman, regarded test items as having in common one **general factor,** or "**g,**" but acknowledged the existence of **specific factors,** or "**s.**" The second, supporting Thurstone, viewed intelligence as a set of distinct **primary mental abilities.**

■ Modern factor analysts have extended the work of Spearman and Thurstone. Cattell's distinction between **crystallized** and **fluid intelligence** has influenced attempts to create culture-fair tests. Carroll's **three-stratum theory of intelligence** is the most comprehensive classification of mental abilities to be confirmed by factor-analytic research.

## RECENT ADVANCES IN DEFINING INTELLIGENCE

*Why have researchers conducted componential analyses of intelligence test scores, and how have Sternberg's triarchic theory and Gardner's theory of multiple intelligences expanded contemporary definitions of intelligence?*

■ To provide process-oriented explanations of mental test performance, some researchers conduct **componential analyses** of children's scores by correlating them with laboratory measures of information processing. Findings reveal that basic efficiency of thinking and effective strategy use are related to measures of general intelligence. Sternberg's **triarchic theory of intelligence** extends these efforts. It views intelligence as a complex interaction of information-processing skills, specific experiences, and contextual (or cultural) influences.

■ According to Gardner's **theory of multiple intelligences,** mental abilities should be defined in terms of unique sets of processing operations applied in culturally meaningful activities. His eight distinct intelligences have been influential in efforts to understand and nurture children's special talents, although they have yet to be firmly grounded in research.

## REPRESENTATIVE INTELLIGENCE TESTS FOR CHILDREN

*Cite commonly used intelligence tests for children, and discuss prediction of later IQ from infant tests.*

■ **The Stanford-Binet Intelligence Scale** and the **Wechsler Intelligence Scale for Children–III (WISC–III)** are most often used to identify highly intelligent children and diagnose those with learning problems. Each provides a measure of general intelligence as well as a profile of subtest scores. However, these tests provide less accurate assessments in early childhood than at older ages.

■ Traditional infant tests, which consist largely of perceptual and motor responses, predict childhood IQ poorly because they do not represent the same aspects of intelligence assessed at older ages. The Fagan Test of Infant Intelligence, made up entirely of items assessing habituation/recovery to visual stimuli, taps important aspects of cognitive processing and is an effective predictor of childhood IQ.

## THE COMPUTATION AND DISTRIBUTION OF IQ SCORES

*How are IQ scores computed and distributed?*

■ Scores on intelligence tests are arrived at by computing an **intelligence quotient (IQ).** It compares a child's raw score to the scores of a large, representative sample of same-age children, which form a normal, or bell-shaped, curve.

## WHAT AND HOW WELL DO INTELLIGENCE TESTS PREDICT?

*Discuss the stability of IQ and its prediction of academic achievement, occupational attainment, and psychological adjustment.*

■ IQs obtained after age 6 show substantial correlational stability. The older the child at time of first testing and the closer in time the testings are, the stronger the relationship between the scores. Nevertheless, most children display considerable age-related change in the absolute value of their IQ. Ethnic minority children and other children who live in poverty often experience declines due to an **environmental cumulative deficit,** or the compounding effects of underprivileged rearing conditions.

■ IQ is an effective predictor of academic achievement, occupational attainment, and certain aspects of psychological adjustment. However, the underlying causes of these correlational findings are complex. In addition to IQ, home background, personality, motivation, education, and **practical intelligence** contribute substantially to academic and life success.

## ETHNIC AND SOCIOECONOMIC VARIATIONS IN IQ

*Describe ethnic and socioeconomic variations in IQ, including evidence on Jensen's Level I– Level II theory.*

■ Black children and children of low **socioeconomic status (SES)** score lower on intelligence tests than do white and middle-SES children, findings responsible for kindling the IQ nature–nurture debate. Jensen's **Level I–Level II theory** attributes the poorer scores of these children largely to a genetic deficiency in abstract reasoning and problem solving, tapped by items strongly correlated with "g." However, the theory has been challenged by subsequent research.

## EXPLAINING INDIVIDUAL AND GROUP DIFFERENCES IN IQ

*Describe and evaluate the contributions of heredity and environment to individual and group differences in IQ.*

■ Heritability estimates support a moderate role for heredity in IQ individual differences. Kinship studies comparing IQ correlations of identical and fraternal twins indicate that the contribution of heredity strengthens with development. However, heritabilities cannot be used to explain ethnic and SES differences in test scores.

■ Adoption studies indicate that advantaged rearing conditions can raise the absolute value of children's IQs substantially. At the same time, adopted children's scores correlate more strongly with those of their biological rather than adoptive relatives, providing support for the influence of heredity. However, black children reared in economically well-off white homes attain IQs substantially above average by middle childhood. No evidence supports the assumption that heredity underlies the ethnic differences that have been the focus of the IQ nature–nurture debate.

*Evaluate evidence on whether IQ is a biased measure of the intelligence of ethnic minority children, and discuss efforts to reduce test bias.*

■ Experts disagree on whether intelligence tests yield biased measures of the mental abilities of low-income minority children. IQ predicts academic achievement equally well for majority and minority children. However, language customs, lack of familiarity with test content, and reactions to testing conditions can lead test scores to underestimate minority children's intelligence.

■ Assessments of children's adaptive behaviour can serve as a safeguard against test scores that underestimate minority children's intelligence. By introducing purposeful teaching into the testing situation, **dynamic testing** narrows the gap between a child's actual and potential performance.

*Summarize the impact of shared and non-shared environmental influences on IQ.*

- **Shared** and **nonshared environmental influences** contribute to individual differences in intelligence. Research with the **Home Observation for Measurement of the Environment (HOME)** indicates that overall quality of the home—a shared environmental influence—consistently predicts language progress and IQ. Although the HOME–IQ relationship partly results from parent–child genetic similarity, a warm, stimulating family environment does foster mental ability. Family beliefs about the importance of intellectual success also exert a powerful impact on academic performance.

- Kinship research suggests that nonshared environmental factors are more powerful than shared influences and strengthen in adolescence and adulthood. Although once thought to be influential, birth order and spacing are unrelated to IQ. The most potent nonshared factors may be unpredictable, one-time events. Understanding the role of nonshared factors requires intensive case studies of children growing up in the same family.

## EARLY INTERVENTION AND INTELLECTUAL DEVELOPMENT

*Discuss the impact of early intervention on intellectual development.*

- Research on high-quality university-based early interventions as well as **Project Head Start** programs located in U.S. communities show that immediate IQ gains **wash out** with time. However, lasting benefits occur in school adjustment. Participants are less likely to be placed in special education classes or retained in grade and more likely to graduate from high school.

- To induce larger and longer-lasting cognitive gains, intervention must start earlier, last longer, and be more intensive. In addition, it must be followed by high-quality public school education. Two-generation programs with developmental goals for both parents and children are being tried to see if they lead to more powerful long-term outcomes.

## DEVELOPMENT OF CREATIVITY

*Describe and evaluate evidence on the development of creativity, including the psychometric view and the multifaceted approach of investment theory.*

- Recognition that intelligence tests do not sample the full range of human mental skills has expanded conceptions of giftedness to include **creativity.** The psychometric approach to creativity, which emphasizes the distinction between

divergent and convergent thinking, is too narrow an approach to predict real-life creative accomplishment. Consequently, it has given way to new, multifaceted approaches. People usually demonstrate creativity in one or a few related areas; consequently, creativity is usually manifested as **talent.**

- According to Sternberg and Lubart's **investment theory of creativity,** a wide variety of intellectual, personality, motivational, and environmental resources are necessary to catalyze creative projects and bring them to fruition. Highly talented children have parents and teachers who nurture their exceptional ability. However, extreme giftedness often results in social isolation, and gifted youths often report emotional and social difficulties. Gifted children are best served by educational programs that grant them opportunities to interact with like-minded peers, take intellectual risks, reflect on ideas, and acquire skills relevant to their talents.

# *important terms and concepts*

Aboriginal Head Start (p. 342)
CANSTART (p. 342)
componential analysis (p. 317)
convergent thinking (p. 346)
creativity (p. 345)
crystallized intelligence (p. 314)
divergent thinking (p. 346)
dynamic testing (p. 339)
emotional intelligence (p. 320)
environmental cumulative deficit hypothesis (p. 325)
factor analysis (p. 313)
fluid intelligence (p. 314)
Flynn effect (p. 335)

general factor, or "g" (p. 313)
Home Observation for Measurement of the Environment (HOME) (p. 340)
intelligence quotient (IQ) (p. 324)
investment theory of creativity (p. 346)
Level I–Level II theory (p. 330)
nonshared environmental influences (p. 339)
practical intelligence (p. 328)
primary mental abilities (p. 313)
Project Head Start (p. 342)
psychometric approach (p. 312)
shared environmental influences (p. 339)

socioeconomic status (SES) (p. 329)
specific factor, or "s" (p. 313)
Stanford-Binet Intelligence Scale (p. 322)
talent (p. 346)
theory of multiple intelligences (p. 318)
three-stratum theory of intelligence (p. 315)
triarchic theory of intelligence (p. 317)
washout effect (p. 343)
Wechsler Intelligence Scale for Children–III (WISC–III) (p. 322)

"A Telephone"
Yukiko S.
6 years, Switzerland

Already, the 6-year-old creator of this painting is a competent speaker of her native tongue. In just a few years, she mastered subtle rules of pronunciation, a rich and varied vocabulary, an intricate grammar, and many strategies for effective communication. Chapter 9 discusses these extraordinary accomplishments.

Reprinted with permission from The International Museum of Children's Art, Oslo, Norway

# *nine*

## Language Development

"DONE!" EXCLAIMED 1-YEAR-old Erin, wriggling in her high chair.

André and Marilyn looked at each other and remarked at once, "Did she say, 'Done'?" Lifting Erin down, Marilyn responded, "Yes! You're done," to her daughter's first clear word. In the next few weeks, more words appeared—among them, "Mama," "Papa," "please," "thanks," and "sure."

Marilyn spoke to Erin in English. André, however, resolved that his second child would become bilingual, so he used only French, his native tongue. As Erin reached the 18-month mark, her vocabulary grew rapidly, and she mixed the two languages. "Book!" she called out, thrusting her favourite picture book toward André in a gesture that meant, "Read this!" As father and daughter "read" together, Erin labelled: "Nez" (nose). "Bouche" (mouth). "Tête" (head). "Yeux" (eyes). "Chien" (dog). "Gros!" (referring to the dog's large size). On reaching the last page, she exclaimed, "Merci!" and slipped off André's lap.

By her second birthday, Erin had a vocabulary of several hundred words, and often combined them: "So big!" "Très gros" (very big). "More cookie." "Donne gallete" (give me cookie), and "Veux pas" (I don't want to). Amused by Erin's willingness to imitate almost anything, her 11-year-old brother François taught her a bit of slang. During mealtime discussions, Erin would interject, "Geta picture" (get the picture). And when asked a question, she sometimes casually answered, "Whatever."

© LAURA DWIGHT

To engage in effective verbal communication, these preschoolers must combine four components of language that have to do with sound, meaning, overall structure, and everyday use. How children accomplish this feat so rapidly raises some of the most puzzling questions about development.

At age 2½, Erin conversed easily. After the family returned from an excursion to the aquarium, Marilyn asked, "What did you see?"

"A big turtle put his head in the shell," Erin replied.

"Why did he do that?" Marilyn inquired.

"He goed away. He's sleepy."

If François interrupted, Erin would cleverly recapture her mother's attention. On one occasion, she commanded in a parental tone of voice, "François, go do your homework!"

Language—the most awesome of universal human achievements—develops with extraordinary speed during early childhood. At age 1, Erin used single words to name familiar objects and convey her desires. A brief year and a half later, she had a diverse vocabulary and combined words into grammatically correct sentences. Even her mistakes, such as "goed," revealed an active, rule-oriented approach to language. Before her third birthday, Erin creatively used language to satisfy her desires, converse with others, and experiment with social roles. And she easily moved between her two native tongues, speaking English with her mother and brother and French with her father.

Children's amazing linguistic accomplishments raise puzzling questions about development. How are a vast vocabulary and intricate grammar system acquired in such a short time? Is language a separate capacity, with its own prewired, special-purpose neural system in the brain? Or is it governed by powerful general cognitive abilities that humans also apply to other aspects of their physical and social worlds? Do all children acquire language in the same way, or do individual and cultural differences exist?

Our discussion opens with the fiery theoretical debate of the 1950s between behaviourist B. F. Skinner and linguist Noam Chomsky, which inspired a burst of research into language development. Next we turn to infant preparatory skills that set the stage for the child's first words. Then, to fully appreciate the diverse linguistic skills children master, our discussion follows the common practice of dividing language into four components. For each, we first consider what develops and then treat the more controversial question of how children acquire so much in so little time. We conclude with the challenges and benefits of bilingualism—mastering two languages—in childhood.

## Components of Language

LANGUAGE CONSISTS OF several subsystems that have to do with sound, meaning, overall structure, and everyday use. Knowing language entails mastering each of these aspects and combining them into a flexible communication system.

The first component, **phonology,** refers to the rules governing the structure and sequence of speech sounds. If you have ever visited a foreign country in which you did not know the language, you probably wondered how anyone could analyze the rapid flow of speech into organized strings of words. Yet in English, you easily apply an intricate set of rules to comprehend and produce complicated sound patterns. How you acquired this ability is the story of phonological development.

**Semantics,** the second component, involves vocabulary, or the way underlying concepts are expressed in words and word combinations. As we will see later, when young children first use a word, it often does not mean the same thing as it does to an adult. To build a versatile vocabulary, preschoolers must refine the meanings of thousands of words and connect them into elaborate networks of related terms.

Once mastery of vocabulary is under way, children combine words and modify them in meaningful ways. **Grammar,** the third component of language, consists of two main parts:

**phonology**
The component of language concerned with the rules governing the structure and sequence of speech sounds.

**semantics**
The component of language concerned with understanding the meaning of words and word combinations.

**grammar**
The component of language concerned with *syntax*, the rules by which words are arranged into sentences, and *morphology*, the use of grammatical markers that indicate number, tense, case, person, gender, active or passive voice, and other meanings.

*syntax,* the rules by which words are arranged into sentences; and *morphology,* the use of grammatical markers that indicate number, tense, case, person, gender, active or passive voice, and other meanings (the "-s" and "-ed" endings are examples in English).

Finally, **pragmatics** refers to the rules for engaging in appropriate and effective communication. To converse successfully, children must take turns, stay on the same topic, and state their meaning clearly. They also must figure out how gestures, tone of voice, and context clarify meaning. Furthermore, pragmatics involves *sociolinguistic knowledge,* since society dictates how language should be spoken. Children must acquire certain interaction rituals, such as verbal greetings and leave-takings. They must also adjust their speech to mark important social relationships, such as differences in age and status.

As we take up the four components of language, you will see that they are interdependent. Acquisition of each facilitates mastery of the others.

## Theories of Language Development

DURING THE FIRST HALF of this century, research on language development identified milestones that applied to children around the globe: all babbled around 6 months, said their first words at about 1 year, combined words at the end of the second year, and had mastered a vast vocabulary and most grammatical constructions by 4 to 5 years of age. The regularity of these achievements suggested a process largely governed by maturation. Yet at the same time, language seemed to be learned, since without exposure to language, children born deaf or severely neglected did not acquire verbal communication. This apparent contradiction set the stage for an intense nature–nurture debate. By the end of the 1950s, two major figures had taken opposite sides.

### THE BEHAVIOURIST PERSPECTIVE

Behaviourist B. F. Skinner (1957) proposed that language, just like other behaviour, is acquired through *operant conditioning.* As the baby makes sounds, parents reinforce those that are most like words with smiles, hugs, and speech in return. For example, at 12 months, my older son, David, often babbled like this: "book-a-book-a-dook-a-dook-a-book-a-nook-a-book-aaa." One day while he babbled away, I held up his picture book and said, "Book!" Very soon, David was saying "book-aaa" in the presence of books.

Some behaviourists say children rely on *imitation* to rapidly acquire complex utterances, such as whole phrases and sentences (Moerk, 1992). And imitation can combine with reinforcement to promote language, as when a parent coaxes, "Say 'I want a cookie,'" and delivers praise and a treat after the child responds, "Wanna cookie!"

Although reinforcement and imitation contribute to early language development, only a few researchers cling to the behaviourist perspective today. Think, for a moment, about the process of language development just described. Adults would have to engage in intensive language tutoring—continuously modelling and reinforcing to yield the extensive vocabulary and complex sentences of the typical 6-year-old. This seems like a physically impossible task, even for the most conscientious parents. Furthermore, children create novel utterances that are not reinforced by or copied from others, such as Erin's use of "goed" at the beginning of this chapter. This suggests that instead of learning specific sentences, young children develop a working knowledge of grammatical rules.

Nevertheless, the ideas of Skinner and other behaviourists should not be dismissed entirely. Throughout this chapter, we will see how adult responsiveness and example support children's language learning, even though they do not fully explain it. Behaviourist principles are also valuable to speech and language therapists in their efforts to help children overcome serious language delays and disabilities (Ratner, 2001).

**pragmatics**
The component of language concerned with the rules for engaging in effective and appropriate communication with others.

*cultural influences*

**CHILDREN INVENT LANGUAGE:
HOMESIGN AND HAWAIIAN CREOLE ENGLISH**

Can children develop complex language systems with only minimal language input? If so, this evidence would serve as strong support for Chomsky's idea that humans are born with a biological program for language development.

### DEAF CHILDREN INVENT SIGN LANGUAGE

In a series of studies, Susan Goldin-Meadow and her colleagues followed deaf preschoolers whose parents discouraged manual signing and addressed them verbally. None of the children made progress in acquiring spoken language or used even the most common gestures of their nation's sign language. Nevertheless, they spontaneously produced a gestural communication system, called *homesign,* that is strikingly similar in basic structure to hearing children's verbal language.

The deaf children developed gestural vocabularies with distinct forms for nouns and verbs that they combined into novel sentences conforming to grammatical rules that were not necessarily those of their parents' spoken language (Goldin-Meadow, Mylander, & Butcher, 1995; Goldin-Meadow et al., 1994). For example, to describe a large bubble he had just blown, one child first pointed at a bubble jar and then used two open palms with fingers spread to denote the act of "blowing up big." Furthermore, by age 4 children produced more complex gestural sentences than did their mothers (Goldin-Meadow & Mylander, 1998). Children seemed to be taking the lead in creating these gesture systems.

Language becomes a flexible means of communicating when it is used to talk about nonpresent objects and events. In referring to the nonpresent, the deaf children followed the same sequence of development as did hearing children—first denoting objects and events in the recent past or anticipated but immediate future, next the more remote past and future, and finally hypothetical and fantasized events (Goldin-Meadow, 1999; Morford & Goldin-Meadow, 1997). Homesigning children conversed in the nonpresent far more often than their parents did. One homesigning child pointed over his shoulder to signify the past, then pointed to a picture of a poodle, and finally pointed to the floor in front of him, saying, "I used to have a poodle!"

Hearing children reach language milestones earlier than do children acquiring homesign, indicating that a rich language environment fosters the attainments just mentioned. But without access to conventional language, deaf children generate their own language system. In Nicaragua, educators brought deaf children and adolescents, each with a unique homesign, together to form a community. Although they had no shared language, in less than two decades they developed one—Nicaraguan Sign Language—that matched other human languages in structural complexity (Senghas & Coppola, 2001).

### THE NATIVIST PERSPECTIVE

Linguist Noam Chomsky (1957) first convinced the scientific community that children assume much responsibility for their own language learning. In contrast to behaviourists, he proposed a nativist account that regards language as a uniquely human accomplishment, etched into the structure of the brain.

Focusing on grammar, Chomsky reasoned that the rules for sentence organization are too complex to be directly taught to or discovered by a young child. Instead, he argued, all children have a **language acquisition device (LAD),** an innate system that permits children, as soon as they have acquired sufficient vocabulary, to combine words into grammatically consistent, novel utterances and to understand the meaning of sentences they hear.

How can a single LAD account for children's mastery of diverse languages around the world? According to Chomsky (1976), within the LAD is a *universal grammar,* a built-in storehouse of rules that apply to all human languages. Young children use this knowledge to decipher grammatical categories and relationships in any language to which they are exposed. Because the LAD is specifically suited for language processing, sophisticated cognitive capacities are not required to master the structure of language. Instead, children do so spontaneously, with only limited language exposure. Therefore, in sharp contrast to the behav-

**language acquisition device (LAD)**
In Chomsky's theory, an innate system for picking up language that permits children, as soon as they have acquired sufficient vocabulary, to combine words into grammatically consistent, novel utterances and to understand the meaning of sentences they hear.

These children are descendants of immigrants who came from many parts of the world to work in the sugar industry in Hawaii in the 1870s. The multilingual population began to speak Hawaiian Pidgin English, a simplified communication system that permitted them to "get by" in everyday life. Yet the next generation spoke a new complex language, Hawaiian Creole English, believed to have been invented by children. The existence of creoles is among the most powerful evidence for Chomsky's idea that humans are born with a biological program for language development.

JOE CARINI/PACIFIC STOCK

### IMMIGRANT CHILDREN INVENT HAWAIIAN CREOLE ENGLISH

*Creoles* are languages that arise rapidly from *pidgins,* which are minimally developed "emergency" tongues that result when several language communities migrate to the same area and no dominant language exists to support interaction between them. In 1876, immigrants from China, Japan, Korea, the Philippines, Puerto Rico, and Portugal came to Hawaii to work in the sugar industry. Out of this melting pot, Hawaiian Pidgin English emerged, a communication system with a minimal vocabulary and grammar that permitted new immigrants to "get by" in everyday life. Yet within

20 to 30 years, a new complex language, Hawaiian Creole English, which borrowed vocabulary from its pidgin and foreign-language predecessors, became widespread. How could this have occurred?

Derek Bickerton (1981, 1999) concludes that the next generation of children must have invented the language, relying on innate mechanisms. Support for this conclusion is of two kinds. First, the structure of creole languages is similar around the world, suggesting that a common genetic program underlies them. Second, creole grammar resembles the linguistic structures children first use when acquiring any language. For example, expressions like "He no bite you" and

"Where he put the toy?" are perfectly correct in Hawaiian Creole English.

According to Bickerton, the child's biological language is always ready to re-emerge when cultural language is shattered. However, no one has yet been able to observe directly language development in first-generation creole children. Therefore, some researchers note, we cannot be sure what role adult input plays in the creation of creole. Others question whether children's capacity to invent language results from a language-specific biological program (Bates, 1999; Tomasello, 1995). These researchers believe that nonlinguistic cognitive capacities, applied to the task of communicating, are responsible.

iourist view, the nativist perspective regards deliberate training by parents as unnecessary for language development. Instead, the LAD ensures that language will be acquired early and swiftly, despite its complexity (Pinker, 1994).

**SUPPORT FOR THE NATIVIST PERSPECTIVE.** Are children biologically primed to acquire language? Research reviewed in the Cultural Influences box above, which suggests that children have a remarkable ability to invent new language systems, provides some of the most powerful support for this perspective. And three additional sets of evidence—efforts to teach animals language, localization of language functions in the human brain, and investigations into whether a sensitive period for language development exists—are consistent with Chomsky's view. Let's look at each in turn.

***Can Animals Acquire Language?*** Is the ability to master a grammatically complex language system uniquely human? To find out, many attempts have been made to teach language to animals. The most impressive results have been achieved with dolphins and chimpanzees.

In the 1980s, Louis Herman (1987) gave two bottle-nosed dolphins, Ake and Phoenix, lessons in understanding artificial languages. Trainers communicated with Ake through

In the photo on the left, bottle-nosed dolphins Ake and Phoenix participate in a language training session. Here, a trainer tests Ake to see if she can distinguish the sentence, "Bring the surfboard to the person," from the sentence, "Bring the person to the surf-board." In the photo on the right, Bonobo chimp Kanzi uses an artificial language, in which he expresses meanings by pressing keys on a symbol board to communicate with a trainer.

gestures and with Phoenix through click-like word sounds using an underwater speaker. Each language had a vocabulary of 35 to 40 words, referring to object names, actions, and object locations. The trainers taught Ake and Phoenix to respond to two kinds of sentences. In one, they had to act on a single object (as in "Touch the hoop on the left"). In the other, they had to carry one object to another (as in "Put the ball in the basket on the left"). When Ake and Phoenix performed correctly, the trainer gave them a food reward.

To test the dolphins' language ability, the trainers gave them novel sentences. Some involved placing known words into familiar grammatical structures not yet used with those words. Others presented novel structures—for example, two joined sentences, as in "Touch the basket on the left and leap over the gate." Ake and Phoenix responded correctly to nearly half these commands (Herman & Morel-Samuels, 1996). Although they required months of training and their knowledge remained imperfect, they grasped the basics of grammar—that the order in which symbols are presented affects the meanings expressed.

Many attempts have been made to teach language to chimpanzees, who are closest to humans in the evolutionary hierarchy. The species most often studied is the common chimp, native to Central Africa. In some instances, researchers used artificial languages in which a computer keyboard generates visual symbols. In others, they used American Sign Language, a gestural communication system used by the deaf that is as elaborate as any spoken language. After years of training, the chimps acquired vocabularies of several hundred words and produced two-word utterances (Miles, 1999). But sign strings longer than two did not follow a rule-based structure. For example, one chimp named Nim produced nonsensical expressions like this: "Eat Nim eat" and "Play me Nim play" (Terrace et al., 1980).

Michael Tomasello (1999) believes that common chimps' language limitations are partly due to a lack of understanding that others are intentional beings who want to share information with them through symbols. In the wild, common chimps' vocal and gestural behaviours are limited to signalling their immediate desires (Tomasello & Camaioni, 1997). For example, a young chimp might push on his mother's back to lower it so he can climb on. The next time he touches her back, she anticipates his desire by lowering her body. But a touch on the back is not the same as a symbol used in conversation, which a speaker intentionally uses to convey meaning. In a study involving novel symbols in which human 2- and 3-year-olds and adult apes were asked to indicate which of three covers hid a reward, children mastered symbolic meanings quickly and easily. But as Figure 9.1 shows, apes (both common chimps and orangutans) had great difficulty, even after three times as many trials (Tomasello, Call, & Gluckman, 1997).

Recently, researchers began to study Bonobo chimps, a species native to the Congo, who are more intelligent and social than the common chimpanzee. The linguistic attainments of a Bonobo named Kanzi are particularly impressive (Savage-Rumbaugh, 2001). While young, Kanzi picked up his mother's artificial language by observing trainers interact with her. Then Kanzi's caregivers encouraged his language further by communicating both in the artificial

(a)

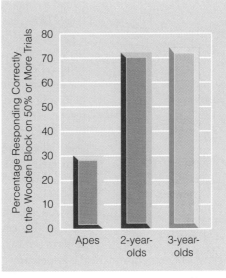

(b)

**FIGURE** 9.1

**Game used to test the ability of adult apes to interpret novel symbols.** (a) The ape sat in front of three distinct containers. After the ape was taught that a piece of orange or sweet potato would be hidden in one of them, an adult "communicator" used one of three types of gestures (pointing, placing a wooden block on top of the correct container, or holding up an exact model of the correct container) to indicate where the reward was hidden. (b) Compared with 2- and 3-year-old children who played a similar game, apes did poorly. No chimp or orangutan demonstrated above-chance responding for the wooden block (shown at left) or any other novel sign, whereas the children performed well. (Adapted from Tomasello, Call, & Gluckman, 1997.)

language and in English. Kanzi rarely combined words because he preferred to join a word to a gesture, such as "carry + [gesture to person]," meaning "you carry Kanzi." But he acquired remarkable comprehension of English. He could act out unusual sentences he had not heard before, such as "Put the money in the mushroom." And most of the time, he could detect the difference between novel, reversed sentences, such as "Take the potato outdoors" and "Go outdoors and get the potato" (Savage-Rumbaugh et al., 1993).

In sum, when extensively trained, encouraged, and rewarded, dolphins and chimps learn the meanings of symbols, and dolphins and Bonobo chimps grasp basic grammar (Kako, 1999). Because the brain organization of dolphins differs greatly from primates', and because neither dolphins nor apes use grammar naturally, researchers think these achievements are due to animal intelligence rather than a brain specialized for language (Herman & Uyeyama, 1999).

Still, researchers disagree on the extent of Kanzi's linguistic achievements. Some argue that his grasp of language symbols is no better than that of the common chimp—that he uses them to get what he wants (a strawberry to eat) rather than to share information (talk about strawberries) (Seidenberg & Petitto, 1987). And Kanzi's comprehension of grammar is at about the level of a human 2-year-old, who (as we will see) is not far along in grammatical development. Overall, Chomsky's assumption of a uniquely human capacity for an elaborate grammar receives support. No evidence exists that dolphins and Bonobo chimps can comprehend and produce complex, novel sentences.

***Language Areas in the Brain.*** Humans have evolved specialized regions in the brain that support language skills. Recall from Chapter 5 that for most individuals, language is housed in the left hemisphere of the cerebral cortex. Within it are two language-specific structures (see Figure 9.2 on page 360). **Broca's area,** located in the frontal lobe, controls language production. Damage to it results in a specific *aphasia,* or communication disorder, in which the person has good comprehension but speaks in a slow, laboured, ungrammatical, and emotionally flat fashion. **Wernicke's area,** located in the temporal lobe, is largely responsible for interpreting language. When it is damaged, speech is fluent and grammatical, but it contains many nonsense words. Comprehension of others' speech is also impaired.

Broca's and Wernicke's areas fit with Chomsky's notion of an LAD. But rather than being fully formed at birth, dedicated language areas in the brain *develop* over time (Bates, 1999; Mills, Coffey-Corina, & Neville, 1997). Recall from Chapter 5 that at birth, the brain is not fully lateralized; it is highly plastic. Although the left hemisphere is biased for language processing, if it is injured in the early years, other regions take over its language functions. Furthermore, as non-brain-damaged children acquire language, the left hemisphere

**Broca's area**
A language structure located in the frontal lobe of the left hemisphere of the cerebral cortex that controls language production.

**Wernicke's area**
A language structure located in the temporal lobe of the left hemisphere of the cerebral cortex that is responsible for interpreting language.

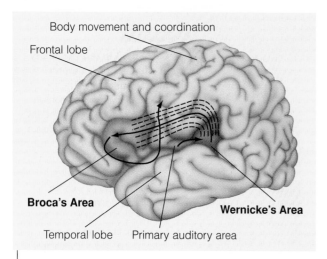

Body movement and coordination

Frontal lobe

Broca's Area

Temporal lobe    Primary auditory area

Wernicke's Area

**FIGURE** 9.2

**Language-specific structures in the left hemisphere of the cerebral cortex.** *Broca's area* controls language production by creating a detailed program for speaking, which it sends to the face area of the cortical region that controls body movement and coordination. *Wernicke's area* interprets language by receiving impulses from the primary auditory area, where sensations from the ears are sent. To produce a verbal response, Wernicke's area communicates with Broca's area through a bundle of nerve fibres, represented by dotted lines in the figure.

becomes increasingly specialized for language functions (see pages 183–184).

In sum, although other areas of the brain support language processing, it is usually concentrated in the left cerebral hemisphere. Recall from Chapter 5 (see page 183) that deaf adults who learned sign language at an early age depend more on the right hemisphere for language processing than do their hearing counterparts. But research by Laura Ann Petitto and her colleagues (2000) conducted at McGill University showed that deaf signers also make use of left-hemisphere regions previously thought to be dedicated to processing speech sounds. Apparently, parts of the left hemisphere are specialized for making sense of language, regardless of its perceptual modality. Furthermore, in most older children and adults, grammatical functions, especially, are localized on the left. In studies of patients who had their left hemispheres removed because of disease or abnormalities that caused severe seizures, grammatical competence suffered much more than semantic and pragmatic abilities, which seem to draw more on right-hemispheric regions (Baynes & Gazzaniga, 1988). Similarly, in older children with left-hemispheric brain damage, grammar is more impaired than other language functions (Stromswold, 2000).

***A Sensitive Period for Language Development.*** Erik Lenneberg (1967) first proposed that children must acquire language during the age span of brain lateralization, which he believed to be complete by puberty. If this idea is correct, it further supports the nativist position that language development has unique biological properties.

To test the sensitive-period notion, researchers tracked the recovery of severely abused children who experienced little human contact in childhood. The most thoroughly studied is Genie, a normally developing child who said her first words just before she was isolated in the back room of her parents' house at 1½ years of age. Until she was found at 13½, no one talked to her, and she was beaten when she made any noise. With several years of training by dedicated teachers, Genie's language developed to some extent. She acquired a large vocabulary and good comprehension of conversation, but her grammar and communication skills were limited (Curtiss, 1977, 1989). Genie's case and others like it fit with the existence of a sensitive period, although a precise age cutoff for a decline in language competence has not been established.

What about acquiring a second language? Is this task harder after a sensitive period for language development has passed? In a study of Chinese and Korean adult immigrants, those who began learning English between ages 3 and 7 scored as well as native speakers on a test of grammar (see Figure 9.3). As age of arrival increased, grammar scores declined. Similar results exist for deaf adults who learned American Sign Language at different ages (Mayberry, 1994; Newport, 1991). Furthermore, brain-wave (ERP) and brain-imaging (fMRI) measures of neural activity indicate that second-language processing is less lateralized in older than in younger learners (Neville & Bruer, 2001). But second-language competence does not drop sharply at adolescence, as Lenneberg predicted. Rather, a continuous, age-related decrease occurs (Bialystok & Hakuta, 1999; Hakuta, 2001). As with first-language acquisition, the sensitive-period boundary for second-language acquisition remains unclear.

Nevertheless, recent research at McGill University suggests that timing of first language acquisition affects the ability to learn a second language (Mayberry, Lock, & Kazmi, 2002). A lifelong capacity to learn language develops when a first language, sign or spoken, is acquired at a young age.

**LIMITATIONS OF THE NATIVIST PERSPECTIVE.** Chomsky's theory has had a major impact on current views of language development. It is now widely accepted that humans have a unique, biological predisposition to acquire language. Still, Chomsky's account of development has been challenged on several grounds.

First, researchers have had great difficulty identifying the universal grammar that Chomsky believes underlies the vastly different grammatical systems of human languages. Even seemingly simple grammatical distinctions, such as use of *the* versus *a* in English, are made in quite different ways around the world. For example, several African languages rely on tone patterns to express these articles. In Japanese and Chinese, they are inferred entirely from sentence context. Critics of Chomsky's theory doubt the existence of a universal grammar that can account for all existing grammatical forms (Maratsos, 1998; Tomasello, 1995).

Second, Chomsky's assumption that grammatical knowledge is innately determined does not fit with certain observations of language development. Although children make extraordinary strides during preschool years, they acquire many sentence constructions gradually. Complete mastery of some forms (such as the passive voice) is not achieved until well into middle childhood (Tager-Flusberg, 2001). This suggests that more learning and discovery are involved than Chomsky assumed.

Dissatisfaction with Chomsky's theory has also arisen from its lack of comprehensiveness. For example, it cannot explain how children weave statements together into connected discourse and sustain meaningful conversations. Perhaps because Chomsky did not dwell on the pragmatic side of language, his theory grants little attention to quality of language input and social experience in supporting language progress. Furthermore, the nativist perspective does not regard children's cognitive capacities as important. Yet in Chapter 6, we saw that cognitive development is involved in children's early vocabulary growth. And studies of children with mental retardation (see the Biology & Environment box on page 362) show that cognitive competence also influences children's grammatical mastery.

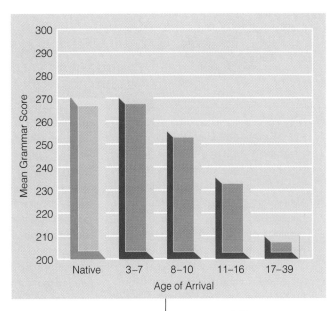

**FIGURE** 9.3

**Relationship between age of arrival of Chinese and Korean immigrants in the United States and performance on a test of English grammar.** Individuals who began learning English in early childhood attained the competence of native speakers. With increasing age, scores declined. (Adapted from Johnson & Newport, 1989.)

## THE INTERACTIONIST PERSPECTIVE

In recent years, new theories of language development have arisen, emphasizing *interactions* between inner predispositions and environmental influences, replacing the dichotomy of the Skinner–Chomsky debate. Although several interactionist theories exist, all stress the social context of language learning. An active child, well endowed for acquiring language, observes and participates in social exchanges. From these experiences, children build a communication system that relates the content and structure of language to its social meanings. According to this view, native capacity, a strong desire to interact with others, and a rich language and social environment combine to assist children in discovering the functions and regularities of language. And because genetic and environmental contributions vary across children, the interactionist perspective predicts individual differences in language learning (Bohannon & Bonvillian, 2001; Chapman, 2000).

Even among interactionists, debate continues over the precise nature of innate language abilities. Some theorists accept a modified view of Chomsky's position. They believe that children are primed to acquire language but that they form and refine hypotheses about its structure based on language experience (Slobin, 1985, 1997). Others believe that children make sense of their complex language environments by applying powerful cognitive strategies rather than ones specifically tuned to language (Bates, 1999; MacWhinney, 1999; Tomasello & Brooks, 1999).

As we chart the course of language development, we will describe some of these new views. But even interactionist theories have not escaped the critical eye of contemporary researchers. Interactionists assume that language competence grows out of communication, yet some children show large disparities between pragmatics and other aspects of language. For example, conversational skills of children with mental retardation often lag behind other language achievements (Levy, 1996). In reality, biology, cognition, and social experience may operate in different balances with respect to each component of language. Today, we still know much more about the course of language development than precisely how it takes place.

# *biology & environment*

## LANGUAGE DEVELOPMENT IN CHILDREN WITH WILLIAMS SYNDROME

illiams syndrome is a rare disorder caused by deletion of genetic material on the seventh chromosome. Affected individuals have facial, heart, and kidney abnormalities and mild to serious mental retardation. With IQ scores typically ranging from 50 to 70, they are just as mentally impaired as individuals with Down syndrome (Tassabehji et al., 1996). Yet compared to children with Down syndrome, children with Williams syndrome are far more advanced in language skills (Bellugi & Wang, 1999). For many years, researchers have taken this apparent "decoupling" of cognition and language as evidence that language is controlled by an innate LAD. To see if this conclusion is warranted, let's look at language attainments linked to this disorder.

Infants with Williams syndrome are strongly oriented toward the social world—extremely gregarious and fascinated by faces and voices (Jones et al., 2000). Although their language development is delayed, it is impressive. During the preschool years, children with Williams syndrome have larger vocabularies and produce grammatically more complex sentences than do children with Down syndrome (Harris et al., 1997; Mervis & Robinson, 2000). For example, the longest sentence of one Williams syndrome 3-year-old was, "Please have some grapes in my cup right now." Her Down syndrome counterpart said, "Here-ya-go" and "Hold me" (Jarrold, Baddeley, & Hewes, 1998, p. 361). By adolescence, the vocabularies of individuals with Williams syndrome contain many unusual words. When asked to name as many animals as possible,

one teenager said "weasel, newt, salamander, Chihuahua, ibex, yak" (Bellugi et al., 1992, p. 11).

Yet affected individuals have trouble with highly challenging grammatical rules. For example, French-speaking adolescents with Williams syndrome do poorly on grammatical gender assignment—matching masculine and feminine articles (such as *un* versus *une*) with nouns by attending to word endings and noting exceptions. Yet normally developing French children master this gender system by age 4 (Karmiloff-Smith et al., 1997). In a study of English-speaking adults, difficulties with subtle verb forms (*he struggled with the dog*, not *he struggle the dog*) appeared (Karmiloff-Smith et al., 1998).

Why does Williams syndrome lead to an uneven language profile—areas of both strength and weakness? According to Annette Karmiloff-Smith (1997), the cognitive deficits of Williams syndrome profoundly affect language development, altering its course. Children with the disorder are relatively good at memorizing but poor at rule learning. To compensate for this weakness, they capitalize on their social strengths, attending closely to faces and voices and acquiring as much language by rote as they can.

In support of this rote approach to language learning, infants with Williams syndrome do not build their early vocabularies on intentional gestures (such as pointing) and advances in categorization, as normally developing children do (Mervis et al., 1999). Instead, they seem to rely heavily on mimicking others. According to some parent reports, children with the disor-

COURTESY OF THE WILLIAMS SYNDROME ASSOCIATION

The impish smile and facial features of this child, who has Williams syndrome, suggest that she is strongly oriented toward the social world. In keeping with their sociability, children with Williams syndrome display impressive language skills given their mild to serious mental retardation. Yet the cognitive deficits of Williams syndrome impair children's ability to master the most complex rules of language.

der even speak without fully comprehending what they are saying.

In sum, although the language of individuals with Williams syndrome is impressive in view of their cognitive limitations, it is impaired in significant ways. These findings indicate that language is not as separate from other human mental abilities as Chomsky's concept of the LAD assumes.

**review**  Summarize outcomes of attempts to teach language to animals. Are results consistent with the nativist assumption that human children are uniquely endowed with an LAD? Explain.

**review**  How does the interactionist perspective on language development differ from behaviourist and nativist views? Why is it attractive to many contemporary researchers?

**apply**  Describe evidence that supports the existence of a sensitive period for second-language learning. What practical implications do these findings have for teaching children a second language in school?

**connect**  Cite research in this chapter and in Chapter 5 indicating that with age, areas of the cortex become increasingly specialized for language. Relate these findings to the concept of brain plasticity.

# Prelinguistic Development: Getting Ready to Talk

FROM THE VERY beginning, infants are prepared to acquire language. During the first year of life, inborn capabilities, cognitive and social milestones, and environmental supports pave the way for the onset of verbal communication.

## RECEPTIVITY TO LANGUAGE

Recall from Chapter 4 that newborns are especially sensitive to the pitch range of the human voice and find speech more pleasing than other sounds. In addition, they have an astonishing ability to make fine-grained distinctions between the sounds of virtually any human language. Because this skill may help them crack the phonological code of their native tongue, let's look at it more closely.

**LEARNING NATIVE-LANGUAGE SOUND CATEGORIES AND PATTERNS.** As adults, we analyze the speech stream into **phonemes,** the smallest sound units that signal a change in meaning, such as the difference between the consonant sounds in "pa" and "ba." Phonemes are not the same across all languages. For example, "ra" and "la" are distinct sounds to English speakers, but Japanese individuals hear them as the same. Similarly, English speakers have trouble perceiving the difference between two "p" sounds—a soft "p" and a sharp "p" with a burst of air—used to distinguish meaning in the Thai language. This tendency to perceive as identical a range of sounds that belong to the same phonemic class is called **categorical speech perception.** Like adults, newborns are capable of it. But they are sensitive to a much wider range of categories than exists in their own language (Aslin, Jusczyk, & Pisoni, 1998).

Within the first few days after birth, babies distinguish and prefer the overall sound pattern of their native tongue to that of other languages (Moon, Cooper, & Fifer, 1993). As infants listen actively to the talk of people around them, they focus on meaningful sound variations. By 6 months, long before they are ready to talk, they organize speech into the phonemic categories of their own language. That is, they stop attending to sounds that will not be useful in mastering their native tongue (Kuhl et al., 1992; Polka & Werker, 1994).

In the second half of the first year, infants focus on larger speech units. They recognize familiar words in spoken passages (Jusczyk & Aslin, 1995; Jusczyk & Hohne, 1997). They also can detect clauses and phrases in sentences. In one study, researchers recorded two versions of a mother telling a story. In the first, she spoke naturally, with pauses occurring between clauses: "Cinderella lived in a great big house [pause], but it was sort of dark...." In the second version, the mother inserted pauses in unnatural places—in the middle of clauses: "Cinderella lived in

---

**phoneme**
The smallest sound unit that signals a change in meaning.

**categorical speech perception**
The tendency to perceive as identical a range of sounds that belong to the same phonemic class.

This Chinese mother speaks to her baby daughter in short, clearly pronounced sentences with high-pitched, exaggerated intonation. Adults in many countries use this form of language, called child-directed speech, with infants and toddlers. It eases the task of early language learning.

a great big house, but it was [pause] sort of dark. . . ." Like adults, 7-month-olds preferred speech with natural breaks to speech with unnatural ones (Hirsh-Pasek et al., 1987).

Around 7 to 9 months, infants extend this rhythmic sensitivity to individual words. They listen much longer to speech with stress patterns and phoneme sequences that are common in their own language (Mattys & Jusczyk, 2001; Morgan & Saffran, 1995). And they divide the speech stream into wordlike segments. Seven-month-olds can distinguish sound patterns that typically begin words from those that do not (Jusczyk, Houston, & Newsome, 1999). For example, English learners often rely on the onset of a strong syllable to indicate a new word, as in "<u>an</u>imal" and "<u>pud</u>ding." By 10 months, infants can detect words that start with weak syllables, such as "sur<u>prise</u>" (Jusczyk, 2001). As Janet Werker and Richard Tees (1999) of the University of British Columbia point out, taken together, these findings reveal that in the second half of the first year, infants have begun to detect the internal structure of sentences and words—information that will be vital for linking speech units with their meanings.

How do babies accomplish these feats? Research reveals that they are vigilant *statistical analyzers* of sound patterns. At birth, they detect differences between broad categories of words—specifically, grammatical words (such as prepositions) versus words conveying wide variations in meaning (such as nouns and verbs) (Shi, Werker, & Morgan, 1999). By 6 months, babies prefer to listen to the second category of words, suggesting that they are trying to make sense of them (Shi & Werker, 2001). And in discriminating between individual words, infants distinguish syllables that frequently occur together (signalling that they belong to the same word) from those that seldom occur together (signalling a word boundary). Consider the sound sequence "pretty baby." In English, "pre" is followed by "ty" far more often than "ty" is followed by "ba." In one study, researchers presented 8-month-olds with a speech stream consisting of four three-syllable nonsense words repeated in random order. After just 2 minutes of exposure, the infants discriminated the words from nonwords (Saffran, Aslin, & Newport, 1996). They could do so only by distinguishing frequent from infrequent syllable patterns.

Furthermore, babies of this age are budding *rule learners;* they notice the structure of short, nonsense-word sequences. In another study, 7-month-olds discriminated the ABA structure of "ga ti ga" and "li na li" from the ABB structure of "wo fe fe" and "ta la la" (Marcus et al., 1999). The infants seemed to detect a simple word-order pattern—a capacity that may later help them grasp the basic syntax of their language.

**ADULT SPEECH TO YOUNG LANGUAGE LEARNERS.** Certain features of adult talk assist babies in making sense of a complex speech stream. Adults in many countries speak to infants and toddlers in **child-directed speech (CDS),** a form of communication made up of short sentences with high-pitched, exaggerated expression, clear pronunciation, distinct pauses between speech segments, and repetition of new words in a variety of contexts ("See the *ball.*" "The *ball* bounced!" "I love that *ball!*") (Fernald et al., 1989; Kuhl, 2000). Deaf mothers show a similar style of communication when signing to their babies (Masataka, 1996).

Parents do not seem to be deliberately trying to teach infants to talk when they use CDS, since many of the same speech qualities appear when adults communicate with foreigners. CDS probably arises from adults' desire to keep young children's attention and ease their task of understanding, and it works effectively in these ways. From birth on, infants prefer to listen to CDS over other kinds of adult talk (Cooper & Aslin, 1994). By 5 months, they are more emotionally responsive to it and can discriminate the tone quality of CDS with different meanings—for example, approving versus soothing utterances (Moore, Spence, & Katz, 1997; Werker, Pegg, & McLeod, 1994).

Parents constantly fine-tune CDS, adjusting the length and content of their utterances to fit children's needs. In a study carried out in four cultures, American, Argentinean, French, and Japanese mothers tended to speak to 5-month-olds in emotion-laden ways, emphasizing greetings, repeated sounds, and affectionate names. At 13 months, when toddlers understood much more, a greater percentage of maternal speech was information laden—concerned with giving directions, asking questions, and describing what was happening at

**child-directed speech (CDS)**
The form of language adults use to speak to infants and toddlers that consists of short sentences with high-pitched, exaggerated expression, clear pronunciation, distinct pauses between speech segments, and repetition of new words in a variety of contexts.

the moment (Bornstein et al., 1992a). The more effectively parents modify speech complexity over the first year, the better their children's language comprehension at 18 months of age (Murray, Johnson, & Peters, 1990).

## FIRST SPEECH SOUNDS

Around 2 months, babies begin to make vowel-like noises, called **cooing** because of their pleasant "oo" quality. Gradually, consonants are added, and around 4 months **babbling** appears, in which infants repeat consonant–vowel combinations in long strings, such as "babababababa" and "nanananana."

The timing of early babbling seems to be due to maturation, since babies everywhere (even those who are deaf) start babbling at about the same age and produce a similar range of early sounds (Stoel-Gammon & Otomo, 1986). But for babbling to develop further, infants must hear human speech. Around 7 months, babbling starts to include the sounds of mature spoken languages. However, if a baby is hearing impaired, these speechlike sounds are greatly delayed, and in the case of deaf infants, are totally absent (Eilers & Oller, 1994; Oller, 2000). When deaf infants are exposed to sign language from birth, they babble with their hands in much the same way hearing infants do through speech (Petitto & Marentette, 1991). Furthermore, hearing babies of deaf, signing parents produce babblelike hand motions with the rhythmic patterns of natural language (Petitto et al., 2001). Infants' sensitivity to language rhythm, evident in both spoken and signed babbling, may help them discover and produce meaningful language units.

At first, babies produce a limited number of babbled sounds, which expand to a much broader range (Oller et al., 1997). By 10 months, babbling reflects the consonant–vowel and intonation patterns of the child's language community, some of which are transferred to their first words (Boysson-Bardies & Vihman, 1991). Listen to an older baby babble, and notice that certain sounds appear in particular contexts—for example, when exploring objects, looking at books, and walking upright (Blake & Boysson-Bardies, 1992). Infants seem to be experimenting with the sound system and meaning of language before they speak in conventional ways. Babbling continues for 4 or 5 months after infants say their first words.

## BECOMING A COMMUNICATOR

At birth, infants are prepared for some aspects of conversational behaviour. For example, newborn babies can initiate interaction by making eye contact and terminate it by looking away. Around 4 months, they start to gaze in the same direction adults are looking, a skill that increases and becomes more accurate between 12 and 15 months of age (Tomasello, 1999). Adults also follow the baby's line of vision and, after establishing **joint attention,** comment on what the infant sees. In this way, they label the baby's environment. Researchers believe that joint attention contributes greatly to early language development. Infants and toddlers who often experience it comprehend more language, produce meaningful gestures and words earlier, and show faster vocabulary development (Carpenter, Nagell, & Tomasello, 1998; Marcus et al., 2000).

By 3 months, the beginnings of conversation can be seen. At first, the mother vocalizes at the same time as the baby—an event that may help infants realize that others attend to their speech sounds (Elias & Broerse, 1996). Between 4 and 6 months, interaction between parent and baby begins to include give-and-take, as in turn-taking games such as pat-a-cake and peekaboo. At first, the parent starts the game and the baby is an amused observer. Nevertheless, 4-month-olds are sensitive to the structure and timing of these interactions, smiling more to an organized than a disorganized peekaboo exchange (Rochat, Querido, & Striano, 1999). By 12 months, babies actively participate, exchanging roles with the parent. As they do so, they practise the turn-taking pattern of human conversation, a vital context for acquiring language and communication skills. Infants' play maturity and vocalizations during games predict advanced language progress between 1 and 2 years of age (Rome-Flanders & Cronk, 1995; Vibbert & Bornstein, 1989).

At the end of the first year, as infants become capable of intentional behaviour, they use two types of preverbal gestures to influence the behaviour of others. The first is the **protodeclarative,**

This 14-month-old uses the protodeclarative to attract her mother's attention to a fascinating sight. As the mother labels her daughter's pointing gesture, she promotes the transition to verbal language.

© LAURA DWIGHT

**cooing**
Pleasant vowel-like noises made by infants beginning around 2 months of age.

**babbling**
Repetition of consonant–vowel combinations in long strings, beginning around 4 months of age.

**joint attention**
A state in which two conversational partners attend to the same object or event.

**protodeclarative**
A preverbal gesture through which infants make an assertion about an object by touching it, holding it up, or pointing to it while looking at others to make sure they notice.

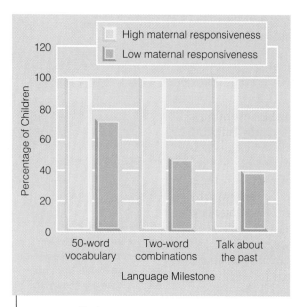

**FIGURE 9.4**

**Relationship of maternal responsiveness at 13 months to attainment of language milestones at 21 months.** Mothers high in responsiveness fell in the top 10 percent in responding to their toddler's vocalizations with verbal prompts, imitations, and expansions. Mothers low in maternal responsiveness fell in the bottom 10 percent. Toddlers of highly responsive mothers were advanced in attaining major language milestones. (Adapted from Tamis-LeMonda, Bornstein, & Baumwell, 2001.)

**protoimperative**
A preverbal gesture in which infants point, reach, and make sounds to get another person to do something.

in which the baby touches an object, holds it up, or points to it while looking at others to make sure they notice. In the second, the **proto-imperative,** the infant gets another person to do something by reaching, pointing, and often making sounds at the same time (Carpenter, Nagell, & Tomasello, 1998; Fenson et al., 1994). Over time, some of these gestures become explicitly symbolic—much like those in children's early make-believe play (see Chapter 6). For example, a 1- to 2-year-old might raise her arms to indicate "big" or flap them to refer to a butterfly (Goldin-Meadow, 1999).

Early in the second year, turn-taking and gestural communication come together, especially in situations in which children's messages do not communicate clearly. When adults label toddlers' reaching and pointing gestures ("Oh, you want a cookie!"), toddlers learn that using language quickly leads to desired results. Soon they integrate words with gestures, using the gesture to expand their verbal message, as in pointing to a toy while saying "give." Gradually, the gestures recede, and words become the dominant symbolic form (Iverson, Capirci, & Caselli, 1994; Namy & Waxman, 1998). Nevertheless, these word–gesture combinations contribute to language development. The earlier toddlers produce them, the sooner they combine words at the end of the second year (Goldin-Meadow & Butcher, 1998).

Throughout our discussion, we have stressed that progress toward spoken language is encouraged by caregivers who respond sensitively to infants and involve them in dialogue-like exchanges. Yet in some cultures, such as the Kaluli of Papua New Guinea and the people of Western Samoa, adults rarely communicate with infants and never play social games with them. Not until infants crawl and walk do siblings take charge, talk to toddlers, and respond to their vocalizations. Yet Kaluli and Samoan children acquire language within the normal time frame (Ochs, 1988).

These findings suggest that adult moulding of communication during the first year may not be essential. But by the second year, caregiver–child interaction contributes greatly to the transition to language. In observations of mother–child play at 9 and 13 months, the frequency with which mothers joined in the child's activity, offered verbal prompts, and imitated and expanded on the child's vocalizations predicted earlier attainment of major language milestones, including first words, 50-word vocabulary, 2-word combinations, and use of language to talk about the past. The relation of maternal responsiveness to language progress was particularly strong at 13 months (see Figure 9.4) (Tamis-LeMonda, Bornstein, & Baumwell, 2001). And as the From Research to Practice box on page 367 illustrates, when a child's disability makes it difficult for parents to engage in responsive communication, children show profound delays in both language and cognitive development.

**ASK YOURSELF**

**review**   Cite findings indicating that both infant capacities and the language environment contribute to prelinguistic development.

**apply**   Fran frequently corrects her 17-month-old son Jeremy's attempts to talk and refuses to respond to his gestures, fearing that he won't use words. How might Fran be contributing to Jeremy's slow language progress? What should she do to encourage his language development?

**connect**   Explain how parents' use of child-directed speech illustrates Vygotsky's zone of proximal development. (See Chapter 6, page 258.)

# from research to practice

## PARENT–CHILD INTERACTION: IMPACT ON LANGUAGE AND COGNITIVE DEVELOPMENT OF DEAF CHILDREN

*a*bout 1 in every 2000 Canadian infants is born with profound hearing loss (Feldman, 1994). When a deaf child cannot participate fully in communication with parents and other caregivers, development is severely compromised. Yet the consequences of deafness for children's language and cognition vary with social context, as comparisons of deaf children of hearing parents with deaf children of deaf parents reveal.

Over 90 percent of deaf children have hearing parents. During toddlerhood and early childhood, these children often are delayed in language and complex make-believe play. In middle childhood, many achieve poorly in school and are deficient in social skills. Yet deaf children of deaf parents escape these difficulties! Their language (use of sign) and play maturity are on a par with hearing children's. After school entry, deaf children of deaf parents learn easily and get along well with adults and peers (Bornstein et al., 1999; Spencer & Lederberg, 1997).

These differences can be traced to early parent–child communication. Beginning in infancy, hearing parents of deaf children are less positive, less effective at achieving joint attention and turn-taking, and more directive and intrusive (Meadow-Orlans & Steinberg, 1993; Spencer & Meadow-Orlans, 1996). While helping their deaf preschoolers solve a challenging puzzle, hearing parents have trouble adjusting their verbal and nonverbal assistance to the child's needs (Jamieson, 1995). In contrast, the quality of interaction between deaf children and deaf parents is similar to that of hearing children and hearing parents.

Children with limited and less sensitive parental communication are behind their agemates in achieving ver-

bal control over their behaviour—in thinking before they act and in planning. Deaf children of hearing parents frequently display impulse-control problems (Arnold, 1999).

Hearing parents are not at fault for their deaf child's problems. Instead, they lack experience with visual communication, which enables deaf parents to respond readily to a deaf child's needs. Deaf parents know they must wait for the child to turn toward them before interacting (Spencer, Bodner-Johnson, & Gutfreund, 1992). Hearing parents tend to speak or gesture while the child's attention is directed elsewhere—a strategy that works with a hearing but not with a deaf partner. When the child is confused or unresponsive, hearing parents often feel overwhelmed and become more controlling (Jamieson, 1995). Furthermore, learning sign language is an immense task, and few hearing parents become fluent.

The impact of deafness on language and cognitive development can best be understood by considering its effects on parents and other significant people in the child's life. Deaf children need access to language models—deaf adults and peers—to create a natural language-learning situation. And their hearing parents benefit from social support along with training in how to interact sensitively with a nonhearing partner. In sum, research on deaf children underscores the vital role of the following adult communicative behaviours in fostering all aspects of language competence, in hearing and deaf children alike:

- Respond to coos and babbles with speech sounds (for hearing infants) and gestures (for deaf infants).

- Establish joint attention and comment on what the child sees (for deaf children, with gestures after re-establishing eye contact).

- Play turn-taking games with infants, such as pat-a-cake, peekaboo, and back-and-forth imitation of sounds and gestures.

- Engage toddlers in frequent conversation—during everyday activities, joint make-believe play (see Chapter 6), and book reading (see Chapter 7).

© DAVID YOUNG-WOLFF/PHOTOEDIT

A teacher fluent in sign language interacts with this deaf toddler, born to hearing parents. Through early access to rich, natural language-learning experiences, he will be protected from serious developmental problems—delayed language, impulse-control difficulties, poor school achievement, and deficits in social skills.

# Phonological Development

IF YOU LISTENED IN on a 1- or 2-year-old trying out her first handful of words, you probably would hear an assortment of interesting pronunciations, such as "nana" for banana, "oap" for soap, and "weddy" for ready, as well as some wordlike utterances that do not resemble adult forms. For "translations" of these, you must ask the child's parent. Phonological development is a complex process that depends on the child's ability to attend to sound sequences, produce sounds, and combine them into understandable words and phrases. Between 1 and 4 years of age, children make great progress at this task. In trying to talk like people around them, they adopt temporary strategies for producing sounds that bring adult words within their current range of physical and cognitive capabilities (Menn & Stoel-Gammon, 2001). Let's see how they do so.

## THE EARLY PHASE

Children's first words are partly influenced by the small number of sounds they can pronounce (Hura & Echols, 1996; Vihman, 1996). The easiest sound sequences start with consonants, end with vowels, and include repeated syllables, as in "Mama," "Dada," "bye-bye," and "nigh-nigh" (for "night-night"). Sometimes young speakers may use the same sound to represent a variety of words, a feature that makes their speech hard to understand (Ingram, 1999). For example, one toddler substituted "bat" for as many as 12 different words, including "bad," "bark," "bent," and "bite."

These observations reveal that early phonological and semantic development are related. Languages cater to young children's phonological limitations. Throughout the world, sounds resembling "mama," "dada," and "papa" refer to parents, so it is not surprising that these are among the first words children everywhere produce. Also, in child-directed speech, adults often use simplified words to talk about things of interest to toddlers. For example, rabbit becomes "bunny" and train becomes "choo-choo." These word forms support the child's first attempts to talk.

## APPEARANCE OF PHONOLOGICAL STRATEGIES

By the middle of the second year, children move from trying to pronounce whole syllables and words to trying to pronounce each phoneme within a word. As a result, they can be heard experimenting with phoneme patterns. One 21-month-old pronounced "juice" as "du," "ju," "dus," "jus," "sus," "zus," "fus," "tfus," "jusi," and "tfusi" within a single hour (Fee, 1997). This marks an intermediate phase of development in which pronunciation is partly right and partly wrong. A close look reveals that children apply systematic strategies to words so they fit with their pronunciation capacities yet resemble adult utterances. Although individual differences exist in the precise strategies children adopt (see Table 9.1 for examples), they follow a general developmental pattern (Vihman, 1996).

At first, children produce *minimal words,* in which they focus on the stressed syllable and try to pronounce its consonant–vowel combination ("du" or "ju" for "juice"). Soon they add ending consonants ("jus"), adjust vowel length ("beee" for "please"), and add unstressed syllables ("mae-do" for "tomato"). Finally, they produce the full word with a correct stress pattern, although they may still need to refine its sounds ("timemba" for "remember," "pagetti" for "spaghetti") (Demuth, 1996; Salidis & Johnson, 1997).

The errors children make are similar across a range of languages, including Cantonese, Czech, English, French, Italian, Quiché (a Mayan language), Spanish, and Swedish. However, differences in rate of phonological progress exist, depending on the complexity of a language's sound system and the importance of certain sounds for conveying meaning. Cantonese-speaking children, for example, develop more quickly than English-speaking children. In Cantonese, many words are single syllables. Although a change in tone of a syllable can lead to a change in meaning, Chinese children master this tone system by age 2 (So

**TABLE** 9.1

Common Phonological Strategies Used by Young Children to Simplify Pronunciation of Adult Words

| STRATEGY | EXAMPLE |
|---|---|
| Repeating the first consonant-vowel in a multisyllable word | "TV" becomes "didi," "cookie" becomes "gege." |
| Deleting unstressed syllables in a multisyllable word | "Banana" becomes "nana," "giraffe" becomes "raffe." |
| Replacing fricatives (hissing sounds) with stop consonant sounds | "Sea" becomes "tea," "say" becomes "tay." |
| Replacing consonant sounds produced in the rear and palate area of the vocal tract with ones produced in the frontal area | "Shoe" becomes "zue," "goose" becomes "doose." |
| Replacing liquid sounds ("l" or "r") with glides ("y" or "w") | "Lap" becomes "yap," "ready" becomes "weddy." |
| Reducing consonant-vowel-consonant words to a consonant-vowel form by deleting the final consonant | "Bike" becomes "bai," "more" becomes "muh." |
| Replacing an ending consonant syllable with a vowel | "Apple" becomes "appo," "bottom" becomes "bada." |
| Reducing a consonant cluster to a single consonant | "Clown" becomes "cown," "play" becomes "pay." |

*Source:* Ingram, 1986.

& Dodd, 1995). Among children acquiring English, "v" is a late-appearing sound, whereas Swedish children master it early. In English, "v" is relatively infrequent; in Swedish, it is common and vital for distinguishing words (Ingram, 1999).

Over the preschool years, children's pronunciation improves greatly. Maturation of the vocal tract and the child's active problem-solving efforts are largely responsible, since children's phonological errors are very resistant to adult correction. One father tried repeatedly to get his 2½-year-old daughter to pronounce the word "music," but each time she persisted with "ju-jic." When her father made one last effort, she replied, "Wait 'til I big. Then I say ju-jic, Daddy!"

### LATER PHONOLOGICAL DEVELOPMENT

Although phonological development is largely complete by age 5, a few syllable stress patterns that signal subtle differences in meaning are acquired in middle childhood and adolescence. For example, when shown pairs of pictures and asked to identify which is the "greenhouse" and which is the "green house," most children recognized the correct label by grade 3 and produced it between grades 4 and 6 (Atkinson-King, 1973). Changes in syllabic stress after certain abstract words take on endings—for example, "humid" to "humidity" and "method" to "methodical"—are not mastered until adolescence (Camarata & Leonard, 1986).

These late attainments are probably affected by the semantic complexity of the words. Throughout development, pronunciation is best for easily understood words. Working simultaneously on the sound and meaning of a new word may overload the cognitive system, leading children to sacrifice sound temporarily until they better understand the word's meaning.

## Semantic Development

WORD COMPREHENSION begins in the middle of the first year. When 6-month-olds listened to the words "mommy" and "daddy" while looking at side-by-side videos of their parents, they looked longer at the video of the named parent (Tincoff & Jusczyk, 1999). At 9 months, after hearing a word paired with an object, babies looked longer at other objects from the same category than at those in a different category (Balaban & Waxman, 1997). On the average, children say their first word around 12 months. By age 6, they have a vocabulary of about 10 000 words. To accomplish this feat, children learn about five new words each day (Bloom, 1998).

**TABLE** 9.2

Types of Words Appearing in Toddlers' 50-Word Vocabularies

| WORD TYPE | DESCRIPTION | TYPICAL EXAMPLES | PERCENTAGES OF TOTAL WORD[a] |
|---|---|---|---|
| Object words | Words used to refer to the "thing world" | *Apple, ball, bird, boat, book, car, cookie, Dada, doggie, kitty, milk, Mama, shoe, snow, truck* | 66 |
| Action words | Words that describe, demand, or accompany action or that express attention or demand attention | *Bye-bye, go, hi, look, more, out, up* | 13 |
| State words (modifiers) | Words that refer to properties or qualities of things or events | *All gone, big, dirty, hot, mine, pretty, outside, red, uh-oh, wet* | 9 |
| Personal/social words | Words that express emotional states and social relationships | *No, ouch, please, want, yes, thank you* | 8 |
| Function words | Words that fill a solely grammatical function | *For, is, to, what, where* | 4 |

[a]Average percentages are given, based on a sample of 18 toddlers.

*Source:* Nelson, 1973.

As these achievements reveal, children's **comprehension,** the language they understand, develops ahead of **production,** the language they use. For example, toddlers follow many simple directions, such as "Bring me your book" or "Don't touch the lamp," even though they cannot yet express all these words in their own speech. A 5-month lag exists between children's comprehension of 50 words (at about 13 months) and production of 50 words (around 18 months) (Menyuk, Liebergott, & Schultz, 1995).

Why is comprehension ahead of production? Think back to the distinction made in Chapter 7 between two types of memory—recognition and recall. Comprehension requires only that children recognize the meaning of a word, whereas production demands that they recall, or actively retrieve from their memories, the word as well as the concept for which it stands. Failure to say a word does not mean that toddlers do not understand it. If we rely only on what children say, we will underestimate their language progress.

### THE EARLY PHASE

To learn words, children must identify which concept each label picks out in their language community. Ask several parents to list their toddlers' first words. Notice how the words build on the sensorimotor foundations Piaget described and on categories children form during their first 2 years (see Chapter 6). First words refer to important people ("Mama," "Dada"), objects that move ("ball," "car," "cat," "shoe"), familiar actions ("bye-bye," "more," "up"), or outcomes of familiar actions ("dirty," "hot," "wet"). As Table 9.2 reveals, in their first 50 words, toddlers rarely name things that just sit there, like "table" or "vase" (Nelson, 1973).

In Chapter 6, we noted that certain early words are linked to specific cognitive achievements. Recall that about the time children master advanced object permanence problems, they use disappearance terms, like "all gone." And success and failure expressions, such as "There!" and "Uh-oh!", appear when toddlers can solve sensorimotor problems suddenly. According to one pair of researchers, "Children seem motivated to acquire words that are relevant to the particular cognitive problems they are working on at the moment" (Gopnik & Meltzoff, 1986, p. 1057).

Besides cognition, emotion influences early word learning. At first, when acquiring a new word for an object, person, or event, 1½-year-olds say it neutrally; they need to listen carefully to learn, and strong emotion diverts their attention. As words become better learned, toddlers integrate talking and expressing feelings (Bloom, 1998). "Shoe!" said one enthusiastic 22-month-old as her mother tied her shoelaces before an outing. At the end of the second year, toddlers label their emotions with words like "happy," "mad," and "sad"—a development we will consider further in Chapter 10.

**comprehension**
In language development, the words and word combinations that children understand.

**production**
In language development, the words and word combinations that children use.

Young toddlers add to their vocabularies slowly, at a rate of 1 to 3 words a month. Over time, the number of words learned accelerates. As Figure 9.5 shows, between 18 and 24 months, a spurt in vocabulary often takes place (Fenson et al., 1994). Many children add 10 to 20 new words a week. An improved ability to categorize experience (see Chapter 6), retrieve words from memory, and pronounce them supports this "naming explosion" (Dapretto & Bjork, 2000; Gershoff-Stowe & Smith, 1997). Also, older toddlers can use language to represent a wider range of experiences as they talk about nonpresent objects and events (Morford & Goldin-Meadow, 1997). Furthermore, a better grasp of others' intentions, evident in toddlers' imitation around 18 months (see page 225), might foster this rapid word learning because it helps toddlers figure out what others are talking about (Bloom, 2000).

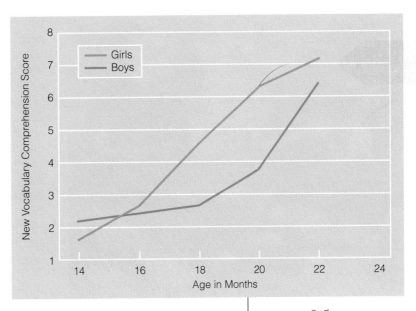

How do children build their vocabularies so quickly? Researchers have discovered that they can connect a new word with an underlying concept after only a brief encounter, a process called **fast-mapping.** When an adult labelled an oddly shaped plastic ring with the nonsense word "koob" during a game, children as young as 2 picked up the word's meaning (Dollaghan, 1985). Even 14-month-olds comprehend new labels remarkably quickly (Werker et al., 1998). But Janet Werker and her colleagues (2002) of the University of British Columbia showed that before 17 to 18 months, toddlers often confuse the meanings of similar-sounding words. And 1- and 2-year-olds need more repetitions of a word's use across several situations than do preschoolers, who better remember and categorize speech-based information (Akhtar & Montague, 1999; Woodward, Markman, & Fitzsimmons, 1994).

**INDIVIDUAL AND CULTURAL DIFFERENCES.** Although the average age at which the first word is spoken is 12 months, the range is large, from 8 to 18 months—variation that results from a complex blend of genetic and environmental influences. Many studies show that girls are slightly ahead of boys in vocabulary growth until 2 years of age, when boys gradually catch up. (Look again at Figure 9.5 to see these trends.) The most common explanation is girls' faster rate of physical maturation, believed to promote earlier development of the left cerebral hemisphere. Besides the child's sex, temperament makes a difference. Toddlers who are very reserved and cautious often wait until they understand a great deal before trying to speak (Nelson, 1973). When they finally do speak, their vocabularies increase rapidly.

But these child characteristics are also related to the surrounding language environment. For example, mothers talk much more to toddler-age girls than boys (Leaper, Anderson, & Sanders, 1998). The more words caregivers use when talking to young children, the greater the number integrated into the child's vocabulary (Hart, 1991; Huttenlocher et al., 1991). Because lower-SES children experience less verbal stimulation in their homes than do higher-SES children, their vocabularies tend to be smaller, regardless of the child's sex and ethnicity (Hart & Risley, 1995; Hoff-Ginsberg, 1994).

Striking individual differences also exist in style of early language learning. Most toddlers use a **referential style;** their vocabularies consist mainly of words that refer to objects. A smaller number of toddlers use an **expressive style.** Compared with referential children, they produce many more social formulas and pronouns, such as "stop it," "thank you," "done," and "I want it." Return to the opening of this chapter, and note Erin's early use of largely expressive-style words. Toddlers' language styles reflect early ideas about the functions of language. Referential children think words are for naming things. In contrast, expressive-style children

**FIGURE** 9.5

**Spurt in vocabulary growth between 18 and 24 months, averaged over 24 English-speaking children.** Although the graph is based on a measure of language comprehension, a similar spurt appears when language production is assessed. Boys lag behind girls in size of their early vocabularies and in timing of the spurt. (From J. S. Reznick & B. A. Goldfield, 1992, "Rapid Change in Lexical Development in Comprehension and Production," *Developmental Psychology, 28,* p. 410. Copyright © 1992 by the American Psychological Association. Reprinted by permission.)

**fast-mapping**
Connecting a new word with an underlying concept after only a brief encounter.

**referential style**
A style of early language learning in which toddlers use language mainly to label objects.

**expressive style**
A style of early language learning in which toddlers use language mainly to talk about people's feelings and needs. Initial vocabulary emphasizes social formulas and pronouns.

In Western societies, many mothers stress object labels to young language learners. In contrast, these African mothers of Botswana respond verbally to their toddlers' glances and vocalizations to other people, not to exploration of objects.

believe words are for talking about people's feelings and needs. The vocabularies of referential-style children grow faster, since all languages contain many more object labels than social phrases (Bates et al., 1994; Nelson, 1973).

What accounts for a toddler's choice of a particular language style? Rapidly developing, referential-style children often have an especially active interest in exploring objects and parents who eagerly respond by naming things. Also, these children freely imitate words they hear, and their parents imitate back—behaviours that support swift vocabulary growth because they help children remember new labels (Masur, 1995; Masur & Rodemaker, 1999). Expressive-style children tend to have highly sociable personalities, and their parents more often use verbal routines ("How are you?" "It's no trouble") designed to support social relationships (Goldfield, 1987).

The two language styles are also linked to culture. When speaking to infants and toddlers, North American mothers label objects more frequently than do Japanese mothers. In contrast, Japanese mothers more often engage young children in social routines, perhaps because their culture stresses the importance of membership in the social group (Fernald & Morikawa, 1993). An African mother of Mali, Mauritania, or Senegal responds verbally to her infant's glances and vocalizations to other people, not to the baby's exploration of objects (Jamin, 1994). When we consider these findings as a whole, early vocabulary development supports the interactionist's emphasis on the combined impact of children's inner dispositions and their linguistic and social worlds.

**TYPES OF WORDS.** Three types of words—object, action, and state—are most common in young children's vocabularies. Careful study of each provides important information about the course of semantic development.

*Object and Action Words.* Many young language learners have more object than action words in their beginning vocabularies (Au, Dapretto, & Song, 1994; Caselli et al., 1995). If actions are an especially important means through which infants find out about their world, then why this early emphasis on naming objects?

One reason is that nouns refer to concepts (such as *table, bird,* or *dog*) that are easy to perceive. As a result, when young children start to talk, they readily match objects with their appropriate labels. In contrast, verbs require more complex understandings—of relationships between objects and actions (Gentner & Rattermann, 1991). For example, "go" involves a person going somewhere, "fix" a person fixing something.

Nevertheless, the linguistic environment affects toddlers' relative use of object and action words. As mentioned earlier, North American mothers often talk about objects with their children. In one study, they rarely prompted 20-month-olds to produce verbs. But they often used verbs to get toddlers to perform actions ("Can you *spin* that wheel?"). Consequently, the toddlers comprehended many more verbs than they produced (Goldfield, 2000). In Chinese, Japanese, and Korean, nouns are often omitted entirely from adult sentences, and verbs are stressed. As a result, Asian toddlers typically produce action words first and use them far more often than do their English-speaking counterparts (Gopnik & Choi, 1995; Kim, McGregor, & Thompson, 2000; Tardif, Gelman, & Xu, 1999).

*State Words.* Between 2 and 2½ years, children's use of state (or modifier) words expands to include labels for attributes of objects, such as size and colour ("big," "red") as well as possession ("my toy," "Mommy purse"). Words referring to the functions of objects appear soon after (for example, "dump truck," "pickup truck") (Nelson, 1976).

When state words are related in meaning, general distinctions (which are easier) appear before more specific ones. For example, among words referring to the size of objects, children acquire "big–small," followed by "tall–short," "high–low," and "long–short," and finally "wide–narrow" and "deep–shallow." The same is true for temporal terms. Between ages 3 and 5, children first master "now" versus "then" and "before" versus "after," followed by "today" versus "yesterday" and "tomorrow" (Stevenson & Pollitt, 1987).

State words referring to the location of objects provide additional examples of how cognition influences vocabulary development. Before age 2, children can easily imitate an adult's action in putting an object "in" or "on" another object, but they have trouble imitating the placement of one object "under" another. These terms appear in children's vocabularies in just this order, with all three achieved around 2½ years of age (Clark, 1983).

Because state words refer to qualities of objects and actions, children can use them to express many more concepts. As preschoolers master these words, their language becomes increasingly flexible.

© LAURA DWIGHT

Cognitive development influences young children's mastery of state (or modifier) words. This toddler is likely to say "in" the bucket and "on" the floor before he says "under" the bucket. Adult labelling of object locations will help him master these terms by age 2½.

**UNDEREXTENSIONS AND OVEREXTENSIONS.** When young children first learn words, they often do not use them just the way we do. Sometimes they apply them too narrowly, an error called **underextension.** For example, at 16 months, my younger son used the word "bear" to refer only to a special teddy bear to which he had become attached. A more common error between 1 and 2½ years is **overextension**—applying the word to a wider collection of objects and events than is appropriate. For example, a toddler might use the word "car" for buses, trains, trucks, and fire engines.

Toddlers' overextensions reflect a remarkable sensitivity to categorical relations. They do not overextend randomly. Instead, they apply a new word to a group of similar experiences, such as "dog" to refer to furry, four-legged animals and "open" to mean opening a door, peeling fruit, and untying shoe laces. Furthermore, the toddler who refers to trucks, trains, and bikes as "cars" is likely to point to these objects correctly when given their names in a comprehension task (Naigles & Gelman, 1995). This suggests that children often overextend deliberately because they have difficulty recalling or have not acquired a suitable word. In addition, when a word is hard to pronounce, toddlers frequently substitute a related one they can say (Elsen, 1994). As vocabulary and pronunciation improve, overextensions gradually disappear.

**WORD COINAGES AND METAPHORS.** To fill in for words they have not yet learned, children as young as age 2 coin new words based on ones they already know. At first, children use the technique of compounding. For example, a child might say "plant-man" for a gardener. Later they convert verbs into nouns and nouns into verbs, as in one child's use of "needle it" for mending something. Soon after, children discover more specialized word coinage techniques, such as adding "-er" to identify the doer of an action—for example, "crayoner" for a child using crayons. Children give up coined words as soon as they acquire conventional labels for their intended meanings (Clark, 1995). Still, these expressions reveal a remarkable, rule-governed approach to language.

Preschoolers also extend language meanings through metaphor. For example, one 3-year-old used the expression "fire engine in my tummy" to describe a stomach ache (Winner, 1988). Not surprisingly, the metaphors young preschoolers use and understand are based largely on concrete, sensory comparisons, such as "clouds are pillows" and "leaves are dancers." Once their vocabulary and knowledge of the world expand, they make nonsensory comparisons, such as "Friends are like magnets" (Karadsheh, 1991; Keil, 1986). Metaphors permit children to communicate in especially vivid and memorable ways.

---

### LATER SEMANTIC DEVELOPMENT

Between the start and end of elementary school, vocabulary increases fourfold, eventually exceeding 40 000 words. On average, about 20 new words are learned each day—a rate of growth that exceeds that of early childhood (see Figure 9.6 on page 374). Jeremy Anglin

**underextension**
An early vocabulary error in which a word is applied too narrowly, to a smaller number of objects or events than is appropriate.

**overextension**
An early vocabulary error in which a word is applied too broadly, to a wider collection of objects and events than is appropriate.

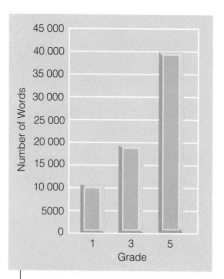

**FIGURE** 9.6

**Estimated vocabulary size of Canadian children at grades 1, 3, and 5.** Rate of vocabulary growth during the school years exceeds that of early childhood. (Adapted from Anglin, 1993.)

(1993) of the University of Waterloo showed that in addition to fast-mapping, school-age children enlarge their vocabularies through analyzing the structure of complex words. From "happy," "wise," and "decide," they quickly derive the meanings of "happiness," "wisdom," and "decision." They also figure out many more word meanings from context, especially while reading (Nagy & Scott, 2000). Because written language contains a richer vocabulary than spoken language, reading contributes greatly to vocabulary growth in middle childhood and adolescence.

As their knowledge base becomes better organized (see Chapter 7), school-age children think about and use words more precisely. Word definitions offer examples of this change. Five- and 6-year-olds give very concrete descriptions that refer to functions or appearance—for example, knife: "when you're cutting carrots"; bicycle: "it's got wheels, a chain, and handlebars." By the end of elementary school, synonyms and explanations of categorical relationships appear—for example, knife: "Something you could cut with. A saw is like a knife. It could also be a weapon" (Wehren, De Lisi, & Arnold, 1981). This advance reflects the ability to deal with word meanings on an entirely verbal plane. Older children can add new words to their vocabulary simply by being given a definition (Dickinson, 1984).

School-age children's more reflective, analytical approach to language permits them to appreciate the multiple meanings of words. For example, they recognize that many words, such as "cool" or "neat," have psychological as well as physical meanings: "What a cool shirt!" or "That movie was really neat!" This grasp of double meanings permits 8- to 10-year-olds to comprehend subtle, mental metaphors, such as "sharp as a tack," "spilling the beans," and "left high and dry" (Nippold, Taylor, & Baker, 1996; Wellman & Hickling, 1994). It also leads to a change in children's humour. By the mid-elementary school years, riddles and puns that go back and forth between different meanings of a key word are common, such as: "Hey, did you take a bath?" "No! Why, is one missing?" (Ely & McCabe, 1994).

The capacity for abstract reasoning permits adolescents to add such words as "counterintuitive" and "philosophy" to their vocabularies. They can also understand subtle nonliteral word meanings. As a result, they become masters of sarcasm and irony (Winner, 1988). When his mother fixed a dish for dinner that he disliked, one 16-year-old quipped, "Oh boy, my favourite!" School-age children sometimes realize that a sarcastic remark is insincere if it is said in a very exaggerated, mocking tone of voice (Capelli, Nakagawa, & Madden, 1990). And they can generate endings to stories that strongly suggest irony, such as a character who discovers that the game she wants for her birthday is very boring (Lucariello & Mindolovich, 1995). But adolescents and adults need only notice the discrepancy between a statement and its context to grasp sarcasm. And they can comprehend and produce irony in a wide range of circumstances.

## IDEAS ABOUT HOW SEMANTIC DEVELOPMENT TAKES PLACE

Research shows that adult feedback facilitates semantic development. When adults go beyond correcting to explain ("That's not a car. It's a truck. See, it has a place to put things in"), toddlers are more likely to move toward conventional word meanings (Chapman, Leonard, & Mervis, 1986). Still, adults cannot tell children exactly what concept each new word picks out. For example, if an adult points to a dog and calls it a "doggie," the word may refer to four-legged animals, the dog's shaggy ears, or its barking sound. Therefore, the child's cognitive processing must play a major role.

**THE INFLUENCE OF MEMORY.** A special part of working memory, a **phonological store** that permits us to retain speech-based information, supports young children's fast-mapping. The more rapidly 4-year-olds can recall a just-presented sequence of nonsense words (a measure of phonological memory skill), the larger their current vocabulary and the greater their vocabulary growth over the following year (Gathercole, 1995; Gathercole et al., 1999). This suggests that a child with good phonological memory has a better chance of transferring new words to long-term memory and linking them with relevant concepts.

**phonological store**
A special part of working memory that permits us to retain speech-based information. Supports early vocabulary development.

But phonological memory does not provide a full account of word learning. After age 5, semantic knowledge affects the speed with which children form phonological traces, and both factors influence vocabulary growth (Gathercole et al., 1997). And even at younger ages (as we will see next), children rely heavily on words they already know to detect the meanings of new ones.

**STRATEGIES FOR WORD LEARNING.** To explain semantic development, Eve Clark (1990, 1993, 1995) proposed **lexical contrast theory.** It assumes that two principles govern vocabulary growth. The first is *conventionality,* children's natural desire to acquire the words and word meanings of their language community. The second is *contrast,* which explains how new word meanings are added. According to Clark, children assume that the meaning of each word they hear is unique. Therefore, when they hear a new label, they try to figure out its meaning by contrasting it with words they know and assigning it to a gap in their vocabulary.

Many researchers have criticized lexical contrast theory for not being specific about the hypotheses young children use to determine new word meanings (Golinkoff et al., 1992). Ellen Markman (1989, 1992) believes that in the early phases of vocabulary growth, children adopt a **principle of mutual exclusivity.** They assume that words refer to entirely separate (nonoverlapping) categories. The principle of mutual exclusivity works well as long as available referents are perceptually very distinct. For example, when 2-year-olds are told the names of two very different novel objects (a clip and a horn), they assign each label correctly (Waxman & Senghas, 1992).

© MICHAEL NEWMAN/PHOTOEDIT

Young children rely on any useful information available to figure out the meanings of new words. For example, this boy might be attending to how his mother uses the word in the structure of sentences. Or he might be noticing social cues, such as his mother's eye movements and actions on the object.

But mutual exclusivity cannot account for what young children do when adults call a single object by more than one name. Children often call on other components of language for help in these instances. According to one proposal, children figure out many word meanings by observing how words are used in syntax, or the structure of sentences—a hypothesis called **syntactic bootstrapping** (Gleitman, 1990). Consider an adult who says, "This is a *citron* one," while showing a child a yellow car. As early as age 21 months, children interpret a new word used as an adjective as referring to a property of the object (Hall & Graham, 1999; Waxman & Markow, 1998).

Furthermore, drawing on their ability to infer others' intentions and perspectives, preschoolers often rely on social cues to identify word meanings (Baldwin & Tomasello, 1998). In one study, an adult performed an action on an object and then used a new label while looking back and forth between the child and the object, as if to invite the child to play. Two-year-olds capitalized on this social information to conclude that the label referred to the action, not the object (Tomasello & Akhtar, 1995).

Adults also provide direct information about the meaning of words. Consider an adult who says, "That soap is *made of* lye." Relying on the phrase *made of,* preschoolers interpret lye to refer to the soap's material qualities rather than the dish on which the soap rests (Deák, 2000). When no social cues or direct information is available, children as young as age 2 demonstrate remarkable flexibility in their word-learning strategies. They treat a new word applied to an already-labelled object as a second name for the object (Deák & Maratsos, 1998; Mervis, Golinkoff, & Bertrand, 1994).

Children acquire vocabulary so efficiently and accurately that some theorists believe that they are innately biased to induce word meanings using certain principles, such as mutual exclusivity (Woodward & Markman, 1998). Critics point out that a small set of built-in, fixed principles are not sufficient to account for the varied, flexible manner in which children draw on any useful information available to master vocabulary (Deák, 2000). Furthermore, many word-learning strategies cannot be innate, since children acquiring different languages use different approaches to mastering the same meanings. For example, English-speaking children rely on syntactic bootstrapping to tell the difference between one object ("This is *a dax*"), multiple objects of the same category ("Those are *daxes*"), and a proper name ("This is *Dax*") (Hall, Lee, & Belanger, 2001). In Japanese, all nouns are treated the same syntactically ("This is *dax*"). Nevertheless, Japanese preschoolers find ways to compensate for the missing syntactic cues, learning just as quickly as their English-speaking agemates (Imai & Haryu, 2001).

**lexical contrast theory**
A theory that assumes two principles govern semantic development: *conventionality,* children's natural desire to acquire the words and word meanings of their language community; and *contrast,* children's discovery of meanings by contrasting new words with ones they know and assigning them to gaps in their vocabulary.

**principle of mutual exclusivity**
The assumption by children in the early stages of vocabulary growth that words refer to entirely separate (nonoverlapping) categories.

**syntactic bootstrapping**
Observing how words are used syntactically, in the structure of sentences, to figure out their meanings.

An alternative perspective is that word learning is governed by the same cognitive strategies that children apply to nonlinguistic stimuli (Merriman, 1999; Smith, 1999). These strategies become more effective as children's knowledge of categories, vocabulary size, and sensitivity to social cues improve (Hollich, Hirsh-Pasek, & Golinkoff, 2000). In sum, we still have much to discover about how children's inner capacities join with diverse patterns of information in the environment to yield the phenomenal pace of semantic development.

## ASK YOURSELF

**review**   Using your knowledge of phonological and semantic development, explain why "Mama" and "Dada" are usually among children's first words.

**review**   Cite examples of how semantic development parallels advances in children's thinking.

**apply**    Katy's first words included "see," "give," and "thank you," and her vocabulary grew slowly during the second year. What style of language learning did she display, and what factors might have contributed to it?

**connect**  Explain how children's strategies for word learning support the interactionist perspective on language development.

# Grammatical Development

GRAMMAR REQUIRES THAT children use more than one word in an utterance. In studying grammatical development, researchers have puzzled over the following questions, prompted by Chomsky's theory: Does a consistent grammar, resembling that of adults, emerge quickly and easily in young children? What is the role of adult teaching—in particular, corrective feedback for grammatical errors? If a nativist account is plausible, then grammar should appear early, and the role of adult input should be minimal. As we chart the course of grammatical development, we will consider evidence on these issues.

## FIRST WORD COMBINATIONS

Sometime between 1½ and 2½ years, shortly after the vocabulary spurt, children combine two words, such as "Mommy shoe," "go car," and "more cookie," in **telegraphic speech.** Like a telegram, they focus on high-content words and leave out smaller, less important ones, such as "can," "the," and "to." For children learning languages that emphasize word order (such as English and French), endings like "-s" and "-ed" are not yet present. In languages in which word order is flexible and small grammatical markers are stressed, children's first sentences include them from the start (de Villiers & de Villiers, 1999).

Even though the two-word utterance is very limited, children the world over use it to express a wide variety of meanings (see Table 9.3). Are they applying a consistent grammar? According to one view, a more complete, and perhaps adultlike, grammar lies behind these two-word sentences (Gleitman et al., 1988; Pinker, 1994; Valian, 1991). Consistent with this idea, children often use the same construction to express different propositions. For example, a child might say "Mommy cookie" when he sees his mother eating a cookie and also when he wants his mother to give him a cookie. Perhaps the more elaborate structures are present in the child's mind, but he cannot yet produce the longer word string.

Other researchers disagree, arguing that two-word sentences are made up of simple formulas, such as "eat + X" and "more + X," with many different words inserted in the X position. These usually copy adult word pairings, as when an adult says, "How about some *more sandwich?*" and "Let's see if you can *eat the berries*" (Tomasello & Brooks, 1999). When toddlers entering the two-word phase were taught several noun and verb nonsense words (for example, "meek" for a doll and "gop" for a snapping action), they easily combined the new nouns

**telegraphic speech**
Children's two-word utterances that, like a telegram, leave out smaller and less important words.

**grammatical morphemes**
Small markers that change the meaning of sentences, as in "John's dog" and "he *is* eating."

**TABLE** 9.3

Common Meanings Expressed by Children's Two-Word Utterances

| MEANING | EXAMPLE |
|---|---|
| Agent–action | "Tommy hit" |
| Action–object | "Give cookie" |
| Agent–object | "Mommy truck" (meaning Mommy push the truck) |
| Action–location | "Put table" (meaning put X on the table) |
| Entity–location | "Daddy outside" |
| Possessor–possession | "My truck" |
| Attribution–entity | "Big ball" |
| Demonstrative–entity | "That doggie" |
| Notice–noticed object | "Hi mommy," "Hi truck" |
| Recurrence | "More milk" |
| Nonexistence–nonexistent or disappeared object | "No shirt," "No more milk" |

*Source:* Brown, 1973.

with words they knew well, as in "more meek." But as Figure 9.7 shows, they seldom formed word combinations with the new verbs (Tomasello et al., 1997). This suggests that they did not yet grasp subject–verb and verb–object relations, which are the foundation of grammar.

In sum, children starting to combine words are absorbed in figuring out word meanings and using their limited vocabularies in whatever way possible to get their thoughts across (Maratsos, 1998). However, children soon grasp the basic structure of their language.

## FROM SIMPLE SENTENCES TO COMPLEX GRAMMAR

In the third year, three-word sentences appear in which English-speaking children follow a subject–verb–object word order. Children learning other languages adopt the word orders of the adult speech to which they are exposed (Maratsos, 1998). For example, for "It is broken," a German child says, "Kaputt is der" (literally translated as "Broken is it"). Between ages 2½ and 3, children create sentences in which adjectives, articles, nouns, verbs, and prepositional phrases conform to an adult structure (Valian, 1986). They have begun to master the grammatical categories of their language.

**DEVELOPMENT OF GRAMMATICAL MORPHEMES.** As children form three-word sentences, a grammatical explosion takes place. They add **grammatical morphemes**[1]— small markers that change the meaning of sentences, as in "John*'s* dog" and "he *is* eating." English-speaking 2- and 3-year-olds acquire these morphemes in a regular sequence, shown in Table 9.4 on page 378 (Brown, 1973; de Villiers & de Villiers, 1973). Although children make mistakes in applying morphemes for months or years after they first appear, their errors are surprisingly few given the difficulty of the task (Maratsos, 1998).

Why does this sequence of development occur? Two characteristics of morphemes play important roles. The first is *structural complexity.* For example, adding the endings "-ing" or "-s" is structurally less complex than using forms of the verb "to be." In these, the child has to express correct tense and also make the subject and verb agree (for example, "I am coming" versus "They are coming"). And children learning English express location (the prepositions "in" and "on") sooner than do children learning Serbo-Croatian, in which structures

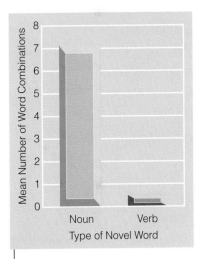

**FIGURE** 9.7

**Number of word combinations with novel nouns and verbs produced by 18- to 23-month-olds.** After learning the meaning of several noun and verb nonsense words, toddlers often combined the new nouns with other words. They seldom formed word combinations with the verbs, suggesting that their two-word utterances were not based on subject–verb and verb–object structures, which are the foundation of grammar. (Adapted from Tomasello et al., 1997.)

---

[1]A *morpheme* is the smallest unit of meaning in speech; any further division violates the meaning or produces meaningless units. Both "dog" and "-s" are morphemes; "-s" is a *grammatical morpheme.*

**TABLE** 9.4

Order of Acquisition of English Grammatical Morphemes

| MORPHEME | EXAMPLE |
|---|---|
| 1. Verb present progressive ending ("-ing") | "He singing." |
| 2. Preposition "on" | "On horsie." |
| 3. Preposition "in" | "In wagon." |
| 4. Noun plural ("-s") | "Cats." |
| 5. Verb irregular past tense | "He ran." "It broke." |
| 6. Noun possessive | "Daddy's hat." |
| 7. Verb uncontractible "be" form used with adjective, preposition, or noun phrase | "Are kitties sleepy?" |
| 8. Articles "a" and "the" | "A cookie." "The bunny." |
| 9. Verb regular past tense ending ("-ed") | "He kicked it." |
| 10. Verb present tense, third person singular irregular ending | "He likes it." |
| 11. Verb present tense, third person singular irregular ending | "She has [from *have*] a cookie." "He does [from *do*] a good job." |
| 12. Auxiliary verb uncontractible "be" forms | "Are you eating?" |
| 13. Verb contractible "be" forms used with adjective, preposition, or noun phrase | "He's inside." "They're sleepy." |
| 14. Auxiliary verb contractible "be" forms | "He's coming." "Doggie's eating." |

*Source:* Brown, 1973.

for location are more complex (Johnston & Slobin, 1979). Second, grammatical morphemes differ in *semantic complexity,* or the number and difficulty of the meanings they express. For example, adding "-s" to a word requires only one semantic distinction—the difference between one and more than one. In contrast, using "to be" involves many more, including an understanding of person, number, and time of occurrence (Brown, 1973; Slobin, 1982).

Look again at Table 9.4, and you will see that some morphemes with irregular forms are acquired before those with regular forms. For example, children use past tense irregular verbs, such as "ran" and "broke," before they acquire the regular "-ed" ending. But once children grasp a regular morphological rule, they extend it to words that are exceptions, a type of error called **overregularization.** "My toy car breaked" and "We each have two foots" are expressions that start to appear between 2 and 3 years of age. Children overregularize only occasionally, in about 5 to 8 percent of instances in which they use irregular words, a rate that remains constant into middle childhood (Marcus, 1995; Marcus et al., 1992). Overregularization shows that children apply grammatical rules creatively, since they do not hear mature speakers use these forms.

You may be wondering, Why do children use some correct irregular forms before they overregularize? In all languages, irregular forms are assigned to important, frequently used words. Since young children hear these often, they probably learn them by rote memory. But when they grasp a morphological rule, they apply it broadly, making their language more orderly than it actually is. Sometimes children even impose the rule on well-learned exceptions—for example, when they say "ated," "felled," or "feets" (Bybee & Slobin, 1982). At other times, children's memory for an irregular morpheme may fail. Then they call on the rule to generate the form, and overregularization results (Marcus, 1995).

**overregularization**
Application of regular grammatical rules to words that are exceptions.

## DEVELOPMENT OF COMPLEX GRAMMATICAL FORMS

Once children master the auxiliary verb "to be," the door is open to a variety of new expressions. Negatives and questions are examples.

**NEGATIVES.** Three types of negation exist, which appear in the following order in 2½- to 3-year-olds learning languages as different as English and Tamil (spoken in India and Sri Lanka): (1) *nonexistence,* in which the child remarks on the absence of something, such as "no cookie" or "all gone crackers"; (2) *rejection,* in which the child expresses opposition to something, such as "no take bath"; and (3) *denial,* in which the child denies the truthfulness of something, such as "That not my kitty" (Bloom, 1970; Clancy, 1985; Vaidyanathan, 1991).

These early constructions probably result from imitating parental speech. When parents express nonexistence or rejection, they often put "no" at the beginning of the sentence, as in "No more cookies" or "No, you can't have another cracker." Around 3 to 3½ years, children add auxiliary verbs and become sensitive to the way they combine with negatives. As a result, correct negative forms appear, as in, "There aren't any more cookies" (nonexistence), "I don't want a bath" (rejection), and "That isn't my kitty" (denial) (Tager-Flusberg, 2001).

© DANA WHITE/PHOTOEDIT

Like English-speaking children, these Korean-speaking preschoolers will master yes/no questions before *wh-* questions, which are both semantically and structurally more difficult.

**QUESTIONS.** Like negatives, questions first appear during the early preschool years and develop in an orderly sequence. English-speaking children can use rising intonation to convert an utterance into a yes/no question, as in "Mommy baking cookies?" As a result, they produce them earlier than do children learning languages in which the structure of yes/no questions is more complex (Bowerman, 1973).

Correct question form requires that children invert the subject and auxiliary verb. And in the case of *wh-* questions—ones that begin with "what," "where," "which," "who," "when," "why," and "how"—the *wh-* word must be placed at the beginning of the sentence. When first creating questions, English-speaking children cling to the subject–verb–object word order. As a result, they do not make the inversion. A 2-year-old is likely to say, "What you doing?" and "Where Daddy going?" (Stromswold, 1995). A little later, children include the auxiliary without inverting, as in "What you are doing?" Finally, they can apply all the rules for producing questions. Among English-, Korean-, and Tamil-speaking preschoolers, correct question form appears first for yes/no questions and later for *wh-* questions, which are semantically and structurally more difficult (Clancy, 1989; Vaidyanathan, 1988).

**OTHER COMPLEX CONSTRUCTIONS.** Between ages 3 and 6, children use increasingly complex grammatical forms. First, connectives appear that join whole sentences ("Mom picked me up, *and* we went to the park") and verb phrases ("I got up *and* ate breakfast"). The most general connective, "and," is used first, followed by connectives expressing more specific meanings, such as "then" and "when" for temporal relations, "because" and "so" for causal relations, "if" for conditionals, and "but" for opposition (Bloom et al., 1980).

Later, children produce embedded sentences ("I think *he will come*"), tag questions ("Dad's going to be home soon, *isn't he?*"), indirect object–direct object structures ("He showed *his friend* the present"), and passive sentences ("The dog *was patted by* the girl"). As the preschool years draw to a close, children use most of the grammatical structures of their native language competently (Tager-Flusberg, 2001).

## LATER GRAMMATICAL DEVELOPMENT

During the school years, children's mastery of complex grammatical constructions improves. The passive voice is an example. At all ages, children produce more abbreviated passives ("It got broken" or "They got lost") than full passives ("The glass was broken by Mary"). During middle childhood and early adolescence, children use the passive voice—including full passive statements—more often (Horgan, 1978).

Older children also apply the passive voice to a wider range of nouns and verbs. Preschoolers comprehend the passive best when the subject of the sentence is an animate being and the verb is an action word ("The *boy is kissed* by the girl"). Over the school years, the passive form extends to inanimate subjects, such as *hat* ("The *hat* was worn by the man") and experiential verbs, such as *see* or *know* ("The dog *was seen* by the cat") (Lempert, 1990; Pinker, Lebeaux, & Frost, 1987).

What accounts for this developmental trend? Recall that action is salient to young children in mastering vocabulary, a bias that may affect their mastery of complex grammar as well. But language input is also influential. English-speaking adults rarely use full and experiential passives in everyday conversation. However, in languages in which adults use these forms often, such as Inuktitut (spoken by the Inuit people of Arctic Canada), children produce them earlier (Allen & Crago, 1996). Furthermore, with training, English-speaking preschoolers readily produce full passives. However, because the passive structure is difficult, children younger than 3½ do not use it flexibly (Brooks & Tomasello, 1999).

Another grammatical achievement of middle childhood is advanced understanding of infinitive phrases, such as the difference between "John is eager to please" and "John is easy to please" (Chomsky, 1969). Like gains in vocabulary, appreciation of these subtle grammatical distinctions is supported by children's improved capacity to analyze and reflect on language and to attend to multiple linguistic and situational cues.

## IDEAS ABOUT HOW GRAMMATICAL DEVELOPMENT TAKES PLACE

Preschoolers' mastery of most of the grammar of their language is truly astounding. Explaining this feat is perhaps the most disputed issue in the study of language development.

**STRATEGIES FOR ACQUIRING GRAMMAR.** Evidence that grammatical development is an extended rather than sudden process has raised questions about Chomsky's strict nativist account. Some experts have concluded that grammar is a product of general cognitive development, or children's tendency to search the environment for consistencies and patterns of all sorts (Bates & MacWhinney, 1987; Bloom, 1991; Budwig, 1995; Maratsos, 1998). Return to page 364, and review infants' capacity to statistically analyze sound patterns and detect the structure of nonsense-word sequences—evidence that they are remarkable cognitive processors of language. Yet among cognitive theorists, there is intense debate about just how children master grammar.

According to one view, young children rely on other properties of language to detect basic grammatical regularities. In **semantic bootstrapping,** for example, they use word meanings to figure out sentence structure. For example, children might begin by grouping together words with "agent qualities" (entities that cause actions) as subjects and words with "action qualities" as verbs and then merge these semantic categories with observations of how words are used in sentences (Bates & MacWhinney, 1987; Braine, 1994). In this way, children lay down a basic grammatical framework, which they modify over time to take exceptions into account. A major problem for semantic bootstrapping is that in some languages, semantic categories (such as "agent") and basic grammatical structures (such as "subject") do not match up. In Tagalog, a language spoken in the Philippines, certain agents can be subjects, but others cannot! Yet Tagalog-speaking children acquire the main grammar of their language by age 3 (Maratsos, 1998).

Other theorists believe that children master grammar through direct observation of the structure of language. That is, they notice which words appear in the same positions in sentences, take the same morphological endings, and are similarly combined with other words. Over time, they group words into grammatical categories and use them appropriately in sentences (Braine, 1992; Maratsos & Chalkley, 1980; Tomasello, 2000). Connectionist models, discussed in Chapter 7 (see pages 273–274), have tested this idea by seeing whether artificial neural networks exposed to language input resembling the input children receive show a similar course of grammatical development. So far, neural-network mastery of some grammatical morphemes and aspects of syntax comes close to children's patterns of learning (Plunkett & Marchman, 1993, 1996). But the correspondence is not perfect, and no current neural-network system offers a comprehensive account of grammatical development (Klahr & MacWhinney, 1998).

**semantic bootstrapping**
Relying on semantics, or word meanings, to figure out sentence structure.

**expansions**
Adult responses that elaborate on a child's utterance, increasing its complexity.

**recasts**
Adult responses that restructure a child's grammatically incorrect speech into correct form.

©BOB DAEMMRICH/STOCK BOSTON

Still other theorists, while also focusing on processing mechanisms, agree with the essence of Chomsky's position that children are specially tuned for language learning. One idea accepts semantic bootstrapping but proposes that the grammatical categories into which children group word meanings are innately given—present at the outset (Bloom, 1999; Pinker, 1989). Critics, however, point out that toddlers' two-word utterances do not show a grasp of grammar.

According to another theory, although children do not start with innate knowledge, they have a special *language-making capacity*—a built-in set of procedures for analyzing language, which supports the discovery of grammatical regularities. Research on children learning more than 40 different languages reveals common patterns, consistent with a basic set of strategies (Slobin, 1985, 1997). Yet controversy persists over whether there is a universal, built-in language-processing device or whether children who hear different languages develop unique strategies (de Villiers & de Villiers, 1999; Maratsos, 1998).

**ENVIRONMENTAL SUPPORT FOR GRAMMATICAL DEVELOPMENT.** Besides investigating the child's capacities, researchers have been interested in aspects of the language environment that might ease the task of mastering grammar. Although adults correct children's semantics, they rarely provide direct feedback about grammar. For example, an early study reported that when a child said, "There's an animal farmhouse," the parent explained that the building was really a lighthouse. In contrast, the statement "her curling my hair" was met with an approving response because the parent was, in fact, curling the child's hair (Brown & Hanlon, 1970). These findings confirm that young children must figure out the intricacies of grammar largely on their own.

Nevertheless, adults could be offering subtle, indirect feedback about grammatical errors through two techniques, generally used in combination: **expansions** and **recasts.** For example, if a child says, "I gotted new red shoes," the parent might respond, "Yes, you got a pair of new red shoes," *expanding* the complexity of the child's statement as well as *recasting* its incorrect features. Parents and nonparents alike tend to respond in these ways after children make errors. When sentences are well formed, adults usually continue the topic of conversation or repeat exactly what the child just said (Bohannon & Stanowicz, 1988; Penner, 1987).

However, the impact of such feedback has been challenged. It is not provided to all children in all cultures. And even when adults provide it, they may not offer it frequently enough and across a broad enough range of mistakes to prompt grammatical development (Marcus, 1993; Valian, 1999). Furthermore, whereas some studies report that parents' reformulations have a corrective effect, others show no impact (Morgan, Bonama, & Travis, 1995; Strapp & Federico, 2000). Rather than eliminating specific errors, perhaps expansions and recasts serve the broader purpose of modelling grammatical alternatives and encouraging children to experiment with them.

In sum, virtually all investigators agree that young children are amazing processors of linguistic structure. But the extent to which factors in the language environment help them correct errors and take the next grammatical step forward remains a hotly contested issue in child language research.

As this preschooler selects a new dress on a shopping trip, her father might be expanding her short sentences and recasting them into grammatically correct form. Researchers are divided over the impact of adult feedback on grammatical development. Nevertheless, expansions and recasts demonstrate good grammar and may encourage children to experiment with new forms.

## ASK YOURSELF

**review**  Do young children use a consistent grammar in their telegraphic speech? Cite evidence to support your answer.

**review**  Cite examples of how both semantic and structural complexity underlie English-speaking children's mastery of grammatical morphemes.

**apply**  Three-year-old Jason's mother explained that the family would take a vacation in Miami. The next morning Jason announced, "I gotted my bags packed. When are we going to Your-ami?" What do Jason's errors reveal about his approach to mastering grammar?

**connect**  Explain why similarities between children's and artificial neural networks' mastery of grammatical structures are at odds with a nativist view of grammatical development.

# Pragmatic Development

BESIDES PHONOLOGY, vocabulary, and grammar, children must learn to use language effectively in social contexts. For a conversation to go well, participants must take turns, stay on the same topic, state their messages clearly, and conform to cultural rules that govern how individuals are supposed to interact. During the preschool years, children make considerable headway in mastering the pragmatics of language.

 **ACQUIRING CONVERSATIONAL SKILLS**

At the beginning of early childhood, children are already skilled conversationalists. In face-to-face interaction, they initiate verbal exchanges, make eye contact, respond appropriately to their partner's remarks, and take turns (Bloom et al., 1996; Pan & Snow, 1999). The number of turns over which children can sustain interaction and their ability to maintain a topic over time increases with age, but even 2-year-olds are capable of effective conversation (Snow et al., 1996).

Additional conversational strategies are added in early childhood. One of these is the **turnabout,** in which the speaker not only comments on what has just been said but also adds a request to get the partner to respond again. Two-year-olds cannot generate many words in each turn; hence, they seldom use turnabouts, which increase over the next few years (Goelman, 1986). Between ages 5 and 9, more advanced conversational strategies appear, such as **shading,** in which a change of topic is initiated gradually by modifying the focus of discussion (Wanska & Bedrosian, 1985).

Effective conversation also depends on understanding **illocutionary intent**—that is, what a speaker means to say, even if the form of the utterance is not perfectly consistent with it. By age 3, children comprehend a variety of requests for action not directly expressed that way, such as "I need a pencil" or "Why don't you tickle me?" (Garvey, 1974). During middle childhood, illocutionary knowledge develops further. For example, after forgetting to do his chores, an 8-year-old understands that his mother's statement, "The garbage is beginning to smell" really means "Take that garbage out!" Appreciating form–intention pairings like this one requires children to make subtle inferences that are beyond preschoolers' cognitive capacities (Ackerman, 1978).

Still, surprisingly advanced conversational abilities are present at a very early age, and adults' patient, sensitive interactions with young children encourage and sustain them. In fact, opportunities to converse with adults, either at home or in preschool, are consistently related to general measures of language progress (Hart & Risley, 1995; NICHD Early Childhood Research Network, 2000). Dialogues about picture books are particularly effective. They expose children to great breadth of language knowledge, including how to communicate in a clear, coherent narrative style—a skill that undoubtedly contributes to the association between joint storybook reading and literacy development (see Chapter 7, page 298).

Low-SES preschoolers benefit especially. Those who experience daily reading at home or in child care, compared with those who do not, are greatly advanced in language comprehension and production (Whitehurst et al., 1994). Shared reading with parents is particularly powerful, perhaps because parents are better able than teachers to read to the child often and tailor conversations to the child's interests and abilities (Lonigan & Whitehurst, 1998).

Finally, the presence of a sibling enhances young children's conversational skills. Toddlers closely monitor interactions between their twin or older sibling and parent, and they often try to join in. When they do, conversations last longer, with each participant taking more turns (Barton & Strosberg, 1997; Barton & Tomasello, 1991). Toddler–parent–sibling dialogues offer especially challenging practice in conversation, since toddlers must adapt to a partner who may not accommodate to their needs.

**turnabout**
A conversational strategy in which the speaker not only comments on what has just been said but also adds a request to get the partner to respond again.

**shading**
A conversational strategy in which a change of topic is initiated gradually by modifying the focus of discussion.

**illocutionary intent**
What a speaker means to say, even if the form of the utterance is not perfectly consistent with it.

**referential communication skills**
The ability to produce clear verbal messages and to recognize when the meaning of others' messages is unclear.

© MYRLEEN FERGUSON CATE/PHOTOEDIT

### COMMUNICATING CLEARLY

To communicate effectively, we must produce clear verbal messages as well as recognize when messages we receive are unclear so we can ask for more information. These aspects of language are called **referential communication skills.**

Laboratory tasks designed to assess children's ability to communicate clearly typically present them with challenging situations in which they must describe one object among a group of very similar objects to a listener. For example, in one study, 3- to 10-year-olds were shown several eight-object arrays. In each, objects were similar in size, shape, and colour. Most 3-year-olds gave ambiguous descriptions. When asked for clarification, they relied heavily on gestures, such as pointing. The ability to send clear messages improved steadily with age (Deutsch & Pechmann, 1982).

These findings may remind you of Piaget's notion of *egocentric speech*—that young children have difficulty taking the perspective of others (see Chapter 6). However, when preschoolers are given simpler communication tasks or engage in face-to-face interaction with familiar people, they adjust their speech to their listener's perspective quite well. In contrast, consider what happens when young children talk on the phone. Here is an excerpt of one 4-year-old's phone conversation with his grandfather:

Parent–toddler–sibling dialogues seem to offer a unique context for acquiring the pragmatics of language. The toddler in this family may become especially skilled at joining in conversations and adapting her speech to the needs of her listeners.

*Grandfather:* "How old will you be?"

*John:* "Dis many." *[Holding up four fingers.]*

*Grandfather:* "Huh?"

*John:* "Dis many." *[Again holding up four fingers.]*

(Warren & Tate, 1992, pp. 259–260)

Preschoolers' referential communication is less mature in highly demanding situations in which they cannot see their listeners' reactions or rely on typical conversational aids, such as gestures and objects to talk about. Nevertheless, when asked to tell a listener how to solve a simple puzzle, 3- to 6-year-olds' directions are more specific over the phone than in person, indicating that they realize that more verbal description is necessary to direct another in the phone context (Cameron & Lee, 1997). Between ages 4 and 8, both conversing and giving directions over the phone improve greatly. Telephone talk provides an excellent example of how preschoolers' communication skills depend on the demands of the situation.

Children's ability to evaluate the adequacy of messages they receive also improves with age. Around age 3, preschoolers start to ask others to clarify ambiguous messages (Revelle, Karabenick, & Wellman, 1981). At first, children recognize when a message provides a poor description of a concrete object (Ackerman, 1993). Only later can they tell when a message contains inconsistencies. For example, when researchers showed 4- and 5-year-olds the scene in Figure 9.8 on page 384 and instructed, "Put the frog on the book in the box," preschoolers could not resolve the ambiguity. Most put a frog on the empty book rather than in the box, even though they used similar embedded phrases in their own speech ("The frog *on the book* went to Mrs. Squid's house") (Hurewitz et al., 2000). This task requires the listener to attend to and integrate two competing representations. Yet recall from Chapter 6 that preschoolers tend to focus only on one aspect of a situation (here, the

© OSCAR BURRIEL/SCIENCE PHOTO LIBRARY/PHOTO RESEARCHERS

Context affects young children's referential communication skills. When talking on the telephone, this 4-year-old is likely to have trouble communicating clearly because she lacks the supports available in face-to-face interaction, such as visual access to her partner's reaction and to objects that are topics of conversation.

FIGURE 9.8

**Scene used to test for referential communication.** When an adult instructed, "Put the frog on the book in the box," 4- and 5-year-olds could not resolve the ambiguity between the phrases "on the book" and "in the box." They stuck to their first inference and put one of the frogs on the empty book. Not until middle childhood can children integrate the two competing representations by selecting the frog on the book and placing it in the box. (Adapted from Hurewitz et al., 2000.)

first prepositional phrase). Furthermore, to succeed, children must engage in *comprehension monitoring* (see Chapter 7)—a skill that improves during middle childhood and adolescence.

## SOCIOLINGUISTIC UNDERSTANDING

Language adaptations to social expectations are called **speech registers.** As early as the preschool years, children are sensitive to them. In one study, 4- to 7-year-olds were asked to act out roles with hand puppets. Even the youngest children showed that they understood the stereotypic features of different social positions. They used more commands when playing socially dominant and male roles, such as teacher, doctor, and father. In contrast, they spoke more politely and used more indirect requests when playing less dominant and feminine roles, such as pupil, patient, and mother (Anderson, 1992).

The importance of register adjustments is reflected in how often parents teach social routines, such as politeness. Infants are encouraged to wave "bye-bye" before they can grasp the gesture's meaning. By age 2, when children fail to say "please," "thank you," or "hi" and "goodbye," parents usually model and demand an appropriate response (Becker, 1990).

Some cultures have an elaborate system of polite language. In Japan, for example, politeness affects many aspects of verbal and nonverbal communication, which vary with gender, age, social status, and familiarity of speaker and listener. Japanese mothers and preschool teachers constantly model and teach these expressions. Consequently, children acquire a large repertoire of polite forms early in the preschool years (Nakamura, 2001). For example, while playing store, even 1-year-olds use the polite greeting "irasshaimase!" ("welcome!") when greeting customers. Two- and 3-year-olds use more complicated polite speech, such as "mata oide-kudasai" ("please come again"). And 3- and 4-year-olds make considerable headway in acquiring the complex honorific/humble language of Japanese society.

Although cultures vary in their emphasis on polite language, parents everywhere seem to realize that a child can get by without perfectly correct pronunciation, grammar, and a large vocabulary. But failing to use socially acceptable speech can lead to scorn and rejection, causing a child's message not to be received at all.

**speech registers**
Language adaptations to social expectations.

**ASK YOURSELF** www

**review** Summarize findings indicating that patient, sensitive interactions with adults foster preschoolers' conversational skills as well as general language progress.

**apply** What pragmatic skills are reflected in Erin's utterances in the opening to this chapter? How did Erin's parents and brother encourage her pragmatic development?

**connect** Cite examples of cognitive advances that contribute to development of referential communication.

# Development of Metalinguistic Awareness

IN PREVIOUS SECTIONS, we noted that older children's more reflective and analytical approach to language is involved in their linguistic achievements. The ability to think about language as a system is called **metalinguistic awareness.** Researchers have been especially interested in when it emerges and the role it plays in a variety of language-related accomplishments.

Consider the following exchange between a mother and her 4-year-old child:

*Child:* What's that?

*Mother:* It's a typewriter.

*Child: (frowning)* No, you're the typewriter, that's a typewrite.

(Karmiloff-Smith et al., 1996)

As the child's remark illustrates, the beginnings of metalinguistic awareness are present in early childhood. This preschooler is conscious of word endings; she expected "-er" to signify an animate agent, like "baker" and "dancer."

By age 4, children also know that word labels are arbitrary and not part of the objects to which they refer. When asked whether an object could be called by a different name in a new language, they respond "yes." Four-year-olds can also make some conscious syntactic judgments—for example, that a puppet who says, "Nose your touch" or "Dog the pat," is saying his sentences backward (Chaney, 1992). And by age 5, children have a good sense of the word concept. When an adult reads a story and stops to ask, "What was the last word I said?" they almost always answer correctly for all parts of speech. They do not say "on-the-floor" instead of "floor" or "isa" instead of "a" (Karmiloff-Smith et al., 1996). These early metalinguistic understandings are good predictors of vocabulary and grammatical development during the preschool years (Smith & Tager-Flusberg, 1982).

Nevertheless, full flowering of metalinguistic skills does not take place until middle childhood. For example, around age 8, children can identify phonemes (all the sounds in a word) (Tunmer & Nesdale, 1982). They also can judge the grammatical correctness of a sentence even if its meaning is false or senseless (Bialystok, 1986). School-age children's metalinguistic knowledge is also evident in their improved ability to define words and appreciate their multiple meanings in puns, riddles, and metaphors—skills that continue to be refined into adolescence.

Metalinguistic awareness emerges as language use becomes more automatic, freeing children from the immediate linguistic context so they can think about how messages are communicated. During the preschool and early school years, *phonological awareness*—the ability to segment spoken words into smaller units of sound segments, including phonemes and syllables—predicts success at reading and spelling alphabetic languages, in which letters stand for speech sounds (Blachman, 2000). Training children in phonological awareness is a promising technique for encouraging early literacy development.

**metalinguistic awareness**
The ability to think about language as a system.

# milestones
## LANGUAGE DEVELOPMENT

| AGE | PHONOLOGY | SEMANTICS |
|---|---|---|
| Birth–1 year | ♪ Has categorical speech perception.<br><br>♪ Organizes speech sounds into phonemic categories of native language.<br><br>♪ Babbles using intonation and sound patterns resembling those of native language. | ♪ Prefers sound pattern of native language.<br><br>♪ Detects words in speech stream.<br><br>♪ Uses preverbal gestures. |
| 1–2 years | ♪ Uses systematic strategies to simplify word pronunciation. | ♪ Says first words.<br><br>♪ Vocabulary grows to several hundred words. |
| 3–5 years | ♪ Shows great improvement in pronunciation. | ♪ Coins words to fill in for words not yet mastered.<br><br>♪ Understands metaphors based on concrete, sensory comparisons. |
| 6–10 years | ♪ Masters syllable stress patterns signalling subtle differences in meaning. | ♪ At school entry, has vocabulary of about 10 000 words.<br><br>♪ Grasps meanings of words on the basis of definitions.<br><br>♪ Appreciates multiple meanings of words, which enhances understanding of metaphors and humour. |
| 11 years–adulthood | ♪ Masters syllable stress patterns of abstract words. | ♪ Has vocabulary of over 40 000 words that includes many abstract terms.<br><br>♪ Understands subtle, nonliteral word meanings, as in irony and sarcasm. |

As we will see in the final section of this chapter, bilingual children are advanced in metalinguistic awareness (as well as other cognitive skills). But before we conclude with this topic, refer to the Milestones table above, which provides an overview of the many aspects of language development we have considered.

# Bilingualism: Learning Two Languages in Childhood

SINCE 1969, WHEN the Official Languages Act was established, Canada has been a bilingual country, meaning that both English and French have equal status, rights, and privileges at the federal level. For example, Canadians can receive the services

| GRAMMAR | PRAGMATICS | METALINGUISTIC AWARENESS |
|---|---|---|
| Begins to develop sensitivity to natural phrase units.  | Establishes joint attention.<br><br>Engages in vocal exchanges and turn-taking games. |  |
| Combines two words in telegraphic speech.<br><br>As three-word sentences appear, gradually adds grammatical morphemes. | Engages in conversational turn-taking and topic maintenance.  | |
| Forms sentences that reflect adult grammatical categories.<br><br>Continues to add grammatical morphemes in a regular order.<br><br>Masters many complex grammatical structures. | Masters additional conversational strategies, such as the turnabout.<br><br>Begins to grasp illocutionary intent.<br><br>Adjusts speech in accord with social expectations. | Shows the beginnings of metalinguistic awareness.  |
| Refines complex grammatical structures, such as the passive voice and infinitive phrases. | Uses advanced conversational strategies, such as shading.<br><br>Continues to refine understanding of illocutionary intent.<br><br>Engages in effective referential communication in highly demanding contexts. | Displays rapid development of metalinguistic awareness.  |
| Continues to refine complex grammatical structures.  | Referential communication continues to improve. | Continues to refine metalinguistic awareness.  |

of federal institutions in either official language. In addition, the federal, provincial, and territorial governments recognize some nonofficial or heritage languages, particularly Aboriginal ones. Although heritage languages do not have special legal status, government programs encourage their continued use by subsidizing initiatives such as language schools, festivals, and local newspapers.

While the proportion of the Canadian population with fluency in both official languages has risen over the past 30 years, the increase has been most marked among young people. According to the 1996 census, 4.8 million Canadians, or 17 percent of the population, are French–English bilingual (Statistics Canada, Population, 2001). That the younger generation is the most bilingual in Canada's history demonstrates the impact of school-based and other

Approximately 4.8 million Canadians, or 17 percent of the population, are French–English bilingual, compared with slightly over 13 percent in 1971 (Statistics Canada, 1996 Census, 1997). These children and their parents gather to attend a film in Quebec. Many are bilingual—a capacity that enhances cognitive development and metalinguistic skills.

**French immersion**
An education program in which English-speaking students are taught entirely in French.

programs initiated by the provinces and territories with the federal government's support (Canadian Heritage, 2001).

Children can become bilingual in two ways: (1) by acquiring both languages at the same time in early childhood, as Erin did, or (2) by learning a second language after mastering the first. Children of bilingual parents who teach them both languages in early childhood show no special problems with language development. Although initially their vocabularies in each language are smaller than those of monolingual children, they readily catch up. Also, toddlers mix the two languages. But this is not a sign of confusion, since bilingual parents rarely maintain strict language separation. And Fred Genesse of McGill University and others report that by age 2, children use each language more with the parent who customarily speaks that language (Bhatia & Ritchie, 1999; Genesse, 2001).

Early language mixing reflects young children's strong desire to use any means available to communicate. Bilingual preschoolers acquire normal native ability in the language of their surrounding community and good to native ability in the second language, depending on their exposure to it. When school-age children acquire a second language after they already speak a first one, it generally takes them 3 to 5 years to become as competent in the second language as native-speaking agemates (Ramirez et al., 1991).

A large body of carefully conducted investigations shows that bilingualism has positive consequences for development. Children who are fluent in two languages are advanced in cognitive development. They do better than others on tests of selective attention, analytical reasoning, concept formation, and cognitive flexibility (Bialystok, 1999; Hakuta, Ferdman, & Diaz, 1987). Also, their metalinguistic skills are particularly well developed. Studies carried out by Ellen Bialystok of York University and others reveal that bilingual children are more aware that words are arbitrary symbols, more conscious of some aspects of language sounds, and better at noticing errors of grammar and meaning—capacities that enhance reading achievement (Bialystok, 2001; Bialystok & Herman, 1999; Campbell & Sais, 1995).

The advantages of bilingualism provide strong justification for bilingual education programs in schools. Bilingualism provides one of the best examples of how language, once learned, becomes an important tool of the mind and fosters cognitive development. From this perspective, the goals of schooling could reasonably be broadened to include helping all children become bilingual, thereby fostering the cognitive, language, and cultural enrichment of the entire nation. Bilingual education programs in Canada are largely for the English-speaking majority and are intended to promote functional competence in French and English, as well as an appreciation of French-Canadian culture. In contrast, U.S. programs largely serve low-SES ethnic minority students, who benefit from instruction in their native language with gradual introduction of English (Ovando & Collier, 1998). Genesse & Gandara (1999) argue that bilingual education for both cultural majority *and* minority children can help reduce prejudice and foster intergroup harmony. The Social Issues: Education box on the following page examines the Canadian invention of **French immersion** schooling.

## ASK YOURSELF www

**review**  Explain why metalinguistic awareness expands greatly in middle childhood. What might account for bilingual children's advanced metalinguistic skills?

**apply**  Reread the examples of Erin's language at the beginning of this chapter. Were Marilyn and André wise to teach Erin both English and French? Does Erin's mixing of the two languages indicate confusion? Justify your answers with research findings.

# social issues: education

## FRENCH IMMERSION SCHOOLING

ducation in Canada is the responsibility of the provinces and territories, so the curriculum for teaching anglophone children both official languages varies from one province to the next. Approximately 50 percent of Canadian school children learn English or French as a second language (Canadian Heritage, 2001). The majority learn their second language through core programs, meaning that French is taught in a separate class like any other subject. Some students, however, are taught through French immersion schooling (Canadian Heritage, 1996; Lapkin, 1998). In 1998–1999, nearly 200 000 children were enrolled in elementary school French immersion programs, and over 130 000 were in secondary school immersion programs (Statistics Canada, Education, 2001).

In early immersion programs, the approach most frequently offered, English-speaking students typically receive all instruction in French from kindergarten to grade 2, with English introduced in grade 3 (Canadian Heritage, 1999b). Late immersion programs begin in grade 6 or 7. Studies show mixed results when comparing the linguistic accomplishments of children in late and early immersion programs (Hamers & Blanc, 2000; Turnbull et al., 1998). And although neither group of immersion students achieves full competence in reading, comprehending, and communicating in French, both attain high levels of proficiency (Harley & Jean, 1999; Holobow, Genesse, & Lambert, 1991).

French immersion began as a pilot project in St. Lambert, Quebec, in 1965. It has been described as the "glamour story" of the past 30 years of second-language instruction in Canada, representing a determined attempt on the part of anglophones to overcome long-standing difficulties and inhibitions in learning French as a second language. In Quebec, however, where English is *not* an official language, precisely parallel immersion programs are not used to teach English to French-speaking children because of the historic vulnerability of the majority French language (Canadian Heritage, 1999a).

Research shows an initial lag in development of English-language reading and writing skills for those children enrolled in early French immersion, but by the end of grade 3, when English is introduced, French immersion students perform as well or better than those educated entirely in English. And this finding applies regardless of SES and ethnicity (Cummins, 1999; Holobow, Genesse, & Lambert, 1991; Swain & Lapkin, 1991). Collectively, then, the results refute the early prevailing views that children who participate in French immersion are disadvantaged in school performance and that only higher-SES

DICK HEMINGWAY

These Canadian children attend a French immersion program in which they receive instruction entirely in French. After several years, they will also study in English. In French immersion classrooms, children gain not only a functional competence in both French and English but also an appreciation of French-Canadian culture, which helps to build ethnic harmony.

children benefit. Indeed, in response to the success of Canada's French immersion programs, numerous countries have adopted the immersion method for the teaching of French, Spanish, and other languages (Canadian Heritage, 1999b).

# summary

## COMPONENTS OF LANGUAGE

*What are the four components of language?*

- Language consists of four subsystems that children combine into a flexible communication system: (1) **phonology,** the rules governing the structure and sequence of speech sounds; (2) **semantics,** the way underlying concepts are expressed in words; (3) **grammar,** the rules by which words are arranged in sentences and modified to vary their meaning; and (4) **pragmatics,** the rules for engaging in appropriate and effective conversation.

## THEORIES OF LANGUAGE DEVELOPMENT

*Describe and evaluate three major theories of language development.*

- According to the behaviourist perspective, language is learned through operant conditioning and imitation. Behaviourism has difficulty accounting for the speed of language progress and for children's novel, rule-based utterances. However, it has been helpful in treating children with language delays and disabilities.

- Chomsky's nativist perspective proposes a **language acquisition device (LAD)** containing a universal grammar, or storehouse of rules that apply to all languages. The LAD permits children, as soon as they have sufficient vocabulary, to speak grammatically and comprehend sentences in any language to which they are exposed.

- Consistent with Chomsky's ideas, although bottle-nosed dolphins and Bonobo chimps can attain a basic grasp of grammar, a complex language system is unique to humans. Furthermore, language functions are housed in **Broca's** and **Wernicke's areas;** grammatical competence, especially, is localized in the left cerebral hemisphere; and a sensitive period for first- and second-language learning exists. These findings support the notion that language has special biological properties. However, vast diversity among the world's languages and children's gradual mastery of many constructions challenge the nativist perspective.

- Interactionist theories stress that innate abilities, a strong desire to interact with others, and a rich language and social environment combine to promote language development. But debate continues over the precise nature of children's innate abilities. In reality, biology, cognition, and social experience may operate in different balances for each component of language.

## PRELINGUISTIC DEVELOPMENT: GETTING READY TO TALK

*Describe receptivity to language, development of speech sounds, and conversational skills during infancy.*

- Infants are specially prepared for language learning. Newborns are capable of **categorical speech perception** and sensitive to a wider range of **phonemes** than are children and adults. By 6 months, infants focus more intently on the sound categories of their own language. In the second half of the first year, they have begun to analyze the internal structure of sentences and words. **Child-directed speech (CDS)** eases the young child's task of making sense of language.

- Infants begin **cooing** at about 2 months; **babbling,** around 4 months. Over the first year, the range of babbled sounds expands. Then, as infants get ready to talk, intonation and sound patterns start to resemble those of the child's native language. Certain patterns of babbles appear in particular contexts, suggesting that infants are experimenting with the semantic function of language.

- Conversational behaviour emerges in the first few months, as infants and caregivers establish **joint attention** and the adult comments on what the baby sees. Turn-taking is present in early vocal exchanges. By the end of the first year, babies become active participants in turn-taking games and use two preverbal gestures, the **protodeclarative** and **protoimperative,** to influence others' behaviour. Soon, words are uttered and gestures diminish as children make the transition to verbal communication. By the second year, caregiver–child interaction contributes greatly to the transition to language.

## PHONOLOGICAL DEVELOPMENT

*Describe the course of phonological development.*

- First words are influenced partly by what children can pronounce. When learning to talk, children experiment with sounds, sound patterns, and speech rhythms and apply systematic phonological strategies to simplify adult pronunciations. Gradually, minimal words are refined into full words with correct stress patterns. Individual differences in rate of phonological progress exist, depending on the complexity of a language's sound system and the importance of certain sounds for conveying meaning.

- Pronunciation improves greatly as the vocal tract matures and preschoolers engage in active problem solving. Accent patterns signalling subtle differences in meaning are not mastered until middle childhood and adolescence.

## SEMANTIC DEVELOPMENT

*Describe the course of semantic development, noting individual differences.*

- Vocabulary increases rapidly in early childhood; language **comprehension** develops ahead of **production.** First words build on early cognitive and emotional foundations. Between 18 and 24 months, a vocabulary spurt usually takes place. To build vocabulary quickly, children engage in **fast-mapping.**

- Girls show faster early vocabulary growth than do boys, and reserved, cautious toddlers may wait for a time before beginning to speak. Because lower-SES children experience less verbal stimulation, their vocabularies tend to be smaller. Most toddlers use a **referential style** of language learning, in which early words consist largely of names for objects. A few use an

**expressive style,** in which social formulas are common and vocabularies grow more slowly.

- Early vocabularies typically emphasize object words; action and state words appear soon after, an order influenced by cognitive development and adult speech to children. When first learning new words, children make errors of **underextension** and **overextension.** Word coinages and metaphors permit children to expand the range of meanings they can express.

- Vocabulary growth in middle childhood exceeds that of the preschool years. School-age children can grasp word meanings from definitions, and comprehension of metaphor and humour expands. Adolescents' ability to reason abstractly leads to an enlarged vocabulary and appreciation of subtle meanings, as in irony and sarcasm.

*Discuss ideas about how semantic development takes place, including the influence of memory and strategies for word learning.*

- A special part of working memory, a **phonological store** that permits us to retain speech-based information, supports vocabulary growth in early childhood. After age 5, semantic knowledge influences how quickly children form phonological traces, and both factors influence word learning.

- According to **lexical contrast theory,** children figure out the meaning of a new word by contrasting it with ones they already know and assigning it to a gap in their vocabulary. The **principle of mutual exclusivity** explains children's acquisition of some, but not all, early words. In addition, preschoolers engage in **syntactic bootstrapping,** observing how words are used in the structure of sentences to figure out word meanings. They also make use of adults' social cues and directly provided information. Intense disagreement exists over whether children are innately biased to induce word meanings or whether they use the same cognitive strategies they apply to nonlinguistic stimuli.

## GRAMMATICAL DEVELOPMENT

*Describe the course of grammatical development.*

- Between 1½ and 2½ years, children combine two words to express a variety of

meanings. These first sentences are called **telegraphic speech,** since they leave out smaller, less important words. Early two-word combinations probably do not reflect adult grammatical rules.

- As children move beyond two-word utterances, a grammatical explosion takes place. Their speech conforms to the grammatical categories of their language. English-speaking children add **grammatical morphemes** in a consistent order that is a product of both structural and semantic complexity. Once children acquire a regular morphological rule, they occasionally **overregularize,** or extend it to words that are exceptions. Expressions based on auxiliary verbs, such as negatives and questions, are soon mastered.

- Between ages 3 and 6, a variety of complex constructions are added. Still, certain forms, such as the passive voice and subtle pronoun reference, continue to be refined in middle childhood.

*Discuss ideas about how grammatical development takes place, including strategies and environmental supports for mastering new structures.*

- Some experts believe that grammar is a product of general cognitive development. According to one view, children rely on other properties of language to figure out basic grammatical regularities. In **semantic bootstrapping,** they use word meanings to figure out sentence structure.

- Others believe that children master grammar through direct observation of language structure. Connectionist models have tested this idea, but no current artificial neural-network system fully accounts for grammatical development.

- Still others agree with the essence of Chomsky's theory that children are specially tuned for language learning. One idea accepts semantic bootstrapping but proposes that grammatical categories are innately given. Another speculation is that children have a built-in set of procedures for analyzing language, which supports the discovery of grammatical regularities.

- Adults provide children with indirect feedback about grammatical errors through **expansions** and **recasts.** However, the

impact of such feedback on grammatical development has been challenged.

## PRAGMATIC DEVELOPMENT

*Describe the course of pragmatic development, including social influences.*

- Young children are effective conversationalists, and these early skills are fostered through caregiver–child interaction. Conversations with adults consistently predict general measures of language progress.

- Strategies that help sustain interaction, such as **turnabout** and **shading,** are added in early and middle childhood. During this time, children's understanding of **illocutionary intent** improves, and they also acquire more effective **referential communication skills.** Preschoolers are sensitive to **speech registers.** Parents tutor children in politeness routines at an early age, emphasizing the importance of adapting language to social expectations.

## DEVELOPMENT OF METALINGUISTIC AWARENESS

*Describe the development of metalinguistic awareness, noting its influence on language and literacy skills.*

- Preschoolers show the beginnings of **metalinguistic awareness,** and their understandings are good predictors of vocabulary and grammatical development. Major advances in metalinguistic skills take place in middle childhood. Phonological awareness predicts reading and spelling achievement.

## BILINGUALISM: LEARNING TWO LANGUAGES IN CHILDHOOD

*How does bilingualism affect language and cognitive development, and what evidence supports bilingual education?*

- Children fluent in two languages score higher in analytical reasoning, concept formation, cognitive flexibility, and metalinguistic awareness. These advantages provide strong justification for bilingual education, including **French immersion.**

# important terms and concepts

babbling (p. 365)
Broca's area (p. 359)
categorical speech perception (p. 363)
child-directed speech (CDS) (p. 364)
comprehension (p. 370)
cooing (p. 365)
expansions (p. 380)
expressive style (p. 371)
fast-mapping (p. 371)
French immersion (p. 388)
grammar (p. 354)
grammatical morphemes (p. 376)
illocutionary intent (p. 382)
joint attention (p. 365)

language acquisition device (LAD)
   (p. 356)
lexical contrast theory (p. 375)
metalinguistic awareness (p. 385)
overextension (p. 373)
overregularization (p. 378)
phoneme (p. 363)
phonological store (p. 374)
phonology (p. 354)
pragmatics (p. 355)
principle of mutual exclusivity (p. 375)
production (p. 370)
protodeclarative (p. 365)
protoimperative (p. 366)

recasts (p. 380)
referential communication skills
   (p. 382)
referential style (p. 371)
semantic bootstrapping (p. 380)
semantics (p. 354)
shading (p. 382)
speech registers (p. 384)
syntactic bootstrapping (p. 375)
telegraphic speech (p. 376)
turnabout (p. 382)
underextension (p. 373)
Wernicke's area (p. 359)

"My Father"
A. Same
12 years, Afghanistan

Reprinted by permission from
The International Museum of
Children's Art, Oslo, Norway.

When parents care for infants and toddlers with love and sensitivity, the baby's feelings of security and competence build quickly. The importance of early relationships for emotional and social development is a major theme of Chapter 10.

# *ten*

# Emotional
# Development

ON A SPRING DAY, 4-month-old Zach, cradled in the arms of his father, followed by 13-month-old Emily and 23-month-old Brenda, led by their mothers, arrived at the door of my classroom, which had been transformed into a playroom for the morning. My students and I spent the next hour watching closely. Especially captivating were the children's emotional reactions to people and objects. As Zach's dad lifted him in the air, Zach responded with a gleeful grin. A tickle followed by a lively kiss on the tummy produced an excited giggle. When I offered Zach a rattle, his brows knit, his face sobered, and he eyed it intently as he mobilized all his energies to reach for it.

Transferred to my arms and then to the laps of students, Zach remained at ease (although he reserved a particularly broad smile for his father). In contrast, Emily and Brenda were wary of this roomful of strangers. I held out a toy and coaxed Emily toward it. She pulled back and glanced at her mother, as if to check whether the new adult and tantalizing object were safe to explore. When her mother encouraged, Emily approached cautiously and accepted the toy. A greater capacity to understand the situation, combined with her mother's explanations, helped Brenda adjust, and soon she was engrossed in play. During the hour, Brenda displayed a wide range of emotions, including embarrassment at seeing chocolate on her chin in a mirror and pride as I remarked on the tall block tower she had built.

Until recently, research on the emotional side of development was overshadowed by cognition, but today great excitement surrounds the topic. Our discussion brings together several lines of evidence. First, we discuss the functions of emotions and chart age-related changes in emotional expression and understanding. As we do, we will account for Zach, Emily, and Brenda's expanding emotional capacities. Next, our attention turns to individual differences in temperament and personality. We examine biological and environmental contributions to these differences and their consequences for future development. Finally, we take up attachment to the caregiver, the infant's first affectional tie. We will see how the feelings of security that grow out of this bond provide a vital source of support for the child's exploration, sense of independence, and expanding social relationships.

# The Functions of Emotions

CONSIDER EVENTS IN YOUR LIFE that generate emotion. In the past day or so, you may have felt happy, sad, fearful, or angry in response to a grade on a test or a conversation with a friend. These events, and others, generate emotion because, at least for the moment, you care about their outcome. The emotion, in turn, prepares you for action. For example, happiness leads you to approach a situation, sadness to passively withdraw, fear to actively move away, and anger to overcome obstacles. An **emotion,** then, expresses your readiness to establish, maintain, or change your relation to the environment on a matter of importance to you (Saarni, Mumme, & Campos, 1998).

New theories, gathered under the **functionalist approach,** emphasize that the broad function of emotions is to prompt action in the service of personal goals (Barrett & Campos, 1987; Frijda, 2000; Izard, 1991; Saarni, Mumme, & Campos, 1998). Events can become personally relevant in several ways. First, you may already have a goal in mind, such as doing well on a test, so the test situation prompts strong emotion. Second, others' social behaviour may alter a situation's significance for you, as when your friend visits and you respond warmly to her friendly greeting. Third, a sensation or a state of mind—any sight, sound, taste, smell, touch, memory, or imagining—can become personally relevant, yielding positive emotion if it is pleasant and negative emotion if it is unpleasant. Your emotional reaction affects your desire to repeat the experience. Functionalist theorists view emotions as central in all aspects of human activity—cognitive processing, social behaviour, and even physical health. To clarify this idea, let's examine the functions of emotions—the way they organize and regulate experience in each domain.

## EMOTIONS AND COGNITIVE PROCESSING

Emotional reactions can lead to learning that is essential for survival. For example, a newly walking toddler does not need to receive a shock from an electric outlet or fall down a staircase to learn to avoid these dangers. Instead, the caregiver's highly charged command prompts the child to acquire these self-protective behaviours.

To illustrate further, think about your own feelings on occasions in which you did poorly on a test even though you spent many hours preparing. Did anxiety affect your performance? Among children and adults, very high or low anxiety impairs thinking, whereas moderate anxiety can be facilitating (Sarason, 1980). Emotions also have powerful effects on memory. For example, children highly upset by an inoculation at the doctor's office tend to remember the event more clearly than do less stressed children (Goodman et al., 1991). At the same time, an agitated child is less likely to be aware of happenings in her broader surroundings (Bugental et al., 1992).

Most functionalist theorists view the relationship between emotion and cognition as bidirectional—a dynamic interplay that is evident in the first half-year of life (Lewis, 1999). In one study, 2- to 8-month-olds were trained to pull a string attached to their wrists, which produced a slide of a smiling baby and a recording of a children's song. As the infants learned the task, they responded with interest, happiness, and surprise—expressions reflecting pleasure at mastering a new contingency. Next, a short period followed in which pulling the string no

**emotion**
An expression of readiness to establish, maintain, or change one's relation to the environment on a matter of personal importance.

**functionalist approach**
A perspective emphasizing that the broad function of emotions is to prompt action in the service of personal goals and that emotions are central forces in all aspects of human activity.

longer activated the attractive stimuli. The babies' emotional reactions quickly changed—mostly to anger but occasionally to sadness. When the contingency was restored, infants who had reacted angrily showed renewed interest and enjoyment, pulling eagerly to produce the stimuli. In contrast, sad babies withdrew, displaying reduced involvement in the task (Lewis, Sullivan, & Ramsay, 1992). Emotions were interwoven with cognitive processing. They served both as outcomes of mastery and as the foundation for infants' next learning phase.

## EMOTIONS AND SOCIAL BEHAVIOUR

Children's emotional signals, such as smiling, crying, and attentive interest, affect others' behaviour in powerful ways. Similarly, emotional reactions of others regulate children's social behaviour.

For example, careful analyses of caregiver–infant interaction reveal that by 3 months, a complex communication system is in place in which each partner responds in an appropriate and carefully timed fashion to the other's cues (Tronick & Cohn, 1989; Weinberg et al., 1999). In several studies, researchers disrupted this exchange of emotional signals by having the parent assume either a still-faced, unreactive pose or a depressed emotional state. Infants tried facial expressions, vocalizations, and body movements to get their mother or father to respond again. When these efforts failed, they turned away, frowned, and cried (Hernandez & Carter, 1996; Moore, Cohn, & Campbell, 2001). At Queen's University researchers found that the still-face reaction is identical in U.S., Canadian, and Chinese babies, suggesting that it might be a built-in withdrawal response to caregivers' lack of communication (Kisilevsky et al., 1998). To find out more about the powerful impact of maternal depression on children's functioning, refer to the From Research to Practice box on page 398.

## EMOTIONS AND HEALTH

Much research indicates that emotions influence children's physical well-being. For example, in Chapter 5 we discussed two childhood growth disorders—nonorganic failure to thrive and psychosocial dwarfism—that result from emotional deprivation. And many other studies indicate that persistent psychological stress is associated with a variety of health difficulties from infancy into adulthood. For example, stress elevates heart rate and blood pressure and depresses the immune response—reactions that may explain its relationship with cardiovascular disease, infectious illness, and several forms of cancer. Stress also reduces digestive activity as blood flows to the brain, heart, and extremities to mobilize the body for action. Consequently, it can cause gastrointestinal difficulties, including constipation, diarrhea, colitis, and ulcers (Donatelle & Davis, 2000; Friedman, 2002).

In a dramatic demonstration of the emotion–health relationship, researchers studied children adopted into Canadian homes who had been exposed to chronic stress as a result of at least 8 months of early rearing in extremely deprived Romanian orphanages. When compared with agemates adopted shortly after birth, the children showed heightened reactivity to stress, as indicated by elevated concentration of the stress hormone cortisol in their saliva—a physiological response linked to illness and behaviour problems. The longer children spent in orphanage care, the higher their cortisol levels (Gunnar, 2000).

Furthermore, even after catching up in height and weight in a caring adoptive home, some orphanage children display highly anxious food-related behaviours that persist for years. These include hoarding, difficulty responding to physical cues of fullness, and extreme distress when their access to food is temporarily threatened (Gunnar, Bruce, & Grotevant, 2000; Johnson, 2000).

Fortunately, sensitive adult care reduces stress reactivity in emotionally traumatized children. In one study, researchers devised a special intervention for difficult-to-manage preschoolers with disrupted home lives. For 10 weeks, a therapist worked with the children in a weekly playgroup, and their foster parents received extensive social support and coaching in parenting skills. After 5 weeks, the children's cortisol levels and behaviour problems declined. In contrast, children in regular foster care who received no intervention showed a rise in cortisol production and difficult behaviours (Fisher et al., 2000).

DAVID J. SAMS/STOCK BOSTON

Emotions profoundly affect cognitive processing. This toddler's interest and delight at the sight, sound, and feel of autumn leaves motivate him to approach, explore, and learn about his surroundings.

## *from research to practice*

### MATERNAL DEPRESSION AND CHILD DEVELOPMENT

*a*pproximately 8 to 10 percent of women experience chronic depression—mild to severe feelings of sadness, distress, and withdrawal that continue for months or years. Often the beginnings of this emotional state cannot be pinpointed; it simply becomes a part of the person's daily life. In other instances, it emerges or strengthens after childbirth but fails to subside as the new mother adjusts to hormonal changes in her body and gains confidence in caring for her baby. Stella experienced this type—called *postpartum depression.* Although genetic makeup increases the risk of depressive illness, social and cultural factors are also involved (Cooper & Murray, 1998; Swendsen & Mazure, 2000).

During Stella's pregnancy, her husband Kyle's lack of interest in the baby caused her to worry that having a child might be a mistake. Shortly after Lucy was born, Stella's mood plunged. She was anxious and weepy, overwhelmed by Lucy's needs, and angry that she no longer had control over her own schedule. When Stella approached Kyle about her own fatigue and his unwillingness to help with the baby, he snapped that she overreacted to every move he made. Stella's friends, who did not have children, stopped by once to see Lucy and did not call again.

Stella's depressed mood quickly affected her baby. In the weeks after birth, infants of depressed mothers sleep poorly, are less attentive and responsive to their surroundings, and show continuously elevated stress hormone levels (Field, 1998). The more extreme the depression and the greater the number of stressors in a mother's life (such as marital discord, little or no social support, and poverty), the more the parent–child relationship suffers (Goodman et al., 1993). Stella, for example, rarely smiled and talked to

Lucy, who responded to her mother's sad, vacant gaze by turning away, crying, and often looking sad or angry herself (Campbell, Cohn, & Meyers, 1995; Murray & Cooper, 1997). Each time this happened, Stella felt guilty and inadequate, and her depression deepened. By 6 months of age, Lucy showed emotional symptoms common in babies of depressed mothers—a negative, irritable mood and attachment difficulties (Martins & Gaffan, 2000).

When maternal depression persists, the parent–child relationship worsens. Depressed mothers view their infants more negatively than do independent observers—a bias that endures through the preschool years (Hart, Field, & Roitfarb, 1999). Furthermore, parents with depression use inconsistent discipline—sometimes lax, at other times too forceful—a pattern that reflects their disengaged as well as hostile behaviour (Zahn-Waxler et al., 1990). As we will see in later chapters, children who experience these maladaptive parenting practices often have serious adjustment problems. To avoid their parent's insensitivity, they sometimes withdraw into a depressed mood themselves. Or they mimic their parent's anger and become impulsive and antisocial (Conger, Patterson, & Ge, 1995; Murray et al., 1999).

Over time, the parenting behaviours just described lead children to develop a negative world view—one in which they lack confidence in themselves and perceive their parents and other people as threatening. Children who constantly feel in danger are likely to become overly aroused in stressful situations, easily losing control in the face of cognitive and social challenges (Cummings & Davies, 1994b). Although children of depressed parents may inherit this tendency for emotional and behav-

ioural problems, quality of parenting is a major factor in their adjustment.

Early treatment of maternal depression is vital to prevent the disorder from interfering with the parent–child relationship and harming children. Stella described her tearfulness, fatigue, and inability to comfort Lucy to her doctor. He referred her to a special program for depressed mothers and their babies. A counsellor worked with the family for several months, helping Stella and Kyle with their marital problems and encouraging them to be more sensitive and patient with Lucy. At times, antidepressant medication is prescribed. In most cases, short-term treatment is successful (Steinberg & Bellavance, 1999). When mothers do not respond easily to treatment, a warm relationship with the father or another caregiver can safeguard children's development.

Depression disrupts parents' capacity to engage with children. This infant tries hard to get his despondent mother to react. If her unresponsiveness continues, the baby is likely to turn away, cry, and become negative and irritable himself. Over time, this disruption in the parent–child relationship leads to serious emotional and behavioural problems.

PHOTOEDIT

### OTHER FEATURES OF THE FUNCTIONALIST APPROACH

According to the functionalist approach, emotions are also important in the emergence of self-awareness. For example, the interest and excitement babies display when acting on novel objects help them develop a *sense of self-efficacy*—an awareness that they can affect events in their surrounding world (Harter, 1998). Once a sense of self appears, the door opens to new emotional reactions. Recall Brenda's expressions of pride and embarrassment—two feeling states that have to do with evaluations of the self's goodness or badness (Saarni, Mumme, & Campos, 1998).

Finally, the functionalist approach points out that to adapt to their physical and social worlds, children must gradually control their emotions, just as they do their motor, cognitive, and social behaviour. And they learn when it is acceptable to communicate feelings in their culture. As a result, by late childhood few emotions are expressed as openly and freely as they were in the early years of life. With these factors in mind, let's chart the course of emotional development.

## ASK YOURSELF

**review**    Cite a research-based example of the impact of emotions on children's (1) cognitive processing, (2) social behaviour, and (3) physical health.

**apply**    Jeannine's husband recently moved out. Lonely, depressed, and anxious about finances, Jeannine spends most of her days caring for 3-month-old Jacob. How might Jeannine's state of mind affect Jacob's emotional development? What can be done to help Jacob?

# Development of Emotional Expression

SINCE INFANTS CANNOT DESCRIBE their feelings, determining exactly which emotions they are experiencing is a challenge. Although vocalizations and body movements provide some information, facial expressions offer the most reliable cues. Cross-cultural evidence reveals that people around the world associate photographs of different facial gestures with emotions in the same way (Ekman & Friesen, 1972). These findings, which suggest that emotional expressions are built-in social signals, inspired researchers to analyze infants' facial patterns to determine the range of emotions they display at different ages. A commonly used method for doing so, the MAX System, is illustrated in Figure 10.1.

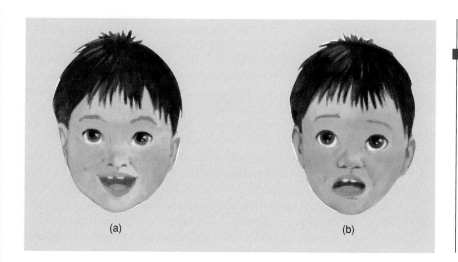

(a)                              (b)

**FIGURE 10.1**

**Which emotions are these babies displaying?**
The MAX (Maximally Discriminative Facial Movement) System is a widely used method for classifying infants' emotional expressions. Facial muscle movements are carefully rated to determine their correspondence with basic feeling states, since people around the world associate different facial gestures with emotions in the same way. For example, cheeks raised and corners of the mouth pulled back and up signal happiness (a). Eyebrows raised, eyes widened, and mouth opened with corners pulled straight back denote fear (b). (From Izard, 1979.)

Basic emotions have a long evolutionary history of adaptation. Nonhuman primates also display them. This mother chimpanzee relaxes with a blissful expression of happiness as she cuddles her 8-day-old infant. Like human infants, baby chimps respond positively to their mother's happy emotional messages, which foster a warm, supportive parent–infant bond.

Do infants come into the world with the ability to express **basic emotions**—those that can be directly inferred from facial expressions, such as happiness, interest, surprise, fear, anger, sadness, and disgust? Basic emotions are universal both in humans and our primate ancestors and have a long evolutionary history of adaptation. Although signs of some basic emotions are present, babies' earliest emotional life consists of little more than two global arousal states: attraction to pleasant stimulation and withdrawal from unpleasant stimulation (Fox, 1991; Sroufe, 1979). Over time, emotions become clear, well-organized signals.

The *dynamic systems perspective* helps us understand how this happens. According to this view, children coordinate separate skills into more effective systems as the central nervous system develops and the child's goals and experiences change (see Chapter 4). Videotaping the facial expressions of her daughter from 6 to 14 weeks, Linda Camras (1992) found that in the early weeks, the infant displayed a fleeting angry face as she was about to cry and a sad face as her crying waned. These expressions first appeared on the way to or away from full-blown distress and were not clearly linked to the baby's experiences and desires. With age, she was better able to sustain an angry signal as she encountered a blocked goal and a sad signal when she could not overcome an obstacle.

Around 6 months, face, gaze, voice, and posture form distinct, coherent patterns that vary meaningfully with environmental events. For example, babies typically respond to their mother's playful interaction with a joyful face, positive vocalizations, and mouthing of body parts. In contrast, an unresponsive mother often evokes a sad face, fussy vocalizations, and a drooping body (sending the message, "I'm despondent") or an angry face, crying, and "pick-me-up" gestures (as if to say, "Change this unpleasant event!"). In sum, by the middle of the first year, emotional expressions are well organized and specific—and therefore able to tell us a great deal about the infant's internal state (Weinberg & Tronick, 1994).

Four emotions—happiness, anger, sadness, and fear—have received the most research attention. Let's see how they develop.

## HAPPINESS

Happiness—first in terms of blissful smiles and later through exuberant laughter—contributes to many aspects of development. Infants smile and laugh when they achieve new skills, expressing their delight in cognitive and motor mastery. The smile also encourages caregivers to be affectionate and stimulating, so the baby smiles even more. Happiness binds parent and baby into a warm, supportive relationship that fosters the infant's developing competence.

During the early weeks, newborn babies smile when full, during REM sleep, and in response to gentle touches and sounds, such as stroking of the skin, rocking, and the mother's soft, high-pitched voice. By the end of the first month, infants smile at interesting sights, but these must be dynamic and eye-catching, such as a bright object jumping suddenly across the baby's field of vision. Between 6 and 10 weeks, the human face evokes a broad grin called the **social smile,** which is soon accompanied by pleasurable cooing (Sroufe & Waters, 1976). These changes parallel the development of infant perceptual capacities—in particular, babies' increasing sensitivity to visual patterns, including the human face (see Chapter 4).

By 2 to 3 months, infants smile and coo when they discover a contingency between their behaviour and an event, such as a foot kick that makes a mobile move or a nod that results in a knee bounce (Watson, 1972). Soon babies smile most when interacting with people. In a Canadian study, 3-month-olds were presented with four facial stimuli, each of which responded contingently to their behaviour: an unfamiliar adult and three hand puppets that varied in resemblance to the human face. Although infants looked with just as much interest at each stimulus, they reserved frequent grins (as well as vocalizations) for the adult (see Figure 10.2)

**basic emotions**
Emotions that can be directly inferred from facial expressions (such as happiness, interest, surprise, fear, anger, sadness, and disgust), that are universal in humans and in our primate ancestors, and that have a long evolutionary history of adaptation.

**social smile**
The smile evoked by the stimulus of the human face. First appears between 6 and 10 weeks.

(Ellsworth, Muir, & Hains, 1993). They clearly identified human beings as having unique, social qualities.

Laughter, which appears around 3 to 4 months, reflects faster processing of information than does smiling. But like smiling, the first laughs occur in response to very active stimuli, such as the parent saying playfully, "I'm gonna get you!" and kissing the baby's tummy. As infants understand more about their world, they laugh at events that contain subtler elements of surprise, such as a soundless game of peek-aboo (Sroufe & Wunsch, 1972).

By the middle of the first year, infants smile and laugh more when interacting with familiar people, a preference that strengthens the parent–child bond. Like adults, 10- to 12-month-olds have several smiles, which vary with context. They show a broad, cheek-raised smile to a parent's greeting, a reserved, muted smile to a friendly stranger, and a mouth-open smile during stimulating play (Dickson, Fogel, & Messinger, 1998). During the second year, the smile becomes a deliberate social signal. Toddlers break their play with an interesting toy to communicate their delight to an attentive adult (Jones & Raag, 1989).

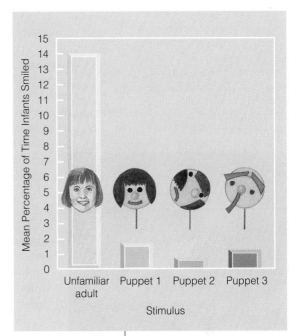

FIGURE 10.2

**Three-month-old infants' smiling at an unfamiliar adult and three hand puppets varying in resemblance to the human face.** Researchers at Queen's University found that although equally interested in each stimulus, infants spent much more time smiling at the human face. By 3 months, they smile most often when interacting with people. (From C. P. Ellsworth, D. W. Muir, & S. M. J. Hains, 1993, "Social Competence and Person–Object Differentiation: An Analysis of the Still-Face Effect," *Developmental Psychology, 29,* p. 70. Copyright © 1993 by the American Psychological Association. Reprinted by permission.)

## ANGER AND SADNESS

Newborn babies respond with generalized distress to a variety of unpleasant experiences, including hunger, painful medical procedures, changes in body temperature, and too much or too little stimulation (see Chapter 4). From 4 to 6 months into the second year, angry expressions increase in frequency and intensity. Older infants react with anger in a wider range of situations—for example, when an interesting object or event is removed, their arms are restrained, the caregiver leaves for a brief time, or they are put down for a nap (Camras et al., 1992; Stenberg & Campos, 1990).

Why do angry reactions increase with age? Cognitive and motor development are intimately involved. As infants acquire the capacity for intentional behaviour (see Chapter 6), they value control over their own actions and the effects they produce (Alessandri, Sullivan, & Lewis, 1990). Older infants can also better identify the agent of a painful stimulus or blocked goal. Consequently, their anger is particularly intense when a caregiver from whom they have come to expect warm behaviour causes discomfort (Stenberg, Campos, & Emde, 1983). The rise in anger is also adaptive. New motor capacities permit babies to use the energy mobilized by anger to defend themselves or overcome obstacles (Izard & Ackerman, 2000). At the same time, anger motivates caregivers to ease a baby's distress, and in the case of separation, may discourage them from leaving again soon.

Expressions of sadness also occur in response to pain, removal of an object, and brief separations, but they are less frequent than anger (Alessandri, Sullivan, & Lewis, 1990; Izard, Hembree, & Huebner, 1987; Shiller, Izard, & Hembree, 1986). In contrast, sadness is common when infants are deprived of a familiar, loving caregiver or when caregiver–infant communication is seriously disrupted (refer again to the From Research to Practice box on page 398).

## FEAR

Like anger, fear rises during the second half of the first year. Older infants hesitate before playing with a new toy that they would have grasped immediately at an earlier age. And as we saw in Chapter 4, newly crawling infants soon show fear of heights. But the most frequent expression of fear is to unfamiliar adults, a reaction called **stranger anxiety.**

Many infants and toddlers are quite wary of strangers, although the reaction does not always occur. It depends on several factors: the infant's temperament (some babies are generally more fearful), past experiences with strangers, and the current situation (Thompson & Limber, 1991). When an unfamiliar adult picks up the infant in a new setting, stranger anxiety is likely. But if the adult sits still while the baby moves around and a parent remains

**stranger anxiety**
The infant's expression of fear in response to unfamiliar adults. Appears in many babies after 6 months of age.

This newly walking 1-year-old explores unfamiliar territory confidently, as long as his mother serves as a secure base to which he can return should he become uneasy or frightened. The rise in fear after 6 months of age holds in check infants' compelling urge to venture away from a caregiver.

PHOTOEDIT

nearby, infants often show positive and curious behaviour (Horner, 1980). The stranger's style of interaction—expressing warmth, holding out an attractive toy, playing a familiar game, and approaching slowly rather than abruptly—reduces the baby's fear.

Culture can modify stranger anxiety through infant-rearing practices. Maternal deaths are high among the Efe hunters and gatherers of Zaire, Africa. To ensure infant survival, a collective caregiving system exists in which, beginning at birth, Efe babies are passed from one adult to another. Consequently, Efe infants show little stranger anxiety (Tronick, Morelli, & Ivey, 1992). In contrast, in Israeli kibbutzim (cooperative agricultural settlements), living in an isolated community subject to terrorist attacks has led to widespread wariness of strangers. By the end of the first year, when infants look to others for cues about how to respond emotionally, kibbutz babies display far greater stranger anxiety than do their city-reared counterparts (Saarni, Mumme, & Campos, 1998).

The rise in fear after 6 months of age keeps newly crawling and walking babies' enthusiasm for exploration in check. Once wariness develops, babies use the familiar caregiver as a **secure base** from which to explore and a haven of safety when distress occurs. As part of this adaptive system, encounters with strangers lead to two conflicting tendencies in the baby: approach (indicated by interest and friendliness) and avoidance (indicated by fear). The infant's behaviour is a matter of a balance between the two.

Eventually, stranger anxiety and other fears decline as cognitive development permits toddlers to discriminate more effectively between threatening and non-threatening people and situations. This change is also adaptive, since adults other than caregivers will soon be important in children's development. Fear also wanes as children acquire a wider array of strategies for coping with it, as we will see shortly when we discuss emotional self-regulation.

## SELF-CONSCIOUS EMOTIONS

Besides basic emotions, humans are capable of a second, higher-order set of feelings, including shame, embarrassment, guilt, envy, and pride. These are called **self-conscious emotions** because each involves injury to or enhancement of our sense of self. For example, when we are ashamed or embarrassed, we feel negatively about our behaviour or accomplishments, and we want to retreat so others will no longer notice our failings. Guilt occurs when we know that we have harmed someone and we want to correct the wrongdoing and repair the relationship. In contrast, pride reflects delight in the self's achievements, and we are inclined to tell others what we have accomplished and take on further challenges (Saarni, Mumme, & Campos, 1998).

Self-conscious emotions appear at the end of the second year, as the sense of self emerges. Shame and embarrassment can be seen as 18- to 24-month-olds lower their eyes, hang their heads, and hide their faces with their hands. Guiltlike reactions are also evident; one 22-month-old returned a toy she had grabbed and patted her upset playmate. Pride emerges around this time, and envy is present by age 3 (Barrett, 1998; Lewis et al., 1989).

Besides self-awareness, self-conscious emotions require an additional ingredient: adult instruction in when to feel proud, ashamed, or guilty. The situations in which adults encourage these feelings vary from culture to culture. In most of North America, children are taught to feel pride over personal achievement, such as winning a game or getting good grades. Among the Zuni Indians, shame and embarrassment occur in response to purely individual success, whereas pride is evoked by generosity, helpfulness, and sharing (Benedict, 1934b). In Japan, lack of concern for others—a parent, a teacher, or an employer—is cause for intense shame (Lewis, 1992).

By 3 years of age, self-conscious emotions are clearly linked to self-evaluation (Lewis, 1995; Stipek, 1995). Preschoolers show much more pride when they succeed on difficult rather than easy tasks and much more shame when they fail simple rather than hard tasks (Lewis, Alessandri, & Sullivan, 1992). Parenting behaviour influences these early self-evaluative reactions. Parents who repeatedly give feedback about the worth of the child and

**secure base**
The use of the familiar caregiver as a base from which the infant confidently explores the environment and to which the infant returns for emotional support.

**self-conscious emotions**
Emotions that involve injury to or enhancement of the sense of self. Examples are shame, embarrassment, guilt, envy, and pride.

her performance ("That's a bad job! I thought you were a good girl") have children who experience self-conscious emotions intensely—more shame after failure and pride after success. In contrast, parents who focus on how to improve performance ("You did it this way; you should have done it that way") induce moderate, more adaptive levels of shame and pride and greater persistence on difficult tasks (Kelley, Brownell, & Campbell, 2000; Lewis, 1998).

Beginning in early childhood, intense shame is associated with feelings of personal inadequacy ("I'm stupid," "I'm a terrible person") and is linked to maladjustment—withdrawal and depression as well as intense anger and aggression at others who participated in the shame-evoking situation (Lindsay-Hartz, de Rivera, & Mascolo, 1995; Reimer, 1996). In contrast, guilt—as long as it occurs in appropriate circumstances and shame does not accompany it—is related to good adjustment, perhaps because guilt helps children resist harmful impulses. Guilt also motivates a misbehaving child to repair the damage and behave more considerately in the future (Ferguson et al., 1999; Tangney, 2001).

The conditions under which children feel proud or guilty change as they develop inner standards of excellence and good behaviour. Unlike preschoolers, school-age children experience these emotions without adult monitoring and encouragement. An adult need not be present for an accomplishment to spark pride and a transgression to arouse guilt (Harter & Whitesell, 1989). Also, school-age children do not report guilt for any mishap, as they did at younger ages, but only for intentional wrongdoing, such as ignoring responsibilities, cheating, or lying (Ferguson, Stegge, & Damhuis, 1991). These changes reflect the older child's more mature sense of morality, a topic we will take up in Chapter 12.

CELIA ROBERTS/EARTH IMAGES

Self-conscious emotions appear at the end of the second year. This Guatemalan 2-year-old undoubtedly feels a sense of pride as she helps care for her elderly grandmother—an activity highly valued in her culture.

## EMOTIONAL SELF-REGULATION

Besides expressing a wider range of emotions, children learn to manage their emotional experiences. **Emotional self-regulation** refers to the strategies we use to adjust our emotional state to a comfortable level of intensity so we can accomplish our goals. It requires several cognitive capacities we discussed in Chapter 7—attention focusing and shifting as well as the ability to inhibit thoughts and behaviour (Eisenberg et al., 1995b; Thompson, 1994). If you ever reminded yourself that an anxiety-provoking event would be over soon or decided not to see a horror movie because it might frighten you, you were engaging in emotional self-regulation.

**INFANCY.** In the early months of life, infants have only a limited capacity to regulate their emotional states. Although they can turn away from unpleasant stimulation and can mouth and suck when their feelings get too intense, they are easily overwhelmed by internal and external stimuli. As a result, they depend on the soothing interventions of caregivers—lifting the distressed infant to the shoulder, rocking, and talking softly.

Rapid development of the cerebral cortex increases the baby's tolerance for stimulation. Between 2 and 4 months, caregivers build on this capacity by initiating face-to-face play and attention to objects. In these interactions, parents arouse pleasure in the baby while adjusting the pace of their behaviour so the infant does not become overwhelmed and distressed. As a result, the baby's tolerance for stimulation increases further (Field, 1994). By 4 months, the ability to shift attention helps infants control emotion. Babies who more readily turn away from unpleasant events are less prone to distress (Axia, Bonichini, & Benini, 1999). At the end of the first year, crawling and walking enable infants to regulate feelings by approaching or retreating from various stimuli.

**emotional self-regulation**
Strategies for adjusting our emotional state to a comfortable level of intensity so we can accomplish our goals.

As caregivers help infants regulate emotion, they contribute to the child's style of self-regulation. Parents who read and respond contingently and sympathetically to the baby's emotional cues have infants who are less fussy, more easily soothed, and more interested in exploration. In contrast, parents who wait to intervene until the infant has become extremely agitated reinforce the baby's rapid rise to intense distress (Eisenberg, Cumberland, & Spinrad, 1998). This makes it harder for parents to soothe the baby in the future—and for the baby to learn to calm herself. When caregivers fail to regulate stressful experiences for infants, brain structures that buffer stress may fail to develop properly, resulting in an anxious, reactive temperament (Nelson & Bosquet, 2000).

By the end of the second year, gains in representation and language lead to new ways of regulating emotion. Although children of this age often redirect their attention for short periods when they are distressed, they are not yet good at using language to comfort themselves (Grolnick, Bridges, & Connell, 1996). But once they can describe their internal states, they can guide caregivers to help them. For example, while listening to a story about monsters, one 22-month-old whimpered, "Mommy, scary." Her mother put down the book and gave her a consoling hug.

we are in this together!

Chris

Many Canadian children felt fearful after witnessing television reports of the September 11, 2001, terrorist attacks on the World Trade Center. Parents and teachers helped them regulate their emotions by talking with them about the events, reassuring them of their safety, and suggesting ways they could help. By drawing portraits and writing messages on boxes, the children involved in this project express their sympathy. The boxes of apple pie were later sent to children in the United States.

**EARLY CHILDHOOD.** After age 2, children frequently talk about their feelings and engage in active efforts to control them. By age 3 to 4, they verbalize a variety of emotional self-regulation strategies. For example, they know they can blunt emotions by restricting sensory input (covering their eyes or ears to block out an unpleasant sight or sound), talking to themselves ("Mommy said she'll be back soon"), or changing their goals (deciding that they don't want to play anyway after being excluded from a game). Children's increasing use of these strategies means fewer emotional outbursts over the preschool years (Thompson, 1990a).

Nevertheless, preschoolers' vivid imaginations, combined with their difficulty separating appearance from reality, make fears of monsters, ghosts, darkness, thunder, and lightning common in early childhood. Parents may need to limit exposure to frightening stories in books and on TV, keep a night-light burning, and offer extra emotional support until the child can better distinguish appearance from reality (see Chapter 6, pages 238–239).

As these interventions suggest, the social environment powerfully affects children's capacity to cope with stress. By watching adults handle their own feelings, preschoolers pick up strategies for regulating emotion. When parents have difficulty controlling anger and hostility, particularly when reacting to their preschoolers' negative emotions, children have continuing problems with regulating emotion that seriously interfere with psychological adjustment (Eisenberg et al., 1999). Adult–child conversations also provide techniques for regulating feelings. When parents prepare children for difficult experiences by describing what to expect and ways to handle anxiety, they offer coping strategies that children can apply.

Besides parenting, temperament affects the development of emotional self-regulation. Children who experience negative emotion very intensely find it harder to inhibit their feelings and shift their focus of attention away from disturbing events. As early as the preschool years, they are more likely to respond with irritation to others' distress and to get along poorly with peers (Eisenberg et al., 1997; Fabes et al., 1999; Walden, Lemerise, & Smith, 1999). As we will see later when we turn to the topic of temperament, because emotionally reactive children are difficult to rear, they often evoke ineffective parenting, which compounds their poor emotional self-regulation.

**MIDDLE CHILDHOOD AND ADOLESCENCE.** Rapid gains in emotional self-regulation occur after school entry. As children compare their accomplishments with their classmates' and care more about peer approval, they must learn to manage negative emotion that threatens their sense of self-worth. Common fears of the school years include poor academic performance and rejection by classmates. And as children begin to understand the realities of the wider world, the possibility of personal harm (being robbed or shot) and media events (wars and disasters) often trouble them (Gullone, 2000).

School-age children's fears are shaped in part by their culture. For example, in China, where self-restraint and complying with social standards are highly valued, more children mention failure and adult criticism as salient fears than in Western countries. Chinese children, however, are not more fearful overall. The number and intensity of fears they report resemble those of Western children (Ollendick et al., 1996).

By age 10, most children have an adaptive set of techniques for managing emotion (Kliewer, Fearnow, & Miller, 1996). In situations where they have some control over an outcome (a difficult test or a friend who is angry at them), they view problem solving and seeking social support as the best strategies. When outcomes are beyond their control (having received a bad grade or awaiting a painful injection at the doctor's office), they opt for distraction or redefine the situation to help them accept current conditions ("Things could be worse. There'll be another test"). Compared with preschoolers, school-age children and adolescents more often use internal strategies to manage emotion, a change due to an improved ability to reflect on their thoughts and feelings (Brenner & Salovey, 1997). Consequently, fears decline steadily (Gullone, 2000).

When emotional self-regulation has developed well, young people acquire a sense of *emotional self-efficacy*—a feeling of being in control of their emotional experience (Saarni, 1999). This fosters a favourable self-image and an optimistic outlook, which further assist them in the face of emotional challenges.

## ACQUIRING EMOTIONAL DISPLAY RULES

In addition to regulating internal emotional states, children must learn to control what they communicate to others. Young preschoolers have some ability to modify their expressive behaviour. For example, when denied a cookie before dinnertime, one 2-year-old paused, picked up her blanket, and walked from the hard kitchen floor to the soft family-room carpet where she could comfortably throw herself and howl loudly!

At first, children modify emotional expressions to serve personal needs, and they exaggerate their true feelings (as this child did to get attention and a cookie). Soon, they damp down their expressive behaviour and substitute other reactions, such as smiling when feeling anxious or disappointed. All societies have **emotional display rules** that specify when, where, and how it is appropriate to express emotions.

As early as the first few months of life, parents encourage infants to suppress negative emotion by often imitating their expressions of interest, happiness, and surprise and rarely imitating their expressions of anger and sadness. Boys get more of this training in controlling unhappiness than do girls, in part because boys have a harder time regulating negative emotion. As a result, the well-known sex difference—females as emotionally expressive and males as emotionally controlled—is promoted at a tender age (Malatesta et al., 1986; Weinberg et al., 1999).

Although caregiver shaping of emotional behaviour begins early, only gradually are children able to conform to display rules. Not until age 3 can they pose an expression they do not feel. These emotional "masks" are largely limited to positive feelings of happiness and surprise. Children of all ages (and adults as well) find it harder to act angry, sad, or disgusted than pleased (Lewis, Sullivan, & Vasen, 1987). Social pressures are responsible for these trends. To foster harmonious relationships, most cultures teach children to communicate positive feelings and inhibit unpleasant emotional displays.

Cultures that stress collectivism place particular emphasis on emotional display rules. For example, compared with North Americans, Japanese and Asian Indian adults place greater importance on masking negative feelings, and they are more emotionally controlled (Matsumoto, 1990; Roland, 1988). Cultures also vary in how adults teach children to control negative emotion. In rural Nepal, Tamang 6- to 9-year-olds, who are steeped in the Buddhist value of inner peace, often say they would feel *tiken* ( "just OK," or calm) in an emotionally charged situation, such as peer aggression or parents arguing. In contrast, Hindu children, who are taught to recognize and suppress negative feelings, are more likely to say they would be upset but would try to hide their emotions (see Figure 10.3) (Cole & Tamang, 1998).

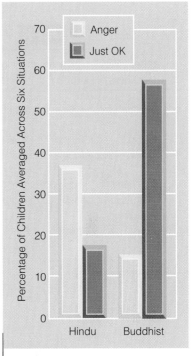

**FIGURE** 10.3

**Hindu and Buddhist children's reports of feeling angry and calm in response to emotionally charged situations.** Hindu children, who are taught to recognize and suppress negative feelings, reported that they would feel more anger. Buddhist children, whose religion values a calm, peaceful disposition, more often stated that they would feel "just OK" and had to engage in less effort to conform to the emotional display rules of masking negative feelings. (Adapted from Cole & Tamang, 1998.)

**emotional display rules**
Rules that specify when, where, and how it is culturally appropriate to express emotions.

As these findings suggest, school-age children become consciously aware of display rules. At first, they say they obey the rules to avoid punishment and gain approval from others. Gradually, they understand the value of display rules for ensuring social harmony (Jones, Abbey, & Cumberland, 1998). School-age children who justify emotional display rules by referring to concern for others' feelings are rated as especially helpful, cooperative, and socially responsive by their teachers and as more likeable by their peers (Garner, 1996; McDowell & Parke, 2000).

## ASK YOURSELF

**review**    Why do many infants show stranger anxiety in the second half of the first year? What factors can increase or decrease wariness of strangers?

**review**    Explain how parenting, language, and temperament contribute to the development of emotional self-regulation.

**apply**    At age 14 months, Reggie built a block tower and gleefully knocked it down. At 2 years of age, Reggie called to his mother and pointed proudly to his tall block tower. What explains this change in Reggie's emotional behaviour?

**connect**    How do children of depressed mothers fare in regulating emotion? (See page 398.) What implications does their self-regulation competence have for handling cognitive and social challenges?

# Understanding and Responding to the Emotions of Others

CHILDREN'S EMOTIONAL EXPRESSIVENESS is intimately tied to their ability to interpret the emotional cues of others. Already we have seen that in the first few months, infants match the feeling tone of the caregiver in face-to-face communication. Early on, babies detect others' emotions through a fairly automatic process of *emotional contagion,* just as we tend to feel happy or sad when we sense these emotions in others. Resonating in this way to another's feelings suggests that babies are beginning to discriminate emotional states.

Between 7 and 10 months, infants perceive facial expressions as organized patterns, and they can match the emotion in a voice with the appropriate face of a speaking person (see Chapter 4). Responding to emotional expressions as organized wholes indicates that these signals have become meaningful to babies. As skill at establishing joint attention improves (see Chapter 9), infants realize that an emotional expression not only has meaning but is a meaningful reaction to a specific object or event (Tomasello, 1999; Walker-Andrews, 1997). Once these understandings are in place, infants actively seek emotional information from trusted caregivers.

## SOCIAL REFERENCING

**Social referencing** involves relying on another person's emotional reaction to appraise an uncertain situation. Beginning at 8 to 10 months, when infants start to evaluate objects and events in terms of their safety and security, social referencing occurs often. Many studies show that a caregiver's emotional expression (happy, angry, or fearful) influences whether a 1-year-old will be wary of strangers, play with an unfamiliar toy, or cross the deep side of the visual cliff (Repacholi, 1998; Sorce et al., 1985; Striano & Rochat, 2000).

Mothers and fathers are equally effective sources of emotional information for babies. When parents are absent, infants and toddlers turn to other familiar adults, especially those who interact with them in an emotionally expressive way (Camras & Sachs, 1991). In fact, a caregiver's emotional cues during moments of uncertainty may be a major reason that she

**social referencing**
Relying on another person's emotional reaction to appraise an uncertain situation.

serves as a secure base for exploration. In an unfamiliar playroom, babies show a strong desire to remain within "eyeshot" of the caregiver. If she turns away, they will leave an attractive set of toys to relocate so they have access to her facial and vocal cues (Carr, Dabbs, & Carr, 1975).

Parents can capitalize on social referencing to teach their youngster how to react to a great many everyday events. Social referencing also permits toddlers to compare their own assessments of events with those of others. By the middle of the second year, they appreciate that others' emotional reactions may differ from their own. Consider a study in which an experimenter showed 14- and 18-month-olds broccoli and crackers. In one condition, she acted delighted with the taste of broccoli but disgusted with the taste of crackers. In the other condition, she showed the reverse preference. When asked to share the food, 14-month-olds offered only the type of food they themselves preferred—usually crackers. In contrast, 18-month-olds gave the experimenter whichever food they saw she liked, regardless of their own preferences (Repacholi & Gopnik, 1997).

In sum, social referencing helps young children move beyond simply reacting to others' emotional messages. They use those signals to find out about others' internal states and preferences and to guide their own actions (Saarni, Mumme, & Campos, 1998).

## EMOTIONAL UNDERSTANDING IN CHILDHOOD

During the preschool years, children's emotional understanding expands rapidly, as their everyday talk about emotions reveals:

*Two-year-old: (After father shouted at child, she became angry, shouting back)* "I'm mad at you, Daddy. I'm going away. Goodbye."

*Two-year-old: (Commenting on another child who refused to take a nap and cried)* "Mom, Annie cry. Annie sad."

*Six-year-old: (In response to mother's comment, "It's hard to hear the baby crying")* "Well, it's not as hard for me as it is for you." *(When mother asked why)* "Well, you like Johnny better than I do! I like him a little, and you like him a lot, so I think it's harder for you to hear him cry."

*Six-year-old: (Trying to comfort a small boy in church whose mother had gone up to communion)* "Aw, that's all right. She'll be right back. Don't be afraid. I'm here." (Bretherton et al., 1986, pp. 536, 540, 541)

**COGNITIVE DEVELOPMENT AND EMOTIONAL UNDERSTANDING.** As the above examples show, early in the preschool years, children refer to causes, consequences, and behavioural signs of emotion, and over time their understanding becomes more accurate and complex (Stein & Levine, 1999). By age 4 to 5, children correctly judge the causes of many basic emotional reactions. When asked why a nearby playmate is happy, sad, or angry, they describe events similar to those identified by adults, such as "He's happy because he's swinging very high" or "He's sad because he misses his mother."

Preschoolers are also good at predicting what a playmate expressing a certain emotion might do next. Four-year-olds know that an angry child might hit someone and that a happy child is more likely to share (Russell, 1990). And they realize that thinking and feeling are interconnected—that a person reminded of a previous sad experience is likely to feel sad (Lagattuta, Wellman, & Flavell, 1997). Furthermore, they come up with effective ways to relieve others' negative feelings, such as hugging to reduce sadness (Fabes et al., 1988). Overall, preschoolers have an impressive ability to interpret, predict, and change others' feelings.

Nevertheless, when asked to explain another's emotional reaction, they are likely to emphasize external factors over internal states as explanations—a balance that changes with age (Levine, 1995; Strayer, 1993). In Chapter 11, we will see that after age 4, children better appreciate that both desires and beliefs motivate behaviour. Once these understandings are in place, children's grasp of how internal factors can trigger emotion expands.

An improved ability to consider conflicting cues when explaining others' emotions develops during middle childhood. For example, when asked what might be happening in a picture showing a happy-faced child with a broken bicycle, 4- and 5-year-olds had difficulty making sense of what was going on. They tended to rely only on the emotional expression ("He's happy because he likes to ride his bike"). By age 8 to 9, children more often reconciled the two cues ("He's happy because his father promised to help fix his broken bike") (Gnepp, 1983; Hoffner & Badzinski, 1989).

Similarly, older children recognize that people can experience more than one emotion at a time—in other words, that they can have "mixed feelings" (Wintre & Vallance, 1994). Preschoolers staunchly deny that two emotions can occur at once, in much the same way that they do not integrate two variables (height and width) in a Piagetian conservation-of-liquid task. When asked about the feelings of a child who pushed a playmate off a swing to get a turn, 4-year-olds report positive emotions—"happy" or "good" because he got what he wanted. By age 8, children explain that in addition to feeling good, the child also feels "sad," "bad," or "angry" because he did harm to another (Arsenio & Kramer, 1992).

This appreciation of mixed emotions helps school-age children realize that people's expressions may not reflect their true feelings (Saarni, 1997). It also promotes awareness of self-conscious emotions. When we feel proud, we combine two sources of happiness—joy over accomplishment and joy that a significant person recognized that accomplishment. When we feel ashamed, we are angry with ourselves for a personal inadequacy and sad at having disappointed another. Many 8- and 9-year-olds understand self-conscious emotions in these ways (Harter, 1999). Notice how thinking about emotions resembles the development of metacognition, or thinking about thought, discussed in Chapter 7. Striking gains in both domains take place in middle childhood.

**SOCIAL EXPERIENCE AND EMOTIONAL UNDERSTANDING.** Although cognitive development fosters emotional understanding, social experience also contributes. The more mothers label emotions and explain them in conversing with preschoolers, the more emotion words children use. Maternal prompting of emotional thoughts, as in "What makes him afraid?" is a good predictor of 2-year-olds' emotion language. Explanations—"He's sad because his dog ran away"—are more important for older preschoolers (Cervantes & Callanan, 1998). Does this remind you of the concept of *scaffolding*—that to be effective, adult teaching must adjust to children's increasing competence?

Preschoolers growing up in families that frequently talk about feelings are better at judging others' emotions when tested at later ages (Denham, Zoller, & Couchoud, 1994; Dunn et al., 1991). Discussions in which family members disagree about feelings are particularly helpful. These dialogues seem to help children step back from the experience of emotion and reflect on its causes and consequences. Furthermore, mothers who establish a warm, relaxed relationship with their 3- to 5-year-old (a secure attachment bond) have children who are advanced in emotional understanding. And such mothers engage in richer conversations about emotions with their preschoolers than do mothers who establish less secure parent–child relationships (Laible & Thompson, 1998, 2000). As preschoolers learn more about emotion from conversing with adults, they transfer this knowledge to other contexts, engaging in more emotion talk with siblings and friends, especially during sociodramatic play (Brown, Donelan-McCall, & Dunn, 1996; Hughes & Dunn, 1998). Make-believe, in turn, contributes to emotional understanding, especially when children play with siblings (Youngblade & Dunn, 1995). The intense nature of the sibling relationship, combined with frequent acting out of feelings in make-believe, makes this an excellent context for early learning about emotions.

Emotion knowledge helps children greatly in their efforts to get along with others. As early as 3 to 5 years of age, it is related to friendly, considerate behaviour, willingness to make amends after harming another, and peer acceptance (Cassidy et al., 1992; Dunn, Brown, & Maguire, 1995; Garner, Jones, & Miner, 1994).

## EMPATHY AND SYMPATHY

In **empathy,** understanding and expression of emotions are interwoven, since both awareness of the emotions of another and the vicarious experience of those emotions are required for an empathic response. Current theorists agree that empathy involves a complex interaction of cognition and affect: the ability to detect different emotions, to take another's perspective, and to *feel with* that person, or respond emotionally in a similar way (Zahn-Waxler & Radke-Yarrow, 1990).

Beginning in the preschool years, empathy is an important motivator of **prosocial,** or **altruistic, behaviour**—actions that benefit another person without any expected reward for the self (Eisenberg & Fabes, 1998). Yet empathy does not always yield acts of kindness and helpfulness. In some children, empathizing with an upset adult or peer escalates into personal distress. In trying to reduce these feelings, the child focuses on himself rather than the person in need. Consequently, empathy does not give way to **sympathy**—feelings of concern or sorrow for another's plight.

### DEVELOPMENT OF EMPATHY.
Empathy has roots early in development. Newborn babies tend to cry in response to the cry of another baby, a reaction that may be the primitive beginnings of an empathic response (Dondi, Simion, & Caltran, 1999). In sensitive, face-to-face communication, infants "connect" emotionally with their caregivers—experiences believed to be the foundation for empathy and concern for others (Zahn-Waxler, 1991).

Like self-conscious emotions, true empathy requires children to understand that the self is distinct from other people. As self-awareness develops, children nearing 2 years of age begin to empathize. They not only sense another's unhappiness but often try to relieve it. For example, one 21-month-old reacted to his mother's simulated sadness by offering comforting words, giving her a hug, trying to distract her with a hand puppet, and asking the experimenter to help (Zahn-Waxler & Radke-Yarrow, 1990).

As language develops, children rely more on words to console others, a change that indicates a more reflective level of empathy. A 6-year-old said this to his mother after noticing her distress at not being able to find a motel after a long day's travel: "You're pretty upset, aren't you, Mom? You're pretty sad. Well, I think it's going to be all right. I think we'll find a nice place and it'll be all right" (Bretherton et al., 1986, p. 540).

Empathic responding increases over the elementary school years because children understand a wider range of emotions and can take multiple cues into account in assessing others' feelings (Ricard & Kamberk-Kilicci, 1995). During late childhood and adolescence, advances in perspective taking permit an empathic response not just to people's immediate distress but also to their general life condition. According to Martin Hoffman (2000), the ability to empathize with the poor, oppressed, and sick is the most mature form of empathy. It requires an advanced form of perspective taking in which the child understands that people lead continuous emotional lives beyond the current situation.

### INDIVIDUAL DIFFERENCES.
Whether empathy occurs and prompts sympathetic, prosocial behaviour or a personally distressed, self-focused response is related to temperament. Hence, twin studies reveal a modest genetic influence (Zahn-Waxler et al., 2001). Children who are sociable, assertive, and good at regulating emotion are most likely to help, share, and comfort others in distress. In contrast, children who are poor emotion regulators less often display sympathetic concern and prosocial behaviour (Eisenberg et al., 1996, 1998).

These differences are evident in children's facial and psychophysiological responses. In a series of studies, children watched videotapes of people in need, such as two children lying on the ground, crying. Children who reacted with facial or physiological markers of sympathy—

During a field trip to the seashore with her preschool classmates, this Australian 3-year-old bursts into tears, and her friend offers comfort. As young children's language skills expand and their ability to take the perspective of others improves, empathy increases and becomes an important motivator of prosocial, or altruistic, behaviour.

ROBERT VAN DER HILST/STONE

**empathy**
The ability to detect different emotions, to take another's perspective and to feel with that person, or respond emotionally in a similar way.

**prosocial,** or **altruistic, behaviour**
Actions that benefit another person without any expected reward for the self.

**sympathy**
An extension of empathy that involves feelings of concern or sorrow for another's plight.

a concerned expression or a decrease in heart rate, suggesting orienting and attention—usually behaved prosocially when offered a chance to help. Children who showed evidence of facial and physiological distress—frowning, lip biting, and a rise in heart rate—were less prosocial (Fabes et al., 1994; Miller et al., 1996). Similarly, empathy is related to brain-wave activity—a mild increase in the left hemisphere (which houses positive emotion) among children showing facial signs of empathy, and a sharp increase in the right hemisphere (which houses negative emotion) among children who lack empathy to another's emotional needs (Jones, Field, & Davalos, 2000; Pickens, Field, & Nawrocki, 2001).

Parenting profoundly influences empathy and sympathy. Parents who are warm and encouraging and who show sensitive, empathic concern for their preschoolers have children who are likely to react in a concerned way to the distress of others—relationships that persist into adolescence and young adulthood (Eisenberg & McNally, 1993; Koestner, Franz, & Weinberger, 1990). Besides modelling sympathy, parents can teach children the importance of kindness and can intervene when they display inappropriate emotion, which predicts high levels of sympathetic responding (Eisenberg et al., 1991; Zahn-Waxler & Radke-Yarrow, 1990).

In contrast, angry, punitive parenting disrupts empathy and sympathy at an early age. In one study, researchers observed physically abused toddlers at a child-care centre to see how they reacted to other children's distress. Compared with nonabused agemates, they rarely showed signs of concern. Instead, they responded with fear, anger, and physical attacks (Klimes-Dougan & Kistner, 1990). The children's reactions resembled the behaviour of their parents, since both responded insensitively to others' distress.

These findings—as well as others discussed so far—reveal wide variations in children's emotional dispositions. As we look closely at these differences, we will discover that they are the combined result of biological and environmental influences. But before we delve into the topic of temperament, turn to the Milestones table on the following page for an overview of the emotional attainments just considered.

## ASK YOURSELF www

**review** What do preschoolers understand about emotion, and how do cognition and social experience contribute to their understanding?

**review** How does empathy change from infancy to adolescence?

**apply** While running, 15-month-old Ellen fell down. She looked at her mother, who smiled and exclaimed, "Oh, wasn't that a funny tumble!" How is Ellen likely to respond emotionally, and why?

**connect** Explain why good emotional self-regulation is vital for empathy to result in sympathy and prosocial behaviour. How can parents promote emotional self-regulation, empathy, and sympathy at the same time?

# Temperament and Development

WHEN WE DESCRIBE ONE PERSON as cheerful and upbeat, another as active and energetic, and still others as calm, cautious, or prone to angry outbursts, we are referring to **temperament**—stable individual differences in quality and intensity of emotional reaction, activity level, attention, and emotional self-regulation (Rothbart & Bates, 1998). Researchers have become increasingly interested in temperamental differences among children, since the psychological traits that make up temperament are believed to form the cornerstone of the adult personality.

The New York Longitudinal Study, initiated in 1956 by Alexander Thomas and Stella Chess, is the most comprehensive study of temperament to date. A total of 141 children were followed from early infancy well into adulthood. Results showed that temperament increases the chances that a child will experience psychological problems or, alternatively, be protected from the effects of a highly stressful home life. However, Thomas and Chess (1977) also found that parenting practices can modify children's emotional styles considerably.

**temperament**
Stable individual differences in quality and intensity of emotional reaction, activity level, attention, and emotional self-regulation.

# milestones

**EMOTIONAL DEVELOPMENT**

| AGE | EMOTIONAL EXPRESSIVENESS | EMOTIONAL UNDERSTANDING |
|-----|--------------------------|--------------------------|
| Birth–6 months | • Signs of almost all basic emotions are present.<br><br>• Social smile emerges.<br><br>• Laughter appears.<br><br>• Expressions of happiness are greater when interacting with familiar people.<br><br>• Emotional expressions are well organized and clearly related to environmental events. | • Capacity to match the feeling tone of the caregiver in face-to-face communication is present.<br><br> |
| 7–12 months | • Anger and fear, especially stranger anxiety, increase.<br><br>• Caregiver is used as a secure base.<br><br>• Emotional self-regulation improves as crawling and walking permit approach and retreat from stimulation. | • Ability to detect the meaning of others' emotional signals emerges.<br><br>• Social referencing develops. |
| 1–2 years | • Self-conscious emotions appear but depend on the monitoring and encouragement of adults.<br><br> | • Appreciation that others' emotional reactions may differ from one's own emerges.<br><br>• Vocabulary of words for talking about feelings expands.<br><br>• Empathy appears. |
| 3–6 years | • Self-conscious emotions are clearly linked to self-evaluation.<br><br>• As representation and language improve, active strategies for regulating emotion develop.<br><br>• Conformity to display rules is indicated by the ability to pose a positive emotion one does not feel. | • Understanding of causes, consequences, and behavioural signs of emotion improves in accuracy and complexity.<br><br>• As language develops, empathy becomes more reflective.<br><br> |
| 7–11 years | • Self-conscious emotions become integrated with inner standards of excellence and good behaviour.<br><br>• Strategies for engaging in emotional self-regulation become more internal and are adjusted to situational demands.<br><br>• Conformity to and conscious awareness of emotional display rules improve. | • Ability to consider conflicting cues when explaining others' emotions emerges.<br><br>• Awareness that people can have mixed feelings and that their expressions may not reflect their true feelings emerges.<br><br>• Empathy increases as emotional understanding improves. |

*Note:* These milestones represent overall age trends. Individual differences exist in the precise age at which each milestone is attained.

10.1

Two Models of Temperament

| THOMAS AND CHESS | | ROTHBART | |
|---|---|---|---|
| **DIMENSION** | **DESCRIPTION AND EXAMPLE** | **DIMENSION** | **DESCRIPTION** |
| Activity level | Proportion of active periods to inactive ones. Some babies are always in motion. Others move about very little. | Activity level | Level of gross motor activity |
| Rhythmicity | Regularity of body functions. Some infants fall asleep, wake up, get hungry, and have bowel movements on a regular schedule, whereas others are much less predictable. | Soothability | Reduction of fussing, crying, or distress in response to soothing techniques by the caregiver or baby |
| Distractibility | Degree to which stimulation from the environment alters behaviour. Some hungry babies stop crying temporarily if offered a pacifier or a toy to play with. Others continue to cry until fed. | Attention span/ persistence | Duration of orienting or interest |
| Approach/ withdrawal | Response to a new object or person. Some babies accept new foods and smile and babble at strangers, whereas others pull back and cry on first exposure. | Fearful distress | Wariness and distress in response to intense or novel stimuli, including time taken to adjust to new situations |
| Adaptability | Ease with which the child adapts to changes in the environment. Although some infants withdraw when faced with new experiences, they quickly adapt, accepting the new food or person on the next occasion. Others continue to fuss and cry. | Irritable distress | Extent of fussing, crying, and showing distress when desires are frustrated |
| Attention span and persistence | Amount of time devoted to an activity. Some babies watch a mobile or play with a toy for a long time, whereas others lose interest after a few minutes. | Positive affect | Frequency of expression of happiness and pleasure |
| Intensity of reaction | Intensity or energy level of response. Some infants laugh and cry loudly, whereas others react only mildly. | | |
| Threshold of responsiveness | Intensity of stimulation required to evoke a response. Some babies startle at the slightest change in sound or lighting. Others take little notice of these changes in stimulation. | | |
| Quality of mood | Amount of friendly, joyful behaviour as opposed to unpleasant, unfriendly behaviour. Some babies smile and laugh frequently when playing and interacting with people. Others fuss and cry often. | | |

*Sources:* Left, Thomas & Chess, 1977; Right, Rothbart, 1981; Rothbart, Ahadi, & Evans, 2000.

These findings stimulated a growing body of research on temperament, including its stability, biological roots, and interaction with child-rearing experiences. Let's begin to explore these issues by looking at the structure, or makeup, of temperament and how it is measured.

### THE STRUCTURE OF TEMPERAMENT

Thomas and Chess's nine dimensions, listed in Table 10.1, served as the first influential model of temperament, inspiring all others that followed. When detailed descriptions of infants' and children's behaviour obtained from parent interviews were rated on these dimensions, certain characteristics clustered together, yielding three types of children:

**easy child**
A child whose temperament is such that he quickly establishes regular routines in infancy, is generally cheerful, and adapts easily to new experiences.

- The **easy child** (40 percent of the sample). This child quickly establishes regular routines in infancy, is generally cheerful, and adapts easily to new experiences.

- The **difficult child** (10 percent of the sample). This child has irregular daily routines, is slow to accept new experiences, and tends to react negatively and intensely.

- The **slow-to-warm-up child** (15 percent of the sample). This child is inactive, shows mild, low-key reactions to environmental stimuli, is negative in mood, and adjusts slowly to new experiences.

Note that 35 percent of the children did not fit any of these categories. Instead, they showed unique blends of temperamental characteristics.

Of the three types, the difficult pattern has sparked the most interest, since it places children at high risk for adjustment problems—both anxious withdrawal and aggressive behaviour in early and middle childhood (Bates, Wachs, & Emde, 1994; Thomas, Chess, & Birch, 1968). Compared with difficult children, slow-to-warm-up children present fewer problems. However, they tend to show excessive fearfulness and slow, constricted behaviour in the late preschool and school years, when they are expected to respond actively and quickly in classrooms and peer groups (Chess & Thomas, 1984; Schmitz et al., 1999).

A second model of temperament, devised by Mary Rothbart (1981), is also shown in Table 10.1. It combines overlapping dimensions of Thomas and Chess and other researchers. For example, "distractibility" and "attention span and persistence" are considered opposite ends of the same dimension and called "attention span/persistence." It also includes a dimension not identified by Thomas and Chess—"irritable distress"—that taps emotional self-regulation. And it deletes overly broad dimensions, such as "rhythmicity," "intensity of reaction," and "threshold of responsiveness" (Rothbart, Ahadi, & Evans, 2000). A child who is rhythmic in sleeping is not necessarily rhythmic in eating or bowel habits. And a child who smiles and laughs quickly and intensely is not necessarily quick and intense in fear or irritability.

Notice how Rothbart's six dimensions represent three underlying components of temperament: (1) emotion ("fearful distress," "irritable distress," "positive affect," and "soothability"); (2) attention ("attention span/persistence"); and (3) action ("activity level"). According to Rothbart, these components form an integrated system of capacities and limitations. Overall, the characteristics shown in Table 10.1 provide a fairly complete picture of the temperamental traits most often studied.

This mother wants her 3-year-old son to put his toys away and turn to another activity—perhaps lunch time or an errand. Transitions seem like crises for this difficult child, who reacts negatively and intensely to disruptions and new experiences.

## MEASURING TEMPERAMENT

Temperament is often assessed through interviews or questionnaires given to parents. Behaviour ratings by pediatricians, teachers, and others familiar with the child, as well as laboratory observations by researchers, have also been used. And researchers are turning to psychophysiological measures for insights into the biological basis of temperament.

Parent reports have been emphasized because of their convenience and parents' depth of knowledge about the child. At the same time, information from parents has been criticized for being biased. For example, parents' prebirth expectations for their infant's temperament affect their later reports (Diener, Goldstein, & Mangelsdorf, 1995). And mothers who are anxious, depressed, and low in self-esteem tend to regard their babies as more difficult (Mebert, 1991; Vaughn et al., 1987). Nevertheless, parent reports are moderately related to laboratory observations of children's behaviour (Rothbart & Bates, 1998). And parent perceptions are useful for understanding the way parents view and respond to their child.

Although they avoid the subjectivity of parent reports, laboratory observations can distort assessments of temperament in other ways. Distress-prone children may become too upset to complete the session. Furthermore, the unfamiliar setting with its restricted range of possible behaviours may lead to biased conclusions. A child who calmly avoids certain experiences at home may become upset if the lab does not permit avoidance (Goldsmith & Rothbart, 1991). Still, researchers can better control children's experiences in the lab. And they can conveniently combine observations of behaviour with psychophysiological measures to gain insight into the origins of temperament.

Most psychophysiological assessments have focused on **inhibited,** or **shy, children,** who react negatively to and withdraw from novel stimuli, and **uninhibited,** or **sociable, children,**

**difficult child**
A child whose temperament is such that she is irregular in daily routines, is slow to accept new experiences, and tends to react negatively and intensely.

**slow-to-warm-up child**
A child whose temperament is such that he is inactive, shows mild, low-key reactions to environmental stimuli, is negative in mood, and adjusts slowly to new experiences.

**inhibited,** or **shy, child**
A child whose temperament is such that she reacts negatively to and withdraws from novel stimuli.

**uninhibited,** or **sociable, child**
A child whose temperament is such that he displays positive emotion to and approaches novel stimuli.

# biology & environment

## BIOLOGICAL BASIS OF SHYNESS AND SOCIABILITY

at age 4 months, Larry and Mitch visited the laboratory of Jerome Kagan, who observed their reactions to a variety of unfamiliar experiences. When exposed to new sights and sounds, such as a moving mobile decorated with colourful toys, Larry tensed his muscles, moved his arms and legs with agitation, and began to cry. Mitch's body remained relaxed and quiet, and he smiled and cooed pleasurably at the excitement around him.

Larry and Mitch returned to the laboratory as toddlers. This time, each experienced procedures designed to induce uncertainty. For example, electrodes were placed on their bodies and blood pressure cuffs on their arms to measure heart rate; toy robots, animals, and puppets moved before their eyes; and unfamiliar people behaved in atypical ways or wore novel costumes. Larry whimpered and quickly withdrew, seeking his mother's protection. Mitch watched with interest, laughed, and approached the toys and strangers.

On a third visit, at age 4½, Larry barely talked or smiled during an interview with an unfamiliar adult. In contrast, Mitch asked questions and communicated his pleasure at each intriguing activity. In a playroom with two unfamiliar peers, Larry pulled back. Mitch made friends quickly.

In longitudinal research on several hundred Caucasian children, Kagan (1998a) found that about 20 percent of 4-month-old babies were easily upset by novelty (like Larry), whereas 40 percent were comfortable, even delighted, with new experiences (like Mitch). About 30 percent of these extreme groups retained their temperamental styles as they grew older (Kagan & Saudino, 2001). Those resembling Larry tended to become fearful, inhibited toddlers and preschoolers; those resembling Mitch developed into outgoing, uninhibited youngsters.

### PHYSIOLOGICAL CORRELATES OF SHYNESS AND SOCIABILITY

Kagan believes that individual differences in arousal of the *amygdala,* an inner brain structure that controls avoidance reactions, contribute to these contrasting temperaments. In shy, inhibited children, novel stimuli easily excite the amygdala and its connections to the cerebral cortex and sympathetic nervous system, which prepares the body to act in the face of threat. The same level of stimulation evokes minimal neural excitation in highly sociable, uninhibited children. In support of this theory, several physiological responses of shy children resemble those of highly timid animals and are known to be mediated by the amygdala:

- *Heart rate.* As early as the first few weeks of life, the heart rates of shy children are consistently higher than those of sociable youngsters, and they speed up further in response to unfamiliar events (Snidman et al., 1995).

- *Cortisol.* Saliva concentration of cortisol, a hormone that regulates blood pressure and is involved in resistance to stress, tends to be higher in shy than sociable children (Gunnar & Nelson, 1994; Kagan & Snidman, 1991).

who display positive emotion to and approach novel stimuli. As the Biology & Environment box reveals, heart rate, hormone levels, and brain waves in the frontal region of the cerebral cortex differentiate children with inhibited and uninhibited temperaments. Investigators do not yet know how or when these measures become interrelated. And as we will see in the following sections, more research is needed to clarify how brain mechanisms combine with experience to support consistency and change in children's temperamental styles.

## STABILITY OF TEMPERAMENT

Many studies provide support for the long-term stability of temperament. Infants and young children who score low or high on attention span, irritability, sociability, or shyness are likely to respond similarly when assessed again several months to a few years later and, occasionally, even into the adult years (Caspi & Silva, 1995; Kochanska & Radke-Yarrow, 1992; Pedlow et al., 1993; Rothbart, Ahadi, & Evans, 2000; Ruff & Rothbart, 1996).

When the evidence as a whole is examined carefully, however, temperamental stability is generally low to moderate (Rothbart & Bates, 1998). Although quite a few children remain the same, a good number change. In fact, some characteristics, such as shyness and

- *Pupil dilation, blood pressure, and skin surface temperature.* Compared with sociable children, shy children show greater pupil dilation, rise in blood pressure, and cooling of the fingertips when faced with novelty (Kagan et al., 1999).

Yet another physiological correlate of approach–withdrawal to people and objects is the pattern of EEG waves in the frontal region of the cerebral cortex. Recall from Chapter 5 that the left cortical hemisphere is specialized to respond with positive emotion, the right hemisphere with negative emotion. Shy infants and preschoolers show greater right than left frontal brain-wave activity; their sociable counterparts show the opposite pattern (Calkins, Fox, & Marshall, 1996; Fox, Calkins, & Bell, 1994). Neural activity in the amygdala is transmitted to the frontal lobes and may influence these patterns.

### LONG-TERM CONSEQUENCES

According to Kagan (1998a), extremely shy or sociable children inherit a physiology that biases them toward a particular temperamental style. Yet heritability research indicates that genes contribute only modestly to shyness and sociability. They share power with experience. When early inhibition persists, it leads to excessive cautiousness, social withdrawal, and loneliness (Caspi & Silva, 1995; Rubin, Stewart, & Coplan, 1995). At the same time, many inhibited infants and children cope with novelty more effectively as they get older.

Child-rearing practices affect the chances that an emotionally reactive baby will become a fearful child. Warm, supportive parenting reduces cortisol production in inhibited babies, buffering the child's fear, whereas cold, intrusive parenting heightens the cortisol response (Gunnar, 1998). In addition, when parents protect infants who dislike novelty from minor stresses, they make it harder for the child to overcome an urge to retreat from unfamiliar events. In contrast, parents who make appropriate demands for their baby to approach new experiences help the child overcome fear (Rubin et al., 1997). In sum, for children to develop at their best, parenting must be tailored to their temperaments— a theme we will encounter again in this and later chapters.

ROBERT BRENNER/PHOTOEDIT

A strong physiological response to uncertain situations prompts this 2-year-old's withdrawal when a friend of her parents bends down to chat with her. Her mother's patient but insistent encouragement can modify her physiological reactivity and help her overcome her urge to retreat from unfamiliar events.

sociability, are stable over the long term only in children at the extremes—those who are very shy or very outgoing to begin with (Kagan & Saudino, 2001; Woodward et al., 2000).

Why is temperament not more stable? A major reason is that temperament itself develops with age. To illustrate, let's look at irritability and activity level. Recall from Chapter 4 that the early months are a period of fussing and crying for most babies. As infants better regulate their attention and emotions, many who seemed irritable become calm and content. In the case of activity level, the meaning of the behaviour changes. At first, an active, wriggling infant tends to be highly aroused and uncomfortable, whereas an inactive baby is often alert and attentive. As infants move on their own, the reverse is so! An active crawler is usually alert and interested in exploration, whereas a very inactive baby might be fearful and withdrawn.

These inconsistencies help us understand why long-term predictions about early temperament are best achieved after the second year of life, when styles of responding are better established (Caspi, 1998; Lemery et al., 1999). At the same time, the changes shown by many youngsters suggest that biologically based temperamental traits can be modified by experience (although children rarely change from one extreme to another—that is, a shy toddler practically never becomes highly sociable). With these ideas in mind, let's turn to genetic and environmental contributions to temperament and personality.

## GENETIC AND ENVIRONMENTAL INFLUENCES

The word *temperament* implies a genetic foundation for individual differences in personality. Many kinship studies have compared individuals with various genetic relationships to determine the extent to which temperament and personality are heritable. As with the heritability of intelligence, the most common approach has been to compare identical and fraternal twins.

**HERITABILITY.** Identical twins are more similar than fraternal twins across a wide range of temperamental traits (activity level, shyness/sociability, irritability, attention span, and persistence) and personality measures (introversion/extroversion, anxiety, agreeableness, and impulsivity) (Caspi, 1998; DiLalla, Kagan, & Reznick, 1994; Emde et al., 1992; Goldsmith, Buss, & Lemery, 1997; Goldsmith et al., 1999). Table 10.2 reveals that twin resemblance for temperament and personality is considerably lower than for intelligence. Nevertheless, when heritability estimates are computed by comparing the correlations of identical and fraternal twins, they are moderate, averaging around .50 (Rothbart & Bates, 1998).

**NONSHARED ENVIRONMENT.** Recall from earlier chapters that adoption research is useful in unravelling the relative contribution of heredity and environment. The few such studies available for temperament and personality report low correlations for both biological and nonbiological siblings, even when reared in the same family (see Table 10.2).

In Chapter 8, we discussed a similar pattern of correlations for IQ. To explain it, we distinguished *shared environmental influences* from *nonshared environmental influences* (see page 341). That siblings growing up in the same family show little or no resemblance in temperament and personality suggests that shared environmental factors, such as the overall climate of the home, do not make an important contribution. Instead, behavioural geneticists believe that nonshared factors—those that bring out each child's uniqueness—are especially salient in personality development (Braungart et al., 1992; Emde et al., 1992; Plomin, 1994d).

How might these nonshared influences operate? Behavioural geneticists claim that parents look for and emphasize personality differences in their children. This is reflected in the comparisons many parents make: "She's a lot more active," or "He's more sociable." In a study of 3-year-old identical twins, mothers treated each twin differently, and this differential treatment predicted twin differences in psychological adjustment. The twin who received more warmth and less punitive parenting was more positive in mood and prosocial behaviour and lower in behaviour problems (Deater-Deckard et al., 2001). Each child, in turn, evokes responses from caregivers that are consistent with parents' beliefs and the child's actual temperamental style.

Besides different experiences within the family, siblings have unique experiences with peers, teachers, and others in their community that profoundly affect development (Caspi, 1998). Furthermore, as they get older, siblings often actively seek ways to differ from one another. For these reasons, both identical and fraternal twins tend to become more distinct

---

**TABLE** 10.2

Kinship Correlations for Temperament, Personality, and Intelligence

| KINSHIP PAIR | TEMPERAMENT IN INFANCY | PERSONALITY IN CHILDHOOD AND ADULTHOOD | INTELLIGENCE |
|---|---|---|---|
| Identical twins reared together | .36 | .52 | .86 |
| Fraternal twins reared together | .18 | .25 | .55 |
| Biological siblings reared together | .18 | .20 | .47 |
| Nonbiological siblings (adopted–natural pairings) | −.03 | .05 | .29 |

*Note:* Correlations are averages across a variety of temperament and personality characteristics.

*Sources:* Braungart et al. (1992) and Emde et al. (1992) for temperament in infancy; Nichols (1978) and Plomin, Chipuer, & Loehlin (1990) for personality in childhood and adulthood; and Scarr (1997) for intelligence.

in personality in adulthood (McCartney, Harris, & Bernieri, 1990). The less contact twins have with one another, the stronger this effect—additional support for the power of the nonshared environment.

However, not everyone agrees that nonshared influences are supreme in personality development. In Chapter 14, we will see that researchers who have studied shared factors like family stress and child-rearing styles directly report that they do affect children's personalities. As Lois Hoffman (1994) points out, we must think of temperament and personality as resulting from many inputs. For some qualities, child-specific experiences may be important. For others, the general family environment may be important. And for still others, both nonshared and shared factors may be involved.

**CULTURAL VARIATIONS.** Consistent ethnic differences in early temperament exist. Compared with Caucasian infants, Chinese and Japanese babies tend to be less active, irritable, and vocal, more easily soothed when upset, and better at quieting themselves (Kagan et al., 1994; Lewis, Ramsay, & Kawakami, 1993). And some Asian infants are more emotionally restrained. Chinese 1-year-olds, for example, smile and cry less than do Western babies (Camras et al., 1998).

Although these variations may have biological roots, cultural beliefs and practices support them. Japanese mothers usually say that babies come into the world as independent beings who must learn to rely on their mothers through close physical contact. North American mothers are likely to believe just the opposite—that they must wean the baby away from dependence into autonomy. Consistent with these beliefs, Asian mothers interact gently, soothingly, and gesturally and discourage strong emotion in their babies, whereas Caucasian mothers use a more active, stimulating, verbal approach (Rothbaum et al., 2000b). These behaviours enhance early temperamental differences between their infants.

Taken together, research on the nature–nurture issue in the realm of temperament and personality indicates that heredity cannot be ignored. At the same time, individual differences can be understood only in terms of complex interdependencies between genetic and environmental factors.

## TEMPERAMENT AS A PREDICTOR OF CHILDREN'S BEHAVIOUR

In the first part of this chapter, we saw many examples of how emotions powerfully affect cognitive and social functioning. Since temperament represents an individual's emotional style, it should predict behaviours that emotions organize and regulate.

Temperamental characteristics of interest and persistence are related to learning and cognitive performance almost as soon as they can be measured. For example, persistence during the first year correlates with infant mental test scores and preschool IQ (Matheny, 1989). During middle childhood, persistence, in the form of teacher-rated task orientation, continues to predict IQ as well as grades in school. In contrast, distractibility, high activity level, and difficult temperament are associated with poor school achievement (Martin, Olejnik, & Gaddis, 1994; Strelau, Zawadzki, & Piotrowska, 2001).

Temperament also predicts important variations in social behaviour. For example, highly active preschoolers are very sociable with peers, but they also become involved in more conflict than do their less active agemates. Shy, inhibited children often watch classmates and engage in anxious behaviours that discourage interaction, such as hovering around play activities and rarely speaking (Rubin & Coplan, 1998). And as we will see in Chapter 12, inhibited children's high anxiety leads to more discomfort after wrongdoing and a greater sense of responsibility to others. As a result, early fearfulness protects children against the development of aggression. In contrast, irritable, impulsive children are at risk for aggressive and antisocial conduct (Shelton et al., 1998).

In some cases, social behaviour seems to be a direct result of temperament, as is the case with shy children. In other instances, it is due to the way people respond to the child's emotional style (Seifer, 2000). For example, active and impulsive children are often targets of negative interaction, which leads to conflict. As Chapter 12 will make clear, the link between early

GEORGE F. MOBLEY/NATIONAL GEOGRAPHIC IMAGE COLLECTION

At birth, Chinese infants are calmer, more easily soothed when upset, and better at quieting themselves than are Caucasian infants. Although these differences may have biological roots, cultural variations in child rearing support them.

The adaptiveness of temperament varies with cultural circumstances. When a famine swept the homeland of the Masai people of Kenya and Tanzania, many more difficult babies than easy babies survived. The irritable behaviour of the difficult infants may have ensured that they were better fed.

impulsivity and later lawbreaking and aggressive acts has much to do with the inept parenting that distractible, headstrong children often evoke. In sum, temperamental styles often stimulate certain reactions in other people, which, in turn, mould the child's development.

## TEMPERAMENT AND CHILD REARING: THE GOODNESS-OF-FIT MODEL

We have already indicated that the temperaments of many children change with age. This suggests that environments do not always sustain or intensify a child's existing temperament. If a child's disposition interferes with learning or getting along with others, adults must gently but consistently counteract the child's maladaptive behaviour.

Thomas and Chess (1977) proposed a **goodness-of-fit model** to describe how temperament and environmental pressures can together produce favourable outcomes. Goodness of fit involves creating child-rearing environments that recognize each child's temperament while encouraging more adaptive functioning.

Goodness of fit helps explain why children with difficult temperaments are at high risk for later behaviour problems. These children, at least in Western middle-SES families, frequently experience parenting that fits poorly with their dispositions. Without encouragement to try new experiences, their dislike of novelty can lead to overwhelming anxiety in the face of academic and social challenges. In addition, difficult infants are less likely to receive sensitive caregiving (van den Boom & Hoeksma, 1994). By the second year, their parents often resort to angry, punitive discipline. In response, the child reacts with defiance and disobedience. Then parents often behave inconsistently, rewarding the child's noncompliant behaviour by giving in (Lee & Bates, 1985). The difficult child's temperament, combined with harsh, inconsistent child rearing, forms a poor fit that maintains and even increases the child's irritable, conflict-ridden style. In contrast, when parents are positive and involved and engage in the sensitive, face-to-face play that helps infants regulate emotion, difficultness declines by age 2 (Feldman, Greenbaum, & Yirmiya, 1999).

According to the goodness-of-fit model, caregiving is not just responsive to the child's temperament. It also depends on life conditions and cultural values. During a famine in Africa, difficult temperament was associated with infant survival—probably because difficult babies demanded and received more maternal attention and food (deVries, 1984). In low-SES Puerto Rican families, difficult children are treated with sensitivity and patience; they are not at risk for adjustment problems (Gannon & Korn, 1983).

In Western nations, shy, withdrawn children are regarded as socially incompetent, yet Chinese adults evaluate such children positively—as advanced in social maturity and understanding (Chen, Rubin, & Li, 1995). In line with this view, in a study comparing Canadian and Chinese children, the Chinese children scored much higher in inhibition. Furthermore, Canadian mothers of shy children reported more protection and punishment and less acceptance and encouragement of achievement. Chinese mothers of shy children indicated just the opposite—less punishment and more acceptance and encouragement (Chen et al., 1998).

In cultures where particular temperamental styles are linked to adjustment problems, an effective match between rearing conditions and child temperament is best accomplished early, before unfavourable temperament–environment relationships produce maladjustment. Both difficult and shy children benefit from warm, accepting parenting that makes firm but reasonable demands for mastering new experiences. In the case of reserved, inactive toddlers, highly stimulating parental behaviour (questioning, instructing, and pointing out objects) fosters exploration. Yet these same parental behaviours have a negative impact on active babies, dampening their curiosity (Gandour, 1989; Miceli et al., 1998).

The goodness-of-fit model reminds us that infants come into the world with unique dispositions that adults have to accept. Parents can neither take full credit for their children's virtues nor be blamed for all their faults. But parents can turn an environment that exaggerates a child's problems into one that builds on the youngster's strengths. In the following sections, we will see that goodness of fit is also at the heart of infant–caregiver attachment. This first intimate relationship grows out of interaction between parent and baby, to which the emotional styles of both partners contribute.

**goodness-of-fit model**
Thomas and Chess's model, which states that an effective match, or "good fit," between child-rearing practices and a child's temperament leads to favourable development and psychological adjustment. When a "poor fit" exists, the outcome is distorted development and maladjustment.

**review**    Why is the stability of temperament only low to moderate?

**review**    How do genetic and environmental factors work together to promote a child's temperament? Cite examples from research on shyness, nonshared environmental influences, and cultural variations.

**apply**    Eighteen-month-old, highly active Jake, who climbed out of his high chair, had a temper tantrum when his father made him sit at the table until the meal was finished. Using the concept of goodness of fit, suggest another way of handling Jake.

**connect**    Compared with their agemates, shy, inhibited 2-year-olds are less likely to respond with sympathetic, prosocial behaviour to an unfamiliar, upset person (Young, Fox, & Zahn-Waxler, 1999). Using the distinction between empathy and sympathy on page 409, explain why.

MARTIN ROGERS/STOCK BOSTON

# Development of Attachment

ATTACHMENT IS THE STRONG, AFFECTIONAL TIE we have with special people in our lives that leads us to feel pleasure when we interact with them and to be comforted by their nearness during times of stress. By the second half of the first year, infants have become attached to familiar people who have responded to their needs. Watch babies of this age, and notice how they single out their parents for special attention. For example, when the mother enters the room, the baby breaks into a broad, friendly smile. When she picks him up, he pats her face, explores her hair, and snuggles against her body. When he feels anxious, he crawls into her lap and clings closely.

Freud first suggested that the infant's emotional tie to the mother provides the foundation for all later relationships. We will see shortly that research on the consequences of attachment is consistent with Freud's idea. But attachment has also been the subject of intense theoretical debate. Return to Chapter 1, and notice how *psychoanalytic theory* regards feeding as the central context in which caregivers and babies build this close emotional bond. *Behaviourism,* too, emphasizes the importance of feeding, but for different reasons. According to a well-known behaviourist *drive-reduction explanation,* as the caregiver satisfies the baby's hunger (primary drive), infants learn to prefer her soft caresses, warm smiles, and tender words of comfort (secondary drive) because these events have been paired with tension relief.

Although feeding is an important context in which mothers and babies build a close relationship, attachment does not depend on hunger satisfaction. In the 1950s, a famous experiment showed that rhesus monkeys reared with terrycloth and wire mesh "surrogate mothers" clung to the soft terrycloth substitute, even though the wire mesh "mother" held the bottle and infants had to climb on it to be fed (Harlow & Zimmerman, 1959). Similarly, human infants become attached to family members who seldom feed them, including fathers, siblings, and grandparents. And perhaps you have noticed that toddlers in Western cultures who sleep alone and experience frequent daytime separations from their parents sometimes develop strong emotional ties to cuddly objects, such as blankets or teddy bears (Passman, 1987). Yet such objects have never played a role in infant feeding!

Another problem with drive reduction and psychoanalytic accounts of attachment is that a great deal is said about the caregiver's contribution to the attachment relationship. But little attention is given to the importance of the infant's characteristics.

Baby monkeys reared with "surrogate mothers" from birth preferred to cling to a soft terrycloth "mother" instead of a wire mesh "mother" that held a bottle. These findings reveal that the drive-reduction explanation of attachment, which assumes that the mother–infant relationship is based on feeding, is incorrect.

**attachment**
The strong affectional tie that humans have with special people in their lives.

**ethological theory of attachment**
A theory formulated by Bowlby, which views the infant's emotional tie to the familiar caregiver as an evolved response that promotes survival through ensuring both safety and competence.

## BOWLBY'S ETHOLOGICAL THEORY

Today, **ethological theory of attachment** is the most widely accepted view of the infant's emotional tie to the caregiver. Recall from Chapter 1 that according to ethology, many human behaviours have evolved over the history of our species because they promote survival. John Bowlby (1969), who first applied this idea to the infant–caregiver bond, was originally a psychoanalyst. In his theory, he retained the psychoanalytic idea that quality of attachment

FIGURE 10.4

**Development of separation anxiety.** In cultures around the world, separation anxiety emerges in the second half of the first year, increasing until about 15 months and then declining. (Reprinted by permission of the publisher from *Infancy: Its Place in Human Development* by Jerome Kagan, Richard B. Kearsley, and Philip Zelazo. Cambridge, Mass.: Harvard University Press. Copyright © 1978 by the President and Fellows of Harvard College.)

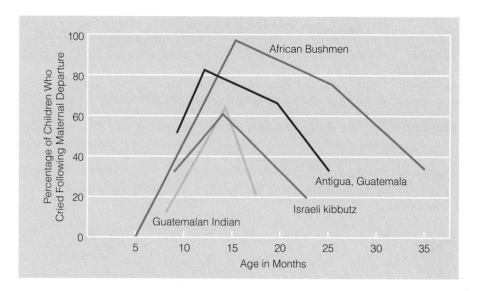

to the caregiver has profound implications for the child's feelings of security and capacity to form trusting relationships.

At the same time, Bowlby was inspired by Konrad Lorenz's studies of imprinting (see Chapter 1). He believed that the human infant, like the young of other animal species, is endowed with a set of built-in behaviours that help keep the parent nearby to protect the infant from danger and to provide support for exploring and mastering the environment (Waters & Cummings, 2000). Contact with the parent also ensures that the baby will be fed, but Bowlby pointed out that feeding is not the basis for attachment. Instead, the attachment bond has strong biological roots. It can best be understood within an evolutionary framework in which survival of the species—through ensuring both safety and competence—is of utmost importance.

According to Bowlby, the infant's relationship with the parent begins as a set of innate signals that call the adult to the baby's side. Over time, a true affectional bond develops, supported by new emotional and cognitive capacities as well as a history of warm, sensitive care. Attachment develops in four phases:

1.  The *preattachment phase* (birth to 6 weeks). Built-in signals—grasping, smiling, crying, and gazing into the adult's eyes—help bring newborn babies into close contact with other humans. Once an adult responds, infants encourage her to remain nearby, since closeness comforts them. Babies of this age recognize their own mother's smell and voice (see Chapter 4). However, they are not yet attached to her, since they do not mind being left with an unfamiliar adult.

2.  The "*attachment-in-the-making*" phase (6 weeks to 6–8 months). During this phase, infants respond differently to a familiar caregiver than to a stranger. For example, the baby smiles, laughs, and babbles more freely with the mother and quiets more quickly when she picks him up. As infants interact with the parent and experience relief from distress, they learn that their own actions affect the behaviour of those around them. They begin to develop a sense of trust—the expectation that the caregiver will respond when signalled. But even though they recognize the parent, babies still do not protest when separated from her.

3.  The *phase of "clear-cut" attachment* (6–8 months to 18 months–2 years). Now attachment to the familiar caregiver is evident. Babies display **separation anxiety**—they become upset when the adult on whom they have come to rely leaves. Separation anxiety does not always occur; like stranger anxiety (see page 401), it depends on infant temperament, context, and the adult's behaviour. But around the world, separation anxiety increases between 6 and 15 months (see Figure 10.4). Its appearance suggests the understanding that the caregiver continues to exist when not in view.

**separation anxiety**
An infant's distressed reaction to the departure of the familiar caregiver.

Consistent with this idea, babies who have not yet mastered Piagetian object permanence usually do not become anxious when separated from their mothers (Lester et al., 1974).

Besides protesting the parent's departure, older infants and toddlers try hard to maintain her presence. They approach, follow, and climb on her in preference to others. And they use her as a secure base from which to explore, as indicated earlier in this chapter.

4. *Formation of a reciprocal relationship* (18 months–2 years and on). By the end of the second year, rapid growth in representation and language permits toddlers to understand some of the factors that influence the parent's coming and going and to predict her return. As a result, separation protest declines. Now children start to negotiate with the caregiver, using requests and persuasion to alter her goals rather than clinging to her. For example, one 2-year-old asked her parents to read a story before leaving her with a baby-sitter. The extra time, along with a better understanding of where they were going ("to have dinner with Uncle Charlie") and when they would be back ("right after you go to sleep"), helped this child withstand her parents' absence.

Although separation anxiety increases between 6 and 15 months of age, its occurrence depends on infant temperament, context, and adult behaviour. This mother spends a few moments with her 9-month-old son and his caregiver before leaving the child-care centre for work. By helping her baby get acclimated, the mother limits his separation anxiety.

According to Bowlby (1980), out of their experiences during these four phases, children construct an enduring affectional tie to the caregiver that they can use as a secure base in the parents' absence. This inner representation becomes a vital part of personality. It serves as an **internal working model,** or set of expectations about the availability of attachment figures, their likelihood of providing support during times of stress, and the self's interaction with those figures. This image becomes the model, or guide, for all future close relationships (Bretherton, 1992).

## MEASURING THE SECURITY OF ATTACHMENT

Although virtually all family-reared babies become attached to a familiar caregiver by the second year, the quality of this relationship differs from child to child. Some infants appear secure in the presence of the caregiver; they know they can count on her for protection and support. Others seem anxious and uncertain.

A widely used technique for measuring the quality of attachment between 1 and 2 years of age is the **Strange Situation.** In designing it, Mary Ainsworth and her colleagues (1978) reasoned that if the development of attachment has gone well, infants and toddlers should use the parent as a secure base from which to explore an unfamiliar playroom. In addition, when the parent leaves, an unfamiliar adult should be less comforting than the parent. As summarized in Table 10.3 on page 422, the Strange Situation takes the baby through eight short episodes in which brief separations from and reunions with the parent occur.

Observing the responses of infants to these episodes, researchers have identified a secure attachment pattern and three patterns of insecurity; a few babies cannot be classified (Ainsworth et al., 1978; Barnett & Vondra, 1999; Main & Solomon, 1990). Although separation anxiety varies between the groups, the baby's reunion responses define attachment quality.

- **Secure attachment.** These infants use the parent as a secure base. When separated, they may or may not cry, but if they do, it is due to the parent's absence, since they show a strong preference for her over the stranger. When the parent returns, they actively seek contact, and their crying is reduced immediately. About 65 percent of North American infants show this pattern.

- **Avoidant attachment.** These infants seem unresponsive to the parent when she is present. When she leaves, they are usually not distressed, and they react to the stranger in much the same way as to the parent. During reunion, they avoid or are slow to greet the parent, and when picked up, they often fail to cling. About 20 percent of North American infants show this pattern.

**internal working model**
A set of expectations derived from early caregiving experiences concerning the availability of attachment figures, their likelihood of providing support during times of stress, and the self's interaction with those figures. Becomes a model, or guide, for all future close relationships.

**Strange Situation**
A research procedure involving short separations from and reunions with the parent that assesses the quality of the attachment bond.

**secure attachment**
The quality of attachment characterizing infants who use the parent as a secure base from which to explore and, when separated, are easily comforted by the parent when she returns.

**avoidant attachment**
The quality of insecure attachment characterizing infants who are usually not distressed by parental separation and who avoid the parent when she returns.

**TABLE** 10.3

Episodes in the Strange Situation

| EPISODE | EVENTS | ATTACHMENT BEHAVIOURS OBSERVED |
|---|---|---|
| 1 | Experimenter introduces parent and baby to playroom and then leaves. | |
| 2 | Parent is seated while baby plays with toys. | Parent as a secure base |
| 3 | Stranger enters, is seated, and talks to parent. | Reaction to unfamiliar adult |
| 4 | Parent leaves room. Stranger responds to baby and offers comfort if upset. | Separation anxiety |
| 5 | Parent returns, greets baby, and offers comfort if necessary. Stranger leaves room. | Reaction to reunion |
| 6 | Parent leaves room. | Separation anxiety |
| 7 | Stranger enters room and offers comfort. | Ability to be soothed by stranger |
| 8 | Parent returns, greets baby, offers comfort if necessary, and tries to reinterest baby in toys. | Reaction to reunion |

*Note:* Episode 1 lasts about 30 seconds; the remaining episodes each last about 3 minutes. Separation episodes are cut short if the baby becomes very upset. Reunion episodes are extended if the baby needs more time to calm down and return to play.
*Source:* Ainsworth et al., 1978.

**resistant attachment**
The quality of insecure attachment characterizing infants who often remain close to the parent and fail to explore and, when separated, display angry, resistive behaviour when she returns.

**disorganized/disoriented attachment**
The quality of insecure attachment characterizing infants who respond in a confused, contradictory fashion when reunited with the parent.

**Attachment Q-Sort**
An efficient method for assessing the quality of the attachment bond, in which a parent or an expert informant sorts a set of 90 descriptors of attachment-related behaviours on the basis of how well they characterize the child. A score is then computed that assigns children to securely or insecurely attached groups.

■ **Resistant attachment.** Before separation, these infants often seek closeness to the parent and fail to explore. When she returns, they display angry, resistive behaviour, sometimes hitting and pushing. In addition, many continue to cry and cling after being picked up and cannot be comforted easily. About 10 to 15 percent of North American infants show this pattern.

■ **Disorganized/disoriented attachment.** This pattern reflects the greatest insecurity. At reunion, these infants show confused, contradictory behaviours. They might look away while being held by the parent or approach her with flat, depressed emotion. Most communicate their disorientation with a dazed facial expression. A few cry out after having calmed down or display odd, frozen postures. About 5 to 10 percent of North American infants show this pattern.

Infants' reactions in the Strange Situation closely resemble their use of the parent as a secure base and their response to separation and reunion at home (Blanchard & Main, 1979; Pederson & Moran, 1996). For this reason, the procedure is a powerful tool for assessing attachment security.

A more efficient method—the **Attachment Q-Sort**—is also available (Waters et al., 1995). It is suitable for children between 1 and 5 years of age. An observer—the parent or an expert informant—sorts a set of 90 descriptors of attachment-related behaviours (such as "Child greets mother with a big smile when she enters the room" and "If mother moves very far, child follows along") into nine categories, ranging from highly descriptive to not at all descriptive of the child. Then a score is computed that assigns children to securely or insecurely attached groups. According to University of Western Ontario researchers David Pederson and Greg Moran, Q-Sort responses of expert observers correspond well with Strange Situation attachment classifications (Pederson et al., 1998). And when mothers are carefully trained and supervised, their responses are reasonably consistent with those of expert observers (Seifer et al., 1996; Teti & McGourty, 1996).

### STABILITY OF ATTACHMENT

Studies assessing the stability of attachment patterns between 1 and 2 years of age yield a wide range of findings. In some, the percentage of children whose reactions to parents remain the same is as low as 30 to 40 percent; in others, it is as high as 70 to 90 percent (Thompson, 1998).

A closer look at which infants change and which ones stay the same yields a more consistent picture. Quality of attachment is usually secure and stable for middle-SES babies experiencing favourable life conditions. And infants who move from insecurity to security typically have well-adjusted mothers with positive family and friendship ties. Perhaps many of these mothers became parents before they were psychologically ready but, with social support, grew into the role. In contrast, for low-SES families with many daily stresses, little social support, and parental psychological problems, attachment status generally moves away from security or changes from one insecure pattern to another (Owen et al., 1984; Vaughn et al., 1979; Vondra, Hommerding, & Shaw, 1999).

These findings indicate that securely attached babies more often maintain their attachment status than do insecure babies, whose relationship with the caregiver is, by definition, fragile and uncertain. The exception to this trend is disorganized/disoriented attachment—an insecure pattern that is as stable as attachment security, with nearly 70 percent retaining this classification over the second year (Barnett, Ganiban, & Cicchetti, 1999; Hesse & Main, 2000). As we will see, many disorganized/disoriented infants experience extremely negative caregiving—a circumstance that may disrupt emotional self-regulation so severely that the baby's confused behaviour persists.

Overall, many children show short-term instability in attachment quality. Yet research reveals high long-term stability. Between 70 and 80 percent of children tested in infancy responded similarly in middle childhood and also (when interviewed about their relationships with parents) in adolescence and young adulthood (Hamilton, 2000; Howes, Hamilton, & Phillipsen, 1998; Waters et al., 2000). But these participants came from middle-SES homes, and most probably had stable family lives or parents with the capacity to maintain a stable relationship with the child despite family stress. In a study of poverty-stricken children, many moved from secure attachment in infancy to insecure attachment in young adulthood. Child maltreatment, maternal depression, and poor family functioning in early adolescence distinguished these young people from the few who stayed securely attached (Weinfield, Sroufe, & Egeland, 2000).

## CULTURAL VARIATIONS

Cross-cultural evidence indicates that attachment patterns may have to be interpreted differently in other cultures. For example, as Figure 10.5 reveals, German infants show considerably more avoidant attachment than U.S. babies do. But German parents encourage their infants to be nonclingy and independent, so the baby's behaviour may be an intended outcome of cultural beliefs and practices (Grossmann et al., 1985). An unusually high number of Japanese infants display a resistant response, but the reaction may not represent true insecurity. Japanese mothers rarely leave their babies in the care of unfamiliar people, so the Strange Situation probably creates greater stress for them than it does for infants who frequently experience maternal separations (Takahashi, 1990). Also, Japanese parents value the infant clinginess and attention seeking that are part of the resistant response. Rather than equating these behaviours with insecurity, they consider them to be normal indicators of infant closeness and dependency. As one group of researchers pointed out, "The path of relying on others, so often devalued in the West, is often favored, even prescribed, in Japan" (Rothbaum et al., 2000a, p. 1097).

Despite these cultural variations and others, the secure pattern is still the most common attachment classification in all societies studied to date (van IJzendoorn & Sagi, 1999). And when the Attachment Q-Sort is used to assess conceptions of the ideal child, mothers from diverse cultures—China, Germany, Israel, Japan, Norway, and the United States—prefer that their young children behave in a securely attached fashion (Posada et al., 1995).

**FIGURE** 10.5

**A cross-cultural comparison of infants' reactions in the Strange Situation.** A high percentage of German babies seem avoidantly attached, whereas a substantial number of Japanese infants appear resistantly attached. Note that these responses may not reflect true insecurity. Instead, they are probably due to cultural differences in values and child-rearing practices. (Adapted from van IJzendoorn & Kroonenberg, 1988.)

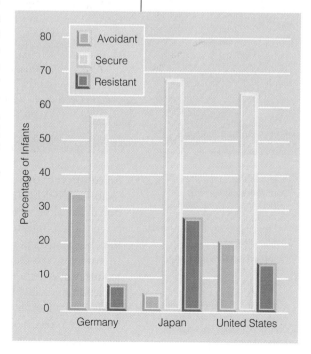

## FACTORS THAT AFFECT ATTACHMENT SECURITY

What factors might influence attachment security? Researchers have looked closely at four important influences: (1) opportunity to establish a close relationship; (2) quality of caregiving; (3) infants' characteristics; and (4) family context, including parents' internal working models.

**OPPORTUNITY FOR ATTACHMENT.** The powerful effect of the baby's affectional tie to the familiar caregiver is most evident when it is absent. In a series of studies, René Spitz (1946) observed institutionalized infants who had been given up by their mothers between 3 and 12 months of age. The babies were placed on a large ward where they shared a nurse with at least seven other babies. In contrast to the happy, outgoing behaviour they had shown before separation, they wept and withdrew from their surroundings, lost weight, and had difficulty sleeping. If a consistent caregiver did not replace the mother, the depression deepened rapidly.

These institutionalized infants experienced emotional difficulties because they were prevented from forming a bond with one or a few adults (Rutter, 1996). Another study supports this conclusion. Researchers followed the development of infants reared in an institution that offered a good caregiver–child ratio and a rich selection of books and toys. However, staff turnover was so rapid that the average child had a total of 50 caregivers by the age of 4½! Many of these children became "late adoptees" who were placed in homes after age 4. Most developed deep ties with their adoptive parents, indicating that a first attachment bond can develop as late as 4 to 6 years of age (Tizard & Rees, 1975).

But these youngsters were more likely to display emotional and social problems, including an excessive desire for adult attention, "overfriendliness" to unfamiliar adults and peers, and few friendships. Adopted children who spent their first 8 months or more in deprived Romanian institutions often display these same difficulties (Hodges & Tizard, 1989; Zeanah, 2000). Although follow-ups into adulthood are necessary to be sure, these results leave open the possibility that fully normal development depends on establishing close bonds with caregivers during the early years of life.

This mother and baby engage in a sensitively tuned form of communication called interactional synchrony in which they match emotional states, especially the positive ones. Interactional synchrony may support the development of secure attachment, but it does not characterize mother–infant interaction in all cultures.

PHOTOEDIT

**QUALITY OF CAREGIVING.** **Sensitive caregiving** distinguishes securely from insecurely attached infants. Combining dozens of studies including thousands of mother–infant pairs, investigators reported that the extent to which mothers responded promptly, consistently, and appropriately to infants and held them tenderly and carefully was moderately related to attachment security (Atkinson et al., 2000; De Wolff & van IJzendoorn, 1997). In contrast, insecurely attached infants tend to have mothers who engage in less physical contact, handle them awkwardly, behave in a "routine" manner, and are sometimes negative, resentful, and rejecting (Ainsworth et al., 1978; Isabella, 1993; Pederson & Moran, 1996).

Also, in several studies, a special form of communication called **interactional synchrony** separated the experiences of secure from insecure babies (Isabella & Belsky, 1991; Kochanska, 1998). It is best described as a sensitively tuned "emotional dance," in which caregiver–infant interaction appears to be mutually rewarding. The caregiver responds to infant signals in a well-timed, rhythmic, appropriate fashion. In addition, both partners match emotional states, especially the positive ones.

Earlier we saw that sensitive face-to-face play, in which interactional synchrony occurs, helps infants regulate emotion. But only 30 percent of the time are exchanges between mothers and babies emotionally "in sync" (Tronick, 1989). Indeed, a recent study showed that moderate adult–infant coordination, rather than "tight" coordination (which may present the baby with too much social influence), predicts attachment security (Jaffe et al., 2001). Perhaps warm, sensitive caregivers use a relaxed, flexible style of communication in which they comfortably accept

**sensitive caregiving**
Caregiving involving prompt, consistent, and appropriate responding to infant signals and tender, careful handling.

**interactional synchrony**
A sensitively tuned "emotional dance," in which the caregiver responds to infant signals in a well-timed, rhythmic, appropriate fashion and both partners match emotional states, especially the positive ones.

and easily repair interactive errors, returning to a synchronous state. Furthermore, finely tuned, coordinated interaction does not characterize mother–infant interaction everywhere. Among the Gusii people of Kenya, mothers rarely cuddle, hug, and interact playfully with their babies, although they are very responsive to their infants' needs (LeVine et al., 1994). This suggests that secure attachment depends on attentive caregiving, but its association with moment-by-moment contingent interaction is probably limited to certain cultures.

Compared with securely attached infants, avoidant babies tend to receive overstimulating, intrusive care. Their mothers might, for example, talk energetically to them while they are looking away or falling asleep. By avoiding the mother, these infants try to escape from overwhelming interaction. Resistant infants often experience inconsistent care. Their mothers are minimally involved in caregiving and unresponsive to infant signals. Yet when the baby begins to explore, these mothers interfere, shifting the infant's attention back to themselves. As a result, the baby shows exaggerated dependence as well as anger and frustration at the mother's lack of involvement (Cassidy & Berlin, 1994; Isabella & Belsky, 1991).

When caregiving is highly inadequate, it is a powerful predictor of disruptions in attachment. Child abuse and neglect (topics we will consider in Chapter 14) are associated with all three forms of attachment insecurity. Among maltreated infants, the most worrisome classification—disorganized/disoriented attachment—is especially high (Barnett, Ganiban, & Cicchetti, 1999). Depressed mothers and parents suffering from a traumatic event (such as loss of a loved one) also tend to promote the uncertain behaviours of this pattern (Teti et al., 1995; van IJzendoorn, 1995). How do they do so? Research indicates that they often display frightening, contradictory, and unpleasant behaviours, such as looking scared, mocking or teasing the baby, holding the baby stiffly at a distance, or seeking reassurance from the upset child (Lyons-Ruth, Bronfman, & Parsons, 1999; Schuengel, Bakermans-Kranenburg, & van IJzendoorn, 1999).

**INFANT CHARACTERISTICS.** Since attachment is the result of a *relationship* that builds between two partners, infant characteristics should affect how easily it is established. In Chapter 3, we saw that prematurity, birth complications, and newborn illness make caregiving more taxing. In poverty-stricken, stressed families, these infant conditions are linked to attachment insecurity (Wille, 1991). But when parents have the time and patience to care for a baby with special needs and view their infants positively, at-risk newborns fare quite well in attachment security (Cox, Hopkins, & Hans, 2000; Pederson & Moran, 1995).

Infants also vary considerably in temperament, but the role of temperament in attachment security has been intensely debated. Some researchers believe that infants who are irritable and fearful may simply react to brief separations with intense anxiety, regardless of the parent's sensitivity to the baby (Kagan, 1998a). Consistent with this view, emotionally reactive, difficult babies are more likely to develop later insecure attachments (Seifer et al., 1996; Vaughn & Bost, 1999).

But other evidence argues for temperament as only a modest influence. Although quality of attachment to the mother and the father is often similar, quite a few infants establish distinct attachment relationships with each parent and with their professional caregivers (Goossens & van IJzendoorn, 1990; van IJzendoorn & De Wolff, 1997). If infant temperament were very powerful, we would expect attachment classification to be more constant across familiar adults than it is.

Furthermore, caregiving seems to be involved in the relationship between difficultness and attachment insecurity. In a study of disorganized/disoriented 1-year-olds (many of whom were maltreated), emotional reactivity increased sharply over the second year (see Figure 10.6) (Barnett, Ganiban, & Cicchetti, 1999). Attachment disorganization was not caused by difficult temperament but rather seemed to promote it. Furthermore, an intervention that taught mothers how to respond sensitively to their irritable 6-month-olds led to gains in maternal responsiveness and children's attachment security, exploration, cooperativeness, and sociability that were still present at 3½ years of age (van den Boom, 1995).

**FIGURE 10.6**

**Mean vocal distress (ranging from brief frustration sounds to continuous crying and screaming) in the Strange Situation by disorganized/disoriented babies and babies with other attachment patterns.** Babies were rated at two ages: 12 months and 18 months. At 12 months, the disorganized/disoriented infants appeared to suppress their distress, perhaps out of fear of their mother's response; they scored lower than did infants with other attachment patterns. By 18 months, the distress of disorganized/disoriented toddlers had risen sharply, whereas the distress of other toddlers had declined. A disorganized/disoriented attachment pattern appeared to promote an emotionally reactive temperament. (Adapted from Barnett, Ganiban, & Cicchetti, 1999.)

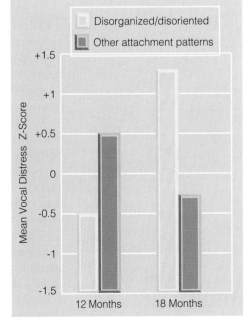

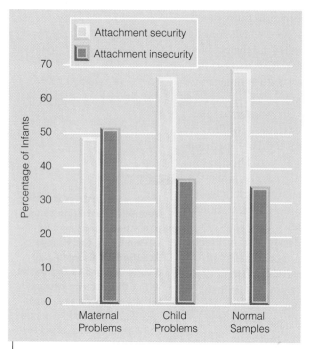

**FIGURE** 10.7

**Comparison of the effects of maternal and child problem behaviours on the attachment bond.** Maternal problems were associated with increased attachment insecurity. In contrast, child problems had little impact on the rate of attachment security and insecurity, which resembled that of normal samples. (Adapted from van IJzendoorn et al., 1992.)

Indeed, extensive research confirms that caregiving can override the impact of infant characteristics on attachment security. When researchers combined data from over 34 studies including more than 1000 mother–infant pairs, they found that maternal problems—such as mental illness, teenage parenthood, and child abuse—were associated with a sharp rise in attachment insecurity (see Figure 10.7). In contrast, child problems—ranging from prematurity and developmental delays to serious physical disabilities and psychological disorders—had little impact on attachment quality (van IJzendoorn et al., 1992).

A major reason that temperament and other child characteristics do not show strong relationships with attachment quality may be that their influence depends on goodness of fit. From this perspective, *many* child attributes can lead to secure attachment as long as the caregiver sensitively adjusts her behaviour to fit the baby's needs (Seifer & Schiller, 1995; Sroufe, 1985). But when a parent's capacity to do so is strained—for example, by her own personality or by stressful living conditions—then infants with illnesses, disabilities, and difficult temperaments are at risk for attachment problems.

**FAMILY CIRCUMSTANCES.** We have already indicated, in this and previous chapters, that quality of caregiving can be fully understood only in terms of the larger social environment. Job loss, a failing marriage, financial difficulties, and other stressors can undermine attachment by interfering with the sensitivity of parental care. Or they can affect babies' sense of security directly, by exposing them to angry adult interactions or unfavourable child-care arrangements (Thompson, 1998).

The arrival of a new sibling illustrates how family circumstances can affect attachment quality. In one study, firstborn preschoolers who declined in attachment security after the birth of a baby had mothers who were depressed, anxious, or hostile before the birth. These symptoms were associated with marital friction (which the firstborns probably sensed) as well as with unfavourable mother–firstborn interaction. When mothers had cooperative marriages, coped well with the second birth, and stayed involved with their older child, preschoolers maintained a secure attachment bond (Teti et al., 1996). The availability of social supports, especially a good mother–father relationship and mutual assistance with caregiving, reduces family stress and predicts greater attachment security (Owen & Cox, 1997).

**PARENTS' INTERNAL WORKING MODELS.** Parents bring to the family context a long history of attachment experiences, out of which they construct internal working models that they apply to the bonds established with their babies. To assess parents' "state of mind" with respect to attachment, Carol George, Nancy Kaplan, and Mary Main (1985) devised the Adult Attachment Interview, which asks adults to recall and evaluate childhood attachment experiences.

As Table 10.4 shows, quality of maternal working models is clearly related to attachment in infancy and early childhood—results replicated in Canada, Germany, Great Britain, the Netherlands, and the United States. Parents who show objectivity and balance in discussing their childhoods tend to have securely attached infants. In contrast, parents who dismiss the importance of early relationships or describe them in angry, confused ways usually have insecurely attached babies (Steele, Steele, & Fonagy, 1996; van IJzendoorn, 1995). Caregiving behaviour helps explain these associations. Mothers with autonomous/secure representations are warmer and more sensitive with their babies. They are also more likely to be supportive and to encourage learning and mastery in their older children, who, in turn, are more affectionate and comfortably interactive with them (Cohn et al., 1992; Pederson et al., 1998).

But we must be careful not to assume any direct transfer of parents' childhood experiences to quality of attachment with their own children. Internal working models are *reconstructed memories* affected by many factors, including relationship experiences over the life course, per-

**TABLE** 10.4

Relationship of Mothers' Internal Working Models to Infant Attachment Security

| TYPE OF MATERNAL WORKING MODEL | DESCRIPTION | INFANT ATTACHMENT CLASSIFICATION |
|---|---|---|
| Autonomous/ secure | These mothers show objectivity and balance in discussing their childhood experiences, whether they were positive or negative. They neither idealize their parents nor feel angry about the past. Their explanations are coherent and believable. | Secure |
| Dismissing | These mothers devalue the importance of their attachment relationships. They tend to idealize their parents without being able to recall specific experiences. What they do recall is discussed intellectually, with little emotion. | Avoidant |
| Overinvolved | These mothers talk about their childhood experiences with highly charged emotion, sometimes expressing anger toward their parents. They appear overwhelmed and confused about their early attachments and cannot discuss them coherently. | Resistant |
| Unresolved | These mothers show characteristics of any of the three other patterns. At the same time, they reason in a disorganized and confused way when loss of a loved one or experiences of physical or sexual abuse are discussed. | Disorganized/ disoriented |

*Note:* Correspondences between type of maternal working model and infant attachment classification hold for 60 to 70 percent of mother–infant pairs.

*Sources:* Benoit & Parker, 1994; Main & Goldwyn, 1994; Pederson et al., 1998.

sonality, and current life satisfaction. According to longitudinal research, certain negative life events can weaken the link between an individual's own attachment security in infancy and a secure internal working model in adulthood. And insecurely attached babies who become adults with insecure internal working models often have lives that, based on adulthood self-reports, are fraught with family crises (Waters et al., 2000; Weinfield, Sroufe, & Egeland, 2000).

In sum, our early rearing experiences do not destine us to become sensitive or insensitive parents. Rather, the way we *view* our childhoods—our ability to come to terms with negative events, to integrate new information into our working models, and to look back on our own parents in an understanding, forgiving way—is much more influential in how we rear our children than is the actual history of care we received (Main, 2000).

### MULTIPLE ATTACHMENTS: THE FATHER'S SPECIAL ROLE

We have already indicated that babies develop attachments to a variety of familiar people—not just mothers, but fathers, siblings, grandparents, and professional caregivers. Although Bowlby (1969) made room for multiple attachments in his theory, he believed that infants are predisposed to direct their attachment behaviours to a single special person, especially when they are distressed. For example, when an anxious, unhappy 1-year-old is permitted to choose between the mother and the father as a source of comfort and security, the infant usually chooses the mother. But this preference declines over the second year of life. And when babies are not distressed, they approach, ask to be held by, vocalize to, and smile at both parents equally (Lamb, 1997).

Fathers are salient figures in the lives of babies, building relationships with them shortly after birth. Observations of and interviews with fathers reveal that most are overjoyed at the infant's arrival; characterize the experience as "awesome," "indescribable," or "unforgettable"; and display intense involvement with their newborn child (Bader, 1995; Rose, 2000).

Like mothers', fathers' sensitive caregiving predicts secure attachment—an effect that becomes stronger the more time they spend with their babies (van IJzendoorn & De Wolff, 1997). Also, fathers of 1- to 5-year-olds enrolled in full-time child care report feeling just as much anxiety as mothers about separating from their child and just as much concern about the impact of these daily separations on the child's welfare (Deater-Deckard et al., 1994, p. 346).

As infancy progresses, mothers from a variety of cultures—Australia, Israel, India, Italy, Japan, the United States, and Canada—relate to babies in different ways from fathers. Mothers

When playing with their infants, especially sons, fathers in many cultures tend to engage in highly physical bouncing and lifting games.

devote more time to physical care and expressing affection. Fathers spend more time in playful interaction (Lamb, 1987; Roopnarine et al., 1990). Mothers and fathers also play differently. Mothers more often provide toys, talk to infants, and initiate conventional games, such as pat-a-cake and peekaboo. In contrast, fathers tend to engage in more exciting, highly physical bouncing and lifting games, especially with their infant sons (Yogman, 1981).

However, this picture of "mother as caregiver" and "father as playmate" has changed in some families due to the revised work status of women. Employed mothers tend to engage in more playful stimulation of their babies than do unemployed mothers, and their husbands are somewhat more involved in caregiving (Cox et al., 1992). When fathers are the primary caregivers, they retain their arousing play style (Lamb & Oppenheim, 1989). Such highly involved fathers are less gender stereotyped in their beliefs; have sympathetic, friendly personalities; and regard parenthood as an especially enriching experience (Lamb, 1987; Levy-Shiff & Israelashvili, 1988).

Paternal involvement with babies takes place within a complex system of family attitudes and relationships. When mothers and fathers believe that men are capable of nurturing infants and they value being involved, fathers devote more time to caregiving (Beitel & Parke, 1998). A warm, gratifying marital relationship supports both parents' involvement with babies, but it is particularly important for fathers (Braungart-Rieker, Courtney, & Garwood, 1999; Frosch, Mangelsdorf, & McHale, 2000). See the Cultural Influences box on the following page for cross-cultural evidence that supports this conclusion.

## ATTACHMENT AND LATER DEVELOPMENT

According to psychoanalytic and ethological theories, the inner feelings of affection and security that result from a healthy attachment relationship support all aspects of psychological development. Many researchers have addressed the link between infant–mother attachment and cognitive, emotional, and social development.

In the most comprehensive longitudinal study of this kind, Alan Sroufe and his collaborators reported that preschoolers who were securely attached as babies showed more elaborate make-believe play and greater enthusiasm, flexibility, and persistence in problem solving by 2 years of age. Preschool teachers rated these children at age 4 as high in self-esteem, socially competent, and empathic. In contrast, the teachers viewed avoidantly attached agemates as isolated and disconnected and resistantly attached agemates as disruptive and difficult. Studied again at age 11 in summer camp, children who had been secure as infants had more favourable relationships with peers, closer friendships, and better social skills, as judged by camp counsellors (Elicker, Englund, & Sroufe, 1992; Matas, Arend, & Sroufe, 1978; Shulman, Elicker, & Sroufe, 1994).

A host of investigations report positive associations between infant attachment security and later emotional and social functioning that agree with Sroufe's results (see, for example, Bohlin, Hagekull, & Rydell, 2000; Schneider, Atkinson, & Tardif, 2001). However, other studies yield a mixed picture. Secure infants do not always show more favourable development than do their insecure counterparts (Belsky & Cassidy, 1994). And one long-term study revealed that secure, avoidant, and resistant attachment at age 1 did not predict psychological adjustment at age 18 (Lewis, 1997). Disorganized/disoriented attachment, however, seems to be an exception. It is consistently related to high hostility and aggression in early and middle childhood (Lyons-Ruth, 1996; Lyons-Ruth, Easterbrooks, & Cibelli, 1997).

Why, overall, is research on the consequences of attachment quality as yet unclear? Michael Lamb and his colleagues (1985) suggest that *continuity of caregiving* determines whether attachment security is linked to later development. When parents respond sensitively not just in infancy but during later years, children are likely to develop favourably. In contrast, children of parents who react insensitively for a long time are at increased risk for maladjustment.

Several findings support this interpretation. Recall that many mothers of disorganized/disoriented infants have serious psychological difficulties and engage in highly maladaptive caregiving—problems that usually persist and are strongly linked to children's maladjustment

# *cultural influences*

## FATHER–INFANT RELATIONSHIPS AMONG THE AKA

BARRY HEWLETT

among the Aka hunters and gatherers of Central Africa, fathers devote more time to infants than in any other known society. Observations reveal that Aka fathers are within arm's reach of their babies more than half the day. They pick up and cuddle their babies at least five times more often than do fathers in other hunting-and-gathering societies in Africa and elsewhere in the world.

Why are Aka fathers so involved with their babies? Research shows that when husband and wife help each other with many tasks, fathers assist more with infant care. The relationship between Aka husband and wife is unusually cooperative and intimate. Throughout the day, they share hunting, food preparation, and social and leisure activities. Babies are brought along on hunts, and mothers find it hard to carry them long distances. This explains, in part, why fathers spend so much time holding their infants. But when the Aka return to the campground, fathers continue to devote many hours to infant caregiving. The more Aka parents are together, the greater the father's interaction with his baby (Hewlett, 1992).

This Aka father spends much time in close contact with his baby. In Aka society, husband and wife share many tasks of daily living and have an unusually cooperative and intimate relationship. Infants are generally within arm's reach of their fathers, who devote many hours to caregiving.

(Lyons-Ruth, Bronfman, & Parsons, 1999). Furthermore, a close look at Sroufe's longitudinal study reveals that the few securely attached infants who did develop later behaviour problems had mothers who became less positive and supportive in early childhood. Similarly, the handful of insecurely attached babies who became well-adjusted preschoolers had mothers who were sensitive and provided their young children with clear structure and guidance (Egeland et al., 1990; Thompson, 2000).

Do these trends remind you of our discussion of *resiliency* in Chapter 1? A child whose parental caregiving improves or who has other compensating affectional ties can bounce back from adversity. In contrast, a child who experiences tender care in infancy but who lacks sympathetic ties later is at risk for problems. In sum, efforts to create warm, sensitive environments are not just important in infancy and toddlerhood; they are crucial throughout childhood and adolescence.

## **ASK** YOURSELF

**review**   What factors explain stability in attachment quality for some children and change for others? Are the same factors involved in the link between infant–mother attachment and later development? Explain.

**review**   What contributions do quality of caregiving and infant characteristics make to attachment security? Which influence is more powerful, and why?

**apply**   In evaluating her childhood attachment experiences, Monica recalls her mother as tense and distant. Is Monica's newborn daughter likely to develop an insecure infant–mother attachment? Explain, drawing on research into adults' internal working models.

**connect**   Review research on emotional self-regulation on pages 403–404. How do the caregiving experiences of securely attached infants promote development of emotional self-regulation?

social issues: health

## DOES CHILD CARE IN INFANCY THREATEN ATTACHMENT SECURITY AND LATER ADJUSTMENT?

Some research suggests that infants placed in full-time child care before 12 months of age are more likely than home-reared babies to display insecure attachment—especially avoidance—in the Strange Situation (Belsky, 1989, 1992). Does this mean that infants who experience daily separations from their employed parents and early placement in child care are at risk for developmental problems? A close look at the evidence reveals that we should be cautious about coming to this conclusion.

### ATTACHMENT QUALITY

In studies reporting a child care–attachment association, the rate of insecurity is somewhat higher among child-care infants than non-child-care infants (36 versus 29 percent), but it nevertheless resembles the overall rate of insecurity reported for children in industrialized countries (Lamb, Sternberg, & Prodromidis, 1992). In fact, most infants of employed mothers are securely attached! Furthermore, not all investigations report a difference in attachment quality between child-care and home-reared infants (McKim et al., 1999; NICHD Early

Child Care Research Network, 1997; Roggman et al., 1994).

### FAMILY CIRCUMSTANCES

We have seen that family conditions affect attachment security. Many employed women find the pressures of handling two full-time jobs (work and motherhood) stressful. Some respond less sensitively to their babies because they receive little caregiving assistance from the child's father and are fatigued and harried, thereby risking the infant's security (Stifter, Coulehan, & Fish, 1993). Other employed parents probably value and encourage their infants' independence. Or their babies are unfazed by brief separations in the Strange Situation because they are used to separating from their parents. In these cases, avoidance in the Strange Situation may represent healthy autonomy rather than insecurity (Lamb, 1998).

### QUALITY AND EXTENT OF CHILD CARE

Poor-quality child care and many hours in child care may contribute to a higher rate of insecure attachment among infants of employed mothers.

In the National Institute of Child Health and Development (NICHD) Study of Early Child Care—the largest longitudinal study to date, including more than 1300 infants and their mothers—child care alone did not contribute to attachment insecurity. But when babies were exposed to combined home and child-care risk factors—insensitive caregiving at home with insensitive caregiving in child care, long hours in child care, or more than one child-care arrangement—the rate of insecurity increased. Overall, mother–child interaction was more favourable when children attended higher-quality child care and were in child care for fewer hours (NICHD Early Child Care Research Network, 1997, 1999).

Furthermore, when the NICHD sample reached 4½ to 5 years of age, children who spent more time in child care were rated by their mothers, caregivers, and kindergarten teachers as showing more behaviour problems, especially aggression. Specifically, 17 percent of children who averaged more than 30 hours of child care per week during their first 4 years were seen as more assertive, defiant, and disobedient,

## Attachment, Parental Employment, and Child Care

OVER THE PAST THREE DECADES, women have entered the labour force in record numbers. Today, more than 90 percent of Canadian working mothers return to work within 2 years of giving birth (Statistics Canada, Employment after childbirth, 1999). In response to this trend, researchers and lay people alike have raised questions about the impact of child care and daily separations of infant from parent on the attachment bond.

© B. MAHONEY/THE IMAGE WORKS

This child-care centre meets rigorous, professionally established standards of quality. A generous caregiver–child ratio, a limited number of children in each room, an environment with appropriate equipment and toys, and training in child development enable caregivers to respond to infants' and toddlers' needs to be held, comforted, and stimulated.

whereas only 6 percent of children in child care for less than 10 hours per week were rated this way. Quality of care slightly reduced the link between child-care hours and aggression but did not eliminate it (NICHD Early Childhood Research Network, 2001). These findings do not necessarily mean that child care causes behaviour problems. Children prone to be aggressive may have parents who leave them in child care for long hours.

Overall, findings of the NICHD Study indicate that parenting has a far stronger impact on preschoolers' problem behaviour than does early, extensive child care (NICHD Early Child Care Research Network, 1998). Indeed, having the opportunity to form a warm bond with a stable professional caregiver seems to be particularly helpful to infants whose relationship with one or both parents is insecure. When fol-

lowed into the preschool and early school years, such children show higher self-esteem and socially skilled behaviour than do their insecurely attached agemates who did not attend child care (Egeland & Hiester, 1995).

## CONCLUSIONS

Taken together, research suggests that some infants may be at risk for attachment insecurity due to inadequate child care and the joint pressures of full-time employment and parenthood experienced by their mothers. However, using this as evidence to justify a reduction in infant child-care services is inappropriate. When family incomes are limited or mothers who want to work are forced to stay at home, children's emotional security is not promoted.

Instead, it makes sense to increase the availability of high-quality child

care and to educate parents about the vital role of sensitive caregiving in early emotional development. Refer to the signs of developmentally appropriate child care for infants and toddlers, listed in Table 10.5 on page 433. For child care to foster attachment security, the professional caregiver's relationship with the baby is vital. When caregiver–child ratios are generous, group sizes are small, environments are stimulating, and caregivers are educated about child development and child rearing, caregivers' interactions are more positive (NICHD Early Child Care Research Network, 1996, 2000). Child care with these characteristics can become part of an ecological system that relieves rather than intensifies parent and child stress, thereby promoting healthy attachment and development.

The Social Issues: Health box above reviews the current controversy over whether child care threatens the emotional security of young children. As you will see, the weight of evidence suggests that *quality of care,* both at home and in the child-care setting, rather than child care itself is the important factor. Research shows that infants and young children exposed to poor-quality child care, whether they come from middle- or low-SES homes, score lower on measures of cognitive and social skills (Canadian Child Care Federation, 1999; Doherty, 1998; Hausfather et al., 1997; NICHD Early Child Care Research Network, 2001).

In contrast, good child care can reduce the negative impact of a stressed, poverty-stricken home life, and it sustains the benefits of growing up in an economically advantaged family (Lamb, 1998). This conclusion is strengthened by longitudinal research in Sweden, where child care is nationally regulated and liberally funded to ensure its high quality. Compared with children reared fully at home, Swedish children enrolled in out-of-home child care before their second birthday scored higher in cognitive, emotional, and social competence during middle childhood and adolescence (Andersson, 1989, 1992; Broberg et al., 1997). Similar findings confirm the importance of high-quality child care for Canadian children. In the Victoria Day Care Research Project, a team of researchers at the University of British Columbia and the University of Victoria followed a group of preschoolers through adolescence, exploring the contribution of child-care experiences to their development. Those receiving sensitive, stimulating child care were advanced in language competence in early childhood. Early childhood language competence, in turn, was associated with greater cognitive competence, peer sociability, and self-esteem during the teenage years (Kohen et al., 2000).

Yet in Canada, high-quality child care is in short supply. Although child-care centres must be licensed, in most provinces and territories home-care programs need not be. Unlicensed home care is regulated only on the number of children that may be served in each home—typically, no more than five or six children younger than age 6, including no more than two to three infants and toddlers. Licensing ensures that in addition to a generous caregiver–child ratio and a limited group size, programs meet basic health and safety standards. And in child-care centres, licensing also guarantees that one staff person with each group of children will have specialized post-secondary training in early childhood education.

Nevertheless, no Canadian licensing standards require child-care programs to provide daily experiences known to enhance children's development (Child Care Resource and Research Unit, 2002; Doherty, 1996). As Nina Howe and Ellen Jacobs (1995) of Concordia University point out, licensing ensures minimally acceptable care, but it does not guarantee developmentally appropriate care. Furthermore, a minority of Canadian children are granted this minimal standard through licensing. At present, Canada offers only about 500 000 licensed child-care spaces, leaving 900 000 children in unlicensed programs (Canadian Child Care Federation, 2000).

Two extensive studies—one of 231 child-care homes and the other of 234 child-care centres across Canada—confirm that Canadian child-care quality is cause for deep concern. Although observations revealed that most home and centre caregivers were warm and attentive, too few provided stimulating, engaging daily activities (Doherty et al., 2000; Goelman et al., 2000). The quality of infant/toddler care was particularly dire. As Figure 10.8 shows, only about one-fourth of centre classrooms provided these very young children with stimulating experiences; most offered only minimal- to mediocre-quality care. Preschoolers fared only slightly better;

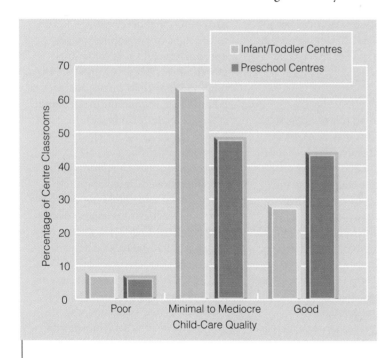

**FIGURE** 10.8

**Quality of centre-based infant/toddler and preschool child care in Canada.** On the basis of classroom observations of children's experiences, researchers rated quality of child care as *poor* (inadequate to marginally custodial), *minimal to mediocre* (custodial to some developmentally stimulating activities), or *good* (many developmentally stimulating activities). The majority of classrooms granted minimal to mediocre care. Infant/toddler child care was particularly low in quality, with only about 29 percent of centre classrooms assessed as providing good care. (From H. Goelman, G. Doherty, D. S. Lero, A. LaGrange, & J. Tougas, 2000, *You Bet I Care! Caring and learning environments: Quality in child care centres across Canada,* Guelph: Centre for Families, Work and Well-Being, University of Guelph, pp. 44–45. Adapted by permission.)

TABLE 10.5

Signs of Developmentally Appropriate Infant and Toddler Child Care

| PROGRAM CHARACTERISTIC | SIGNS OF QUALITY |
|---|---|
| Physical setting | Indoor environment is clean, in good repair, well lighted, and well ventilated. Fenced outdoor play space is available. Setting does not appear overcrowded when children are present. |
| Toys and equipment | Play materials are appropriate for infants and toddlers and stored on low shelves within easy reach. Cribs, highchairs, infant seats, and child-sized tables and chairs are available. Outdoor equipment includes small riding toys, swings, slide, and sandbox. |
| Caregiver–child ratio | In child-care centres, caregiver–child ratio is no greater than 1 to 3 for infants and 1 to 6 for toddlers. Group size (number of children in one room) is no greater than 6 infants with 2 caregivers and 12 toddlers with 2 caregivers. In child-care homes, caregiver is responsible for no more than 6 children; within this group, no more than 2 are infants and toddlers. Staffing is consistent, so infants and toddlers can form relationships with particular caregivers. |
| Daily activities | Daily schedule includes times for active play, quiet play, naps, snacks, and meals. It is flexible rather than rigid, to meet the needs of individual children. Atmosphere is warm and supportive, and children are never left unsupervised. |
| Interactions between adults and children | Caregivers respond promptly to infants' and toddlers' distress; hold, talk to, sing, and read to them; and interact with them in a manner that respects the individual child's interests and tolerance for stimulation. |
| Caregiver qualifications | Centre-based caregivers have early childhood education diplomas. Home-based caregivers have some training in child development, first aid, and safety. |
| Relationships with parents | Parents are welcome any time. Caregivers talk frequently with parents about children's behaviour and development. |
| Licensing | Child-care setting, whether a centre or home, is licensed by the province. |

Sources: Bredekamp & Copple, 1997; Canadian Child Care Federation, 1994; Howe & Jacobs, 1995; National Association for the Education of Young Children, 1998.

44 percent of preschool classrooms had stimulating learning opportunities. Finally, more than 7 percent of classrooms for both age groups provided child care so low in quality that the researchers judged it to compromise development (refer again to Figure 10.8).

Table 10.5 lists signs of high-quality care that can be used in choosing a child-care setting for an infant or toddler based on standards devised by the Canadian Child Care Federation (1994) and the U.S. National Association for the Education of Young Children (Bredekamp & Copple, 1997). These program characteristics meet the developmental and individual needs of young children, based on current research and the consensus of experts. Child care in Canada is affected by a macrosystem of individualistic values and weak government regulation and funding. Furthermore, many parents who place their children in child care think that their children's experiences are higher quality than they really are (Helburn, 1995). Inability to identify good care means that many parents do not demand it.

Although Canada lacks a national child-care policy, a recent poll revealed that 80 percent of Canadians support government plans to improve child care (Canadian Council on Social Development, 2000b). The Canadian federal government is working on its National Children's Agenda, which includes steps for improving the quality, affordability, and accessibility of child care. This is a hopeful sign, since good child care is a cost-effective means for supporting the well-being of all children, and it can serve as effective early intervention for children whose development is at risk, much like the programs we discussed in Chapter 8. We will revisit the topics of parental employment and child care in Chapter 14, when we take up additional research on the family.

**ASK YOURSELF** www

**review**    Cite evidence that high-quality infant and toddler child care supports development, whereas poor-quality care undermines it.

**apply**    Randi and Mike are worried that placing their 6-month-old baby, Lucinda, in child care may disrupt the development of attachment. List steps that Randi and Mike can take to ensure that Lucinda's experiences—at home and in child care—support attachment security.

# summary

## THE FUNCTIONS OF EMOTIONS

*Describe the functionalist approach to emotional development.*

- According to the **functionalist approach,** the broad function of **emotions** is to prompt action in the service of personal goals. Functionalist theorists regard emotions as central, adaptive forces in all aspects of human activity, including cognitive processing, social behaviour, and physical health. In addition, emotions are viewed as important in the emergence of self-awareness, which opens the door to new, self-evaluative emotions. Furthermore, to adapt to their physical and social worlds, children must gradually gain voluntary control over their emotions.

## DEVELOPMENT OF EMOTIONAL EXPRESSION

*How does the expression of happiness, anger, sadness, and fear change during infancy?*

- During the first half-year, **basic emotions** are gradually coordinated into more effective systems. By the middle of the first year, they are well-organized signals that vary meaningfully with environmental events.

- Happiness strengthens the parent–child bond and reflects as well as supports cognitive and physical mastery. As infants' sensitivity to visual patterns improves between 6 and 10 weeks, the **social smile** appears. By 3 months, infants smile most often when interacting with familiar people. Soon laughter, associated with faster information processing, emerges.

- Anger and fear, especially in the form of **stranger anxiety,** increase in the second half of the first year as infants can better evaluate objects and events. These emotions have special adaptive value as infants' motor capacities improve. Once fear develops, infants use the familiar caregiver as a **secure base** from which to explore. Expressions of sadness appear in response to pain, removal of an object, brief separations, and disruptions of caregiver–infant communication, but they are less frequent than anger.

*Describe the development of self-conscious emotions, emotional self-regulation, and conformity to emotional display rules.*

- At the end of the second year, self-awareness and adult instruction provide the foundation for **self-conscious emotions,** such as shame, embarrassment, guilt, envy, and pride. With age, self-conscious emotions become more internally governed. Whereas guilt is often related to good adjustment, intense shame is associated with feelings of personal inadequacy. Parents who repeatedly give feedback about the worth of the child and her performance have children who experience overly high, maladaptive levels of shame and pride.

- **Emotional self-regulation** emerges as caregivers sensitively assist infants in adjusting their emotional reactions. As motor, cognitive, and language development proceed, children gradually acquire more effective self-regulatory strategies. Adult modelling and conversations with children about emotional challenges foster emotional self-regulation. Children who experience negative emotion intensely find it harder to inhibit their feelings.

- During the preschool years, children start to conform to the **emotional display rules** of their culture, but only gradually do they become adept at doing so. In middle childhood, they become consciously aware of these rules and come to understand their value for ensuring social harmony.

## UNDERSTANDING AND RESPONDING TO THE EMOTIONS OF OTHERS

*Describe the development of emotional understanding from infancy into adolescence.*

- As infants develop the capacity to meaningfully interpret emotional expressions, they actively seek emotional information from trusted caregivers. **Social referencing** appears at the end of the first year. By the middle of the second year, toddlers begin to appreciate that others' emotional reactions may differ from their own.

- Preschoolers have an impressive understanding of the causes, consequences, and behavioural signs of emotion. The capacity to consider conflicting cues when explaining others' feelings develops during middle childhood. Older children also realize that people can experience mixed emotions.

- Both cognitive development and social experience contribute to emotional understanding. A warm, relaxed parent–child relationship, conversations with family members and friends, and make-believe play are excellent contexts for learning about emotions.

*Distinguish empathy and sympathy, and describe the development of empathy from infancy into adolescence, noting individual differences.*

- The development of **empathy** involves a complex interaction of cognition and affect. Empathy is an important motivator of **prosocial, or altruistic, behaviour.** Yet if the emotion aroused by an upset other escalates into personal distress, empathy is unlikely to prompt **sympathy** and resulting acts of kindness and helpfulness.

- As self-awareness emerges, toddlers begin to empathize. Gains in language, emotional understanding, and perspective taking support an increase in empathic responding during childhood and adolescence. Eventually, empathy is evoked not just by people's immediate distress but by their general life condition.

- Temperament affects whether empathy gives way to sympathy. Children who are sociable, assertive, and good at regulating emotion are more likely to behave prosocially than are children who often display negative emotion. Parents who are nurturant, display empathic concern, and set clear limits on children's display of inappropriate emotion foster the development of empathy and sympathy. In contrast, angry, punitive parenting disrupts these capacities at an early age.

## TEMPERAMENT AND DEVELOPMENT

*What is temperament, and how is it measured?*

- Children differ greatly in **temperament,** or quality and intensity of emotion, activity level, attention, and emotional self-regulation. Three patterns of temperament—the **easy child,** the **difficult child,** and the **slow-to-warm-up child**—were identified in the New York Longitudinal Study. Rothbart's dimensions of temperament represent three underlying components—emotion, attention, and action—that form an integrated system of capacities and limitations.

- Temperament is most often assessed through parent reports. Although laboratory observations avoid the subjectivity of parent reports, the unfamiliar setting introduces other biases. Researchers have begun to combine laboratory observations with psychophysiological measures to distinguish temperamental styles, such as **inhibited, or shy, children** from **uninhibited, or sociable, children.**

*Discuss the role of heredity and environment in the stability of temperament, the relationship of temperament to cognitive and social functioning, and the goodness-of-fit model.*

- Because temperament itself develops with age and can be modified by experience, stability from one age period to the next is generally low to moderate. Long-term prediction from early temperament is best achieved after the second year of life, when styles of responding are better established.

- Kinship studies reveal that temperament is moderately heritable. They also suggest that nonshared environmental influences are more important than are shared influences in contributing to temperament. Although ethnic differences in temperament may have biological roots, cultural beliefs and practices support them.

- Temperament is consistently related to cognitive performance and social behaviour. The **goodness-of-fit model** describes how temperament and environmental pressures work together to affect later development. Parenting practices that create a good fit with the child's temperament help difficult, shy, and highly active children achieve more adaptive functioning.

## DEVELOPMENT OF ATTACHMENT

*What are the unique features of ethological theory of attachment?*

- The development of **attachment,** the strong affectional tie we feel for special people in our lives, has been the subject of intense theoretical debate. Although psychoanalytic and drive-reduction (behaviourist) explanations exist, the most widely accepted perspective is **ethological theory of attachment.** It views babies as biologically prepared to contribute to ties established with their caregivers, which promote survival through ensuring both safety and competence.

- In early infancy, a set of built-in behaviours encourages the parent to remain close to the baby. Around 6 to 8 months, **separation anxiety** and use of the parent as a secure base indicate that a true attachment bond has formed. As representation and language develop, preschoolers better understand the parent's goals, and separation anxiety declines. Out of early caregiving experiences, children construct an **internal working model** that serves as a guide for all future close relationships.

*Cite the four attachment patterns assessed by the Strange Situation and the Attachment Q-Sort, and discuss factors that affect the development of attachment.*

- A widely used technique for measuring the quality of attachment between 1 and 2 years of age is the **Strange Situation.** A more efficient method is the **Attachment Q-Sort,** suitable for children between 1 and 5 years of age. Four attachment patterns have been identified: **secure, avoidant, resistant,** and **disorganized/disoriented.**

- Quality of attachment is usually secure and stable for infants reared in middle-SES families with favourable life conditions. For infants in low-SES families with many daily stresses and for children who encounter serious family problems, quality of attachment often changes. Cultural conditions must be considered in interpreting the meaning of attachment patterns.

- A variety of factors affect attachment security. Infants deprived of affectional ties with one or a few adults show lasting emotional and social problems. **Sensitive caregiving** is moderately related to secure attachment. **Interactional synchrony** also separates the experiences of secure from insecure babies, but its importance is probably limited to certain cultures.

- Even ill and emotionally reactive, difficult infants are likely to become securely attached if parents adapt their caregiving to suit the baby's needs. Family circumstances influence caregiving behaviour and attachment security. Parents' internal working models show substantial correspondence with their own children's attachment status in infancy and early childhood. Internal working models are reconstructed memories; transfer of parents' childhood experiences to quality of attachment with their own children is indirect and affected by many factors.

*Discuss fathers' attachment relationships with their infants and the role of early attachment quality in later development.*

■ Infants develop strong affectional ties to fathers, whose sensitive caregiving predicts secure attachment. Fathers in a variety of cultures devote more time to stimulating, playful interaction than mothers, who focus on physical care and expressing affection.

■ Evidence for the impact of early attachment quality on cognitive, emotional, and social competence in later years is mixed. Continuity of parental care may be the crucial factor that determines whether attachment security is linked to later development.

## ATTACHMENT, PARENTAL EMPLOYMENT, AND CHILD CARE

*Discuss the effects of parental employment and child care on attachment security and early psychological development.*

■ The majority of mothers with children under age 2 are employed. The combination of many hours in poor-quality child care and insensitive caregiving at home is associated with insecure attachment. Furthermore, substandard child care results in less favourable cognitive, emotional, and social development.

■ Many Canadian infants and toddlers receive some out-of-home child care, the majority in unregulated settings. When child-care settings meet professionally accepted standards for developmentally appropriate practice, children's learning opportunities and the warmth, sensitivity, and stability of their caregivers are especially high.

 *important terms and concepts*

attachment (p. 419)
Attachment Q-Sort (p. 422)
avoidant attachment (p. 421)
basic emotions (p. 400)
difficult child (p. 413)
disorganized/disoriented attachment (p. 422)
easy child (p. 412)
emotion (p. 396)
emotional display rules (p. 405)
emotional self-regulation (p. 403)
empathy (p. 409)

ethological theory of attachment (p. 419)
functionalist approach (p. 396)
goodness-of-fit model (p. 418)
inhibited, or shy, child (p. 413)
interactional synchrony (p. 424)
internal working model (p. 421)
prosocial, or altruistic, behaviour (p. 409)
resistant attachment (p. 422)
secure attachment (p. 421)
secure base (p. 402)

self-conscious emotions (p. 402)
sensitive caregiving (p. 424)
separation anxiety (p. 420)
slow-to-warm-up child (p. 413)
social referencing (p. 406)
social smile (p. 400)
Strange Situation (p. 421)
stranger anxiety (p. 401)
sympathy (p. 409)
temperament (p. 410)
uninhibited, or sociable, child (p. 413)

How did this artist construct a multifaceted sense of self, imbued with personality traits, competencies, limitations, values, and life plans—each laced with imprints of her culture? Developing selfhood is a major focus of Chapter 11.

# eleven

## Self and Social Understanding

"GRANDPA, LOOK AT MY NEW shirt!" exclaimed 4-year-old Ellen at her family's annual reunion. "See, it's got Barney and Baby Bop on it and ..."

Ellen's voice trailed off as she realized all eyes were turned toward her 1-year-old cousin, who was about to take his first steps. As little David tottered forward, the grownups laughed and cheered. No one, not even Grandpa, who was usually so attentive and playful, took note of Ellen and her new shirt.

Ellen retreated to the bedroom, where she threw a blanket over her head. Arms outstretched, she peered through the blanket's loose weave and made her way back to the living room, where she saw Grandpa leading David about the room. "Here I come, the scary ghost," announced Ellen as she purposefully bumped into David, who toppled over and burst into tears.

Pulling off the blanket, Ellen quickly caught her mother's disapproving expression. "I couldn't see him, Mom! The blanket was over my face," Ellen sheepishly explained.

Ellen's mother insisted that Ellen help David up and apologize at once. At the same time, she marvelled at Ellen's skilful capacity for trickery.

This chapter addresses the development of **social cognition,** or how children come to understand their multifaceted social world. Like our discussion of cognitive development in Chapters 6 and 7, this chapter is concerned with thinking about and interpreting experience. But the experience of interest is no longer the child's physical surroundings. Instead, it is the characteristics of the self and other people.

Researchers interested in social cognition seek answers to questions like these: When do infants discover they are separate beings, distinct from other people and objects? How does children's understanding of their own and others' mental lives change with age? For example, what new realizations underlie Ellen's creative act of deception? When children and adolescents are asked to describe their own and others' characteristics, what do they say?

As we answer these and other questions, you will see that the trends we have already identified for cognitive development also apply to children's developing understanding of their social world. First, social cognition develops from *concrete* to *abstract.* Children first notice observable characteristics—the appearance and behaviour of themselves and other people. Soon after, they become aware of internal processes—the existence of desires, beliefs, intentions, abilities, and attitudes. Second, social cognition becomes *better organized* with age as children integrate separate behaviours into an appreciation of their own and others' personalities and identities. Third, children revise their ideas about the causes of behaviour—from *simple, one-sided explanations* to *complex interacting relationships* that take into account both person and situation. Finally, social cognition moves toward *metacognitive understanding.* As children get older, their thinking is no longer limited to social reality. They also think about their own and other people's social thoughts.

Although nonsocial and social cognition share many features, they also differ. Consider how much easier it is to predict the motions of physical objects, such as a rolling ball, than the actions of people. Movements of things can be fully understood from the physical forces that act on them. In contrast, the behaviour of people is not just the result of others' actions toward them. It is also affected by inner states that cannot be observed directly.

In view of this complexity, we might expect social cognition to develop more slowly than nonsocial cognition. Yet surprisingly, it does not. Unique features of social experience probably help children make early sense of its complexity. First, because people are animated beings and objects of deep emotional investment, they are especially interesting to think about. Second, social experience continually presents children with discrepancies between behaviours they expect and those that occur, which prompts them to revise their thoughts about social concerns. Finally, children and the people with whom they interact are all human beings, with the same basic nervous system and a background of similar experiences. This means that interpreting behaviour from the self's point of view often helps us understand others' actions. When it does not, humans are equipped with a powerful capacity—*perspective taking*—that permits us to imagine what another's thoughts and feelings might be.

Our discussion is organized around three aspects of development: thinking about the self, thinking about other people, and thinking about relationships between people. Perhaps you have noticed that we have already considered some social-cognitive topics in previous chapters—for example, referential communication skills in Chapter 9 and emotional understanding in Chapter 10. Children's sense of morality is another important social-cognitive topic, but research on it is so extensive that it merits a chapter of its own. We will consider the development of moral reasoning in Chapter 12.

# Emergence of Self and Development of Self-Concept

VIRTUALLY ALL INVESTIGATORS agree that the self has two distinct aspects, identified by philosopher William James (1890/1963) over a century ago:

- The **I-self,** a sense of self as *knower* and *actor.* It includes the following realizations: *self-awareness,* that the self is separate from the surrounding world and has a private, inner life not accessible to others; *self-continuity,* that the self remains the same person over time; *self-coherence,* that the self is a single, consistent, bounded entity; and *self-agency,* that the self controls its own thoughts and actions.

---

**social cognition**
Thinking about the characteristics of the self and other people.

**I-self**
A sense of self as knower and actor. Includes self-awareness, self-continuity, self-coherence, and self-agency.

**me-self**
A sense of self as object of knowledge and evaluation. Consists of all qualities that make the self unique, including material, psychological, and social characteristics.

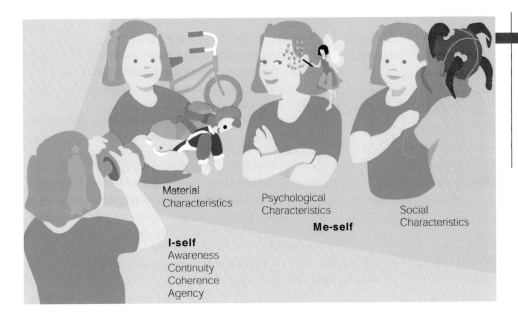

**The I-self and the me-self.**
The I-self is a sense of self as knower and actor. It is the active observer. The me-self is a sense of self as object of knowledge and evaluation. It is made up of the cognitive representations that arise from the observing process.

Material Characteristics

Psychological Characteristics

**Me-self**

Social Characteristics

**I-self**
Awareness
Continuity
Coherence
Agency

- The **me-self,** a sense of self as *object of knowledge and evaluation.* The me-self consists of all qualities that make the self unique—*material characteristics,* such as physical appearance and possessions; *psychological characteristics,* including desires, attitudes, beliefs, thought processes, and personality traits; and *social characteristics,* such as roles and relationships with others.

The I-self and the me-self are complementary. The I-self can be thought of as the *active observer;* it emerges first. The me-self follows and is made up of the *cognitive representations* that arise from the observing process (see Figure 11.1) (Harter, 1999; Lewis, 1994). In sum, self-development begins with the dawning of self-awareness in infancy and gradually evolves into a rich, multifaceted, organized view of the self's characteristics and capacities during childhood and adolescence.

### SELF-AWARENESS

As early as the first few months of life, infants smile and return friendly behaviours to their reflection in a mirror. When do they realize that the charming baby gazing and grinning back is the self?

**BEGINNINGS OF THE I-SELF.** To answer this question, researchers have exposed infants and toddlers to images of themselves in mirrors, on videotapes, and in photos. When shown two side-by-side video images of their kicking legs, one from their own perspective (camera behind the baby) and one from an observer's perspective (camera in front of the baby), 3-month-olds looked longer at the observer's view (see Figure 11.2a). In another video-image comparison, they looked longer at a reversal of their leg positions than at a normal view (see Figure 11.2b) (Rochat, 1998). Furthermore, when shown their videotaped image next to that of a peer, 3-month-olds (who in Western cultures have seen their image in mirrors) look longer at the peer's image (Bahrick, Moss, & Fadil, 1996). Within the first few months, then, infants seem to have a budding I-self—some sense of their own body as a distinct entity, since they have habituated to it, as indicated by their interest in novel images.

How do infants develop this awareness? According to many theorists, the beginnings of the I-self lie in infants' recognition that their own actions cause objects and people to react in predictable ways. In support of this idea, parents who encourage babies to explore and who respond to their signals consistently and sensitively (as indicated by a secure attachment

Baby's View    Observer's View
(a)

Left    Right    Right    Left
Normal View    Reversed View
(b)

**Three-month-olds' emerging self-awareness, as indicated by reactions to video images.**
(a) When shown two side-by-side views of their kicking legs, babies looked longer at the novel, observer's view than at their own view. (b) When shown a normal view of their leg positions alongside a reversed view, infants looked longer at the novel, reversed view. (Adapted from Rochat, 1998.)

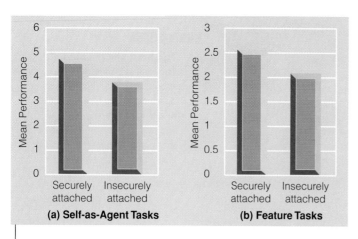

**FIGURE** 11.3

**Relationship of attachment quality to toddlers' performance on self-as-agent and self-knowledge tasks.** Compared with insecure toddlers, securely attached toddlers displayed (a) more complex, self-related actions during pretend play and (b) more complex knowledge of the self's features. (Adapted from Pipp, Easterbrooks, & Harmon, 1992.)

This 1-year-old notices the correspondence between her own movements and the movements of the image in the mirror, a cue that helps her figure out that the grinning baby is really herself.

bond) are advanced in constructing a sense of self as agent (see Figure 11.3a). For example, between 1 and 2 years of age, they display more complex, self-related actions during pretend play (such as making a doll labelled as the self take a drink or kiss a teddy bear) (Pipp, Easterbrooks, & Harmon, 1992).

As infants act on the environment, they notice effects that help them sort out self from other people and objects (Rochat, 2001). For example, batting a mobile and seeing it swing in a pattern different from the infant's own actions informs the baby about the relation between self and physical world. Smiling and vocalizing at a caregiver who smiles and vocalizes back helps specify the relation between self and social world. And watching the movements of one's own hand provides still another kind of feedback—one under much more direct control than other people or objects. The contrast between these experiences may help infants build an image of self as separate from external reality.

**BEGINNINGS OF THE ME-SELF.** During the second year, toddlers start to construct the me-self. Consequently, they become consciously aware of the self's physical features. In one study, 9- to 24-month-olds were placed in front of a mirror. Then, under the pretext of wiping the baby's face, each mother was asked to rub red dye on her child's nose. Younger infants touched the mirror as if the red mark had nothing to do with them. But by 15 months, toddlers rubbed their strange-looking noses, a response indicating awareness of their unique appearance—the "me" in the mirror (Lewis & Brooks-Gunn, 1979). In addition, some toddlers act silly or coy in front of the mirror, playfully experimenting with the way the self looks (Bullock & Lutkenhaus, 1990).

Around age 2, **self-recognition**—perception of the self as a physically distinct being—is well established. Children recognize themselves in photos, and almost all use their name or a personal pronoun ("I" or "me") to refer to themselves (Lewis & Brooks-Gunn, 1979). Like the I-self, the me-self seems to be fostered by sensitive caregiving. Securely attached toddlers display more complex featural knowledge (such as labelling their own and their parents' body parts) than do their insecurely attached agemates (see Figure 11.3b) (Pipp, Easterbrooks, & Brown, 1993).

**SELF-AWARENESS AND EARLY EMOTIONAL AND SOCIAL DEVELOPMENT.** Self-awareness quickly becomes a central part of children's emotional and social lives. Recall from Chapter 10 that self-conscious emotions depend on toddlers' emerging sense of self. Self-awareness also leads to first efforts to appreciate another's perspective. For example, it is associated with the beginnings of empathy (see page 409) and self-conscious behaviour—bashfulness and embarrassment. Furthermore, mirror self-recognition precedes the appearance of sustained, mutual peer imitation—a partner banging an object, the toddler copying the behaviour, the partner imitating back, and the toddler copying again (Asendorpf, Warkentin, & Baudonniere, 1996). These exchanges indicate that the toddler not only is interested in the playmate but realizes that the playmate is interested in him or her.

Two-year-olds' consciousness of their unique features is linked to the emergence of a sense of ownership. The stronger 2-year-olds' self-definitions, the more possessive they tend to be, claiming objects as "Mine!" (Levine, 1983; Fasig, 2000). Nevertheless, the ability to identify objects as belonging to the self suggests another advance—a beginning grasp of self-continuity, or sameness over time.

A firmer sense of self also permits children to cooperate in resolving disputes over objects, playing games, and solving simple problems (Brownell & Carriger, 1990; Caplan et al., 1991). Accordingly, when trying to promote friendly peer interaction, parents and teachers can accept the young child's possessiveness as a sign of self-assertion ("Yes, that's your toy") and then encourage compromise ("but in a little while, would you give someone else a turn?"), rather than simply insisting on sharing.

## THE CATEGORICAL AND REMEMBERED SELVES

Language is a powerful tool in self-development (Lewis, 1994). Because it permits children to represent and express the me-self more clearly, it greatly enhances young preschoolers' self-awareness.

Between 18 and 30 months, children develop a **categorical self** as they classify themselves and others on the basis of age ("baby," "boy," or "man"), sex ("boy" versus "girl" and "woman" versus "man"), physical characteristics ("big," "strong"), and even goodness and badness ("I good girl." "Tommy mean!"). They also start to refer to the self's competencies ("Did it!" "I can't") (Stipek, Gralinski, & Kopp, 1990).

In Chapter 7, we noted that conversations with adults about the past and the beginnings of a "psychological self" lead to an autobiographical memory. This life-story narrative grants the child a **remembered self**—a more coherent and enduring portrait than offered by the isolated, episodic memories of the first few years. As early as age 2, both working-class and middle-class parents use these discussions to impart rules and standards and include much descriptive and evaluative information about the child ("We made mashed potatoes, and you shook the salt and pepper all over them. That's a very important job!") (Burger & Miller, 1999). Consequently, personal storytelling serves as a rich source of self-knowledge. And as the Cultural Influences box on page 444 reveals, these narratives are a major means through which parents imbue the young child's me-self with cultural values.

## THE INNER SELF: YOUNG CHILDREN'S THEORY OF MIND

As children think more about themselves and others, they form a naive *theory of mind*—a coherent understanding of their own and others' rich mental lives. Recall from Chapter 7 that after age 2½, children refer to mental states, such as "want," "think," and "pretend," frequently and appropriately in everyday language. Although they confuse certain mental terms (see page 294), young preschoolers are clearly aware of an **inner self** of private thoughts and imaginings.

How does the young child view this inner self, and how does this view change with age? Investigators are interested in this question because ideas about the mind are powerful tools in predicting and explaining our own and others' everyday behaviour.

**EARLY UNDERSTANDINGS OF MENTAL STATES.** Over the first year of life, infants build an implicit appreciation of people as animate beings whose behaviour is governed by intentions, desires, and feelings. This sets the stage for the verbalized mental understandings that blossom in early childhood. At York University, researchers found that as early as age 2 months, infants distinguish animate beings from inanimate objects; they imitate people's actions but not objects' simulations of those actions (Legerstee, 1991). In Chapter 10, we saw that 3-month-olds smile more at people than objects, and they become upset when people fail to communicate, posing a still face. By 6 months, when infants see people talk, they expect the talk to be directed at other people and not at inanimate objects (Legerstee, Barna, & Diadamo, 2000). At the end of the first year, infants' capacity for joint attention, social referencing, and preverbal gestures (see Chapters 9 and 10) suggest that they realize that people can share and influence each other's mental states. The second year brings a clearer grasp of people's emotions and desires, as reflected in toddlers' capacity to empathize.

As language for talking about the mind expands in the third year, children appreciate the connections between perceiving, feeling, and desiring. For example, seeing that a person peeking inside a box is *happy*, 2½-year-olds predict that the box contains a *desirable* rather than an *undesirable* snack. In addition, they often talk about links between perception and desire ("I *want see* beaver") and emotion and desire ("I *like* celery, so I *want* celery"). Occasionally, they link all three ("You *want* to *see* how he *cried*") (Wellman, Phillips, & Rodriguez, 2000). But

**self-recognition**
Perception of the self as a separate being, distinct from other people and objects.

**categorical self**
Early classification of the self according to salient ways people differ, such as age, sex, physical characteristics, and goodness and badness.

**remembered self**
The life story constructed from conversations with adults about the past that leads to an autobiographical memory.

**inner self**
Awareness of the self's private thoughts and imaginings.

# cultural influences

## CULTURAL VARIATIONS IN PERSONAL STORYTELLING: IMPLICATIONS FOR EARLY SELF-CONCEPT

Preschoolers of many cultural backgrounds participate in personal storytelling with their parents. Striking cultural differences exist in parents' selection and interpretation of events in these early narratives, affecting the way children come to view themselves.

In ethnographic research, Peggy Miller and her colleagues spent hundreds of hours over a 2-year period studying the storytelling practices of six middle-SES Irish-American families in Chicago and six middle-SES Chinese families in Taiwan. From extensive videotapes of adults' conversations with 2½-year-olds, the researchers identified personal stories and coded them for content, quality of their endings, and evaluation of the child (Miller, Fung, & Mintz, 1996; Miller et al., 1997).

Parents in both cultures discussed pleasurable holidays and family excursions about as often and in similar ways. Chinese parents, however, more often told lengthy stories about the child's misdeeds, such as using impolite language, writing on the wall, or playing in an overly rowdy way. These narratives were conveyed with warmth and caring, stressed the impact of misbehaviour on others ("You made

Mama lose face"), and often ended with direct teaching of proper behaviour ("Saying dirty words is not good"). In the few instances in which Irish-American stories referred to transgressions, parents downplayed their seriousness, attributing them to the child's spunk and assertiveness.

Early narratives about the child seem to launch preschoolers' self-concepts on culturally distinct paths. Influenced by Confucian traditions of strict discipline and social obligations, Chinese parents integrated these values into their personal stories, affirming the importance of not disgracing the family and explicitly teaching proper behaviour in the story's conclusion. Although Irish-American parents disciplined their children, they rarely dwelt on misdeeds in storytelling.

This Chinese child on an outing with her mother was about to eat a sweet treat she had been told to save until later. Her mother stops the bike and speaks gently to her. Chinese parents often tell preschoolers stories about the child's misdeeds, emphasizing their negative impact on others. The Chinese child's self-concept, in turn, emphasizes social obligations.

© OWEN FRANKLIN/STOCK BOSTON

Rather, they cast the child's shortcomings in a positive light, perhaps to encourage a positive sense of self. Hence, the Chinese child's self-image emphasizes obligations to others, whereas the U.S. child's is more autonomous (Markus, Mullally, & Kitayama, 1997).

---

**desire theory of mind**
The theory of mind of 2- and 3-year-olds, who understand the relation of desire to perception and emotion but who assume that people's behaviour is merely a reflection of their desires. Fails to take account of the influence of interpretive mental states, such as beliefs, on behaviour.

**belief–desire theory of mind**
The theory of mind that emerges around age 4 in which both beliefs and desires determine behaviour. Closely resembles the everyday psychology of adults.

although 2-year-olds have started to integrate mental states, their understanding is limited to a simplistic **desire theory of mind** (Bartsch & Wellman, 1995). They think that people always act in ways consistent with their desires and do not understand that less obvious, more interpretive mental states, such as beliefs, also affect behaviour.

**DEVELOPMENT OF BELIEF–DESIRE REASONING.** According to Henry Wellman, from age 4 on, children realize that both *beliefs* and *desires* determine *actions*, and they understand the relationship between these constructs (Gopnik & Wellman, 1994). Turn back to the beginning of this chapter, and notice how 4-year-old Ellen deliberately tried to alter her mother's *belief* about the motive behind her pretending—in hopes of warding off any *desire* on her mother's part to punish her. Wellman labels Ellen's more sophisticated view of the mind a **belief–desire theory**—a conception of mentality that closely resembles the everyday psychology of adults.

A dramatic illustration of belief–desire reasoning comes from games that test whether preschoolers know that *false beliefs*—ones that do not represent reality accurately—can guide people's actions. To test for a grasp of false belief, researchers present situations that test for children's understanding that a person will look for an object in a certain location based on where she believes the object to be, regardless of its true location. For example: Show a child two small closed boxes, one a familiar Band-Aid box and the other a plain, unmarked box (see Figure 11.4). Then say, "Pick the box you think has the Band-Aids in it." Almost always, children pick the marked container. Next, ask the child to look inside both boxes; when she does, contrary to her own belief, she finds that the marked one is empty and the unmarked one contains the Band-Aids. Finally, introduce the child to a hand puppet and explain, "Here's Pam. She has a cut, see? Where do you think she'll look for Band-Aids? Why would she look in there? Before you looked inside, did you think that the (unmarked) box contained Band-Aids? Why?" (Bartsch & Wellman, 1995; Gopnik & Welman, 1994). Only a handful of 3-year-olds but many 4-year-olds can explain Pam's and their own false beliefs.

Many studies confirm that children's understanding of their own and others' susceptibility to false belief strengthens over the preschool years, becoming more secure between ages 4 and 6 (Flavell & Miller, 1998; Wellman, Cross, & Watson, 2001). Mastery of false belief signals a change in representation—the ability to view beliefs as *interpretations,* not just reflections, of reality. Does this remind you of school-age children's more active view of the mind, discussed in Chapter 7? Belief–desire reasoning may mark the very beginnings of this overall change.

**CONSEQUENCES OF BELIEF–DESIRE REASONING.** As soon as it emerges, the capacity to use both beliefs and desires to predict people's behaviour seems to help children interact more favourably with others. The better 3- to 6-year-olds perform on false-belief tasks, the more advanced they are in social skills, as rated by their teachers (Watson et al., 1999). False-belief understanding also predicts gains in 3- and 4-year-olds' sociodramatic play—specifically, the capacity to engage in joint planning, to negotiate pretend roles, and to imagine verbally, without the support of real objects (Jenkins & Astington, 2000).

Once children grasp the relation between beliefs and behaviour, they refine their understanding, applying it to a wider range of situations. For example, the eyewitness memories of children who pass false-belief tasks are more accurate than those of children who do not, because children who understand false belief are less suggestible (Templeton & Wilcox, 2000). They realize that one person can present misinformation to another, which can affect the second individual's beliefs. Consequently, in reporting observed events, such children are more likely to resist attempts to mislead them. Development of a belief–desire theory may be a major reason that children's eyewitness memories become more dependable after age 6, when appreciation of the belief–reality distinction is more secure (see Chapter 7, page 292).

School-age children soon apply their grasp of the relation between beliefs and behaviour in their own efforts to persuade others. Third graders are more adept than kindergartners and first graders in considering people's beliefs when trying to convince them to do something. They know, for example, that a boy who wants a kitten but whose mother believes that cats scratch furniture should focus on telling his mother that the cat is declawed rather than litter trained (Bartsch & London, 2000).

In sum, the development of a belief–desire theory strengthens children's sensitivity to people's beliefs and fosters their reasoned attempts to change these beliefs. As a result, it contributes to diverse social competencies.

**FACTORS CONTRIBUTING TO YOUNG CHILDREN'S THEORY OF MIND.** How do children develop a theory of mind at such a young age? Although great controversy surrounds this question, research suggests that language, cognitive abilities, make-believe play, and social experiences contribute.

*Language.* Understanding the mind requires the ability to reflect on thoughts, made possible by language. A grasp of false belief is related to language ability equivalent to that of

**FIGURE 11.4**

**Example of a false-belief task.**
(a) An adult shows a child the contents of a Band-Aid box and an unmarked box. The Band-Aids are in the unmarked container. (b) The adult introduces the child to a hand puppet named Pam, asks the child to predict where Pam would look for the Band-Aids and to explain Pam's behaviour. The task reveals whether children understand that without having seen that the Band-Aids are in the unmarked container, Pam will hold a false belief.

an average 4-year-old or higher (Jenkins & Astington, 1996). More specifically, use of complex sentences involving mental-state words, as in, "I thought the sock was in the drawer," is linked to false-belief understanding (de Villiers & de Villiers, 2000). Among the Quechua of the Peruvian highlands, adults refer to mental states such as "think" and "believe" indirectly, since their language lacks mental-state terms. Quechua children have difficulty with false-belief tasks for years after children in industrialized nations have mastered them (Vinden, 1996).

***Cognitive Abilities.*** The ability of 3- and 4-year-olds to inhibit inappropriate responses, think flexibly, and plan predicts current performance on false-belief tasks as well as improvements over time (Carlson & Moses, 2001; Hughes, 1998). Like language, these cognitive skills are thought to enhance children's capacity to reflect on their experiences and mental states.

***Make-Believe Play.*** Earlier we noted that theory of mind fosters children's sociodramatic play. But make-believe also offers a rich context for thinking about the mind. As children act out various roles, they notice that the mind can change what objects and events mean. Often they create situations they know to be untrue in the real world and reason about their implications (Harris & Leevers, 2000). These experiences may increase children's awareness that belief influences behaviour. In support of this idea, preschoolers who engage in extensive fantasy play are more advanced in understanding of false belief and other aspects of the mind (Astington & Jenkins, 1995). And the better 3- and 4-year-olds are at reasoning about situations that contradict a real-world state of affairs, the more likely they are to pass false-belief tasks (Riggs & Peterson, 2000).

***Social Interaction.*** Preschoolers with older siblings are advanced in performance on false-belief tasks (Ruffman et al., 1998). Having older siblings may allow for many interactions that highlight the influence of beliefs on behaviour—through teasing, trickery, make-believe play, and discussing feelings.

Preschool friendships also may foster mental understanding. The more 3- and 4-year-olds engage in mental-state talk with friends, the better their performance on false-belief tasks more than a year later (Hughes & Dunn, 1998).

© TONY FREEMAN/PHOTOEDIT

Having older siblings fosters an understanding of false belief, probably because sibling interactions often highlight the influence of beliefs on behaviour—through teasing, trickery, make-believe play, and discussing feelings.

Interacting with more mature members of society is also helpful. In a study of Greek preschoolers with large networks of extended family and neighbours, daily contact with many adults and older children predicted mastery of false belief (Lewis et al., 1996). These encounters probably offer extra opportunities to talk about the reasons for people's behaviour, speculate about what they might do in the future, and observe different points of view.

Some nativist theorists believe that for children to profit from the social experiences just described, the human brain must be specialized for "reading" people's minds, just as it is prewired to make sense of physical reality and language (see Chapters 6 and 9). To support this view, nativists point out that reasoning about beliefs is unique to humans. Chimpanzees fail tasks assessing false belief and the mental understandings that precede it (Povinelli & Giambrone, 2000). Nativists also claim that children with *autism,* who do not grasp false belief, are deficient in the brain mechanism that enables humans to detect mental states. See the Biology & Environment box on the following page to examine these fascinating findings—and to critically evaluate their implications for the biological basis of theory of mind.

# biology & environment

## "MINDBLINDNESS" AND AUTISM

Sidney stood at the water table in his preschool classroom, repeatedly filling a plastic cup and dumping out its contents. Dip-splash, dip-splash he went, until his teacher came over and redirected his actions. Without looking at his teacher's face, Sidney moved to a new repetitive pursuit: pouring water from one cup into another and back again. As other children entered the play space and conversed, Sidney hardly noticed. He rarely spoke, and when he did, he usually used words to get things he wanted, not to exchange ideas.

Sidney has *autism*, the most severe behaviour disorder of childhood. The term *autism* means "absorbed in the self," an apt description of Sidney. Like other children with the disorder, Sidney is impaired in emotional and gestural (nonverbal) behaviours required for successful social interaction. In addition, his language is delayed and stereotyped; some autistic children do not speak at all. Sidney's interests, which focus on the physical world, are narrow and overly intense. For example, one day he sat for more than an hour making a toy ferris wheel go round and round.

Researchers agree that the disorder stems from abnormal brain functioning, usually due to genetic or prenatal environmental causes. Growing evidence suggests that one psychological factor involved is a severely deficient or absent theory of mind. Long after they reach the intellectual level of an average 4-year-old, autistic children have great difficulty with false-belief tasks. Most cannot attribute mental states to others or to themselves. Such words as "believe," "think," "know," "feel," and "pretend" are rarely part of their vocabularies (Happé, 1995; Yirmiya, Solomonica-Levi, & Shulman, 1996).

As early as the second year, autistic children show deficits in skills believed to lead to an understanding of mentality. For example, they less often establish joint attention, engage in social referencing, or imitate an adult's novel behaviours than do other children (Charman et al., 1997; Leekam, Lopez, & Moore, 2000). Furthermore, they are relatively insensitive to a speaker's gaze as a cue to what he is talking about (Baron-Cohen, Baldwin, & Crowson, 1997). Finally, autistic children engage in much less make-believe play than do age- and mental-ability-matched comparison groups—both normal children and children with other developmental problems (Baron-Cohen, Baldwin, & Crowson, 1997; Hughes, 1998).

Do these findings indicate that autism is due to an impairment in an innate social-cognitive brain module, which leaves the child "mindblind" and therefore unable to engage in human sociability? Some researchers think so (Baron-Cohen, 1995; Scholl & Leslie, 2000). But others point out that autistic individuals are not alone in poor performance on tasks assessing mental understanding; nonautistic, mentally retarded individuals also show it (Yirmiya et al., 1998). This suggests that some kind of general intellectual impairment may be involved.

Another conjecture is that autism is due to a memory deficit, which makes it hard to retain the parts of complex tasks (Bennetto, Pennington, & Rogers, 1996). Perhaps this explains autistic children's preoccupation with simple, repetitive acts. It also may contribute to their difficulty with tasks that require them to integrate several parts into a coherent whole to solve a problem (Jarold et al., 2000; Yirmiya & Shulman, 1996). These memory and integration deficits would interfere with understanding the social world, since social interaction takes place quickly and requires combining information from various sources.

At present, it is not clear which of these hypotheses is correct. Although researchers agree that the disorder stems from abnormal brain functioning, psychophysiological research has not yet pinpointed a specific brain region (Tsai, 1999). Rather than a specific impairment in "mind-reading," one or more nonsocial-cognitive deficits might underlie the tragic social isolation of children like Sidney. However, much more research is needed to verify these alternative claims.

This autistic girl does not take note of a speaker's gaze as a cue to what he or she is talking about. For this reason, the girl's teacher takes extra steps to capture her attention in a science lesson. Researchers disagree on whether autistic children's "mindblindness" is due to an impairment in an innate social-cognitive brain module or to a general memory deficit.

© WILL HART

## SELF-CONCEPT

As children develop an appreciation of their inner mental world, they think more intently about themselves. During early childhood, the me-self expands as children begin to construct a **self-concept,** the set of attributes, abilities, attitudes, and values that an individual believes defines who he or she is.

**EARLY CHILDHOOD.** Ask a 3- to 5-year-old to tell you about him- or herself, and you are likely to hear something like this: "I'm Tommy. See, I got this new red T-shirt. I'm 4 years old. I can brush my teeth, and I can wash my hair all by myself. I have a new Tinkertoy set, and I made this big, big tower." As these statements indicate, preschoolers' self-concepts are very concrete. Usually they mention observable characteristics, such as their name, physical appearance, possessions, and everyday behaviours (Harter, 1996; Watson, 1990).

By age 3½, children also describe themselves in terms of typical emotions and attitudes, as in "I'm happy when I play with my friends" or "I don't like being with grownups" (Eder, 1989). This suggests a beginning understanding of their unique psychological characteristics. As further support for this budding grasp of personality, when someone is given a trait label, such as "shy" or "mean," 4-year-olds infer appropriate motives and feelings. For example, they know that a shy person doesn't like to be with unfamiliar people (Heyman & Gelman, 1999). But preschoolers do not refer directly to traits, by making such statements as "I'm helpful," "I'm shy," or "I'm usually truthful." This capacity must wait for greater cognitive maturity.

**MIDDLE CHILDHOOD.** Over time, children organize their observations of typical behaviours and internal states into general dispositions that they verbalize to others, with a major shift taking place between ages 8 and 11. The following response from an 11-year-old reflects this change:

My name is A. I'm a human being. I'm a girl. I'm a truthful person. I'm not pretty. I do so-so in my studies. I'm a very good cellist. I'm a very good pianist. I'm a little bit tall for my age. I like several boys. I like several girls. I'm old-fashioned. I play tennis. I am a very good swimmer. I try to be helpful. I'm always ready to be friends with anybody. Mostly I'm good, but I lose my temper. I'm not well-liked by some girls and boys. I don't know if I'm liked by boys or not. (Montemayor & Eisen, 1977, pp. 317–318)

Notice that instead of specific behaviours, this child emphasizes competencies, as in "I'm a very good cellist" (Damon & Hart, 1988). In addition, she clearly describes personality traits and mentions both positive and negative attributes—"truthful" but "not pretty," a "good cellist [and] pianist" but only "so-so in my studies." Older school-age children are far less likely to describe themselves in unrealistically positive, all-or-none ways (Harter, 1996).

A major reason for these qualified self-descriptions is that school-age children often make **social comparisons**—that is, judge their appearance, abilities, and behaviour in relation to those of others. Although 4- to 6-year-olds can compare their own performance to that of one peer and use that information as a basis for self-evaluation, older children can compare multiple individuals, including themselves. Consequently, they conclude that they are "very good" at some things, "so-so" at others, and not good at still others (Butler, 1998; Ruble & Frey, 1991).

**ADOLESCENCE.** In early adolescence, young people unify separate traits, such as "smart" and "talented," into higher-order, abstract descriptors, such as "intelligent." But these generalizations about the self are not interconnected, and often they are contradictory. For example, 12- to 14-year-olds might mention such opposing traits as "intelligent" and "airhead" or "shy" and "outgoing." These disparities result from social pressures to display

Preschoolers' self-concepts emphasize observable characteristics—the child's name, physical appearance, possessions, and everyday behaviours. If asked to tell about himself, this 4-year-old might say, "I can help my dad load the dishwasher!" In a few years, he will begin to mention personality traits, such as "I'm helpful and responsible."

**self-concept**
The set of attributes, abilities, attitudes, and values that an individual believes defines who she is.

**social comparisons**
Judgments of one's own abilities, behaviour, and appearance in relation to those of others.

different selves in different relationships—with parents, classmates, close friends, and romantic partners. As adolescents' social world expands, contradictory self-descriptions increase, and teenagers frequently agonize over "which is the real me" (Harter, 1999; Harter & Monsour, 1992).

By middle to late adolescence, teenagers combine their various traits into an organized system. And they begin to use qualifiers ("I have a *fairly* quick temper," "I'm not *thoroughly* honest"), which reveal their awareness that psychological qualities often change from one situation to the next. Older adolescents also add integrating principles, which make sense of formerly troublesome contradictions. For example, one young person remarked, "I'm very adaptable. When I'm around my friends, who think that what I say is important, I'm very talkative; but around my family I'm quiet because they're never interested enough to really listen to me" (Damon, 1990, p. 88).

Compared with school-age children, teenagers also place more emphasis on social virtues, such as being friendly, considerate, kind, and cooperative. Adolescents are very preoccupied with being liked and viewed positively by others, and their statements about themselves reflect this concern. In addition, personal and moral values appear as key themes in older adolescents' self-concepts. For example, here is how 16-year-old Ben described himself in terms of honesty to himself and others:

> I like being honest like with yourself and with everyone.... [A person] could be, in the eyes of everyone else the best person in the world, but if I knew they were lying or cheating, in my eyes they wouldn't be.... When I'm friendly, it's more to tell people that it's all right to be yourself. Not necessarily don't conform, but just whatever you are, you know, be happy with that.... So I'm not an overly bubbly person that goes around, "Hi, how are you?" ... But if someone wants to talk to me, you know, sure. I wouldn't like, not talk to someone. (Damon & Hart, 1988, pp. 120–121)

Ben's account of his personal traits and values forms a coherent narrative. As adolescents revise their views of themselves to include enduring beliefs and plans, they move toward the kind of unity of self that is central to identity development.

## COGNITIVE, SOCIAL, AND CULTURAL INFLUENCES ON SELF-CONCEPT

What factors are responsible for these revisions in self-concept? Cognitive development certainly affects the changing *structure* of the self. School-age children, as we saw in Chapter 6, can better coordinate several aspects of a situation in reasoning about their physical world. They show improved ability to relate separate observations in the social realm as well. Consequently, they combine typical experiences and behaviours into stable psychological dispositions, blend positive and negative characteristics, and compare their own characteristics with those of many other peers (Harter, 1998, 1999). In middle childhood, children also gain a clearer understanding of traits as linked to specific desires (a "generous" person *wants* to share) and, therefore, as causes of behaviour (Yuill & Pearson, 1998). For this reason, they may mention traits more often. And formal operational thought transforms the adolescent's vision of the self into a complex, well-organized, internally consistent picture (Harter, 1998, 1999).

The changing *content* of the self is a product of both cognitive capacities and feedback from others. Early in this century, sociologist George Herbert Mead (1934) described the self as a blend of what we imagine important people in our lives think of us. He believed that a psychological self emerges when the child's *I-self* adopts a view of the *me-self* that resembles the attitudes of significant others. Mead called this reflected self the **generalized other.** In other words, *perspective-taking skills*—in particular, an improved ability to infer what other people are thinking—are crucial in the development of a self-concept based on personality traits. During middle childhood and adolescence, young people become better at "reading" messages they receive from others and incorporating these into their self-definitions. As

**generalized other**
A blend of what we imagine important people in our lives think of us. Contributes to a self-concept comprising personality traits.

During the school years, children's self-concepts expand to include feedback from a wider range of people as they spend more time in settings beyond the home. As part of a club activity, these boys wrap holiday presents for poverty-stricken young children. Helpfulness and kindness are probably important aspects of their self-definitions.

school-age children internalize others' expectations, they form an *ideal self* (what they hope to become) that they use to evaluate their *real self*. As we will see shortly, a large discrepancy between the ideal and real selves can greatly affect self-esteem, leading to feelings of sadness, hopelessness, and depression.

During middle childhood, children look to more people for information about themselves as they enter a wider range of settings in school and community. This is reflected in children's frequent reference to social groups in their self-descriptions (Livesley & Bromley, 1973). "I'm a Boy Scout, a paper boy, and a Prairie City soccer player," one 10-year-old remarked. Gradually, as children move into adolescence, their sources of self-definition become more selective. Although parents remain influential, between ages 8 and 15, peers become more important. And over time, self-concept becomes increasingly vested in feedback from close friends (Oosterwegel & Oppenheimer, 1993).

Keep in mind, however, that these changes are based on interviews with North American and Western European children. Development of self-concept does not follow the same path in all societies. Recall from earlier chapters that Asian parents stress harmonious interdependence, whereas Western parents emphasize the person's separateness and the importance of asserting the self. Consequently, in China and Japan, the self is defined in relation to the social group. In Canada and the United States, the self usually becomes the "property" of a self-contained individual (Markus & Kitayama, 1991). Turn back to page 444, and notice this difference in mothers' personal storytelling with their young children.

A strong collectivist theme is also reflected in the values of many subcultures in Western nations. In one study, children in a Puerto Rican fishing village more often described themselves as "polite," "nice," "respectful," and "obedient" than did children in a U.S. town. Puerto Rican children justified these social traits by noting the positive reactions they evoke from others. In contrast, the U.S. children more often mentioned individualistic traits, such as interests, preferences, and skills (Damon, 1988). In characterizing themselves, children from individualistic cultures seem to be more egoistic and competitive, those from collectivist cultures more concerned with the welfare of others—a finding that underscores the powerful impact of the social environment on the makeup of self-concept.

Now pause to review. The Milestones table on the following page summarizes the vast changes in self-conceptions from infancy through adolescence, considered in the first part of this chapter.

## ASK YOURSELF

**review**    What factors contribute to development of a belief–desire theory of mind, and why is each influential?

**review**    Describe major changes in self-concept from early childhood to adolescence. What factors lead self-descriptions to change in these ways?

**apply**    List indicators of healthy self-development in the first 2 years, and suggest ways that parents can promote a sturdy sense of self in infants and toddlers.

**connect**    Recall from Chapter 6 (see page 237) that between 4 and 8 years, children figure out who is really behind the activities of Santa Claus and the Tooth Fairy, and they realize that magicians use trickery. How might these understandings relate to their developing theory of mind?

# milestones

## EMERGENCE OF SELF AND DEVELOPMENT OF SELF-CONCEPT

| AGE | MILESTONES |
|---|---|
| 1–2 years  | ♪ Self-recognition becomes well established. |
| | ♪ Categorical self develops. |
| 3–5 years | ♪ Remembered self, in the form of a life story, develops. |
| | ♪ Desire theory of mind expands into a belief–desire theory, as indicated by mastery of false-belief tasks. |
| | ♪ Self-concept emphasizes observable characteristics and typical emotions and attitudes. |
| 6–10 years | ♪ Self-concept emphasizes personality traits and includes both positive and negative attributes. |
| | ♪ Social comparisons among multiple individuals appear. |
| 11 years–adulthood | ♪ Self-concept includes higher-order, abstract descriptors that unify separate traits (for example, "smart" and "talented" into "intelligent"). |
| | ♪ Traits making up self-concept are combined into an organized system. |

*Note:* These milestones represent overall age trends. Individual differences exist in the precise age at which each milestone is attained.

# Self-Esteem: The Evaluative Side of Self-Concept

SO FAR, WE HAVE focused on how the general structure and content of self-concept change with age. Another component of self-concept is **self-esteem,** the judgments we make about our own worth and the feelings associated with those judgments. According to Morris Rosenberg (1979), "a person with high self-esteem is fundamentally satisfied with the type of person he is, yet he may acknowledge his faults while hoping to overcome them" (p. 31). High self-esteem implies a realistic evaluation of the self's characteristics and competencies, coupled with an attitude of self-acceptance and self-respect.

Self-esteem ranks among the most important aspects of self-development, since evaluations of our own competencies affect emotional experiences, future behaviour, and long-term psychological adjustment. As soon as a categorical self with features that can be judged positively or negatively is in place, children become self-evaluative beings. Around age 2, they call a parent's attention to an achievement, such as completing a puzzle, by pointing and saying something like "Look, Mom!" In addition, 2-year-olds are likely to smile when they succeed at a task set for them by an adult and look away or frown when they fail (Stipek, Recchia, & McClintic, 1992). Self-esteem originates early, and its structure becomes increasingly elaborate with age.

**self-esteem**
The aspect of self-concept that involves judgments about one's own worth and the feelings associated with those judgments.

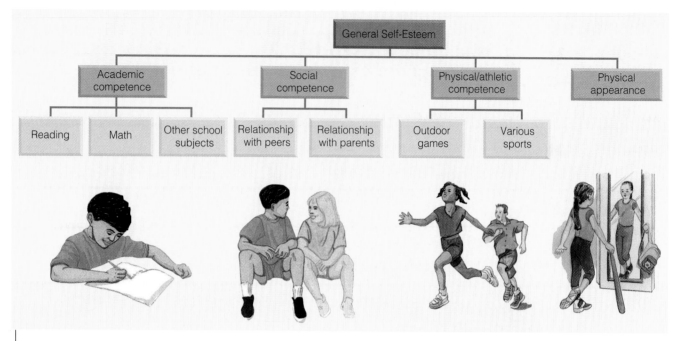

**FIGURE 11.5**

**Hierarchical structure of self-esteem in the mid-elementary school years.** From their experiences in different settings, children form at least four separate self-esteems: academic competence, social competence, physical/athletic competence, and physical appearance. These differentiate into additional self-evaluations and combine to form a general sense of self-esteem.

## ONE SELF-ESTEEM OR MANY?

Take a moment to think about your own self-esteem. Besides a global appraisal of your worth as a person, you have a variety of separate self-judgments concerning how well you perform at different activities.

Researchers have studied the multifaceted nature of self-esteem by applying *factor analysis*[1] to children's ratings of the extent to which such statements as "I am good at homework," "I'm usually the one chosen for games," and "Most kids like me," are true (Harter, 1982, 1986). Findings reveal that preschoolers have several self-esteems related to such activities as learning well in school, trying hard at challenging tasks, making friends, and treating others kindly (Marsh, Craven, & Debus, 1998). However, compared with older children, their understanding is restricted.

The structure of self-esteem depends on information available to children and the ability to process that information. By 6 to 7 years, children have formed at least four self-esteems—academic competence, social competence, physical/athletic competence, and physical appearance—that become more refined with age (Marsh, 1990). Furthermore, the capacity to view the self in terms of stable dispositions permits school-age children to combine their separate self-evaluations into a general psychological image of themselves—an overall sense of self-esteem (Harter, 1998, 1999). Consequently, self-esteem takes on the hierarchical structure shown in Figure 11.5.

Separate self-evaluations, however, do not contribute equally to general self-esteem. Instead, as children attach greater importance to some aspects, those self-judgments are weighted more heavily in the total picture. Although individual differences exist in aspects of the self deemed most important, at all ages perceived physical appearance correlates more strongly with global self-worth than any other self-esteem factor (Hymel et al., 1999). The emphasis that society and the media place on appearance has major implications for young people's overall satisfaction with themselves.

With the arrival of adolescence, several new dimensions of self-esteem are added—close friendship, romantic appeal, and job competence—that reflect important concerns of this period (Harter, 1990, 1999). Furthermore, adolescents become more discriminating in the people to whom they look for validation of their self-esteem. Some rely more on parents,

[1]Return to Chapter 8, page 313, to review the meaning of *factor analysis*.

others on teachers, and still others on peers—differences that reflect the extent to which teenagers believe that people in each context are interested in and respect them as individuals (Harter, Waters, & Whitesell, 1998).

## CHANGES IN LEVEL OF SELF-ESTEEM: THE ROLE OF SOCIAL COMPARISONS

Longitudinal and cross-sectional evidence shows that self-esteem is very high during early childhood. Then it drops over the first few years of elementary school as children increasingly engage in social comparison (Marsh, Craven, & Debus, 1998; Wigfield et al., 1997). Consequently, self-esteem adjusts to a more realistic level that matches the opinions of others as well as objective performance.

To protect their self-worth, most children eventually balance social comparison information with personal achievement goals (Ruble & Flett, 1988). Perhaps for this reason, the drop in self-esteem in the early school years is not great enough to be harmful. Then, from grade 4 on, self-esteem rises and remains high for the majority of young people, especially if they feel good about their peer relationships and athletic capabilities (Twenge & Campbell, 2001; Zimmerman et al., 1997). The only exception to this trend is a decline in self-worth for some adolescents after transition to junior high and high school. Entry into a new school, accompanied by new teacher and peer expectations, may temporarily interfere with the ability to make realistic judgments about behaviour and performance. In Chapter 15, we will take up these school transition effects. For most young people, however, becoming an adolescent leads to feelings of pride and self-confidence.

## INFLUENCES ON SELF-ESTEEM

Up to this point, we have discussed general trends in the development of self-esteem. Wide individual differences exist that correlate strongly with everyday behaviour. For example, academic self-esteem predicts children's school achievement and their willingness to try hard at challenging tasks (Marsh, Smith, & Barnes, 1985). Children with high social self-esteem are better liked by their peers (Harter, 1982). And as we saw in Chapter 5, boys come to believe they have more athletic talent than do girls, and they are more advanced in a variety of physical skills.

By adolescence, young people vary greatly in their self-esteem profiles. Whereas some evaluate themselves similarly in all areas, others are more satisfied in one or two than in others. A profile of all favourable self-evaluations is not associated with better adjustment than is a profile that is generally positive. But teenagers who feel much better about their peer relations than their academic competence and family relations tend to have adjustment difficulties. And a profile of low self-regard in all areas is linked to anxiety, depression, and increasing antisocial behaviour over time (DuBois et al., 1998, 1999).

From age 5 on, children know self-esteem is influential; they say that people who like themselves would do better at a challenging task and cope more easily with a peer's rebuff (Daniels, 1998). Because self-esteem is associated with many important outcomes, researchers have been intensely interested in identifying factors that cause it to be high for some children and low for others.

**CULTURE.** Cultural forces profoundly affect self-esteem. For example, gender-stereotyped expectations for physical attractiveness and achievement have a detrimental effect on the self-esteem of many girls. In adolescence, they score slightly lower than boys in overall sense of self-worth, partly because girls worry more about their appearance and partly because they feel more insecure about their abilities (Crain, 1996). Also, a widely accepted cultural belief is that boys have much higher self-esteem

Self-esteem rises during adolescence. These teenagers organized and carried out a car wash to raise money for their school. They appear optimistic about life and proud of their new competencies.

Children from collectivist cultures rarely call on social comparison to enhance their self-esteem. In a masquerade dance at their annual village carnival, these Caribbean children of St. Kitts display a strong sense of connection with their social group. Compared with children in individualistic societies, they are likely to be less concerned with whether another child is better at a skill than they are.

Jason, a bright adolescent growing up in a well-to-do Canadian family, earned C's and D's in academic courses because he seldom turned in homework or studied for exams. Jason's parents tried paying him for good grades, but to no avail. Next, they threatened to ground him. But when Jason's report card again showed no improvement, his parents gave in to his pleas for weekend privileges.

"If only Jason liked himself better," his father reasoned, "he'd work harder in school." Over the next 6 months, Jason's grades dropped further, and he and two of his friends were arrested for property destruction at a shopping mall. Will parenting that boosts children's self-esteem help young people like Jason, who lack character and direction? Or is Jason's parents' indulgence at the heart of his problems?

Since the 1970s, our cultural values have increasingly emphasized individualism and a focus on the self. Over the past two decades, much popular literature for parents advised promoting children's self-esteem, and special school programs were devised to boost it (Haney & Durlak, 1998). In line with these trends, the self-esteem of children and adolescents rose during this time (see Figure 11.6) (Twenge & Campbell, 2001).

According to William Damon (1995), the self-esteem movement has led many parents to conclude, incorrectly, that a child cannot develop meaningful goals and respect others without first coming to love himself. This idea is based on the assumption that self-esteem *precedes* healthy development. In other words, it must be built before anything else, through generous praise and unconditional acceptance. As a result of this belief, many parents became more indulgent. Instead of insisting on mastery of meaningful skills, many assured their children, regardless of circumstances, that they were "O.K." in every way.

Yet during the period that young people's self-esteem rose, many indicators suggested that compared to previous generations, they were actually doing less well—achieving more poorly in school and displaying more antisocial behaviour. Children and adolescents with highly inflated self-esteem—self-perceptions much more favourable than the judgments of others—often have serious adjustment problems. In one study, school-age children identified by their teachers as aggressive (frequently teasing, starting fights, telling mean lies, or excluding others) were far more likely than their classmates to rate themselves as perfect on a self-esteem measure. Individuals who feel superior frequently encounter threats to their self-worth (Hughes, Cavell, & Grossman, 1997). When a person or an event challenges their overblown self-image, they tend to lash out in anger, repudiating any sign that they are less admirable than they thought they were (Baumeister, Smart, & Boden, 1996).

than girls, yet the gender difference is small. Girls may think less well of themselves because they internalize this negative cultural message (Kling et al., 1999).

Furthermore, the role of social comparison in self-esteem varies from culture to culture. An especially strong emphasis on social comparison in school may underlie the finding that Chinese and Japanese children score lower in self-esteem than do North American children, despite their higher academic achievement (Chiu, 1992–1993; Hawkins, 1994). In Asian classrooms, competition is tough and achievement pressure is high. At the same time, Asian children less often call on social comparisons to bolster their own self-esteem. Because their culture places a high value on modesty and social harmony, they tend to be reserved about judging themselves positively but generous in their praise of others (Falbo et al., 1997; Heine & Lehman, 1995).

Finally, Caucasian-American children and adolescents have slightly lower self-esteem than do African Americans, who benefit from warm, extended families and a strong sense of ethnic pride (Gaines et al., 1997; Gray-Little & Hafdahl, 2000). Also, white girls are far more likely to show declines in self-esteem in early adolescence than are black girls, who are more satisfied with their physical appearance and peer relations (Brown et al., 1999; Eccles et al., 1999). And teenagers who attend schools or live in neighbourhoods where their SES or ethnic group is well represented have fewer self-esteem problems, perhaps because these contexts offer many opportunities for like-minded friendships and promote a stronger sense of belonging (Gray-Little & Carels, 1997).

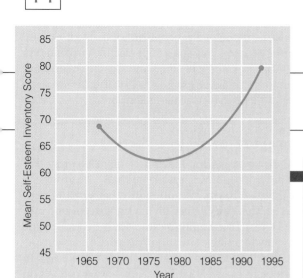

**FIGURE** 11.6

**Cohort effects for junior-high school students' self-esteem from 1965 to 1995.** Self-esteem dropped slightly during the late 1960s and 1970s. From 1980 on, the period of considerable public attention to boosting children's self-esteem, average self-esteem rose sharply. Self-esteem scores for elementary school and university students show a similar rise. (From J. M. Twenge & W. Keith Campbell, 2001, "Age and Birth Cohort Differences in Self-Esteem: A Cross-Temporal Meta-Analysis," *Personality and Social Psychology Review, 5,* p. 336. Adapted by permission.)

In Damon's view, self-esteem that fosters favourable development cannot be gained through its own pursuit; it must be earned through socially useful commitment and responsibility. Compliments, such as "you're great," "you're terrific," that have no basis in real attainment disrupt children's potential for development. Sooner or later children see through them, come to mistrust the adults who repeat them, and doubt themselves.

Cross-cultural evidence supports the view that genuine self-esteem is the product (not the producer) of real accomplishment. As we will see in Chapter 15, the academic achievement of children in North America falls behind that of children in Asian nations, such as Japan and Taiwan. Yet even though Japanese and Taiwanese high school students report higher parental expectations for school performance, they feel less stress and anxiety than do their North American agemates and display low rates of deviant behaviour. Strong parental support for achievement seems to contribute to Asian students' ability to meet rigorous academic standards while remaining well adjusted (Chen & Stevenson, 1995; Crystal et al., 1994).

In sum, parents serve children best when they guide them toward worthwhile activities and goals that result in credible self-esteem. Parents serve children poorly when they promote in them a false sense of self-regard. Had Jason's parents helped him sustain effort in the face of difficulty and insisted that he meet his responsibilities years earlier, they might have prevented the current situation.

**CHILD-REARING PRACTICES.** Children and adolescents whose parents are warm and accepting and who provide reasonable expectations for mature behaviour feel especially good about themselves (Carlson, Uppal, & Prosser, 2000; Feiring & Taska, 1996). Warm, positive parenting lets young people know that they are accepted as competent and worthwhile. And firm but appropriate expectations, backed up with explanations, help them make sensible choices and evaluate themselves against reasonable standards.

Also, when parental support is *conditional* (withheld unless the young person meets very high standards), adolescents frequently engage in behaviours they consider "false." Although most teenagers report acting "phony" from time to time, they usually do so to win temporary approval or to experiment with new roles. Those who display false-self behaviour—"expressing things you don't really believe" or "putting on an act"—because others (and therefore they) devalue their true self suffer from low self-esteem, depression, and pessimism about the future (Harter et al., 1996).

When parents help or make decisions for their youngsters when they do not need assistance, children and adolescents often suffer from low self-esteem. These controlling parents communicate a sense of inadequacy to children—that their behaviour needs to be controlled by adults because they are ineffective in managing it themselves (Pomerantz & Eaton, 2000). Finally, overly tolerant, indulgent parenting is linked to unrealistically high self-esteem, which also undermines development (see the From Research to Practice box above).

Most preschoolers are "learning optimists" who believe they can succeed if they keep on trying. Their attributions support initiative in the face of challenging tasks.

**attributions**
Common, everyday explanations for the causes of behaviour.

**achievement motivation**
The tendency to persist at challenging tasks.

**mastery-oriented attributions**
Attributions that credit success to high ability and failure to insufficient effort. Leads to high expectancies of success and a willingness to approach challenging tasks.

**incremental view of ability**
The view that ability can be improved through effort.

**learned helplessness**
Attributions that credit success to external factors, such as luck, and failure to low ability. Leads to low expectancies of success and anxious loss of control in the face of challenging tasks.

**entity view of ability**
The view that ability is a fixed characteristic that cannot be improved through trying hard.

Although warmth and maturity demands are undoubtedly ingredients of high self-esteem, we cannot tell the extent to which child-rearing practices are causes of or reactions to children's characteristics and behaviour. Research on the precise content of adults' messages to children has been far more successful at isolating factors that affect children's sense of self-worth. Let's see how these messages mould children's evaluations of themselves in achievement contexts.

## ACHIEVEMENT-RELATED ATTRIBUTIONS

**Attributions** are our common, everyday explanations for the causes of behaviour—the answers we provide to the question "Why did I (or another person) do that?" We group the causes of our own and others' behaviour into two broad categories: external, environmental causes and internal, psychological causes. Then we further divide the category of psychological causes into two types: ability and effort. In assigning a cause, we use certain rules. If a behaviour occurs for many people but only in a single situation (the whole class gets A's on Mrs. Apple's French test), we conclude that it is externally caused (the test was easy). In contrast, if an individual displays a behaviour in many situations (Sally always gets A's on French tests), we judge the behaviour to be internally caused—by ability, effort, or both.

In Chapter 8, we showed that although intelligence predicts school achievement, the relationship is far from perfect. Differences among children in **achievement motivation**—the tendency to persist at challenging tasks—explain why some less intelligent pupils do better in school than their more intelligent classmates. Today, researchers regard achievement-related attributions as the main reason some children are competent learners who display initiative when faced with obstacles to success, whereas others give up easily.

### EMERGENCE OF ACHIEVEMENT-RELATED ATTRIBUTIONS.
In earlier chapters, we showed that infants express great pleasure at acquiring new skills—satisfaction that reinforces their efforts. Babies are naturally driven to master activities that support their development (White, 1959). Achievement motivation is believed to have roots in this early drive.

By the end of the second year, children turn to adults for evaluations of their accomplishments, picking up information about the meaning of competence in their culture (Stipek, Recchia, & McClintic, 1992). And around age 3, they begin making attributions about their successes and failures. These attributions affect their expectancies of success. Expectancies, in turn, influence the extent to which children try hard in the future.

Many studies show that preschoolers are "learning optimists" who rate their own ability very high, often underestimate task difficulty, and hold positive expectancies of success. When asked to react to a situation in which one person does worse on a task than another, young children indicate that the lower-scoring person can still succeed if she keeps on trying (Schuster, Ruble, & Weinert, 1998). One reason that young children's attributions are usually optimistic is that cognitively, they cannot yet distinguish the precise cause of their successes and failures. Instead, they view all good things as going together: A person who tries hard is also a smart person who is going to succeed (Nichols, 1978).

Nevertheless, by age 3, some children give up easily when faced with a challenge, such as working a hard puzzle. They conclude that they cannot do the task and express shame and despondency after failing. These nonpersisters have a history of critical maternal feedback about their worth and performance. In contrast, their enthusiastic, highly motivated agemates have mothers who patiently encourage while offering information about how to succeed. When preschool nonpersisters use dolls to act out an adult's reaction to failure, they expect disapproval. For example, they say, "He's punished because he can't do the puzzle," whereas persisters say, "He worked hard but just couldn't finish. He wants to try again" (Burhans & Dweck, 1995).

Preschoolers readily internalize adult evaluations. Whereas persisters view themselves as "good," nonpersisters see themselves as "bad" and deserving of negative feedback (Heyman, Dweck, & Cain, 1992). Already, nonpersisters seem to base their self-worth entirely on others' judgments, not on inner standards. Consequently, they show early signs of maladaptive achievement behaviours that become more common during the school years, when performance evaluations increase.

**MASTERY-ORIENTED VERSUS LEARNED-HELPLESS CHILDREN.** During middle childhood, children begin to distinguish ability, effort, and external factors in explaining their performance (Skinner, 1995). Those who are high in achievement motivation develop **mastery-oriented attributions.** They believe their successes are due to ability—a characteristic they can improve through trying hard and can count on when faced with new challenges. This **incremental view of ability**—that it can be altered through effort—influences the way mastery-oriented children interpret negative events (Heyman & Dweck, 1998). When failure hits, they attribute it to factors that can be changed or controlled, such as insufficient effort or a very difficult task. So whether these children succeed or fail, they take an industrious, persistent approach to learning.

Unfortunately, children who develop **learned helplessness** give very discouraging explanations for their performance. They attribute their failures, not their successes, to ability. When they succeed, they are likely to conclude that external events, such as luck, are responsible. Furthermore, unlike their mastery-oriented counterparts, they hold an **entity view of ability**—that it is fixed and cannot be improved by trying hard. So when a task is difficult, these children are overwhelmed by anxiety. They quickly give up, saying "I can't do this," before they have really tried (Elliott & Dweck, 1988).

Children's attributions affect their goals. Mastery-oriented children focus on *learning goals*—increasing ability through effort and seeking information on how to do so. In contrast, learned-helpless children focus on *performance goals*—obtaining positive and avoiding negative evaluations of their fragile sense of ability.

Over time, the ability of learned-helpless children no longer predicts their performance. In one study, the more fourth to sixth graders held self-critical attributions, the lower they rated their competence, the less they knew about study techniques that would help them succeed, the more they avoided challenge, and the poorer their academic performance. These outcomes solidified their entity view of ability (that effort won't make them smarter) (Pomerantz & Saxon, 2001). Because learned-helpless children fail to connect effort with success, they do not develop the metacognitive and self-regulatory skills necessary for high achievement (see Chapter 7). Lack of effective learning strategies, reduced persistence, and a sense of loss of control sustain one another in a vicious cycle (Heyman & Dweck, 1998).

In adolescence, young people attain a fully differentiated understanding of the relation between ability and effort. They realize that people varying in ability can achieve the same outcome with different degrees of effort (Butler, 1999). When adolescents view their own ability as fixed and low, they conclude that mastering a challenging task is not worth the cost—extremely high effort. To protect themselves from painful feelings of failure, these learned-helpless young people select less demanding courses and careers. As Figure 11.7 shows, learned helplessness prevents children from realizing their potential.

Repeated negative evaluations of their ability can cause children to develop learned helplessness. While his classmates raise their hands eagerly, this boy has difficulty with the assignment and is overcome by frustration and debilitating anxiety. He seems to have concluded that he can do little to improve his performance.

**FIGURE** 11.7

**Consequences of mastery-oriented and learned-helpless attributional styles.**

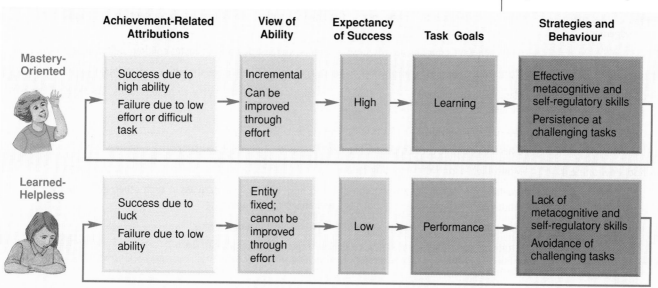

| | Achievement-Related Attributions | View of Ability | Expectancy of Success | Task Goals | Strategies and Behaviour |
|---|---|---|---|---|---|
| **Mastery-Oriented** | Success due to high ability · Failure due to low effort or difficult task | Incremental · Can be improved through effort | High | Learning | Effective metacognitive and self-regulatory skills · Persistence at challenging tasks |
| **Learned-Helpless** | Success due to luck · Failure due to low ability | Entity fixed; cannot be improved through effort | Low | Performance | Lack of metacognitive and self-regulatory skills · Avoidance of challenging tasks |

**INFLUENCES ON ACHIEVEMENT-RELATED ATTRIBUTIONS.** What accounts for the different attributions of mastery-oriented and learned-helpless children? As with preschoolers, adult communication plays a key role in school-age children's achievement motivation. Children with a learned-helpless style tend to have parents who set unusually high standards yet believe that their child is not very capable and has to work harder than others to succeed (Parsons, Adler, & Kaczala, 1982; Phillips, 1987). When the child fails, the adult might say, "You can't do that, can you? It's okay if you quit" (Hokoda & Fincham, 1995). And when the child succeeds, the adult might respond, "Gee, I'm surprised you got that A," or the adult might give feedback evaluating the child's traits, as in "You're so smart." When used often, trait statements promote an entity view of ability, which encourages children to question their competence in the face of setbacks and respond helplessly (Erdley et al., 1997).

Teachers' messages also affect children's attributions. When teachers are caring and helpful and emphasize learning over performance goals, they tend to have mastery-oriented students (Anderman et al., 2001; Daniels, Kalkman, & McCombs, 2001). A study following 1600 children in grades 3 to 8 over a three-year period highlights the power of teacher communication (Skinner, Zimmer-Gembeck, & Connell, 1998). Students who viewed their teachers as warm and fair (for example, clarifying expectations, checking that the child understands) worked harder on assignments and participated more in class. Trying hard, in turn, predicted better academic performance, which sustained the child's belief in the role of effort. In contrast, children who experienced their teachers as unsupportive were more likely to regard their performance as externally controlled (by teachers or luck). This predicted withdrawal from learning activities and declining achievement. These negative outcomes led children to doubt their ability and believe even more strongly in the power of external forces.

Some children are especially likely to have their performance undermined by adult feedback. Girls more often than boys blame their ability for poor performance. Girls also tend to receive messages from teachers and parents that their ability is at fault when they do not do well (Ruble & Martin, 1998). Low-SES, ethnic minority children also are at risk for learned helplessness. In several studies, African-American and Mexican-American children received less favourable teacher feedback than did other children (Aaron & Powell, 1982; Irvine, 1986; Losey, 1995). Furthermore, when ethnic minority children observe that adults in their own family are not rewarded by society for their achievement efforts, they may give up themselves (Ogbu, 1997).

**TABLE** 11.1

Ways to Foster a Mastery-Oriented Approach to Learning

| TECHNIQUE | DESCRIPTION |
|---|---|
| Provision of tasks | Select tasks that are meaningful, responsive to a diversity of pupil interests, and appropriately matched to current competence so that the child is challenged but not overwhelmed. |
| Parent and teacher encouragement | Communicate warmth, confidence in the child's abilities, the value of achievement, and the importance of effort in success. |
| | (For teachers) Communicate often with parents, suggesting ways to foster children's effort and progress. |
| | (For parents) Monitor schoolwork; promote knowledge of effective strategies and self-regulation. |
| Performance evaluations | Make evaluations private; avoid publicizing success or failure through wall posters, stars, privileges to "smart" children, and prizes for "best" performance. |
| | Stress individual progress and self-improvement. |
| | Offer small classes, which permit teachers to provide individualized support for mastery. |
| School environment | Model high effort in overcoming failure. |
| | Provide for cooperative learning and peer tutoring, in which children assist each other; avoid ability grouping, which makes evaluations of children's progress public. |
| | Accommodate individual and cultural differences in styles of learning. |
| | Create an atmosphere that sends a clear message that all pupils can learn. |

*Sources:* Ames, 1992; Eccles, Wigfield, & Schiefele, 1998.

# milestones
## DEVELOPMENT OF SELF-ESTEEM

| AGE | MILESTONES |
|---|---|
| 1–2 years | ❧ Expressions of pleasure in mastery are evident. <br> ❧ Sensitivity to adults' evaluations appear. |
| 3–5 years | ❧ Self-esteem is typically high and consists of several separate self-evaluations. <br> ❧ Achievement-related attributions appear but are undifferentiated; for example, a person who tries hard is smart and will succeed. |
| 6–10 years | ❧ Self-esteem becomes hierarchically organized; separate self-evaluations (academic, social, and physical competence, physical appearance) are integrated into an overall self-image. <br> ❧ Self-esteem declines as children make social comparisons, then rises. <br> ❧ Achievement-related attributions differentiate into ability, effort, and external factors. |
| 11 years–adulthood | ❧ New dimensions of self-esteem are added (close friendship, romantic appeal, job competence). <br> ❧ Self-esteem continues to rise. <br> ❧ Achievement-related attributions reflect full differentiation of ability and effort. |

*Note:* These milestones represent overall age trends. Individual differences exist in the precise age at which each milestone is attained.

Finally, cultural values affect the likelihood that children will develop learned helplessness. Compared with North Americans, Chinese and Japanese parents and teachers believe that success in school depends much more on effort than ability—a message they transmit to children (Tuss, Zimmer, & Ho, 1995). And Israeli children growing up on *kibbutzim* (cooperative agricultural settlements) are shielded from learned helplessness by classrooms that emphasize mastery and interpersonal harmony rather than ability and competition (Butler & Ruzany, 1993).

**FOSTERING A MASTERY-ORIENTED APPROACH.** Attribution research suggests that at times, well-intended messages from adults undermine children's competence. **Attribution retraining** is an effective approach to intervention that encourages learned-helpless children to believe they can overcome failure by exerting more effort. Most often, children are given tasks that are hard enough that they will experience some failure. Then they get repeated feedback that helps them revise their attributions, such as "You can do it if you try harder." Children are also taught to view their success as due to both ability and effort rather than chance factors, by giving them additional feedback after they succeed, such as "You're really good at this" or "You really tried hard on that one" (Schunk, 1994). Another successful approach is to teach low-effort students to focus less on grades and more on learning for its own sake (Ames, 1992). Instruction in metacognition and self-regulation is also helpful, to make up for development lost in this area and to ensure that renewed effort will pay off (Borkowski & Muthukrisna, 1995).

To work well, attribution retraining is best begun early, before children's views of themselves become hard to change (Eccles, Wigfield, & Schiefele, 1998). Table 11.1 on the previous page, lists a variety of ways to foster a mastery-oriented approach to learning. Consult the Milestones table above for an overview of the development of self-esteem.

**attribution retraining**
An approach to intervention that uses adult feedback to modify the attributions of learned-helpless children, thereby encouraging them to believe that they can overcome failure by exerting more effort.

## ASK YOURSELF

**review**    Describe and explain changes in the structure and level of self-esteem from early childhood to adolescence.

**review**    Describe mastery-oriented and learned-helpless children's differing views of ability. What impact do those views have on achievement motivation?

**apply**    Should parents promote children's self-esteem by telling them they're "smart" and "wonderful"? Is it harmful if children do not feel good about everything they do? Why or why not? How would you recommend that parents foster children's self-esteem?

**connect**    Why is the rise in self-esteem during the 1980s and 1990s, depicted in Figure 11.6, called a *cohort effect*? (See Chapter 2, page 58.)

As these adolescents exchange opinions about a recent news event, they become more aware of a diversity of viewpoints. A flexible, open-minded approach to grappling with competing beliefs and values fosters identity development.

© TONY FREEMAN/PHOTOEDIT

# Constructing an Identity: Who Should I Become?

ADOLESCENTS' WELL-ORGANIZED self-descriptions and differentiated sense of self-esteem provide the cognitive foundation for forming an **identity,** first recognized by psychoanalyst Erik Erikson (1950, 1968) as a major personality achievement and a crucial step toward becoming a productive, content adult. Constructing an identity involves defining who you are, what you value, and the directions you choose to pursue in life. One expert described it as an explicit theory of oneself as a rational agent—one who acts on the basis of reason, takes responsibility for those actions, and can explain them (Moshman, 1999). This search for what is true and real about the self is the driving force behind many commitments—to a sexual orientation (see Chapter 5); a vocation; interpersonal relationships; community involvement; ethnic group membership; and moral, political, religious, and gender-role ideals.

Erikson believed that successful psychosocial outcomes in infancy and childhood pave the way toward a coherent, positive identity. (Return to Chapter 1, page 18, to review Erikson's stages.) Although the seeds of identity formation are planted early, not until adolescence do young people become absorbed in this task. According to Erikson, in complex societies, teenagers experience an *identity crisis*—a temporary period of distress as they experiment with alternatives. During this period, adolescents question what they once took for granted. Those who go through a process of inner soul-searching eventually arrive at a mature identity. They sift through characteristics that defined the self in childhood and combine them with new commitments. Then they mould these into a solid inner core that provides a sense of sameness as they move through different roles in daily life.

Current theorists agree with Erikson that questioning of values, plans, and priorities is necessary for a mature identity, but they no longer refer to this process as a "crisis" (Grotevant, 1998). The term suggests a sudden, intense upheaval of the self. For some young people, identity development is traumatic and disturbing, but for most it is not. "Exploration" better describes the typical adolescent's gradual approach to identity formation. By trying out various life possibilities and moving toward making enduring decisions, young people forge an organized self-structure (Arnett, 2000a; Moshman, 1999).

Erikson described the negative outcome of adolescence as *identity confusion*. Some young people appear shallow and directionless, either because earlier conflicts have been resolved negatively or society restricts their choices to ones that do not match their abilities and desires. As a result, they are unprepared for the psychological challenges of adulthood. Does research support Erikson's ideas about identity development? In the following sections, we will see that adolescents go about the task of defining the self in ways that closely match Erikson's description.

**identity**
A well-organized conception of the self made up of values, beliefs, and goals to which the individual is solidly committed.

## PATHS TO IDENTITY

Using a clinical interviewing procedure devised by James Marcia (1966, 1980) of Simon Fraser University, researchers group adolescents into four categories, called *identity statuses,*

**TABLE** 11.2

The Four Identity Statuses

| IDENTITY STATUS | DESCRIPTION | EXAMPLE |
|---|---|---|
| Identity achievement | Having already explored alternatives, identity-achieved individuals are committed to a clearly formulated set of self-chosen values and goals. They feel a sense of psychological well-being, of sameness through time, and of knowing where they are going. | When asked how willing she would be to change her career goal if something better came along, Darla responded, "Well, I might, but I doubt it. I've thought long and hard about law as a career. I'm pretty certain it's for me." |
| Moratorium | *Moratorium* means "delay or holding pattern." These individuals have not yet made definite commitments. They are in the process of exploring—gathering information and trying out activities, with the desire to find values and goals to guide their life. | When asked if he had ever had doubts about his religious beliefs, Ray said, "Yes, I guess I'm going through that right now. I just don't see how there can be a God and yet so much evil in the world." |
| Identity foreclosure | Identity-foreclosed individuals have committed themselves to values and goals without exploring alternatives. They accept a ready-made identity that authority figures (usually parents but sometimes teachers, religious leaders, or romantic partners) have chosen for them. | When asked if she had ever reconsidered her political beliefs, Hillary answered, "No, not really, our family is pretty much in agreement on these things." |
| Identity diffusion | Identity-diffused individuals lack clear direction. They are not committed to values and goals, or trying to reach them. They may have never explored alternatives, or they may have tried to do so but found the task too threatening and overwhelming. | When asked about his attitude toward nontraditional gender roles—a husband staying home to care for children while the wife works, for example—Joel responded, "Oh, I don't know. It doesn't make much difference to me. I can take it or leave it." |

which show the progress they have made toward forming a mature identity. Table 11.2 summarizes these identity statuses: **identity achievement, moratorium, identity foreclosure,** and **identity diffusion.**

Identity development follows many paths. Some adolescents remain in one status, whereas others experience many status transitions. And the pattern often varies across identity domains, such as sexual orientation, vocation, and religious, political, and other world views. Most young people change from "lower" statuses (foreclosure or diffusion) to "higher" statuses (moratorium or achievement) by the time they reach their twenties, but some move in the reverse direction (Kroger, 1995; Meeus, 1996).

Because college and university students have many opportunities to explore career options and lifestyles, they make more progress toward formulating an identity than they did in high school (Meeus et al., 1999). And in the years following university, many young people continue to obtain a broad range of life experiences before choosing a life course. For example, some take short-term volunteer jobs or travel extensively on their own. Young people who go to work after high school graduation often settle on a self-definition earlier than do college- or university-educated youths (Munro & Adams, 1977). However, those who find it difficult to realize their occupational goals because of lack of training or vocational choices are at risk for identity foreclosure or diffusion (Archer, 1989).

At one time, researchers thought that adolescent girls postponed the task of establishing an identity and, instead, focused their energies on Erikson's next stage, intimacy development. Some girls do show more sophisticated reasoning in identity areas related to intimacy, such as sexuality and family–career priorities. In this respect, they are actually ahead of boys in identity development. Otherwise, adolescents of both sexes typically make progress on identity concerns before experiencing genuine intimacy in relationships (Kroger, 2000; Meeus et al., 1999).

## IDENTITY STATUS AND PSYCHOLOGICAL WELL-BEING

Identity achievement and moratorium are psychologically healthy routes to a mature self-definition, whereas foreclosure and diffusion are maladaptive. Young people who are

**identity achievement**
The identity status of individuals who have explored and committed themselves to self-chosen values and goals.

**moratorium**
The identity status of individuals who are exploring alternatives in an effort to find values and goals to guide their life.

**identity foreclosure**
The identity status of individuals who have accepted ready-made values and goals that authority figures have chosen for them.

**identity diffusion**
The identity status of individuals who do not have firm commitments to values and goals and are not actively trying to reach them.

# social issues: health

## ADOLESCENT SUICIDE: ANNIHILATION OF THE SELF

the suicide rate increases over the lifespan. As Figure 11.8 shows, it is lowest in childhood and jumps sharply at adolescence. Currently, suicide is the second-leading cause of death among young people in Canada, surpassed only by motor vehicle injuries. Suicide rates have been relatively stable in Canada over the past 20 years, although they are double the rates of 30 years ago (Langlois & Morrison, 2002; Statistics Canada, 1999). The adolescent suicide rate varies widely among industrialized nations. Japan and most of Western Europe have low rates; the United States and Australia, like Canada, have intermediate rates; and Finland, New Zealand, and Estonia have high rates (Johnson, Krug, & Potter, 2000). Although many theories exist, international differences remain unexplained.

### FACTORS RELATED TO ADOLESCENT SUICIDE

Striking sex differences in suicidal behaviour exist. The number of boys who kill themselves exceeds the number of girls by 4 or 5 to 1. This may seem surprising, since girls show higher rates of depression. Yet the findings are not inconsistent. Girls make more unsuccessful suicide attempts and use methods from which they can more likely be revived, such as a sleeping pill overdose. Girls are hospitalized for suicide attempts at one and a half times the rate for boys (Langlois & Morrison, 2002). In contrast, boys tend to select more active techniques that lead to instant death, such as firearms or hanging. Gender-role expectations may account for these differences. Less tolerance exists for feelings of helplessness and failed efforts in males than females (Canetto & Sakinofsky, 1998).

In the United States, compared with the white majority, nonwhite, ethnic minority teenagers (including African Americans, Hispanics, and Native Americans) have slightly lower suicide rates. Higher levels of support through extended families may be responsible (Borowsky, Ireland, & Resnick, 2001). In contrast, when stress is overwhelming and social support lacking, the suicide rate rises. For example, the suicide rate among the Aboriginal population in Canada is two to seven times higher than in the general population and is most acute for young Aboriginals (Quantz, 1997). Some proposed explanations include living on reserves in remote, isolated areas, alcohol consumption, and culture clashes with non-Aboriginals. Similarly, gay, lesbian, and bisexual youths are at high risk for suicide, making attempts at a rate three times higher than other adolescents. Those who have tried to kill themselves report more family conflict, inner turmoil about their sexuality, problems in romantic relationships, and peer victimization due to their sexual orientation (Hershberger, Pilkington, & D'Augelli, 1997).

Suicidal adolescents often show signs of extreme despondency during the period before the suicidal act. Many verbalize the wish to die, lose interest in school and friends, neglect their personal appearance, and give away treasured possessions. These warning signs appear in two types of young people. In the first group are highly intelligent teenagers who are solitary, withdrawn, and unable to meet their own high standards or those of important people in their lives. A second, larger group show antisocial tendencies. These young people express their unhappiness through bullying, fighting, stealing, and increased risk taking and drug use (Fergusson, Woodward, & Horwood, 2000). Besides turning their anger and disappointment inward, they are hostile and destructive toward others.

Parental emotional problems and family turmoil are common in the backgrounds of suicidal adolescents

identity achieved or actively exploring have a higher sense of self-esteem, are more likely to engage in abstract and critical thinking, report greater similarity between their ideal self and their real self, and are more advanced in moral reasoning (Josselson, 1994; Marcia et al., 1993). Although adolescents in moratorium are often anxious about the challenges that lie before them, they join with identity-achieved individuals in using an autonomous, information-gathering style when making decisions and solving problems (Berzonsky & Kuk, 2000; Kroger, 1995).

Adolescents who get stuck in either foreclosure or diffusion have adjustment difficulties. Foreclosed individuals tend to be dogmatic, inflexible, and intolerant. Some regard any difference of opinion as a threat. Most are afraid of rejection by people on whom they depend

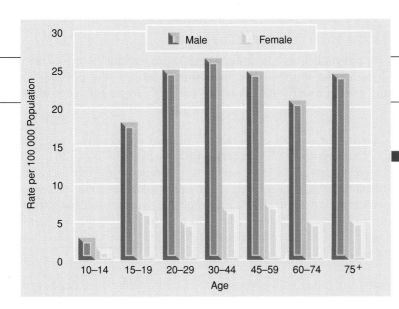

**FIGURE** 11.8

**Suicide rates over the lifespan in Canada.**
Although teenagers do not commit suicide as often as adults and the aged, the suicide rate rises sharply from childhood to adolescence. Rates are greater for males than females. (Created from the Statistics Canada website, http://www.statcan.ca/english/pgdg/People/ Health/health01.htm, and the Statistics Canada publication "Suicide deaths and suicide attempts," Catalogue no. 82-003, vol. 13, no. 2, January 2002.)

(Gould & Kramer, 2001). The fragile self-esteem of these teenagers quickly disintegrates in the face of stressful life events. Common circumstances just before a suicide include the breakup of an important peer relationship or the humiliation of having been caught engaging in irresponsible, antisocial acts.

Why is suicide rare in childhood but on the rise in adolescence? Teenagers' improved ability to plan ahead seems to be involved. Although some act impulsively, many young people at risk take purposeful steps toward killing themselves (McKeown et al., 1998). Other cognitive changes also contribute. Belief in the personal fable (see Chapter 6) leads many depressed young people to conclude that no one could possibly understand the intense pain they feel. As a result, their despair, hopelessness, and isolation deepen.

## PREVENTION AND TREATMENT

Picking up on the signals that a troubled teenager sends is a crucial first step in suicide prevention. Parents and teachers must be trained to see warning signs. Schools can help by providing sympathetic counsellors, peer support groups, and information about telephone hotlines. Once a teenager takes steps toward suicide, staying with the young person, listening, and expressing sympathy and concern until professional help can be obtained is essential.

Treatments for depressed and suicidal adolescents take many forms, from anti-depressant medication to individual, family, and group therapy. Sometimes hospitalization is necessary to ensure the teenager's safety. Until the adolescent improves, parents are usually advised to remove weapons, knives, razors, scissors, and drugs from the home.

After a suicide, family and peer survivors need support to assist them in coping with grief, anger, and guilt for not having been able to help the victim. Teenage suicides often take place in clusters. When one occurs, it increases the likelihood of others among peers who knew the young person or heard about the death through the media (Grossman & Kruesi, 2000). In view of this trend, an especially watchful eye must be kept on vulnerable adolescents after a suicide happens. Restraint by journalists is also important, since publicity given to suicides increases suicide contagion among teenagers (Velting & Gould, 1997).

for affection and self-esteem (Berzonsky, 1993; Kroger, 1995). A few foreclosed teenagers who are alienated from their families and society may join cults or other extremist groups, uncritically adopting a way of life that is different from their past.

Long-term diffused teenagers are the least mature in identity development. They typically entrust themselves to luck or fate, have an "I don't care" attitude, and tend to passively go along with whatever the "crowd" is doing at the moment. As a result, they often experience time-management and academic difficulties (Berzonsky & Kuk, 2000). And they are most likely to use and abuse drugs. Often at the heart of their apathy is a sense of hopelessness about the future (Archer & Waterman, 1990). Many of these young people are at risk for serious depression and suicide—problems that rise sharply during adolescence (see the Social Issues: Health box above).

# INFLUENCES ON IDENTITY DEVELOPMENT

Adolescent identity formation begins a lifelong, dynamic process that blends personality and context. Whenever the individual or the context changes, the possibility for reformulating identity exists (Yoder, 2000). A wide variety of factors influence identity development.

**PERSONALITY.** Identity status, as we saw in the previous section, is both cause and consequence of personality characteristics. Adolescents who assume that absolute truth is always attainable tend to be foreclosed, whereas those who lack confidence in the prospect of ever knowing anything with certainty are more often identity diffused. Adolescents who appreciate that they can use rational criteria to choose among alternatives are more likely to be in a state of moratorium or identity achievement (Berzonsky & Kuk, 2000; Boyes & Chandler, 1992). This flexible, open-minded approach assists them greatly in defining educational, career, and other life goals.

**FAMILY.** Recall that infants and toddlers who develop a healthy sense of agency have parents who provide both emotional support and freedom to explore. A similar link between parenting and identity exists at adolescence. When the family serves as a "secure base" from which teenagers can confidently move out into the wider world, identity development is enhanced. Adolescents who feel attached to their parents but who are also free to voice their own opinions tend to be identity achieved or in a state of moratorium (Grotevant & Cooper, 1998; Hauser, Powers, & Noam, 1991). Foreclosed teenagers usually have close bonds with parents, but they lack opportunities for healthy separation. And diffused young people report the lowest levels of warm, open communication at home (Papini, 1994).

**PEERS.** As adolescents interact with a diversity of peers, their exposure to ideas and values expands. Close friends assist each other in exploring options by providing emotional support and role models of identity development (Josselson, 1992). Within friendships, adolescents also learn much about themselves. In one study, late adolescents' attachment to friends predicted exploration of careers and progress in choosing one (Felsman & Blustein, 1999). In sum, friends—like parents—can serve as a "secure base" as adolescents grapple with possibilities.

**SCHOOL AND COMMUNITY.** Schools and communities that offer rich and varied opportunities for exploration also support identity development. Erikson (1968, p. 132) noted that it is "the inability to settle on an occupational identity which most disturbs young people." Schools can foster identity development in many ways—through classrooms that promote high-level thinking; extracurricular and community activities that enable teenagers to take on responsible roles; teachers and counsellors who encourage low-SES and ethnic minority students to go to university; and vocational training programs that immerse adolescents in the real world of adult work (Cooper, 1998; Hart, Atkins, & Ford, 1998).

Regional variations in opportunity can lead to differences in identity development. For example, between ages 13 and 17, exploration increases among Australian adolescents living in urban environments, whereas it decreases among youths in rural areas. Lack of educational and vocational options in Australian rural regions is probably responsible (Nurmi, Poole, & Kalakoski, 1996). Regardless of where they live, young people benefit from a chance to talk with adults and older peers who have worked through identity questions.

**LARGER SOCIETY.** The larger cultural context and historical time period affect identity development. Among contemporary adolescents, exploration and commitment take place earlier in the identity domains of gender-role preference and vocational choice than in religious and political values. Societal forces are also responsible for the special problems that gay, lesbian, and bisexual youths (see Chapter 5) and ethnic minority adolescents face in forming a secure identity, as the Cultural Influences box on the following page describes.

---

**ethnic identity**
An enduring aspect of the self that includes a sense of ethnic group membership and attitudes and feeling associated with that membership.

**bicultural identity**
The identity constructed by adolescents who explore and adopt values from both their subculture and the dominant culture.

# cultural influences

## IDENTITY DEVELOPMENT AMONG ETHNIC MINORITY ADOLESCENTS

most adolescents are aware of their cultural ancestry, but it is not a matter of intense concern for them. But for teenagers who are members of minority groups, **ethnic identity**—an enduring aspect of the self that includes a sense of ethnic-group membership and attitudes and feelings associated with that membership—is central to the quest for identity. Although ethnic identity increases with age, it presents complex challenges (Phinney, Ferguson, & Tate, 1997). As they develop cognitively and become more sensitive to feedback from the social environment, minority youths become painfully aware that they are targets of discrimination and inequality. This discovery complicates their efforts to develop a sense of cultural belonging and a set of personally meaningful life goals.

Minority adolescents often feel caught between the standards of the larger society and the traditions of their culture of origin. Aboriginal youths in Canada frequently face the dilemma of not knowing where they fit in society (Quantz, 1997). In many immigrant families, adolescents' commitment to obeying their parents and fulfilling family obligations lessens as time passes (Phinney, Ong, & Madden, 2000). Moreover, young people sometimes reject aspects of their ethnic background. In one study, 15- to 17-year-old Asian immigrants were more likely than blacks and Hispanics to hold negative attitudes toward their subcultural group (Phinney, 1989). Perhaps the absence of a social movement stressing ethnic pride of the kind available to black and Hispanic teenagers underlies this finding.

Some immigrant parents overly restrict their teenagers out of fear that assimilation into the larger society will undermine their cultural traditions, and their youngsters rebel. One Southeast-Asian refugee described his daughter's behaviour: "She complains about going to the Lao temple on the weekend and instead joined a youth group in a neighborhood Christian Church. She refused to wear traditional dress on the Lao New Year. The girl is setting a very bad example for her younger sisters and brothers" (Nidorf, 1985, pp. 422–423).

Other minority teenagers react to years of shattered self-esteem, school failure, and barriers to success by defining themselves in contrast to majority values. A minority teenager, responding to the question of what it takes to be a successful adult, pointed to his uncle, leader of a local gang, as an example (Matute-Bianchi, 1986, pp. 250–251).

Because it is painful and confusing, minority high school students often dodge the task of forming an ethnic identity. Many are diffused or foreclosed on ethnic identity issues (Markstrom-Adams & Adams, 1995). Yet some do not react this way. A case study of six poverty-stricken African-American adolescents who were high-achieving and optimistic about the future revealed that they were intensely aware of oppression but believed in striving to alter their social position. How did they develop this sense of agency? Parents, relatives, and teachers had convinced them through discussion and example that injustice should not be tolerated and that together, blacks could overcome it. David, whose family was on welfare and lived in rundown housing, illustrates the experiences of these ethnically identified, achieving young people:

> My 20-year-old brother, he talks about it a lot. The way that Blacks have been treated as time went on. And he stress . . . never forget where you came from. Make our selves one—make Whites stand up and take notice—'cause that's the only way we [Blacks] going to get out of the situation we always been in. (O'Connor, 1997, p. 618)

Adolescents who use a proactive style to deal with prejudice and discrimination, including self-affirmation and attempts to disprove stereotypes, are more likely to have a committed sense of their ethnic group membership (Phinney & Chavira, 1995).

How can society help minority adolescents resolve identity conflicts constructively? A variety of efforts are relevant, including

- reducing poverty;
- promoting effective parenting, in which children and adolescents benefit from family ethnic pride yet are encouraged to explore the meaning of ethnicity in their own lives;
- ensuring that schools respect minority youths' native language, unique learning styles, and right to a high-quality education; and
- fostering contact among peers of the same ethnicity along with respect between ethnic groups (García-Coll & Magnuson, 1997).

A secure ethnic identity is associated with higher self-esteem, optimism, sense of mastery over the environment, and more positive attitudes toward one's own ethnic group (Carlson, Uppal, & Prosser, 2000; Phinney, Ferguson, & Tate, 1997; Smith et al., 1999). But forming a **bicultural identity**—by exploring and adopting values from both the adolescent's subculture and the dominant culture—offers added benefits. Biculturally identified adolescents tend to be achieved in other areas of identity as well. And their relations with members of other ethnic groups are especially favourable (Phinney & Kohatsu, 1997). In sum, ethnic-identity achievement enhances many aspects of emotional and social development.

These East Indian adolescents dress in traditional costumes for a folk dancing demonstration at a town festival. When minority youths encounter respect for their cultural heritage in schools and communities, they are more likely to retain ethnic values and customs as an important part of their identities.

© RUDI VON BRIEL/PHOTOEDIT

The identity explorations of young people make the late teens and early twenties an especially full and intense time of life. Experiences are not always agreeable; many encounter disappointments, must revise their goals, and are disturbed by conditions in their society and the world (Arnett, 2000b). Nevertheless, almost all are optimistic about the future. According to results from the National Longitudinal Survey of Children and Youth, 93 percent of teens reported that they are happy with their lives and 95 percent reported that their futures look good (Statistics Canada, National Longitudinal Survey, 1999).

## ASK YOURSELF

**review**    Explain how the four identity statuses are linked to psychological adjustment.

**review**    Cite personal and contextual factors that contribute to identity development.

**apply**    Frank and Vera worry that their 18-year-old son Jules will waste time at university because he is unsure about his major and career goals. Explain why Jules's uncertainty might be advantageous for his identity development.

**connect**    Return to pages 448–449 and 452 to review changes in self-concept and self-esteem at adolescence. How might these changes pave the way for constructing an identity?

# Thinking About Other People

CHILDREN'S UNDERSTANDING of other people—the inferences they make about others' behaviour, personality traits, and viewpoints—has much in common with their developing understanding of themselves. These facets of social cognition also become increasingly differentiated and well organized with age.

## UNDERSTANDING INTENTIONS

Accurately interpreting others' behaviour and deciding how to react to it often depend on distinguishing actions that are intentional from those that are accidental. During the first year, infants pick up much information about how people's gaze, movements, and emotional expressions signal their goals (Woodward, Sommerville, & Guajardo, 2001). Toddlers display an even clearer appreciation of people as intentional beings—as deliberately engaging in actions to reach a goal. When adults engage in intentional and accidental actions that have interesting effects on objects, 14- to 18-month-olds are twice as likely to imitate their intentional behaviours (Carpenter, Akhtar, & Tomasello, 1998). And as noted in Chapter 6, toddlers of this age can imitate an adult's intended behaviour, even when the adult fails to complete it (see page 225).

By age 2, children say "gonna," "hafta," and "wanna" to announce behaviours they are about to perform. Soon they rely on this grasp of purposefulness to defend themselves. After being scolded for bumping into a playmate or spilling a glass of milk, 3-year-olds exclaim, "It was an accident!" or "I didn't do it on purpose!" (Wellman & Phillips, 2001).

Between 2½ and 3 years, this understanding extends to others. Preschoolers become sensitive to behavioural cues that help them tell if another person is acting intentionally. At first, they focus on the person's statements. If a person says he is going to do something and then succeeds at doing it, 3-year-olds judge the behaviour as deliberate. If statements and the outcomes of actions do not match, then the behaviour was not intended (Astington, 1993).

Around age 4, children move beyond this fusion of intention with behaviour. They appreciate intention as an internal mental state that is distinct from other mental states and from the outcomes of actions. Consequently, they realize that a desired outcome can be achieved intentionally or accidentally. They also know that intending to do something (such as clean the bathroom) is not the same as desiring to do it (Astington, 2001). In one study, preschoolers played a game in which they had to indicate which of several buckets they wanted to hit with a beanbag. If the bucket they hit contained a picture, they stuck it on a scorecard, winning the game when their card was full. When children's intention was not fulfilled (they accidentally hit a bucket they hadn't targeted), 3-year-olds nevertheless claimed that they intended this result, especially when their desire was satisfied (the accidentally hit bucket contained a picture). Not until age 4 could children consistently distinguish intentions and desires (Schult, 1999).

In everyday interactions, people may conceal their intentions. For example, we can deliberately refrain from doing something but pretend that we simply forgot about it. Older preschoolers have some understanding that intentions can be disguised. They say that an involuntary behaviour (sneezing, coughing, or yawning) is intentional if someone is pretending to do it (Joseph, 1998). Between ages 5 and 9, children rely increasingly on a *verbal–nonverbal consistency rule* to evaluate the sincerity of people's statements about their intentions. For example, older children know that telling another person you intended an outcome when you look neutral, disappointed, or surprised probably means you are not telling the truth (Rotenberg, Simourd, & Moore, 1989).

Finally, children differ in how accurately they interpret others' intentions. Those who get along well with adults and peers make these judgments easily. In contrast, highly aggressive children often see hostility where it does not exist (Dodge & Price, 1994). As we will see in Chapter 12, such children require special help in learning how to evaluate and respond appropriately to others' behaviour.

## PERSON PERCEPTION

**Person perception** concerns how we size up the attributes of people with whom we are familiar. To study it, researchers use methods similar to those that focus on children's self-concepts: asking them to describe people they know, such as "Can you tell me what kind of person _____ is?"

**UNDERSTANDING PEOPLE AS PERSONALITIES.** Like their self-descriptions, before age 8, children's descriptions of others focus on commonly experienced emotions and attitudes, concrete activities, and behaviours. Over time, children discover consistencies in the actions of people they know and mention personality traits.

At first, these references are closely tied to behaviour and consist of implied dispositions, such as "He is always fighting with people" or "She steals and lies" (Rholes, Newman, & Ruble, 1990). Later, children mention traits directly, but they are vague and stereotyped—for example, "good," "nice," or "acts smart." Gradually, sharper trait descriptions appear, such as "honest," "trustworthy," "generous," "polite," and "selfish," and children become more convinced of the stability of such dispositions (Droege & Stipek, 1993; Ruble & Dweck, 1995).

During adolescence, as abstract thinking becomes better established, inferences about others' personalities are drawn together into organized character sketches (O'Mahoney, 1989). As a result, between ages 14 and 16, teenagers present rich accounts of people they know that integrate physical traits, typical behaviours, and inner dispositions.

**UNDERSTANDING ETHNICITY AND SOCIAL CLASS.** Person perception also includes making sense of diversity and inequality among people. Most 3- and 4-year-olds have formed basic concepts of race and ethnicity, in that they can apply labels of black and white to pictures, dolls, and people. Indicators of social class—education and occupational prestige—are not accessible to young children. Nevertheless, they can distinguish rich from poor on the basis of physical characteristics, such as clothing, residence, and possessions (Ramsey, 1991).

By the early school years, children absorb prevailing societal attitudes toward social groups. Since race, ethnicity, and social class are closely related in North America, children connect power and privilege with white people, and poverty and inferior status with people of colour

**person perception**
The way individuals size up the attributes of people with whom they are familiar.

Contact with members of other races and ethnic groups reduces the chances that children will classify the social world on the basis of race and ethnicity. When children sort people in these ways, they are likely to rate members of their own group positively and members of out-groups negatively. This tendency is one of the beginning signs of prejudice.

(Ramsey, 1995). How do children acquire these attitudes? They do not necessarily do so by directly adopting the attitudes of parents and friends. In a Canadian study, although white school-age children assumed that parents' and friends' racial attitudes would resemble their own, no similarities in attitudes were found (Aboud & Doyle, 1996). Perhaps white parents are reluctant to discuss their racial views with children, and children's friends say little as well. Faced with limited or ambiguous information, children may fill in the gaps and then rely on their own attitudes as the basis for inferring others'.

Other evidence suggests that children pick up much information about group status from implicit messages in their environments. In a recent experiment, 7- to 12-year-olds attending a summer school program were randomly assigned to social groups, denoted by coloured T-shirts (yellow or blue) the children wore in the classroom. The researchers hung posters in the classroom that depicted unfamiliar yellow-group members as having higher status—for example, as having won more athletic and spelling competitions. When teachers recognized the social groups by using them as the basis for seating arrangements, task assignments, and bulletin-board displays, children in the high-status group evaluated their own group more favourably than the other group. And children in the low-status group appeared to view their own group less favourably. But no prejudices emerged when teachers ignored the social groupings (Bigler, Brown, & Markell, 2001). These findings indicate that children do not necessarily form stereotypes when some basis for them exists (the posters). But when an authority figure indirectly grants validity to a status hierarchy, children develop biased attitudes.

In their everyday worlds, children are more likely to hold positive attitudes toward groups to which they themselves belong and negative attitudes toward out-groups—a bias that also characterizes adults. Yet recall that with age, children pay more attention to dispositions and make finer distinctions between people. The capacity to classify the social world in multiple ways permits school-age children to understand that people can be both "the same" and "different"—that those who look different need not think, feel, or act differently (Bigler & Liben, 1993; Doyle & Aboud, 1995). Consequently, prejudice declines in middle childhood.

Nevertheless, children vary in the extent to which they hold racial, ethnic, and social-class biases. Although adults with intolerant personalities (who hold a wide array of negative stereotypes) exist, traitlike prejudice is rare among children. Five- to 12-year-olds' ethnic bias does not predict their gender bias or their dislike of overweight people (Powlishta et al., 1994). This suggests that childhood prejudice is the product of specific learning experiences. The following three factors are influential:

- *A fixed view of personality traits.* Children who come to believe that personality is fixed tend to make rigid judgments of people as good or bad and ignore the intentions behind their behaviour. These trait-stability endorsers, compared with children who see personality as changeable, are more likely to agree that "a new girl at school who makes up a lie to try to get other kids to like her" is a bad kid and that "if someone is really friendly and shares her toys with other kids, she will always act this way" (Heyman & Dweck, 1998).

- *High self-esteem.* A surprising finding is that children (and adults) with very high self-esteem are more likely to hold unfair racial and ethnic biases (Bigler, Brown, & Markell, 2001; Gagnon & Morasse, 1995). Individuals who think well of themselves seem to compare themselves with lower-status, less advantaged individuals or groups as a way of confirming their favourable self-evaluation. As yet, researchers are not sure what motivates people to use this means of maintaining a positive self-image.

■ *A social world in which people are sorted into groups.* The more adults highlight group distinctions for children, the greater the chances that children will display own-group preference and out-group discrimination (Bigler, Brown, & Markell, 2001; Kowalski & Lo, 1999).

Children assigned to cooperative learning groups, in which they work toward joint goals with children of diverse backgrounds and characteristics, show low levels of prejudice in peer preferences and interactions. Still, once biases against racial groups form, they are hard to undo. Although children experiencing cooperative learning relate to other-race children more positively, they continue to hold racial stereotypes (Hewstone, 1996). Long-term contact and collaboration among neighbourhood, school, and community groups may be the best ways to overcome these prejudices (Ramsey, 1995).

## PERSPECTIVE TAKING

In this and previous chapters, we have emphasized that **perspective taking**—the capacity to imagine what other people may be thinking and feeling—is important for a wide variety of social-cognitive achievements: understanding others' emotions (Chapter 10); appreciating false belief; developing referential communication skills (Chapter 9), self-concept, self-esteem, and person perception; and inferring intentions.

Recall that Piaget regarded egocentrism—preschoolers' inability to take the viewpoint of another—as the major feature responsible for the immaturity of their thought, in both the physical and social domains. Yet we have seen that young children have some capacity for perspective taking as soon as they become consciously self-aware in the second year of life. Nevertheless, Piaget's ideas inspired a wealth of research on children's capacity to take another's perspective, which improves steadily over childhood and adolescence.

**SELMAN'S STAGES OF PERSPECTIVE TAKING.** Robert Selman developed a five-stage model of children's perspective-taking skill. He asked preschool through adolescent youngsters to respond to social dilemmas in which characters have differing opinions about an event. These dilemmas differ from tasks used to assess children's understanding of false belief. Here, differences in perspectives are not determined by the immediate situation (for example, who has seen what's really inside a Band-Aid box). Instead, all characters are presented with the same situation. But they arrive at it with different *pre-existing knowledge and beliefs,* which cause them to interpret the situation differently. Consider this example:

> Holly is an 8-year-old girl who likes to climb trees. She is the best tree climber in the neighborhood. One day while climbing down from a tall tree she falls off the bottom branch but does not hurt herself. Her father sees her fall. He is upset and asks her to promise not to climb trees anymore. Holly promises. Later that day, Holly and her friends meet Sean. Sean's kitten is caught up in a tree and cannot get down. Something has to be done right away or the kitten may fall. Holly is the only one who climbs trees well enough to reach the kitten and get it down, but she remembers her promise to her father. (Selman & Byrne, 1974, p. 805)

After the dilemma is presented, children answer questions that highlight their ability to interpret the story from varying points of view, such as,

Does Sean know why Holly cannot decide whether or not to climb the tree?

What will Holly's father think? Will he understand if she climbs the tree?

Does Holly think she will be punished for climbing the tree? Should she be punished for doing so?

Table 11.3 on page 470 summarizes Selman's five stages of perspective taking. Longitudinal and cross-sectional findings reveal that at first, children have only a limited idea of

These third graders' perspective-taking skills enable them to understand that each person can interpret this sculpture differently. By this age, they probably can engage in self-reflective perspective taking—viewing their own attitude toward the sculpture from another person's perspective. For example, one child might be saying to herself, "My friend probably thinks I'm pretty weird because I like this sculpture!"

**perspective taking**
The capacity to imagine what other people may be thinking and feeling.

**TABLE** 11.3

Selman's Stages of Perspective Taking

| STAGE | APPROXIMATE AGE RANGE | DESCRIPTION | TYPICAL RESPONSE TO "HOLLY DILEMMA" |
|---|---|---|---|
| Level 0: Undifferentiated perspective taking | 3–6 | Children recognize that self and other can have different thoughts and feelings, but they frequently confuse the two. | The child predicts that Holly will save the kitten because she does not want it to get hurt and believes that Holly's father will feel just as she does. |
| Level 1: Social-informational perspective taking | 4–9 | Children understand that different perspectives may result because people have access to different information. | When asked how Holly's father will react when he finds out that she climbed the tree, the child responds, "If he didn't know anything about the kitten, he would be angry. But if Holly shows him the kitten, he might change his mind." |
| Level 2: Self-reflective perspective taking | 7–12 | Children can "step in another person's shoes" and view their own thoughts, feelings, and behaviour from the other person's perspective. They also recognize that others can do the same. | When asked whether Holly thinks she will be punished, the child says, "No. Holly knows that her father will understand why she climbed the tree." |
| Level 3: Third-party perspective taking | 10–15 | Children can step outside a two-person situation and imagine how the self and other are viewed from the perspective of a third, impartial party. | When asked whether Holly should be punished, the child says, "No, because Holly thought it was important to save the kitten. But she also knows that her father told her not to climb the tree. So she'd think she shouldn't be punished only if she could get her father to understand why she had to climb the tree." |
| Level 4: Societal perspective taking | 14–adult | Individuals understand that third-party perspective taking can be influenced by one or more systems of larger societal values. | When asked if Holly should be punished, the individual responds, "No. The value of humane treatment of animals justifies Holly's action. Her father's appreciation of this value will lead him not to punish her." |

*Sources:* Selman, 1976; Selman & Byrne, 1974.

what other people might be thinking and feeling. Over time, they become more aware that people can interpret the same event quite differently. Soon, they can "step in another person's shoes" and reflect on how that person might regard their own thoughts, feelings, and behaviour. Finally, they can evaluate two people's perspectives simultaneously, at first from the vantage point of a disinterested spectator and later by making reference to societal values (Gurucharri & Selman, 1982; Selman, 1980).

Cognitive development contributes to advances in perspective taking. Children who fail Piaget's concrete operational tasks tend to be at Selman's Level 0; those who pass concrete but not formal operational tasks tend to be at Levels 1 and 2; and young people who are increasingly formal operational tend to be at Levels 3 and 4 (Keating & Clark, 1980; Krebs & Gillmore, 1982). Furthermore, each set of Piagetian tasks tends to be mastered somewhat earlier than its related perspective-taking level (Walker, 1980). These findings suggest that gains in perspective taking require additional cognitive and social capacities.

**OTHER ASSESSMENTS OF PERSPECTIVE TAKING.** According to several theorists, preschoolers' limited capacity to take another's perspective is largely due to their passive view of the mind—their assumption that what a person knows results from observing rather than actively interpreting experience (Chandler & Carpendale, 1998; Pillow, 1995). To explore this idea, researchers have devised gamelike tasks that assess children's realization that people's pre-existing knowledge and beliefs affect their viewpoints.

One approach is to see whether children realize that younger, and therefore less knowledgeable, individuals view new information differently than older individuals do. In one such study, 4- to 8-year-olds were asked whether a baby and an adult would know the location of an object after seeing where it had been placed or, alternatively, being told where it had been placed (Montgomery, 1993). Children of all ages judged correctly that both the baby and the adult would know through directly perceiving. But 4-year-olds (even though they said that babies don't know what most words mean) incorrectly thought the baby could learn from the verbal message. As Figure 11.9 shows, performance improved between ages 6 and 8.

Other research confirms that not until age 6 do children understand that a person's *prior knowledge* affects their ability to understand new information. Between 6 and 8 years, children also realize that people's *pre-existing beliefs* can affect their viewpoints. And around this time, they understand that two people can interpret the same ambiguous information differently (Miller, 2000).

Perspective-taking tasks for older children and adolescents have focused on **recursive thought,** the form of perspective taking that involves thinking about what another person is thinking. Selman's stages suggest that thinking recursively (Levels 3 and 4) improves from middle childhood to adolescence, a trend that is supported by research. When first through sixth graders were asked to describe cartoons like those in Figure 11.10, only 50 percent of sixth graders succeeded on one-loop recursions, and few could handle two-loop recursions. Not until midadolescence do young people grasp complex, recursive understanding (Flavell et al., 1968).

Recursive thought makes human interaction truly reciprocal. People often call on it to clear up misunderstandings, as when they say, "I thought you would think I was just kidding when I said that." Recursive thinking is also involved in clever attempts to disguise our real thoughts and feelings, when we reason in ways like this: "He'll think I'm jealous if I tell him I don't like his new car, so I'll act like I do" (Perner, 1988). Finally, the capacity to think recursively contributes to the intense self-focusing and concern with the imaginary audience typical of early adolescence (see Chapter 6). "Often to their pain, adolescents are much more gifted at this sort of wondering than first graders are" (Miller, Kessel, & Flavell, 1970, p. 623).

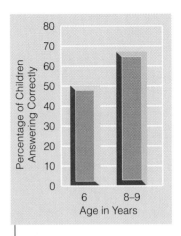

**FIGURE 11.9**

**Development of children's understanding that a person's prior knowledge affects their understanding of new information.** When asked whether a baby and an adult would know the location of an object after being told where it had been placed, 4-year-olds did not realize that a baby could not learn from a verbal message. Performance on this perspective-taking task improved between ages 6 and 8. (Adapted from Montgomery, 1993.)

**One-loop recursion**
"The boy is thinking that he is thinking about himself."

**Two-loop recursion**
"The boy is thinking that the girl is thinking of the father thinking of the mother."

**FIGURE 11.10**

**Cartoon drawings depicting recursive thought.** Not until midadolescence do young people master the complexities of this self-embedded form of perspective taking. (From P. H. Miller, F. S. Kessel, & J. H. Flavell, 1970, "Thinking About People Thinking About People Thinking About . . . A Study of Social Cognitive Development," *Child Development, 41,* p. 616. © The Society for Research in Child Development, Inc. Reprinted by permission.)

**recursive thought**
The self-embedded form of perspective taking that involves thinking about what another person is thinking.

Although it improves with age, perspective-taking skill varies among children of the same age. Experiences in which adults and peers explain their viewpoints, encouraging children to consider another's perspective, contribute to these individual differences (Dixon & Moore, 1990). Consistent with this idea, children in collectivist cultures, which emphasize cooperation and group harmony, do better on perspective-taking tasks than do children in individualistic cultures (Keats & Fang, 1992).

**PERSPECTIVE TAKING AND SOCIAL BEHAVIOUR.** Perspective-taking skills help children get along with others. When we anticipate people's points of view, we can also respond to their needs more effectively. Good perspective takers are more likely to display empathy and sympathy, and they are better at thinking of effective ways to handle difficult social situations (Eisenberg, Murphy, & Shepard, 1997; Marsh, Serafica, & Barenboim, 1981). For these reasons, they tend to be especially well liked by peers (LeMare & Rubin, 1987).

Although good perspective taking is crucial for mature social behaviour, situational and personal factors determine whether it will lead to prosocial acts. In a competitive task, skilled perspective takers are often as good at defending their own viewpoint as they are at cooperating. Also, even when children appreciate another person's thoughts and feelings, temperament influences their behaviour. Recall from Chapter 10 that children who are good at regulating emotion are more likely to help others in distress and to handle social conflicts constructively. Assertive, sociable children also engage in higher rates of prosocial responding.

Finally, children and adolescents with poor social skills—in particular, the angry, aggressive styles we will take up in Chapter 12—have great difficulty imagining the thoughts and feelings of others. They often mistreat adults and peers without experiencing the guilt and remorse prompted by awareness of another's point of view. Interventions that provide coaching and practice in perspective taking help reduce antisocial behaviour and increase prosocial responding (Chalmers & Townsend, 1990; Chandler, 1973).

## ASK YOURSELF

**review** Describe changes in children's understanding of intention over the preschool years.

**review** What factors account for variations in perspective-taking skills among children of the same age? How does perspective taking contribute to social development?

**apply** Ten-year-old Marla is convinced that her classmate, Bernadette, who gets poor grades, is lazy. In contrast, Jane thinks Bernadette tries but can't concentrate because her parents are getting a divorce. Why is Marla more likely than Jane to harbour social prejudices?

**connect** Children pass *false-belief* tasks around age 4, long before they understand that people's *pre-existing beliefs* affect their viewpoints, between ages 6 to 8. Why is the latter understanding more difficult? (Hint: Note the difference between false-belief and perspective-taking tasks, described on page 469.)

# Thinking About Relations Between People: Understanding Conflict

AS CHILDREN DEVELOP, they apply their insights about themselves and others to an understanding of relations between people. Most research on this aspect of social cognition has to do with friendship and conflicts. We will reserve the topic of friendship for Chapter 15. Here we focus on how children think about and resolve situations in which their goals and the goals of agemates are at odds.

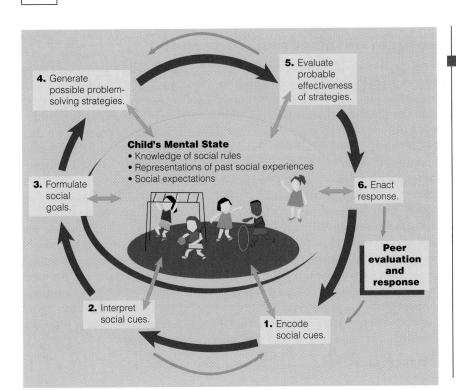

**FIGURE 11.11**

**Dodge's information-processing model of social problem solving.** The model is circular, since children often engage in several information-processing activities at once—for example, interpreting information as they encode it and continuing to consider the meaning of another's behaviour while they generate and evaluate problem-solving strategies. The model also takes into account the impact of mental state on social information processing—in particular, children's knowledge of social rules, their representations of past social experiences, and their expectations for future experiences. Peer evaluations and responses to enacted strategies, along with the way children think about those responses, are also important factors in social problem solving. (Adapted from N. R. Crick & K. A. Dodge, 1994, "A Review and Reformulation of Social Information-Processing Mechanisms in Children's Social Adjustment," *Psychological Bulletin, 115,* 74–101. Copyright © 1994 by the American Psychological Association. Adapted by permission.)

## SOCIAL PROBLEM SOLVING

Children, even good friends, sometimes come into conflict. Yet even preschoolers seem to handle most quarrels constructively; only rarely do their disagreements result in hostile encounters. Overall, conflicts are not very frequent when compared with children's friendly, cooperative interactions (Hay, 1984).

Nevertheless, peer conflicts are important. Watch children engage in disputes over play objects ("That's mine!" "I had it first!"), entry into and control over play activities ("I'm on your team, Jerry." "No, you're not!"), and disagreements over facts, ideas, and beliefs ("I'm taller than he is." "No, you aren't!"). You will see that they take these matters quite seriously. In Chapter 6, we noted that resolution of conflict, rather than conflict per se, promotes development. Social conflicts offer children invaluable learning opportunities for **social problem solving**. In their efforts to resolve conflicts effectively—in ways that are both acceptable to others and beneficial to the self—children must bring together diverse social understandings.

Nicki Crick and Kenneth Dodge (1994) organize the steps of social problem solving into the circular model shown in Figure 11.11. Notice how this flowchart takes an *information-processing approach,* clarifying exactly what a child must do to grapple with a social problem and arrive at a solution. Once this is known, then processing deficits can be identified and intervention can be tailored to children's individual needs.

Social problem solving profoundly affects social competence. Children who get along well with agemates interpret social cues accurately, formulate goals that enhance relationships (such as being helpful to peers), and have a repertoire of effective problem-solving strategies that they apply adaptively. In contrast, children with peer difficulties often hold biased social expectations. Consequently, they attend selectively to social cues (such as hostile acts) and misinterpret others' behaviour (an unintentional jostle as hostile). Their social goals (getting even with or avoiding a peer) often lead to strategies that damage relationships (Erdley & Asher, 1999; Youngstrom et al., 2000).

**social problem solving**
Resolving social conflicts in ways that are both acceptable to others and beneficial to the self. Involves encoding and interpreting social cues, clarifying a social goal, generating and evaluating strategies, and enacting a response.

## DEVELOPMENT OF SOCIAL PROBLEM SOLVING

Most research on social problem solving focuses on strategy generation—by asking young children to think of ways to deal with hypothetical conflicts, such as wanting to play with a toy someone else has. Findings reveal that the quantity and quality of children's strategies improve with age. Younger children, as well as children with poor peer relations, describe strategies that impulsively meet their needs, such as grabbing, hitting, or ordering another child to obey. Older children and those with good peer relations assert their needs in ways that take into account the needs of others. They rely on friendly persuasion and compromise, sometimes suggesting that a conflict be solved by creating new mutual goals. In doing so, they recognize that solutions to problems have an enduring impact on the relationship (Downey & Walker, 1989; Yeates, Schultz, & Selman, 1991).

Other researchers have expanded the study of social problem solving to find out at what points, besides strategy generation, socially competent children differ from less competent children. Dodge and his collaborators (1986) assessed school-age children's skilfulness at five of the problem-solving steps shown in Figure 11.11. A videotape dramatized a problem involving entry into a play group. In the first scene, two children played a board game, and the researchers measured each participant's ability to *encode and interpret social cues* about the video characters' willingness to let the third child join the game. Then children *generated strategies* for joining the game, and their responses were coded as follows:

- *Competent:* polite requests to play and other friendly comments

- *Aggressive:* threats, physical force, and barging in without asking

- *Self-centred:* statements about the self, such as "Hey, I know how to play that!"

- *Passive:* shy, hovering responses, such as waiting and "hanging around"

- *Appeals to authority:* for example, "The teacher said I could play"

Next, participants viewed five more scenes in which a child tried to enter the game using each of these strategies, and they engaged in *strategy evaluation* by indicating whether or not the technique would succeed. Finally, participants *enacted a response* by demonstrating a way of joining the game.

In a separate session, the investigators assessed children's actual social competence by having them gain entry into a real peer group activity in the laboratory. Results showed that all five social problem-solving skills were related to children's performance. Each social-cognitive measure also predicted how effectively children joined play activities on their school playground.

Over the early elementary school years, the components of social problem solving become more strongly associated with socially competent behaviour. As children move through the first few years of schooling, they confront increasingly complex social situations, which demand more sophisticated social information-processing skills. These, in turn, become increasingly important for getting along with others (Dodge & Price, 1994).

## TRAINING SOCIAL PROBLEM SOLVING

Intervening with children who have weak social problem-solving skills can enhance development in several ways. Besides improving peer relations, effective social problem solving is linked to better academic performance. And it fosters a sense of mastery in the face of stressful life events, reducing the risk of adjustment difficulties in children from low-income and troubled families (Dubow et al., 1991; Goodman, Gravitt, & Kaslow, 1995).

In one widely applied social problem-solving training program, preschoolers and kindergartners discuss how to resolve social problems acted out with puppets in daily sessions over several months. In addition, teachers intervene as conflicts arise in the classroom, point out consequences of children's behaviour, and suggest alternative strategies. In several studies, trained children, in contrast to untrained controls, improved in their ability to think about social problems and in teacher-rated adjustment—gains still evident months after the program ended (Shure, 1997). School-age children benefit from similar interventions (Gettinger, Doll, & Salmon, 1994).

Practice in enacting responses may strengthen these positive outcomes. Often children know how to solve a social problem effectively, but they do not apply their knowledge (Rudolph & Heller, 1997). Also, for children who have enacted maladaptive responses repeatedly, rehearsal of alternatives may be necessary to overcome their habitual behaviours, change their expectations, and spark more adaptive social information processing.

RICHARD HUTCHINGS/PHOTOEDIT

Although infrequent when compared with friendly interaction, conflicts between children do occur. To solve their social problem effectively, these boys must bring together a variety of social-cognitive skills. These include accurately encoding and interpreting social cues, formulating social goals that take into account both their own and others' needs, generating and evaluating problem-solving strategies, and enacting an adaptive response.

On a final note, social-cognitive training is not the only means for helping socially incompetent children. Because their parents often model poor social problem-solving skills and use ineffective child-rearing practices, family intervention may be necessary—a topic we will return to several times in later chapters.

## ASK YOURSELF

**review**   Using the social problem-solving steps in Figure 11.11, distinguish effective from ineffective social problem solvers.

**connect**   Does improved perspective taking contribute to gains in social problem solving from early to middle childhood? Explain.

# summary

## What is social cognition, and how does it differ from nonsocial cognition?

■ Researchers interested in the development of **social cognition** study how children's understanding of themselves, other people, and relationships between people changes with age. Compared with nonsocial cognition, social cognition involves the challenge of comprehending how both inner states and external forces affect people's behaviour.

## EMERGENCE OF SELF AND DEVELOPMENT OF SELF-CONCEPT

*Describe the development of self-awareness in infancy and toddlerhood and its consequences for young children's emotional and social capacities.*

■ The earliest aspect of the self to emerge is the **I-self,** a sense of self as knower and actor. Its beginnings lie in infants' recognition that their own actions cause objects and people to react in predictable ways. During the second year, toddlers start to construct the **me-self,** a reflective observer who treats the self as an object of knowledge and evaluation. Parents who respond to infants' and toddlers' signals consistently and sensitively (as indicated by secure attachment) are advanced in early self-development.

■ By the end of the second year, **self-recognition** is well established, as revealed by reactions of toddlers to their own image and use of language to refer to themselves. Self-awareness underlies the emergence of self-conscious emotions, perspective tak-

ing, empathy, sustained imitative play, peer competition for objects, and cooperation.

*Describe the development of the categorical, remembered, and inner selves, and cite consequences of and contributors to preschoolers' belief–desire theory of mind.*

■ Language development permits young preschoolers to construct a **categorical self** as they classify themselves and others on the basis of age, sex, physical characteristics, and goodness and badness. Conversations with adults about the past lead to an autobiographical memory—a life-story narrative that grants the child a **remembered self** imbued with cultural values.

■ Infants' implicit appreciation of people as animate beings whose behaviour is governed by intentions, desires, and feelings and who can share inner states sets the stage for an **inner self** of private thoughts and imaginings. As 2-year-olds talk about mental states, they form a **desire theory of mind,** in which they integrate desire with perception and emotion. Around age 4, children's theory of mind becomes a **belief–desire theory,** as mastery of false-belief tasks reveals their understanding that both beliefs and desires determine actions.

■ Belief–desire reasoning is related to advances in social skills. Among children who pass false-belief tasks, sociodramatic play is more mature and eyewitness memories more accurate.

■ Many factors contribute to the development of belief–desire reasoning, including language development; cognitive skills of inhibition, flexible thinking, and planning; make-believe play; and social interaction with siblings, friends, and adults. Some researchers believe that the human brain is biologically prepared to develop a belief–desire theory. Others think that belief–desire is supported by general cognitive development.

*Discuss the development of self-concept from early childhood through adolescence, noting cognitive, social, and cultural influences.*

■ The me-self expands as preschoolers construct a **self-concept,** or set of beliefs about their own characteristics. In middle childhood, self-concept changes from a focus on observable characteristics and typical emotions and attitudes to an emphasis on personality traits, positive and negative characteristics, and **social comparisons.** In adolescence, self-descriptions become more abstract and form an organized system that places greater emphasis on social virtues and personal and moral values.

■ Changes in self-concept are supported by cognitive development, perspective-taking skills (as suggested by Mead's concept of the **generalized other**), and feedback from others. In describing themselves, children tend to be more egoistic and competitive in individualistic cultures, more concerned with the welfare of others in collectivist cultures.

## SELF-ESTEEM: THE EVALUATIVE SIDE OF SELF-CONCEPT

*Discuss development of and influences on self-esteem from early childhood through adolescence.*

■ **Self-esteem,** the judgments we make about our own worth, differentiates, becomes hierarchically organized, and declines over the first few years of elementary school as children start to make social comparisons. Except for a temporary drop associated with school transition, self-esteem rises from grade 4 on, and new dimensions are added in adolescence. For most young people, becoming an adolescent leads to feelings of pride and self-confidence.

■ Various aspects of self-esteem are strongly correlated with everyday behaviours. A generally positive profile is associated with positive adjustment, a profile of low self-regard in all areas with poor adjustment. Cultural forces affect self-esteem, as illustrated by cultural differences in the role of social comparison. Child-rearing practices that are warm and accepting and that provide reasonable expectations for mature behaviour are consistently related to high self-esteem.

*Discuss the development of achievement-related attributions, noting the influence of cognitive development and adults' messages to children, and suggest ways to foster a mastery-oriented style.*

■ Research on achievement-related **attributions** has identified adult messages that affect children's self-esteem and **achievement motivation.** During middle childhood, children begin to distinguish ability, effort, and external factors in attributions for success and failure.

■ Children with **mastery-oriented attributions** credit their successes to high ability and failures to insufficient effort. They hold an **incremental view of ability**—that it can be improved through trying hard. In contrast, children with **learned helplessness** attribute their successes to luck and their failures to low ability. They hold an **entity view of ability**—that it is fixed and cannot be changed.

■ Adolescents have a fully differentiated understanding of the relation between ability and effort. Those with learned helplessness quickly conclude that mastering a challenging task is not worth the cost—extremely high effort. In this way, they fail to realize their potential.

■ Children who experience negative feedback about their ability, messages that evaluate their traits, pressure to focus on performance goals, and unsupportive teachers are likely to develop learned helplessness. Teachers who are caring and helpful, who emphasize learning over performance goals, and who stress effort and interpersonal harmony in their classrooms foster a mastery orientation.

■ **Attribution retraining,** which encourages learned-helpless children to believe they can overcome failure if only they exert more effort, has improved the self-evaluations and task performance of learned-helpless children. Teaching children to focus less on grades and more on mastering tasks for their own sake and providing instruction in metacognition and self-regulation also are effective.

## CONSTRUCTING AN IDENTITY: WHO SHOULD I BECOME?

*Describe the quest for identity, the four identity statuses, and factors that influence identity development.*

■ Erikson first recognized **identity**—the construction of a solid self-definition consisting of self-chosen values and goals—as the major personality achievement of adolescence. In complex societies, a period of exploration is necessary to form a personally meaningful identity. Because university students have many opportunities to explore career options and lifestyles, they make more progress toward achieving an identity than they did in high school.

■ **Identity achievement** and **moratorium** (exploration) are psychologically healthy identity statuses. Long-term **identity foreclosure** (commitment without exploration) and **identity diffusion** (absence of clear direction) are related to adjustment difficulties.

- Adolescents who have a flexible, open-minded approach to grappling with competing beliefs and values and who feel attached to parents but free to voice their own opinions are likely to be advanced in identity development. Close friendships offer emotional support and role models of identity development. Schools and communities that provide young people with rich and varied options for exploration support the search for identity. Ethnic minority youths who construct a **bicultural identity** are advantaged in many aspects of emotional and social development.

## THINKING ABOUT OTHER PEOPLE

*Discuss gains in understanding intentions and in person perception, including children's appreciation of others' personalities, ethnicity, and social class.*

- During the first few years, children become increasingly skilled at distinguishing intentional from unintentional acts. By age 4, they move beyond a fusion of intention with behaviour to an understanding of intention as an internal mental state that is distinct from other mental states and from the outcomes of actions. During middle childhood, they can better detect people's efforts to conceal their intentions.

- **Person perception** concerns how we size up the attributes of people with whom we are familiar. Like their self-concepts, children's descriptions of other people place greater emphasis on personality traits and become more differentiated and organized with age.

- Basic concepts of race and ethnicity emerge in the preschool years, and children distinguish rich from poor on the basis of physical characteristics. By the early school years, children absorb prevailing attitudes toward social groups. But they do not necessarily directly adopt the attitudes of parents and friends; rather, they seem to pick up information about group status from implicit messages in their environments.

- The capacity to classify the social world in multiple ways leads prejudice to decline in middle childhood. Children who view personality as fixed, have high self-esteem, and experience a social world in which people are sorted into groups are more likely to harbour prejudices.

*Cite major changes in perspective taking from early childhood into adolescence, and explain the role of perspective-taking skill in children's social behaviour.*

- **Perspective taking** improves greatly from childhood to adolescence, as Selman's five-stage sequence indicates. Mastery of Piagetian tasks and a view of the mind as an active interpreter of experience are related to advances in perspective taking. Around age 6, children understand that prior knowledge affects people's ability to understand new information. Between 6 and 8 years, they realize that people's pre-existing beliefs can affect their viewpoints. During adolescence, **recursive thought** is mastered.

- The ability to understand the viewpoints of others contributes to diverse social skills. Angry, aggressive young people have great difficulty imagining the thoughts and feelings of others. Interventions that teach perspective-taking skills reduce antisocial behaviour and increase prosocial responding.

## THINKING ABOUT RELATIONS BETWEEN PEOPLE: UNDERSTANDING CONFLICT

*Describe the components of social problem solving, the development of social problem-solving skills, and ways to help children who are poor social problem solvers.*

- With age, children become better at resolving conflict through **social problem solving**. Components of the social problem-solving process—encoding and interpreting social cues, clarifying social goals, generating and evaluating strategies, and enacting responses—become more strongly linked to socially competent behaviour in middle childhood. Training in social problem solving leads to improved peer relations and academic performance.

# *important terms and concepts*

"Beauty of Nature"
Prabath Nuwan
12 years, Sri Lanka

Children's morality includes respect for the welfare of the environment and all its living creatures. Chapter 12 takes up the emotional, cognitive, and behavioural sides of moral development, including children's reasoning about the close link between humans and nature.

# *twelve*

## Moral Development

THREE-YEAR-OLD LISE grabbed a toy from Anna, a little neighbour girl who had come to play. Anna cried, "Give it back! I had it first!" Lise's mother bent down and explained, "Look! Anna's about to cry. She just wants a turn. Let's give Anna the teddy bear." Lise's mother gently freed the toy from Lise's hands and returned it to Anna. For a moment, Lise looked hurt, but she soon busied herself with her blocks and called out, "Anna, want some of these blocks?"

Now consider Lise at age 11, as she reacted to a newspaper article about an elderly woman, soon to be evicted from her crumbling home because city inspectors judged it a fire and health hazard. "Look at what they're trying to do to this poor lady," exclaimed Lise. "They wanna throw her out of her house. You don't just knock someone's home down! Where're her friends and neighbours? Why aren't they over there fixing up that house?" Lise has come a long way from the preschool child just beginning to appreciate the rights and feelings of others. That beginning, however, is an important one. Preschooler Lise's prosocial invitation to her visiting playmate is not unique and is part of an emerging picture.

In cultures as diverse as the Canadian middle class, a community of Southeast Asian immigrants in Vancouver, and the Fiji Islands of the South Pacific, children undergo a profound change in the latter half of the second year. They react with distress to actions that are aggressive or that might endanger their own or another's welfare. By age 2, they use words to evaluate behaviour as "good" or "bad" (Kochanska, Casey, &

479

Fukumoto, 1995). Empathy and sympathetic concern also emerge around this time (see Chapter 10). And children of this age start to share toys, help others, and cooperate in games (see Chapter 11)—early indicators of a considerate, responsible attitude.

As these observations reveal, accompanying the emergence of self-awareness and new representational capacities in the second year is another crowning achievement: The child becomes a moral being. As cognition and language develop, children express more elaborate moral thoughts accompanied by intense emotion that, at times, escalates to moral outrage—as with 11-year-old Lise.

What accounts for the early emergence of morality and children's expanding appreciation of standards of conduct? Philosophers have pondered this question for centuries, and modern investigators have addressed it with such intensity that research on moral development exceeds that on all other aspects of social development.

The determinants of morality can be found at both societal and individual levels. In all cultures, morality is promoted by an overarching social organization that specifies rules for good conduct. At the same time, morality has roots in each major aspect of our psychological makeup. First, morality has an *emotional component,* since powerful feelings cause us to empathize with another's distress or feel guilty when we are the cause of it. Second, morality has an important *cognitive component.* Children's developing social understanding permits them to make more profound judgments about actions they believe to be right or wrong. Third, morality has a vital *behavioural component,* since experiencing morally relevant thoughts and feelings only increases the chances, but does not guarantee, that people will act in accord with them.

Traditionally, these three facets of morality have been studied separately: biological and psychoanalytic theories focus on emotions, cognitive-developmental theory on moral thought, and social learning theory on moral behaviour. Today, a growing body of research reveals that all three facets are interrelated. Still, major theories disagree on which is primary. We will see that the aspect a theory emphasizes has major implications for how it conceptualizes the basic trend of moral development: the shift from externally controlled responses to behaviour that is based on inner standards or moral understanding. Truly moral individuals do not just do the right thing for the sake of social conformity or the expectations of authority figures. Instead, they have developed compassionate concerns and ideals of good conduct, which they follow in a wide variety of situations.

Our discussion of moral development begins by highlighting the strengths and limitations of the theories just mentioned, based on recent research. Then we consider the important related topic of self-control. The development of a personal resolve to keep the self from doing anything it feels like doing is crucial for translating moral commitments into action. We conclude with a discussion of the "other side" of self-control—the development of aggression.

# Morality as Rooted in Human Nature

DURING THE 1970S, biological theories of human social behaviour suggested that many morally relevant behaviours and emotions have roots in our evolutionary history (Wilson, 1975). This view was supported by the work of ethologists, who observed animals aiding other members of their species, often at great risk to themselves. For example, ants, bees, and termites show extremes of self-sacrifice. Large numbers will sting or bite an animal that threatens the hive, a warlike response that often results in their own death. Dogs who breach a master's prohibition by damaging furniture or defecating indoors sometimes display intense regret, in the form of distress and submission (Lorenz, 1983).

Among primates, chimpanzees (who are genetically closest to humans) conform to moral-like rules, which group members enforce in one another. For example, when males attack females, they avoid using their sharp canine teeth. If a male does harm a female, the entire colony responds with a chorus of indignant barks, sometimes followed by a band of females chasing off the aggressor (de Waal, 1991, 1996). Chimps also reciprocate favours; they generously groom and share food with those who have done the same for them. And they engage in kind and comforting acts. Juveniles sometimes soothe frightened or injured peers, and adult females practise adoption when a baby loses its mother (Goodall, 1990). On the basis of this evidence, researchers reasoned that evolution must have made similar biologically based provisions for moral acts in human beings.

How might genes influence behaviours that support the social group and, thereby, the survival of the species? Many researchers believe that prewired emotional reactions are involved (Haidt, 2001; Hoffman, 2000; Trivers, 1971). In Chapter 10, we noted that newborns cry when they hear another baby cry, a possible precursor of empathy. By the second year, empathic concern is present, and toddlers react with distress to behaviours that threaten not just their own well-being but that of others. Perhaps these emotions underlie human prosocial acts.

Furthermore, researchers have identified an area within the frontal region of the cerebral cortex (the ventromedial area, located just behind the bridge of the nose) as vital for emotional responsiveness to the suffering of others and to one's own misdeeds. Adults experiencing damage to this area do not react negatively to images of extreme human harm, although they know they should feel something. And they show less concern than others with conforming to social norms (Damasio, 1994). When the brain damage occurs early, it seems to severely disrupt social learning; in two such cases, antisocial behaviour was extreme (Anderson et al., 1999). Furthermore, brain-wave and brain-imaging studies reveal that psychopaths, who inflict severe harm on others without any trace of empathy or guilt, show reduced activity in this brain region (Raine, 1997).

According to sociobiologists, many morally relevant prosocial behaviours, such as helping, sharing, and cooperating, are rooted in the genetic heritage of our species. These chimpanzees retreat to a safe, secluded spot in a tree to share meat after a cooperative hunt.

But, like most other human behaviours, morality cannot be fully explained by its biological foundations. Recall from Chapter 10 that morally relevant emotions, such as pride, guilt, empathy, and sympathy, require strong caregiving supports to develop. And their mature expression depends on cognitive development. Furthermore, although emotion is one basis for moral action, it is not a complete account, since following our empathic feelings is not always moral. For example, most of us would question the behaviour of a parent who decides not to take a sick child to the doctor out of empathy with the child's fear and anxiety over doctor visits.

Still, the biological perspective reminds us of morality's value. Because the capacity to serve the self's needs is present early, humans, along with other highly social species, have evolved a brain-based moral substrate that counteracts self-centred motives and promotes concern for others.

## Morality as the Adoption of Societal Norms

THE TWO PERSPECTIVES we are about to discuss—psychoanalytic theory and social learning theory—offer quite different accounts of how children become moral beings. Yet both regard moral development as a matter of **internalization:** adopting societal standards for right action as one's own. In other words, both focus on how morality moves from society to individual—that is, how children acquire norms, or prescriptions for good conduct, widely held by members of their social group.

Our examination of these theories will reveal that several factors jointly affect the child's willingness to adopt societal standards:

- parental discipline, which varies with the type of misdeed;
- the child's characteristics, including age and temperament;
- the parent's characteristics; and
- the child's view of both the misdeed and the reasonableness of parental demands.

**internalization**
The process of adopting societal standards for right action as one's own.

As this list indicates, internalization results from a combination of influences within the child and the rearing environment. When the process goes well, external forces foster the child's positive inclinations (Turiel, 1998) and counteract the child's negative inclinations. In the following sections, we will see many examples of this idea.

## ■ PSYCHOANALYTIC THEORY

According to Sigmund Freud, morality emerges between ages 3 and 6, the period when the well-known Oedipus and Electra conflicts arise (see Chapter 1, page 17). Young children desire to possess the parent of the other sex, but they give up this wish because they fear punishment and loss of parental love. To maintain the affection of parents, children form a *superego,* or conscience, by *identifying* with the same-sex parent, whose moral standards they take into their personality. Finally, children are thought to internalize, along with moral standards, some intense emotion. They turn the hostility previously aimed at the same-sex parent toward themselves, and that internalized hostility leads to painful feelings of guilt each time they disobey the superego (Freud, 1925/1961). Freud viewed moral development as largely complete by age 5 or 6, with some strengthening of the superego in middle childhood.

**IS FREUD'S THEORY SUPPORTED BY RESEARCH?** Today, most researchers disagree with Freud's account of conscience development. First, Freud's view of guilt as a hostile impulse redirected toward the self is no longer accepted. As we will see, high levels of self-blame are not associated with moral internalization. Instead, school-age children experience guilt when they intentionally engage in an unacceptable act and feel personally responsible for the outcome (see Chapter 10).

Second, notice how Freud's theory assumes that discipline promoting fear of punishment and loss of parental love motivates conscience formation and moral behaviour (Kochanska, 1993; Tellings, 1999). Yet children whose parents frequently use threats, commands, or physical force tend to violate standards often and feel little guilt after harming others. In the case of love withdrawal—for example, when a parent refuses to speak to or actually states a dislike for the child—children often respond with high levels of self-blame after misbehaving. They might think to themselves, "I'm no good" or "Nobody loves me." Eventually, these children may protect themselves from overwhelming feelings of guilt by denying the emotion when they do something wrong. So they, too, develop a weak conscience (Kochanska, 1991; Zahn-Waxler et al., 1990).

***The Power of Inductive Discipline.*** In contrast to Freud's focus on punishment and love withdrawal as initiating the superego, a type of discipline called **induction**—which spurs the child to notice others' feelings—supports conscience formation. Induction involves pointing out the effects of the child's misbehaviour on others, noting especially their distress and making clear that the child caused it. For example, at younger ages, the parent might say, "She's crying because you won't give back her doll." Notice how Lise's mother did something similar in the introduction to this chapter. Later, parents can explain why the child's action was inappropriate, perhaps by referring to the other person's intentions: "Don't yell at him. That makes him feel sad. He was trying to help you!" And with further cognitive advances, more subtle psychological explanations can be given: "He felt proud of his tower, and you hurt his feelings by knocking it down" (Hoffman, 2000).

As long as generally warm parents provide explanations that match the child's ability to understand and firmly insist that the child listen and comply, induction is effective as early as 2 years of age. In one study, mothers who used inductive reasoning had preschoolers who were more likely to make up for their misdeeds, as Lise did when she invited Anna to play with her blocks. Children exposed to induction also showed more prosocial behaviour, in that they spontaneously gave hugs, toys, and verbal sympathy to others in distress (Zahn-Waxler, Radke-Yarrow, & King, 1979).

The success of induction may lie in its power to cultivate children's active commitment to moral norms (Turiel, 1998). How does it do so? First, induction tells children how to

**induction**
A type of discipline in which the effects of the child's misbehaviour on others are communicated to the child.

behave so they can call on this information in future situations. Second, by pointing out the impact of the child's actions on others, parents encourage empathy and sympathetic concern, which motivate use of the inductive information in prosocial behaviour (Krevans & Gibbs, 1996). Third, providing children with reasons for changing their behaviour invites them to judge the appropriateness of parental expectations, which fosters adoption of standards because they make sense. When children experience induction consistently, they may form a *script* for the negative emotional consequences of harming others: child harms, inductive message points out harm, child feels empathy for victim, child makes amends. The script deters future transgressions (Hoffman, 2000).

In contrast, discipline that relies too heavily on threats of punishment or love withdrawal produces such high levels of fear and anxiety that children cannot think clearly enough to figure out what they should do. And in the long run, these practices do not get children to internalize moral norms. However, warnings, disapproval, and commands are sometimes necessary to get children to listen to an inductive message (Hoffman, 2000).

Furthermore, Freud's theory places a heavy burden on parents, who must ensure through their disciplinary practices that children develop an internalized conscience. The research we have reviewed indicates that parental discipline is vitally important. Yet parent–child interaction is a two-way street; children's characteristics can affect the success of parenting techniques. Twin studies suggest a modest genetic contribution to empathy (Zahn-Waxler, Robinson, & Emde, 1992). A more empathic child requires less power assertion and is likely to be more responsive to induction. Turn to the From Research to Practice box on page 484 for recent findings on temperament and moral internalization.

***The Role of Guilt.*** Although there is little support for Freudian conceptions of guilt or conscience development, Freud was correct that guilt is an important motivator of moral action. *Inducing empathy-based guilt* (expressions of personal responsibility and regret, such as "I'm sorry I hurt him") by explaining to children that their behaviour is causing pain or distress to a victim and has disappointed the parent is a means of influencing them without using coercion. Empathy-based guilt reactions are consistently associated with stopping harmful actions, repairing damage caused by misdeeds, and engaging in future prosocial behaviour (Baumeister, 1998). Still, parents must help children deal with guilt feelings constructively. They must ensure that children lessen guilty feelings by doing their best to make up for immoral behaviour, not by minimizing or excusing wrongful acts (Bybee, Merisca, & Velasco, 1998).

Despite the effectiveness of guilt in prompting moral action, Freud's theory is one-sided in viewing it as the only force that compels us to act morally. In addition, a wealth of research we will review later in this chapter indicates that contrary to what Freud believed, moral development is not largely complete by the end of the preschool years. Instead, it is far more gradual, beginning in the second year of life and extending into adulthood.

**RECENT PSYCHOANALYTIC IDEAS.** Responding to the limitations of Freud's theory, recent psychoanalytic research underscores the importance of a positive parent–child relationship, emphasizing attachment as a vital foundation for acquiring moral standards. Toddlers who feel a secure sense of connection with the parent are more likely to respond to adult messages about how to behave (Emde et al., 1991; Kochanska & Aksan, 1995). (See the From Research to Practice box on page 484, and notice the strong role of attachment in impulsive children's moral internalization.)

This teacher uses inductive discipline to explain to a child the impact of her transgression on others. Induction supports conscience development by clarifying how the child should behave, encouraging empathy and sympathetic concern, and permitting the child to grasp the reasons behind parental expectations.

*from research to practice*

## TEMPERAMENT AND MORAL INTERNALIZATION IN YOUNG CHILDREN

When her mother reprimanded her sharply for pouring water on the floor as she played in her bath, 3-year-old Katherine burst into tears. An anxious, sensitive child, Katherine was so distressed that it took her mother 10 minutes to calm her down. The next day, Katherine's mother watched as a neighbour patiently asked her 3-year-old son not to pick tulips in the garden. Alex, an active, adventurous child, paid no attention. As he pulled at another tulip, Alex's mother grabbed him, scolded him harshly, and carried him inside. Alex responded by kicking, hitting, and screaming, "Let me down, let me down!"

What explains Katherine and Alex's very different reactions to firm parental discipline? Grazyna Kochanska (1995) points out that children's temperaments affect the parenting practices that best promote responsibility and concern for others. She found that for temperamentally inhibited 2- and 3-year-olds, gentle maternal discipline—reasoning, polite requests, suggestions, and distractions—predicted conscience development at age 4, measured in terms of not cheating in games and completing stories about moral issues with prosocial themes (saying "I'm sorry," not taking someone else's toys, helping a child who is hurt). In contrast, for relatively fearless, impulsive children, mild disciplinary tactics showed no relationship to moral internalization. Instead secure attachment with the mother predicted mature conscience (Fowles & Kochanska, 2000; Kochanska, 1997a).

According to Kochanska, inhibited children like Katherine, who are prone to anxiety, are easily overcome by intense psychological discipline. Mild, patient tactics are sufficient to motivate them to internalize parental messages. But impulsive children, such as Alex, may not respond to gentle interventions with enough discomfort to promote internalization. Yet frequent use of power-assertive methods is not effective either, since these techniques spark anger and resentment, which interfere with the child's processing of parental messages.

Why does secure attachment predict conscience development in nonanxious children? Kochanska suggests that when children are so low in anxiety that typically effective disciplinary practices fail, a close, emotionally positive bond with the caregiver provides an alternative foundation for conscience formation. It motivates children unlikely to experience negative emotion to internalize rules as a means of preserving a spirit of affection and cooperation with the parent.

To foster early moral development, parents must tailor their child-rearing strategies to their child's temperament. In Katherine's case, a soft-spoken correction would probably be effective. For Alex, taking extra steps to build a warm, caring relationship during times when he behaves well is likely to promote moral internalization. In addition, Alex's parents need to use firmer and more frequent discipline than do Katherine's. Without consistent parental controls, children who repeatedly resist parental directives become more unruly with age (Bates et al., 1998). At the same time, extensive power assertion is counterproductive for both children. Do these findings remind you of the notion of *goodness of fit,* discussed in Chapter 10? Return to page 418 to review this idea.

---

Furthermore, current psychoanalytic theorists believe that the superego children build from parental teachings consists not just of prohibitions or "don'ts" (as Freud emphasized), but also of positive guidelines for behaviour, or "do's." After formulating a punitive superego, Freud acknowledged that conscience includes a set of ideals based on love rather than threats of punishment, but he said little about this aspect. Erik Erikson, in his psychosocial theory, placed greater emphasis on the superego as a positive, constructive force that leads to initiative, a sense of ambition and purpose (see Chapter 1, page 18). The positive side of conscience probably emerges first, out of toddlers' participation in morally relevant activities with caregivers, such as helping to wipe up spilled milk or move a delicate object from one place to another. In these situations, parents offer generous praise, and the small child smiles broadly with pride—an early sign of internalization of parental moral standards.

A short time later, parents' warnings and disapproval of forbidden acts evoke "hurt feelings" that may be the forerunners of guilt. Soon, toddlers use their capacity for social referencing to check back with the parent, searching for emotional information to guide their behaviour. With a disapproving glance or shake of the head, parents offer subtle but powerful messages about the moral meaning of the child's actions (see Chapter 10) (Emde & Oppenheim, 1995). Notice how recent psychoanalytic formulations retain continuity with Freud's theory in regarding emotion as the basis for moral development—as the platform on which mature commitment to moral norms is built.

## SOCIAL LEARNING THEORY

The social learning perspective does not regard morality as a special human activity with a unique course of development. Instead, moral behaviour is acquired just like any other set of responses: through reinforcement and modelling.

**THE IMPORTANCE OF MODELLING.** Operant conditioning—following up children's "good behaviour" with reinforcement in the form of approval, affection, and other rewards—is not enough for children to acquire moral responses. For a behaviour to be reinforced, it must first occur spontaneously. Yet many prosocial acts, such as sharing, helping, or comforting an unhappy playmate, do not occur often enough at first for reinforcement to explain their rapid development in early childhood. Instead, social learning theorists believe that children largely learn to behave morally through *modelling*—observing and imitating adults who demonstrate appropriate behaviour (Bandura, 1977; Grusec, 1988). Once children acquire a moral response, such as sharing or telling the truth, reinforcement in the form of praising the act ("That was a nice thing to do") and the child's character ("You're a very kind and considerate boy") increases its frequency (Mills & Grusec, 1989).

Many studies show that models who behave helpfully or generously increase young children's prosocial responses. The following characteristics of models affect children's willingness to imitate:

- *Warmth and responsiveness.* Preschoolers are more likely to copy the prosocial actions of an adult who is warm and responsive than one who is cold and distant (Yarrow, Scott, & Waxler, 1973). Warmth seems to make children more attentive and receptive to the model, and is itself a model of a prosocial response.

- *Competence and power.* Children admire and therefore tend to select competent, powerful models to imitate—the reason they are especially willing to copy the behaviour of older peers and adults (Bandura, 1977).

- *Consistency between assertions and behaviour.* When models say one thing and do another—for example, announce that "it's important to help others" but rarely engage in helpful acts—children generally choose the most lenient standard of behaviour that adults demonstrate (Mischel & Liebert, 1966).

Models exert their strongest influence during the preschool years. At the end of early childhood, children who have a history of consistent exposure to caring adults tend to behave prosocially regardless of whether a model is present. By that time, they have internalized prosocial and other rules for good conduct from repeated observations of and encouragement by others (Mussen & Eisenberg-Berg, 1977).

**EFFECTS OF PUNISHMENT.** Many parents are aware that yelling at, slapping, or spanking children for misbehaviour are ineffective disciplinary tactics. Sharp reprimands or physical force to restrain or move a child are justified when immediate obedience is necessary—for example, when a 3-year-old is about to run into the street. In fact, parents are most likely to use forceful methods under these conditions. When they wish to foster long-term goals, such as acting kindly toward others, they tend to rely on warmth and reasoning (Kuczynski, 1984). Furthermore, according to Joan Grusec of the University of Toronto, parents often combine power assertion with reasoning in response to very serious transgressions, such as lying and stealing (Grusec & Goodnow, 1994).

However, when used frequently, punishment promotes only momentary compliance, not lasting changes in children's behaviour. Children who are repeatedly criticized, shouted at, or

**FIGURE** 12.1

**Prevalence of corporal punishment by child's age.** Estimates are based on the percentage of parents in a U.S. nationally representative sample of nearly 1000 reporting one or more instances of spanking, slapping, pinching, shaking, or hitting with a hard object in the past year. Punishment increases sharply during early childhood and then declines, but it is high at all ages. (From M. A. Straus & J. H. Stewart, 1999, "Corporal Punishment by American Parents: National Data on Prevalence, Chronicity, Severity, and Duration, in Relation to Child and Family Characteristics," *Clinical Child and Family Psychology Review, 2,* p. 59. Adapted by permission.)

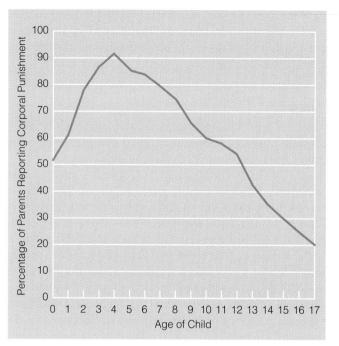

One alternative to harsh punishment is time out, in which children are removed from the immediate setting until they are ready to act appropriately. Time out is useful when a child is out of control and other methods of discipline cannot be applied at the moment. But the best way to motivate good conduct is to let children know ahead of time how to act and praise them when they behave well. Then time out will seldom be necessary.

hit are likely to display the unacceptable response again as soon as adults are out of sight and they can get away with it. In fact, children of highly punitive parents are known to be especially aggressive and defiant outside the home (Strassberg et al., 1994). And several longitudinal studies indicate that the more physical punishment children experience, the greater the rise in maladaptive behaviour, including depression, antisocial acts, and poor academic performance (Brezina, 1999; Gunnoe & Mariner, 1997).

Harsh punishment also has undesirable side effects. First, when parents spank, they often do so in response to children's aggression (Holden, Coleman, & Schmidt, 1995). Yet the punishment itself models aggression! Second, children who are frequently punished soon learn to avoid the punishing adult. As a result, those adults have little opportunity to teach desirable behaviours. Finally, as punishment "works" to stop children's misbehaviour temporarily, it offers immediate relief to adults, and they are reinforced for using coercive discipline. For this reason, a punitive adult is likely to punish with greater frequency over time, a course of action that can spiral into serious abuse.

In view of these findings, the widespread use of corporal punishment by Canadian parents is cause for concern. According to Joan Durrant (2000) of the University of Manitoba, over 70 percent have used physical punishment. A U.S. survey of nearly 1000 households revealed that although corporal punishment increases from infancy to age 5 and then declines, it is high at all ages (see Figure 12.1). An alarming 35 to 50 percent of infants—who are not yet capable of complying with adult directives—get spanked or hit. Parents are most likely to physically punish toddlers and preschoolers repeatedly. And even though use of corporal tactics drops off in middle childhood, 5- to 12-year-olds are more likely than other age groups to be targets of severe forms, such as spanking with brushes and belts; slapping on the face, head, or ears; and pinching (Straus & Stewart, 1999).

A prevailing belief in North American culture is that corporal punishment, if implemented by caring parents, is harmless (Straus & Mathur, 1996). Evidence documenting negative outcomes for children exposed to frequent harsh physical discipline indicates that parents are wise to restrict its use. The Social Issues: Health box on the following page explores the debate on spanking in Canada.

**ALTERNATIVES TO HARSH PUNISHMENT.** Several alternatives to criticism, slaps, and spankings exist. A technique called **time out** involves removing children from the immediate setting—for example, by sending them to their rooms—until they are ready to act appropriately. Time out is useful when a child is out of control (Betz, 1994). It usually requires only a few minutes to change children's behaviour, and it also offers a "cooling off" period for angry parents. Another approach is *withdrawal of privileges,* such as getting an allowance or going to the movies. Removing privileges often generates some resentment in children, but it allows parents to avoid harsh techniques that could easily intensify into violence.

Although its usefulness is limited, punishment can play a valuable role in moral development. Earlier we noted that mild warnings and disapproval are occasionally necessary to get the

## social issues: health

### SHOULD PARENTS BE PERMITTED TO SPANK THEIR CHILDREN?

a tourist from Chicago was charged with assault in London, Ontario, for spanking his daughter on her exposed behind. A witness reported that the father had pulled his daughter out of the family car and spanked her for misbehaving. The father was later acquitted in provincial court under Section 43 of the Canadian Criminal Code. This statute, which dates back to 1892, allows parents and teachers to use reasonable force to correct a child. More recently, six Ontario children were removed from their home by the Children's Aid Society because their fundamentalist Christian parents, who spanked them frequently with a paddle, refused to promise not to hit the children again. This case has yet to be heard.

While most parents say they don't approve of spanking, 22 percent have spanked more than once a week (Durrant, Broberg, & Rose-Krasnor, 2000). A recent Ontario study revealed that children who are spanked often are twice as likely as children who are not spanked to develop psychiatric illnesses, substance abuse problems, and antisocial behaviours (MacMillan et al., 1999).

Is spanking an acceptable form of discipline, or is it child abuse? This has been the topic of heated debate in Canada for years. The Canadian Paediatric Society discourages spanking as a primary method of discipline, but says more research is needed. In a recent Ontario court case, the Superior Court of Justice ruled that striking a child does not violate the child's constitutional rights. This ruling was reinforced in January 2002, when the Ontario Court of Appeal upheld Section 43, which allows reasonable force. The court noted that criminalizing nonabusive physical punishment would interfere with parents' and educators' ability to carry out their responsibilities.

Although a recent poll showed that about 70 percent of Canadians oppose making spanking illegal (McKenzie, 2002), the United Nations has criticized Canada for condoning "reasonable force" in the discipline of children. In Germany, parents and teachers can no longer use physical punishment. Sweden banned all forms of corporal punishment in 1979, the first country to do so. Durrant (1999) evaluated the effectiveness of the ban and found that public attitudes in support of corporal punishment have declined markedly in Sweden. Should Canada criminalize all forms of physical discipline, or should parents and teachers be permitted to use limited, corrective force?

---

child to attend to the parent's inductive teaching. And recall William Damon's (1995) argument, discussed in Chapter 11, that parents must be willing to assert their authority to avoid the dangers of excessive child-centredness (see page 450).

When parents do decide to use punishment, they can increase its effectiveness in several ways:

- *Consistency.* When parents scold children on some occasions but permit them to act inappropriately on others, children are confused about how to behave, and the unacceptable act persists. In a study in which researchers had mothers carry on a telephone conversation while their toddlers played, reprimanding half the children's inappropriate demands for attention ("Please don't interrupt") and giving in to the other half led to a dramatic increase in children's negative emotion and unruly behaviour (see Figure 12.2 on page 488) (Acker & O'Leary, 1996).

- *A warm parent–child relationship.* Children of involved, caring parents find the interruption in parental affection that accompanies punishment to be especially unpleasant. As a result, they want to regain the warmth and approval of parents as quickly as possible.

- *Explanations.* Explanations help children recall the misdeed and relate it to expectations for future behaviour. Consequently, providing reasons for mild punishment (such as time out) leads to a far greater reduction in misbehaviour than using punishment alone (Larzelere et al., 1996).

**time out**
A form of mild punishment in which children are removed from the immediate setting until they are ready to act appropriately.

**FIGURE** 12.2

**How does inconsistent punishment affect children's behaviour?** To find out, researchers conducted an experiment in which they had mothers talk on the telephone while their toddlers played. Mothers in the "reprimand/give in" condition (who reprimanded half of their child's inappropriate demands and gave in to the other half) had toddlers with far higher rates of negative emotion and unruly behaviour than did mothers in the "reprimand" condition (who reprimanded every inappropriate demand) and mothers in the "reprimand/ignore" condition (who reprimanded half of the inappropriate demands and ignored the other half). (Adapted from Acker & O'Leary, 1996.)

[Bar chart: Percentage of Intervals Behaviours Were Observed (y-axis, 0–60) by Condition (x-axis: Reprimand/Give In, Reprimand, Reprimand/Ignore). Legend: Negative emotion, Unruly behaviour.]

Sensitivity, cooperation, and shared positive affect between parent and child support conscience development. This boy feels a sense of commitment to the relationship with his father. This eases the parent's task of encouraging competent behaviour.

© ARIEL SKELLEY/THE STOCK MARKET

**POSITIVE RELATIONSHIPS, POSITIVE DISCIPLINE.** The most effective forms of discipline encourage good conduct. Instead of waiting for children to misbehave, parents can build a positive, cooperative relationship with the child, serve as good examples, let children know ahead of time how to act, and praise children when they behave well (Zahn-Waxler & Robinson, 1995).

When sensitivity, cooperation, and shared positive emotion are evident in joint activities between mothers and their toddlers or preschoolers, children show firmer conscience development—in the form of empathy after transgressing, responsible behaviour, fair play in games, and consideration for others' welfare (Kochanska, 1997b; Kochanska, Forman, & Coy, 1999). Longitudinal research reveals that an early, mutually responsive and pleasurable mother–child tie continues to predict a firmer conscience into the early school years (Kochanska & Murray, 2000). Parent–child closeness leads children to heed parental demands because children feel a sense of commitment to the relationship.

Parents who use positive discipline also reduce opportunities for misbehaviour. For example, on a long car trip, they bring back-seat activities that relieve children's restlessness and boredom. At the supermarket, where exciting temptations abound, they engage preschoolers in conversation and encourage them to help with shopping (Holden & West, 1989). Adults who help children acquire acceptable behaviours that they can use to replace forbidden acts greatly reduce the need for punishment.

## LIMITATIONS OF "MORALITY AS THE ADOPTION OF SOCIETAL NORMS" PERSPECTIVE

As previously noted, both psychoanalytic and social learning theories view moral development as a process of adopting societal norms. Personal commitment to societal norms is, without question, an essential aspect of moral development. Without an internalized, shared moral code and the cultivation of empathy through inductive discipline, people would disregard each other's rights whenever their desires conflict and transgress as soon as others could not observe their behaviour.

Nevertheless, theories that regard morality as entirely a matter of internalizing norms have been criticized because prevailing standards sometimes are at odds with important ethical principles and social goals. Under these conditions, deliberate violation of norms is not immoral. It is justifiable and courageous. Think, for a moment, about historical figures who rose to greatness because they refused to accept certain societal norms. Louis Riel's struggles for the rights of the Métis, Nellie McClung's leadership in the crusade for women's suffrage, and Martin Luther King, Jr.'s campaign to end racial prejudice are examples.

With respect to children, internalization is often accompanied by other parental goals. At times, parents regard noncompliance as acceptable if the child provides a reasonable justification (Kuczynski & Hildebrandt, 1997). Consider a boy who violates a parental prohibition by cutting a cake reserved for a family celebration and giving a piece to a hungry playmate. As the parent begins to reprimand, the boy explains that the playmate had not eaten all day and that the refrigerator was nearly empty, leaving no alternative. In this instance, many parents would value the morality of the boy's claims along with his reasoning and negotiation skills.

Cognitive-developmental theorists believe that neither identification with parents nor teaching, modelling, and reinforcement are the major means through which children become moral. Instead of internalizing existing rules and expectations, the cognitive-developmental approach assumes that individuals develop morally through **construction**—actively attending to and interrelating multiple perspectives on situations in which social conflicts arise and thereby deriving new moral understandings. In other words, children make moral judgments on the basis of concepts they construct about justice and fairness. As these concepts become increasingly adequate with age, children experience them as having a rational basis—as something that *must be true* in the social world, just as conservation *must be true* in the physical world (Gibbs, 1991, 2002).

In sum, the cognitive-developmental position on morality is unique in its view of the child as a thinking moral being who wonders about right and wrong and searches for moral truth. These theorists regard changes in children's reasoning as the heart of moral development.

**ASK YOURSELF**

**review** Describe evidence suggesting that many morally relevant behaviours have roots in our evolutionary history.

**review** Summarize the main features of the psychoanalytic and social learning perspectives on moral development. Why has each been criticized?

**apply** Alice and Wayne want their two young children to develop a strong, internalized conscience and to become generous, caring individuals. Recommend parenting practices that would promote these goals, explaining why each is effective.

**connect** What social-cognitive capacities discussed in Chapter 11 are probably fostered by inductive discipline? Explain.

# Morality as Social Understanding

ACCORDING TO THE cognitive-developmental perspective, cognitive maturity and social experience lead to advances in moral understanding, from a superficial orientation to physical power and external consequences toward a more profound appreciation of interpersonal relationships, societal institutions, and lawmaking systems (Gibbs, 1995, 2002). As their grasp of social cooperation expands, children's ideas about what ought to be done when the needs and desires of people conflict also change, toward increasingly just, fair, and balanced solutions to moral problems.

## PIAGET'S THEORY OF MORAL DEVELOPMENT

Piaget's (1932/1965) early work on children's moral judgments was the original inspiration for the cognitive-developmental perspective. To study children's ideas about morality, Piaget relied on open-ended clinical interviews, questioning 5- to 13-year-old Swiss children about their understanding of rules in the game of marbles. In addition, he gave children stories in which characters' intentions to engage in right or wrong action and the consequences of their behaviour varied. In the best known of these stories, children were asked which of two boys—well-intentioned John, who breaks 15 cups while on his way to dinner, or ill-intentioned Henry, who breaks 1 cup while stealing some jam—is naughtier and why. From children's responses, Piaget identified two broad stages of moral understanding.

**construction**
The process of actively attending to and interrelating multiple perspectives on situations in which social conflicts arise, and thereby deriving new moral understandings.

**HETERONOMOUS MORALITY (ABOUT 5 TO 10 YEARS).** *Heteronomous* means under the authority of another. As the term **heteronomous morality** suggests, children of this stage view rules as handed down by authorities (God, parents, and teachers), as having a permanent existence, as unchangeable, and as requiring strict obedience. For example, young children state that the rules of the game of marbles cannot be changed, explaining that "God didn't teach [the new rules]," "you couldn't play any other way," or "it would be cheating.... A fair rule is one that is in the game" (Piaget, 1932/1965, pp. 58, 59, 63).

According to Piaget, two factors limit children's moral understanding: (1) the power of adults to insist that children comply, which promotes unquestioning respect for rules and those who enforce them; and (2) cognitive immaturity, especially their limited capacity to imagine other perspectives. Because young children think that all people view rules the same way, their moral understanding is characterized by **realism**—that is, they regard rules as external features of reality rather than as cooperative principles that can be modified at will.

Together, adult power, egocentrism, and realism result in superficial moral understandings. In judging an act's wrongness, younger children focus on outcomes rather than on intent to do harm. For example, in the story about John and Henry mentioned earlier, they regard John as naughtier because he broke more cups, despite his innocent intentions.

**AUTONOMOUS MORALITY, OR THE MORALITY OF COOPERATION (ABOUT 10 YEARS AND OLDER).** Cognitive development, gradual release from adult control, and peer interaction lead children to make the transition to **autonomous morality.** Piaget regarded peer disagreements as especially facilitating (see Chapter 6). Through them, children realize that people's perspectives on moral action can differ and that intentions, not concrete consequences, should serve as the basis for judging behaviour.

Furthermore, as children interact as equals with peers, they learn to settle conflicts in mutually beneficial ways. Gradually, they start to use a standard of fairness called *reciprocity,* in which they express the same concern for the welfare of others as they do for themselves. Piaget found that at first, children's grasp of reciprocity is a "crude," tit-for-tat understanding: "You scratch my back and I'll scratch yours." It defines the beginning of the morality of cooperation.

Older children and adolescents move beyond this payback morality to a view of reciprocity as mutuality of expectations. This advanced understanding is called **ideal reciprocity.** Most of us are familiar with it in the form of the Golden Rule: "Do unto others as you would have them do unto you." Ideal reciprocity helps young people realize that rules are flexible, socially agreed-on principles that can be reinterpreted and revised to take into account individual circumstances, thereby ensuring just outcomes for all.

## EVALUATION OF PIAGET'S THEORY

Follow-up research indicates that Piaget's theory accurately describes the general direction of change in moral judgment. In many studies, as children get older, outer features, such as physical damage or getting punished, give way to subtler considerations, such as the actor's intentions or the needs and wishes of others. Also, much evidence confirms Piaget's conclusion that moral understanding is supported by cognitive maturity, gradual release from adult control, and peer interaction. We will consider these findings when we turn to extensions of Piaget's work by Lawrence Kohlberg and his followers. Nevertheless, several aspects of Piaget's theory have been questioned because they underestimate the moral capacities of young children.

**INTENTIONS AND MORAL JUDGMENTS.** Look again at the story about John and Henry on page 489. Because bad intentions are paired with little damage and good intentions with a great deal of damage, Piaget's method yields a conservative picture of young

**heteronomous morality**
Piaget's first stage of moral development, in which children view rules as handed down by authorities, as having a permanent existence, as unchangeable, and as requiring strict obedience.

**realism**
A view of rules as external features of reality rather than as cooperative principles that can be modified at will. Characterizes Piaget's heteronomous stage.

**autonomous morality**
Piaget's second stage of moral development, in which children view rules as flexible, socially agreed-on principles that can be revised to suit the will of the majority.

**ideal reciprocity**
A standard of fairness based on mutuality of expectations, in which individuals express the same concern for the welfare of others as they would have others grant to them. Captured by the Golden Rule.

children's ability to appreciate intentions. When questioned about moral issues in a way that makes a person's intent stand out as strongly as the harm he does, preschool and early school-age children are quite capable of judging ill-intentioned people as naughtier and more deserving of punishment than well-intentioned ones (Helwig, Zelazo, & Wilson, 2001; Jones & Thomson, 2001).

As further evidence, by age 4, children clearly recognize the difference between two morally relevant intentional behaviours: truthfulness and lying. They approve of telling the truth and disapprove of lying, even when a lie remains undetected (Bussey, 1992). And by age 7, earlier than one might expect from Piaget's findings, children integrate their judgments of lying and truth telling with prosocial and antisocial intentions. For example, influenced by collectivist values of social harmony and self-effacement, Chinese children are more likely than Canadian children to rate lying favourably when an intention involves modesty—for example, when a student who generously picks up the garbage in the schoolyard says, "I didn't do it." In contrast, both Chinese and Canadian children rate lying about antisocial acts as "very naughty" (Lee et al., 1997).

Nevertheless, an advanced understanding of the morality of intentions does await autonomous morality. Young elementary school children interpret statements of intention in a rigid, heteronomous fashion. They believe that once you say you will do something, you are obligated to follow through, even if uncontrollable circumstances (such as an accident) make it difficult or impossible for you to do so. By age 9 or 10, children realize that not keeping your word is much worse in some situations than in others—namely, when you are able to do so and permit another person to count on your actions (Mant & Perner, 1988). In sum, Piaget was partly right and partly wrong about this aspect of moral reasoning.

**REASONING ABOUT AUTHORITY.** Research on young children's understanding of authority reveals that they do not regard adults with the unquestioning respect Piaget assumed. Even preschoolers judge certain acts, such as hitting and stealing, to be wrong regardless of the opinions of authorities. When asked to explain, 3- and 4-year-olds express concerns about harming other people rather than obeying adult dictates (Nucci & Turiel, 1978; Smetana, 1981, 1985).

By age 4, children have differentiated notions about the legitimacy of authority figures that they refine during the school years. In several studies, children in kindergarten through grade 6 were asked questions designed to assess their view of how broad an adult's authority should be. Practically none regarded adults as having general authority. For example, most rejected a principal's right to set rules and issue directives in settings other than his own school (Laupa, 1995).

With respect to nonmoral concerns, such as the rules to be followed in a game, children judge legitimacy of authority on a person's knowledge of the situation, not her social position. And when a directive is fair and caring (for example, telling children to stop fighting or share candy), children view it as right, regardless of who states it—a principal, a teacher, a class president, or a child. This is even true for Korean children, whose culture places a high value on respect for and deference to adults. Korean 7- to 11-year-olds evaluate negatively a teacher's or principal's order to keep fighting, to steal, or to refuse to share—a response that strengthens with age (Kim, 1998; Kim & Turiel, 1996).

As these findings reveal, adult status is not required for preschool and school-age children to view someone as an authority. Peers who are very knowledgeable or who act to

These fourth graders listen attentively and seriously as their principal discusses the importance of obeying school rules. Yet they do not have an unquestioning respect for adult authority. They recognize the principal's right to govern in her school. But if she ordered them to behave immorally—to fight, steal, or refuse to share—the children would probably resist.

DICK HEMINGWAY

protect others' rights are regarded as just as legitimate. In reasoning about authority, preschool and young elementary school children place somewhat greater weight on power and status than do older children. Nevertheless, several factors are coordinated at a much earlier age than Piaget anticipated—the attributes of the individual, the type of behaviour to be controlled, and the context in which it occurs.

**STAGEWISE PROGRESSION.** An additional point about Piaget's theory is that many children display both heteronomous and autonomous reasoning, which raises questions about whether a stage is a general, unifying organization of moral judgment responses. But in fairness, Piaget (1932/1965) also observed this mixture in children he interviewed, and he viewed the two moralities as fluid, overlapping phases rather than tightly knit stages.

Finally, moral development is currently regarded as a more extended process than Piaget believed. In fact, Kohlberg's six-stage sequence, to which we now turn, identifies three stages beyond the first appearance of autonomous morality. Nevertheless, Kohlberg's theory is a direct continuation of the research that Piaget began.

## KOHLBERG'S EXTENSION OF PIAGET'S THEORY

Like Piaget, Kohlberg used a clinical interviewing procedure to study moral development. But whereas Piaget asked children to judge the naughtiness of a character who had already chosen a course of action, Kohlberg presented people with moral dilemmas and asked them what the main actor should do and why.

**THE CLINICAL INTERVIEW.** In Kohlberg's **Moral Judgment Interview**, individuals resolve dilemmas that present conflicts between two moral values. The best known of these is the "Heinz dilemma," which pits the value of obeying the law (not stealing) against the value of human life (saving a dying person):

> In Europe, a woman was near death from cancer. There was one drug the doctors thought might save her. A druggist in the same town had discovered it, but he was charging ten times what the drug cost him to make. The sick woman's husband, Heinz, went to everyone he knew to borrow the money, but he could only get together half of what it cost. The druggist refused to sell it cheaper or let Heinz pay later. So Heinz got desperate and broke into the man's store to steal the drug for his wife. Should Heinz have done that? Why or why not? (paraphrased from Colby et al., 1983, p. 77)

In addition to justifying their decisions, participants are asked to evaluate the conflicting moral values on which the dilemma is based. Scoring of responses is intricate and demanding—perhaps the most complex of any interview scoring system (Gibbs, Basinger, & Grime, 2002; Miller, 1998).

Kohlberg emphasized that the *way an individual reasons about the dilemma* and not the *content of the response* (whether or not to steal) determines moral maturity. Individuals who believe that Heinz should take the drug and those who think he should not can be found at each of Kohlberg's first four stages. At the highest two stages, moral reasoning and content come together. Individuals do not just agree on why certain actions are justified; they also agree on what people ought to do when faced with a moral dilemma. Given a choice between obeying the law and preserving individual rights, the most advanced moral thinkers support individual rights (in the Heinz dilemma, stealing the drug to save a life). As we look at development in Kohlberg's scheme, we will see that moral reasoning and content are at first independent, but eventually they are integrated into a coherent ethical system (Kohlberg, Levine, & Hewer, 1983).

**A QUESTIONNAIRE APPROACH.** For more efficient gathering and scoring of moral reasoning, researchers have devised short-answer questionnaires. The most recent is the

**moral judgment interview**
A clinical interviewing procedure for assessing moral understanding, in which people are given moral dilemmas that present conflicts between two moral values and are asked what the main actor should do and why.

**Sociomoral Reflection Measure–Short Form (SRM–SF).** Like Kohlberg's clinical interview, the SRM–SF asks individuals to evaluate the importance of moral values and produce moral reasoning. Here are four of its eleven questions:

- Let's say a friend of yours needs help and may even die, and you're the only person who can save him or her. How important is it for a person (without losing his or her own life) to save the life of a friend?

- What about saving the life of anyone? How important is it for a person (without losing his or her own life) to save the life of a stranger?

- How important is it for people not to take things that belong to other people?

- How important is it for people to obey the law? (Gibbs, Basinger, & Fuller, 1992, pp. 151–152)

After reading each question, participants rate the importance of the value it addresses (as "very important," "important," or "not important") and write a brief explanation of their rating. The explanations are coded according to a revised rendition of Kohlberg's stages.

The SRM–SF is far less time consuming than the Moral Judgment Interview because it does not require people to read and think about lengthy moral dilemmas. Instead, participants merely evaluate moral values and justify their evaluations. Nevertheless, scores on the SRM–SF correlate well with those obtained from the Moral Judgment Interview and show similar age trends (Basinger, Gibbs, & Fuller, 1995; Gibbs, Bassinger, & Grime, 2002). Apparently, moral reasoning can be measured without using dilemmas—a discovery that is likely to ease the task of conducting moral development research.

**KOHLBERG'S STAGES OF MORAL UNDERSTANDING.** Kohlberg organized his six stages into three general levels and made strong statements about this sequence. First, he regarded the stages as invariant and universal—a sequence of steps that people everywhere move through in a fixed order. Second, he viewed each new stage as building on reasoning of the preceding stage, resulting in a more logically consistent and morally adequate concept of justice. Finally, he saw each stage as an organized whole—a qualitatively distinct structure of moral thought that a person applies across a wide range of situations (Colby & Kohlberg, 1987). Recall from Chapter 6 that these characteristics are the very ones Piaget used to describe his cognitive stages.

Furthermore, Kohlberg believed that moral understanding is promoted by the same factors that Piaget thought were important for cognitive development: (1) disequilibrium, or actively grappling with moral issues and noticing weaknesses in one's current thinking; and (2) gains in perspective taking, which permit individuals to resolve moral conflicts in more complex and effective ways. As we examine Kohlberg's developmental sequence and illustrate it with responses to the Heinz dilemma, look for changes in cognition and perspective taking that each stage assumes.

*The Preconventional Level.* At the **preconventional level,** morality is externally controlled. As in Piaget's heteronomous stage, children accept the rules of authority figures, and actions are judged by their consequences. Behaviours that result in punishment are viewed as bad, and those that lead to rewards are seen as good.

- *Stage 1: The punishment and obedience orientation.* Children at this stage find it difficult to consider two points of view in a moral dilemma. As a result, they ignore people's intentions and instead focus on fear of authority and avoidance of punishment as reasons for behaving morally.

*Prostealing:* "If you let your wife die, you will get in trouble. You'll be blamed for not spending the money to help her, and there'll be an investigation of you and the druggist for your wife's death." (Kohlberg, 1969, p. 381)

**Sociomoral Reflection Measure–Short Form (SRM–SF)**
A questionnaire for assessing moral understanding, in which individuals rate the importance of moral values addressed by brief questions and explain their ratings. Does not require research participants to read and think about lengthy moral dilemmas.

**preconventional level**
Kohlberg's first level of moral development, in which moral understanding is based on rewards, punishment, and the power of authority figures.

*Antistealing:* "You shouldn't steal the drug because you'll be caught and sent to jail if you do. If you do get away, [you'd be scared that] the police would catch up with you any minute." (Kohlberg, 1969, p. 381)

- *Stage 2: The instrumental purpose orientation.* Children become aware that people can have different perspectives in a moral dilemma, but this understanding is, at first, very concrete. They view right action as flowing from self-interest. Reciprocity is understood as equal exchange of favours—"You do this for me and I'll do that for you."

*Prostealing:* "The druggist can do what he wants and Heinz can do what he wants to do. . . . But if Heinz decides to risk jail to save his wife, it's his life he's risking; he can do what he wants with it. And the same goes for the druggist; it's up to him to decide what he wants to do." (Rest, 1979, p. 26)

*Antistealing:* "[Heinz] is running more risk than it's worth [to save a wife who is near death]." (Rest, 1979, p. 27)

**The Conventional Level.** At the **conventional level,** individuals continue to regard conformity to social rules as important, but not for reasons of self-interest. They believe that actively maintaining the current social system ensures positive human relationships and societal order.

- *Stage 3: The "good boy–good girl" orientation, or the morality of interpersonal cooperation.* The desire to obey rules because they promote social harmony first appears in the context of close personal ties. Stage 3 individuals want to maintain the affection and approval of friends and relatives by being a "good person"—trustworthy, loyal, respectful, helpful, and nice. The capacity to view a two-person relationship from the vantage point of an impartial, outside observer supports this new approach to morality. At this stage, the individual understands *ideal reciprocity,* as expressed in the Golden Rule.

*Prostealing:* "No one will think you're bad if you steal the drug, but your family will think you're an inhuman husband if you don't. If you let your wife die, you'll never be able to look anyone in the face again." (Kohlberg, 1969, p. 381)

*Antistealing:* "It isn't just the druggist who will think you're a criminal, everyone else will too. After you steal it, you'll feel bad thinking how you brought dishonor on your family and yourself." (Kohlberg, 1969, p. 381)

- *Stage 4: The social-order-maintaining orientation.* At this stage, the individual takes into account a larger perspective—that of societal laws. Moral choices no longer depend on close ties to others. Instead, rules must be enforced in the same evenhanded fashion for everyone, and each member of society has a personal duty to uphold them. The Stage 4 individual believes that laws cannot be disobeyed under any circumstances because they are vital for ensuring societal order.

*Prostealing:* "He should steal it. Heinz has a duty to protect his wife's life; it's a vow he took in marriage. But it's wrong to steal, so he would have to take the drug with the idea of paying the druggist for it and accepting the penalty for breaking the law later."

*Antistealing:* "It's a natural thing for Heinz to want to save his wife but. . . . Even if his wife is dying, it's still his duty as a citizen to obey the law. No one else is allowed to steal, why should he be? If everyone starts breaking the law in a jam, there'd be no civilization, just crime and violence." (Rest, 1979, p. 30)

**The Postconventional or Principled Level.** Individuals at the **postconventional level** move beyond unquestioning support for the rules and laws of their own society. They define morality in terms of abstract principles and values that apply to all situations and societies.

- *Stage 5: The social-contract orientation.* At Stage 5, individuals regard laws and rules as flexible instruments for furthering human purposes. They can imagine alternatives to

**conventional level**
Kohlberg's second level of moral development, in which moral understanding is based on conforming to social rules to ensure positive human relationships and societal order.

**postconventional level**
Kohlberg's highest level of moral development, in which individuals define morality in terms of abstract principles and values that apply to all situations and societies.

their social order, and they emphasize fair procedures for interpreting and changing the law. When laws are consistent with individual rights and the interests of the majority, each person follows them because of a *social-contract orientation*—free and willing participation in the system because it brings about more good for people than if it did not exist.

*Prostealing:* "Although there is a law against stealing, the law wasn't meant to violate a person's right to life. Taking the drug does violate the law, but Heinz is justified in stealing in this instance. If Heinz is prosecuted for stealing, the law needs to be reinterpreted to take into account situations in which it goes against people's natural right to keep on living."

Young people make up a large sector of public demonstrations over moral issues. These students express a principled level of morality as they protest the meeting of the World Trade Organization in downtown Seattle in November 1999. Despite the police crackdown, the Seattle demonstrators continued to object peacefully to a world market that benefits corporations at the expense of low-paid workers and farmers.

- *Stage 6: The universal ethical principle orientation.* At this highest stage, right action is defined by self-chosen ethical principles of conscience that are valid for all humanity, regardless of law and social agreement. These values are abstract, not concrete moral rules like the Ten Commandments. Stage 6 individuals typically mention such principles as equal consideration of the claims of all human beings and respect for the worth and dignity of each person.

*Prostealing:* "If Heinz does not do everything he can to save his wife, then he is putting some value higher than the value of life. It doesn't make sense to put respect for property above respect for life itself. [People] could live together without private property at all. Respect for human life and personality is absolute, and accordingly [people] have a mutual duty to save one another from dying." (Rest, 1979, p. 37)

## RESEARCH ON KOHLBERG'S STAGES

Is there support for Kohlberg's developmental sequence? If so, movement through the stages should be related to age, cognitive development, and gains in perspective taking. Also, moral reasoning should conform to the strict stage properties that Kohlberg assumed.

### AGE-RELATED CHANGE AND INVARIANT STAGES.

A wealth of research reveals that progress through Kohlberg's stages is consistently related to age. The most convincing evidence comes from a 20-year continuation of Kohlberg's first study of adolescent boys, in which participants were reinterviewed at 3- to 4-year intervals. The correlation between age and moral judgment maturity was strong, at .78. In addition, the stages formed an invariant sequence. Almost all participants moved through them in the predicted order, without skipping steps or returning to less mature reasoning once a stage had been attained (Colby et al., 1983). Other longitudinal findings confirm the invariance of Kohlberg's stages (Rest, 1986; Walker, 1989; Walker & Taylor, 1991b).

A striking finding is that development of moral reasoning is very slow and gradual. Figure 12.3 on page 496 shows the extent to which individuals used each stage of moral reasoning between ages 10 and 36 in the longitudinal study just described. Notice how Stages 1 and 2 decrease in early adolescence, whereas Stage 3 increases through midadolescence and then declines. Stage 4 rises over the teenage years until, by early adulthood, it is the typical response. Few people move beyond it to Stage 5. In fact, postconventional morality is so rare that there is no clear evidence that Kohlberg's Stage 6 actually follows Stage 5. The highest stage of moral development is a matter of speculation.

### ARE KOHLBERG'S STAGES ORGANIZED WHOLES?

If each of Kohlberg's stages forms an organized whole, then people should use the same level of moral reasoning across many tasks and situations—not just in hypothetical dilemmas but in everyday moral problems as well. In focusing on hypothetical dilemmas, Kohlberg emphasized the rational weighing of

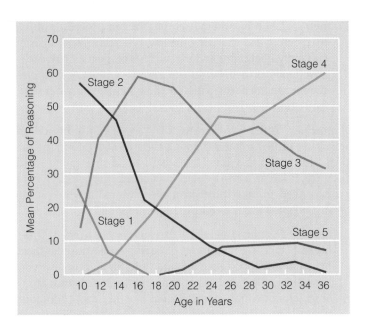

**FIGURE** 12.3

**Longitudinal trends in moral reasoning at each stage in Kohlberg's 20-year study of adolescent boys.** (From A. Colby, L. Kohlberg, J. C. Gibbs, & M. Lieberman, 1983, "A Longitudinal Study of Moral Judgment," *Monographs of the Society for Research in Child Development, 48* [1–2, Serial No. 200], p. 46. © The Society for Research in Child Development, Inc. Reprinted by permission.)

Will the 14-year-old girls on the right decide to accept a peer's offer of a cigarette? How will they justify their decision? Real-life moral dilemmas bring out the motivational and emotional side of moral judgment along with a variety of strategies for resolving conflicts. These teenagers may talk the matter through with each other or call on intuition, since they must make an on-the-spot decision.

alternatives, and he neglected other influences on moral judgment. When Lawrence Walker of the University of British Columbia and others had adolescents and adults recall and discuss a real-life moral dilemma, participants most often focused on relationships—whether to continue helping a friend when she's taking advantage of you, whether to live with mother or with father after their separation. Although participants mentioned reasoning as the most frequent strategy for resolving these dilemmas, they also posed other strategies, such as talking through issues with others, relying on intuition that their decision was right, and calling on notions of religion and spirituality. Especially striking were expressions of anguish in working through everyday dilemmas. People mentioned feeling drained, confused, and torn by temptation—a motivational and emotional side of moral judgment not tapped by hypothetical situations (Walker et al., 1995, 1999).

Although everyday moral reasoning corresponds to Kohlberg's scheme, it typically falls at a lower stage than do responses to hypothetical dilemmas (Walker & Moran, 1991). Real-life problems seem to elicit reasoning below a person's actual capacity because they bring out many practical considerations. Hypothetical situations, in contrast, evoke the upper limits of adolescents' and adults' moral thought because they allow reflection without the interference of personal risks. As one participant in a study involving both types of dilemmas observed, "It's a lot easier to be moral when you have nothing to lose" (Walker et al., 1995, pp. 381–382).

The influence of situational factors on moral reasoning suggests that like Piaget's cognitive stages, Kohlberg's moral stages are loosely organized. Rather than developing in a neat, stepwise fashion, people seem to draw on a range of moral responses that vary with context. With age, this range shifts upward as less mature moral reasoning is gradually replaced by more advanced moral thought (Siegler, 1996).

**COGNITIVE PREREQUISITES FOR MORAL REASONING.** Moral maturity, whether based on Piaget's or Kohlberg's theories, is positively correlated with IQ, performance on Piagetian cognitive tasks, and perspective-taking skill (Lickona, 1976; Walker & Hennig, 1997). Kohlberg (1976) argued that each moral stage requires certain cognitive and perspective-taking capacities, but these are not enough to ensure moral advances. In addition,

TABLE 12.1

Relations among Kohlberg's Moral, Piaget's Cognitive, and Selman's Perspective-Taking Stages

| KOHLBERG'S MORAL STAGE | DESCRIPTION | PIAGET'S COGNITIVE STAGE | SELMAN'S PERSPECTIVE-TAKING STAGE[a] |
|---|---|---|---|
| Punishment and obedience orientation | Fear of authority and avoidance of punishment are reasons for behaving morally. | Preoperational, early concrete operational | Social-informational |
| Instrumental purpose orientation | Satisfying personal needs determines moral choice. | Concrete operational | Self-reflective |
| "Good boy–good girl" orientation | Maintaining the affection and approval of friends and relatives motivates good behaviour. | Early formal operational | Third-party |
| Social-order-maintaining orientation | A duty to uphold laws and rules for their own sake justifies moral conformity. | Formal operational | Societal |
| Social-contract orientation | Fair procedures for changing laws to protect individual rights and the needs of the majority are emphasized. | | |
| Universal ethical principle orientation | Abstract universal principles that are valid for all humanity guide moral decision making. | | |

[a]To review these stages, return to Chapter 11, page 470.

reorganization of thought unique to the moral domain is necessary. In other words, Kohlberg hypothesized that cognitive and perspective-taking attainments are *necessary but not sufficient conditions* for each moral stage.

Consistent with Kohlberg's predictions, children and adolescents at each moral stage score either at a higher stage or the matching stage of cognition and perspective taking, shown in Table 12.1 (Krebs & Gillmore, 1982; Selman, 1976; Walker, 1980). Furthermore, attempts to increase moral reasoning reveal that it cannot be stimulated beyond the stage for which an individual has the appropriate cognitive prerequisites (Walker & Richards, 1979).

Finally, Kohlberg's stage order makes sense to adolescents and adults who have not studied his theory. When Russian high school and Dutch university students were asked to sort statements typical of Kohlberg's stages, overall they ranked reasoning at each consecutive stage as more sophisticated. However, the higher the stage, the more participants disagreed in their ranking of its statements because they had difficulty ordering statements beyond their own current stage (Boom, Brugman, & van der Heijden, 2001).

## ARE THERE SEX DIFFERENCES IN MORAL REASONING?

As we have just seen, in real-life moral dilemmas, emotion often contributes to moral judgment. Return to Lise's moral reasoning in the opening to the chapter and notice how her argument focuses on caring and commitment to others. Carol Gilligan (1982) is the most well-known figure among those who have argued that Kohlberg's theory—originally formulated on the basis of interviews with males—does not adequately represent the morality of girls and women. She believes that feminine morality emphasizes an "ethic of care" that is devalued in Kohlberg's system. Lise's reasoning falls at Kohlberg's Stage 3 because it is based on interpersonal obligations. In contrast, Stages 4 to 6 stress justice—an abstract, rational commitment to moral ideals. According to Gilligan, a concern for others is a *different,* not less valid, basis for moral judgment than a focus on impersonal rights.

Many studies have tested Gilligan's claim that Kohlberg's approach underestimates the moral maturity of females, and most do not support it (Turiel, 1998). On hypothetical dilemmas as well as everyday moral problems, adolescent and adult females display reasoning at the same or higher stages as do their male counterparts. Also, themes of justice and caring appear in the responses of both sexes, and when girls do raise interpersonal concerns, they are not downscored in Kohlberg's system (Jadack et al., 1995; Kahn, 1992; Walker, 1995).

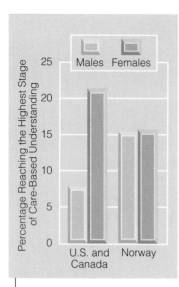

**FIGURE** 12.4

**Complex reasoning about care issues among U.S. and Canadian versus Norwegian males and females.** In this study of 17- to 26-year-olds, North American females scored much higher than males in complex care-based understanding. In contrast, Norwegian males and females displayed equally advanced care-based understanding. (Adapted from Skoe, 1998.)

These findings suggest that although Kohlberg emphasized justice rather than caring as the highest of moral ideals, his theory does include both sets of values.

Still, Gilligan makes a powerful claim that research on moral development has been limited by too much attention to rights and justice (a "masculine" ideal) and too little attention to care and responsiveness (a "feminine" ideal). Some evidence shows that although the morality of males and females taps both orientations, females do tend to stress care, or empathic perspective taking, whereas males either stress justice or use justice and care equally (Galotti, Kozberg, & Farmer, 1991; Garmon et al., 1996; Wark & Krebs, 1996).

The difference in emphasis appears most often in real-life rather than hypothetical dilemmas. Consequently, it may be largely a function of women's greater involvement in daily activities involving care and concern for others. In one study, U.S. and Canadian 17- to 26-year-old females showed more complex reasoning about care issues than their male counterparts. But as Figure 12.4 shows, Norwegian males were just as advanced as Norwegian females in care-based understanding (Skoe, 1998). Perhaps Norwegian culture, which explicitly endorses gender equality at home, at school, and in the workplace, induces boys and men to think deeply about interpersonal obligations.

Although current evidence indicates that justice and caring are not gender-specific moralities, Gilligan's work has expanded our conception of the highly moral person—to one who engages in "reasoned and deliberate judgments that ensure justice be accorded each person while maintaining a passionate concern for the well-being and care of each individual" (Brabeck, 1983, p. 289). Perhaps Piaget (1932/1965) himself said it best: "Between the more refined forms of justice . . . and love properly so called, there is no longer any real conflict" (p. 324).

## INFLUENCES ON MORAL REASONING

Earlier we mentioned Kohlberg's belief that actively grappling with moral issues is vital for moral change. As we will see in the following sections, many factors are related to moral understanding, including the young person's personality and a wide range of social experiences—peer interaction, child-rearing practices, schooling, and aspects of culture. Growing evidence suggests that these experiences work by inducing disequilibrium—presenting young people with cognitive challenges, which stimulate them to think about moral problems in more complex ways.

**PERSONALITY.** A flexible, open-minded approach to new information and experiences is linked to gains in moral reasoning, just as it is to identity development (Hart et al., 1998; Matsuba & Walker, 1998). Because open-minded young people are more socially skilled, they have more opportunities for social participation (Block & Block, 1980). A richer social life enhances exposure to others' perspectives, and open-mindedness helps adolescents derive moral insights from the exposure. In contrast, adolescents who have difficulty adapting to new experiences are less likely to be interested in others' moral ideas and justifications.

**PEER INTERACTION.** Research supports Piaget's belief that interaction with agemates can promote moral understanding. For example, adolescents who report more close friendships, who more often participate in leisure activities and conversations with their friends, and who are viewed as leaders by their classmates score higher in moral reasoning (Schonert-Reichl, 1999). Studies conducted in Africa underline the importance of exposure to diverse peer value systems for stimulating moral thought. Kenyan and Nigerian students enrolled in ethnically and racially mixed high schools and universities were advanced in moral development compared with those enrolled in homogeneous settings (Edwards, 1978; Maqsud, 1977).

As Piaget suggested, peer conflict probably contributes to gains in moral reasoning by making children aware of others' perspectives. But as noted in Chapter 6, conflict resolution, rather than conflict per se, may be the feature of peer disagreements that stimulates cognitive development—nonmoral and moral alike. When children engage in negotiation and compromise, they realize that social life can be based on cooperation between equals rather than authority relations (Damon, 1988; Killen & Nucci, 1995). Within children's friendships, conflicts often arise but are worked out collaboratively. The mutuality and intimacy of friendship, which foster decisions based on consensual agreement, may contribute to moral development.

Peer experiences have provided the framework for many interventions aimed at improving moral understanding. Most involve peer discussion and role playing of moral problems. In a study with particularly impressive findings, after sixth and tenth graders participated in either teacher- or student-led classroom discussions of moral dilemmas for one semester, many moved partially or totally to the next moral stage, a change not found in students who did not receive the intervention (Blatt & Kohlberg, 1975). A year later, group differences were still evident.

Which aspects of peer discussion stimulate moral development? Once again, give-and-take and compromise, involving efforts to comprehend another's viewpoint, appear important. Observations of university students discussing moral dilemmas revealed that those who confronted, critiqued, and attempted to clarify one another's statements gained in moral maturity. In contrast, nongainers made assertions, told personal anecdotes, or expressed confusion about the task (Berkowitz & Gibbs, 1983). However, because moral development is a gradual process, many peer interaction sessions over weeks or months typically are necessary to produce moral change.

© BOB DAEMMRICH/STOCK BOSTON

Discussions about moral issues in which peers confront, critique, and attempt to clarify one another's statements lead to gains in moral understanding.

**CHILD-REARING PRACTICES.** Child-rearing practices associated with mature moral reasoning combine warmth with exchange of ideas. In moral discussions with children and adolescents, parents who listen sensitively, ask clarifying questions, present higher-level reasoning, and use praise and humour have youngsters who gain most in moral understanding in succeeding years. In contrast, parents who lecture, use threats, or make sarcastic remarks have children who change little or not at all (Pratt et al., 1999; Walker & Taylor, 1991a).

Other research reveals that parents who use low levels of power assertion and high levels of warmth and inductive discipline and who encourage participation in family decision making have morally mature children (Boyes & Allen, 1993; Parikh, 1980). In sum, the kind of parent who facilitates moral understanding is verbal, rational, and affectionate and promotes a cooperative style of family life. Notice that these are the very characteristics, discussed earlier in this chapter, that foster moral internalization in young children.

**SCHOOLING.** Years of schooling completed is one of the most powerful predictors of moral understanding. Moral reasoning advances in late adolescence and young adulthood only as long as a person remains in school (Rest & Narvaez, 1991; Speicher, 1994). Perhaps higher education has a strong impact on moral development because it introduces young people to social issues that extend beyond personal relationships to entire political or cultural groups. Consistent with this idea, university students who report more academic perspective-taking opportunities (for example, classes that emphasize open discussion of opinions) and who indicate that they have become more aware of social diversity tend to be advanced in moral reasoning (Mason & Gibbs, 1993a, 1993b).

**CULTURE.** Cross-cultural research reveals that individuals in technologically advanced, urban cultures move through Kohlberg's stages more rapidly and advance to a higher level than do individuals in nonindustrialized, village societies. Members of these small, collectivist communities do not reach Stage 4 and above, whereas high school- and university-educated adolescents and adults in developed nations do (Snarey, 1995). (Keep in mind, however, that only a few adults in industrialized nations reach Stages 5 and 6.)

Young people growing up on Israeli kibbutzim receive training in the governance of their society at an early age. As a result, they understand the role of societal laws and rules in resolving moral conflict and are advanced in moral reasoning.

One explanation of these cultural differences focuses on the role of societal institutions in advanced moral understanding. In village societies, moral cooperation is based on direct relations between people. Yet Stage 4 to 6 reasoning depends on understanding the role of laws and government institutions in resolving moral conflict (Snarey, 1995). In support of this view, in cultures where young people participate in the institutions of their society at early ages, moral reasoning is advanced. For example, on *kibbutzim,* small but technologically complex agricultural settlements in Israel, children receive training in the governance of their community in middle childhood. By grade 3, they mention more concerns about societal laws and rules when discussing moral conflicts than do Israeli city-reared or North American children (Fuchs et al., 1986). During adolescence and adulthood, a greater percentage of kibbutz than North American individuals reach Kohlberg's Stages 4 and 5 (Snarey, Reimer, & Kohlberg, 1985).

A second possible reason for cultural variation is that responses to dilemmas in some cultures cannot be scored in Kohlberg's scheme. Recall from Chapter 11 that self-concepts in collectivist cultures (including village societies) are more other-directed than in Western Europe and North America. This very difference seems to characterize moral reasoning as well (Miller, 1994, 1997). In village societies, moral statements that portray the individual as vitally connected to the social group are common. For example, one New Guinea village leader placed the blame for the Heinz dilemma on the entire community, stating, "If I were the judge, I would give him only light punishment because he asked everybody for help but nobody helped him" (Tietjen & Walker, 1985, p. 990).

Similarly, members of Eastern collectivist nations grant obligations to others more weight than do people in Western individualistic societies. East Indians, for example, are far more likely than North Americans to view interpersonal transgressions, such as a son refusing to care for his elderly parents, as moral offences rather than matters of personal choice (Miller & Luthar, 1989). At the same time, East Indians less often hold individuals accountable for moral violations. In their view, the self and its physical and social surroundings are inseparable. Therefore, they often explain behaviour in contextual rather than personal terms (Miller, 1994; Miller & Bersoff, 1995). This perspective is evident even among well-educated adults, who would be expected to be at Kohlberg's higher stages. In discussing the Heinz dilemma, they resist choosing a course of action, explaining that a moral solution should be the burden of the entire society. As one woman explained,

> The problems that Heinz is up against are not individual problems that are affecting one or two Heinzes of the world. These are social problems. Forget Heinz in Europe, just come to India.... Heinz's story is being repeated all around us all the time with wives dying, with children dying, and there is no money to save them.... So Heinz in his individual capacity—yes, okay, steal the drug, but it's not going to make any difference on a large scale.... I don't think in the final analysis a solution can be worked out on an individual basis.... It will probably have to be tackled on a macro level. (Vasudev & Hummel, 1987, p. 110)

These findings raise the question of whether Kohlberg's highest stages represent a culturally specific rather than universal way of thinking—one limited to Western societies that emphasize individual rights and an appeal to an inner, private conscience.

## MORAL REASONING AND BEHAVIOUR

A central assumption of the cognitive-developmental perspective is that moral understanding should affect moral motivation. As young people grasp the moral "logic" of human social cooperation, they are upset when this logic is violated. As a result, they gradually realize that behaving in line with the way one thinks is vital for creating and maintaining a just social world (Gibbs, 1995). On the basis of this idea, Kohlberg predicted that moral thought and behaviour should come together at the higher levels of moral understanding (Blasi, 1994). Consistent with this idea, higher-stage adolescents more often act prosocially by helping, sharing, and defending victims of injustice (Carlo et al., 1996; Comunian & Gielan, 2000). They also less often engage in cheating, aggression, and other antisocial behaviours (Gregg, Gibbs, & Fuller, 1994; Taylor & Walker, 1997).

Yet even though a clear connection between moral thought and action exists, it is only moderate. We have already seen that moral behaviour is influenced by a great many factors besides cognition, including the emotions of empathy, sympathy, and guilt; individual differences in temperament; and a long history of experiences that affect moral choice and decision making.

Also, **moral self-relevance**—the degree to which morality is central to self-concept—affects moral behaviour. In a study of low-SES African-American and Hispanic teenagers, those who emphasized moral traits and goals in their self-descriptions displayed exceptional levels of community service. These highly prosocial young people, however, did not differ from their agemates in moral reasoning (Hart & Fegley, 1995). That a synthesis of moral concern with sense of self can motivate moral action also is supported by a study of people who have made outstanding contributions to moral causes, such as civil rights, the fight against poverty, medical ethics, and religious freedom. Interviews with these moral exemplars revealed that their most distinguishing characteristic is "seamless integration" of moral vision with personal identity (Colby & Damon, 1992, p. 309).

Researchers have yet to uncover just how moral reasoning combines with other influences to foster moral commitment. Still, as the Social Issues: Education box on pages 502–503 reveals, promoting civic responsibility in young people can help them see the connection between their personal interests and the public interest—an insight that may foster all aspects of morality.

## FURTHER QUESTIONS ABOUT KOHLBERG'S THEORY

Although there is much support for Kohlberg's theory, it continues to face challenges. The most important of these concerns Kohlberg's conception of moral maturity and the appropriateness of his stages for characterizing the moral reasoning of young children.

A key controversy has to do with Kohlberg's belief that moral maturity is not achieved until the postconventional level. Yet if people had to reach Stages 5 and 6 to be considered truly morally mature, few individuals anywhere would measure up! John Gibbs (1991, 2002) argues that "postconventional morality" should not be viewed as the standard against which other levels are judged immature. Instead, he regards postconventional reasoning as a highly reflective endeavour, achieved only by individuals with advanced education, usually with training in philosophy.

Gibbs finds maturity in a revised understanding of Stages 3 and 4. These stages are not "conventional" or based on social conformity, as Kohlberg assumed. Instead, they require vital moral constructions—an understanding of ideal reciprocity as the basis for relationships between people (Stage 3) and for widely accepted moral standards, set forth in rules and laws (Stage 4). As Gibbs points out, these constructions—not those of Stages 5 and 6—are the profound, universal attainments required for a highly moral life.

Finally, Kohlberg's stages largely describe changes in moral reasoning during adolescence and adulthood. They tell us little about moral understanding in early and middle childhood. Indeed, Kohlberg's moral dilemmas are remote from the experiences of most children and may not be clearly understood by them. When children are given moral dilemmas related to their everyday lives, their responses indicate that Kohlberg's preconventional level, much like Piaget's heteronomous morality, underestimates their moral reasoning. Nancy Eisenberg created dilemmas that do not make reference to laws but instead pit satisfying one's own desires against acting prosocially—for example, going to a birthday party versus taking time to help an injured peer and missing the party (Eisenberg, 1986; Eisenberg et al., 1991, 1995). Children and adolescents' *prosocial moral reasoning* about such dilemmas is clearly advanced when compared with Kohlberg's stages. Furthermore, research suggests that empathic

**moral self-relevance**
The degree to which morality is central to self-concept.

# social issues: education

## DEVELOPMENT OF CIVIC RESPONSIBILITY

uring the summer, Jodie and Jim joined other high school students in a Habitat for Humanity project, building a home for the needy. Throughout the year, Sasha volunteered on Saturday mornings at a nursing home, conversing with bedridden elders. In the months before a provincial election, all three young people attended special youth meetings with candidates, where they raised concerns. "What's your view on preserving our environment?" Jim asked. "How would you prevent the proposed tax cut from mostly benefiting the rich?" Sasha chimed in. At school, Jodie and Jim formed an organization devoted to promoting ethnic and racial tolerance.

Already, these young people have a strong sense of civic responsibility—a complex capacity that combines cognition, emotion, and behaviour. Civic responsibility involves *knowledge* of political issues and the means through which citizens can resolve differing views fairly; *feelings* of attachment to the community, of wanting to make a difference in its welfare; and *skills* for achieving civic goals, such as how to contact and question public officials and conduct meetings so that all participants have a voice (Flanagan & Faison, 2001). New research reveals that family, school, and community experiences contribute to adolescents' civic responsibility.

### FAMILY INFLUENCES

Canadian research shows that parents who bring up controversial issues and encourage their children to form opinions have teenagers who are more knowledgeable, more interested in civic issues, and better able to see them from more than one perspective (Santoloupo & Pratt, 1994). Also, adolescents who report that their families emphasize compassion for the less fortunate tend to hold socially responsible values. When asked what causes such social ills as unemployment, poverty, and homelessness, these teenagers more often mention situational and societal factors (such as lack of education, government policies, or insufficient job opportunities) than individual factors (such as low intelligence or personal problems). Youths who endorse situational and societal causes, in turn, have more altruistic life goals, such as working to eradicate poverty or preserve the earth for future generations (Flanagan & Tucker, 1999).

### SCHOOL AND COMMUNITY INFLUENCES

A democratic climate at school—one in which teachers hold the same high academic and moral standards for all students, express respect for students' ideas, and insist that students listen to and respect one another—fosters a sense of civic responsibility. Teenagers who say that their teachers engage in these practices are more aware of political issues, better able to critically analyze

---

perspective taking strengthens prosocial moral thought and its realization in everyday behaviour (Eisenberg, Zhoe, & Koller, 2001; Lasoya & Eisenberg, 2001).

In sum, Kohlberg's belief in an early, externally governed morality meant that he failed to uncover young children's internally based judgments of right and wrong. We take a close look at additional evidence on children's moral reasoning in the following sections.

## ASK YOURSELF 🌐

**review**   Compare and contrast the moral development theories of Piaget and Kohlberg. Cite major criticisms of each.

**review**   How does an understanding of *ideal reciprocity* contribute to moral development? Why might Kohlberg's Stages 3 and 4 be morally mature constructions? At which stage is Lise's reasoning about the elderly woman to be evicted from her home, presented in the introduction to this chapter? Explain.

**apply**   Tam grew up in a small village culture, Lydia in a large industrial city. At age 15, Tam reasons at Kohlberg's Stage 2, Lydia at Stage 4. What factors probably account for the difference? Is Lydia's reasoning morally mature? Explain.

**connect**   What experiences that promote mature moral reasoning are also likely to foster identity development? Explain. (See Chapter 11, page 464.)

them, and more committed to social causes (Flanagan & Faison, 2001).

Participation in extracurricular activities at school and in youth organizations is also associated with civic commitment that persists into adulthood (Verba, Schlozman, & Brady, 1995). Researchers believe that two aspects of these involvements account for their lasting impact.

First, they introduce adolescents to the vision and skills required for mature civic engagement. Within clubs, teams, and other groups, young people see how their actions affect the wider school and community. They realize that collectively, they can achieve results greater than any one person can achieve alone. And to reach these goals, they learn to work together, balancing strong convictions with compromise.

Second, while producing a weekly newspaper, participating in a dramatic production, or implementing a service project, young people explore political

During adolescence, young people develop a stronger sense of connection to their community. These teenagers test a polluted tributary for signs of life. Teenagers' involvement in community service grows out of a sense of civic responsibility, which is supported by family, school, and community experiences.

and moral ideals, selecting those they find meaningful. In one study, researchers tracked high school students' changing views during a year of volunteering at a soup kitchen. The students gradually gave up stereotypes of the "homeless," replacing them with images of people with complex life histories and problems. At the same time, they redefined themselves as more fortunate citizens with a responsibility to combat others' misfortunes (Youniss, McClellan, & Yates, 1997).

Current evidence points to growing self-interest and materialism among North American high school students (Rahn & Transue, 1998). Granting young people many opportunities to think in terms of *we* rather than *I* and to work with others toward a common good can combat this trend. The power of family, school, and community to promote civic responsibility may lie in discussions, educational practices, and activities that jointly foster moral thought, emotion, and behaviour.

## Moral Reasoning of Young Children

RESEARCHERS FOCUSING ON children's moral understanding have addressed (1) their ability to distinguish moral obligations from social conventions and matters of personal choice, and (2) their ideas about fair distribution of rewards. Findings reveal surprisingly advanced moral judgments.

### DISTINGUISHING MORAL, SOCIAL-CONVENTIONAL, AND PERSONAL DOMAINS

As early as age 3, children have a beginning grasp of justice. Many studies reveal that preschool and young grade-school children distinguish **moral imperatives,** which protect people's rights and welfare, from two other domains of action: **social conventions,** customs determined solely by consensus, such as table manners, dress styles, and rituals of social interaction; and **matters of personal choice,** which do not violate rights or harm others, are not socially regulated, and therefore are up to the individual (Nucci, 1996; Smetana, 1995; Tisak, 1995).

**moral imperatives**
Standards that protect people's rights and welfare.

**social conventions**
Customs determined solely by consensus, such as table manners, dress styles, and rituals of social interaction.

**matters of personal choice**
Concerns that do not violate rights or harm others, are not socially regulated, and therefore are up to the individual.

**MORAL VERSUS SOCIAL-CONVENTIONAL DISTINCTIONS.** In one study, 2- and 3-year-olds were interviewed about drawings depicting familiar moral and social-conventional violations. For example, a moral picture showed a child stealing an agemate's apple; a social-conventional picture showed a child eating ice cream with fingers. By 34 months, children viewed moral transgressions as more generalizably wrong (not OK, regardless of the setting in which they are committed). And by 42 months, they indicated that moral (but not social-conventional) violations would still be wrong if an adult did not see them and no rules existed to prohibit them (Smetana & Braeges, 1990). As these findings illustrate, the distinction between moral and social-conventional transgressions sharpens during early childhood.

How do young children arrive at these distinctions? According to Elliott Turiel (1998), they do so by actively making sense of their experiences. They observe that after a moral offence, peers react with strong negative emotion, describe their own injury or loss, tell another child to stop, or retaliate. And an adult who intervenes is likely to call attention to the rights and feelings of the victim. In contrast, peers seldom react to violations of social convention. And in these situations, adults tend to demand obedience without explanation or point to the importance of keeping order (Turiel, Smetana, & Killen, 1991).

As their ideas about justice advance, children clarify and link moral imperatives and social conventions. Over time, their understanding becomes more complex, taking into account an increasing number of variables, including the purpose of the rule; people's intentions, knowledge, and beliefs; and the context of their behaviour.

School-age children distinguish social conventions with a clear *purpose* (not running in school hallways because doing so might cause an accident) from ones with no obvious justification (crossing a "forbidden" line on the playground). They regard violations of purposeful social conventions as closer to moral transgressions (Buchanan-Barrow & Barrett, 1998).

Furthermore, children age 6 and older realize that people's *intentions* and the *context* of their actions affect the moral implications of social-conventional transgressions—understandings that improve with age. In a Canadian study, 8- to 10-year-olds judged that because of a flag's symbolic value, burning it to express disapproval of a country or to start a cooking fire is worse than burning it accidentally. Older school-age children also stated that public flag-burning is worse than private flag-burning. When asked to explain, they referred to the emotional harm inflicted on others. At the same time, they recognized that burning a flag is a form of freedom of expression. Most acknowledged that in an unfair country, burning a flag would be acceptable (Helwig & Prencipe, 1999).

In middle childhood, children also realize that people whose *knowledge* differs may not be equally responsible for moral transgressions. Many 7-year-olds are tolerant of a teacher's decision to give more snack to girls than boys because she thinks (incorrectly) that girls need more food. But when a teacher gives girls more snack because she holds an *immoral belief* ("it's all right to be nicer to girls than boys"), almost all children judge her actions negatively (Wainryb & Ford, 1998).

**ARE MORAL VERSUS SOCIAL-CONVENTIONAL DISTINCTIONS CULTURALLY UNIVERSAL?** Children and adolescents in many societies—not just Western nations, but diverse non-Western cultures, such as Brazil, Korea, Indonesia, Nigeria, and Zambia—use the same criteria to separate moral concerns from social conventions (Bersoff & Miller, 1993; Nucci, Camino, & Sapiro, 1996; Tisak, 1995). Still, certain behaviours are classified differently across cultures. For example, East Indian Hindu children believe that eating chicken the day after a father's death is morally wrong because Hindu religious teachings specify that it prevents the father's soul from reaching salvation. North American children, in contrast, regard this practice as an arbitrary convention (Shweder, Mahapatra, & Miller, 1990). But when asked about acts that obviously lead to harm or violate rights, such as breaking promises, destroying another's property, or kicking harmless animals, cultural differences diminish (Turiel, 1998).

We are reminded, once again, that justice considerations appear to be a universal feature of moral thought.

**RELATION OF PERSONAL AND MORAL DOMAINS.** In Western and non-Western cultures, children and adolescents identify a unique domain of personal matters. For example, they are likely to argue that hairstyle, choice of friends, and the contents of a diary are up to the individual—a view that strengthens between ages 8 and 16 (Nucci, 1996; Nucci, Camino, & Sapiro, 1996). Even in collectivist societies that place a high value on obedience to adult authority, children distinguish personal from moral and social issues and vehemently defend their right to personal control. As one Colombian child remarked about the legitimacy of a teacher telling a student where to sit during circle time: "She should be able to sit wherever she wants" (Ardila-Rey & Killen, 2001, p. 249).

The personal domain emerges with self-awareness in the early preschool years. By age 2, children engage in efforts to establish boundaries between the self and others through claims of ownership (see Chapter 11, page 488). And they quickly learn that parents and teachers are willing to compromise on personal issues and, at times, on social-conventional matters, but not on moral concerns. Likewise, when children and adolescents challenge adult authority, they typically do so within the personal domain (Nucci & Weber, 1995). As insistence that parents not intrude on the personal arena strengthens at adolescence, disputes over personal issues increase. Disagreements are sharpest on matters that are both personal and social-conventional and therefore subject to interpretation—for example, a messy bedroom, which can be viewed as individual and communal space (Smetana & Asquith, 1994).

According to Larry Nucci (1996), children's grasp of the personal contributes to moral development because it leads to concepts of rights and freedom. By adolescence, young people in both individualistic and collectivistic cultures think more intently about conflicts between personal freedom and community obligation—for example, whether, and under what conditions, it is permissible for governments to restrict speech, religion, marriage, childbearing, and other individual rights (Helwig, 1995; Wainryb, 1997). Although answers vary, personal, social-conventional, and moral matters coexist and interact in all societies.

## DISTRIBUTIVE JUSTICE

In everyday life, children frequently experience situations that involve **distributive justice**—beliefs about how to divide material goods fairly. Heated discussions take place over how much weekly allowance is to be given to siblings of different ages, who has to sit where in the family car on a long trip, and in what way an eight-slice pizza is to be shared by six hungry playmates. William Damon (1977, 1988) has traced children's concepts of distributive justice over early and middle childhood.

Preschoolers recognize the importance of sharing, but their reasons often seem self-serving: "I shared because if I didn't, she wouldn't play with me" or "I let her have some, but most are for me because I'm older." These explanations are consistent with preschoolers' "undifferentiated perspective-taking" responses to such problems as Selman's "Holly dilemma" (see Chapter 11, page 469). As children enter middle childhood, they express more mature notions of distributive justice (see Table 12.2 on page 506). At first, fairness is based on *equality*. Children in the early school grades are intent on making sure that each person gets the same amount of a treasured resource, such as money, turns in a game, or a delicious treat. This strict-equality approach resembles young children's less flexible thinking in other areas.

A short time later, children view fairness in terms of *merit*. Extra rewards should be given to someone who has worked especially hard or otherwise performed in an exceptional way. Finally, around 8 years, children can reason on the basis of *benevolence*. They recognize that special consideration should be given to those at a disadvantage. Older children say that an

Children in diverse cultures use the same criteria to separate moral concerns from social conventions. Certain behaviours are classified differently across cultures because of the intentions behind those practices. This East Indian Hindu girl is likely to say that eating chicken the day after a father's death is an immoral act. In her world view, doing so would inflict harm on the father by preventing his soul from receiving salvation.

**distributive justice**
Beliefs about how to divide material goods fairly.

**TABLE** 12.2

Damon's Sequence of Distributive Justice Reasoning

| BASIS OF REASONING | AGE | DESCRIPTION |
|---|---|---|
| Equality | 5–6 | Fairness involves strictly equal distribution of goods. Special considerations, such as merit and need, are not considered. |
| Merit | 6–7 | Fairness is based on deservingness. Children recognize that some people should get more because they have worked harder. |
| Benevolence | 8 | Fairness includes special consideration for those who are disadvantaged. More should be given to people in need. |

*Source:* Damon, 1977, 1988.

These fourth-grade boys are figuring out how to divide a handful of penny candy fairly among themselves. Already, they have a well-developed sense of distributive justice.

© JEFF GREENBERG/PHOTOEDIT

extra amount might be given to a child who cannot produce as much or does not get any allowance from his parents. They also adapt their basis of fairness to the situation—for example, relying more on merit when interacting with strangers and more on benevolence when interacting with friends (McGillicuddy-De Lisi, Watkins, & Vinchur, 1994).

According to Damon (1988), parental advice and encouragement support these developing standards of justice, but the give-and-take of peer interaction is especially important (Kruger, 1993). Advanced distributive justice reasoning, in turn, is associated with more effective social problem solving and a greater willingness to help and share with others (Blotner & Bearison, 1984; McNamee & Peterson, 1986).

The research reviewed in the preceding sections reveals that moral understanding in childhood is a rich, diverse phenomenon. Children's responses to a wide range of moral problems are needed to comprehensively represent the development of moral thought. To review changes in children's moral internalization and construction, consult the Milestones table on the following page.

# Development of Self-Control

THE STUDY OF MORAL judgment tells us what people think they should do and why when faced with a moral problem. But people's good intentions often fall short. Whether children and adults act in accord with their beliefs depends in part on characteristics we call willpower, firm resolve, or, put more simply, **self-control.** Self-control in the moral domain involves inhibiting an impulse to engage in behaviour that violates a moral standard. Sometimes it is called *resistance to temptation.* In the first part of this chapter, we noted that inductive discipline and modelling foster children's self-controlled behaviour. But these practices become effective only when children have the ability to resist temptation. When and how does this capacity develop?

**self-control**
Inhibiting an impulse to engage in behaviour that violates a moral standard.

# milestones

## INTERNALIZATION OF MORAL NORMS AND DEVELOPMENT OF MORAL UNDERSTANDING

| AGE | INTERNALIZATION OF MORAL NORMS | MORAL UNDERSTANDING |
|---|---|---|
| 2–5 years | ⚮ Models many morally relevant behaviours | ⚮ Shows sensitivity to intentions when making moral judgments |
| | ⚮ Shows empathy-based guilt reactions to transgressions  | ⚮ At the end of this period, displays differentiated understanding of authority figures' legitimacy |
| | | ⚮ Distinguishes moral rules, social conventions, and matters of personal choice |
| | | ⚮ At the end of this period, bases distributive justice on equality |
| 6–11 years | ⚮ Internalizes many norms of good conduct, including prosocial standards | ⚮ Gives preconventional responses to Kohlberg's moral dilemmas |
| | | ⚮ Understands ideal reciprocity |
| | | ⚮ Takes more variables into account in distinguishing moral rules, social conventions, and matters of personal choice |
| | | ⚮ Includes merit and, eventually, benevolence, in distributive justice reasoning; adapts concept of fairness to each situation |
| 12 years–adulthood | | ⚮ Increasingly gives conventional responses to Kohlberg's moral dilemmas; they become the dominant, morally mature form of reasoning |
| | | ⚮ Postconventional responses to Kohlberg's moral dilemmas appear among a few highly educated individuals |
| | | ⚮ The link between moral reasoning and behaviour strengthens |

*Note:* These milestones represent overall age trends. Individual differences exist in the precise age at which each milestone is attained. See Chapter 10, page 507, for additional milestones related to the morally relevant emotions of empathy and guilt.

## BEGINNINGS OF SELF-CONTROL

The beginnings of self-control are supported by achievements of the second year, discussed in earlier chapters. To behave in a self-controlled fashion, children must have some ability to think of themselves as separate, autonomous beings who can direct their own actions. And they must have the representational and memory skills to recall a caregiver's directive and apply it to their own behaviour. Cognitive inhibition, supported by development of the frontal lobes of the cortex (see Chapter 7), is also essential (Rothbart & Bates, 1998). And as we will see shortly, emotional self-regulation—strategies children acquire that prevent them from being overwhelmed by negative emotion—is intimately involved in self-control (see Chapter 10).

As these capacities emerge, the first glimmerings of self-control appear in the form of **compliance.** Between 12 and 18 months, children start to show clear awareness of caregivers' wishes and expectations and can voluntarily obey simple requests and commands (Kaler & Kopp, 1990). Parents are usually delighted at toddlers' newfound ability to comply,

**compliance**
Voluntary obedience to requests and commands.

© LAURA DWIGHT

How will this 5-year-old resist temptation? If she focuses on the delicious taste of the cookies, she is likely to give in quickly. But if she diverts her attention away from the cookies by covering her eyes, engaging in another activity, or imagining the cookies to be wheels, Frisbees, or large pennies, she will be able to wait much longer.

since it indicates that they are ready to learn the rules of social life. Nevertheless, control of the child's actions during the second year depends heavily on caregiver support. According to Vygotsky (1934/1986), children cannot guide their own behaviour until they integrate standards represented in adult–child dialogues into their own self-directed speech (see Chapter 6). The development of compliance quickly leads to toddlers' first consciencelike verbalizations—for example, correcting the self by saying "no, can't" before touching a light socket or jumping on the sofa (Kochanska, 1993).

Researchers typically study self-control by creating situations in the laboratory much like the ones just mentioned. Notice how each calls for **delay of gratification**—waiting for a more appropriate time and place to engage in a tempting act or obtain a desired object. In one study, toddlers were given three delay-of-gratification tasks. In the first, they were asked not to touch an interesting toy telephone that was within arm's reach. In the second, raisins were hidden under cups, and the toddlers were instructed to wait until the experimenter said it was all right to pick up a cup and eat a raisin. In the third, they were told not to open a gift until the experimenter had finished her work. On all problems, the ability to wait increased steadily between 18 and 30 months. Children who were especially self-controlled were advanced in language development (Vaughn, Kopp, & Krakow, 1984).

Mothers who are sensitive and supportive have toddlers who show more rapid development of self-control (Kochanska, Murray, & Harlan, 2000). Such parenting seems to encourage as well as model patient, nonimpulsive behaviour. As self-control improves, mothers gradually increase the rules they require toddlers to follow, from safety and respect for property and people to family routines, manners, and simple chores (Gralinski & Kopp, 1993). Overall, mothers' expectations dovetail nicely with toddlers' emerging capacity.

## DEVELOPMENT OF SELF-CONTROL IN CHILDHOOD AND ADOLESCENCE

Although the capacity for self-control is in place by the third year, it is not complete. Cognitive development—in particular, gains in attention and mental representation—permits children to use a variety of effective self-instructional strategies to resist temptation. As a result, delay of gratification improves during childhood and adolescence.

**STRATEGIES FOR SELF-CONTROL.** Walter Mischel (1996) has studied what children think and say to themselves that promotes resistance to temptation. In several studies, preschoolers were shown two rewards: a highly desirable one that they would have to wait for and a less desirable one that they could have any time. The most self-controlled preschoolers used any technique they could to divert their attention from the desired objects: covering their eyes, singing, and even trying to go to sleep!

In everyday situations, preschoolers find it difficult to keep their minds off tempting activities and objects for long. When their thoughts do turn to an enticing but prohibited goal, the way they mentally represent it has much to do with their success at self-control. Mischel found that teaching children to transform the stimulus in ways that de-emphasize its arousing qualities promotes delay of gratification. In one study, some preschoolers were told to think about marshmallows imaginatively as "white and puffy clouds." Others were asked to focus on their realistic, "sweet and chewy properties." Children in the stimulus-transforming, imaginative condition waited much longer before eating the marshmallow reward (Mischel & Baker, 1975).

Beginning in the elementary school years, children become better at thinking up their own strategies for resisting temptation. By this time, self-control has been transformed into a flexible capacity for **moral self-regulation**—the ability to monitor one's own conduct, constantly adjusting it as circumstances present opportunities to violate inner standards (Bandura, 1991).

**delay of gratification**
Waiting for a more appropriate time and place to engage in a tempting act or obtain a desired object.

**moral self-regulation**
The ability to monitor one's own conduct, constantly adjusting it as circumstances present opportunities to violate inner standards.

**KNOWLEDGE OF STRATEGIES.**  In Chapter 7, we indicated that metacognitive knowledge, or awareness of strategies, plays an important role in the development of self-regulation. When interviewed about situational conditions and self-instructions likely to help delay gratification, over middle childhood, children suggested a broader array of arousal-reducing strategies. But not until the late elementary school years did they mention techniques involving transformations of rewards or their own arousal states. For example, one 11-year-old recommended saying, "The marshmallows are filled with an evil spell." Another said he would tell himself, "I hate marshmallows; I can't stand them. But when the grown-up gets back, I'll tell myself 'I love marshmallows' and eat it" (Mischel & Mischel, 1983, p. 609).

Perhaps awareness of transforming ideation appears late in development because it requires the abstract, hypothetical reasoning powers of formal operational thought. But once this advanced metacognitive understanding emerges, it facilitates moral self-regulation (Rodriguez, Mischel, & Shoda, 1989).

**INDIVIDUAL DIFFERENCES.**  Longitudinal research reveals modest stability in children's capacity to manage their behaviour in a morally relevant fashion. Mischel and his collaborators found that toddlers who could divert their attention and wait patiently during a short separation from their mother tended to perform better during a delay-of-gratification task at age 5 (Sethi et al., 2000). And in a series of studies, 4-year-olds better at delaying gratification were especially adept as adolescents in applying metacognitive skills to their behaviour. Their parents saw them as more responsive to reason, as better at concentrating and planning ahead, and as coping with stress more maturely. When applying to university in the United States, those who had been self-controlled preschoolers scored somewhat higher on the Scholastic Aptitude Test (SAT), although they were no more intelligent than other individuals (Mischel, Shoda, & Peake, 1988; Shoda, Mischel, & Peake, 1990). Furthermore, children who are better at delaying gratification can wait long enough to interpret social cues accurately, which supports effective social problem solving and positive peer relations (Gronau & Waas, 1997).

Janet Metcalfe and Walter Mischel (1999) propose that the interaction of two processing systems—*hot* and *cool*—governs the development of self-control and accounts for individual differences. Table 12.3 displays the characteristics of each. With age, the emotional, reactive hot system becomes interconnected with the cognitive, reflective cool system. When an arousing experience occurs, interconnections between the systems permit individuals to divert energy away from hot processing to cool thinking, as in the resistance-to-temptation strategies and metacognitive awareness of such strategies just considered.

**TABLE** 12.3

Characteristics of Metcalfe and Mischel's Hot and Cool Processing Systems Governing Development of Self-Control

| HOT SYSTEM | COOL SYSTEM |
|---|---|
| Emotional | Cognitive |
| "Go" | "Know" |
| Simple | Complex |
| Reflexive | Reflective |
| Fast | Slow |
| Develops early | Develops later |
| Accentuated by stress | Attenuated by stress |
| Stimulus control | Self-control |

*Source:* J. Metcalfe & W. Mischel, 1999, "A Hot/Cool-System Analysis of Delay of Gratification: Dynamics of Willpower," *Developmental Review, 106,* p. 4. Copyright © by the American Psychological Association. Reprinted by permission of the publisher and author.

# milestones

## DEVELOPMENT OF SELF-CONTROL AND AGGRESSION

| AGE | SELF-CONTROL | AGGRESSION | |
|-----|--------------|------------|---|
| 1½–5 years | § Compliance and delay of gratification emerge and improve | § Instrumental aggression declines<br><br>§ Physical aggression is gradually replaced by verbal aggression<br><br>§ Hostile aggression increases, in the form of overt aggression among boys and relational aggression among girls |  |
| 6–11 years | § Strategies for self-control expand<br><br>§ Awareness of ideation that transforms rewards and arousal state emerges<br><br>§ Flexible capacity for moral self-regulation is present | § Hostile aggression—overt aggression among boys and relational aggression among girls—continues to increase | |
| 12–20 years | § Moral self-regulation continues to improve  | § Teacher- and peer-rated aggression decline<br><br>§ Delinquent acts increase, then decline at the end of this period | |

*Note:* These milestones represent overall age trends. Individual differences exist in the precise age at which each milestone is attained.

Both individual dispositions and environmental factors affect the extent to which cool-system representations come to dominate hot-system reactivity. When temperamentally vulnerable children are exposed to highly power-assertive, inconsistent discipline, the cool system develops poorly or fails to function, permitting the hot system to prevail. Such children display hostile, unruly behaviour and serious deficits in moral conduct. Refer to the Milestones table above for a summary of changes in self-control and aggression—our next topic.

## ASK YOURSELF www

**review**    What experiences help children differentiate moral imperatives, social conventions, and matters of personal choice? How does children's understanding change from early to middle childhood?

**apply**    Parker Elementary School will give a cash award to the classroom that sells the most raffle tickets for the school fundraiser. Children in the winning classroom will decide how to divide the award fairly. How are first through third graders likely to differ in their decision making?

**connect**    Explain how school-age children's understanding of moral imperatives, social conventions, and distributive justice takes into account an increasing number of variables. What cognitive and social-cognitive changes, discussed in Chapters 6 and 11, probably support these advances?

# The Other Side of Self-Control: Development of Aggression

BEGINNING IN LATE infancy, all children display aggression from time to time, and as interactions with siblings and peers increase, aggressive outbursts occur more often. Although at times aggression serves prosocial ends (for example, stopping a victimizer from harming others), the large majority of human aggressive acts are clearly antisocial (Coie & Dodge, 1998).

As early as the preschool years, some children show abnormally high rates of hostility. They verbally and physically assault others with little or no provocation. Allowed to continue, their belligerent behaviour can lead to lasting delays in moral development and deficits in self-control, resulting in an antisocial lifestyle. To understand this process, let's see how aggression develops during childhood and adolescence.

## EMERGENCE OF AGGRESSION

During the second half of the first year, infants develop the cognitive capacity to identify sources of anger and frustration and the motor skills to lash out at them (see Chapter 10). By the early preschool years, two general types of aggression emerge. The most common is **instrumental aggression.** In this form, children want an object, privilege, or space, and in trying to get it, they push, shout at, or otherwise attack a person who is in the way. The other type, **hostile aggression,** is meant to hurt another person.

Hostile aggression comes in at least two varieties. The first is **overt aggression,** which harms others through physical injury or the threat of such injury—for example, hitting, kicking, or threatening to beat up a peer. The second is **relational aggression,** which damages another's peer relationships, as in social exclusion or rumour spreading.

## AGGRESSION IN EARLY AND MIDDLE CHILDHOOD

Both the form of aggression and the way it is expressed change during the preschool years. On the basis of observation and parental reports, Richard Tremblay of the Université de Montréal found that physical aggression, present in most toddlers by the middle of the second year, is gradually replaced by verbal aggression after age 2 (Tremblay et al., 1999). Rapid language development contributes to this change, but it is also due to adults' and peers' strong negative reactions to pushing, hitting, and biting. Furthermore, for most preschoolers, instrumental aggression declines with age as improved ability to delay gratification helps them avoid grabbing others' possessions (Shantz, 1987). In contrast, hostile outbursts rise over early and middle childhood (Tremblay, 2000). Older children are better able to recognize malicious intentions and, as a result, more often retaliate in hostile ways.

On average, boys are more overtly aggressive than girls, a trend that appears in many cultures (Whiting & Edwards, 1988a). In Chapter 13, when we take up sex-related differences in aggression in greater detail, we will see that biological factors—in particular, male sex hormones, or androgens—are influential. At the same time, the development of gender roles is important. As soon as 2-year-olds become dimly aware of gender stereotypes—that males and females are expected to behave differently—overt aggression drops off more sharply for girls than for boys (Fagot & Leinbach, 1989).

But preschool and school-age girls are not less aggressive than boys! Instead, they are likely to express their hostility differently—through relational aggression (Crick, Casas, & Mosher, 1997; Crick & Grotpeter, 1995). When trying to harm a peer, children seem to do so in ways especially likely to thwart that child's social goals. Boys more often attack physically to block the dominance goals that are typical of boys. Girls resort to relational aggression because it interferes with the intimate bonds especially important to girls.

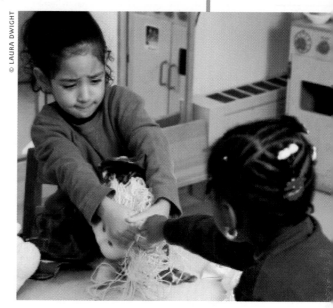

An occasional expression of aggression is normal among young children. These preschoolers display instrumental aggression as they struggle over an attractive toy. Instrumental aggression declines with age as preschoolers' improved ability to delay gratification helps them avoid grabbing others' possessions.

**instrumental aggression**
Aggression aimed at obtaining an object, privilege, or space, with no deliberate intent to harm another person.

**hostile aggression**
Aggression intended to harm another person.

**overt aggression**
A form of hostile aggression that harms others through physical injury or the threat of such injury—for example, hitting, kicking, or threatening to beat up a peer.

**relational aggression**
A form of hostile aggression that damages another's peer relationships, as in social exclusion or rumour spreading.

## AGGRESSION AND DELINQUENCY IN ADOLESCENCE

Although most young people decline in teacher- and peer-rated aggression in adolescence, the teenage years are accompanied by a rise in delinquent acts. Despite a drop in Canadian youth crime over the past decade, young people under the age of 18 continue to account for a large proportion of police arrests—about 21 percent in the year 2000 (Statistics Canada, Crime Statistics in Canada, 2001). When teenagers are asked directly, and confidentially, about lawbreaking, almost all admit that they are guilty of an offence of one sort or another (Farrington, 1987). Most of the time, they do not commit major crimes. Instead, they engage in petty theft and disorderly conduct.

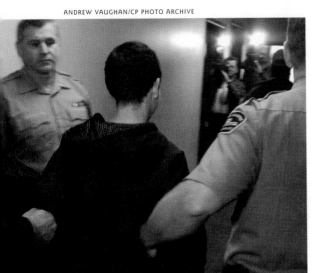

ANDREW VAUGHAN/CP PHOTO ARCHIVE

Delinquency rises during the early teenage years and remains high during middle adolescence. Although most of the time it involves petty theft and disorderly conduct, a small percentage of young people engage in repeated, serious offences and are at risk for a life of crime.

Both police arrests and self-reports show that acts of delinquency rise over the early teenage years, remain high during middle adolescence, and then decline into young adulthood. What accounts for this trend? The desire for peer approval increases antisocial behaviour among young teenagers. Over time, peers become less influential, moral reasoning improves, and young people enter social contexts (such as marriage, work, and career) that are less conducive to lawbreaking.

For most adolescents, a brush with the law does not forecast long-term antisocial behaviour. But repeated arrests are cause for concern. In the year 2000, teenagers in Canada were responsible for 16 percent of violent crime (homicide, sexual assault, robbery, and assault) and 27 percent of property crimes (breaking and entering, theft, and possession of stolen goods) (Statistics Canada, Crime Statistics in Canada, 2001). A small percentage of youth commit most crimes, developing into recurrent offenders. Some enter a life of crime.

In adolescence, the gender gap in overt aggression widens (Chesney-Lind, 2001). Depending on the estimate, about three to eight times as many boys as girls commit major crimes. Although SES and ethnicity are strong predictors of arrests, they are only mildly related to teenagers' self-reported antisocial acts. The difference is due to biases in the juvenile justice system—in particular, the tendency to arrest, charge, and punish low-SES, ethnic minority youths more often than their higher-SES white and Asian counterparts (Elliot, 1994). Fortunately, changes to the Young Offenders Act (to be superseded in 2003 by the Youth Criminal Justice Act) have permitted many nonviolent but delinquent youths to be dealt with outside the formal justice system. This has improved the situation of low-SES and minority youths somewhat.

## STABILITY OF AGGRESSION

A small number of youths sustain a high level of aggression from middle childhood to adolescence, whereas others show declines. Examining aggression from ages 6 to 15 among more than 1000 boys from Canada, New Zealand, and the United States, Tremblay and his colleagues identified four groups with different patterns of change, shown in Figure 12.5 (Brame, Nagin, & Tremblay, 2001; Nagin & Tremblay, 1999). The group with high-level physical aggression in kindergarten was the smallest (only 4 percent of the sample). But children in that group were more likely than others to move to high-level adolescent aggression, becoming involved in violent delinquency. When kindergarten boys high in oppositional behaviour (such as disobedience and inconsiderateness) but not physical aggression were considered (7 percent of the sample), they were also prone to adolescent delinquency, but in less violent forms (such as theft). And an investigation of nearly 900 Canadian girls revealed a similar link between disruptive behaviour in childhood (characterizing only 1.4 percent of the sample) and conduct problems in adolescence (Coté et al., 2001).

As the Biology & Environment box on page 514 confirms, conduct problems that develop in childhood are far more likely to persist than are conduct problems that emerge in adolescence. In recent years, researchers have made considerable progress in identifying personal and environmental factors that sustain aggressive behaviour. Although some children—especially those who are impulsive and overactive—are clearly at risk for high aggression, whether or not they become so depends on child-rearing conditions. Strife-ridden families, poor parenting practices, aggressive peers, and televised violence are strongly linked to antisocial acts. In this chapter, we focus on family and peer influences, reserving the topic of television for Chapter 15. We will also see that community and cultural influences can heighten or reduce children's risk of sustaining a hostile interpersonal style.

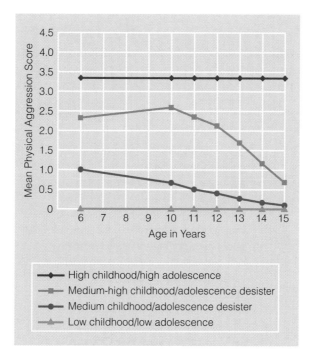

**FIGURE** 12.5

**Longitudinal trends in boys' physical aggression from 6 to 15 years of age.** The patterns are based on a sample of more than 1000 boys from Canada, New Zealand, and the United States. Boys with high-level childhood physical aggression were especially likely to sustain their aggressive style. In contrast, boys with medium-high and medium levels of aggression showed declines in aggressive responding after age 10. And boys who rarely displayed aggression in childhood usually remained nonaggressive in adolescence. (From R. E. Tremblay, 2000, "The Development of Aggressive Behaviour during Childhood: What Have We Learned in the Past Century?" *International Journal of Behavioral Development, 24,* p. 136. Reprinted by permission.)

## THE FAMILY AS TRAINING GROUND FOR AGGRESSIVE BEHAVIOUR

The same child-rearing practices that undermine moral internalization and self-control are related to aggression. Love withdrawal, power assertion, physical punishment, and inconsistent discipline are linked to antisocial behaviour from early childhood through adolescence, in children of both sexes (Coie & Dodge, 1998; Stormshak et al., 2000).

Home observations of aggressive children reveal that anger and punitiveness quickly create a conflict-ridden family atmosphere and an "out-of-control" child. As Figure 12.6 shows, the pattern begins with forceful discipline, which occurs more often with stressful life

**FIGURE** 12.6

**Coercive interaction pattern that promotes and sustains aggression between family members.**

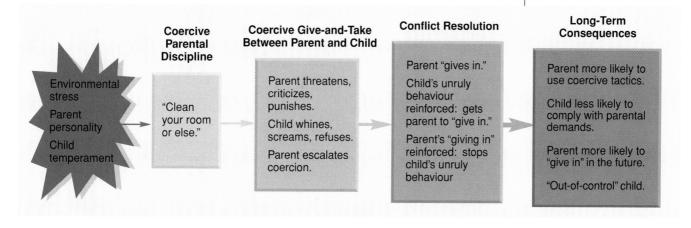

# biology & environment

## TWO ROUTES TO ADOLESCENT DELINQUENCY

Persistent adolescent delinquency follows two paths of development, one with an onset of conduct problems in childhood, the second with an onset in adolescence. Longitudinal research reveals that the early-onset type is far more likely to lead to a life-course pattern of aggression and criminality. The late-onset type usually does not persist beyond the transition to young adulthood (Farrington & Loeber, 2000).

Childhood-onset and adolescent-onset youths both engage in serious offences; associate with deviant peers; participate in substance abuse, unsafe sex, and dangerous driving; and spend time in correctional facilities. Why does antisocial activity more often persist and escalate into violence in the first group than in the second? Longitudinal research extending from childhood into early adulthood sheds light on this question. So far, investigations have focused only on boys because of their greater rate of delinquency.

### EARLY-ONSET TYPE

A difficult temperament distinguishes these boys; they are emotionally negative, restless, and wilful as early as age 3. In addition, they show subtle deficits in cognitive functioning that seem to contribute to disruptions in the development of language, memory, and cognitive and emotional self-regulation (Loeber et al., 1999; Moffitt et al., 1996). Some have attention-deficit hyperactivity disorder (ADHD), which compounds their learning and self-control problems (see Chapter 7, page 282) (White et al., 1996).

Yet these biological risks are not sufficient to sustain antisocial behaviour, since most early-onset boys do not display serious delinquency followed by adult criminality. Among those who follow the life-course path, inept parenting transforms their undercontrolled style into hostility and defiance. As they fail academically and are rejected by peers, they befriend other deviant youths, who provide the attitudes and

motivations for violent behaviour (see Figure 12.7). Compared with their adolescent-onset counterparts, early-onset teenagers feel distant from their families and leave school early (Moffitt et al., 1996). Their limited cognitive and social skills result in high rates of unemployment, contributing further to their antisocial involvements. Often these boys experience their first arrest before age 14—a strong predictor of becoming a chronic offender by age 18 (Patterson et al., 1998).

### LATE-ONSET TYPE

Other youths begin to display antisocial behaviour around the time of puberty, gradually increasing their involvement. Their conduct problems arise from the peer context of early adolescence, not from biological deficits and a history of unfavourable development. For some, quality of parenting may decline for a time, perhaps due to family stresses or the challenges of disciplining an unruly

experiences (such as economic hardship or an unhappy marriage), a parent's unstable personality, or a temperamentally difficult child. Once the parent threatens, criticizes, and punishes, then the child whines, yells, and refuses until the parent "gives in." The sequence is likely to be repeated, since at the end of each exchange, both parent and child get relief for stopping the unpleasant behaviour of the other. The next time the child misbehaves, the parent is even more coercive and the child more defiant until one member of the pair "begs off" (Dodge, Pettit, & Bates, 1994; Patterson, 1995, 1997).

As these cycles become more frequent, they generate anxiety and irritability among other family members, who soon join in the hostile interactions. Compared with siblings in typical families, preschool siblings who have critical, punitive parents are more verbally and physically aggressive toward one another. Destructive sibling conflict, in turn, contributes to a rise in poor impulse control and antisocial behaviour by the early school years (Garcia et al., 2000).

Boys are more likely than girls to be targets of angry, inconsistent discipline because they are more active and impulsive and therefore harder to control. When children extreme in these characteristics are exposed to inept parenting, aggression rises during childhood and persists into adulthood (refer again to the Biology & Environment box).

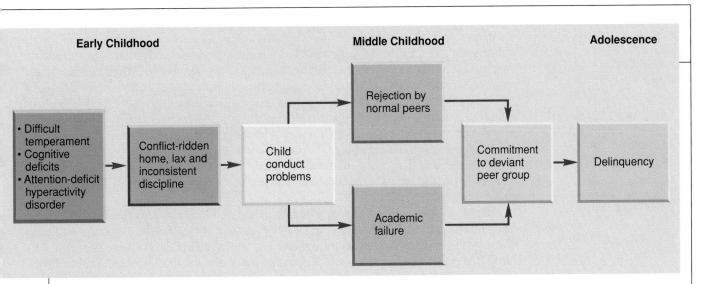

**FIGURE** 12.7

**Path to chronic delinquency for adolescents with childhood-onset antisocial behaviour.** Difficult temperament and cognitive deficits characterize many of these youths in early childhood; some have attention-deficit hyperactivity disorder. Inept parenting transforms biologically based self-control difficulties into hostility and defiance. (Adapted from Patterson, DeBaryshe, & Ramsey, 1989.)

teenager. When age brings gratifying adult privileges, they draw on prosocial skills mastered before adolescence and give up their antisocial ways (Moffitt et al., 1996).

A few late-onset youths, however, continue to engage in antisocial acts. The seriousness of their adolescent offences seems to act as a "snare," trapping them in situations that close off opportunities for responsible behaviour. In one study, finding a steady, well-paying job and entering a happy marriage led to a large reduction in repeat offending (Sampson & Laub, 1993).

These findings suggest a need for a fresh look at policies aimed at stopping youth crime. Keeping adolescent and young adult offenders locked up for many years disrupts their vocational and marital lives during a crucial period of development, committing them to a bleak future.

Besides fostering aggression directly, parents can encourage it indirectly, through poor supervision of children (Vitaro, Brendgen, & Tremblay, 2000). Unfortunately, children from conflict-ridden homes who already display serious antisocial tendencies are most likely to experience inadequate parental monitoring. As a result, few if any limits are placed on out-of-home activities and association with antisocial friends, who further the child's hostile style of responding.

### SOCIAL-COGNITIVE DEFICITS AND DISTORTIONS

Children who are products of the family processes just described soon acquire a violent and callous view of the social world. Aggressive children often see hostile intent where it does not exist—in situations where a peer's intentions are unclear, where harm is accidental, and even where a peer is trying to be helpful (Dodge, 1985; Dodge & Somberg, 1987). As a result, they make many unprovoked attacks, which trigger aggressive retaliations.

Furthermore, compared with their nonaggressive agemates, aggressive children are convinced that there are more benefits and fewer costs for engaging in hostile acts. They are more likely to think that aggression "works" to produce tangible rewards and reduce teasing, taunting, and other unpleasant behaviours by others (Perry, Perry, & Rasmussen, 1986). And when tempted to aggress, they are more concerned about achieving control and less concerned about a victim's suffering or being disliked by peers (Boldizar, Perry, & Perry, 1989).

Yet another biased feature of many aggressive children's social cognition is overly high self-esteem (see Chapter 11, page 454). Despite their academic and social failings, chronic aggressors commonly believe that they are superior, competent beings. When their arrogant, cocky behaviour inevitably results in challenges to their inflated but vulnerable self-image, they react with anger and lash out at others (Baumeister, Smart, & Boden, 1996). Furthermore, antisocial young people may neutralize their basic biological capacity for empathy by using such cognitive distortion techniques as blaming their victims. As a result, they retain a positive self-evaluation after behaving aggressively (Liau, Barriga, & Gibbs, 1998). Looking back on his burglaries, one delinquent reflected, "If I started feeling bad, I'd say to myself, 'Tough rocks for him. He should have had his house locked better and the alarm on'" (Samenow, 1984, p. 115).

Recall, also, that antisocial young people are delayed in moral-judgment maturity. And they are low in moral self-relevance as well. In a study of 16- to 19-year-old college students, those with immature moral reasoning and low moral–self-relevance were prone to self-serving cognitive distortions (such as blaming the victim and minimizing the harm done), which predicted high levels of acting-out behaviour. Compared with boys, girls scored higher in moral self-relevance and lower in self-serving cognitive distortions—likely contributors to their lower rates of antisocial activity (Barriga et al., 2001).

## COMMUNITY AND CULTURAL INFLUENCES

Children's tendency to engage in destructive, injurious behaviour increases under certain environmental conditions. When the peer group atmosphere is tense and competitive, hostility is more likely (DeRosier et al., 1994). These group characteristics are more common in poverty-stricken neighbourhoods with a wide range of stressors, including poor-quality schools, limited recreational and employment opportunities, and adult criminal subcultures (Pagani et al., 1999).

Such neighbourhoods predict aggression beyond family influences (Farrington & Loeber, 2000). Children and adolescents have easy access to deviant peers, drugs, and firearms, all of which are linked to violence. And they are especially likely to be recruited into antisocial gangs, whose members commit the vast majority of violent delinquent acts (Thornberry, 1998). Furthermore, schools in these locales typically fail to meet students' developmental needs. Large classes, weak instruction, and rigid rules are associated with higher rates of law-breaking, even after other influences are controlled (Hawkins & Lam, 1987).

Ethnic and political prejudices further magnify the risk of angry, combative responses. In inner-city ghettos and in war-torn areas of the world, large numbers of children live in the midst of constant danger, chaos, and deprivation. As the Cultural Influences box on the following page reveals, these youngsters are at risk for severe emotional stress, deficits in moral reasoning, and behaviour problems.

## HELPING CHILDREN AND PARENTS CONTROL AGGRESSION

Help for aggressive children must break the cycle of hostilities between family members and promote effective ways of relating to others. Interventions with preschool and school-age children have been most successful. Once antisocial patterns persist into adolescence, so many factors act to sustain them that treatment is far more difficult.

**COACHING, MODELLING, AND REINFORCING ALTERNATIVE BEHAVIOURS.** Procedures based on social learning theory have been devised to interrupt destructive family interaction. Several parent-training programs have been developed in which a therapist

# cultural influences

## IMPACT OF ETHNIC AND POLITICAL VIOLENCE ON CHILDREN

Violence stemming from ethnic and political tensions is being felt increasingly around the world. Most conflicts are civil wars in the developing world, in which well-established ways of life are threatened or destroyed. Children's experiences under armed conflict are diverse. Some may participate in the fighting, either because they are forced or because they want to please adults. Others are kidnapped, terrorized, or tortured. Those who are bystanders often come under direct fire and may be killed or physically maimed for life. And many watch in horror as family members and friends flee, are wounded, or die. In the past decade, wars have left 4 to 5 million children physically disabled, 12 million homeless, and more than 1 million separated from their parents (Stichick, 2001).

When war and social crises are temporary, most children are comforted by caregivers' reassuring messages and do not show long-term emotional difficulties. But chronic danger requires children to make substantial adjustments, and their psychological functioning can be seriously impaired. Many children of war lose their sense of safety, become desensitized to violence, are haunted by terrifying memories, and build a pessimistic view of the future. Aggressive and antisocial behaviour often increases (Muldoon & Cairns, 1999).

The extent to which children are negatively affected by war depends on mediating factors. Closeness to wartime events increases the chances of maladjustment. For example, the greater Cambodian children's exposure to war-related events, the more emotional and behaviour problems their parents reported (Mollica et al., 1997). Parental affection and reassurance are the best protection against lasting problems. When children are separated from parents, the child's community can step in. For example, 4- to 7-year-old orphans in Eritrea placed in residential settings where they could form close emotional ties with at least one adult showed much less emotional stress at a 5-year follow-up than did orphans placed in impersonal settings (Wolff & Fesseha, 1999). Education programs are powerful safeguards, too, providing children with a sense of predictability and security along with teacher and peer supports.

The September 11, 2001 terrorist attacks on the World Trade Center and the Pentagon led children across North America to witness wartime violence and devastation on television. Children in Public School 31 in Brooklyn, New York, however, experienced these events firsthand. They stared out windows as planes rushed toward the towers, the towers were engulfed in flames, and they crumbled. Many worried about the safety of family members, and some lost them. In the aftermath, most expressed intense fears—for example, that terrorists were infiltrating their neighbourhoods and that planes flying overhead might smash into nearby buildings.

Unlike many war-traumatized children in the developing world, P.S. 31 students received immediate intervention—a "trauma curriculum" in which they grappled with their emotions through writing, drawing, and discussion and participated in experiences aimed at restoring trust and tolerance (Lagnado, 2001). Older children learned about the feelings of their Muslim classmates, the dire condition of children in Afghanistan, and ways to help victims as a means of overcoming a sense of helplessness.

These traumatized, displaced children eat in a refugee camp along the India–Pakistan border. Because of civil unrest, their families left their homes. Most have seen their neighbourhood severely damaged or destroyed and witnessed violence toward people they know. Without special support from caring adults, they may show lasting emotional problems.

When wartime drains families and communities of resources, international organizations must step in and help children. Until we know how to prevent war, efforts to preserve children's physical, psychological, and educational well-being may be the best way to stop transmission of violence to the next generation.

observes inept practices, models alternatives, and has parents practise them (McMahon, 1999). Parents learn not to give in to an acting-out child and not to escalate forceful attempts to control misbehaviour. In addition, they are taught to pair commands with reasons and to replace verbal insults and spankings with more effective punishments, such as time out and withdrawal of privileges. After several weeks of such training, antisocial behaviour declines and parents view their children more positively—benefits still evident 1 to 4 years later.

On the child's side, interventions that teach nonaggressive ways of resolving conflict are helpful. Sessions in which children model and role-play cooperation and sharing and see that these behaviours lead to rewarding social outcomes reduce aggression and increase positive social behaviour. Many aggressive children also need help with language delays and deficits that interfere with the development of self-control. Encouraging parents to converse with their young children, especially about how to regulate strong negative emotion, helps children develop internalized controls. Once aggressive children begin to change, parents must be reminded to give them attention and approval for prosocial acts. The coercive cycles of parents and aggressive children are so pervasive that these children often get punished even when they do behave appropriately (Strassberg, 1995).

**SOCIAL-COGNITIVE INTERVENTIONS.** The social-cognitive deficits and distortions of aggressive children prevent them from sympathizing with another person's pain and suffering—an important inhibitor of aggressive behaviour. Furthermore, since aggressive children have few opportunities to witness family members acting in sensitive, caring ways, they miss early experiences that are vital for promoting empathy and sympathy (see Chapter 10). In such children, these responses may have to be directly taught.

Social-cognitive treatments focus on improving social information processing in antisocial youths. In one, adolescents were taught to attend to relevant, nonhostile social cues; seek additional information before acting; and evaluate potential responses in terms of their effectiveness. The intervention led to increased skill in solving social problems, decreased endorsement of beliefs supporting aggression, and reduced hostile, impulsive behaviours (Guerra & Slaby, 1990). Furthermore, training in perspective taking is helpful (see Chapter 11) because it promotes more accurate interpretation of social cues and sympathetic concern for others.

**COMPREHENSIVE APPROACHES.** According to some researchers, effective treatment for antisocial children and adolescents must be multifaceted, encompassing parent training, social understanding, relating to others, and self-control. In a program called EQUIP, *positive peer culture*—an adult-guided but youth-conducted small-group approach designed to create a climate in which prosocial acts replace antisocial behaviour—served as the basis for treatment. By themselves, peer-culture groups do not reduce antisocial behaviour, and in one study they increased it (Guerra, Attar, & Weissberg, 1997). But in EQUIP, the approach is supplemented with social skills training, anger management training, training to correct cognitive distortions, and moral discussions to promote "catch-up" in moral reasoning (Gibbs, Potter, & Goldstein, 1995; Potter, Gibbs, & Goldstein, 2001). Juvenile delinquents who participated in EQUIP displayed improved social skills and conduct during the following year relative to controls receiving no intervention. Also, the more advanced moral reasoning that emerged during group meetings appeared to have a long-term impact on antisocial youths' ability to inhibit law-breaking behaviour (Leeman, Gibbs, & Fuller, 1993).

Yet even multidimensional treatments can fall short if young people remain embedded in hostile home lives, antisocial peer groups, and violent neighbourhoods. Intensive efforts to create nonaggressive environments—at the family, community, and cultural levels—are needed to support the interventions just described and to foster healthy development of all children. We will return to this theme in later chapters.

## ASK YOURSELF

**review** Cite factors that contribute to an improved ability to delay gratification from early to middle childhood, and explain why each makes a difference.

**review** What temperamental, child-rearing, and social-cognitive factors are associated with persistence of high-level childhood aggression into adolescence?

**apply** Zack had been a well-behaved child in elementary school, but around age 13, he started spending time with the "wrong crowd." At age 16, he was arrested for property damage. Is Zack likely to become a long-term offender? Why or why not?

**connect** Reread the section on adolescent parenthood in Chapter 5 (pages 208–211) and the section on adolescent suicide in Chapter 11 (pages 462–463). How would you explain the finding that teenagers who experience one of these difficulties are likely to display others?

# summary

## MORALITY AS ROOTED IN HUMAN NATURE

*Describe and evaluate the biological perspective on morality.*

■ The biological perspective on moral development assumes that morality is grounded in the genetic heritage of our species, perhaps through prewired emotional reactions. Humans share many morally relevant behaviours with other species, and the ventromedial area of the frontal region of the cerebral cortex is vital for emotional responsiveness to others' suffering. Nevertheless, human morality cannot be fully explained in this way, since morally relevant emotions require strong caregiving supports and cognitive attainments for their mature expression.

## MORALITY AS THE ADOPTION OF SOCIETAL NORMS

*Describe and evaluate the psychoanalytic perspective on moral development.*

■ Both psychoanalytic and social learning theories regard moral development as a matter of **internalization:** the adoption of societal standards for right action as one's own. Internalization is not just a straightforward process of taking over externally imposed prescriptions. Instead, it is the combined result of factors within the child and the rearing environment.

■ According to Freud, morality emerges with the resolution of the Oedipus and Electra conflicts during the preschool years. Fear of punishment and loss of parental love lead children to form a superego through identification with the same-sex parent and to redirect hostile impulses toward the self in the form of guilt.

■ Although guilt is an important motivator of moral action, Freud's interpretation of it is no longer widely accepted. In contrast to Freudian predictions, power assertion and love withdrawal do not foster conscience development. Instead, **induction** is far more effective and seems to cultivate children's active commitment to moral norms. Recent psychoanalytic ideas place greater emphasis on a positive parent–child relationship and earlier beginnings of morality. However, they retain continuity with Freud's theory in regarding emotion as the basis for moral development.

*Describe and evaluate the social learning perspective on moral development, including the importance of modelling, the effects of punishment, and alternatives to harsh discipline.*

■ Social learning theory views moral behaviour as acquired in the same way as other responses: through modelling and reinforcement. Effective models are warm and powerful and display consistency between what they say and what they do. By middle childhood, children have internalized many prosocial and other rules for good conduct.

■ Harsh punishment does not promote moral internalization and socially desirable behaviour. Instead, it provides children with aggressive models, leads them to avoid the punishing adult, and can spiral into serious abuse. Alternatives, such as **time out** and withdrawal of privileges, can reduce these undesirable side effects, as long as parents apply them consistently, maintain a warm relationship with the child, and offer explanations that fit the transgression.

■ The most effective forms of discipline encourage good conduct. Parents who build a positive relationship with the child have children who want to adopt parental standards because they feel a sense of commitment to the relationship.

## MORALITY AS SOCIAL UNDERSTANDING

*Describe Piaget's theory of moral development, and evaluate its accuracy.*

■ Piaget's cognitive-developmental perspective assumes that morality develops through **construction**—actively thinking about multiple aspects of situations in which social conflicts arise and deriving new moral understandings.

■ Piaget's work was the original inspiration for the cognitive-developmental perspective. He identified two stages of moral understanding: **heteronomous morality,** in which children view moral rules in terms of **realism** and as fixed dictates of authority figures; and **autonomous morality,** in which children base fairness on **ideal reciprocity** and regard rules as flexible, socially agreed-on principles.

■ Although Piaget's theory describes the general direction of moral development, it underestimates the moral capacities of young children. Preschool and early school-age children take intentions into account in making moral judgments, although they interpret intentions in a rigid fashion. Furthermore, they have differentiated notions about the legitimacy of authority figures. With respect to nonmoral issues, they base authority on knowledge, not social position. When a directive is morally valid, they view it as important, regardless of whether an authority figure endorses it.

*Describe Kohlberg's extension of Piaget's theory, methods for assessing moral reasoning, and evidence on the accuracy of his stages.*

■ According to Kohlberg, moral development is a gradual process that extends beyond childhood into adolescence and adulthood. Using **Moral Judgment Interview,** Kohlberg found that moral reasoning advances through three levels, each of which contains two stages: (1) the **preconventional level,** in which morality is viewed as controlled by rewards, punishments, and the power of authority figures; (2) the **conventional level,** in which conformity to laws and rules is regarded as necessary to preserve positive human relationships and societal order; and (3) the **postconventional level,** in which individuals define morality in terms of abstract, universal principles of justice. Besides Kohlberg's clinical interview, efficient questionnaires for assessing moral understanding exist. The most recently devised is the **Sociomoral Reflection Measure–Short Form (SRM–SF).**

■ Kohlberg's stages are strongly related to age and form an invariant sequence. In focusing on hypothetical moral dilemmas, however, Kohlberg's theory assesses only the rational weighing of alternatives and overlooks other strategies that affect moral judgment. Because situational factors affect moral reasoning, Kohlberg's stages are best viewed in terms of a loose rather than strict concept of stage. Piaget's cognitive and Selman's perspective-taking stages are necessary but not sufficient conditions for each advance in moral reasoning.

■ Contrary to Gilligan's claim, Kohlberg's theory does not underestimate the moral maturity of females. Instead, justice and caring moralities coexist but vary in prominence between males and females, from one situation to the next, and across cultures.

*Describe influences on moral reasoning, its relationship to moral behaviour, and continuing challenges to Kohlberg's theory.*

■ A flexible, open-minded approach to new information and experiences is linked to gains in moral reasoning. Among experiences that contribute are peer interactions that resolve conflict through negotiation and compromise; warm, rational child-rearing practices; and years of schooling.

■ Cross-cultural research indicates that a certain level of societal complexity is required for Kohlberg's higher stages. Although his theory does not encompass the full range of moral reasoning, a common justice morality is evident in individuals from vastly different cultures.

■ Maturity of moral reasoning is moderately related to a wide variety of moral behaviours. Many other factors also influence moral behaviour, including emotions, temperament, personality, history of morally relevant experiences, and **moral self-relevance**—the degree to which morality is central to self-concept.

■ Moral judgment maturity appears to be achieved at Stages 3 and 4, as young people grasp ideal reciprocity. Because Kohlberg's dilemmas are remote from the experiences of children and not clearly understood by them, his theory overlooks moral-reasoning capacities that develop in early and middle childhood.

## MORAL REASONING OF YOUNG CHILDREN

*Explain how children separate moral imperatives from social conventions and matters of personal choice, and trace changes in*

their understanding from childhood into adolescence.

■ Even preschoolers have a beginning grasp of justice in that they distinguish **moral imperatives** from **social conventions** and **matters of personal choice.** From actively making sense of people's everyday social experiences and emotional reactions, children in diverse cultures come to view moral transgressions as wrong in any context, regardless of whether rules or authorities prohibit them. Gradually, children clarify and link moral imperatives and social conventions, taking into account more variables, including the purpose of the rule; people's intentions, knowledge, and beliefs; and the context of their behaviour.

■ The personal domain emerges with self-awareness in the early preschool years and strengthens from middle childhood into adolescence. It supports young people's moral concepts of rights and freedom.

*Describe the development of distributive justice reasoning, noting factors that foster mature understanding.*

■ Children's concepts of **distributive justice** change over middle childhood, from equality to merit to benevolence. Peer disagreements, along with efforts to resolve them, make children more sensitive to others' perspectives, which fosters their developing ideas of fairness.

## DEVELOPMENT OF SELF-CONTROL

*Trace the development of **self-control** from early childhood into adolescence, noting the implications of individual differences for cognitive and social competencies.*

■ The emergence of self-control is supported by self-awareness and by the representational and memory capacities of the second year. The first glimmerings of self-control appear in the form of **compliance.** The ability to **delay gratification** increases steadily over the third year. Language development and sensitive, supportive parenting foster self-control.

■ During the preschool years, children profit from adult-provided self-control strategies. Over middle childhood, they produce an increasing variety of strategies themselves and become consciously aware of which ones work well and why, leading to a flexible capacity for **moral self-regulation**.

■ Individual differences in delay of gratification predict diverse cognitive and social competencies. Development of self-control appears to be governed by two processing systems: an emotional, reactive hot system that eventually is dominated by a cognitive, reflective cool system.

## THE OTHER SIDE OF SELF-CONTROL: DEVELOPMENT OF AGGRESSION

*Discuss the development of aggression from infancy into adolescence, noting individual, family, community, and cultural influences, and describe successful interventions.*

■ Aggression first appears in late infancy. Physical forms are soon replaced by verbal forms. Whereas **instrumental aggression** declines, **hostile aggression** increases over early and middle childhood. Two types of hostile aggression are evident: **overt aggression,** more common among boys, and **relational aggression,** more common among girls.

■ Although teacher- and peer-reported aggression decline in adolescence, delinquent acts increase, especially for boys. However, only a few youths sustain a high level of aggression from childhood to adolescence, becoming involved in violent crime.

■ Impulsive, overactive children are at risk for high aggression, but whether or not they become so depends on child-rearing conditions. Strife-ridden family environments and power-assertive, inconsistent discipline promote self-perpetuating cycles of aggressive behaviour. Children who are products of these family processes develop social-cognitive deficits and distortions that add to the long-term maintenance of aggression. Widespread poverty, harsh living conditions, and schools that fail to meet students' developmental needs increase antisocial acts among children and adolescents.

■ Among interventions designed to reduce aggression, training parents in child discipline and teaching children alternative ways of resolving conflict are helpful. Social-cognitive interventions that focus on improving social information processing and perspective taking have yielded benefits as well. However, the most effective treatments are comprehensive, addressing multiple factors that sustain antisocial behaviour.

## important terms and concepts

autonomous morality (p. 490)
compliance (p. 507)
construction (p. 489)
conventional level (p. 494)
delay of gratification (p. 508)
distributive justice (p. 505)
heteronomous morality (p. 490)
hostile aggression (p. 511)
ideal reciprocity (p. 490)

induction (p. 482)
instrumental aggression (p. 511)
internalization (p. 481)
matters of personal choice (p. 503)
moral judgment interview (p. 492)
moral imperatives (p. 503)
moral self-regulation (p. 508)
moral self-relevance (p. 501)
overt aggression (p. 511)

postconventional level (p. 494)
preconventional level (p. 493)
realism (p. 490)
relational aggression (p. 511)
self-control (p. 506)
social conventions (p. 503)
Sociomoral Reflection Measure–Short Form (SRM–SF) (p. 493)
time out (p. 487)

"With My Dolls"
Amrita Kochar
6 years, India

This 6-year-old depicts herself as a sunny, contented caregiver, out for a stroll with a carriage full of dolls. Chapter 13 explains how biology and environment jointly contribute to her firmly "feminine" gender-role behaviour.

# thirteen

## Development of Sex Differences and Gender Roles

ON A TYPICAL MORNING, I observed the following scene during a free-play period at our university laboratory preschool:

Four-year-old Jenny eagerly entered the housekeeping corner and put on a frilly long dress and high heels. Karen, setting the table nearby, produced whimpering sound effects for the baby doll in the crib. Jenny lifted the doll, sat in the rocking chair, gently cradled the baby in her arms, and whispered, "You're hungry, aren't you?" A moment later, Jenny announced to Karen, "This baby won't eat. I think she's sick. Ask Rachel if she'll be the nurse." Karen ran off to find Rachel, who was colouring at the art table.

Meanwhile, Nathan called to Tommy, "Wanna play traffic?" Both boys dashed energetically toward the cars and trucks in the block corner. Soon David joined them. "I'll be policeman first!" announced Nathan, who climbed on a chair in the block area. "Green light, go!" shouted the young police officer. With this signal, Tommy and David scurried on all fours around the chair, each pushing a large wooden truck. "Red light," exclaimed Nathan, and the trucks screeched to a halt.

"My truck beat yours," announced Tommy to David.

"Only 'cause I need gas," David responded.

"Let's build a runway for the trucks," suggested Nathan. The three construction engineers began to gather large blocks and boards for the task.

At an early age, children adopt many of the gender-linked standards of their culture. Jenny, Karen, and Rachel use dresses, dolls, and household props to act out a stereotypically feminine scene of nurturance. In contrast, Nathan, Tommy, and David's play is active, competitive, and masculine in theme. And both boys and girls interact more with agemates of their own sex.

What causes young children's play and social preferences to become so strongly gender typed, and how do these attitudes and behaviours change with age? Do societal expectations affect the way children think about themselves as masculine and feminine beings, thereby limiting their potential? To what extent do widely held beliefs about the characteristics of males and females reflect reality? Is it true that the average boy is aggressive, competitive, and good at spatial and mathematical skills, whereas the average girl is passive, nurturant, and good at verbal skills? How large are differences between the sexes, and in what ways do heredity and environment contribute to them? These are the central questions asked by researchers who study gender typing, and we will answer each of them in this chapter.

Perhaps more than any other area of child development, the study of gender typing has responded to societal change. Largely because of progress in women's rights, over the past 30 years major shifts have occurred in how psychologists view sex differences. Until the early 1970s, they regarded the adoption of gender-typed beliefs and behaviour as essential for healthy adjustment. Today, many people recognize that some gender-typed characteristics, such as extreme aggressiveness and competitiveness on the part of males and passivity and conformity on the part of females, are serious threats to mental health.

Consistent with this realization, theoretical revision marks the study of gender typing. Social learning theory, with its emphasis on modelling and reinforcement, and cognitive-developmental theory, with its focus on children as active thinkers about their social world, are major current approaches to gender typing. However, neither is sufficient by itself. We will see that an information-processing view, *gender schema theory,* combines elements of both theories to explain how children acquire gender-typed knowledge and behaviour.

Along with new theories have come new terms. Considerable controversy surrounds the labels *sex* and *gender.* Some researchers use these words interchangeably. Others use the term *sex* for biologically based differences, *gender* for socially influenced differences. Still others object to this convention because our understanding of many differences is still evolving. Also, it perpetuates too strong a dichotomy between nature and nurture (Halpern, 2000). In this book, I use the term *sex* when simply referring to a difference between males and females, without inferring the source of the difference. In contrast, I use *gender* when discussing genetic or environmental influences, or both (Deaux, 1993).

Additional terms are central to our discussion. Two of them involve the public face of gender in society. **Gender stereotypes** are widely held beliefs about characteristics deemed appropriate for males and females. **Gender roles** are the reflection of these stereotypes in everyday behaviour. **Gender identity** is the private face of gender. It refers to perception of the self as relatively masculine or feminine in characteristics. Finally, **gender typing,** a term already mentioned, is the process of developing gender-linked beliefs, gender roles, and a gender identity. As we explore this process, you will see that biological, cognitive, and social factors are involved.

**gender stereotypes**
Widely held beliefs about characteristics deemed appropriate for males and females.

**gender roles**
The reflection of gender stereotypes in everyday behaviour.

**gender identity**
The perception of oneself as relatively masculine or feminine in characteristics.

**gender typing**
The process of developing gender-linked beliefs, gender roles, and a gender identity.

# Gender Stereotypes and Gender Roles

GENDER STEREOTYPES HAVE appeared in religious, philosophical, and literary works for centuries. Consider the following literary excerpts, from ancient times to the present:

- "Woman is more compassionate than man and has a greater propensity to tears.... But the male ... is more disposed to give assistance in danger, and is more courageous than the female." (Aristotle, cited in Miles, 1935)

- "A man will say what he knows, a woman says what will please." (Jean-Jacques Rousseau, *Emile,* 1762)

- "Man with the head and woman with the heart:
  Man to command and woman to obey;
  All else confusion." (Alfred, Lord Tennyson, *The Princess*,
  Canto V, 1847)

- "Love is a mood—no more—to a man,
  And love to a woman is life or death." (Ella Wheeler
  Wilcox, *Blind*, 1882)

- "Women ask: How do you get a man to open up? Men
  ask: Why does she always want to talk about the relationship?" (John Gray, *Mars and Venus on a Date*, 1997)

Although the past three decades have brought a new level
of awareness about the wide range of roles possible for each
gender, strong beliefs about sex differences remain. In the
1960s, researchers began to ask people what personality characteristics they consider typical of men and women. Widespread agreement emerged in many studies. As Table 13.1
illustrates, **instrumental traits,** reflecting competence, rationality, and assertiveness, were regarded as masculine;
**expressive traits,** emphasizing warmth, caring, and sensitivity, were viewed as feminine. Despite intense political activism
over gender equality during the 1970s and 1980s, these stereotypes have remained essentially the same (Lueptow, Garovich,
& Lueptow, 2001; Lutz & Ruble, 1995; Martin, 1995). Furthermore, cross-cultural research conducted in 30 nations
reveals that the instrumental–expressive dichotomy is a widely
held stereotype around the world (Williams & Best, 1990).

Besides personality traits, other gender stereotypes exist. These include physical characteristics (tall, strong, and sturdy for men; soft, dainty, and graceful for women), occupations (truck
driver, insurance agent, and chemist for men; elementary school teacher, secretary, and nurse
for women), and activities or behaviours (good at fixing things and leader in groups for men;
good at child care and decorating the home for women) (Biernat, 1991; Powlishta et al., 2001).

The variety of attributes consistently identified as masculine or feminine, their broad
acceptance, and their stability over time suggest that gender stereotypes are deeply ingrained
patterns of thinking. Indeed, adults seem to stereotype children particularly intensely. In a
study in which 20- to 40-year-olds were shown photos of children and adults and asked to
rate each for "masculine," "feminine," and "neutral" personality traits, adults differentiated
boys from girls more sharply than they did men from women (see Figure 13.1) (Powlishta,
2000). Given that many adults view children through a gender-biased lens, perhaps it is not
surprising that by the second year, children have begun to absorb these messages.

**TABLE 13.1**

Personality Traits Regarded as Stereotypically
Masculine or Feminine

| MASCULINE TRAITS | FEMININE TRAITS |
| --- | --- |
| Active | Aware of others' feelings |
| Acts as a leader | Considerate |
| Adventurous | Cries easily |
| Aggressive | Devotes self to others |
| Ambitious | Emotional |
| Competitive | Excitable in a major crisis |
| Doesn't give up easily | Feelings hurt easily |
| Dominant | Gentle |
| Feels superior | Home oriented |
| Holds up well under pressure | Kind |
| Independent | Likes children |
| Makes decisions easily | Neat |
| Not easily influenced | Needs approval |
| Outspoken | Passive |
| Rough | Tactful |
| Self-confident | Understanding of others |
| Takes a stand | Warm in relations with others |

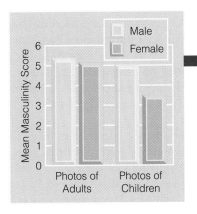

**FIGURE 13.1**

**Masculinity ratings by adults of photos depicting adults
and children.** Adult raters indicated little difference in the adult
photos but a sharp difference in the child photos, rating boys as
far more "masculine" in personality traits than girls. A similar
pattern emerged for "feminine" personality traits (not shown);
adults reported a much greater difference between boys and girls
than between men and women. Adults may act in line with their
gender-biased perceptions of children, encouraging gender typing
at an early age. (Adapted from Powlishta, 2000.)

**instrumental traits**
Masculine-stereotyped personality traits that reflect competence,
rationality, and assertiveness.

**expressive traits**
Feminine-stereotyped personality
traits that reflect warmth, caring,
and sensitivity.

FIGURE 13.2

**Girls' and boys' looking times at vehicles and dolls at 12, 18, and 23 months.** At 12 months, boys and girls showed similar visual preferences; both looked much longer at dolls than vehicles, perhaps because of their interest in the human face. At 18 months, gender-stereotyped preferences emerged; boys looked longer than girls at vehicles, whereas girls looked longer than boys at dolls. At 23 months, this difference was more pronounced; boys spent practically no time attending to the dolls. (From L. A. Serbin, D. Poulin-Dubois, K. A. Colburne, M. G. Sen, & J. A. Eichstedt, 2001, "Gender Stereotyping in Infancy: Visual Preferences for and Knowledge of Gender-Stereotyped Toys in the Second Year," *International Journal of Behavioural Development, 25,* p. 11. Reprinted by permission.)

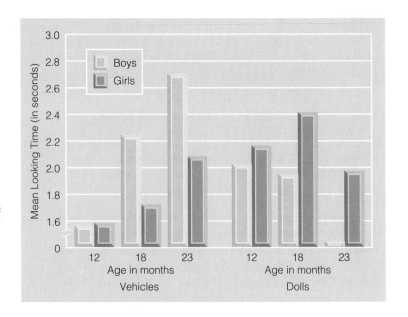

By age 1½, gender-stereotyped game and toy choices are present, becoming increasingly consistent with age. Already, these 3-year-olds play in highly gender-stereotyped ways.

© E. ZUCKERMAN/PHOTOEDIT

## GENDER STEREOTYPING IN EARLY CHILDHOOD

To find out how early children form gender stereotypes, Lisa Serbin of Concordia University and her colleagues showed 12-, 18-, and 23-month-olds paired photos of gender-stereotyped toys (vehicles and dolls) to see if they would look longer at the one stereotyped for their own gender. As Figure 13.2 indicates, 12-month-old boys and girls differed very little in their visual preference. But at 18 months, boys looked much longer than girls at vehicles, whereas girls looked much longer than boys at dolls. At 23 months, boys' stereotyping increased even further (Serbin et al., 2001). Even before children can label their own sex consistently, they stereotype their play world.

Recall from Chapter 11 that between 18 months and 3 years, children label their own and others' sex, using such words as "boy" and "girl" and "woman" and "man." Once these categories are in place, children sort out what they mean in terms of activities and behaviours. Consequently, gender stereotypes expand and strengthen rapidly. Preschoolers associate many toys, articles of clothing, tools, household items, games, occupations, and even colours (pink and blue) with one sex as opposed to the other (Ruble & Martin, 1998). They have even acquired gender-stereotyped metaphors, such as "bears are for boys" and "butterflies are for girls"(Leinbach, Hort, & Fagot, 1997).

A striking feature of preschoolers' gender stereotypes is that they operate like blanket rules rather than flexible guidelines. In several studies, researchers labelled a target child as a boy or girl and then provided either gender-typical or gender-atypical information about the target's characteristics. Next, children rated the target on additional gender-stereotypic attributes. Preschoolers usually relied on only the gender label in making these judgments, ignoring the specific information. For example, when told, "Tommy is a boy. Tommy's best friend is a girl, and Tommy likes to play house," children under age 6 nevertheless said that Tommy would much prefer to play with cars and train engines than sewing machines and dolls (Biernat, 1991; Martin, 1989).

The rigidity of preschoolers' gender stereotypes helps us understand some commonly observed everyday behaviours. Shown a picture of a Scottish bagpiper wearing a kilt, a North American 4-year-old is likely to say, "Men don't wear skirts!" At preschool, children exclaim that girls can't be police officers and boys can't take care of babies. These one-sided judgments are a joint product of gender stereotyping in the environment and young children's cognitive limitations—in particular, their difficulty integrating conflicting sources of information. Most preschoolers do not yet realize that characteristics *associated with* one's sex—activities, toys, occupations, hairstyle, and clothing—do not *determine* whether a person is male or female. They have trouble understanding that males and females can be different in terms of their bodies but similar in many other ways.

## GENDER STEREOTYPING IN MIDDLE CHILDHOOD AND ADOLESCENCE

By age 5, gender stereotyping of activities and occupations is well established. During middle childhood and adolescence, knowledge of stereotypes increases in the less obvious areas of personality traits and achievement (Signorella, Bigler, & Liben, 1993). At the same time, older children realize that gender-stereotypic attributes are associated, not defining, features of gender. As a result, beliefs about characteristics and capacities possible for males and females become more flexible.

**PERSONALITY TRAITS.** To assess stereotyping of personality traits, researchers ask children to assign "masculine" adjectives (such as *tough, rational,* and *cruel*) and "feminine" adjectives (such as *gentle, affectionate,* and *dependent*) to either a male or female stimulus figure. Recall from Chapter 11 that not until middle childhood are children good at sizing up people's dispositions. This same finding carries over to awareness of gender stereotypes.

Research in many countries reveals that stereotyping of personality traits increases steadily in middle childhood, becoming adultlike around age 11 (Beere, 1990; Best, 2001). A large Canadian study examined the pattern of children's trait learning and found that the stereotypes acquired first reflected "own-sex favouritism." Kindergartners through second graders had greatest knowledge of trait stereotypes that portrayed their own gender in a positive light. Once trait stereotyping was well under way, elementary school students were most familiar with "positive feminine" traits and "negative masculine" traits (Serbin, Powlishta, & Gulko, 1993). In addition to learning specific traits, children of both sexes seemed to pick up a widely held general impression—that of girls as "sugar and spice and everything nice" and boys as "snakes and snails and puppy dog tails."

**ACHIEVEMENT AREAS.** Shortly after entering elementary school, children figure out which academic subjects and skill areas are "masculine" and which are "feminine." They regard reading, spelling, art, and music as more for girls and mathematics, athletics, and mechanical skills as more for boys (Eccles, Jacobs, & Harold, 1990; Jacobs & Weisz, 1994). These stereotypes influence children's preferences for and sense of competence at certain subjects. For example, boys feel more competent than girls at math and science, whereas girls feel more competent than boys at reading and spelling—even when children of equal skill level are compared (Andre et al., 1999; Freedman-Doan et al., 2000).

Furthermore, girls seem to adopt a more general stereotype of males as smarter than females, which they apply to themselves. In a study of more than 2000 students grade 2 to 6 from diverse cultures (Eastern and Western Europe, Japan, Russia, and the United States), girls consistently had higher school grades than boys. Yet they did not report stronger beliefs in their own ability despite being aware of their performance standing. Compared with boys, girls discounted their talent (Stetsenko et al., 2000). Recall from Chapter 11 that when girls have difficulty with school tasks, parents and teachers are likely to tell them that they lack ability. Apparently, gender stereotyping of academic talent occurs in many parts of the world.

**TOWARD GREATER FLEXIBILITY.** Clearly, school-age children are knowledgeable about a wide variety of gender stereotypes. At the same time, they develop a more open-minded view of what males and females *can do,* a trend that continues into adolescence.

In studying gender stereotyping, researchers often use a forced-choice procedure in which children must assign a characteristic to either one gender or the other. But sometimes they ask children whether both genders can display a personality trait or activity—a response that

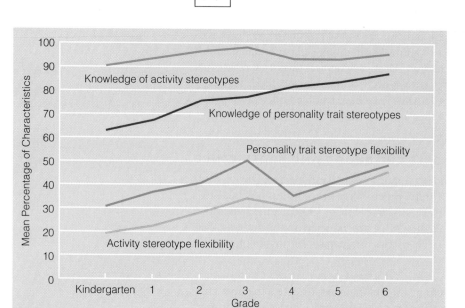

**FIGURE** 13.3

**Changes in gender-stereotype knowledge and flexibility from kindergarten to grade 6.** More than 300 Canadian school-age children responded to a questionnaire assessing their gender-stereotyped knowledge and the flexibility of their gender-stereotyped beliefs (whether or not they thought both genders could display a personality trait or activity). Both stereotype knowledge and flexibility increased from kindergarten to grade 6. (From L. A. Serbin, K. K. Powlishta, & J. Gulko, 1993, "The Development of Sex Typing in Middle Childhood," *Monographs of the Society for Research in Child Development*, 58 [2, Serial No. 232], p. 35. © The Society for Research in Child Development, Inc. Adapted by permission.)

**gender-stereotype flexibility**
Belief that both genders can display a gender-stereotyped personality trait or activity.

measures **gender-stereotype flexibility,** or overlap in the characteristics of males and females. In the Canadian study mentioned on page 526, stereotype knowledge and flexibility were assessed, and as Figure 13.3 reveals, both increased from kindergarten to grade 6 (Serbin, Powlishta, & Gulko, 1993).

Gender stereotypes become more flexible as children develop the cognitive capacity to integrate conflicting social cues. They realize that a person's sex is not a certain predictor of his or her personality traits, activities, and behaviour. Consequently, they no longer rely on only a gender label to predict what a person will be like; they also consider the individual's unique characteristics.

Accompanying this change is a greater tendency to view gender differences as socially rather than biologically influenced. In one study, 4- to 10-year-olds and adults were told stories about hypothetical boy and girl babies reared on an island either by members of their own sex or of the other sex. Then they were asked what "masculine" and "feminine" properties each child would develop. As Figure 13.4 shows, preschool and younger school-age children believed that gender-stereotyped characteristics would emerge, regardless of rearing environment. But by the end of middle childhood, children thought that a child reared by the other sex would be nonstereotyped in many ways (Taylor, 1996).

Nevertheless, acknowledging that boys and girls *can* cross gender lines does not mean that children always *approve* of doing so. Children and adults are fairly tolerant of girls' violations of gender roles. But they judge boys' violations (such as wearing a dress or playing with dolls) harshly—as just as bad as a moral transgression! Clearly, evaluations of certain "cross-gender" behaviours on the part of males are negative at all ages—a finding that reflects greater social pressure on boys and men to conform to gender roles (Levy, Taylor, & Gelman, 1995).

## INDIVIDUAL AND GROUP DIFFERENCES IN GENDER STEREOTYPING

Almost all children acquire extensive knowledge of gender stereotypes by middle childhood. But they differ widely in the makeup of their understanding. The various components of gender stereotyping—activities, behaviours, occupations, and personality traits—do not correlate highly. A child very knowledgeable in one area may not be very knowledgeable in the others (Serbin, Powlishta, & Gulko, 1993). This suggests that gender typing is like "an intricate puzzle that the child pieces together in a rather idiosyncratic way" (Hort, Leinbach, & Fagot, 1991, p. 196). To build a coherent notion of gender, children must assemble many elements. The precise pattern in which they acquire the pieces, the rate at which they do so, and the flexibility of their beliefs vary greatly from child to child.

Group differences in gender stereotyping also exist. The strongest of these is sex related: boys from a variety of nations hold more rigid gender-stereotyped views throughout childhood and adolescence (Archer, 1992; Levy, Taylor, & Gelman, 1995; Turner, Gervai, & Hinde, 1993). However, a few studies found no differences between boys and girls (Serbin, Powlishta, & Gulko, 1993; Taylor, 1996). And in one study, adolescents of both sexes responded to vignettes about hypothetical high-achieving peers with greater liking for the high-achieving girls (Quatman, Sokolik, & Smith, 2000). One

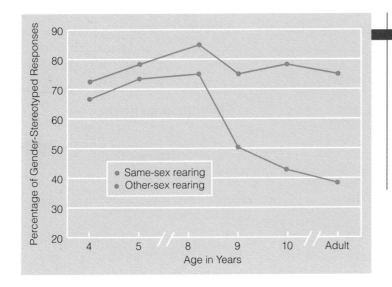

**FIGURE 13.4**

**Gender-stereotyped responses of 4- to 10-year-olds and adults to stories about hypothetical boy and girl babies reared on an island either by members of their own sex or by members of the other sex.** Younger children thought that gender-stereotyped characteristics would emerge, regardless of rearing environment. Beginning at ages 9 and 10, children viewed gender typing as socially rather than biologically influenced. They thought that other-sex rearing would produce far less stereotyped children than would same-sex rearing. (Adapted from Taylor, 1996.)

heartening possibility is that boys are beginning to view gender roles as encompassing more varied possibilities.

In adolescence and adulthood, higher-SES individuals tend to hold more flexible gender-stereotyped views than their lower-SES counterparts (Lackey, 1989; Serbin, Powlishta, & Gulko, 1993). Years of schooling along with a wider array of life options may contribute to this difference.

## GENDER STEREOTYPING AND GENDER-ROLE ADOPTION

Do children's gender-stereotyped patterns of thinking influence gender-role adoption, thereby restricting their experiences and potential? The evidence on this issue is mixed. Gender-typed preferences and behaviours increase sharply over the preschool years—the same period in which children rapidly acquire stereotypes. In addition, boys—the more stereotyped of the two sexes—show greater conformity to their gender role (Bussey & Bandura, 1992; Ruble & Martin, 1998).

But these parallel patterns do not tell us for sure that gender stereotyping shapes children's behaviour. Indeed, research suggests that children may be well versed in gender-related expectations but not highly gender typed in everyday life (Downs & Langlois, 1988; Serbin, Powlishta, & Gulko, 1993; Weinraub et al., 1984). Why might this be so? First, some gender-role preferences, such as the desire to play with "gender-appropriate" toys and same-sex playmates, are acquired before children know much about stereotypes. Second, we have seen that children master the components of gender-stereotyped knowledge in diverse ways, each of which may have different implications for their behaviour. Finally, by middle childhood, virtually all children know a great deal about gender stereotypes—knowledge so universal that it cannot predict variations in their behaviour.

Rather than stereotype knowledge, stereotype flexibility is a good predictor of children's gender-role adoption in middle childhood. Children who believe that many stereotyped characteristics are appropriate for both sexes (for example, that playing with trucks is okay for girls) are more likely to cross gender lines in the activities, playmates, and occupational roles they choose for themselves (Serbin, Powlishta, & Gulko, 1993; Signorella, Bigler, & Liben, 1993). This suggests that gender stereotypes affect behaviour only when children incorporate those beliefs into their own gender identities—self-perceptions of what they can and should do at play, in school, and as future participants in society. But the development of gender identity is a topic we treat later in this chapter. Let's turn now to various influences that promote children's gender-typed beliefs and behaviours.

## ASK YOURSELF www

**review**    Explain how gender stereotyping in the environment and young children's cognitive limitations contribute to rigid gender stereotypes in early childhood.

**review**    What factors allow for greater gender-stereotype flexibility in middle childhood and adolescence? How is gender-stereotyped flexibility related to gender-typed preferences and behaviour?

**apply**    Dennis is the only boy in his grade 7 home-economics cooking class. His friends Tom and Bill tease him relentlessly. Cite evidence that explains this negative reaction to Dennis's "cross-gender" behaviour.

**connect**    Cite parallels between the development of gender stereotyping and children's understanding of ethnicity and social class (see Chapter 11, pages 467–468).

# Influences on Gender Stereotyping and Gender-Role Adoption

ACCORDING TO SOCIAL learning theorists, gender-stereotyped knowledge and behaviours are transmitted to children through direct teaching. We will see shortly that much research is consistent with this view. Nevertheless, others argue that biological makeup leads each sex to be uniquely suited to particular roles and that most societies do little more than encourage gender differences that are genetically based. Is there evidence to support this idea?

## THE CASE FOR BIOLOGY

Although practically no modern theorist would argue that "biology is destiny," serious questions about biological influences on gender typing remain. According to the evolutionary perspective, the adult life of our male ancestors was largely oriented toward competing for mates, that of our female ancestors toward rearing children. Therefore, males became genetically primed for dominance and females for intimacy, responsiveness, and cooperativeness. These sex differences in behaviour exist in 97 percent of mammalian species, including chimpanzees, our closest evolutionary relative (Clutton-Brock, 1991; de Waal, 1993). Evolutionary theorists claim that family and cultural forces can influence the intensity of biologically based sex differences, leading some individuals to be much more gender typed than others. But experience cannot eradicate those aspects of gender typing etched into our biological makeup because they served adaptive functions in human history (Geary, 1999; Maccoby, 2002).

Two sources of evidence have been used to support the role of biology: (1) cross-cultural similarities in gender stereotypes and gender-role adoption, and (2) the influence of hormones on gender-role behaviour. Let's examine each in turn.

**HOW MUCH CROSS-CULTURAL SIMILARITY EXISTS IN GENDER TYPING?**
Earlier in this chapter, we noted that the instrumental–expressive dichotomy is reflected in the gender stereotyping of many national groups. Although this finding fits with the idea that social influences simply build on genetic differences between the sexes, we must be cautious in drawing this conclusion.

A close look at cross-cultural findings reveals that most societies promote instrumental traits in males and expressive traits in females, although great diversity exists in the magnitude of this difference (Whiting & Edwards, 1988b). Consider Nyansongo, a small agricultural settlement in Kenya. Nyansongo mothers, who work 4 to 5 hours a day in the gardens, assign the care of young

Great diversity exists in the extent to which societies promote instrumental traits in males and expressive traits in females. These boys of the Dinka tribe in Kenya are assigned "feminine" tasks—grinding corn and looking after younger siblings. Consequently, they are less likely to be gender stereotyped in personality traits than are most boys in other cultures.

AKHTAR HUSSEIN/WOODFIN CAMP & ASSOCIATES

# cultural influences

## SWEDEN'S COMMITMENT TO GENDER EQUALITY

Of all nations in the world, Sweden is unique in its valuing of gender equality. More than a century ago, Sweden's ruling political party adopted equality as a central goal. One social class was not to exploit another, nor one gender another. In the 1960s, Sweden's expanding economy required that women enter the labour force in large numbers. When the question arose as to who would help sustain family life, the Swedish people called on the principle of equality and answered: fathers, just like mothers.

The Swedish "equal roles family model" maintains that husband and wife should have the same opportunity to pursue a career and be equally responsible for housework and child care. To support this goal, child-care centres had to be made available outside the home. Otherwise, a class of less privileged women might be exploited for caregiving and domestic work—an outcome that would contradict the principle of equality. And since full-time employment for both parents often strains a family with young children, Sweden mandated that mothers and fathers with children under age 8 could reduce the length of their working day to 6 hours, with a corresponding reduction in pay but not in benefits (Sandqvist, 1992).

According to several indicators, Sweden's family model is very successful. Maternal employment is extremely high; over 80 percent of mothers with infants and preschoolers are employed. Child-care centres are numerous, of high quality, and heavily subsidized by the government (Kallós & Broman, 1997). Although Swedish fathers do not yet share housework and child care equally with mothers, they are more involved than fathers in North America and other Western European nations.

Has Sweden's progressive family policy affected the gender beliefs and behaviours of its youths? A study of Swedish and U.S. adolescents found that valuing the "masculine" role over the "feminine" was less pronounced in Sweden than in the United States. Swedish young people regarded each gender as a blend of instrumental and expressive traits. Furthermore, Swedish girls felt considerably better about their gender. Finally, compared with

Sweden places a high value on gender equality. Compared with fathers in North America and other Western European nations, Swedish fathers are more involved in housework and child care. This father enjoys a paid paternity leave during the first 15 months of his child's life (see Chapter 3, page 113).

U.S. adolescents, Swedish young people more often viewed gender roles as a matter of learned tasks and domains of expertise than inborn traits or rights and duties (Intons-Peterson, 1988).

Traditional gender typing is not eradicated in Sweden. But great progress has been made as a result of steadfastly pursuing a program of gender equality for several decades.

children, the tending of the cooking fire, and the washing of dishes to older siblings. Since children of both sexes perform these duties, girls are relieved of total responsibility for "feminine" tasks and have more time to interact with agemates. Their greater freedom and independence lead them to score higher than girls of other tribal and village cultures in dominance, assertiveness, and playful roughhousing. In contrast, boys' caregiving responsibilities mean that they often display help-giving and emotional support (Whiting & Edwards, 1988a). Among industrialized nations, Sweden is widely recognized as a society in which traditional gender beliefs and behaviours are considerably reduced (see the Cultural Influences box above).

These examples indicate that experience can have a profound impact on gender typing. Nevertheless, it can be argued that reversals of traditional gender roles are rare (Daly & Wilson, 1988). Because cross-cultural findings are inconclusive, scientists have turned to a more direct test of the importance of biology: research on the impact of sex hormones on gender typing.

Beginning in the preschool years, children seek out playmates of their own sex. Sex hormones are believed to influence children's play styles, leading to calm, gentle actions in girls and rough, noisy movements in boys. Then preschoolers naturally choose same-sex partners who share their interests and behaviour. Social pressures for "gender-appropriate" play and the tendency to evaluate members of one's own sex more positively are also believed to promote gender segregation.

**SEX HORMONES AND GENDER TYPING.** In Chapters 3 and 5, we discussed how genetic makeup, mediated by hormones, regulates sexual development and body growth. Sex hormones also affect brain development and neural activity in many animal species, and they do so in humans as well (Hines & Green, 1991). Are hormones, which so pervasively affect body structures, also important in gender-role adoption?

***Play Styles and Preference for Same-Sex Peers.*** Experiments with animals reveal that exposure to sex hormones during certain sensitive periods does affect behaviour. For example, prenatally administered androgens (male sex hormones) increase active play in both male and female mammals. Androgens also promote male-typical sexual behaviour and aggression and suppress maternal caregiving in a wide variety of species (Beatty, 1992).

Eleanor Maccoby (1998) argues that at least some of these hormonal effects extend to humans. Recall from the introduction to this chapter that as early as the preschool years, children seek out playmates of their own sex—a preference observed in many cultures and mammalian species (Beatty, 1992; Whiting & Edwards, 1988a). At age 4, children already spend three times as much time with same-sex as with other-sex playmates. By age 6, this ratio climbs to 11 to 1 (Maccoby & Jacklin, 1987). Throughout the school years, children continue to show a strong preference for same-sex peers.

Why is gender segregation so widespread and persistent? According to Maccoby, early on, hormones affect play styles, leading to rough, noisy movements among boys and calm, gentle actions among girls. Then, as children interact with peers, they choose partners whose interests and behaviours are compatible with their own. By age 2, girls already appear overwhelmed by boys' rambunctious behaviour. When paired with a boy in a laboratory play session, the girl is likely to stand idly by while he explores the toys (Benenson, Apostoleris, & Parnass, 1997; Maccoby & Jacklin, 1987). Nonhuman primates react similarly. When a male juvenile initiates rough, physical play, male peers join in, whereas females withdraw (Beatty, 1992).

During the preschool years, girls increasingly seek out other girls and like to play in pairs because of a common preference for quieter activities involving cooperative roles (Benenson, 1993). And boys come to prefer larger-group play with other boys, who respond positively to one another's desire to run, climb, play-fight, and build up and knock down (Benenson, Apostoleris, & Parnass, 1997).

Social pressures for "gender-appropriate" play and cognitive factors—in particular, gender stereotyping, the tendency to evaluate members of one's own sex more positively, and expectations of negative reactions from others for play with other-sex children—may also contribute to gender segregation. But sex hormones are involved, a conclusion supported by studies of exceptional sexual development in humans.

***Exceptional Sexual Development.*** For ethical reasons, we cannot experimentally manipulate hormones to see how they affect human behaviour. But cases exist in which hormone levels varied naturally or were modified for medical reasons.

John Money, Anke Ehrhardt, and their collaborators conducted research on children with *congenital adrenal hyperplasia (CAH)*, a disorder in which a genetic defect causes the adrenal system to produce unusually high levels of androgens from the prenatal period onward. Although the physical development of boys remains unaffected, CAH girls are usually born with masculinized external genitals. Most undergo surgical correction in infancy or childhood and receive continuous drug therapy to overcome the hormone imbalance (Ehrhardt & Baker, 1974; Money & Ehrhardt, 1972).

Interviewing CAH children and their family members, the researchers found that girls liked cars, trucks, and blocks better than dolls; preferred boys as playmates; were uninterested in fantasizing about traditional feminine roles (such as bride and mother); and were less concerned with matters of physical appearance (clothing, jewellery, and hairstyle) than were non-CAH girls. Also, both boys and girls with CAH showed higher activity levels, as indicated by greater participation in active sports and outdoor games.

Recent interview and observational studies lend additional weight to the conclusion that prenatal androgen exposure supports certain aspects of "masculine" gender-role behaviour. Compared with controls, CAH women asked to reflect on their childhoods recall less comfort with their sense of femininity and more "masculine" toy, peer, and fantasy-role preferences (Zucker et al., 1996). Similarly, observations confirmed that CAH girls prefer vehicle and building toys and, to a lesser extent, boys as play partners (Berenbaum & Hines, 1992; Berenbaum & Snyder, 1995; Hines & Kaufman, 1994). The greater CAH girls' exposure to prenatal androgens, the more "masculine" their play preferences (Berenbaum, Duck, & Bryk, 2000).

Critics point out that subtle environmental pressures may contribute to the "masculine" play styles and interests of CAH girls. One speculation is that genital abnormalities, in some cases not corrected until after infancy, may have caused family members to perceive affected girls as boyish and unfeminine and to treat them accordingly. However, in the studies just described, CAH girls with masculinized genitals were not more "masculine" in toy or playmate preferences than other CAH girls. And as CAH girls get older and have more opportunities for adults to influence them in a "feminine" direction, they nevertheless continue to express greater interest than their non-CAH female siblings in "masculine" activities and careers (Berenbaum, 1999).

Other research on individuals reared as members of the other sex because they had ambiguous genitals indicates that sexual identity (feeling comfortable about being a boy or girl) usually is consistent with gender of rearing, regardless of genetic sex (Slijper et al., 1998; Zucker, 2001). But in these cases, children's biological sex and prenatal hormone exposure (which caused the ambiguous genitals) are discrepant—circumstances that might foster successful assignment to either gender. What about children whose genetic sex and prenatal hormone exposure are congruent but whose genitals are ambiguous due to injury? Turn to the Biology & Environment box on page 534 for a case study of a Canadian boy who lost his penis in an accident during circumcision. It suggests that when biological makeup and sex of rearing are at odds, children experience serious problems with sexual identity and psychological adjustment.

Taken together, research suggests that sex hormones affect gender typing. The most uniform findings involve activity level and a related preference for "gender-appropriate" play and toys (Collaer & Hines, 1995). But we must be careful not to minimize the role of experience. As we will see next, a wide variety of environmental forces build on genetic influences to promote children's awareness and adoption of gender roles.

# biology & environment

### DAVID: A BOY REARED AS A GIRL

*a* happily married father of three children, David Reimer talks freely about his everyday life: his interest in auto mechanics, his problems at work, and the challenges of child rearing. But when asked about his first 15 years of life, his smile fades and he distances himself, speaking as if the child of his early life was another person. In essence, she was.

David—named Bruce at birth— underwent the first infant sex reassignment ever reported on a genetically and hormonally normal child. To find out about David's development, Milton Diamond and Keith Sigmundson (1999) intensively interviewed him and studied his medical and psychotherapy records. Later, John Colapinto (2001) extended this effort.

At age 8 months, Bruce's penis was accidentally severed during circumcision. At that time, phallic reconstruction surgery was in its infancy and local doctors could offer little hope. Bruce's desperate parents saw psychologist John Money on CBC television's *This Hour Has Seven Days* and learned of his success in assigning a sex to children with ambiguous genitals. They travelled

from their home in Manitoba to Johns Hopkins University in Baltimore, where under Money's supervision, 22-month-old Bruce had surgery to remove his testicles and sculpt his genitals to look like those of a girl. The operation complete, Bruce's parents named their daughter Brenda.

As it happened, Bruce had an identical twin brother, Brian. Altering one twin, while having the other twin as a control, provided a unique opportunity for Money to test his theory on reassignment of gender. He hoped to show that biology is not destiny, that if gender is reassigned before the age of 18 months, a child will make a complete adjustment to the reassigned role.

Previous research on infants with ambiguous genitals indicated that a parent-chosen sex assignment usually works out. But because of an imbalance in prenatal sex hormones, the organization of those children's central nervous systems might also be ambiguous, thereby permitting development as either a male or a female. Brenda's outcome, in contrast, was tragic. From the outset, she resisted her parents' efforts to steer her in a "feminine" direction.

Brian recalled that Brenda looked like a delicate, pretty girl, but as soon as she moved or spoke, this impression evaporated. "She walked like a guy. Sat with her legs apart. She talked about guy things…. She played with my toys: Tinkertoys, dump trucks" (Colapinto, 2001, p. 57). Brian was quiet and gentle in personality, showing little interest in the war toys his parents gave him. Brenda, in contrast, was a dominant, rough-and-tumble child who picked fights with other children and usually won. Former teachers and classmates agreed that Brenda was the more traditionally masculine of the two children.

At school, Brenda's boyish behaviour, combined with her unhappy demeanour, led classmates to taunt and tease her. When she played with girls, she tried organizing large-group, active games, such as cowboys and Indians, but they weren't interested. Uncomfortable as a girl and without friends, Brenda's behaviour problems increased and her school performance deteriorated. During periodic medical follow-ups, she drew pictures of herself as a boy and refused additional surgery to create a vagina and relocate her urethra. Reflecting back on

---

## THE CASE FOR ENVIRONMENT

A wealth of evidence reveals that environmental factors provide powerful support for gender-role development. As we will see in the following sections, adults view boys and girls differently, and they treat them differently. In addition, children's social contexts— home, school, and community—offer many opportunities to observe people behaving in ways consistent with gender stereotypes. And as soon as children enter the world of the peer group, their agemates encourage conformity to gender roles.

**PERCEPTIONS AND EXPECTATIONS OF ADULTS.** When adults are asked to observe neutrally dressed infants who are labelled as either boy or girl, they "see" qualities that fit with the baby's artificially assigned sex. In research of this kind, adults tend to rate infants' physical features and (to a lesser extent) their personality traits in a gender-stereotyped fashion (Stern & Karraker, 1989; Vogel et al., 1991). Boys, for example, are viewed as firmer, larger, better coordinated, and hardier and girls as softer, finer featured, more delicate, and less alert.

Brenda's elementary school years, David explained that she realized she was not a girl and never would be.

As adolescence approached, Brenda's parents moved her from school to school and therapist to therapist, in an effort to help her fit in socially and accept a female identity. Brenda reacted with increased anxiety and insecurity, and conflict with her parents increased. At puberty, Brenda's shoulders broadened and her body added muscle, so her parents insisted that she begin estrogen therapy to feminize her appearance. Soon she grew breasts and added fat around her waist and hips. Repelled by her own feminizing shape, Brenda began overeating to hide it. Her classmates reacted with stepped-up brutality to her confused appearance.

At last, Brenda was transferred to a therapist who recognized her despair and encouraged her parents to tell her about her infancy. When Brenda was 14, her father explained the circumcision accident. David recalled reacting with mixed emotions, but mostly with relief. "Suddenly it all made sense why I felt the way I did" (Colapinto, 2001, p. 180). Immediately deciding to return to his biological

sex, he chose for himself the name David, after the biblical lad who slew a giant and overcame adversity. David soon started injections of testosterone to masculinize his body, and he underwent surgery to remove his breasts and to construct a penis. Although his adolescence continued to be troubled, in his twenties he fell in love with Jane, a single mother of three children, and married her.

David's case confirms the impact of genetic sex and prenatal hormones on a person's inner sense of self as male or female. At the same time, his childhood highlights the importance of experience. David expressed outrage at adult encouragement of dependency and passivity in girls, having experienced it first-hand. And he realized that had Brenda not been ostracized by peers for her "masculine" traits, she might have had an easier time reverting to her biological sex. In adulthood, David worked in a slaughterhouse with all male employees, who were extreme in their gender stereotyping. At one point he wondered—if he had had a typical childhood, would he have become like them? Of course, he can never know the

Because of a tragic medical accident when he was a baby, David Reimer underwent the first sex reassignment on a genetically and hormonally normal baby: He was reared as a girl. His case shows the overwhelming impact of biology on gender identity. David is pictured here as he is today—a happily married man and father of three children.

answer to that question, but his case does clarify one issue: His gender reassignment failed because his male biology overwhelmingly demanded a consistent sexual identity.

During their children's childhood and adolescence, parents continue to hold different perceptions and expectations of their sons and daughters. They interpret children's behaviour in stereotyped ways, want their preschoolers to play with "gender-appropriate" toys, and say that boys and girls should be reared differently. For example, when asked about their child-rearing values, parents describe achievement, competition, and control of emotion as important for sons and warmth, "ladylike" behaviour, and closely supervised activities as important for daughters (Brody, 1999; Turner & Gervai, 1995). Furthermore, when asked for their attitudes toward "cross-gender" behaviour, parents of preschoolers responded more negatively to the idea of "cross-gender" boys than girls. And they predicted that "cross-gender" children of both sexes would grow up to be slightly less well adjusted than "typical" children (Sandnabba & Ahlberg, 1999).

**TREATMENT BY PARENTS.** Do adults actually treat children in accord with their stereotypical beliefs? A combined analysis of 172 studies reported that on the whole, differences in the way parents socialize boys and girls are not large (Lytton & Romney, 1991). However, this does not mean that parental treatment is unimportant. It simply says that if we generalize across age periods and behaviours, we find only a few clear trends. When the evidence is examined closely, consistent age effects emerge. Younger children receive more direct training in gender roles than do older children—a finding that is not surprising, since gender typing takes place especially rapidly during early childhood (Fagot & Hagan, 1991). And wide variation from study to study suggests that some parents practise differential treatment much more intensely than do others.

***Infancy and Early Childhood.*** In infancy and early childhood, parents encourage a diverse array of "gender-appropriate" play activities and behaviours. As early as the first few months of life—before children can express their own preferences—parents create different environments for boys and girls. Bedrooms are decorated with distinct colours and themes. Parents give toys that stress action and competition (such as guns, cars, tools, and footballs) to boys. They give toys that emphasize nurturance, cooperation, and physical attractiveness (dolls, tea sets, jewellery, and jump ropes) to girls (Leaper, 1994).

Parents also actively reinforce independence in boys and closeness and dependency in girls. For example, parents react more positively when a son plays with cars and trucks, demands attention, runs and climbs, or tries to take toys from others. In contrast, they more often direct play activities, provide help, encourage participation in household tasks, and refer to emotions when interacting with a daughter (Fagot & Hagan, 1991; Kuebli, Butler, & Fivush, 1995). Furthermore, mothers more often *label emotions* when talking to girls. In doing so, they seem to teach daughters to "tune in" to others' feelings. In contrast, mothers more often *explain emotions,* noting causes and consequences, when talking to boys—an approach that emphasizes why it is important to control the expression of emotion (Cervantes & Callanan, 1998; Fivush, 1989).

Early in development, then, parents provide experiences—through play materials and social interaction—that encourage assertiveness, exploration, engagement with the physical world, and emotional control in boys. In contrast, they promote imitation, reliance on others, and emotional sensitivity in girls (Leaper, 2000).

***Middle Childhood.*** During middle childhood, as children's skills expand, issues of achievement become more salient to parents. Observations of mothers and fathers interacting with their school-age children in teaching situations reveal that parents continue to demand greater independence from boys. For example, when a child requests help, parents more often ignore or refuse to respond to a son, whereas they offer help right away to a daughter (Rothbart & Rothbart, 1976). And the way parents provide help to each sex differs. They behave in a more mastery-oriented fashion with sons, setting higher standards and pointing out important features of the task. In contrast, they frequently stray from task goals to joke and play with daughters (Block, Block, & Harrington, 1975). During conversations, parents are likely to interrupt daughters but permit sons to finish their statements, subtly delivering the message that what a boy has to say is more important (Greif, 1979).

Parents also hold gender-differentiated perceptions of and expectations for children's competencies in various school subjects. In longitudinal research on more than 2100 families with school-age children, Jacqueline Eccles, Janis Jacobs, and Rena Harold (1990) found that parents rated daughters as more competent in English than sons; the reverse was true for mathematics and sports. These beliefs were stronger than actual skill differences between boy and girl participants, who performed equally well in the two academic areas. Parents' gender-typed judgments, in turn, influenced children's self-perceptions of ability, the effort they devoted to mastering particular skills, and their later performance (Eccles et al., 2000). The researchers speculated that this chain of events affects the occupations that males and females seek out and qualify for. Indeed, women's progress in entering male-dominated professions has been slow. For example, in Canada, only 5.5 percent of engineers, 14 percent of police officers, 29 percent of doctors, and 26 percent of university faculty are women (Canadian Council of Professional Engineers, 1998; Canadian Institute for Health Information, 2000; Statistics Canada, Full-time University Faculty, 2000; Statistics Canada, Police Resources, 2000).

Differential treatment by parents extends to the freedom granted children in their everyday lives. Parents use more directive speech (imperatives and specific suggestions) with girls than with boys (Leaper, Anderson, & Sanders, 1998). Furthermore, when insisting that children meet

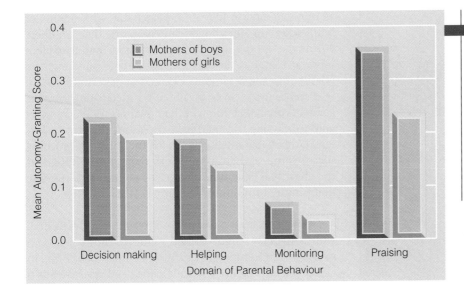

FIGURE 13.5

**Mothers' autonomy granting in the context of control tactics aimed at getting 6- to 11-year-olds to meet their daily responsibilities.** Autonomy granting was assessed in four domains of parental behaviour: *decision making, helping* (with homework and other projects), *monitoring* (overseeing completion of homework, out-of-school projects, and chores), and *praising* (communicating confidence in the child). In each, mothers granted boys more autonomy. (Adapted from Pomerantz & Ruble, 1998b.)

their daily responsibilities, mothers of sons more often pair control with autonomy granting. That is, they tend to ask boys to make decisions ("When do you think would be a good time for you to do your music practice?"), whereas they tend to decide for girls ("Do your practising right after dinner"). And mothers more often communicate confidence in boys when praising them for meeting a standard, as in "you must enjoy your work" (see Figure 13.5) (Pomerantz & Ruble, 1998b). Although school-age children interpret parental control without autonomy granting as well-intentioned guidance, they also say it makes them feel incompetent (Pomerantz & Ruble, 1998a).

Yet another sign of boys' greater freedom is parental willingness to let them range farther from home without supervision. Assignment of chores also reflects this trend. In many cultures, girls are given tasks, such as food preparation, cleaning, and baby-sitting, that keep them close to home, whereas boys are given responsibilities that take them into the surrounding world, such as yard work and errands (Whiting & Edwards, 1988a). As noted earlier, when cultural circumstances require children to perform "cross-gender" chores (as in Nyansongo), the range of behaviours practised expands.

Although these findings might be taken to suggest that children in Western cultures should be assigned more gender-atypical tasks, the consequences of doing so are not so straightforward. For example, when fathers hold stereotypical views and their sons engage in "feminine" housework, boys experience strain in the father–child relationship, feel stressed by their responsibilities, and judge themselves to be less competent (McHale et al., 1990).

In contrast, a match between parental values and nontraditional child-rearing practices leads to benefits for children. In one study, 6-year-olds growing up in countercultural families that were committed to gender equality were compared with agemates living in conventional homes or experiencing other countercultural alternatives (for example, communes emphasizing spiritual and pro-nature values). Children in gender-countercultural homes were less likely to classify objects and occupations in stereotypical ways, and girls more often aspired to nontraditional careers (Weisner & Wilson-Mitchell, 1990).

***Mothers versus Fathers.*** In most aspects of differential treatment of boys and girls, fathers discriminate the most. For example, in Chapter 10 we saw that fathers tend to engage in more physically stimulating play with their infant sons than with their daughters, where-

This Lapp boy of Norway wanders far from home as he tends his family's sled reindeer. The freedom he is granted promotes independence and self-reliance. Because his sisters are given household tasks, they spend much more time under the watchful eye of adults.

Parents' expectations and treatment of their children affect gender-role development. This father helps his daughter with a project in which she designed and constructed a solar-powered vehicle. His encouragement bolsters her interest in and self-confidence at tackling complex problems in physical science.

as mothers tend to play in a quieter way with infants of both sexes. In childhood, fathers more than mothers encourage "gender-appropriate" behaviour, and they place more pressure to achieve on sons than on daughters (Gervai, Turner, & Hinde, 1995; Lytton & Romney, 1991).

Parents also seem especially committed to ensuring the gender typing of children of their own sex. While mothers go on shopping trips and bake cookies with their daughters, fathers play catch, help coach the Saturday morning soccer game, and go fishing with their sons. This same-sex-child bias is another aspect of gender-role training that is more pronounced for fathers (Parke, 1996).

**TREATMENT BY TEACHERS.** In some ways, preschool and elementary school teachers reinforce children of both sexes for "feminine" rather than "masculine" behaviour. In classrooms, obedience is usually valued and assertiveness is discouraged—by male and female teachers alike (Fagot, 1985a; Oettingen, 1985). This "feminine bias" is believed to promote discomfort for boys in school, but it may be equally or even more harmful for girls, who willingly conform, with possible long-term negative consequences for their sense of independence and self-esteem.

Teachers also act in ways that maintain and even extend gender roles taught at home. They often segregate children by sex, as when they say, "Will the girls line up on one side and the boys on the other?" and "Boys, I wish you'd quiet down like the girls!" (Thorne, 1993). At the same time, teachers (like parents) interrupt girls more than boys during conversation, thereby promoting boys' social dominance and girls' passivity. By age 4, children react in kind: Boys interrupt their female teachers more than girls do (see Figure 13.6) (Hendrick & Stange, 1991).

At older ages, teachers praise boys for their knowledge, girls for their obedience. And although they discourage aggression and other forms of misbehaviour in all children, they do so more frequently and forcefully in boys. Teachers' greater scolding of boys seems to result from an expectation that boys will misbehave more often than girls—a belief based partly on boys' actual behaviour and partly on gender stereotypes. When teachers reprimand girls, it is usually for giving a wrong answer (Good & Brophy, 1996).

Just as teachers can promote gender typing, they can do the opposite by modifying the way they communicate with children. For example, when teachers introduce new materials in a non-gender-biased fashion, praise all students for independence and persistence, and ignore attention seeking and dependency, children's activity choices and behaviours change accordingly (Serbin, Connor, & Citron, 1978; Serbin, Connor, & Iler, 1979). But most of the time, changes in behaviour are short lived. As soon as the usual interaction patterns resume in the classroom, children return to their prior ways of responding. Like nontraditional families, schools that are successful in modifying gender typing have clearly articulated philosophies about gender equality that pervade all aspects of classroom life (Gash & Morgan, 1993).

**OBSERVATIONAL LEARNING.** In addition to direct pressures from adults, numerous gender-typed models are available in children's environments. Although Canadian society has changed to some degree, children come in contact with many real people who conform to traditional gender roles. In school, for example, women are more likely to be teachers, especially in the early grades, whereas men more often hold administrative positions.

Reflections of gender in the media are also stereotyped. As we will see in Chapter 15, portrayal of gender roles in television programs—especially in children's programs and commercials—has changed very little in recent years. And gender stereotyping is rampant in video games (Dietz, 1998; Huston & Wright, 1998). In addition, analyses of the content of children's storybooks and textbooks reveal that gender-equitable reading materials are increasing, but many continue to portray males and females stereotypically. Boys and men more often are mentioned in titles, serve as main characters, take centre stage in exciting and adventurous plot activities, and display assertiveness and creativity. Girls and women tend to be pictured as passive and dependent (Tepper & Cassidy, 1999; Turner-Bowker, 1996).

When children are exposed to nonstereotyped models, they are less traditional in their beliefs and behaviours. Children who often see their parents cross traditional gender lines—mothers who are employed or who engage in "masculine" household tasks (repairing appliances, washing the car) and fathers who engage in "feminine" household tasks (ironing, cooking, child care)—less often endorse gender stereotypes (Turner & Gervai, 1995; Updegraff, McHale, & Crouter, 1996). Girls with career-oriented mothers show special benefits. They more often engage in typically masculine activities (such as physically active play), have higher educational aspirations, and hold nontraditional vocational goals (Hoffman, 2000).

Furthermore, among children of divorced parents, boys in father-absent homes and girls in mother-absent homes are less gender typed, perhaps because they have fewer opportunities to observe traditional gender roles than they would in a two-parent household (Brenes, Eisenberg, & Helmstadter, 1985; Williams, Radin, & Allegro, 1992). Besides displaying less stereotyped beliefs and activities, children from single-parent homes are more likely to have at least one other-sex friend than are agemates in two-parent families (Kovacs, Parker, & Hoffman, 1996).

In sum, relationships between exposure to gender stereotyping and children's preferences and behaviours suggest that modelling is important in gender typing. Nevertheless, children do not imitate same-sex models indiscriminately. Instead, they imitate models whose behaviours they judge to be gender-typical. For example, they are more likely to copy a same-sex adult's behaviour if that person acts like other same-sex adults (Perry & Bussey, 1979). In most cases, multiple models acting similarly or a warm, powerful model acting consistently for a long period seem necessary to influence children's gender typing.

**PEERS.** Earlier we noted that children's preference for same-sex peers is widespread. Once formed, sex-segregated peer associations strengthen traditional beliefs and behaviours.

By age 3, same-sex peers positively reinforce one another for "gender-appropriate" play by praising, approving, imitating, or joining in. In contrast, when preschoolers engage in "gender-inappropriate" activities—for example, when boys play with dolls or girls with cars and trucks—peers criticize them. Boys are especially intolerant of cross-gender play in their male companions (Carter & McCloskey, 1984; Fagot, 1984). A boy who frequently crosses gender lines is likely to be ignored by other boys, even when he does engage in "masculine" activities!

Over time, children form strong beliefs about the acceptability of gender-segregated play, and those beliefs strengthen gender-segregation and the stereotyped activities associated with it. In one study, 3- to 5-year-olds believed that peers would be more likely to approve of their behaviour if they played with same-sex agemates—a conviction that predicted children's actual association with same-sex peers at their child-care centre (Martin et al., 1999). As boys and girls separate, "own-sex favouritism"—the tendency to evaluate one's own group more positively— becomes yet another factor that sustains the separate social worlds of boys and girls.

Once in place, gender-segregated peer groups promote different styles of social influence in boys and girls. To get their way with male peers, boys more often rely on commands, threats, and physical force. In contrast, girls use polite requests and persuasion. These strategies succeed with other girls but not with boys, who start to ignore girls' gentle tactics (Leaper, 1994; Leaper, Tenenbaum, & Shaffer, 1999). Consequently, girls may have an additional reason to prefer girls; they find boys to be unresponsive, unrewarding social partners.

Some educators believe that fostering mixed-sex interaction in classrooms—by teaching nonstereotyped values and forming mixed-sex activity groups—is a vital means for reducing gender stereotyping and broadening developmental possibilities for both sexes (Lloyd &

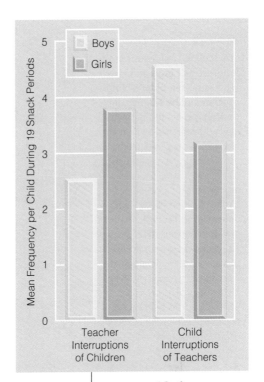

**FIGURE** 13.6

**Interruptions by teachers of children and by children of teachers at snack time in preschool.** Children were observed in groups of two boys and two girls at a table with a female teacher. Teachers interrupted girls' conversations more often than boys'. Boys responded in kind; compared to girls, they more often interrupted teachers. (Adapted from Hendrick & Stange, 1991.)

FIGURE 13.7

**"Masculine" behaviour scores for preschool boys and girls with same-sex older siblings, other-sex older siblings, and no siblings.** In this British study in which more than 5000 mothers reported on the play and other behaviours of their 3-year-olds, children with same-sex older siblings were more gender typed than children with no siblings, who were more gender typed than children with other-sex older siblings. Notice how boys with the lowest masculine behaviour scores have older sisters, whereas girls with highest masculine behaviour scores have older brothers. (Adapted from Rust et al., 2000.)

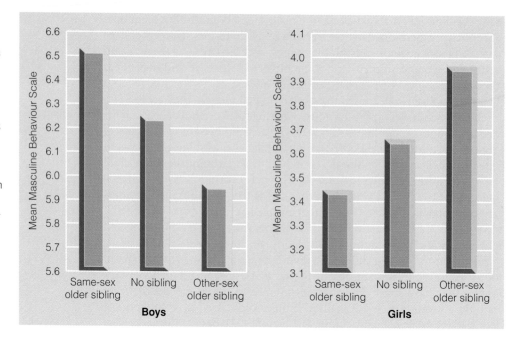

**Boys**

**Girls**

When siblings are the same sex, they are more likely to be assigned "cross-gender" chores. These brothers help with dishes after a family meal—a responsibility typically reserved for girls.

Smith, 1985). However, to be successful, interventions may have to modify the styles of social influence learned in same-sex peer relations. Otherwise, boys are likely to dominate and girls to react passively, thereby strengthening traditional gender roles and the stereotypes each sex holds of the other.

By secondary school, athletics becomes a major context in which gender stereotypes are fostered (Eder & Parker, 1987). The high status of male athletes and female cheerleaders leads the peer culture to value competition and toughness for boys and physical attractiveness and support of male prowess for females.

**SIBLINGS.** Growing up with siblings of the same or other sex also affects gender typing. But compared with peer influences, sibling effects are more complex because their impact depends on birth order and family size (Wagner, Schubert, & Schubert, 1993).

Whereas younger siblings have little impact on older siblings' gender typing, older siblings serve as powerful models for younger siblings. In a British study, more than 5000 mothers provided information on the play and other behaviours of their 3-year-old children, each of whom either had one older sibling or no siblings. As Figure 13.7 shows, children with same-sex siblings were more gender typed than children with no siblings, who were more gender typed than children with other-sex older siblings (Rust et al., 2000). Older siblings' influence expands during the school years, affecting younger siblings' sex-stereotyped attitudes, personality traits, and leisure pursuits (McHale et al., 2001).

But curiously, other research contradicts these findings, indicating that children with same-sex siblings are less stereotyped in their interests and personality traits than are those from mixed-sex families (Grotevant, 1978; Tauber, 1979). How can these conflicting results be explained? Recall from Chapter 10 that siblings often strive to be different from one another. This effect is strongest when children are of the same sex and come from large families, in which they may feel a greater need to stand out. A close look reveals that studies reporting a *modelling and reinforcement effect* (an increase in gender typing among same-sex siblings) focus on children from two-child families. In contrast, those reporting a *differentiation effect* include children from larger families.

In addition, parents may sometimes relax pressures toward gender typing when their children are all of the same sex. Consistent with this idea, mothers are more willing to give their child a gender-atypical toy as a gift if a child has an older, same-sex sibling (Stoneman, Brody, & MacKinnon, 1986). Also, in all-girl and all-boy families, children are more likely to be assigned "cross-gender" chores because no "gender-appropriate" child is available to do the job. Therefore, families in which siblings are all of the same sex may provide some special opportunities to step out of traditional gender roles.

In sum, older siblings are influential models in the gender typing of young siblings. But aspects of the family context, including family size and parental pressures, can alter this modelling effect.

## ASK YOURSELF

**review**  Cite research indicating that biology influences gender-role adoption.

**review**  Summarize parent, peer, and sibling influences on gender-role adoption. Why are sibling influences more complex than parent and peer influences?

**apply**  Pat and Chris had to do a science project. Pat's mother said, "You can go to the library tonight to choose your topic." Chris's mother said, "You'd better get started right away. We have some books on whales, so you can do it on that." Is Pat more likely to be a boy or a girl? How about Chris? Explain, using research findings.

**connect**  Girls are more susceptible than boys to learned helplessness in achievement situations. Explain why this is so, using research in this chapter (see page 536) and in Chapter 11 (see pages 457–459).

# Gender Identity

BESIDES BIOLOGICAL AND environmental influences, another factor eventually influences gender stereotyping and gender-role behaviour: *gender identity,* a person's perception of the self as relatively masculine or feminine in characteristics. Researchers measure gender identity in middle childhood by asking children to rate themselves on personality traits, since at that time, self-concepts begin to emphasize psychological dispositions over concrete behaviours (see Chapter 11). Table 13.2 on page 542 shows some sample items from a gender identity questionnaire for school-age children, who evaluate each statement on a four-point scale, from "very true of me" to "not at all true of me" (Boldizar, 1991).

Individuals vary considerably in the way they respond to these questionnaires. A child or adult with a "masculine" identity scores high on traditionally masculine items (such as ambitious, competitive, and self-sufficient) and low on traditionally feminine ones (such as affectionate, cheerful, and soft-spoken). Someone with a "feminine" identity does just the reverse. Although most people view themselves in gender-typed terms, a substantial minority (especially females) have a type of gender identity called **androgyny.** They score high on *both* masculine and feminine personality characteristics.

Gender identity is a good predictor of psychological adjustment. Masculine and androgynous children and adults have a higher sense of self-esteem, whereas feminine individuals often think poorly of themselves (Alpert-Gillis & Connell, 1989; Boldizar, 1991). In line with their flexible self-definitions, androgynous individuals are more adaptable in behaviour—for example, able to show masculine independence or feminine sensitivity, depending on the situation (Taylor & Hall, 1982). They also show greater maturity of moral judgment than do individuals with other gender-role orientations (Bem, 1977).

However, a close look at these findings reveals that the masculine component of androgyny is largely responsible for the superior psychological health of androgynous women over those with traditional identities (Taylor & Hall, 1982; Whitley, 1983). Feminine women seem to have adjustment difficulties because many of their traits are not valued highly by society. Nevertheless, the existence of an androgynous identity demonstrates that children can acquire a mixture of positive qualities traditionally associated with each gender—an orientation that may best help them realize their potential. And in a future society in which feminine characteristics are

**androgyny**
A type of gender identity in which the person scores high on both masculine and feminine personality characteristics.

**TABLE 13.2**

Sample Items from a Gender Identity Questionnaire for School-Age Children

| PERSONALITY TRAIT | ITEM |
|---|---|
| *Masculine* | |
| Ambitious | I'm willing to work hard to get what I want. |
| Assertive | It's easy for me to tell people what I think, even when I know they will probably disagree with me. |
| Competitive | When I play games, I really like to win. |
| Self-sufficient | I can take care of myself. |
| *Feminine* | |
| Affectionate | When I like someone, I do nice things for them to show them how I feel. |
| Cheerful | I am a cheerful person. |
| Soft-spoken | I usually speak softly. |
| Yielding | When there's a disagreement, I usually give in and let others have their way. |

*Source:* J. P. Boldizar, 1991, "Assessing Sex Typing and Androgyny in Children: The Children's Sex Role Inventory," *Developmental Psychology, 27,* p. 509. Copyright © 1991 by the American Psychological Association. Reprinted by permission.

socially rewarded to the same extent as masculine ones, androgyny may very well represent the ideal personality.

### EMERGENCE OF GENDER IDENTITY

How do children develop a gender identity? Both social learning and cognitive-developmental answers exist. According to *social learning theory,* behaviour comes before self-perceptions. Preschoolers first acquire gender-typed responses through modelling and reinforcement. Only later do they organize these behaviours into gender-linked ideas about themselves. In contrast, *cognitive-developmental theory* emphasizes that self-perceptions come before behaviour. Over the preschool years, children first acquire a cognitive appreciation of the permanence of their sex. They develop **gender constancy,** the understanding that sex is biologically based and remains the same even if clothing, hairstyle, and play activities change. Then children use this idea to guide their behaviour. Let's trace the development of gender constancy during the preschool years.

**DEVELOPMENT OF GENDER CONSTANCY.** Lawrence Kohlberg (1966) proposed that before age 6 or 7, children cannot maintain the constancy of their gender, just as they cannot pass Piagetian conservation problems. Only gradually do they attain this understanding, by moving through three stages of development:

1. **Gender labelling.** During the early preschool years, children can label their own sex and that of others correctly. But when asked such questions as "When you (a girl) grow up, could you ever be a daddy?" or "Could you be a boy if you wanted to?" young children freely answer yes (Slaby & Frey, 1975). In addition, when shown a doll whose hairstyle and clothing are transformed before their eyes, children indicate that the doll's sex is no longer the same (McConaghy, 1979).

2. **Gender stability.** At this stage, children have a partial understanding of the permanence of sex. They grasp its stability over time. But even though they know that male and female babies will eventually become boys and girls and men and women, they continue to insist that changing hairstyle, clothing, or "gender-appropriate" activities will lead a person to switch sexes as well (Fagot, 1985b; Slaby & Frey, 1975).

3. **Gender consistency.** During the late preschool and early school years, children become certain of the situational consistency of sex. They know that sex remains

**gender constancy**
The understanding that sex is biologically based and remains the same even if clothing, hairstyle, and play activities change.

**gender labelling**
Kohlberg's first stage of gender understanding, in which preschoolers can label the gender of themselves and others correctly.

**gender stability**
Kohlberg's second stage of gender understanding, in which preschoolers have a partial understanding of the permanence of sex; they grasp its stability over time.

**gender consistency**
Kohlberg's final stage of gender understanding, in which children in the late preschool and early school years master gender constancy.

constant even if a person decides to dress in "cross-gender" clothes or engage in non-traditional activities (Emmerich, 1981; McConaghy, 1979).

Many studies confirm that gender constancy emerges in the sequence just described. And as Kohlberg assumed, mastery of gender constancy is associated with attainment of conservation (De Lisi & Gallagher, 1991). However, in Western cultures, many young children do not see members of the other sex naked. Therefore, they distinguish males and females using the only information they do have—hairstyle, clothing, and behaviour. But providing children with information about genital differences does not result in a full understanding of gender constancy. Preschoolers who have such knowledge usually answer gender constancy questions correctly (Bem, 1989). But when asked to justify their responses, they still do not refer to sex as an innate, unchanging quality of people (Szkrybalo & Ruble, 1999). This suggests that cognitive immaturity, not social experience, is largely responsible for preschoolers' difficulty in grasping the permanence of sex.

**HOW WELL DOES GENDER CONSTANCY PREDICT GENDER-ROLE ADOPTION?** Is cognitive-developmental theory correct that gender constancy is responsible for children's gender-typed behaviour? From findings discussed earlier in this chapter, perhaps you have already concluded that evidence for this assumption is weak. "Gender-appropriate" behaviour appears so early in the preschool years that modelling and reinforcement must contribute to its initial appearance, as social learning theory suggests.

Although gender constancy does not initiate gender-role conformity, the cognitive changes that lead up to it do seem to facilitate gender typing. Preschoolers who reach the stage of gender labelling early show especially rapid development of "gender-appropriate" play preferences and are more knowledgeable about gender stereotypes than are their late-labelling peers (Fagot & Leinbach, 1989; Fagot, Leinbach, & O'Boyle, 1992). Similarly, understanding of gender stability is related to gender stereotyping, preference for same-sex playmates, and choice of "gender-consistent" toys (Martin & Little, 1990). These findings suggest that as soon as children acquire basic gender categories, they use them for acquiring gender-relevant information and modifying their own behaviour.

At present, investigators disagree on how a complete understanding of gender constancy contributes to gender typing (Bussey & Bandura, 1992; Lutz & Ruble, 1995). But overall, research indicates that its impact is not great. As we will see next, gender-role adoption is more powerfully affected by children's beliefs about how tight the connection must be between their own gender and behaviour.

## GENDER IDENTITY DURING MIDDLE CHILDHOOD

During middle childhood, boys' and girls' gender identities follow different paths. Self-ratings on personality traits reveal that from grade 3 to grade 6, boys strengthen their identification with the "masculine" role. In contrast, girls' identification with "feminine" characteristics declines. Although girls still lean toward the feminine side, they are clearly the more androgynous of the sexes (Boldizar, 1991; Serbin, Powlishta, & Gulko, 1993). This difference also is apparent in the activities children choose in middle childhood. Whereas boys usually stick to "masculine" pursuits, girls experiment with a wider range of options. Besides cooking, sewing, and baby-sitting, they join organized sports teams, take up science projects, and build forts in the backyard.

These changes are due to a mixture of cognitive and social forces. During the school years, children of both sexes are aware that society attaches greater prestige to "masculine" characteristics. For example, they rate "masculine" occupations as having higher status than "feminine" occupations. And by age 11, they regard a novel job (such as *clipster*, "a person who tests batteries") portrayed with a male worker as having higher status than the identical job portrayed with a female worker (see Figure 13.8 on page 544) (Liben, Bigler, &

During middle childhood, girls feel freer than boys to engage in "cross-gender" activities. This 10-year-old perfects her lasso technique.

© BOB DAEMMRICH/STOCK BOSTON

**FIGURE 13.8**

**Eleven-year-olds' status ratings of novel jobs portrayed with male and female workers.** Although children had no prior knowledge of these jobs and therefore had not previously stereotyped them as "masculine" or "feminine," simply portraying the job with a male worker resulted in higher status ratings. (Adapted from Liben, Bigler, & Krogh, 2001.)

Krogh, 2001). Given the strong association of males' activities with high status, it is not surprising that girls start to identify with "masculine" traits and are attracted to some typically masculine activities.

Messages from adults and agemates are also influential. Parents (especially fathers) are far less tolerant when sons as opposed to daughters cross gender lines. Similarly, a tomboyish girl can make her way into boys' activities without losing the approval of her female peers, but a boy who hangs out with girls is likely to be ridiculed and rejected.

### GENDER IDENTITY DURING ADOLESCENCE

Early adolescence is a period of **gender intensification**—increased gender stereotyping of attitudes and behaviour and movement toward a more traditional gender identity (Basow & Rubin, 1999; Galambos, Almeida, & Petersen, 1990). Gender intensification occurs in both sexes, but it is stronger for girls, who were more androgynous during middle childhood. Although overall, young teenage girls continue to be less gender typed than boys, they feel less free to experiment with "other-gender" activities and behaviour than they did earlier (Huston & Alvarez, 1990).

What accounts for gender intensification? Biological, social, and cognitive factors are involved. Puberty magnifies sex differences in appearance, causing teenagers to spend more time thinking about themselves in gender-linked ways. Pubertal changes also prompt gender-typed pressures from others. Parents—especially those with traditional gender-role beliefs—may encourage "gender-appropriate" activities and behaviour to a greater extent than they did when their children were younger (Crouter, Manke, & McHale, 1995). And when adolescents start to date, they often become more gender typed as a way of increasing their attractiveness to other-sex peers (Maccoby, 1998). For example, in encounters with boys, girls frequently use disclaimers, such as "I may be wrong" and "sort of"—a tentative speech style their male partners prefer (Carli, 1995). Finally, cognitive changes—in particular, greater concern with what others think—make young teenagers more responsive to gender-role expectations.

As young people move toward a mature personal identity, they become less concerned with others' opinions of them and more involved in finding meaningful values to include in their self-definitions (see Chapter 11). As a result, highly stereotypic self-perceptions decline, especially when parents and teachers encourage adolescents to question the value of gender stereotypes for themselves and their society.

### GENDER SCHEMA THEORY

Currently, researchers recognize that children's gender identities arise from their gender-linked experiences (as social learning theory assumes). Then these self-perceptions guide behaviour (as cognitive-developmental theory predicts). **Gender schema theory** is an

Early adolescence is a period of gender intensification. Puberty magnifies gender differences in appearance, causing teenagers to think about themselves in gender-linked ways. And when adolescents start to date, they often become more gender typed as a way of increasing their attractiveness to the other sex.

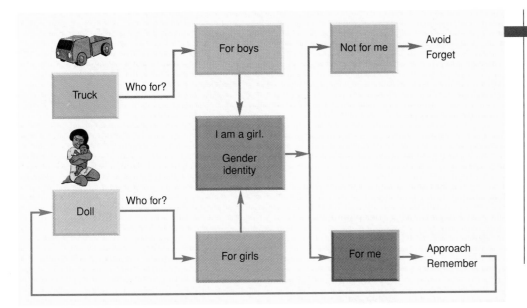

**FIGURE** 13.9

**Effect of gender schemas on gender-stereotyped preferences and behaviour.** Mandy's network of gender schemas leads her to approach and explore "feminine" toys, such as dolls, and to avoid "masculine" ones, such as trucks. (From C. L. Martin & C. F. Halverson, 1981, "A Schematic Processing Model of Sex Typing and Stereotyping in Children," *Child Development, 52,* p. 1121. © The Society for Research in Child Development, Inc. Adapted by permission.)

information-processing approach to gender typing that combines social learning and cognitive-developmental features. It also integrates the various elements of gender typing—stereotyping, gender identity, and gender-role adoption—into a unified picture of how masculine and feminine orientations emerge and are often strongly maintained (Martin, 1993; Martin & Halverson, 1987).

At an early age, children respond to instruction from others, picking up gender-typed preferences and behaviours. At the same time, they start to organize their experiences into *gender schemas,* or masculine and feminine categories, that they use to interpret their world. A young child who says, "Only boys can be doctors" or "Cooking is a girl's job" already has some well-formed gender schemas. As soon as preschoolers can label their own sex, they select gender schemas that are consistent with it, applying those categories to themselves. As a result, self-perceptions become gender typed and serve as additional gender schemas that children use to process information and guide their own behaviour.

Let's look at the example in Figure 13.9 to see exactly how this network of gender schemas strengthens gender-typed preferences and behaviours. Mandy has been taught that "dolls are for girls" and "trucks are for boys." She also knows that she is a girl. Mandy uses this information to make decisions about how to behave. Because her schemas lead her to conclude that "dolls are for me," when given a doll she approaches it, explores it, and learns more about it. In contrast, on seeing a truck, she uses her gender schemas to conclude that "trucks are not for me" and responds by avoiding the "gender-inappropriate" toy.

In research examining this pattern of reasoning, 4- and 5-year-olds were shown gender-neutral toys varying in attractiveness. An adult labelled some as boys' toys and others as girls' toys and left a third group unlabelled. Children engaged in gender-based reasoning, preferring toys labelled for their gender and predicting that same-sex peers would also like those toys. Highly attractive toys, especially, lost their appeal when they were labelled as for the other gender (Martin, Eisenbud, & Rose, 1995).

Gender schema theory explains why gender stereotypes and gender-role preferences are self-perpetuating and how they restrict children's alternatives. Children attend to and approach schema-consistent information, whereas they ignore, misinterpret, or reject schema-inconsistent information. For example, when shown a picture of a boy cooking at a stove, many children recall the picture as a girl rather than a boy. And when shown a film that includes a male nurse, they remember him as a doctor (Liben & Signorella, 1993; Martin & Halverson, 1983). Over time, children increase their knowledge of "things for me" that fit with their gender schemas, but they learn much less about "cross-gender" activities and behaviours.

Would these children continue playing if an adult labelled marbles as a boys' toy or a girls' toy? Powerful gender schemas lead children to like a toy or game less if they believe it is for the other gender.

**gender intensification**
Increased stereotyping of attitudes and behaviour and movement toward a more traditional gender identity. Often occurs in early adolescence.

**gender schema theory**
An information-processing approach to gender typing that combines social learning and cognitive-developmental features to explain how social pressures and cognitions work together to affect stereotyping, gender-role identity, and gender-role adoption.

## *from research to practice*

### REDUCING GENDER-SCHEMATIC THINKING WITH COGNITIVE INTERVENTIONS

On the first day of school, Mrs. Brown taped blue tags with boys' names and pink tags with girls' names to the corner of each desk in her grade 2 classroom. When explaining classroom routines, she told boys and girls to form separate lines at lunch and recess. During daily lessons, Mrs. Brown made frequent reference to gender. "All the boys should be sitting down!" she exclaimed when the class got too noisy. And as an art activity was about to begin, she directed, "Leanne, please get paper for the girls. Jack, I'd like you to be a good helper for the boys."

Rebecca Bigler (1995) had some teachers create "gender classrooms" like Mrs. Brown's by emphasizing gender categories. Other teachers in "control classrooms" were told to refer to children only by their names or treat the class as a unit. After 4 weeks, 6- to 10-year-olds in "gender classrooms" endorsed more gender stereotypes than did controls. They also had a more homogeneous view of each gender group in that they judged all or most members as very similar in personality traits and abilities. An additional consequence of group labelling is a positive view of one's own group and a negative view of the out-group (see Chapter 11, page 468).

Yet as Figure 13.10 shows, the impact of "gender classrooms" was largely limited to rigid thinkers—children who had trouble understanding that a person can belong to more than one social category at once. According to gender schema theory, environmental influences on gender typing are sustained by cognitive forces. When children who are one-dimensional thinkers encounter an exception to their gender schemas (such as a girl who is good at baseball), they are unlikely to process it because they cannot separate the activity category "baseball" from the gender category "male." Recall that operational thought enables children to classify flexibly by the end of middle childhood (see Chapter 6, page 241).

Bigler's findings suggest that it is especially important for teachers to avoid grouping children on the basis of gender during the early years of schooling, when classification skills are limited and gender stereotypes are forming. At the same time, training in multiple classification can reduce gender-biased thinking. When 5- to 10-year-olds were taught that ability and interest, not gender, determine whether a person can do a job well, they gained in stereotype flexibility and memory for "gender-inconsistent" information (story characters engaged in "cross-gender" tasks). Interestingly, classification train-

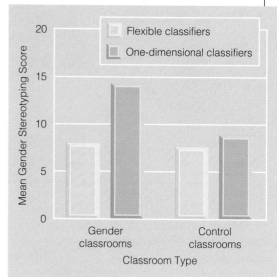

**FIGURE 13.10**

**Children's gender stereotyping in "gender" and "control classrooms."** "Gender classrooms" had a powerful impact on 6- to 10-year-olds who were one-dimensional thinkers—unable to see that a person can belong to more than one social category at once. These children endorsed many more stereotypes than did classmates who could classify flexibly. (Adapted from Bigler, 1995.)

ing with gender-neutral stimuli that required children to sort objects into two categories at once had the same effect (Bigler & Liben, 1992). Interventions that promote logical reasoning about gender and other aspects of the world can help children develop more gender-equitable beliefs.

---

Among children with strong stereotypical beliefs, self-perceptions, and activity preferences, gender-schematic thinking is especially extreme (Carter & Levy, 1991). But gender-schematic thinking could not operate so forcefully to restrict knowledge and learning opportunities if society did not teach children a wide variety of gender-linked associations. Currently, researchers are experimenting with ways to reduce children's tendency to view the world in gender-schematic terms. As the From Research to Practice box above reveals, training in cognitive skills that counteract powerful social messages about gender has produced some impressive results. The Milestones table on the following page provides an overview of the changes in gender stereotyping, gender identity, and gender-role adoption we have considered.

# milestones

## GENDER TYPING

| AGE | GENDER STEREOTYPING AND GENDER-ROLE ADOPTION | GENDER IDENTITY |
|-----|----------------------------------------------|-----------------|
| 1–5 years | ♒ "Gender-appropriate" toy preferences emerge and strengthen. <br><br> ♒ Gender stereotyping of activities, occupations, and behaviours expands. <br><br> ♒ Gender segregation in peer interaction emerges and strengthens. <br><br> ♒ Girls' preference for play in pairs, boys for play in larger groups, appears. | ♒ Gender constancy develops in a three-stage sequence: gender labelling, gender stability, and gender consistency. <br><br>  |
| 6–11 years | ♒ Gender-stereotyped knowledge expands, especially for personality traits and achievement areas. <br><br> ♒ Gender stereotyping becomes more flexible. | ♒ "Masculine" gender identity strengthens among boys; girls' gender identity becomes more androgynous. |
| 12–20 years | ♒ Gender-role conformity increases in early adolescence and then declines. <br><br> ♒ Gender segregation becomes less pronounced. <br><br>  | ♒ Gender identity becomes more traditional in early adolescence, after which highly stereotypic self-perceptions decline. |

*Note:* These milestones represent overall age trends. Individual differences exist in the precise age at which each milestone is attained and in the extent of gender typing.

## ASK YOURSELF

**review**    Define androgyny. Which of the two sexes is more androgynous in middle childhood, and why?

**review**    Describe the general path of gender-identity development, from early childhood through adolescence.

**apply**    When 4-year-old Roger was in the hospital, he was cared for by a male nurse named Wilson. After Roger recovered, he told his friends about Dr. Wilson. Using gender schema theory, explain why Roger remembered Wilson as a doctor, not a nurse.

**connect**    Describe gains in perspective taking that lead young teenagers to be very concerned with what others think, thereby contributing to gender intensification. (See Chapter 11, page 471.)

# To What Extent Do Boys and Girls *Really* Differ in Gender-Stereotyped Attributes?

SO FAR, WE HAVE examined the relationship of biological, social, and cognitive factors to children's gender-typed preferences and behaviour. But we have said little about the extent to which boys and girls actually differ in mental abilities and personality traits. Over the past several decades, thousands of studies have measured sex differences in these characteristics. At the heart of these efforts is the age-old nature–nurture debate. Researchers have looked for stable differences between males and females and, from there, have searched for the biological and environmental roots of each variation.

To avoid basing conclusions on single studies and small, potentially biased samples, researchers often use a technique called *meta-analysis,* in which they reanalyze the data of many investigations together. Besides telling us whether a sex difference exists, this method provides an estimate of its size. Table 13.3 summarizes differences between boys and girls in mental abilities and personality traits, based on current evidence. The majority of findings listed in the table are small to moderate. And as Figure 13.11 shows, the distributions for males and females usually overlap greatly. Sex differences usually account for only 5 to 10 percent of individual differences, leaving most to be explained by other factors. Consequently, males and females are actually more alike than different in developmental potential. Nevertheless, as we will see shortly, a few sex differences are substantial (Eagly, 1995; Hyde & Plant, 1995).

**TABLE** 13.3

Sex Differences in Mental Abilities and Personality Traits

| CHARACTERISTIC | SEX-RELATED DIFFERENCE |
| --- | --- |
| Verbal abilities | Girls are advantaged in early language development and reading achievement in the school years. |
| Spatial abilities | Boys outperform girls in certain spatial skills, a difference that persists throughout the lifespan. |
| Mathematical abilities | Beginning in adolescence, boys do better than girls on tests of mathematical reasoning. The difference is greatest among high-achieving pupils. Many more boys perform exceptionally well in math. |
| School achievement | Girls get better grades than boys in all academic subjects in elementary school, after which the difference declines. In junior high, boys start to show an advantage in mathematics. |
| Achievement motivation | Sex-related differences in achievement motivation are linked to type of task. Boys perceive themselves as more competent and have higher expectancies of success in "masculine" achievement areas, such as mathematics, sports, and mechanical skills. Girls have higher expectancies and set higher standards for themselves in "feminine" areas, such as reading, writing, literature, and art. |
| Emotional sensitivity | Girls are more effective senders and receivers of emotional information and score higher on self-report measures of empathy and sympathy. Girls' advantage in prosocial behaviour is greatest for kindness and considerateness, very small for helping behaviour. |
| Fear, timidity, and anxiety | Girls are more fearful and timid than boys, a difference that is present in the first year of life. In school, girls are more anxious about failure and try harder to avoid it. In contrast, boys are greater risk takers, a difference reflected in their higher injury rates throughout childhood and adolescence. |
| Compliance and dependency | Girls more readily comply with directives from adults or peers. They also seek help from adults more often and score higher in dependency on personality tests. |
| Activity level | Boys are more active than girls. |
| Depression | Adolescent girls are more likely to show depressive symptoms than are adolescent boys. |
| Aggression | Boys display more overt aggression, girls more relational aggression. Adolescent boys are far more likely than girls to become involved in antisocial behaviour and violent crime. |
| Developmental problems | Problems more common among boys include speech and language disorders, reading disabilities, and behaviour problems such as hyperactivity, hostile acting-out behaviour, and emotional and social immaturity. More boys than girls are born with genetic disorders, physical disabilities, and mental retardation. |

In considering the size of sex differences, we must keep in mind that some have changed over time. For example, during the past several decades, the gender gap has narrowed in all areas of mental ability for which differences have been identified except upper-level mathematics, where boys' advantage has remained constant (Feingold, 1993). This trend is a reminder that sex differences are not fixed for all time. The general picture of how boys and girls differ may not be the same in a few decades as it is today.

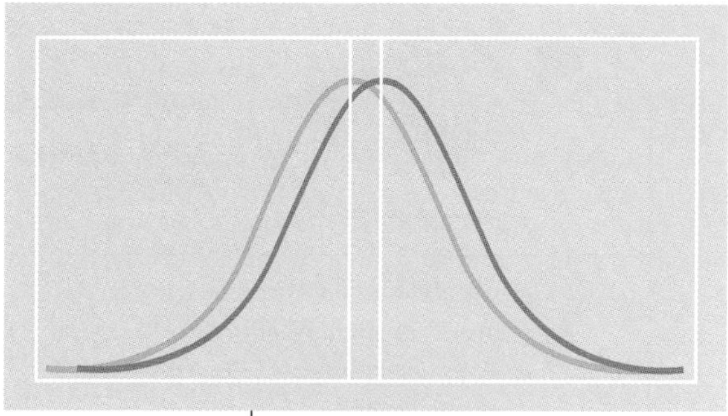

## MENTAL ABILITIES

Sex differences in mental abilities have sparked almost as much controversy as the ethnic and SES differences in IQ considered in Chapter 8. Although boys and girls do not differ in general intelligence, they do vary in specific mental abilities. Many researchers believe that heredity is involved in the disparities, and they have attempted to identify the specific biological processes responsible. But no biological factor operates in an experiential vacuum. For each ability we will consider, environment plays an important role.

**VERBAL ABILITIES.** Early in development, girls are ahead in language progress. They begin to talk earlier and show faster vocabulary growth during the second year, after which boys catch up (see Chapter 9). Throughout the school years, girls attain higher scores on reading and writing achievement tests and account for a lower percentage of children referred for remedial reading instruction (Campbell, Hombo, & Mazzeo, 2000; Halpern, 2000). Girls' advantage on tests of general verbal ability is still present in adolescence. However, it has declined over time and currently is so slight that it is not meaningful (Hyde & Linn, 1988).

In Chapter 9, we noted that girls' early advantage in language skills may be fostered by their faster rate of physical maturation, believed to promote earlier development of the left hemisphere of the cerebral cortex, where language functions usually are localized (see Chapter 5). In animals and humans, the left side of the cerebral cortex is slightly larger and more mature in females than in males (Diamond et al., 1983).

Although biology may contribute to girls' superior language and reading performance, experience also seems to be important. Recall that mothers talk much more to toddler-age girls than to toddler-age boys (see Chapter 9). Furthermore, children think of reading as a feminine subject, parents rate daughters as more competent at it, and elementary school classrooms are feminine-biased settings in which boys' greater activity level and noncompliance lead them to be targets of teacher disapproval. Perhaps girls write more fluently than boys because they spend more time reading and generalize what they learn to written expression (Hedges & Nowell, 1995).

**MATHEMATICAL ABILITIES.** Sex differences in mathematical ability are apparent by grade 2 among academically talented students. By adolescence, an overall difference between boys and girls exists (Bielinski & Davison, 1998; Linn & Hyde, 1989). When all students are considered, the size of the difference is small. But among the most capable, the gender gap is considerable. In some widely publicized research on more than 40 000 bright seventh and eighth graders who were invited to take the Scholastic Aptitude Test (SAT) long before they needed to do so for college admission, boys outscored girls on the mathematics subtest year after year. Twice as many boys as girls had scores above 500; 13 times as many scored over 700 (Benbow & Stanley, 1983; Lubinski & Benbow, 1994). However, sex differences show up only on some test items. Boys and girls do equally well in basic math knowledge, and girls do better in computational skills. The difference appears in abstract reasoning, primarily on complex word problems and geometry (Hyde, Fenema, & Lamon, 1990).

A subgroup of the academically talented students just mentioned—those whose SAT math scores were in the top 1 percent for 12- to 14-year-olds—were followed into adulthood. Both sexes demonstrated high achievement, earning bachelor's, master's, and doctoral degrees at far higher rates than in the general population. But the occupations they chose were consistent with early sex differences in math ability. Men entered engineering, math,

**FIGURE 13.11**

**Typical distributions of scores in studies comparing males and females on mental abilities and personality traits.** For most characteristics, the distributions overlap greatly. This means that males and females are actually much more alike than different.

# biology & environment

## SEX DIFFERENCES IN SPATIAL ABILITIES

Spatial abilities have become a key focus of researchers' efforts to explain sex differences in mathematical reasoning. Clear sex differences on some spatial tasks exist by age 4 (Levine et al., 1999). From middle childhood on, the gender gap favouring males is large for *mental rotation tasks,* in which individuals must rotate a three-dimensional figure rapidly and accurately inside their heads (see Figure 13.12). In addition, males do considerably better on *spatial perception tasks,* in which people must determine spatial relationships by considering the orientation of the surrounding environment. Sex differences on *spatial visualization tasks,* involving analysis of complex visual forms, are weak or nonexistent, perhaps because many strategies can be used to solve them. Both sexes may come up with effective procedures (Linn & Petersen, 1985; Voyer, Voyer, & Bryden, 1995).

Sex differences in spatial abilities emerge by middle childhood and persist throughout the lifespan (Kerns & Berenbaum, 1991). The pattern is consistent enough to suggest a biological explanation. One hypothesis is that heredity, through prenatal exposure to androgen hormones, enhances right hemispheric functioning, granting males a spatial advantage. (Recall that for

This girl is probably the only female enrolled in her high school metal shop class. Experience with manipulative activities, including model building and carpentry, contribute to gender differences in spatial abilities. Superior spatial skills and confidence at doing math, in turn, contribute to the ease with which young people solve complex math problems.

© BOB DAEMMRICH/STOCK BOSTON

most people, spatial skills are housed in the right hemisphere of the cerebral cortex.) Consistent with this idea, girls and women whose prenatal androgen levels were abnormally high show superior performance on mental rotation tasks (Berenbaum, 2001; Collaer & Hines, 1995). And people with severe prenatal deficits in either male or female hormones have difficulty with spatial reasoning (Hier & Crowley, 1982; Temple & Carney, 1995).

Research on hormone variations within normal range is less clear. Although many studies report a relation between androgens and spatial abilities, not all do. And when a relationship is found, it is not always straightforward (Geary, 1998). But consistent with a biological contribution, boys show more rapid development of the right hemisphere of the cerebral cortex than do girls (Breedlove, 1994).

Why might a biologically based gender difference in spatial abilities exist? Evolutionary theorists point out that mental rotation skill predicts rapid, accurate map drawing and interpretation, in which males are advantaged. During human evolution, the cognitive abilities of males became adapted for hunting, which required generating mental representations of large-scale spaces to find one's way within those

physical science, and computer science careers at higher rates than women, who surpassed men in entering medicine and other health professions (Benbow et al., 2000).

Some researchers believe that the gender gap in mathematics—especially the tendency for many more boys to be extremely talented in math—is genetic. Accumulating evidence suggests that sex differences in mathematical ability are rooted in boys' biologically based superior spatial reasoning. See the Biology & Environment box above for a discussion of this issue.

Although heredity is involved, social pressures have also contributed to girls' underrepresentation among the mathematically talented. The mathematics gender gap is related to student attitudes and self-esteem. Earlier in this chapter, we noted that long before sex differences in math achievement are present, children often view math as a masculine subject, and many parents believe boys are better at it. Furthermore, girls regard math as less useful environments (Moffat, Hampson, & Hatzipantelis, 1998).

Although biology is involved in males' superior spatial performance, experience also makes a difference. Children who engage in manipulative activities, such as block play, model building, and carpentry, do better on spatial tasks (Baenninger & Newcombe, 1995). Furthermore, playing video games that require rapid mental rotation of visual images enhances spatial scores of boys and girls alike (Okagaki & Frensch, 1996; Subrahmanyam & Greenfield, 1996). Boys spend far more time at all these pursuits than do girls. At the same time, research suggests a genetic–environmental correlation—that is, young people with a spatial skill advantage more often seek out spatial activities. When girls with one or more left-handed close relatives (suggesting a genetic, right-hemispheric bias) grow up with brothers and, therefore, in homes rich in spatial activities, they excel at mental rotation tasks (Casey, Nuttall, & Pezaris, 1999).

Do superior spatial skills contribute to the greater ease with which males solve complex math problems? Research indicates that they do (Casey et al., 1995). Yet in a study of high-ability university-bound adolescents, *both* mental rotation ability and self-confidence

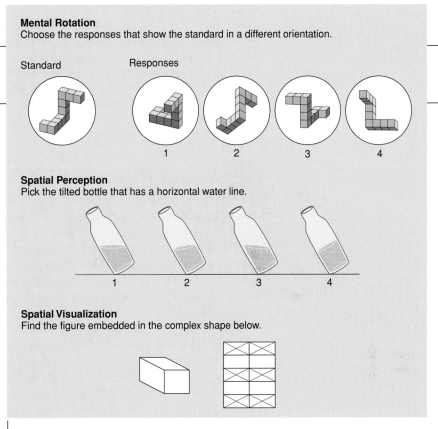

**Mental Rotation**
Choose the responses that show the standard in a different orientation.

Standard    Responses
1  2  3  4

**Spatial Perception**
Pick the tilted bottle that has a horizontal water line.

1  2  3  4

**Spatial Visualization**
Find the figure embedded in the complex shape below.

**FIGURE** 13.12

**Types of spatial tasks.** Large sex differences favouring males appear on mental rotation, and males do considerably better than females on spatial perception. In contrast, sex differences on spatial visualization are weak or nonexistent. (From M. C. Linn & A. C. Petersen, 1985, "Emergence and Characterization of Sex Differences in Spatial Ability: A Meta-Analysis," *Child Development, 56,* pp. 1482, 1483, 1485. © The Society for Research in Child Development, Inc. Reprinted by permission.)

at doing math predicted higher scores on the math subtest of the SAT (Casey, Nuttall, & Pezaris, 1997). Boys are advantaged not only in mental rotation but in math self-confidence. Even when their grades are poorer than girls', boys judge themselves to be better at math (Eccles et al., 1993a). In sum, biology and environment *jointly* determine variations in spatial and math performance—within and between the sexes.

for their future lives, perceive themselves as having to work harder at it to do well, and more often blame their errors on lack of ability. These beliefs, in turn, lead girls to become less interested in math and to be less likely to consider math- or science-related careers (Byrnes & Takahira, 1993; Catsambis, 1994). The result of this chain of events is that girls—even those who are highly talented academically—are less likely to develop abstract mathematical concepts and effective problem-solving strategies.

A positive sign, however, is that sex differences in mathematical reasoning, as in the verbal arena, have declined steadily over the past several decades. Paralleling this change is an increase in girls' enrolment in advanced math and science courses. Today, boys and girls reach advanced levels of high school math and science study in equal proportions—a crucial factor in reducing sex differences in knowledge and skill (Campbell, Hombo, & Mazzeo, 2000).

Clearly, extra steps must be taken to promote girls' interest in and confidence at math and science. By the end of high school, sex differences in attitudes are much larger than in test performance. When parents hold nonstereotyped values, daughters are less likely to show declines in math and science achievement at adolescence (Updegraff, McHale, & Crouter, 1996). In schools, teachers must demonstrate the relevance of math and science to everyday life. Girls, especially, respond positively to math and science taught from an applied, hands-on perspective (Eccles, 1994). At the same time, teachers must ensure that girls participate fully in hands-on group activities and are not reduced to a passive role by boys' more assertive style of peer interaction (Jovanovic & King, 1998).

## PERSONALITY TRAITS

Sex differences in personality are in line with gender stereotypes. Traits most often studied include emotional sensitivity, compliance and dependency, depression, and aggression.

**EMOTIONAL SENSITIVITY.** Females are more emotionally sensitive than are males, a difference that appears quite early. Beginning in the preschool years, girls perform slightly better than boys when asked to judge others' emotional states using nonverbal cues (Hall, 1978). Except for anger, girls also express feelings more freely and intensely in everyday interaction (Geary, 1998).

It would be reasonable to expect these differences to extend to empathy, sympathy, and prosocial behaviour, but so far the evidence is mixed. On self-report measures, girls and women consistently score higher than boys and men. When observed for behavioural signs, however, 1- to 2-year-old girls display greater concern for a distressed person than do boys, but youngsters from preschool age through adolescence show no difference. Girls show a slight advantage in prosocial responding. It is greatest for being kind and considerate, very small for helping another (Eisenberg & Fabes, 1998). And in line with their greater motivation to be nice to others, after being given an undesirable gift, school-age girls more often than boys hide their negative feelings and act pleased (McDowell, O'Neil, & Parke, 2000).

As with other attributes, both biological and environmental explanations for sex differences in emotional sensitivity exist. One evolutionary account is that females are genetically prewired to be more emotionally sensitive as a way of ensuring that they will be well prepared for the caregiving role. Yet research suggests that girls are not naturally more nurturant. Before age 5, boys and girls spend equal amounts of time talking to and playing with babies (Fogel et al., 1987). In middle childhood, Caucasian boys' willingness to relate to infants declines. Yet African-American boys, who endorse fewer gender stereotypes, smile, touch, and look at babies as much as girls do (Reid & Trotter, 1993). Furthermore, sex differences in emotional sensitivity are not present in adulthood when parents interact with their babies. In Chapter 10, we saw that fathers are very affectionate with infants and are just as competent at caregiving as mothers. And in Chapter 4, we noted that men and women react similarly to the sound of a crying baby.

Cultural expectations that girls be warm and expressive and boys be distant and controlled seem largely responsible for the gender gap in emotional sensitivity. In infancy, mothers respond more often to a girl's happiness and distress than to a boy's (Malatesta et al., 1986). And during childhood, parents are more likely to rely on inductive discipline with girls (which promotes sympathetic concern) and to pressure girls to be thoughtful and caring (Block, 1978; Zahn-Waxler, Cole, & Barrett, 1991). In addition, recall that parents spend more time talking about emotions when conversing with daughters. Taken together, these findings suggest that girls receive far more encouragement to express and reflect on feelings than boys do.

© CAMILLE TOKERUD/PHOTO RESEARCHERS, INC.

Girls' greater emotional sensitivity is probably environmentally determined, since boys are just as caring and affectionate in certain situations—for example, when interacting with a cherished pet.

**COMPLIANCE AND DEPENDENCY.** Begin-ning in the preschool years, girls are more com-pliant than are boys, to both adult and peer demands. Girls also seek help and information from adults more often and score higher in dependency on personality tests (Feingold, 1994). There is widespread agreement that these patterns of behaviour are learned, and they have much to do with the activity environments in which boys and girls spend their time.

From an early age, girls are encouraged into adult-structured activities at home and school and, consequently, spend more time near adults. In contrast, boys are attracted to activities in which adults are minimally involved or entirely absent (Powlishta, Serbin, & Moller, 1993). Compliance and bids for help and attention appear more often in adult-structured contexts, whereas assertiveness, leadership, and creative use of materials occur more often in unstructured pursuits (Carpenter, 1983).

Ideally, boys and girls should experience a balanced array of activities to develop the capacity to lead and assert as well as to comply with others' directives. In one study, the assertive and compliant tendencies of preschoolers of both sexes were easily modified by assigning them to classroom activities that differed in adult structure (Carpenter, Huston, & Holt, 1986).

**DEPRESSION.** Depression—feeling sad, frustrated, and hopeless about life, accompanied by loss of pleasure in most activities and disturbances in sleep, appetite, concentration, and energy—is the most common psychological problem of adolescence. About 15 to 20 percent of teenagers have had one or more major depressive episodes (a rate comparable to that of adults). From 2 to 8 percent are chronically depressed—gloomy and self-critical for many months and sometimes years (Birmaher et al., 1996; Kessler et al., 1994). As Figure 13.13 shows, depressive symptoms increase sharply around the time of puberty. They occur twice as often in adolescent girls as in adolescent boys—a difference sustained throughout the lifespan. And if allowed to persist, depression seriously impairs social, academic, and vocational func-tioning (Nolen-Hoeksema, 2001).

Researchers believe that diverse combinations of biological and environmental factors lead to depression; the precise blend differs from one individual to the next. As we saw in Chapter 3, kinship studies of identical and fraternal twins reveal that heredity plays an important role. Genes can promote depression by affecting the balance of neurotransmitters in the brain, the development of brain regions involved in inhibiting negative emotion, or the body's hormonal response to stress (Cicchetti & Toth, 1998a).

But experience can also activate depression, promoting any of the biological changes just described. Parents of depressed children and adolescents have a high incidence of depression and other psychological disorders. Although a genetic risk may be passed from parent to child, in earlier chapters we saw that depressed or otherwise stressed parents often engage in maladaptive parenting. As a result, their child's emotional self-regulation, attachment, and self-esteem may be impaired, with serious consequences for many cognitive and social skills (Garber, Braafladt, & Weiss, 1995; Garber et al., 1991). Depressed youths usually display a learned-helpless attributional style, in which they view positive academic and social out-comes as beyond their control. Consequently, myriad events can spark depression in a vul-nerable young person—for example, failing at something important, parental divorce, or the end of a close friendship or romantic partnership.

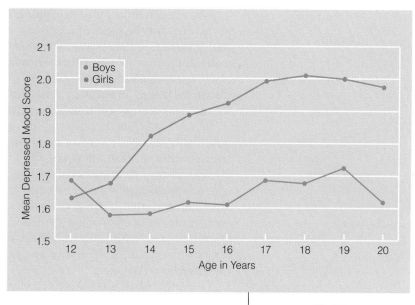

**FIGURE** 13.13

**Change in depressive symp-toms from age 12 to 20 in a cross-sectional study of more than 12,000 Norwegian adolescents.** Girls showed a more rapid rise in depression around the time of puberty than did boys. Sim-ilar trends occur in other industrial-ized nations. (From L. Wichstrøm, 1999, "The Emergence of Gender Difference in Depressed Mood During Adolescence: The Role of Intensified Gender Socialization," *Developmental Psychology, 35*, p. 237. Copyright © 1999 by the American Psychological Associa-tion. Reprinted by permission of the publisher and author.)

Why are girls more prone to depression? Biological changes associated with puberty cannot account for the gender gap, since it is limited to industrialized nations. In developing countries, rates of depression are similar for males and females and occasionally higher for males (Culbertson, 1997). Even in countries with a gender difference, its size varies considerably. For example, the gender difference favouring depression in females is smaller in China than in the United States. Decades of efforts by the Chinese government to eliminate gender inequalities may have contributed to this finding (Greenberger et al., 2000).

Research suggests that stressful life events and gender-typed coping styles account for girls' higher rates of depression. Early maturing girls are especially prone to depression, particularly when they face other stressful life events (Ge, Conger, & Elder, 2001). The gender intensification girls experience at puberty often strengthens passivity and dependency—maladaptive approaches to the challenges teenagers encounter in complex cultures (Nolen-Hoeksema & Girgus, 1994). Consistent with this explanation, teenagers who identify strongly with "feminine" traits are more depressed, regardless of their sex (Hart & Thompson, 1996; Wichstrøm, 1999). And girls with either an androgynous or masculine gender identity show a much lower rate of depressive symptoms—one no different from that of masculine-identified boys (Wilson & Cairns, 1988).

Currently, researchers believe that biological and environmental factors join in a bidirectional fashion to induce higher rates of depression in adolescent girls and adult women (Nolen-Hoeksema, 2001). As girls experience more stressful life events—due to learned helplessness, gender intensification, reduced power in relationships with romantic partners, and a "feminine" orientation that can lead them to subordinate their own needs to those of others—they develop an overly reactive physiological stress response (Young & Korzun, 1999). When stress occurs in the future, they increasingly feel overwhelmed and cope poorly. In this way, stressful experiences and stress reactivity feed on one another, thereby sustaining depression.

Unfortunately teachers and parents tend to minimize the seriousness of teenagers' depressive symptoms. Because of the popular stereotype of adolescence as a period of storm and stress, many adults interpret adolescent depression as just a passing phase. Yet without intervention that improves coping strategies and reduces hyperresponsiveness to stress, adolescent depression is likely to evolve into a lifelong pattern.

**AGGRESSION.** Aggression has attracted more research attention than any other sex difference. In Chapter 12, we noted that boys are more overtly aggressive than are girls. But recall that preschool and school-age girls exceed boys in another form of hostility—relational aggression. As Figure 13.14 shows, the percentage of girls who often engage in rumour spreading and exclusion, in an effort to disrupt the closeness of other girls' friendships, is just as great as the percentage of boys who frequently engage in direct attacks (Crick & Grotpeter, 1995). Since most research focuses on physical and verbal assaults, it underestimates girls' aggressiveness.

Look again at Figure 13.14, and you will see that a few children are gender-atypical: girls who display high overt aggression, boys who display high relational aggression. As we saw in Chapter 12, gender-typical aggressive boys suffer from peer and academic difficulties. But gender-atypical aggressors have more severe emotional and behaviour problems (Crick, 1997). Children who violate their gender role in the realm of aggression may be targets of especially intolerant

**FIGURE** 13.14

**Percentage of boys and girls who often used overt and relational aggression in a study of third through sixth graders.** Boys expressed their antagonism directly, through physical and verbal attacks. In contrast, girls used indirect forms of aggression aimed at damaging another's peer relationships. When both types of aggression are considered, girls are just as aggressive as boys. (Adapted from Crick & Grotpeter, 1995.)

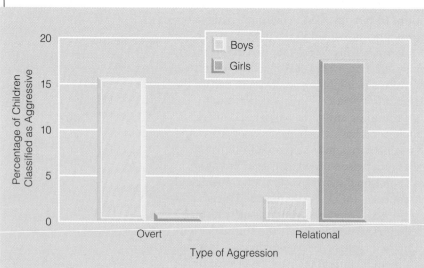

and rejecting feedback from adults and peers—reactions that compound their adjustment difficulties.

Our discussion of the origins of sex differences in aggression focuses on overt verbal and physical acts. At present, little is known about factors that contribute to relational aggression.

*Biological Influences.* Because males' greater overt aggression is evident early in life, generalizes across cultures, and is found in many animal species, almost all researchers agree that biology must be involved. Earlier we mentioned that androgen hormones are related to aggression in animals; they are also believed to play a role in humans. But think back to our discussion of children with CAH. Although they were exposed prenatally to abnormally high androgen levels, they were not more aggressive. This suggests that in humans, only a predisposition for aggression results from androgen exposure. Researchers believe that the impact of male sex hormones is indirect. That is, androgens affect certain behaviours that, when combined with situational influences, lead to a higher likelihood of aggressive outcomes.

One possibility is that prenatal androgens promote physical activity, which may or may not be translated into aggression, depending on the situation (Archer, 1994). For example, an active, competitive child who often participates in large-group activities might become more overtly aggressive than a child who participates in small-group pursuits. To explore this idea, researchers brought kindergartners and first graders to a laboratory where some played a game in same-sex pairs and others in same-sex tetrads (groups of four). In the game, children rolled a die, which indicated how many beads they could take, and they could choose to take them from either a common pile (a noncompetitive move) or another player (a competitive move). Group size had no impact on girls' competitive behaviour. In contrast, boys displayed nearly twice as many competitive moves in tetrads as in dyads (Benenson et al., 2001). Recall that compared with girls, boys spend much more time playing in large groups—an attraction, according to evolutionary theorists, adapted to preparing them for the competitive adult life of their male ancestors. Large groups, in turn, serve as contexts in which competition may promote aggression.

Another hypothesis is that sex hormones influence brain functioning in ways that affect children's emotional reactions. According to this view, hormone levels might induce more frequent displays of excitement, anger, or anxiety, which might result in aggression in the presence of certain environmental conditions. In line with this idea, adolescent boys with high androgen levels are more dominant and, perhaps for this reason, likely to respond with aggression when provoked by peers (Olweus et al., 1988; Tremblay et al., 1997). In one study, higher estrogens and androgens were linked to more frequent expressions of anger by adolescent girls in a laboratory discussion session with their parents (Inoff-Germain et al., 1988).

Although more research is needed, current evidence suggests that multiple pathways exist between sex hormones and overt aggression, and that each involves several steps. It is also clear that environmental conditions have much to do with whether hormonally induced responses are channelled into aggressive acts.

*Environmental Influences.* In Chapter 12, we showed how coercive child-rearing practices and strife-ridden families promote aggressive behaviour. For several reasons, boys are more likely to be affected by these interaction patterns than girls. Parents more often use physical punishment with boys, which encourages boys to adopt the same tactics in their own relationships. In addition, parents are less likely to interpret fighting as aggressive when it occurs among boys. The stereotype reflected in the saying "Boys will be boys" may lead many adults to overlook male hostility unless it is extreme. This sets up conditions in which it is encouraged, or at least tolerated (Condry & Ross, 1985). In view of these findings, it is not surprising that school-age boys expect less parental disapproval and report feeling less guilty for overt aggression than do girls (Perry, Perry, & Weiss, 1989).

Furthermore, arguing between husband and wife, although stimulating aggression among all family members, more often triggers hostility in boys. In a study in which 2-year-olds overheard angry verbal exchanges between adults while playing with a familiar peer in a laboratory, girls tended to show fearful, withdrawing reactions, such as freezing in place and covering or hiding their faces. In contrast, boys engaged in more aggression, lashing out at their playmates (Cummings, Iannotti, & Zahn-Waxler, 1985). During the school years, boys report feeling more hostile than do girls after observing adults' angry exchanges (Hennessy, Rabideau, & Cicchetti, 1994).

Putting together all the evidence, we can see that boys have a higher likelihood of becoming embroiled in circumstances that serve as a training ground for aggressive and antisocial behaviour. Biological predispositions and encouragement from the social environment are jointly responsible.

# Developing Non-Gender-Stereotyped Children

WE HAVE SEEN THAT children's developmental possibilities can be seriously limited by persistent gender stereotypes in their culture. Although many researchers and lay people recognize the importance of rearing children who feel free to express their human qualities without fear of violating gender-role expectations, no easy recipe exists for accomplishing this difficult task. It must be tackled on many fronts—in the home, at school, and in the wider society.

Biology clearly affects children's gender typing, channelling boys toward active, competitive play and girls toward quieter, more intimate interaction—a difference that leads each sex, on the average, to seek out activities and social experiences consistent with those predispositions. But the substantial revisions in gender roles and relationships between the sexes over previous generations—along with wide individual, family, and cultural variations in gender typing—reveal that most aspects of gender typing are not built into human nature as a result of evolution (Maccoby, 2000). And a long human childhood ensures that experiences can greatly influence biologically based differences between the sexes (Geary & Bjorklund, 2000).

Throughout our discussion, we have mentioned ways in which gender stereotyping and gender-role adoption can be reduced. But even children who are fortunate enough to grow up in homes and schools that minimize stereotyping will eventually encounter it in the media and in what men and women typically do in their communities. Consequently, children need early experiences that repeatedly counteract their readiness to absorb our culture's extensive network of gender-linked associations.

Sandra Bem (1993, 1998) suggests that parents and teachers make a special effort to delay young children's learning of gender-stereotyped messages, since preschoolers readily assume that cultural practices determine a person's gender. Adults can begin by eliminating traditional gender roles from their own behaviour and from the alternatives they provide for children. For example, mothers and fathers can take turns making dinner, bathing children, and driving the family car, and they can provide sons and daughters with both trucks and dolls and pink and blue clothing. Teachers can make sure that all children spend some time each day in adult-structured and unstructured activities. Also, efforts can be made to shield children from media presentations that indicate males and females differ in what they can do.

Once children notice the wide array of gender stereotypes in their society, parents and teachers can point out exceptions. For example, they can arrange for children to see men and women pursuing nontraditional careers. And they can reason with children, explaining that interests and skills, not sex, should determine a person's occupation. Furthermore, older children can be told about the historical roots and current consequences of gender inequalities—why, for example, there have been few female prime ministers and presidents, why fathers rarely stay home with their children, and why stereotyped views of men and women are hard to change. As these efforts help children build concepts of themselves and their social world that are not limited by a masculine–feminine dichotomy, they contribute to the transformation of societal values. And they bring us closer to a time when people will be released from the constraints of traditional gender roles.

## ASK YOURSELF

**review** Cite evidence indicating that both biological and environmental factors contribute to girls' early advantage in verbal abilities and boys' superior performance in mathematical reasoning.

**review** Explain the *indirect* link between androgen hormones and boys' greater overt aggression, noting the influence of both family and peer-group experiences.

**apply** Thirteen-year-old Donna reached puberty early and feels negatively about her physical appearance. She also has a feminine gender identity. Explain why Donna is at risk for depression.

**connect** Using Bronfenbrenner's ecological systems theory (see Chapter 1, page 28), describe steps that can be taken at each level of the environment to reduce gender stereotyping in children.

# summary

*Explain how the study of gender typing has responded to societal change.*

■ Largely because of progress in women's rights, the adoption of gender-typed beliefs and behaviour is no longer regarded as essential for healthy psychological development. Researchers are more interested in how children might be released from gender-based definitions of appropriate behaviour.

## GENDER STEREOTYPES AND GENDER ROLES

*Cite examples of gender stereotypes, and describe the development of gender stereotyping from early childhood into adolescence.*

■ Despite recent progress in women's rights, gender stereotypes have remained essentially the same. **Instrumental traits** continue to be regarded as masculine, **expressive traits** as feminine—a dichotomy that is widely held around the world. Stereotyping of physical characteristics, occupations, and activities is also common.

■ Children begin to acquire **gender stereotypes** and **gender roles** early in the preschool years. As gender categories form, gender-stereotyped beliefs and behaviours

increase rapidly. By middle childhood, children are aware of many stereotypes, including those that focus on activities, occupations, personality traits, and achievement areas. Because of cognitive limitations, preschoolers' understanding of gender stereotypes is inflexible. Gains in **gender-stereotype flexibility** occur during middle childhood and adolescence; children develop a more open-minded view of what males and females can do, although they often do not approve of males who violate gender-role expectations.

*Cite individual and group differences in gender stereotyping, and discuss the relationship of gender stereotyping to gender-role adoption.*

■ Children acquire the components of gender stereotyping—activities, behaviours, occupations, and personality traits—in different patterns and to different degrees. Boys hold more rigid gender-stereotyped views than do girls, and middle-SES adolescents and adults hold more flexible views than do their lower-SES counterparts.

■ Awareness of gender stereotypes is only weakly related to gender-role adoption. Stereotype flexibility, however, is a moderately good predictor of children's willingness to cross gender lines during the school years.

## INFLUENCES ON GENDER STEREOTYPING AND GENDER-ROLE ADOPTION

*Discuss the role of biology in gender stereotyping and gender-role adoption, including cross-cultural evidence and the influence of hormones.*

■ According to an evolutionary perspective, human history led males to be genetically primed for dominance and females for intimacy, responsiveness, and cooperation. Cross-cultural similarities in gender stereotypes and gender-role adoption have been used to support the role of biology in **gender typing.** However, great diversity exists in the extent to which cultures endorse the instrumental–expressive dichotomy and encourage conformity to traditional gender roles.

■ Prenatal androgen levels contribute to gender differences in play styles and children's preference for same-sex playmates. Research on children with congenital adrenal hyperplasia (CAH) supports the role of androgens in certain aspects of "masculine" gender-role adoption. CAH girls prefer vehicle and building toys and boys as play partners. However, other gender-role preferences of CAH children seem responsive to environmental pressures. In instances in which children are reared as members of the other sex because of ambiguous genitals caused by a prenatal hormone imbalance, gender typing is usually consistent with sex of rearing, regardless of genetic sex. However, when biological makeup and sex of rearing are at odds, children seem to experience serious adjustment problems.

*Discuss environmental influences on gender stereotyping and gender-role adoption, including expectations and treatment by parents, teachers, and peers; observational learning; and the impact of siblings.*

■ Beginning in infancy, adults hold gender-stereotyped perceptions and expectations of boys and girls and create different environments for them. By the preschool years, parents reinforce their children for many "gender-appropriate" play activities and behaviours. During middle childhood, they demand greater independence from boys in achievement situations, hold gender-stereotyped beliefs about children's abilities in various school subjects, and grant boys more freedom in their everyday lives. Fathers differentiate between boys and girls more than mothers do. Also, each parent takes special responsibility for the gender typing of the same-sex child.

■ Teachers reinforce children of both sexes for "feminine" behaviour and also act in ways that promote traditional gender roles. Besides direct pressure from adults, children have many opportunities to observe gender-typed models in the surrounding environment. When children are exposed to nonstereotyped models, such as parents who cross traditional gender lines in household tasks or career choice, they are less traditional in their beliefs and behaviours.

■ When interacting with children of their own sex, boys and girls receive further reinforcement for "gender-appropriate" play, come to believe in the appropriateness of having same-sex playmates, and develop different styles of social influence. Boys more often rely on commands, threats, and physical force, girls on polite requests and persuasion—differences that strengthen gender segregation.

■ The impact of siblings on gender typing varies with birth order and family size. In small, two-child families, younger children tend to imitate the gender-role behaviour of their older sibling. In larger families, same-sex siblings often strive to be different from one another. Consequently, they are likely to be less stereotyped in their interests and personality traits.

## GENDER IDENTITY

*Explain the meaning of androgyny, and describe and evaluate the accuracy of social learning and cognitive-developmental views of the development of gender identity in early childhood.*

■ Researchers measure **gender identity** by asking children and adults to rate themselves on "masculine" and "feminine" personality traits. Although most people have traditional identities, some are **androgynous,** scoring high on both masculine and feminine characteristics. At present, the masculine component of androgyny is largely responsible for its association with superior psychological adjustment.

■ According to social learning theory, preschoolers first acquire gender-typed responses through modelling and reinforcement and only later organize the responses into cognitions about themselves. Cognitive-developmental theory suggests that **gender constancy** must be achieved before children can develop gender-typed behaviour.

■ Children master gender constancy by moving through three stages: **gender labelling, gender stability,** and **gender consistency.** Understanding of gender constancy is associated with attainment of conservation and opportunities to learn about genital differences between the sexes. In contrast to cognitive-developmental predictions, "gender-appropriate" behaviour is acquired long before gender constancy. However, other cognitive attainments—gender labelling and gender stability—strengthen preschoolers' gender-role adoption.

*What changes in gender identity typically occur in middle childhood and adolescence?*

■ During middle childhood, boys strengthen their identification with the "masculine"

role, whereas girls become more androgynous. The greater prestige of "masculine" characteristics makes them attractive to girls. At the same time, parents and peers are more tolerant of girls as opposed to boys crossing gender lines.

■ Early adolescence is a period of **gender intensification:** the gender identities of both sexes become more traditional. Physical and cognitive changes prompt young teenagers to spend more time thinking about themselves in gender-linked ways, and gender-typed pressures from parents and peers increase. As young people move toward a mature personal identity, highly stereotypic self-perceptions decline. Individual differences in gender identity persist that are moderately related to gender-role behaviour.

*Explain how gender schema theory accounts for the persistence of gender stereotypes and gender-role preferences.*

■ **Gender schema theory** is an information-processing approach to gender typing that combines social learning and cognitive-developmental features. As children learn gender-typed preferences and behaviours, they form masculine and feminine categories, or gender schemas, that they apply to themselves and use to interpret their world. Schema-consistent information is attended to and approached, whereas schema-inconsistent information is ignored, misinterpreted, or actively rejected. As a result, children learn much more about "gender-appropriate" than "gender-inappropriate" activities and behaviours.

## TO WHAT EXTENT DO BOYS AND GIRLS *REALLY* DIFFER IN GENDER-STEREOTYPED ATTRIBUTES?

*Describe sex differences in mental abilities and personality attributes, noting factors that contribute to those differences.*

■ Most sex differences in mental abilities and personality traits are small to moderate. Girls are ahead in early language development, score better in reading and writing achievement, are more prone to depression, and are more relationally aggressive. Boys are advantaged in certain spatial skills and complex mathematical reasoning. Boys also display more overt aggression, whereas girls engage in more relational aggression.

- Biological factors contribute to differences between boys and girls in language development and spatial and math performance. At the same time, adult encouragement and learning opportunities play strong roles. Girls' greater emotional sensitivity, compliance, and dependency are largely due to gender-stereotyped expectations and child-rearing practices.

- Depression is the most common psychological problem of the teenage years. The higher rate of severe depression in adolescent girls is the combined result of the challenges of adolescence and gender-typed coping styles. Gender intensification in early adolescence often strengthens passivity, dependency, and selflessness in girls, which interfere with their mastery of developmental tasks and their ability to handle stressful life events.

- Androgen hormones contribute to greater overt aggression in males. However, hormones exert their effects indirectly, by influencing activity level, emotional reactions, or dominance, which increase the likelihood of aggression under certain conditions. Powerful environmental influences on aggression include coercive child-rearing practices and strife-ridden families. Parents are more likely to use physical punishment with boys and to overlook their aggressive acts. In addition, boys react with greater hostility to parental arguments than do girls.

## DEVELOPING NON-GENDER-STEREOTYPED CHILDREN

*Cite ways to reduce gender stereotyping in children.*

- Most aspects of gender typing are not built into human nature. And for those that are genetically influenced, a long human childhood ensures that experience can greatly influence their intensity. Parents and teachers can counteract young children's readiness to absorb gender-linked associations by eliminating traditional gender roles from their own behaviour and from the alternatives they provide for children. They can also shield children from gender-stereotyped media messages. Once children notice gender stereotypes, adults can point out exceptions and discuss the arbitrariness of many gender inequalities in society.

# important terms and concepts

androgyny (p. 541)
expressive traits (p. 525)
gender consistency (p. 542)
gender constancy (p. 542)
gender identity (p. 524)

gender intensification (p. 545)
gender labelling (p. 542)
gender roles (p. 524)
gender schema theory (p. 545)
gender stability (p. 542)

gender-stereotype flexibility (p. 528)
gender stereotypes (p. 524)
gender typing (p. 524)
instrumental traits (p. 525)

"The Family and I"
Zeng Kaifeng
6 years, India

Reprinted with permission from
The International Museum of
Children's Art, Oslo, Norway

The warmth and closeness of family ties are central to this young artist's animated, expressive creation. As you will see in Chapter 14, parents and siblings exert powerful influences on all aspects of psychological development.

# *f*ourteen

## The Family

"I CAN'T REMEMBER MUCH family togetherness when I was a kid," 19-year-old Hannah reflected over dinner with Aunt Eva and Uncle Charlie. "Our parents couldn't talk things out with each other, and they rarely talked things out with us. We almost never sat down to a meal together or went places together; we each went our own way. Mom took me to Girl Guides, swimming, piano, and other lessons. I enjoyed the activities and the friends I made, but they couldn't compensate for warm, family time."

When Hannah was 9 years old, her parents divorced, and she moved with her mother from Saint John to Edmonton. Her father remained behind, and Hannah visited him once a year. To make ends meet, her mother worked weekdays, evenings, and most weekends. Many nights, Hannah opened a can of spaghetti, had dinner alone, and spent hours daydreaming and looking at old family pictures. She had difficulty concentrating, and her grades suffered. In high school, stormy relationships with several boyfriends left Hannah feeling rejected.

"I was at sea," Hannah recalled. "I didn't have any confidence in myself, and I didn't think I could do anything." When she got her driver's licence, Hannah began visiting her Aunt Eva and Uncle Charlie, who lived two hours away. They didn't need to do anything special to entertain her; she simply hungered to be part of their family. During these visits, Eva and Charlie helped Hannah think through her course schedule and advised on time management and peer problems. Hannah graduated a year later, attributing her turnabout in motivation and self-confidence to the connection forged with her aunt and uncle.

The family is the child's first, and longest lasting, context for development. Compared with other species, human children develop slowly, requiring years of support and teaching before they are ready to be independent. Our gradual journey to maturity has left an imprint on human social organization everywhere: Families are pervasive, and parents are universally important in children's lives. Many children without a satisfying, supportive family crave it. Some, like Hannah, find what they seek in extended family or another special adult.

Of course, other contexts also mould children's development, but in power and breadth of influence, none equals the family. The attachments children form with parents and siblings usually last a lifetime, and they serve as models for relationships in the wider world of neighbourhood and school. Within the family, children experience their first social conflicts. Discipline by parents and arguments with siblings provide important lessons in compliance and cooperation and opportunities to learn how to influence the behaviour of others. Finally, within the family, children learn the language, skills, and social and moral values of their culture.

We begin our discussion of the family by examining the reasons that this social unit came into being and has survived for thousands of years. Then we describe the current view of the family as a *social system* with many interacting influences on the child. Next, we look closely at the family as the core socializing agent of society. We consider child-rearing styles, the many factors that shape them, and their consequences for children's development.

In the second half of this chapter, we take up recent social changes that have led to a diversity of family lifestyles. Finally, the contemporary family is especially vulnerable to a breakdown in protective, emotionally supportive parent–child relationships. We conclude by considering the origins and consequences of child maltreatment.

# Evolutionary Origins

THE FAMILY IN ITS most common form—a lifelong commitment between a man and woman who feed, shelter, and nurture their children until they reach maturity—arose tens of thousands of years ago among our hunting-and-gathering ancestors. Many other species live in social groups, but rarely do they organize into family-like units. Only 3 percent of birds and mammals, for example, form families (Emlen, 1995). Even among monkeys and apes, our closest evolutionary ancestors, families are almost nonexistent (Lancaster & Witten, 1980).

Anthropologists believe that bipedalism—the ability to walk upright on two legs—was an important evolutionary step that led to the human family unit. Once arms were freed to carry things, our ancestors found it easier to cooperate and share, especially in providing for the young. Men usually travelled in search of game; women gathered fruit and vegetables as a temporary food supply when hunting was unsuccessful. The human family pattern in which a man and woman assumed special responsibility for their own children emerged because it enhanced survival. It ensured a relatively even balance of male hunters and female gatherers within a social group, thereby creating the greatest possible protection against starvation during times when game was scarce (Lancaster & Whitten, 1980).

Kinship groups expanded to include ties with other relatives, such as grandparents, aunts, uncles, and cousins, because larger kin networks offered greater chances for successful competition with other humans for resources. Within these clans, elders helped their children and other younger relatives reproduce by assisting with mate selection and child care. In this way, they increased the likelihood that their own genetic

A lifelong commitment between a man and woman who care for their young until they reach maturity arose tens of thousands of years ago among our hunting-and-gathering ancestors because it enhanced survival. This modern hunting-and-gathering mother of Central Africa cracks recently gathered nuts with her children while the father hunts for game.

© I. DEVORE/ANTHRO-PHOTO

heritage would continue (Geary, 1998). And because economic and social obligations among family members were so important for survival, strong emotional bonds evolved to foster long-term commitment among parents, children, and other relatives (Nesse, 1990; Williams, 1997).

##  Functions of the Family

BESIDES PROMOTING SURVIVAL of its members, the family unit of our evolutionary ancestors performed the following vital services for society:

- *Reproduction:* Replacing dying members.

- *Economic services:* Producing and distributing goods and services.

- *Social order:* Devising procedures for reducing conflict and maintaining order.

- *Socialization:* Training the young to become competent, participating members of society.

- *Emotional support:* Helping others surmount emotional crises and fostering in each person a sense of commitment and purpose.

In the early history of our species, families probably served all or most of these functions. But as societies became more complex, the demands placed on the family became too much for it to sustain alone. Consequently, other institutions developed to assist with certain functions, and families became linked to larger social structures. For example, political and legal institutions assumed responsibility for ensuring societal order, and schools built on the family's socialization function. Religious institutions supplemented both child-rearing and emotional support functions by offering family members educational services and a set of common beliefs that enhanced their sense of purpose (Parke & Kellam, 1994).

Finally, although some family members still carry out economic tasks together (as in family-run farms and businesses), this function has largely been taken over by institutions that make up the world of work. The modern family consumes far more goods and services than it produces. Consequently, whereas children used to contribute to families' economic well-being, today they are economic liabilities. According to 1996 Canadian census data, new parents will spend about $154 000 to rear a child from birth to age 18 and another $20 000 for university tuition—one factor that has contributed to the declining birth rate in industrialized nations (Vanier Institute of the Family, 2001).

Although some functions are shared with other institutions, three important ones especially concerned with children—reproduction, socialization, and emotional support—remain primarily the province of the family. Researchers interested in finding out how families fulfill these functions take a **social systems perspective,** viewing the family as a complex set of interacting relationships influenced by the larger social context.

##  The Family as a Social System

THE SOCIAL SYSTEMS perspective on family functioning grew out of researchers' efforts to describe and explain the complex patterns of interaction between family members. As we review its features, you will see that it has much in common with Bronfenbrenner's ecological systems theory, discussed in Chapter 1. Family systems theorists recognize that parents do not mechanically shape their children. You already know from earlier chapters that *bidirectional influences* exist, in which family members mutually influence one another. The very term *family system* implies that the responses of all family members are interrelated (Hart et al., 1997; Parke & Buriel, 1998). These system influences operate both directly and indirectly.

**social systems perspective**
A view of the family as a complex set of interacting relationships influenced by the larger social context.

## DIRECT INFLUENCES

Recently, as I passed through the checkout counter at the supermarket, I witnessed the following two episodes, in which parents and children directly influenced each other:

■ Little Danny stood next to tempting rows of candy as his mother lifted groceries from the cart onto the counter. "Pleeeease, can I have it, Mom?" begged Danny, holding up a large package of bubble gum. "Do you have a dollar? Just one?"

"No, not today," his mother answered softly. "Remember, we picked out your special cereal. That's what I need the dollar for." Danny's mother handed him the cereal while gently taking the bubble gum from his hand. "Here, let's pay the man," she said, as she lifted Danny so he could see the checkout counter.

■ Three-year-old Meg sat in the cart while her mother transferred groceries to the counter. Meg turned around, grabbed a bunch of bananas, and started to pull them apart.

"Stop it, Meg!" shouted her mom, who snatched the bananas from Meg's hand. Meg reached for a chocolate bar from a nearby shelf while her mother swiped her debit card. "Meg, how many times have I told you, DON'T TOUCH!" Loosening the candy from Meg's tight little grip, Meg's mother slapped her hand. Meg's face turned red with anger as she began to wail.

These observations fit with a wealth of research on the family system. Many studies show that when parents are firm but patient (like Danny's mom), children tend to comply with their requests. And when children cooperate, their parents are likely to be warm and gentle in the future. In contrast, parents who discipline with harshness and impatience (like Meg's mom) have children who refuse and rebel (Stormshak et al., 2000). And because children's misbehaviour is stressful for parents, they may increase their use of punishment, leading to more unruliness by the child (Dodge, Pettit, & Bates, 1994). In these examples, the behaviour of one family member helps sustain a form of interaction in another that either promotes or undermines children's well-being.

## INDIRECT INFLUENCES

The impact of family relationships on child development becomes even more complicated when we consider that interaction between any two members is affected by others present in the setting. Recall from Chapter 1 that Bronfenbrenner called these indirect influences the effect of *third parties*. Researchers have become intensely interested in how a range of relationships—mother with father, parent with sibling, grandparent with parent—modifies the child's direct experiences in the family (Hart et al., 1997). In fact, as the From Research to Practice box on page 565 reveals, a child's birth can have a third-party impact on parents' interaction, which may affect the child's development and well-being.

Third parties can serve as supports for children's development, or they can undermine it. For example, when parents' marital relationship is warm and considerate, mothers and fathers praise and stimulate their children more and nag and scold them less. In contrast, when a marriage is tense and hostile, parents tend to be less responsive to their children's needs and to criticize, express anger, and punish (Cox, Paley, & Harter, 2001; Erel & Burman, 1995). Children chronically exposed to parental conflict show myriad behaviour problems—both internalizing difficulties (especially among girls), such as blaming themselves, feeling worried and fearful, and trying to repair their parents' relationship; and externalizing difficulties (especially among boys), including feeling threatened and displaying more overt and relational aggression (Davies, Myers, & Cummings, 1996; Hart et al., 1998).

Yet even when parental arguments strain children's adjustment, other family members may help restore effective interaction. Grandparents are a case in point. As we will see later, they can promote children's development in many ways—both directly, by responding warmly and assisting with caregiving, and indirectly, by providing parents with child-rearing advice, models of child-rearing skill, and even financial assistance (Drew, Richard, & Smith, 1998). Of

# from research to practice

## THE TRANSITION TO PARENTHOOD

the early weeks after a baby enters the family are full of profound changes—disrupted sleep schedules, new caregiving and household tasks, less time for couples to devote to each other, and added financial responsibilities. In addition, the roles of husband and wife often become more traditional, even for couples who are strongly committed to gender equality and were used to sharing household tasks. Mothers spend more time at home with the baby, whereas fathers focus more on their provider role (Cowan & Cowan, 1997; Huston & Vangelisti, 1995). In one study, these changes were associated with a mild decline in marital happiness—one that exceeded that of childless couples, who also decline slightly in satisfaction as their marriage "settles in" (Cowan & Cowan, 2000).

For most new parents, however, the arrival of a baby does not cause significant marital strain. Marriages that are gratifying and supportive tend to remain so (Miller, 2000). In contrast, troubled marriages can become even more distressed after a baby is born. In a study of newlyweds who were interviewed annually for 6 years, the husband's affection, expression of "we-ness" (values and goals similar to his wife's), and awareness of his wife's daily life predicted mothers' stable or increasing marital satisfaction after childbirth. In contrast, the husband's negativity and the couples' out-of-control conflict predicted a drop in the mother's satisfaction (Shapiro, Gottman, & Carrere, 2000).

Also, the larger the difference in men's and women's caregiving responsibilities, the greater the rise in conflict and decline in marital satisfaction and mental health after childbirth, especially for women—with negative consequences for parent–infant interaction

(Hawkins et al., 1993; Levy-Shiff, 1994). In contrast, sharing caregiving tasks predicts greater sensitivity by both parents to their baby (Feldman, 2000).

Postponing childbearing until the late twenties or thirties eases the transition to parenthood. Waiting permits couples to pursue occupational goals and gain life experience (Taniguchi, 1999). Under these circumstances, men are more enthusiastic about becoming fathers and therefore more willing to participate. And women whose careers are under way are more likely to encourage their husbands to share housework and child care (Coltrane, 1990).

Special interventions exist to ease the transition to parenthood. For those who are not high risk for problems, couples' groups led by counsellors are highly effective (Cowan & Cowan, 1995). In one program, first-time expectant couples gathered once a week for 6 months to discuss their dreams for the family and changes in relationships sparked by the baby's arrival. Eighteen months after the program ended, participating fathers described themselves as more involved with their children than did fathers assigned to a no-intervention condition. Perhaps because of fathers' caregiving assistance, participating mothers maintained their prebirth satisfaction with family and work roles. Three years after the birth, the marriages of all participating couples were still intact and just as happy as they had been before parenthood. In contrast, 15 percent of couples receiving no intervention had divorced (Cowan & Cowan, 1997).

For high-risk parents struggling with poverty or the birth of a child with disabilities, interventions must be more intensive. Programs in which a trained intervenor visits the home and enhances social supports and the parent–child relationship have resulted

These parents settle their newborn daughter into her car seat for the trip home from the hospital. The transition to parenthood can enrich a warm, gratifying marriage or worsen a tense, unhappy marriage. Sharing caregiving tasks enhances marital satisfaction and is related to both parents' sensitivity toward their new baby.

in improved parent–infant interaction and benefits for children's cognitive and social development up to 5 years after the intervention (Meisels, Dichtelmiller, & Liaw, 1993).

Recent improvements to the Canadian government's parental leave policy should help ease the transition to parenthood (see Chapter 3, page 113). Flexible work hours are also helpful. When favourable workplace policies exist and couples try to support each other's needs, the stress caused by the birth of a baby stays at manageable levels. Family relationships are worked out after a few months, and most infants flourish, bringing great satisfaction to their parents and making the sacrifices of this period worthwhile.

course, like any indirect influence, grandparents can sometimes be harmful. When quarrelsome relations exist between grandparents and parents, children may suffer.

## ADAPTING TO CHANGE

Think back to the *chronosystem* in Bronfenbrenner's theory (see page 29). To make matters more complicated, the interplay of forces within the family must constantly adapt to the development of its members, since each changes throughout the lifespan.

As children acquire new skills, parents adjust the way they treat their more competent youngsters. To cite just one example, turn back to Chapter 4, page 139, and review how babies' mastery of crawling leads parents to engage in more game playing and expressions of affection as well as restriction of the child's activities. Then changes in child rearing pave the way for new achievements and further modifications in family relationships. Can you think of other illustrations of this idea, discussed in earlier chapters?

Parents' development affects children as well. Later we will see that the mild increase in parent–child conflict that often occurs in early adolescence is not solely due to teenagers' striving for independence and desire to explore new values and goals. Most parents are conscious that their adolescent youngsters will soon leave home and establish their own lives (Grotevant, 1998). Consequently, while the adolescent presses for greater autonomy, the parent may press for more togetherness. This imbalance promotes friction until parent and teenager accommodate to one another (Collins, 1997). In sum, no social unit other than the family is required to adjust to such vast changes in its members.

## THE FAMILY SYSTEM IN CONTEXT

The social systems perspective, as we noted earlier, views the family as affected by surrounding social contexts. As the *mesosystem* and *exosystem* in Bronfenbrenner's model make clear, connections to the neighbourhood and the larger community—in terms of *formal organizations,* such as school, workplace, child-care centre, and church or synagogue, as well as *informal social networks* of relatives, friends, and neighbours—influence parent–child relationships.

For example, child adjustment problems are highest in inner-city neighbourhoods where families move often, parks and playgrounds are in disarray, and community centres do not exist (Human Resources Development Canada, 2001). When lack of neighbourhood organization combines with little or no parent involvement, youth antisocial activity is especially high (Elliott et al., 1996; Sampson, 2000). In contrast, when family ties to the surrounding social context are strong—as indicated by regular church attendance and frequent contact with friends and relatives—family stress and child adjustment problems are reduced (Garbarino & Kostelny, 1993).

How do neighbourhood and community ties reduce stress and foster child development? One answer lies in their provision of social support, which leads to the following benefits:

■ *Parental interpersonal acceptance.* A neighbour or relative who listens and tries to relieve a parent's concern enhances her self-esteem. The parent, in turn, is likely to behave more sensitively toward her children. In one study of families experiencing economic strain, social networks affected parenting indirectly by reducing mothers' feelings of depression (Simons et al., 1993).

■ *Parental access to valuable information and services.* A friend who suggests where a job or housing might be found or who looks after children while the parent attends to other pressing needs helps make the multiple roles of spouse, provider, and caregiver easier to fulfill.

■ *Child-rearing controls and role models.* Friends, relatives, and other community members may encourage and demonstrate effective ways of interacting with children and discourage ineffective practices (Cochran, 1993).

■ *Direct assistance with child rearing.* As children participate in their parents' social networks and in child-oriented community activities, other adults can influence children directly through warmth, stimulation, and exposure to a wider array of competent

models. Those adults can also intervene when they see young people skipping school or behaving antisocially.

Neighbourhood resources have a greater impact on young people growing up in economically disadvantaged than well-to-do areas (Leventhal & Brooks-Gunn, 2000). Affluent families are not as dependent on their immediate surroundings for social support. They can afford to reach beyond the streets near their homes, transporting their children to lessons and entertainment and, if necessary, to better-quality schools (Elliott et al., 1996). In low-income neighbourhoods, after-school programs that substitute for lack of resources by providing enrichment activities are associated with improved school performance and psychological adjustment in middle childhood (Posner & Vandell, 1994; Vandell & Posner, 1999). Neighbourhood organizations and informal social activities predict many aspects of adolescents' psychological well-being, including self-confidence, school performance, and educational aspirations (Gonzales et al., 1996).

No researcher could possibly study all aspects of the social systems perspective on the family at once. But throughout this chapter, we will continually see examples of how its many interlocking parts combine to influence development.

According to the social systems perspective, ties to the community are essential for families to function at their best. These parents and children participate in a municipal project in which they plant trees along an expressway. As they beautify their community, they also form networks of social support.

## ASK YOURSELF

**review**   In our evolutionary history, why was the family adaptive?

**review**   Explain how, in the social systems perspective, the responses of all family members are interrelated.

**apply**   On a trip to a shopping centre, you see a father getting angry with his young son. Using the social systems perspective, list as many factors as you can that might account for the father's behaviour.

**connect**   How does the goodness-of-fit model, discussed in Chapter 10 (see page 418), illustrate central features of the social systems perspective on family functioning?

# Socialization Within the Family

AMONG FUNCTIONS OF THE family, socialization has been of greatest interest to child development researchers. Socialization begins in earnest during the second year, once children are first able to comply with parental directives (see Chapter 12). Effective caregivers pace their demands so they fit with children's capacities. For example, they do not impose a range of "don'ts" on infants. Instead, they put away breakable objects, place barriers across steep staircases, and physically remove babies when they behave in ways that endanger themselves or disturb others. As socialization pressures increase in early childhood, parents vary greatly in how they go about the task.

In previous chapters, we discussed many ways parents can foster children's competence—for example, through warmth and sensitivity to children's needs; by serving as models and reinforcers of mature behaviour; by using reasoning and inductive discipline; and by guiding and encouraging children's mastery of new skills. Now let's combine the various practices we have considered into an overall view of effective parenting.

## STYLES OF CHILD REARING

**Child-rearing styles** are constellations of parenting behaviours that occur over a wide range of situations, thereby creating a pervasive and enduring child-rearing climate. In a landmark series of studies, Diana Baumrind gathered information on child rearing by watching parents interact with their preschoolers (Baumrind, 1971; Baumrind & Black, 1967).

**child-rearing styles**
Constellations of parenting behaviours that occur over a wide range of situations, thereby creating a pervasive and enduring child-rearing climate.

This mother uses an authoritative style to discipline her son. She insists on mature behaviour, yet communicates patiently and sensitively. Her son listens carefully, with an expression of regret over his transgression.

Her findings, along with many others that extend her work, reveal three features that consistently differentiate an *authoritative parenting style* from less effective *authoritarian* and *permissive parenting styles*. They are (1) *acceptance* of the child and *involvement* in the child's life to establish emotional connection with the child; (2) *control* of the child to promote more mature behaviour; and (3) *autonomy granting* to encourage self-reliance (Barber & Olsen, 1997; Gray & Steinberg, 1999; Hart, Newell, & Olsen, 2002). Table 14.1 shows how child-rearing styles differ in these features. Let's discuss each style in turn.

**AUTHORITATIVE CHILD REARING.** The **authoritative style** is the most successful approach to child rearing. Authoritative parents are high in *acceptance* and *involvement*—warm, responsive, attentive, patient, and sensitive to their child's needs. They establish an enjoyable, emotionally fulfilling parent–child relationship that draws the child into close connection and interaction.

At the same time, authoritative parents use adaptive *control* techniques. They make reasonable demands for maturity and consistently enforce those demands. In doing so, they place a premium on communication. They give reasons for their expectations and use disciplinary encounters as "teaching moments" to promote the child's self-regulation of behaviour.

Finally, authoritative parents engage in gradual, appropriate *autonomy granting*. They allow the child to make decisions in areas where he is ready to make choices. They also encourage the child to express his thoughts, feelings, and desires. When parent and child disagree, authoritative parents engage in joint decision making when possible (Russell, Mize, & Bissaker, 2002). And according to Leon Kuczynski and Susan Lollis (2002) at the University of Guelph authoritative parents' willingness to accommodate to the child's perspective increases the chances that the child will listen to their perspective in situations where compliance is vital.

Studies show that throughout childhood and adolescence, authoritative parenting is linked to many aspects of competence. These include an upbeat mood, self-control, task persistence, and cooperativeness during the preschool years and, at older ages, responsiveness to parents' views in social interaction and high self-esteem, social and moral maturity, achievement motivation, and school performance (Baumrind & Black, 1967; Eccles et al., 1997a; Herman et al., 1997; Kaisa, Stattin, & Nurmi, 2000; Luster & McAdoo, 1996; Mackey, Arnold, & Pratt, 2001; Steinberg, Darling, & Fletcher, 1995).

**AUTHORITARIAN CHILD REARING.** Parents who use an **authoritarian style** are low in *acceptance and involvement*. They appear cold and rejecting, frequently degrading their child by mocking and putting her down. And although authoritarian parents focus heavily on

**TABLE** 14.1

Features of Child-Rearing Styles

| CHILD-REARING STYLE | ACCEPTANCE AND INVOLVEMENT | CONTROL | AUTONOMY GRANTING |
|---|---|---|---|
| Authoritative | Is warm, responsive, attentive, patient, and sensitive to the child's needs | Makes reasonable demands for maturity, and consistently enforces and explains them | Permits the child to make decisions in accord with readiness<br><br>Encourages the child to express thoughts, feelings, and desires<br><br>When parent and child disagree, engages in joint decision making when possible |
| Authoritarian | Is cold and rejecting and frequently degrades the child | Makes many demands coercively, by yelling, commanding, and criticizing | Makes decisions for the child<br><br>Rarely listens to the child's point of view |
| Permissive | Is warm but overindulgent or inattentive | Makes few or no demands | Permits the child to make many decisions before the child is ready |
| Uninvolved | Is emotionally detached and withdrawn | Makes few or no demands | Is indifferent to the child's decision making and point of view |

*control* of their child's behaviour, they do so coercively, by yelling, commanding, and criticizing. "Do it because I say so!" is the attitude of these parents. If the child disobeys, authoritarian parents resort to force and punishment. In addition, authoritarian parents are low in *autonomy granting.* They make decisions for their child and expect the child to accept their word in an unquestioning manner. If the child does not, authoritarian parents resort to force and punishment. The authoritarian style is clearly biased in favour of parents' needs; children's self-expression and independence are suppressed.

Research shows that children with authoritarian parents often are anxious and unhappy. Girls, especially, appear dependent, lacking in exploration, and overwhelmed in the face of challenging tasks. When playing with peers, children reared in an authoritarian climate react with hostility when frustrated. Like their parents, they resort to force when they do not get their way. Boys, especially, show high rates of anger, defiance, and aggression (Baumrind, 1967, 1971; Hart et al., 1998b, 2002; Nix et al., 1999).

In adolescence, young people with authoritarian parents continue to be less well adjusted than those with authoritative parents (Steinberg et al., 1994). Nevertheless, because of authoritarian parents' concern with controlling their child's behaviour, teenagers experiencing this style do better in school and are less likely to engage in antisocial acts than are those with undemanding parents—that is, parents who use the two styles we are about to discuss (Baumrind, 1991; Kurdek & Fine, 1994; Lamborn et al., 1991).

**PERMISSIVE CHILD REARING.** The **permissive style** of child rearing is warm and accepting. But rather than being involved, such parents are overindulging or inattentive. Permissive parents engage in little *control* of their children's behaviour. Most of the time, they avoid making demands or imposing limits. And rather than engaging in effective *autonomy granting,* permissive parents allow children to make many of their own decisions at an age when they are not yet capable of doing so. They can eat meals and go to bed when they feel like it and watch as much television as they want. They do not have to learn good manners or do any household chores. Although some permissive parents truly believe that this approach is best, many others lack confidence in their ability to influence their child's behaviour.

Children of permissive parents have great difficulty controlling their impulses and are disobedient and rebellious when asked to do something. They are also overly demanding and dependent on adults, and they show less persistence at tasks than do children of parents who exert more control. The link between permissive parenting and dependent, nonachieving behaviour is especially strong for boys (Baumrind, 1971).

In adolescence, parental indulgence continues to be related to poor self-control. Permissively reared teenagers do less well academically, are more defiant of authority figures, and display more antisocial behaviour than do teenagers whose parents communicate clear standards for behaviour (Barber & Olsen, 1997; Baumrind, 1991; Kurdek & Fine, 1994; Lamborn et al., 1991).

**UNINVOLVED CHILD REARING.** The **uninvolved style** combines low acceptance and involvement with little control and general indifference to issues of autonomy. Uninvolved parents' child rearing barely exceeds the minimum effort required to feed and clothe the child. Often these parents are emotionally detached and depressed and so overwhelmed by the many stresses in their lives that they have no time and energy to spare for children. As a result, they may respond to the child's demands for easily accessible objects, but any parenting strategies that involve long-term goals, such as establishing and enforcing rules about homework and social behaviour, listening to the child's point of view, and providing guidance on appropriate choices, are weak and fleeting (Maccoby & Martin, 1983).

At its extreme, uninvolved parenting is a form of child maltreatment called *neglect.* It is likely to characterize depressed parents with many stresses in their lives, such as marital conflict, little or no social support, and poverty. Especially when it begins early, it disrupts virtually all aspects of development, including attachment, cognition, play, and emotional and social skills (see Chapter 10, page 398).

Even when parental disengagement is less extreme, it is linked to adjustment problems. Adolescents whose parents rarely interact with them, take little interest in their life at school,

**authoritative style**
A child-rearing style that is high in acceptance and involvement, emphasizes firm control with explanations, and includes gradual, appropriate autonomy granting.

**authoritarian style**
A child-rearing style that is low in acceptance and involvement, is high in coercive control, and restricts rather than grants autonomy.

**permissive style**
A child-rearing style that is high in acceptance but overindulging and inattentive, low in control, and lax rather than appropriate in autonomy granting.

**uninvolved style**
A child-rearing style that combines low acceptance and involvement with little control and effort to grant autonomy. Reflects minimal commitment to parenting.

**TABLE** 14.2

Relationship of Child-Rearing Styles to Development and Adjustment

| CHILD-REARING STYLE | OUTCOMES | |
| --- | --- | --- |
| | CHILDHOOD | ADOLESCENCE |
| Authoritative | Upbeat mood; high self-esteem, self-control, task-persistence, and cooperativeness | High self-esteem, social and moral maturity, and academic achievement |
| Authoritarian | Anxious, withdrawn, and unhappy mood; hostile when frustrated | Less well adjusted than agemates reared with the authoritative style, but better school performance and less antisocial behaviour than agemates reared with permissive or uninvolved styles |
| Permissive | Impulsive, disobedient, and rebellious; demanding and dependent on adults; poor persistence at tasks | Poor self-control and school performance; defiance and antisocial behaviour |
| Uninvolved | Deficits in attachment, cognition, play, and emotional and social skills | Poor emotional self-regulation; low academic self-esteem and school performance; antisocial behaviour |

and do not monitor their whereabouts show poor emotional self-regulation, low academic self-esteem and school performance, and frequent antisocial behaviour (Aunola, Stattin, & Nurmi, 2000; Baumrind, 1991; Kurdek & Fine, 1994; Lamborn et al., 1991).

## WHAT MAKES THE AUTHORITATIVE STYLE EFFECTIVE?

Table 14.2 summarizes outcomes associated with each child-rearing style just considered. But like other correlational findings, the relationship between the authoritative style and children's competence is open to interpretation. Perhaps parents of well-adjusted children use demanding tactics because their youngsters have cooperative, obedient dispositions, not because firm control is an essential ingredient of effective parenting.

Children's characteristics do contribute to the ease with which parents can apply the authoritative style. To illustrate, recall from Chapter 10 that temperamentally difficult children require a combination of warmth and firm control to modify their intense, negative behaviour. Yet they are more likely to receive coercive discipline. And when children resist, some parents respond inconsistently, at first by being punitive and later by giving in, thereby reinforcing the child's unruly behaviour. Over time, the relationship between parenting and children's characteristics becomes increasingly bidirectional. An impulsive, noncompliant child makes it very hard for parents to be warm, firm, rational, and consistent. Nevertheless, longitudinal research reveals that authoritative child rearing reduces difficult children's intense, negative behaviour, whereas parental coercion intensifies their difficultness (Stice & Barrera, 1995; Woodward, Taylor, & Dowdney, 1998).

How might authoritative child rearing support children's competence and help bring children's recalcitrant behaviour under control? It seems to create an *emotional context* for positive parental influence, in the following ways:

- Control that appears fair and reasonable to the child, not arbitrary, is far more likely to be complied with and internalized (see Chapter 12).

- Warm, involved parents who are secure in the standards they hold for their children provide models of caring concern as well as confident, self-controlled behaviour. Perhaps for this reason, children of such parents are advanced in emotional self-regulation and emotional and social understanding—factors linked to social competence with peers (Lindsey & Mize, 2000; Parke, 1994).

- Parents who combine warmth with rational and reasonable control are likely to be more effective reinforcing agents, praising children for striving to meet their expectations and making good use of disapproval, which works best when applied by an adult who has been warm and caring (see Chapter 12).

- Authoritative parents make demands and engage in autonomy granting that fits with children's ability to take responsibility for their own behaviour. As a result, these parents let children know that they are competent individuals who can do things successfully for themselves, thereby fostering high self-esteem and cognitive and social maturity (see Chapter 11).

- Supportive aspects of the authoritative style, including parental acceptance, involvement, and rational control, help protect children from the negative effects of family stress and poverty (Pettit, Bates, & Dodge, 1997).

Still, a few theorists are convinced that parenting has little impact on children's development. Instead, they claim that parents and children share genes, leading parents to provide children with genetically influenced child rearing that does little more than enhance the child's built-in propensities. Yet this conclusion has been rebutted with a host of findings indicating that parenting contributes crucially to children's competence. See the Biology & Environment box on page 572 for discussion of the controversial question, Does parenting really matter?

## ADAPTING CHILD REARING TO CHILDREN'S DEVELOPMENT

Since authoritative parents continually adapt to children's growing competence, their practices change with their child's age. In the following sections, we will see that a gradual lessening of direct control and increase in autonomy granting supports development.

**PARENTING IN MIDDLE CHILDHOOD: COREGULATION.** In middle childhood, the amount of time children spend with parents declines dramatically. The child's growing independence means that parents must deal with new issues. As one mother commented, "I've struggled with how many chores to assign, how much allowance to give, whether their friends are good influences, and what to do about problems at school. And then there's the challenge of how to keep track of them when they're out of the house or even when they're home and I'm not there to see what's going on."

Although parents face new concerns, child rearing becomes easier for those who established an authoritative style during the early years. As children demonstrate that they can manage daily activities and responsibilities, effective parents gradually shift responsibilities from adult to child. This does not mean that they let go entirely. Instead, they engage in **coregulation,** a transitional form of supervision in which parents exercise general oversight while permitting children to be in charge of moment-by-moment decision making.

Coregulation grows out of a cooperative relationship between parent and child—one based on give-and-take and mutual respect. Parents must guide and monitor from a distance and effectively communicate expectations when with their children. And children must inform parents of their whereabouts, activities, and problems so parents can intervene when necessary (Maccoby, 1984). Coregulation supports and protects children while preparing them for adolescence, when they will make many important decisions themselves.

Although school-age children often press for greater independence, they know how much they need their parents' continuing support. In one study, fifth and sixth graders described parents as the most influential people in their lives (Furman & Buhrmester, 1992). Further exploring this theme, researchers from Laurentian University interviewed second to eighth graders about what they liked and disliked about how their parents treated them (Bigelow, Levin, & Cunning, 1994). The children particularly liked their parents' small caregiving gestures, such as tucking them in at night or giving them a good-bye kiss, and disliked it when their parents were too busy for them. Even the older children said that they liked to feel that their parents were keeping an eye on them.

**coregulation**
A transitional form of supervision in which parents exercise general oversight while permitting children to be in charge of moment-by-moment decision making.

# biology & environment

## DO PARENTS REALLY MATTER?

according to Judith Harris (1998), parents are minor players in children's development; they are overshadowed by children's genetic makeup and peer culture. Harris's conclusion is largely based on evidence that siblings reared in the same family show little resemblance in temperament and personality (see Chapter 10, page 416, to review). The reason, she argued, is that parents largely *react* to children's genetic dispositions; their socialization efforts do not change children in any appreciable way. No wonder, Harris continued, that many studies show no more than weak to moderate parenting effects on development. She also noted that children and adolescents resemble their friends more strongly than their siblings. Therefore, she claimed, peers are far more powerful influences on children than are parents.

Harris's assertions have been refuted by a host of experts, who believe that parents, while not the sole influence, exert a profound impact. Let's examine the evidence more closely:

■ *Recent, well-designed research reveals that the relation between parenting and children's development is sometimes substantial.* For example, in one large-scale study, the correlation between authoritative parenting and adolescents' social responsibility was .76 for mothers, .49 for fathers (Hetherington et al., 1999). Similarly, when parents engage in joint problem solving with their adolescent youngster; establish firm, consistent control; and monitor the adolescent's whereabouts, research shows strong negative relationships with antisocial behaviour (Patterson & Forgatch, 1995).

■ *Parenting often has different effects on different children.* When weak associations between parenting and children's development are found, they are not necessarily due to the feeble impact of parenting. Instead, some child-rearing practices affect different children in different ways. Much evidence indicates that parents respond differently to children with different temperaments. But the relationship is not just a reactive one. In Chapter 10, we saw that parents can modify the behaviour of difficult and shy, inhibited children. As Eleanor Maccoby (2000) concluded, "The idea that in a long-standing relation such as one between parent and child, the child would be influencing the parent but the parent would not be influencing the child is absurd" (p. 18).

■ *Longitudinal research suggests that parenting affects children's development.* Many longitudinal studies indicate that the influence of parenting on children's development holds even after controlling for children's earlier characteristics (see, for example, Bornstein et al., 1996; Carlson, 1998; Pettit, Bates, & Dodge, 1997). These findings suggest that the influence of parents is long lasting.

■ *Parenting interventions show that when child rearing improves, children's development changes accordingly.* The most powerful evidence that parents matter comes from intervention experiments (Collins et al., 2000). For example, in one study, recently divorced single mothers who were randomly assigned to a year of parent training and support had school-age sons who showed fewer behaviour problems than did sons of mothers in a control group (Forgatch & DeGarmo, 1999).

■ *Parents profoundly influence children's peer relations.* Children and adolescents resemble their friends because young people choose friends who are similar to themselves. But beginning in the preschool years, parents propel children toward certain peers by managing their social activities. And as we will see in Chapter 15, authoritative child rearing affects the values and inclinations adolescents bring to the peer situation and, therefore, their choice of friends (Steinberg, 2001).

■ *Some parenting influences cannot be measured easily.* Many people report memorable moments with parents that made a lasting impression. In contrast, a parent's broken promise or discovered deception can destroy parent–child trust and change the impact of future parenting (Maccoby, 2000).

In sum, parenting effects combine in complex ways with many other factors, including heredity and peers. Indeed, the contribution of each factor cannot be partitioned from the others, just as nature and nurture are interwoven throughout development. In view of current evidence, what can parents do to ensure the best outcomes for children? Craig Hart (1999) offers four recommendations:

■ Teach moral values, to help children make wise choices in the face of their genetic inclinations and pressures from peers.

■ Adapt parenting to help children overcome unfavourable dispositions. Using coercive control instead of rational firmness with an impulsive child or overprotection instead of encouragement with an inhibited youngster can worsen maladaptive behaviour.

■ Foster children's positive capacities through rich, varied experiences—academic, social, athletic, artistic, musical, and spiritual.

■ Engage in authoritative child rearing, a style that consistently predicts positive outcomes for children.

**PARENTING IN ADOLESCENCE: FOSTERING AUTONOMY.** During adolescence, **autonomy**—establishing oneself as a separate, self-governing individual—becomes a salient task. Autonomy has two vital aspects: (1) an *emotional component*—relying more on oneself and less on parents for support and guidance; and (2) a *behavioural component*—making decisions independently by carefully weighing one's own judgment and the suggestions of others to arrive at a well-reasoned course of action (Hill & Holmbeck, 1986; Steinberg & Silverberg, 1986). Autonomy is closely related to adolescents' quest for identity. Young people who successfully construct personally meaningful values and life goals are autonomous. They have given up childish dependence on parents for a more mature, responsible relationship (Frank, Pirsch, & Wright, 1990).

Autonomy receives support from a variety of changes within the adolescent. In Chapter 5, we saw that puberty triggers psychological distancing from parents. In addition, as young people look more mature, they are granted more independence and responsibility. Cognitive development also paves the way toward autonomy. Abstract thinking permits teenagers to solve problems and foresee the consequences of their actions more effectively. And an improved ability to reason about social relationships leads adolescents to *deidealize* their parents, viewing them as "just people." Consequently, they no longer bend as easily to parental authority as they did at earlier ages.

Warm, supportive parent–child ties that permit young people to explore ideas and social roles foster adolescent autonomy, predicting high self-reliance, work orientation, academic competence, and self-esteem (Allen et al., 1994; Lamborn & Steinberg, 1993). Conversely, parents who are intrusive, coercive, or psychologically controlling (for example, who discount young people's feelings, belittle them, or use love withdrawal) interfere with the development of autonomy. These tactics promote low self-esteem, depression, and antisocial behaviour (Aquilino & Supple, 2001; Barber & Harmon, 2002).

Although promoting autonomy involves granting teenagers more freedom, it also requires high parental involvement in the young person's daily life. Parental monitoring—knowledge of their child's whereabouts, activities, and friends—predicts favourable adjustment. In a study of over 400 seventh to twelfth graders, adolescents experiencing greater parental monitoring committed fewer minor delinquent acts, engaged in less sexual activity, performed better in school, and reported more positive psychological well-being (Jacobson & Crockett, 2000).

Parents often report that living with adolescents is stressful. Why is this so? Recall that the family is a system that must adapt to changes in its members. But when development is very rapid, adjustment is harder. Many parents of adolescents have reached their forties and are changing as well. While teenagers face a boundless future and a wide array of choices, their parents must come to terms with the fact that half their life is over and their own possibilities are narrowing. The pressures experienced by each generation act in opposition (Holmbeck & Hill, 1991). Parents often can't understand why the adolescent wants to skip family activities to be with peers. And teenagers fail to appreciate that parents want the family to be together as often as possible because an important stage in adult life—parenthood—will soon be over.

In addition, young people's interest in making choices about personal matters strengthens in adolescence (see Chapter 12). Yet parents and teenagers—especially young teenagers—differ sharply on the appropriate time young people should be granted certain responsibilities and privileges, such as control over clothing, school courses, and going out with friends (Collins et al., 1997; Smetana, 1995). Parents typically say that the young person is not yet ready for these signs of independence, whereas teenagers think they should have been granted long ago!

As adolescents move closer to adulthood, parents and children must blend togetherness and independence so that parental control gradually relaxes without breaking the parent–child bond. This means establishing guidelines that are flexible and open to discussion. The mild parent–child conflict that typically occurs facilitates adolescent identity and autonomy by helping family members learn to express and tolerate disagreement (Steinberg, 1999, 2001). Conflicts also inform parents of adolescents' changing needs and expectations, signalling that adjustments in the parent–child relationship are necessary. After a temporary decline in early adolescence, positive parent–child interaction is on the rise (Larson et al., 1996).

Adolescent autonomy is best achieved in the context of warm parenting. This mother and father support their daughter's desire to try new experiences, relaxing control in accord with her readiness to take on new responsibilities. The girl's beaming smile as she introduces her prom date suggests a healthy balance of togetherness and independence.

**autonomy**
A sense of oneself as a separate, self-governing individual. An important developmental task of adolescence that is closely related to the quest for identity.

## SOCIOECONOMIC AND ETHNIC VARIATIONS IN CHILD REARING

Research indicates that the authoritative style is the most common and effective approach to child rearing in many ethnic groups and cultures (Rohner & Rohner, 1981; Steinberg, 2001). Nevertheless, consistent variations in parenting are linked to SES and ethnicity.

**SOCIOECONOMIC STATUS.** Recall that SES is an index that combines years of education, prestige and skill required by one's job, and income. As SES rises and falls, parents and children face changing circumstances that profoundly affect family functioning.

When asked about qualities they would like to encourage in their children, lower-SES parents tend to emphasize external characteristics, such as obedience, neatness, and cleanliness. In contrast, higher-SES parents emphasize psychological traits, such as curiosity, happiness, and self-direction. In addition, fathers in higher-SES families tend to play a more supportive role in child rearing. Lower-SES fathers—partly because of their gender-stereotyped beliefs and partly because of necessity—focus more on their provider role (Rank, 2000).

These differences are reflected in parenting behaviours. Parents higher in SES talk to and stimulate their infants more and grant them greater freedom to explore. When their children are older, higher-SES parents use more warmth, explanations, inductive discipline, and verbal praise. In contrast, commands, such as "You do that because I told you to," as well as criticism and physical punishment occur more often in low-SES households (Hoff-Ginsburg & Tardiff, 1995).

The life conditions of families help explain these findings. Lower-SES parents often feel a sense of powerlessness and lack of influence in their relationships beyond the home. For example, at work they must obey the rules of others in positions of power and authority. When they get home, their parent–child interaction seems to duplicate these experiences, with them in the authority role. Higher levels of stress combined with a stronger belief in the value of physical punishment contribute to low-SES parents' greater use of coercive discipline (Pinderhughes et al., 2000). Higher-SES parents, in contrast, have more control over their own lives. At work, they are used to making independent decisions and convincing others of their point of view. At home, they teach these skills to their children (Greenberger, O'Neil, & Nagel, 1994).

Education also contributes to SES differences in child rearing. Higher-SES parents' interest in providing verbal stimulation and nurturing inner traits is supported by years of schooling, during which they learned to think about abstract, subjective ideas (Uribe, LeVine, & LeVine, 1994). Furthermore, the greater economic security of higher-SES parents frees them from worry about making ends meet on a daily basis. They can devote more time, energy, and material resources to furthering their own and their children's psychological characteristics.

**POVERTY.** When families slip into poverty, effective parenting and children's development are seriously threatened. Shirley Brice Heath (1990), an anthropologist who has spent many years studying children and families of poverty, describes the case of Zinnia Mae, who grew up in Trackton, a close-knit black community located in a small southeastern U.S. city. As unemployment struck Trackton in the 1980s and citizens moved away, 16-year-old Zinnia Mae caught a ride to Atlanta. Two years later, Heath visited her there. By then, Zinnia Mae was the mother of three children—a 16-month-old daughter named Donna and 2-month-old twin boys. She had moved into a high-rise in public housing.

Each of Zinnia Mae's days was much the same. She watched TV and talked with her girlfriends on the phone. The children had only one set meal (breakfast) and otherwise ate whenever they were hungry or bored. Their play space was limited to the living-room sofa and a mattress on the floor. Toys consisted of scraps of a blanket, spoons and food cartons, a small rubber ball, a few plastic cars, and a roller skate abandoned in the building. Zinnia Mae's most frequent words were "I'm so tired." She worried about where to find a baby-sitter so she could go to the laundry or grocery, and what she would do if she located the twins' father, who had stopped sending money.

At Heath's request, Zinnia Mae agreed to tape-record her interactions with her children over a 2-year period. In 500 hours of tape (other than simple directions or questions about what the children were doing), Zinnia Mae started a conversation with Donna and the boys only 18 times. Cut off from community ties and preoccupied with day-to-day survival, Zinnia Mae had little energy for her children.

The constant stresses that accompany poverty gradually weaken the family system. Poor families have many daily hassles—bills to pay, the car breaking down, loss of welfare and unemployment payments, something stolen from the house, to name just a few. When daily crises arise, parents become depressed, irritable, and distracted; hostile interactions increase; and children's development suffers (McLoyd, 1998b). These outcomes are especially severe in single-parent families, in families living in poor housing and dangerous neighbourhoods, and in homeless families—conditions that make everyday existence even more difficult while reducing social supports (Brooks-Gunn & Duncan, 1997).

Besides stress and conflict, reduced parental involvement and depleted home learning environments profoundly affect poor children's cognitive and emotional well-being (Duncan & Brooks-Gunn, 2000; Smith, Brooks-Gunn, & Klebanov, 1997). The earlier poverty begins, the deeper it is, and the longer it lasts, the more devastating its effects on children's physical and mental health, intelligence, and school achievement (Duncan et al., 1998).

**ETHNICITY.** Despite broad agreement on the advantages of authoritative child rearing, ethnic groups often have distinct child-rearing beliefs and practices. For example, compared with Caucasian Americans, Chinese adults describe their own parenting techniques and those they experienced as children as more controlling (Berndt et al., 1993). This greater emphasis on control continues to characterize immigrant Chinese parents. In particular, Chinese parents are more directive in teaching and scheduling their children's time beginning in early childhood, as a way of fostering self-control and high achievement (Huntsinger, Jose, & Larson, 1998).

Yet controversy exists over whether high control in Chinese families is coercive and detrimental. According to one view, Chinese parental control can easily be misunderstood by Western observers. That is, it reflects the Confucian belief in strict discipline, respect for elders, and socially desirable behaviour, taught by parents who are deeply concerned and involved in the lives of their children (Chao, 1994). But other investigators, such as Xinyin Chen of the University of Western Ontario, believe that high coerciveness is harmful in Chinese as well as Western culture (Chen, Dong, & Zhou, 1997). Consistent with this perspective, Chen and his colleagues found that authoritative parenting was positively related to academic and social competence, whereas authoritarian parenting predicted poorer academic achievement and increased aggression and peer relationship difficulties among Chinese school-age children (Chen, Dong, & Zhou, 1997; Chen, Liu, & Li, 2000).

In Hispanic and Asian Pacific Island families, firm insistence on respect for parental authority, particularly that of the father, is paired with high parental warmth—a combination suited to promoting competence and strong feelings of family loyalty (Harrison et al., 1994). Consistent with their high valuing of parental commitment, Hispanic fathers are more likely than Caucasian parents to spend time with and monitor their school-age and adolescent youngsters. And although at one time viewed as coercive, contemporary Hispanic fathers are more nurturant than the strict authority figure of the past (Jambunathan, Burts, & Pierce, 2000; Toth & Xu, 1999).

Although wide variation exists, black mothers (especially those who are young, single, and less educated) often expect immediate obedience (Kelley, Power, & Wimbush, 1992). Strict demands for compliance, however, make sense under certain conditions. When parents have few social supports and live in dangerous neighbourhoods, some forceful discipline may protect children from becoming victims of crime or involved in antisocial activities. Other research suggests that black parents use firm child rearing for broader reasons—to promote self-reliance, self-control, and a watchful attitude in risky surroundings (Brody & Flor, 1998).

Consistent with this view, low-SES African-American and Hispanic parents who use more controlling strategies tend to have more cognitively and socially competent children (Baldwin, Baldwin, & Cole, 1990; Brody, Stoneman, & Flor, 1995, 1996). And in several studies, physical discipline in early childhood predicted aggression and other conduct problems during the school years only for Caucasian-American children, not for African-American children (Deater-Deckard & Dodge, 1997; Deater-Deckard et al., 1996). This does not mean that slaps and spankings are effective strategies. But it does suggest that ethnic differences in how children view parental behaviour may modify its consequences. Most African-American parents who use strict, "no-nonsense" discipline refrain from physical punishment. And they typically combine strictness with warmth and reasoning, which predict favourable adjustment, regardless of ethnicity (Bluestone & Tamis-LeMonda, 1999; Pettit, Bates, & Dodge, 1997).

The family structure and child-rearing customs of many ethnic minorities buffer the stress and disorganization caused by poverty. For example, **extended-family households** in which an adult relative lives with the parent–child **nuclear family unit** can offer additional support to a stressed, single parent. Active and involved extended family households also characterize Asian, Aboriginal, and Hispanic subcultures (Harrison et al., 1994). These families illustrate the remarkable ability of the family unit to use its cultural traditions to support its members under conditions of high life stress.

## ASK YOURSELF www

**review**    How do authoritative, authoritarian, and permissive child-rearing styles differ in acceptance and involvement, control, and autonomy granting? Why is authoritative parenting effective?

**review**    Why are lower-SES parents less likely to engage in authoritative child rearing? Is the authoritative style limited to Western middle-SES cultures? Explain.

**apply**    Prepare a short talk for a parent–teacher organization showing that parents matter greatly in children's lives. Support each of your points with research evidence.

**connect**    Explain how factors that support autonomy in adolescence also foster identity development.

# Family Lifestyles and Transitions

FAMILIES IN INDUSTRIALIZED nations have become more diverse. Today, there are fewer births per family unit, more adults who want to adopt, more lesbian and gay parents who are open about their sexual orientation, and more never-married parents. In addition, transitions in family life over the past several decades—a dramatic rise in marital breakup, remarried parents, and employed mothers—have reshaped the family system.

In the following sections, we discuss these changes in the family, emphasizing how each affects family relationships and children's development. In reading about some of these shifts, you may wonder, as many people do, whether the family is in a state of crisis. As you consider this question, think back to the social systems perspective and Bronfenbrenner's ecological model. Notice how children's well-being continues to depend on the quality of family interaction, supportive ties to kin and community, and favourable policies in the larger culture.

## FROM LARGE TO SMALL FAMILIES

In 1959, Canada's birth rate was 3.9 live births per woman of childbearing age. Today, the birth rate is 1.6, a downward trend expected to continue (Dateno, 1998). In other developed countries, the birth rate is also low—for example, 1.8 in the United States; 1.7 in Australia; 1.6 in Austria, Great Britain, and Sweden; 1.5 in the Netherlands and Japan; and 1.3 in Germany (Bellamy, 2000; Pearce, Cantisani, & Laihonen, 1999).

In addition to improved contraception, a major reason for this decline is that many women are reaping the economic and personal rewards of a career. A family size of one or two children is more compatible with the decision of many women to divide their energies between family and work. Furthermore, more couples are delaying the birth of their first child until they are well established professionally and secure economically (see Chapter 3).

**extended-family household**
A household in which parent and child live with one or more adult relatives.

**nuclear family unit**
The part of the family that consists of parents and their children.

Adults who postpone parenthood are likely to have fewer children. Finally, marital instability is another reason families are smaller. More couples today get divorced before their child-bearing plans are complete.

**FAMILY SIZE AND CHILD REARING.** Overall, a smaller family size enhances parent–child interaction. Parents of fewer children are more patient and less punitive. They also have more time to devote to each child's activities, schoolwork, and other special needs. Furthermore, in smaller families, siblings are more likely to be widely spaced (born more than 2 years apart), which adds to the attention and resources parents can invest in each child. Together, these findings may account for the fact that children who grow up in smaller families are healthier, have somewhat higher intelligence test scores, do better in school, attain higher levels of education, and engage in lower rates of antisocial behaviour (Grant, 1994; Powell & Steelman, 1993).

However, these findings require an important qualification. Large families are usually less well off economically. Factors associated with low SES—crowded housing, inadequate nutrition, and poorly educated and stressed parents—may contribute to the negative relationship between family size and children's well-being. Indeed, research supports this idea. Parents with lower intelligence test scores (many of whom are poorly educated) tend to have larger families (Rodgers et al., 2000). And when children of bright, stimulating, economically advantaged parents grow up in large families, unfavourable outcomes associated with large family size are eliminated (Guo & VanWey, 1999).

**GROWING UP WITH SIBLINGS.** Despite a declining family size, 80 percent of Canadian children still grow up with at least one sibling. Siblings exert important influences on development, both directly, through relationships with each other, and indirectly, through the effects an additional child has on the behaviour of parents. In previous chapters, we examined some consequences of having brothers and sisters, including effects on language development, personality, self and social understanding, and gender typing. Now let's look more closely at the quality of the sibling relationship.

***Emergence of Sibling Relationships.*** The arrival of a baby brother or sister is a difficult experience for most preschoolers, who quickly realize that now they must share their parents' attention and affection. They often become demanding and clingy for a time and engage in deliberate naughtiness. And their security of attachment may decline, especially if they are over age 2 (old enough to feel threatened and displaced) and the mother is under stress due to marital or psychological problems (Teti et al., 1996).

Yet resentment is only one feature of a rich emotional relationship that starts to build between siblings after baby's birth. The older child can also be seen kissing, patting, and calling out "Mom, he needs you" when the baby cries—signs of affection and sympathetic concern. By the end of the baby's first year, siblings typically spend much time together, with the preschooler helping, sharing toys, imitating, and expressing friendliness in addition to anger and ambivalence. And during the second year, toddlers often imitate and join in play with the older child (Dunn & Kendrick, 1982).

Because of their frequency and emotional intensity, sibling interactions become unique contexts in which social competence expands. Between their second and fourth birthdays, younger siblings take a more active role in play. As a result, sibling conversations increase. And when they are close in age, siblings relate to one another on a more equal footing than do parents and children. They often talk about emotions in playful ways and call attention to their own wants and needs when conflicts arise (Brown & Dunn, 1992). The skills acquired during sibling interaction contribute to perspective taking, moral maturity, and competence in relating to other children. Consistent with these outcomes, positive sibling ties predict favourable adjustment, even among hostile children at risk for social difficulties (Dunn et al., 1994; Stormshak et al., 1996).

Nevertheless, individual differences in the quality of sibling relationships appear shortly after birth. In Chapter 10, we noted that temperament affects how positive or conflict-ridden sibling interaction will be. Parenting also makes a difference. Secure infant–mother attachment and warmth toward both children are related to positive sibling interaction (MacKinnon-Lewis et al.,

BARRY HEWLETT

Sibling interactions become unique contexts in which social competence expands. This 3-year-old is actively involved in play with her 5-year-old sister, and both derive pleasure from the interaction.

1997; Stocker & McHale, 1992). Nina Howe and William Bukowski of Concordia University and Jasmin Aquan-Assee of Kings College, London, England found that mothers who frequently play with their children and head off potential conflicts by explaining the toddler's wants and needs to the preschool sibling foster cooperative sibling ties. In contrast, lack of maternal involvement and use of coercive control to manage sibling conflict are associated with increasingly antagonistic sibling relationships (Howe, Aquan-Assee, & Bukowski, 2001).

***Sibling Relationships in Middle Childhood and Adolescence.*** During middle childhood, sibling rivalry tends to increase. At times, it is evoked by one child making new friends, sparking jealousy in a sibling who feels left out (Dunn, 1996). Also, as children participate in more activities, parents often compare siblings' traits and accomplishments. The child who gets less parental affection, more disapproval, or fewer material resources is likely to be resentful (Brody, Stoneman, & McCoy, 1994; McHale et al., 1995).

When siblings are close in age and the same sex, parental comparisons are more frequent, resulting in more quarrelling, antagonism, and poorer adjustment. This effect is particularly strong when parenting is cold or harsh (Feinberg & Hetherington, 2001). It is also strengthened when fathers prefer one child. Perhaps because fathers spend less time with children, their favouritism is more noticeable and triggers greater anger (Brody, Stoneman, & McCoy, 1992; Brody et al., 1992).

Of course, disagreements occur between virtually all siblings, but the extent to which siblings work them out in agreeable ways depends on the quality of the sibling relationship. In a study of sibling conflict by Avigal Ram and Hildy Ross (2001) of the University of Waterloo, siblings rated their relationship quality. Then they were asked to negotiate the division of six attractive toys. In cases where siblings rated their relationship as negative, negotiations were more destructive and often resulted in a failure to reach agreement. Their interactions included refusals, such as "No, I'm not giving you the ball!" and verbal aggression, as in "You're a beggar! You beg for everything!" In contrast, when the sibling relationship was positive, negotiations usually were constructive and led to fair approaches to conflict resolution, as in, "I'll pick one, then you pick one" or "How about we'll share?"

Although conflict is common during the school years, siblings continue to rely on each other for companionship, emotional support, and assistance with everyday tasks. In another study, siblings reported on their shared daily activities in evening telephone interviews, and participants mentioned that older siblings often assisted younger siblings with academic and peer challenges. And both pair members offered one another assistance with family issues (Tucker, McHale, & Crouter, 2001). When parents are distant and uninvolved with their school-age children, siblings may fill in and become more intensely supportive of one another (Bank, Patterson, & Reid, 1996).

Like parent–child relationships, sibling interactions adapt to development at adolescence. As younger children mature and become more self-sufficient, they are no longer willing to accept as much direction from their older brothers and sisters. Consequently, older siblings' influence declines during the teenage years. Furthermore, as teenagers become more involved in friendships and romantic partnerships, they invest less time and energy in siblings, who are part of the family from which they are trying to establish autonomy (Furman & Buhrmester, 1992; Stocker & Dunn, 1994). As a result, sibling relationships often become less intense in adolescence, in both positive and negative feelings (Hetherington, Henderson, & Reiss, 1999).

Despite a drop in companionship, attachment between siblings, like closeness to parents, remains strong for most young people. Quality of sibling relationships is fairly stable over time. Brothers and sisters who established a positive bond in early childhood are more likely to display affection and caring during the teenage years (Dunn, Slomkowski, & Beardsall, 1994).

Sibling interaction at adolescence continues to be affected by other relationships, both within and outside the family. Teenagers whose parents are warm and supportive have more positive sibling ties (Bussell et al., 1999). And adolescents experiencing strains in peer relationships may turn to siblings. For example, when young people have difficulty making friends, siblings can compensate (East & Rook, 1992; Seginer, 1998). Adolescents without close bonds with either siblings or friends have more adjustment problems than do those with either positive sibling or positive friendship ties (Updegraff & Obeidallah, 1999).

© MARC BERNHEIM/WOODFIN CAMP & ASSOCIATES

Limiting family size is a basic national policy in the People's Republic of China. In urban areas, the majority of couples have no more than one child.

**TABLE** 14.3

Advantages and Disadvantages of a One-Child Family

| ADVANTAGES | | DISADVANTAGES | |
| --- | --- | --- | --- |
| **MENTIONED BY PARENTS** | **MENTIONED BY CHILDREN** | **MENTIONED BY PARENTS** | **MENTIONED BY CHILDREN** |
| Having time to pursue one's own interests and career | Avoiding sibling rivalry | Walking a "tightrope" between family attention and overindulgence | Not getting to experience the closeness of a sibling relationship |
| Less financial pressure | Having more privacy | Having only one chance to "make good" as a parent | Feeling too much pressure from parents to succeed |
| Not having to worry about "playing favourites" among children | Enjoying greater affluence | Being left childless in case of the child's death | Having no one to help care for parents when they get old |
| | Having a closer parent–child relationship | | |

*Source:* Hawke & Knox, 1978.

## ONE-CHILD FAMILIES

Sibling relationships bring many benefits, but they are not essential for healthy development. Contrary to popular belief, only children are not spoiled. Instead, they are just as well-adjusted as other children, and advantaged in some respects. Children in one-child families score higher in self-esteem and achievement motivation. Consequently, they do better in school and attain higher levels of education (Falbo, 1992). A major reason may be that they have somewhat closer relationships with their parents, who exert more pressure for mastery (Falbo & Polit, 1986).

Favourable development also characterizes only children in China, where a one-child family policy has been strictly enforced for two decades to control overpopulation. Compared with agemates who have siblings, Chinese only children are advanced in performance on a variety of cognitive tasks and in academic achievement (Falbo & Poston, 1993; Jiao, Ji, & Jing, 1996). They also feel more emotionally secure, perhaps because government disapproval promotes tension in families with more than one child (Falbo & Poston, 1993; Yang et al., 1995). Although many Chinese adults remain convinced that the one-child family policy breeds self-centred "little emperors," Chinese only children do not differ from children with siblings in social skills and peer acceptance (Chen, Rubin, & Li, 1995).

Nevertheless, the one-child family has both pros and cons, as does every family lifestyle. In a survey in which only children and their parents were asked what they liked and disliked about living in a single-child family, each mentioned a set of advantages and disadvantages, which are summarized in Table 14.3.

This Chinese girl, transracially adopted at birth, plays with her Caucasian older sisters. Will she develop an identity that is a healthy blend of her birth and rearing backgrounds? The answer depends on the extent to which her adoptive parents expose her to her Chinese heritage.

## ADOPTIVE FAMILIES

Adults who are infertile, who are likely to pass along a genetic disorder, or who are older and single but want a family are turning to adoption in increasing numbers. Adoption agencies try to find parents of the same ethnic and religious background as the child. Where possible, they also try to choose parents who are the same age as most natural parents. Because the availability of healthy babies has declined (since fewer young unwed mothers give up their babies than in the past), more people are adopting from foreign countries or taking children who are older or who have developmental problems.

Adopted children and adolescents—whether born in a foreign country or the country of their adoptive parents—have more learning and emotional difficulties than do other

FIGURE 14.1

**Percentage of 15-year-olds with high maladjustment scores who were adopted, placed in foster homes, or returned to their biological mothers shortly after birth, according to a Swedish longitudinal study.** All adolescents had been candidates for adoption when they were born. Compared with the other two groups, adopted young people were rated by teachers as having far fewer problems, including anxiety, withdrawal, aggression, inability to concentrate, peer difficulties, and poor school motivation. (Adapted from Bohman & Sigvardsson, 1990.)

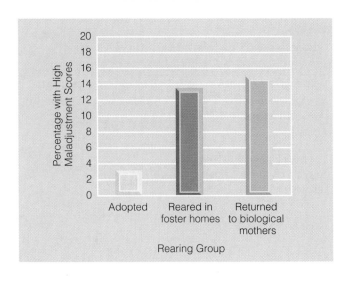

Homosexual parents are as committed to and as effective at child rearing as are heterosexual parents—and sometimes more so. Their children are well adjusted, and the large majority develop a heterosexual orientation.

MARK RICHARDS/PHOTOEDIT

children (Levy-Shiff, 2001; Peters, Atkins, & McKay, 1999). There are many reasons for this trend. The biological mother may have been unable to care for the child because of problems believed to be partly genetic, such as alcoholism or severe depression, and she may have passed this tendency to her offspring. Or perhaps she experienced stress, poor diet, or inadequate medical care during pregnancy. Furthermore, children adopted after infancy often lacked parental affection or experienced conflict-ridden family relationships. Finally, adoptive parents and children, who are genetically unrelated, are less alike in intelligence and personality than are biological relatives—differences that may threaten family harmony.

But despite these risks, most adopted children fare well. In a Swedish longitudinal study, researchers followed more than 600 infant adoption candidates into adolescence and young adulthood. Some were adopted shortly after birth; some were reared in foster homes; and some were reared by their biological mothers, who changed their minds about giving them up. As Figure 14.1 shows, adoptees developed much more favourably than the other two groups (Bohman & Sigvardsson, 1990). Furthermore, children with special needs usually benefit, even when they are adopted at older ages. From 70 to 80 percent of their parents report high satisfaction with the adoptive experience (Rosenthal, 1992).

By adolescence, adoptees' lives are often complicated by unresolved curiosity about their roots. Some have difficulty accepting the possibility that they may never know their birth parents. Others worry about what they would do if their birth parents suddenly reappeared (Grotevant & Kohler, 1999). Despite concerns about their origins, most adoptees appear optimistic and well adjusted as adults. And as long as their parents took steps to help them learn about their heritage in childhood, transracially or transculturally adopted young people generally develop identities that are healthy blends of their birth and rearing backgrounds (Simon, Altstein, & Melli, 1994).

Clearly, adoption is a satisfying family alternative for most parents and children who experience it. The outcomes are good because of careful pairing of children with parents and guidance provided to adoptive families by well-trained social service professionals.

## GAY AND LESBIAN FAMILIES

Several million gay men and lesbians are parents, most through heterosexual marriages that ended in divorce, a few through adoption or reproductive technologies (Bigner, 2000). In the past, laws assuming that homosexuals could not be adequate parents led those who divorced a heterosexual partner to lose custody of their children. Today, several jurisdictions hold that sexual orientation is irrelevant to custody. In others, fierce prejudice against homosexual parents still prevails.

Research on homosexual parents and children is limited and based on small samples. Nevertheless, findings consistently indicate that gay and lesbian parents are as committed to and effective at child rearing as are heterosexual parents (Patterson, 2001). Some evidence suggests that gay fathers are more consistent in setting limits and more responsive to their children's needs than are heterosexual fathers, perhaps because gay men's less traditional gender identity fosters involvement with children (Bigner & Jacobsen, 1989). In lesbian families, quality of mother–child interaction is as positive as in heterosexual families. And children of lesbian mothers regard their mother's partner as very much a parent (Brewaeys et al., 1997). Whether born to or adopted by their parents or conceived through donor insemination, children in homosexual families seem as well-adjusted as other children. Also the large majority are heterosexual (Allen & Burrell, 1996; Chan, Raboy, & Patterson, 1998; Golombok & Tasker, 1996).

## DIVORCE

Parental separation and divorce are extremely common in the lives of Canadian children. In 1987, the divorce rate in Canada rose dramatically after amendments to the Divorce Act shortened the necessary waiting period from 3 years of separation to 1 year. After its peak in 1987, the divorce rate in Canada declined and then stabilized. Currently, Canada has the fourth highest divorce rate in the world (see Figure 14.2). Estimates indicate that more than 30 percent of Canadian marriages will end in divorce. At any given time, about 20 percent of Canadian children live in single-parent households. Although the large majority reside with their mothers, the percentage of fathers has increased steadily, to about 10 percent (Statistics Canada, Divorces, 1999, 2000; Statistics Canada, Family Studies Kit, 2002).

The average child of divorce spends 5 years in a single-parent home, or almost one-third of childhood. For many, divorce eventually leads to new family relationships. About two-thirds of divorced parents marry a second time. Half the children in this situation eventually experience a third major change—the end of their parents' second marriage (Hetherington & Henderson, 1997).

These figures reveal that divorce is not a single event in the lives of parents and children. Instead, it is a transition that leads to a variety of new living arrangements, accompanied by changes in housing, income, and family roles and responsibilities. Since the 1960s, many studies have reported that marital breakup is quite stressful for children (Amato & Booth, 2000). But the research also reveals wide individual differences. How well children fare depends on many factors: the custodial parent's psychological health, the child's characteristics, and social supports within the family and surrounding community.

Our understanding of the impact of divorce has been enriched by many longitudinal studies as well as many short-term investigations. As we consider current evidence, you may find it helpful to refer to the summary in Table 14.4 on page 582.

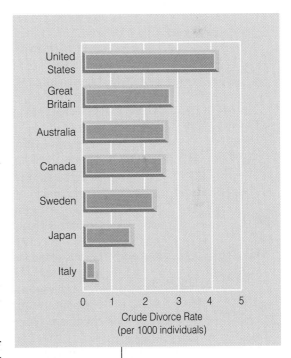

**FIGURE** 14.2

**Divorce rate in seven industrialized nations.** The divorce rate in Canada is the fourth highest in the world, following the United States, Great Britain, and Australia. (From Statistics Canada, 2000; Australia Bureau of Statistics, 2000; U.S. Bureau of the Census, 2001; United Nations, 1999.)

**TABLE** 14.4

Factors Related to Children's Adjustment to Divorce

| FACTOR | DESCRIPTION |
|---|---|
| Custodial parents' psychological health | A mature, well-adjusted parent is better able to handle stress, shield the child from conflict, and engage in authoritative parenting. |
| Children's characteristics | |
|    Age | Preschool and early school-age children often blame themselves and show intense separation anxiety. Older children and adolescents may also react strongly by engaging in disruptive, anti-social acts. However, some display unusually mature, responsible behaviour. |
|    Temperament | Children with difficult temperaments are less able to withstand stress and show longer-lasting difficulties. |
|    Sex | Boys in mother-custody homes experience more severe and longer-lasting problems than do girls. |
| Social supports | The ability of parents to set aside their hostilities; contact with the noncustodial parent; and positive relationships with extended-family members, teachers, and friends lead to improved outcomes for children. |

**IMMEDIATE CONSEQUENCES.** Family conflict often rises around the time of divorce as parents try to settle disputes over children, finances, and personal belongings. Once one parent moves out, additional events threaten supportive interaction between parents and children. Mother-headed households typically experience a sharp drop in income. Lone mothers in Canada are five to six times more likely to be living in poverty than are mothers raising their children with a partner (Statistics Canada, Robert Glossop, 2002). Divorced mothers often have to move to new housing for economic reasons, reducing supportive ties to neighbours and friends.

Longitudinal research shows that the transition from marriage to divorce often leads to high maternal stress, depression, and anxiety and to a disorganized family situation called "minimal parenting" (Hope, Power, & Rodgers, 1999; Marks & Lambert, 1998; Wallerstein & Kelly, 1980). Predictable events and routines—scheduled meals and bedtimes, household chores, and joint parent–child activities—usually disintegrate. As children react with distress and anger to their less secure home lives, discipline may become harsh and inconsistent. Contact with noncustodial fathers decreases over time (Hetherington, Bridges, & Insabella, 1998; Lamb, 1999). When fathers see their children only occasionally, they are inclined to be permissive and indulgent. This often conflicts with the mother's style of parenting and makes her task of managing the child on a day-to-day basis even more difficult.

In view of these changes, it is not surprising that children experience painful emotional reactions. But the intensity of their feelings and the way they are expressed vary with the child's age, temperament, and sex.

***Children's Age.*** The cognitive immaturity of preschool and early school-age children makes it difficult for them to grasp the reasons behind their parents' separation. Younger children often blame themselves and take the marital breakup as a sign that both parents may abandon them. They may whine and cling, displaying intense separation anxiety. Preschoolers are especially likely to fantasize that their parents will get back together (Hetherington, 1989; Wallerstein, Corbin, & Lewis, 1988).

Older children are better able to understand the reasons behind their parents' divorce. They recognize that strong differences of opinion, incompatible personalities, and lack of caring for one another are responsible (Mazur, 1993). The ability to accurately assign blame may reduce some of the pain children feel. Still, many school-age and adolescent youngsters react strongly to the end of their parents' marriage, particularly when family conflict is high and parental supervision of children is low. Escaping into undesirable peer activities—

running away, truancy, early sexual activity, and delinquent behaviour—and dropping out of school are common (Hetherington & Stanley-Hagan, 1999; Simons & Chao, 1996).

However, not all older children react this way. For some—especially the oldest child in the family—divorce can trigger more mature behaviour. These youngsters may willingly take on extra burdens, such as household tasks, care and protection of younger siblings, and emotional support of a depressed, anxious mother. But if these demands are too great, older children may eventually become resentful and withdraw from the family into some of the more destructive behaviour patterns just described (Hetherington, 1995, 1999b).

*Children's Temperament and Sex.* When temperamentally difficult children are exposed to stressful life events and inadequate parenting, their problems are magnified (Lengua et al., 2000). In contrast, easy children are less often targets of parental anger and are also better at coping with adversity when it hits. After a moderately stressful divorce, some easy children (usually girls) actually emerge with enhanced coping skills (Hetherington, 1995).

These findings help us understand sex differences in children's response to divorce. Girls sometimes respond with internalizing reactions, such as crying, self-criticism, and withdrawal. More often, they show demanding, attention-getting behaviour. But in mother-custody families, boys typically experience more serious adjustment problems. Recall from Chapter 13 that boys are more active and noncompliant—behaviours that increase with exposure to parental conflict and inconsistent discipline. Research reveals that long before the marital breakup, many sons of divorcing couples were impulsive and defiant—behaviours that may have contributed to, as well as been caused by, their parents' marital problems (Cherlin et al., 1991; Hetherington, 1999b). As a result, these boys entered the period of turmoil surrounding divorce with a reduced capacity to cope with family stress.

Perhaps because their behaviour is so unruly, boys of divorcing parents receive less emotional support from mothers, teachers, and peers. Furthermore, the coercive cycles of interaction that boys often establish with their divorced mothers soon spread to sibling relations (MacKinnon, 1989). These outcomes compound boys' difficulties. After divorce, children with pre-existing behaviour problems generally get worse (Hanson, 1999; Morrison & Coiro, 1999).

**LONG-TERM CONSEQUENCES.** Most children show improved adjustment by 2 years after divorce. Yet for a few, persisting emotional distress and declines in school achievement contribute to serious adjustment difficulties into young adulthood (Chase-Lansdale, Cherlin, & Kiernan, 1995). And a host of studies indicate that overall, children of divorced parents score slightly lower than children with continuously married parents in self-esteem, social competence, and emotional and behaviour problems (Amato, 2000).

Boys and children with difficult temperaments are especially likely to drop out of school and display antisocial behaviour in adolescence. For both sexes, divorce is linked to problems with adolescent sexuality and with development of intimate ties. Young people who experienced parental divorce—especially more than once—display higher rates of early sexual activity and adolescent parenthood (Booth, 1999; Cherlin, Kiernan, & Chase-Lansdale, 1995; Hetherington, 1997).

The overriding factor in positive adjustment following divorce is effective parenting—in particular, how well the custodial parent handles stress and shields the child from family conflict, and the extent to which each parent engages in authoritative child rearing (Amato & Gilbreth, 1999; Whiteside & Becker, 2000). In a study of 8- to 15-year-olds whose parents had divorced in the previous 2 years, children reporting high maternal warmth and consistency of discipline were better able than other children to withstand divorce stressors and had the fewest adjustment problems (Wolchik et al., 2000).

Contact with fathers also is important. For girls, a good father–child relationship appears to protect against early sexual activity and unhappy romantic involvements. For boys, it seems to affect overall psychological well-being. In fact, several studies indicate that outcomes for sons are better when the father is the custodial parent (Camara & Resnick,

© SPENCER GRANT/PHOTOEDIT

This divorced father welcomes his daughters for a visit. Keeping fathers involved in parenting and in assisting with financial support has great benefits for children's development. And when parents set aside their disagreements and support one another in their child-rearing roles, children of divorce have the best chance of growing up competent, stable, and happy.

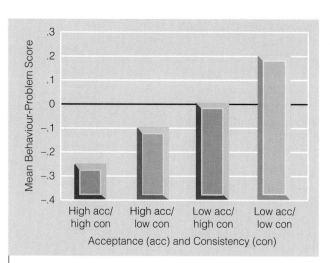

**FIGURE** 14.3

**Relationship of child-rearing styles to adjustment following divorce.** High parental acceptance and consistency in discipline yielded a low level of behaviour problems. As child rearing diminished in quality, behaviour problems increased. When both parental acceptance and consistency in discipline were low, problems were severe. These children and adolescents had each experienced a highly stressful divorce. Under those conditions, effective child rearing is particularly powerful in limiting adjustment difficulties. (Adapted from Wolchik et al., 2000.)

**divorce mediation**
A series of meetings between divorcing couples and a trained professional, who tries to help them settle disputes. Aimed at avoiding legal battles that intensify family conflict.

**joint custody**
A child custody arrangement following divorce in which the court grants both parents equal say in important decisions about the child's upbringing.

1988; Clarke-Stewart & Hayward, 1996). Fathers are more likely to praise a boy's good behaviour and less likely to ignore his disruptiveness. The father's image of greater power and authority may also help him obtain more compliance from a son. Furthermore, boys in father-custody families may benefit from greater involvement of both parents, since noncustodial mothers participate more in their children's lives than do noncustodial fathers.

A few studies indicate that children who remain in a high-conflict, intact family fare worse in adjustment than do children who make the transition to a low-conflict, single-parent household (Emery, 1999; Hetherington, 1999a). Does this mean that divorce is ultimately beneficial for children? Although it can offer an escape from chronic parental conflict, only a minority of divorces are preceded by intense parental strife (Amato & Booth, 2000). As one expert summed up, "For this reason, divorce probably helps fewer children than it hurts" (Amato, 2000, p. 1278).

When divorcing parents put aside their disagreements and support one another in their child-rearing roles, children have the best chance of growing up competent, stable, and happy. As Figure 14.3 shows, in a study of 8- to 15-year-olds, young people who experienced both high parental acceptance and high consistency of discipline had the lowest levels of adjustment problems (Wolchik et al., 2000). Caring extended-family members, teachers, siblings, and friends also reduce the likelihood that divorce will result in long-term disruption (DeGarmo & Forgatch, 1999; Grych & Fincham, 1997).

**DIVORCE MEDIATION, JOINT CUSTODY, AND CHILD SUPPORT.** Awareness that divorce is highly stressful for parents and children has led to community-based services aimed at helping them through this difficult time. One such service is **divorce mediation.** It consists of a series of meetings between divorcing couples and a trained professional, who tries to help them settle disputes, such as property division and child custody. Its purpose is to avoid legal battles that intensify family conflict. Research reveals that mediation increases out-of-court settlements, compliance with these agreements, cooperation between parents in child rearing, and feelings of well-being reported by divorcing parents and their children (Emery, 2001; Walton, Oliver, & Griffin, 1999).

A relatively recent child custody option tries to keep both parents involved with children. In **joint custody,** the court grants the mother and father equal say in important decisions about the child's upbringing. In Canada, joint custody orders are now granted in slightly more than one-quarter of cases (Statistics Canada, Divorces, 1999). In most instances, children reside with one parent and see the other on a fixed schedule, much like the typical sole-custody situation. But in other cases, parents share physical custody and children move between homes and sometimes schools and peer groups. The success of joint custody requires a cooperative relationship between divorced parents. If they continue to quarrel, it prolongs children's exposure to a hostile family atmosphere (Emery, 1999).

Finally, many single-parent families depend on child support from the absent parent to relieve financial strain. Procedures have been established for withholding wages from parents, usually fathers, who fail to make these court-ordered payments. Although child support is usually not enough to lift a single-parent family out of poverty, it can ease the burden substantially. An added benefit is that noncustodial fathers are more likely to maintain contact with children if they pay child support (Garfinkel & McLanahan, 1995).

## BLENDED FAMILIES

Life in a single-parent family is often temporary. Many parents remarry within a few years. Others *cohabit,* or share a sexual relationship and a residence with a partner outside of

**TABLE** 14.5

Factors Related to Children's Adjustment to Blended Families

| FACTOR | DESCRIPTION |
|---|---|
| Form of blended family | Children living in father–stepmother families display more adjustment difficulties than do those in mother–stepfather families, perhaps because father-custody children start out with more problems. |
| Children's characteristics | |
| *Age* | Early adolescents find it harder to adjust, perhaps because they view the presence of a step-parent as a threat to their freedom. Also, they are more likely to notice and challenge negative aspects of stepfamily living. |
| *Sex* | Girls adjust less well than boys due to interruptions in close bonds with custodial parents and greater conflict with stepmothers. |
| Repeated marital transitions | The more marital transitions, the greater the risk of severe and long-lasting adjustment problems. |
| Social supports | (See Table 14.4 on page 582.) |

marriage. Parent, step-parent, and children form a new family structure called the **blended, or reconstituted, family.**

For some children, this expanded family network is positive and brings greater adult attention. But for most, it presents difficult adjustments. Step-parents often introduce new child-rearing practices, and having to switch to new rules and expectations can be stressful. In addition, children often regard steprelatives as "intruders." But how well they adapt is, once again, related to the overall quality of family functioning (Hetherington & Kelly, 2002). This often depends on which parent forms a new relationship and on the child's age and sex. As we will see, older children and girls seem to have the hardest time (refer to Table 14.5).

**MOTHER–STEPFATHER FAMILIES.** The most frequent form of blended family is a mother–stepfather arrangement, since mothers generally retain custody of the child. Boys usually adjust quickly. They welcome a stepfather who is warm and involved, who refrains from exerting his authority too quickly, and who offers relief from the coercive cycles of interaction that tend to build with their divorced mothers. Mothers' friction with sons also declines due to greater economic security, another adult to share household tasks, and an end to loneliness (Stevenson & Black, 1995). In contrast, girls adapt less favourably. Stepfathers disrupt the close ties many girls have established with their mothers in the single-parent family, and girls often react to the new arrangement with sulky, resistant behaviour (Hetherington, 1993).

Note, however, that age affects these findings. Older school-age children and adolescents of both sexes display more irresponsible, acting out, and antisocial behaviour than do their agemates in nonstepfamilies. Parenting in stepfamilies—particularly families with stepsiblings—is highly challenging. Often parents are warmer and more involved with their biological children than with their stepchildren (Hetherington, Henderson, & Reiss, 1999). Older children are more likely to notice and challenge unfair treatment and other negative consequences of stepfamily living, sparking conflict-ridden family interaction. And adolescents are more likely to view the new step-parent as a threat to their freedom, especially if they experienced little monitoring in the single-parent family (Hetherington & Stanley-Hagan, 2000).

About one-third of adolescent boys and one-fourth of adolescent girls disengage from their stepfamilies, spending little time at home. Instead, they may turn to a friend's family (as a "surrogate"), extracurricular activities, a job, or peers. When disengagement leads to positive relationships with adults and constructive pursuits, teenagers fare quite well. When it results in involvement with antisocial peers and little adult supervision, it is linked to serious difficulties (Hetherington & Jodl, 1994). For some teenagers, problems extend into adulthood. Adults from remarried families are more likely to have lower SES and to experience escalating marital conflict than are those from first-marriage families (Hetherington, 1999b).

**blended,** or **reconstituted, family**
A family structure resulting from cohabitation or remarriage that includes parent, step-parent, and children.

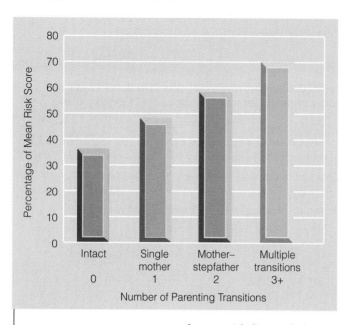

FIGURE 14.4

**Boys' risk for poor adjustment by number of parenting transitions.** Risk was determined by averaging seven adjustment measures: antisocial behaviour, drug use, deviant peer associations, peer rejection, poor academic skills, low self-esteem, and depression. The greater the number of transitions, the higher the risk score. (Adapted from Capaldi & Patterson, 1991.)

**FATHER–STEPMOTHER FAMILIES.** Remarriage of non-custodial fathers often leads to reduced contact, as they tend to withdraw from their "previous" families, more so if they have daughters than sons (Hetherington & Henderson, 1997). Research, however, reveals there is more confusion for children in father–stepmother families. When fathers have custody, children typically react negatively to remarriage. One reason is that children living with fathers often start out with more problems. Perhaps the biological mother could no longer handle the unruly child (usually a boy), so the father and his new wife are faced with a youngster who has serious behaviour problems. In other instances, the father is granted custody because of a very close relationship with the child, and his remarriage disrupts this bond (Buchanan, Maccoby, & Dornbusch, 1996).

Girls, especially, have a hard time getting along with their stepmothers. Sometimes (as just mentioned) this occurs because the girl's relationship with her father is threatened by the remarriage. In addition, girls often become entangled in loyalty conflicts between their two mother figures. But the longer girls live in father–stepmother households, the more positive their interaction with stepmothers becomes (Hetherington & Jodl, 1994). With time and patience they do adjust, and eventually girls benefit from the support of a second mother figure.

**SUPPORT FOR BLENDED FAMILIES.** In blended families, as in divorce, multiple pathways lead to diverse outcomes. Family life education and therapy can help parents and children adapt to the complexities of their new circumstances. Effective approaches encourage step-parents to move into their new roles gradually by first building a friendly relationship with the child. Active parenting can begin only when a warm bond has formed between step-parents and stepchildren (Ganong & Colman, 2000). In addition, therapy can offer couples help in forming a "parenting coalition" through which they cooperate and provide consistency in child rearing. By limiting loyalty conflicts, this allows children to benefit from step-parent relationships and increased diversity in their lives.

**REPEATED MARITAL TRANSITIONS.** Unfortunately, many children do not have a chance to settle into a happy blended family, since the divorce rate for second marriages is higher than for first marriages. In a study of boys in grade 4, the more marital transitions children experienced, the more severe and prolonged their adjustment difficulties (see Figure 14.4). Furthermore, parents with poor child-rearing skills and antisocial tendencies (as indicated by arrest records, drug use, and personality tests) were particularly likely to undergo several divorces and remarriages. In the process, they exposed their children to recurring episodes of high family conflict and inconsistent parenting (Capaldi & Patterson, 1991).

## MATERNAL EMPLOYMENT AND DUAL-EARNER FAMILIES

For many years, divorce has been associated with a high rate of maternal employment, due to financial strains experienced by single mothers. But over the last several decades, women of all sectors of the population—not just those who are single and poor—have gone to work in increasing numbers. Today, 55 percent of single mothers and 69 percent of married mothers work during their children's preschool years. These figures rise to 75 percent of single mothers and 79 percent of married mothers who work once their children are in school (Vanier Institute of the Family, 2001).

As in infancy (see Chapter 10), the consequences of maternal employment for children and adolescents depend on the parent–child relationship. In addition, the mother's work satisfaction, the support she receives from her partner, the child's sex, and the quality of child care have a bearing on how children fare.

**MATERNAL EMPLOYMENT AND CHILD DEVELOPMENT.** Children of mothers who enjoy their work and remain committed to parenting show very favourable adjustment—a higher sense of self-esteem, more positive family and peer relations, less gender-stereotyped beliefs, and better grades in school. Girls, especially, profit from the image of female competence. Overall, daughters of employed mothers perceive the woman's role as involving more freedom of choice and satisfaction and are more achievement and career oriented (Hoffman, 2000).

These benefits undoubtedly result from parenting practices. Employed mothers who value their parenting role are more likely to use authoritative child rearing and coregulation—granting their child independence with oversight. Also, children in dual-earner households devote more daily hours to doing homework under parental guidance and participate more in household chores. And maternal employment results in more time with fathers, who take on greater child-care responsibility (Gottfried et al., 1999; Hoffman & Youngblade, 1999). More paternal contact is related to higher intelligence and achievement, mature social behaviour, and gender-stereotype flexibility (Gottfried, 1991; Radin, 1994).

However, when employment places heavy demands on the mother's schedule, children are at risk for ineffective parenting. Working long hours and spending little time with children are associated with less favourable adjustment (Moorehouse, 1991). In contrast, part-time employment seems to have benefits for children of all ages, probably because it prevents work overload, thereby helping mothers meet children's needs (Hart et al., 1997).

**SUPPORT FOR EMPLOYED PARENTS AND THEIR FAMILIES.** In dual-earner families, the husband's willingness to share responsibilities helps mothers engage in effective parenting. If the father helps very little or not at all, the mother carries a double load, at home and at work, leading to fatigue, distress, and reduced time and energy for children.

Employed mothers and dual-earner parents need assistance from work settings and communities in their child-rearing roles. Part-time employment, flexible schedules, job-sharing, and paid leave when children are ill help parents juggle the demands of work and child rearing. Equal pay and equal employment opportunities for women are also important. Because these policies enhance financial status and morale, they improve the way mothers feel and behave when they arrive home at the end of the working day.

As long as this employed mother enjoys her job, remains committed to parenting, and finds satisfactory child-care arrangements, her child is likely to develop high self-esteem, positive family and peer relations, and flexible beliefs about gender. But when employment places heavy demands on the mother's schedule and she receives little or no help from the father, children are at risk for ineffective parenting and less favourable cognitive and social outcomes.

## CHILD CARE

Over the last 30 years, the number of young children in child care has steadily increased. Figure 14.5 shows where Canadian preschoolers spend their days. Although most children are cared for at home by a parent, 40 percent spend part of their week in some form of child-care arrangement while their parents work, study, or train (Kohen & Hertzman, 1998). Children of higher-SES parents and children of very low-SES parents are especially likely to be in regulated care centres (Human Resources, 1997). Lower-income working parents more often use informal home care because they are not eligible for subsidized centre-based care (Howes & James, 2002).

**CHILD-CARE QUALITY AND CHILDREN'S DEVELOPMENT.** Recall from Chapter 8 that early intervention can enhance the development of economically disadvantaged children. Preschoolers in poor-quality child care, regardless of their SES level, score lower on measures of cognitive and social skills. In contrast, high-quality child care enhances development, especially among low-SES children (Hausfather et al., 1997; Howes & James, 2002; Lamb, 1998). And recall from longitudinal research reported in Chapter 10 (see page 432) that Canadian preschoolers in high-quality child care scored higher in language competence than their agemates receiving less sensitive, stimulating care. This early advantage in language competence was associated with more favourable cognitive and social development through adolescence (Kohen et al., 2000).

© JONATHAN NOUROK/STONE/GETTY IMAGES

**FIGURE** 14.5

**Who's minding Canada's 4- and 5-year-olds?** Although most children are cared for at home by their parents, 40 percent spend part of their week in some type of outside care arrangement while their parents work, study, or train. Most children in child care are enrolled in an unlicensed setting outside the home. (Adapted from Kohen & Hertzman, 1998. Reprinted by permission of Human Resources Development Canada and Government Works, 2002.)

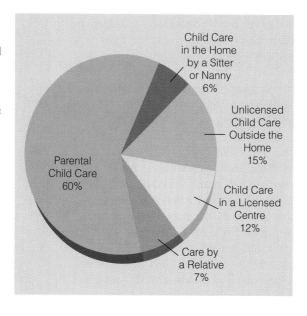

Child Care in the Home by a Sitter or Nanny 6%

Unlicensed Child Care Outside the Home 15%

Parental Child Care 60%

Child Care in a Licensed Centre 12%

Care by a Relative 7%

What are the ingredients of high-quality child care for preschoolers? Large-scale studies of child-care centres and child-care homes reveal that the following factors are important: group size (number of children in a single space), caregiver–child ratio, caregivers' educational preparation, and caregivers' personal commitment to learning about and caring for children. When these characteristics are favourable, adults are more verbally stimulating and sensitive to preschoolers' needs. Children, in turn, do especially well on measures of cognitive, language, and social skills—effects that persist into the early school years for children of a wide range of family backgrounds (Burchinal et al., 2000; Helburn, 1995; Peiser-Feinberg, 1999). Other research shows that spacious, well-equipped environments and activities that meet the educational needs and interests of preschool children also contribute to positive outcomes (Howes, 1988b).

**CHILD-CARE POLICIES.** Table 14.6 summarizes characteristics of high-quality child care for preschoolers, based on standards devised by the U.S. National Association for

**TABLE** 14.6

High-Quality Child Care for Preschool Children

| PROGRAM CHARACTERISTICS | SIGNS OF QUALITY |
|---|---|
| Physical setting | Indoor environment is clean, in good repair, and well ventilated. Classroom space is divided into richly equipped activity areas, including make-believe play, blocks, science, math, games and puzzles, books, art, and music. Fenced outdoor play space is equipped with swings, climbing equipment, tricycles, and sandbox. |
| Group size | In preschools and child-care centres, group size is no greater than 18 to 20 children with 2 teachers. |
| Caregiver–child ratio | In child-care centres, teacher is responsible for no more than 8 to 10 children. In child-care homes, caregiver is responsible for no more than 6 children. |
| Daily activities | Most of the time, children work individually or in small groups. Children select many of their own activities and learn through experiences relevant to their own lives. Teachers facilitate children's involvement, accept individual differences, and adjust expectations to children's developing capacities. |
| Interactions between adults and children | Teachers move between groups and individuals, asking questions, offering suggestions, and adding more complex ideas. They use positive guidance techniques, such as modelling and encouraging expected behaviour and redirecting children to more acceptable activities. |
| Teacher qualifications | Teachers have post-secondary specialized preparation in early childhood development, early childhood education, or a related field. |
| Relationships with parents | Parents are encouraged to observe and participate. Teachers talk frequently with parents about children's behaviour and development. |
| Licensing and accreditation | Program is licensed. |

*Sources:* Bredekamp & Copple, 1997; Canadian Child Care Federation, 1994; Howe and Jacobs, 1995; National Association for the Education of Young Children, 1998.

the Education of Young Children. (Return to Chapter 10, page 433, to review the signs of high-quality child care for infants and toddlers.) When these ingredients are absent, children's well-being is compromised.

Just over one-third of child-care centres in Canada are licensed (Canadian Child Care Federation, 2000). Recall from Chapter 10 that government licensing does not guarantee high-quality care; it merely ensures adequate safety, child-to-adult ratio, and staff-training standards (Kohen & Hertzman, 1998). The child-care situation in Canada is compromised by the absence of a national policy on child care. Licensing regulations are uneven across provinces and territories (Childcare Resource and Research Unit, 2000). Consequently, most centres provide only minimal- to mediocre-quality care (refer to Figure 10.8 on page 432).

In Australia and Western Europe, child care that meets rigorous standards is widely available, and caregivers are paid on the same salary scale as elementary school teachers. Regardless of family income, in Denmark, up to 80 percent of child-care costs are government supported; in Sweden, nearly 90 percent; and in France, 100 percent (Waldfogel, 2001). Because Canada, like the United States, does not yet have a national child-care policy, it lags behind other industrialized nations in supply, quality, and affordability of child care.

---

### SELF-CARE

High-quality child care is vital for parents' peace of mind and children's well-being, even during middle childhood. However, increasing numbers of children are expected to care for themselves in the after-school hours. Provincial guidelines vary with respect to the age a child can be left alone and/or in charge of others. Generally, children may not be left alone under age 10.

Clearly, parents must consider children's maturity before deciding on self-care. According to University of Victoria professor Nancy Galambos, children should not be left unsupervised before 8 or 9 years of age because most are not yet competent to handle emergencies (Galambos & Maggs, 1991). Unfortunately, even when children are not mature enough to handle self-care, many employed parents resort to it because they have few alternatives.

Research on these **self-care children** reveals inconsistent findings. Some studies report that they suffer from low self-esteem, antisocial behaviour, poor academic achievement, and fearfulness, whereas others show no such effects. Children's maturity and the way they spend their time seem to explain these contradictions. Among younger school-age children, those who spend more hours alone have more adjustment difficulties (Vandell & Posner, 1999). As children become old enough to look after themselves, those who have a history of authoritative child rearing, are monitored from a distance by parental telephone calls, and have regular after-school chores appear responsible and well adjusted. In contrast, those left to their own devices are more likely to bend to peer pressures and engage in antisocial behaviour (Steinberg, 1986).

When school-age children experience "after care" with a staff trained in child development; a generous adult–child ratio; positive adult–child communication; and stimulating, varied activities, they show better social skills and psychological adjustment (Pettit et al., 1997; Pierce, Hamm, & Vandell, 1999). Low-SES children in high-quality after-school programs who otherwise would have few opportunities for enrichment activities, such as scouting, music lessons, and organized sports, display broader benefits. These include better work habits, school grades, and peer relations and fewer behaviour problems (Posner & Vandell, 1994, 1999).

In this after-school nature club in Toronto, children spend time productively and enjoyably while their parents are at work. A community volunteer assists children as they explore nature. Children who attend after-school programs display better school grades, work habits, and peer relations.

TONY FREEMAN/PHOTOEDIT

**self-care children**
Children who regularly look after themselves during after-school hours.

## ASK YOURSELF (www)

**review**    Describe and explain changes in sibling relationships from early childhood to adolescence. How does parenting influence the quality of sibling ties?

**review**    Under what conditions do maternal employment and child care lead to benefits for preschool and school-age children?

**apply**    What advice would you give divorcing parents of two school-age sons about how to help their children adapt to life in a single-parent family?

**connect**    Review research on resilient children in Chapter 1 (see page 10). Are factors that foster resiliency similar to those that promote favourable adjustment to divorce and remarriage? Explain.

# Vulnerable Families: Child Maltreatment

FAMILIES CONTRIBUTE TO THE maintenance of society by serving as contexts in which children are loved, protected, and encouraged to develop into competent, caring adults. Throughout our discussion of family transitions, we encountered examples of many factors, both within and outside the family, that contribute to parents' capacity to be warm, consistent, and appropriately demanding. As we turn now to the topic of child maltreatment, we will see that when these vital supports for effective child rearing break down, children as well as their parents can suffer terribly.

## INCIDENCE AND DEFINITIONS

Child maltreatment is as old as the history of humankind, but only recently has the problem been recognized and research been directed at understanding it. Perhaps public concern has increased because child maltreatment is especially common in large industrialized nations. A Canadian survey revealed that in 1997, children were the victims of 23 percent of assaults reported to police. In about one-fourth of these cases, a family member committed the offence (Statistics Canada, Family Violence, 1999).

In Canada, child maltreatment is categorized into the following forms (Trocmé et al., 2001a; MacMillan, 2000):

- *Physical abuse:* assaults on children, such as kicking, biting, shaking, punching, or stabbing, that produce pain, cuts, welts, bruises, burns, broken bones, and other injuries

- *Sexual abuse:* sexual comments, fondling, intercourse, and other forms of sexual exploitation

- *Physical neglect:* living conditions in which children do not receive enough food, clothing, medical attention, or supervision

- *Psychological abuse:* failure of caregivers to meet children's needs for affection and emotional support, and actions, such as ridicule, humiliation, scapegoating, or terrorizing, that damage children's cognitive, emotional, or social functioning

To provide a more complete picture of reported child maltreatment cases, the first Canada-wide study of the incidence and characteristics of child abuse was recently completed (Trocmé et al., 2001b). In 1998, approximately 22 child abuse investigations were conducted per 1000 Canadian children. Physical neglect was the primary concern in 40 percent of these investigations, with physical abuse identified in 30 percent, psychological abuse in

**TABLE** 14.7

Factors Related to Child Maltreatment

| FACTOR | DESCRIPTION |
| --- | --- |
| Parent characteristics | Psychological disturbance; alcohol and drug abuse; history of abuse as a child; belief in harsh, physical discipline; desire to satisfy unmet emotional needs through the child; unreasonable expectations for child behaviour; young age (most under 30); low educational level |
| Child characteristics | Premature or very sick baby; difficult temperament; inattentiveness and overactivity; other developmental problems |
| Family characteristics | Low income; poverty; homelessness; marital instability; social isolation; physical abuse of mother by husband or boyfriend; frequent moves; large family with closely spaced children; overcrowded living conditions; disorganized household; lack of steady employment |
| Community | Few parks, child-care centres, preschool programs, recreation centres, and churches to serve as family supports; violent neighbourhood |
| Culture | Approval of physical force and violence as ways to solve problems |

*Source:* Cicchetti & Toth, 1993.

19 percent, and sexual abuse in 11 percent. However, the true figures for all types of abuse are likely higher, since most cases go unreported.

Although all experts recognize that these types of child maltreatment exist, they do not agree on how frequent and intense an adult's actions must be to be called maltreatment. The greatest problems arise in the case of subtle, ambiguous behaviours. All of us can agree that broken bones, cigarette burns, and bite marks are abusive, but the decision is harder to make in instances in which an adult touches or makes degrading comments to a child.

Some investigators regard psychological and sexual abuse as the most destructive forms, but psychological abuse may be the most common, since it accompanies most other types. Yet definitions of psychological abuse are especially complex and serious in their consequences. If they are too narrow and include only the most severe instances of mental cruelty, they allow many harmful actions toward children to continue unchecked and untreated. If they are too lenient, they can result in arbitrary, disruptive legal intrusions into family life.

Child sexual abuse is examined in the Social Issues: Health box on page 592.

## ORIGINS OF CHILD MALTREATMENT

Early findings suggested that child maltreatment was rooted in adult psychological disturbance (Kempe et al., 1962). But it soon became clear that although child abuse was more common among disturbed parents, a single "abusive" personality type does not exist. Sometimes, even "normal" parents harm their children! Perhaps more surprising, parents who were abused as children do not necessarily repeat the cycle with their own children (Buchanan, 1996; Simons et al., 1991).

For help in understanding child maltreatment, researchers turned to the social systems perspective on family functioning. They discovered that many interacting variables—at the family, community, and cultural levels—promote child abuse and neglect. Table 14.7 summarizes factors associated with child maltreatment. The more of these risks that are present, the greater the likelihood that abuse or neglect will occur. Let's examine each set of influences in turn.

**THE FAMILY.** Within the family, certain children—those whose characteristics make them more of a challenge to rear—are more likely to become targets of abuse. These include premature or very sick babies and children who are temperamentally difficult, are inattentive

*social issues: health*

### CHILD SEXUAL ABUSE

Until recently, child sexual abuse was viewed as a rare occurrence. When children came forward to report it, adults rarely took their claims seriously. In the 1970s, efforts by professionals along with media attention brought child sexual abuse into focus as a serious and widespread problem.

#### CHARACTERISTICS OF ABUSERS AND VICTIMS

Sexual abuse is committed against children of both sexes but more often against girls. Most cases are reported in middle childhood, but sexual abuse also occurs at younger and older ages. For some victims, the abuse begins early in life and continues for many years (Trickett & Putnam, 1998).

Generally the abuser is a male—a parent or someone the parent knows well. Often it is a father, stepfather, or live-in boyfriend; somewhat less often, an uncle or older brother. In a few instances, mothers are the offenders, more often with sons (Kolvin & Trowell, 1996). In the overwhelming majority of cases, the abuse is serious—vaginal or anal intercourse, oral–genital contact, fondling, and forced stimulation of the adult. Abusers make the child comply

in a variety of distasteful ways, including deception, bribery, verbal intimidation, and physical force.

You may be wondering how any adult—especially a parent or close relative—could possibly violate a child sexually. Many offenders deny their own responsibility. They blame the abuse on the willing participation of a seductive youngster. Yet children are not capable of making a deliberate, informed decision to enter into a sexual relationship! Even at older ages, they are not free to say yes or no. Instead, the responsibility lies with abusers, who tend to have characteristics that predispose them toward sexual exploitation of children. They have great difficulty controlling their impulses and may suffer from alcohol and drug abuse. Often they pick out children who are unlikely to defend themselves— children who are physically weak, emotionally deprived, and socially isolated (Bolen, 2001).

Reported cases of child sexual abuse are strongly linked to poverty, marital instability, and resulting weakening of family ties. Children who live in homes with a history of constantly changing characters—repeated marriages, separations, and new partners—are espe-

cially vulnerable. But community surveys reveal that children in economically advantaged, stable families are also victims: there, the perpetrators are simply more likely to escape detection (Gomez-Schwartz, Horowitz, & Cardarelli, 1990).

#### CONSEQUENCES OF SEXUAL ABUSE

The adjustment problems of child sexual abuse victims are often severe. Depression, low self-esteem, mistrust of adults, and anger and hostility can persist for years after the abusive episodes. Younger children react with sleep difficulties, loss of appetite, and generalized fearfulness. Reactions of adolescents include severe depression, suicidal impulses, substance abuse, early sexual activity with more partners, running away, and delinquency. At all ages, persistent abuse accompanied by force and violence has a more severe impact (Feiring, Taska, & Lewis, 1999; Wolfe, 1998).

Sexually abused children frequently display sexual knowledge and behaviour beyond their years. They have learned from their abusers that sexual overtures are acceptable ways to get attention and rewards. As they move toward young adulthood, many abused girls

or overactive, or have other developmental problems (Kotch, Muller, & Blakely, 1999). But whether such children actually are maltreated depends on parents' characteristics.

Maltreating parents are less skilful than other parents in handling discipline confrontations and getting children to cooperate in working toward common goals. They also suffer from biased thinking about their child. For example, they often evaluate transgressions as worse than they are and attribute their child's misdeeds to a stubborn or bad disposition— perspectives that lead them to move quickly toward physical force (Milner, 1993; Rogosch et al., 1995).

Once abuse gets started, it quickly becomes part of a self-sustaining relationship. The small irritations to which abusive parents react—a fussy baby, a preschooler who knocks over her milk, or a child who will not mind immediately—soon become bigger ones. Then the harshness increases. By the preschool years, abusive and neglectful parents seldom interact

This poster for Keeping Ourselves Safe, New Zealand's national, school-based child abuse prevention program, illustrates the importance of teaching children to recognize abusive adult behaviours so they can take steps to protect themselves. Parents are informed about children's classroom learning experiences and encouraged to support and extend them at home.

NEW ZEALAND POLICE

become promiscuous, believing that their bodies are for others to use. Women are likely to choose partners who abuse both them and their children (Faller, 1990). As mothers, they often show poor parenting skills, abusing and neglecting their youngsters (Pianta, Egeland, & Erickson, 1989). In these ways, the harmful impact of sexual abuse is transmitted to the next generation.

## PREVENTION AND TREATMENT

Treating child sexual abuse is difficult. Since it typically appears in the midst of other serious family problems, long-term therapy with both children and parents usually is necessary (Olafson & Boat, 2000). The best way to reduce the suffering of victims is to prevent it from continuing. Today, courts are prosecuting abusers

(especially nonrelatives) more vigorously and taking children's testimony more seriously (see Chapter 7). Special efforts are needed to help sexually abused boys, who are less likely than girls to speak about the experience and receive therapy and court protection (Holmes & Slap, 1998).

Educational programs can teach children to recognize inappropriate sexual advances and show them where to go for help. Yet because of controversies over teaching children about sexual abuse, few schools offer these

interventions. New Zealand is the only country in the world with a national, school-based prevention program targeting sexual abuse. In *Keeping Ourselves Safe,* children and adolescents learn that abusers are rarely strangers. Parent involvement ensures that home and school work together in teaching children self-protection skills. Evaluations reveal that virtually all New Zealand parents and children support the program and that it has helped many children avoid or report abuse (Briggs & Hawkins, 1996, 1999).

with their children. When they do, they rarely express pleasure and affection; the communication is almost always negative (Wolff, 1999).

Most parents, however, have enough self-control not to respond to their children's misbehaviour or developmental problems with abuse. Other factors must combine with these conditions to prompt an extreme parental response. Abusive parents react to stressful situations with high emotional arousal. At the same time, such factors as low income and education (less than a high school diploma), unemployment, young maternal age, alcohol and drug use, marital conflict, overcrowded living conditions, frequent moves, and extreme household disorganization are common in abusive homes (Gelles, 1998; Kotch, Muller, & Blakely, 1999). These personal and situational conditions increase the chances that parents will be too overwhelmed to meet basic child-rearing responsibilities or will vent their frustrations by lashing out at their children.

**THE COMMUNITY.** The majority of abusive and neglectful parents are isolated from both formal and informal social supports. This social isolation has at least two causes. First, because of their own life histories, many of these parents have learned to mistrust and avoid others. They do not have the skills necessary for establishing and maintaining positive relationships with friends and relatives (Polansky et al., 1985). Second, maltreating parents are more likely to live in unstable, run-down neighbourhoods that provide few links between family and community, such as parks, child-care centres, preschool programs, recreation centres, and churches (Coulton, Korbin, & Su, 1999; Garbarino & Kostelny, 1993). For these reasons, they lack "lifelines" to others and have no one to turn to for help during stressful times.

Also, the negative conditions and stress associated with living in a violent neighbourhood seem to heighten violent responses to conflict in the home. In a study carried out at a summer day camp, school-age children who reported hearing about, experiencing, or witnessing a greater number of neighbourhood violent acts (such as shootings, stabbings, and sexual assaults) were more likely to have been physically abused and severely neglected (Lynch & Cicchetti, 1998).

**THE LARGER CULTURE.** One final set of factors—cultural values, laws, and customs—profoundly affects the chances that child maltreatment will occur when parents feel overburdened. Societies that view violence, and even physical punishment, as an appropriate way to solve problems set the stage for child abuse. Research indicates that in countries where physical punishment is not accepted, such as Luxembourg and Sweden, rates of child abuse are low (U.S. Department of State, 1999). In Canada, laws are designed to protect children from maltreatment, yet physical force is still used. On the positive side, the percentage of Canadian parents who refrain from using physical punishment with their children has increased. In 1994, 56 percent of children had parents who never used physical discipline. In 1996 that group rose to 64 percent (Minister of Public Works and Government Services Canada, 2002).

## CONSEQUENCES OF CHILD MALTREATMENT

The family circumstances of maltreated children impair the development of emotional self-regulation, empathy and sympathy, self-concept, social skills, and academic motivation. Over time, these youngsters show serious learning and adjustment problems, including school failure, severe depression, aggressive behaviour, peer difficulties, substance abuse, and delinquency (Bolger & Patterson, 2001; Shonk & Cicchetti, 2001). In a study of Canadian high school students, those reporting high levels of child maltreatment had engaged in more violent crime, carried concealed weapons, and threatened or physically abused others (Wolfe et al., 2001).

How do these damaging consequences occur? Think back to our discussion in Chapter 12 of the effects of hostile cycles of parent–child interaction. Indeed, a family characteristic strongly associated with child abuse is spouse abuse, in which physical and psychological brutality permeate the parents' relationship (Margolin, 1998). Clearly, the home lives of abused children overflow with opportunities to learn to use aggression as a way of solving problems.

Furthermore, demeaning parental messages, in which children are ridiculed, humiliated, rejected, or terrorized, result in low self-esteem, high anxiety, self-blame, opposition, aggression, and efforts to escape from extreme psychological pain—at times severe enough to prompt a suicide attempt in adolescence (Kaplan, Pelcovitz, & Labruna, 1999; Wolfe, 1999). At school, maltreated children are serious discipline problems. Their noncompliance, poor motivation, and cognitive immaturity interfere with academic achievement—an outcome that further undermines their chances for life success (Margolin & Gordis, 2000).

Finally, the trauma of repeated abuse can lead to psychophysiological changes, including abnormal brain-wave activity and heightened production of stress hormones (Ito et al., 1998;

Nelson & Carver, 1998). By school age, abused children are hyperaroused by angry faces, as indicated by an elevated EEG response—a reaction that primes them to lash out when challenged (Cicchetti & Toth, 2000). These effects on brain functioning increase the chances that emotional self-regulation and adjustment problems will endure.

### PREVENTING CHILD MALTREATMENT

Since child maltreatment is embedded within families, communities, and society as a whole, efforts to prevent it must be directed at each of these levels. Many approaches have been suggested, including interventions that teach high-risk parents effective child-rearing and disciplinary strategies, high school child development courses that include direct experience with children, and broad social programs aimed at bettering economic conditions for low-SES families.

We have seen that providing social supports to families is very effective in easing parental stress. This approach sharply reduces child maltreatment as well (Azar & Wolfe, 1998). Research also indicates that a trusting relationship with another person is the most important factor in preventing mothers with childhood histories of abuse from repeating the cycle with their own youngsters (Egeland, Jacobvitz, & Sroufe, 1988). Parents Anonymous, an organization that has as its main goal helping child-abusing parents learn constructive parenting practices, does so largely through providing social supports such as self-help group meetings, daily phone calls, and regular home visits to relieve social isolation and teach alternative child-rearing skills.

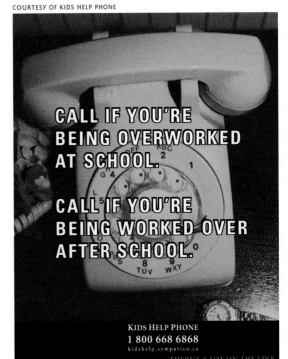

This poster informs children that help is available by phone 24 hours a day, 7 days a week, for those suffering from abuse. Public service announcements like this one help prevent child abuse by educating people about the problem and telling them where they can find help.

Other preventive approaches include announcements in the media that educate people about child maltreatment and tell them where to seek help. The Kids Help Phone line is a Canadian toll-free national counselling service for children and adolescents. It offers assistance 24 hours a day, 7 days a week and answers 800 to 1000 calls per day on issues pertaining to relationships, health, abusive behaviours, violence, sexuality, substance abuse, and suicide (Kids Help Phone, 2002). The Parent Help Line began operations in 2000 as an offshoot of the Kids Help Phone, and it offers recorded messages on a variety of parenting topics, such as child abuse. Counsellors are available as well.

Besides these efforts, changes are needed in our culture. Many experts believe that child maltreatment cannot be eliminated as long as violence is widespread and corporal punishment is regarded as an acceptable child-rearing alternative. In addition, combatting poverty and its diverse correlates—family stress and disorganization, inadequate food and medical care, teenage parenthood, low-birth-weight babies, and parental hopelessness—would reduce child maltreatment.

Although more cases reach the courts than in decades past, child maltreatment remains a crime that is difficult to prove. Most of the time, the only witnesses are the child victims or other loyal family members. Even in court cases in which the evidence is strong, judges hesitate to impose the ultimate safeguard against further harm: permanently removing the child from the family.

There are two reasons for this reluctant attitude. First, in Canadian society, government intervention in family life is viewed as a last resort. Second, despite destructive family relationships, maltreated children and their parents are usually attached to one another. Most of the time, neither desires separation.

Even with intensive treatment, some adults persist in their abusive acts. In 1997, 96 youth under the age of 18 were victims of homicide, representing 17 percent of all homicides in Canada. More than half of these cases were children younger than 3. Family members, mostly parents, were responsible for 76 percent of these homicides

(Statistics Canada, Family Violence, 1999). When parents are unlikely to change their behaviour, the drastic step of separating parent from child and legally terminating parental rights is the only reasonable course of action.

Individuals who work with children, such as teachers, social workers, and psychologists, have a legal obligation to report suspected child abuse to their local children's aid society. Except for the Yukon, all jurisdictions in Canada have a "duty to report" statute, although each jurisdiction varies in the level of certainty required for a report (Evans, 1997).

Child maltreatment is a distressing and horrifying topic. When we consider how often it occurs in Canada, a society that claims to place a high value on the dignity and worth of the individual, it is even more appalling. Yet there is reason to be optimistic. Great strides have been made over the past several decades in understanding and preventing child maltreatment.

## ASK YOURSELF

**review**    How do personal and situational factors that contribute to child maltreatment illustrate the social systems perspective on family functioning?

**review**    Explain how the consequences of maltreatment for children's development can increase the chances of further maltreatment and lead to lasting adjustment problems.

**apply**    Claire told her 6-year-old daughter to be very careful never to talk to or take candy from strangers. Why will Claire's directive not protect her daughter from sexual abuse?

**connect**    After reviewing factors linked to adolescent parenthood (Chapter 5, pages 209–210), explain why it places children at risk for abuse and neglect.

# summary

## EVOLUTIONARY ORIGINS

*Discuss the evolutionary origins and adaptive value of the family among our hunting-and-gathering ancestors.*

■ The human family in its most common form can be traced to our hunting-and-gathering ancestors. When bipedalism evolved and arms were freed to carry things, our ancestors found it easier to cooperate and share, especially in providing food for the young. A man and woman assumed special responsibility for their own children because the arrangement enhanced survival. Kinship groups expanded, offering greater success at competing with other humans for resources.

## FUNCTIONS OF THE FAMILY

*Cite the functions modern families perform for society.*

■ Responsibilities of contemporary families are largely restricted to reproduction, socialization, and emotional support. As societies became more complex, other institutions developed to assist with certain essential functions, such as educating children and ensuring societal order.

## THE FAMILY AS A SOCIAL SYSTEM

*Describe the social systems perspective on family functioning, including its view of family interaction and the influence of surrounding social contexts.*

■ Contemporary researchers view the family from a **social systems perspective**—as a complex set of interacting relationships affected by the larger social context. Bidirectional influences exist in which the behaviours of each family member affect those of others—an interplay of forces that must constantly adapt to the development of its members. Connections to the community—through formal organizations and informal social networks—grant parents and children social support, thereby promoting effective family interaction and children's development.

## SOCIALIZATION WITHIN THE FAMILY

*Discuss the features that differentiate major child-rearing styles, and explain how effective parents adapt child rearing to children's growing competence during middle childhood and adolescence.*

■ Three features differentiate major **child-rearing styles:** (1) acceptance and involvement in the child's life to establish emotional connection; (2) control of the child to promote mature behaviour; and (3) autonomy granting to encourage self-reliance. The **authoritative style** is high in acceptance and involvement, emphasizes firm control with explanations, and includes gradual, appropriate autonomy granting. It promotes cognitive, emotional, and social competence from early childhood into adolescence.

- The **authoritarian style** is low in acceptance and involvement, high in coercive control, and restricts instead of granting autonomy. It is associated with anxious, withdrawn, dependent child behaviour, especially among girls, and high rates of anger, defiance, and aggression, especially among boys. The **permissive style** is high in acceptance, low in control, and lax rather than appropriate in autonomy granting. Children who experience it typically show poor self-control and achievement and, in adolescence, are defiant and antisocial. The **uninvolved style** combines low acceptance and involvement with little control or effort to grant autonomy. When it begins early, it disrupts virtually all aspects of development. Children's characteristics contribute to the ease with which parents can apply an authoritative style.

- In middle childhood, effective parents engage in **coregulation,** exerting general oversight while permitting children to be in charge of moment-by-moment decision making. During adolescence, mature **autonomy** is fostered by parenting that grants young people independence in accord with their readiness while maintaining a warm, supportive relationship.

*Describe socioeconomic and ethnic variations in child rearing, including the impact of poverty.*

- The authoritative style is the most common pattern of child rearing in many ethnic groups and cultures. Nevertheless, consistent variations in child rearing exist that are linked to SES and ethnicity. Higher-SES parents are more verbal and stimulating and rely more on warmth and explanations; low-SES parents use more commands, criticism, and physical punishment. Certain ethnic groups, including Chinese, Hispanic, Asian Pacific Island, and African American, rely on high levels of parental control. Research on Chinese children reveals that when such control is highly coercive, it impairs academic and social competence.

- Effective parenting, along with children's development, is seriously undermined by the stress and disorganization of living in poverty. **Extended-family households,** in which one or more adult relatives live with the parent–child **nuclear family unit,** are common among ethnic minorities and protect children's development under conditions of high life stress.

## FAMILY LIFESTYLES AND TRANSITIONS

*Describe the influence of family size on child rearing, and explain how sibling relationships change with age and affect development.*

- The trend toward smaller families has positive consequences for child rearing, in terms of attention, patience, and resources invested in children. However, factors associated with low SES seem largely responsible for negative relationships between family size and children's health and adjustment.

- Most children still grow up with at least one sibling. Because of their frequency and emotional intensity, sibling interactions promote many aspects of social competence. Parental warmth fosters cooperative sibling ties; lack of parental involvement, coercive control, and favouritism increase sibling rivalry. During adolescence, sibling relationships become less intense, but attachment to siblings remains strong for most young people.

- Contrary to popular belief, only children are as well adjusted as are children with siblings, and they are advantaged in self-esteem, school achievement, and educational attainment.

*How do children fare in adoptive families, gay and lesbian families, and single-parent families?*

- Infertile couples and older, single individuals often turn to adoption as a way of starting a family. Although adopted children have more learning and emotional difficulties than do their nonadopted agemates, by adulthood this difference disappears. Most parents who adopt children with physical or psychological problems report high satisfaction with the adoptive experience. When parents help them learn about their heritage, transracially or trans-

culturally adopted young people typically develop healthy identities that combine their birth and rearing backgrounds.

- Although limited and based on small samples, research on gay and lesbian parents indicates that they are as committed to and effective at child rearing as are heterosexuals. Their children seem as well adjusted as other children, and most are heterosexual.

*What factors influence children's adjustment to divorce and blended-family arrangements?*

- Divorce is common in the lives of Canadian children. Although painful emotional reactions usually accompany the period surrounding divorce, children with difficult temperaments and boys in mother-custody homes are more likely to show continuing school-performance difficulties and antisocial behaviour. For children of both sexes, divorce is linked to problems with adolescent sexuality and development of intimate ties.

- The overriding factor in positive adjustment following divorce is effective parenting. Contact with fathers reduces the risk of lasting problems. Because **divorce mediation** helps parents resolve their disputes and cooperate in child rearing, it can help children through the difficult period surrounding divorce. The success of **joint custody** requires a cooperative relationship between divorced parents.

- When divorced parents enter new relationships through cohabitation or remarriage, children must adapt to a **blended,** or **reconstituted, family.** How well children do depends on which parent forms a new relationship and on the age and sex of the child. Girls, older children, and children in father–stepmother families experience more difficulties. Step-parents who move into their roles gradually and form a "parenting coalition" with the natural parent help children adjust. Because repeated marital transitions expose children to recurring episodes of family conflict and inconsistent parenting, they severely disrupt development.

*How do maternal employment and life in dual-earner families affect children's development?*

- When mothers enjoy their work and remain committed to parenting, maternal employment is associated with favourable consequences for children, including a higher sense of self-esteem, more positive family and peer relations, less gender-stereotyped beliefs, and better grades in school. In dual-earner families, the father's willingness to share child rearing is linked to many positive outcomes for children. The availability of workplace supports, such as part-time employment and paid parental leave, helps mothers juggle the demands of work and child rearing.

*Discuss the influence of child-care quality on preschoolers' development, the status of child care in Canada compared with other industrialized nations, and the impact of self-care on school-age children's adjustment.*

■ Canadian children experience a diverse array of child-care arrangements while their parents are at work. Other than parental care, unlicensed care settings outside the home are the most common form during the preschool years. When group size is small, caregiver–child ratios are generous, and caregivers are well educated and personally committed to caring for children, adults communicate in more stimulating and responsive ways. As a result, children do especially well on measures of cognitive, language, and social skills.

■ **Self-care children** who are old enough to look after themselves, are monitored from a distance, and have a history of authoritative parenting appear responsible and well adjusted. In contrast, children left to their own devices are at risk for antisocial behaviour. Children in high-quality after-school programs reap academic and social benefits.

## VULNERABLE FAMILIES: CHILD MALTREATMENT

*Discuss the multiple origins of child maltreatment, its consequences for development, and prevention strategies.*

■ Child maltreatment is related to factors within the family, community, and larger culture. Child and parent characteristics often feed on one another to produce abusive behaviour. Unmanageable parental stress, social isolation, and neighbourhood violence greatly increase the chances that abuse and neglect will occur. When a society approves of force and violence as appropriate means for solving problems, child abuse is promoted.

■ Maltreated children are impaired in the development of emotional self-regulation, empathy and sympathy, self-concept, social skills, and learning in school. In addition, the trauma of abuse is associated with abnormal brain-wave activity and a heightened stress response. Over time, children show a wide variety of serious adjustment problems. Successful prevention of child maltreatment requires efforts at the family, community, and cultural levels, including social supports for parents, public education about the problem and how to seek help, and a reduction in societal violence and poverty.

# important terms and concepts

authoritarian style (p. 569)
authoritative style (p. 569)
autonomy (p. 573)
blended, or reconstituted, family
   (p. 585)

child-rearing styles (p. 567)
coregulation (p. 571)
divorce mediation (p. 584)
extended-family household (p. 576)
joint custody (p. 584)

nuclear family unit (p. 576)
permissive style (p. 569)
self-care children (p. 589)
social systems perspective (p. 563)
uninvolved style (p. 569)

"My Favourite Game"
Alia Nemir Ahmed
9 years, United Arab Emirates

With age, children enter into an increasingly elaborate network of peers, where they learn to cooperate in groups and forge close friendships. The role of peers in promoting emotional security, self- and social understanding, and skills for relating to others is a vital part of Chapter 15.

# fifteen

## Peers, Media, and Schooling

STU AND PETE BECAME friends in their school's Connections program, which assists seventh graders with the transition to junior high by assigning a group of students to the same classes and lunch hour. The program aims to help students feel "connected" in their new, large-school environment. During a discussion in health class, Mrs. Stevens asked what their new-school experiences had been like.

Stu began, "When we started the year, people were bouncing around, trying to find friends they felt comfortable with, and it wasn't so easy. I wasn't sure I was going to fit in. In the past few weeks, though, Pete and I clicked."

"Same with Marie and me," Denise chimed in. "I used to have another group of friends in grade 6, but I lost interest. I mean, when they got here, they were trying too hard to be popular."

"Can you explain that a little?" Mrs. Stevens inquired.

"Well, every time they talked to someone, they acted like a different person—kinda two-faced. It was annoying. So I looked for new friends."

"How do you know someone's going to be a good friend?" Mrs. Stevens asked.

"You've gotta have the same interests, and Stu and me, we've got similar personalities," Pete responded. "For example, we both like computer stuff like playing games and chatting on instant messaging. But it can take a while to become friends. You have to feel the person cares about you. And a friend should make you feel good about yourself. I wouldn't be friends with someone who's always making me feel bad."

"Yeah," Marie agreed. "I know kids who'll say they're a friend but are nasty and backbiting, who don't show any kindness or understanding. Mostly, everyone dislikes them."

Outside the family, what forces strongly influence children and adolescents? The answer is clear: peers, with whom they share countless play, classroom, and extracurricular activities; media, such as television and computers, which consume a substantial portion of their free time; and finally, school, which assists the family in transmitting culturally valued knowledge to the next generation.

In the first part of this chapter, we take a close look at the development of peer sociability, friendship, and peer acceptance and their profound significance for psychological adjustment. Next we turn to television and computers, reviewing the impact of these captivating electronic devices on children's cognitive and social skills. Finally, our discussion turns to the school, established to assist the family in transmitting culturally valued knowledge to the next generation. We consider how class and school size, educational philosophy, teacher–student interaction, and the ability mix of students affect students' educational experiences and learning. We conclude with a look at schooling and achievement in international perspective, with special attention to how well Canadian schools prepare young people for productive work lives.

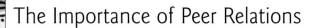

## The Importance of Peer Relations

ARE PEER RELATIONS CRUCIAL for development, and how do they add to children's experiences with caring adults? To find out for sure, we would need to study a group of children reared only by parents, comparing them to children growing up under typical conditions. In humans, these circumstances rarely occur naturally and are unethical to arrange experimentally. But scientists who have conducted such studies with nonhuman primates report that although peer bonds usually are not as intense as attachments to parents, they are vital for social competence. For example, maternally reared rhesus monkeys with no peer contact show immature play, excessive aggression and fearfulness, and less cooperation at maturity (Harlow, 1969).

Parent and peer relations seem to complement one another. Parents provide affection and guidance, granting children the security and social skills they need to enter the world of peers. Peer interaction, in turn, permits children to expand their social skills further. Peers can also fill in, at least to some extent, for the early parent–child bond. After rearing rhesus monkeys in groups without adults, researchers let them choose between their preferred peer (the one they sought closeness to during rearing), a familiar peer, and an unfamiliar peer. The monkeys spent most time near their preferred peer, who served as a source of security (Higley et al., 1992).

Nevertheless, peer-only reared monkeys do not fare as well as monkeys with a typical upbringing. In novel environments, they spend much time anxiously clinging to their preferred agemate. And as they get older, they display behaviour problems, including dominant and submissive (as opposed to friendly) interaction with unfamiliar peers (Goy & Goldfoot, 1974).

Do these findings generalize to human children? A unique parallel to peer-only rearing research suggests that in large measure, they do. In the 1940s, Anna Freud and Sophie Dann (1951) studied six young German-Jewish orphans whose parents had been murdered in the Nazi gas chambers shortly after the children's birth. The children remained together in a concentration camp for several years, without close ties to adults. When World War II ended, they were brought to England and cared for as a group. Observations revealed that they were passionately attached, becoming upset whenever separated. They were also intensely prosocial, freely sharing with, comforting, and helping one another. Nevertheless, they displayed many anxious symptoms, including intense thumb sucking, restlessness, immature play, and aggression toward as well as excessive dependency on their caregivers. As they built trusting relationships with adults, the children's play, language, and exploration developed rapidly.

In sum, peers serve as vital sources of security in threatening situations and contribute greatly to development. But they do so more effectively when combined with warm, supportive ties to parents.

# Development of Peer Sociability

IN CULTURES WHERE infants and toddlers have regular contact with agemates, peer sociability begins early, gradually evolving into the complex, well-coordinated exchanges of childhood and adolescence. Development of peer sociability is supported by and contributes to cognitive, emotional, and social milestones discussed in previous chapters.

## INFANT AND TODDLER BEGINNINGS

When pairs of infants are brought together in a laboratory, looking accompanied by touching is present at 3 to 4 months, peer-directed smiles and babbles by 6 months. These isolated social acts increase until, by the end of the first year, an occasional reciprocal exchange occurs in which babies grin, gesture, or otherwise imitate a playmate's behaviour (Vandell & Mueller, 1995; Vandell, Wilson, & Buchanan, 1980).

Between 1 and 2 years, coordinated interaction occurs more often, largely in the form of mutual imitation involving jumping, chasing, or banging a toy. Through these imitative, turn-taking games, children create joint understandings that aid in verbal communication. Around age 2, toddlers begin to use words to talk about and influence a peer's behaviour, as when they say, "Let's play chase," and after the game gets going, "Hey, good running!" (Eckerman & Didow, 1996; Eckerman & Whitehead, 1999). Hildy Ross of the University of Waterloo and others (1992) observed that reciprocal play and positive emotion are especially frequent in toddlers' interactions with familiar agemates, suggesting that they are building true peer relationships.

Although quite limited, peer sociability is present in the first 2 years, and it is fostered by the early caregiver–child bond. From interacting with sensitive adults, babies learn how to send and interpret emotional signals in their first peer associations (Vandell & Mueller, 1995). Consistent with this idea, toddlers with a warm parental relationship engage in more extended peer exchanges. These children, in turn, display more socially competent behaviour as preschoolers (Howes, 1988a; Howes & Matheson, 1992).

## THE PRESCHOOL YEARS

As children become increasingly self-aware, more effective at communicating, and better at understanding the thoughts and feelings of others, the amount and quality of peer interaction change greatly. Observing 2- to 5-year-olds in preschool, Mildred Parten (1932) noticed a dramatic rise with age in joint, interactive play. She concluded that social development proceeds in a three-step sequence. It begins with **nonsocial activity**—unoccupied, onlooker behaviour and solitary play. Then it shifts to a form of limited social participation called **parallel play,** in which a child plays near other children with similar materials but does not try to influence their behaviour. At the highest level are two forms of true social interaction. One is **associative play,** in which children engage in separate activities, but they exchange toys and comment on one another's behaviour. The second is **cooperative play**—a more advanced type of interaction in which children orient toward a common goal, such as acting out a make-believe theme.

Recent longitudinal evidence indicates that these play forms emerge in the order suggested by Parten, but they do not form a developmental sequence in which later-appearing ones replace earlier ones (Howes & Matheson, 1992). Instead, all types coexist during the preschool years. Furthermore, although nonsocial activity declines with age, it is still the

© NANCY SHEEHAN

The beginnings of peer sociability emerge in infancy, in the form of touches, smiles, and babbles that gradually develop into coordinated interaction in the second year. Early peer sociability is fostered by a warm, sensitive caregiver–child bond.

**nonsocial activity**
Unoccupied, onlooker behaviour and solitary play.

**parallel play**
A form of limited social participation in which the child plays near other children with similar materials but does not try to influence their behaviour.

**associative play**
A form of true social participation in which children engage in separate activities but interact by exchanging toys and commenting on one another's behaviour.

**cooperative play**
A form of true social participation in which children's actions are directed toward a common goal.

These children are engaged in parallel play. Although they sit side by side and use similar materials, they do not try to influence one another's behaviour. Parallel play remains frequent and stable over the preschool years. Working puzzles or engaging in other similar activities encourages it.

most frequent form among 3- to 4-year-olds. Even among kindergartners it continues to take up as much as a third of children's free-play time. Also, solitary and parallel play remain fairly stable from 3 to 6 years, accounting for as much of the young child's play as highly social, cooperative interaction.

We now understand that it is the *type*, rather than the amount, of solitary and parallel play that changes during early childhood. In studies of preschoolers' play, researchers rated the *cognitive maturity* of nonsocial, parallel, and cooperative play by applying the categories shown in Table 15.1. Within each of Parten's play types, older children engaged in more cognitively mature behaviour than did younger children (Pan, 1994; Rubin, Watson, & Jambor, 1978).

Often parents wonder if a young child who spends much time playing alone is developing normally. Only *certain kinds* of nonsocial activity—aimless wandering, hovering near peers, and functional play involving immature, repetitive motor action—are cause for concern. Children who behave in these ways are usually temperamentally inhibited, anxious preschoolers who have not learned to regulate their high social fearfulness. Often their parents have overprotected rather than encouraged them to approach other children (Burgess et al., 2001).

But not all preschoolers with low rates of peer interaction are socially anxious. To the contrary, most like to play by themselves, and their solitary activities are positive and constructive. Teachers encourage such play when they set out art materials, puzzles, and building toys. Children who spend much time in these activities are not maladjusted (Rubin et al., 1995). Instead, they are bright children who, when they do play with peers, show socially skilled behaviour.

As noted in Chapter 6, *sociodramatic play* becomes especially common during the preschool years. This advanced form of cooperative play supports both cognitive and social development. In joint make-believe, preschoolers act out and respond to one another's pretend feelings. They also explore and gain control of fear-arousing experiences when they play doctor or pretend to search for monsters in a magical forest. As a result, they are better able to understand others' feelings and regulate their own. Finally, to create and manage complex plots, preschoolers must resolve their disputes through negotiation and compromise (Howes, 1992).

**TABLE** 15.1

Developmental Sequence of Cognitive Play Categories

| PLAY CATEGORY | DESCRIPTION | EXAMPLES |
|---|---|---|
| Functional play | Simple, repetitive motor movements with or without objects. Especially common during the first 2 years of life. | Running around a room, rolling a car back and forth, kneading clay with no intent to make something |
| Constructive play | Creating or constructing something. Especially common between 3 and 6 years. | Making a house out of toy blocks, drawing a picture, putting together a puzzle |
| Make-believe play | Acting out everyday and imaginary roles. Especially common between 2 and 6 years. | Playing house, school, or police officer; acting out storybook or television characters |
| Games with rules | Understanding and following rules in play activities. | Playing board games, cards, hopscotch, baseball |

*Source:* Rubin, Fein, & Vandenberg, 1983.

## MIDDLE CHILDHOOD AND ADOLESCENCE

When formal schooling begins, children are exposed to agemates who differ in many ways, including achievement, ethnicity, religion, interests, and personality. Contact with a wider variety of peers probably contributes to school-age children's increasing awareness that others have viewpoints different from their own (see Chapter 11). Peer communication, in turn, profits from improved perspective taking. Children of this age can better interpret others' emotions and intentions and take them into account in peer dialogues. In addition, their ability to understand the complementary roles of several players in relation to a set of rules permits the transition to rule-oriented games in middle childhood (refer again to Table 15.1).

School-age children apply their greater awareness of prosocial norms to peer interaction. Recall from Chapter 12 that sharing, helping, and other prosocial acts increase in middle childhood. In addition, younger and older children differ in how they help agemates. Kindergartners move right in and give assistance, regardless of whether it is desired. In contrast, school-age children offer help and wait for a peer to accept it before behaving prosocially. During adolescence, agemates work on tasks more cooperatively—staying on task, exchanging ideas freely, asking for opinions, and acknowledging one another's contributions (Hartup, 1983).

As children enter middle childhood, another form of peer interaction becomes common. Watch children at play in a public park or schoolyard, and you will see that they sometimes wrestle, roll, hit, and run after one another while smiling and laughing. This friendly chasing and play-fighting is called **rough-and-tumble play.** Research indicates that it is a good-natured, sociable activity that is quite distinct from aggressive fighting. Children in many cultures engage in it with peers they like especially well, and they continue interacting after a rough-and-tumble episode rather than separating as they do after an aggressive encounter (Smith & Hunter, 1992).

Children's rough-and-tumble play is similar to the social behaviour of young mammals of many species. It seems to originate in parents' physical play with babies, especially fathers with sons (see Chapter 10). Similarly, childhood rough-and-tumble is more common among boys, although girls also display it. Girls' rough-and-tumble largely consists of running, chasing, and brief physical contact. Boys engage in more playful wrestling, restraining, and hitting (Boulton, 1996).

In our evolutionary past, rough-and-tumble play may have been important for the development of fighting skill. Consistent with this idea, by age 11, children choose rough-and-tumble partners who are similar in strength to themselves, permitting safer physical contact (Humphreys & Smith, 1987). Another possibility is that rough-and-tumble play assists children, especially boys, in establishing a **dominance hierarchy**—a stable ordering of group members that predicts who will win when conflict arises. Observations of arguments, threats, and physical attacks between children reveal a consistent lineup of winners and losers that becomes increasingly stable during middle childhood and adolescence, especially among boys. Through rough-and-tumble play, children can assess their own and others' strength before challenging a peer's dominance (Pellegrini & Smith, 1998).

Dominance relations among children, like those among nonhuman animals, serve the adaptive function of limiting aggression. Once a dominance hierarchy is clearly established, hostility is rare. As adolescents reach physical maturity, individual differences in strength become clear, and rough-and-tumble play along with dominance based on physical prowess declines.

Over middle childhood, children interact increasingly often with peers until, by mid-adolescence, more time is spent with them than with any other social partners. Common interests, novel play activities, and opportunities to interact on an equal footing make peer interaction especially gratifying. As adolescence draws to a close, most young people are proficient in many complex social behaviours.

© TONY FREEMAN/PHOTOEDIT

Rough-and-tumble play can be distinguished from aggression by its good-natured quality. In our evolutionary past, it may have been important for the development of fighting skill and dominance relations.

**rough-and-tumble play**
A form of peer interaction involving friendly chasing and play-fighting that, in our evolutionary past, may have been important for the development of fighting skill.

**dominance hierarchy**
A stable ordering of group members that predicts who will win when conflict arises.

# Influences on Peer Sociability

CHILDREN FIRST ACQUIRE skills for interacting with peers within the family. Parents influence children's peer sociability both *directly,* through attempts to influence children's peer relations, and *indirectly,* through their child-rearing practices and play behaviours (Ladd & Pettit, 2002). Situational factors that adults can influence, such as age mix of children, also make a difference. And cultural values are influential as well.

## DIRECT PARENTAL INFLUENCES

Outside preschool and child care, young children are limited in their ability to find playmates. They depend on parents to help them establish rewarding peer associations. Parents affect children's peer associations through the neighbourhood they live in. Safe areas with sidewalks and playgrounds and closely spaced homes increase the ease with which children can gather (Medrich et al., 1992).

When children live some distance from one another, parents must act as social planners and "booking agents," scheduling play at home, taking children to community settings such as the library or pool, and enrolling them in organized activities (Parke et al., 1994). Parents who frequently arrange informal peer contact tend to have preschoolers with larger peer networks and who are more socially skilled (Ladd, LeSieur, & Profilet, 1993). And when parents permit preschoolers to assist in setting up play experiences, children master skills for managing peer activities and more often initiate their own play dates (Ladd & Hart, 1992).

Parents also influence children's social relations by offering guidance on how to act toward others. Their skilful advice on how to solve peer problems—such as managing conflict, discouraging teasing, keeping a relationship going, and entering an ongoing play group—is associated with preschoolers' social competence and peer acceptance (Laird et al., 1994; Mize & Pettit, 1997).

Finally, recall from Chapter 14 that parental monitoring of their youngsters' whereabouts and activities protects older children and adolescents from involvement in antisocial activities. But teenagers' disclosure of information is vital for successful monitoring. The extent to which young people tell parents about their whereabouts and companions is an especially strong predictor of adjustment (Stattin & Kerr, 2000). Disclosure depends on a well-functioning parent–child relationship, which (as we will see next) also fosters positive peer relations.

Parents influence children's peer interaction skills by offering advice, guidance, and examples of how to behave. This father teaches his 3-year-old son how to offer a present as a guest at a birthday party.

## INDIRECT PARENTAL INFLUENCES

In previous chapters, we discussed many child-rearing variables not directly aimed at promoting peer sociability but that nevertheless spill over into peer relations. For example, inductive discipline and authoritative parenting offer a firm foundation for competence in relating to agemates. In contrast, coercive control and harsh discipline are linked to poor social skills and aggressive behaviour (see Chapters 12 and 14).

Furthermore, Barry Schneider of the University of Ottawa and others found that secure attachments to parents are linked to more responsive, harmonious peer interactions, larger peer networks, and rewarding friendships during the preschool years (Bost et al., 1998; Schneider, Atkinson, & Tardif, 2001). The emotionally expressive and supportive communication that underlies secure attachment may be responsible for this finding. In one study, researchers observed parent–child conversations, rating them for the strength of the mother–child bond, as indicated by exchange of positive emotion and parental sensitivity to the child's statements and feelings. Kindergartners who were more emotionally "connected" to their mothers displayed more empathy and prosocial behaviour toward their classmates. This empathic orientation, in turn, was linked to more positive peer ties (Clark & Ladd, 2000).

Parent–child play seems to be a particularly effective context for promoting peer-interaction skills. During play, parents interact with their child on a "level playing field," in much the way peers do. Consequently, they are especially likely to provide opportunities for acquiring social skills that generalize to peer-play contexts (Russell, Pettit, & Mize, 1998). Highly involved, emotionally positive, and cooperative play between parents and preschoolers is associated with more positive peer relations. And perhaps because parents play more with children of their own sex, mothers' play is more strongly linked with daughters' competence, fathers' play with sons' competence (Lindsey & Mize, 2000; Pettit et al., 1998).

## AGE MIX OF CHILDREN

When observed in age-graded settings, such as child-care centres, schools, and summer camps, children typically interact with others close in age. Yet in the neighbourhood, more than half their contacts are with children who differ in age by at least a year (Ellis, Rogoff, & Cromer, 1981). And in cultures where children are not segregated by age for schooling and recreation, cross-age interaction is even more common.

The theories of Piaget and Vygotsky, discussed in Chapter 6, suggest different benefits from same-age versus mixed-age interaction. Piaget emphasized experiences with children equal in status who challenge one another's viewpoints, thereby fostering cognitive, social, and moral development. In contrast, Vygotsky believed that children profit from interacting with older, more capable peers, who encourage more advanced skills.

Among preschoolers, the play of younger children is more cognitively and socially mature in mixed-age classrooms than in single-age classrooms. Furthermore, as early as age 3 or 4, children can modify their behaviour to fit the needs of a less advanced child, simplifying their rate of communication and assuming more responsibility for the task (Brody, Graziano, & Musser, 1983; Howes & Farver, 1987). Nevertheless, the oldest school-age children in mixed-age settings prefer same-age companions, perhaps because they have more compatible interests and experience more cooperative interaction. Younger children's interaction with same-age partners is also more intense and harmonious, but they often turn to older peers because of their superior knowledge and exciting play ideas.

Children clearly profit from both same-age and mixed-age relationships. From interacting with equals, they learn to cooperate and resolve conflicts, and they develop important moral notions of reciprocity and justice (see Chapters 11 and 12). In mixed-age settings, younger children acquire new competencies from their older companions. And when more mature youngsters help their less mature counterparts, they practise nurturance, guidance, and other prosocial behaviours.

## CULTURAL VALUES

Peer sociability in collectivist societies, which stress group harmony, differs from that in Western individualistic cultures. For example, children in India generally play in large groups that require high levels of cooperation. Much of their behaviour during sociodramatic play and early games is imitative, occurs in unison, and involves close physical contact. In a game called Atiya Piatiya, children sit in a circle, join hands, and swing while they recite a jingle. In Bhatto Bhatto, they act out a script about a trip to the market, touching each other's elbows and hands as they pretend to cut and share a tasty vegetable (Roopnarine et al., 1994).

Cultural beliefs about the importance of play also affect early peer associations. Adults who view play as mere entertainment are less likely to provide props and encourage pretending than those who value its cognitive and social benefits (Farver & Wimbarti, 1995a, 1995b). Korean-American parents, who emphasize task persistence as the means to academic success, have preschoolers who spend less time at joint make-believe and more time unoccupied and in parallel play than do their Caucasian-American counterparts (Farver, Kim, & Lee, 1995).

Return to the description of Yucatec Mayan preschoolers' daily lives on page 264 of Chapter 6. Mayan parents do not promote children's play, and when it interferes with important cultural activities, they discourage it. Yet even though they spend little time pretending, Mayan children are socially

These Chinese girls demonstrate an intricate hand-clapping game in which they must respond quickly and in unison. Preschoolers in the People's Republic of China frequently perform such games for classmates and parents. Their play reflects the value their culture places on group harmony.

© JEFF GREENBERG/PHOTOEDIT

competent (Gaskins, 2000). Perhaps Western-style sociodramatic play, with its elaborate materials and wide-ranging themes, is particularly important for social development in societies where child and adult worlds are distinct. It may be less crucial when children participate in adult activities from an early age.

In all societies, peer contact rises in adolescence, a trend that is particularly strong in industrialized nations, where young people spend most of each weekday with agemates in school. Teenagers also spend much out-of-class time together. North American teenagers average 18 nonschool hours per week with peers, compared with 12 hours for Japanese and 9 hours for Taiwanese adolescents. Less demanding academic standards probably account for this difference (Fuligni & Stevenson, 1995; Larson & Verma, 1999).

## ASK YOURSELF

**review**     Cite major changes in children's peer sociability during early and middle childhood. Why do children engage in rough-and-tumble play?

**review**     How do parents contribute, both directly and indirectly, to children's peer sociability?

**apply**     Roger's mother is worried about his social development because he likes to play alone, working puzzles, painting, and looking at books. Is Roger likely to be deficient in social skills? Explain.

**connect**     What aspects of parent–child interaction probably contribute to the relationship between attachment security and children's peer sociability? (See Chapter 10, pages 424–425.)

# Friendship

CHILDREN HAVE ENCOUNTERS and relationships with many peers. But they prefer some peers over others as playmates and, beginning in toddlerhood, they form **friendships**—close relationships involving companionship in which each partner wants to be with the other. Observations of 1- and 2-year-olds reveal that they initiate play, exchange expressions of positive emotion, and engage in more complex interactions with selected, familiar peers (Howes, 1998). These early mutual relationships may lay the groundwork for deeper, more meaningful friendship ties during childhood and adolescence.

To study friendship, researchers ask the child or a knowledgeable adult to name friends and check whether nominated friends return the choice. They also observe friendship interactions, comparing these with other peer relationships (Hartup, 1996). And they interview children about what friendship means. Findings reveal that with age, children's ideas about friendship change, as do certain features of friendships. And from the preschool years on, friendship contributes uniquely to children's psychological adjustment.

###  THINKING ABOUT FRIENDSHIP

To an adult, friendship is a consensual relationship involving companionship, sharing, understanding of thoughts and feelings, and caring for and comforting one another in times of need. In addition, mature friendships endure over time and survive occasional conflicts. To a child, however, friendship begins as something far more concrete, based on pleasurable activity. Gradually it evolves into a more abstract relationship based on mutual consideration and psychological satisfaction. William Damon (1977, 1988) has combined the work of several investigators into the following three-stage sequence, which has been confirmed by both cross-sectional and longitudinal research:

**LEVEL 1: FRIENDSHIP AS A HANDY PLAYMATE[1] (ABOUT 4 TO 7 YEARS).** Preschoolers understand something about the uniqueness of friendship. They know that a friend is someone

[1]I have provided titles for each of the stages to help you remember them.

**friendship**
A close relationship involving companionship in which each partner wants to be with the other.

"who likes you," with whom you spend a lot of time playing, and with whom you share toys. Because friendship is viewed concretely, young children regard it as easily begun—for example, by meeting in the neighbourhood and saying, "Hi." As yet, friendship does not have a long-term, enduring quality. Level 1 children say that a friendship can dissolve when one partner refuses to share, hits, or is not available to play. A 5-year-old's answer to the question "What makes a good friend?" sums up the young child's view of friendship: "Boys play with boys, trucks play with trucks, dogs play with dogs." When the interviewer probed, "Why does that make them good friends?" the child answered, "Because they do the same things" (Selman, 1980, p. 136).

**LEVEL 2: FRIENDSHIP AS MUTUAL TRUST AND ASSISTANCE (ABOUT 8 TO 10 YEARS).** During middle childhood, children's understanding of friendship becomes more complex and psychologically based. Consider the following 8-year-old's ideas:

*Why is Shelly your best friend?* Because she helps me when I'm sad, and she shares.... *What makes Shelly so special?* I've known her longer, I sit next to her and got to know her better.... *How come you like Shelly better than anyone else?* She's done the most for me. She never disagrees, she never eats in front of me, she never walks away when I'm crying, and she helps me on my homework.... *How do you get someone to like you?*... If you're nice to [your friends], they'll be nice to you. (Damon, 1988, pp. 80–81)

As these responses show, friendship has become a mutually agreed-on relationship in which children like each other's personal qualities and respond to one another's needs and desires. Since friendship is a matter of both children wanting to be together, getting it started takes more time and effort than it did at earlier ages.

Once a friendship forms, *trust* becomes its defining feature. School-age children state that a good friendship is based on acts of kindness that signify that each person can be counted on to support the other. Consequently, older children regard violations of trust, such as not helping when others need help, breaking promises, and gossiping behind the other's back, as serious breaches of friendship—as Marie did in the chapter introduction. Once a rift occurs, it cannot be patched up as easily as it could at younger ages—by playing nicely after a conflict. Instead, apologies and explanations are necessary (Damon, 1977; Selman, 1980).

**LEVEL 3: FRIENDSHIP AS INTIMACY AND LOYALTY (11 TO 15 YEARS AND OLDER).** When asked about the meaning of friendship, teenagers stress two characteristics. The first, and most important, is *intimacy.* Adolescents seek psychological closeness and mutual understanding from their friends. Second, more than younger children, teenagers want their friends to be *loyal*—to stick up for them and not to leave them for somebody else (Buhrmester, 1996).

As friendship takes on these deeper features, adolescents regard it as a relationship formed over time by "getting to know someone." In addition, friends are viewed as important in relieving psychological distress, such as loneliness, sadness, and fear. And because true mutual understanding implies forgiveness, only an extreme falling out can terminate a friendship. Here is how one teenager described his best friendship:

Well, you need someone you can tell anything to, all kinds of things that you don't want to spread around. That's why you're someone's friend. *Is that why Jimmy is your friend? Because he can keep a secret?* Yes, and we like the same kinds of things. We speak the same language. My mother says we're two peas in a pod.... *Do you ever get mad at Jimmy?* Not really. *What if he did something that got you really mad?* He'd still be my best friend. I'd tell him what he did wrong and maybe he'd understand. I could be wrong too, it depends. (Damon, 1977, p. 163)

## CHARACTERISTICS OF FRIENDSHIPS

Changes in children's thinking about friendships are linked to characteristics of their real friendships. Let's look closely at friendship stability, interaction, and resemblance.

During middle childhood, concepts of friendship become more psychologically based. Although these boys enjoy playing baseball, they want to spend time together because they like each other's personal qualities. Mutual trust is a defining feature of their friendship. Each child counts on the other to provide support and assistance.

**FIGURE** 15.1

**Age changes in reported self-disclosure to parents and peers, based on data from several studies.** Self-disclosure to friends increases steadily during adolescence, reflecting intimacy as a major basis of friendship. Self-disclosure to romantic partners also rises. However, not until the university years does it surpass intimacy with friends. Self-disclosure to parents declines in early adolescence, a time of mild parent–child conflict. As family relationships readjust to the young person's increasing autonomy, self-disclosure to parents rises. (From D. Buhrmester, 1996, "Need Fulfillment, Interpersonal Competence, and the Developmental Contexts of Early Adolescent Friendship," in W. M. Bukowski, A. F. Newcomb, & W. W. Hartup, Eds., *The Company They Keep: Friendship during Childhood and Adolescence,* New York: Cambridge University Press, p. 168. Reprinted by permission of Cambridge University Press.)

**FRIENDSHIP SELECTIVITY AND STABILITY.** We would expect greater friendship selectivity and stability as mutual trust and loyalty become more important in children's friendship expectations. Indeed, school-age children grow more selective about their friendships. Preschoolers say they have lots of friends—sometimes everyone in their class! But by age 8 or 9, children name only a handful of good friends. As teenagers focus on friendship quality, this narrowing continues. Number of best friends declines from four to six in early adolescence to one or two in young adulthood (Hartup & Stevens, 1999). Girls, especially, are more exclusive in their friendships because (as we will see shortly) they typically demand greater closeness than do boys (Parker & Asher, 1993).

Although friendship stability increases with age, friendships are remarkably stable at all ages. However, stability for younger children is largely a function of the constancy of social environments, such as preschool and neighbourhood. At older ages, friendships endure for psychological reasons, although they often undergo temporary shifts in the strength of each partner's commitment (Degirmencioglu et al., 1998). As young people transfer to middle or junior high school, varying rates of pubertal development and encounters with new peers often lead to a temporary period of change in choice of friends.

**INTERACTION BETWEEN FRIENDS.** At all ages, friends have special ways of interacting with each other. Preschoolers, for example, give twice as much reinforcement, in the form of greetings, praise, and compliance, to children they identify as friends, and they also receive more from them. Friends are also more emotionally expressive—talking, laughing, and looking at each other more often—than are nonfriends (Hartup, 1996; Vaughn et al., 2001). Apparently, spontaneity, intimacy, and sensitivity characterize rewarding friendships very early, although children are not able to express these ideas until much later.

But a more mature understanding of friendship seems to spark greater prosocial behaviour between friends. When working on a task together, school-age friends help, share, refer to each other's comments, and spend more time focused than preschool friends do (Hartup, 1996; Newcomb & Bagwell, 1995). Cooperation, generosity, mutual affirmation, and self-disclosure (see Figure 15.1) continue to rise into adolescence—trends that may reflect greater effort and skill at preserving the relationship and increased sensitivity to a friend's needs (Phillipsen, 1999). Teenagers are also less possessive of their friends than they were in childhood. They recognize that friends need a certain degree of autonomy, which they also desire for themselves (Rubin, Bukowski, & Parker, 1998).

Friends do not just behave more prosocially. They disagree and compete with each other more than do nonfriends. Since children regard friendship as based on equality, they seem especially concerned about losing a contest to a friend. Also, when children hold differing opinions, friends are more likely to voice them than are nonfriends (Fonzi et al., 1997). As early as middle childhood, friends realize that close relationships can survive disagreements if both parties are secure in their liking for one another (Rose & Asher, 1999). As a result, friendship provides an important context in which children learn to tolerate criticism and resolve disputes.

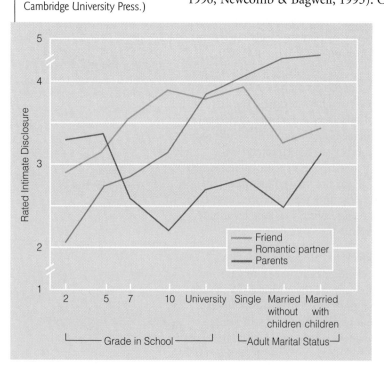

Yet the impact that friendships have on children's development depends on the nature of those friends. Children who bring kindness and compassion to their friendships strengthen each other's prosocial tendencies. When aggressive children make friends, the relationship often becomes a context for magnifying antisocial acts. The friendships of aggressive girls are high in self-disclosure but full of relational hostility, including jealousy, conflict, and betrayal (Grotpeter & Crick, 1996). Among boys, talk between aggressive friends contains frequent coercive statements and attacks, even during videotaping in a laboratory (Dishion, Andrews, & Crosby, 1995). These findings indicate that the social problems of aggressive children operate within their closest peer ties.

**RESEMBLANCE BETWEEN FRIENDS.** The value adolescents attach to feeling "in sync" with their friends suggests that friends will become increasingly similar in attitudes and values with age. Actually, the attributes in which friends are most alike throughout childhood and adolescence are sex, ethnicity, and SES. But friends also resemble one another in personality (sociability, shyness, aggression, and depression), peer popularity, academic achievement, and prosocial behaviour (Haselager et al., 1998; Kupersmidt, DeRosier, & Patterson, 1995). And by adolescence, they tend to be alike in identity status, educational aspirations, political beliefs, and willingness to try drugs and engage in minor lawbreaking acts (Akers, Jones, & Coyl, 1998). Perhaps children and adolescents choose companions like themselves to increase the supportiveness of friendship. Once they do, friends become more alike in attitudes, values, school grades, and social behaviour over time (Berndt & Keefe, 1995).

Nevertheless, as adolescents enter a wider range of school and community settings, they choose some friends who differ from themselves. Young teenagers often sacrifice similarity in favour of admiration for superficial features—whether a potential friend is popular, physically attractive, or athletically skilled. And in early adolescence, both boys and girls are attracted to high-status, aggressive boys as friends—a trend that contributes to a rise in antisocial behaviour in early adolescence (Bukowski, Sippola, & Newcomb, 2000).

As adolescents forge a personal identity, at times they befriend agemates with differing attitudes and values. This permits them to explore new perspectives within the security of a compatible relationship.

**SEX DIFFERENCES IN FRIENDSHIPS.** During middle childhood, children start to report a consistent sex difference in friendships. Research on Montreal children ranging from preschool to post-secondary age confirms that emotional closeness is more common between girls than boys (Markovits, Benenson, & Dolensky, 2001). Whereas girls frequently get together in pairs to "just talk," boys more often gather in groups for an activity—usually sports and competitive games that foster control, power, and excitement. When boys talk, their discussions often focus on recognition and mastery issues, such as the accomplishments of sports figures or their own achievements in sports and school (Buhrmester, 1998).

Because of gender-role expectations, boys and girls seem to enter friendships with different social needs. Then their friendships nurture those needs further—girls toward communal concerns, boys toward achievement and status concerns. This does not mean that boys rarely form close friendship ties. They often do, but the quality of their friendships is more variable. The intimacy of boys' friendships is related to gender identity. Androgynous boys are just as likely as girls to form

During adolescence, intimacy and loyalty become defining features of friendship. Yet girls place a higher value on emotional closeness than do boys. Girls more often get together to "just talk," and they rate their friendships as higher in self-disclosure and emotional support.

© CINDY CHARLES/PHOTOEDIT

intimate same-sex ties, whereas boys who identify strongly with the traditional masculine role are less likely to do so (Jones & Dembo, 1989).

In early adolescence, young people who are either very popular or very unpopular with agemates are more likely to have other-sex friends. Boys have more other-sex friends than do girls, whose desire for closeness leads to a preference for same-sex friendships (Sippola, Bukowski, & Noll, 1997). Teenagers not accepted by their own sex sometimes look to the other sex for friends. Among boys without same-sex friends, having an other-sex friend is associated with feelings of competence. Among girls who lack same-sex friends, other-sex friendships are linked to less positive well-being (Bukowski, Sippola, & Hoza, 1999). Perhaps these girls are especially likely to befriend boys with negative traits, such as aggression.

## FRIENDSHIP AND ADJUSTMENT

Warm, gratifying childhood and adolescent friendships are related to many aspects of psychological health and competence into early adulthood (Bagwell et al., 2001; Bukowski, 2001). The reasons are several:

- *Close friendships provide opportunities to explore the self and develop a deep understanding of another.* Through open, honest communication, friends become sensitive to each other's strengths and weaknesses, needs and desires. They get to know themselves and their friend especially well, a process that supports the development of self-concept, perspective taking, and identity (Savin-Williams & Berndt, 1990).

- *Close friendships provide a foundation for future intimate relationships.* Look again at Figure 15.1 (on page 610), and you will see that self-disclosure to friends precedes disclosure to romantic partners. The lengthy, often emotionally laden psychological discussions between adolescent friends appear to prepare the young person for love relationships (Sullivan, 1953). Sexuality and romance are common topics of discussion between teenage friends—conversations that, along with the intimacy of friendship itself, may help adolescents establish and work out problems in romantic partnerships (Connolly & Goldberg, 1999).

- *Close friendships provide support in dealing with the stresses of everyday life.* Because supportive friendship enhances sensitivity to and concern for another, it increases the likelihood of empathy, sympathy, and prosocial behaviour. Adolescents with supportive friendships report fewer daily hassles (Kanner et al., 1987). As a result, anxiety and loneliness are reduced while self-esteem is fostered. Adolescents experiencing family stress who manage to develop close friendships show the same high level of well-being as do children from better-functioning families (Gauze et al., 1996).

- *Close friendships can improve attitudes toward and involvement in school.* Close friendship ties promote good school adjustment in both middle- and low-SES students. When children and adolescents enjoy interacting with friends at school, perhaps they begin to view all aspects of school life more positively (Berndt & Keefe, 1995; Vandell & Hembree, 1994).

At the same time, some friendships are linked to poor adjustment. Longitudinal research shows that aggressive friends grant each other positive attention for deviant acts and become increasingly antisocial (Berndt, 1998; Dishion, Poulin, & Burraston, 2001). Finally, children who have no friends usually have undesirable personal styles; they may be easily angered, shy and anxious, or self-centred (less caring and honest) (Ladd, 1999). Without supportive friendship as a context for acquiring more adaptive social behaviours, their maladaptive behaviours tend to persist.

## ASK YOURSELF

**review** Describe unique qualities of interaction between close friends, and explain how they contribute to development.

**review** Why are aggressive children's friendships likely to magnify their antisocial behaviour?

**apply** In his junior year of high school, Ralph, of Irish-Catholic background, befriended Jonathan, a Chinese-Canadian of the Buddhist faith. Both boys are from middle-SES homes and are good students. What might explain Ralph's desire for a friend both similar to and different from himself?

**connect** Cite similarities in development of self-concept and concepts of friendship. (See Chapter 11, pages 448–449.) Explain how Stu's, Pete's, Denise's, and Marie's discussion in the introduction to this chapter reflects understandings that typically emerge at adolescence.

## Peer Acceptance

**PEER ACCEPTANCE** REFERS TO likeability—the extent to which a child is viewed by a group of agemates, such as classmates, as a worthy social partner. It differs from friendship in that it is not a mutual, two-person relationship. Rather, it is a one-sided perspective, involving the group's view of an individual. Although friendship and peer acceptance are distinct, we will see that some social skills that contribute to friendship also enhance peer acceptance. Consequently, better-accepted children have more friends and more positive relationships with them (Gest, Graham-Bermann, & Hartup, 2001). As with friendship, peer acceptance contributes uniquely to children's adjustment.

Researchers usually assess peer acceptance with self-report measures called **sociometric techniques.** For example, children may be asked to nominate several peers in their class whom they especially like or dislike, to indicate for all possible pairs of classmates which one they prefer to play with, or to rate each peer on a scale from "like very much" to "like very little" (Cillessen & Bukowski, 2000).

Sociometric techniques yield four categories of peer acceptance: **popular children,** who get many positive votes; **rejected children,** who are actively disliked; **controversial children,** who get a large number of positive and negative votes; and **neglected children,** who are seldom chosen, either positively or negatively. About two-thirds of students in a typical elementary school classroom fit one of these categories. The remaining one-third are *average* in peer acceptance; they do not receive extreme scores (Coie, Dodge, & Coppotelli, 1982).

Peer acceptance is a powerful predictor of psychological adjustment. Rejected children, especially, are unhappy, alienated, poorly achieving children with a low sense of self-esteem. Both teachers and parents view them as having a wide range of emotional and social problems. Peer rejection in middle childhood is also strongly associated with poor school performance, absenteeism, dropping out, antisocial behaviour, and delinquency in adolescence and criminality in young adulthood (Bagwell, Newcomb, & Bukowski, 1998; Laird et al., 2001; Parker & Asher, 1987).

Preceding influences—children's characteristics, parenting practices, or some combination of the two—may largely explain the link between peer relations and psychological adjustment. In one study, 9-year-olds identified by their teachers as having peer-relationship problems were more likely to come from low-SES families and to have experienced parental changes (divorce, remarriage, death), insensitive caregiving, and punitive discipline. These children also showed high rates of childhood conduct problems—the strongest predictor of adolescent adjustment difficulties (Woodward & Fergusson, 1999a).

Nevertheless, rejected children evoke distinct reactions from peers that contribute to their unfavourable development. Let's turn to factors in the peer situation that increase the chances that a child will fall into a particular peer-acceptance category.

**peer acceptance**
Likeability, or the extent to which the child is viewed by a group of agemates (such as classmates) as a worthy social partner.

**sociometric techniques**
Self-report measures that ask peers to evaluate one another's likeability.

**popular children**
Children who get many positive votes on sociometric measures of peer acceptance.

**rejected children**
Children who are actively disliked and get many negative votes on sociometric measures of peer acceptance.

**controversial children**
Children who get a large number of positive and negative votes on sociometric measures of peer acceptance.

**neglected children**
Children who are seldom chosen, either positively or negatively, on sociometric measures of peer acceptance.

## ORIGINS OF ACCEPTANCE IN THE PEER SITUATION

What causes one child to be liked and another to be rejected? A wealth of research reveals that social behaviour plays a powerful role.

**POPULAR CHILDREN.** Although many popular children are kind and considerate, others are admired for their socially sophisticated yet belligerent behaviour. Two subtypes of popular children exist:

- **Popular-prosocial children.** Most popular children combine academic and social competence. They are good students and communicate with peers in sensitive, friendly, and cooperative ways. They are appropriately assertive. When they do not understand another child's reaction, they ask for an explanation. If they disagree with a play partner in a game, they go beyond voicing their displeasure; they suggest what the other child could do instead. When they want to enter an ongoing play group, they adapt their behaviour to the flow of the activity (Dodge, McClaskey, & Feldman, 1985; Newcomb, Bukowski, & Pattee, 1993).

- **Popular-antisocial children.** This smaller subtype largely consists of "tough" boys who are athletically skilled but poor students. Popular-antisocial children are highly aggressive, often getting into fights, causing other trouble, and defying adult authority with nonchalance. Yet their peers view them as "cool," perhaps because of their athletic ability and sophisticated but devious social skills, through which they exploit others (Parkhurst & Hopmeyer, 1998; Rodkin et al., 2000).

Although popular-antisocial children are ethnically diverse, many are members of low-SES ethnic minorities. Recall from our discussion of achievement-related attributions that such children may conclude that they cannot succeed academically. Perhaps for this reason, their peer culture encourages troublemaking behaviour. Consistent with this view, in classrooms with greater numbers of aggressive children, peers are more likely to rate such children as "most liked" (Stormshak et al., 1999). So far, we do not know whether popular-antisocial children's likeability protects them from future adjustment difficulties. But their antisocial activities require intervention, and positive classroom climates where they can succeed academically may be particularly helpful.

**REJECTED CHILDREN.** Rejected children display a wide range of negative social behaviours. But like popular children, not all of these disliked children look the same. At least two subtypes exist:

- **Rejected-aggressive children,** the largest subgroup, show severe conduct problems—high rates of conflict, hostility, and hyperactive, inattentive, and impulsive behaviour. These children are also deficient in social understanding and regulation of negative emotion. For example, they are more likely than others to be poor perspective takers, to misinterpret the innocent behaviours of peers as hostile, to blame others for their social difficulties, and to act on their angry feelings (Crick & Ladd, 1993; Deković & Gerris, 1994). Both boys' overt aggression and girls' relational aggression predict peer rejection (Crick, 1996).

- **Rejected-withdrawn children,** a smaller subgroup, are passive and socially awkward. These inhibited, timid children are poor emotion regulators; overwhelmed by social anxiety, they withdraw in the face of social challenges (Hart et al., 2000; Rubin et al., 1995). As a result, they feel lonely, hold negative expectations for how peers will treat them, and are very concerned about being scorned and attacked (Boivin & Hymel, 1997; Ladd & Burgess, 1999). Because of their inept, submissive style, rejected-withdrawn children are at risk for **peer victimization** (see the Biology & Environment box on the following page).

**popular-prosocial children**
A subgroup of popular children who combine academic and social competence.

**popular-antisocial children**
A subgroup of popular children largely made up of "tough" boys who are athletically skilled, highly aggressive, defiant of adult authority, and poor students.

**rejected-aggressive children**
A subgroup of rejected children who engage in high rates of conflict, hostility, and hyperactive, inattentive, and impulsive behaviour.

**rejected-withdrawn children**
A subgroup of rejected children who are passive and socially awkward.

**peer victimization**
A destructive form of peer interaction in which certain children become frequent targets of verbal and physical attacks or other forms of abuse.

# biology & environment

## PEER VICTIMIZATION

In March 2002, a 16-year-old Vancouver girl was convicted of criminal harassment after a classmate hanged herself. A note left by the grade 9 victim cited threats from girls at school as the reason for her suicide. This case is an extreme example of **peer victimization,** a particularly destructive form of interaction that emerges during middle childhood, in which certain children become frequent targets of verbal and physical attacks or other forms of abuse. What sustains repeated assault–retreat cycles between pairs of children?

Debra Pepler of York University and Wendy Craig of Queen's University outline individual characteristics as well as family factors that contribute to victimization (Pepler & Craig, 2000). The majority of victims reinforce bullies by giving in to their demands, crying, assuming defensive postures, and failing to fight back. Victimized boys are passive when active behaviour is expected; on the playground, they hang around chatting or wander on their own (Boulton, 1999). Biologically based traits—an inhibited, fearful temperament and a frail physical appearance—contribute to their behaviour. But victimized children also have histories of resistant attachment; overly intrusive, controlling parenting; and (among boys) maternal overprotectiveness. These parenting behaviours prompt anxiety, low self-esteem, and dependency, resulting in a fearful demeanour that radiates vulnerability (Ladd & Ladd, 1998; Olweus, 1993).

About 10 percent of children and adolescents are harassed by aggressive agemates (Nansel et al., 2001). Peers expect these victims to give up desirable objects, show signs of distress, and fail to retaliate. In addition, children (espe-

cially those who are aggressive) feel less discomfort at the thought of causing pain and suffering to victims than non-victims (Perry, Williard, & Perry, 1990). Although bullies and victims are most often boys, girls are also aggressors and targets, as the tragic case of the Vancouver suicide victim illustrates. Girls most often harass vulnerable classmates with relational hostility (Crick & Grotpeter, 1996). As early as kindergarten, frequent victimization leads to a variety of adjustment difficulties, including depression, loneliness, low self-esteem, anxiety, and avoidance of school. And children who stop being victims do not necessarily show prompt improvements in loneliness and social satisfaction (Hawker & Boulton, 2000; Kochenderfer-Ladd & Wardrop, 2001).

Aggression and victimization are not polar opposites. A small number of extreme victims are also aggressive—picking arguments and fights or retaliating with relational aggression (Boulton & Smith, 1994; Crick & Bigbee, 1998). Perhaps these children foolishly provoke stronger agemates, who then prevail over them. Among rejected children, these bully/victims are the most despised, and they often experience extremely maladaptive parenting, including child abuse (Smith & Myron-Wilson, 1998). These home and peer influences place them at severe risk for maladjustment.

Interventions that change victimized children's negative opinions of themselves and that teach them to respond in nonreinforcing ways to their attackers are vital. Nevertheless, victimized children's behaviour should not be taken to mean that they are to blame for their abuse. Developing a school code against bullying, teaching child bystanders to intervene when it occurs,

© MICHAEL NEWMAN/PHOTOEDIT

Children who are victimized by bullies have characteristics that make them easy targets. They are physically weak, rejected by their peers, and afraid to defend themselves. Both temperament and child-rearing experiences contribute to their cowering behaviour, which reinforces their attackers' abusive acts.

enlisting parents' assistance in changing both bullies' and victims' behaviour, and moving aggressive children to another class or school can greatly reduce bully–victim problems, which account for a substantial portion of peer aggression in middle childhood (Olweus, 1995; Pepler & Craig, 2000).

Another way to help victimized children is to assist them with the social skills to form and maintain a gratifying friendship. Anxious, withdrawn children who have a best friend seem better equipped to withstand peer attacks. They show fewer adjustment problems than do victims with no close friends (Hodges et al., 1999).

Longitudinal research shows that beginning in kindergarten, peers exclude rejected children. As a result, rejected children's classroom participation declines, their feelings of loneliness rise, their academic achievement falters, and they want to avoid school (Buhs & Ladd, 2001). In addition to being disliked by many peers, rejected children usually have few friends, and occasionally none. They are likely to befriend others who are also unpopular, and their friendships are less caring and more conflict-ridden than are those of their peers (George & Hartmann, 1996; Parker & Asher, 1993).

**CONTROVERSIAL CHILDREN.** Consistent with the mixed peer opinion they engender, controversial children display a blend of positive and negative social behaviours. Like rejected-aggressive children, they are hostile and disruptive, but they also engage in high rates of positive, prosocial acts. Even though some peers dislike them, controversial children have qualities that protect them from social exclusion. As a result, they have as many friends as popular children do and are happy with their peer relationships. The social status of controversial children often changes over time (Newcomb, Bukowski, & Pattee, 1993; Parkhurst & Asher, 1992).

**NEGLECTED CHILDREN.** Perhaps the most surprising finding on peer acceptance is that neglected children, once thought to be in need of treatment, are usually well adjusted. Although they engage in low rates of interaction and are considered shy by their classmates, they are not less socially skilled than average children. They do not report feeling lonely or unhappy about their social life, and when they want to, they can break away from their usual pattern of playing by themselves (Harrist et al., 1997; Ladd & Burgess, 1999). Perhaps for this reason, neglected status (like controversial status) is usually temporary.

Neglected children remind us that there are other paths to emotional well-being besides the outgoing, gregarious personality style so highly valued in our culture. In Chapter 10, we noted that in China, adults view restrained, cautious children as advanced in social maturity! Perhaps because shyness is consistent with a cultural emphasis on not standing out from the collective, shyness and sensitivity are associated with peer acceptance and teacher-rated social competence and leadership among Chinese 8- to 10-year-olds (Chen, 2002; Chen, Rubin, & Li, 1995).

## HELPING REJECTED CHILDREN

A variety of interventions exist to improve the peer relations and psychological adjustment of rejected children. Most involve coaching, modelling, and reinforcing positive social skills, such as how to begin interacting with a peer, cooperate in games, and respond to another child with friendly emotion and approval. Although not always effective, several programs have produced gains in social competence and peer acceptance still present from several weeks to a year later (Asher & Rose, 1997; Lochman et al., 1993; Mize & Ladd, 1990).

Combining social-skills training with other treatments increases their effectiveness. Often rejected-aggressive children's impulsivity contributes to a maladaptive learning style, including distractibility and poor planning and organization. As early as grade 1, many are poor students, and their low academic self-esteem magnifies their negative reactions to teachers and classmates (O'Neil et al., 1997). Intensive academic tutoring improves both school achievement and social acceptance (Coie & Krehbiel, 1984). In addition, techniques aimed at reducing rejected-aggressive children's antisocial behaviour are helpful. In one study, including verbal prohibitions against antisocial acts and negative consequences for engaging in them in a social-skills coaching program led to better social acceptance than a program focusing only on teaching positive social behaviours (Bierman, Miller, & Stabb, 1987).

Social-cognitive interventions, such as training in perspective taking and social problem solving (see Chapter 11), are often essential. Many rejected-aggressive children fail to accurately interpret social cues and generate impulsive, ineffective social problem-solving strategies. They are also unaware of their own social ineffectiveness and do not take responsibility for their social failures (Coie & Dodge, 1998; Mrug, Hoza, & Gerdes, 2001). Rejected-withdrawn children, on the other hand, are likely to develop a *learned helpless* approach to peer acceptance. They conclude, after repeated rebuffs, that no matter how hard they try, they will never be liked (Rubin, Bukowski, & Parker, 1998). Both types of youngsters need help attributing their peer difficulties to internal, changeable causes.

Finally, we have seen that rejected children's socially incompetent behaviours often originate in a poor fit between the child's temperament and parenting practices. Therefore, interventions that focus on the child alone may not be sufficient. If the quality of parent–child interaction does not change, rejected children may soon return to their old behaviour patterns. When interventions on the child's and the parents' sides lead either to improved peer reputation or to close friendships, they enhance children's development and well-being (Asher, Parker, & Walker, 1998).

## ASK YOURSELF

**review**   Why are rejected children at risk for maladjustment? What experiences with peers probably contribute to their serious, long-term adjustment problems?

**review**   What factors make some children susceptible to peer victimization? What consequence does victimization have for adjustment, and how can it be prevented?

**connect**   Cite parenting influences on children's social skills, and explain why interventions that focus only on the rejected child are unlikely to produce lasting changes in peer acceptance. (See page 606.) What changes in parent–child relationships are probably necessary?

# Peer Groups

WATCH CHILDREN IN THE schoolyard or neighbourhood, and you will see that groups of three to a dozen often gather. The organization of these collectives changes greatly with age. By the end of middle childhood, children display a strong desire for group belonging. Together, group members generate values and standards for behaviour. They also create a social structure of leaders and followers that ensures group goals will be met. When these characteristics are present, a **peer group** is formed.

Whereas friendships contribute to the development of trust, sensitivity, and intimacy, peer groups grant young people practice in cooperation, leadership, followership, and loyalty to collective goals. Through these experiences, children experiment with and learn about the functioning of social organizations.

Peer groups form by the end of middle childhood. These boys have probably established a social structure of leaders and followers as they gather often for joint activities. Their body language suggests that they feel a strong sense of group belonging.

© ROBERT E. DAEMMRICH/STONE/GETTY IMAGES

## FIRST PEER GROUPS

Peer groups organize on the basis of proximity (being in the same classroom) and similarity in sex, ethnicity, and popularity, and they are moderately stable. When tracked for 3 to 6 weeks, membership changes very little. When observed for a year or longer, substantial change can occur, depending on whether children are reshuffled into different classrooms and loyalties change within the group. When children remain together as a unit, 50 to 70 percent of groups consist mostly of the same children from year to year (Cairns, Xie, & Leung, 1998).

The practices of these informal groups lead to a "peer culture" that typically consists of a specialized vocabulary, dress code, and place to "hang out" during leisure hours. As children develop these exclusive associations, the codes of dress and behaviour that grow out of them become more broadly influential. At school, children who deviate are often rebuffed. "Kissing up" to teachers, wearing the wrong kind of shirt or shoes, tattling on classmates, or carrying a

**peer group**
Peers who form a social unit by generating unique values and standards of behaviour and a social structure of leaders and followers.

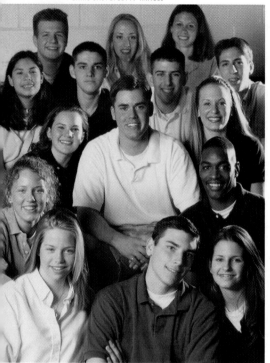

These high school yearbook club members form a crowd. Unlike the more intimate clique, the larger, more loosely organized crowd grants adolescents an identity within the larger social structure of the school.

strange-looking lunchbox are grounds for critical glances and comments. These customs bind peers together, creating a sense of group identity.

The beginning of peer group ties also is a time when some of the "nicest children begin to behave in the most awful way" (Redl, 1966, p. 395). From grade 3 on, relational aggression—gossip, rumour spreading, and exclusion—toward the "outgroup" rises among girls (Crick & Grotpeter, 1995). Boys are more straightforward in their outgroup hostility. Overt aggression, in the form of verbal insults and pranks—toilet-papering a front yard or ringing a doorbell and running away—occurs among small groups of boys, who provide one another with temporary social support for these mildly antisocial behaviours.

Unfortunately, peer groups—at the instigation of their leaders, who are sometimes aggressive children—often direct their hostilities toward their own members, excluding no-longer "respected" children. These cast-outs are profoundly wounded, and many find new group ties hard to establish. Their previous behaviour toward the outgroup, including expressed contempt for less popular children, reduces their chances of being included elsewhere. As one fifth grader explained, "I think they didn't like me because when I was in the popular group we'd make fun of everyone.... I had been too mean to them in the past" (Adler & Adler, 1998, p. 70). Peer-rejected children often turn to other low-status peers for group belonging. As they associate with other children who have poor social skills, they reduce their opportunities to learn socially competent behaviour (Bagwell et al., 2001).

The school-age child's desire for group belonging can also be satisfied through formal group ties—scouting, guides, religious youth groups, and other associations. Adult involvement holds in check the negative behaviours associated with children's informal peer groups. And as children work on joint projects and help in their communities, they gain in social and moral maturity (Killen & Nucci, 1995; Vandell & Shumow, 1999).

## CLIQUES AND CROWDS

The peer groups of the early teenage years are more tightly structured than those of middle childhood. They are organized around **cliques,** small groups of about five to seven members who are friends and, therefore, usually resemble one another in family background, attitudes, and values.

In early adolescence, cliques are limited to same-sex members. Being in one predicts girls' academic and social competence, but not boys'. Clique membership is more important to girls, who often exchange expressions of emotional closeness and support (Henrich et al., 2000). By the midadolescent years, mixed-sex cliques become common. The cliques within a typical high school can be identified by their interests and social status, as the well-known "popular" and "unpopular" groups reveal (Cairns et al., 1995; Gillmore et al., 1997).

Often several cliques with similar values form a larger, more loosely organized group called a **crowd**. Unlike the more intimate clique, membership in a crowd is based on reputation and stereotype. Whereas the clique serves as the main context for direct interaction, the crowd grants the adolescent an identity within the larger social structure of the school. Prominent crowds in a typical high school are the "studious" kids, or nonathletes who enjoy academics; the "jocks," who are very involved in athletics; the "preppies," who have a boyfriend or girlfriend, are physically attractive, and wear brand-name clothes; the "headbangers," who use drugs, listen to heavy-metal rock music, skip school, and get into fights; the "partyers," who value partying and popularity and care little about schoolwork; and the "normals," average students who get along with students in most other crowds (Kinney, 1999; Stone & Brown, 1999).

What influences sorting of teenagers into cliques and crowds? In addition to adolescent personality and interests, family factors are important. In a study of 8000 ninth to twelfth graders, adolescents who described their parents as authoritative tended to be members of "studious," "jock," and "preppie" groups that accepted both the adult and peer reward systems of the school. In contrast, boys with permissive parents valued interpersonal relationships

**clique**
A small group of about five to seven peers who are friends.

**crowd**
A large, loosely organized peer group in which membership is based on reputation and stereotype.

and aligned themselves with the "partyer" crowd. And teenagers who viewed their parents as uninvolved more often affiliated with "partyer" and "headbanger" crowds, suggesting lack of identification with adult reward systems (Durbin et al., 1993).

These findings indicate that many peer group values are extensions of ones acquired at home. But once adolescents join a clique or crowd, it can modify their beliefs and behaviours. For example, when adolescents associate with peers who have authoritative parents, their friends' academic and social competence "rubs off" on them (Fletcher et al., 1995). However, the positive impact of having academically and socially skilled peers is greatest for teenagers whose own parents are authoritative. And the negative impact of having antisocial, drug-using friends is strongest for teenagers whose parents use less effective child-rearing styles (Mounts & Steinberg, 1995). In sum, family experiences affect the extent to which adolescents become like their peers over time.

In early adolescence, boys' and girls' cliques come together. Jennifer Connolly of York University and others found that the merger takes place slowly. At junior high school dances and parties, clusters of boys and girls can be seen standing on opposite sides of the room, watching but seldom interacting. As mixed-sex cliques form, they provide a supportive context for boys and girls to get to know each other. Cliques offer models of how to interact with the other sex and opportunities to do so without having to be intimate. In addition, members can check with one another to find out if their attraction to someone is likely to be returned (Brown, 1999). Gradually, the larger group divides into couples, several of whom spend time together, going to parties and movies. By late adolescence, boys and girls feel comfortable enough approaching each other directly that the mixed-sex clique disappears (Connolly, Furman, & Konarski, 2000; Connolly & Goldberg, 1999).

Crowds also decline in importance. As adolescents formulate their own personal values and goals, they no longer feel a strong need to broadcast, through dress, language, and preferred activities, who they are. And about half of young people switch crowds from tenth to twelfth grade, mostly in favourable directions. "Studious" and "normal" crowds grow and deviant crowds lose members as teenagers focus more on their future (Brown, Freedman, & Huang, 1992; Strouse, 1999). Strong, prosocial friendships and positive self-esteem are associated with these changes.

# Peer Relations and Socialization

PEER INTERACTION CONTRIBUTES to a wide variety of skills that help children and adolescents adapt successfully to their social worlds. Just how do peers socialize one another? As we will see in the following sections, they use some of the same techniques that parents do: reinforcement, modelling, and direct pressure to conform.

## PEER REINFORCEMENT AND MODELLING

Children's responses to one another serve as reinforcers, modifying the extent to which they display certain behaviours. Turn back to Chapter 13, page 539, to review how peers reinforce gender-role behaviour. Peer reinforcement begins early and increases with age. Children often use it for positive ends. Those who engage in attentive, approving, and affectionate social acts are likely to receive similar behaviours in return (Kindermann, 1998).

Children are just as receptive to peer reinforcement for antisocial behaviour as they are for prosocial acts. In the Biology & Environment box on page 615, we showed that the hostile acts of bullies are reinforced by their victims' passivity. Children who retaliate punish an aggressor's actions. At the same time, their retaliatory behaviour is rewarded. Research reveals a steady increase in aggression by initially nonaggressive children who counterattack in the face of peer hostility (Patterson, Littman, & Bricker, 1967). Peer feedback is an important means through which children's aggression is enhanced as well as controlled, and even mild-mannered children can learn to behave aggressively from being targets of peer hostility.

Besides dispensing reinforcers, peers model a broad array of social behaviours. Peer imitation occurs more often between familiar than unfamiliar peers. Being imitated, in turn, fosters feelings of connection to others and may be an important means through which peer ties form and strengthen (Kindermann, 1998).

The powerful effects of peer reinforcement and modelling have led researchers to experiment with peers as agents of behaviour change. Socially competent children can be trained to encourage social skills in less competent peers, and both show gains in social maturity (Strain, 1977). Peers can also tutor less knowledgeable children at school, teaching, modelling, and reinforcing academic skills. Carefully planned peer tutoring programs, in which tutors are trained and supervised by adult teachers, lead to benefits in academic achievement and self-esteem for both tutors and their pupils (Renninger, 1998).

### PEER CONFORMITY

Conformity to peer pressure is greater during adolescence than in childhood or young adulthood—a finding that is not surprising when we consider how much time teenagers spend together. But contrary to popular belief, adolescence is not a period in which young people blindly do what their peers ask. Peer conformity is a complex process that varies with the adolescent's age and need for social approval, and with the situation.

In one study of nearly 400 junior and senior high students, adolescents felt greatest pressure to conform to the most obvious aspects of the peer culture—dressing and grooming like everyone else and participating in social activities, such as dating and going to parties. Peer pressure to engage in proadult behaviour, such as getting good grades and cooperating with parents, was also strong. Although pressure toward misconduct rose in early adolescence, it was low. Many teenagers said that their friends actively discouraged antisocial acts. These findings show that peers and parents often act in concert, toward desirable ends! Finally, peer pressures correlated only modestly with teenagers' actual values and behaviours (Brown, Lohr, & McClenahan, 1986).

Perhaps because of their greater concern with what their friends think of them, early adolescents are more likely than younger or older individuals to give in to peer pressure. Yet when parents and peers disagree, even young teenagers do not consistently rebel against the family. Instead, parents and peers differ in their spheres of greatest influence. Parents have more impact on teenagers' basic life values and educational plans. Peers are more influential in short-term, day-to-day matters, such as type of dress, taste in music, and choice of friends (Steinberg, 2001). Adolescents' personal characteristics also make a difference. Young people who feel competent and worthwhile are less likely to fall in line behind peers who engage in early sex, delinquency, and frequent drug use (see the From Research to Practice box on page 622).

Finally, authoritative parenting is consistently related to resistance to unfavourable peer pressure (Fletcher et al., 1995; Mason et al., 1996). Adolescents whose parents are supportive and exert appropriate oversight hold their parents in high regard, and this attitude of respect acts as an antidote to antisocial peer pressure (Sim, 2000). In contrast, teenagers who experience extremes of parental behaviour—either too much or too little control and monitoring—tend to be highly peer oriented. They more often rely on friends for advice about their personal lives and future and are more willing to break their parents' rules, ignore their schoolwork, and hide their talents to be popular (Fuligni & Eccles, 1993). Under conditions of high life stress, such as poverty and divorce, supportive ties to parents or other caring, involved adults are an especially powerful antidote to unfavourable peer pressures (Masten, 2001).

© DAVID YOUNG WOLFF/PHOTOEDIT

Peer conformity rises in early adolescence. But it is greatest for the most obvious aspects of the peer culture, such as dress and grooming. These boys' parents are probably more influential than their peers on matters of lasting impact, such as life values and educational plans.

# milestones

## DEVELOPMENT OF PEER RELATIONS

| AGE | PEER SOCIABILITY | FRIENDSHIP | PEER GROUPS |
|-----|-----------------|------------|-------------|
| Birth–2 years | ⚬ Isolated social acts increase and are gradually replaced by coordinated interaction. | ⚬ Mutual relationships with familiar peers emerge. | |
| 2½–6 years | ⚬ Parallel play appears, remains stable, and becomes more cognitively advanced.<br>⚬ Cooperative play increases, especially sociodramatic play.<br>⚬ Rough-and-tumble play emerges. | ⚬ Friendship is viewed concretely, in terms of play and sharing toys. | |
| 7–11 years | ⚬ Peer communication skills improve, including interpreting and responding to the emotions and intentions of others.<br>⚬ Ability to understand the complementary roles of several players improves, permitting the transition to rule-oriented games.<br>⚬ Peer interaction becomes more prosocial.<br>⚬ Rough-and-tumble play becomes more common. | ⚬ Friendship is based on mutual trust and assistance.<br>⚬ Interaction between friends becomes more prosocial.<br>⚬ Number of close friends declines. | ⚬ Peer groups emerge. |
| 12–20 years | ⚬ Peer interaction becomes more cooperative.<br>   ⚬ Rough-and-tumble play declines.<br>   ⚬ More time is spent with peers than any other social partners. | ⚬ Friendship is based on intimacy and loyalty.<br>⚬ Friends become more alike in attitudes and values.<br>⚬ Young people choose some friends who differ from themselves.<br>⚬ Number of close friends declines further. | ⚬ Peer groups become more tightly structured, organized around cliques.<br>⚬ Crowds form, based on reputation and stereotype.<br>⚬ As interest in dating increases, mixed-sex cliques form.<br>⚬ Conformity to peer pressure increases and gradually declines. |

Before we turn to the impact of media on children and adolescents, you may find it helpful to examine the Milestones table above, which summarizes the development of peer relations.

## *from research to practice*

### ADOLESCENT SUBSTANCE USE AND ABUSE

In Canada and other industrialized nations, teenage alcohol and drug use is pervasive (Bauman & Phongsavan, 1999). The longest on-going study of adolescent substance use in Canada examines adolescents in Ontario. By age 12, 5 percent of Ontario youths have tried smoking, 36 percent drinking, and 11 percent at least one illegal drug. By the end of high school, 36 percent report smoking during the previous year, 80 percent have become regular or occasional drinkers, 27 percent have engaged in heavy drinking at least once, and 44 percent have experimented with illegal drugs (Adlaf & Paglia, 2001).

These figures represent a decline in alcohol and drug use in the late 1980s, followed by a resurgence in the mid-1990s, and little fluctuation in recent years (see Figure 15.2). Why do so many young people subject themselves to the health risks of these substances? Part of the reason is cultural. Adolescents live in drug-dependent contexts. They see adults using caffeine to wake up in the morning, cigarettes to cope with daily hassles, a drink to calm down in the evening, and other remedies to relieve stress, depression, and physical illness. Reduced focus on the hazards of drugs by parents, schools, and media, followed by renewed public

attention, may explain recent trends in adolescent drug taking.

For most young people substance use simply reflects their intense curiosity about "adultlike" behaviours. Research reveals that many teenagers dabble in alcohol as well as tobacco and marijuana. These minimal *experimenters* are not headed for a life of decadence and addiction. Instead, they are psychologically healthy, sociable, curious young people (Shedler & Block, 1990). In a society in which substance abuse is commonplace, some involvement with drugs appears to be normal.

Yet adolescent drug experimentation should not be taken lightly. Because most drugs impair perception and thought processes, a single heavy dose can lead to permanent injury or death. And a worrisome minority of teenagers move from substance *use* to *abuse*—taking drugs regularly, requiring increasing amounts to achieve the same effect, and using enough to impair their ability to meet school, work, or other responsibilities.

### CORRELATES AND CONSEQUENCES OF ADOLESCENT SUBSTANCE ABUSE

In contrast to experimenters, drug abusers are seriously troubled young people who are inclined to express their

unhappiness through antisocial acts. Longitudinal evidence reveals that their impulsive, disruptive, sensation-seeking style often is evident in early childhood. Compared with other young people, their drug-taking starts earlier (Chassin & Ritter, 2001). Although it probably has genetic roots, a wide range of environmental factors promote it. These include low SES, family mental health problems, parental and older sibling drug abuse, lack of parental warmth and involvement, physical and sexual abuse, and poor school performance. Peer encouragement—friends who engage in high levels of deviant talk (including rule-breaking), who use drugs, and who provide access to illegal substances—predicts increased substance abuse and other antisocial behaviours (Baron, 1999; Kilpatrick et al., 2000; Patterson, Dishion, & Yoerger, 2000).

Adolescent substance abuse often has lifelong consequences. When teenagers depend on alcohol and hard drugs to deal with daily stresses, they fail to learn responsible decision-making skills and alternative coping techniques. These young people show serious adjustment problems, including depression and antisocial behaviour (Luthar & Cushing, 1997). They often enter into marriage, childbearing, and the work world prematurely and fail at them readily.

## ASK YOURSELF

**review**    What positive functions do group ties serve in young people's development? What factors lead some peer groups to have harmful consequences?

**review**    Do adolescents indiscriminately bend to peer pressures? Explain.

**apply**    Thirteen-year-old Mattie's parents are warm, firm in their expectations, and consistent in monitoring her peer activities. What type of crowd is Mattie likely to belong to, and why?

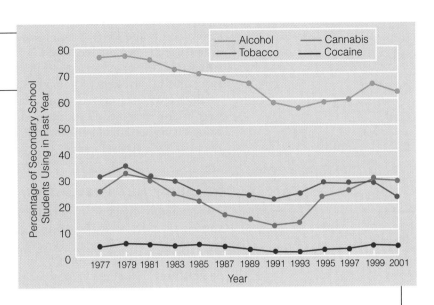

**FIGURE** 15.2

**Percentages of Ontario secondary school students (grades 7 to 13) reporting use of alcohol, cigarettes, and illegal drugs in the past year, 1977–2001.** According to the Ontario Student Drug Use Survey, drug use declined in the 1980s, showed a resurgence in the 1990s, and did not increase significantly in 2001. (Adapted from Adlaf & Paglia, 2001. Reprinted with permission from the Centre for Addiction and Mental Health © 2002.)

## PREVENTION AND TREATMENT

Programs that promote effective parenting (including clear standards against drug use and monitoring of teenagers' activities) and that teach adolescents skills for resisting peer pressure reduce drug experimentation (Kosterman et al., 2000). But some drug taking seems inevitable. Therefore, interventions that prevent adolescents from endangering themselves and others when they do experiment are essential, such as on-call transportation services that any young person can contact for a safe ride home, with no questions asked. And educating teenagers about the dangers of drugs and alcohol is vital, since an increase in perceived risk

closely paralleled the decline in substance use in the 1980s and early 1990s (Adlaf & Paglia, 2001; O'Malley, Johnston, & Bachman, 1995).

Drug abuse, as we have seen, occurs for quite different reasons than does occasional use. Therefore, different prevention strategies are required. One approach is to work with parents early, reducing family adversity and improving parenting skills, before children are old enough to become involved with drugs (Luthar, Cushing, & McMahon, 1997). Programs that teach at-risk teenagers strategies for handling life stressors and that build competence through community service have been found to reduce alcohol and drug use, just as they reduce teenage pregnancy

(see Chapter 5) (Richards-Colocino, McKenzie, & Newton, 1996).

When an adolescent becomes a drug abuser, hospitalization is often a necessary and even lifesaving first step. Once the young person is weaned from the drug, family and individual therapy to treat maladaptive parent–child relationships, low self-esteem, anxiety, and impulsivity are generally needed. Academic and vocational training to improve life success make a difference as well. Not much is known about the best way to treat adolescent drug abuse. Even the most comprehensive programs have relapse rates that are alarmingly high—from 35 to 85 percent (Gilvarry, 2000).

# Television

EXPOSURE TO TELEVISION IS almost universal in Canada and other industrialized nations. Nearly all Canadian homes have at least one television set, and more than half have two or more (Statistics Canada, Selected Dwelling Characteristics, 2001). In 1999, the typical Canadian household had the television switched on for about 3 hours a day (Statistics Canada, Television Viewing, 2001). Although television viewing is decreasing in Canada, there continues to be good reason for concern about television's impact on children and adolescents. Tannis MacBeth (née Williams) of the University of British Columbia carried out a unique study on the impact of television on a small Canadian town. Residents were studied just before TV reception became available in their community and then 2 years later. School-age children showed a decline in reading ability and creative thinking, a rise in gender-stereotyped beliefs, and an increase in verbal and physical aggression during play. In addition, a sharp drop in adolescents' community participation occurred (Williams, 1986).

But television has as much potential for good as for ill. If the content of TV programming were improved and adults capitalized on it to enhance children's interest in their everyday worlds, television could be a powerful, cost-effective means of strengthening cognitive, emotional, and social development.

## HOW MUCH TELEVISION DO CHILDREN VIEW?

The amount of time Canadian children devote to watching television is substantial. Regular viewing typically begins between 2 and 3 years of age. In 1999, children and adolescents between ages 2 and 17 watched an average of 2 hours of television per day (Statistics Canada, Television Viewing, 2001). In early and middle childhood, boys watch slightly more TV than do girls. Low-SES, ethnic minority children and children from large families are also more frequent viewers, perhaps because their parents are less able to pay for out-of-home entertainment or their neighbourhoods provide few alternative activities. And if parents tend to watch a lot of TV, their children usually do (Comstock & Scharrer, 1999; Huston & Wright, 1998). Excessive TV viewing is associated with family and peer difficulties. Parents and children with high life stress often escape into it (Anderson et al., 1996).

## DEVELOPMENT OF TELEVISION LITERACY

When watching TV programs, children are confronted with a rapid stream of people, objects, places, words, and sounds. Television, or film, has its own specialized code of conveying information. Researchers liken the task of cracking this code to that of learning to read, calling it **television literacy.** Although the symbolic learning required to understand television is not as great as that demanded by reading, it is still considerable.

Television literacy has two interrelated parts. The first involves understanding the form of the message. Children must master the meaning of visual and auditory effects, such as camera zooms, panoramic views, fade-outs, and split screens. Second, they must use those effects in processing the content of the message, constructing an accurate story line by integrating scenes, character behaviour, and dialogue (Fitch, Huston, & Wright, 1993).

During early and middle childhood, children are captivated by TV's salient perceptual features. When a program contains quickly paced character movement, special effects, loud music, nonhuman speech, or children's voices, they become highly attentive. At other times, they look away, play with toys, and talk to others (Rice, Huston, & Wright, 1982). While involved in other activities, preschoolers follow the TV soundtrack. They turn back to the set when they hear cartoon characters and puppets speaking and certain words, such as "Big Bird" and "cookie," that signal the content is likely to be interesting to them (Alwitt et al., 1980). Clearly, young children are selective and strategic processors of televised information, but how much do they really understand? Not a great deal.

Young children find it hard to judge the reality of TV material. At ages 2 and 3, they do not discriminate televised images from real objects; they say a bowl of popcorn on television would spill if the TV were turned upside down (Flavell et al., 1990). By age 4, they have mastered this distinction, and they judge TV reality according to whether the images resemble people and objects in their everyday world. Consequently, they consider human actors "real" and cartoon characters "unreal." Around age 5, children make finer discriminations. They say that news and documentaries depict real events and that fictional programs are "just for TV."

**television literacy**
The task of learning television's specialized symbolic code of conveying information.

But not until age 7 do they fully grasp the unreality of TV fiction—that characters do not retain their roles in real life and that their behaviour is scripted (Wright et al., 1994).

Furthermore, before age 8, children have difficulty connecting separate scenes into a meaningful story line. Consequently, they often fail to detect motives or consequences (Collins, 1983). A villain who gets what he wants by punching, shooting, and killing may not be a "bad guy" to a young child, who fails to notice that the character was brought to justice in the end. Consequently, they evaluate the character and his actions overly favourably (Collins, 1983).

In sum, preschool and early school-age children have an incomplete grasp of TV reality, assimilate televised information piecemeal, and cannot critically evaluate it. These misunderstandings increase the chances that they will imitate and believe what they see on the screen. Let's look at the impact of TV on children's social learning.

## TELEVISION AND SOCIAL LEARNING

Since the 1950s, researchers and public citizens have been concerned about the attitudes and behaviours that television cultivates in young viewers. Most studies have focused on TV violence and development of antisocial conduct. Still others have addressed the power of TV to teach undesirable gender and ethnic stereotypes. And growing evidence illustrates TV's potential to contribute to children's cognitive and social competence.

**AGGRESSION.** Although Canadian television features made-in-Canada programs as well as governmental regulations on television content, the majority of Canadians have direct access to U.S. TV signals. Two-thirds of Canadians' viewing time is devoted to U.S. programs (Statistics Canada, Television Viewing, 2001).

The U.S. National Television Violence Study, a recent large-scale survey of the amount, nature, and context of TV violence, concluded that violence pervades U.S. TV (see Figure 15.3). Fifty-seven percent of programs between 6 A.M. and 11 P.M. contain violent scenes, often in the form of repeated aggressive acts against a victim that go unpunished. In fact, few violent portrayals show victims experiencing any serious physical harm, and few condemn violence or depict alternative ways of solving problems. Violent content in

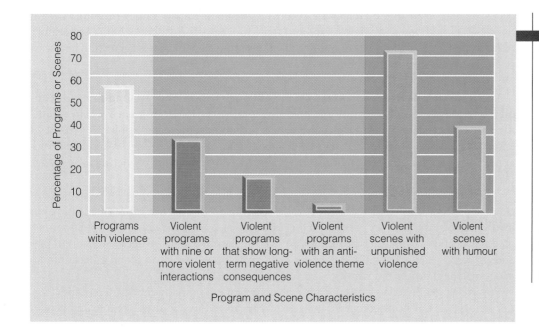

**FIGURE 15.3**

**Violent characteristics of U.S. television, based on a representative sample of more than 3000 programs broadcast between 6 A.M. and 11 P.M.** Violence occurs in the majority of programs. It often consists of repeated aggressive acts that go unpunished and that are embedded in humour. Only rarely do programs show long-term negative consequences of violence or present it in the context of an antiviolence theme. (Center for Communication and Social Policy, 1998.)

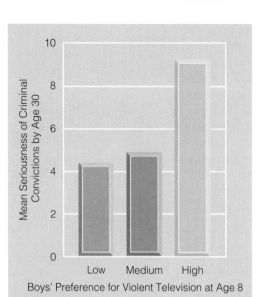

**FIGURE 15.4**

**Relationship between boys' violent television viewing at age 8 and seriousness of criminal convictions by age 30.** Longitudinal research showed that boys who watched many violent programs were more likely to commit serious criminal acts in adolescence and early adulthood. (From L. R. Huesmann, 1986, "Psychological Processes Promoting the Relation Between Exposure to Media Violence and Aggressive Behavior by the Viewer," *Journal of Social Issues, 42,* p. 129. Reprinted by permission.)

children's programming is 9 percent above the average for all TV, and cartoons are the most violent (Center for Communication and Social Policy, 1998).

Reviewers of thousands of studies conducted in many countries, including Canada, have concluded that television violence provides children with "an extensive how-to course in aggression" (Slaby et al., 1995, p. 163; see also Comstock & Scharrer, 1999). The case is strengthened by the fact that research using a wide variety of research designs, methods, and participants has yielded similar findings. In addition, the relationship of TV violence to hostile behaviour remains the same after many factors—including family background and child characteristics—are controlled.

Because of their difficulty distinguishing fantasy from reality, preschool and young school-age children are more likely to imitate TV violence. In addition, aggressive children have a greater appetite for violent TV. As they watch more, they become increasingly likely to resort to hostile ways of solving problems, a spiralling pattern of learning that contributes to serious antisocial acts by adolescence and young adulthood (Slaby et al., 1995). In one longitudinal study, boys who watched many violent programs at age 8 were more likely to be rated by peers as highly aggressive at age 19 and to have committed serious crimes by age 30 (see Figure 15.4) (Huesmann, 1986). Nevertheless, violent TV sparks hostile thoughts and behaviour even in non-aggressive children; its impact is simply less intense (Bushman & Huesmann, 2001).

Furthermore, television violence "hardens" children to aggression, making them more willing to tolerate it in others. Heavy TV viewers believe that there is much more violence and danger in society, an effect that is especially strong for children who perceive televised aggression as relevant to their own lives (Donnerstein, Slaby, & Eron, 1994). As these responses indicate, violent television modifies children's attitudes toward social reality so they increasingly match what children see on TV.

The television industry has countered these findings, claiming that they are weak and affect few individuals. But the correlation between media violence and aggression is nearly as high as the correlation between smoking and lung cancer. And it is higher than correlations between other widely accepted health effects and outcomes (see Figure 15.5 on the following page). Because exposure to violent TV is so widespread, its impact can be profound even if only a small percentage of viewers are affected (Anderson & Bushman, 2002). Laboratory research shows that 15 minutes of mildly violent programming increases aggression in at least one-quarter of viewers (Bushman, 1995).

**ETHNIC AND GENDER STEREOTYPES.** Although educational programming for children is sensitive to issues of equity and diversity, commercial entertainment TV conveys ethnic and gender stereotypes. Ethnic minorities are underrepresented; only 33 percent of entertainment shows include a main character from a minority group. When minorities appear, they are usually depicted in subservient roles or as villains or victims of violence (Williams & Cox, 1995).

Similarly, women appear less often than men, filling only one-third or less of main-character roles. Compared with two decades ago, today women are more often shown as involved in careers. But they continue to be portrayed as young, attractive, caring, emotional, victimized, and in romantic and family contexts. In contrast, men are depicted as dominant and powerful (Signorielli, 2001). Gender roles are especially stereotypic in entertainment programs for children and youths.

TV viewing is linked to gains in children's endorsement of many gender stereotypes (Signorielli, 1993). But nonstereotypic images on TV can reduce children's ethnic and gender biases. For example, positive portrayals of ethnic minorities lead to more favourable views and greater willingness to form ethnically diverse friendships (Graves, 1993).

**CONSUMERISM.** Television commercials directed at children "work" by increasing product sales. Although children can distinguish a TV program from a commercial as early as 3 years of age, below age 8 they seldom grasp the selling purpose of the ad. They think that commercials are meant to help viewers (Levin, Petros, & Petrella, 1982). Around age 8 or 9, most children understand that commercials are meant to persuade, and by age 11, they realize that advertisers will resort to clever techniques to sell their products. As a result, children become increasingly skeptical of commercial messages (Kunkel, 2001).

Nevertheless, even older children and adolescents find many commercials alluring. In a study of 8- to 14-year-old boys, celebrity endorsement of a racing toy made the product more attractive, and live racetrack images led to exaggerated estimates of the toy's positive features (Ross et al., 1984). The ease with which television advertising can manipulate children's beliefs and preferences has raised questions about the ethics of child-directed commercials.

In 1963, Advertising Standards Canada (formerly the Canadian Advertising Foundation) established a broadcasting code for children's advertising. Under the Canadian Code of Advertising Standards, which is reviewed and revised periodically to keep it contemporary, those who advertise for children must refrain from transmitting messages below the threshold of awareness, must not exaggerate the features of the product, cannot repeat the same commercial within a half-hour, and cannot play more than four minutes of advertising within each half-hour. If a violation occurs, the advertiser is asked to amend the advertisement in question, or withdraw it. When an advertiser is reluctant to take corrective action, the broadcasters carrying the advertisement are notified, and the broadcaster usually drops the advertisement in question (Media Awareness Network, 2000).

**PROSOCIAL BEHAVIOUR.** Many TV programs include acts of cooperating, helping, and comforting. A large-scale review leaves little doubt that television with prosocial content can increase children's prosocial behaviour (Hearold, 1986). But the review also highlights some important qualifications. Almost all the findings are short term and limited to situations quite similar to those shown on TV. In addition, television programs often mix prosocial and antisocial intentions and behaviour. Recall that young children have difficulty integrating these elements. Prosocial TV has positive effects only when it is free of violent content (Liss, Reinhardt, & Fredriksen, 1983).

Finally, parents who use authoritative child rearing have children who watch more prosocial programs (Abelman, 1985). Consequently, children from families that already promote social and moral maturity probably benefit most from prosocial television.

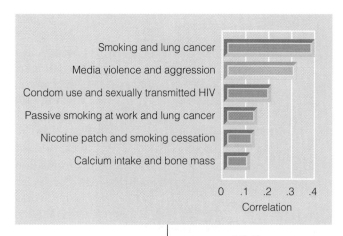

**FIGURE** 15.5

**Comparison of the consequences of media violence with other widely accepted health effects.** The media violence–aggression correlation is almost as high as the correlation between smoking and lung cancer. It is higher than the correlation between other health effects and outcomes. (Adapted from B. J. Bushman & C. A. Anderson, 2001, "Media Violence and the American Public," *American Psychologist, 56*, p. 481. Copyright © 2001 by the American Psychological Association. Reprinted by permission of the publisher and author.)

## TELEVISION, ACADEMIC LEARNING, AND IMAGINATION

Since the early days of television, educators have been interested in its potential for strengthening school performance, especially among low-SES children. Research shows that preschoolers from low- to moderate-income families who spend more time watching age-appropriate educational programs perform better on tests of diverse academic skills at age 5 (Wright et al., 2001). *Sesame Street,* especially, was created with the goal of boosting low-SES children's learning. It uses lively visual and sound effects to stress basic literacy and number concepts, and puppet and human characters to teach general knowledge, emotional and social understanding, and social skills. The Canadian version, *Sesame Park,* also offers an introduction to the French language and Aboriginal culture. Today, the majority of preschoolers watch *Sesame Street* (or *Sesame Park*) at least once a week, and it is broadcast in more than 40 countries (Zill, Davies, & Daly, 1994).

Although television has the potential to support development, too often it teaches negative lessons. Heavy viewers learn that aggression is an acceptable way to solve problems and are taken in by TV advertising. Boys, especially, are attracted to shows with violent content.

*Sesame Street* works well as an academic tutor. The more children watch, the higher they score on tests designed to measure the program's learning goals (Fisch, Truglio, & Cole, 1999). One study reported a link between preschool viewing of *Sesame Street* and other similar educational programs and getting higher grades, reading more books, placing more value on achievement, and scoring higher on a divergent thinking test (a measure of creativity) in high school (Anderson et al., 2001). In recent years, however, *Sesame Street* has reduced its rapid-paced, adlike format in favour of leisurely episodes with a clear story line (Truglio, 2000). Children's programs with slow-paced action and easy-to-follow narratives, such as *Caillou, Mr. Rogers' Neighborhood,* and *Barney and Friends,* lead to more elaborate make-believe play than do programs that present quick, disconnected bits of information (Singer, 1999; Tower et al., 1979).

Yet another program that enhances children's cognitive development is *Blue's Clues,* in which a host named Joe invites preschoolers to help solve various problems, provides time for them to come up with solutions, and gives them feedback on strategies and answers. Children who regularly watched *Blue's Clues,* compared with children of similar backgrounds living in areas where it was not broadcast, showed greater gains on tests of vocabulary, pattern identification, and problem solving over a 2-year period (Anderson et al., 2000).

Does entertainment TV take children away from activities that promote cognitive development? Some evidence suggests that it does. The more preschool and school-age children watch prime-time shows and cartoons, the less time they spend reading and interacting with others and the more poorly they perform on tests of academic skills (Huston et al., 1999; Wright et al., 2001). In sum, whereas educational programs lead to diverse cognitive benefits, entertainment TV—especially heavy viewing—detracts from children's cognitive progress and success in school.

### REGULATING CHILDREN'S TELEVISION

The regulation of media violence in Canada began in 1987, when the Canadian Association of Broadcasters introduced the Violence Code. Although appropriate to its time, as early as the 1990s the Violence Code was viewed as insufficient. A new violence code came into effect in 1994, partly in response to a Quebec teenager named Virginie Larivière, who believed that her 11-year-old sister's murder was influenced by media violence. In 1992, Larivière brought the prime minister a petition to reduce violent television programming, signed by 1.3 million Canadians. The new code bans gratuitous or glamorized violence and prohibits violence intended for adult audiences from being shown before 9 P.M. However, implementation of the ban has proved difficult. Although the Canadian government can regulate its own broadcasting, programs received from the United States are exempt from Canadian control. In other words, young viewers who cannot find a violent show on Canadian networks before 9 P.M. can simply switch channels and watch one on U.S. television (Canadian Broadcast Standards Council, 2001; Primero, 1993).

In response, the Canadian Radio-television and Telecommunications Commission (CRTC) mandated the adoption of the V-Chip, also called the Violence-Chip. This device, invented by Tim Collings of Simon Fraser University, allows parents to block out certain programs. However, licensing laws prevent Canadian cable operators from making any V-chip changes to purchased programming, so the V-Chip plan has been delayed (Canadian Broadcast Standards Council, 2001; Primero, 1993).

But the Violence Code and the V-Chip are far from complete solutions. Ratings indicating violent, sexual, and offensive-language content may make shows more appealing to some young people—an outcome supported for boys (Cantor & Harrison, 1997). And children may go to other homes to watch programs forbidden by their own parents. Until children's television improves, parents must be informed about the dangers of TV viewing and how to control it. Table 15.2 lists some strategies they can use.

**TABLE** 15.2

Regulating Children's TV Viewing

| STRATEGY | DESCRIPTION |
|---|---|
| Limit TV viewing. | Avoid using TV as a baby-sitter. Provide clear rules that limit what children can watch—for example, an hour a day and only certain programs—and stick to the rules. Do not place a TV in the child's bedroom, where TV viewing is difficult to monitor. |
| Refrain from using TV as a reinforcer. | Do not use television to reward or punish children, a practice that increases its attractiveness. |
| Encourage child-appropriate viewing. | Encourage children to watch programs that are child-appropriate, informative, and prosocial. |
| Explain televised information to children. | As much as possible, watch with children, helping them understand what they see. When adults express disapproval of on-screen behaviour, raise questions about the realism of televised information, and encourage children to discuss it, they teach children to evaluate TV content rather than accept it uncritically. |
| Link televised content to everyday learning experiences. | Build on TV programs in constructive ways, encouraging children to move away from the set into active engagement with their surroundings. For example, a program on animals might spark a trip to the zoo, a visit to the library for books about animals, or new ways of observing and caring for the family pet. |
| Model good viewing practices. | Avoid excess television viewing, especially violent programs, yourself. Parental viewing patterns influence children's viewing patterns. |
| Use a warm, rational approach to child rearing. | Respond to children with warmth and reasonable demands for mature behaviour. Children who experience these practices prefer programs with prosocial content and are less attracted to violent TV. |

*Source:* Slaby et al., 1995.

# Computers

TODAY, COMPUTERS ARE a familiar fixture in the everyday lives of children and adolescents, offering a wide range of learning and entertainment tools. Almost all Canadian public schools integrate computers into their instructional programs. Fifty-five percent of Canadian households report owning a computer and nearly 7 out of 10 families with children have access to the Internet through home and school, or various other locations such as the library (Statistics Canada, Household Internet Use, 2001; Statistics Canada, Selected Dwelling Statistics, 2001). Higher-income households are more likely to use the Internet, although with access available through various locations, Internet use is growing among low-SES households (Statistics Canada, Household Internet Use, 2001).

In a survey of children and adolescents in the United States, the percentage who reported using a computer on the previous day rose with age, from 26 percent of 2- to 7-year-olds to 44 percent of 14- to 18-year-olds. Higher SES also predicted increased use. Boys were heavier users of computer games and more often visited websites than did girls, but no gender differences emerged for chatting, using e-mail, or doing schoolwork on the computer (Roberts et al., 1999). And teenage boys and girls express equal confidence in their computer skills (National Science Foundation, 1997).

Parents estimate that, on the average, their school-age children and adolescents use the computer about 1½ hours per day (Stanger & Gridina, 1999). Although they say they buy computers to enrich their children's education, parents express concern about the influence of the Internet and violent computer games (Turow, 1999). Let's see how computers affect academic and social development.

## COMPUTERS AND ACADEMIC LEARNING

Computers can have rich cognitive and social benefits. Children as young as 3 years of age like computer activities and can type in simple commands on a standard keyboard

(Campbell & Schwartz, 1986). Furthermore, in classrooms, small groups often gather around the machine, and children more often collaborate when working with the computer than with paper and pencil (Clements, Nastasi, & Swaminathan, 1993).

As soon as children begin to read and write, they can use the computer for word processing. It permits them to write without having to struggle with handwriting. In addition, they can revise the text's meaning and style as well as check their spelling. As a result, they worry less about making mistakes, and their written products tend to be longer and of higher quality (Clements, 1995). However, computers by themselves do not help children master the mechanics of writing. According to Keith Stanovich of the Ontario Institute for Studies in Education, children learn to spell better without a computer than they do with one (Cunningham & Stanovich, 1990). So it is best to use computers to build on and enhance, not replace, other classroom writing experiences.

Specially designed computer languages introduce children to programming skills. As long as adults support children's efforts, computer programming leads to improved concept formation, problem solving, and creativity (Clements, 1995; Clements & Nastasi, 1992). Also, since children must detect errors in their programs to get them to work, programming helps them reflect on their thought processes, leading to gains in metacognitive knowledge and self-regulation (Clements, 1990). Furthermore, while programming, children are especially likely to collaborate, persist in the face of challenge, and display positive attitudes toward learning (Nastasi & Clements, 1992, 1994). In sum, consistent with Vygotsky's theory, social interaction supporting children's mastery of challenging computer tasks fosters a wide variety of higher cognitive processes.

Adolescents report that they often use the computer for schoolwork, largely through word processing and searching the Web to find information. In one study, secondary-school students who used the computer more earned higher grades in math and English and did better on a test of scientific knowledge (Rocheleau, 1995). However, only certain kinds of computer use are related to school performance. For example, academically "unsuccessful" children and adolescents spend more time playing computer games than do their academically "successful" agemates (Madden, Bruekman, & Littlejohn, 1997).

In view of the computer's benefits for academic development, low-SES children's limited home access can place them at an educational disadvantage. Therefore, schools should take extra steps to ensure that these children have many opportunities to benefit from the cognitively enriching aspects of computer technology.

## COMPUTERS AND SOCIAL LEARNING

Children and adolescents spend much time using home computers for entertainment purposes. Among 8- to 14-year-old boys, interactive games are an alluring pursuit. And surfing the Net and communicating through e-mail, chat rooms, and instant messaging rise sharply in adolescence (Roberts et al., 1999).

**COMPUTER GAMES.** Most computer games emphasize speed and action in violent plots in which players advance by shooting at and evading the enemy. Children also play more complex exploratory and adventure games with themes of conquest and aggression and sports games, such as football and soccer. And they enjoy simulation games, involving caring for virtual pets (which require attention to "stay alive"), entering virtual realities (such as an ecosystem where the player mutates plants and animals into new species), and role-playing characters (for example, a cowboy, a seductive woman, a furry animal).

Speed-and-action computer games foster attentional and spatial skills in boys and girls alike (Okagaki & Frensch, 1996; Subrahmanyam & Greenfield, 1996). Yet game software is unappealing to girls because of its themes of violence and male-dominated sports. And a growing number of studies indicate that playing violent games has effects similar to those of

Computers in classrooms provide learning environments that are cognitively stimulating and socially interactive. Children are far more likely to collaborate when working with the computer than when working with paper and pencil.

violent TV—that is, promotes hostility and aggression and reduces prosocial behaviour (Anderson & Bushman, 2001). Furthermore, computer games are full of ethnic and gender stereotypes (Dietz, 1998).

While offering opportunities for learning, extensive playing of simulation games risks blurring the distinction between virtual and real life (Turkle, 1995). For example, one 10-year-old described the creatures in a virtual reality as "a little alive" and stated that as long as the modem remained on, they could "get out of your computer and go to America Online" (p. 169). A 15-year-old indicated that by role-playing characters, he turned parts of his mind on and off: "'rl' [real life] is just one more window, and it's not usually my best one" (p. 13).

Compared with infrequent users, "passionate" game players spend time less productively, more often watching cartoons, and less often reading (Wright & Huston, 1995). When game simulations are violent, they may contribute—along with disengaged parents, antisocial peers, and alienation from school—to heinous acts in at-risk young people. News reports indicated that the Columbine High School teenage murderers were obsessed with a game called *Doom,* in which players try to rack up the most kills (Subrahmanyam et al., 2001).

**THE INTERNET AND COMMUNICATION.** Using the computer to communicate is a popular activity among adolescents. They report that after homework, e-mail and chat rooms are their most frequent Internet activities (Turow, 1999).

Yet debate surrounds the implications of home-based Internet access for social development (Kraut et al., 1998a). Are social relationships on the Internet similar in quality to social ties in other settings? To find out, researchers provided over 90 families, many of whom had teenagers, with their first Internet experience by giving each a computer, a telephone line, and free Internet access in exchange for allowing automatic tracking of their Internet use (Kraut et al., 1998b). Before gaining access and 1 to 2 years later, participants completed a questionnaire assessing social involvement and psychological well-being.

Findings revealed that teenagers used the Internet for more hours than did adults. Regardless of age, greater Internet use predicted a drop in time spent communicating with family members and in size of nearby and distant social networks. Also, those who used the Internet more reported feeling lonelier and more depressed at a later date. Because initial social involvement and psychological well-being were unrelated to time on-line, the investigators concluded that heavy Internet use negatively affected emotional and social adjustment. It probably did so by displacing face-to-face social activity with relatives, friends, and neighbours—stronger, more supportive ties than typically form through e-mail or in chat rooms.

The Internet's potential for causing disengagement from real life must be weighed against its value for acquiring computer skills and information and enabling convenient communication. Parents are wise to oversee how much their children use the home computer—and when they use the Internet, just how they spend their time.

## ASK YOURSELF www

**review**   Why are preschool and young school-age children more likely than older children and adolescents to imitate TV violence?

**review**   Describe research that supports the academic and social benefits of educational television and computer use.

**apply**   Eleven-year-old Tommy spends hours each afternoon surfing the Net and playing computer games. Using research findings, explain why his parents should intervene in both activities.

**connect**   Which of the following children is most likely to be attracted to watching violent TV: Jane, a popular child; Mack, a rejected child; or Tim, a neglected child? Explain.

# Schooling

UNLIKE THE INFORMAL WORLD of peer relations, the school is a formal institution designed to transmit knowledge and skills children need to become productive members of society. Children spend many hours in school—6 hours a day, 5 days a week, 36 weeks of the year—totalling, altogether, about 14 000 hours by high school graduation. Although school attendance is not compulsory until grade 1, the trend in Canada is to begin school before this time, so the majority of children attend kindergarten programs, and some attend junior kindergarten, both of which are publicly funded. See the Social Issues: Education box on the following page for research on school readiness and early retention.

In earlier chapters, we noted that schools are vital forces in children's development, affecting their motivation to learn and modes of remembering, reasoning, problem solving, and social and moral understanding. How do schools exert such a powerful impact? Research looking at schools as complex social systems—their class and student body size, educational philosophies, teacher–student relationships, and cultural context—provides important insights.

## CLASS AND STUDENT BODY SIZE

The physical plants of all schools are similar: Each has classrooms, hallways, a playground, and a lunchroom. But they also vary widely in the number of students they accommodate in each class and in the school as a whole.

Is there an optimal class size? In a large-scale field experiment, over 6000 kindergartners in 79 elementary schools were randomly assigned to three class types: small (13 to 17 students), regular (22 to 25 students) with only a teacher to supervise, and regular with a teacher plus a full-time teacher's aide. These arrangements continued into grade 3. Small-class students scored higher in reading and math achievement each year, an effect that was particularly strong for minority students. Placing teacher's aides in regular-size classes had no consistent impact (Mosteller, 1995). Finally, even after returning to regular-size classes, children who had been in small classes remained ahead in academic progress. Consistently being in small classes from kindergarten through grade 3 was associated with substantially higher achievement from grades 4 through 9 (see Figure 15.6) (Finn et al., 2001; Nye, Hedges, & Konstantopoulos, 2001).

Why is small class size beneficial? Teachers of fewer children spend less time disciplining and more time giving individual attention, and children's interactions with one another are more positive and cooperative. Also, when class size is small, children learn in smaller groups and are more satisfied with their school experiences. And teachers report better concentration and higher-quality contributions to group discussion by their students (Blatchford et al., 2001).

By the time students reach secondary school, they move from class to class and have access to many activities outside regular instruction. As a result, the relevant physical context is the school as a whole. Student body size profoundly affects school life. Members of smaller schools consistently report more social support and caring. As one teacher at a large high school commented, "A huge problem here is our size. It breeds anonymity. It breeds disconnection.... There is no sense of identification" (Lee et al., 2000, p. 159).

Furthermore, schools with 500 to 700 students or fewer have fewer people to ensure that clubs, sports events, and social activities will function. As a result, young people enter a greater number and variety of activities and hold more positions of responsibility and leadership. In contrast, plenty of students are available to fill activity slots in large schools, so only a small elite are genuinely active (Barker & Gump, 1964).

In view of these findings, it is not surprising that adolescents in small schools report a greater sense of personal responsibility, competence, and challenge from their extracurricular experiences. This is true even for "marginal" students—those with low IQs, academic difficulties, and poverty-stricken backgrounds. A special advantage of small schools is that potential dropouts

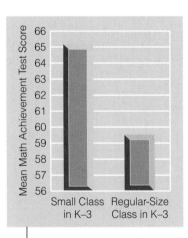

**FIGURE** 15.6

**Relationship of consistently being in small classes from kindergarten through grade 3 to grade-9 math achievement.** In this longitudinal study of thousands of Tennessee students, small class size in the early grades continued to be associated with higher academic achievement 6 years later, in grade 9. Here, findings for math scores are shown. (Adapted from Nye, Hedges, & Konstantopoulos, 2001.)

## SCHOOL READINESS AND EARLY RETENTION

the majority of Canadian children attend kindergarten at age 5, and some attend junior kindergarten, if available, at age 4. In some Canadian school districts, children start school as early as age 3 because the entry requirement states only that they must have their fourth birthday by December 31 of their first school year.

At what age should children begin school? Although some parents wonder whether they should delay their child's entry into kindergarten, research reveals no benefits from doing so. Many studies indicate that younger children make just as much academic progress as do older children in the same grade (Cameron & Wilson, 1990; Graue & DiPerna, 2000; Jones & Mandeville, 1990). And as Jeff Bisanz of the University of Alberta and others showed, younger first graders reap academic gains from on-time enrolment; they outperform same-age children a year behind them in school (Bisanz, Morrison, & Dunn, 1995; Morrison, Griffith, & Alberts, 1997). Furthermore, children who are delayed in entering school show no advantage in self-esteem, peer acceptance, or teacher ratings of behaviour (Spitzer, Cupp, & Parke, 1995). Delaying kindergarten entry does not seem to prevent or solve emotional and social problems. To the contrary, children usually are aware that their school entry has been delayed, and some worry that they have failed (Graue, 1993).

A related dilemma concerns whether to retain a student not progressing well for a second year in kindergarten or one of the primary grades. A wealth of research reveals no learning benefits and suggests negative consequences for motivation, self-esteem, peer relations,

and attitudes toward school as early as kindergarten (Carlton & Winsler, 1999). In a Canadian study, students retained between kindergarten and grade 2—regardless of the academic and social characteristics they brought to the situation—showed worsening academic performance, anxiety, and (among boys) disruptiveness throughout elementary school. These unfavourable trends did not characterize non-retained students (Pagani et al., 2001). Retaining students may have even longer-term consequences. Additional Canadian research revealed that high school dropouts were more than five times as likely as graduates to have repeated a grade in elementary school (see Figure 15.7) (Bowlby & McMullen, 2002).

To address some of these concerns, Marvin Simner (1999) of the University of Western Ontario developed a screening tool that teachers can use with preschoolers to identify students at risk for school failure. He also devised a series of activities that address language, problem-solving, and reading difficulties—teaching that increases the chances of school success.

Those who believe that younger children should be held back from starting school and those who believe that poorly performing children should be retained for a second year in kindergarten or grade 1 share the view that readiness for school largely results from biological maturation. An alternative

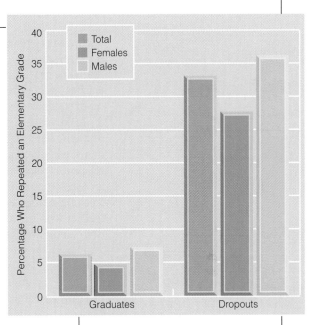

FIGURE 15.7

**Incidence of elementary grade repetition based on Canada's Longitudinal Youth in Transition survey.** Overall, high school dropouts were more than five times as likely as graduates to have failed an elementary school grade. Males were more likely than females to have repeated a grade, whether they are graduates or dropouts. (From J.W. Bowlby & K. McMullen, 2002, *At a Crossroads: First Results for the 18- to 20-Year-Old Cohort of the Youth in Transition Survey*, Ottawa: Human Resources Development Canada and Statistics Canada, p. 34. Reprinted by permission of Statistics Canada and Government Works, 2002.)

perspective, based on Vygotsky's sociocultural theory, is that children acquire the knowledge, skills, and attitudes for school success through the assistance of parents and teachers. Research supports this idea. School readiness is not something to wait for; it can be cultivated.

are far more likely to join in activities, gain recognition, and remain until graduation (Mahoney & Cairns, 1997). The sense of social obligation engendered in small high schools seems to carry over to better achievement, especially for low-SES students (Lee & Smith, 1995).

## EDUCATIONAL PHILOSOPHIES

Each teacher brings to the classroom an educational philosophy that plays a major role in children's learning experiences. Two philosophical approaches—traditional and open classrooms—have received much research attention. They differ in what children are taught, the way they are believed to learn, and how their progress is evaluated.

**TRADITIONAL VERSUS OPEN CLASSROOMS.** In a **traditional classroom,** the teacher is the sole authority for knowledge, rules, and decision making and does most of the talking. Students are relatively passive, listening, responding when called on, and completing teacher-assigned tasks. Their progress is evaluated by how well they keep pace with a uniform set of standards for all students in their grade.

In contrast, in an **open classroom,** students are viewed as active agents in their own development. The teacher assumes a flexible authority role, sharing decision making with students, who learn at their own pace. Students are evaluated by considering their progress in relation to their own prior development. How well they compare to other same-age students is of less importance. A glance inside the door of an open classroom reveals richly equipped learning centres, small groups of students working on tasks they choose themselves, and a teacher who moves from one area to another, guiding and supporting in response to children's individual needs.

During the past few decades, the pendulum has swung back and forth between these two views. In the 1960s and early 1970s, open education gained in popularity, inspired by Piaget's vision of the child as an active, motivated learner. Then, as concerns over the academic progress of children and youths became widespread, a "back to basics" movement arose. Classrooms returned to traditional, teacher-directed instruction, a style still prevalent today.

The combined results of many studies reveal that older students in traditional classrooms have a slight edge in academic achievement. But open settings are associated with other benefits. Open-classroom students have more advanced critical-thinking skills, and they value and respect individual differences in their classmates more. Students in open environments also like school better than do those in traditional classrooms (Walberg, 1986).

Whole-class, teacher-directed instruction has filtered down to preschools and kindergartens. When young children spend much time passively sitting and doing worksheets as opposed to being actively engaged in learning centres, they display more stress behaviours, such as wiggling, withdrawal, and talking out. Follow-ups reveal that traditional-classroom kindergartners show poorer study habits and achieve less well in grade school (Burts et al., 1992; Hart et al., 1998). These outcomes are strongest for low-SES children. Yet teachers tend to prefer a traditional approach for economically disadvantaged students, despite its negative impact on motivation and learning (Stipek & Byler, 1997).

**VYGOTSKY-INSPIRED DIRECTIONS.** The philosophies of some teachers fall between traditional and open. They want to foster high achievement as well as critical thinking, positive social relationships, and excitement about learning. Approaches to elementary education, grounded in Vygotsky's sociocultural theory, represent this point of view. In Chapter 6, we considered two Vygotsky-inspired educational innovations: reciprocal teaching and cooperative learning (see pages 262–264). Each is consistent with one or more of the following themes:

- *Teachers and children as partners in learning.* A classroom rich in both teacher–child and child–child collaboration transfers culturally valued ways of thinking to children.

- *Experience with many types of symbolic communication in meaningful activities.* As children master reading, writing, and quantitative reasoning, they become aware of their culture's communication systems, reflect on their own thinking, and bring it under voluntary control.

**traditional classroom**
A classroom based on the educational philosophy that children are passive learners who acquire information presented by teachers. Children's progress is evaluated on the basis of how well they keep pace with a uniform set of standards for all students in their grade.

**open classroom**
A classroom based on the educational philosophy that children are active agents in their own development and learn at different rates. Teachers share decision making with students. Children's progress is evaluated in relation to their own prior development.

■ *Teaching adapted to each child's zone of proximal development.* Assistance that is responsive to current understandings but that encourages children to take the next step forward helps ensure that each student will make the best progress possible.

The most well-known and extensive educational reform effort based on these principles is the *Kamehameha Elementary Education Program* (KEEP). Thousands of low-SES minority children in the United States have attended KEEP classrooms in the public schools of Hawaii, on a Navajo reservation in Arizona, and in Los Angeles. To foster development, KEEP instruction is organized around activity settings specially designed to enhance teacher–child and child–child interaction. In each setting, small groups of students work on a project that ensures that their learning will be active and directed toward a meaningful goal.

All children enter a focal activity setting, called "Center One," at least once each morning for scaffolding of challenging literacy skills. Teachers carefully select text content to relate to children's experiences and engage them in discussion that builds on their ideas. The precise organization of each KEEP classroom is adjusted to fit the unique learning styles of its students, creating culturally responsive environments (Au, 1997; Tharp, 1993, 1994).

In KEEP schools, minority students performed at their expected grade level in reading achievement, much better than children of the same background enrolled in traditional schools. As the KEEP model becomes more widely applied, perhaps it will prove successful with all types of children because of its comprehensive goals and effort to meet the learning needs of a wide range of students.

© WILL HART

Active engagement in learning centres in preschool and kindergarten fosters a relaxed, confident approach to challenging problems and better achievement in grade school, especially for low-SES children.

## SCHOOL TRANSITIONS

Besides size and educational philosophy, an additional structural feature of schooling affects students' achievement and psychological adjustment: the timing of transitions from one school level to the next. Entering kindergarten is a major milestone. Children must accommodate to new physical settings, adult authorities, daily schedules, peer companions, and academic challenges.

**EARLY ADJUSTMENT TO SCHOOL.** In a study of factors that predict effective transition to kindergarten, Gary Ladd and Joseph Price (1987) gathered observational and interview data on children at the end of preschool and during their kindergarten year. Children who engaged in cooperative play and friendly interaction with agemates in preschool seemed to transfer these skills to kindergarten. They were better liked by peers and more involved in classroom life. The presence of preschool friends in kindergarten also enhanced adaptation. The continuity of these ties may have provided children with a sense of stability in their otherwise changing social environments.

In further longitudinal research extending over the kindergarten year, children with more preschool experience scored higher on school readiness tests and showed increasingly positive school attitudes. Liking for school predicted greater classroom participation. And participation, in turn, predicted higher achievement. Furthermore, children with friendly, prosocial behavioural styles more easily made new friends, gained peer acceptance, and formed a warm bond with their teacher. These favourable relationships also predicted high achievement, perhaps by energizing cooperation and initiative in the classroom (Birch & Ladd, 1998; Ladd, Birch, & Buhs, 1999; Ladd, Buhs, & Seid, 2000; Ladd, Kochenderfer, & Coleman, 1997).

| Preschool Experience<br><br>Presence of Preschool Friends in Kindergarten<br><br>Prosocial Behavioural Style | → | Favourable Peer Acceptance<br><br>New Kindergarten Friends<br><br>Warm Teacher–Child Bond | → | Positive Attitude Toward School | → | High Classroom Participation | → | High Achievement |

**FIGURE** 15.8

**Factors linked to favourable adaptation to kindergarten.**

In contrast, kindergartners with antisocial styles (who are argumentative and aggressive) tend to establish conflict-ridden relationships with teachers and peers, which impair their liking for school, classroom participation, and achievement. And peer-avoidant kindergartners often become overly dependent on teachers, clinging and asking for help when they do not need it (Birch & Ladd, 1998). These early, poor-quality teacher–child relationships predict academic and behaviour problems throughout elementary school (Hamre & Pianta, 2001).

Figure 15.8 summarizes factors linked to favourable adaptation to kindergarten. A look at these factors suggests that parents can foster good school adjustment by encouraging positive social skills and arranging for their child to attend preschool. In planning the composition of kindergarten classrooms, educators might also consider grouping children to maximize contact with friends. And positive teacher–child ties, while important for all children, are crucial for preventing long-lasting school difficulties in poorly adjusted kindergartners.

**SCHOOL TRANSITIONS IN ADOLESCENCE.** Early adolescence is a second important period of school transition, when students typically move from an intimate, self-contained elementary school classroom to a much larger, impersonal secondary school in which they must shift from one class to the next. Research reveals that with each school change—from elementary to junior high and then to high school—adolescents' course grades decline. The drop is partly due to tighter academic standards. At the same time, the transition to secondary school often brings less personal attention, more whole-class instruction, and fewer opportunities to participate in classroom decision making.

In view of these changes, it is not surprising that many students rate their junior-high learning experiences less favourably than their elementary school experiences (Wigfield & Eccles, 1994). They also report that their junior-high teachers care less about them, are less friendly, grade less fairly, and stress competition more and mastery and improvement less. Consequently, many young people feel less academically competent and show a drop in motivation (Anderman & Midgley, 1997; Eccles et al., 1993c).

Inevitably, the transition to junior high and then to high school requires students to readjust their feelings of self-confidence and self-worth as academic expectations are revised and students enter a more complex social world. A comprehensive study revealed that the timing of school transition is important, especially for girls (Simmons & Blyth, 1987). More than 300 adolescents were followed from grade 6 to grade 10. Some were enrolled in school districts with a 6–3–3 grade organization (a K–6 elementary school, a 3-year junior high, and a 3-year high school). These students made two school changes, one to junior high and one to high school. A comparison group attended schools with an 8–4 grade organization. They made only one school transition, from a K–8 elementary school to high school.

For the sample as a whole, grade point average dropped and feelings of anonymity increased after each transition. Participation in extracurricular activities declined more in the 6–3–3 than in the 8–4 arrangement, although the drop was greater for

Moving from a small, self-contained elementary school classroom to a large, impersonal secondary school is stressful for adolescents. As this cafeteria line suggests, feelings of anonymity increase, and school grades and extracurricular participation also decline. The stress of school transition can be particularly harmful to adolescents with academic and emotional difficulties, increasing the risk of school failure and dropout.

© JOHN MAHER/STOCK BOSTON

girls. Furthermore, in 8–4 schools, school transition led to gains in self-esteem. In contrast, in 6–3–3 schools, sex differences in self-esteem were striking. Whereas boys remained stable, girls showed a sharp drop with each school change (see Figure 15.9).

These findings show that any school transition is likely to temporarily depress adolescents' psychological well-being, but the earlier it occurs, the more dramatic and long lasting its impact. Girls in 6–3–3 schools fared poorest, the researchers argued, because movement to junior high tended to coincide with other life changes—namely, the onset of puberty and dating. In support of this idea, Patricia McDougall and Shelley Hymel (1998) of the University of British Columbia found that students with poor social adjustment and school attitudes in grade 6 experienced a more difficult junior-high transition. Adolescents who face added strains, such as family disruption, parental unemployment, or learned helplessness with respect to academic performance at the time they enter junior high, are at greatest risk for emotional difficulties (Flanagan & Eccles, 1993; Rudolph et al., 2001).

Distressed young people whose school performance drops sharply often show a persisting pattern of poor self-esteem, motivation, and achievement. In another study, researchers compared "multiple-problem" youths (those with both academic and mental-health problems), youths having difficulties in just one area (either academic or mental health), and well-adjusted youths (doing well in both areas) across the transition to high school. Although all groups declined in grade point average, well-adjusted students continued to get high marks and multiple-problem youths low marks, with the other groups falling in between. And as Figure 15.10 on page 638 shows, the multiple-problem youths showed a far greater rise in truancy and out-of-school problem behaviours (Roeser, Eccles, & Freedman-Doan, 1999). For some, school transition initiates a downward spiral in academic performance and school involvement that leads to dropping out (Eccles et al., 1997b).

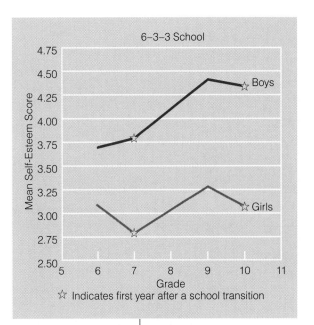

**FIGURE 15.9**

**Self-esteem from grade 6 to grade 10 in 6–3–3 schools.** In this longitudinal study of more than 300 adolescents, boys' self-esteem remained stable after school transition. In contrast, girls' self-esteem dropped sharply in the year after each school change. (Adapted from Simmons & Blyth, 1987.)

**HELPING ADOLESCENTS ADJUST TO SCHOOL TRANSITIONS.** Consider the findings just reviewed, and you will see that school transitions often lead to environmental changes that fit poorly with adolescents' developmental needs. They disrupt close relationships with teachers at a time when adolescents need adult support. They emphasize competition during a period of heightened self-focusing. They reduce decision making and choice as the desire for autonomy is increasing. And they interfere with peer networks at a time of increased concern with peer acceptance.

Enhanced support from parents, teachers, and peers eases the strain of school transition. Parent involvement, monitoring, and autonomy granting are associated with better adjustment after entering junior high (Grolnick et al., 2000). Since most students do better in an 8–4 school arrangement, school districts thinking about reorganization should seriously consider this plan.[2] Also, smaller social units can be formed within large schools, permitting closer relations with teachers and peers and greater extracurricular involvement (Seidman & French, 1997). And students can be assigned to classes with several familiar peers or a constant group of new peers—arrangements that promote emotional security and social support.

Finally, teenagers' perceptions of the sensitivity and flexibility of their school learning environments contribute substantially to their adjustment. When schools minimize competition and differential treatment by ability, students are less likely to feel angry and

[2]Recall from Chapter 5 (page 202) that girls who reach puberty early fare better in K–6 schools, where they are relieved of pressures from older adolescents to become involved in dating, sexual activity, and drug experimentation. Although the 8–4 organization is best for the majority of adolescents, early maturing girls require special support under these conditions.

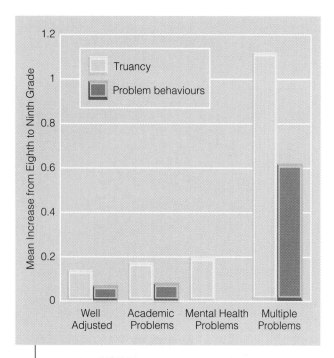

FIGURE 15.10

**Increase in truancy and out-of-school problem behaviours across the transition to high school in four groups of students.** Well-adjusted students, students with only academic problems, and students with only mental health problems showed little change. (Good students with mental health problems actually declined in problem behaviours, so no purple bar is shown for them.) In contrast, multiple-problem students—with both academic and mental health difficulties—increased sharply in truancy and problem behaviours after changing schools from grade 8 to grade 9. (Adapted from Roeser, Eccles, & Freedman-Doan, 1999.)

**educational self-fulfilling prophecy**
The idea that students may adopt teachers' positive or negative attitudes toward them and start to live up to these views.

depressed, to be truant, and to show declines in academic values, self-esteem, and achievement during junior high school (Roeser, Eccles, & Sameroff, 2000). School rules that strike young people as fair rather than punitive also foster satisfaction with school life (Eccles et al., 1993b).

### ■ TEACHER–STUDENT INTERACTION

The classroom is a complex social system, in which teachers engage in as many as 1000 exchanges with students each day (Jackson, 1968). A vast amount of research exists on teacher–student interaction, most focusing on its significance for academic achievement.

Elementary and secondary school students describe good teachers as caring, helpful, and stimulating—characteristics positively associated with learning (Daniels, Kalkman, & McCombs, 2001; Sanders & Jordan, 2000). Yet with respect to stimulation, a disappointing finding is that many teachers emphasize rote, repetitive drill more than higher-level thinking, such as analyzing, synthesizing, and applying ideas (Campbell, Hombo, & Mazzeo, 2000). In a study of grade 5 social studies and math lessons, students were far more attentive when teachers emphasized high-level thinking (Stodolsky, 1988). And in a longitudinal investigation of over 5000 seventh graders, those attending schools with a more demanding academic climate showed better attendance and larger gains in math achievement during the following 2 years (Phillips, 1997).

As we have already seen, teachers do not interact in the same way with all children. Some students get more attention, encouragement, and praise than others. Well-behaved, high-achieving students typically get more encouragement and praise, whereas unruly students are often criticized and rarely called on to contribute to class discussion. When they seek special help or permission, their requests are usually denied (Good & Brophy, 1996).

Unfortunately, once teachers' attitudes toward students are established, they can become more extreme than is warranted by children's behaviour. A special concern is that an **educational self-fulfilling prophecy**[3] can be set in motion: Children may adopt teachers' positive or negative views and start to live up to them. This effect is particularly strong when teachers emphasize competition and make public comparisons between children (Weinstein et al., 1987).

When teachers hold inaccurate views, poorly achieving students are more affected. In longitudinal research on more than 1500 middle-school students, teacher overestimates and underestimates of sixth graders' math talent, effort, and performance (determined by comparing teacher ratings to the previous year's math achievement) had a greater impact on future math achievement for low than high achievers (Madon, Jussim, & Eccles, 1997). High-achieving students have less room to improve when teachers think well of them, and they can fall back on their long history of success experiences when a teacher is critical.

In the study just described, teacher overestimates had a stronger impact on achievement than did teacher underestimates (see Figure 15.11). When teachers are optimistic, many children respond with improved performance. Unfortunately, biased teacher judgments are usually slanted in a negative direction. Recall from Chapter 11 that compared with Caucasian children, low-SES, ethnic minority children tend to receive less favourable feedback from teachers, a circumstance that undermines their achievement motivation.

[3]Most research on self-fulfilling prophecies focuses on the teacher–student relationship, but the effect can occur in other social contexts, such as parent–child and peer interaction.

## GROUPING PRACTICES

In many schools, students are ability grouped or tracked into classes in which children of similar achievement levels are taught together. The practice is designed to ease teachers' task of having to meet a wide range of academic needs.

**GROUPING IN ELEMENTARY SCHOOL.** In many elementary schools, children are assigned to *homogeneous* groups or classes, which can be a potent source of self-fulfilling prophecies (Smith et al., 1998). Group labels quickly result in stereotyping. As a result, low-group students get more drill on basic facts and skills, less discussion, and a slower learning pace. Gradually, such children show a drop in self-esteem, are viewed by themselves and others as "not smart," and have friends only within their own group. Not surprisingly, homogeneous grouping widens the gap between high and low achievers (Dornbusch, Glasgow, & Lin, 1996; Fuligni, Eccles, & Barber, 1995).

Partly because of these findings, some schools have increased the *heterogeneity* of students taught together. In *multigrade classrooms,* students of different grades are placed in the same classroom. When academic achievement differs between multigrade and single-grade classrooms, it favours the multigrade arrangement. Self-esteem and attitudes toward school are also more positive, perhaps because multigrade classrooms decrease competition and increase harmony (Lloyd, 1999). The opportunity multigrade grouping affords for peer tutoring (see page 620) may also contribute to its favourable outcomes.

Yet multigrade classrooms may not work well if principals create them for convenience (for example, to deal with uneven enrolments) rather than for philosophical reasons (Burns & Mason, 1998). Under these circumstances, they tend to place higher-ability and more independent students in the multigrade settings, producing an alternative form of homogeneous grouping!

Finally, recall from our discussion of Vygotsky's theory that more-expert children can foster learning in less-expert children, as long as participants resolve conflicts, share responsibility, and consider one another's ideas (see Chapter 6). In many classrooms, however, heterogeneous groups yield poorer-quality interaction (less accurate explanations and answers) than do homogeneous groups of above-average students (Fuchs et al., 1998). For collaboration between heterogeneous peers to succeed, children need extensive training and guidance.

When teachers provide this assistance, heterogeneous classes are desirable into junior high school. They do not stifle more able students, and they have cognitive and social benefits for poorly performing youngsters (Oakes, Gamoran, & Page, 1992).

**GROUPING IN HIGH SCHOOL.** By high school, some homogeneous grouping is unavoidable because certain aspects of instruction must dovetail with the young person's educational and vocational plans. High school students are typically counselled into university,

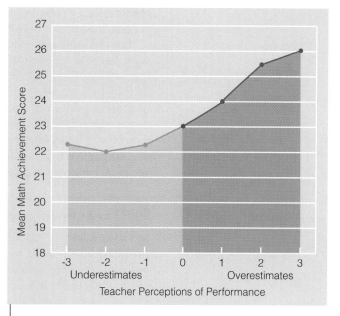

**FIGURE 15.11**

**Teacher overestimates and underestimates of sixth graders' math talent, effort, and performance in relation to later math achievement.** Overestimates of capacity led to substantial gains in achievement; underestimates led to a slight decline. These findings illustrate how believing in students' ability to succeed can inspire them to work harder and improve. (Adapted from S. Madon, L. Jussim, & J. Eccles, 1997, "In search of the powerful self-fulfilling prophecy," *Journal of Personality and Social Psychology, 72,* p. 800. Copyright © by the American Psychological Association. Reprinted by permission of the publisher and author.)

Grouping practices can affect the quality of teachers' interactions with students. In this heterogeneous group, children receive warm, stimulating teaching that emphasizes high-level thinking. As a result, each student is attentive and involved in learning.

© STEVE WARMOWSK/JOURNAL COURIER/THE IMAGE WORKS

vocational, or general education tracks. Unfortunately, this sorting tends to perpetuate educational inequalities of earlier years.

Low-SES minority students are assigned in large numbers to nonuniversity tracks. One study found that a good student from an economically disadvantaged family had only half as much chance of ending up in an academically oriented program as did a student of equal ability from a middle-SES background (Vanfossen, Jones, & Spade, 1987). Furthermore, teachers of nonuniversity-track classes are less likely to communicate with parents about what they can do to support their adolescents' learning (Dornbusch & Glasgow, 1997). Longitudinal research following the school performance of thousands of students from grade 8 to grade 12 revealed that assignment to an academic track accelerates academic progress, whereas assignment to a vocational or general education track decelerates it (Hallinan & Kubitschek, 1999).

## TEACHING STUDENTS WITH SPECIAL NEEDS

So far, we have seen that effective teachers flexibly adjust their teaching strategies to accommodate students with a wide range of characteristics. These adjustments, however, are especially challenging when children have learning difficulties. Extra steps must be taken to create appropriate learning environments for these students.

**CHILDREN WITH LEARNING DIFFICULTIES.** Provincial legislation mandates that schools place children who require special supports for learning in the "least restrictive" environments that meet their educational needs. The law led to an increase in **mainstreaming,** or placement of students with learning difficulties in regular classrooms for part of the school day, a practice designed to better prepare them for participation in society. Largely due to parental pressures, in some schools mainstreaming has been extended to **full inclusion**—placement in regular classrooms full time.

Some mainstreamed students are **mildly mentally retarded**—children whose IQs fall between 55 and 70 and who also show problems in adaptive behaviour, or skills of everyday living (American Psychiatric Association, 1994). But the largest number have **learning disabilities.** Learning-disabled students, who constitute 5 to 10 percent of school-age children, obtain average or above-average IQ scores but have great difficulty with one or more aspects of learning, usually reading. As a result, their achievement is considerably behind what would be expected on the basis of their IQ. Their problems cannot be traced to any obvious physical or emotional difficulty or to environmental disadvantage. Instead, subtle deficits in brain functioning appear to be involved. Some disorders run in families, suggesting a genetic influence (Kibby & Hynd, 2001). In most instances, the cause is unknown.

**HOW EFFECTIVE ARE MAINSTREAMING AND FULL INCLUSION?** Does placement of these students in regular classes accomplish its two goals—providing more appropriate academic experiences and integrated participation in classroom life? At present, the evidence is not positive on either of these points.

Although some mainstreamed and fully included students benefit academically, many do not. Achievement gains depend both on the severity of the disability and the support services available in the regular classroom (Klingner et al., 1998; Waldron & McLeskey, 1998). Furthermore, children with disabilities often are rejected by regular-classroom peers. Students who are mentally retarded are overwhelmed by the social skills of their classmates; they cannot interact quickly or adeptly in a conversation or game. And the processing deficits of learning-disabled students lead to problems in social awareness and responsiveness (Gresham & MacMillan, 1997; Sridhar & Vaughn, 2001).

Does this mean that children with special needs cannot be served in regular classrooms? Often these children do best when they receive instruction in a resource room for part of the day and in the regular classroom for the remainder—an arrangement the majority of school-age children with learning disabilities say they prefer (Vaughn & Klingner, 1998). In the resource room, a special education teacher works with students on an individual and small-group basis. Then, depending on their abilities, children are mainstreamed for different subjects

**mainstreaming**
Placement of students with learning difficulties in regular classrooms for part of the school day.

**full inclusion**
Placement of students with learning difficulties in regular classrooms for the entire school day.

**mild mental retardation**
The condition that characterizes children whose IQs fall between 55 and 70 and who also show problems in adaptive behaviour.

**learning disability**
Great difficulty with one or more aspects of learning (usually reading) that results in poor school achievement, despite an average or above-average IQ.

and amounts of time. This flexible approach helps ensure that the unique academic needs of each child will be served (Hocutt, 1996).

Once children enter the regular classroom, special steps must be taken to promote peer acceptance. Cooperative learning and peer-tutoring experiences in which mainstreamed children and their classmates work together lead to friendly interaction and improved social acceptance (Scruggs & Mastropieri, 1994; Siegel, 1996). Teachers can also prepare children for the arrival of a special-needs student. Under these conditions, mainstreaming and full inclusion may foster gains in emotional sensitivity and prosocial behaviour among regular classmates.

## PARENT–SCHOOL PARTNERSHIPS

Regardless of students' abilities, parent involvement in education—keeping tabs on the child's progress, communicating often with teachers, and assuring that the child is enrolled in challenging, well-taught classes—is crucial for optimum learning. Parents who are in frequent contact with the school send a message to their child about the value of education, model constructive solutions to academic problems, and (as children get older) promote wise educational decisions. Involved parents can also prevent school personnel from placing a bright student not working up to potential in unstimulating learning situations (Grolnick & Slowiaczek, 1994).

Schools can increase parent involvement in the following ways:

- fostering frequent communication between parents and teachers;

- showing parents how to support their child's education at home;

- building bridges between minority home cultures and the culture of the school;

- developing assignments that give parents a meaningful role to play, such as having students find out about their parents' experiences while growing up; and

- including parents in basic planning and governance to ensure that they are invested in school goals.

Community characteristics affect the ease with which schools can involve parents. In ethnic minority neighbourhoods, value conflicts and misunderstandings between parents and school personnel are common. Parents in poverty-stricken, inner-city areas are often more preoccupied with protecting their children from danger than with developing their talents. And since these parents face many daily stresses, they are particularly hard for schools to reach (Christenson & Sheridan, 2001). Yet schools could relieve some of this stress by forging stronger home–school links. Parents who are highly involved in their child's education exist in every minority group and neighbourhood.

RICHARD HUTCHINGS/PHOTOEDIT

The student in the centre, who has a learning disability, has been fully included in a regular classroom. Because his teacher takes special steps to encourage peer acceptance, individualizes instruction, minimizes comparisons with classmates, and promotes cooperative learning, this boy looks forward to school and is doing well.

# How Well Educated Are Canadian Young People?

OUR DISCUSSION HAS FOCUSED largely on what teachers can do to support the education of children and adolescents. Yet we have also seen, in this and earlier chapters, that many factors—both within and outside schools—affect children's learning. Societal values, school resources, quality of teaching, and parent involvement all play important roles. The combined impact of these influences becomes strikingly apparent when schooling is examined in cross-national perspective.

# *cultural influences*

## EDUCATION IN JAPAN, TAIWAN, AND NORTH AMERICA

**W**hy do Asian children perform so well academically? Research examining societal, school, and family conditions in Japan, Taiwan, and North America provides some answers.

### CULTURAL VALUING OF ACADEMIC ACHIEVEMENT

In Japan and Taiwan, natural resources are limited. Progress in science and technology is essential for economic well-being. Since a well-educated work force is necessary to meet this goal, children's mastery of academic skills is vital. Compared with Western countries, Japan, Taiwan, and other East Asian nations invest more in education, including paying higher salaries to teachers and granting them more prestige (Lewis, 1995; Rohlen, 1997). In Canada and the United States, attitudes toward academic achievement are far less unified. Many believe that it is more important to encourage children to feel good about themselves and to explore various areas of knowledge than to perform well in school.

### EMPHASIS ON EFFORT AND PARENT INVOLVEMENT IN EDUCATION

Japanese and Taiwanese parents and teachers believe that all children have the potential to master challenging academic tasks if they work hard enough. In contrast, U.S. parents and teachers tend to regard native ability as key in academic success (Stevenson, 1992). These differences in attitude may contribute to the fact that U.S. parents are less inclined to encourage activities at home that might enhance school performance. Japanese and Taiwanese parents promote their children's commitment to academics, and they devote many more hours to helping with homework than do U.S. parents. As a result, Asian children spend far more free time studying, reading, and playing academic-related games than do children in the United States (Huntsinger, Jose, & Larson, 1998; Stevenson & Lee, 1990).

Furthermore, effort takes on different meaning in Asian collectivist societies than in individualistic Western societies.

Japanese and Chinese youth strive to achieve in school because effort is a moral obligation—part of one's responsibility to family and community. In contrast, U.S. young people regard working hard academically as a matter of individual choice—of fulfilling personal goals (Bempechat & Drago-Severson, 1999). In high school, Asian students continue to devote more time to academic pursuits than do U.S. students, who spend more time socializing with peers, pursuing sports and other leisure activities, and working at part-time jobs (Larson & Verma, 1999). When asked what factors influence academic success, U.S. students most often mention "having a good teacher," whereas Asian students most often say "studying hard" (Stevenson, Lee, & Mu, 2000).

### HIGH-QUALITY EDUCATION FOR ALL

In Japanese and Taiwanese elementary schools, separate ability groups do not exist. Instead, all students receive the same high-quality instruction. Academic

### CROSS-NATIONAL RESEARCH ON ACADEMIC ACHIEVEMENT

Canadian students fare well when their achievement is compared with students in other industrialized nations. In 2000, Canada participated in the Programme for International Student Assessment (PISA), sponsored by the Organization for Economic Cooperation and Development. Designed to assess the skill level of 15-year-olds nearing the completion of their compulsory education, the study included about 30 000 Canadian students from over 1000 schools. The goal of the study was to identify whether students have the necessary skills to prepare them for economic and technological change and to determine the factors that influence the development of these skills at home and at school. Reading, science, and mathematical literacy levels were measured and compared across 32 industrialized countries (Organization for Economic Cooperation and Development, 1999).

The result? Canadian students fared best in reading, ranking second among the participating countries. In science, Canadian students ranked fifth; in mathematics, they ranked sixth. Perhaps most encouraging, the average score of Canadian students from the bottom SES quartile was above the international mean (Statistics Canada, Measuring Student Knowledge, 2001).

Japanese children achieve considerably better than their North American counterparts for a variety of reasons. A longer school day permits frequent alternation of academic instruction with pleasurable activity, an approach that fosters learning. During a break from academic subjects, these Japanese elementary-school children enjoy a class in the art of calligraphy.

lessons are particularly well organized and presented in ways that capture children's attention and involve them actively. Topics in mathematics are treated in greater depth, and there is less repetition of material taught the previous year. Also, the complexity of academic topics and the frequency and depth of teachers' explanations are considerably greater in Asian classrooms (Perry, 2000).

## MORE TIME DEVOTED TO INSTRUCTION

In Japan and Taiwan, the school year is over 50 days longer than in Canada. When one U.S. elementary school experimented by adding 30 days to its school year, extended-year students scored higher in reading, general-knowledge, and (especially) math achievement than did pupils in similar-quality schools with a traditional calendar (Frazier & Morrison, 1998).

Furthermore, on a day-to-day basis, Japanese and Taiwanese teachers devote much more of the school day to academic pursuits, especially mathematics. However, Asian schools are not regimented places, as many believe. An 8-hour school day permits extra recesses and a longer lunch period, with plenty of time for play, social interaction, field trips, and extracurricular activities. Frequent breaks may increase children's capacity to learn (Pellegrini & Smith, 1998; Stevenson, 1994).

## COMMUNICATION BETWEEN TEACHERS AND PARENTS

Japanese and Taiwanese teachers get to know their students especially well. They teach the same children for 2 or 3 years and make visits to the home once or twice a year. Continuous communication between teachers and parents takes place with the aid of small notebooks that children carry back and forth every day with messages about assignments, academic performance, and behaviour (Stevenson & Lee, 1990). No such formalized system of frequent teacher–parent communication exists in Canada.

Do Japanese and Taiwanese children pay a price for the pressure placed on them to succeed? By high school, academic work often displaces other experiences, since Asian adolescents must pass a highly competitive entrance exam to gain admission to university. Yet Asian parenting practices that encourage academic competence do not undermine children's adjustment. In fact, high-performing Asian students are socially competent (Crystal et al., 1994; Huntsinger, Jose, & Larson, 1998).

Japanese and Korean students scored significantly higher on mathematics compared with the Canadian students. Several Asian nations are well known for their high-achieving students and focused learning environments. The Cultural Influences box above examines a variety of social forces that combine to foster a strong commitment to learning in many Asian families and schools.

In a second international study of mathematical literacy, Canadian students in their final year of high school placed 10th out of 21 participating nations, scoring just above the average (see Figure 15.12 on page 644) (U.S. Department of Education, 1998). Although Canada's performance ranked higher than that of many other industrialized nations, there is room for improvement.

An increasing number of jobs are demanding high levels of literacy and technical knowledge. School reforms are currently under way in many provinces to help young people master the language, math, and science skills necessary to meet work-force needs. Effective educational change must take into account the life backgrounds and future goals of students. Simply toughening academic standards could discourage low-SES young people, who might fall farther behind under these conditions. As we will see next, besides strengthening academic instruction, special efforts are needed in vocational education to help non-university-bound youths prepare for productive work roles.

FIGURE 15.12

**Performance of students in the final year of high school from 21 countries on the math general knowledge test in the most recent international study of mathematics and science achievement.** Canada scored just above the international average, ranking 10th of 21 countries. (Adapted from Mullis, 1998.)

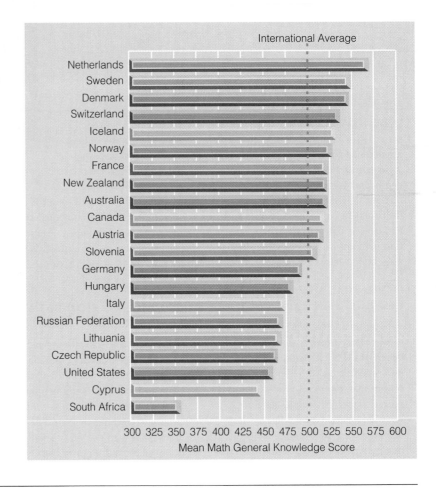

## MAKING THE TRANSITION FROM SCHOOL TO WORK

Approximately 30 percent of Canadian adolescents graduate from high school without plans to pursue post-secondary education. Although they are more likely to find employment than those who drop out, they have fewer opportunities than they did several decades ago. About 15 percent of recent high school graduates who do not continue their education are unemployed (Bowlby & McMullen, 2002). When they do find work, most are limited to low-paid, unskilled jobs. In addition, they lack access to vocational counselling and job placement as they make the transition from school to work (Bailey, 1993).

Canadian employers regard the recent high school graduate as poorly prepared for a demanding, skilled occupation. Indeed, there is some truth to this conclusion. During the final year of high school, just over 60 percent of Canadian students have jobs. But most of these are middle-SES students in pursuit of spending money rather than vocational exploration and training (Bowlby & McMullen, 2002).

Furthermore, the jobs adolescents hold are limited to low-level, repetitive tasks that provide little contact with adult supervisors. A heavy commitment to such jobs is actually harmful. High school students who work more than 15 hours a week have poorer school attendance, lower grades, and less time for extracurricular activities. They also report more drug and alcohol use and feel more distant from their parents. Although young people whose school performance is already compromised are more likely to work long hours, doing so makes a bad situation worse. And perhaps because of the menial nature of their jobs, employed teenagers tend to become cynical about work life. Many admit to having stolen from their employers (Barling, Rogers, & Kelloway, 1995; Steinberg & Dornbusch, 1991; Steinberg, Fegley, & Dornbusch, 1993).

When work experiences are specially designed to meet educational and vocational goals and involve responsibility and challenge, outcomes are different. Participation in work-study programs is related to positive school and work attitudes, improved achievement, lower dropout rates, and continued work in the occupational area after high school graduation (Hamilton & Hamilton, 2000; Steinberg, 1984). Yet unlike some European nations, Canada has no widespread training system to prepare its youth for skilled business and industrial occupations and manual trades. For the same reason, many high school graduates in the United States and Great Britain also experience a "floundering period" (Grubb, 1999; Heinz, 1999). The Canadian federal and provincial governments do support some job-training programs, but most are too short to make a difference in the lives of poorly skilled adolescents, who need intensive training and academic remediation before they are ready to enter the job market.

Inspired by successful programs in Europe, youth apprenticeship strategies that coordinate on-the-job training with classroom instruction are being considered as an important dimension of educational reform. Bringing together the worlds of schooling and work offers many benefits. These include helping non-university-bound adolescents establish productive lives right after graduation, motivating at-risk youths to stay in school, and contributing to the nation's economic growth (Hamilton, 1993; Safyer, Leahy, & Colan, 1995).

Nevertheless, implementing an apprenticeship system poses major challenges. Among these are overcoming the reluctance of employers to assume part of the responsibility for youth vocational training; creating institutional structures that ensure cooperation between schools and businesses; and preventing low-SES youth from being concentrated in the lowest-skilled apprenticeship placements, a circumstance that would perpetuate current social inequalities (Hamilton & Hamilton, 2000). Pilot apprenticeships are underway, in an effort to solve these problems and build bridges for young people between learning and working.

## ASK YOURSELF

**review** List educational practices that promote children's satisfaction with school life and academic achievement, explaining why each is effective.

**review** Why is homogeneous grouping in elementary school likely to induce educational self-fulfilling prophecies?

**apply** Tom and Sandy want to do everything possible to foster their 5-year-old son's favourable transition to kindergarten and high academic achievement in elementary school. Provide a list of suggestions.

**connect** What common factors contribute to the high academic achievement of children and adolescents in Asian nations and to the academic success of immigrant youths, discussed on page 50 of Chapter 2?

# summary

## THE IMPORTANCE OF PEER RELATIONS

*Discuss evidence indicating that both parental and peer relationships are vital for children's development.*

■ Research on nonhuman primates suggests that parent and peer relations complement one another. The parent–child bond provides children with the security to enter the world of peers. Peer interaction, in turn, permits children to expand social skills acquired within the family. Studies of peer-only reared monkeys and human children reveal that peer relations can, to some extent, fill in for the early parent–child bond. However, subjects do not develop as well as their counterparts with typical parental and peer upbringing.

## DEVELOPMENT OF PEER SOCIABILITY

*Trace the development of peer sociability from infancy into adolescence.*

■ Peer sociability begins in infancy with isolated social acts that are gradually replaced by coordinated exchanges in the second year of life. During the preschool years, interactive play with peers increases. According to Parten, it begins with **nonsocial activity,** shifts to **parallel play,** and then becomes **associative** and **cooperative play.** However, preschoolers do not follow this straightforward developmental sequence. Solitary play and parallel play remain common throughout early childhood. Sociodramatic play becomes especially frequent and enhances cognitive, emotional, and social skills.

■ During middle childhood, peer interaction is more sensitively tuned to others' perspectives and increasingly governed by prosocial norms, and play emphasizes rule-oriented games. Also, **rough-and-tumble play** becomes more common. In our evolutionary past, this friendly chasing and play-fighting may have been important for the development of fighting skill and **dominance hierarchies.** Adolescents show greater skill at working on tasks cooperatively.

## INFLUENCES ON PEER SOCIABILITY

*How do parental encouragement, age mix of children, and cultural values influence peer sociability?*

- Parents influence children's peer sociability both directly, through attempts to influence their children's peer relations, and indirectly, through their child-rearing practices and play behaviours. Preschoolers tend to be more socially competent when their parents often arrange informal peer contact and offer guidance on how to act toward others. Parental monitoring of young people's peer activities predicts favourable adjustment. Secure attachment, authoritative child rearing, inductive discipline, and emotionally positive and cooperative parent–child play also foster positive peer relations.

- Although same-age peers engage in more intense and harmonious exchanges, mixed-age interaction has benefits. It provides older children with practice in prosocial behaviour and younger children with opportunities to learn from their older companions.

- In collectivist societies, large-group imitative play involving highly scripted activities is common. When caregivers value the cognitive and educational benefits of make-believe and stress individuality and self-expression, sociodramatic play occurs more often. Sociodramatic play may be particularly important for social development in societies where child and adult worlds are distinct.

## FRIENDSHIP

*Describe children's developing concepts of friendship, characteristics of friendships in childhood and adolescence, and implications of friendship for psychological adjustment.*

- Preschool and young school-age children view **friendship** as a concrete relationship based on shared activities and material goods. During middle childhood, children come to understand friendship as a mutual relationship based on trust. Teenagers stress intimacy and loyalty as the basis of friendship.

- With age, children become more selective about their friendships; number of best friends declines during middle childhood and adolescence. In addition, friendships are characterized by greater stability and prosocial responding with age. At the same time, close friends are more likely than nonfriends to disagree and compete, providing contexts in which children learn to tolerate criticism and resolve disputes. However, for aggressive children, friendships often magnify hostility and antisocial acts.

- Throughout childhood and adolescence, friends tend to be alike in sex, ethnicity, SES, and personality. By adolescence, they resemble one another in attitudes and values. Nevertheless, young teenagers are often attracted to a peer's superficial features (such as physical attractiveness and athletic skill) and to high-status, aggressive boys—a trend that contributes to antisocial behaviour. As adolescents forge a personal identity, they explore new perspectives by befriending agemates with differing attitudes and values.

- Girls emphasize emotional closeness in their friendships more than boys do. However, androgynous boys are just as likely as girls to form intimate friendships. In early adolescence, very popular or very unpopular agemates are more likely to have other-sex friends. Compared with girls, boys have more other-sex friends and benefit in terms of feelings of competence.

- Warm, gratifying friendships foster self-concept, perspective taking, and identity development; provide a foundation for intimate relationships; offer support in dealing with everyday stresses; and promote positive attitudes toward and involvement in school. Aggressive friend-ships, however, seriously undermine development and adjustment.

## PEER ACCEPTANCE

*Describe major categories of peer acceptance, the relationship of physical appearance and social behaviour to likeability, and ways to help rejected children.*

- **Sociometric techniques** distinguish four types of **peer acceptance:** (1) **popular children,** who are liked by many agemates; (2) **rejected children,** who are actively disliked; (3) **controversial children,** who are both liked and disliked; and (4) **neglected children,** who are seldom chosen, either positively or negatively. As with friendship, peer acceptance contributes uniquely to children's adjustment. Rejected children often experience lasting adjustment problems.

- Two subtypes of popular children exist: **popular-prosocial children,** who are academically and socially competent, and **popular-antisocial children,** who generally are athletically skilled, highly aggressive boys who are poor students. Rejected children also divide into at least two subtypes: **rejected-aggressive** children, who show severe conduct problems, and **rejected-withdrawn** children, who are passive and socially awkward and at risk for **peer victimization.** Controversial children display a blend of positive and negative social behaviours. Although neglected children often choose to play by themselves, they are usually socially competent and well adjusted.

- Interventions that lead to gains in rejected children's peer acceptance include coaching in social skills; intensive academic tutoring; and social-cognitive interventions, such as training in perspective taking and social problem solving. Teaching rejected children to attribute peer difficulties to internal, changeable causes motivates them to improve their peer relations. Nevertheless, because socially incompetent behaviour often originates in maladaptive parent–child interaction, interventions focusing only on the rejected child are usually not sufficient.

## PEER GROUPS

*Describe peer groups in middle childhood and adolescence and their consequences for development.*

- By the end of middle childhood, **peer groups** with shared values and standards for behaviour and a social structure of leaders and followers emerge. They organize on the basis of proximity (being in the same classroom) and similarity in sex, ethnicity, and popularity. Within peer groups, children practise cooperation, leadership, followership, and loyalty to collective goals.

- Early adolescent peer groups are organized around **cliques,** or small groups of friends with common interests and similar social status. Often several cliques form a larger, more loosely organized group called a **crowd** that grants the adolescent an identity within the larger social structure of the school. Parenting styles influence teenagers' choice of peer groups and the impact of group membership on their beliefs and behaviour. As interest in dating increases, boys' and girls' cliques come together, providing a supportive context for interacting with the other sex.

- As boys and girls feel comfortable approaching each other directly, the mixed-sex clique disappears. Crowds also decline in importance as adolescents formulate their own personal values and goals.

## PEER RELATIONS AND SOCIALIZATION

*What techniques do peers use to socialize one another?*

- Peers serve as socialization agents through reinforcement, modelling, and direct pressures to conform to social behaviours. Peer conformity is strongest during early adolescence. However, peers seldom demand total conformity, and most peer pressures focus on short-term, day-to-day matters (such as dress and taste in music) and do not conflict with important adult values.

## TELEVISION

*Cite factors that affect how much time children devote to TV viewing, and describe age-related changes in television literacy.*

- Canadian children spend too much time watching TV. Low-SES, ethnic minority children and children from large families tend to be more frequent viewers. Excessive TV watching is linked to family and peer difficulties.

- Cognitive development and experience in watching TV gradually lead to gains in **television literacy.** Before age 8, children do not fully grasp the unreality of TV fiction, assimilate televised information piecemeal, and cannot critically evaluate it.

*Discuss the influence of television on children's development, including aggression, ethnic and gender stereotypes, consumerism, prosocial behaviour, and academic learning and imagination.*

- Studies with a wide variety of research designs indicate that televised violence promotes aggressive behaviour, tolerance of aggression in others, and a violent and dangerous view of the world. TV also conveys stereotypes that affect children's beliefs about ethnicity and gender. Children are easily manipulated by TV commercials. Not until age 8 or 9 do they understand the selling purpose of the ads.

- Television can foster prosocial behaviour as long as it is free of violent content. Children pick up many cognitive academic skills from educational television programs such as *Sesame Street* and *Blue's Clues.* Programs with slow-paced action and easy-to-follow story lines foster more elaborate make-believe play. Heavy TV viewers of prime-time shows and cartoons spend less time reading and interacting with others and achieve less well in school.

## COMPUTERS

*Discuss children's computer use, noting benefits and concerns.*

- Computers can have rich cognitive benefits. In classrooms, students often use computers collaboratively. When young children use the computer for word processing, they produce longer, higher-quality written products. Programming promotes a wide variety of higher cognitive processes, and adolescents who use the computer and Web for schoolwork perform better in school. Low-SES children's limited home access to computers is among factors that place them at an educational disadvantage.

- Although boys' extensive use of computers for game play fosters attentional and spatial skills, violent games promote hostility and aggression and desensitize children to violence. Extensive playing of simulation games risks blurring children's distinction between virtual and real life. Heavy Internet use at home undermines adolescents' social involvement and psychological well-being.

## SCHOOLING

*Discuss the influence of class and student body size and teachers' educational philosophies on academic and social development.*

- Schools powerfully influence many aspects of development. Smaller classes in the early elementary grades lead to lasting gains in academic achievement. In small high schools, adolescents are more actively involved in extracurricular activities and develop a sense of social obligation that carries over to better achievement.

- Teachers' educational philosophies play a major role in children's learning experiences. Older students in **traditional classrooms** have a slight edge in academic achievement. Students in **open classrooms** tend to be critical thinkers who respect individual differences and have more positive attitudes toward school. Preschool and kindergarten children in traditional classrooms display more stress behaviours, followed by poorer study habits and achievement in grade school.

- Philosophical approaches based on Vygotsky's sociocultural theory emphasize the importance of rich, socially communicative environments and teaching adapted to each child's zone of proximal development. The Kamehameha Elementary Education Program (KEEP), based on these principles, resulted in substantial achievement gains for low-SES minority children.

*Cite factors that affect adjustment to school transitions in early childhood and adolescence.*

■ Experience in preschool; a friendly, prosocial behavioural style; positive school attitudes; supportive ties to peers and teachers; and classroom participation predict high achievement in kindergarten. In contrast, kindergartners with antisocial and peer-avoidant styles establish conflict-ridden relationships with teachers, which predict academic and behaviour problems.

■ School transitions in adolescence can also be stressful. As school environments become larger and more impersonal, grades and feelings of competence decline. Girls experience more adjustment difficulties after the elementary to junior high transition, since other life changes (puberty and the beginning of dating) tend to occur at the same time. Emotionally distressed, poorly achieving young people whose school performance drops sharply are at greatest risk for continuing academic difficulties and alienation from school.

*Discuss the role of teacher–student interaction and grouping practices in academic achievement.*

■ Patterns of teacher–student interaction affect children's academic progress.

Instruction that encourages higher-level thinking promotes student interest and involvement in classroom activities. **Educational self-fulfilling prophecies** are most likely to occur in classrooms that emphasize competition and public evaluation, and they have a greater impact on low achievers.

■ Ability grouping in elementary school is linked to poorer-quality instruction and a drop in self-esteem and achievement for children in low-ability groups. In contrast, multigrade classrooms promote self-esteem and positive school attitudes. However, teachers must provide extensive training and assistance for collaboration between heterogeneous peers to succeed.

■ By high school, separate educational tracks that dovetail with adolescents' future plans are necessary. Unfortunately, high school tracking usually extends the educational inequalities of earlier years.

*Under what conditions is placement of mildly mentally retarded and learning-disabled children in regular classrooms successful, and how can schools increase parent involvement in education?*

■ Students with **mild mental retardation** and **learning disabilities** are often placed in regular classrooms, usually through **mainstreaming** but also through **full inclusion.** The success of regular classroom placement depends on tailoring learning experiences to children's academic needs and promoting positive peer relations.

■ Schools can increase parent involvement by fostering communication between parents and teachers, building bridges between minority home cultures and the culture of the school, and involving parents in school governance. Reaching out to ethnic minority parents and parents in poverty-stricken, inner-city areas is especially important.

## HOW WELL EDUCATED ARE CANADIAN YOUNG PEOPLE?

*How do Canadian students fare on international assessments of academic achievement, and what factors are important in making an effective school-to-work transition?*

■ In cross-national comparisons of reading, math, and science achievement, Canadian students have been scoring above the mean. Asian students are consistently among the top performers, because a strong cultural commitment to learning pervades homes and schools.

■ Non-university-bound high school graduates need assistance in making an effective transition from school to work.

# important terms and concepts

associative play (p. 603)
clique (p. 618)
controversial children (p. 613)
cooperative play (p. 603)
crowd (p. 618)
dominance hierarchy (p. 605)
educational self-fulfilling prophecy
    (p. 638)
friendship (p. 608)
full inclusion (p. 640)

learning disability (p. 640)
mainstreaming (p. 640)
mild mental retardation (p. 640)
neglected children (p. 613)
nonsocial activity (p. 603)
open classroom (p. 634)
parallel play (p. 603)
peer acceptance (p. 613)
peer group (p. 617)
peer victimization (p. 614)

popular children (p. 613)
popular-antisocial children (p. 614)
popular-prosocial children (p. 614)
rejected children (p. 613)
rejected-aggressive children (p. 614)
rejected-withdrawn children (p. 614)
rough-and-tumble play (p. 605)
sociometric techniques (p. 613)
television literacy (p. 624)
traditional classroom (p. 634)

# lossary

**Aboriginal Head Start** A Canadian Head Start program designed for Aboriginal children under age 6 operated by local nonprofit Aboriginal organizations.

**accommodation** In Piaget's theory, that part of adaptation in which an individual adjusts old schemes and creates new ones to produce a better fit with the environment. Distinguished from *assimilation*.

**achievement motivation** The tendency to persist at challenging tasks.

**adaptation** In Piaget's theory, the process of building schemes through direct interaction with the environment. Consists of two complementary activities: *assimilation* and *accommodation*.

**adolescent initiation ceremony** A ritual, or rite of passage, announcing to the community that a young person is ready to make the transition from childhood into adolescence or full adulthood.

**affordances** The action possibilities a situation offers an organism with certain motor capabilities. Discovery of affordances plays a major role in perceptual differentiation.

**age of viability** The age at which the fetus can first survive if born early. Occurs sometime between 22 and 26 weeks.

**allele** Each of two or more forms of a gene located at the same place on the chromosomes.

**amnion** The inner membrane that forms a protective covering around the prenatal organism and encloses it in amniotic fluid, which helps keep temperature constant and provides a cushion against jolts caused by the mother's movement.

**analogical problem solving** Taking a solution strategy from one problem and applying it to other relevant problems.

**androgens** Hormones produced chiefly by the testes, and in smaller quantities by the adrenal glands, that influence the pubertal growth spurt, the appearance of body hair, and male sex characteristics.

**androgyny** A type of gender identity in which the person scores high on both masculine and feminine personality characteristics.

**animistic thinking** The belief that inanimate objects have lifelike qualities, such as thoughts, wishes, feelings, and intentions.

**anorexia nervosa** An eating disorder in which individuals (usually females) starve themselves because of a compulsive fear of getting fat.

**A-not-B search error** The error made by 8- to 12-month-olds after an object is moved from hiding place A to hiding place B. Infants in Piaget's Substage 4 search for it in only the first hiding place (A).

**Apgar Scale** A rating system used to assess the newborn baby's physical condition immediately after birth.

**assimilation** In Piaget's theory, that part of adaptation in which an individual uses current schemes to interpret the external world. Distinguished from *accommodation*.

**associative play** A form of true social participation in which children engage in separate activities but interact by exchanging toys and commenting on one another's behaviour. Distinguished from *nonsocial activity, parallel play,* and *cooperative play*.

**attachment** The strong affectional tie that humans have with special people in their lives.

**Attachment Q-Sort** An efficient method for assessing the quality of the attachment bond, in which a parent or an expert informant sorts a set of 90 descriptors of attachment-related behaviours on the basis of how well they characterize the child. A score is then computed that assigns children to securely or insecurely attached groups.

**attention-deficit hyperactivity disorder** A childhood disorder involving inattention, impulsivity, and excessive motor activity. Often leads to academic failure and social problems.

**attribution retraining** An approach to intervention that uses adult feedback to modify the attributions of learned-helpless children, thereby encouraging them to believe that they can overcome failure by exerting more effort.

**attributions** Common, everyday explanations for the causes of behaviour.

**authoritarian style** A child-rearing style that is low in acceptance and involvement, is high in coercive control, and restricts rather than grants autonomy. Distinguished from *authoritative, permissive,* and *uninvolved styles*.

**authoritative style** A child-rearing style that is high in acceptance and involvement, emphasizes firm control with explanations, and includes gradual,

appropriate autonomy granting. Distinguished from *authoritarian, permissive,* and *uninvolved styles*.

**autobiographical memory** Representations of special, one-time events that are long lasting and particularly meaningful in terms of the life story each of us creates.

**autonomous morality** Piaget's second stage of moral development, in which children view rules as flexible, socially agreed-on principles that can be revised to suit the will of the majority.

**autonomy** A sense of oneself as a separate, self-governing individual. An important developmental task of adolescence that is closely related to the quest for identity.

**autosomes** The 22 matching chromosome pairs in each human cell.

**avoidant attachment** The quality of insecure attachment characterizing infants who are usually not distressed by parental separation and who avoid the parent when she returns. Distinguished from *secure, resistant,* and *disorganized/ disoriented attachment*.

**babbling** Repetition of consonant–vowel combinations in long strings, beginning around 4 months of age.

**basic emotions** Emotions that can be directly inferred from facial expressions (such as happiness, interest, surprise, fear, anger, sadness, and disgust), that are universal in humans and in our primate ancestors, and that have a long evolutionary history of adaptation.

**basic-skills approach** An approach to beginning reading instruction that emphasizes training in phonics—the basic rules for translating written symbols into sounds—and simplified reading materials. Distinguished from *whole-language approach*.

**behaviour modification** Procedures that combine conditioning and modelling to eliminate undesirable behaviours and increase desirable responses.

**behavioural genetics** A field of study devoted to uncovering the hereditary and environmental origins of individual differences in human traits and abilities.

**behaviourism** An approach that views directly observable events—stimuli and responses—as the appropriate focus of study, and the development of behaviour as taking place through classical and operant conditioning.

**belief–desire theory of mind** The theory of mind that emerges around age 4 in which both beliefs and desires determine behaviour. Closely resembles the everyday psychology of adults.

**biased sampling** Failure to select participants who are representative of the population of interest in a study.

**bicultural identity** The identity constructed by adolescents who explore and adopt values from both their subculture and the dominant culture.

**binocular depth cues** Depth cues that rely on each eye receiving a slightly different view of the visual field; the brain blends the two images, creating three-dimensionality.

**blended,** or **reconstituted, family** A family structure resulting from cohabitation or remarriage that includes parent, step-parent, and children.

**body image** Conception of and attitude toward one's physical appearance.

**brain plasticity** The ability of other parts of the brain to take over functions of damaged regions.

**breech position** A position of the baby in the uterus that would cause the buttocks or feet to be delivered first.

**Broca's area** A language structure located in the frontal lobe of the left hemisphere of the cerebral cortex that controls language production.

**bulimia nervosa** An eating disorder in which individuals (mainly females) engage in strict dieting and excessive exercise accompanied by binge eating; often followed by deliberate vomiting and purging with laxatives.

**canalization** The tendency of heredity to restrict the development of some characteristics to just one or a few outcomes.

**CANSTART** A Canadian program with the principal goal of providing teachers with information on research-based procedures to help identify, and then assist, children at risk for early school failure.

**cardinality** A principle specifying that the last number in a counting sequence indicates the quantity of items in a set.

**carrier** A heterozygous individual who can pass a recessive trait to his or her offspring.

**catch-up growth** Physical growth that returns to its genetically determined path after being delayed by environmental factors.

**categorical self** Early classification of the self according to salient ways people differ, such as age, sex, physical characteristics, and goodness and badness.

**categorical speech perception** The tendency to perceive as identical a range of sounds that belong to the same phonemic class.

**central conceptual structures** In Case's neo-Piagetian theory, networks of concepts and relations that permit children to think about a wide range of situations in more advanced ways. Formation of new central conceptual structures marks the transition to a new Piagetian stage.

**central executive** The part of working memory that directs the flow of information by coordinating information coming from the environment with information already in the system, allocating attention to cognitive tasks, and selecting, applying, and monitoring the effectiveness of strategies.

**centration** The tendency to focus on one aspect of a situation to the neglect of other important features.

**cephalocaudal trend** An organized pattern of physical growth and motor control that proceeds from head to tail.

**cerebellum** A brain structure that aids in balance and control of body movements.

**cerebral cortex** The largest structure of the human brain; accounts for the highly developed intelligence of the human species.

**child development** A field of study devoted to understanding human constancy and change from conception through adolescence.

**child-directed speech (CDS)** The form of language adults use to speak to infants and toddlers that consists of short sentences with high-pitched, exaggerated expression, clear pronunciation, distinct pauses between speech segments, and repetition of new words in a variety of contexts.

**childhood social indicators** Periodic measures of children's health, living conditions, and psychological well-being that lend insight into their overall status in a community, region, or nation.

**child-rearing styles** Constellations of parenting behaviours that occur over a wide range of situations, thereby creating a pervasive and enduring child-rearing climate.

**chorion** The outer membrane that forms a protective covering around the prenatal organism. It sends out tiny hairlike villi, from which the placenta begins to emerge.

**chromosomes** Rodlike structures in the cell nucleus that store and transmit genetic information.

**chronosystem** In ecological systems theory, temporal changes in children's environments, which produce new conditions that affect development. These changes can be imposed externally or arise from within the child. Distinguished from *microsystem, mesosystem, exosystem,* and *macrosystem.*

**circular reaction** In Piaget's theory, a means of building schemes in which infants try to repeat a chance event caused by their own motor activity.

**classical conditioning** A form of learning that involves associating a neutral stimulus with a stimulus that leads to a reflexive response.

**clinical interview** A method in which the researcher uses flexible, open-ended questions to probe for the participant's point of view.

**clinical**, or **case study**, **method** A method in which the researcher attempts to understand the unique individual child by combining interview data, observations, test scores, and sometimes psychophysiological assessments.

**clique** A small group of about five to seven peers who are friends.

**codominance** A pattern of inheritance in which both alleles, in a heterozygous combination, are expressed.

**cognitive inhibition** The ability to control internal and external distracting stimuli, preventing them from capturing attention and cluttering working memory with irrelevant information.

**cognitive maps** Mental representations of large-scale spaces.

**cognitive self-regulation** The process of continuously monitoring progress toward a goal, checking outcomes, and redirecting unsuccessful efforts.

**cognitive-developmental theory** An approach introduced by Piaget that views children as actively constructing knowledge as they manipulate and explore their world, and cognitive development as taking place in stages.

**cohort effects** The effects of cultural-historical change on the accuracy of findings: Children developing in the same time period who are influenced by particular cultural and historical conditions make up a cohort.

**collectivist societies** Societies in which people define themselves as part of a group and stress group over individual goals. Distinguished from *individualistic societies.*

**compliance** Voluntary obedience to requests and commands.

**componential analysis** A research procedure in which researchers look for relationships between aspects (or components) of information processing and children's intelligence test performance. Aims to clarify the cognitive processes responsible for test scores.

**comprehension** In language development, the words and word combinations that children understand. Distinguished from *production.*

**concordance rate** The percentage of instances in which both twins show a trait when it is present in one twin.

**concrete operational stage** Piaget's third stage, during which thought is logical, flexible, and organized in its application to concrete information. However, the capacity for abstract thinking is not yet present. Spans the years from 7 to 11.

**conditioned response (CR)** In classical conditioning, a new response produced by a conditioned stimulus (CS) that resembles the unconditioned response (UCR).

**conditioned stimulus (CS)** In classical conditioning, a neutral stimulus that through pairing with an unconditioned stimulus (UCS) leads to a new, conditioned response (CR).

**connectionist**, or **artificial neural network, models** Models of mental functioning that focus on the most basic information-processing units and their connections, using computer simulations to imitate the workings of neurons in the brain. If the network's responses resemble those of people, then researchers conclude that it is a good model of human learning.

**conservation** The understanding that certain physical characteristics of objects remain the same, even when their outward appearance changes.

**construction** The process of actively attending to and interrelating multiple perspectives on situations in which social conflicts arise, and thereby deriving new moral understandings.

**constructivist approach** An approach to cognitive development in which children discover virtually all knowledge about their world through their own activity. Consistent with Piaget's theory.

**contexts** Unique combinations of genetic and environmental circumstances that can result in markedly different paths of development.

**continuous development** A view that regards development as a cumulative process of gradually adding more of the same types of skills that were there to begin with. Distinguished from *discontinuous development.*

**contrast sensitivity** Ability to detect contrast, or differences in the amount of light between adjacent regions in a pattern.

**control deficiency** The failure to execute a mental strategy effectively. Distinguished from *production* and *utilization deficiencies.*

**controversial children** Children who get a large number of positive and negative votes on sociometric measures of peer acceptance. Distinguished from *popular, rejected,* and *neglected children.*

**conventional level** Kohlberg's second level of moral development, in which moral understanding is based on conforming to social rules to ensure positive human relationships and societal order.

**convergent thinking** The generation of a single correct answer to a problem; the type of cognition emphasized on intelligence tests. Distinguished from *divergent thinking.*

**cooing** Pleasant vowel-like noises made by infants beginning around 2 months of age.

**cooperative learning** A learning environment in which groups of peers work toward common goals.

**cooperative play** A form of true social participation in which children's actions are directed toward a common goal. Distinguished from *nonsocial activity, parallel play,* and *associative play.*

**core knowledge perspective** A view that assumes that infants begin life with innate special-purpose knowledge systems, or core domains of thought, each of which permits a ready grasp of new, related information and therefore supports early, rapid development of certain aspects of cognition.

**coregulation** A transitional form of supervision in which parents exercise general oversight while permitting children to be in charge of moment-by-moment decision making.

**corpus callosum** The large bundle of fibres that connects the two hemispheres of the brain.

**correlation coefficient** A number, ranging from +1.00 to −1.00, that describes the strength and direction of the relationship between two variables.

**correlational design** A research design in which the investigator gathers information without altering participants' experiences and examines relationships between variables. Does not permit inferences about cause and effect.

**creativity** The ability to produce work that is original (that others have not thought of before) and that is appropriate (sensible or useful in some way).

**crossing over** Exchange of genes between chromosomes next to each other during meiosis.

**cross-sectional design** A research design in which groups of participants of different ages are studied at the same point in time. Distinguished from *longitudinal design*.

**crowd** A large, loosely organized peer group in which membership is based on reputation and stereotype.

**crystallized intelligence** In Cattell's theory, a form of intelligence that consists of accumulated knowledge and skills and that depends on culture and learning opportunities. Distinguished from *fluid intelligence*.

**debriefing** Providing a full account and justification of research activities to participants in a study in which deception was used.

**deferred imitation** The ability to remember and copy the behaviour of models who are not present.

**delay of gratification** Waiting for a more appropriate time and place to engage in a tempting act or obtain a desired object.

**deoxyribonucleic acid (DNA)** Long, double-stranded molecules that make up chromosomes.

**dependent variable** The variable the researcher expects to be influenced by the independent variable in an experiment.

**desire theory of mind** The theory of mind of 2- and 3-year-olds, who understand the relation of desire to perception and emotion but who assume that people's behaviour is merely a reflection of their desires. Fails to take account of the influence of interpretive mental states, such as beliefs, on behaviour.

**developmental psychology** A branch of psychology devoted to understanding all changes that human beings experience throughout the lifespan.

**differentiation theory** The view that perceptual development involves the detection of increasingly fine-grained, invariant features in the environment.

**difficult child** A child whose temperament is such that she is irregular in daily routines, is slow to accept new experiences, and tends to react negatively and intensely. Distinguished from *easy child* and *slow-to-warm-up child*.

**discontinuous development** A view in which new ways of understanding and responding to the world emerge at specific times. Distinguished from *continuous development*.

**disorganized/disoriented attachment** The quality of insecure attachment characterizing infants who respond in a confused, contradictory fashion when reunited with the parent. Distinguished from *secure, avoidant,* and *resistant attachment*.

**distance curve** A growth curve that plots the average height and weight of a sample of children at each age. Shows typical yearly progress toward mature body size. Distinguished from *velocity curve*.

**distributive justice** Beliefs about how to divide material goods fairly.

**divergent thinking** The generation of multiple and unusual possibilities when faced with a task or problem; associated with creativity. Distinguished from *convergent thinking*.

**divorce mediation** A series of meetings between divorcing couples and a trained professional, who tries to help them settle disputes. Aimed at avoiding legal battles that intensify family conflict.

**dominance hierarchy** A stable ordering of group members that predicts who will win when conflict arises.

**dominant cerebral hemisphere** The hemisphere of the brain responsible for skilled motor action. The left hemisphere is dominant in right-handed individuals. In left-handed individuals, the right hemisphere may be dominant, or motor and language skills may be shared between the hemispheres.

**dominant–recessive inheritance** A pattern of inheritance in which, under heterozygous conditions, the influence of only one allele is apparent.

**dual representation** Viewing a symbolic object as both an object in its own right and a symbol.

**dynamic systems perspective** A view of development that regards the child's mind, body, and physical and social worlds as a dynamic, integrated system. A change in any part of the system leads the child to reorganize his behaviour so the components of the system work together again but in a more complex, effective way.

**dynamic systems theory of motor development** A theory that views new motor skills as reorganizations of previously mastered skills that lead to more effective ways of exploring and controlling the environment. Each new skill is a product of central nervous system development, movement

possibilities of the body, the goal the child has in mind, and environmental supports for the skill.

**dynamic testing** An approach to testing consistent with Vygotsky's concept of the zone of proximal development, in which purposeful teaching is introduced into the testing situation to find out what the child can attain with social support.

**easy child** A child whose temperament is such that he quickly establishes regular routines in infancy, is generally cheerful, and adapts easily to new experiences. Distinguished from *difficult child* and *slow-to-warm-up child*.

**ecological systems theory** Bronfenbrenner's approach, which views the child as developing within a complex system of relationships affected by multiple levels of the surrounding environment, from immediate settings of family and school to broad cultural values and programs.

**educational self-fulfilling prophecy** The idea that students may adopt teachers' positive or negative attitudes toward them and start to live up to these views.

**effective strategy use** Consistent use of a mental strategy that leads to improvement in performance. Distinguished from *production, control,* and *utilization deficiencies*.

**egocentrism** The tendency to focus on one's own viewpoint and ignore others' perspectives.

**elaboration** The memory strategy of creating a relationship between two or more pieces of information that are not members of the same category.

**embryo** The prenatal organism from 2 to 8 weeks after conception, during which time the foundations of all body structures and internal organs are laid down.

**emergent literacy** Young children's active efforts to construct literacy knowledge through informal experiences.

**emotion** An expression of readiness to establish, maintain, or change one's relation to the environment on a matter of personal importance.

**emotional display rules** Rules that specify when, where, and how it is culturally appropriate to express emotions.

**emotional intelligence** A set of abilities that includes accurately perceiving emotions, expressing emotion appropriately, understanding the causes and consequences of emotions, and managing one's own and others' feelings to facilitate thinking and social interaction.

**emotional self-regulation** Strategies for adjusting our emotional state to a comfortable level of intensity so we can accomplish our goals.

**empathy** The ability to detect different emotions, to take another's perspective and to feel with that person, or respond emotionally in a similar way.

**entity view of ability** The view that ability is a fixed characteristic that cannot be improved through trying hard. Distinguished from *incremental view of ability*.

**environmental cumulative deficit hypothesis** A view that attributes the age-related decline in IQ among ethnic minority and other children who live in poverty to the cumulative effects of underprivileged rearing conditions.

**epigenesis** Development resulting from ongoing bidirectional exchanges between heredity and all levels of the environment.

**epiphyses** Growth centres in the bones where new cartilage cells are produced and gradually harden.

**episodic memory** Memory for personally experienced events.

**equilibration** In Piaget's theory, back-and-forth movement between cognitive equilibrium and disequilibrium that leads to more effective schemes.

**estrogens** Hormones produced chiefly by the ovaries that cause the breasts, uterus, and vagina to mature and the body to take on feminine proportions, and that influence the pubertal growth spurt.

**ethnic identity** An enduring aspect of the self that includes a sense of ethnic group membership and attitudes and feeling associated with that membership.

**ethnography** A method by which the researcher attempts to understand the unique values and social processes of a culture or a distinct social group by living with its members and taking field notes for an extended period.

**ethological theory of attachment** A theory formulated by Bowlby, which views the infant's emotional tie to the familiar caregiver as an evolved response that promotes survival through ensuring both safety and competence.

**ethology** An approach concerned with the adaptive, or survival, value of behaviour and its evolutionary history.

**event sampling** An observational procedure in which the researcher records all instances of a particular behaviour during a specified time period.

**evolutionary developmental psychology** An approach that seeks to understand the adaptive value of species-wide cognitive, emotional, and social competencies as those competencies change over time.

**exosystem** In ecological systems theory, social settings that do not contain children but nevertheless affect their experiences in immediate settings. Examples are parents' workplace and health and welfare services in the community, as well as parents' social networks. Distinguished from *microsystem, mesosystem, macrosystem,* and *chronosystem.*

**expansions** Adult responses that elaborate on a child's utterance, increasing its complexity.

**experimental design** A research design in which the investigator randomly assigns participants to two or more treatment conditions and studies the effect that manipulating an independent variable has on a dependent variable. Permits inferences about cause and effect.

**expressive style** A style of early language learning in which toddlers use language mainly to talk about people's feelings and needs. Initial vocabulary emphasizes social formulas and pronouns. Distinguished from *referential style.*

**expressive traits** Feminine-stereotyped personality traits that reflect warmth, caring, and sensitivity. Distinguished from *instrumental traits.*

**extended-family household** A household in which parent and child live with one or more adult relatives. Distinguished from *nuclear family unit.*

**extinction** In classical conditioning, decline of the conditioned response (CR), as a result of presenting the conditioned stimulus (CS) enough times without the unconditioned stimulus (UCS).

**factor analysis** A statistical procedure that combines scores from many separate test items into a few factors, which substitute for the separate scores. Used to identify mental abilities that contribute to successful performance on intelligence tests.

**fast-mapping** Connecting a new word with an underlying concept after only a brief encounter.

**fetal alcohol effects (FAE)** The condition of children who display some but not all of the defects of fetal alcohol syndrome. Usually their mothers drank alcohol in smaller quantities or less often during pregnancy.

**fetal alcohol syndrome (FAS)** A set of defects that results when pregnant women consume large amounts of alcohol during most or all of pregnancy. Includes mental retardation; impaired motor coordination, attention, memory, language, planning, and problem solving; overactivity; slow physical growth; and facial abnormalities.

**fetus** The prenatal organism from the beginning of the third month to the end of pregnancy, during which time completion of body structures and dramatic growth in size take place.

**field experiment** A research design in which participants are randomly assigned to treatment conditions in natural settings.

**fluid intelligence** In Cattell's theory, a form of intelligence that involves the ability to see relationships among stimuli. Believed to depend largely on conditions in the brain. Distinguished from *crystallized intelligence.*

**Flynn effect** The large gains in IQ that have occurred over successive generations, from 1930 to the present.

**fontanels** Six soft spots that separate the bones of the skull at birth.

**formal operational stage** Piaget's highest stage, in which adolescents develop the capacity for abstract, scientific thinking. Begins around age 11.

**fraternal, or dizygotic, twins** Twins that result from the release and fertilization of two ova. They are genetically no more alike than ordinary siblings. Distinguished from *identical,* or *monozygotic, twins.*

**French immersion** An education program in which English-speaking students are taught entirely in French.

**friendship** A close relationship involving companionship in which each partner wants to be with the other.

**full inclusion** Placement of students with learning difficulties in regular classrooms for the entire school day.

**functionalist approach** A perspective emphasizing that the broad function of emotions is to prompt action in the service of personal goals and that emotions are central forces in all aspects of human activity.

**fuzzy-trace theory** A theory that proposes two types of encoding, one that automatically reconstructs information into a fuzzy version called a *gist,* which is especially useful for reasoning; and a second, verbatim version that is adapted for answering questions about specifics.

**gametes** Human sperm and ova, which contain half as many chromosomes as a regular body cell.

**gender consistency** Kohlberg's final stage of gender understanding, in which children in the late preschool and early school years master gender constancy.

**gender constancy** The understanding that sex is biologically based and remains the same even if clothing, hairstyle, and play activities change.

**gender identity** The perception of oneself as relatively masculine or feminine in characteristics.

**gender intensification** Increased stereotyping of attitudes and behaviour and movement toward a more traditional gender identity. Often occurs in early adolescence.

**gender labelling** Kohlberg's first stage of gender understanding, in which preschoolers can label the gender of themselves and others correctly.

**gender roles** The reflection of gender stereotypes in everyday behaviour.

**gender schema theory** An information-processing approach to gender typing that combines social learning and cognitive-developmental features to explain how social pressures and cognitions work together to affect stereotyping, gender-role identity, and gender-role adoption.

**gender stability** Kohlberg's second stage of gender understanding, in which preschoolers have a partial understanding of the permanence of sex; they grasp its stability over time.

**gender stereotypes** Widely held beliefs about characteristics deemed appropriate for males and females.

**gender typing** The process of developing gender-linked beliefs, gender roles, and a gender identity.

**gender-stereotype flexibility** Belief that both genders can display a gender-stereotyped personality trait or activity.

**gene** A segment of a DNA molecule that contains instructions for production of various proteins that contribute to growth and functioning of the body.

**general factor, or "g"** In Spearman's theory of intelligence, a common factor representing abstract reasoning power that underlies a wide variety of test items.

**general growth curve** Curve that represents changes in overall body size—rapid growth during infancy, slower gains in early and middle childhood, and rapid growth again during adolescence.

**generalized other** A blend of what we imagine important people in our lives think of us. Contributes to a self-concept comprising personality traits.

**genetic counselling** A communication process designed to help couples assess their chances of giving birth to a baby with a hereditary disorder and choose the best course of action in view of risks and family goals.

**genetic imprinting** A pattern of inheritance in which alleles are imprinted, or chemically marked, in such a way that one pair member is activated, regardless of its makeup.

**genetic–environmental correlation** The idea that heredity influences the environments to which individuals are exposed.

**genotype** The genetic makeup of an individual.

**gist** A fuzzy representation of information that preserves essential content without details, is less likely to be forgotten than a verbatim version, and requires less working-memory capacity to use.

**glial cells** Cells responsible for myelinization of neural fibres.

**goodness-of-fit model** Thomas and Chess's model, which states that an effective match, or "good fit," between child-rearing practices and a child's temperament leads to favourable development and psychological adjustment. When a "poor fit" exists, the outcome is distorted development and maladjustment.

**grammar** The component of language concerned with *syntax,* the rules by which words are arranged into sentences, and *morphology,* the use of grammatical markers that indicate number, tense, case, person, gender, active or passive voice, and other meanings.

**grammatical morphemes** Small markers that change the meaning of sentences, as in "John*'s* dog" and "he *is* eating."

**growth hormone (GH)** A pituitary hormone that affects the development of all body tissues except the central nervous system and the genitals.

**guided participation** A concept that accounts for cultural variations in children's opportunities to learn through involvement with others. Calls attention to both adult and child contributions to a cooperative dialogue, without specifying the precise features of communication.

**habituation** A gradual reduction in the strength of a response due to repetitive stimulation.

**heritability estimate** A statistic that measures the extent to which individual differences in complex traits in a specific population are due to genetic factors.

**heteronomous morality** Piaget's first stage of moral development, in which children view rules as handed down by authorities, as having a permanent existence, as unchangeable, and as requiring strict obedience.

**heterozygous** Having two different alleles at the same place on a pair of chromosomes. Distinguished from *homozygous.*

**hierarchical classification** The organization of objects into classes and subclasses on the basis of similarities and differences.

**Home Observation for Measurement of the Environment (HOME)** A checklist for gathering information about the quality of children's home lives through observation and parental interviews. Infancy, preschool, and middle childhood versions exist.

**homozygous** Having two identical alleles at the same place on a pair of chromosomes. Distinguished from *heterozygous.*

**horizontal décalage** Development within a Piagetian stage. Gradual mastery of logical concepts during the concrete operational stage is an example.

**hostile aggression** Aggression intended to harm another person. Distinguished from *instrumental aggression.*

**human development** An interdisciplinary field devoted to understanding all changes that human beings experience throughout the lifespan.

**hypothalamus** A structure located at the base of the brain that initiates and regulates pituitary secretions.

**hypothesis** A prediction about behaviour drawn from a theory.

**hypothetico-deductive reasoning** A formal operational problem-solving strategy in which adolescents begin with a general theory of all possible factors that could affect an outcome in a problem, and deduce specific hypotheses, which they test in an orderly fashion.

**ideal reciprocity** A standard of fairness based on mutuality of expectations, in which individuals express the same concern for the welfare of others as they would have others grant to them. Captured by the Golden Rule.

**identical,** or **monozygotic, twins** Twins that result when a zygote that has started to duplicate separates into two clusters of cells that develop into two individuals with the same genetic makeup. Distinguished from *fraternal,* or *dizygotic, twins.*

**identity** A well-organized conception of the self made up of values, beliefs, and goals to which the individual is solidly committed.

**identity achievement** The identity status of individuals who have explored and committed themselves to self-chosen values and goals. Distinguished from *moratorium, identity foreclosure,* and *identity diffusion.*

**identity diffusion** The identity status of individuals who do not have firm commitments to values and goals and are not actively trying to reach them. Distinguished from *identity achievement, moratorium,* and *identity foreclosure.*

**identity foreclosure** The identity status of individuals who have accepted ready-made values and goals that authority figures have chosen for them. Distinguished from *identity achievement, moratorium,* and *identity diffusion.*

**illocutionary intent** What a speaker means to say, even if the form of the utterance is not perfectly consistent with it.

**imaginary audience** Adolescents' belief that they are the focus of everyone else's attention and concern.

**imitation** Learning by copying the behaviour of another person. Also called *modelling* or *observational learning.*

**incremental view of ability** The view that ability can be improved through trying hard. Distinguished from *entity view of ability.*

**independent variable** The variable manipulated by the researcher in an experiment. Distinguished from *dependent variable.*

**individualistic societies** Societies in which people think of themselves as separate entities and are largely concerned with their own personal needs. Distinguished from *collectivist societies.*

**induction** A type of discipline in which the effects of the child's misbehaviour on others are communicated to the child.

**infant mortality** The number of deaths in the first year of life per 1000 live births.

**infantile amnesia** The inability of older children and adults to remember experiences that happened before age 3.

**information processing** An approach that views the human mind as a symbol-manipulating system through which information flows and that regards cognitive development as a continuous process.

**informed consent** The right of research participants, including children, to have explained to them, in language they can understand, all aspects of a study that may affect their willingness to participate.

**inhibited,** or **shy, child** A child whose temperament is such that she reacts negatively to and withdraws from novel stimuli. Distinguished from *uninhibited,* or *sociable, child.*

**inner self** Awareness of the self's private thoughts and imaginings.

**instrumental aggression** Aggression aimed at obtaining an object, privilege, or space, with no deliberate intent to harm another person. Distinguished from *hostile aggression.*

**instrumental traits** Masculine-stereotyped personality traits that reflect competence, rationality, and assertiveness. Distinguished from *expressive traits.*

**intelligence quotient (IQ)** A score that indicates the extent to which an individual's raw score (number of items passed) on an intelligence test deviates from the typical performance of same-age individuals.

**intentional,** or **goal-directed, behaviour** A sequence of actions in which schemes are deliberately combined to solve a problem.

**interactional synchrony** A sensitively tuned "emotional dance," in which the caregiver responds to infant signals in a well-timed, rhythmic, appropriate fashion and both partners match emotional states, especially the positive ones.

**intermodal perception** Perception that combines information from more than one modality, or sensory system.

**internal working model** A set of expectations derived from early caregiving experiences concerning the availability of attachment figures, their likelihood of providing support during times of stress, and the self's interaction with those figures. Becomes a model, or guide, for all future close relationships.

**internalization** The process of adopting societal standards for right action as one's own.

**intersubjectivity** A process whereby two participants who begin a task with different understandings arrive at a shared understanding.

**invariant features** Features that remain stable in a constantly changing perceptual world.

**investment theory of creativity** Sternberg and Lubart's theory, in which investing in novel projects depends on diverse cognitive, personality, motivational, and environmental resources, each of which must be present to catalyze creativity.

**I-self** A sense of self as knower and actor. Includes self-awareness, self-continuity, self-coherence, and self-agency. Distinguished from *me-self.*

**joint attention** A state in which two conversational partners attend to the same object or event.

**joint custody** A child custody arrangement following divorce in which the court grants both parents equal say in important decisions about the child's upbringing.

**kinetic depth cues** Depth cues created by movements of the body or of objects in the environment.

**kinship studies** Studies comparing the characteristics of family members to determine the importance of heredity in complex human characteristics.

**kwashiorkor** A disease usually appearing between 1 and 3 years of age that is caused by a diet low in protein. Symptoms include an enlarged belly, swollen feet, hair loss, skin rash, and irritable, listless behaviour.

**laboratory experiment** An experiment conducted in the laboratory, permitting the maximum possible control over treatment conditions.

**language acquisition device (LAD)** In Chomsky's theory, an innate system for picking up language that permits children, as soon as they have acquired sufficient vocabulary, to combine words into grammatically consistent, novel utterances and to understand the meaning of sentences they hear.

**lanugo** A white, downy hair that covers the entire body of the fetus, helping the vernix stick to the skin.

**lateralization** Specialization of functions of the two hemispheres of the cerebral cortex.

**learned helplessness** Attributions that credit success to external factors, such as luck, and failure to low ability. Leads to low expectancies of success and anxious loss of control in the face of challenging tasks. Distinguished from *mastery-oriented attributions.*

**learning disability** Great difficulty with one or more aspects of learning (usually reading) that results in poor school achievement, despite an average or above-average IQ.

**Level I–Level II theory** Jensen's controversial theory, which states that ethnic and SES differences in IQ are due to genetic differences in abstract reasoning and problem-solving abilities (Level II) rather than basic memory skills (Level I).

**lexical contrast theory** A theory that assumes two principles govern semantic development: *conventionality,* children's natural desire to acquire the words and word meanings of their language community; and *contrast,* children's discovery of meanings by contrasting new words with ones they know and assigning them to gaps in their vocabulary.

**logical necessity** A basic property of propositional thought, which specifies that the accuracy of conclusions drawn from premises rests on the rules of logic, not on real-world confirmation. A grasp of logical necessity permits individuals to reason from premises that contradict reality or their own beliefs.

**longitudinal design** A research design in which one group of participants is studied repeatedly at different ages. Distinguished from *cross-sectional design*.

**longitudinal-sequential design** A research design with both longitudinal and cross-sectional components in which groups of participants born in different years are followed over time.

**long-term memory** The part of the mental system that contains our permanent knowledge base. Distinguished from *microsystem, mesosystem, exosystem,* and *chronosystem*.

**macrosystem** In ecological systems theory, cultural values, laws, customs, and resources that influence experiences and interactions at inner levels of the environment. Distinguished from *microsystem, mesosystem, exosystem,* and *chronosystem*.

**mainstreaming** Placement of students with learning difficulties in regular classrooms for part of the school day.

**make-believe play** A type of play in which children pretend, acting out everyday and imaginary activities.

**marasmus** A disease usually appearing in the first year of life that is caused by a diet low in all essential nutrients. Leads to a wasted condition of the body.

**mastery-oriented attributions** Attributions that credit success to high ability and failure to insufficient effort. Leads to high expectancies of success and a willingness to approach challenging tasks. Distinguished from *learned helplessness*.

**matching** A procedure in which participants are measured ahead of time on the factor in question, enabling researchers to assign participants with similar characteristics in equal numbers to each treatment condition in an experiment. Ensures that groups will be equivalent on factors likely to distort the results.

**matters of personal choice** Concerns that do not violate rights or harm others, are not socially regulated, and therefore are up to the individual. Distinguished from *moral imperatives* and *social conventions*.

**maturation** A genetically determined, naturally unfolding course of growth.

**meiosis** The process of cell division through which gametes are formed and in which the number of chromosomes in each cell is halved.

**memory span** The longest sequence of items a person can recall, a measure of working-memory capacity.

**menarche** First menstruation.

**mental representation** Internal depiction of information that the mind can manipulate. The most powerful mental representations are images and concepts.

**mental strategies** Learned procedures that operate on and transform information, thereby increasing the efficiency and flexibility of thinking and the chances that information will be retained.

**me-self** A sense of self as object of knowledge and evaluation. Consists of all qualities that make the self unique, including material, psychological, and social characteristics. Distinguished from *I-self*.

**mesosystem** In ecological systems theory, connections between children's immediate settings. Distinguished from *microsystem, exosystem, macrosystem,* and *chronosystem*.

**metacognition** Awareness and understanding of various aspects of thought.

**metalinguistic awareness** The ability to think about language as a system.

**microgenetic design** A research design in which researchers present children with a novel task and follow their mastery over a series of closely spaced sessions.

**microsystem** In ecological systems theory, the activities and interaction patterns in the child's immediate surroundings. Distinguished from *mesosystem, exosystem, macrosystem,* and *chronosystem*.

**mild mental retardation** The condition that characterizes children whose IQs fall between 55 and 70 and who also show problems in adaptive behaviour.

**mitosis** The process of cell duplication, in which each new cell receives an exact copy of the original chromosomes.

**model of strategy choice** Siegler's evolutionary theory of cognitive development, which states that variation and selection characterize children's mental strategies, yielding adaptive problem-solving techniques and an overlapping-waves pattern of cognitive development.

**modifier genes** Genes that can enhance or dilute the effects of alleles controlling particular traits.

**moral imperatives** Standards that protect people's rights and welfare. Distinguished from *social conventions* and *matters of personal choice*.

**moral judgment interview** A clinical interviewing procedure for assessing moral understanding, in which people are given moral dilemmas that present conflicts between two moral values and are asked what the main actor should do and why.

**moral self-regulation** The ability to monitor one's own conduct, constantly adjusting it as circumstances present opportunities to violate inner standards.

**moral self-relevance** The degree to which morality is central to self-concept.

**moratorium** The identity status of individuals who are exploring alternatives in an effort to find values and goals to guide their life. Distinguished from *identity achievement, identity foreclosure,* and *identity diffusion*.

**mutation** A sudden but permanent change in a segment of DNA.

**myelinization** A process in which neural fibres are coated with an insulating fatty sheath (called myelin) that improves the efficiency of message transfer.

**natural experiment** A research design in which the investigator studies already existing treatments in natural settings by carefully selecting groups of participants with similar characteristics.

**natural,** or **prepared, childbirth** An approach designed to reduce pain and medical intervention and to make childbirth a rewarding experience for parents.

**naturalistic observation** A method by which the researcher goes into the natural environment to observe the behaviour of interest. Distinguished from *structured observation*.

**nature–nurture controversy** Disagreement among theorists about whether genetic or environmental factors are more important determinants of development and behaviour.

**neglected children** Children who are seldom chosen, either positively or negatively, on sociometric measures of peer acceptance. Distinguished from *popular, rejected,* and *controversial children*.

**Neonatal Behavioural Assessment Scale (NBAS)** A test developed to assess the behavioural status of the newborn.

**neo-Piagetian theory** A theory that reinterprets Piaget's stages within an information-processing framework.

**neurons** Nerve cells that store and transmit information in the brain.

**niche-picking** A type of genetic–environmental correlation in which individuals actively choose environments that complement their heredity.

**noble savage** Rousseau's view of the child as naturally endowed with a sense of right and wrong and with an innate plan for orderly, healthy growth.

**nonorganic failure to thrive** A growth disorder usually present by 18 months of age that is caused by lack of affection and stimulation.

**non-rapid-eye-movement (NREM) sleep** A "regular" sleep state in which the body is almost motionless and heart rate, breathing, and brain-wave activity are slow and regular. Distinguished from *rapid-eye-movement (REM) sleep*.

**nonshared environmental influences** Environmental influences that make siblings living in the same home different from one another. Distinguished from *shared environmental influences*.

**nonsocial activity** Unoccupied, onlooker behaviour and solitary play. Distinguished from *parallel play, associative play,* and *cooperative play*.

**normative approach** A child-study approach in which age-related averages are computed to represent typical development.

**nuclear family unit** The part of the family that consists of parents and their children. Distinguished from *extended-family household*.

**obesity** A greater-than-20-percent increase over average body weight, based on the child's age, sex, and physical build.

**object permanence** The understanding that objects continue to exist when they are out of sight.

**observer bias** The tendency of observers who are aware of the purposes of a study to see and record what is expected rather than participants' actual behaviours.

**observer influence** The tendency of participants to react to the presence of an observer and behave in unnatural ways.

**open classroom** A classroom based on the educational philosophy that children are active agents in their own development and learn at different rates. Teachers share decision making with students. Children's progress is evaluated in relation to their own prior development. Distinguished from *traditional classroom*.

**operant conditioning** A form of learning in which a spontaneous behaviour is followed by a stimulus that changes the probability that the behaviour will occur again.

**operations** In Piaget's theory, mental representations of actions that obey logical rules.

**optical flow** Movements in the visual field signalling that the body is in motion, leading to postural adjustments so the body remains upright.

**oral rehydration therapy (ORT)** A treatment for diarrhea, in which sick children are given a glucose, salt, and water solution that quickly replaces fluids the body loses.

**ordinality** A principle specifying order (more-than and less-than) relationships between quantities.

**organization** In Piaget's theory, the internal rearrangement and linking together of schemes so that they form a strongly interconnected cognitive system. In *information processing*, the memory strategy of grouping together related information.

**overextension** An early vocabulary error in which a word is applied too broadly, to a wider collection of objects and events than is appropriate. Distinguished from *underextension.*

**overregularization** Application of regular grammatical rules to words that are exceptions.

**overt aggression** A form of hostile aggression that harms others through physical injury or the threat of such injury—for example, hitting, kicking, or threatening to beat up a peer.

**parallel play** A form of limited social participation in which the child plays near other children with similar materials but does not try to influence their behaviour. Distinguished from *nonsocial activity, associative play,* and *cooperative play.*

**peer acceptance** Likeability, or the extent to which the child is viewed by a group of agemates (such as classmates) as a worthy social partner.

**peer group** Peers who form a social unit by generating unique values and standards of behaviour and a social structure of leaders and followers.

**peer victimization** A destructive form of peer interaction in which certain children become frequent targets of verbal and physical attacks or other forms of abuse.

**permissive style** A child-rearing style that is high in acceptance but overindulging and inattentive, low in control, and lax rather than appropriate in autonomy granting. Distinguished from *authoritative, authoritarian,* and *uninvolved styles.*

**person perception** The way individuals size up the attributes of people with whom they are familiar.

**personal fable** Adolescents' belief that they are special and unique. Leads them to conclude that others cannot possibly understand their thoughts and feelings. By convincing teenagers of their invulnerability, may contribute to adolescent risk taking.

**perspective taking** The capacity to imagine what other people may be thinking and feeling.

**phenotype** The individual's physical and behavioural characteristics, which are determined by both genetic and environmental factors.

**phoneme** The smallest sound unit that signals a change in meaning.

**phonological store** A special part of working memory that permits us to retain speech-based information. Supports early vocabulary development.

**phonology** The component of language concerned with the rules governing the structure and sequence of speech sounds.

**pictorial depth cues** Depth cues such as those that artists use to make a painting look three-dimensional, including receding lines, texture changes, and overlapping objects.

**pincer grasp** The well-coordinated grasp emerging at the end of the first year, in which thumb and forefinger are used opposably.

**pituitary gland** A gland located near the base of the brain that releases hormones affecting physical growth.

**placenta** The organ that separates the mother's bloodstream from the embryo's or fetus's bloodstream but permits exchange of nutrients and waste products.

**planning** Thinking out a sequence of acts ahead of time and allocating attention accordingly to reach a goal.

**polygenic inheritance** A pattern of inheritance involving many genes that applies to characteristics that vary continuously among people.

**popular children** Children who get many positive votes on sociometric measures of peer acceptance. Distinguished from *rejected, controversial,* and *neglected children.*

**popular-antisocial children** A subgroup of popular children largely made up of "tough" boys who are athletically skilled, highly aggressive, defiant of adult authority, and poor students. Distinguished from *popular-prosocial children.*

**popular-prosocial children** A subgroup of popular children who combine academic and social competence. Distinguished from *popular anti-social children.*

**postconventional level** Kohlberg's highest level of moral development, in which individuals define morality in terms of abstract principles and values that apply to all situations and societies.

**practical intelligence** Mental abilities apparent in the real world but not in testing situations.

**practice effects** Changes in participants' natural responses as a result of repeated testing.

**pragmatics** The component of language concerned with the rules for engaging in effective and appropriate communication with others.

**preconventional level** Kohlberg's first level of moral development, in which moral understanding is based on rewards, punishment, and the power of authority figures.

**preformationism** Medieval view of the child as a miniature adult.

**prenatal diagnostic methods** Medical procedures that permit detection of developmental problems before birth.

**preoperational stage** Piaget's second stage, in which rapid development of representation takes place. However, thought is not yet logical. Spans the years from 2 to 7.

**prereaching** The well-aimed but poorly coordinated primitive reaching movements of newborn babies.

**preterm** Infants born several weeks or more before their due date.

**primary mental abilities** In Thurstone's theory of intelligence, seven distinct mental abilities identified through factor analysis: verbal meaning, perceptual speed, reasoning, number, rote memory, word fluency, and spatial visualization.

**primary sexual characteristics** Physical features that involve the reproductive organs (ovaries, uterus, and vagina in females; penis, scrotum, and testes in males). Distinguished from *secondary sexual characteristics.*

**principle of mutual exclusivity** The assumption by children in the early stages of vocabulary growth that words refer to entirely separate (nonoverlapping) categories.

**private speech** Self-directed speech that children use to guide their thinking and behaviour.

**production** In language development, the words and word combinations that children use. Distinguished from *comprehension.*

**production deficiency** The failure to produce a mental strategy when it could be helpful. Distinguished from *control* and *utilization deficiencies.*

**programmed cell death** Death of many surrounding neurons during the peak period of development in any brain area, to make room for growth of neural fibres that form synaptic connections.

**Project Head Start** A U.S. federal program that provides low-income children with a year or two of preschool education, along with nutritional and medical services, and that encourages parent involvement in children's development.

**propositional thought** A type of formal operational reasoning in which adolescents evaluate the logic of verbal statements without referring to real-world circumstances.

**prosocial, or altruistic, behaviour** Actions that benefit another person without any expected reward for the self.

**protection from harm** The right of research participants to be protected from physical or psychological harm.

**protodeclarative** A preverbal gesture through which infants make an assertion about an object by touching it, holding it up, or pointing to it while looking at others to make sure they notice.

**protoimperative** A preverbal gesture in which infants point, reach, and make sounds to get another person to do something.

**proximodistal trend** An organized pattern of physical growth and motor control that proceeds from the centre of the body outward.

**psychoanalytic perspective** An approach to personality development introduced by Freud that assumes children move through a series of stages in which they confront conflicts between biological drives and social expectations. The way these conflicts are resolved determines psychological adjustment.

**psychometric approach** A product-oriented approach to cognitive development that focuses on the construction of tests to assess mental abilities.

**psychophysiological methods** Methods that measure the relationship between physiological processes and behaviour. Among the most common are measures of autonomic nervous system activity (such as heart rate, respiration, and stress hormone levels) and measures of brain functioning (such as the electroencephalogram [EEG], event-related potentials [ERPs], and functional magnetic resonance imaging [fMRI]).

**psychosexual theory** Freud's theory, which emphasizes that how parents manage their child's sexual and aggressive drives during the first few years is crucial for healthy personality development.

**psychosocial dwarfism** A growth disorder observed between 2 and 15 years of age. Characterized by substantially below-average stature, weight that is usually appropriate for height, immature skeletal age, and decreased GH secretion. Caused by severe emotional deprivation.

**psychosocial theory** Erikson's theory, which emphasizes that at each Freudian stage, individuals not only develop a unique personality, but also acquire attitudes and skills that help them become active, contributing members of their society. Recognizes the lifespan nature of development and the impact of culture.

**puberty** Biological changes during adolescence that lead to an adult-sized body and sexual maturity.

**public policy** Laws and government programs aimed at improving current conditions.

**punishment** In operant conditioning, removing a desirable stimulus or presenting an unpleasant one to decrease the occurrence of a response.

**random assignment** An evenhanded procedure for assigning participants to treatment groups, such as drawing numbers out of a hat or flipping a coin. Increases the chances that participants' characteristics will be equally distributed across treatment conditions in an experiment.

**range of reaction** Each person's unique, genetically determined response to a range of environmental conditions.

**rapid-eye-movement (REM) sleep** An "irregular" sleep state in which brain-wave activity is similar to that of the waking state; eyes dart beneath the lids; heart rate, blood pressure, and breathing are uneven; and slight body movements occur. Distinguished from *non-rapid-eye-movement (NREM) sleep.*

**realism** A view of rules as external features of reality rather than as cooperative principles that can be modified at will. Characterizes Piaget's heteronomous stage.

**recall** A type of memory that involves generating a mental representation of an absent stimulus. Distinguished from *recognition.*

**recasts** Adult responses that restructure a child's grammatically incorrect speech into correct form.

**reciprocal teaching** A method of teaching based on Vygotsky's theory in which a teacher and two to four pupils form a collaborative learning group. Dialogues occur that create a zone of proximal development in which reading comprehension improves.

**recognition** A type of memory that involves noticing whether a stimulus is identical or similar to one previously experienced. Distinguished from *recall.*

**reconstruction** A type of memory in which complex, meaningful material is reinterpreted in terms of existing knowledge.

**recovery** Following habituation, increase in responsiveness to a new stimulus.

**recursive thought** The self-embedded form of perspective taking that involves thinking about what another person is thinking.

**referential communication skills** The ability to produce clear verbal messages and to recognize when the meaning of others' messages is unclear.

**referential style** A style of early language learning in which toddlers use language mainly to label objects. Distinguished from *expressive style.*

**reflex** An inborn, automatic response to a particular form of stimulation.

**rehearsal** The memory strategy of repeating information.

**reinforcer** In operant conditioning, a stimulus that increases the occurrence of a response.

**rejected children** Children who are actively disliked and get many negative votes on sociometric measures of peer acceptance. Distinguished from *popular, controversial,* and *neglected children.*

**rejected-aggressive children** A subgroup of rejected children who engage in high rates of conflict, hostility, and hyperactive, inattentive, and impulsive behaviour. Distinguished from *rejected-withdrawn children.*

**rejected-withdrawn children** A subgroup of rejected children who are passive and socially awkward. Distinguished from *rejected-aggressive children.*

**relational aggression** A form of hostile aggression that damages another's peer relationships, as in social exclusion or rumour spreading.

**reliability** The consistency, or repeatability, of measures of behaviour.

**remembered self** The life story constructed from conversations with adults about the past that leads to an autobiographical memory.

**resiliency** The ability to adapt effectively in the face of threats to development.

**resistant attachment** The quality of insecure attachment characterizing infants who often remain close to the parent and fail to explore and, when separated, display angry, resistive behaviour when she returns. Distinguished from *secure, avoidant,* and *disorganized/disoriented attachment.*

**reticular formation** A structure in the brain stem that maintains alertness and consciousness.

**reversibility** The ability to mentally go through a series of steps and then reverse direction, returning to the starting point. In Piaget's theory, part of every logical operation.

**Rh factor** A protein that, when present in the fetus's blood but not in the mother's, can cause the mother to build up antibodies if the fetus's blood enters the mother's bloodstream. If these antibodies return to the fetus's system, they destroy red blood cells, reducing the oxygen supply to organs and tissues.

**risks-versus-benefits ratio** A comparison of the costs of a research study to participants in terms of inconvenience and possible psychological or physical injury against its value for advancing knowledge and improving conditions of life. Used in assessing the ethics of research.

**rough-and-tumble play** A form of peer interaction involving friendly chasing and play-fighting that, in our evolutionary past, may have been important for the development of fighting skill.

**scaffolding** A changing quality of support over a teaching session, in which adults adjust the assistance they provide to fit the child's current level of performance. Direct instruction is offered when a task is new; less help is provided as competence increases.

**scheme** In Piaget's theory, a specific structure, or organized way of making sense of experience, that changes with age.

**scripts** General representations of what occurs and when it occurs in a particular situation. A basic means through which children organize and interpret familiar everyday experiences.

**secondary sexual characteristics** Features visible on the outside of the body that serve as signs of sexual maturity but do not involve the reproductive organs (for example, breast development in females, appearance of underarm and pubic hair in both sexes). Distinguished from *primary sexual characteristics.*

**secular trends in physical growth** Changes in body size and rate of growth from one generation to the next.

**secure attachment** The quality of attachment characterizing infants who use the parent as a secure base from which to explore and, when separated, are easily comforted by the parent when she returns. Distinguished from *avoidant, resistant,* and *disorganized/disoriented attachment.*

**secure base** The use of the familiar caregiver as a base from which the infant confidently explores the environment and to which the infant returns for emotional support.

**selective attrition** Selective loss of participants during an investigation, resulting in a biased sample.

**self-care children** Children who regularly look after themselves during after-school hours.

**self-concept** The set of attributes, abilities, attitudes, and values that an individual believes defines who he is.

**self-conscious emotions** Emotions that involve injury to or enhancement of the sense of self. Examples are shame, embarrassment, guilt, envy, and pride.

**self-control** Inhibiting an impulse to engage in behaviour that violates a moral standard.

**self-esteem** The aspect of self-concept that involves judgments about one's own worth and the feelings associated with those judgments.

**self-recognition** Perception of the self as a separate being, distinct from other people and objects.

**semantic bootstrapping** Relying on semantics, or word meanings, to figure out sentence structure.

**semantic memory** The vast, intricately organized knowledge system in long-term memory.

**semantics** The component of language concerned with understanding the meaning of words and word combinations.

**sensitive caregiving** Caregiving involving prompt, consistent, and appropriate responding to infant signals and tender, careful handling.

**sensitive period** A time that is optimal for certain capacities to emerge because the individual is especially responsive to environmental influences.

**sensorimotor stage** Piaget's first stage, during which infants and toddlers build schemes through sensorimotor action patterns.

**sensory register** The first part of the mental system, where sights and sounds are represented directly but held only briefly.

**separation anxiety** An infant's distressed reaction to the departure of the familiar caregiver.

**seriation** The ability to arrange items along a quantitative dimension, such as length or weight.

**sex chromosomes** The twenty-third pair of chromosomes, which determines the sex of the child. In females, this pair is called XX; in males, it is called XY.

**shading** A conversational strategy in which a change of topic is initiated gradually by modifying the focus of discussion.

**shape constancy** Perception of an object's shape as stable, despite changes in the shape of its retinal image when seen from different vantage points.

**shared environmental influences** Environmental influences that pervade the general atmosphere of the home and, therefore, similarly affect all children living in it. Distinguished from *nonshared environmental influences*.

**size constancy** Perception of an object's size as stable, despite changes in the size of its retinal image caused by changes in distance.

**skeletal age** An estimate of physical maturity based on development of the bones of the body.

**slow-to-warm-up child** A child whose temperament is such that he is inactive, shows mild, low-key reactions to environmental stimuli, is negative in mood, and adjusts slowly to new experiences. Distinguished from *difficult child* and *easy child*.

**small for date** Infants whose birth weight is below normal when length of pregnancy is taken into account. May be full term or preterm.

**social cognition** Thinking about the characteristics of the self and other people.

**social comparisons** Judgments of one's own abilities, behaviour, and appearance in relation to those of others.

**social conventions** Customs determined solely by consensus, such as table manners, dress styles, and rituals of social interaction. Distinguished from *moral imperatives* and *matters of personal choice*.

**social learning theory** An approach that emphasizes the role of modelling, or observational learning, in the development of behaviour. Its most recent revision stresses the importance of thinking in social learning and is called *social-cognitive theory*.

**social policy** Any planned set of actions directed at solving a social problem or attaining a social goal.

**social problem solving** Resolving social conflicts in ways that are both acceptable to others and beneficial to the self. Involves encoding and interpreting social cues, clarifying a social goal, generating and evaluating strategies, and enacting a response.

**social referencing** Relying on another person's emotional reaction to appraise an uncertain situation.

**social smile** The smile evoked by the stimulus of the human face. First appears between 6 and 10 weeks.

**social systems perspective** A view of the family as a complex set of interacting relationships influenced by the larger social context.

**sociocultural theory** Vygotsky's theory, in which children acquire the ways of thinking and behaving that make up a community's culture through cooperative dialogues with more knowledgeable members of society.

**sociodramatic play** The make-believe play with other children that is under way by age 2½.

**socioeconomic status (SES)** A measure of a family's social position and economic well-being that combines three interrelated, but not completely overlapping, variables: (1) years of education and (2) the prestige of and skill required by one's job, both of which measure social status; and (3) income, which measures economic status.

**sociometric techniques** Self-report measures that ask peers to evaluate one another's likeability.

**Sociomoral Reflection Measure–Short Form (SRM–SF)** A questionnaire for assessing moral understanding, in which individuals rate the importance of moral values addressed by brief questions and explain their ratings. Does not require research participants to read and think about lengthy moral dilemmas.

**specific factor, or "s"** In Spearman's theory of intelligence, a mental ability factor that is unique to a task.

**specimen record** An observational procedure in which the researcher records a description of the participant's entire stream of behaviour for a specified time period.

**speech registers** Language adaptations to social expectations.

**spermarche** First ejaculation of seminal fluid.

**stage** A qualitative change in thinking, feeling, and behaving that characterizes a specific period of development.

**Stanford-Binet Intelligence Scale** An individually administered intelligence test that is the modern descendant of Alfred Binet's first successful test for children. Measures general intelligence and four factors: verbal reasoning, quantitative reasoning, abstract/visual (spatial) reasoning, and short-term memory.

**states of arousal** Different degrees of sleep and wakefulness.

**store model** A model of mental functioning that views information as being held in three parts of the mental system for processing: the sensory register; working, or short-term, memory; and long-term memory.

**Strange Situation** A research procedure involving short separations from and reunions with the parent that assesses the quality of the attachment bond.

**stranger anxiety** The infant's expression of fear in response to unfamiliar adults. Appears in many babies after 6 months of age.

**structured interview** A method in which the researcher asks each participant the same questions in the same way.

**structured observation** A method by which the researcher sets up a situation that evokes the behaviour of interest and observes it in a laboratory. Distinguished from *naturalistic observation*.

**sudden infant death syndrome (SIDS)** The unexpected death, usually during the night, of an infant younger than 1 year of age that remains unexplained after thorough investigation.

**sympathy** An extension of empathy that involves feelings of concern or sorrow for another's plight.

**synapse** The gap between neurons, across which chemical messages are sent.

**synaptic pruning** Loss of connective fibres by seldom-stimulated neurons, thereby returning them to an uncommitted state so they can support the development of future skills.

**syntactic bootstrapping** Observing how words are used syntactically, in the structure of sentences, to figure out their meanings.

**tabula rasa** Locke's view of the child as a blank slate whose character is shaped by experience.

**talent** Outstanding performance in a specific field.

**telegraphic speech** Children's two-word utterances that, like a telegram, leave out smaller and less important words.

**television literacy** The task of learning television's specialized symbolic code of conveying information.

**temperament** Stable individual differences in quality and intensity of emotional reaction, activity level, attention, and emotional self-regulation.

**teratogen** Any environmental agent that causes damage during the prenatal period.

**theory** An orderly, integrated set of statements that describes, explains, and predicts behaviour.

**theory of mind** A coherent understanding of people as mental beings, which children revise as they encounter new evidence. Includes knowledge of mental activity and awareness that people can have different perceptions, feelings, desires, and beliefs.

**theory of multiple intelligences** Gardner's theory, which identifies eight intelligences on the basis of distinct sets of processing operations applied in culturally valued activities (linguistic, logico-mathematical, musical, spatial, bodily-kinesthetic, naturalist, interpersonal, intrapersonal).

**theory theory** A theory that assumes that children build on innate concepts to form naive theories, or explanations of everyday events, in each core domain of thought. Then they test their theory against experience, revising it when it cannot adequately account for new information. Preschoolers have naive physical and biological theories and a psychological theory, or theory of mind.

**three-stratum theory of intelligence** Carroll's theory, which represents the structure of intelligence as a pyramid, with "g" at the top; eight broad, biologically based abilities at the second stratum; and narrower manifestations of these abilities at the lowest stratum that result from experience with particular tasks. The most comprehensive classification of mental abilities to be confirmed by factor-analytic research.

**thyroxine** A hormone released by the thyroid gland that is necessary for central nervous system development and body growth.

**time out** A form of mild punishment in which children are removed from the immediate setting until they are ready to act appropriately.

**time sampling** An observational procedure in which the researcher records whether certain behaviours occur during a sample of short time intervals.

**traditional classroom** A classroom based on the educational philosophy that children are passive learners who acquire information presented by teachers. Children's progress is evaluated on the basis of how well they keep pace with a uniform set of standards for all students in their grade. Distinguished from *open classroom.*

**transitive inference** The ability to seriate—or arrange items along a quantitative dimension—mentally.

**triarchic theory of intelligence** Sternberg's theory, which states that information-processing skills, prior experience with tasks, and contextual (or cultural) factors combine to influence intelligent behaviour.

**turnabout** A conversational strategy in which the speaker not only comments on what has just been said but also adds a request to get the partner to respond again.

**ulnar grasp** The clumsy grasp of the young infant, in which the fingers close against the palm.

**umbilical cord** The long cord connecting the prenatal organism to the placenta that delivers nutrients and removes waste products.

**unconditioned response (UCR)** In classical conditioning, a reflexive response that is produced by an unconditioned stimulus (UCS).

**unconditioned stimulus (UCS)** In classical conditioning, a stimulus that leads to a reflexive response.

**underextension** An early vocabulary error in which a word is applied too narrowly, to a smaller number of objects or events than is appropriate. Distinguished from *overextension.*

**uninhibited, or sociable, child** A child whose temperament is such that he displays positive emotion to and approaches novel stimuli. Distinguished from *inhibited, or shy, child.*

**uninvolved style** A child-rearing style that combines low acceptance and involvement with little control and effort to grant autonomy. Reflects minimal commitment to parenting. Distinguished from *authoritative, authoritarian,* and *permissive styles.*

**utilization deficiency** Consistent use of a mental strategy, with little or no improvement in performance. Distinguished from *production* and *control deficiencies.*

**validity** The extent to which methods in a research study accurately measure what the investigator set out to measure.

**velocity curve** A growth curve that plots the average amount of growth at each yearly interval for a sample of children. Reveals the timing of growth spurts.

**vernix** A white, cheeselike substance covering the fetus and preventing the skin from chapping due to constant exposure to the amniotic fluid.

**violation-of-expectation method** A method for finding out about infants' understanding of physical experience, in which researchers habituate babies to a physical event and then determine whether they recover to (look longer at) a possible event (a variation of the first event that conforms to physical laws) or an impossible event (a variation that violates physical laws). Recovery to the impossible event suggests surprise at a deviation from reality and, therefore, an understanding of that aspect of the physical world.

**visual acuity** Fineness of visual discrimination.

**visual cliff** An apparatus used to study depth perception in infants. Consists of a Plexiglas-covered table and a central platform, from which babies are encouraged to crawl. Checkerboard patterns placed beneath the Plexiglas create the appearance of a shallow and deep side.

**washout effect** The loss of IQ and achievement gains resulting from early intervention within a few years after the program ends.

**Wechsler Intelligence Scale for Children–III (WISC–III)** An individually administered intelligence test that includes a measure of general intelligence and a variety of verbal and performance scores.

**Wernicke's area** A language structure located in the temporal lobe of the left hemisphere of the cerebral cortex that is responsible for interpreting language.

**whole-language approach** An approach to beginning reading instruction that parallels children's natural language learning and keeps reading materials whole and meaningful. Distinguished from *basic-skills approach.*

**working, or short-term, memory** The conscious part of the mental system, where we actively "work" on a limited amount of information to ensure that it will be retained.

**X-linked inheritance** A pattern of inheritance in which a recessive gene is carried on the X chromosome. Males are more likely to be affected.

**zone of proximal development** In Vygotsky's theory, a range of tasks that the child cannot yet handle alone but can do with the help of more skilled partners.

**zygote** The union of sperm and ovum at conception.

# references

Aaron, R., & Powell, G. (1982). Feedback practices as a function of teacher and pupil race during reading groups instruction. *Journal of Negro Education, 51,* 50–59.

Aarons, S. J., Jenkins, R. R., Raine, T. R., El-Khorazaty, M. N., Woodward, K. M., Williams, R. L., Clark, M. C., & Wingrove, B. K. (2000). Postponing sexual intercourse among urban junior high school students—a randomized controlled trial. *Journal of Adolescent Health, 27,* 236–247.

Abbott, S. (1992). Holding on and pushing away: Comparative perspectives on an eastern Kentucky child-rearing practice. *Ethos, 20,* 33–65.

Abelman, R. (1985). Styles of parental disciplinary practices as a mediator of children's learning from prosocial television portrayals. *Child Study Journal, 15,* 131–145.

Aboud, F. E., & Doyle, A. (1996). Parental and peer influences on children's racial attitudes. *International Journal of Intercultural Relations, 20,* 371–383.

Abramovitch, R., Freedman, J. L., Henry, K., & Van Brunschot, M. (1995). Children's capacity to agree to psychological research: Knowledge of risks and benefits and voluntariness. *Ethics and Behavior, 5,* 25–48.

Achenbach, T. M., Phares, V., Howell, C. T., Rauh, V. A., & Nurcombe, B. (1990). Seven-year outcome of the Vermont intervention program for low-birthweight infants. *Child Development, 61,* 1672–1681.

Acker, M. M., & O'Leary, S. G. (1996). Inconsistency of mothers' feedback and toddlers' misbehavior and negative affect. *Journal of Abnormal Child Psychology, 24,* 703–714.

Ackerman, B. P. (1978). Children's understanding of speech acts in unconventional frames. *Child Development, 49,* 311–318.

Ackerman, B. P. (1993). Children's understanding of the speaker's meaning in referential communication. *Journal of Experimental Child Psychology, 55,* 56–86.

Adams, M. J., Treiman, R., & Pressley, M. (1998). Reading, writing, and literacy. In I. E. Sigel & K. A. Renninger (Eds.), *Handbook of child psychology: Vol. 4. Cognition, perception, and language* (5th ed., pp. 275–355). New York: Wiley.

Adams, R. J., & Courage, M. L. (1998). Human newborn color vision: Measurement with chromatic stimuli varying in excitation purity. *Journal of Experimental Child Psychology, 68,* 22–34.

Adams, R., & Laursen, B. (2001). The organization and dynamics of

adolescent conflict with parents and friends. *Journal of Marriage and the Family, 63,* 97–110.

Addis, A., Moretti, M., Syed, F., Einarson, T., & Koren, G. (2001). Fetal effects of cocaine: An updated meta-analysis. *Reproductive Toxicology, 15,* 341–369.

Adlaf, E. M., & Paglia, A. (2001). Drug use among Ontario students, 1997–2001: Findings from the OSDUS. *CAMH Research Document Series No. 10.* Toronto: Centre for Addiction and Mental Health.

Adler, P. A., & Adler, P. (1998). *Peer power.* New Brunswick, NJ: Rutgers University Press.

Adolph, K. E. (1997). Learning in the development of infant locomotion. *Monographs of the Society for Research in Child Development, 62*(3, Serial No. 251).

Adolph, K. E. (2000). Specificity of learning: Why infants fall over a veritable cliff. *Psychological Science, 11,* 290–295.

Adolph, K. E., & Eppler, M. A. (1998). Development of visually guided locomotion. *Ecological Psychology, 10,* 303–321.

Adolph, K. E., & Eppler, M. A. (1999). Obstacles to understanding: An ecological approach to infant problem solving. In E. Winograd, R. Fivush, & W. Hirst (Eds.), *Ecological approaches to cognition* (pp. 31–58). Mahwah, NJ: Erlbaum.

Adolph, K. E., Vereijken, B., & Denny, M. A. (1998). Learning to crawl. *Child Development, 69,* 1299–1312.

Aguiar, A., & Baillargeon, R. (1999). 2.5-month-old infants' reasoning about when objects should and should not be occluded. *Cognitive Psychology, 39,* 116–157.

Ahlsten, G., Cnattingius, S., & Lindmark, G. (1993). Cessation of smoking during pregnancy improves fetal growth and reduces infant morbidity in the neonatal period: A population-based prospective study. *Acta Paediatrica, 82,* 177–181.

Ahmed, A., & Ruffman, T. (1998). Why do infants make A not B errors in a search task, yet show memory for the location of hidden objects in a nonsearch task? *Developmental Psychology, 34,* 441–453.

Ainsworth, M. D. S., Blehar, M., Waters, E., & Wall, S. (1978). *Patterns of attachment.* Hillsdale, NJ: Erlbaum.

Akers, J. F., Jones, R. M., & Coyle, D. D. (1998). Adolescent friendship pairs: Similarities in identity status development, behaviors,

attitudes, and intentions. *Journal of Adolescent Research, 13,* 178–201.

Akhtar, N., & Montague, L. (1999). Early lexical acquisition: The role of cross-situational learning. *First Language, 19,* 347–358.

Alan Guttmacher Institute. (1998). *Facts in brief—teen sex and pregnancy.* New York: Author.

Albert, R. S. (1994). The achievement of eminence: A longitudinal study of exceptionally gifted boys and their families. In R. F. Subotnik & K. D. Arnold (Eds.), *Beyond Terman: Contemporary studies of giftedness and talent* (pp. 282–315). Norwood, NJ: Ablex.

Alessandri, S. M., Bendersky, M., & Lewis, M. (1998). Cognitive functioning in 8- to 18-month-old drug-exposed infants. *Developmental Psychology, 34,* 565–573.

Alessandri, S. M., Sullivan, M. W., & Lewis, M. (1990). Violation of expectancy and frustration in early infancy. *Developmental Psychology, 26,* 738–744.

Alexander, J. M., Lucas, M. J., Ramin, S. M., McIntire, D. D., & Leveno, K. J. (1998). The course of labor with and without epidural analgesia. *American Journal of Obstetrics and Gynecology, 178,* 516–520.

Alexander, J. M., & Schwanenflugel, P. J. (1996). Development of metacognitive concepts about thinking in gifted and nongifted children: Recent research. *Learning and Individual Differences, 8,* 305–325.

Alfieri, T., Ruble, D. N., & Higgins, E. T. (1996). Gender stereotypes during adolescence: Developmental changes and the transition to junior high school. *Developmental Psychology, 32,* 1129–1137.

Alibali, M. W. (1999). How children change their minds: Strategy change can be gradual or abrupt. *Developmental Psychology, 35,* 127–145.

Alibali, M. W., & Goldin-Meadow, S. (1993). Gesture–speech mismatch and mechanisms of learning: What the hands reveal about a child's state of mind. *Cognitive Psychology, 25,* 468–523.

Allen, J. P., Hauser, S. T., Bell, K. L., & O'Connor, T. G. (1994). Longitudinal assessment of autonomy and relatedness in adolescent–family interactions as predictors of adolescent ego development and self-esteem. *Child Development, 65,* 179–194.

Allen, J. P., Philliber, S., Herrling, S., & Kuperminc, G. P. (1997). Preventing teen pregnancy and academic failure: Experimental

evaluation of a developmentally based approach. *Child Development, 64,* 729–742.

Allen, M., & Burrell, N. (1996). Comparing the impact of homosexual and heterosexual parents on children: Meta-analysis of existing research. *Journal of Homosexuality, 32,* 19–35.

Allen, S. E. M., & Crago, M. B. (1996). Early passive acquisition in Inuktitut. *Journal of Child Language, 23,* 129–156.

Alpert-Gillis, L. J., & Connell, J. P. (1989). Gender and sex-role influences on children's self-esteem. *Journal of Personality, 57,* 97–114.

Alsaker, F. D. (1995). Timing of puberty and reactions to pubertal changes. In M. Rutter (Ed.), *Psychosocial disturbances in young people* (pp. 37–82). New York: Cambridge University Press.

Alwitt, L. F., Anderson, D. R., Lorch, E. P., & Levin, S. R. (1980). Preschool children's visual attention to attributes of television. *Human Communication Research, 7,* 52–67.

Amabile, T. M. (1982). Children's artistic creativity: Detrimental effects of competition in a field setting. *Personality and Social Psychology Bulletin, 8,* 573–578.

Amato, P. R. (2000). The consequences of divorce for adults and children. *Journal of Marriage and the Family, 62,* 1269–1287.

Amato, P. R., & Booth, A. (2000). *A generation at risk: Growing up in an era of family upheaval.* Cambridge, MA: Harvard University Press.

Amato, P. R., & Gilbreth, J. (1999). Nonresident fathers and children's well-being: A meta-analysis. *Journal of Marriage and the Family, 61,* 557–573.

American Academy of Pediatrics. (1999). Contraception and adolescents. *Pediatrics, 104,* 1161–1166.

American Academy of Pediatrics. (2000). Changing concepts of sudden infant death syndrome: Implications for infant sleeping environment and sleep position. *Pediatrics, 105,* 650–656.

American Psychiatric Association. (1994). *Diagnostic and statistical manual of mental disorders* (4th ed.). Washington, DC: Author.

American Psychological Association. (1992). Ethical principles of psychologists and code of conduct. *American Psychologist, 44,* 1597–1611.

Ames, C. (1992). Classrooms: Goals, structures, and student motivation. *Journal of Educational Psychology, 84,* 261–271.

Ananth, C. V., Berkowitz, G., Savitz, D. A., & Lapinski, R. H. (1999). Placental abruption and adverse perinatal outcomes. *Journal of the American Medical Association, 282,* 1646–1651.

Anderman, E. M., Eccles, J. S., Yoon, K. S., Roeser, R., Wigfield, A., & Blumenfeld, P. (2001). Learning to value mathematics and reading: Relations to mastery and performance-oriented instructional practices. *Contemporary Educational Psychology, 26,* 76–95.

Anderman, E. M., & Midgley, C. (1997). Changes in achievement goal orientations, perceived academic competence, and grades across the transition to middle-level schools. *Contemporary Educational Psychology, 22,* 269–298.

Andersen, R. E. (2000). The spread of the childhood obesity epidemic. *Canadian Medical Association Journal, 163,* 1461–1462.

Anderson, C. A., & Bushman, B. J. (2001). Effects of violent video games on aggressive behavior, aggressive cognition, aggressive affect, physiological arousal, and prosocial behavior: A meta-analytic review of the scientific literature. *Psychological Science, 12,* 353–359.

Anderson, C. A., & Bushman, B. J. (2002). The effects of media violence on society. *Science, 295,* 2377–2379.

Anderson, D. M., Huston, A. C., Schmitt, K. L., Linebarger, D. L., & Wright, J. C. (2001). Early childhood television viewing and adolescent behavior. *Monographs of the Society for Research in Child Development, 66*(1, Serial No. 264).

Anderson, D. R., Bryant, J., Wilder, A., Santomero, A., Williams, M., & Crawley, A. M. (2000). Researching Blue's Clues: Viewing behavior and impact. *Media Psychology, 2,* 179–194.

Anderson, D. R., Collins, P. A., Schmitt, K. L., & Jacobvitz, R. S. (1996). Stressful life events and television viewing. *Communication Research, 23,* 243–260.

Anderson, E. (1992). *Speaking with style: The sociolinguistic skills of children.* London: Routledge.

Anderson, J. W., Johnstone, B. M., & Remley, D. T. (1999). Breast-feeding and cognitive development: A meta-analysis. *American Journal of Clinical Nutrition, 70,* 525–535.

Anderson, S. W., Bechara, A., Damasio, H., Tranel, D., & Damasio, A. R. (1999). Impairment of social and moral behavior related to early damage in human prefrontal cortex. *Nature Neuroscience, 2,* 1032–1037.

Andersson, B.-E. (1989). Effects of public day care—A longitudinal study. *Child Development, 60,* 857–866.

Andersson, B.-E. (1992). Effects of day-care on cognitive and socio-emotional competence of thirteen-year-old Swedish schoolchildren. *Child Development, 63,* 20–36.

Andre, T., Whigham, M., Hendrickson, A., & Chambers, S. (1999). Competence beliefs, positive affect, and gender stereotypes of elementary students and their parents about science versus other school subjects. *Journal of Research in Science Teaching, 36,* 719–747.

Andrews, G., & Halford, G. S. (1998). Children's ability to make transitive inferences: The importance of premise integration and structural complexity. *Cognitive Development, 13,* 479–513.

Andrews, L. B., & Elster, N. (2000). Regulating reproductive technologies. *Journal of Legal Medicine, 21,* 35–65.

Anglin, J. M. (1993). Vocabulary development: A morphological analysis. *Monographs of the Society for Research in Child Development, 58*(10, Serial No. 238).

Anhalt, K., & Morris, T. L. (1998). Developmental and adjustment issues of gay, lesbian, and bisexual adolescents: A review of the empirical literature. *Clinical Child and Family Psychology Review, 1,* 215–230.

Anisfeld, M., Turkewitz, G., Rose, S. A., Rosenberg, F. R., Shelber, F. J., Couturier-Fagan, D. A., Ger, J. S., & Sommer, I. (2001). No compelling evidence that newborns imitate oral gestures. *Infancy, 2,* 111–122.

Annett, M. (1994). Handedness as a continuous variable with dextral shift: Sex, generation, and family handedness in subgroups of left- and right-handers. *Behavioral Genetics, 24,* 51–63.

Annett, M. (1999). Left-handedness as a function of sex, maternal versus paternal inheritance, and report bias. *Behavior Genetics, 29,* 103–114.

Apgar, V. (1953). A proposal for a new method of evaluation in the newborn infant. *Current Research in Anesthesia and Analgesia, 32,* 260–267.

Aquilino, W. S., & Supple, A. J. (2001). Long-term effects of parenting practices during adolescence on well-being outcomes in young adulthood. *Journal of Family Issues, 22,* 289–308.

Archer, J. (1992). Childhood gender roles: Social content and organization. In H. McGurk (Ed.), *Childhood social development* (pp. 31–62). Hillsdale, NJ: Erlbaum.

Archer, J. (1994). Testosterone and aggression: A theoretical review. *Journal of Offender Rehabilitation, 21,* 3–39.

Archer, S. L. (1989). The status of identity: Reflections on the need for intervention. *Journal of Adolescence, 12,* 345–359.

Archer, S. L., & Waterman, A. S. (1990). Varieties of identity diffusions and foreclosures: An exploration of subcategories of the identity statuses. *Journal of Adolescent Research, 5,* 96–111.

Ardila-Rey, A., & Killen, M. (2001). Middle class Colombian children's evaluations of personal, moral, and social-conventional interactions in the classroom. *International Journal of Behavioral Development, 25,* 246–255.

Ariès, P. (1962). *Centuries of childhood.* New York: Random House.

Armstrong, K. L., Quinn, R. A., & Dadds, M. R. (1994). The sleep patterns of normal children. *Medical Journal of Australia, 161,* 202–206.

Arnett, J. J. (1999). Adolescent storm and stress reconsidered. *American Psychologist, 54,* 317–326.

Arnett, J. J. (2000a). Emerging adulthood: A theory of development from the late teens through the twenties. *American Psychologist, 55,* 469–480.

Arnett, J. J. (2000b). High hopes in a grim world: Emerging adults' views of their futures and of "Generation X." *Youth and Society, 31,* 267–286.

Arnold, P. (1999). Emotional disorders in deaf children. In V. L. Schwean & D. H. Saklofske (Eds.), *Handbook of psychosocial characteristics of exceptional children* (pp. 493–522). New York: Kluwer.

Aronson, M., Hagberg, B., & Gillberg, C. (1997). Attention deficits and autistic spectrum problems in children exposed to alcohol during gestation: A follow-up study. *Developmental Medicine and Child Neurology, 39,* 583–587.

Arora, S., McJunkin, C., Wehrer, J., & Kuhn, P. (2000). Major factors influencing breastfeeding rates: Mother's perception of father's attitude and milk supply. *Pediatrics, 106,* e67.

Arsenio, W., & Kramer, R. (1992). Victimizers and their victims: Children's conceptions of the mixed emotional consequences of moral transgressions. *Child Development, 63,* 915–927.

Arterberry, M. E. (1993). Development of spatial temporal integration in infancy. *Infant Behavior and Development, 16,* 343–364.

Arterberry, M. E., Craton, L. G., & Yonas, A. (1993). Infants' sensitivity to motion-carried information for depth and object properties. In C. E. Granrud (Ed.), *Visual perception and cognition in infancy* (pp. 215–234). Hillsdale, NJ: Erlbaum.

Artman, L., & Cahan, S. (1993). Schooling and the development of transitive inference. *Developmental Psychology, 29,* 753–759.

Asendorpf, J. B., Warkentin, V., & Baudonniere, P. (1996). Self-awareness and other-awareness II: Mirror self-recognition, social contingency awareness, and synchronic imitation. *Developmental Psychology, 32,* 313–321.

Asher, S. R., Parker, J. G., & Walker, D. L. (1998). Distinguishing friendship from acceptance: Implications for intervention and assessment. In W. M. Bukowski, A. F. Newcomb, & W. W. Hartup (Eds.), *The company they keep: Friendship in childhood and adolescence* (pp. 366–405). New York: Cambridge University Press.

Asher, S. R., & Rose, A. J. (1997). Promoting children's social-emotional adjustment with peers. In P. Salovey & D. J. Sluyter (Eds.), *Emotional development and emotional intelligence* (pp. 193–195). New York: Basic Books.

Ashley-Koch, A., Robinson, H., Glicksman, A. E., Nolin, S. L., Schwartz, C. E., & Brown, W. T. (1998). Examination of factors associated with instability of the FMR1 CGG repeat. *American Journal of Human Genetics, 63,* 776–785.

Ashley-Koch, A., Yang, Q., & Olney, R. S. (2000). Sickle hemoglobin (HbS) allele and sickle cell disease: A HuGE review. *American Journal of Epidemiology, 151,* 839–845.

Ashmead, D. H., McCarty, M. E., Lucas, L. S., & Belvedere, M. C. (1993). Visual guidance in infants' reaching toward suddenly displaced targets. *Child Development, 64,* 1111–1127.

Ashmead, D. H., & Perlmutter, M. (1980). Infant memory in every-day life. In M. Perlmutter (Ed.), *New directions for child development* (Vol. 10, pp. 1–16). San Francisco: Jossey-Bass.

Aslin, R. N. (2000). Why take the cog out of infant cognition? *Infancy, 1,* 463–470.

Aslin, R. N., Jusczyk, P. W., & Pisoni, D. B. (1998). Speech and auditory processing during infancy: Constraints on and precursors to language. In D. Kuhn & R. S. Siegler (Eds.), *Handbook of child psychology: Vol. 2. Cognition, perception, and language* (5th ed., pp. 147–198). New York: Wiley.

Aslin, R. N., & Smith, L. B. (1988). Perceptual development. *Annual Review of Psychology, 39,* 435–473.

Astington, J. W. (1993). *The child's discovery of the mind.* Cambridge: Cambridge University Press.

Astington, J. W. (1995). Commentary: Talking it over with my brain. In J. H. Flavell, F. L. Green, & E. R. Flavell, Young children's knowledge about thinking. *Monographs of the Society for Research in Child Development, 60*(1, Serial No. 243).

Astington, J. W. (2001). The paradox of intention: Assessing children's metarepresentational understanding. In B. F. Malle, L. J. Moses, & D. A. Baldwin (Eds.),

*Intentions and intentionality* (pp. 85–103). Cambridge, MA: MIT Press.

Astington, J. W., & Jenkins, J. M. (1995). Theory of mind development and social understanding. *Cognition and Emotion, 9,* 151–165.

Astley, S. J., Clarren, S. K., Little, R. E., Sampson, P. D., & Daling, J. R. (1992). Analysis of facial shape in children gestationally exposed to marijuana, alcohol, and/or cocaine. *Pediatrics, 89,* 67–77.

Atkinson, L., Niccols, A., Paglia, A., Coolbear, J., Parker, K. C. H., Poulton, L., Guger, S., & Sitarenios, G. (2000). A meta-analysis of time between maternal sensitivity and attachment assessments: Implications for internal working models in infancy/toddlerhood. *Journal of Social and Personal Relationships, 17,* 791–810.

Atkinson, R. C., & Shiffrin, R. M. (1968). Human memory: A proposed system and its control processes. In K. W. Spence & J. T. Spence (Eds.), *Advances in the psychology of learning and motivation* (Vol. 2, pp. 90–195). New York: Academic Press.

Atkinson-King, K. (1973). Children's acquisition of phonological stress contrasts. *UCLA Working Papers in Phonetics, 25.*

Atlas, R. S., & Pepler, D. J. (1998). Observations of bullying in the classroom. *Journal of Educational Research, 92,* 86–99.

Attie, I., & Brooks-Gunn, J. (1996). The development of eating regulation across the life span. In D. Cicchetti & D. J. Cohen (Eds.), *Developmental psychology: Vol. 2. Risk, disorder, and adaptation* (pp. 332–368). New York: Wiley.

Au, K. H. (1997). A sociocultural model of reading instruction: The Kamehameha Elementary Education Program. In S. A. Stahl & D. A. Hayes (Eds.), *Instructional models in reading* (pp. 181–202). Mahwah, NJ: Erlbaum.

Au, T. K., Dapretto, M., & Song, Y.-K. (1994). Input vs. constraints: Early word acquisition in Korean and English. *Journal of Memory and Language, 33,* 567–582.

Au, T. K., Sidle, A. L., & Rollins, K. B. (1993). Developing an intuitive understanding of conservation and contamination: Invisible particles as a plausible mechanism. *Developmental Psychology, 29,* 286–299.

Aunola, K., Stattin, H., & Nurmi, J.-E. (2000). Parenting styles and adolescents' achievement strategies. *Journal of Adolescence, 23,* 205–222.

Australian Bureau of Statistics. (2000). *Divorce rates.* [On-line]. Available: www.abus.gov.au

Axia, G., Bonichini, S., & Benini, F. (1999). Attention and reaction to distress in infancy: A longitudinal study. *Developmental Psychology, 35,* 500–504.

Azar, S. T., & Wolfe, D. A. (1998). Child physical abuse and neglect. In E. J. Mash & R. A. Barkley (Eds.), *Treatment of childhood disorders* (2nd ed., pp. 501–504). New York: Guilford.

Azmitia, M. (1988). Peer interaction and problem solving: When are two heads better than one? *Child Development, 59,* 87–96.

Bacharach, V. R., & Baumeister, A. A. (1998). Direct and indirect effects of maternal intelligence, maternal age, income, and home environment on intelligence of preterm, low-birth-weight children. *Journal of Applied Developmental Psychology, 19,* 361–375.

Baddeley, A. (1993). Working memory and conscious awareness. In A. F. Collins, S. E. Gathercole, M. A. Conway, & P. E. Morris (Eds.), *Theories of memory* (pp. 11–28). Hove, UK: Erlbaum.

Baddeley, A. (2000). Short-term and working memory. In E. Tulving & R. I. M. Craik (Eds.), *The Oxford handbook of memory* (pp. 77–92). New York: Oxford University Press.

Bader, A. P. (1995). Engrossment revisited: Fathers are still falling in love with their newborn babies. In J. L. Shapiro, M. J. Diamond, & M. Greenberg (Eds.), *Becoming a father* (pp. 224–233). New York: Springer.

Baenninger, M., & Newcombe, N. (1995). Environmental input to the development of sex-related differences in spatial and mathematical ability. *Learning and Individual Differences, 7,* 363–379.

Bagwell, C. L., Newcomb, A. F., & Bukowski, W. M. (1998). Preadolescent friendship and peer rejection as predictors of adult adjustment. *Child Development, 69,* 140–153.

Bagwell, C. L., Schmidt, M. E., Newcomb, A. F., & Bukowski, W. M. (2001). Friendship and peer rejection as predictors of adult adjustment. In D. W. Nangle & C. A. Erdley (Eds.), *The role of friendship in psychological adjustment* (pp. 25–49). San Francisco: Jossey-Bass.

Bahrick, L. E. (1983). Infants' perception of substance and temporal synchrony in multimodal events. *Infant Behavior and Development, 6,* 429–451.

Bahrick, L. E. (1988). Intermodal learning in infancy: Learning on the basis of two kinds of invariant relations in audible and visible events. *Child Development, 59,* 197–209.

Bahrick, L. E. (1992). Infants' perceptual differentiation of amodal and modality-specific audio-visual relations. *Journal of Experimental Child Psychology, 53,* 180–199.

Bahrick, L. E. (2001). Increasing specificity in perceptual development: Infants' detection of nested levels of multimodal stimulation. *Journal of Experimental Child Psychology, 79,* 253–270.

Bahrick, L. E., Moss, L., & Fadil, C. (1996). Development of visual self-recognition in infancy. *Ecological Psychology, 8,* 189–208.

Bahrick, L. E., Netto, D., & Hernandez-Reif, M. (1998). Intermodal perception of adult and child faces and voices by infants. *Child Development, 69,* 1263–1275.

Bai, D. L., & Bertenthal, B. I. (1992). Locomotor status and the development of spatial search skills. *Child Development, 63,* 215–226.

Bailey, J. M., Bobrow, D., Wolfe, M., & Mikach, S. (1995). Sexual orientation of adult sons of gay fathers. *Developmental Psychology, 31,* 124–129.

Bailey, J. M., & Pillard, R. C. (1991). A genetic study of male sexual orientation. *Archives of General Psychiatry, 43,* 808–812.

Bailey, J. M., Pillard, R. C., Neale, M. C., & Agyei, Y. (1993). Heritable factors influence sexual orientation in women. *Archives of General Psychiatry, 50,* 217–223.

Bailey, R. C. (1990). Growth of African pygmies in early childhood. *New England Journal of Medicine, 323,* 1146.

Bailey, T. (1993). Can youth apprenticeship thrive in the United States? *Educational Researcher, 22* (3), 4–10.

Baillargeon, R. (1994). Physical reasoning in infancy. In M. S. Gazzaniga (Ed.), *The cognitive neurosciences* (pp. 181–204). Cambridge, MA: MIT Press.

Baillargeon, R. (2000). Reply to Bogartz, Shinskey, and Schilling; Schilling; and Cashon and Cohen. *Infancy, 1,* 447–462.

Baillargeon, R., & DeVos, J. (1991). Object permanence in young infants: Further evidence. *Child Development, 62,* 1227–1246.

Bakeman, R., Adamson, L. B., Konner, M., & Barr, R. G. (1990). !Kung infancy: The social context of object exploration. *Child Development, 61,* 794–809.

Baker-Ward, L., Ornstein, P. A., & Holden, D. J. (1984). The expression of memorization in early childhood. *Journal of Experimental Child Psychology, 37,* 555–575.

Balaban, M. T., & Waxman, S. R. (1997). Do words facilitate object categorization in 9-month-old infants? *Journal of Experimental Child Psychology, 64,* 3–26.

Baldwin, A., Baldwin, C., & Cole, R. E. (1990). Stress-resistant families and stress-resistant children. In J. E. Rolf, A. S. Masten, D. Cicchetti, K. N. Wechterlein, & S. Weintraub (Eds.), *Risk and protective factors in the development of psychopathology* (pp. 257–280). New York: Cambridge University Press.

Baldwin, D. A., & Tomasello, M. (1998). Word learning: A window on early pragmatic understanding. In E. V. Clark (Ed.), *Proceedings of the Twenty-Ninth Annual Child Language Research Forum* (pp. 3–23). Stanford, CA: Center for the Study of Language and Information.

Baldwin, J. M. (1895). *Mental development in the child and the race: Methods and processes.* New York: Macmillan.

Baldwin, J. M. (1897). *Social and ethnic interpretations in mental development: A study in social psychology.* New York: Macmillan.

Ballard, B. D., Gipson, M. T., Guttenberg, W., & Ramsey, K. (1980). Palatability of food as a factor influencing obese and normal-weight children's eating habits. *Behavior Research and Therapy, 18,* 598–600.

Bandura, A. (1977). *Social learning theory.* Englewood Cliffs, NJ: Prentice-Hall.

Bandura, A. (1986). *Social foundations of thought and action: A social cognitive theory.* Englewood Cliffs, NJ: Prentice-Hall.

Bandura, A. (1989). Social cognitive theory. In R. Vasta (Ed.), *Annals of child development* (Vol. 6, pp. 1–60). Greenwich, CT: JAI Press.

Bandura, A. (1991). Social cognitive theory of moral thought and action. In W. M. Kurtines & J. L. Gewirtz (Eds.), *Handbook of moral behavior and development* (Vol. 1, pp. 45–103). Hillsdale, NJ: Erlbaum.

Bandura, A. (1992). Perceived self-efficacy in cognitive development and functioning. *Educational Psychologist, 28,* 117–148.

Bandura, A. (1999). Social cognitive theory of personality. In L. A. Pervin & O. P. John (Eds.), *Handbook of personality: Theory and research* (2nd ed., pp. 154–196). New York: Guilford.

Banish, M. T. (1998). Integration of information between the cerebral hemispheres. *Current Directions in Psychological Science, 7,* 32–37.

Banish, M. T., & Heller, W. (1998). Evolving perspectives on lateralization of function. *Current Directions in Psychological Science, 7,* 1–2.

Bank, L., Patterson, G. R., & Reid, J. B. (1996). Negative sibling interaction patterns as predictors of later adjustment problems in adolescent and young adult males. In G. H. Brody (Ed.), *Sibling relationships: Their causes and consequences* (pp. 197–229). Norwood, NJ: Ablex.

Banks, M. S. (1980). The development of visual accommodation during early infancy. *Child Development, 51,* 646–666.

Banks, M. S., & Bennett, P. J. (1988). Optical and photoreceptor immaturities limit the spatial and chromatic vision of human neonates. *Journal of the Optical Society of America, 5,* 2059–2079.

Banks, M. S., & Ginsburg, A. P. (1985). Early visual preferences: A review and new theoretical treatment. In H. W. Reese (Ed.), *Advances in child development and behavior* (Vol. 19, pp. 207–246). New York: Academic Press.

Banks, M. S., & Salapatek, P. (1983). Infant visual perception. In M. M. Haith & J. J. Campos (Eds.), *Handbook of child psychology: Vol. 2. Infancy and developmental psychobiology* (4th ed., pp. 436–571). New York: Wiley.

Barber, B. K., & Harmon, E. L. (2002). Violating the self: Parental psychological control of children and adolescents. In B. K. Barber (Ed.), *Parental psychological control of children and adolescents* (pp. 15–52). Washington, DC: American Psychological Association.

Barber, B. K., & Olsen, J. A. (1997). Socialization in context: Connection, regulation, and autonomy in the family, school, and neighborhood, and with peers. *Journal of Adolescent Research, 12,* 287–315.

Bardwell, J. R., Cochran, S. W., & Walker, S. (1986). Relationship of parental education, race, and gender to sex role stereotyping in five-year-old kindergartners. *Sex Roles, 15,* 275–281.

Barker, D. J. P. (1994). *Mothers, babies, and disease in later life.* London: British Medical Journal Publishing.

Barker, R. G., & Gump, P. V. (1964). *Big school, small school: High school size and student behavior.* Stanford, CA: Stanford University Press.

Barkley, R. A. (1997). Behavioral inhibition, sustained attention, and executive functions: Constructing a unifying theory of ADHD. *Psychological Bulletin, 121,* 65–94.

Barkley, R. A. (1999). Theories of attention-deficit/hyperactivity disorder. In H. C. Quay & A. E. Hogan (Eds.), *Handbook of disruptive behavior disorders* (pp. 295–313). New York: Kluwer.

Barling, J., Rogers, K., & Kelloway, K. (1995). Some effects of teenagers' part-time employment: The quantity and quality of work make the differences. *Journal of Organizational Behavior, 16,* 143–154.

Barnes-Josiah, D., & Augustin, A. (1995). Secular trend in the age at menarche in Haiti. *American Journal of Human Biology, 7,* 357–362.

Barnett, D., Ganiban, J., & Cicchetti, D. (1999). Maltreatment, negative expressivity, and the development of Type D attachments from 12 to 24 months of age. In J. I. Vondra & D. Barnett (Eds.), Atypical attachment in infancy and early childhood among children at developmental risk. *Monographs of the Society for Research in Child Development, 64*(3, Serial No. 258), 97–118.

Barnett, D., & Vondra, J. I. (1999). Atypical patterns of early attachment: Theory, research, and current directions. In J. I. Vondra & D. Barnett (Eds.), Atypical attachment in infancy and early childhood among children at developmental risk. *Monographs of the Society for Research in Child Development, 64*(3, Serial No. 258), 1–24.

Barnett, W. S. (1998). Long-term cognitive and academic effects of early childhood education on children in poverty. *Preventive Medicine, 27,* 204–207.

Baron, S. W. (1999). Street youths and substance use: The role of background, street lifestyle and economic factors. *Youth and Society, 31,* 3–26.

Baron-Cohen, S. (1995). *Mindblindness: An essay on autism and theory of mind.* Cambridge, MA: Cambridge University Press.

Baron-Cohen, S., Baldwin, D. A., & Crowson, M. (1997). Do children with autism use the speaker's direction of gaze strategy to crack the code of language? *Child Development, 68,* 48–57.

Barr, H. M., Streissguth, A. P., Darby, B. L., & Sampson, P. D. (1990). Prenatal exposure to alcohol, caffeine, tobacco, and aspirin: Effects on fine and gross motor performance in 4-year-old children. *Developmental Psychology, 26,* 339–348.

Barr, R. G., Chen, S., Hopkins, B., & Westra, T. (1996). Crying patterns in preterm infants. *Developmental Medicine and Child Neurology, 38,* 345–355.

Barr, R. G., & Gunnar, M. (2000). Colic: The 'transient responsivity' hypothesis. In R. G. Barr, B. Hopkins, & J. A. Green (Eds.), *Crying as a sign, a symptom, and a signal* (pp. 41–66). New York: Cambridge University Press.

Barr, R., & Hayne, H. (1999). Developmental changes in imitation from television during infancy. *Child Development, 70,* 1067–1081.

Barr, R. G., Konner, M., Bakeman, R., & Adamson, L. (1991). Crying in !Kung San infants: A test of the cultural specificity hypothesis. *Developmental Medicine and Child Neurology, 33,* 601–610.

Barratt, M. S., Roach, M. A., & Leavitt, L. A. (1996). The impact of low-risk prematurity on maternal behaviour and toddler outcomes. *International Journal of Behavioral Development, 19,* 581–602.

Barrett, K. C. (1998). The origins of guilt in early childhood. In J. Bybee (Ed.), *Guilt and children* (pp. 75–90). San Diego: Academic Press.

Barrett, K. C., & Campos, J. J. (1987). Perspectives on emotional development II: A functionalist approach to emotions. In J. D. Osofsky (Ed.), *Handbook of infant development* (2nd ed., pp. 555–578). New York: Wiley.

Barriga, A. Q., Morrison, E. M., Liau, A. K., & Gibbs, J. C. (2001). Moral cognition: Explaining the gender difference in antisocial behavior. *Merrill-Palmer Quarterly, 47,* 532–562.

Barron, F. (1988). Putting creativity to work. In R. J. Sternberg (Ed.), *The nature of creativity: Contemporary psychological perspectives* (pp. 76–98). New York: Cambridge University Press.

Bartlett, F. C. (1932). *Remembering.* Cambridge: Cambridge University Press.

Barton, M. E., & Strosberg, R. (1997). Conversational patterns of two-year-old twins in mother–twin–twin triads. *Journal of Child Language, 24,* 257–269.

Barton, M. E., & Tomasello, M. (1991). Joint attention and conversation in mother-infant-sibling triads. *Child Development, 62,* 517–529.

Bartrip, J., Morton, J., & de Schonen, S. (2001). Responses to mother's face in 3-week to 5-month-old infants. *British Journal of Developmental Psychology, 19,* 219–232.

Bartsch, K., & London, K. (2000). Children's use of mental state information in selecting persuasive arguments. *Developmental Psychology, 36,* 352–365.

Bartsch, K., & Wellman, H. M. (1995). *Children talk about the mind.* New York: Oxford University Press.

Basinger, K. S., Gibbs, J. C., & Fuller, D. (1995). Context and the measurement of moral judgment. *International Journal of Behavioral Development, 18,* 537–556.

Basow, S. A., & Rubin, L. R. (1999). Gender influences on adolescent development. In N. G. Johnson & M. C. Roberts (Eds.), *Beyond appearance: A new look at adolescent girls* (pp. 25–52). Washington, DC: American Psychological Association.

Bates, E. (1999). Plasticity, localization, and language development. In S. H. Broman & J. M. Fletcher (Eds.), *The changing nervous system: Neurobehavioral consequences of early brain disorders* (pp. 214–247). New York: Oxford University Press.

Bates, E., Elman, J., Johnson, M. C., Karmiloff-Smith, A., Parisi, D., & Plunkett, K. (1998). Innateness and emergentism. In W. Bechtel & G. Graham (Eds.), *A companion to cognitive science* (pp. 590–601). New York: Oxford University Press.

Bates, E., & MacWhinney, B. (1987). Competition, variation, and language learning. In B. MacWhinney (Ed.), *Mechanisms of language acquisition* (pp. 157–193). Hillsdale, NJ: Erlbaum.

Bates, E., Marchman, V., Thal, D., Fenson, L., Dale, P., Reznick, J. S., Reilly, J., & Hartung, J. (1994). Developmental and stylistic variation in the composition of early vocabulary. *Journal of Child Language, 21,* 85–123.

Bates, J. E., Pettit, G. S., Dodge, K. A., & Ridge, B. (1998). Interaction of temperamental resistance to control and restrictive parenting in the development of externalizing behavior. *Developmental Psychology, 34,* 982–995.

Bates, J. E., Wachs, T. D., & Emde, R. N. (1994). Toward practical uses for biological concepts. In J. E. Bates & T. D. Wachs (Eds.), *Temperament: Individual differences at the interface of biology and behavior* (pp. 275–306). Washington, DC: American Psychological Association.

Bauer, P. J. (1996). What do infants recall of their lives? Memory for specific events by one- to two-year-olds. *American Psychologist, 51,* 29–41.

Bauer, P. J. (1997). Development of memory in early childhood. In N. Cowan (Ed.), *The development of memory in childhood* (pp. 83–111). Hove, UK: Psychology Press.

Bauman, A., & Phongsavan, P. (1999). Epidemiology of substance use in adolescence: Trends and policy implications. *Drug and Alcohol Dependence, 55,* 187–207.

Baumeister, R. F. (1998). Inducing guilt. In J. Bybee (Ed.), *Guilt and children* (pp. 185–213). San Diego: Academic Press.

Baumeister, R. F., Smart, L., & Boden, J. M. (1996). Relation of threatened egotism to violence and aggression: The dark side of high self-esteem. *Psychological Review, 103,* 5–33.

Baumrind, D. (1967). Child care practices anteceding three patterns of preschool behavior. *Genetic Psychology Monographs, 75,* 43–88.

Baumrind, D. (1971). Current patterns of parental authority. *Developmental Psychology Monograph, 4*(1, Pt. 2).

Baumrind, D. (1991). The influence of parenting style on adolescent competence and substance use. *Journal of Early Adolescence, 11,* 56–95.

Baumrind, D., & Black, A. E. (1967). Socialization practices associated with dimensions of competence in preschool boys and girls. *Child Development, 38,* 291–327.

Bayley, N. (1969). *Bayley Scales of Infant Development.* New York: Psychological Corporation.

Bayley, N. (1993). *Bayley Scales of Infant Development* (2nd ed.). New York: Psychological Corporation.

Baynes, K., & Gazzaniga, M. S. (1988). Right hemisphere language: Insights into normal language mechanisms. In F. Plum (Ed.), *Language, communication, and the brain* (pp. 117–126). New York: Raven.

Beal, C. R. (1990). The development of text evaluation and revision skills. *Child Development, 61,* 247–258.

Bearison, D. J. (1998). Pediatric psychology and children's medical problems. In I. G. Sigel & K. A. Renninger (Eds.), *Handbook of child psychology: Vol. 4. Child psychology in practice* (5th ed., pp. 635–711). New York: Wiley.

Beatty, W. W. (1992). Gonadal hormones and sex differences in nonreproductive behaviors. In A. A. Gerall, H. Moltz, & I. L. Ward (Eds.), *Handbook of behavioral neurobiology: Vol. 11. Sexual differentiation* (pp. 85–128). New York: Plenum.

Beauchamp, G. K., Cowart, B. J., Mennella, J. A., & Marsh, R. R. (1994). Infant salt taste: Developmental, methodological, and contextual factors. *Developmental Psychobiology, 27,* 353–365.

Beausang, C. C., & Razor, A. G. (2000). Young Western women's experiences of menarche and menstruation. *Health Care for Women International, 21,* 517–528.

Becker, H. J. (2000). Who's wired and who's not: Children's access to and use of computer technology. *Future of Children, 10,* 44–75.

Becker, J. (1990). Processes in the acquisition of pragmatic competence. In G. Conti-Ramsden & C. Snow (Eds.), *Children's language* (Vol. 7, pp. 7–24). Hillsdale, NJ: Erlbaum.

Beere, C. A. (1990). *Gender roles: A handbook of tests and measures.* New York: Greenwood Press.

Begley, S. (1995, February 13). Surprising new lessons from the controversial science of race. *Newsweek,* pp. 67–68.

Behrman, R. D., Kliegman, R. M., & Arvin, A. M. (Eds.). (1996). *Nelson textbook of pediatrics* (15th ed.). Philadelphia: Saunders.

Behrman, R. E., Kiegman, R. M., & Jenson, H. B. (2000). *Nelson textbook of pediatrics* (16th ed.). Philadelphia: Saunders.

Beilin, H. (1992). Piaget's enduring contribution to developmental psychology. *Developmental Psychology, 28,* 191–204.

Beitel, A. H., & Parke, R. D. (1998). Paternal involvement in infancy: The role of maternal and paternal attitudes. *Journal of Family Psychology, 12,* 268–288.

Bell, A., Weinberg, M., & Hammersmith, S. (1981). *Sexual preference: Its development in men and women.* Bloomington: Indiana University Press.

Bell, K. L., Allen, J. P., Hauser, S. T., & O'Connor, T. G. (1996). Family factors and young adult transitions: Educational attainment and occupational prestige. In J. A. Graber, J. Brooks-Gunn, & A. C. Petersen (Eds.), *Transitions through adolescence: Interpersonal domains and contexts* (pp. 345–366). Mahwah, NJ: Erlbaum.

Bell, M. A. (1998). Frontal lobe function during infancy: Implications for the development of cognition and attention. In J. E. Richards (Ed.), *Cognitive neuroscience of attention: A developmental perspective* (pp. 327–362). Mahwah, NJ: Erlbaum.

Bell, M. A., & Fox, N. A. (1994). Brain development over the first year of life: Relations between EEG frequency and coherence and cognitive and affective behaviors. In G. Dawson & K. W. Fischer (Eds.), *Human behavior and the developing brain* (pp. 314–345). New York: Guilford.

Bell, M. A., & Fox, N. A. (1996). Crawling experience is related to changes in cortical organization during infancy: Evidence from EEG coherence. *Developmental Psychobiology, 29,* 551–561.

Bell, M. A., & Fox, N. A. (1998). Crawling experience is related to changes in cortical organization during infancy: Evidence from EEG coherence. *Developmental Psychology, 29,* 551–561.

Bell, S. M., & Ainsworth, M. D. S. (1972). Infant crying and maternal responsiveness. *Child Development, 43,* 1171–1190.

Bellamy, C. (1998). *The state of the world's children 1998.* New York: Oxford University Press (in cooperation with UNICEF).

Bellamy, C. (2000). *The state of the world's children 2000.* New York: Oxford University Press (in cooperation with UNICEF).

Bell-Dolan, D. J., & Wessler, A. E. (1994). Ethical administration of sociometric measures: Procedures in use and suggestions for improvement. *Professional Psychology—Research and Practice, 25,* 23–32.

Bell-Dolan, D. J., Foster, S. L., & Sikora, D. M. (1989). Effects of sociometric testing on children's behavior and loneliness in school. *Developmental Psychology, 25,* 306–311.

Belle, D. (1997). A qualitative look at children's experiences in the after-school hours. *Merrill-Palmer Quarterly, 43,* 478–496.

Bellugi, U., Bihrle, A., Neville, H., Jernigan, T., & Doherty, S. (1992). Language, cognition, and brain organization in a neurodevelopmental disorder. In M. Gunnar & C. Nelson (Eds.), *Developmental behavioral neuroscience* (pp. 201–232). Hillsdale, NJ: Erlbaum.

Bellugi, U., & Wang, P. P. (1999). Williams syndrome: From cognition to brain to gene. In *Encyclopaedia of Neuroscience.* Amsterdam: Elsevier Science.

Belsky, J. (1989). Infant-parent attachment and day care: In defense of the Strange Situation. In J. Lande, S. Scarr, & N. Gunzenhauser (Eds.), *Caring for children: Challenge to America* (pp. 23–48). Hillsdale, NJ: Erlbaum.

Belsky, J. (1992). Consequences of child care for children's development: A deconstructionist view. In A. Booth (Ed.), *Child care in the 1990s: Trends and consequences* (pp. 83–85). Hillsdale, NJ: Erlbaum.

Belsky, J., & Cassidy, J. (1994). Attachment: Theory and evidence. In M. Rutter & D. Hay (Eds.), *Development through life* (pp. 373–402). Oxford, England: Blackwell.

Bem, S. L. (1977). On the utility of alternative procedures for assessing psychological androgyny. *Journal of Consulting and Clinical Psychology, 45,* 196–205.

Bem, S. L. (1989). Genital knowledge and gender constancy in preschool children. *Child Development, 60,* 649–662.

Bem, S. L. (1993). *The lenses of gender: Transforming the debate on sexual inequality.* New Haven, CT: Yale University Press.

Bem, S. L. (1998). *An unconventional family.* New Haven, CT: Yale University Press.

Bempechat, J., & Drago-Severson, E. (1999). Cross-national differences in academic achievement: Beyond etic conceptions of children's understandings. *Review of Educational Research, 69,* 287–314.

Benbow, C. P., Lubinski, D., Shea, D. L., & Eftekhara-Sanjani, H. (2000). Sex differences in mathematical reasoning ability at age 13: Their status 20 years later. *Psychological Science, 11,* 474–480.

Benbow, C. P., & Stanley, J. C. (1983). Sex differences in mathematical reasoning: More facts. *Science, 222,* 1029–1031.

Bender, S. L., Word, C. O., DiClemente, R. J., Crittenden, M. R., Persaud, N. A., & Ponton, L. (1995). The developmental implications of prenatal and/or postnatal crack cocaine exposure in preschool children: A preliminary report. *Developmental and Behavioral Pediatrics, 16,* 418–424.

Bendersky, M., & Lewis, M. (1994). Environmental risk, biological risk, and developmental outcome. *Developmental Psychology, 30,* 484–494.

Benedict, R. (1934). *Patterns of culture.* Boston: Houghton Mifflin.

Benenson, J. F. (1993). Greater preference among females than males for dyadic interaction in early childhood. *Child Development, 64,* 544–555.

Benenson, J. F., Apostoleris, N. H., & Parnass, J. (1997). Age and sex differences in dyadic and group interaction. *Developmental Psychology, 33,* 538–543.

Benenson, J. F., Nicholson, C., Waite, A., Roy, R., & Simpson, A. (2001). The influence of group size on children's competitive behavior. *Child Development, 72,* 921–928.

Benjamin, W., Schneider, B., Greenman, P., & Hum, M. (2001). Conflict and childhood friendship in Taiwan and Canada. *Canadian Journal of Behavioural Science, 33,* 203–211.

Bennetto, L., Pennington, B. F., & Rogers, S. J. (1996). Intact and impaired memory functions in autism. *Child Development, 67,* 1816–1835.

Benoit, D., & Parker, K. C. H. (1994). Stability and transmission of attachment across three generations. *Child Development, 65,* 1444–1456.

Berenbaum, S. A. (1999). Effects of early androgens on sex-typed activities and interests in adolescents with congenital adrenal hyperplasia. *Hormones and Behavior, 35,* 102–110.

Berenbaum, S. A. (2001). Cognitive function in congenital adrenal hyperplasia. *Endocrinology and Metabolism Clinics of North America, 30,* 173–192.

Berenbaum, S. A., Duck, S. C., & Bryk, K. (2000). Behavioral effects of prenatal versus postnatal androgen excess in children with 21-hydroxylase-deficient congenital adrenal hyperplasia. *Journal of Clinical Endocrinology and Metabolism, 85,* 727–733.

Berenbaum, S. A., & Hines, M. (1992). Early androgens are related to childhood sex-typed toy preferences. *Psychological Science, 3,* 203–206.

Berenbaum, S. A., & Snyder, E. (1995). Early hormonal influences on childhood sex-typed activity and playmate preferences: Implications for the development of sexual orientation. *Developmental Psychology, 31,* 31–42.

Bergen, D., & Mauer, D. (2000). Symbolic play, phonological awareness, and literacy skills at three age levels. In K. A. Roskos & J. F. Christie (Eds.), *Play and literacy in early childhood: Research from multiple perspectives* (pp. 45–62). Mahwah, NJ: Erlbaum.

Berk, L. E. (1985). Relationship of caregiver education to child-oriented attitudes, job satisfaction, and behaviors toward children. *Child Care Quarterly, 14,* 103–129.

Berk, L. E. (1992). Children's private speech: An overview of theory and the status of research. In R. M. Diaz & L. E. Berk (Eds.), *Private speech: From social interaction to* self-regulation (pp. 17–53). Hillsdale, NJ: Erlbaum.

Berk, L. E. (2001a). *Awakening children's minds: How parents and teachers can make a difference.* New York: Oxford University Press.

Berk, L. E. (2001b). Private speech and self-regulation in children with impulse-control difficulties: Implications for research and practice. *Journal of Cognitive Education and Psychology, 2,* 1–21.

Berk, L. E. (2002). Development. In J. Halonen & S. Davis (Eds.), *The many faces of psychological research in the twenty-first century.* Society for Teachers of Psychology. [On-line]. Available: teachpsych. lemoyne.edu/teachpsych/faces/facesindex. html

Berk, L. E., & Landau, S. (1993). Private speech of learning disabled and normally achieving children in classroom academic and laboratory contexts. *Child Development, 64,* 556–571.

Berk, L. E., & Spuhl, S. T. (1995). Maternal interaction, private speech, and task performance in preschool children. *Early Childhood Research Quarterly, 10,* 145–169.

Berk, L. E., & Winsler, A. (1995). *Scaffolding children's learning: Vygotsky and early childhood education.* Washington, DC: National Association for the Education of Young Children.

Berkey, C. S., Wang, X., Dockery, D. W., & Ferris, B. G., Jr. (1994). Adolescent height growth of U.S. children. *Annals of Human Biology, 21,* 435–442.

Berkowitz, M. W., & Gibbs, J. C. (1983). Measuring the developmental features of moral discussion. *Merrill-Palmer Quarterly, 29,* 399–410.

Berlin, L. J., Brooks-Gunn, J., McCarton, C., & McCormick, M. C. (1998). The effectiveness of early intervention: Examining risk factors and pathways to enhanced development. *Preventive Medicine, 27,* 238–245.

Berman, P. (1980). Are women more responsive than men to the young? A review of developmental and situational variables. *Psychological Bulletin, 88,* 668–695.

Bermejo, V. (1996). Cardinality development and counting. *Developmental Psychology, 32,* 263–268.

Berndt, T. J. (1998). Exploring the effects of friendship quality on social development. In W. M. Bukowski, A. F. Newcomb, & W. W. Hartup (Eds.), *The company they keep: Friendship in childhood and adolescence* (pp. 346–365). New York: Cambridge University Press.

Berndt, T. J., Cheung, P. C., Lau, S., Hau, K.-T., & Lew, W. J. F. (1993). Perceptions of parenting in mainland China, Taiwan, and Hong Kong: Sex differences and societal differences. *Developmental Psychology, 29,* 156–164.

Berndt, T. J., & Keefe, K. (1995). Friends' influence on adolescents' adjustment to school. *Child Development, 66,* 1312–1329.

Bernier, J. C., & Siegel, D. H. (1994). Attention-deficit hyperactivity disorder: A family ecological systems perspective. *Families in Society, 75,* 142–150.

Bersoff, D. M., & Miller, J. G. (1993). Culture, context, and the development of moral accountability judgments. *Developmental Psychology, 29,* 664–676.

Bertenthal, B. I. (1993). Infants' perception of biomechanical motions: Instrinsic image and knowledge-based constraints. In C. Granrud (Ed.), *Visual perception and cognition in infancy* (pp. 175–214). Hillsdale, NJ: Erlbaum.

Bertenthal, B. I. (1996). Origins and early development of perception, action, and representation. *Annual Review of Psychology, 47,* 431–459.

Bertenthal, B. I., Campos, J. J., & Barrett, K. (1984). Self-produced locomotion: An organizer of emotional, cognitive, and social development in infancy. In R. Emde & R. Harmon (Eds.), *Continuities and discontinuities in development* (pp. 174–210). New York: Plenum.

Bertenthal, B. I., & Clifton, R. K. (1998). Perception and action. In D. Kuhn & R. S. Siegler (Eds.), *Handbook of child psychology: Vol. 2. Cognition, perception, and language* (pp. 51–102). New York: Wiley.

Bertenthal, B. I., Proffitt, D. R., Kramer, S. J., & Spetner, N. B. (1987). Infants' encoding of kinetic displays varying in relative coherence. *Developmental Psychology, 23,* 171–178.

Bertenthal, B. I., Proffitt, D. R., Spetner, N. B., & Thomas, M. A. (1985). The development of infant sensitivity to biomechanical motions. *Child Development, 56,* 531–543.

Bertenthal, B. I., Rose, J. L., & Bai, D. L. (1997). Perception–action coupling in the development of visual control of posture. *Journal of Experimental Psychology: Human Perception and Performance, 23,* 1631–1643.

Bertenthal, B., & von Hofsten, C. (1998). Eye, head and trunk control: The foundation for manual development. *Neuroscience and Biobehavioral Reviews, 22,* 515–520.

Berzonsky, M. D. (1993). A constructivist view of identity development: People as postpositivist self-theorists. In J. Kroger (Ed.), *Discussions on ego identity* (pp. 169–203). Hillsdale, NJ: Erlbaum.

Berzonsky, M. D., & Kuk, L. S. (2000). Identity status, identity processing style, and the transition to university. *Journal of Adolescent Research, 15,* 81–98.

Best, D. L. (2001). Gender concepts: Convergence in cross-cultural research and methodologies. *Cross-cultural Research: The Journal of Comparative Social Science, 35,* 23–43.

Betz, C. (1994). Beyond time-out: Tips from a teacher. *Young Children, 49*(3), 10–14.

Beyth-Marom, R., & Fischhoff, B. (1997). Adolescents' decisions about risks: A cognitive perspective. In J. Schulenberg, J. L. Maggs, & K. Hurrelmann (Eds.), *Health risks and developmental transitions during adolescence* (pp. 110–135). New York: Cambridge University Press.

Bhatia, T. K., & Ritchie, W. C. (1999). The bilingual child: Some issues and perspectives. In W. C. Ritchie & T. K. Bhatia (Eds.), *Handbook of child language acquisition* (pp. 569–643). San Diego: Academic Press.

Bhatt, R. S., Rovee-Collier, C. K. & Weiner, S. (1994). Developmental changes in the interface between perception and memory retrieval. *Developmental Psychology, 30,* 151–162.

Bialystok, E. (1986). Factors in the growth of linguistic awareness. *Child Development, 57,* 498–510.

Bialystok, E. (1999). Cognitive complexity and attentional control in the bilingual mind. *Child Development, 70,* 636–644.

Bialystok, E. (2001). *Bilingualism in development: Language, literacy, and cognition.* New York: Cambridge University Press.

Bialystok, E., & Hakuta, K. (1999). Confounded age: Linguistic and cognitive factors in age differences in second language acquisition. In D. Birdsong (Ed.), *Second language acquisition and the critical period hypothesis* (pp. 161–181). Mahwah, NJ: Erlbaum.

Bialystok, E., & Herman, J. (1999). Does bilingualism matter for early literacy? *Language and Cognition, 2,* 35–44.

Bianco, A., Stone, J., Lynch, L., Lapinski, R., Berkowitz, G., & Berkowitz, R. L. (1996). Pregnancy outcome at age 40 and older. *Obstetrics and Gynecology, 87,* 917–922.

Bibace, R., & Walsh, M. E. (1980). Development of children's concepts of illness. *Pediatrics, 66,* 912–917.

Bickerton, D. (1981). *Roots of language.* Ann Arbor, MI: Karoma.

Bickerton, D. (1999). Creole languages, the language bioprogram hypothesis, and language acquisition. In W. C. Ritchie (Ed.), *Handbook of child language acquisition* (pp. 195–220). San Diego, CA: Academic Press.

Bidell, T. R., & Fischer, K. W. (1992). Cognitive development in educational contexts: Implications for skill learning. In A. Demetriou, M. Shayer, & A. Efklides (Eds.), *Neo-Piagetian theories of cognitive development* (pp. 11–31). London: Routledge & Kegan Paul.

Biederman, J., & Spencer, T. J. (2000). Genetics of childhood disorders: XIX. ADHD, part 3: Is ADHD a noradrenergic disorder? *Journal of the American Academy of Child and Adolescent Psychiatry, 39,* 1330–1333.

Bielinski, J., & Davison, M. L. (1998). Gender differences by item difficulty interactions in multiple-choice mathematics items. *American Educational Research Journal, 35,* 455–476.

Bierman, K. L., Miller, C. L., & Stabb, S. D. (1987). Improving the social behavior and peer acceptance of rejected boys: Effects of social skill training with instructions and prohibitions. *Journal of Consulting and Clinical Psychology, 55,* 194–200.

Biernat, M. (1991). A multi-component, developmental analysis of sex-typing. *Sex Roles, 24,* 567–586.

Bigelow, A. (1992). Locomotion and search behavior in blind infants. *Infant Behavior and Development, 15,* 179–189.

Bigelow, B., Levin, E., & Cunning, S. (1994). Support and control in parent-child relations from childhood to early adolescence. The Maccoby-Minuchin hypothesis. In E. Porter, G. Tesson, & J. Lewko (Eds.), *Sociological studies of children* (pp. 197–219). Greenwich, CT: JAI Press.

Bigler, R. S. (1995). The role of classification skill in moderating environmental influences on children's gender stereotyping: A study of the functional use of gender in the classroom. *Child Development, 66,* 1072–1087.

Bigler, R. S., Brown, C. S., & Markell, M. (2001). When groups are not created equal: Effects of group status on the formation of intergroup attitudes in children. *Child Development, 72,* 1151–1162.

Bigler, R. S., & Liben, L. S. (1992). Cognitive mechanisms in children's gender stereotyping: Theoretical and educational implications of a cognitive-based intervention. *Child Development, 63,* 1351–1363.

Bigler, R. S., & Liben, L. S. (1993). A cognitive-developmental approach to racial stereotyping and reconstructive memory in Euro-American children. *Child Development, 64,* 1507–1518.

Bigner, J. J. (2000). Gay and lesbian families. In W. C. Nichols & M. A. Pace-Nichols (Eds.), *Handbook of family development and intervention* (pp. 279–298). New York: Wiley.

Bigner, J. J., & Jacobsen, R. B. (1989). Parenting behaviors of homosexual and heterosexual fathers. *Journal of Homosexuality, 18,* 173–186.

Bijeljac-Babic, R., Bertoncini, J., & Mehler, J. (1993). How do 4-day-old infants categorize multisyllable utterances? *Developmental Psychology, 29,* 711–721.

Birch, E. E. (1993). Stereopsis in infants and its developmental relation to visual acuity. In K. Simons (Ed.), *Early visual development: Normal and abnormal* (pp. 224–236). New York: Oxford University Press.

Birch, L. L. (1998). Psychological influences on the childhood diet. *Journal of Nutrition, 128,* 407S–410S.

Birch, L. L., & Fisher, J. A. (1995). Appetite and eating behavior in children. *Pediatric Clinics of North America, 42,* 931–953.

Birch, L. L., Zimmerman, S., & Hind, H. (1980). The influence of social-affective context on preschool children's food preferences. *Child Development, 51,* 856–861.

Birch, S. H., & Ladd, G. W. (1997). The teacher–child relationship and children's early school adjustment. *Journal of School Psychology, 35,* 61–79.

Birch, S. H., & Ladd, G. W. (1998). Children's interpersonal behaviors and the teacher–child relationship. *Developmental Psychology, 34,* 934–946.

Biringen, Z., Emde, R. N., Campos, J. J., & Appelbaum, M. I. (1995). Affective reorganization in the infant, the mother, and the dyad: The role of upright locomotion and its timing. *Child Development, 66,* 499–514.

Birmaher, B., Ryan, N., Williamson, D., Brent, D., & Kaufman, J. (1996). Childhood and adolescent depression: A review of the past 10 years. Part II. *Journal of the American Academy of Child and Adolescent Psychiatry, 35,* 1575–1583.

Biro, F. M., McMahon, R. P., Striegel-Moore, R., Crawford, P. B., Obarzanek, E., & Morrison, J. A. (2001). Impact of timing of pubertal maturation on growth in black and white female adolescents: The National Heart, Lung, and Blood Institute Growth and Health Study. *Journal of Pediatrics, 138,* 636–643.

Bisanz, J., Morrison, F. J., & Dunn, M. (1995). Effects of age and schooling on the acquisition of elementary quantitative skills. *Developmental Psychology, 31,* 221–236.

Bischofshausen, S. (1985). Developmental differences in schema dependency for temporally ordered story events. *Journal of Psycholinguistic Research, 14,* 543–556.

Bivens, J. A., & Berk, L. E. (1990). A longitudinal study of the development of elementary school children's private speech. *Merrill-Palmer Quarterly, 36,* 443–463.

Bjorklund, D. F. (1997). The role of immaturity in human development. *Psychological Bulletin, 122,* 153–169.

Bjorklund, D. F. (2000). *Children's thinking* (3rd ed.). Belmont, CA: Wadsworth.

Bjorklund, D. F., Cassel, W. S., Bjorklund, B. R., Brown, R. D., Park, C. L., Ernst, K., & Owen, F. A. (2000). Social demand characteristics in children's and adults' eyewitness memory and suggestibility: The effect of different interviewers on free recall and recognition. *Applied Cognitive Psychology, 14,* 421–423.

Bjorklund, D. F., & Coyle, T. R. (1995). Utilization deficiencies in the development of memory strategies. In F. E. Weinert & W. Schneider (Eds.), *Research on memory development: State of the art and future directions* (pp. 161–180). Hillsdale, NJ: Erlbaum.

Bjorklund, D. F., & Douglas, R. N. (1997). The development of memory strategies. In N. Cowan (Ed.), *The development of memory in childhood* (pp. 83–111). Hove, UK: Psychology Press.

Bjorklund, D. F., & Harnishfeger, K. K. (1995). The evolution of inhibition mechanisms and their role in human cognition and behavior. In M. L. Howe & R. Pasnak (Eds.), *Emerging themes in cognitive development: Vol. 1. Foundations* (pp. 141–173). New York: Springer-Verlag.

Bjorklund, D. F., & Pellegrini, A. D. (2000). Child development and evolutionary psychology. *Child Development, 71,* 1687–1708.

Bjorklund, D. F., Schneider, W., Cassel, W. S., & Ashley, E. (1994). Training and extension of a memory strategy: Evidence for utilization deficiencies in high- and low-IQ children. *Child Development, 65,* 951–965.

Blachman, B. A. (2000). Phonological awareness. In M. L. Kamil & P. B. Mosenthal (Eds.), *Handbook of reading research* (Vol. 3, pp. 483–502). Mahwah, NJ: Erlbaum.

Blake, I. K. (1994). Language development and socialization in young African-American children. In P. M. Greenfield & R. R. Cocking (Eds.), *Cross-cultural roots of minority child development* (pp. 167–195). Hillsdale, NJ: Erlbaum.

Blake, J., & de Boysson-Bardies, B. (1992). Patterns in babbling: A cross-linguistic study. *Journal of Child Language, 19,* 51–74.

Blanchard, B., & Bogaert, A. F. (1996). Homosexuality in men and number of older brothers. *American Journal of Psychiatry, 153,* 27–31.

Blanchard, M., & Main, M. (1979). Avoidance of the attachment figure and social-emotional adjustment in day-care infants. *Developmental Psychology, 15,* 445–446.

Blanchard, R., Zucker, K. J., Bradley, S. J., & Hume, C. S. (1995). Birth order and sibling sex ratio in homosexual male adolescents and probably prehomosexual feminine boys. *Developmental Psychology, 31,* 22–30.

Blasi, A. (1994). Bridging moral cognition and moral action: A critical review of the literature. In B. Puka (Ed.), *Fundamental research in moral development: A compendium* (Vol. 2, pp. 123–167). New York: Garland.

Blass, E. M. (1999). Savoring sucrose and suckling milk: Easing pain, saving calories, and learning about mother. In M. Lewis & D. Ramsay (Eds.), *Soothing and stress* (pp. 79–107). Mahwah, NJ: Erlbaum.

Blass, E. M., Ganchrow, J. R., & Steiner, J. E. (1984). Classical conditioning in newborn humans 2–48 hours of age. *Infant Behavior and Development, 7,* 223–235.

Blatchford, P., Baines, E., Kutnick, P., & Martin, C. (2001). Classroom contexts: Connections between class size and within class grouping. *British Journal of Educational Psychology, 71,* 283–302.

Blatt, M., & Kohlberg, L. (1975). The effects of classroom moral discussion upon children's level of moral judgment. *Journal of Moral Education, 4,* 129–161.

Blewitt, P. (1994). Understanding categorical hierarchies: The earliest levels of skill. *Child Development, 65,* 1279–1298.

Block, J., & Block, J. H. (1980). *The California Child Q-Set.* Palo Alto, CA: Consulting Psychologists Press.

Block, J. H. (1978). Another look at sex differentiation in the socialization behaviors of mothers and fathers. In J. Sherman & F. L. Denmark (Eds.), *Psychology of women: Future directions for research* (pp. 29–87). New York: Psychological Dimensions.

Block, J. H., Block, J., & Harrington, D. (1975). *Sex role typing and instrumental behavior: A developmental study.* Paper presented at the annual meeting of the Society for Research in Child Development, Denver.

Bloom, L. (1970). *Language development: Form and function in emerging grammars.* Cambridge, MA: MIT Press.

Bloom, L. (1991). *Language development from two to three.* New York: Cambridge University Press.

Bloom, L. (1998). Language acquisition in its developmental context. In D. Kuhn & R. S. Siegler (Eds.), *Handbook of child psychology: Vol. 2. Cognition, perception, and language* (5th ed., pp. 309–370). New York: Wiley.

Bloom, L. (2000). The intentionality model of language development: How to learn a word, any word. In R. Golinkoff, K. Hirsh-Pasek, N. Akhtar, L. Bloom, G. Hollich, L. Smith, M. Tomasello, & A. Woodward (Eds.), *Becoming a word learner: A debate on lexical acquisition.* New York: Oxford University Press.

Bloom, L., Lahey, M., Liften, K., & Fiess, K. (1980). Complex sentences: Acquisition of syntactic connections and the semantic relations they encode. *Journal of Child Language, 7,* 235–256.

Bloom, L., Margulis, C., Tinker E., & Fujita, N. (1996). Early conversations and word learning: Contributions from child and adult. *Child Development, 67,* 3154–3175.

Bloom, P. (1999). The role of semantics in solving the bootstrapping problem. In R. Jackendoff & P. Bloom (Eds.), *Language, logic, and concepts* (pp. 285–309). Cambridge, MA: MIT Press.

Blotner, R., & Bearison, D. J. (1984). Developmental consistencies in socio-moral knowledge: Justice reasoning and altruistic behavior. *Merrill-Palmer Quarterly, 30,* 349–367.

Bluestone, C., & Tamis-LeMonda, C. S. (1999). Correlates of parenting styles in predominantly working- and middle-class African-American mothers. *Journal of Marriage and the Family, 61,* 881–893.

Blum, N. J., & Carey, W. B. (1996). Sleep problems among infants and young children. *Pediatrics in Review, 17,* 87–93.

Blumberg, M. S., & Lucas, D. E. (1996). A developmental and component analysis of active sleep. *Developmental Psychobiology, 29,* 1–22.

Blyth, D. A., Simmons, R. G., & Zakin, D. F. (1985). Satisfaction with body image for early adolescent females: The impact of pubertal timing within different school environments. *Journal of Youth and Adolescence, 14,* 207–225.

Bock, G. R., & Goode, J. A. (Eds.). (1996). *Genetics of criminal and antisocial behavior, Ciba Foundation Symposium 194.* Chichester, England: Wiley.

Bogartz, R. S., Shinskey, J. L., & Schilling, T. H. (2000). Object permanence in five-and-a-half-month-old infants. *Infancy, 1,* 403–428.

Bohannon, J. N., III, & Bonvillian, J. D. (2001). Theoretical approaches to language acquisition. In J. Berko Gleason (Ed.), *The development of language* (5th ed., pp. 254–314). Boston: Allyn and Bacon.

Bohannon, J. N., III, & Stanowicz, L. (1988). The issue of negative evidence: Adult responses to children's language errors. *Developmental Psychology, 24,* 684–689.

Bohlin, G., Hagekull, B., & Rydell, A. (2000). Attachment and social functioning: A longitudinal study from infancy to middle childhood. *Social Development, 9,* 24–39.

Bohman, M. (1996). Predispositions to criminality: Swedish adoption studies in retrospect. In G. R. Bock & J. A. Goode (Eds.), *Genetics of criminal and antisocial behavior, Ciba Foundation Symposium 194* (pp. 99–114). Chichester, England: Wiley.

Bohman, M., & Sigvardsson, S. (1990). Outcome in adoption: Lessons from longitudinal studies. In D. M. Bordzkinsky & M. D. Schechter (Eds.), *The psychology of adoption* (pp. 93–106). New York: Oxford University Press.

Boivin, M., & Hymel, S. (1997). Peer experiences and social self-perceptions: A sequential model. *Developmental Psychology, 33,* 135–145.

Boldizar, J. P. (1991). Assessing sex typing and androgyny in children: The children's sex role inventory. *Developmental Psychology, 27,* 505–515.

Boldizar, J. P., Perry, D. G., & Perry, L. C. (1989). Outcome values and aggression. *Child Development, 60,* 571–579.

Bolen, R. M. (2001). *Child sexual abuse.* New York: Kluwer Academic.

Bolger, K. E., & Patterson, C. J. (2001). Developmental pathways from child maltreatment to peer rejection. *Child Development, 72,* 549–568.

Boom, J., Brugman, D., & van der Heijden, P. G. M. (2001). Hierarchical structure of moral stages assessed by a sorting task. *Child Development, 72,* 535–548.

Booth, A. (1999). Causes and consequences of divorce: Reflections on recent research. In R. A. Thompson & P. R. Amato (Eds.), *The postdivorce family: Children, parenting, and society* (pp. 29–48). Thousand Oaks, CA: Sage.

Borke, H. (1975). Piaget's mountains revisited: Changes in the egocentric landscape. *Developmental Psychology, 11,* 240–243.

Borkowski, J. G., & Muthukrisna, N. (1995). Learning environments and skill generalization: How contexts facilitate regulatory processes and efficacy beliefs. In F. Weinert & W. Schneider (Eds.), *Memory performances and competence: Issues in growth and development* (pp. 283–300). Hillsdale, NJ: Erlbaum.

Bornstein, M. H. (1989). Sensitive periods in development: Structural characteristics and causal

interpretations. *Psychological Bulletin, 105,* 179–197.

Bornstein, M. H., Haynes, O. M., Pascual, L., Painter, K. M., & Galperin, C. (1999). Play in two societies: Pervasiveness of process, specificity of structure. *Child Development, 70,* 317–331.

Bornstein, M. H., Selmi, A. M., Haynes, O. M., Painter, K. M., & Marx, E. S. (1999). Representational abilities and the hearing status of child/mother dyads. *Child Development, 70,* 833–852.

Bornstein, M. H., Tal, J., Rahn, C., Galperín, C. Z., Pàcheux, M., Lamour, M., Toda, S., Azuma, H., Ogino, M., & Tamis-LeMonda, C. S. (1992a). Functional analysis of the contents of maternal speech to infants of 5 and 13 months in four cultures: Argentina, France, Japan, and the United States. *Developmental Psychology, 28,* 593–603.

Bornstein, M. H., Vibbert, M., Tal, J., & O'Donnell, K. (1992b). Toddler language and play in the second year: Stability, covariation, and influences of parenting. *First Language, 12,* 323–338.

Bornstein, P., Duncan, P., D'Ari, A., Pieniadz, J., Fitzgerald, M., Abrams, C. L., Frankowski, B., Franco, O., Hunt, C., & Oh Cha, S. (1996). Family and parenting behaviors predicting middle school adjustment: A longitudinal study. *Family Relations, 45,* 415–425.

Borowski, I. W., Ireland, M., & Resnick, M. D. (2001). Adolescent suicide attempts: Risks and protectors. *Pediatrics, 107,* 485–493.

Borst, C. G. (1995). *Catching babies: The professionalization of childbirth, 1870–1920.* Cambridge, MA: Harvard University Press.

Borstelmann, L. J. (1983). Children before psychology: Ideas about children from antiquity to the late 1800s. In W. Kessen (Ed.), *Handbook of child psychology: Vol. 1. History, theory, and methods* (4th ed., pp. 1–40). New York: Wiley.

Bortolus, R., Parazzini, F., Chatenoud, L., Benzi, G., Bianchi, M. M., & Marini, A. (1999). The epidemiology of multiple births. *Human Reproduction Update, 5,* 179–187.

Bost, K. K., Vaughn, B. E., Washington, W. N., Cielinski, K. L., & Bradbard, M. R. (1998). Social competence, social support, and attachment: Demarcation of construct domains, measurement, and paths of influence for preschool children attending Head Start. *Child Development, 69,* 192–218.

Bouchard, C. (1994). *The genetics of obesity.* Boca Raton, FL: CRC Press.

Bouchard, T. J., Jr. (1997). IQ similarity in twins reared apart: Findings and responses to critics. In

R. J. Sternberg & E. L. Grigorenko (Eds.), *Intelligence, heredity, and environment* (pp. 126–160). New York: Cambridge University Press.

Bouchard, T. J., Jr., Lykken, D. T., McGue, M., Segal, N. L., & Tellegen, A. (1990). Sources of human psychological differences: The Minnesota Study of Twins Reared Apart. *Science, 250,* 223–228.

Bouchard, T. J., Jr., & McGue, M. (1981). Familial studies of intelligence: A review. *Science, 212,* 1055–1058.

Boukydis, C. F. Z., & Burgess, R. L. (1982). Adult physiological response to infant cries: Effects of temperament of infant, parental status and gender. *Child Development, 53,* 1291–1298.

Boukydis, C. F. Z., & Lester, B. M. (1998). Infant crying, risk status and social support in families of preterm and term infants. *Early Development and Parenting, 7,* 31–39.

Boulton, M. J. (1996). A comparison of 8- and 11-year-old girls' and boys' participation in specific types of rough-and-tumble play and aggressive fighting: Implications for functional hypotheses. *Aggressive Behavior, 22,* 271–287.

Boulton, M. J. (1999). Concurrent and longitudinal relations between children's playground behavior and social preference, victimization, and bullying. *Child Development, 70,* 944–954.

Boulton, M. J., & Smith, P. K. (1994). Bully/victim problems in middle-school children: Stability, self-perceived competence, peer perceptions and peer acceptance. *British Journal of Developmental Psychology, 12,* 315–329.

Bowerman, M. (1973). *Early syntactic development: A cross-linguistic study with special reference to Finnish.* Cambridge: Cambridge University Press.

Bowlby, J. (1969). *Attachment and loss: Vol. 1. Attachment.* New York: Basic Books.

Bowlby, J. (1980). *Attachment and loss: Vol. 3. Loss.* New York: Basic Books.

Bowlby, J. W., & McMullen, K. (2002). At a crossroads: First results for the 18 to 20-year-old cohort of the *Youth in Transition Survey.* Human Resources Development Canada. Ottawa, ON: Author.

Boyer, K., & Diamond, A. (1992). Development of memory for temporal order in infants and young children. In A. Diamond (Ed.), *Development and neural bases of higher cognitive function* (pp. 267–317). New York: New York Academy of Sciences.

Boyes, M. C., & Allen, S. G. (1993). Styles of parent–child interaction and moral reasoning in adoles-

cence. *Merrill-Palmer Quarterly, 39,* 551–570.

Boyes, M. C., & Chandler, M. (1992). Cognitive development, epistemic doubt, and identity formation in adolescence. *Journal of Youth and Adolescence, 21,* 277–304.

Boysson-Bardies, B. de, & Vihman, M. M. (1991). Adaptation to language: Evidence from babbling and first words in four languages. *Language, 67,* 297–319.

Brabeck, M. (1983). Moral judgment: Theory and research on differences between males and females. *Developmental Review, 3,* 274–291.

Brackbill, Y., McManus, K., & Woodward, L. (1985). *Medication in maternity: Infant exposure and maternal information.* Ann Arbor: University of Michigan Press.

Bradley, R. H., & Caldwell, B. M. (1979). Home Observation for Measurement of the Environment: A revision of the preschool scale. *American Journal of Mental Deficiency, 84,* 235–244.

Bradley, R. H., Caldwell, B. M., & Rock, S. L. (1988). Home environment and school performance: A ten-year follow-up and examination of three models of environmental action. *Child Development, 59,* 852–867.

Bradley, R. H., Caldwell, B. M., Rock, S. L., Hamrick, H. M., & Harris, P. (1988). Home Observation for Measurement of the Environment: Development of a home inventory for use with families having children 6 to 10 years old. *Contemporary Educational Psychology, 13,* 58–71.

Bradley, R. H., Caldwell, B. M., Rock, S. L., Ramey, C. T., Barnard, K. E., Gray, C., Hammond, M. A., Mitchell, S., Gottfried, A., Siegel, L., & Johnson, D. L. (1989). Home environment and cognitive development in the first 3 years of life: A collaborative study involving six sites and three ethnic groups in North America. *Developmental Psychology, 25,* 217–235.

Bradley, R. H., Whiteside, L., Mundfrom, D. J., Casey, P. H., Kelleher, K. J., & Pope, S. K. (1994). Contribution of early intervention and early caregiving experiences to resilience in low-birthweight, premature children living in poverty. *Journal of Clinical Child Psychology, 23,* 425–434.

Bradley-Johnson, S. (2001). Cognitive assessment for the youngest children: A critical review of tests. *Journal of Psychoeducational Assessment, 19,* 19–44.

Braet, C., Mervielde, I., & Vandereycken, W. (1997). Psychological aspects of childhood obesity: A controlled study in a clinical and nonclinical sample. *Journal of Pediatric Psychology, 22,* 59–71.

Braine, M. D. S. (1992). What sort of innate structure is needed to "bootstrap" into syntax? *Cognition, 45*, 77–100.

Braine, M. D. S. (1994). Is nativism sufficient? *Journal of Child Language, 21*, 1–23.

Brainerd, C. J., & Gordon, L. L. (1994). Development of verbatim and gist memory for numbers. *Developmental Psychology, 30*, 163–177.

Brainerd, C. J., & Reyna, V. F. (1993). Memory independence and memory interference in cognitive development. *Psychological Review, 100*, 42–67.

Brainerd, C. J., & Reyna, V. F. (1995). Learning rate, learning opportunities, and the development of forgetting. *Developmental Psychology, 31*, 251–262.

Brainerd, C. J., & Reyna, V. F. (2001). Fuzzy-trace theory: Dual processes in memory, reasoning, and cognitive neuroscience. In H. W. Reese (Ed.), *Advances in child development and behavior* (Vol. 28). San Diego, CA: Academic Press.

Brainerd, C. J., Reyna, V. F., & Poole, D. A. (2000). Fuzzy-trace theory and false memory: Memory theory in the courtroom. In D. F. Bjorklund (Ed.), *Research and theory in false-memory creation in children and adults* (pp. 93–127). Mahwah, NJ: Erlbaum.

Brame, B., Nagin, D. S., & Tremblay, R. E. (2001). Developmental trajectories of physical aggression from school entry to late adolescence. *Journal of Child Psychology and Psychiatry, 42*, 503–512.

Braungart, J. M., Fulker, D. W., & Plomin, R. (1992). Genetic mediation of the home environment during infancy: A sibling adoption study of the HOME. *Developmental Psychology, 28*, 1048–1055.

Braungart, J. M., Plomin, R., DeFries, J. C., & Fulker, D. W. (1992). Genetic influence on tester-rated infant temperament as assessed by Bayley's Infant Behavior Record: Nonadoptive and adoptive siblings and twins. *Developmental Psychology, 28*, 40–47.

Braungart-Rieker, J., Courtney, S., & Garwood, M. M. (1999). Mother– and father–infant attachment: Families in context. *Journal of Family Psychology, 13*, 535–553.

Bray, J. H. (1999). From marriage to remarriage and beyond: Findings from the Developmental Issues in Stepfamilies Research Project. In E. M. Hetherington (Ed.), *Coping with divorce, single parenting, and remarriage: A risk and resiliency perspective* (pp. 295–319). Mahwah, NJ: Erlbaum.

Brazelton, T. B., Koslowski, B., & Tronick, E. Z. (1976). Neonatal behavior among urban Zambians and Americans. *Journal of the American Academy of Child Psychiatry, 15*, 97–107.

Brazelton, T. B., & Nugent, J. K. (1995). *Neonatal Behavioral Assessment Scale.* London: Mac Keith Press.

Brazelton, T. B., Nugent, J. K., & Lester, B. M. (1987). Neonatal Behavioral Assessment Scale. In J. D. Osofsky (Ed.), *Handbook of infant development* (2nd ed., pp. 780–817). New York: Wiley.

Bredekamp, S., & Copple, C. (Eds.). (1997). *Developmentally appropriate practice in early childhood programs* (rev. ed.). Washington, DC: National Association for the Education of Young Children.

Breedlove, S. M. (1994). Sexual differentiation of the human nervous system. *Annual Review of Psychology, 45*, 389–418.

Bremner, J. G. (1998). From perception to action: The early development of knowledge. In F. Simion & G. Butterworth (Eds.), *Development of sensory, motor, and cognitive capacities in early infancy* (pp. 239–255). East Sussex, UK: Psychology Press.

Brenes, M. E., Eisenberg, N., & Helmstadter, G. C. (1985). Sex role development of preschoolers from two-parent and one-parent families. *Merrill-Palmer Quarterly, 31*, 33–46.

Brennan, W. M., Ames, E. W., & Moore, R. W. (1966). Age differences in infants' attention to patterns of different complexities. *Science, 151*, 354–356.

Brenner, E., & Salovey, P. (1997). Emotion regulation during childhood: Developmental, interpersonal, and individual considerations. In P. Salovey & D. Sluyter (Eds.), *Emotional literacy and emotional development* (pp. 168–192). New York: Basic Books.

Brent, R. L. (1999). Utilization of developmental basic science principles in the evaluation of reproductive risks from pre- and postconception environmental radiation exposures. *Teratology, 59*, 182–204.

Bretherton, I. (1992). The origins of attachment theory: John Bowlby and Mary Ainsworth. *Developmental Psychology, 28*, 759–775.

Bretherton, I., Fritz, J., Zahn-Waxler, C., & Ridgeway, D. (1986). Learning to talk about emotions: A functionalist perspective. *Child Development, 57*, 529–548.

Brewaeys, A., Ponjaert, I., Van Hall, E. V., & Golombok, S. (1997). Donor insemination: Child development and family functioning in lesbian mother families. *Human Reproduction, 12*, 1349–1359.

Brezina, T. (1999). Teenage violence toward parents as an adaptation to family strain: Evidence from a national survey of male adolescents. *Youth and Society, 30*, 416–444.

Brien, M. J., & Willis, R. J. (1997). Costs and consequences for the fathers. In R. A. Maynard (Ed.), *Kids having kids* (pp. 95–144). Washington, DC: Urban Institute.

Briggs, F., & Hawkins, R. (1996). *Keeping ourselves safe: Who benefits?* Wellington, New Zealand: New Zealand Council for Educational Research.

Briggs, F., & Hawkins, R. (1999). The importance of parent involvement in child protection curricula. In L. E. Berk (Ed.), *Landscapes of development* (pp. 321–335). Belmont, CA: Wadsworth.

Broberg, A. G., Wessels, H., Lamb, M. E., & Hwang, C. P. (1997). Effects of day care on the development of cognitive abilities in 8-year-olds: A longitudinal study. *Developmental Psychology, 33*, 62–69.

Brody, G. H., & Flor, D. L. (1998). Maternal resources, parenting practices, and child competence in rural, single-parent African American families. *Child Development, 69*, 803–816.

Brody, G. H., Graziano, W. G., & Musser, L. M. (1983). Familiarity and children's behavior in same-age and mixed-age peer groups. *Developmental Psychology, 19*, 568–576.

Brody, G. H., Stoneman, Z., & Flor, D. (1995). Linking family processes and academic competence among rural African American youths. *Journal of Marriage and the Family, 57*, 567–570.

Brody, G. H., Stoneman, Z., & Flor, D. (1996). Parental religiosity, family processes, and youth competence in rural, two-parent African American families. *Developmental Psychology, 32*, 696–706.

Brody, G. H., Stoneman, Z., & McCoy, J. K. (1992). Associations of maternal and paternal direct and differential behavior with sibling relationships: Contemporaneous and longitudinal analyses. *Child Development, 63*, 82–92.

Brody, G. H., Stoneman, Z., & McCoy, J. K. (1994). Forecasting sibling relationships in early adolescence from child temperaments and family processes in middle childhood. *Child Development, 65*, 771–784.

Brody, G. H., Stoneman, Z., McCoy, J. K., & Forehand, R. (1992). Contemporaneous and longitudinal associations of sibling conflict with family relationship assessments and family discussions about sibling problems. *Child Development, 63*, 391–400.

Brody, L. (1999). *Gender, emotion, and the family.* Cambridge, MA: Harvard University Press.

Brody, N. (1987). Jensen, Gottfredson, and the black–white difference in intelligence test scores. *Behavioral and Brain Sciences, 10*, 507–508.

Brody, N. (1997). *Intelligence* (2nd ed.). San Diego: Academic Press.

Brody, N. (2000). History of theories and measurements of intelligence. In R. J. Sternberg (Ed.), *Handbook of intelligence* (pp. 17–33). Cambridge: Cambridge University Press.

Bronfenbrenner, U. (1995). The bioecological model from a life course perspective: Reflections of a participant observer. In P. Moen, G. H. Elder, Jr., & K. Lüscher (Eds.), *Examining lives in context* (pp. 599–618). Washington, DC: American Psychological Association.

Bronfenbrenner, U., & Ceci, S. J. (1994). Nature–nurture reconceptualized in developmental perspective: A bioecological model. *Psychological Review, 101*, 568–586.

Bronfenbrenner, U., & Evans, G. W. (2000). Developmental science in the 21st century: Emerging theoretical models, research designs, and empirical findings. *Social Development, 9*, 115–125.

Bronfenbrenner, U., & Morris, P. A. (1998). The ecology of developmental processes. In R. M. Lerner (Ed.), *Handbook of child psychology: Vol. 1. Theoretical models of human development* (5th ed., pp. 535–584). New York: Wiley.

Bronson, G. W. (1991). Infant differences in rate of visual encoding. *Child Development, 62*, 44–54.

Bronson, M. B. (1995). *The right stuff for children birth to 8.* Washington, DC: National Association for the Education of Young Children.

Brooks, P. J., & Tomasello, M. (1999). Young children learn to produce passives with nonce verbs. *Developmental Psychology, 35*, 29–44.

Brooks-Gunn, J. (1988a). Antecedents and consequences of variations in girls' maturational timing. *Journal of Adolescent Health Care, 9*, 365–373.

Brooks-Gunn, J. (1988b). The impact of puberty and sexual activity upon the health and education of adolescent girls and boys. *Peabody Journal of Education, 64*, 88–113.

Brooks-Gunn, J., & Chase-Lansdale, P. L. (1995). Adolescent parenthood. In M. H. Bornstein (Ed.), *Handbook of parenting: Vol. 3. Status and social conditions of parenting* (pp. 113–149). Mahwah, NJ: Erlbaum.

Brooks-Gunn, J., & Duncan, G. J. (1997). The effects of poverty on children. *Future of Children, 7*, 55–71.

Brooks-Gunn, J., McCarton, C. M., Casey, P. H., McCormick, M. C., Bauer, C. R., Bernbaum, J. C.,

Tyson, J., Swanson, M., Bennett, F. C., Scott, D. T., Tonascia, J., & Meinert, C. L. (1994). Early intervention in low-birth-weight premature infants. *Journal of the American Medical Association, 272,* 1257–1262.

Brooks-Gunn, J., & Ruble, D. N. (1980). Menarche: The interaction of physiology, cultural, and social factors. In A. J. Dan, E. A. Graham, & C. P. Beecher (Eds.), *The menstrual cycle: A synthesis of interdisciplinary research* (pp. 141–159). New York: Springer-Verlag.

Brooks-Gunn, J., & Ruble, D. N. (1983). The experience of menarche from a developmental perspective. In J. Brooks-Gunn & A. C. Peterson (Eds.), *Girls at puberty* (pp. 155–177). New York: Plenum.

Brooks-Gunn, J., Warren, M. P., Samelson, M., & Fox, R. (1986). Physical similarity of and disclosure of menarcheal status to friends: Effects of grade and pubertal status. *Journal of Early Adolescence, 6,* 3–14.

Brown, A. L., & Campione, J. C. (1972). Recognition memory for perceptually similar pictures in preschool children. *Journal of Experimental Psychology, 95,* 55–62.

Brown, A. L., Smiley, S. S., Day, J. D., Townsend, M., & Lawton, S. Q. C. (1977). Intrusion of a thematic idea in children's recall of prose. *Child Development, 48,* 1454–1466.

Brown, A. L., Smiley, S. S., & Lawton, S. Q. C. (1978). The effects of experience on the selection of suitable retrieval cues for studying texts. *Child Development, 49,* 829–835.

Brown, B. B. (1999). "You're going out with who?": Peer group influences on adolescent romantic relationships. In W. Furman, B. B. Brown, & C. Feiring (Eds.), *The development of romantic relationships in adolescence* (pp. 291–329). New York: Cambridge University Press.

Brown, B. B., Freedman, H., & Huang, B. (1992). *"Crowd hopping": Incidence, correlates, and consequences of change in crowd affiliation during adolescence.* Paper presented at the biennial meeting of the Society for Research on Adolescence, Washington, DC.

Brown, B. B., Lohr, M. J., & McClenahan, E. L. (1986). Early adolescents' perceptions of peer pressure. *Journal of Early Adolescence, 6,* 139–154.

Brown, D. (1991). *Human universals.* New York: McGraw-Hill.

Brown, J. M., & Mehler, P. S. (2000). Medical complications occurring in adolescents with anorexia nervosa. *Western Journal of Medicine, 172,* 189–193.

Brown, J. R., & Dunn, J. (1992). Talk with your mother or your sibling? Developmental changes in early family conversations about feelings. *Child Development, 63,* 336–349.

Brown, J. R., Donelan-McCall, N., & Dunn, J. (1996). Why talk about mental states? The significance of children's conversations with friends, siblings and mothers. *Child Development, 67,* 836–849.

Brown, K. M., McMahon, R. P., Biro, F. M., Crawford, P., Schreiber, G. B., & Similo, S. L. (1999). Changes in self-esteem in black and white girls between the ages of 9 and 14 years: The NHLBI Growth and Health Study. *Journal of Adolescent Health, 23,* 7–19.

Brown, R. (1973). *A first language: The early stages.* Cambridge, MA: Harvard University Press.

Brown, R., & Hanlon, C. (1970). Derivational complexity and order of acquisition in child speech. In J. R. Hayes (Ed.), *Cognition and the development of language* (pp. 11–53). New York: Wiley.

Brown, R. T., Reynolds, C. R., & Whitaker, J. S. (1999). Bias in mental testing since *Bias in Mental Testing. School Psychology Quarterly, 14,* 208–238.

Brownell, C. A., & Carriger, M. S. (1990). Changes in cooperation and self-other differentiation during the second year. *Child Development, 61,* 1164–1174.

Bruce, D., Dolan, A., & Phillips-Grant, K. (2000). On the transition from childhood amnesia to recall of personal memories. *Psychological Science, 11,* 360–364.

Bruch, H. (2001). *The golden cage: The enigma of anorexia nervosa.* Cambridge, MA: Harvard University Press.

Bruck, M., Ceci, S. J., & Hembrooke, H. (1998). Reliability and credibility of young children's reports. *American Psychologist, 53,* 136–151.

Bruck, M., Treiman, R., Caravolas, M., Genesee, F., & Cassar, M. (1998). Spelling skills of children in whole language and phonics classrooms. *Applied Psycholinguistics, 19,* 669–684.

Bruer, J. T., & Greenough, W. T. (2001). The subtle science of how experience affects the brain. In D. B. Bailey, Jr., J. T. Bruer, F. J. Symons, & J. W. Lichtman (Eds.), *Critical thinking about critical periods* (pp. 209–232). Baltimore: Paul H. Brookes.

Bruner, J. S. (1983). The acquisition of pragmatic commitments. In R. M. Golinkoff (Ed.), *The transition from prelinguistic to linguistic communication* (pp. 27–42). Hillsdale, NJ: Erlbaum.

Bryan, Y. E., & Newman, J. D. (1988). Influence of infant cry structure on the heart rate of the listener. In J. D. Newman (Ed.), *The physiological control of mammalian vocalization* (pp. 413–432). New York: Plenum.

Buchanan, A. (1996). *Cycles of child maltreatment.* Chichester, UK: Wiley.

Buchanan, C. M., Eccles, J. S., & Becker, J. B. (1992). Are adolescents the victims of raging hormones? Evidence for activational effects of hormones on moods and behavior at adolescence. *Psychological Bulletin, 111,* 62–107.

Buchanan, C. M., & Holmbeck, G. N. (1998). Measuring beliefs about adolescent personality and behavior. *Journal of Youth and Adolescence, 27,* 609–629.

Buchanan, C. M., Maccoby, E. E., & Dornbusch, S. M. (1996). *Adolescents after divorce.* Cambridge, MA: Harvard University Press.

Buchanan-Barrow, E., & Barrett, M. (1998). Children's rule discrimination within the context of the school. *British Journal of Developmental Psychology, 16,* 539–551.

Buckingham, D., & Shultz, T. R. (2000). The developmental course of distance, time, and velocity concepts: A generative connectionist model. *Journal of Cognition and Development, 1,* 305–345.

Budwig, N. (1995). *A developmental-functionalist approach to child language.* Mahwah, NJ: Erlbaum.

Bugental, D. B., Blue, J., Cortez, V., Fleck, K., & Rodriquez, A. (1992). Influences of a witnessed affect of information processing in children. *Child Development, 63,* 774–786.

Buhrmester, D. (1996). Need fulfillment, interpersonal competence, and the developmental contexts of early adolescent friendship. In W. M. Bukowski, A. F. Newcomb, & W. W. Hartup (Eds.), *The company they keep: Friendship during childhood and adolescence* (pp. 158–185). New York: Cambridge University Press.

Buhrmester, D. (1998). Need fulfillment, interpersonal competence, and the developmental contexts of early adolescent friendship. In W. M. Bukowski, A. F. Newcomb, & W. W. Hartup (Eds.), *The company they keep: Friendship in childhood and adolescence* (pp. 158–185). New York: Cambridge University Press.

Buhrmester, D., & Furman, W. (1990). Perceptions of sibling relationships during middle childhood and adolescence. *Child Development, 61,* 1387–1398.

Buhs, E. S., & Ladd, G. W. (2001). Peer rejection as antecedent of young children's school adjustment: An examination of mediating processes. *Developmental Psychology, 37,* 550–560.

Bukowski, W. M. (2001). Friendship and the worlds of childhood. In D. W. Nangle & C. A. Erdley (Eds.), *The role of friendship in psychological adjustment* (pp. 93–105). San Francisco: Jossey-Bass.

Bukowski, W. M., Sippola, L. K., & Hoza, B. (1999). Same and other: Interdependency between participation in same- and other-sex friendships. *Journal of Youth and Adolescence, 28,* 439–459.

Bukowski, W. M., Sippola, L. K., & Newcomb, A. F. (2000). Variations in patterns of attraction of same- and other-sex peers during early adolescence. *Developmental Psychology, 36,* 147–154.

Bullock, M., & Lutkenhaus, P. (1990). Who am I? The development of self-understanding in toddlers. *Merrill-Palmer Quarterly, 36,* 217–238.

Burchinal, M. R., Peisner-Feinberg, E., Bryant, D. M., & Clifford, R. (2000). Children's social and cognitive development and child-care quality: Testing for differential associations related to poverty, gender, or ethnicity. *Applied Developmental Science, 4,* 149–165.

Burger, L. K., & Miller, P. J. (1999). Early talk about the past revisited: Affect in working-class and middle-class children's co-narrations. *Journal of Child Language, 26,* 133–162.

Burgess, K. B., Rubin, K. H., Chea, C. S. L., & Nelson, L. J. (2001). Behavioral inhibition, social withdrawal, and parenting. In R. Crozier & L. Alden (Eds.), *International handbook of social anxiety* (pp. 137–158). New York: Wiley.

Burhans, K. K., & Dweck, C. S. (1995). Helplessness in early childhood: The role of contingent worth. *Child Development, 66,* 1719–1738.

Burns, R. B., & Mason, D. A. (1998). Class formation and composition in elementary schools. *American Educational Research Journal, 35,* 739–772.

Burts, D. C., Hart, C. H., Charlesworth, R., Fleege, P. O., Mosley, J., & Thomasson, R. H. (1992). Observed activities and stress behaviors of children in developmentally appropriate and inappropriate kindergarten classrooms. *Early Childhood Research Quarterly, 7,* 297–318.

Bushman, B. J. (1995). The moderating role of trait aggressiveness in the effects of violent media on aggression. *Journal of Personality and Social Psychology, 69,* 950–960.

Bushman, B. J., & Anderson, C. A. (2001). Media violence and the American public: Scientific facts versus media misinformation. *American Psychologist, 56,* 477–489.

Bushman, B. J., & Huesmann, L. R. (2001). Effects of televised violence on aggression. In D. G. Singer & J. L. Singer (Eds.), *Handbook of children and the media* (pp. 223–254). Thousand Oaks, CA: Sage.

Bushnell, E. W., & Boudreau, J. P. (1993). Motor development and the mind: The potential role of motor abilities as a determinant of aspects of perceptual development. *Child Development, 64,* 1005–1021.

Bussell, D. A., Neiderhiser, J. M., Pike, A., Plomin, R., Simmens, S., Howe, G. W., Hetherington, E. M., Carroll, E., & Reiss, D. (1999). Adolescents' relationships to siblings and mothers: A multivariate genetic analysis. *Developmental Psychology, 35,* 1248–1259.

Bussey, K. (1992). Lying and truthfulness: Children's definitions, standards, and evaluative reactions. *Child Development, 63,* 129–137.

Bussey, K., & Bandura, A. (1992). Self-regulatory mechanisms governing gender development. *Child Development, 63,* 1236–1250.

Butler, R. (1998). Age trends in the use of social and temporal comparison for self-evaluation: Examination of a novel developmental hypothesis. *Child Development, 69,* 1054–1073.

Butler, R. (1999). Information seeking and achievement motivation in middle childhood and adolescence: The role of conceptions of ability. *Developmental Psychology, 35,* 146–163.

Butler, R., & Ruzany, N. (1993). Age and socialization effects on the development of social comparison motives and normative ability assessment in kibbutz and urban children. *Child Development, 64,* 532–543.

Butterworth, G. (1999). Neonatal imitation: Existence, mechanisms and motives. In J. Nadel & G. Butterworth (Eds.), *Imitation in infancy* (pp. 63–88). Cambridge: Cambridge University Press.

Bybee, J., & Slobin, D. (1982). Rules and schemes in the development and use of the English past tense. *Language, 58,* 265–289.

Bybee, J., Merisca, R., & Velasco, R. (1998). The development of reactions to guilt-producing events. In J. Bybee (Ed.), *Guilt and children* (pp. 185–213). San Diego: Academic Press.

Byrnes, J. P., & Takahira, S. (1993). Explaining gender differences on SAT-math items. *Developmental Psychology, 29,* 805–810.

Caine, N. (1986). Behavior during puberty and adolescence. In G. Mitchell & J. Erwin (Eds.), *Comparative primate biology: Vol. 2A. Behavior, conservation, and ecology* (pp. 327–361). New York: Alan R. Liss.

Cairns, R. B. (1992). The making of a developmental science: The contributions and intellectual heritage of James Mark Baldwin. *Developmental Psychology, 28,* 17–24.

Cairns, R. B. (1998). The making of developmental psychology. In R. M. Lerner (Ed.), *Handbook of child psychology: Vol. 1. Theoretical models of human development* (5th ed., pp. 25–105). New York: Wiley.

Cairns, R. B., Leung, M.-C., Buchanan, L., & Cairns, B. D. (1995). Friendships and social networks in childhood and adolescence: Fluidity, reliability, and interrelations. *Child Development, 66,* 1330–1345.

Cairns, R., Xie, H., & Leung, M.-C. (1998). The popularity of friendship and the neglect of social networks: Toward a new balance. In W. M. Bukowski & A. H. Cillessen (Eds.), *Sociometry then and now: Building on six decades of measuring children's experiences with the peer group* (pp. 25–53). San Francisco: Jossey-Bass.

Caldwell, B. M., & Bradley, R. H. (1994). Environmental issues in developmental follow-up research. In S. L. Friedman & H. C. Haywood (Eds.), *Developmental follow-up* (pp. 235–256). San Diego: Academic Press.

Caldwell, C. H., & Antonucci, T. C. (1997). Childbearing during adolescence: Mental health risks and opportunities. In J. Schulenberg, J. L. Maggs, & K. Hurrelmann (Eds.), *Health risks and developmental transitions during adolescence* (pp. 220–245). New York: Cambridge University Press.

Calkins, S. D., Fox, N. A., & Marshall, T. R. (1996). Behavioral and physiological antecedents of inhibited and uninhibited behavior. *Child Development, 67,* 523–540.

Callaghan, T. C. (1999). Early understanding and production of graphic symbols. *Child Development, 70,* 1314–1324.

Callaghan, T. C., & Rankin, M. P. (2002). Emergence of graphic symbol functioning and the question of domain specificity: a longitudinal training study. *Child Development 73,* 359–376.

Camara, K. A., & Resnick, G. (1988). Interparental conflict and cooperation: Factors moderating children's post-divorce adjustment. In E. M. Hetherington & J. D. Arasteh (Ed.), *Impact of divorce, single parenting, and stepparenting on children* (pp. 169–195). Hillsdale, NJ: Erlbaum.

Camarata, S., & Leonard, L. B. (1986). Young children pronounce object words more accurately than action words. *Journal of Child Language, 13,* 51–65.

Cameron, C. A., & Lee, K. (1997). The development of children's telephone communication. *Journal of Applied Developmental Psychology, 18,* 55–70.

Cameron, M. B., & Wilson, B. J. (1990). The effects of chronological age, gender, and delay of entry on academic achievement and retention: Implications for academic redshirting. *Psychology in the Schools, 27,* 260–263.

Campbell, F. A., & Ramey, C. T. (1994). Effects of early intervention on intellectual and academic achievement: A follow-up study of children from low-income families. *Child Development, 65,* 684–698.

Campbell, F. A., & Ramey, C. T. (1995). Cognitive and school outcomes for high-risk African-American students at middle adolescence: Positive effects of early intervention. *American Educational Research Journal, 32,* 743–772.

Campbell, J. R., Hombo, C. M., & Mazzeo, J. (2000). *NAEP 1999: Trends in academic progress.* Washington, DC: U.S. Department of Education.

Campbell, P. F., & Schwartz, S. S. (1986). Microcomputers in the preschool: Children, parents, and teachers. In P. Campbell & G. Fein (Eds.), *Young children and microcomputers* (pp. 45–60). Englewood Cliffs, NJ: Prentice-Hall.

Campbell, R., & Sais, E. (1995). Accelerated metalinguistic (phonological) awareness in bilingual children. *British Journal of Developmental Psychology, 13,* 61–68.

Campbell, S. B., Cohn, J. F., & Meyers, T. (1995). Depression in first-time mothers: Mother–infant interaction and depression chronicity. *Developmental Psychology, 31,* 349–357.

Campos, J. J., Anderson, D. I., Barbu-Roth, M. A., Hubbard, E. M., Hertenstein, J. J., & Witherington, D. (2000). Travel broadens the mind. *Infancy, 1,* 149–219.

Campos, J. J., Kermoian, R., & Zumbahlen, M. R. (1992). Socioemotional transformation in the family system following infant crawling onset. In N. Eisenberg & R. A. Fabes (Eds.), *New directions for child development* (No. 55, pp. 25–40). San Francisco: Jossey-Bass.

Campos, R. G. (1989). Soothing pain-elicited distress in infants with swaddling and pacifiers. *Child Development, 60,* 781–792.

Camras, L. A. (1992). Expressive development and basic emotions. *Cognition and Emotion, 6,* 267–283.

Camras, L. A., Oster, H., Campos, J. J., Miyake, K., & Bradshaw, D. (1992). Japanese and American infants' responses to arm restraint. *Developmental Psychology, 28,* 578–583.

Camras, L. A., Oster, H., Campos, J., Campos, R., Ujie, T., Miyake, K., Wang, L., & Meng, Z. (1998). Production of emotional and facial expressions in European American, Japanese, and Chinese infants. *Developmental Psychology, 34,* 616–628.

Camras, L. A., & Sachs, V. B. (1991). Social referencing and caretaker expressive behavior in a day care setting. *Infant Behavior and Development, 14,* 27–36.

Canadian Broadcast Standards Council. (2001). *Canada deals with media violence* [On-line]. Available: www.cbsc.ca/english/canada.htm

Canadian Child Care Federation. (1994). *National statement on quality child care* [On-line]. Available: www.cfc-efc.ca/docs/cccf/00000111.htm

Canadian Child Care Federation. (1999). *Partners in practice—Successful Canadian mentoring programs* [On-line]. Available: www.cfc-efc.ca/docs/unknown/00000819.htm

Canadian Child Care Federation. (2000). *CICH supports quality child care* [On-line]. Available: www.cccf-fcsge.ca/pressroom/pr_08_en.html

Canadian Council of Professional Engineers. (1998). *National survey of the Canadian engineering profession in 1997: Summary of findings* [On-line]. Available: www.ccpe.ca/ccpe.cfm?page=NatEngSurv

Canadian Council on Social Development. (2000a). *Immigrant youth in Canada: Lifestyle patterns of immigrant youth. In: Cultural diversity: a CCSD research program. Ottawa:* [On-line]. Available: www.ccsd.ca/subsites/cd/docs/iy/lifestyl.htm

Canadian Council on Social Development. (2000b). *The progress of Canada's children: Into the millennium, 1999–2000.* Ottawa, ON: Author.

Canadian Fitness and Lifestyle Research Institute. (2001). *2000 physical activity monitor.* Increasing Physical Activity: Supporting Children's Participation. Ottawa, ON: Author.

Canadian Foundation for the Study of Infant Deaths. (2001). *What is SIDS?* [On-line]. Available: www.sidscanada.org/whatissids.html

Canadian Health Network. (2001). *Childhood obesity: An alarming trend* [On-line]. Available: www.canadian-health-network.ca/html/newnotable/may1_2001e.html

Canadian Heritage. (1996). Second language learning. *Second Language Education-Information Kit* [On-line]. Available: www.pch.gc.ca/offlangoff/publications/kit/EF02b.htm

Canadian Heritage. (1999a). *Bilingualism in Canada* [On-line]. Available: www.pch.gc.ca/offlangoff/publications/facts/bilingualism.html

Canadian Heritage. (1999b). *French immersion in Canada* [On-line]. Available: www.pch.gc.ca/

offlangoff/publications/facts/immersion.html

Canadian Heritage. (2001). *Linguistic duality-second-language instruction* [On-line]. Available: www.pch.gc.ca/offlangoff/publications/2000-01/english/page_03c.html

Canadian Heritage. (2002). *Welcome to Canadian Heritage: Towards a more creative and cohesive Canada* [On-line]. Available: www.pch.gc.ca/

Canadian Institute for Health Information. (2000). *Supply, distribution and migration of Canadian physicians, 1999.* Ottawa: Author.

Canadian Institute of Child Health. (2000). *The health and well being of children – Does it contribute to the bottom line?* [On-line]. Available: www.cich.ca/bottomline.htm

Canadian Paediatric Society. Fetus and Newborn Committee. (1996). Neonatal circumcision revisited. *Canadian Medical Association Journal, 154,* 769–780.

Canadian Psychological Association. (2001). *Canadian code of ethics for psychologists* (3rd ed.). Ottawa, ON: Author.

Canetto, S. S., & Sakinofsky, I. (1998). The gender paradox in suicide. *Suicide and Life-Threatening Behavior, 28,* 1–23.

Canobi, K. H., Reeve, R. A., & Pattison, P. E. (1998). The role of conceptual understanding in children's addition problem solving. *Developmental Psychology, 34,* 882–891.

Cantor, J., & Harrison, K. (1997). Ratings and advisories for television programming. In Center for Communication and Social Policy (Ed.), *National television violence study* (Vol. 2). Newbury Park, CA: Sage.

Capaldi, D. M., & Patterson, G. R. (1991). Relation of parental transitions to boys' adjustment problems: I. A linear hypothesis. II. Mothers at risk for transitions and unskilled parenting. *Developmental Psychology, 27,* 489–504.

Capelli, C. A., Nakagawa, N., & Madden, C. M. (1990). How children understand sarcasm: The role of context and intonation. *Child Development, 61,* 1824–1841.

Caplan, M., Vespo, J., Pedersen, J., & Hay, D. F. (1991). Conflict and its resolution in small groups of one- and two-year-olds. *Child Development, 62,* 1513–1524.

Caracciolo, E., Moderato, P., & Perini, S. (1988). Analysis of some concrete-operational tasks from an interbehavioral standpoint. *Journal of Experimental Child Psychology, 46,* 391–405.

Carey, S. (1995). On the origins of causal understanding. In D. Sperber, D. Premack, & A. J. Premack (Eds.), *Causal cognition*

(pp. 268–308). Oxford, UK: Clarendon Press.

Carey, S. (1999). Sources of conceptual change. In E. K. Scholnick, K. Nelson, S. A. Gelman, & P. H. Miller (Eds.), *Conceptual development: Piaget's legacy* (pp. 293–326). Mahwah, NJ: Erlbaum.

Carey, S., & Markman, E. M. (1999). Cognitive development. In B. M. Bly & D. E. Rumelhart (Eds.), *Cognitive science* (pp. 201–254). San Diego: Academic Press.

Carli, L. L. (1995). No: Biology does not create gender differences in personality. In M. R. Walsh (Ed.), *Women, men, and gender.* New Haven, CT: Yale University Press.

Carlo, G., Koller, S. H., Eisenberg, N., Da Silva, M., & Frohlich, C. (1996). A cross-national study on the relations among prosocial moral reasoning, gender-role orientations, and prosocial behaviors. *Developmental Psychology, 32,* 231–240.

Carlson, C., Uppal, S., & Prosser, E. C. (2000). Ethnic differences in processes contributing to the self-esteem of early adolescent girls. *Journal of Early Adolescence, 20,* 44–67.

Carlson, E. A. (1998). A prospective longitudinal study of attachment disorganization/disorientation. *Child Development, 4,* 1107–1128.

Carlson, S. M., & Moses, L. J. (2001). Individual differences in inhibitory control and children's theory of mind. *Child Development, 72,* 1032–1053.

Carlton, M. P., & Winsler, A. (1999). School readiness: The need for a paradigm shift. *School Psychology Review, 28,* 338–352.

Carmichael, S. L., & Shaw, G. M. (2000). Maternal life stress and congenital anomalies. *Epidemiology, 11,* 30–35.

Carpendale, J. I., & Chandler, M. J. (1996). On the distinction between false belief understanding and subscribing to an interpretive theory of mind. *Child Development, 67,* 1686–1706.

Carpenter, C. J. (1983). Activity structure and play: Implications for socialization. In M. Liss (Ed.), *Social and cognitive skills: Sex roles and children's play* (pp. 117–145). New York: Academic Press.

Carpenter, C. J., Huston, A. C., & Holt, W. (1986). Modification of preschool sex-typed behaviors by participation in adult-structured activities. *Sex Roles, 14,* 603–615.

Carpenter, M., Akhtar, N., & Tomasello, M. (1998). Fourteen-through 18-month-old infants differentially imitate intentional and accidental actions. *Infant Behavior and Development, 21,* 315–330.

Carpenter, M., Nagell, K., & Tomasello, M. (1998). Social cognition, joint attention, and

communicative competence. *Monographs of the Society for Research in Child Development, 63*(4, Serial No. 255).

Carpenter, T. P., Fennema, E., Fuson, K., Hiebert, J., Human, P., & Murray, H. (1999). Learning basic number concepts and skills as problem solving. In E. Fennema & T. A. Romberg (Eds.), *Mathematics classrooms that promote understanding: Studies in mathematical thinking and learning series* (pp. 45–61). Mahwah, NJ: Erlbaum.

Carr, S., Dabbs, J., & Carr, T. (1975). Mother–infant attachment: The importance of the mother's visual field. *Child Development, 46,* 331–338.

Carraher, T., Schliemann, A. D., & Carraher, D. W. (1988). Mathematical concepts in everyday life. In G. B. Saxe & M. Gearhart (Eds.), *New directions for child development* (Vol. 41, pp. 71–87). San Francisco: Jossey-Bass.

Carroll, J. B. (1993). *Human cognitive abilities: A survey of factor-analytic studies.* New York: Cambridge University Press.

Carroll, J. B. (1997). The three-stratum theory of cognitive abilities. In D. P. Flanagan, J. L. Genshaft, & P. Harrison (Eds.), *Contemporary intellectual assessment* (pp. 122–130). New York: Guilford.

Carskadon, M. A., Viera, C., & Acebo, C. (1993). Association between puberty and delayed phase preference. *Sleep, 16,* 258–262.

Carta, J. J., Atwater, J. B., Greenwood, C. R., McConnell, S. R., & McEvoy, M. A. (2001). Effects of cumulative prenatal substance exposure and environmental risks on children's developmental trajectories. *Journal of Clinical Psychology, 30,* 327–337.

Carter, C. A., Bottoms, B. L., & Levine, M. (1996). Linguistic and socioemotional influences on the accuracy of children's reports. *Law and Human Behavior, 20,* 335–358.

Carter, D. B., & Levy, G. D. (1991). Gender schemas and the salience of gender: Individual differences in nonreversal discrimination learning. *Sex Roles, 25,* 555–567.

Carter, D. B., & McCloskey, L. A. (1984). Peers and the maintenance of sex-typed behavior: The development of children's conceptions of cross-gender behavior in their peers. *Social Cognition, 2,* 294–314.

Casaer, P. (1993). Old and new facts about perinatal brain development. *Journal of Child Psychology and Psychiatry, 34,* 101–109.

Case, R. (1992). *The mind's staircase.* Hillsdale, NJ: Erlbaum.

Case, R. (1996). Introduction: Reconceptualizing the nature of children's conceptual structures and their development in middle

childhood. In R. Case & Y. Okamoto (Eds.), The role of central conceptual structures in the development of children's thought. *Monographs of the Society for Research in Child Development, 61*(1–2, Serial No. 246), pp. 1–26.

Case, R. (1998). The development of central conceptual structures. In D. Kuhn & R. Siegler (Eds.), *Handbook of child psychology: Vol. 2. Cognition, perception, and language* (5th ed., pp. 745–800). New York: Wiley.

Case, R., & Okamoto, Y. (Eds.). (1996). The role of central conceptual structures in the development of children's thought. *Monographs of the Society for Research in Child Development, 61*(1–2, Serial No. 246).

Caselli, M. C., Bates, E., Casadio, P., Fenson, J., Fenson, L., Sanderl, L., & Weir, J. (1995). A cross-linguistic study of early lexical development. *Cognitive Development, 10,* 159–199.

Case-Smith, J., Bigsby, R., & Clutter, J. (1998). Perceptual-motor coupling in the development of grasp. *American Journal of Occupational Therapy, 52,* 102–110.

Casey, M. B., Nuttall, R. L., & Pezaris, E. (1997). Mediators of gender differences in mathematics college entrance test scores: A comparison of spatial skills with internalized beliefs and anxieties. *Developmental Psychology, 33,* 669–680.

Casey, M. B., Nuttall, R. L., & Pezaris, E. (1999). Evidence in support of a modal that predicts how biological and environmental factors interact to influence spatial skills. *Developmental Psychology, 35,* 1237–1247.

Casey, M. B., Nuttall, R., Pezaris, E., & Benbow, C. P. (1995). The influence of spatial ability on gender differences in mathematics college entrance test scores across diverse samples. *Developmental Psychology, 31,* 697–705.

Cashon, C. H., & Cohen, L. B. (2000). Eight-month-old infants' perceptions of possible and impossible events. *Infancy, 1,* 429–446.

Caspi, A. (1998). Personality development across the life course. In N. Eisenberg (Ed.), *Handbook of child psychology: Vol. 3. Social, emotional, and personality development* (5th ed., pp. 311–388). New York: Wiley.

Caspi, A., & Silva, P. A. (1995). Temperamental qualities at age three predict personality traits in young adulthood: Longitudinal evidence from a birth cohort. *Child Development, 66,* 486–498.

Caspi, A., Elder, G. H., Jr., & Bem, D. J. (1987). Moving against the world: Life-course patterns of explosive children. *Developmental Psychology, 23,* 308–313.

Caspi, A., Elder, G. H., Jr., & Bem, D. J. (1988). Moving away from the world: Life-course patterns of shy children. *Developmental Psychology, 24,* 824–831.

Caspi, A., Lynam, D., Moffitt, T. E., & Silva, P. A. (1993). Unraveling girls' delinquency: Biological, dispositional, and contextual contributions to adolescent misbehavior. *Developmental Psychology, 29,* 19–30.

Cassia, V. M., Simion, F., & Umiltá, C. (2001). Face preference at birth: The role of an orienting mechanism. *Developmental Science, 4,* 101–108.

Cassidy, J., & Berlin, L. J. (1994). The insecure/ambivalent pattern of attachment: Theory and research. *Child Development, 65,* 971–991.

Cassidy, J., & Berlin, L. J. (1994). The insecure/ambivalent pattern of attachment: Theory and research. *Child Development, 65,* 971–991.

Cassidy, J., Parke, R. D., Butkovsky, L., & Braungart, J. M. (1992). Family–peer connections: The roles of emotional expressiveness within the family and children's understanding of emotions. *Child Development, 63,* 603–618.

Catherwood, D., Crassini, B., & Freiberg, K. (1989). Infant response to stimuli of similar hue and dissimilar shape: Tracing the origins of the categorization of objects by hue. *Child Development, 60,* 752–762.

Catsambis, S. (1994). The path to math: Gender and racial-ethnic differences in mathematics participation from middle school to high school. *Sociology of Education, 67,* 199–215.

Cattell, J. M. (1890). Mental tests and measurements. *Mind, 15,* 373–381.

Cattell, R. B. (1971). *Abilities: Their structure, growth and action.* Boston: Houghton Mifflin.

Cattell, R. B. (1987). *Intelligence: Its structure, growth and action.* Amsterdam: North-Holland.

Cavadini, C., Siega-Riz, A. M., & Popkin, B. M. (2000). U.S. adolescent food intake trends from 1965 to 1996. *Archives of Diseases in Childhood, 83,* 18–24.

Cavalli-Sforza, L. L., Menozzi, P., & Piazza, A. (1994). *The history and geography of human genes.* Princeton, NJ: Princeton University Press.

CBC (Canadian Broadcasting Corporation). (2000). *Witness Presents* [On-line]. Available: www.cbc.ca/programs/sites/features/offspring/off_rights.html

Ceci, S. J. (1991). How much does schooling influence general intelligence and its cognitive components? A reassessment of the evidence. *Developmental Psychology, 27,* 703–722.

Ceci, S. J. (1999). Schooling and intelligence. In S. J. Ceci & W. M.

Williams (Eds.), *The nature–nurture debate: The essential readings* (pp. 168–175). Oxford: Blackwell.

Ceci, S. J., & Bruck, M. (1998). Children's testimony: Applied and basic issues. In I. Sigel & K. A. Renninger (Eds.), *Handbook of child psychology: Vol. 4. Child psychology in practice* (5th ed., pp. 713–774). New York: Wiley.

Ceci, S. J., Bruck, M., & Battin, D. B. (2000). The suggestibility of children's testimony. In D. F. Bjorklund (Ed.), *False-memory creation in children and adults* (pp. 169–201). Mahwah, NJ: Erlbaum.

Ceci, S. J., Leichtman, M. D., & Bruck, M. (1994). The suggestibility of children's eyewitness reports: Methodological issues. In F. Weinert & W. Schneider (Eds.), *Memory development: State of the art and future directions* (pp. 323–347). Hillsdale, NJ: Erlbaum.

Ceci, S. J., Loftus, E. F., Leichtman, M. D., & Bruck, M. (1994). The possible role of source misattributions in the creation of false beliefs among preschoolers. *International Journal of Clinical Experimental Hypnosis, 42,* 304–320.

Ceci, S. J., & Roazzi, A. (1994). The effects of context on cognition: Postcards from Brazil. In R. J. Sternberg (Ed.), *Mind in context* (pp. 74–101). New York: Cambridge University Press.

Ceci, S. J., Rosenblum, T. B., & Kumpf, M. (1998). The shrinking gap between high- and low-scoring groups: Current trends and possible causes. In U. Neisser (Ed.), *The rising curve* (pp. 287–302). Washington, DC: American Psychological Association.

Ceci, S. J., & Williams, W. M. (1997). Schooling, intelligence, and income. *American Psychologist, 52,* 1051–1058.

Center for Communication and Social Policy. (Ed.). (1998). *National television violence study* (Vol. 2). Newbury Park, CA: Sage.

Central Intelligence Agency. (2001). *The world factbook.* Washington, DC: Author.

Cermak, S. A., & Daunhauer, L. A. (1997). Sensory processing in the post-institutionalized child. *American Journal of Occupational Therapy, 51,* 500–507.

Cernoch, J. M., & Porter, R. H. (1985). Recognition of maternal axillary odors by infants. *Child Development, 56,* 1593–1598.

Cervantes, C. A., & Callanan, M. A. (1998). Labels and explanations in mother–child emotion talk: Age and gender differentiation. *Developmental Psychology, 34,* 88–98.

Chalmers, J. B., & Townsend, M. A. R. (1990). The effects of training in social perspective taking on so-

cially maladjusted girls. *Child Development, 61,* 178–190.

Chan, R. W., Raboy, B., & Patterson, C. J. (1998). Psychosocial adjustment among children conceived via donor insemination by lesbian and heterosexual mothers. *Child Development, 69,* 443–457.

Chandler, M. J. (1973). Egocentrism and antisocial behavior: The assessment and training of social perspective-taking skills. *Developmental Psychology, 9,* 326–332.

Chandler, M. J., & Carpendale, J. I. (1998). Inching toward a mature theory of mind. In M. Ferrari & R. J. Sternberg (Eds.), *Self-awareness: Its nature and development* (pp. 148–190). New York: Guilford.

Chandra, R. K. (1991). Interactions between early nutrition and the immune system. In *Ciba Foundation Symposium* (No. 156, pp. 77–92). Chichester, England: Wiley.

Chaney, C. (1992). Language development, metalinguistic skills, and print awareness in 3-year-old children. *Applied Psycholinguistics, 13,* 485–514.

Chao, R. K. (1994). Beyond parental control and authoritarian parenting style: Understanding Chinese parenting through the cultural notion of training. *Child Development, 65,* 1111–1119.

Chapman, K. L., Leonard, L. B., & Mervis, C. B. (1986). The effect of feedback on young children's inappropriate word usage. *Journal of Child Language, 13,* 101–117.

Chapman, R. S. (2000). Children's language learning: An interactionist perspective. *Journal of Child Psychology and Psychiatry, 41,* 33–54.

Chapman, R. S., & Hesketh, L. J. (2000). Behavioral phenotype of individuals with Down syndrome. *Mental Retardation and Developmental Disabilities Research Reviews, 6,* 84–95.

Charman, T., Baron-Cohen, S., Swettenham, J., Baird, G., Cox, A., & Drew, A. (2001). Testing joint attention, imitation, and play as infancy precursors to language and theory of mind. *Cognitive Development, 15,* 481–498.

Charman, T., Swettenham, J., Baron-Cohen, S., Cox, A., Baird, G., & Drew, A. (1997). Infants with autism: An investigation of empathy, pretend play, joint attention, and imitation. *Developmental Psychology, 33,* 781–789.

Chase, C., Teele, D. W., Klein, J. O., & Rosner, B. A. (1995). Behavioral sequelae of otitis media for infants at one year of age and their mothers. In D. J., Lim, C. D. Bluestone, J. O. Klein, J. D. Nelson, & P. L. Ogra (Eds.), *Recent advances in otitis media.* Ontario: Decker.

Chase-Lansdale, P. L., Brooks-Gunn, J., & Zamsky, E. S. (1994). Young African-American multigenerational families in poverty: Quality of mothering and grandmothering. *Child Development, 65,* 373–393.

Chase-Lansdale, P. L., Cherlin, A. J., & Kiernain, K. E. (1995). The long-term effects of parental divorce on the mental health of young children. *Child Development, 66,* 1614–1634.

Chase-Lansdale, P. L., Gordon, R., Brooks-Gunn, J., & Klebanov, P. K. (1997). Neighborhood and family influences on the intellectual and behavioral competence of preschool and early school-age children. In J. Brooks-Gunn, G. Duncan, & J. L. Aber (Eds.), *Neighborhood poverty: Context and consequences for development* (pp. 79–118). New York: Russell Sage Foundation.

Chassin, L., & Ritter, J. (2001). Vulnerability to substance use disorders in childhood and adolescence. In R. E. Ingram & J. M. Price (Eds.), *Vulnerability to psychopathology: Risk across the lifespan* (pp. 107–134). New York: Guilford.

Chatkupt, S., Mintz, M., Epstein, L. G., Bhansali, D., & Koenigsberger, M. R. (1989). Neuroimaging studies in children with human immunodeficiency virus type 1 infection. *Annals of Neurology, 26,* 453.

Chen, C., & Stevenson, H. W. (1995). Motivation and mathematics achievement: A comparative study of Asian-American, Caucasian-American, and East Asian high school students. *Child Development, 66,* 1215–1234.

Chen, X. (2002). Peer relationships and networks and socio-emotional adjustment: A Chinese perspective. In B. Cairns & T. Farmer (Eds.), *Social networks from a developmental perspective.* New York: Cambridge University Press.

Chen, X., Dong, Q., & Zhou, H. (1997). Authoritative and authoritarian parenting practices and social and school performance in Chinese children. *International Journal of Behavioral Development, 21,* 855–873.

Chen, X., Hastings, P. D., Rubin, K. H., Chen, H., Cen, G., & Stewart, S. L. (1998). Child-rearing attitudes and behavioral inhibition in Chinese and Canadian toddlers: A cross-cultural study. *Developmental Psychology, 34,* 677–686.

Chen, X., Liu, M., & Li, D. (2000). Parental warmth, control, and indulgence and their relations to adjustment in Chinese children: A longitudinal study. *Journal of Family Psychology, 14,* 401–419.

Chen, X., Rubin, K. H., & Li, D. (1997). Relation between academic achievement and social adjustment: Evidence from Chinese children. *Developmental Psychology, 33,* 518–525.

Chen, X., Rubin, K. H., & Li, Z. (1995). Social functioning and adjustment in Chinese children: A longitudinal study. *Developmental Psychology, 31,* 531–539.

Chen, Y.-C., Yu, M.-L., Rogan, W., Gladen, B., & Hsu, C.-C. (1994). A 6-year follow-up of behavior and activity disorders in the Taiwan Yu-cheng children. *American Journal of Public Health, 84,* 415–421.

Chen, Y.-J., & Hsu, C.-C. (1994). Effects of prenatal exposure to PCBs on the neurological function of children: A neuropsychological and neurophysiological study. *Developmental Medicine and Child Neurology, 36,* 312–320.

Chen, Z., & Siegler, R. S. (2000). Across the great divide: Bridging the gap between understanding of toddlers' and older children's thinking. *Monographs of the Society for Research in Child Development, 65*(2, Serial No. 261).

Chen, Z., Sanchez, R. P., & Campbell, T. (1997). From beyond to within their grasp: The rudiments of analogical problem solving in 10- to 13-month-olds. *Developmental Psychology, 33,* 790–801.

Cherlin, A. J., Furstenberg, F. F., Jr., Chase-Lansdale, P. L., Kiernan, K. E., Robins, P. K., Morrison, D. R., & Teitler, J. O. (1991). Longitudinal studies of effects of divorce on children in Great Britain and the United States. *Science, 252,* 1386–1389.

Cherlin, A. J., Kiernan, K. E., & Chase-Lansdale, P. L. (1995). Parental divorce in childhood and demographic outcomes in young adulthood. *Demography, 32,* 299–318.

Cherny, S. S. (1994). Home environmental influences on general cognitive ability. In J. C. DeFries, R. Plomin, & D. W. Fulker (Eds.), *Nature and nurture during middle childhood* (pp. 262–280). Cambridge, MA: Blackwell.

Chesney-Lind, M. (2001). Girls, violence, and delinquency: Popular myths and persistent problems. In S. O. White (Ed.), *Handbook of youth and justice* (pp. 135–158). New York: Kluwer Academic.

Chess, S., & Thomas, A. (1984). *Origins and evolution of behavior disorders.* New York: Brunner/Mazel.

Chi, M. T. H. (1978). Knowledge structures and memory development. In R. S. Siegler (Ed.), *Children's thinking: What develops?* (pp. 73–96). Hillsdale, NJ: Erlbaum.

Childcare Resource and Research Unit, University of Toronto. (2000). The big picture, Tables 9–15. In *Early childhood education and care in Canada: Provinces and territories, 1998* (pp. 109–114). Toronto, ON: Author.

Children's Defense Fund. (1998). *The state of America's children: Yearbook 1998.* Washington, DC: Author.

Children's Defense Fund. (2001). *The state of America's children: Yearbook 2001.* Washington, DC: Author.

Childs, C. P., & Greenfield, P. M. (1982). Informal modes of learning and teaching: The case of Zinacanteco weaving. In N. Warren (Ed.), *Advances in cross-cultural psychology* (Vol. 2, pp. 269–316). London: Academic Press.

Chin, D. G., Schonfeld, D. J., O'Hare, L. L., Mayne, S. T., Salovey, P., Showalter, D. R., & Cicchetti, D. V. (1998). Elementary school-age children's developmental understanding of the causes of cancer. *Developmental and Behavioral Pediatrics, 19,* 397–403.

Chisholm, J. S. (1989). Biology, culture, and the development of temperament: A Navajo example. In J. K. Nugent, B. M. Lester, & T. B. Brazelton (Eds.), *Biology, culture, and development* (Vol. 1, pp. 341–364). Norwood, NJ: Ablex.

Chiu, L.-H. (1992–1993). Self-esteem in American and Chinese (Taiwanese) children. *Current Psychology: Research and Reviews, 11,* 309–313.

Chodirker, B., Cadrin, C., Davies, G., Summers, A., Wilson, R., Winsor, E., & Young, D. (2001). Genetic indications for prenatal diagnosis. *Journal of the Society of Obstetricians and Gynaecologists of Canada, 23,* 525–531.

Chomsky, C. (1969). *The acquisition of syntax in children from 5 to 10.* Cambridge, MA: MIT Press.

Chomsky, N. (1957). *Syntactic structures.* The Hague: Mouton.

Chomsky, N. (1976). *Reflections on language.* London: Temple Smith.

Christenson, S. L., & Sheridan, S. M. (2001). *Schools and families.* New York: Guilford.

Church, R. B. (1999). Using gesture and speech to capture transitions in learning. *Cognitive Development, 14,* 313–342.

Cicchetti, D., & Aber, J. L. (1986). Early precursors of later depression: An organizational perspective. In L. P. Lipsitt & C. Rovee-Collier (Eds.), *Advances in infancy research* (Vol. 4, pp. 87–137). Norwood, NJ: Ablex.

Cicchetti, D., & Toth, S. L. (1993). *Child abuse, child development, and social policy.* Norwood, NJ: Ablex.

Cicchetti, D., & Toth, S. L. (1998). The development of depression in children and adolescents. *American Psychologist, 53,* 221–241.

Cicchetti, D., & Toth, S. L. (2000). Developmental processes in maltreated children. In D. J. Hansen (Ed.), *Nebraska Symposium on Motivation* (Vol. 46, pp. 85–160). Lincoln, NB: University of Nebraska Press.

Cillessen, A. H. N., & Bukowski, W. M. (2000). *Recent advances in the measurement of acceptance and rejection in the peer system.* San Francisco: Jossey-Bass.

Clancy, P. (1985). Acquisition of Japanese. In D. I. Slobin (Ed.), *The crosslinguistic study of language acquisition: Vol. 1. The data* (pp. 323–524). Hillsdale, NJ: Erlbaum.

Clancy, P. (1989). Form and function in the acquisition of Korean wh- questions. *Journal of Child Language, 16,* 323–347.

Clark, E. V. (1983). Meanings and concepts. In P. H. Mussen (Ed.), *Handbook of child psychology: Vol. 3. Cognitive development* (pp. 787–840). New York: Wiley.

Clark, E. V. (1990). On the pragmatics of contrast. *Journal of Child Language, 17,* 417–431.

Clark, E. V. (1993). *The lexicon in acquisition.* Cambridge: Cambridge University Press.

Clark, E. V. (1995). The lexicon and syntax. In J. L. Miller & P. D. Eimas (Eds.), *Speech, language, and communication* (pp. 303–337). San Diego: Academic Press.

Clark, K. E., & Ladd, G. W. (2000). Connectedness and autonomy support in parent–child relationships: Links to children's socioemotional orientation and peer relationships. *Developmental Psychology, 36,* 485–498.

Clark, R., Hyde, J. S., Essex, M. J., & Klein, M. H. (1997). Length of maternity leave and quality of mother–infant interaction. *Child Development, 68,* 364–383.

Clarke-Stewart, K. A. (1998). Historical shifts and underlying themes in ideas about rearing young children in the United States: Where have we been? Where are we going? *Early Development and Parenting, 7,* 101–117.

Clarke-Stewart, K. A., & Hayward, C. (1996). Advantages of father custody and contact for the psychological well-being of school-age children. *Journal of Applied Developmental Psychology, 17,* 239–270.

Claude, D., & Firestone, P. (1995). The development of ADHD boys: A 12-year follow-up. *Canadian Journal of Behavioural Science, 27,* 226–249.

Clausen, J. A. (1975). The social meaning of differential physical and sexual maturation. In S. E. Dragastin & G. H. Elder (Eds.), *Adolescence in the life cycle: Psychological change and the social context* (pp. 25–47). New York: Halsted.

Clements, D. H. (1990). Metacomponential development in a Logo programming environment. *Journal of Educational Psychology, 82,* 141–149.

Clements, D. H. (1995). Teaching creativity with computers. *Educational Psychology Review, 7,* 141–161.

Clements, D. H., & Nastasi, B. K. (1992). Computers and early childhood education. In M. Gettinger, S. N. Elliott, & T. R. Kratochwill (Eds.), *Advances in school psychology: Preschool and early childhood treatment directions* (pp. 187–246). Hillsdale, NJ: Erlbaum.

Clements, D. H., Nastasi, B. K., & Swaminathan, S. (1993). Young children and computers: Crossroads and directions from research. *Young Children, 48*(2), 56–64.

Clifton, R. K., Rochat, P., Robin, D. J., & Berthier, N. E. (1994). Multimodal perception in the control of infant reaching. *Journal of Experimental Psychology: Human Perception and Performance, 20,* 876–886.

Clinton, H. R. (1996). *It takes a village: And other lessons children teach us.* New York: Simon & Schuster.

Clutton-Brock, T. H. (1991). *The evolution of parental care.* Princeton, NJ: Princeton University Press.

Coakley, J. (1990). *Sport and society: Issues and controversies* (4th ed.). St. Louis: Mosby.

Cochran, M. (1993). Personal networks in the ecology of human development. In M. Cochran, M. Larner, D. Riley, L. Gunnarsson, & C. R. Henderson, Jr. (Eds.), *Extending families: The social networks of parents and their children* (pp. 1–33). New York: Cambridge University Press.

Cohen, F. L. (1993). HIV infection and AIDS: An overview. In F. L. Cohen & J. D. Durham (Eds.), *Women, children, and HIV/AIDS* (pp. 3–30). New York: Springer.

Cohen, K. M., & Savin-Williams, R. C. (1996). Developmental perspectives on coming out to self and others. In W. R. Savin, K. M. Cohen, & R. C. Savin-Williams (Eds.), *The lives of lesbians, gays, and bisexuals: Children to adults* (pp. 113–151). Ft. Worth, TX: Harcourt Brace.

Cohen, L. B., & Cashon, C. H. (2001). Infant object segregation implies information integration. *Journal of Experimental Child Psychology, 78,* 75–83.

Cohen, S., & Williamson, G. M. (1991). Stress and infectious disease in humans. *Psychological Bulletin, 109,* 5–24.

Cohn, D. A., Cowan, P. A., Cowan, C. P., & Pearson, J. (1992). Mothers' and fathers' working models of childhood attachment relationships, parenting styles, and child behavior. *Development and Psychopathology, 4,* 417–432.

Coie, J. D., & Dodge, K. A. (1998). Aggression and antisocial behavior. In N. Eisenberg (Ed.), *Handbook of child psychology: Vol. 3. Social, emotional, and personality development* (5th ed., pp. 779–862). New York: Wiley.

Coie, J. D., Dodge, K. A., & Coppotelli, H. (1982). Dimensions and types of social status: A cross-age perspective. *Developmental Psychology, 18,* 557–570.

Coie, J. D., & Krehbiel, G. (1984). Effects of academic tutoring on the social status of low-achieving, socially rejected children. *Child Development, 55,* 1465–1478.

Colapinto, J. (2001). *As nature made him: The boy who was raised as a girl.* New York: Perennial.

Colby, A., & Damon, W. (1992). *Some do care: Contemporary lives of moral commitment.* New York: Free Press.

Colby, A., & Kohlberg, L. (1987). *The measurement of moral judgment: Theoretical foundations and research validation* (Vol. 1). Cambridge: Cambridge University Press.

Colby, A., Kohlberg, L., Gibbs, J. C., & Lieberman, M. (1983). A longitudinal study of moral judgment. *Monographs of the Society for Research in Child Development, 48*(1–2, Serial No. 200).

Cole, M. (1990). Cognitive development and formal schooling: The evidence from cross-cultural research. In L. C. Moll (Ed.), *Vygotsky and education* (pp. 89–110). New York: Cambridge University Press.

Cole, P. M., & Tamang, B. L. (1998). Nepali children's ideas about emotional displays in hypothetical challenges. *Developmental Psychology, 34,* 640–646.

Cole, T. J. (2000). Secular trends in growth. *Proceedings of the Nutrition Society, 59,* 317–324.

Coley, R. L. (1998). Children's socialization experiences and functioning in single-mother households: The importance of fathers and other men. *Child Development, 69,* 219–230.

Coley, R. L., & Chase-Lansdale, P. L. (1998). Adolescent pregnancy and parenthood: Recent evidence and future directions. *American Psychologist, 53,* 152–166.

Collaer, M. L., & Hines, M. (1995). Human behavioral sex differences: A role for gonadal hormones during early development? *Psychological Bulletin, 118,* 55–107.

Collie, R., & Hayne, H. (1999). Deferred imitation by 6- and 9-month-old infants: More evidence for declarative memory. *Developmental Psychobiology, 35,* 83–90.

Collins, M. A., & Amabile, T. M. (1999). Motivation and creativity. In R. J. Sternberg (Ed.), *Handbook of creativity* (pp. 297–312). Cambridge: Cambridge University Press.

Collins, W. A. (1983). Children's processing of television content: Implications for prevention of negative effects. *Prevention in Human Services, 2,* 53–66.

Collins, W. A. (1997). Relationships and development during adolescence: Interpersonal adaptation to individual change. *Personal Relationships, 4,* 1–14.

Collins, W. A., Laursen, B., Mortensen, N., Luebker, C., & Ferreira, M. (1997). Conflict processes and transitions in parent and peer relationships: Implications for autonomy and regulation. *Journal of Adolescent Research, 12,* 178–198.

Collins, W. A., Maccoby, E. E., Steinberg, L., Hetherington, E. M., & Bornstein, M. H. (2000). Contemporary research on parenting: The case for nature and nurture. *American Psychologist, 55,* 218–232.

Colombo, J. (1995). On the neural mechanisms underlying developmental and individual differences in visual fixation in infancy. *Developmental Review, 15,* 97–135.

Coltrane, S. (1990). Birth timing and the division of labor in dual-earner families. *Journal of Family Issues, 11,* 157–181.

Common, R., & Frost, L. (1988). The implications of the mismeasurement of Native students' intelligence through the use of standardized intelligence tests. *Canadian Journal of Native Education, 15,* 18–30.

Comstock, G. A., & Scharrer, E. (1999). *Television: What's on, who's watching, and what it means.* San Diego: Academic Press.

Comstock, G. A., & Scharrer, E. (2001). The use of television and other film-related media. In D. G. Singer & J. L. Singer (Eds.), *Handbook of children and the media* (pp. 47–72). Thousand Oaks, CA: Sage.

Comunian, A. L, & Gielan, U. P. (2000). Sociomoral reflection and prosocial and antisocial behavior: Two Italian studies. *Psychological Reports, 87,* 161–175.

Condry, J. C., & Ross, D. F. (1985). Sex and aggression: The influence of gender label on the perception of aggression in children. *Child Development, 56,* 225–233.

Conger, R. D., Patterson, G. R., & Ge, X. (1995). It takes two to replicate: A mediational model for the impact of parents' stress on adolescent adjustment. *Child Development, 66,* 80–97.

Conner, D. B., Knight, D. K., & Cross, D. R. (1997). Mothers' and fathers' scaffolding of their 2-year-olds during problem-solving and literacy interactions. *British Journal of Developmental Psychology, 15,* 323–338.

Connolly, J., Furman, W., & Konarski, R. (2000). The role of peers in the emergence of heterosexual romantic relationships in adolescence. *Child Development, 71,* 1395–1408.

Connolly, J. A., & Doyle, A. B. (1984). Relations of social fantasy play to social competence in preschoolers. *Developmental Psychology, 20,* 797–806.

Connolly, J. A., & Goldberg, A. (1999). Romantic relationships in adolescence: The role of friends and peers in their emergence and development. In W. Furman, B. B. Brown, & C. Feiring (Eds.), *The development of romantic relationships in adolescence* (pp. 266–290). Cambridge: Cambridge University Press.

Connor, P. D., Sampson, P. D., Bookstein, F. L., Barr, H. M., & Streissguth, A. P. (2001). Direct and indirect effects of prenatal alcohol damage on executive function. *Developmental Neuropsychology, 18,* 331–354.

Connor, S. K., & McIntyre, L. (1998, October). *How tobacco and alcohol affect newborn children.* W-98-34Es. Paper presented at Investing in Children: A National Research Conference, Ottawa.

Connors, L. J., & Epstein, J. L. (1996). Parent and school partnerships. In M. H. Bornstein (Ed.), *Handbook of parenting: Vol. 4. Applied and practical parenting* (pp. 437–458). Mahwah, NJ: Erlbaum.

Conti-Ramsden, G., & Pérez-Pereira, M. (1999). Conversational interactions between mothers and their infants who are congenitally blind, have low vision, or are sighted. *Journal of Visual Impairment and Blindness, 93,* 691–703.

Coon, H., Fulker, D. W., DeFries, J. C., & Plomin, R. (1990). Home environment and cognitive ability of 7-year-old children in the Colorado Adoption Project: Genetic and environmental etiologies. *Developmental Psychology, 26,* 459–468.

Cooper, C. R. (1998). *The weaving of maturity: Cultural perspectives on adolescent development.* New York: Oxford University Press.

Cooper, P. J., & Murray, L. (1998). Postnatal depression. *British Medical Journal, 316,* 1884–1886.

Cooper, R. P., & Aslin, R. N. (1994). Developmental differences in infant attention to the spectral properties of infant-directed speech. *Child Development, 65,* 1663–1677.

Coplan, R. J., Gavinski-Molina, M-H., Lagacé-Séguin, D. G., & Wichmann, C. (2001). When girls versus boys play alone: Nonsocial play and adjustment in kindergarten. *Developmental Psychology, 37,* 464–474.

Corah, N. L., Anthony, E. J., Painter, P., Stern, J. A., & Thurston, D. L. (1965). Effects of perinatal anoxia after seven years. *Psychological Monographs, 79*(3, No. 596).

Cornelius, M. D., Day, N. L., Richardson, G. A., & Taylor, P. M. (1999). Epidemiology of substance abuse during pregnancy. In P. J. Ott & R. E. Tarter (Eds.), *Sourcebook on substance abuse: Etiology, epidemiology, assessment, and treatment* (pp. 1–13). Boston, MA: Allyn and Bacon.

Cornelius, M. D., Ryan, C. M., Day, N. L., Goldschmidt, L., & Willford, J. A. (2001). Prenatal tobacco effects on neuropsychological outcomes among preadolescents. *Developmental and Behavioral Pediatrics, 22,* 217–225.

Corrigan, R. (1987). A developmental sequence of actor-object pretend play in young children. *Merrill-Palmer Quarterly, 33,* 87–106.

Cosden, M., Peerson, S., & Elliott, K. (1997). Effects of prenatal drug exposure on birth outcomes and early child development. *Journal of Drug Issues, 27,* 525–539.

Costello, E. J., & Angold, A. (1995). Developmental epidemiology. In D. Cicchetti & D. Cohen (Eds.), *Developmental psychopathology: Vol. 1. Theory and method* (pp. 23–56). New York: Wiley.

Coté, S., Zoccolillo, M., Tremblay, R., Nagin, D., & Vitaro, F. (2001). Predicting girls' conduct disorder in adolescence from childhood trajectories of disruptive behaviors. *Journal of the American Academy of Child and Adolescent Psychiatry, 40,* 678–684.

Coulton, C. J., Korbin, J. E., & Su, M. (1999). Neighborhoods and child maltreatment: A multi-level study. *Child Abuse and Neglect, 23,* 1019–1040.

Couper, R. T., & Couper, J. J. (2000). Prader-Willi Syndrome. *Lancet, 356,* 673–675.

Covell, K., & Howe, R. B. (1999). Working adolescents in economically depressed areas of Canada. *Canadian Journal of Behavioural Science, 31,* 229–239.

Cowan, C. P., & Cowan, P. A. (1995). Interventions to ease the transition to parenthood: Why they are needed and what they can do. *Family Relations, 44,* 412–423.

Cowan, C. P., & Cowan, P. A. (1997). Working with couples during stressful transitions. In S. Dreman (Ed.), *The family on the threshold of the 21st century* (pp. 17–47). Mahwah, NJ: Erlbaum.

Cowan, C. P., & Cowan, P. A. (2000). *When partners become parents.* Mahwah, NJ: Erlbaum.

Cowan, N., Nugent, L. D., Elliott, E. M., Ponomarev, I., & Saults, J. S. (1999). The role of attention in the development of short-term memory: Age differences in the verbal span of apprehension. *Child Development, 70,* 1082–1097.

Cowan, P. A., Powell, D., & Cowan, C. P. (1998). Parenting interventions: A family systems perspective. In I. E. Sigel & K. A. Renninger (Eds.), *Handbook of child psychology: Vol. 4. Child psychology in practice* (5th ed., pp. 3–72). New York: Wiley.

Cox, M. J., Owen, M. T., Henderson, V. K., & Margand, N. A. (1992). Prediction of infant–father and infant–mother attachment. *Developmental Psychology, 28,* 474–483.

Cox, M. J., Paley, B., & Harter, K. (2001). Interparental conflict and parent–child relationships. In J. H. Grych & F. D. Fincham (Eds.), *Interparental conflict and child development: Theory, research, and applications* (pp. 249–272). New York: Cambridge University Press.

Cox, M., & Littleton, K. (1995). Children's use of converging obliques in their perspective drawings. *Educational Psychology, 15,* 127–139.

Cox, S. M., Hopkins, J., & Hans, S. L. (2000). Attachment in preterm infants and their mothers: Neonatal risk status and maternal representations. *Infant Mental Health Journal, 21,* 464–480.

Coyle, T. R., & Bjorklund, D. F. (1997). Age differences in, and consequences of, multiple- and variable-strategy use on a multitrial sort-recall task. *Developmental Psychology, 33,* 372–380.

Craig, W., & Pepler, D. J. (1997). Observations of bullying and victimization on the schoolyard. *Canadian Journal of School Psychology, 13,* 41–59.

Crain, R. M. (1996). The influence of age, race, and gender on child and adolescent multidimensional self-concept. In B. A. Bracken (Ed.), *Handbook of self-concept: Developmental, social, and clinical considerations* (pp. 395–420). New York: Wiley.

Cratty, B. J. (1986). *Perceptual and motor development in infants and children* (3rd ed.). Englewood Cliffs, NJ: Prentice-Hall.

Crawford, J. (1995). *Bilingual education: History, politics, theory, and practice.* Los Angeles: Bilingual Education Services.

Crawford, J. (1997). *Best evidence: Research foundations of the Bilingual Education Act.* Washington, DC: National Clearinghouse for Bilingual Education.

Creasey, G. L., Jarvis, P. A., & Berk, L. E. (1998). Play and social competence. In O. N. Saracho & B. Spodek (Eds.), *Multiple perspectives on play in early childhood education* (pp. 116–143). Albany: State University of New York Press.

Creatsas, G. K., Vekemans, M., Horejsi, J., Uzel, R., Lauritzen, C., & Osler, M. (1995). Adolescent sexuality in Europe: A multicentric study. *Adolescent and Pediatric Gynecology, 8,* 59–63.

Crick, N. R. (1996). The role of overt aggression, relational aggression, and prosocial behavior in the prediction of children's future social adjustment. *Child Development, 67,* 2317–2327.

Crick, N. R. (1997). Engagement in gender normative versus nonnormative forms of aggression: Links to social-psychological adjustment. *Developmental Psychology, 33,* 610–617.

Crick, N. R., & Bigbee, M. A. (1998). Relational and overt forms of peer victimization: A multi-informant approach. *Journal of Consulting and Clinical Psychology, 66,* 337–347.

Crick, N. R., Casas, J. F., & Mosher, M. (1997). Relational and overt aggression in preschool. *Developmental Psychology, 33,* 579–588.

Crick, N. R., & Dodge, K. A. (1994). A review and reformulation of social information-processing mechanisms in children's social adjustment. *Psychological Bulletin, 115,* 74–101.

Crick, N. R., & Grotpeter, J. K. (1995). Relational aggression, gender, and social-psychological adjustment. *Child Development, 66,* 710–722.

Crick, N. R., & Grotpeter, J. K. (1996). Children's treatment by peers: Victims of relational and overt aggression. *Development and Psychopathology, 8,* 367–380.

Crick, N. R., & Ladd, G. W. (1993). Children's perceptions of their peer experiences: Attributions, loneliness, social anxiety, and social avoidance. *Developmental Psychology, 29,* 244–254.

Crosby, R., Leichliter, J. S., & Brackbill, R. (2000). Longitudinal prediction of sexually transmitted diseases among adolescents. *American Journal of Preventive Medicine, 18,* 312–317.

Cross, D. R., & Paris, S. G. (1988). Developmental and instructional analyses of children's metacognition and reading comprehension. *Journal of Educational Psychology, 80,* 131–142.

Crouter, A. C., Manke, B. A., & McHale, S. M. (1995). The family context of gender intensification in early adolescence. *Child Development, 66,* 317–329.

Crowe, H. P., & Zeskind, P. S. (1992). Psychophysiological and perceptual responses to infant cries varying in pitch: Comparison of adults with low and high scores on the child abuse potential inventory. *Child Abuse and Neglect, 16,* 19–29.

Crystal, D. S., Chen, C., Fuligni, A. J., Stevenson, H. W., Hsu, C.-C., Ko, H.-J., Kitamura, S., & Kimura, S. (1994). Psychological maladjustment and academic achievement: A cross-cultural study of Japanese, Chinese, and American high school students. *Child Development, 65,* 738–753.

Csikszentmihalyi, M. (1999). Implications of a systems perspective for the study of creativity. In R. J. Sternberg (Ed.), *Handbook of creativity* (pp. 313–335). Cambridge: Cambridge University Press.

Csikszentmihalyi, M., & Larson, R. (1984). *Being adolescent: Conflict and growth in the teenage years.* New York: Basic Books.

Culbertson, F. M. (1997). Depression and gender: An international review. *American Psychologist, 52,* 25–51.

Culnane, M., Fowler, M. G., Lee, S. S., McSherry, G., Brady, M., & O'Donnell, K. (1999). Lack of long-term effects of in utero exposure to zidovudine among uninfected children born to HIV-infected women. *Journal of the American Medical Association, 281,* 151–157.

Cummings, E. M., & Davies, P. T. (1994). Maternal depression and child development. *Journal of Child Psychology and Psychiatry, 35,* 73–112.

Cummings, E. M., Iannotti, R. J., & Zahn-Waxler, C. (1985). Influence of conflict between adults on the emotions and aggression of young children. *Developmental Psychology, 21,* 495–507.

Cummins, J. (1999). Alternative paradigms in bilingual education research: Does theory have a place? *Educational Researcher, 28*(7), 26–32.

Cunningham, A. E., & Stanovich, K. E. (1990). Early spelling acquisition: Writing beats the computer. *Journal of Educational Psychology, 82,* 159–162.

Currie, J., & Thomas, D. (1997). Can Head Start lead to long term gains in cognition after all? *SRCD Newsletter, 40*(2), 3–5.

Curtin, S. C., & Park, M. M. (1999). Trends in the attendant, place, and timing of births and in the use of obstetric interventions: United States, 1989–1997. *National Vital Statistics Report, 47*(27), 1–12.

Curtiss, S. (1977). *Genie: A psycholinguisitc study of a modern-day "wild child."* New York: Academic Press.

Curtiss, S. (1989). The independence and task-specificity of language. In M. H. Bornstein & J. S. Bruner (Eds.), *Interaction in human development* (pp. 105–137). Hillsdale, NJ: Erlbaum.

Cutrona, C. E., Hessling, R. M., Bacon, P. L., & Russell, D. W. (1998). Predictors and correlates of continuing involvement with the baby's father among adolescent mothers. *Journal of Family Psychology, 12,* 369–387.

D'Agostino, J. A., & Clifford, P. (1998). Neurodevelopmental consequences associated with the premature neonate. *AACN Clinical Issues, 9,* 11–24.

Dahl, R. E., Scher, M. S., Williamson, D. E., Robles, N., & Day, N. (1995). A longitudinal study of prenatal marijuana use. Effects on sleep and arousal at age 3 years. *Archives of Pediatric and Adolescent Medicine, 149,* 145–150.

Daly, K. A., Hunter, L. L., & Giebink, G. S. (1999). Chronic otitis media with effusion. *Pediatrics in Review, 20,* 85–93.

Daly, M., & Wilson, M. (1988). *Homicide.* New York: Aldine de Gruyter.

Damasio, A. R. (1994). *Descartes' error: Emotion, reason, and the human brain.* New York: Putnam.

Damon, W. (1977). *The social world of the child.* San Francisco: Jossey-Bass.

Damon, W. (1988). *The moral child.* New York: Free Press.

Damon, W. (1990). Self-concept, adolescent. In R. M. Lerner, A. C. Petersen, & J. Brooks-Gunn (Eds.), *The encyclopedia of adolescence* (Vol. 2, pp. 67–91) . New York: Garland.

Damon, W. (1995). *Greater expectations: Overcoming the culture of indulgence in America's homes and schools.* New York: Free Press.

Damon, W., & Hart, D. (1988). *Self-understanding in childhood and adolescence.* New York: Cambridge University Press.

Daniels, D. H. (1998). Age differences in concepts of self-esteem. *Merrill-Palmer Quarterly, 44,* 234–259.

Daniels, D. H., Kalkman, D. L., & McCombs, B. L. (2001). Young children's perspectives on learning and teacher practices in different classroom contexts: Implications for motivation. *Early Education and Development, 12,* 253–273.

Dannemiller, J. L. (1989). A test of color constancy in 9- and 20-week-old human infants following simulated illuminant changes. *Developmental Psychology, 25,* 171–184.

Dannemiller, J. L., & Stephens, B. R. (1988). A critical test of infant pattern preference models. *Child Development, 59,* 210–216.

Dapretto, M., & Bjork, E. L. (2000). The development of word retrieval abilities in the second year and its relation to early vocabulary growth. *Child Development, 71,* 635–648.

Darling-Hammond, L., Ancess, J., & Falk, B. (1995). *Authentic assessment: Studies of schools and students at work.* New York: Teachers College Press.

Darnton-Hill, I., & Coyne, E. T. (1998). Feast and famine: Socioeconomic disparities in global nutrition and health. *Public Health and Nutrition, 1,* 23–31.

Darwin, C. (1877). Biographical sketch of an infant. *Mind, 2,* 285–294.

Darwin, C. (1936). *On the origin of species by means of natural selection.* New York: Modern Library. (Original work published 1859)

Dateno, S. (Ed.). (1998). Developed population drops but many eat better despite "crowding." *Population Research Institute Review, 9*(1) [On-line]. Available: www.pop.org/reports/rv019907.html

Datta-Bhutada, S., Johnson, H. L., & Rosen, T. S. (1998). Intrauterine cocaine and crack exposure: Neonatal outcome. *Journal of Perinatology, 18,* 183–188.

Davidson, E., Levine, M., Malvern, J., Niebyl, J., & Tobin, M. (1993). A rebirth of obstetrical care. *Medical World News, 34*(5), 42–47.

Davidson, R. J. (1994). Asymmetric brain function, affective style, and psychopathology: The role of early experience and plasticity. *Development and Psychopathology, 6,* 741–758.

Davies, P. T., Myers, R. L., & Cummings, E. M. (1996). Responses of children and adolescents to marital conflict scenarios as a function of the emotionality of conflict endings. *Merrill-Palmer Quarterly, 42,* 1–21.

Davis, D. L., Gottlieb, M. B., & Stampnitzky, J. R. (1998). Reduced ratio of male to female births in several industrial countries. *Journal of the American Medical Association, 279,* 1018–1023.

Deák, G. O. (2000). Hunting the fox of word learning: Why "constraints" fail to capture it. *Developmental Review, 20,* 29–80.

Deák, G. O., & Maratsos, M. (1998). On having complex representations of things: Preschoolers use multiple words for objects and people. *Developmental Psychology, 34,* 224–240.

Deary, I. J., & Stough, C. (1996). Intelligence and inspection time: Achievements, prospects, and problems. *American Psychologist, 51,* 599–608.

Deater-Deckard, K., & Dodge, K. A. (1997). Externalizing behavior problems and discipline revisited: Nonlinear effects and variation by culture, context, and gender. *Psychological Inquiry, 8,* 161–175.

Deater-Deckard, K., Dodge, K. A., Bates, J. E., & Pettit, G. S. (1996). Physical discipline among African American and European American mothers: Links to children's externalizing behaviors. *Developmental Psychology, 32,* 1065–1072.

Deater-Deckard, K., Pike, A., Petrill, S. A., Cutting, A. L., Hughes, C.,

& O'Connor, T. G. (2001). Non-shared environmental processes in social-emotional development: An observational study of identical twin differences in the preschool period. *Developmental Science, 4,* F1–F6.

Deater-Deckard, K., Scarr, S., McCartney, K., & Eisenberg, M. (1994). Paternal separation anxiety: Relationships with parenting stress, child-rearing attitudes, and maternal anxieties. *Psychological Science, 5,* 341–346.

Deaux, K. (1993). Commentary: Sorry, wrong number—A reply to Gentile's call. *Psychological Science, 4,* 125–126.

DeBerry, K. M., Scarr, S., & Weinberg, R. (1996). Family racial socialization and ecological competence: Longitudinal assessments of African-American transracial adoptees. *Child Development, 67,* 2375–2399.

DeCasper, A. J., & Spence, M. J. (1986). Prenatal maternal speech influences newborns' perception of speech sounds. *Infant Behavior and Development, 9,* 133–150.

DeGarmo, D. S., & Forgatch, M. S. (1999). Contexts as predictors of changing maternal parenting practices in diverse family structures: A social interactional perspective of risk and resilience. In E. M. Hetherington (Ed.), *Coping with divorce, single parenting, and remarriage: A risk and resiliency perspective* (pp. 227–252). Mahwah, NJ: Erlbaum.

Degirmencioglu, S. M., Urberg, K. A., Tolson, J. M., & Richard, P. (1998). Adolescent friendship networks: Continuity and change over the school year. *Merrill-Palmer Quarterly, 44,* 313–337.

DeGroot, A. D. (1951). War and the intelligence of youth. *Journal of Abnormal and Social Psychology, 46,* 596–597.

Dejin-Karlsson, E., Hanson, B. S., Estergren, P.-O., Sjoeberg, N.-O., & Marsal, K. (1998). Does passive smoking in early pregnancy increase the risk of small-for-gestational-age infants? *American Journal of Public Health, 88,* 1523–1527.

Deković, M., & Gerris, J. R. M. (1994). Developmental analysis of social cognitive and behavioral differences between popular and rejected children. *Journal of Applied Developmental Psychology, 15,* 367–386.

Deković, M., Noom, M. J., & Meeus, W. (1997). Expectations regarding development during adolescence: Parent and adolescent perceptions. *Journal of Youth and Adolescence, 26,* 253–271.

Delaney-Black, V., Covington, C., Ostrea, E., Jr., Romero, A., Baker, D., Tagle, M., & Nordstrom-Klee, B. (1996). Prenatal cocaine and

neonatal outcome: Evaluation of dose-response relationship. *Pediatrics, 98,* 735–740.

De Lisi, R., & Gallagher, A. M. (1991). Understanding gender stability and constancy in Argentinean children. *Merrill-Palmer Quarterly, 37,* 483–502.

Dell, D. L. (2001). Adolescent pregnancy. In N. L. Stotland & D. E. Stewart (Eds.), *Psychological aspects of women's health care* (pp. 95–116). Washington, DC: American Psychiatric Association.

DeLoache, J. S. (1987). Rapid change in symbolic functioning of very young children. *Science, 238,* 1556–1557.

DeLoache, J. S. (1991). Symbolic functioning in very young children: Understanding of pictures and models. *Child Development, 62,* 736–752.

DeLoache, J. S. (2000). Dual representation and young children's use of scale models. *Child Development, 71,* 329–338.

DeLoache, J. S., Perralta de Mendoza, O. A., & Anderson, K. N. (1999). Multiple factors in early symbol use: Instructions, similarity, and age in understanding a symbol-referent relation. *Cognitive Development, 14,* 299–312.

DeLoache, J. S., & Todd, C. M. (1988). Young children's use of spatial categorization as a mnemonic strategy. *Journal of Experimental Child Psychology, 46,* 1–20.

DeMarie-Dreblow, D., & Miller, P. H. (1988). The development of children's strategies for selective attention: Evidence for a transitional period. *Child Development, 59,* 1504–1513.

Demianczuk, N., (1999). Guidelines for ultrasound as part of routine prenatal care. *Journal of the Society of Obstetricians and Gynaecologists of Canada, 21,* 874–879.

Dempster, F. N. (1995). Interference and inhibition in cognition: An historical perspective. In F. N. Dempster & C. J. Brainerd (Eds.), *Interference and inhibition in cognition* (pp. 3–26). San Diego: Academic Press.

Dempster, F. N., & Corkill, A. J. (1999). Interference and inhibition in cognition and behavior: Unifying themes for educational psychology. *Educational Psychology Review, 11,* 1–88.

Demuth, K. (1996). The prosodic structure of early words. In J. Morgan & K. Demuth (Eds.), *From signal to syntax* (pp. 171–184). Mahwah, NJ: Erlbaum.

Denckla, M. B. (1996). Biological correlates of learning and attention: What is relevant to learning disability and attention-deficit hyperactivity disorder? *Developmental and Behavioral Pediatrics, 17,* 114–119.

Denham, S. A., Zoller, D., & Couchoud, E. (1994). Socialization of preschoolers' emotion understanding. *Developmental Psychology, 30,* 928–936.

Dennis, W. (1960). Causes of retardation among institutionalized children: Iran. *Journal of Genetic Psychology, 96,* 47–59.

Derom, C., Thiery, E., Vlietinck, R., Loos, R., & Derom, R. (1996). Handedness in twins according to zygosity and chorion type: A preliminary report. *Behavior Genetics, 26,* 407–408.

DeRosier, M. E., Cillessen, A. H. N., Coie, J. D., & Dodge, K. A. (1994). Group social context and children's aggressive behavior. *Child Development, 65,* 1068–1079.

Deutsch, W., & Pechmann, T. (1982). Social interaction and the development of definite descriptions. *Cognition, 11,* 159–184.

de Villiers, J. G., & de Villiers, P. A. (1973). A cross-sectional study of the acquisition of grammatical morphemes in child speech. *Journal of Psycholinguistic Research, 2,* 267–278.

de Villiers, J. G., & de Villiers, P. A. (1999). Language development. In M. H. Bornstein & M. E. Lamb (Eds.), *Developmental psychology: An advanced textbook* (4th ed., pp. 313–373). Mahwah, NJ: Erlbaum.

de Villiers, J. G., & de Villiers, P. A. (2000). Linguistic determinism and the understanding of false beliefs. In P. Mitchell & K. J. Riggs (Eds.), *Children's reasoning and the mind* (pp. 87–99). Hove, UK: Psychology Press.

Devlin, B., Fienberg, S. E., Resnick, D. P., & Roeder, K. (1995). Galton redux: Intelligence, race and society: A review of "The Bell Curve: Intelligence and Class Structure in American Life." *American Statistician, 90,* 1483–1488.

deVries, M. W. (1984). Temperament and infant mortality among the Masai of East Africa. *American Journal of Psychiatry, 141,* 1189–1194.

de Waal, F. (1991). The chimpanzee's sense of social regularity and its relation to the human sense of justice. *American Behavioral Scientist, 34,* 335–349.

de Waal, F. (1996). *Good natured: The origins of right and wrong in humans and other animals.* Cambridge, MA: Harvard University Press.

de Waal, F. B. M. (1993). Sex differences in chimpanzee (and human) behavior: A matter of social values? In M. Hechter, L. Nadel, & R. E. Michod (Eds.), *The origin of values* (pp. 285–303). New York: Aldine de Gruyter.

de Waal, F. B. M. (1999). The end of nature versus nurture. *Scientific American, 281*(6), 94–99.

Dewey, K. G. (2001). Nutrition, growth, and complementary feeding of the breastfed infant. *Pediatric Clinics of North America, 48,* 87–104.

De Wolff, M. S., & van IJzendoorn, M. H. (1997). Sensitivity and attachment: A meta-analysis on parental antecedents of infant attachment. *Child Development, 68,* 571–591.

Dewsbury, D. A. (1992). Comparative psychology and ethology: A reassessment. *American Psychologist, 47,* 208–215.

Diamond, A. (1991). Neuropsychological insights into the meaning of object concept development. In S. Carey & R. Gelman (Eds.), *The epigenesis of mind: Essays on biology and knowledge* (pp. 67–110). Hillsdale, NJ: Erlbaum.

Diamond, A. Cruttenden, L., & Neiderman, D. (1994). AB with multiple wells: 1. Why are multiple wells sometimes easier than two wells? 2. Memory or memory + inhibition. *Developmental Psychology, 30,* 192–205.

Diamond, L. M. (1998). Development of sexual orientation among adolescent and young adult women. *Developmental Psychology, 34,* 1085–1095.

Diamond, L. M., Savin-Williams, R. C., & Dubé, E. M. (1999). Sex, dating, passionate friendships, and romance: Intimate peer relations among lesbian, gay, and bisexual adolescents. In W. Furman & B. B. Brown (Eds.), *The development of romantic relationships in adolescence* (pp. 175–210). New York: Cambridge University Press.

Diamond, M., & Hopson, J. (1999). *Magic trees of the mind.* New York: Plume.

Diamond, M., Johnson, R., Young, D., & Singh, S. (1983). Age-related morphologic differences in the rat cerebral cortex and hippocampus: Male–female; right–left. *Experimental Neurology, 81,* 1–13.

Diamond, M., & Sigmundson, H. K. (1999). Sex reassignment at birth. In S. J. Ceci & W. M. Williams (Eds.), *The nature–nurture debate* (pp. 55–75). Malden, MA: Blackwell.

Dias, M. G., & Harris, P. L. (1990). The influence of imagination on reasoning by young children. *British Journal of Developmental Psychology, 8,* 305–318.

Dick, D. M., Rose, R. J., Viken, R. J., & Kaprio, J. (2000). Pubertal timing and substance use: Associations between and within families across late adolescence. *Developmental Psychology, 36,* 180–189.

Dickens, W. T., & Flynn, J. R. (2001). Heritability estimates versus large environmental effects: The IQ paradox resolved. *Psychological Review, 108,* 346–369.

Dickinson, D. K. (1984). First impressions: Children's knowledge of words gained from a single exposure. *Applied Psycholinguistics, 5,* 359–373.

Dick-Read, G. (1959). *Childbirth without fear.* New York: Harper & Brothers.

Dickson, K. L., Fogel, A., & Messinger, D. (1998). The development of emotion from a social process view. In M. F. Mascolo (Ed.), *What develops in emotional development?* (pp. 253–271). New York: Plenum.

Dickson, S. V., Collins, V. L., Simmons, D. C., & Kameenui, E. J. (1998). Metacognitive strategies: Research bases. In D. C. Simmons & E. J. Kameenui (Eds.), *What reading research tells us about children with diverse learning needs: Bases and basics* (pp. 295–360). Mahwah, NJ: Erlbaum.

Diener, M. L., Goldstein, L. H., & Mangelsdorf, S. C. (1995). The role of prenatal expectations in parents' reports of infant temperament. *Merrill-Palmer Quarterly, 41,* 172–190.

Dietrich, K. N. (1999). Environmental toxicants and child development. In H. Tager-Flusberg (Ed.), *Neurodevelopmental disorders* (pp. 469–490). Boston: MIT Press.

Dietrich, K. N., Berger, O. G., & Succop, P. A. (1993). Lead exposure and the motor developmental status of urban six-year-old children in the Cincinnati Prospective Study. *Pediatrics, 91,* 301–307.

Dietz, T. L. (1998). An examination of violence and gender role portrayals in video games: Implications for gender socialization and aggressive behavior. *Sex Roles, 38,* 425–442.

DiLalla, L. F., Kagan, J., & Reznick, J. S. (1994). Genetic etiology of behavioral inhibition among 2-year-old children. *Infant Behavior and Development, 17,* 405–412.

Dildy, G. A., Jackson, G. M., Fowers, G. K., Oshiro, B. T., Varner, M. W., & Clark, S. L. (1996). Very advanced maternal age. Pregnancy after age 45. *American Journal of Obstetrics and Gynecology, 175,* 668–674.

DiMatteo, M. R., & Kahn, K. L. (1997). Psychosocial aspects of childbirth. In S. J. Gallant, G. P. Keita, & R. Royak-Shaler (Eds.), *Health care for women: Psychological, social, and behavioral influences* (pp. 175–186). Washington, DC: American Psychological Association.

DiPietro, J. A., Hodgson, D. M., Costigan, K. A., & Hilton, S. C. (1996a). Fetal neurobehavioral development. *Child Development, 67,* 2553–2567.

DiPietro, J. A., Hodgson, D. M., Costigan, K. A., & Johnson, T. R. B. (1996b). Fetal antecedents of infant temperament. *Child Development, 67,* 2568–2583.

Dirks, J. (1982). The effect of a commercial game on children's Block Design scores on the WISC-R test. *Intelligence, 6,* 109–123.

Dishion, T. J., Andrews, D. W., & Crosby, L. (1995). Antisocial boys and their friends in early adolescence: Relationship characteristics, quality, and interactional processes. *Child Development, 66,* 139–151.

Dishion, T. J., Poulin, F., & Burraston, B. (2001). Peer group dynamics associated with iatrogenic effects in group interventions with high-risk young adolescents. In D. W. Nangle & C. A. Erdley (Eds.), *The role of friendship in psychological adjustment* (pp. 79–92). San Francisco: Jossey-Bass.

Dixon, J. A., & Moore, C. F. (1990). The development of perspective taking: Understanding differences in information and weighting. *Child Development, 61,* 1502–1513.

Dixon, R. A., & Lerner, R. M. (1999). History and systems in developmental psychology. In M. H. Bornstein & M. E. Lamb (Eds.), *Developmental psychology: An advanced textbook* (4th ed., pp. 3–46). Mahwah, NJ: Erlbaum.

Dodge, K. A. (1985). A social information processing model of social competence in children. In M. Perlmutter (Ed.), *Minnesota Symposia on Child Psychology* (Vol. 18, pp. 77–125). Hillsdale, NJ: Erlbaum.

Dodge, K. A., McClaskey, C. L., & Feldman E. (1985). A situational approach to the assessment of social competence in children. *Journal of Consulting and Clinical Psychology, 53,* 344–353.

Dodge, K. A., Pettit, G. S., & Bates, J. E. (1994). Socialization mediators of the relation between socioeconomic status and child conduct problems. *Child Development, 65,* 649–665.

Dodge, K. A., Pettit, G. S., McClaskey, C. L., & Brown, M. M. (1986). Social competence in children. *Monographs of the Society for Research in Child Development, 51*(2, Serial No. 213).

Dodge, K. A., & Price, J. M. (1994). On the relation between social information processing and socially competent behavior in early school-aged children. *Child Development, 65,* 1385–1397.

Dodge, K. A., & Somberg, D. R. (1987). Hostile attributional biases among aggressive boys are exacerbated under conditions of threats to the self. *Child Development, 58,* 213–224.

Doherty, G., Lero, D. S., Goelman, H., Tougas, J., & LaGrange, A. (2000). *You bet I care! Caring and learning environments: Quality in regulated family child care across Canada.* Guelph, ON: Centre for Families, Work and Well-Being, University of Guelph.

Dolan, B. (1999). From the field: Cognitive profiles of First Nations and Caucasian children referred from psychoeducational assessment. *Canadian Journal of School Psychology, 15,* 63–71.

Dollaghan, C. (1985). Child meets word: "Fast mapping" in preschool children. *Journal of Speech and Hearing Research, 28,* 449–454.

Donatelle, R. J., & Davis, L. G. (2000). *Health: The basics* (4th ed.). Boston: Allyn and Bacon.

Dondi, M., Simion, F., & Caltran, G. (1999). Can newborns discriminate between their own cry and the cry of another newborn infant? *Developmental Psychology, 35,* 418–426.

Donnerstein, E., Slaby, R. G., & Eron, L. D. (1994). The mass media and youth aggression. In L. D. Eron, J. H. Gentry, & P. Schlegel (Eds.), *Reason to hope: A psychosocial perspective on violence and youth* (pp. 219–250). Washington, DC: American Psychological Association.

Donovan, W. L., Leavitt, L. A., & Walsh, R. O. (1997). Cognitive set and coping strategy affect mothers' sensitivity to infant cries: A signal detection approach. *Child Development, 68,* 760–772.

Donovan, W. L., Leavitt, L. A., & Walsh, R. O. (2000). Maternal illusory control predicts socialization strategies and toddler compliance. *Developmental Psychology, 36,* 402–411.

Dornbusch, S. M., & Glasgow, K. L. (1997). The structural context of family–school relations. In A. Booth & J. F. Dunn (Eds.), *Family–school links: How do they affect educational outcomes?* (pp. 35–55). Mahwah, NJ: Erlbaum.

Dornbusch, S. M., Glasgow, K. L., & Lin, I.-C. (1996). The social structure of schooling. *Annual Review of Psychology, 47,* 401–427.

Dorris, M. (1989). *The broken cord.* New York: Harper & Row.

Dossett, D., & Burns, B. (2000). The development of children's knowledge of attention and resource allocation in single and dual tasks. *Journal of Genetic Psychology, 161,* 216–234.

Dougherty, T. M., & Haith, M. M. (1997). Infant expectations and reaction time as predictors of childhood speed of processing and IQ. *Developmental Psychology, 33,* 146–155.

Downey, G., & Walker, E. (1989). Social cognition and adjustment in children at risk for psychopathology. *Developmental Psychology, 25,* 835–845.

Downs, A. C., & Fuller, M. J. (1991). Recollections of spermarche: An exploratory investigation.

Current Psychology: Research and Reviews, 10, 93–102.

Downs, A. C., & Langlois, J. H. (1988). Sex typing: Construct and measurement issues. *Sex Roles, 18*, 87–100.

Doyle, A. B., & Aboud, F. E. (1995). A longitudinal study of white children's racial prejudice as a social-cognitive development. *Merrill-Palmer Quarterly, 41*, 209–228.

Drabman, R. S., Cordua, G. D., Hammer, D., Jarvie, G. J., & Horton, W. (1979). Developmental trends in eating rates of normal and overweight preschool children. *Child Development, 50*, 211–216.

Draper, P., & Cashdan, E. (1988). Technological change and child behavior among the !Kung. *Ethnology, 27*, 339–365.

Drew, L. M., Richard, M. H., & Smith, P. K. (1998). Grandparenting and its relationship to parenting. *Clinical Child Psychology and Psychiatry, 3*, 465–480.

Droege, K. L., & Stipek, D. J. (1993). Children's use of dispositions to predict classmates' behavior. *Developmental Psychology, 29*, 646–654.

Drotar, D., Overholser, J. C., Levi, R., Walders, N., Robinson, J. R., Palermo, T. M., & Riekert, K. A. (2000). Ethical issues in conducting research with pediatric and clinical child populations in applied settings. In D. Drotar (Ed.), *Handbook of research in pediatric and clinical child psychology* (pp. 305–326). New York: Kluwer.

Drotar, D., Pallotta, J., & Eckerle, D. (1994). A prospective study of family environments of children hospitalized for nonorganic failure-to-thrive. *Developmental and Behavioral Pediatrics, 15*, 78–85.

Dryburgh, H. (2001). Teenage pregnancy. *Health Reports, 12*(1). Statistics Canada, cat. no. 82–003.

Dubé, E. M., Savin-Williams, R. C., & Diamond, L. M. (2001). Intimacy development, gender, and ethnicity among sexual-minority youths. In A. R. D'Augelli & C. J. Patterson (Eds.), *Lesbian, gay, and bisexual identities and youth* (pp. 129–152). New York: Oxford University Press.

DuBois, D. L., Bull, C. A., Sherman, M. D., & Roberts, M. (1998). Self-esteem and adjustment in early adolescence: A social-contextual perspective. *Journal of Youth and Adolescence, 27*, 557–583.

DuBois, D. L., Felner, R. D., Brand, S., & George, G. R. (1999). Profiles of self-esteem in early adolescence: Identification and investigation of adaptive correlates. *American Journal of Community Psychology, 27*, 899–932.

Dubow, E. F., Tisak, J., Causey, D., Hryshko, A., & Reid, G. (1991). A two-year longitudinal study of stressful life events, social support, and social problem-solving skills: Contributions to children's behavioral and academic adjustment. *Child Development, 62*, 583–599.

Duncan, G. J., & Brooks-Gunn, J. (2000). Family poverty, welfare reform, and child development. *Child Development, 71*, 188–196.

Duncan, G., Yeung, W. J., Brooks-Gunn, J., & Smith, J. R. (1998). How much does childhood poverty affect the life changes of children? *American Sociological Review, 63*, 406–423.

Duncan, R. M., & Pratt, M. W. (1997). Microgenetic change in the quantity and quality of preschoolers' private speech. *International Journal of Behavioral Development, 20*, 367–383.

Duniz, M., Scheer, P. J., Trojovsky, A., Kaschnitz, W., Kvas, E., & Macari, S. (1996). *European Child and Adolescent Psychiatry, 5*, 93–100.

Dunn, J. (1996). Sibling relationships and perceived self-competence: Patterns of stability between childhood and early adolescence. In A. J. Sameroff & M. M. Haith (Eds.), *The five to seven year shift* (pp. 253–270). Chicago: University of Chicago Press.

Dunn, J., Brown, J. R., & Maguire, M. (1995). The development of children's moral sensibility: Individual differences and emotion understanding. *Developmental Psychology, 31*, 649–659.

Dunn, J., Brown, J., Slomkowski, C. T., & Youngblade, L. (1991). Young children's understanding of other people's feelings and beliefs: Individual differences and their antecedents. *Child Development, 62*, 1352–1366.

Dunn, J., & Kendrick, C. (1982). *Siblings: Love, envy and understanding.* Cambridge, MA: Harvard University Press.

Dunn, J., Slomkowski, C., & Beardsall, L. (1994). Sibling relationships from the preschool period through middle childhood and early adolescence. *Developmental Psychology, 30*, 315–324.

Dunn, J., Slomkowski, C., Beardsall, L., & Rende, R. (1994). Adjustment in middle childhood and early adolescence: Links with earlier and contemporary sibling relationships. *Journal of Child Psychology and Psychiatry, 35*, 491–504.

Durbin, D. L., Darling, N., Steinberg, L., & Brown, B. B. (1993). Parenting style and peer group membership among European-American adolescents. *Journal of Research on Adolescence, 3*, 87–100.

Durrant, J. (1999). Evaluating the success of Sweden's corporal punishment ban. *Child Abuse and Neglect, 23*, 435–448.

Durrant, J. E., Broberg, A., & Rose-Krasnor, L. (1999). Predicting use of physical punishment during mother–child conflicts in Sweden and Canada. In P. Hastings & C. Piotrowski (Eds.), Maternal beliefs about child-rearing. *New Directions for Child Development, 86*, 25–42.

Dwyer, T., Ponsonby, A. L., & Couper, D. (1999). Tobacco smoke exposure at one month of age and subsequent risk of SIDS: A prospective study. *American Journal of Epidemiology, 149*, 593–602.

Dybing, E., & Sanner, T. (1999). Passive smoking, sudden infant death syndrome (SIDS), and childhood infections. *Human Experimental Toxicology, 18*, 202–205.

Dyer, C. (1999). Pathophysiology of phenylketonuria. *Mental Retardation and Developmental Disabilities Research Reviews, 5*, 104–112.

Dye-White, E. (1986). Environmental hazards in the work setting: Their effect on women of child-bearing age. *American Association of Occupational Health and Nursing Journal, 34*, 76–78.

Eagly, A. H. (1995). The science and politics of comparing women and men. *American Psychologist, 50*, 145–158.

East, P. L., & Felice, M. E. (1996). *Adolescent pregnancy and parenting: Findings from a racially diverse sample.* Mahwah, NJ: Erlbaum.

East, P. L., & Rook, K. S. (1992). Compensatory patterns of support among children's peer relationships: A test using school friends, nonschool friends, and siblings. *Developmental Psychology, 28*, 168–172.

Easterbrook, M. A., Kisilevsky, B. S., Muir, D. W., & LaPlante, D. P. (1999). Newborns discriminate schematic faces from scrambled faces. *Canadian Journal of Experimental Psychology, 53*, 231–241.

Ebeling, K. S., & Gelman, S. A. (1994). Children's use of context in interpreting "big" and "little." *Child Development, 65*, 1178–1192.

Eberhart-Phillips, J. E., Frederick, P. D., & Baron, R. C. (1993). Measles in pregnancy: A descriptive study of 58 cases. *Obstetrics and Gynecology, 82*, 797–801.

Ebrahim, S. H., Floyd, R. L., Merritt, R. K., Decoufle, P., & Holtzman, D. (2000). Trends in pregnancy-related smoking rates in the United States, 1987–1996. *Journal of the American Medical Association, 283*, 361–366.

Eccles, J. S. (1994). Understanding women's educational and occupational choices: Applying the Eccles et al. model of achievement-related choices. *Psychology of Women Quarterly, 18*, 585–609.

Eccles, J. S., Barber, B., Jozefowicz, D., Malenchuk, O., & Vida, M. (1999). Self-evaluations of competence, task values, and self-esteem. In N. G. Johnson & M. C. Roberts (Eds.), *Beyond appearance: A new look at adolescent girls* (pp. 53–83). Washington, DC: American Psychological Association.

Eccles, J. S., Early, D., Frasier, K., Belansky, E., & McCarthy, K. (1997a). The relation of connection, regulation, and support for autonomy to adolescents' functioning. *Journal of Adolescent Research, 12*, 263–286.

Eccles, J. S., Freedman-Doan, C., Frome, P., Jacobs, J., & Yoon, K. S. (2000). Gender-role socialization in the family: A longitudinal approach. In T. Eckes & H. M. Trautner (Eds.), *The developmental social psychology of gender* (pp. 333–360). Mahwah, NJ: Erlbaum.

Eccles, J. S., & Harold, R. D. (1991). Gender differences in sport involvement: Applying the Eccles' expectancy-value model. *Journal of Applied Sport Psychology, 3*, 7–35.

Eccles, J. S., Jacobs, J. E., & Harold, R. D. (1990). Gender-role stereotypes, expectancy effects, and parents' role in the socialization of gender differences in self-perceptions and skill acquisition. *Journal of Social Issues, 46*, 183–201.

Eccles, J. S., Lord, S., Roeser, R. W., Barber, B., & Josefowicz-Hernandez, D. (1997b). The association of school transitions in early adolescence with developmental trajectories through high school. In J. Schulenberg, J. Maggs, & K. Hurrelmann (Eds.), *Health risks and developmental transitions during adolescence* (pp. 283–320). New York: Cambridge University Press.

Eccles, J. S., Midgley, C. Wigfield, A., Buchanan, C. M., Reuman, D., Flanagan, C., & Mac Iver, D. (1993b). Development during adolescence: The impact of stage–environment fit on young adolescents' experiences in schools and in families. *American Psychologist, 48*, 90–101.

Eccles, J. S., Wigfield, A., Harold, R. D., & Blumfeld, P. (1993a). Age and gender differences in children's self and task perceptions during elementary school. *Child Development, 64*, 830–847.

Eccles, J. S., Wigfield, A., Midgley, C., Reuman, D., Mac Iver, D., & Feldlaufer, H. (1993c). Negative effects of traditional middle schools on students' motivation. *Elementary School Journal, 93*, 553–574.

Eccles, J. S., Wigfield, A., & Schiefele, U. (1998). Motivation to succeed. In N. Eisenberg (Ed.), *Handbook* of child psychology: Vol. 3. Social, emotional, and personality development (5th ed., pp. 1017–1095). New York: Wiley.

Eckerman, C. O., & Didow, S. M. (1996). Nonverbal imitation and toddlers' mastery of verbal means of achieving coordinated interaction. Developmental Psychology, 32, 141–152.

Eckerman, C. O., & Whitehead, H. (1999). How toddler peers generate coordinated action: A cross-cultural exploration. Early Education and Development, 10, 241–266.

Eder, D., & Parker, S. (1987). The cultural production and reproduction of gender: The effect of extracurricular activities on peer-group culture. Sociology of Education, 60, 200–213.

Eder, R. A. (1989). The emergent personologist: The structure and content of $3^1/2$-, $5^1/2$-, and $7^1/2$-year-olds' concepts of themselves and other persons. Child Development, 60, 1218–1228.

Edwards, C. P. (1978). Social experiences and moral judgment in Kenyan young adults. Journal of Genetic Psychology, 133, 19–30.

Egeland, B., & Hiester, M. (1995). The long-term consequences of infant day-care and mother–infant attachment. Child Development, 66, 474–485.

Egeland, B., Jacobvitz, D., & Sroufe, L. A. (1988). Breaking the cycle of abuse. Child Development, 59, 1080–1088.

Egeland, B., Kalkoske, M., Gottesman, N., & Erickson, M. F. (1990). Preschool behavior problems: Stability and factors accounting for change. Journal of Child Psychology and Psychiatry, 31, 891–909.

Ehrhardt, A. A., & Baker, S. W. (1974). Fetal androgens, human central nervous system differentiation, and behavior sex differences. In R. C. Friedman, R. M. Richart, & R. L. VandeWiele (Eds.), Sex differences in behavior (pp. 33–51). New York: Wiley.

Eiben, B., Hammans, W., Hansen, S., Trawicki, W., Osthelder, B., Stelzer, A., Jaspers, K.-D., & Goebel, R. (1997). On the complication risk of early amniocentesis versus standard amniocentesis. Fetal Diagnosis and Therapy, 12, 140–144.

Eibl-Eibesfeldt, I. (1989). Human ethology. Hawthorne, NY: Aldine.

Eiden, R. D., & Reifman, A. (1996). Effects of Brazelton demonstrations on later parenting: A meta-analysis. Journal of Pediatric Psychology, 21, 857–868.

Eilers, R. E., & Oller, D. K. (1994). Infant vocalizations and the early diagnosis of severe hearing impairment. Journal of Pediatrics, 124, 199–203.

Eisenberg, L. (1999). Experience, brain, and behavior: The importance of a head start. Pediatrics, 103, 1031–1035.

Eisenberg, N. (1986). Altruistic emotion, cognition, and behavior. Hillsdale, NJ: Erlbaum.

Eisenberg, N. (1998). Introduction. In N. Eisenberg (Ed.), Handbook of child psychology: Vol. 3. Social, emotional, and personality development (pp. 1–24). New York: Wiley.

Eisenberg, N., Carlo, G., Murphy, B., & Van Court, P. (1995). Prosocial development in late adolescence: A longitudinal study. Child Development, 66, 1179–1197.

Eisenberg, N., Cumberland, A., & Spinrad, T. L. (1998). Parental socialization of emotion. Psychological Inquiry, 9, 241–273.

Eisenberg, N., & Fabes, R. A. (1998). Prosocial development. In N. Eisenberg (Ed.), Handbook of child psychology: Vol. 3. Social, emotional, and personality development (5th ed., pp. 701–778). New York: Wiley.

Eisenberg, N., Fabes, R. A., Carlo, G., Speer, A. L., Switzer, G., Karbon, M., & Troyer, D. (1993). The relations of empathy-related emotions and maternal practices to children's comforting behavior. Journal of Experimental Child Psychology, 55, 131–150.

Eisenberg, N., Fabes, R. A., Murphy, B., Maszk, P., Smith, M., & Karbon, M. (1995b). The role of emotionality and regulation in children's social functioning: A longitudinal study. Child Development, 66, 1360–1384.

Eisenberg, N., Fabes, R. A., Shepard, S. A., Guthrie, I., Murphy, B. C., & Reiser, M. (1999). Parental reactions to children's negative emotions: Longitudinal relations to quality of children's social functioning. Child Development, 70, 513–534.

Eisenberg, N., Fabes, R. A., Shepard, S. A., Murphy, B. C., Guthrie, I. K., Jones, S., Friedman, J., Poulin, R., & Maszk, P. (1997). Contemporaneous and longitudinal prediction of children's social functioning from regulation and emotionality. Child Development, 68, 642–664.

Eisenberg, N., Fabes, R. A., Shepard, S. A., Murphy, B. C., Jones, S., & Guthrie, I. K. (1998). Contemporaneous and longitudinal prediction of children's sympathy from dispositional regulation and emotionality. Developmental Psychology, 34, 910–924.

Eisenberg, N., Fabes, R., Murphy, B., Karbon, M., Smith, M., & Maszk, P. (1996). The relations of children's dispositional empathy-related responding to their emotionality, regulation, and social functioning. Developmental Psychology, 32, 195–209.

Eisenberg, N., & McNally, S. (1993). Socialization and mothers' and adolescents' empathy-related characteristics. Journal of Research on Adolescence, 3, 171–191.

Eisenberg, N., Miller, P. A., Shell, R., McNalley, S., & Shea, C. (1991). Prosocial development in adolescence: A longitudinal study. Developmental Psychology, 27, 849–857.

Eisenberg, N., Murphy, B. C., & Shepard, S. (1997). The development of empathic accuracy. In W. Ickes (Ed.), Empathic accuracy (pp. 73–116). New York: Guilford.

Eisenberg, N., Zhoe, Q., & Koller, S. (2001). Brazilian adolescents' prosocial moral judgment and behavior: Relations to sympathy, perspective taking, gender-role orientation, and demographic characteristics. Child Development, 72, 518–534.

Ekman, P., & Friesen, W. (1972). Constants across culture in the face of emotion. Journal of Personality and Social Psychology, 17, 124–129.

Elardo, R., Bradley, R. H., & Caldwell, B. M. (1975). The relation of infants' home environments to mental test performance from six to thirty-six months: A longitudinal analysis. Child Development, 46, 71–76.

Elder, G. H., Jr. (1999). Children of the Great Depression (25th anniversary ed.). Boulder, CO: Westview Press.

Elder, G. H., Jr., & Caspi, A. (1988). Human development and social change: An emerging perspective on the life course. In N. Bolger, A. Caspi, G. Downey, & M. Moorehouse (Eds.), Persons in context: Developmental processes (pp. 77–113). Cambridge: Cambridge University Press.

Elder, G. H., Jr., & Hareven, T. K. (1993). Rising above life's disadvantage: From the Great Depression to war. In G. H. Elder, Jr., J. Modell, & R. D. Parke (Eds.), Children in time and place (pp. 47–72). Cambridge, England: Cambridge University Press.

Elder, G. H., Jr., Liker, J. K., & Cross, C. E. (1984). Parent–child behavior in the Great Depression: Life course and intergenerational influences. In P. B. Baltes & O. G. Brim (Eds.), Life-span development and behavior (Vol. 6, pp. 109–158). New York: Academic Press.

Elder, G. H., Jr., Van Nguyen, T., & Caspi, A. (1985). Linking family hardship to children's lives. Child Development, 56, 361–375.

Elias, C. L., & Berk, L. E. (2002). Self-regulation in young children: Is there a role for sociodramatic play? Early Childhood Research Quarterly, 17, 1–17.

Elias, G., & Broerse, J. (1996). Developmental changes in the incidence and likelihood of simultaneous talk during the first two years: A question of function. Journal of Child Language, 23, 201–217.

Elicker, J., Englund, M., & Sroufe, L. A. (1992). Predicting peer competence and peer relationships in childhood from early parent–child relationships. In R. D. Parke & G. W. Ladd (Eds.), Family–peer relationships: Modes of linkage (pp. 77–106). Hillsdale, NJ: Erlbaum.

Elkind, D. (1994). A sympathetic understanding of the child: Birth to sixteen (3rd ed.). Boston: Allyn and Bacon.

Elkind, D., & Bowen, R. (1979). Imaginary audience behavior in children and adolescence. Developmental Psychology, 15, 33–44.

Elliot, D. S. (1994). Serious violent offenders: Onset, developmental course, and termination. Criminology, 32, 1–21.

Elliot, D. S., Wilson, W. J., Huizinga, D., Sampson, R. J., Elliott, A., & Rankin, B. (1996). The effects of neighborhood disadvantage on adolescent development. Journal of Research in Crime and Delinquency, 33, 389–426.

Elliott, E. S., & Dweck, C. S. (1988). Goals: An approach to motivation and achievement. Journal of Personality and Social Psychology, 54, 5–12.

Ellis, B. J., & Garber, J. (2000). Psychosocial antecedents of variation in girls' pubertal timing: Maternal depression, stepfather presence, and marital and family stress. Child Development, 71, 485–501.

Ellis, B. J., McFadyen-Ketchum, S., Dodge, K. A., Pettit, G. S., & Bates, J. E. (1999). Quality of early family relationships and individual differences in the timing of pubertal maturation in girls: A longitudinal test of an evolutionary model. Journal of Personality and Social Psychology, 77, 933–952.

Ellis, S., & Gauvain, M. (1992). Social and cultural influences on children's collaborative interactions. In L. T. Winegar & J. Valsiner (Eds.), Children's development within social context (Vol. 2, pp. 155–180). Hillsdale, NJ: Erlbaum.

Ellis, S., Rogoff, B., & Cromer, C. (1981). Age segregation in children's social interactions. Developmental Psychology, 17, 399–407.

Ellsworth, C. P., Muir, D. W., & Hains, S. M. J. (1993). Social competence and person-object differentiation: An analysis of the still-face effect. Developmental Psychology, 29, 63–73.

Elman, J. L., Bates, E. A., Johnson, M. H., Karmiloff-Smith, A., Parisi, D., & Plunkett, K. (1996). Rethinking innateness: A connectionist perspective on development. Cambridge, MA: MIT Press.

Elsen, H. (1994). Phonological constraints and overextensions. *First Language, 14,* 305–315.

El-Sheikh, M., Cummings, E. M., & Reiter, S. (1996). Preschoolers' responses to ongoing interadult conflict: The role of prior exposure to resolved versus unresolved arguments. *Journal of Abnormal Child Psychology, 24,* 665–679.

Ely, R. (1997). Language and literacy in the school years. In J. Berko Gleason (Ed.), *The development of language* (4th ed., pp. 398–439). Boston: Allyn and Bacon.

Ely, R., & McCabe, A. (1994). The language play of kindergarten children. *First Language, 14,* 19–35.

Emanuel, R. L., Robinson, B. G., Seely, E. W., Graves, S. W., Kohane, I., Saltzman, D., Barbieri, R., & Majzoub, J. A. (1994). Corticotrophin releasing hormone levels in human plasma and amniotic fluid during gestation. *Clinical Endocrinology, 40,* 257–262.

Emde, R. N. (1992). Individual meaning and increasing complexity: Contributions of Sigmund Freud and René Spitz to developmental psychology. *Developmental Psychology, 28,* 347–359.

Emde, R. N., Bioringen, Z., Clyman, R. B., & Oppenheim, D. (1991). The moral self of infancy: Affective core and procedural knowledge. *Developmental Review, 11,* 251–270.

Emde, R. N., & Oppenheim, D. (1995). Shame, guilt, and the Oedipal drama: Developmental considerations concerning morality and the referencing of critical others. In J. P. Tangney & K. W. Fischer (Eds.), *Self-conscious emotions: The psychology of shame, guilt, embarrassment, and pride* (pp. 413–436). New York: Guilford.

Emde, R. N., Plomin, R., Robinson, J., Corley, R., DeFries, J., Fulker, D. W., Reznick, J. S., Campos, J., Kagan, J., & Zahn-Waxler, C. (1992). Temperament, emotion, and cognition at fourteen months: The MacArthur Longitudinal Twin Study. *Child Development, 63,* 1437–1455.

Emery, R. E. (1999). Postdivorce family life for children: An overview of research and some implications for policy. In R. A. Thompson & P. R. Amato (Eds.), *The postdivorce family: Children, parenting, and society* (pp. 3–27). Thousand Oaks, CA: Sage.

Emery, R. E. (2001). Interparental conflict and social policy. In J. H. Grych & F. D. Fincham (2001). *Interparental conflict and child development: Theory, research, and applications* (pp. 417–439). New York: Cambridge University Press.

Emery, R. E., & Laumann-Billings, L. (1998). An overview of the nature, causes, and consequences of abusive family relationships: Toward differentiating maltreatment and violence. *American Psychologist, 53,* 121–135.

Emlen, S. T. (1995). An evolutionary theory of the family. *Proceedings of the National Academy of Sciences, 92,* 8092–8099.

Emmerich, W. (1981). Non-monotonic developmental trends in social cognition: The case of gender constancy. In S. Strauss (Ed.), *U-shaped behavioral growth* (pp. 249–269). New York: Academic Press.

Emory, E. K., Schlackman, L. J., & Fiano, K. (1996). Drug–hormone interactions on neurobehavioral responses in human neonates. *Infant Behavior and Development, 19,* 213–220.

Emory, E. K., & Toomey, K. A. (1988). Environmental stimulation and human fetal responsibility in late pregnancy. In W. P. Smotherman & S. R. Robinson (Eds.), *Behavior of the fetus* (pp. 141–161). Caldwell, NJ: Telford.

Enright, R. D., Lapsley, D. K., & Shukla, D. (1979). Adolescent egocentrism in early and late adolescence. *Adolescence, 14,* 687–695.

Epstein, L. H., Valoski, A. M., Kalarchain, M. A., & McCurley, J. (1995). Do children lose and maintain weight easier than adults: A comparison of child and parent weight changes from six months to ten years. *Obesity Research, 3,* 411–417.

Erdley, C. A., & Asher, S. R. (1999). A social goals perspective on children's social competence. *Journal of Emotional and Behavioral Disorders, 7,* 156–167.

Erdley, C. A., Cain, K. M., Loomis, C. C., Dumas-Hines, F., & Dweck, C. S. (1997). Relations among children's social goals, implicit personality theories, and responses to social failure. *Developmental Psychology, 33,* 263–272.

Erel, O., & Burman, B. (1995). Interrelatedness of marital relations and parent–child relations: A meta-analytic review. *Psychological Bulletin, 118,* 108–132.

Erikson, E. H. (1950). *Childhood and society.* New York: Norton.

Erikson, E. H. (1968). *Identity, youth, and crisis.* New York: Norton.

Eskenazi, B. (1993). Caffeine during pregnancy: Grounds for concern? *Journal of the American Medical Association, 270,* 2973–2974.

Eskenazi, B., Stapleton, A. L., Kharrazi, M., & Chee, W. Y. (1999). Associations between maternal decaffeinated and caffeinated coffee consumption and fetal growth and gestational duration. *Epidemiology, 10,* 242–249.

Espy, K. A., Kaufmann, P. M., & Glisky, M. L. (1999). Neuropsychological function in toddlers exposed to cocaine in utero: A preliminary study. *Developmental Neuropsychology, 15,* 447–460.

Espy, K. A., Molfese, V. J., & DiLalla, L. F. (2001). Effects of environmental measures on intelligence in young children: Growth curve modeling of longitudinal data. *Merrill-Palmer Quarterly, 47,* 42–73.

Evans, D. (1997). *The law, standards of practice, and ethics in the practice of psychology.* Toronto: Emond Montgomery.

Evans, G. W., Bullinger, M., & Hygge, S. (1998). Chronic noise exposure and physiological response: A prospective study of children living under environmental stress. *Psychological Science, 9,* 75–77.

Evans, M. A., Shaw, D., & Bell, M. (2000). Home literacy activities and their influence on early literacy skills. *Canadian Journal of Experimental Psychology, 54,* 65–75.

Eveleth, P. B., & Tanner, J. M. (1990). *Worldwide variation in human growth* (2nd ed.). Cambridge: Cambridge University Press.

Everett, S. A., Warren, C. W., Santelli, J. S., Kann, L., Collins, J. L., & Kolbe, L. J. (2000). Use of birth control pills, condoms, and withdrawal among U.S. high school students. *Journal of Adolescent Health, 27,* 112–118.

Everman, D. B., & Cassidy, S. B. (2000). Genetics of childhood disorders: XII. Genomic imprinting: Breaking the rules. *Journal of the American Academy of Child and Adolescent Psychiatry, 38,* 386–389.

Fabes, R. A., Eisenberg, N., Jones, S., Smith, M., Guthrie, I., Poulin, R., Shepard, S., & Friedman, J. (1999). Regulation, emotionality, and preschoolers' socially competent peer interactions. *Child Development, 70,* 432–444.

Fabes, R. A., Eisenberg, N., Karbon, M., Troyer, D., & Switzer, G. (1994). The relations of children's emotion regulation to their vicarious emotional responses and comforting behavior. *Child Development, 65,* 1678–1693.

Fabes, R. A., Eisenberg, N., McCormick, S. E., & Wilson, M. S. (1988). Preschoolers' attributions of the situational determinants of others' naturally occurring emotions. *Developmental Psychology, 24,* 376–385.

Fabricius, W. V., & Wellman, H. M. (1993). Two roads diverged: Young children's ability to judge distance. *Child Development, 64,* 399–414.

Facchinetti, F., Battaglia, C., Benatti, R., Borella, P., & Genazzani, A. R. (1992). Oral magnesium supplementation improves fetal circulation. *Magnesium Research, 3,* 179–181.

Fagan, J. F., III. (1973). Infant's delayed recognition memory and forgetting. *Journal of Experimental Child Psychology, 16,* 424–450.

Fagan, J. F., III, & Detterman, D. K. (1992). The Fagan Test of Infant Intelligence: A technical summary. *Journal of Applied Developmental Psychology, 13,* 173–193.

Fagan, J. F., III, & Singer, L. T. (1979). The role of simple feature differences in infants' recognition of faces. *Infant Behavior and Development, 2,* 39–45.

Fagan, J. F., III, & Singer, L. T. (1983). Infant recognition memory as a measure of intelligence. In L. P. Lipsitt (Ed.), *Advances in infancy research* (Vol. 2, pp. 31–78). Norwood, NJ: Ablex.

Fagard, J., & Pezé, A. (1997). Age changes in interlimb coupling and the development of bimanual coordination. *Journal of Motor Behavior, 29,* 199–208.

Fagot, B. I. (1984). The child's expectations of differences in adult male and female interactions. *Sex Roles, 11,* 593–600.

Fagot, B. I. (1985a). Beyond the reinforcement principle: Another step toward understanding sex role development. *Developmental Psychology, 21,* 1097–1104.

Fagot, B. I. (1985b). Changes in thinking about early sex role development. *Developmental Review, 5,* 83–98.

Fagot, B. I., & Hagan, R. I. (1991). Observations of parent reactions to sex-stereotyped behaviors: Age and sex effects. *Child Development, 62,* 617–628.

Fagot, B. I., & Leinbach, M. D. (1989). The young child's gender schema: Environmental input, internal organization. *Child Development, 60,* 663–672.

Fagot, B. I., Leinbach, M. D., & O'Boyle, C. (1992). Gender labeling, gender stereotyping, and parenting behaviors. *Developmental Psychology, 28,* 225–230.

Fagot, B. I., Pears, K. C., Capaldi, D. M., Crosby, L., & Lee, C. S. (1998). Becoming an adolescent father: Precursors and parenting. *Developmental Psychology, 34,* 1209–1219.

Fahrmeier, E. D. (1978). The development of concrete operations among the Hausa. *Journal of Cross-Cultural Psychology, 9,* 23–44.

Fairburn, C. G., Doll, H. A., Welch, S. L., Hay, P. J., Davies, B. A., & O'Conner, M. E. (1997). Risk factors for binge eating disorder: A community-based case control study. *Archives of General Psychiatry, 54,* 509–517.

Falbo, T. (1992). Social norms and the one-child family: Clinical and policy implications. In F. Boer & J. Dunn (Eds.), *Children's sibling relationships* (pp. 71–82). Hillsdale, NJ: Erlbaum.

Falbo, T., & Polit, D. (1986). A quantitative review of the only-child literature: Research evidence and theory development. *Psychological Bulletin, 100,* 176–189.

Falbo, T., & Poston, D. L., Jr. (1993). The academic, personality, and physical outcomes of only children in China. *Child Development, 64,* 18–35.

Falbo, T., Poston, D. L., Jr., Triscari, R. S., & Zhang, X. (1997). Self-enhancing illusions among Chinese schoolchildren. *Journal of Cross-Cultural Psychology, 28,* 172–191.

Fall, C. H., Stein, C. E., Kumaran, K., Cox, V., Osmond, C., Barker, D. J., & Hales, C. N. (1998). Size at birth, maternal weight, and type 2 diabetes in South India. *Diabetic Medicine, 15,* 220–227.

Faller, K. C. (1990). *Understanding child sexual maltreatment.* Newbury Park, CA: Sage.

Fancher, R. E. (1998). Alfred Binet, general psychologist. In G. A. Kimble & M. Wertheimer (Eds.), *Portraits of pioneers in psychology* (Vol. 3, pp. 67–83). Washington, DC: American Psychological Association.

Fantz, R. L. (1961). The origin of form perception. *Scientific American, 204,* 66–72.

Faraone, S. V., Biederman, J., Weiffenbach, B., Keith, T., Chu, M. P., & Weaver, A. (1999). Dopamine D-sub-4 gene 7-repeat allele and attention deficit hyperactivity disorder. *American Journal of Psychiatry, 156,* 768–770.

Farrant, K., & Reese, E. (2000). Maternal style and children's |participation in reminiscing: Stepping stones in children's autobiographical memory development. *Journal of Cognition and Development, 1,* 193–225.

Farrar, M. J., & Goodman, G. S. (1992). Developmental changes in event memory. *Child Development, 63,* 173–187.

Farrington, D. P. (1987). Epidemiology. In H. C. Quay (Ed.), *Handbook of juvenile delinquency* (pp. 33–61). New York: Wiley.

Farrington, D. P., & Loeber, R. (2000). Epidemiology of juvenile violence. *Juvenile Violence, 9,* 733–748.

Farver, J. M. (1993). Cultural differences in scaffolding pretend play: A comparison of American and Mexican mother–child and sibling–child pairs. In K. MacDonald (Ed.), *Parent–child play* (pp. 349–366). Albany, NY: SUNY Press.

Farver, J. M., & Branstetter, W. H. (1994). Preschoolers' prosocial responses to their peers' distress. *Developmental Psychology, 30,* 334–341.

Farver, J. M., & Wimbarti, S. (1995a). Indonesian toddlers' social play with their mothers and older siblings. *Child Development, 66,* 1493–1503.

Farver, J. M., & Wimbarti, S. (1995b). Paternal participation in toddlers' pretend play. *Social Development, 4,* 19–31.

Farver, J. M., Kim, Y. K., & Lee, Y. (1995). Cultural differences in Korean- and Anglo-American preschoolers' social interaction and play behaviors. *Child Development, 66,* 1088–1099.

Fasig, L. G. (2000). Toddlers' understanding of ownership: Implications for self-concept development. *Social Development, 9,* 370–382.

Fasouliotis, S. J., & Schenker, J. G. (2000). Ethics and assisted reproduction. *European Journal of Obstetrics, Gynecology, and Reproductive Biology, 90,* 171–180.

Fee, E. J. (1997). The prosodic framework for language learning. *Topics in Language Disorders, 17,* 53–62.

Feinberg, M. E., & Hetherington, E. M. (2001). Differential parenting as a within-family variable. *Journal of Family Psychology, 51,* 22–37.

Feingold, A. (1993). Cognitive gender differences: A developmental perspective. *Sex Roles, 29,* 91–112.

Feingold, A. (1994). Gender differences in personality: A meta-analysis. *Psychological Bulletin, 116,* 429–456.

Feiring, C., & Taska, L. S. (1996). Family self-concept: Ideas on its meaning. In B. Bracken (Ed.), *Handbook of self-concept* (pp. 317–373). New York: Wiley.

Feiring, C., Taska, L., & Lewis, M. (1999). Age and gender differences in children's and adolescents' adaptation to sexual abuse. *Child Abuse and Neglect, 23,* 115–128.

Feldman, D. H. (1999). The development of creativity. In R. J. Sternberg (Ed.), *Handbook of creativity* (pp. 169–186). Cambridge: Cambridge University Press.

Feldman, D. H., & Goldsmith, L. T. (1991). *Nature's gambit.* New York: Teachers College Press.

Feldman, R. (2000). Parents' convergence on sharing and marital satisfaction, father involvement, and parent–child relationship at the transition to parenthood. *Infant Mental Health Journal, 21,* 176–191.

Feldman, R., Greenbaum, C. W., & Yirmiya, N. (1999). Mother–infant affect synchrony as an antecedent of the emergence of self-control. *Developmental Psychology, 35,* 223–231.

Feldman, W. (1994). Well-baby care in the first two years of life. *The Canadian Guide to Clinical Preventive Healthcare* (pp. 257–266). Ottawa: Health Canada, Canadian Task Force on the Periodic Health Examination.

Felsman, D. E., & Blustein, D. L. (1999). The role of peer relatedness in late adolescent career development. *Journal of Vocational Behavior, 54,* 279–295.

Fenson, L., Dale, P. S., Reznick, J. S., Bates, E., Thal, D. J., & Pethick, S. J. (1994). Variability in early communicative development. *Monographs of the Society for Research in Child Development, 59*(5, Serial No. 242).

Ferguson, R. F. (1998). Teachers' perceptions and expectations and the black–white test score gap. In C. Jencks & M. Phillips (Eds.), *The black–white test score gap* (pp. 273–317). Washington, DC: Brookings Institution.

Ferguson, T. J., Stegge, H., & Damhuis, I. (1991). Children's understanding of guilt and shame. *Child Development, 62,* 827–839.

Ferguson, T. J., Stegge, H., Miller, E. R., & Olsen, M. E. (1999). Guilt, shame, and symptoms in children. *Developmental Psychology, 35,* 347–357.

Fergusson, D. M., & Woodward, L. J. (1999). Breast-feeding and later psychosocial adjustment. *Paediatric and Perinatal Epidemiology, 13,* 144–157.

Fergusson, D. M., Woodward, L. J., & Horwood, L. J. (2000). Risk factors and life processes associated with the onset of suicidal behaviour during adolescence and early adulthood. *Psychological Medicine, 30,* 23–39.

Fernald, A., & Morikawa, H. (1993). Common themes and cultural variations in Japanese and American mothers' speech to infants. *Child Development, 64,* 637–656.

Fernald, A., Taeschner, T., Dunn, J., Papousek, M., Boysson-Bardies, B., & Fukui, I. (1989). A cross-language study of prosodic modifications in mothers' and fathers' speech to preverbal infants. *Journal of Child Language, 16,* 477–502.

Fernald, L. C., & Grantham-McGregor, S. M. (1998). Stress response in school-age children who have been growth retarded since early childhood. *American Journal of Clinical Nutrition, 68,* 691–698.

Fernandes, O., Sabharwal, M., Smiley, T., Pastuszak, A., Koren, G., & Einarson, T. (1998). Moderate to heavy caffeine consumption during pregnancy and relationship to spontaneous abortion and abnormal fetal growth: A meta-analysis. *Reproductive Toxicology, 12,* 435–444.

Feuerstein, R. (1979). *Dynamic assessment of retarded performers: The learning potential assessment device: Theory, instruments, and techniques.* Baltimore: University Park Press.

Feuerstein, R. (1980). *Instrumental enrichment.* Baltimore: University Park Press.

Ficca. G., Fagioli, I., Giganti, F., & Salzarulo, P. (1999). Spontaneous awakenings from sleep in the first year of life. *Early Human Development, 55,* 219–228.

Fichter, M. M., & Quadflieg, N. (1999). Six-year course and outcome of anorexia nervosa. *International Journal of Eating Diorders, 16,* 359–385.

Field, T. (1998). Maternal depression effects on infants and early interventions. *Preventive Medicine, 27,* 200–203.

Field, T. (2001). Massage therapy facilitates weight gain in preterm infants. *Current Directions in Psychological Science, 10,* 51–54.

Field, T. M. (1994). The effects of mother's physical and emotional unavailability on emotion regulation. In N. A. Fox (Ed.), The development of emotion regulation: Biological and behavioral considerations. *Monographs of the Society for Research in Child Development, 59*(2–3, Serial No. 240).

Field, T. M. (1998). Massage therapy effects. *American Psychologist, 53,* 1270–1281.

Field, T. M., Schanberg, S. M., Scafidi, F., Bauer, C. R., Vega-Lahr, N., Garcia, R., Nystrom, J., & Kuhn, C. M. (1986). Effects of tactile/kinesthetic stimulation on preterm neonates. *Pediatrics, 77,* 654–658.

Field, T. M., Woodson, R., Greenberg, R., & Cohen, D. (1982). Discrimination and imitation of facial expressions by neonates. *Science, 218,* 179–181.

Finkel, D., & Pedersen, N. L. (2001). Sources of environmental influence on cognitive abilities in adulthood. In E. L. Grigorenko & R. J. Sternberg (Eds.), *Family environment and intellectual functioning: A life-span perspective* (pp. 173–194). Mahwah, NJ: Erlbaum.

Finn, J. D., Gerber, S. B., Achilles, C. M., & Boyd-Zaharias, J. (2001). The enduring effects of small classes. *Teachers College Record, 103,* 145–183.

Fisch, S. M., Truglio, R. T., & Cole, C. (1999). The impact of Sesame Street on preschool children: A review and synthesis of 30 years' research. *Media Psychology, 1,* 165–190.

Fischer, K. W., & Bidell, T. R. (1998). Dynamic development of psychological structures in action and thought. In R. M. Lerner (Ed.), *Handbook of child psychology: Vol. 1. Theoretical models of human development* (5th ed., pp. 467–561). New York: Wiley.

Fischer, K. W., & Hencke, R. W. (1996). Infants' construction of actions in context: Piaget's contribution to research on early development. *Psychological Science, 7,* 204–210.

Fischer, K. W., & Rose, S. P. (1995, Fall). Concurrent cycles in the dynamic development of brain and behavior. *SRCD Newsletter,* pp. 3–4, 15–16.

Fischman, M. G., Moore, J. B., & Steele, K. H. (1992). Children's one-hand catching as a function of age, gender, and ball location. *Research Quarterly for Exercise and Sport, 63,* 349–355.

Fisher, C. B. (1993, Winter). Integrating science and ethics in research with high-risk children and youth. *Social Policy Report of the Society for Research in Child Development, 4*(4).

Fisher, J. A., & Birch, L. L. (1995). 3–5 year-old children's fat preferences and fat consumption are related to parental adiposity. *Journal of the American Dietetic Association, 95,* 759–764.

Fisher, L., Ames, E., Chisholm, K., & Savoie, L. (1997). Problems reported by parents of Romanian orphans adopted to British Columbia. *International Journal of Behavioural Development, 20,* 67–82.

Fisher, P. A., Gunnar, M. R., Chamberlain, P., & Reid, J. B. (2000). Preventive intervention for maltreated preschool children: Impact on children's behavior, neuroendocrine activity, and foster parent functioning. *Journal of the American Academy of Child and Adolescent Psychiatry, 39,* 1356–1364.

Fisher, W. A., Boroditsky, R., & Bridges, M. L. (1999). Special Issue: The 1998 Canadian contraception study. *The Canadian Journal of Human Sexuality, 8,* 161–216.

Fitch, M., Huston, A. C., & Wright, J. C. (1993). From television forms to genre schemata: Children's perceptions of television reality. In G. L. Berry & J. K. Asamen (Eds.), *Children and television* (pp. 38–52). Newbury Park, CA: Sage.

Fivush, R. (1989). Exploring sex differences in the emotional content of mother–child conversations about the past. *Sex Roles, 20,* 675–691.

Fivush, R., Haden, C., & Adam, S. (1995). Structure and coherence of preschoolers' personal narratives over time: Implications for childhood amnesia. *Journal of Experimental Child Psychology, 60,* 32–56.

Fivush, R., & Hamond, N. R. (1990). Autobiographical memory across the preschool years: Toward reconceptualizing childhood amnesia. In R. Fivush & J. A. Hudson (Eds.), *Knowing and remembering in young children* (pp.

223–248). New York: Cambridge University Press.

Fivush, R., Kuebli, J., & Clubb, P. A. (1992). The structure of events and event representations: A developmental analysis. *Child Development, 63,* 188–201.

Flake, A., Roncarolo, M., Puck, J. M., Almeidaporada, G., Evins, M. I., Johnson, M. P., Abella, E. M., Harrison, D. D., & Zanjani, E. D. (1996). Treatment of X-linked severe combined immunodeficiency by in utero transplantation of paternal bone marrow. *New England Journal of Medicine, 335,* 1806–1810.

Flanagan, C. A., & Eccles, J. S. (1993). Changes in parents' work status and adolescents' adjustment at school. *Child Development, 64,* 246–257.

Flanagan, C. A., & Faison, N. (2001). Youth civic development: Implications of research for social policy and programs. *Social Policy Report of the Society for Research in Child Development, 15*(1).

Flanagan, C. A., & Tucker, C. J. (1999). Adolescents' explanations for political issues: Concordance with their views of self and society. *Developmental Psychology, 35,* 1198–1209.

Flannery, K. A., & Liederman, J. (1995). Is there really a syndrome involving the co-occurrence of neurodevelopmental disorder, talent, nonright handedness and immune disorder among children? *Cortex, 31,* 503–515.

Flavell, J. H. (1985). *Cognitive development* (2nd ed.). Englewood Cliffs, NJ: Prentice-Hall.

Flavell, J. H. (1993). The development of children's understanding of false belief and the appearance–reality distinction. *International Journal of Psychology, 28,* 595–604.

Flavell, J. H. (2000). Development of children's knowledge about the mental world. *International Journal of Behavioral Development, 24,* 15–23.

Flavell, J. H., Botkin, P. T., Fry, C. L., Jr., Wright, J. W., & Jarvis, P. E. (1968). *The development of role-taking and communication skills in children.* New York: Wiley.

Flavell, J. H., Flavell, E. R., Green, F. L., & Korfmacher, J. E. (1990). Do young children think of television images as pictures or real objects? *Journal of Broadcasting and Electronic Media, 34,* 399–419.

Flavell, J. H., Green, F. L., & Flavell, E. R. (1987). Development of knowledge about the appearance–reality distinction. *Monographs of the Society for Research in Child Development, 51*(1, Serial No. 212).

Flavell, J. H., Green, F. L., & Flavell, E. R. (1993). Children's understanding of the stream of con-

sciousness. *Child Development, 64,* 387–398.

Flavell, J. H., Green, F. L., & Flavell, E. R. (1995). Young children's knowledge about thinking. *Monographs of the Society for Research in Child Development, 60*(1, Serial No. 243).

Flavell, J. H., Green, F. L., & Flavell, E. R. (2000). Development of children's awareness of their own thoughts. *Journal of Cognition and Development, 1,* 97–112.

Flavell, J. H., & Miller, P. H. (1998). Social cognition. In D. Kuhn & R. S. Siegler (Eds.), *Handbook of child psychology: Vol. 2. Cognition, perception, and language* (4th ed., pp. 851–898). New York: Wiley.

Flavell, J. H., Miller, P. H., & Miller, S. A. (2002). *Cognitive development* (4th ed.). Upper Saddle River, NJ: Prentice Hall.

Flegal, K. M. (1999). The obesity epidemic in children and adults: Current evidence and research issues. *Medicine and Science in Sports and Exercise, 31,* S509–S514.

Fleming, V., M., & Alexander, J. M. (2001). The benefits of peer collaboration: A replication with a delayed posttest. *Contemporary Educational Psychology, 26,* 588–601.

Fletcher, A. C., Darling, N. E., Steinberg, L., & Dornbusch, S. M. (1995). The company they keep: Relation of adolescents' adjustment and behavior to their friends' perceptions of authoritative parenting in the social network. *Developmental Psychology, 31,* 300–310.

Floccia, C., Christophe, A., & Bertoncini, J. (1997). High-amplitude sucking and newborns: The quest for underlying mechanisms. *Journal of Experimental Child Psychology, 64,* 175–198.

Florsheim, P., Tolan, P., & Gorman-Smith, D. (1998). Family relationships, parenting practices, the availability of male family members, and the behavior of inner-city boys in single-mother and two-parent families. *Child Development, 69,* 1437–1447.

Flynn, J. R. (1987). Massive IQ gains in 14 nations: What IQ tests really measure. *Psychological Bulletin, 101,* 171–191.

Flynn, J. R. (1994). IQ gains over time. In R. J. Sternberg (Ed.), *The encyclopedia of human intelligence* (pp. 617–623). New York: Macmillan.

Flynn, J. R. (1996). What environmental factors affect intelligence: The relevance of IQ gains over time. In D. K. Detterman (Ed.), *The environment. Current topics in human intelligence* (Vol. 5, pp. 17–29). Norwood, NJ: Ablex.

Flynn, J. R. (1999). Searching for justice: The discovery of IQ gains

over time. *American Psychologist, 54,* 5–20.

Fogel, A. (2000). Systems, attachment, and relationships. *Human Development, 43,* 314–320.

Fogel, A., Melson, G. F., Toda, S., & Mistry, T. (1987). Young children's responses to unfamiliar infants. *International Journal of Behavioral Development, 10,* 1071–1077.

Foltz, C., Overton, W. F., & Ricco, R. B. (1995). Proof construction: Adolescent development from inductive to deductive problem-solving strategies. *Journal of Experimental Child Psychology, 59,* 179–195.

Fonzi, A., Schneider, B. H., Tani, F., & Tomada, G. (1997). Predicting children's friendship status from their dyadic interaction in structured situations of potential conflict. *Child Development, 68,* 496–506.

Ford, C., & Beach, F. (1951). *Patterns of sexual behavior.* New York: Harper & Row.

Ford-Jones, E., & Tam, T. (1999). Prevention of congenital rubella syndrome. *Paediatrics & Child Health, 4,* 155–157.

Forgatch, M. S., & DeGarmo, D. S. (1999). Parenting through change: An effective prevention program for single mothers. *Journal of Consulting and Clinical Psychology, 67,* 711–724.

Forman, E. A., & McPhail, J. (1993). Vygotskian perspective on children's collaborative problem-solving activities. In E. A. Forman, N. Minick, & C. A. Stone (Eds.), *Contexts for learning* (pp. 323–347). New York: Cambridge University Press.

Forman, R, Klein, J., & Koren, G. (1994). Fetal exposure to cocaine in Toronto: An epidemic. *The Motherisk Newsletter, 3,* 1–4.

Forsén, T., Eriksson, J., Tuomilehto, J., Reunanen, A., Osmond, C., & Barker, D. (2000). The fetal and childhood growth of persons who develop type 2 diabetes. *Annals of Internal Medicine, 133,* 176–182.

Fortier, I., Marcoux, S., & Beaulac-Baillargeon, L. (1993). Relation of caffeine intake during pregnancy to intrauterine growth retardation and preterm birth. *American Journal of Epidemiology, 137,* 931–940.

Fowles, D. C., & Kochanska, G. (2000). Temperament as a moderator of pathways to conscience in children: The contribution of electrodermal activity. *Psychophysiology, 37,* 788–795.

Fox, N. A. (1991). If it's not left, it's right: Electroencephalograph asymmetry and the development of emotion. *American Psychologist, 46,* 863–872.

Fox, N. A., Calkins, S. D., & Bell, M. A. (1994). Neural plasticity and development in the first two years of life: Evidence from cognitive and socioemotional domains of research. *Development and Psychopathology, 6,* 677–696.

Fox, N. A., & Card, J. A. (1998). Psychophysiological measures in the study of attachment. In J. Cassidy & P. Shaver (Eds.), *Handbook of attachment: Theory, research, and clinical applications* (pp. 226–245). New York: Guilford.

Fox, N. A., & Davidson, R. J. (1986). Taste-elicited changes in facial signs of emotion and the asymmetry of brain electrical activity in newborn infants. *Neuropsychologia, 24,* 417–422.

Fox, N. A., Schmidt, L. A., & Henderson, H. A. (2000). Developmental psychophysiology: Conceptual and methodological perspectives. In J. T. Cacioppo & L. G. Tassinary (Eds.), *Handbook of psychophysiology* (2nd ed., pp. 665–686). New York: Cambridge University Press.

Fraiberg, S. (1977). *Insights from the blind: Comparative studies of blind and sighted infants.* New York: Basic Books.

Franco, P., Chabanski, S., Szliwowski, H., Dramaix, M., & Kahn, A. (2000). Influence of maternal smoking on autonomic nervous system in healthy infants. *Pediatric Research, 47,* 215–220.

Frank, S. J., Pirsch, L. A., & Wright, V. C. (1990). Late adolescents' perceptions of their relationships with their parents: Relationships among deidealization, autonomy, relatedness, and insecurity and implications for adolescent adjustment and ego identity status. *Journal of Youth and Adolescence, 19,* 571–588.

Frankel, K. A., & Bates, J. E. (1990). Mother-toddler problem solving: Antecedents in attachment, home behavior, and temperament. *Child Development, 61,* 810–819.

Franklin, C., & Corcoran, J. (2000). Preventing adolescent pregnancy: A review of programs and practices. *Social Work, 45,* 40–52.

Franklin, C., Grant, D., Corcoran, J., O'Dell-Miller, P., & Bultman, L. (1997). Effectiveness of prevention programs for adolescent pregnancy: A meta-analysis. *Journal of Marriage and the Family, 59,* 551–567.

Frazier, J. A., & Morrison, F. J. (1998). The influence of extended-year schooling on growth of achievement and perceived competence in early elementary school. *Child Development, 69,* 495–517.

Fredericks, M., & Miller, S. I. (1997). Some brief notes on the "unfinished business" of qualitative inquiry. *Quality and Quantity, 31,* 1–13.

Freedman, D. G., & Freedman, N. (1969). Behavioral differences between Chinese-American and European-American newborns. *Nature, 224,* 1227.

Freedman, D. S., Khan, L. K., Serdula, M. K., Srinivasan, S. R., & Berenson, G. S. (2000). Secular trends in height among children during 2 decades: The Bogalusa Heart Study. *Archives of Pediatric and Adolescent Medicine, 154,* 155–161.

Freedman-Doan, C., Wigfield, A., Eccles, J. S., Blumenfeld, P., Arbreton, A., & Harold, R. D. (2000). What am I best at? Grade and gender differences in children's beliefs about ability improvement. *Journal of Applied Developmental Psychology, 21,* 379–402.

Freeman, D. (1983). *Margaret Mead and Samoa: The making and unmaking of an anthropological myth.* Cambridge, MA: Harvard University Press.

Freud, A., & Dann, S. (1951). An experiment in group upbringing. *Psychoanalytic Study of the Child, 6,* 127–168.

Freud, S. (1961). Some psychological consequences of the anatomical distinction between the sexes. In J. Strachey (Ed.), *Standard edition of the complete psychological works of Sigmund Freud* (Vol. 19, pp. 248–258). London: Hogarth Press. (Original work published 1925.)

Freud, S. (1974). *The ego and the id.* London: Hogarth. (Original work published 1923.)

Fried, M. N., & Fried, M. H. (1980). *Transitions: Four rituals in eight cultures.* New York: Norton.

Fried, P. A. (1993). Prenatal exposure to tobacco and marijuana: Effects during pregnancy, infancy, and early childhood. *Clinical Obstetrics and Gynecology, 36,* 319–337.

Fried, P. A., & Makin, J. E. (1987). Neonatal behavioral correlates of prenatal exposure to marijuana, cigarettes, and alcohol in a low risk population. *Neurobehavioral Toxicology and Teratology, 9,* 1–7.

Fried, P. A., Watkinson, B., & Gray, R. (1999). Growth from birth to early adolescence in offspring prenatally exposed to cigarettes and marijuana. *Neurotoxicology and Teratology, 21,* 513–525.

Friedman, H. S. (2002). *Health psychology.* Upper Saddle River, NJ: Prentice Hall.

Friedman, J. M. (1996). *The effects of drugs on the fetus and nursing infant: A handbook for health care professionals.* Baltimore: Johns Hopkins University Press.

Frijda, N. (2000). The psychologist's point of view. In M. Lewis & J. M. Haviland-Jones (Eds.), *Handbook of emotions* (pp. 59–74). New York: Guilford.

Frodi, A. (1985). When empathy fails: Aversive infant crying and child abuse. In B. M. Lester & C. F. Z. Boukydis (Eds.), *Infant crying: Theoretical and research perspectives* (pp. 263–277). New York: Plenum.

Frosch, C. A., Mangelsdorf, S. C., & McHale, J. L. (2000). Marital behavior and security of preschooler–parent attachment relationships. *Journal of Family Psychology, 14,* 144–161.

Fry, A. F., & Hale, S. (1996). Processing speed, working memory, and fluid intelligence: Evidence for a developmental cascade. *Psychological Science, 7,* 237–241.

Fuchs, I., Eisenberg, N., Hertz-Lazarowitz, R., & Sharabany, R. (1986). Kibbutz, Israeli city, and American children's moral reasoning about prosocial moral conflicts. *Merrill-Palmer Quarterly, 32,* 37–50.

Fuchs, L. S., Fuchs, D., Hamlett, C. L., & Karns, K. (1998). High-achieving students' interactions and performance on complex mathematical tasks as a function of homogeneous and heterogeneous pairings. *American Educational Research Journal, 35,* 227–267.

Fujinaga, T., Kasuga, T., Uchida, N., & Saiga, H. (1990). Long-term follow-up study of children developmentally retarded by early environmental deprivation. *Genetic, Social and General Psychology Monographs, 116,* 37–104.

Fuligni, A. J. (1997). The academic achievement of adolescents from immigrant families: The roles of family background, attitudes, and behavior. *Child Development, 68,* 261–273.

Fuligni, A. J. (1998a). Authority, autonomy, and parent–adolescent conflict and cohesion: A study of adolescents from Mexican, Chinese, Filipino, and European backgrounds. *Developmental Psychology, 34,* 782–792.

Fuligni, A. J. (1998b). The adjustment of children from immigrant families. *Current Directions in Psychological Science, 7,* 99–103.

Fuligni, A. J., Burton, L., Marshall, S., Perez-Febles, A., Yarrington, J., Kirsh, L. B., & Merriwether-DeVries, C. (1999). Attitudes toward family obligations among American adolescents with Asian, Latin American, and European backgrounds. *Child Development, 70,* 1030–1044.

Fuligni, A. J., & Eccles, J. S. (1993). Perceived parent–child relationships and early adolescents' orientation toward peers. *Developmental Psychology, 29,* 622–632.

Fuligni, A. J., Eccles, J. S., & Barber, B. L. (1995). The long-term effects of seventh-grade ability grouping in mathematics. *Journal of Early Adolescence, 15,* 58–89.

Fuligni, A. J., & Stevenson, H. W. (1995). Time use and mathematics achievement among American, Chinese, and Japanese high school students. *Child Development, 66,* 830–842.

Furman, W., & Buhrmester, D. (1992). Age and sex differences in perceptions of networks of personal relationships. *Child Development, 63,* 103–115.

Furstenberg, F. F., Jr., Brooks-Gunn, J., & Morgan, S. P. (1987). *Adolescent mothers and their children in later life.* Cambridge: Cambridge University Press.

Furstenberg, F. F., Jr., & Harris, K. M. (1993). When and why fathers matter: Impact of father involvement on children of adolescent mothers. In R. I. Lerman & T. J. Ooms (Eds.), *Young unwed fathers* (pp. 117–138). Philadelphia: Temple University Press.

Fuson, K. C. (1990). Issues in place-value and multidigit addition and subtraction learning and teaching. *Journal of Research in Mathematics Education, 21,* 273–280.

Fuson, K. C. (1992). Research on learning and teaching addition and subtraction of whole numbers. In G. Leinhardt, R. T. Putnam, & R. A. Hattrup (Eds.), *The analysis of arithmetic for mathematics teaching* (pp. 53–187). Hillsdale, NJ: Erlbaum.

Fuson, K. C., & Kwon, Y. (1992). Korean children's understanding of multidigit addition and subtraction. *Child Development, 63,* 491–506.

Gaddis, A., & Brooks-Gunn, J. (1985). The male experience of pubertal change. *Journal of Youth and Adolescence, 14,* 61–69.

Gagnon, A., & Morasse, I. (1995, March). *Self-esteem and intergroup discrimination in second-grade schoolchildren.* Paper presented at the biennial meeting of the Society for Research in Child Development, Indianapolis.

Gaillard, W. D., Hertz-Pannier, L., Mott, S. H., Barnett, A. S., LeBihan, D., & Theodore, W. H. (2000). Functional anatomy of cognitive development: fMRI of verbal fluency in children and adults. *Neurology, 54,* 180–185.

Gains, S. O., Jr., Marelich, W. D., Bledsoe, K. L., Steers, W. N., Henderson, M. C., & Granrose, C. S. (1997). Links between race/ethnicity and cultural values as mediated by racial/ethnic identity and moderated by gender. *Journal of Personality and Social Psychology, 72,* 1460–1476.

Galambos, N. L., Almeida, D. M., & Petersen, A. C. (1990). Masculinity, femininity, and sex role attitudes in early adolescence: Exploring gender intensification. *Child Development, 61,* 1904–1914.

Galambos, N. L., & Maggs, J. L. (1991). Children in self-care: Figures, facts, and fiction. In J. V. Lerner & N. L. Galambos (Eds.), *Employed mothers and their* children (pp. 131–157). New York: Garland.

Gale, G., & VandenBerg, K. A. (1998). Kangaroo care. *Neonatal Network, 17*(5), 69–71.

Galler, J. R., Ramsey, C. F., Morley, D. S., Archer, E., & Salt, P. (1990). The long-term effects of early kwashiorkor compared with marasmus. IV. Performance on the National High School Entrance Examination. *Pediatric Research, 28,* 235–239.

Galler, J. R., Ramsey, F., & Solimano, G. (1985a). A follow-up study of the effects of early malnutrition on subsequent development: I. Physical growth and sexual maturation during adolescence. *Pediatric Research, 19,* 518–523.

Galler, J. R., Ramsey, F., & Solimano, G. (1985b). A follow-up study of the effects of early malnutrition on subsequent development: II. Fine motor skills in adolescence. *Pediatric Research, 19,* 524–527.

Galler, J. R., Ramsey, F., Solimano, G., Kucharski, L. T., & Harrison, R. (1984). The influence of early malnutrition on subsequent behavioral development: IV. Soft neurological signs. *Pediatric Research, 18,* 826–832.

Galotti, K. M., Kozberg, S. F., & Farmer, M. C. (1991). Gender and developmental differences in adolescents' conceptions of moral reasoning. *Journal of Youth and Adolescence, 20,* 13–30.

Galton, F. (1883). *Inquiries into human faculty and its development.* London: Macmillan.

Gandour, M. J. (1989). Activity level as a dimension of temperament in toddlers: Its relevance for the organismic specificity hypothesis. *Child Development, 60,* 1092–1098.

Gannon, S., & Korn, S. J. (1983). Temperament, cultural variation, and behavior disorder in preschool children. *Child Psychiatry and Human Development, 13,* 203–212.

Ganong, L. H., & Coleman, M. (1994). *Remarried family relationships.* Thousand Oaks, CA: Sage.

Ganong, L. H., & Coleman, M. (2000). Remarried families. In C. Hendrick & S. S. Hendrick (Eds.), *Close relationships* (pp. 155–168). Thousand Oaks, CA: Sage.

Garbarino, J., & Bedard, C. (2001). *Parents under siege: Why you are the solution and not the problem in your child's life.* New York: Free Press.

Garbarino, J., & Kostelny, K. (1993). Neighborhood and community influences on parenting. In T. Luster & L. Okagaki (1993). *Parenting: An ecological perspective* (pp. 203–226). Hillsdale, NJ: Erlbaum.

Garber, J., Braafladt, N., & Weiss, B. (1995). Affect regulation in depressed and nondepressed children and young adolescents. *Developmental and Psychopathology, 7,* 93–115.

Garber, J., Quiggle, N., Panak, W., & Dodge, K. (1991). Aggression and depression in children: Comorbidity, specificity, and social cognitive processing. In D. Cicchetti & S. L. Toth (Eds.), *Rochester Symposium on Developmental Psychopathology: Vol. 2. Internalizing and externalizing expressions of dysfunction* (pp. 225–264). Hillsdale, NJ: Erlbaum.

Garcia, M. M., Shaw, D. S., Winslow, E. B., & Yaggi, K. E. (2000). Destructive sibling conflict and the development of conduct problems in young boys. *Developmental Psychology, 36,* 44–53.

García-Coll, C., & Magnuson, K. (1997). The psychological experience of immigration: A developmental perspective. In A. Booth, A. C. Crouter, & N. Landale (Eds.), *Immigration and the family* (pp. 91–131). Mahwah, NJ: Erlbaum.

Gardner, H. (1980). *Artful scribbles: The significance of children's drawings.* New York: Basic Books.

Gardner, H. (1983). *Frames of mind.* New York: Basic Books.

Gardner, H. (1993). *Multiple intelligences: The theory in practice.* New York: Basic Books.

Gardner, H. E. (1998a). Are there additional intelligences? The case of the naturalist, spiritual, and existential intelligences. In J. Kane (Ed.), *Educational information and transformation.* Upper Saddle River, NJ: Prentice-Hall.

Gardner, H. E. (1998b). Extraordinary cognitive achievements (ECA): A symbol systems approach. In W. Damon & R. M. Lerner (Eds.), *Handbook of child psychology: Vol. 1. Theoretical models of human development* (5th ed., pp. 415–466). New York: Wiley.

Garfinkel, I., & McLanahan, S. (1995). The effects of child support reform on child well-being. In P. L. Chase-Lansdale & J. Brooks-Gunn (Eds.), *Escape from poverty: What makes a difference for children?* (pp. 211–238). New York: Cambridge University Press.

Garmezy, N. (1993). Children in poverty: Resilience despite risk. *Psychiatry, 56,* 127–136.

Garmon, L. C., Basinger, K. S., Gregg, V. R., & Gibbs, J. C. (1996). Gender differences in stage and expression of moral judgment. *Merrill-Palmer Quarterly, 42,* 418–437.

Garner, D. M., & Garfinkel, P. E. (Eds.). (1997). *Handbook of treatment for eating disorders* (2nd ed.). New York: Guilford.

Garner, P. W. (1996). The relations of emotional role taking, affective/moral attributions, and emotional display rule knowledge to low-income school-age children's social competence. *Journal of Applied Developmental Psychology, 17,* 19–36.

Garner, P. W., Jones, D. C., & Miner, J. L. (1994). Social competence among low-income preschoolers: Emotion socialization practices and social cognitive correlates. *Child Development, 65,* 622–637.

Garner, R. (1990). Children's use of strategies in reading. In D. F. Bjorklund (Ed.), *Children's strategies: Contemporary views of cognitive development* (pp. 245–268). Hillsdale, NJ: Erlbaum.

Garvey, C. (1974). Requests and responses in children's speech. *Journal of Child Language, 2,* 41–60.

Gasden, V. (1999). Black families in intergenerational and cultural perspective. In M. E. Lamb (Ed.), *Parenting and child development in "nontraditional" families* (pp. 221–246). Mahwah, NJ: Erlbaum.

Gash, H., & Morgan, M. (1993). School-based modifications of children's gender-related beliefs. *Journal of Applied Developmental Psychology, 14,* 277–287.

Gaskins, S. (1999). Children's daily lives in a Mayan village: A case study of culturally constructed roles and activities. In R. Göncü (Ed.), *Children's engagement in the world: Sociocultural perspectives* (pp. 25–61). Cambridge: Cambridge University Press.

Gaskins, S. (2000). Children's daily activities in a Mayan village: A culturally grounded description. *Cross-Cultural Research, 34,* 375–389.

Gathercole, S. E. (1995). Is nonword repetition a test of phonological memory or long-term knowledge? It all depends on the nonwords. *Memory and Cognition, 23,* 83–94.

Gathercole, S. E., Hitch, G. J., Service, E., & Martin, A. J. (1997). Phonological short-term memory and new word learning in children. *Developmental Psychology, 33,* 966–979.

Gathercole, S. E., Service, E., Hitch, G. J., Adams, A., & Martin, A. J. (1999). Phonological short-term memory and vocabulary development: Further evidence on the nature of the relationship. *Applied Cognitive Psychology, 13,* 65–77.

Gaub, M., & Carlson, C. L. (1997). Gender differences in ADHD: A meta-analysis and critical review. *Journal of the American Academy of Child and Adolescent Psychiatry, 36,* 1036–1045.

Gauvain, M., & Huard, R. D. (1999). Family interaction, parenting style, and the development of planning: A longitudinal analysis using archival data. *Journal of Family Psychology, 13,* 75–92.

Gauvain, M., & Rogoff, B. (1989). Collaborative problem solving and children's planning skills. *Developmental Psychology, 25,* 139–151.

Gauze, C., Bukowski, W. M., Aquan-Assee, J., & Sippola, L. K. (1996). Interactions between family environment and friendship and associations with self-perceived well-being during early adolescence. *Child Development, 67,* 2201–2216.

Ge, X., Conger, R. D., & Elder, G. H., Jr. (1996). Coming of age too early: Pubertal influences on girls' vulnerability to psychological distress. *Child Development, 67,* 3386–3400.

Ge, X., Conger, R. D., & Elder, G. H., Jr. (2001a). Pubertal transition, stressful life events, and the emergence of gender differences in adolescent depressive symptoms. *Developmental Psychology, 37,* 404–417.

Ge, X., Conger, R. D., & Elder, G. H., Jr. (2001b). The relation between puberty and psychological distress in adolescent boys. *Journal of Research on Adolescence, 11,* 49–70.

Geary, D. C. (1994). *Children's mathematical development.* Washington, DC: American Psychological Association.

Geary, D. C. (1995). *Children's mathematical development: Research and practical applications.* Washington, DC: American Psychological Association.

Geary, D. C. (1996). International differences in mathematics achievement: Their nature, causes, and consequences. *Current Directions in Psychological Science, 5,* 133–137.

Geary, D. C. (1998). *Male, female: The evolution of human sex differences.* Washington, DC: American Psychological Association.

Geary, D. C. (1999). Evolution and developmental sex differences. *Current Directions in Psychological Science, 8,* 115–120.

Geary, D. C. (1999). Evolution and developmental sex differences. *Current Directions in Psychological Science, 8,* 115–120.

Geary, D. C., & Bjorklund, D. F. (2000). Evolutionary developmental psychology. *Child Development, 71,* 57–65.

Geary, D. C., Bow-Thomas, C. C., Liu, F., & Siegler, R. S. (1996). Development of arithmetical competencies in Chinese and American children: Influence of age, language, and schooling. *Child Development, 67,* 2022–2044.

Gelbaugh, S., Ramos, M., Soucar, E., & Urena, R. (2001). Therapy for anorexia nervosa. *Journal of the American Academy of Child and Adolescent Psychiatry, 40,* 129–130.

Gelles, R. J. (1998). The youngest victims: Violence toward children. In R. Bergen & R. Kennedy (Eds.), *Issues in intimate violence* (pp. 5–24). Thousand Oaks, CA: Sage.

Gellin, B. G., Maibach, E. W., & Marcuse, E. K. (2000). Do parents understand immunizations?

A national telephone survey. *Pediatrics, 106*, 1097–1102.

Gelman, R. (1972). Logical capacity of very young children: Number invariance rules. *Child Development, 43*, 75–90.

Gelman, R., & Shatz, M. (1978). Appropriate speech adjustments: The operation of conversational constraints on talk to two-year-olds. In M. Lewis & L. A. Rosenblum (Eds.), *Interaction, conversation, and the development of language* (pp. 27–61). New York: Wiley.

Gelman, S. A., Coley, J. D., Rosengren, K. S., Hartman, E., & Pappas, A. (1998). Beyond labeling: The role of maternal input in the acquisition of richly structured categories. *Monographs of the Society for Research in Child Development, 63*(1, Serial No. 253).

Gelman, S. A., & Wellman, H. M. (1991). Insides and essences: Early understandings of the nonobvious. *Cognition, 38*, 213–244.

Genessee, F., Lambert, W. E., & Holobow, N. E. (1986). The acquisition of second language by immersion: The Canadian approach. *Infancia y Aprendizaje, 33*, 27–36.

Genessee, F. (2001). Portrait of the bilingual child. In V. Cook (Ed.), *Portraits of the second language user* (pp. 170–196). Clevedon, Eng.: Multilingual Matters.

Genessee, F., & Gandara, P. (1999). Bilingual education programs: A cross-national perspective. *Journal of Social Issues, 55*, 665–685.

Genome International Sequencing Consortium. (2001). Initial sequencing and analysis of the human genome. *Nature, 409*, 860–921.

Gentner, D., & Rattermann, M. J. (1991). Language and the career of similarity. In S. A. Gelman & J. P. Byrnes (Eds.), *Perspectives on language and thought: Interrelations in development* (pp. 225–277). Cambridge: Cambridge University Press.

George, C., Kaplan, N., & Main, M. (1985). *The Adult Attachment Interview.* Unpublished manuscript, University of California at Berkeley.

George, T. P., & Hartmann, D. P. (1996). Friendship networks of unpopular, average, and popular children. *Child Development, 67*, 2301–2316.

Georgiewa, P., Rzanny, R., Hopf, J. M., Knab, R., Glauche, V., Kaiser, W. A., & Blanz, B. (1999). fMRI during word processing in dyslexic and normal reading children. *Neuroreport, 10*, 3459–3465.

Gershoff-Stowe, L., & Smith, L. B. (1997). A curvilinear trend in naming errors as a function of

early vocabulary growth. *Cognitive Psychology, 34*, 37–71.

Gervai, J., Turner, P. J., & Hinde, R. A. (1995). Gender-related behaviour, attitudes, and personality in parents of young children in England and Hungary. *International Journal of Behavioral Development, 18*, 105–126.

Geschwind, D. H., Boone, K. B., Miller, B. L., & Swerdloff, R. S. (2000). Neurobehavioral phenotype of Klinefelter syndrome. *Mental Retardation and Developmental Disabilities Research Reviews, 6*, 107–116.

Gesell, A. (1933). Maturation and patterning of behavior. In C. Murchison (Ed.), *A handbook of child psychology.* Worcester, MA: Clark University Press.

Gest, S. D., Graham-Bermann, S. A., & Hartup, W. W. (2001). Peer experience: Common and unique features of number of friendships, social network centrality, and sociometric status. *Social Development, 10*, 23–40.

Getchell, N., & Roberton, M. A. (1989). Whole body stiffness as a function of developmental level in children's hopping. *Developmental Psychology, 25*, 920–928.

Gettinger, M., Doll, B., & Salmon, D. (1994). Effects of social problem solving, goal setting, and parent training on children's peer relations. *Journal of Applied Developmental Psychology, 15*, 141–163.

Getzels, J., & Csikszentmihalyi, M. (1976). *The creative vision: A longitudinal study of problem-finding in art.* New York: Wiley.

Gewirtz, J. L., & Boyd, E. F. (1977). Does maternal responding imply reduced infant crying? A critique of the 1972 Bell and Ainsworth report. *Child Development, 48*, 1200–1207.

Ghim, H. R. (1990). Evidence for perceptual organization in infants: Perception of subjective contours by young infants. *Infant Behavior and Development, 13*, 221–248.

Gibbs, J. C. (1991). Toward an integration of Kohlberg's and Hoffman's theories of morality. In W. M. Kurtines & J. L. Gewirtz (Eds.), *Handbook of moral behavior and development* (Vol. 1, pp. 183–222). Hillsdale, NJ: Erlbaum.

Gibbs, J. C. (1995). The cognitive developmental perspective. In W. M. Kurtines & J. L. Gewirtz (Eds.), *Moral development: An introduction* (pp. 27–48). Boston: Allyn and Bacon.

Gibbs, J. C. (2002). *Moral development and reality: Beyond the theories of Kohlberg and Hoffman.* Thousand Oaks, CA: Sage. [Manuscript in press]

Gibbs, J. C., Basinger, K. S., & Fuller, D. (1992). *Moral maturity: Measuring the development of sociomoral reflection.* Hillsdale, NJ: Erlbaum.

Gibbs, J. C., Basinger, K. S., & Grime, R. L. (2002). Moral judgment maturity: From clinical to standard measures. In S. J. Lopez & C. R. Snyder (Eds.), *Handbook of positive psychological assessment.* Washington, DC: American Psychological Association.

Gibbs, J. C., Potter, G. B., & Goldstein, A. P. (1995). *The EQUIP program: Teaching youth to think and act responsibly through a peer-helping approach.* Champaign, IL: Research Press.

Gibson, E. J. (1970). The development of perception as an adaptive process. *American Scientist, 58*, 98–107.

Gibson, E. J. (2000). Perceptual learning in development: Some basic concepts. *Ecological Psychology, 12*, 295–302.

Gibson, E. J., & Walk, R. D. (1960). The "visual cliff." *Scientific American, 202*, 64–71.

Gibson, F. L., Ungerer, J. A., McMahon, C. A., Leslie, G. I., & Saunders, D. M. (2000). The mother–child relationship following in vitro fertilization (IVF): Infant attachment, responsivity, and maternal sensitivity. *Journal of Child Psychology and Psychiatry, 41*, 1015–1023.

Gibson, J. J. (1979). *The ecological approach to visual perception.* Boston: Houghton Mifflin.

Giedd, J. N., Blumenthal, J., Molloy, E., & Castellanos, F. X. (2001). Brain imaging of attention deficit/hyperactivity disorder. In J. Wasserstein & L. E. Wolf (Eds.), *Adult attention deficit disorder: Brain mechanisms and life outcomes.* Annals of the New York Academy of Sciences (Vol. 931, pp. 33–49). New York: New York Academy of Sciences.

Giedd, J. N., Blumenthal, J., Jeffries, N. O., Rajapakse, J. C., Vaituzis, C., & Liu, H. (1999). Development of the human corpus callosum during childhood and adolescence: A longitudinal MRI study. *Progress in Neuro-Psychopharmacology and Biological Psychiatry, 23*, 571–588.

Gillies, R. M. (2000). The maintenance of cooperative and helping behaviours in cooperative groups. *British Journal of Educational Psychology, 70*, 97–111.

Gilligan, C. F. (1982). *In a different voice.* Cambridge, MA: Harvard University Press.

Gillmore, M. R., Hawkins, J. D., Day, L. E., & Catalano, R. F. (1997). Friendship and deviance: New evidence on an old controversy. *Journal of Early Adolescence, 16*, 80–95.

Gilvarry, E. (2000). Substance abuse in young people. *Journal of Child Psychology and Psychiatry, 41*, 55–80.

Ginsburg, H. P. (1997). *Entering the child's mind: The clinical interview in psychological research and practice.* New York: Cambridge University Press.

Ginsburg, H. P., & Opper, S. (1988). *Piaget's theory of intellectual development* (3rd ed.). Englewood Cliffs, NJ: Prentice-Hall.

Ginsburg, H. P., Klein, A., & Starkey, P. (1998). The development of children's mathematical thinking: Connecting research with practice. In I. E. Sigel & K. A. Renninger (Eds.), *Handbook of child psychology: Vol. 4. Cognition, perception, and language* (5th ed., pp. 401–476). New York: Wiley.

Giusti, R. M., Iwamoto, K., & Hatch, E. E. (1995). Diethylstilbestrol revisited: A review of the long-term health effects. *Annals of Internal Medicine, 122*, 778–788.

Gladwell, M. (1998, February 2). The Pima paradox. *The New Yorker*, pp. 44–57.

Glassman, B. S. (Ed.). (1996). *The new view almanac.* Woodbridge, CT: Blackbirch Press.

Gleitman, L. R. (1990). The structural sources of verb meanings. *Language Acquisition, 1*, 3–55.

Gleitman, L., Gleitman, H., Landau, B., & Wanner, E. (1988). Where learning begins: Initial representations for language learning. In F. Newmeyer (Ed.), *Language: Psychological and biological aspects* (Vol. 3, pp. 150–193). Cambridge: Cambridge University Press.

Glick, J. (1975). Cognitive development in cross-cultural perspective. In F. Horowitz (Ed.), *Review of child development research* (Vol. 4, pp. 595–654). Chicago: University of Chicago Press.

Glick, P. C. (1997). Demographic pictures of African American families. In H. P. McAdoo (Ed.), *Black families* (3rd ed., pp. 118–138). Thousand Oaks, CA: Sage.

Glosten, B. (1998). Controversies in obstetric anesthesia. *Anesthesia and Analgesia, 428*(Suppl.), 32–38.

Glover, J. A. (1977). Risky shift and creativity. *Social Behavior and Personality, 5*, 317–320.

Gnepp, J. (1983). Children's social sensitivity: Inferring emotions from conflicting cues. *Developmental Psychology, 19*, 805–814.

Goelman, H. (1986). The language environments of family day care. In S. Kilmer (Ed.), *Advances in early education and day care* (Vol. 4, pp. 153–179). Greenwich, CT: JAI Press.

Goelman, H., Doherty, G., Lero, D. S., LaGrange, A., & Tougas, J. (2000). *You bet I care! Caring and learning environments: Quality in child care centres across Canada.* Guelph, ON: Centre for Families, Work and Well-Being, University of Guelph.

Goldfield, B. A. (1987). The contributions of child and caregiver to referential and expressive language. *Applied Psycholinguistics, 8,* 267–280.

Goldfield, B. A. (2000). Nouns before verbs in comprehension vs. production: The view from pragmatics. *Journal of Child Language, 27,* 501–520.

Goldin-Meadow, S. (1999). The development of gesture with and without speech in hearing and deaf children. In L. S. Messing & R. Campbell (Eds.), *Gesture, speech, and sign* (pp. 117–132). New York: Oxford University Press.

Goldin-Meadow, S. (2001). Giving the mind a hand: The role of gesture in cognitive change. In J. L. McClelland & R. S. Siegler (Eds.), *Mechanisms of cognitive development* (pp. 5–31). Mahwah, NJ: Erlbaum.

Goldin-Meadow, S., & Butcher, C. (1998). Pointing toward two-word speech in young children. In S. Kita (Ed.), *Pointing: Where language, culture, and cognition meet.* Cambridge: Cambridge University Press.

Goldin-Meadow, S., Butcher, C., Mylander, C., & Dodge, M. (1994). Nouns and verbs in a self-styled gesture system: What's in a name? *Cognitive Psychology, 27,* 259–319.

Goldin-Meadow, S., & Mylander, C. (1998). Spontaneous sign systems created by deaf children in two cultures. *Nature, 391,* 279–281.

Goldin-Meadow, S., Mylander, C., & Butcher, C. (1995). The resilience of combinatorial structure at the word level: Morphology in self-styled gesture systems. *Cognition, 56,* 88–96.

Goldsmith, H. H., Buss, K. A., & Lemery, K. S. (1997). Toddler and childhood temperament: Expanded content, stronger genetic evidence, new evidence for the importance of the environment. *Developmental Psychology, 33,* 891–905.

Goldsmith, H. H., Lemery, K. S., Buss, K. A., & Campos, J. J. (1999). Genetic analyses of focal aspects of infant temperament. *Developmental Psychology, 35,* 972–985.

Goldsmith, H. H., & Rothbart, M. K. (1991). Contemporary instruments for assessing early temperament by questionnaire and in the laboratory. In J. Strelau & A. Angleitner (Eds.), *Explorations in temperament* (pp. 249–272). New York: Plenum.

Goldsmith, L. T. (2000). Tracking trajectories of talent: Child prodigies growing up. In R. C. Friedman & B. M. Shore (Eds.), *Talents unfolding: Cognition and development* (pp. 89–122). Washington, DC: American Psychological Association.

Goleman, D. (1980, February). 1,528 little geniuses and how they grew. *Psychology Today, 13*(9), 28–53.

Goleman, D. (1995). *Emotional intelligence.* New York: Bantam.

Goleman, D. (1998). *Working with emotional intelligence.* New York: Bantam.

Golinkoff, R. M., Hirsh-Pasek, K., Bailey, L. M., & Wenger, N. R. (1992). Young children and adults use lexical principles to learn new nouns. *Developmental Psychology, 28,* 99–108.

Golomb, C., & Galasso, L. (1995). Make believe and reality: Explorations of the imaginary realm. *Developmental Psychology, 31,* 800–810.

Golombok, S., MacCallum, F., & Goodman, E. (2001). The "test-tube" generation: Parent–child relationships and the psychological well-being of in vitro fertilization children at adolescence. *Child Development, 72,* 599–608.

Golombok, S., & Tasker, F. L. (1996). Do parents influence the sexual orientation of their children? Findings from a longitudinal study of lesbian families. *Developmental Psychology, 32,* 3–11.

Golub, M. S. (1996). Labor analgesia and infant brain development. *Pharmacology Biochemistry and Behavior, 55,* 619–628.

Gomez-Schwartz, B., Horowitz, J. M., & Cardarelli, A. P. (1990). *Child sexual abuse: Initial effects.* Newbury Park, CA: Sage.

Göncü, A. (1993). Development of intersubjectivity in the dyadic play of preschoolers. *Early Childhood Research Quarterly, 8,* 99–116.

Gonzales, N. A., Cauce, A. M., Friedman, R. J., & Mason, C. A. (1996). Family, peer, and neighborhood influences on academic achievement among African-American adolescents: One-year prospective effects. *American Journal of Community Psychology, 24,* 365–387.

Good, T. L., & Brophy, J. E. (1996). *Looking in classrooms* (7th ed.). New York: Addison-Wesley.

Goodall, J. (1990). *Through a window: My thirty years with the chimpanzees of Gombe.* Boston: Houghton Mifflin.

Goodfellow, P. N., & Lovell, B. R. (1993). SRY and sex determination in mammals. *Annual Review of Genetics, 27,* 71–92.

Goodlet, C. R., & Johnson, T. B. (1999). Temporal windows of vulnerability within the third trimester equivalent: Why "knowing when" matters. In J. H. Hannigan, L. P. Spear, N. P. Spear, & C. R. Goodlet (Eds.), *Alcohol and alcoholism: Effects on brain and development* (pp. 59–91). Mahwah, NJ: Erlbaum.

Goodlin-Jones, B. L., Burnham, M. M., & Anders, T. F. (2000). Sleep and sleep disturbances: Regulatory processes in infancy. In A. J. Sameroff, M. Lewis, & S. M. Miller (Eds.), *Handbook of developmental psychology* (2nd ed., pp. 309–325). New York: Kluwer.

Goodman, G. S., Hirschman, J. E., Hepps, D., & Rudy, L. (1991). Children's memory for stressful events. *Merrill-Palmer Quarterly, 37,* 109–158.

Goodman, G. S., Quas, J. A., Bulkley, J., & Shapiro, C. (1999). Innovations for child witnesses: A national survey. *Psychology, Public Policy, and Law, 5,* 255–281.

Goodman, S. H., Brogan, D., Lynch, M. E., & Fielding, B. (1993). Social and emotional competence in children of depressed mothers. *Child Development, 64,* 516–531.

Goodman, S. H., Gravitt, G. W., Jr., & Kaslow, N. J. (1995). Social problem solving: A moderator of the relation between negative life stress and depression symptoms in children. *Journal of Abnormal Child Psychology, 23,* 473–485.

Goossens, F. A., & van IJzendoorn, M. H. (1990). Quality of infants' attachments to professional caregivers: Relation to infant–parent attachment and day-care characteristics. *Child Development, 61,* 832–837.

Gopnik, A., & Choi, S. (1995). Names, relational words, and cognitive development in English and Korean speakers: Nouns are not always learned before verbs. In A. Gopnik & S. Choi (Eds.), *Beyond names for things: Children's acquisition of verbs* (pp. 63–80). Hillsdale, NJ: Erlbaum.

Gopnik, A., & Graf, P. (1988). Knowing how you know: Young children's ability to identify and remember the sources of their beliefs. *Child Development, 59,* 1366–1371.

Gopnik, A., & Meltzoff, A. N. (1986). Relations between semantic and cognitive development in the one-word stage: The specificity hypothesis. *Child Development, 57,* 1040–1053.

Gopnik, A., & Meltzoff, A. N. (1987a). The development of categorization in the second year and its relation to other cognitive and linguistic developments. *Child Development, 58,* 1523–1531.

Gopnik, A., & Meltzoff, A. N. (1987b). Language and thought in the young child: Early semantic developments and their relationships to object permanence, means-ends understanding, and categorization. In K. Nelson & A. Van Kleeck (Eds.), *Children's language* (Vol. 6, pp. 191–212). Hillsdale, NJ: Erlbaum.

Gopnik, A., & Wellman, H. M. (1994). The 'theory' theory. In L. A. Hirschfeld & S. A. Gelman (Eds.), *Mapping the mind: Domain specificity in cognition and culture* (pp. 257–293). Cambridge: Cambridge University Press.

Gordon, B. N., Baker-Ward, L., & Ornstein, P. A. (2001). Children's testimony: A review of research on memory for past experiences. *Clinical Child and Family Psychology Review, 4,* 157–181.

Gormally, S., Barr, R. G., Wertheim, L., Alkawaf, R., Calinoiu, N., & Young S. N. (2001). Contact and nutrient caregiving effects on newborn infant pain responses. *Developmental Medicine and Child Neurology, 43,* 28–38.

Gortmaker, S. L., Must, A., Perrin, J. M., Sobol, A. M., & Dietz, W. H., Jr. (1993). Social and economic consequences of overweight in adolescence and young adulthood. *New England Journal of Medicine, 329,* 1008–1012.

Gortmaker, S. L., Must, A., Sobol, A. M., Peterson, K., Colditz, G. A., & Dietz, W. H. (1996). Television viewing as a cause of increasing obesity among children in the United States, 1986–1990. *Archives of Pediatric and Adolescent Medicine, 150,* 356–362.

Goswami, U. (1995). Transitive relational mappings in three- and four-year-olds: The analogy of Goldilocks and the Three Bears. *Child Development, 66,* 877–892.

Goswami, U. (1996). Analogical reasoning and cognitive development. In H. Reese (Ed.), *Advances in child development and behavior* (Vol. 26, pp. 91–138). New York: Academic Press.

Goswami, U., & Brown, A. (1989). Melting chocolate and melting snowmen: Analogical reasoning and causal relations. *Cognition, 35,* 69–95.

Gott, V. L. (1998). Antoine Marfan and his syndrome: One hundred years later. *Maryland Medical Journal, 47,* 247–252.

Gottesman, I. I. (1963). Genetic aspects of intelligent behavior. In N. R. Ellis (Ed.), *Handbook of mental deficiency* (pp. 253–296). New York: McGraw-Hill.

Gottesman, I. I. (1991). *Schizophrenia genetics: The origins of madness.* New York: Freeman.

Gottesman, I. I., Carey, G., & Hanson, D. R. (1983). Pearls and perils in epigenetic psychopathology. In S. B. Guze, E. J. Earls, & J. E. Barrett (Eds.), *Childhood psychopathology and development* (pp. 287–300). New York: Raven Press.

Gottfried, A. E. (1991). Maternal employment in the family setting: Developmental and environmental issues. In J. V. Lerner & N. L. Galambos (Eds.), *Employed mothers and their children* (pp. 63–84). New York: Garland.

Gottfried, A. E., Gottfried, A. W., Bathurst, K., & Killian, C. (1999).

Maternal and dual-earner employment. In. M. E. Lamb (Ed.), *Parenting and child development in "nontraditional" families* (pp. 15–37). Mahwah, NJ: Erlbaum.

Gottlieb, G. (1992). *Individual development and evolution: The genesis of novel behavior.* New York: Oxford University Press.

Gottlieb, G. (1996). Developmental psychobiological theory. In R. B. Cairns, G. H. Elder, Jr., & E. J. Costello (Eds.), *Developmental science: Cambridge studies in social and emotional development* (pp. 63–77). New York: Cambridge University Press.

Gottlieb, G. (1998). Normally occurring environmental and behavioral influences on gene activity: From central dogma to probabilistic epigenesis. *Psychological Review, 105,* 792–802.

Gottlieb, G. (2000). Environmental and behavioral influences on gene activity. *Current Directions in Psychological Science, 9,* 93–97.

Gould, J. L., & Keeton, W. T. (1996). *Biological science* (6th ed.). New York: Norton.

Gould, M. S., & Kramer, R. A. (2001). Youth suicide prevention. *Suicide and Life-Threatening Behavior, 31,* 6–31.

Goy, R. W., & Goldfoot, D. A. (1974). Experiential and hormonal factors influencing development of sexual behavior in the male rhesus monkey. In R. O. Schmitt & F. G. Worden (Eds.), *The neurosciences* (pp. 571–581). Cambridge, MA: MIT Press.

Graber, J. A., Lewinsohn, P. M., Seeley, J. R., & Brooks-Gunn, J. (1997). Is psychopathology associated with the timing of pubertal development? *Journal of the American Academy of Child and Adolescent Psychiatry, 36,* 1768–1776.

Graber, J. A., Petersen, A. C., & Brooks-Gunn, J. (1996). Pubertal processes: Methods, measures, and models. In J. A. Graber, J. Brooks-Gunn, & A. C. Petersen (Eds.), *Transitions through adolescence* (pp. 23–53). Mahwah, NJ: Erlbaum.

Graczyk, P. A., Weikssberg, R. P., Payton, J. W., Elias, M. J., Greenberg, M. T., & Zins, J. E. (2000). Criteria for evaluating the quality of school-based social and emotional learning programs. In R. Bar-On & J. D. A. Parker (Eds.), *Handbook of emotional intelligence* (pp. 391–410). San Francisco: Jossey-Bass.

Graham, S. A., Baker, R. K., & Poulin-Dubois, D. (1998). Infants' expectations about object label reference. *Canadian Journal of Experimental Psychology, 52,* 103–112.

Graham, T. A. (1999). The role of gesture in children's learning to

count. *Journal of Experimental Child Psychology, 74,* 333–355.

Gralinski, J. H., & Kopp, C. B. (1993). Everyday rules for behavior: Mothers' requests to young children. *Developmental Psychology, 29,* 573–584.

Granger, R. C., & Cytron, R. (1999). Teenage parent programs: A synthesis of the long-term effects of the New Chance Demonstration, Ohio's Learning, Earning, and Parenting Program, and the Teenage Parent Demonstration. *Evaluation Review, 23,* 107–145.

Granot, M., Spitzer, A., Aroian, K. J., Ravid, C., Tamir, B., & Noam, R. (1996). Pregnancy and delivery practices and beliefs of Ethiopian immigrant women in Israel. *Western Journal of Nursing Research, 18,* 299–313.

Grant, J. P. (1994). *The state of the world's children 1994.* New York: Oxford University Press for UNICEF.

Grantham-McGregor, S., Powell, C., Walker, S., Chang, S., & Fletcher, P. (1994). The long-term follow-up of severely malnourished children who participated in an intervention program. *Child Development, 65,* 428–439.

Grattan, M. P., De Vos, E., Levy, J., & McClintock, M. K. (1992). Asymmetric action in the human newborn: Sex differences in patterns of organization. *Child Development, 63,* 273–289.

Graue, M. E. (1993). Expectations and ideas coming to school. *Early Childhood Research Quarterly, 8,* 53–75.

Graue, M. E., & DiPerna, J. (2000). Redshirting and early retention: Who gets the "gift of time" and what are its outcomes? *American Educational Research Journal, 37,* 509–534.

Graves, S. B. (1993). Television, the portrayal of African Americans, and the development of children's attitudes. In G. L. Berry & J. K. Asamen (Eds.), *Children and television* (pp. 179–190). Newbury Park, CA: Sage.

Gray, J. (1997). *Mars and Venus on a date.* New York: HarperCollins.

Gray, M. R., & Steinberg, L. (1999). Unpacking authoritative parenting: Reassessing a multidimensional construct. *Journal of Marriage and the Family, 61,* 574–587.

Gray-Little, B., & Carels, R. (1997). The effects of racial and socioeconomic consonance on self-esteem and achievement in elementary, junior high, and high school students. *Journal of Research on Adolescence, 7,* 109–131.

Gray-Little, B., & Hafdahl, A. R. (2000). Factors influencing racial comparisons of self-esteem: A quantitative review. *Psychological Bulletin, 126,* 26–54.

Green, G. E., Irwin, J. R., & Gustafson, G. E. (2000). Acoustic cry analysis, neonatal status and long-term developmental outcomes. In R. G. Barr, B. Hopkins, & J. A. Green (Eds.), *Crying as a sign, a symptom, and a signal* (pp. 137–156). Cambridge: Cambridge University Press.

Green, R. (1987). *The "sissy boy" syndrome and the development of homosexuality.* New Haven, CT: Yale University Press.

Greenberger, E., Chen, C., Tallym, S. R., & Dong, Q. (2000). Family, peer, and individual correlates of depressive symptomology among U. S. and Chinese adolescents. *Journal of Consulting and Clinical Psychology, 68,* 209–219.

Greenberger, E., O'Neil, R., & Nagel, S. K. (1994). Linking workplace and homeplace: Relations between the nature of adults' work and their parenting behaviors. *Developmental Psychology, 30,* 990–1002.

Greendorfer, S. L., Lewko, J. H., & Rosengren, K. S. (1996). Family and gender-based socialization of children and adolescents. In F. L. Smoll & R. E. Smith (Eds.), *Children and youth in sport: A biopsychological perspective* (pp. 89–111). Dubuque, IA: Brown & Benchmark.

Greene, K., Krcmar, M., Walters, L. H., Rubin, D. L., Hale, J., & Hale, L. (2000). Targeting adolescent risk-taking behaviors: The contributions of egocentrism and sensation-seeking. *Journal of Adolescence, 23,* 439–461.

Greenfield, P. (1992, June). *Notes and references for developmental psychology.* Conference on Making Basic Texts in Psychology More Culture-Inclusive and Culture-Sensitive, Western Washington University, Bellingham, WA.

Greenfield, P. M. (1994). Independence and interdependence as developmental scripts: Implications for theory, research, and practice. In P. M. Greenfield & R. R. Cocking (Eds.), *Cross-cultural roots of minority child development* (pp. 1–37). Hillsdale, NJ: Erlbaum.

Greenfield, P. M. (1997). You can't take it with you: Why ability assessments don't cross cultures. *American Psychologist, 52,* 1115–1124.

Greenfield, P. M., & Suzuki, L. (1998). Culture and human development: Implications for parenting education, pediatrics, and mental health. In I. E. Sigel & K. A. Renninger (Eds.), *Handbook of child psychology: Vol. 4. Child psychology in practice* (5th ed., pp. 1059–1109). New York: Wiley.

Greenhill, L. L., Halperin, J. M., & Abikoff, H. (1999). Stimulant medications. *Journal of the American Academy of Child and Adolescent Psychiatry, 38,* 503–512.

Greenhoot, A. F. (2000). Remembering and understanding: The effects of changes in underlying knowledge on children's recollections. *Child Development, 71,* 1309–1328.

Greenough, W. T., & Black, J. E. (1992). Induction of brain structure by experience: Substrates for cognitive development. In M. R. Gunnar & C. A. Nelson (Eds.), *Minnesota Symposia on Child Psychology* (pp. 155–200). Hillsdale, NJ: Erlbaum.

Greenough, W. T., Wallace, C. S., Alcantara, A. A., Anderson, B. J., Hawrylak, N., Sirevaag, A. M., Weiler, I. J., & Withers, G. S. (1993). Development of the brain: Experience affects the structure of neurons, glia, and blood vessels. In N. J. Anastasiow & S. Harel (Eds.), *At-risk infants: Interventions, families, and research* (pp. 173–185). Baltimore: Paul H. Brookes.

Gregg, V., Gibbs, J. C., & Fuller, D. (1994). Patterns of developmental delay in moral judgment by male and female delinquents. *Merrill-Palmer Quarterly, 40,* 538–553.

Greif, E. B. (1979). *Sex differences in parent–child conversations: Who interrupts who?* Paper presented at the annual meeting of the Society for Research in Child Development, Boston.

Gresham, F. M., & MacMillan, D. L. (1997). Social competence and affective characteristics of students with mild disabilities. *Review of Educational Research, 67,* 377–415.

Grigorenko, E. L. (2000). Heritability and intelligence. In R. J. Sternberg (Ed.), *Handbook of intelligence* (pp. 53–91). Cambridge: Cambridge University Press.

Grigorenko, E. L., & Sternberg, R. J. (1998). Dynamic testing. *Psychological Bulletin, 124,* 75–111.

Grody, W. W. (1999). Cystic fibrosis: Molecular diagnosis, population screening, and public policy. *Archives of Pathology and Laboratory Medicine, 123,* 1041–1046.

Groff, J. Y., Mullen, P. D., Mongoven, M., & Burau, K. (1997). Prenatal weight gain patterns and infant birthweight associated with maternal smoking. *Birth, 24,* 234–239.

Grolnick, W. S., Bridges, L. J., & Connell, J. P. (1996). Emotion regulation in two-year-olds: Strategies and emotional expression in four contexts. *Child Development, 67,* 928–941.

Grolnick, W. S., Kurowski, C. O., Dunlap, K. G., & Hevey, C. (2000). Parental resources and the transition to junior high. *Journal of Research on Adolescence, 10,* 465–488.

Grolnick, W. S., & Slowiaczek, M. L. (1994). Parents' involvement in children's schooling: A multidimensional conceptualization and motivational model. *Child Development, 65,* 237–252.

Gronau, R. C., & Waas, G. A. (1997). Delay of gratification and cue utilization: An examination of children's social information processing. *Merrill-Palmer Quarterly, 43,* 305–322.

Groome, L. J., Swiber, M. J., Atterbury, J. L., Bentz, L. S., & Holland, S. B. (1997). Similarities and differences in behavioral state organization during sleep periods in the perinatal infant before and after birth. *Child Development, 68,* 1–11.

Grossman, J. A., & Kruesi, M. J. P. (2000). Innovative approaches to youth suicide prevention: An update of issues and research findings. In R. W. Maris, S. S. Canetto, J. L. McIntosh, & M. M. Silverman (Eds.), *Review of Suicidology, 2000* (pp. 170–201). New York: Guilford.

Grossmann, K., Grossmann, K. E., Spangler, G., Suess, G., & Unzner, L. (1985). Maternal sensitivity and newborns' orientation responses as related to quality of attachment in Northern Germany. In I. Bretherton & E. Waters (Eds.), Growing points of attachment theory and research. *Monographs of the Society for Research in Child Development, 50* (1–2, Serial No. 209).

Grotevant, H. D. (1978). Sibling constellations and sex-typing of interests in adolescence. *Child Development, 49,* 540–542.

Grotevant, H. D. (1998). Adolescent development in family contexts. In N. Eisenberg (Ed.), Handbook of child psychology: Vol. 3. Social, emotional, and personality development (5th ed., pp. 1097–1149). New York: Wiley.

Grotevant, H. D., & Cooper, C. R. (1998). Individuality and connectedness in adolescent development: Review and prospects for research on identity, relationships, and context. In E. Skoe & A. von der Lippe (Eds.), *Personality development in adolescence* (pp. 3–37). London: Routledge & Kegan Paul.

Grotevant, H. D., & Kohler, J. K. (1999). Adoptive families. In M. E. Lamb (Ed.), *Parenting and child development in "nontraditional" families* (pp. 161–190). Mahwah, NJ: Erlbaum.

Grotpeter, J. K., & Crick, N. R. (1996). Relational aggression, overt aggression, and friendship. *Child Development, 67,* 2328–2338.

Grubb, W. N. (1999). The subbaccalaureate labor market in the United States: Challenges for the school-to-work transition. In W. R. Heinz (Ed.), *From education to work: Cross-national perspectives* (pp. 171–193). New York: Cambridge University Press.

Grusec, J. E. (1988). *Social development: History, theory, and research.* New York: Springer-Verlag.

Grusec, J. E., & Goodnow, J. J. (1994). Impact of parental discipline methods on the child's internalization of values: A reconceptualization of current points of view. *Developmental Psychology, 30,* 4–19.

Grych, J. H., & Fincham, F. D. (1997). Children's adaptation to divorce: From description to explanation. In S. A. Wolchik & I. N. Sandler (Eds.), *Handbook of children's coping: Linking theory to intervention* (pp. 159–193). New York: Plenum.

Guerra, N. G., & Slaby, R. G. (1990). Cognitive mediators of aggression in adolescent offenders: 2. Intervention. *Developmental Psychology, 26,* 269–277.

Guerra, N. G., Attar, B., & Weissberg, R. P. (1997). Prevention of aggression and violence among inner-city youths. In D. M. Stoff, J. Breiling, & J. D. Maser (Eds.), *Handbook of antisocial behavior* (pp. 375–383). New York: Wiley.

Guerri, C. (1998). Neuroanatomical and neurophysiological mechanisms involved in central nervous system dysfunctions induced by prenatal alcohol exposure. *Alcoholism: Clinical and Experimental Research, 22,* 304–312.

Guilford, J. P. (1985). The structure-of-intellect model. In B. B. Wolman (Ed.), *Handbook of intelligence* (pp. 225–266). New York: Wiley.

Gullone, E. (2000). The development of normal fear: A century of research. *Clinical Psychology Review, 20,* 429–451.

Gunnar, M. R. (1998). Quality of early care and buffering of neuroendocrine stress reactions: Potential effects on the developing human brain. *Preventive Medicine, 27,* 208–211.

Gunnar, M. R. (2000). Early adversity and the development of stress reactivity and regulation. In C. A. Nelson (Ed.), *Minnesota Symposia on Child Psychology* (Vol. 31, pp. 163–200). Hillsdale, NJ: Erlbaum.

Gunnar, M. R., Bruce, J., & Grotevant, H. D. (2000). International adoption of institutionally reared children: Research and policy. *Development and Psychopathology, 12,* 677–693.

Gunnar, M. R., & Nelson, C. A. (1994). Event-related potentials in year-old infants: Relations with emotionality and cortisol. *Child Development, 65,* 80–94.

Gunnoe, M. L., & Mariner, C. L. (1997). Toward a developmental-contextual model of the effects of parental spanking on children's aggression. *Archives of Pediatric and Adolescent Medicine, 151,* 768–775.

Guo, G., & VanWey, L. K. (1999). Sibship size and intellectual development: Is the relationship causal? *American Sociological Review, 64,* 169–187.

Gurucharri, C., & Selman, F. L. (1982). The development of interpersonal understanding during childhood, preadolescence, and adolescence: A longitudinal follow-up study. *Child Development, 53,* 924–927.

Gustafson, G. E., Green, J. A., & Cleland, J. W. (1994). Robustness of individual identity in the cries of human infants. *Developmental Psychobiology, 27,* 1–9.

Gustafson, G. E., Wood, R. M., & Green, J. A. (2000). Can we hear the causes of infants' crying? In R. G. Barr, B. Hopkins, & J. A. Green (Eds.), *Crying as a sign, a symptom, and a signal* (pp. 8–22). New York: Cambridge University Press.

Guttentag, R. (1997). Memory development and processing resources. In N. Cowan (Ed.), *The development of memory in childhood* (pp. 247–274). Hove, UK: Psychology Press.

Gwiazda, J., & Birch, E. E. (2001). Perceptual development: Vision. In E. B. Goldstein (Ed.), *Blackwell handbook of perception* (pp. 636–668). Oxford: Blackwell.

Hack, M. B., Taylor, H. G., Klein, N., Eiben, R., Schatschneider, C., & Mercuri-Minich, N. (1994). School-age outcomes in children with birth weights under 750 g. *New England Journal of Medicine, 331,* 753–759.

Hack, M., Wright, L. L., Shankaran, S., & Tyson, J. E. (1995). Very low birth weight outcomes of the National Institute of Child Health and Human Development Neonatal Network, November 1989 to October 1990. *American Journal of Obstetrics and Gynecology, 172,* 457–464.

Haden, C. A., Haine, R. A., & Fivush, R. (1997). Developing narrative structure in parent–child reminiscing across the preschool years. *Developmental Psychology, 33,* 295–307.

Hagekull, B., Bohlin, G., & Rydell, A. (1997). Maternal sensitivity, infant temperament, and the development of early feeding problems. *Infant Mental Health Journal, 18,* 92–106.

Haidt, J. (2001). The emotional dog and its rational tail: A social intuitionist approach to moral judgment. *Psychological Review, 108,* 814–834.

Haight, W. L., & Miller, P. J. (1993). *Pretending at home: Early development in a sociocultural context.* Albany, NY: SUNY Press.

Haith, M. M. (1997). The development of future thinking as essential for the emergence of skill in planning. In S. L. Friedman & E. K. Scholnick (Eds.), *The developmental psychology of planning: Why, how, and when do we plan?* (pp. 25–42). Mahwah, NJ: Erlbaum.

Haith, M. M. (1999). Some thoughts about claims for innate knowledge and infant physical reasoning. *Developmental Science, 2,* 153–156.

Haith, M. M., & Benson, J. B. (1998). Infant cognition. In D. Kuhn & R. S. Siegler (Eds.), *Handbook of child psychology: Vol. 2. Cognition, perception, and language* (5th ed., pp. 199–254). New York: Wiley.

Hakuta, K. (2001). A critical period for second language acquisition? In D. B. Bailey, Jr., J. T. Bruer, F. J. Symons, & J. W. Lichtman (Eds.), *Critical thinking about critical periods* (pp. 193–205). Baltimore: Paul H. Brookes.

Hakuta, K., Ferdman, B. M., & Diaz, R. M. (1987). Bilingualism and cognitive development: Three perspectives. In S. Rosenberg (Ed.), *Advances in applied psycholinguistics: Vol. 2. Reading, writing, and language learning* (pp. 284–319). New York: Cambridge University Press.

Hall, D. G., & Graham, S. A. (1999). Lexical form class information guides word-to-object mapping in preschoolers. *Child Development, 70,* 78–91.

Hall, D. G., Lee, S. C., & Belanger, J. (2001). Young children's use of syntactic cues to learn proper names and count nouns. *Developmental Psychology, 37,* 298–307.

Hall, G. S. (1904). *Adolescence* (Vols. 1–2). New York: Appleton-Century-Crofts.

Hall, J. A. (1978). Gender effects in decoding nonverbal cues. *Psychological Bulletin, 85,* 845–857.

Halle, T. G., Kurtz-Costes, B., & Mahoney, J. L. (1997). Family influences on school achievement in low-income, African-American children. *Journal of Educational Psychology, 89,* 527–537.

Halliday, J. L., Watson, L. F., Lumley, J., Danks, D. M., & Sheffield, L. S. (1995). New estimates of Down syndrome risks at chorionic villus sampling, amniocentesis, and live birth in women of advanced maternal age from a uniquely defined population. *Prenatal Diagnosis, 15,* 455–465.

Hallinan, M. T., & Kubitschek, W. N. (1999). Curriculum differentiation and high school achievement. *Social Psychology of Education, 3,* 41–62.

Halpern, C. T., Udry, J. R., Campbell, B., & Suchindran, C. (1999). Effects of body fat on weight concerns, dating, and sexual activity: A longitudinal analysis of black and white adolescent girls. *Developmental Psychology, 35,* 721–736.

Halpern, C. T., Udry, J. R., & Suchindran, C. (1997). Testosterone predicts initiation of coitus in adolescent females. *Psychosomatic Medicine, 59,* 161–171.

Halpern, D. F. (1997). Sex differences in intelligence. *American Psychologist, 52,* 1091–1102.

Halpern, D. F. (2000). *Sex differences in cognitive abilities* (3rd ed.). Mahwah, NJ: Erlbaum.

Halpern, L. F., MacLean, W. E., & Baumeister, A. A. (1995). Infant sleep–wake characteristics: Relation to neurological status and the prediction of developmental outcome. *Developmental Review, 15,* 255–291.

Hamer, D. H., Hu, S., Magnuson, V. L., Hu, N., & Pattatucci, A. M. L. (1993). A linkage between DNA markers on the X chromosome and male sexual orientation. *Science, 261,* 321–327.

Hamers, J. F., & Blanc, M. H. A. (2000). *Bilinguality and bilingualism* (2nd ed.). Cambridge: Cambridge University Press.

Hamilton, C. E. (2000). Continuity and discontinuity of attachment from infancy through adolescence. *Child Development, 71,* 690–694.

Hamilton, S. F. (1993). Prospects for an American-style youth apprenticeship system. *Educational Researcher, 22*(3), 11–16.

Hamilton, S. F., & Hamilton, M. A. (2000). Research, intervention, and social change: Improving adolescents' career opportunities. In L. J. Crockett & R. K. Silbereisen (Eds.), *Negotiating adolescence in times of social change* (pp. 267–283). New York: Cambridge University Press.

Hamm, J. V. (2000). Do birds of a feather flock together? The variable bases for African American, Asian American, and European American adolescents' selection of similar friends. *Developmental Psychology, 36,* 209–219.

Hammersley, M. (1992). *What's wrong with ethnography?* New York: Routledge.

Hamre, B. K., & Pianta, R. C. (2001). Early teacher–child relationships and the trajectory of children's school outcomes through eighth grade. *Child Development, 72,* 625–638.

Han, J. J., Leichtman, M. D., & Wang, Q. (1998). Autobiographical memory in Korean, Chinese, and American children. *Developmental Psychology, 34,* 701–713.

Haney, P., & Durlak, J. A. (1998). Changing self-esteem in children and adolescents: A meta-analytic review. *Journal of Clinical Child Psychology, 27,* 423–433.

Hanson, T. L. (1999). Does parental conflict explain why divorce is negatively associated with child welfare? *Social Forces, 77,* 1283–1316.

Happé, F. G. E. (1995). The role of age and verbal ability in the theory of mind task performance of subjects with autism. *Child Development, 66,* 843–855.

Hardy, J. B., Astone, N. M., Brooks-Gunn, J., Shapiro, S., & Miller, T. L. (1998). Like mother, like child: Intergenerational patterns of age at first birth and associations with childhood and adolescent characteristics and adult outcomes in the second generation. *Developmental Psychology, 34,* 1220–1232.

Harley, B., & Jean, G. (1999). Vocabulary skills of French immersion students in their second language. *Zeitschrift für Interkulturellen Fremdsprachenunterricht, 4*(2) [On-line]. Available: www.ualberta.ca/~german/ejournal/harley2.htm

Harlow, H. F. (1969). Age-mate or peer affectional system. In D. S. Lehrman, R. A. Hinde, & E. Shaw (Eds.), *Advances in the study of behavior* (Vol. 2, pp. 333–383). New York: Academic Press.

Harlow, H. F., & Zimmerman, R. (1959). Affectional responses in the infant monkey. *Science, 130,* 421–432.

Härnqvist, K. (1968). Changes in intelligence from 13 to 18. *Scandinavian Journal of Psychology, 9,* 50–82.

Harris, G. (1997). Development of taste perception and appetite regulation. In G. Bremner, A. Slater, & G. Butterworth (Eds.), *Infant development: Recent advances* (pp. 9–30). East Sussex, UK: Erlbaum.

Harris, I. B. (1996). *Children in jeopardy.* New Haven, CT: Yale University Press.

Harris, J. R. (1998). *The nurture assumption: Why children turn out the way they do.* New York: Free Press.

Harris, K. M. (2000). The health status and risk behavior of adolescents in immigrant families. In D. J. Hernandez (Ed.), *Children of immigrants: Health, adjustment, and public assistance.* Washington, DC: National Academy Press.

Harris, N. G. S., Bellugi, U., Bates, E., Jones, W., & Rossen, M. (1997). Contrasting profiles of language development in children with Williams syndrome. *Developmental Neuropsychology, 13,* 345–370.

Harris, P. L., & Leevers, H. J. (2000). Reasoning from false premises. In P. Mitchell & K. J. Riggs (Eds.), *Children's reasoning and the mind* (pp. 67–99). Hove, UK: Psychology Press.

Harrison, A. O., Wilson, M. N., Pine, C. J., Chan, S. Q., & Buriel, R. (1994). Family ecologies of ethnic minority children. In G. Handel & G. G. Whitchurch (Eds.), *The psychosocial interior of the family* (pp. 187–210). New York: Aldine De Gruyter.

Harrist, A. W., Zaia, A. F., Bates, J. E., Dodge, K. A., & Pettit, G. S. (1997). Subtypes of social withdrawal in early childhood: Sociometric status and social–cognitive differences across four years. *Child Development, 68,* 278–294.

Hart, B. (1991). Input frequency and children's first words. *First Language, 11,* 289–300.

Hart, B., & Risley, T. R. (1995). *Meaningful differences in the everyday experience of young American children.* Baltimore: Paul H. Brookes.

Hart, B. I., & Thompson, J. M. (1996). Gender role characteristics and depressive symptomatology among adolescents. *Journal of Early Adolescence, 16,* 407–426.

Hart, C. H. (1999, November). *Combating the myth that parents don't matter.* Address presented at the World Congress of Families II, Geneva, Switzerland.

Hart, C. H., Burts, D. C., Durland, M. A., Charlesworth, R., DeWolf, M., & Fleege, P. O. (1998a). Stress behaviors and activity type participation of preschoolers in more and less developmentally appropriate classrooms: SES and sex differences. *Journal of Research in Childhood Education, 13,* 176–196.

Hart, C. H., Nelson, D. A., Robinson, C. C., Olsen, S. F., & McNeilly-Choque, M. K. (1998b). Overt and relational aggression in Russian nursery-school-age children: Parenting style and marital linkages. *Developmental Psychology, 34,* 687–697.

Hart, C. H., Nelson, D. A., Robinson, C. C., Olsen, S. F., McNeilly-Choque, M. K., Porter, C. L., & Mckee, T. R. (2002). Russian parenting styles and family processes: Linkages with subtypes of victimization and aggression. In K. A. Kerns, J. M. Contreras, & A. M. Neal-Barnett (Eds.), *Family and peers: Linking two social worlds.* Westport, CT: Praeger.

Hart, C. H., Newell, L. D., & Olsen, S. F. (2002). Parenting skills and social/communicative competence in childhood. In J. O. Greene & B. R. Burleson (Eds.), *Handbook of communication and social interaction skill.* Hillsdale, NJ: Erlbaum.

Hart, C. H., Olsen, S. F., Robinson, C. C., & Mandleco, B. L. (1997). The development of social and communicative competence in childhood: Review and a model of personal, familial, and extrafamilial processes. *Communication Yearbook, 20,* 305–373.

Hart, C. H., Yang, C., Nelson, L. J., Robinson, C. C., Olsen, J. A., Nelson, D. A., Porter, C. L., Jin, S., Olsen, S. F., & Wu, P. (2000). Peer acceptance in early childhood and subtypes of socially withdrawn behaviour in China, Russia, and the United States. *International Journal of Behavioral Development, 24,* 73–81.

Hart, D., Atkins, R., & Ford, D. (1998). Urban America as a context for the development of moral identity in adolescence. *Journal of Social Issues, 54,* 513–530.

Hart, D., & Fegley, S. (1995). Prosocial behavior and caring in adolescence: Relations to self-understanding and social judgment. *Child Development, 66,* 1346–1359.

Hart, D., Keller, M., Edelstein, W., & Hofmann, V. (1998). Childhood personality influences on social-cognitive development: A longitudinal study. *Journal of Personality and Social Psychology, 74,* 1278–1289.

Hart, S., Field, T., & Roitfarb, M. (1999). Depressed mothers' assessments of their neonates' behaviors. *Infant Mental Health Journal, 20,* 200–210.

Harter, S. (1982). The perceived competence scale for children. *Child Development, 53,* 87–97.

Harter, S. (1986). Processes underlying the construction, maintenance, and enhancement of self-concept in children. In S. Suhls & A. Greenwald (Eds.), *Psychological perspectives of the self* (Vol. 3, pp. 136–182). Hillsdale, NJ: Erlbaum.

Harter, S. (1990). Issues in the assessment of the self-concept of children and adolescents. In A. LaGreca (Ed.), *Through the eyes of a child* (pp. 292–325). Boston: Allyn and Bacon.

Harter, S. (1996). Developmental changes in self-understanding across the 5 to 7 shift. In A. J. Sameroff & M. M. Haith (Eds.), *The five to seven year shift* (pp. 207–236). Chicago: University of Chicago Press.

Harter, S. (1998). The development of self-representations. In N. Eisenberg (Ed.), *Handbook of child psychology: Vol. 3. Social, emotional, and personality development* (5th ed., pp. 553–618). New York: Wiley.

Harter, S. (1999). *The construction of self: A developmental perspective.* New York: Guilford.

Harter, S., Marold, D. B., Whitesell, N. R., & Cobbs, G. (1996). A model of the effects of parent and peer support on adolescent false self-behavior. *Child Development, 67,* 360–374.

Harter, S., & Monsour, A. (1992). Developmental analysis of conflict caused by opposing attributes in the adolescent self-portrait. *Developmental Psychology, 28,* 251–260.

Harter, S., Waters, P., & Whitesell, N. R. (1998). Relational self-worth: Differences in perceived worth as a person across interpersonal contexts among adolescents. *Child Development, 69,* 756–766.

Harter, S., & Whitesell, N. (1989). Developmental changes in children's understanding of simple, multiple, and blended emotion concepts. In C. Saarni & P. Harris (Eds.), *Children's understanding of emotion* (pp. 81–116). Cambridge: Cambridge University Press.

Hartshorn, K., Rovee-Collier, C., Gerhardstein, P., Bhatt, R. S., Klein, P. J., Aaron, F., Wondoloski, T. L., & Wurtzel, N. (1998). Developmental changes in the specificity of memory over the first year of life. *Developmental Psychobiology, 33*, 61–78.

Hartup, W. W. (1983). Peer relations. In E. M. Hetherington (Ed.), *Handbook of child psychology: Vol. 4. Socialization, personality, and social development* (4th ed., pp. 103–196). New York: Wiley.

Hartup, W. W. (1996). The company they keep: Friendships and their developmental significance. *Child Development, 67*, 1–13.

Hartup, W. W., & Stevens, N. (1999). Friendships and adaptation across the life span. *Current Directions in Psychological Science, 8*, 76–79.

Haselager, J. T., Hartup, W. W., van Lieshout, C. F. M., & Riksen-Walraven, J. M. A. (1998). Similarities between friends and nonfriends in middle childhood. *Child Development, 69*, 1198–1208.

Hatano, G. (1994). Introduction: Conceptual change—Japanese perspectives. *Human Development, 37*, 189–197.

Hatano, G., & Inagaki, K. (1996). Cognitive and cultural factors in the acquisition of intuitive biology. In D. R. Olson & N. Torrance (Eds.), *Handbook of education and human development* (pp. 683–708). Cambridge, MA: Blackwell.

Hatch, M. C., Shu, X.-O., McLean, D. E., Levin, B., Begg, M., Reuss, L., & Susser, M. (1993). Maternal exercise during pregnancy, physical fitness, and fetal growth. *American Journal of Epidemiology, 137*, 1105–1114.

Hatton, D. D., Bailey, D. B., Jr., Burchinal, M. R., & Ferrell, K. A. (1997). Developmental growth curves of preschool children with vision impairments. *Child Development, 68*, 788–806.

Hauser, S. T., Powers, S. I., & Noam, G. G. (1991). *Adolescents and their families: Paths of ego development.* New York: Free Press.

Hausfather, A., Toharia, A., LaRoche, C., & Engelsmann, F. (1997). Effects of age of entry, day-care quality, and family characteristics on preschool behavior. *Journal of Child Psychology and Psychiatry, 38*, 441–448.

Hauth, J. C., Goldenberg, R. L., Parker, C. R., Cutter, G. R., & Cliver, S. P. (1995). Low-dose aspirin—lack of association with an increase in abruptio placentae or perinatal mortality. *Obstetrics and Gynecology, 85*, 1055–1058.

Hawke, S., & Knox, D. (1978). The one-child family: A new life-style. *The Family Coordinator, 27*, 215–219.

Hawker, D. S. J., & Boulton, M. J. (2000). Twenty years' research on peer victimization and psychosocial maladjustment: A meta-analytic review of cross-sectional studies. *Journal of Child Psychology and Psychiatry, 41*, 441–455.

Hawkins, A. J., Christiansen, S. L., Sargent, K. P., & Hills, E. J. (1993). Rethinking fathers' involvement in child care: A developmental perspective. *Journal of Family Issues, 14*, 531–549.

Hawkins, D. J., & Lam, T. (1987). Teacher practices, social development, and delinquency. In J. D. Burchard & S. N. Burchard (Eds.), *Prevention of delinquent behavior* (pp. 241–274). Newbury Park, CA: Sage.

Hawkins, J. N. (1994). Issues of motivation in Asian education. In H. F. O'Neil, Jr., & M. Drillings (Eds.), *Motivation: Theory and research* (pp. 101–115). Hillsdale, NJ: Erlbaum.

Hay, D. F. (1984). Social conflict in early childhood. In G. Whitehurst (Ed.), *Annals of child development* (Vol. 1, pp. 1–44). Greenwich, CT: JAI Press.

Hayne, H., Boniface, J., & Barr, R. (2000). The development of declarative memory in human infants: Age-related changes in deferred imitation. *Behavioral Neuroscience, 114*, 77–83.

Hayne, H., & Rovee-Collier, C. K. (1995). The organization of reactivated memory in infancy. *Child Development, 66*, 893–906.

Hayne, H., Rovee-Collier, C. K., & Perris, E. E. (1987). Categorization and memory retrieval by three-month-olds. *Child Development, 58*, 750–767.

Hayslip, B., Jr. (1994). Stability of intelligence. In R. J. Sternberg (Ed.), *Encyclopedia of human intelligence* (Vol. 2, pp. 1019–1026). New York: Macmillan.

Head Start Bureau. (2001). *2001 Head Start Fact Sheet.* [On-line]. Available: www.acf.dhhs.gov

Health Canada. (1997). Canadian national report on immunization, 1996. *Canada Communicable Disease Report, 23* (Suppl. 4).

Health Canada. (1998a, March). *Canadian perinatal surveillance system: Infant mortality* [On-line]. Available: www.hc-sc.gc.ca/hpb/lcdc/brch/factshts/alcprg

Health Canada. (1998b, November). *Canadian perinatal surveillance system: Alcohol and pregnancy* [On-line]. Available: www.hc-sc.gc.ca/hbp/lcdc/brch/factshts/mort

Health Canada. (1999a). *National guidelines for the childbearing years* [On-line] Available: www.hc-sc.ca/english/media/releases/1999

Health Canada. (1999b). *Joint statement: Reducing the risk of sudden infant death syndrome in Canda.* Ottawa, ON: Author.

Health Canada. (1999c). Statistical report on the health of Canadians. Prepared by the Federal, Provincial and Territorial Advisory Committee on Population Health for the Meeting of the Ministers of Health. Charlottetown, PEI, September 16–17, 1999. (Cat. No. H39-467/1999E.) [On-line]. Available: www.hc-sc.gc.ca/hppb/phdd/report/stat/pdf/english/all_english.pdf

Health Canada. (1999d). Reproductive and genetic technologies overview paper. [On-line]. Available: www.hc-sc.gc.ca/english/protection/reproduction/rgt/overview_sum.htm

Health Canada. (2000a). *Aboriginal Head Start Urban and Northern Initiative – Biennial report, 1998–2000* [On-line]. Available: www.hc-sc.gc.ca

Health Canada. (2000b). *How much is too much when you're pregnant?* [On-line]. Available: www.hc-sc.gc.ca/english/magazine/2000

Health Canada. (2000c). *Paediatrics and child health: Canadian Report on Immunization, 1997.* [On-line]. Available: www.hc-sc.gc.ca/hppb/childhood-youth/acy/pdf/Biennial.pdf

Health Canada. (2001a). *HIV/AIDs epi update: HIV and AIDS among youth in Canada.* Bureau of HIV/AIDS, STD and TB Update Series, Centre for Infectious Disease Prevention and Control [On-line]. Available: www.hc-sc.gc.ca/hpb/lcdc/bah/epi/youth_e.html

Health Canada. (2001b). *Nutrition for a Healthy Pregnancy.* [On-line]. Available: www.hc-sc.gc.ca/hppb/nutrition/pube/pregnancy/e_10.html

Heath, S. B. (1982). Questioning at home and at school: A comparative study. In G. Spindler (Ed.), *Doing the ethnography of schooling: Educational anthropology in action* (pp. 102–127). New York: Holt.

Heath, S. B. (1989). Oral and literate traditions among black Americans living in poverty. *American Psychologist, 44*, 367–373.

Heath, S. B. (1990). The children of Trackton's children: Spoken and written language and social change. In J. Stigler, G. Herdt, & R. A. Shweder (Eds.), *Cultural psychology: Essays on comparative human development* (pp. 496–519).

New York: Cambridge University Press.

Heckman, J. J. (1995). Lessons from *The Bell Curve. Journal of Political Economy, 193*, 1091–1120.

Hedges, L. V., & Nowell, A. (1995). Sex differences in mental test scores: Variability and numbers of high-scoring individuals. *Science, 269*, 41–45.

Hedges, L. V., & Nowell, A. (1998). Black–white test score convergence since 1995. In C. Jencks & M. Phillips (Eds.), *The black–white test score gap* (pp. 149–181). Washington, DC: Brookings Institution.

Heine, S. J., & Lehman, D. R. (1995). Cultural variation in unrealistic optimism: Does the West feel more invulnerable than the East? *Journal of Personality and Social Psychology, 68*, 595–607.

Heinz, W. R. (1999). Introduction: Transitions to employment in a cross-national perspective. In W. R. Heinz (Ed.), *From education to work: Cross-national perspectives* (pp. 1–21). New York: Cambridge University Press.

Helburn, S. W. (Ed.). (1995). *Cost, quality and child outcomes in child care centers.* Denver: University of Colorado.

Helwig, C. C. (1995). Adolescents' and young adults' conceptions of civil liberties: Freedom of speech and religion. *Child Development, 66*, 152–166.

Helwig, C. C., & Prencipe, A. (1999). Children's judgments of flags and flag-burning. *Child Development, 70*, 132–143.

Helwig, C. C., Zelazo, P. D., & Wilson, M. (2001). Children's judgments of psychological harm in normal and noncanonical situations. *Child Development, 72*, 66–81.

Hendrick, J., & Stange, T. (1991). Do actions speak louder than words? An effect of the functional use of language on dominant sex role behavior in boys and girls. *Early Childhood Research Quarterly, 6*, 565–576.

Hendricks, M., Guilford, J. P., & Hoepfner, R. (1969). *Measuring creative social intelligence.* (Reports from the Psychological Laboratory, University of Southern California No. 42).

Hennessy, K. D., Rabideau, G. J., & Cicchetti, D. (1994). Responses of physically abused and nonabused children to different forms of interadult anger. *Child Development, 65*, 815–828.

Henrich, C. C., Kuperminc, G. P., Sack, A., Blatt, S. J., & Leadbeater, B. J. (2000). Characteristics and homogeneity of early adolescent friendship groups: A comparison of male and female clique and nonclique members. *Applied Developmental Science, 4*, 15–26.

Henry, B., Moffitt, T. E., Caspi, A., Langley, J., & Silva, P. A. (1994). On the "remembrance of things past": A longitudinal evaluation of the retrospective method. *Psychological Assessment, 6,* 92–101.

Hepper, P. G. (1997). Fetal habituation: Another Pandora's box? *Developmental Medicine and Child Neurology, 39,* 274–278.

Herdt, G., & Boxer, A. M. (1993). *Children of horizons: How gay and lesbian teens are leading a new way out of the closet.* Boston: Beacon Press.

Hergenrather, J. R., & Rabinowitz, M. (1991). Age-related differences in the organization of children's knowledge of illness. *Developmental Psychology, 27,* 952–959.

Herman, L. M. (1987). Receptive competencies of language-trained animals. In J. S. Rosenblatt, C. Beer, M.-C. Busnel, & P. J. B. Slater (Eds.), *Advances in the study of behavior* (Vol. 17, pp. 1–60). Orlando, FL: Academic Press.

Herman, L. M., & Morel-Samuels, P. (1996). Knowledge acquisition and asymmetry between language comprehension and production: Dolphins and apes as general models for animals. In M. Bekoff & D. Jamieson (Eds.), *Readings in animal cognition* (pp. 289–306). Cambridge, MA: Cambridge University Press.

Herman, L. M., & Uyeyama, R. K. (1999). The dolphin's grammatical competency: Comments on Kako. *Animal Learning and Behavior, 27,* 18–23.

Herman, M. R., Dornbusch, S. M., Herron, M. C., & Herting, J. R. (1997). The influence of family regulation, connection, and psychological autonomy on six measures of adolescent functioning. *Journal of Adolescent Research, 12,* 34–67.

Hernandez, D. J. (1994, Spring). Children's changing access to resources: A historical perspective. *Social Policy Report of the Society for Research in Child Development, 8* (1).

Hernandez, F. D., & Carter, A. S. (1996). Infant response to mothers and fathers in the still-face paradigm. *Infant Behavior and Development, 19,* 502.

Herrnstein, R. J., & Murray, C. (1994). *The bell curve: Intelligence and class structure in American life.* New York: Free Press.

Hershberger, S. L., Pilkington, N. W., & D'Augelli, A. R. (1997). Predictors of suicide attempts among gay, lesbian, and bisexual youth. *Journal of Adolescent Research, 12,* 477–497.

Hespos, S. J., & Baillargeon, R. (2001). Reasoning about containment events in very young infants. *Cognition, 78,* 207–245.

Hesse, E., & Main, M. (2000). Disorganized infant, child, and adult attachment: Collapse in behavioral and attentional strategies. *Journal of the American Psychoanalytic Association, 48,* 1097–1127.

Hetherington, E. M. (1989). Coping with family transitions: Winners, losers and survivors. *Child Development, 60,* 1–14.

Hetherington, E. M. (1993). An overview of the Virginia Longitudinal Study of Divorce and Remarriage: A focus on early adolescence. *Journal of Family Psychology, 7,* 39–56.

Hetherington, E. M. (1995, April). *The changing American family and the well-being of children.* Master lecture presented at the biennial meeting of the Society for Research in Child Development, Indianapolis.

Hetherington, E. M. (1997). Teenaged childbearing and divorce. In S. Luthar, J. A. Burack, D. Cicchetti, & J. Weisz (Eds.), *Developmental psychopathology: Perspectives on adjustment, risk, and disorders* (pp. 350–373). Cambridge, UK: Cambridge University Press.

Hetherington, E. M. (1999a). Should we stay together for the sake of the children? In E. M. Hetherington (Ed.), *Coping with divorce, single-parenting, and remarriage: A risk and resiliency perspective* (pp. 93–116). Hillsdale, NJ: Erlbaum.

Hetherington, E. M. (1999b). Social capital and the development of youth from nondivorced, divorced, and remarried families. In A. Collins (Ed.), *Minnesota Symposia on Child Psychology* (Vol. 29). Hillsdale, NJ: Erlbaum.

Hetherington, E. M., Bridges, M., & Insabella, G. M. (1998). What matters? What does not? Five perspectives on the association between marital transitions and children's adjustment. *American Psychologist, 53,* 167–184.

Hetherington, E. M., & Henderson, S. H. (1997). Fathers in stepfamilies. In M. E. Lamb (Ed.), *The role of the father in child development* (pp. 212–226). New York: Wiley.

Hetherington, E. M., Henderson, S. H., & Reiss, D. (1999). Adolescent siblings in stepfamilies: Family functioning and adolescent adjustment. *Monographs of the Society for Research in Child Development, 64*(4, Serial No. 259).

Hetherington, E. M., & Jodl, K. M. (1994). Stepfamilies as settings for child development. In A. Booth & J. Dunn (Eds.), *Stepfamilies: Who benefits? Who does not?* (pp. 55–79). Hillsdale, NJ: Erlbaum.

Hetherington, E. M., & Kelly, J. (2002). *For better or for worse: Divorce reconsidered.* New York: Norton.

Hetherington, E. M., & Stanley-Hagan, M. M. (1999). The adjustment of children with divorced parents: A risk and resiliency perspective. *Journal of Child Psychology and Psychiatry, 40,* 129–140.

Hetherington, E. M., & Stanley-Hagan, M. (2000). Diversity among stepfamilies. In D. H. Demo, K. R. Allen, & M. A. Fine (Eds.), *Handbook of family diversity* (pp. 173–196). New York: Oxford University Press.

Hetherington, P. (1995, March). *The changing American family and the well-being of children.* Master lecture presented at the biennial meeting of the Society for Research in Child Development, Indianapolis.

Hewlett, B. S. (1992). Husband–wife reciprocity and the father–infant relationship among Aka pygmies. In B. S. Hewlett (Ed.), *Father–child relations: Cultural and biosocial contexts* (pp. 153–176). New York: Aldine De Gruyter.

Hewlett, S. A., & West, C. (1998). *The war against parents: What we can do for America's beleaguered moms and dads.* Boston: Houghton Mifflin.

Hewstone, M. (1996). Contact and categorization: Social psychological interventions to change intergroup relations. In C. N. Macrae, C. Stangor, & M. Hewstone (Eds.), *Stereotypes and stereotyping* (pp. 323–368). New York: Guilford.

Heyman, G. D., & Dweck, C. S. (1998). Children's thinking about traits: Implications for judgments of the self and others. *Child Development, 69,* 391–403.

Heyman, G. D., Dweck, C. S., & Cain, K. M. (1992). Young children's vulnerability to self-blame and helplessness: Relationship to beliefs about goodness. *Child Development, 63,* 401–415.

Heyman, G. D., & Gelman, S. A. (1999). The use of trait labels in making psychological inferences. *Child Development, 70,* 604–619.

Heyns, B. (1978). *Summer learning and the effects of schooling.* San Diego: Academic Press.

Hickey, T. L., & Peduzzi, J. D. (1987). Structure and development of the visual system. In P. Salapatek & L. Cohen (Eds.), *Handbook of infant perception: Vol. 1. From sensation to perception* (pp. 1–42). New York: Academic Press.

Hier, D. B., & Crowley, W. F. (1982). Spatial ability in androgen-deficient men. *New England Journal of Medicine, 302,* 1202–1205.

High, P., Hopmann, M., LaGasse, L., Sege, R., Moran, J., Guiterrez, C., & Becker, S. (1999). Child centered literacy orientation: A form of social capital? *Pediatrics, 103,* e55.

Higley, J. D., Hopkins, W. D., Thompson, W. W., Byrne, E. A., Hirsch, R. M., & Suomi, S. J. (1992). Peers as primary attachment sources in yearling rhesus monkeys (*Macaca mulatta*).

*Developmental Psychology, 28,* 1163–1171.

Hildebrand, D., & Saklofske, D. (1996). *The Wechsler Adult Intelligence Scale,* Third Edition: A Canadian standardization study. *Canadian Journal of School Psychology, 12,* 75–76.

Hill, J., & Holmbeck, G. N. (1986). Attachment and autonomy during adolescence. In G. Whitehurst (Ed.), *Annals of child development* (Vol. 3, pp. 145–189). Greenwich, CT: JAI Press.

Hinde, R. A. (1989). Ethological and relationships approaches. In R. Vasta (Ed.), *Annals of child development* (Vol. 6, pp. 251–285). Greenwich, CT: JAI Press.

Hines, M., & Green, R. (1991). Human hormonal and neural correlates of sex-typed behaviors. *Review of Psychiatry, 10,* 536–555.

Hines, M., & Kaufman, F. R. (1994). Androgen and the development of human sex-typical behavior: Rough-and-tumble play and sex of preferred playmates in children with congenital adrenal hyperplasia (CAH). *Child Development, 65,* 1042–1053.

Hines, S., & Bennett, F. (1996). Effectiveness of early intervention for children with Down syndrome. *Mental Retardation and Developmental Disabilities Research Reviews, 2,* 96–101.

Hirschfeld, L. A. (1995). Do children have a theory of race? *Cognition, 54,* 209–252.

Hirsh-Pasek, K., Kemler Nelson, D. G., Jusczyk, P. W., Cassidy, K. W., Druss, B., & Kennedy, L. (1987). Clauses are perceptual units for young infants. *Cognition, 26,* 269–286.

Ho, C. S.-H., & Fuson, K. C. (1998). Children's knowledge of teen quantities as tens and ones: Comparisons of Chinese, British, and American kindergartners. *Journal of Educational Psychology, 90,* 536–544.

Hochschild, A. R. (1997). *The time bind: When work becomes home and home becomes work.* New York: Metropolitan Books.

Hock, H. S., Park, C. L., & Bjorklund, D. F. (1998). Temporal organization in children's strategy formation. *Journal of Experimental Child Psychology, 70,* 187–206.

Hocutt, A. M. (1996). Effectiveness of special education: Is placement a critical factor? *Future of Children, 6,* 77–102.

Hodapp, R. M. (1996). Down syndrome: Developmental, psychiatric, and management issues. *Child and Adolescent Psychiatric Clinics of North America, 5,* 881–894.

Hodges, E. V. E., Boivin, M., Vitaro, F., & Bukowski, W. M. (1999). The power of friendship: Protection against an escalating cycle of peer victimization. *Developmental Psychology, 35,* 94–101.

Hodges, J., & Tizard, B. (1989). Social and family relationships of ex-institutional adolescents. *Journal of Child Psychology and Psychiatry, 30,* 77–97.

Hodges, R. M., & French, L. A. (1988). The effect of class and collection labels on cardinality, class-inclusion, and number conservation tasks. *Child Development, 59,* 1387–1396.

Hoff, T. L. (1992). Psychology in Canada one hundred years ago: James Mark Baldwin at the University of Toronto. *Canadian Psychology, 33*(2).

Hoff-Ginsburg, E. (1994). Influences of mother and child on maternal talkativeness. *Discourse Processes, 18,* 105–117.

Hoff-Ginsburg, E., & Tardiff, T. (1995). Socioeconomic status and parenting. In M. Bornstein (Ed.), *Handbook of parenting* (Vol. 2, pp. 161–188). Hillsdale, NJ: Erlbaum.

Hoffman, L. W. (1994). Commentary on Plomin, R. (1994). A proof and a disproof questioned. *Social Development, 3,* 60–63.

Hoffman, L. W. (2000). Maternal employment: Effects of social context. In R. D. Taylor & M. C. Wang (Eds.), *Resilience across contexts: Family, work, culture, and community* (pp. 147–176). Mahwah, NJ: Erlbaum.

Hoffman, L. W., & Youngblade, L. M. (1999). *Mothers at work: Effects on children's well-being.* New York: Cambridge University Press.

Hoffman, M. L. (2000). *Empathy and moral development.* New York: Cambridge University Press.

Hoffman, S., & Hatch, M. C. (1996). Stress, social support and pregnancy outcome: A reassessment based on research. *Paediatric and Perinatal Epidemiology, 10,* 380–405.

Hoffner, C., & Badzinski, D. M. (1989). Children's integration of facial and situational cues to emotion. *Child Development, 60,* 411–422.

Hokoda, A., & Fincham, F. D. (1995). Origins of children's helpless and mastery achievement patterns in the family. *Journal of Educational Psychology, 87,* 375–385.

Holcomb, T. F. (1990). Fourth graders' attitudes toward AIDS issues: A concern for the elementary school counselor. *Elementary School Guidance and Counseling, 25,* 83–90.

Holden, G. W., Coleman, S. M., & Schmidt, K. L. (1995). Why 3-year-old children get spanked: Determinants as reported by college-educated mothers. *Merrill-Palmer Quarterly, 41,* 431–452.

Holden, G. W., & West, M. J. (1989). Proximate regulation by mothers:

A demonstration of how differing styles affect young children's behavior. *Child Development, 60,* 64–69.

Hollich, G. J., Hirsh-Pasek, K., & Golinkoff, R. M. (2000). Breaking the language barrier: An emergentist coalition model for the origins of word learning. *Monographs of the Society for Research in Child Development, 65*(3, Serial No. 262).

Holmbeck, G. N. (1996). A model of family relational transformations during the transition to adolescence: Parent–adolescent conflict and adaptation. In J. A. Graber, J. Brooks-Gunn, & A. C. Petersen (Eds.), *Transitions through adolescence* (pp. 167–199). Mahwah, NJ: Erlbaum.

Holmbeck, G. N., & Hill, J. P. (1991). Conflictive engagement, positive affect, and menarche in families with seventh-grade girls. *Child Development, 62,* 1030–1048.

Holmes, W. C., & Slap, G. B. (1998). Sexual abuse of boys: Definition, prevalence, correlates, sequelae, and management. *Journal of the American Medical Association, 280,* 1855–1862.

Holobow, N., Genessee, F., & Lambert, W. (1991). The effectiveness of a foreign language immersion program for children from different ethnic and social class backgrounds: Report 2. *Applied Psycholinguistics, 12,* 179–198.

Honzik, M. P., Macfarlane, J. W., & Allen, L. (1948). The stability of mental test performance between two and eighteen years. *Journal of Experimental Education, 17,* 309–329.

Hood, B., Carey, S., & Prasada, S. (2000). Predicting outcomes of physical events: Two-year-olds fail to reveal knowledge of solidity and support. *Child Development, 71,* 1540–1554.

Hood, B. M., Murray, L., King, F., Hooper, R., Atkinson, J., & Braddick, O. (1996). Habituation changes in early infancy: Longitudinal measures from birth to 6 months. *Journal of Reproductive and Infant Psychology, 14,* 177–185.

Hope, S., Power, C., & Rodgers, B. (1999). Does financial hardship account for elevated psychological distress in lone mothers? *Social Science and Medicine, 29,* 381–389.

Hopkins, B., & Butterworth, G. (1997). Dynamical systems approaches to the development of action. In G. Bremner, A. Slater, & G. Butterworth (Eds.), *Infant development: Recent advances* (pp. 75–100). East Sussex, UK: Psychology Press.

Hopkins, B., & Westra, T. (1988). Maternal handling and motor development: An intracultural study. *Genetic, Social and General Psychology Monographs, 14,* 377–420.

Horgan, D. (1978). The development of the full passive. *Journal of Child Language, 5,* 65–80.

Horn, J. L. (1994). Theory of fluid and crystallized intelligence. In R. J. Sternberg (Ed.), *Encyclopedia of intelligence* (pp. 443–451). New York: Macmillan.

Horn, J. M. (1983). The Texas Adoption Project: Adopted children and their intellectual resemblance to biological and adoptive parents. *Child Development, 54,* 268–275.

Hornblower, M. (1997, June 9). Great Xpectations. *Time, 149,* 58–68.

Horne, R. S., Sly, D. J., Cranage, S. M., Chau, B., & Adamson, T. M. (2000). Effects of prematurity on arousal from sleep in the newborn infant. *Pediatric Research, 47,* 468–474.

Horner, T. M. (1980). Two methods of studying stranger reactivity in infants: A review. *Journal of Child Psychology and Psychiatry, 21,* 203–219.

Horowitz, F. D. (1992). John B. Watson's legacy: Learning and environment. *Developmental Psychology, 28,* 360–367.

Hort, B. E., Leinbach, M. D., & Fagot, B. I. (1991). Is there coherence among the cognitive components of gender acquisition? *Sex Roles, 24,* 195–207.

Hotz, V. J., McElroy, S. W., & Sanders, S. G. (1997). The costs and consequences of teenage childbearing for mothers. In R. A. Maynard (Ed.), *Kids having kids* (pp. 55–94). Washington, DC: Urban Institute.

Howe, D., Kahn, P. H., Jr., & Friedman, B. (1996). Along the Rio Negro: Brazilian children's environmental views and values. *Developmental Psychology, 32,* 979–987.

Howe, M. J. (1999). Prodigies and creativity. In R. J. Sternberg (Ed.), *Handbook of creativity* (pp. 431–446). Cambridge: Cambridge University Press.

Howe, M. L., & Courage, M. L. (1993). On resolving the enigma of infantile amnesia. *Psychological Bulletin, 113,* 305–326.

Howe, M. L., & Courage, M. L. (1997). The emergence and early development of autobiographical memory. *Psychological Review, 104,* 499–523.

Howe, N., Aquan-Assee, J., & Bukowski, W. M. (2001). Predicting sibling relations over time: Synchrony between maternal management styles and sibling relationship quality. *Merrill-Palmer Quarterly, 47,* 121–141.

Howe, N., & Jacobs, E. (1995). Child care research: A case for Canadian national standards. *Canadian Psychology, 36,* 131–148.

Howes, C. (1988a). Peer interaction of young children. *Monographs of*

the Society for Research in Child Development, 53(1, Serial No. 217).

Howes, C. (1988b). Relations between early child care and schooling. *Developmental Psychology, 24,* 53–57.

Howes, C. (1992). *The collaborative construction of pretend.* Albany, NY: SUNY Press.

Howes, C. (1998). The earliest friendships. In W. M. Bukowski, A. F. Newcomb, & W. W. Hartup (Eds.), *The company they keep: Friendship in childhood and adolescence* (pp. 66–86). New York: Cambridge University Press.

Howes, C., & Farver, J. (1987). Social pretend play in 2-year-olds: Effects of age of partner. *Early Childhood Research Quarterly, 2,* 305–314.

Howes, C., Hamilton, C. E., & Phillipsen, L. C. (1998). Stability and continuity of child–caregiver and child–peer relationships. *Child Development, 69,* 418–426.

Howes, C., & James, J. (2002). Children's social development within the socialization context of child care and early childhood education. In P. Smith & C. H. Hart (Eds.), *Handbook of childhood social development.* New York: Blackwell.

Howes, C., & Matheson, C. C. (1992). Sequences in the development of competent play with peers: Social and social pretend play. *Developmental Psychology, 28,* 961–974.

Hubbard, F. O. A., & van IJzendoorn, M. H. (1991). Maternal unresponsiveness and infant crying across the first 9 months: A naturalistic longitudinal study. *Infant Behavior and Development, 14,* 299–312.

Hudson, J. A., & Fivush, R. (1991). As time goes by: Sixth graders remember a kindergarten experience. *Applied Cognitive Psychology, 5,* 347–360.

Hudson, J. A., Fivush, R., & Kuebli, J. (1992). Scripts and episodes: The development of event memory. *Applied Cognitive Psychology, 6,* 483–505.

Hudson, J. A., Sosa, B. B., & Shapiro, L. R. (1997). Scripts and plans: The development of preschool children's event knowledge and event planning. In S. L. Friedman & E. K. Scholnick (Eds.), *The developmental psychology of planning: Why, how, and when do we plan?* (pp. 77–102). Mahwah, NJ: Erlbaum.

Huesmann, L. R. (1986). Psychological processes promoting the relation between exposure to media violence and aggressive behavior by the viewer. *Journal of Social Issues, 42,* 125–139.

Hughes, C., & Dunn, J. (1998). Understanding mind and emotion: Longitudinal associations with mental-state talk between young friends. *Developmental Psychology, 34,* 1026–1037.

Hughes, F. P. (1998). Play in special populations. In O. N. Saracho & B. Spodek (Eds.), *Multiple perspectives on play in early childhood education* (pp. 171–193). Albany: State University of New York Press.

Hughes, J. N., Cavell, T. A., & Grossman, P. B. (1997). A positive view of self: Risk or protection for aggressive children? *Development and Psychopathology, 9,* 75–94.

Hull, J. (1988). Socioeconomic status and Native education in Canada. *Canadian Journal of Native Education, 15*(2), 1–14.

Hulanicka, B. (1999). Acceleration of menarcheal age of girls from dysfunctional families. *Journal of Reproductive and Infant Psychology, 17,* 119–132.

Human Resources Development Canada. (1997). *Status of day care in Canada, 1995 and 1996: A review of the major findings of the National Day Care Study, 1995 and 1996.* Ottawa: Government of Canada.

Humphrey, L. T. (1998). Growth patterns in the modern human skeleton. *American Journal of Physical Anthropology, 105,* 57–72.

Humphrey, T. (1978). Function of the nervous system during prenatal life. In U. Stave (Ed.), *Perinatal physiology* (pp. 651–683). New York: Plenum.

Humphreys, A. P., & Smith, P. K. (1987). Rough and tumble, friendship, and dominance in schoolchildren: Evidence for continuity and change with age. *Child Development, 58,* 201–212.

Humphreys, L. G. (1989). Intelligence: Three kinds of instability and their consequences for policy. In R. L. Linn (Ed.), *Intelligence* (pp. 193–216). Urbana: University of Illinois Press.

Hunt, E., Streissguth, A. P., Kerr, B., & Olson, H. C. (1995). Mothers' alcohol consumption during pregnancy: Effects on spatial-visual reasoning in 14-year-old children. *Psychological Science, 6,* 339–342.

Hunter, M., Salter-Ling, N., & Glover, L. (2000). Donor insemination: Telling children about their origins. *Child Psychology and Psychiatry Review, 5,* 157–163.

Huntsinger, C. S., Jose, P. E., & Larson, S. L. (1998). Do parent practices to encourage academic competence influence the social adjustment of young European American and Chinese American children? *Developmental Psychology, 34,* 747–756.

Hura, S. L., & Echols, C. H. (1996). The role of stress and articulatory difficulty in children's early productions. *Developmental Psychology, 32,* 165–176.

Hurewitz, F., Brown-Schmidt, S., Thorpe, K., Gleitman, L. R., & Trueswell, J. C. (2000). One frog, two frog, red frog, blue frog: Factors affecting children's syntactic choices in production and comprehension. *Journal of Psycholinguistic Research, 29,* 597–626.

Hursti, U. K. (1999). Factors influencing children's food choice. *Annals of Medicine, 31,* 26–32.

Huston, A. C., & Alvarez, M. M. (1990). The socialization context of gender role development in early adolescence. In R. Montemayor, G. R. Adams, & T. P. Gullotta (Eds.), *From childhood to adolescence: A transitional period?* (pp. 156–179). Newbury Park, CA: Sage.

Huston, A. C., & Wright, J. C. (1998). Mass media and children's development. In I. E. Sigel & K. A. Renninger (Eds.), *Handbook of child psychology: Vol. 4. Child psychology in practice* (5th ed., pp. 999–1058). New York: Wiley.

Huston, A. C., Wright, J. C., Marquis, J., & Green, S. B. (1999). How young children spend their time: Television and other activities. *Developmental Psychology, 35,* 912–925.

Huston, T. L., & Vangelisti, A. L. (1995). How parenthood affects marriage. In M. A. Fitzpatrick & Anita L. Vangelisti (Eds.), *Explaining family interactions* (pp. 147–176). Thousand Oaks, CA: Sage.

Huttenlocher, J., Haight, W., Bryk, A., Seltzer, M., & Lyons, T. (1991). Early vocabulary growth: Relation to language input and gender. *Developmental Psychology, 27,* 236–248.

Huttenlocher, P. R. (1994). Synaptogenesis in human cerebral cortex. In G. Dawson & K. W. Fischer (Eds.), *Human behavior and the developing brain* (pp. 137–152). New York: Guilford.

Huttenlocher, P. R., & Dabholkar, A. S. (1997). Regional differences in synaptogenesis in human cerebral cortex. *Journal of Comparative Neurology, 387,* 167–178.

Huwiler, S. M. S., & Remafedi, G. (1998). Adolescent homosexuality. In L. A. Barness (Ed.), *Advances in pediatrics* (pp. 107–144). St. Louis: Mosby.

Hyde, J. S. (1995). Women and maternity leave: Empirical data and public policy. *Psychology of Women Quarterly, 19,* 299–313.

Hyde, J. S., Fenema, E., & Lamon, S. J. (1990). Gender differences in mathematics performance: A meta-analysis. *Psychological Bulletin, 107,* 139–155.

Hyde, J. S., Klein, M. H., Essex, M. J., & Clark, R. (1995). Maternity leave and women's mental health. *Psychology of Women Quarterly, 19,* 257–285.

Hyde, J. S., & Linn, M. C. (1988). Gender differences in verbal ability: A meta-analysis. *Psychological Bulletin, 104,* 53–69.

Hyde, J. S., & Plant, E. A. (1995). Magnitude of psychological gender differences: Another side to the story. *American Psychologist, 50,* 159–161.

Hymel, S., LeMare, L., Ditner, E., & Woody, E. Z. (1999). Assessing self-concept in children: Variations across self-concept domains. *Merrill-Palmer Quarterly, 45,* 602–623.

Imai, M., & Haryu, E. (2001). Learning proper nouns and common nouns without clues from syntax. *Child Development, 72,* 787–802.

Inagaki, K. (1997). Emerging distinctions between naïve biology and naïve psychology. In H. M. Wellman & K. Inagaki (Eds.), *The emergence of core domains of thought: New directions for child development #75,* (pp. 27–44). San Francisco: Jossey-Bass.

Inagaki, K., & Hatano, G. (1993). Children's understanding of mind–body distinction. *Child Development, 64,* 1534–1549.

Ingram, D. (1986). Phonological development: Production. In P. Fletcher & M. Garman (Eds.), *Language acquisition* (2nd ed., pp. 223–239). Cambridge: Cambridge University Press.

Ingram, D. (1999). Phonological acquisition. In M. Barrett (Ed.), *The development of language* (pp. 73–97). Philadelphia: Psychology Press/Taylor & Francis.

Inhelder, B., & Piaget, J. (1958). *The growth of logical thinking from childhood to adolescence: An essay on the construction of formal operational structures.* New York: Basic Books. (Original work published 1955)

Inoff-Germain, G., Arnold, G. S., Nottelman, E. D., Susman, E. J., Cutler, G. B., Jr., & Crousos, G. P. (1988). Relations between hormone levels and observational measures of aggressive behavior of young adolescents in family interactions. *Developmental Psychology, 24,* 129–139.

Intons-Peterson, M. J. (1988). *Gender concepts of Swedish and American youth.* Hillsdale, NJ: Erlbaum.

Irvine, J. J. (1986). Teacher–student interactions: Effects of student race, sex, and grade level. *Journal of Educational Psychology, 78,* 14–21.

Isabella, R. A. (1993). Origins of attachment: Maternal interactive behavior across the first year. *Child Development, 64,* 605–621.

Isabella, R. A., & Belsky, J. (1991). Interactional synchrony and the origins of infant–mother attachment: A replication study. *Child Development, 62,* 373–384.

Ito, Y., Teicher, M. H., Glod, C. A., & Ackerman, E. (1998). Preliminary evidence for aberrant cortical development in abused children: A quantitative EEG study. *Journal of Neuropsychiatry and Clinical Neuroscience, 10,* 298–307.

Iverson, J. M., Capirci, O., & Caselli, M. C. (1994). From communication to language in two modalities. *Cognitive Development, 9,* 23–43.

Izard, C. E. (1979). *The maximally discriminative facial movement scoring system.* Unpublished manuscript, University of Delaware.

Izard, C. E. (1991). *The psychology of emotions.* New York: Plenum.

Izard, C. E., & Ackerman, B. P. (2000). Motivational, organizational, and regulatory functions of discrete emotions. In M. Lewis & J. M. Haviland-Jones (Eds.), *Handbook of emotions* (2nd ed., pp. 253–264). New York: Guilford.

Izard, C. E., Hembree, E. A., & Huebner, R. R. (1987). Infants' emotion expressions to acute pain. *Developmental Psychology, 23,* 105–113.

Izard, C. E., Porges, S. W., Simons, R. F., Haynes, O. M., Hyde, C., Parisi, M., & Cohen, B. (1991). Infant cardiac activity: Developmental changes and relations with attachment. *Developmental Psychology, 27,* 432–439.

Jackson, P. W. (1968). *Life in classrooms.* New York: Holt, Rinehart & Winston.

Jacobs, J. E., & Weisz, V. (1994). Gender stereotypes: Implications for gifted education. *Roeper Review, 16,* 152–155.

Jacobson, J. L., Jacobson, S. W., Fein, G., Schwartz, P. M., & Dowler, J. (1984). Prenatal exposure to an environmental toxin: A test of the multiple effects model. *Developmental Psychology, 20,* 523–532.

Jacobson, J. L., Jacobson, S. W., Padgett, R. J., Brumitt, G. A., & Billings, R. L. (1992). Effects of prenatal PCB exposure on cognitive processing efficiency and sustained attention. *Developmental Psychology, 28,* 297–306.

Jacobson, K. C., & Crockett, L. J. (2000). Parental monitoring and adolescent adjustment: An ecological perspective. *Journal of Research on Adolescence, 10,* 65–97.

Jacobson, S. W. (1998). Specificity of neurobehavioral outcomes associated with prenatal alcohol exposure. *Alcoholism: Clinical and Experimental Research, 22,* 313–320.

Jadack, R. A., Hyde, J. S., Moore, C. F., & Keller, M. L. (1995). Moral reasoning about sexually transmitted diseases. *Child Development, 66,* 167–177.

Jaffe, J., Beebe, B., Feldstein, S., Crown, C. L., & Jasnow, M. D. (2001). Rhythms of dialogue in infancy. *Monographs of the Society for Research in Child Development, 66*(2, Serial No. 265).

Jaffee, S., Caspi, A., Moffitt, T. E., Belsky, J., & Silva, P. (2001). Why are children born to teen mothers at risk for adverse outcomes in young adulthood? Results of a 20-year longitudinal study. *Development and Psychopathology, 13,* 377–397.

Jambunathan, S., Burts, D. C., & Pierce, S. (2000). Comparisons of parenting attitudes among five ethnic groups in the United States. *Journal of Comparative Family Studies, 31,* 395–406.

James, D. (1998). Recent advances in fetal medicine. *British Medical Journal, 316,* 1580–1583.

James, W. (1963). *Psychology.* New York: Fawcett. (Original work published 1890)

Jameson, S. (1993). Zinc status in pregnancy: The effect of zinc therapy on perinatal mortality, prematurity, and placental ablation. *Annals of the New York Academy of Sciences, 678,* 178–192.

Jamieson, J. R. (1995). Interactions between mothers and children who are deaf. *Journal of Early Intervention, 19,* 108–117.

Jamin, J. R. (1994). Language and socialization of the child in African families living in France. In P. M. Greenfield & R. R. Cocking (Eds.), *Cross-cultural roots of minority child development* (pp. 147–166). Hillsdale, NJ: Erlbaum.

Jarrold, C., Baddeley, A. D., & Hewes, A. K. (1998). Verbal and nonverbal abilities in the Williams syndrome phenotype: Evidence for diverging developmental trajectories. *Journal of Child Psychology and Psychiatry, 39,* 511–523.

Jarrold, C., Butler, D. W., Cottington, E. M., & Jimenez, F. (2000). Linking theory of mind and central coherence bias in autism and in the general population. *Developmental Psychology, 36,* 126–138.

Jencks, C. (1972). *Inequality: A reassessment of the effect of family and schooling in America.* New York: Basic Books.

Jenkins, J. M., & Astington, J. W. (1996). Cognitive factors and family structure associated with theory of mind development in young children. *Developmental Psychology, 32,* 70–78.

Jenkins, J. M., & Astington, J. W. (2000). Theory of mind and social behavior: Causal models tested in a longitudinal study. *Merrill-Palmer Quarterly, 46,* 203–220.

Jensen, A. R. (1969). How much can we boost IQ and scholastic achievement? *Harvard Educational Review, 39,* 1–123.

Jensen, A. R. (1974). Cumulative deficit: A testable hypothesis. *Developmental Psychology, 10,* 996–1019.

Jensen, A. R. (1980). *Bias in mental testing.* New York: Free Press.

Jensen, A. R. (1985). The nature of the black–white difference on various psychometric tests: Spearman's hypothesis. *Behavioral and Brain Sciences, 8,* 193–219.

Jensen, A. R. (1998). *The g factor: The science of mental ability.* New York: Praeger.

Jensen, A. R. (2001). Spearman's hypothesis. In J. M. Collis & S. Messick (Eds.), *Intelligence and personality: Bridging the gap in theory and measurement* (pp. 3–24). Mahwah, NJ: Erlbaum.

Jensen, A. R., & Figueroa, R. A. (1975). Forward and backward digit-span interaction with race and IQ: Predictions from Jensen's theory. *Journal of Educational Psychology, 67,* 882–893.

Jensen, A. R., & Reynolds, C. R. (1982). Race, social class and ability patterns on the WISC-R. *Personality and Individual Differences, 3,* 423–438.

Jensen, A. R., & Whang, P. A. (1994). Speed of accessing arithmetic facts in long-term memory: A comparison of Chinese-American and Anglo-American children. *Contemporary Educational Psychology, 19,* 1–12.

Jensen, P. S., Hoagwood, K., & Trickett, E. J. (1999). Ivory towers or earthen trenches? Community collaboration to foster real-world research. *Applied Developmental Science, 3,* 206–212.

Jessor, R. (1996). Ethnographic methods in contemporary perspective. In R. Jessor, A. Colby, & R. A. Shweder (Eds.), *Ethnography and human development* (pp. 3–14). Chicago: University of Chicago Press.

Jeynes, W. H., & Littell, S. W. (2000). A meta-analysis of studies examining the effect of whole language instruction on the literacy of low-SES students. *Elementary School Journal, 101,* 21–33.

Jiao, S., Ji, G., & Jing, Q. (1996). Cognitive development of Chinese urban only children and children with siblings. *Child Development, 67,* 387–395.

Johnson, D. E. (2000). Medical and developmental sequelae of early childhood institutionalization in Eastern European adoptees. In C. A. Nelson (Ed.), *Minnesota Symposia on Child Psychology* (Vol. 31, pp. 113–162). Mahwah, NJ: Erlbaum.

Johnson, D. E., Albers, L. H., Iverson, S., Mathers, M., Dole, K., Georgieff, M. K., Hostetter, M. K., & Miller, L. C. (1996). Health status of Eastern European orphans referred for adoption. *Pediatric Research, 39,* 134A.

Johnson, G. R., Krug, E. G., & Potter, L. B. (2000). Suicide among adolescents and young adults: A cross-national comparison of 34 countries. *Suicide and Life-Threatening Behavior, 30,* 74–82.

Johnson, J., & Summers, A. (1999). Prenatal genetic screening for Down Syndrome and open neural tube defects using maternal serum marker screening. *Journal of the Society of Obstetricians and Gynaecologists of Canada, 21,* 887–891.

Johnson, J. S., & Newport, E. L. (1989). Critical period effects in second language learning: The influence of maturational state on the acquisition of English as a second language. *Cognitive Psychology, 21,* 60–99.

Johnson, M. H. (1995). The inhibition of automatic saccades in early infancy. *Developmental Psychobiology, 28,* 281–291.

Johnson, M. H. (1998). The neural basis of cognitive development. In D. Kuhn & R. S. Siegler (Ed.), *Handbook of child psychology: Vol. 2. Cognition, perception, and language* (5th ed., pp. 1–49). New York: Wiley.

Johnson, M. H. (1999). Ontogenetic constraints on neural and behavioral plasticity: Evidence from imprinting and face processing. *Canadian Journal of Experimental Psychology, 55,* 77–90.

Johnson, M. H. (2001). The development and neural basis of face recognition: Comment and speculation. *Infant and Child Development, 10,* 31–33.

Johnson, S. L., & Birch, L. L. (1994). Parents' and children's adiposity and eating style. *Pediatrics, 94,* 653–661.

Johnson, S. P. (1996). Habituation patterns and object perception in young infants. *Journal of Reproductive and Infant Psychology, 14,* 207–218.

Johnson, S. P. (1997). Young infants' perception of object unity: Implications for development of attentional and cognitive skills. *Current Directions in Psychological Science, 6,* 5–11.

Johnson, S. P., & Aslin, R. N. (1996). Perception of object unity in young infants: The roles of motion, depth, and orientation. *Cognitive Development, 11,* 161–180.

John-Steiner, V., & Mahn, H. (1996). Sociocultural approaches to learning and development: A Vygotskian framework. *Educational Psychologist, 3,* 191–206.

Johnston, J. R., & Slobin, D. I. (1979). The development of locative expressions in English, Italian, Serbo-Croatian, and Turkish. *Journal of Child Language, 16,* 531–547.

Jones, D. C., Abbey, B. B., & Cumberland, A. (1998). The development of display rule knowledge: Linkages with family expressiveness and social competence. *Child Development, 69,* 1209–1222.

Jones, E. F., & Thomson, N. R. (2001). Action perception and outcome valence: Effects on children's inferences of intentionality and moral and liking judgments. *Journal of Genetic Psychology, 162,* 154–166.

Jones, G. P., & Dembo, M. H. (1989). Age and sex role differences in intimate friendships during childhood and adolescence. *Merrill-Palmer Quarterly, 35,* 445–462.

Jones, G., Ritter, F. E., & Wood, D. J. (2000). Using a cognitive architecture to examine what develops. *Psychological Science, 11,* 93–100.

Jones, J. L., Lopez, A. Wilson, M., Schulkin, J., & Gibbs, R. (2001). Congenital toxoplasmosis: A review. *Obstetrical and Gynecological Survey, 56,* 296–305.

Jones, K. L. (1997). *Smith's recognizable patterns of human malformation* (5th ed.). Philadelphia: Saunders.

Jones, M. C. (1965). Psychological correlates of somatic development. *Child Development, 36,* 899–911.

Jones, M. C., & Mussen, P. H. (1958). Self-conceptions, motivations, and interpersonal attitudes of early- and late-maturing girls. *Child Development, 29,* 491–501.

Jones, M. M., & Mandeville, G. K. (1990). Th effect of age at school entry on reading achievement scores among South Carolina students. *Remedial and Special Education, 11,* 56–62.

Jones, N. A., Field, T., & Davalos, M. (2000). Right frontal EEG asymmetry and lack of empathy in preschool children of depressed mothers. *Child Psychiatry and Human Development, 30,* 189–204.

Jones, N. A., Field, T., Fox, N. A., Lundy, B., & Davalos, M. (1997). EEG activation in 1-month-old infants of depressed mothers. *Development and Psychopathology, 9,* 491–505.

Jones, S. S., & Raag, T. (1989). Smile production in older infants: The importance of a social recipient for the facial signal. *Child Development, 60,* 811–818.

Jones, W., Bellugi, U., Lai, Z., Chiles, M., Reilly, J., Lincoln, A., & Adolphs, R. (2000). Hypersociability in Williams syndrome. *Journal of Cognitive Neuroscience, 12,* 30–46.

Jordan, B. (1993). *Birth in four cultures.* Prospect Heights, IL: Waveland.

Jorgensen, K. M. (1999). Pain assessment and management in the newborn infant. *Journal of Peri-Anesthesia Nursing, 14,* 349–356.

Jorgensen, M., & Keiding, N. (1991). Estimation of spermarche from longitudinal spermaturia data. *Biometrics, 47,* 177–193.

Joseph, R. M. (1998). Intention and knowledge in preschoolers' conception of pretend. *Child Development, 69*, 966–980.

Josselson, R. (1992). *The space between us.* San Francisco: Jossey-Bass.

Josselson, R. (1994). The theory of identity development and the question of intervention. In S. L. Archer (Ed.), *Interventions for adolescent identity development* (pp. 12–25). Thousand Oaks, CA: Sage.

Jouen, F., & Lepecq, J.-C. (1989). Sensitivity to optical flow in neonates. *Psychologie Française, 34*, 13–18.

Jovanovic, J., & King, S. S. (1998). Boys and girls in the performance-based science classroom: Who's doing the performing? *American Educational Research Journal, 35*, 477–496.

Joyner, M. H., & Kurtz-Costes, B. (1997). Metamemory development. In W. Schneider & F. E. Weinert (Eds.), *Memory performance and competencies: Issues in growth and development* (pp. 275–300). Hillsdale, NJ: Erlbaum.

Jusczyk, P. W. (1995). Language acquisition: Speech sounds and phonological development. In J. L. Miller & P. D. Eimas (Eds.), *Handbook of perception and cognition: Vol. 11. Speech, language, and communication* (pp. 263–301). Orlando, FL: Academic Press.

Jusczyk, P. W. (2001). In the beginning, was the word . . . In F. Lacerda & C. von Hofsten (Eds.), *Emerging cognitive abilities in early infancy* (pp. 173–192). Mahwah, NJ: Erlbaum.

Jusczyk, P. W., & Aslin, R. N. (1995). Infants' detection of the sound patterns of words in fluent speech. *Cognitive Psychology, 29*, 1–23.

Jusczyk, P. W., & Hohne, E. A. (1997). Infants' memory for spoken words. *Science, 277*, 1984–1986.

Jusczyk, P. W., Houston, D. M., & Newsome, M. (1999). The beginnings of word segmentation in English-learning infants. *Cognitive Psychology, 39*, 159–207.

Jusczyk, P. W., Johnson, S. P., Spelke, E. S., & Kennedy, L. J. (1999). Synchronous change and perception of object unity: Evidence from adults and infants. *Cognition, 71*, 257–288.

Justice, E. M. (1986). Developmental changes in judgments of relative strategy effectiveness. *British Journal of Developmental Psychology, 4*, 75–81.

Justice, E. M., Baker-Ward, L., Gupta, S., & Jannings, L. R. (1997). Means to the goal of remembering: Developmental changes in awareness of strategy use–performance relations. *Journal of Experimental Child Psychology, 65*, 293–314.

Juul, A. (2001). The effects of oestrogens on linear bone growth. *Human Reproduction Update, 7*, 303–313.

Kagan, J. (1998). Biology and the child. In N. Eisenberg (Ed.), *Handbook of child psychology: Vol. 3. Social, emotional, and personality development* (5th ed., pp. 177–236). New York: Wiley.

Kagan, J., Arcus, D., Snidman, N., Feng, W. Y., Hendler, J., & Greene, S. (1994). Reactivity in infants: A cross-national comparison. *Developmental Psychology, 30*, 342–345.

Kagan, J., Kearsley, R. B., & Zelazo, P. R. (1978). *Infancy: Its place in human development.* Cambridge, MA: Harvard University Press.

Kagan, J., & Saudino, K. J. (2001). Behavioral inhibition and related temperaments. In R. N. Emde & J. K. Hewitt (Eds.), *Infancy to early childhood: Genetic and environmental influences on developmental change* (pp. 111–119). New York: Oxford University Press.

Kagan, J., & Snidman, N. (1991). Temperamental factors in human development. *American Psychologist, 46*, 856–862.

Kagan, J., Snidman, N., Zentner, M., & Peterson, E. (1999). Infant temperament and anxious symptoms in school-age children. *Development and Psychopathology, 11*, 209–224.

Kahn, P. H., Jr. (1992). Children's obligatory and discretionary moral judgments. *Child Development, 63*, 416–430.

Kahn, P. H., Jr. (1997a). Bayous and jungle rivers: Cross-cultural perspectives on children's environmental moral reasoning. In H. D. Saltzstein (Ed.), *New Directions for Child Development* (No. 76, pp. 23–36). San Francisco: Jossey-Bass.

Kahn, P. H., Jr. (1997b). Children's moral and ecological reasoning about the Prince William Sound oil spill. *Developmental Psychology, 33*, 1091–1096.

Kahn, P. H., Jr. (1999). *The human relationship with nature.* Cambridge, MA: MIT Press.

Kahn, P. H., Jr., & Friedman, B. (1995). Environmental views and values of children in an inner-city black community. *Child Development, 66*, 1403–1417.

Kail, R. (1988). Developmental functions for speeds of cognitive processes. *Journal of Experimental Child Psychology, 45*, 339–364.

Kail, R. (1991). Processing time declines exponentially during childhood and adolescence. *Developmental Psychology, 27*, 259–266.

Kail, R. (1993). The role of a global mechanism in developmental change in speed of processing. In M. L. Howe & R. Pasnak (Eds.), *Emerging themes in cognitive development: Vol. 1. Foundations.* New York: Springer-Verlag.

Kail, R. (1997). Processing time, imagery, and spatial memory. *Journal of Experimental Child Psychology, 64*, 67–78.

Kail, R., & Park, Y. (1992). Global developmental change in processing time. *Merrill-Palmer Quarterly, 38*, 525–541.

Kail, R., & Salthouse, T. A. (1994). Processing speed as a mental capacity. *Acta Psychologica, 86*, 199–225.

Kaisa, A., Stattin, H., & Nurmi, J. (2000). Parenting styles and adolescents' achievement strategies. *Journal of Adolescence, 23*, 205–222.

Kaitz, M., Meirov, H., Landman, I., & Eidelman, A. I. (1993a). Infant recognition by tactile cues. *Infant Behavior and Development, 16*, 333–341.

Kaitz, M., Shiri, S., Danziger, S., Hershko, Z., & Eidelman, A. I. (1993b). Fathers can also recognize their newborns by touch. *Infant Behavior and Development, 17*, 205–207.

Kako, E. (1999). Elements of syntax in the systems of three language-trained animals. *Animal Learning and Behavior, 27*, 1–14.

Kaler, S. R., & Kopp, C. B. (1990). Compliance and comprehension in very young toddlers. *Child Development, 61*, 1997–2003.

Kallós, D., & Broman, I. T. (1997). Swedish child care and early childhood education in transition. *Early Education and Development, 8*, 265–284.

Kamerman, S. (2000). Early childhood intervention policies: An international perspective. In J. P. Shonkoff & S. J. Meisels (Eds.), *Handbook of early childhood intervention* (2nd ed., pp. 316–329). New York: Cambridge University Press.

Kamerman, S. B. (1993). International perspectives on child care policies and programs. *Pediatrics, 91*, 248–252.

Kamerman, S. B. (2000). From maternity to parental leave policies: Women's health, employment, and child and family well-being. *Journal of the American Medical Women's Association, 55*, 96–99.

Kandall, S. R., Gaines, J., Habel, L., Davidson, G., & Jessop, D. (1993). Relationship of maternal substance abuse to subsequent sudden infant death syndrome in offspring. *Journal of Pediatrics, 123*, 120–126.

Kane, C. M. (2000). African-American family dynamics as perceived by family members. *Journal of Black Studies, 30*, 691–702.

Kanner, A. D., Feldman, S. S., Weinberger, D. A., & Ford, M. E. (1987). Uplifts, hassles, and adaptational outcomes in early adolescents. *Journal of Early Adolescence, 7*, 371–394.

Kao, G. (2000). Psychological well-being and educational achievement among immigrant youth. In D. J. Hernandez (Ed.), *Children of immigrants: Health, adjustment, and public assistance.* Washington, DC: National Academy Press.

Kao, G., & Tienda, M. (1995). Optimism and achievement: The educational performance of immigrant youth. *Social Science Quarterly, 76*, 1–19.

Kaplan, S. J., Pelcovitz, D., & Labruna, V. (1999). Child and adolescent abuse and neglect research: A review of the past 10 years. Part I: Physical and emotional abuse and neglect. *Journal of the American Academy of Child and Adolescent Psychiatry, 38*, 1214–1222.

Kaprio, J., Rimpela, A., Winter, T., Viken, R. J., Pimpela, M., & Rose, R. J. (1995). Common genetic influence on BMI and age at menarche. *Human Biology, 67*, 739–753.

Karadsheh, R. (1991, March). *This room is a junkyard! Children's comprehension of metaphorical language.* Paper presented at the biennial meeting of the Society for Research in Child Development, Seattle, WA.

Karmiloff-Smith, A. (1992). *Beyond modularity: A developmental perspective on cognitive science.* Cambridge, MA: MIT Press.

Karmiloff-Smith, A. (1997). Crucial differences between developmental cognitive neuroscience and adult neuropsychology. *Developmental Neuropsychology, 13*, 513–524.

Karmiloff-Smith, A. (1999). The connectionist infant: Would Piaget turn in his grave? In A. Slater & D. Muir (Eds.), *The Blackwell reader in developmental psychology* (pp. 43–52). Malden, MA: Blackwell.

Karmiloff-Smith, A., Grant, J., Berthoud, I., Davies, M., Howlin, P., & Udwin, O. (1997). Language and Williams syndrome: How intact is "intact"? *Child Development, 68*, 246–262.

Karmiloff-Smith, A., Grant, J., Sims, K., Jones, M., & Cuckle, P. (1996). Rethinking metalinguistic awareness: Representing and accessing knowledge about what counts as a word. *Cognition, 58*, 197–219.

Karmiloff-Smith, A., Tyler, L. K., Voice, K., Sims, K., Udwin, O., Howlin, P., & Davies, M. (1998). Linguistic dissociations in Williams syndrome: Evaluating receptive syntax in on-line and off-line tasks. *Neuropsychologia, 36*, 343–351.

Katchadourian, H. (1977). *The biology of adolescence.* San Francisco: Freeman.

Kaufman, A. S. (2000). Tests of intelligence. In R. J. Sternberg (Ed.), *Handbook of intelligence* (pp.

445–476). Cambridge: Cambridge University Press.

Kaufman, A. S., Kamphaus, R. W., & Kaufman, N. L. (1985). New directions in intelligence testing: The Kaufman Assessment Battery for Children (K-ABC). In B. B. Wolman (Ed.), *Handbook of intelligence* (pp. 663–698). New York: Wiley.

Kauppi, C. (2001). *From teen mom to cybermom: Supporting pregnant teens and young mothers using the web.* Cybermoms [On-line]. Available: cybermoms.cyber-beach.net

Kavanaugh, R. D., & Engel, S. (1998). The development of pretense and narrative in early childhood. In O. N. Saracho & B. Spodek (Eds.), *Multiple perspectives on play in early childhood education* (pp. 80–99). Albany: State University of New York Press.

Kaye, K., & Marcus, J. (1981). Infant imitation: The sensory-motor agenda. *Developmental Psychology, 17,* 258–265.

Kaye, W. H., Klump, K. L., Frank, G. K. W., & Strober, M. (2000). Anorexia and bulimia nervosa. *Annual Review of Medicine, 51,* 299–313.

Kearins, J. M. (1981). Visual spatial memory in Australian aboriginal children of desert regions. *Cognitive Psychology, 13,* 434–460.

Keating, D. (1979). Adolescent thinking. In J. Adelson (Ed.), *Handbook of adolescent psychology* (pp. 211–246). New York: Wiley.

Keating, D. (1990). Adolescent thinking. In S. S. Feldman & G. R. Elliott (Eds.), *At the threshold* (pp. 54–89). Cambridge, MA: Harvard University Press.

Keating, D., & Clark, L. V. (1980). Development of physical and social reasoning in adolescence. *Developmental Psychology, 16,* 23–30.

Keats, D. M., & Fang, F.-X. (1992). The effect of modification of the cultural content of stimulus materials on social perspective taking ability in Chinese and Australian children. In S. Iwawaki, & Y. Kashina (Eds.), *Innovations in cross-cultural psychology* (pp. 319–327). Amsterdam: Swets & Zeitlinger.

Keil, F. C. (1986). Conceptual domains and the acquisition of metaphor. *Cognitive Development, 1,* 72–96.

Keil, F. C., & Lockhart, K. L. (1999). Explanatory understanding in conceptual development. In E. K. Scholnick, K. Nelson, S. A. Gelman, & P. H. Miller (Eds.), *Conceptual development: Piaget's legacy* (pp. 103–130). Mahwah, NJ: Erlbaum.

Kelley, M. L., Power, T. G., & Wimbush, D. D. (1992). Determinants of disciplinary practices in low-income black mothers. *Child Development, 63,* 573–582.

Kelley, S. A., Brownell, C. A., & Campbell, S. B. (2000). Mastery motivation and self-evaluative affect to toddlers: Longitudinal relations with maternal behavior. *Child Development, 71,* 1061–1071.

Kellman, P. J. (1993). Kinematic foundations of infant visual perception. In C. E. Granrud (Ed.), *Visual perception and cognition in infancy* (pp. 121–173). Hillsdale, NJ: Erlbaum.

Kellman, P. J. (1996). The origins of object perception. In W. Epstein & S. Rogers (Eds.), *Handbook of perception and cognition* (pp. 3–48). New York: Academic Press.

Kelly, F. W., Terry, R., & Naglieri, R. (1999). A review of alternative birthing positions. *Journal of the American Osteopathic Association, 99,* 470–474.

Kempe, C. H., B. F., Steele, P. W., Droegemueller, P. W., & Silver, H. K. (1962). The battered-child syndrome. *Journal of the American Medical Association, 181,* 17–24.

Kennell, J., Klaus, M., McGrath, S., Robertson, S., & Hinkley, C. (1991). Continuous emotional support during labor in a U.S. hospital. *Journal of the American Medical Association, 265,* 2197–2201.

Kerns, K. A., & Berenbaum, S. A. (1991). Sex differences in spatial ability in children. *Behavior Genetics, 21,* 383–396.

Kessen, W. (1967). Sucking and looking: Two organized congenital patterns of behavior in the human newborn. In H. W. Stevenson, E. H. Hess, & H. L. Rheingold (Eds.), *Early behavior: Comparative and developmental approaches* (pp. 147–179). New York: Wiley.

Kessler, R., McGonagle, K., Zhao, S., Nelson, C., Hughes, M., Eshleman, S., Wittchen, H., & Kendler, K. (1994). Lifetime and 12-month prevalence of DSM-III-R psychiatric disorders in the United States: Results from the national comorbidity survey. *Archives of General Psychiatry, 51,* 8–19.

Khattri, N., Reeve, A. L., & Kane, M. B. (1998). *Principles and practices of performance assessment.* Mahwah, NJ: Erlbaum.

Kibby, M. Y., & Hynd, G. W. (2001). Neurobiological basis of learning disabilities. In D. P. Hallahan & B. K. Keogh (Eds.), *Research and global perspectives in learning disabilities* (pp. 25–42). Mahwah, NJ: Erlbaum.

Kids' Help Phone Statistics. (2002). [On-line]. Available: www.kidshelp.sympatico.ca/info/whatwedo/calldata.htm

Kihlstrom, J. F., & Cantor, N. (2000). Social intelligence. In R. J. Sternberg (Ed.), *Handbook of intelligence* (pp. 359–379). Cambridge: Cambridge University Press.

Killen, M., & Nucci, L. P. (1995). Morality, autonomy, and social conflict. In M. Killen & D. Hart (Eds.), *Morality in everyday life: Developmental perspectives* (pp. 52–86). Cambridge: Cambridge University Press.

Kilpatrick, D. G., Acierno, R., Saunders, B., Resnick, H. S., Best, C. L., & Schnurr, P. P. (2000). Risk factors for adolescent substance abuse and dependence: Data from a national sample. *Journal of Consulting and Clinical Psychology, 68,* 19–30.

Kilpatrick, S. W., & Sanders, D. M. (1978). Body image stereotypes: A developmental comparison. *Journal of Genetic Psychology, 132,* 87–95.

Kim, J. M. (1998). Korean children's concepts of adult and peer authority and moral reasoning. *Developmental Psychology, 34,* 947–955.

Kim, J. M., & Turiel, E. (1996). Korean children's concepts of adult and peer authority. *Social Development, 5,* 310–329.

Kim, M., McGregor, K. K., & Thompson, C. K. (2000). Early lexical development in English- and Korean-speaking children: Language-general and language-specific patterns. *Journal of Child Language, 27,* 225–254.

Kindermann, T. (1998). Children's development within peer groups: Using composite social maps to identify peer networks and to study their influences. In W. M. Bukowski & A. H. Cillessen (Eds.), *New directions for child development* (No. 80, pp. 55–82). San Francisco: Jossey-Bass.

King, C. A. (1997). Suicidal behavior in adolescence. In R. W. Maris, M. M. Silverman, & S. S. Canetto (Eds.), *Review of suicidology, 1997* (pp. 61–95). New York: Guilford.

King, C. M., & Johnson, L. M. P. (1999). Constructing meaning via reciprocal teaching. *Reading Research and Instruction, 38,* 169–186.

Kinney, D. (1999). From "head-bangers" to "hippies": Delineating adolescents' active attempts to form an alternative peer culture. In J. A. McLellan & M. J. V. Pugh (Eds.), *The role of peer groups in adolescent social identity: Exploring the importance of stability and change* (pp. 21–35). San Francisco: Jossey-Bass.

Kisilevsky, B. S., & Low, J. A. (1998). Human fetal behavior: 100 years of study. *Developmental Review, 18,* 1–29.

Kisilevsky, B. S., Hains, S. M. J., Lee, K., Muir, D. W., Xu, F., Fu, G., Zhao, Z. Y., & Yang, R. L. (1998). The still-face effect in Chinese and Canadian 3- to 6-month-old infants. *Developmental Psychology, 34,* 629–639.

Klaczynski, P. A. (1997). Bias in adolescents' everyday reasoning and its relationships with intellectual ability, personal theories, and self-serving motivation. *Developmental Psychology, 33,* 273–283.

Klaczynski, P. A., & Narasimham, G. (1998a). Development of scientific reasoning biases: Cognitive versus ego-protective explanations. *Developmental Psychology, 34,* 175–187.

Klaczynski, P. A., & Narasimham, G. (1998b). Representations as mediators of adolescent deductive reasoning. *Developmental Psychology, 34,* 865–881.

Klahr, D., & MacWhinney, B. (1998). Information processing. In D. Kuhn & R. S. Siegler (Eds.), *Information processing.* In D. Kuhn & R. S. Siegler (Eds.), *Handbook of child psychology: Vol. 2. Cognition, perception, and language* (5th ed., pp. 631–678). New York: Wiley.

Klebanov, P. K., Brooks-Gunn, J., McCarton, C., & McCormick, M. C. (1998). The contribution of neighborhood and family income to developmental test scores over the first three years of life. *Child Development, 69,* 1420–1436.

Kleeman, W. J., Schlaud, M., Fieguth, A., Hiller, A. S., Rothamel, T., & Troger, H. D. (1999). Body and head position, covering of the head by bedding, and risk of sudden infant death (SID). *International Journal of Legal Medicine, 112,* 22–26.

Klein, P. J., & Meltzoff, A. N. (1999). Long-term memory, forgetting, and deferred imitation in 12-month-old infants. *Developmental Science, 2,* 102–113.

Kliewer, W., Fearnow, M. D., & Miller, P. A. (1996). Coping socialization in middle childhood: Tests of maternal and paternal influences. *Child Development, 67,* 2339–2357.

Klimes-Dougan, B., & Kistner, J. (1990). Physically abused preschoolers' responses to peers' distress. *Developmental Psychology, 26,* 599–602.

Klineberg, O. (1963). Negro–white differences in intelligence test performance: A new look at an old problem. *American Psychologist, 18,* 198–203.

Kling, K. C., Hyde, J. S., Showers, C. J., & Buswell, B. N. (1999). Gender differences in self-esteem: A meta-analysis. *Psychological Bulletin, 125,* 470–500.

Klingner, J. K., Vaughn, S., Hughes, M. T., Schumm, J. S., & Elbaum, B. (1998). Outcomes for students with and without learning disabilities in inclusive classrooms. *Learning Disabilities Research and Practice, 13,* 153–161.

Klump, K. L., Kaye, W. H., & Strober, M. (2001). The evolving foundations of eating disorders. *Psychiatric Clinics of North America, 24,* 215–225.

Knecht, S., Draeger, B., Deppe, M., Bobe, L., Lohmann, H., Floeel, A., Ringelstein, E.-B., & Henningsen, H. (2000). Handedness and hemispheric language dominance in healthy humans. *Brain, 123,* 2512–2518.

Knobloch, H., & Pasamanick, B. (Eds.). (1974). *Gesell and Amatruda's Developmental Diagnosis.* Hagerstown, MD: Harper & Row.

Knoers, N., van den Ouweland, A., Dreesen, J., Verdijk, M., Monnens, L. S., & van Oost, B. A. (1993). Nephrogenic diabetes insipidus: Identification of the genetic defect. *Pediatric Nephrology, 7,* 685–688.

Kobayashi, Y. (1994). Conceptual acquisition and change through social interaction. *Human Development, 37,* 233–241.

Kochanska, G. (1991). Socialization and temperament in the development of guilt and conscience. *Child Development, 62,* 1379–1392.

Kochanska, G. (1993). Toward a synthesis of parental socialization and child temperament in early development of conscience. *Child Development, 64,* 325–347.

Kochanska, G. (1995). Children's temperament, mothers' discipline, and security of attachment: Multiple pathways to emerging internalization. *Child Development, 66,* 597–615.

Kochanska, G. (1997a) Multiple pathways to conscience for children with different temperaments: From toddlerhood to age 5. *Developmental Psychology, 33,* 228–240.

Kochanska, G. (1997b) Mutually responsive orientation between mothers and their young children: Implications for early socialization. *Child Development, 68,* 94–112.

Kochanska, G. (1998). Mother–child relationship, child fearfulness, and emerging attachment: A short-term longitudinal study. *Developmental Psychology, 34,* 480–490.

Kochanska, G., & Aksan, N. (1995). Mother–child mutually positive affect, the quality of child compliance to requests and prohibitions, and maternal control as correlates of early internalization. *Child Development, 66,* 597–615.

Kochanska, G., Casey, R. J., & Fukumoto, A. (1995). Toddlers' sensitivity to standard violations. *Child Development, 66,* 643–656.

Kochanska, G., Forman, D. R., & Coy, K. C. (1999). Implications of the mother–child relationship in infancy for socialization in the second year of life. *Infant Behavior and Development, 22,* 249–265.

Kochanska, G., & Murray, K. T. (2000). Mother–child mutually responsive orientation and conscience development: From toddler to early school age. *Child Development, 71,* 417–431.

Kochanska, G., Murray, K. T., & Harlan, E. T. (2000). Effortful control in early childhood: Continuity and change, antecedents, and implications for social development. *Developmental Psychology, 36,* 220–232.

Kochanska, G., & Radke-Yarrow, M. (1992). Inhibition in toddlerhood and the dynamics of the child's interaction with an unfamiliar peer at age five. *Child Development, 63,* 325–335.

Kochenderfer-Ladd, B., & Wardrop, J. L. (2001). Chronicity and instability of children's peer victimization experiences as predictors of loneliness and social satisfaction trajectories. *Child Development, 72,* 134–151.

Koestner, R., Franz, C., & Weinberger, J. (1990). The family origins of empathic concern: A 26-year longitudinal study. *Journal of Personality and Social Psychology, 58,* 709–717.

Kohen, D., & Hertzman, C. (1998, October). *The importance of quality child care.* W-98-33Es. Paper presented at Investing in Children: A National Research Conference, Ottawa.

Kohen, D., Hunter, T., Pence, A., & Goelman, H. (2000). The Victoria Day Care Research Project: Overview of a longitudinal study of child care and human development in Canada. *Canadian Journal of Research in Early Childhood Education, 8,* 49–54.

Kohlberg, L. (1966). A cognitive-developmental analysis of children's sex-role concepts and attitudes. In E. E. Maccoby (Ed.), *The development of sex differences* (pp. 82–173). Stanford, CA: Stanford University Press.

Kohlberg, L. (1969). Stage and sequence: The cognitive-developmental approach to socialization. In D. A. Goslin (Ed.), *Handbook of socialization theory and research* (pp. 347–480). Chicago: Rand McNally.

Kohlberg, L. (1976). Moral stages and moralization: The cognitive-developmental approach. In T. Lickona (Ed.), *Moral development and behavior: Theory, research, and social issues* (pp. 31–53). New York: Holt.

Kohlberg, L., Levine, C., & Hewer, A. (1983). *Moral stages: A current formulation and a response to critics.* Basel: Karger.

Kohlendorfer, U., Kiechl, S., & Sperl, W. (1998). Sudden infant death syndrome: Risk factor profiles for distinct subgroups. *American Journal of Epidemiology, 147,* 960–968.

Kolvin, I., & Trowell, J. (1996). Child sexual abuse. In I. Rosen (Ed.), *Sexual deviation* (3rd ed., pp. 337–360). Oxford: Oxford University Press.

Kopp, C. B. (1994). Infant assessment. In C. B. Fisher & R. M. Lerner (Eds.), *Applied developmental psychology* (pp. 265–293). New York: McGraw-Hill.

Korner, A. F. (1996). Reliable individual differences in preterm infants' excitation management. *Child Development, 67,* 1793–1805.

Kosterman, R., Hawkins, J. D., Guo, J., Catalano, R. F., & Abbott, R. D. (2000). The dynamics of alcohol and marijuana initiation: Patterns and predictors of first use in adolescence. *American Journal of Public Health, 90,* 360–366.

Kotch, J. B., Muller, G. O., & Blakely, C. H. (1999). Understanding the origins and incidence of spousal violence in North America. In T. P. Gullotta & S. J. McElhaney (Eds.), *Violence in homes and communities* (pp. 1–38). Thousand Oaks, CA: Sage.

Kotchick, B. A., Shaffer, A., Forehand, R., & Miller, K. S. (2001). Adolescent sexual risk behavior: A multisystem perspective. *Clinical Psychology Review, 21,* 493–519.

Kovacs, D. M., Parker, J. G., & Hoffman, L. W. (1996). Behavioral, affective, and social correlates of involvement in cross-sex friendship in elementary school. *Child Development, 67,* 2269–2286.

Kowaleski-Jones, L., & Mott, F. L. (1998). Sex, contraception and childbearing among high-risk youth: Do different factors influence males and females? *Family Planning Perspectives, 30,* 163–169.

Kowalski, K., & Lo, Y. (1999, April). *The influence of perceptual features and sociocultural information on the development of ethnic/racial bias in young children.* Paper presented at the biennial meeting of the Society for Research in Child Development, Albuquerque, NM.

Kowalski, N., & Allen, R. (1995). School sleep lag is less but persists with a very late starting high school. *Sleep Research, 24,* 124.

Kozulin, A. (1990). *Vygotsky's psychology: A biography of ideas.* Cambridge, MA: Harvard University Press.

Kraemer, H. C., Yesavage, J. A., Taylor, J. L., & Kupfer, D. (2000). How can we learn about developmental processes from cross-sectional studies, or can we? *American Journal of Psychiatry, 157,* 163–171.

Krafft, K., & Berk, L. E. (1998). Private speech in two preschools: Significance of open-ended activities and make-believe play for verbal self-regulation. *Early Childhood Research Quarterly, 13,* 637–658.

Kranzler, J. H. (1997). Educational and policy issues related to the use and interpretation of intelligence tests in the schools. *School Psychology Review, 26,* 150–162.

Krascum, R. M., & Andrews, S. (1998). The effects of theories on children's acquisition of family-resemblance categories. *Child Development, 69,* 333–346.

Krashden, S. D. (1999). *Condemned without trial.* Portsmouth, NH: Heinemann.

Kraut, R., Mukhopadhyay, T., Szczypula, J., Kiesler, S., & Scherlis, W. (1998a). Communication and information: Alternative uses of the Internet in households. In *Proceedings of the CHI '98* (pp. 368–383). New York: ACM.

Kraut, R., Patterson, M., Lundmark, V., Kiesler, S., Mukopadhyay, T., & Scherlis, W. (1998b). Internet paradox: A social technology that reduces social involvement and psychological well-being? *American Psychologist, 53,* 1017–1031.

Krebs, D., & Gillmore, J. (1982). The relationship among the first stages of cognitive development, role-taking abilities, and moral development. *Child Development, 53,* 877–886.

Kreutzer, M. A., Leonard, C., & Flavell, J. H. (1975). An interview study of children's knowledge about memory. *Monographs of the Society for Research in Child Development, 40*(1, Serial No. 159).

Krevans, J., & Gibbs, J. C. (1996). Parents' use of inductive discipline: Relations to children's empathy and prosocial behavior. *Child Development, 67,* 3263–3277.

Kroger, J. (1995). The differentiation of "firm" and "developmental" foreclosure identity statuses: A longitudinal study. *Journal of Adolescent Research, 10,* 317–337.

Kroger, J. (2000). *Identity development: Adolescence through adulthood.* Thousand Oaks, CA: Sage.

Kruger, A. C. (1993). Peer collaboration: Conflict, cooperation, or both? *Social Development, 2,* 165–182.

Krumhansl, C. L., & Jusczyk, P. W. (1990). Infants' perception of phrase structure in music. *Psychological Science, 1,* 70–73.

Kuczynski, L. (1984). Socialization goals and mother–child interaction: Strategies for long-term and short-term compliance. *Developmental Psychology, 20,* 1061–1073.

Kuczynski, L., & Hildebrandt, N. (1997). Models of conformity and resistance in socialization theory. In J. E. Grusec & L. Kuczynski (Eds.), *Parenting and children's internalization of values* (pp. 227–256). New York: Wiley.

Kuczynski, L., & Lollis, S. (2002). Four foundations for a dynamic model of parenting. In J. R. M.

Gerris (Eds.), *Dynamics of parenting*. Hillsdale, NJ: Erlbaum.

Kuebli, J., Butler, S., & Fivush, R. (1995). Mother–child talk about past emotions: relations of maternal language and child gender over time. *Cognition and Emotion, 9,* 265–283.

Kuhl, P. K. (2000). A new view of language acquisition. *Proceedings of the National Academy of Sciences, 97,* 11850–11857.

Kuhl, P. K., Williams, K. A., Lacerda, F., Stevens, K. N., & Lindblom, B. (1992). Linguistic experience alters phonetic perception in infants by 6 months of age. *Science, 255,* 606–608.

Kuhn, D. (1989). Children and adults as intuitive scientists. *Psychological Review, 96,* 674–689.

Kuhn, D. (1993). Connecting scientific and informal reasoning. *Merrill-Palmer Quarterly, 39,* 74–103.

Kuhn, D. (1995). Microgenetic study of change: What has it told us? *Psychological Science, 6,* 133–139.

Kuhn, D. (1999). Metacognitive development. *Current Directions in Psychological Science, 9,* 178–181.

Kuhn, D., Amsel, E., & O'Loughlin, M. (1988). *The development of scientific thinking* skills. Orlando, FL: Academic Press.

Kuhn, D., Garcia-Mila, M., Zohar, A., & Andersen, C. (1995). Strategies of knowledge acquisition. *Monographs of the Society for Research in Child Development, 60* (4, Serial No. 245).

Kuhn, L., & Stein, Z. (1997). Infant survival, HIV infection, and feeding alternatives in less-developed countries. *American Journal of Public Health, 87,* 926–931.

Kunkel, D. (2001). Children and television advertising. In D. G. Singer & J. L. Singer (Eds.), *Handbook of children and the media* (pp. 375–393). Thousand Oaks, CA: Sage.

Kunzinger, E. L., III. (1985). A short-term longitudinal study of memorial development during early grade school. *Developmental Psychology, 21,* 642–646.

Kupersmidt, J. B., DeRosier, M. E., & Patterson, C. P. (1995). Similarity as the basis for children's friendships: The roles of sociometric status, aggressive and withdrawn behavior, academic achievement, and demographic characteristics. *Journal of Social and Personal Relationships, 12,* 439–452.

Kupersmidt, J. B., Griesler, P. C., De Rosier, M. E., Patterson, C. J., & Davis, P. W. (1995). Childhood aggression and peer relations in the context of family and neighborhood factors. *Child Development, 66,* 360–375.

Kurdek, L. A., & Fine, M. A. (1994). Family acceptance and family control as predictors of adjustment in young adolescents: Linear, curvi-

linear, or interactive effects? *Child Development, 65,* 1137–1146.

Lackey, P. N. (1989). Adults' attitudes about assignments of household chores to male and female children. *Sex Roles, 20,* 271–281.

Ladd, G. W. (1999). Peer relationships and social competence during early and middle childhood. *Annual Review of Psychology, 50,* 333–359.

Ladd, G. W., Birch, S. H., & Buhs, E. S. (1999). Children's social and scholastic lives in kindergarten: Related spheres of influence? *Child Development, 70,* 1373–1400.

Ladd, G. W., Buhs, E. S., & Seid, M. (2000). Children's initial sentiments about kindergarten: Is school liking an antecedent of early classroom participation and achievement? *Merrill-Palmer Quarterly, 46,* 255–279.

Ladd, G. W., & Burgess, K. B. (1999). Charting the relationship trajectories of aggressive, withdrawn, and aggressive/withdrawn children during early grade school. *Child Development, 70,* 910–929.

Ladd, G. W., & Hart, C. H. (1992). Creating informal play opportunities: Are parents' and preschoolers' initiations related to children's competence with peers? *Developmental Psychology, 28,* 1179–1187.

Ladd, G. W., Kochenderfer, B. J., & Coleman, C. C. (1997). Classroom peer acceptance, friendship, and victimization: Distinct relational systems that contribute uniquely to children's school adjustment? *Child Development, 68,* 1181–1197.

Ladd, G. W., & Ladd, B. K. (1998). Parenting behaviors and parent-child relationships: Correlates of peer victimization in kindergarten? *Developmental Psychology, 34,* 1450–1458.

Ladd, G. W., LeSieur, K., & Profilet, S. M. (1993). Direct parental influences on young children's peer relations. In S. Duck (Ed.), *Learning about relationships* (Vol. 2, pp. 152–183). London: Sage.

Ladd, G. W., & Pettit, G. S. (2002). Parenting and the development of children's peer relationships. In M. Bornstein (Ed.), *Handbook of parenting* (2nd ed.). Mahwah, NJ: Erlbaum.

Ladd, G. W., & Price, J. M. (1987). Predicting children's social and school adjustment following the transition from preschool to kindergarten. *Child Development, 58,* 1168–1189.

Lagattuta, K. H., Wellman, H. M., & Flavell, J. H. (1997). Preschoolers' understanding of the link between thinking and feeling: Cognitive cuing and emotional change. *Child Development, 68,* 1081–1104.

Lagercrantz, H., & Slotkin, T. A. (1986). The "stress" of being born. *Scientific American, 254,* 100–107.

Lagnado, L. (2001, November 2). Kids confront Trade Center

trauma. *The Wall Street Journal,* pp. B1, B6.

Lahey, B. B., & Loeber, R. (1997). Attention-deficit/hyperactivity disorder, oppositional defiant disorder, conduct disorder, and adult antisocial behavior: A life span perspective. In D. M. Stoff, J. Breiling, & J. D. Maser (Eds.), *Handbook of antisocial behavior* (pp. 51–59). New York: Wiley.

Laible, D. J., & Thompson, R. A. (1998). Attachment and emotional understanding in preschool children. *Developmental Psychology, 34,* 1038–1045.

Laible, D. J., & Thompson, R. A. (2000). Mother–child discourse, attachment security, shared positive affect, and early conscience development. *Child Development, 71,* 1424–1440.

Laird, R. D., Jordan, K. Y., Dodge, K. A., Pettit, G. S., & Bates, J. E. (2001). Peer rejection in childhood, involvement with antisocial peers in early adolescence, and the development of externalizing behavior problems. *Development and Psychopathology, 13,* 337–354.

Laird, R. D., Pettit, G. S., Mize, J., & Lindsey, E. (1994). Mother–child conversations about peers: Contributions to competence. *Family Relations, 43,* 425–432.

Lamaze, F. (1958). *Painless childbirth.* London: Burke.

Lamb, M. E. (1987). *The father's role: Cross-cultural perspectives.* Hillsdale, NJ: Erlbaum.

Lamb, M. E. (1997). The development of father–infant relationships. In M. E. Lamb (Ed.), *The role of the father in child development* (3rd ed., pp. 104–120). New York: Wiley.

Lamb, M. E. (1998). Nonparental child care: Context, quality, correlates, and consequences. In I. E. Sigel & K. A. Renninger (Eds.), *Handbook of child psychology: Vol. 4. Child psychology in practice* (5th ed., pp. 73–133). New York: Wiley.

Lamb, M. E. (1999). Noncustodial fathers and their impact on the children of divorce. In R. A. Thompson & P. R. Amato (Eds.), *The postdivorce family: Children, parenting, and society* (pp. 105–125). Thousand Oaks, CA: Sage.

Lamb, M. E., & Oppenheim, D. (1989). Fatherhood and father–child relationships: Five years of research. In S. H. Cath, A. Gurwitt, & L. Gunsberg (Eds.), *Fathers and their families* (pp. 11–26). Hillsdale, NJ: Erlbaum.

Lamb, M. E., Sternberg, K. J., & Prodromidis, M. (1992). Nonmaternal care and the security of infant–mother attachment: A reanalysis of the data. *Infant Behavior and Development, 15,* 71–83.

Lamb, M. E., Thompson, R. A., Gardner, W., Charnov, E. L., &

Connell, J. P. (1985). *Infant–mother attachment: The origins and developmental significance of individual differences in Strange Situation behavior.* Hillsdale, NJ: Erlbaum.

Lamborn, S. D., & Steinberg, L. (1993). Emotional autonomy redux: Revisiting Ryan and Lynch. *Child Development, 64,* 483–499.

Lamborn, S. D., Mounts, N. S., Steinberg, L., & Dornbusch, S. M. (1991). Patterns of competence and adjustment among adolescents from authoritative, authoritarian, indulgent, and neglectful families. *Child Development, 62,* 1049–1065.

Lancaster, J. B., & Whitten, P. (1980). Family matters. *The Sciences, 20,* 10–15.

Landau, R. (1982). Infant crying and fussing. *Journal of Cross-Cultural Psychology, 13,* 427–443.

Landry, S. H., & Whitney, J. A. (1996). The impact of prenatal cocaine exposure: Studies of the developing infant. *Seminars in Perinatology, 20,* 99–106.

Landry, S. H., Garner, P. W., Swank, P. R., & Baldwin, C. D. (1996). Effects of maternal scaffolding during joint toy play with preterm and full-term infants. *Merrill-Palmer Quarterly, 42,* 177–199.

Lange, G., & Pierce, S. H. (1992). Memory-strategy learning and maintenance in preschool children. *Developmental Psychology, 28,* 453–462.

Lapkin, S. (Ed.) (1998). *French second-language education in Canada: Empirical studies.* Toronto: University of Toronto Press.

Lapointe, A. E., Askew, J. M., & Mead, N. A. (1992). *Learning mathematics.* Princeton, NJ: Educational Testing Service.

Lapsley, D. K. (1993). Toward an integrated theory of adolescent ego development: The "new look" at adolescent egocentrism. *American Journal of Orthopsychiatry, 63,* 562–571.

Lapsley, D. K., Jackson, S., Rice, K., & Shadid, G. (1988). Self-monitoring and the "new look" at the imaginary audience and personal fable: An ego-developmental analysis. *Journal of Adolescent Research, 3,* 17–31.

Lapsley, D. K., Milstead, M., Quintana, S., Flannery, D., & Buss, R. (1986). Adolescent egocentrism and formal operations: Tests of a theoretical assumption. *Developmental Psychology, 22,* 800–807.

Larson, D. E. (1996). *Mayo Clinic family health book.* New York: Morrow.

Larson, R. W., & Verma, S. (1999). How children and adolescents spend time across the world: Work, play, and developmental opportunities. *Psychological Bulletin, 25,* 701–736.

Larson, R. W., Richards, M. H., Moneta, G., Holmbeck, G., & Duckett, E. (1996). Changes in adolescents' daily interactions with their families from ages 10 to 18: Disengagement and transformation. *Developmental Psychology, 32,* 744–754.

Larson, R., & Ham, M. (1993). Stress and "storm and stress" in early adolescence: The relationship of negative events with dysphoric affect. *Developmental Psychology, 29,* 130–140.

Larson, R., & Lampman-Petraitis, C. (1989). Daily emotional states as reported by children and adolescents. *Child Development, 60,* 1250–1260.

Larson, R., & Richards, M. (1998). Waiting for the weekend: Friday and Saturday night as the emotional climax of the week. In A. C. Crouter & R. Larson (Eds.), *Temporal rhythms in adolescence: Clocks, calendars, and the coordination of daily life* (pp. 37–51). San Francisco: Jossey-Bass.

Larzelere, R. E., Schneider, W. N., Larson, D. B., & Pike, P. L. (1996). The effects of discipline responses in delaying toddler midbehavior recurrences. *Child and Family Behavior Therapy, 18,* 35–57.

Lasoya, S. H., & Eisenberg, N. (2001). Affective empathy. In J. A. Hall & F. A. Bernieri (Eds.), *Interpersonal sensitivity: Theory and measurement* (pp. 21–43). Mahwah, NJ: Erlbaum.

Latz, S., Wolf, A. W., & Lozoff, B. (1999). Sleep practices and problems in young children in Japan and the United States. *Archives of Pediatric and Adolescent Medicine, 153,* 339–346.

Laupa, M. (1995). "Who's in charge?" Preschool children's concepts of authority. *Early Childhood Research Quarterly, 9,* 1–7.

Laursen, B., Coy, K., & Collins, W. A. (1998). Reconsidering changes in parent–child conflict across adolescence: A meta-analysis. *Child Development, 69,* 817–832.

Lazar, I., & Darlington, R. (1982). Lasting effects of early education: A report from the Consortium for Longitudinal Studies. *Monographs of the Society for Research in Child Development, 47*(2–3, Serial No. 195).

Leach, C. E. A., Blair, P. S., Fleming, P. J., Smith, I. J., Platt, M. W., & Berry, P. J. (1999). Epidemiology of SIDS and explained sudden infant deaths. *Pediatrics, 104,* e43.

Leach, P. (1997). *Your baby and child.* Toronto: Random House.

Leaper, C. (1994). Exploring the correlates and consequences of gender segregation: Social relationships in childhood, adolescence, and adulthood. In C.

Leaper (Ed.), *New directions for child development* (No. 65, pp. 67–86). San Francisco: Jossey-Bass.

Leaper, C. (2000). Gender, affiliation, assertion, and the interactive context of parent–child play. *Developmental Psychology, 36,* 381–393.

Leaper, C., Anderson, K. J., & Sanders, P. (1998). Moderators of gender effects on parents' talk to their children: A meta-analysis. *Developmental Psychology, 34,* 3–27.

Leaper, C., Tenenbaum, H. R., & Shaffer, T. G. (1999). Communication patterns of African-American girls and boys from low-income, urban backgrounds. *Child Development, 70,* 1489–1503.

Lederer, J. M. (2000). Reciprocal teaching of social studies in inclusive elementary classrooms. *Journal of Learning Disabilities, 33,* 91–106.

Lee, C. L., & Bates, J. E. (1985). Mother–child interaction at age two years and perceived difficult temperament. *Child Development, 56,* 1314–1325.

Lee, K., Cameron, C., Xu, F., Fu, G., & Board, J. (1997). Chinese and Canadian children's evaluations of lying and truth telling: Similarities and differences in the context of pro- and antisocial behaviors. *Child Development, 68,* 924–934.

Lee, S. H., Ewert, D. P., Frederick, P. D., & Mascola, L. (1992). Resurgence of congenital rubella syndrome in the 1990s. *Journal of the American Medical Association, 267,* 2616–2620.

Lee, V. E., Smerdon, B. A., Alfeld-Liro, C., & Brown, S. L. (2000). Inside large and small high schools: Curriculum and social relations. *Educational Evaluation and Policy Analysis, 22,* 147–171.

Lee, V. E., & Smith, J. B. (1995). Effects of high school restructuring and size on early gains in achievement and engagement. *Sociology of Education, 68,* 241–270.

Leekam, S. R., Lopez, B., & Moore, C. (2000). Attention and joint attention in preschool children with autism. *Developmental Psychology, 36,* 261–273.

Leeman, L. W., Gibbs, J. C., & Fuller, D. (1993). Evaluation of a multicomponent group treatment program for juvenile delinquents. *Aggressive Behavior, 19,* 281–292.

Legerstee, M. (1991). The role of people and objects in early imitation. *Journal of Experimental Child Psychology, 51,* 423–433.

Legerstee, M., Barna, J., & DiAdamo, C. (2000). Precursors to the development of intention at 6 months: Understanding people and their actions. *Developmental Psychology, 36,* 627–634.

Lehman, D. R., & Nisbett, R. E. (1990). A longitudinal study of the effects of undergraduate

training on reasoning. *Developmental Psychology, 26,* 952–960.

Leichtman, M. D., & Ceci, S. J. (1993). The problem of infantile amnesia: Lessons from fuzzy-trace theory. In M. L. Howe & R. Pasnak (Eds.), *Emerging themes in cognitive development: Vol. 1. Foundations.* New York: Springer-Verlag.

Leichtman, M. D., & Ceci, S. J. (1995). The effect of stereotypes and suggestions on preschoolers' reports. *Developmental Psychology, 31,* 568–578.

Leinbach, M. D., Hort, B. E., & Fagot, B. I. (1997). Bears are for boys: Metaphorical associations in young children's gender stereotypes. *Cognitive Development, 12,* 107–130.

LeMare, L. J., & Rubin, K. H. (1987). Perspective taking and peer interaction: Structural and developmental analyses. *Child Development, 58,* 306–315.

LeMare, L. J., Vaughan, K., Warford, L., & Fernyhough, L. (2001, April). *Intellectual and academic performance of Romanian orphans 10 years after being adopted to Canada.* Poster session presented at the Biennial Meeting of the Society for Research in Child Development, Minneapolis, MN.

Lemery, K. S., Goldsmith, H. H., Klinnert, M. D., & Mrazek, D. A. (1999). Developmental models of infant and childhood temperament. *Developmental Psychology, 35,* 189–204.

Lemery, K. S., Goldsmith, H. H., Klinnert, M. D., & Mrazek, D. A. (1999). Developmental models of infant and childhood temperament. *Developmental Psychology, 35,* 189–204.

Lempert, H. (1990). Acquisition of passives: The role of patient animacy, salience, and lexical accessibility. *Journal of Child Language, 17,* 677–696.

Lengua, L. J., Wolchik, S., Sandler, I. N., & West, S. G. (2000). The additive and interactive effects of parenting and temperament in predicting problems of children of divorce. *Journal of Clinical Psychology, 29,* 232–244.

Lenneberg, E. H. (1967). *Biological foundations of language.* New York: Wiley.

Lerner, R. M., Fisher, C. B., & Weinberg, R. A. (2000). Toward a science for and of the people: Promoting civil society through the application of developmental science. *Child Development, 71,* 11–20.

Lester, B. M. (1985). Introduction: There's more to crying than meets the ear. In B. M. Lester & C. F. Z. Boukydis (Eds.), *Infant crying* (pp. 1–27). New York: Plenum.

Lester, B. M. (2000). Prenatal cocaine exposure and child outcome: A

model for the study of the infant at risk. *Israel Journal of Psychiatry and Related Sciences, 37,* 223–235.

Lester, B. M., & Dreher, M. (1989). Effects of marijuana use during pregnancy on newborn cry. *Child Development, 60,* 765–771.

Lester, B. M., Kotelchuck, M., Spelke, E., Sellers, M. J., & Klein, R. E. (1974). Separation protest in Guatemalan infants: Cross-cultural and cognitive findings. *Developmental Psychology, 10,* 79–85.

LeVay, S. (1993). *The sexual brain.* Cambridge, MA: MIT Press.

Leventhal, T., & Brooks-Gunn, J. (2000). The neighborhoods they live in: The effects of neighborhood residence on child and adolescent outcomes. *Psychological Bulletin, 126,* 309–337.

Levesque, R. J. R. (1996). International children's rights: Can they make a difference in American family policy? *American Psychologist, 51,* 1251–1256.

Levin, S. R., Petros, T. V., & Petrella, F. W. (1982). Preschoolers' awareness of television advertising. *Child Development, 53,* 933–937.

Levine, J. A., Pollack, H., & Comfort, M. E. (2001). Academic and behavioral outcomes among the children of young mothers. *Journal of Marriage and the Family, 63,* 355–367.

Levine, L. E. (1983). Mine: Self-definition in 2-year-old boys. *Developmental Psychology, 19,* 544–549.

Levine, L. J. (1995). Young children's understanding of the causes of anger and sadness. *Child Development, 66,* 697–709.

LeVine, R. A., Dixon, S., LeVine, S., Richman, A., Leiderman, P. H., Keefer, C. H., & Brazelton, T. B. (1994). *Child care and culture: Lessons from Africa.* New York: Cambridge University Press.

Levine, S. C., Huttemlocher, J., Taylor, A., & Langrock, A. (1999). Early sex differences in spatial skill. *Developmental Psychology, 35,* 940–949.

Levitsky, D. A., & Strupp, B. J. (1995). Malnutrition and the brain: Changing concepts, changing concerns. *Journal of Nutrition, 125,* 2245S–2254S.

Levtzion-Korach, O., Tennenbaum, A., Schnitzer, R., & Ornoy, A. (2000). Early motor development of blind children. *Journal of Paediatric and Child Health, 36,* 226–229.

Levy, G. D., Taylor, M. G., & Gelman, S. A. (1995). Traditional and evaluative aspects of flexibility in gender roles, social conventions, moral rules, and physical laws. *Child Development, 66,* 515–531.

Levy, Y. (1996). Modularity of language reconsidered. *Brain and Language, 55,* 240–263.

Levy-Shiff, R. (1994). Individual and contextual correlates of marital change across the transition to parenthood. *Developmental Psychology, 30,* 591–601.

Levy-Shiff, R. (2001). Psychological adjustment of adoptees in adulthood: Family environment and adoption-related correlates. *International Journal of Behavioral Development, 25,* 97–104.

Levy-Shiff, R., & Israelashvili, R. (1988). Antecedents of fathering: Some further exploration. *Developmental Psychology, 24,* 434–440.

Lew, A. R., & Butterworth, G. (1997). The development of hand–mouth coordination in 2- to 5-month-old infants: Similarities with reaching and grasping. *Infant Behavior and Development, 20,* 59–69.

Lewis, C. C. (1995). *Educating hearts and minds.* New York: Cambridge University Press.

Lewis, C., Freeman, N. H., Kyriadidou, C., Maridakikassotaki, K., & Berridge, D. M. (1996). Social influences on false belief access—specific sibling influences or general apprenticeship? *Child Development, 67,* 2930–2947.

Lewis, M. (1992). *Shame: The exposed self.* New York: Free Press.

Lewis, M. (1994). Myself and me. In S. T. Parker, R. W. Mitchell, & M. L. Boccia (Eds.), *Self-awareness in animals and humans: Developmental perspectives* (pp. 20–34). New York: Cambridge University Press.

Lewis, M. (1995). Cognition-emotion feedback and the self-organization of developmental paths. *Human Development, 38,* 71–102.

Lewis, M. (1997). *Altering fate: Why the past does not predict the future.* New York: Guilford.

Lewis, M. (1998). Emotional competence and development. In D. Pushkar, W. M. Bukowski, A. E. Schwartzman, E. M. Stack, & D. R. White (Eds.), *Improving competence across the lifespan* (pp. 27–36). New York: Plenum.

Lewis, M. (1999). The role of the self in cognition and emotion. In T. Dalgleish & M. J. Power (Eds.), *Handbook of cognition and emotion* (pp. 125–142). Chichester, UK: Wiley.

Lewis, M. D. (2000). The promise of dynamic systems approaches for an integrated account of human development. *Child Development, 71,* 36–43.

Lewis, M., Alessandri, S. M., & Sullivan, M. W. (1992). Differences in shame and pride as a function of children's gender and task difficulty. *Child Development, 63,* 630–638.

Lewis, M., & Brooks-Gunn, J. (1979). *Social cognition and the acquisition of self.* New York: Plenum.

Lewis, M., Ramsay, D. S., & Kawakami, K. (1993). Differences between Japanese infants and Caucasian American infants in behavioral and cortisol response to inoculation. *Child Development, 64,* 1722–1731.

Lewis, M., Sullivan, M. W., & Ramsay, D. S. (1992). Individual differences in anger and sad expressions during extinction: Antecedents and consequences. *Infant Behavior and Development, 15,* 443–452.

Lewis, M., Sullivan, M. W., & Vasen, A. (1987). Making faces: Age and emotion differences in the posing of emotional expressions. *Developmental Psychology, 23,* 690–697.

Lewis, M., Sullivan, M. W., Stanger, C., & Weiss, M. (1989). Self development and self-conscious emotions. *Child Development, 60,* 146–156.

Lewkowicz, D. J. (1996). Infants' response to the audible and visible properties of the human face: I. Role of lexical syntactic content, temporal synchrony, gender, and manner of speech. *Developmental Psychology, 32,* 347–366.

Lewontin, R. C. (1976). Race and intelligence. In N. J. Block & G. Dworkin (Eds.), *The IQ controversy* (pp. 78–92). New York: Pantheon Books.

Liau, A. K., Barriga, A. Q., & Gibbs, J. C. (1998). Relations between self-serving cognitive distortion and overt vs. covert antisocial behavior in adolescents. *Aggressive Behavior, 24,* 335–346.

Liaw, F., & Brooks-Gunn, J. (1993). Patterns of low-birth-weight children's cognitive development. *Developmental Psychology, 29,* 1024–1035.

Liben, L. S. (1999). Developing an understanding of external spatial representations. In I. E. Sigel (Ed.), *Development of mental representation* (pp. 297–321). Mahwah, NJ: Erlbaum.

Liben, L. S., Bigler, R. S., & Krogh, H. R. (2001). Pink and blue collar jobs: Children's judgments of job status and job aspirations in relation to sex of worker. *Journal of Experimental Child Psychology, 79,* 346–363.

Liben, L. S., & Downs, R. M. (1993). Understanding person-space-map relations: Cartographic and developmental perspectives. *Developmental Psychology, 29,* 739–752.

Liben, L. S., & Signorella, M. L. (1993). Gender-schematic processing in children: The role of initial interpretations of stimuli. *Developmental Psychology, 29,* 141–149.

Lickliter, R., & Bahrick, L. E. (2000). The development of infant intersensory perception: Advantages of a comparative convergent-operations approach. *Psychological Bulletin, 126,* 260–280.

Lickona, T. (1976). Research on Piaget's theory of moral development. In T. Lickona (Ed.), *Moral development and behavior* (pp. 219–240). New York: Holt, Rinehart & Winston.

Lidz, C. S. (1991). *Practitioner's guide to dynamic assessment.* New York: Guilford.

Lidz, C. S. (1997). Dynamic assessment: Psychoeducational assessment with cultural sensitivity. *Journal of Social Distress and the Homeless, 6,* 95–111.

Lidz, C. S. (2001). Multicultural issues and dynamic assessment. In L. A. Suzuki & J. G. Ponterotto (Eds.), *Handbook of multicultural assessment: Clinical, psychological, and educational applications* (2nd ed., pp. 523–539). San Francisco: Jossey-Bass.

Light, P., & Perrett-Clermont, A. (1989). Social context effects in learning and testing. In A. R. H. Gellatly, D. Rogers, & J. Sloboda (Eds.), *Cognition and social worlds* (pp. 99–112). Oxford: Clarendon Press.

Lillard, A. S. (1998). Playing with a theory of mind. In O. N. Saracho & B. Spodek (Eds.), *Multiple perspectives on play in early childhood education* (pp. 11–33). Albany: State University of New York Press.

Lillard, A. S. (2001). Pretending, understanding pretense, and understanding minds. In S. Reifel (Ed.), *Theory in context and out: Play and culture studies, Vol. 3* (pp. 233–254). Westport, CT: Ablex.

Lin, C. C., Hsiao, C. K., & Chen, W. J. (1999). Development of sustained attention assessed using the continuous performance test among children 6–15 years. *Journal of Abnormal Child Psychology, 27,* 403–412.

Lindsay-Hartz, J., de Rivera, J., & Mascolor, M. F. (1995). Differentiating guilt and shame and their effects on motivation. In J. P. Tangney & K. W. Fischer (Eds.), *Self-conscious emotions* (pp. 274–300). New York: Guilford.

Lindsey, E. W., & Mize, J. (2000). Parent–child physical and pretense play: Links to children's social competence. *Merrill-Palmer Quarterly, 46,* 565–591.

Link, S. C., & Ancoli-Israel, S. (1995). Sleep and the teenager. *Sleep Research, 24a,* 184.

Linn, M. C., & Hyde, J. S. (1989). Gender, mathematics, and science. *Educational Researcher, 18,* 17–27.

Linn, M. C., & Petersen, A. C. (1985). Emergence and characterization of sex differences in spatial ability: A meta-analysis. *Child Development, 56,* 1479–1498.

Liss, M. B., Reinhardt, L. C., & Fredriksen, S. (1983). TV heroes: The impact of rhetoric and deeds. *Journal of Applied Developmental Psychology, 4,* 175–187.

Lissens, W., & Sermon, K. (1997). Preimplantation genetic diagnosis—current status and new developments. *Human Reproduction, 12,* 1756–1761.

Litovsky, R. Y., & Ashmead, D. H. (1997). Development of binaural and spatial hearing in infants and children. In R. H. Gilkey & T. R. Anderson (Eds.), *Binaural and spatial hearing in real and virtual environments* (pp. 571–592). Mahwah, NJ: Erlbaum.

Livesley, W. J., & Bromley, D. B. (1973). *Person perception in childhood and adolescence.* New York: Wiley.

Livson, N., & Peshkin, H. (1980). Perspectives on adolescence from longitudinal research. In J. Adelson (Ed.), *Handbook of adolescent psychology* (pp. 47–98). New York: Wiley.

Lloyd, B., & Smith, C. (1985). The social representation of gender and young children's play. *British Journal of Developmental Psychology, 3,* 65–73.

Lloyd, L. (1999). Multi-age classes and high ability students. *Review of Educational Research, 69,* 187–212.

Lochman, J. E., Coie, J. D., Underwood, M. K., & Terry, R. (1993). Effectiveness of a social relations intervention program for aggressive and nonaggressive, rejected children. *Journal of Consulting and Clinical Psychology, 61,* 1053–1058.

Locke, J. (1892). Some thoughts concerning education. In R. H. Quick (Ed.), *Locke on education* (pp. 1–236). Cambridge: Cambridge University Press. (Original work published 1690)

Lockhart, R. S., & Craik, F. I. M. (1990). Levels of processing: A retrospective commentary on a framework for memory research. *Canadian Journal of Psychology, 44,* 87–112.

Loeber, R. L., Farrington, D. P., Stouthamer-Loeber, M., Moffitt, T. E., & Caspi, A. (1999). The development of male offending: Key findings from the first decade of the Pittsburgh Youth Study. *Studies on Crime and Crime Prevention, 8,* 245–263.

Loehlin, J. C. (1992). *Genes and environment in personality development.* Newbury Park, CA: Sage.

Loehlin, J. C. (2000). Group differences in intelligence. In R. J. Sternberg (Ed.), *Handbook of intelligence* (pp. 176–193). New York: Cambridge University Press.

Loehlin, J. C., Horn, J. M., & Willerman, L. (1997). Heredity, environment, and IQ in the Texas Adoption Project. In R. J. Sternberg & E. L. Grigorenko (Eds.), *Intelligence, heredity, and environment* (pp. 105–125). New York: Cambridge University Press.

Loehlin, J. C., Willerman, L., & Horn, J. M. (1988). Human behavior genetics. *Annual Review of Psychology, 38,* 101–133.

Lonigan, C. J., & Whitehurst, G. J. (1998). Relative efficacy of parent and teacher involvement in a shared-reading intervention for preschool children from low-income backgrounds. *Early Childhood Research Quarterly, 13,* 263–290.

Lorenz, K. Z. (1943). Die angeborenen Formen möglicher Erfahrung. *Zeitschrift für Tierpsychologie, 5,* 235–409.

Lorenz, K. Z. (1952). *King Solomon's ring.* New York: Crowell.

Lorenz, K. Z. (1983). *So Kam der Mensch auf den Hund.* Munich: DTV.

Losey, K. M. (1995). Mexican-American students and classroom interaction: An overview and critique. *Review of Educational Research, 65,* 283–318.

Louis, J., Cannard, C., Bastuji, H., & Challamel, M.-J. (1997). Sleep ontogenesis revisited: A longitudinal 24-hour home polygraphic study on 15 normal infants during the first two years of life. *Sleep, 20,* 323–333.

Lozoff, B., Askew, G. L., & Wolf, A. W. (1996). Cosleeping and early childhood sleep problems: Effects of ethnicity and socioeconomic status. *Developmental and Behavioral Pediatrics, 17,* 9–15.

Lozoff, B., Klein, N. K., Nelson, E. C., McClish, D. K., Manuel, M., & Chacon, M. E. (1998). Behavior of infants with iron-deficiency anemia. *Child Development, 69,* 24–36.

Lozoff, B., Wolf, A., Latz, S., & Paludetto, R. (1995, March). *Cosleeping in Japan, Italy, and the U.S.: Autonomy versus interpersonal relatedness.* Paper presented at the biennial meeting of the Society for Research in Child Development, Indianapolis.

Lubart, T. I. (1994). Creativity. In R. J. Sternberg (Ed.), *Thinking and problem solving* (pp. 289–332). San Diego: Academic Press.

Lubinski, D., & Benbow, C. P. (1994). The study of mathematically precocious youth: The first three decades of a planned 50-year study of intellectual talent. In R. F. Subotnik & K. D. Arnold (Eds.), *Beyond Terman: Contemporary longitudinal studies of giftedness and talent* (pp. 255–281). Norwood, NJ: Ablex.

Lucariello, J., Kyratzis, A., & Nelson, K. (1992). Taxonomic knowledge: What kind and when? *Child Development, 63,* 978–998.

Lucariello, J., & Mindolovich, C. (1995). The development of complex metarepresentations reasoning: The case of situational irony. *Cognitive Development, 10,* 551–576.

Ludemann, P. M. (1991). Generalized discrimination of positive facial expressions by seven- and ten-month-old infants. *Child Development, 62,* 55–67.

Lueptow, L. B., Garovich, L., & Lueptow, M. B. (2001). Social change and the persistnce of sex typing: 1974–1997. *Social Forces, 80,* 1–36.

Luria, A. R. (1976). *Cognitive development: Its cultural and social foundations.* Cambridge, MA: Harvard University Press.

Luster, T., & Dubow, E. (1992). Home environment and maternal intelligence as predictors of verbal intelligence: A comparison of preschool and school-age children. *Merrill-Palmer Quarterly, 38,* 151–175.

Luster, T., & McAdoo, H. (1996). Family and child influences on educational attainment: A secondary analysis of the High/Scope Perry Preschool data. *Developmental Psychology, 32,* 26–39.

Luthar, S. S., & Cushing, G. (1997). Substance use and personal adjustment among disadvantaged teenagers: A six-month prospective study. *Journal of Youth and Adolescence, 26,* 353–372.

Luthar, S. S., Cushing, T. J., & McMahon, T. J. (1997). Interdisciplinary interface: Developmental principles brought to substance abuse research. In S. S. Luthar, J. A. Burack, D. Cicchetti, & J. R. Weisz, *Developmental psychopathology* (pp. 437–456). Cambridge: Cambridge University Press.

Lutz, D. J., & Sternberg, R. J. (1999). Cognitive development. In M. H. Bornstein & M. E. Lamb (Eds.), *Developmental psychology: An advanced textbook* (4th ed., pp. 275–311). Mahwah, NJ: Erlbaum.

Lutz, S. E., & Ruble, D. N. (1995). Children and gender prejudice: Context, motivation, and the development of gender conception. In R. Vasta (Ed.), *Annals of child development* (Vol. 10, pp. 131–166). London: Jessica Kingsley.

Lynch, M., & Cicchetti, D. (1998). An ecological-transactional analysis of children and contexts: The longitudinal interplay among child maltreatment, community violence, and children's symptomatology. *Development and Psychopathology, 10,* 235–257.

Lyon, T. D., & Flavell, J. H. (1994). Young children's understanding of "remember" and "forget." *Child Development, 65,* 1357–1371.

Lyons-Ruth, K. (1996). Attachment relationships among children with aggressive behavior problems: The role of disorganized early attachment patterns. *Journal of Consulting and Clinical Psychology, 64,* 64–73.

Lyons-Ruth, K., Bronfman, E., & Parsons, E. (1999). Maternal frightened, frightening, or atypical behavior and disorganized infant attachment patterns. *Monographs of the Society for Research in Child Development, 64*(3, Serial No. 258), 67–96.

Lyons-Ruth, K., Easterbrooks, A., & Cibelli, C. (1997). Infant attachment strategies, infant mental lag, and maternal depressive symptoms: Predictors of internalizing and externalizing problems at age 7. *Developmental Psychology, 33,* 681–692.

Lytle, L. A., Seifert, S., Greenstein, J., & McGovern, P. (2000). How do children's eating patterns and food choices change over time? Results from a cohort study. *American Journal of Health Promotion, 14,* 222–228.

Lytton, H., & Romney, D. M. (1991). Parents' sex-related differential socialization of boys and girls: A meta-analysis. *Psychological Bulletin, 109,* 267–296.

Maccoby, E. E. (1984). Socialization and developmental change. *Child Development, 55,* 317–328.

Maccoby, E. E. (1998). *The two sexes: Growing up apart, coming together.* Cambridge, MA: Belknap/Harvard University Press.

Maccoby, E. E. (2000a). Parenting and its effects on children: On reading and misreading behavior genetics. *Annual Review of Psychology, 51,* 1–27.

Maccoby, E. E. (2000b). Perspectives on gender development. *International Journal of Behavioral Development, 24,* 398–406.

Maccoby, E. E. (2000c). Gender and group process: A developmental perspective. *Current Dorections in Psychological Science, 11,* 54–58.

Maccoby, E. E., & Jacklin, C. N. (1987). Gender segregation in childhood. In E. H. Reese (Ed.), *Advances in child development and behavior* (Vol. 20, pp. 239–287). New York: Academic Press.

Maccoby, E. E., & Martin, J. A. (1983). Socialization in the context of the family. In E. M. Hetherington (Ed.), *Handbook of Child Psychology: Vol. 4. Socialization, personality, and social development* (pp. 1–101). New York: Wiley.

MacDorman, M. F., & Atkinson, J. O. (1999). Infant mortality statistics from the 1997 period linked birth/infant death data set. *National Vital Statistics Report, 47*(23), 1–23.

Macfarlane, J. (1971). From infancy to adulthood. In M. C. Jones, N. Bayley, J. W. Macfarlane, & M. P. Honzik (Eds.), *The course of human development* (pp. 406–410). Waltham, MA: Xerox College Publishing.

Mackey, K., Arnold, M. K., & Pratt, M. W. (2001). Adolescents' stories of decision making in more and less authoritative families: Representing the voices of parents in narrative. *Journal of Adolescent Research, 16,* 243–268.

MacKinnon, C. E. (1989). An observational investigation of sibling interactions in married and divorced families. *Developmental Psychology, 25,* 36–44.

MacKinnon-Lewis, C., Starnes, R., Volling, B., & Johnson, S. (1997). Perceptions of parenting as predictors of boys' sibling and peer relations. *Developmental Psychology, 33,* 1024–1031.

MacMillan, H. (2000). Child maltreatment: What we know in the year 2000. *Canadian Journal of Psychiatry, 45,* 702–711.

MacMillan, H., Walsh, C., Jamieson, E., Crawford, A., & Boyle, M. (2002). Children's health. *First Nations and Inuit Regional Health Surveys.* First Nations and Inuit Regional Health Survey National Steering Committee.

MacMillan, H. L., Boyle, M. H., Wong, M. Y.-Y., Duku, E. K., Fleming, J. E., & Walsh, C. A. (1999). Slapping and spanking in childhood and its association with lifetime prevalence of psychiatric disorders in a general population sample. *Canadian Medical Association Journal, 16,* 805–812.

MacWhinney, B. (Ed.). (1999). *The emergence of language.* Mahwah, NJ: Erlbaum.

Madden, D., Bruekman, J., & Littlejohn, K. V. (1997). *A contrast of amount and type of activity in elementary school years between academically successful and unsuccessful youth.* Champaign, IL: Educational Resources Information Center. (ERIC Document Reproduction Service No. ED 411 067)

Madon, S., Jussim, L., & Eccles, J. (1997). In search of the powerful self-fulfilling prophecy. *Journal of Personality and Social Psychology, 72,* 791–809.

Maggs, J. L., Schulenberg, J., & Hurrelmann, K. (1997). Developmental transitions during adolescence: Health promotion implications. In J. Schulenberg, J. L. Maggs, & K. Hurrelmann (Eds.), *Health risks and developmental transitions during adolescence* (pp. 522–546). New York: Cambridge University Press.

Magnusson, D., & Stattin, H. (1998). Person-context interaction theories. In R. M. Lerner (Ed.), *Handbook of child psychology: Vol. 1. Theoretical models of human development* (5th ed., pp. 685–759). New York: Wiley.

Mahoney, J. L., & Cairns, R. B. (1997). Do extracurricular activities protect against early school dropout? *Developmental Psychology, 33,* 241–253.

Main, M. (1995). Recent studies in attachment: Overview with selected implications for clinical work. In S. Goldberg & R. Muir (Eds.), *Attachment theory: Social, developmental, and clinical perspectives* (pp. 407–474). Hillsdale, NJ: Erlbaum.

Main, M. (2000). The organized categories of infant, child, and adult attachment: Flexible vs. inflexible attention under attachment-related stress. *Journal of the American Psychoanalytic Association, 48,* 1055–1096.

Main, M., & Goldwyn, R. (1994). *Interview-based adult attachment classifications: Related to infant–mother and infant–father attachment.* Unpublished manuscript, University of California, Berkeley.

Main, M., & Solomon, J. (1990). Procedures for identifying infants as disorganized/disoriented during the Ainsworth Strange Situation. In M. Greenberg, D. Cicchetti, & M. Cummings (Eds.), *Attachment in the preschool years: Theory, research, and intervention* (pp. 121–160). Chicago: University of Chicago Press.

Makin, J. W., Fried, P. A., & Watkinson, B. (1991). A comparison of active and passive smoking during pregnancy: Long-term effects. *Neurotoxicology and Teratology, 13,* 5–12.

Malatesta, C. Z., Grigoryev, P., Lamb, C., Albin, M., & Culver, C. (1986). Emotion socialization and expressive development in preterm and full-term infants. *Child Development, 57,* 316–330.

Malina, R. M. (1975). *Growth and development: The first twenty years in man.* Minneapolis: Burgess Publishing.

Malina, R. M., & Bouchard, C. (1991). *Growth, maturation, and physical activity.* Champaign, IL: Human Kinetics.

Malloy, M. H., & Hoffman, H. J. (1995). Prematurity, sudden infant death syndrome, and age of death. *Pediatrics, 96,* 464–471.

Maloni, J. A., Cheng, C. Y., Liebl, C. P., & Maier, J. S. (1996). Transforming prenatal care: Reflections on the past and present with implications for the future. *Journal of Obstetrics, Gynecology, and Neonatal Nursing, 25,* 17–23.

Mandler, J. M. (1984). *Stories, scripts, and scenes: Aspects of schema theory.* Hillsdale, NJ: Erlbaum.

Mandler, J. M. (1998). Representation. In D. Kuhn & R. S. Siegler (Eds.), *Handbook of child psychology: Vol. 2. Cognition, perception, and language* (5th ed., pp. 255–308). New York: Wiley.

Mandler, J. M. (2000). What global-before-basic trend? Comment on perceptually based approaches to early categorization. *Infancy, 1,* 99–110.

Mandler, J. M., & McDonough, L. (1993). Concept formation in infancy. *Cognitive Development, 8,* 291–318.

Mandler, J. M., & McDonough, L. (1996). Drinking and driving don't mix: Inductive generalization in infancy. *Cognition, 59,* 307–335.

Mandler, J. M., & McDonough, L. (1998). On developing a knowledge base in infancy. *Developmental Psychology, 34,* 1274–1288.

Mandler, J. M., & Robinson, C. A. (1978). Developmental changes in picture recognition. *Journal of Experimental Child Psychology, 26,* 122–136.

Mange, E. J., & Mange, A. P. (1998). *Basic human genetics* (2nd ed.). Sunderland, MA: Sinauer Associates.

Manion, V., & Alexander, J. M. (1997). The benefits of peer collaboration on strategy use, metacognitive causal attribution, and recall. *Journal of Experimental Child Psychology, 67,* 268–289.

Mant, C. M., & Perner, J. (1988). The child's understanding of commitment. *Developmental Psychology, 24,* 343–351.

Maqsud, M. (1977). The influence of social heterogeneity and sentimental credibility on moral judgments of Nigerian Muslim adolescents. *Journal of Cross-Cultural Psychology, 8,* 113–122.

Maratsos, M. (1998). The acquisition of grammar. In D. Kuhn & R. S. Siegler (Eds.), *Handbook of child psychology: Vol. 2. Cognition, perception and language* (5th ed., pp. 421–466). New York: Wiley.

Maratsos, M. P., & Chalkley, M. A. (1980). The internal language of children's syntax: The ontogenesis and representation of syntactic categories. In K. Nelson (Ed.), *Children's language* (Vol. 2, pp. 127–214). New York: Gardner Press.

March of Dimes. (2001). *International comparisons of infant mortality rates.* White Plains, NY: March of Dimes Birth Defects Foundation.

Marcia, J. E. (1966). Development and validation of ego-identity status. *Journal of Personality and Social Psychology, 3,* 551–558.

Marcia, J. E. (1980). Identity in adolescence. In J. Adelson (Ed.), *Handbook of adolescent psychology* (pp. 159–187). New York: Wiley.

Marcia, J. E., Waterman, A. S., Matteson, D. R., Archer, S. L., & Orlofsky, J. L. (1993). *Ego identity: A handbook for psychosocial research.* New York: Springer-Verlag.

Marcon, R. A. (1999). Positive relationships between parent–school involvement and public school inner-city preschoolers' development and academic performance. *School Psychology Review, 28,* 395–412.

Marcus, G. F. (1993). Negative evidence in language acquisition. *Cognition, 46,* 53–85.

Marcus, G. F. (1995). Children's overregularization of English plurals: A quantitative analysis. *Journal of Child Language, 22,* 447–459.

Marcus, G. F., Pinker, S., Ullman, M., Hollander, M., Rosen, T. J., & Xu, F. (1992). Overregularization in language acquisition. *Monographs of the Society for Research in Child Development, 57*(4, Serial No. 228).

Marcus, G. F., Vijayan, S., Rao, S. B., & Vishton, P. M. (1999). Rule learning by seven-month-old infants. *Science, 283,* 77–80.

Marcus, J., Mundy, P., Morales, M., Delgado, C. E. F., & Yale, M. (2000). Individual differences in infant skills as predictors of child-caregiver joint attention and language. *Social Development, 9,* 302–315.

Margolin, G. (1998). Effects of domestic violence on children. In P. K. Trickett & C. J. Schellenbach (Eds.), *Violence against children in the family and community* (pp. 57–102). Washington, DC: American Psychological Association.

Margolin, G., & Gordis, E. B. (2000). The effects of family and community violence on children. *Annual Review of Psychology, 51,* 445–479.

Markman, E. M. (1989). *Categorization and naming in children.* Cambridge, MA: MIT Press.

Markman, E. M. (1992). Constraints on word learning: Speculations about their nature, origins, and domain specificity. In M. R. Gunnar & M. P. Maratsos (Eds.), *Minnesota Symposia on Child Psychology* (Vol. 25, pp. 59–101). Hillsdale, NJ: Erlbaum.

Markovits, H., Benenson, J., & Dolensky, E. (2001). Evidence that children and adolescents have internal models of peer interactions that are gender differentiated. *Child Development, 72,* 879–886.

Markovits, H., & Bouffard-Bouchard, T. (1992). The belief-bias effect in reasoning: The development and activation of competence. *British Journal of Developmental Psychology, 10,* 269–284.

Markovits, H., Dumas, C., & Malfait, N. (1995). Understanding transitivity of a spatial relationship: A developmental analysis. *Journal of Experimental Child Psychology, 59,* 124–141.

Markovits, H., Fleury, M. L., Quinn, S., & Venet, M. (1998). The development of conditional reasoning and the structure of semantic memory. *Child Development, 69,* 742–755.

Markovits, H., Schleifer, M., & Fortier, L. (1989). Development of elementary deductive reasoning in young children. *Developmental Psychology, 25,* 787-793.

Markovits, H., & Vachon, R. (1989). Reasoning with contrary-to-fact propositions. *Journal of Experimental Child Psychology, 47,* 398–412.

Markovits, H., & Vachon, R. (1990). Conditional reasoning, representation, and level of abstraction. *Developmental Psychology, 26,* 942–951.

Marks, N. F., & Lambert, J. D. (1998). Marital status continuity and change among young and midlife adults. *Journal of Family Issues, 19,* 652–686.

Markstrom-Adams, C., & Adams, G. R. (1995). Gender, ethnic group, and grade differences in psychosocial functioning during middle adolescence? *Journal of Youth and Adolescence, 24,* 397–417.

Markus, H. R., & Kitayama, S. (1991). Culture and the self: Implications for cognition, emotion, and motivation. *Psychological Review, 98,* 224–253.

Markus, H. R., Mullally, P. R., & Kitayama, S. (1997). Selfways: Diversity in modes of cultural participation. In U. Neisser & D. Jopling (Eds.), *The conceptual self in context* (pp. 13–61). New York: Cambridge University Press.

Marlier, L., & Schaal, B. (1997). La perception de la familiarité olfactive chez le nouveau-né: Influence différentielle du mode d'alimentation? [The perception of olfactory familiarity in the neonate: Differential influence of the mode of feeding?] *Enfance, 1,* 47–61.

Marlier, L., Schaal, B., & Soussignan, R. (1998). Neonatal responsiveness to the odor of amniotic and lacteal fluids: A test of perinatal chemosensory continuity. *Child Development, 69,* 611–623.

Marsh, D. T., Serafica, F. C., & Barenboim, C. (1981). Interrelationships among perspective taking, interpersonal problem solving, and interpersonal functioning. *Journal of Genetic Psychology, 138,* 37–48.

Marsh, H. W. (1990). The structure of academic self-concept: The Marsh/Shavelson model. *Journal of Educational Psychology, 82,* 623–636.

Marsh, H. W., Craven, R., & Debus, R. (1998). Structure, stability, and development of young children's self-concepts: A multicohort-multioccasion study. *Child Development, 69,* 1030–1053.

Marsh, H. W., Smith, I. D., & Barnes, J. (1985). Multidimensional self-concepts: Relations with sex and academic achievement. *Journal of Educational Psychology, 77,* 581–596.

Marshall-Baker, A., Lickliter, R. & Cooper, R. P. (1998). Prolonged exposure to a visual pattern may promote behavioral organization in preterm infants. *Journal of Perinatal and Neonatal Nursing, 12*, 50–62.

Martin, C. L. (1989). Children's use of gender-related information in making social judgments. *Developmental Psychology, 25*, 80–88.

Martin, C. L. (1993). New directions of investigating children's gender knowledge. *Developmental Review, 13*, 184–204.

Martin, C. L. (1995). Stereotypes about children with traditional and nontraditional gender roles. *Sex Roles, 33*, 727–751.

Martin, C. L., Eisenbud, L., & Rose, H. (1995). Children's gender-based reasoning about toys. *Child Development, 66*, 1453–1471.

Martin, C. L., Fabes, R. A., Evans, S. M., & Wyman, H. (1999). Social cognition on the playground: Children's beliefs about playing with girls versus boys and their relations to sex segregated play. *Journal of Social and Personal Relationships, 16*, 751–771.

Martin, C. L., & Halverson, C. F., Jr. (1981). A schematic processing model of sex typing and stereotyping in children. *Child Development, 52*, 1119–1134.

Martin, J. C., & Halverson, C. F., Jr. (1983). The effects of sex-typing schemas on young children's memory. *Child Development, 54*, 563–574.

Martin, C. L., & Halverson, C. F., Jr. (1987). The role of cognition in sex role acquisition. In D. B. Carter (Ed.), *Current conceptions of sex roles and sex typing: Theory and research* (pp. 123–137). New York: Praeger.

Martin, J. A. (1981). A longitudinal study of the consequences of early mother-infant interaction: A microanalytic approach. *Monographs of the Society for Research in Child Development, 46*(3, Serial No. 190).

Martin, J. C., Barr, H. M., Martin, D. C., & Streissguth, A. P. (1996). Neonatal exposure to cocaine. *Neurotoxicology and Teratology, 18*, 617–625.

Martin, R. P., Olejnik, S., & Gaddis, L. (1994). Is temperament an important contributor to schooling outcomes in elementary school? Modeling effects of temperament and scholastic ability on academic achievement. In W. B. Carey & S. C. McDevitt (Eds.), *Prevention and early intervention* (pp. 59–68). New York: Brunner/Mazel.

Martin, R. P., Olejnik, S., & Gaddis, L. (1994). Is temperament an important contributor to schooling outcomes in elementary school? Modeling effects of temperament and scholastic ability on academic achievement. In W. B. Carey & S. C. McDevitt (Eds.), *Prevention and early intervention* (pp. 59–68). New York: Brunner/Mazel.

Martins, C., & Gaffan, E. A. (2000). Effects of maternal depression on patterns of infant–mother attachment: A meta-analytic investigation. *Journal of Child Psychology and Psychiatry, 41*, 737–746.

Martlew, M., & Connolly, K. J. (1996). Human figure drawings by schooled and unschooled children in Papua New Guinea. *Child Development, 67*, 2743–2762.

Martorell, R. (1980). Interrelationships between diet, infectious disease, and nutritional status. In L. S. Greene & F. E. Johnston (Eds.), *Social and biological predictors of nutritional status, physical growth, and neurological development* (pp. 81–106). New York: Academic Press.

Marzolf, D. P., & DeLoache, J. S. (1994). Transfer in young children's understanding of spatial representations. *Child Development, 65*, 1–15.

Masataka, N. (1996). Perception of motherese in a signed language by 6-month-old deaf infants. *Developmental Psychology, 32*, 874–879.

Mason, C. A., Cauce, A. M., Gonzales, N., & Hiraga, Y. (1996). Neither too sweet nor too sour: Problem peers, maternal control, and problem behavior in African American adolescents. *Child Development, 67*, 2115–2130.

Mason, M. G., & Gibbs, J. C. (1993a). Role-taking opportunities and the transition to advanced moral judgment. *Moral Education Forum, 18*, 1–12.

Mason, M. G., & Gibbs, J. C. (1993b). Social perspective taking and moral judgment among college students. *Journal of Adolescent Research, 8*, 109–123.

Masten, A. S. (2001). Ordinary magic: Resilience processes in development. *American Psychologist, 56*, 227–238.

Masten, A. S., & Coatsworth, J. D. (1998). The development of competence in favorable and unfavorable environments: Lessons from research on successful children. *American Psychologist, 53*, 205–220.

Masten, A. S., Coatsworth, J. D., Neemann, J., Gest, S. D., Tellegen, A., & Garmezy, N. (1995). The structure and coherence of competence from childhood through adolescence. *Child Development, 66*, 1635–1659.

Masten, A. S., Hubbard, J. J., Gest, S. D., Tellegen, A., Garmezy, N., & Ramirez, M. (1999). Adaptation in the context of adversity: Pathways to resilience and maladaptation from childhood to late adolescence. *Development and Psychopathology, 11*, 143–169.

Mastropieri, D., & Turkewitz, G. (1999). Prenatal experience and neonatal responsiveness to vocal expressions of emotion. *Developmental Psychobiology, 35*, 204–214.

Masur, E. F. (1995). Infants' early verbal imitation and their later lexical development. *Merrill-Palmer Quarterly, 41*, 286–306.

Masur, E. F., & Rodemaker, J. E. (1999). Mothers' and infants' spontaneous vocal, verbal, and action imitation during the second year. *Merrill-Palmer Quarterly, 45*, 392–412.

Masur, E. F., McIntyre, C. W., & Flavell, J. H. (1973). Developmental changes in apportionment of study time among items in a multi-trial free recall task. *Journal of Experimental Child Psychology, 15*, 237–246.

Matas, L., Arend, R., & Sroufe, L. A. (1978). Continuity of adaptation in the second year: The relationship between quality of attachment and later competence. *Child Development, 49*, 547–556.

Matheny, A. P., Jr. (1989). Temperament and cognition: Relations between temperament and mental test scores. In G. A. Kohnstamm, J. E. Bates, & M. K. Rothbart (Eds.), *Temperament in childhood* (pp. 263–282). New York: Wiley.

Mathews, F., Yudkin, P., & Neil, A. (1999). Influence of maternal nutrition on outcome of pregnancy: Prospective cohort study. *British Medical Journal, 319*, 339–343.

Matsuba, M. K., & Walker, L. J. (1998). Moral reasoning in the context of ego functioning. *Merrill-Palmer Quarterly, 44*, 464–483.

Matsumoto, D. (1990). Cultural similarities and differences in display rules. *Motivation and Emotion, 14*, 195–214.

Mattson, S. N., Riley, E. P., Delis, D. C., & Jones, K. L. (1998). Neuropsychological comparison of alcohol-exposed children with or without physical features of fetal alcohol syndrome. *Neuropsychology, 12*, 146–153.

Mattys, S. L., & Jusczyk, P. W. (2001). Phonotactic cues for segmentation of fluent speech by infants. *Cognition, 78*, 91–121.

Matute-Bianchi, M. E. (1986). Ethnic identities and patterns of school success and failure among Mexican-descent and Japanese-American students in a California high school: An ethnographic analysis. *American Journal of Education, 95*, 233–255.

Mayberry, R. I. (1994). The importance of childhood to language acquisition: Evidence from American Sign Language. In J. C. Goodman & H. C. Nusbaum (Eds.), *The development of speech perception: The transition from speech sounds to spoken words* (pp. 57–90). Cambridge, MA: MIT Press.

Mayberry, R., Lock, E., & Kazmi, H. (2002). Development: Linguistic ability and early language exposure. *Nature, 417*, 38.

Mayer, J. D., Caruso, D., & Salovey, P. (1999). Emotional intelligence meets traditional standards for an intelligence. *Intelligence, 27*, 267–298.

Mayer, J. D., Salovey, P., & Caruso, D. R. (2000). Selecting a measure of emotional intelligence: The case for ability scales. In R. Bar-On & J. D. A. Parker (Eds.), *Handbook of emotional intelligence* (pp. 320–342). San Francisco: Jossey-Bass.

Mayes, L. C. (1999). Reconsidering the concept of vulnerability in children using the model of prenatal cocaine exposure. In T. B. Cohen & E. M. Hossein (Eds.), *The vulnerable child* (Vol. 3, pp. 35–54). Madison, CT: International Universities Press.

Mayes, L. C., & Bornstein, M. H. (1997). Attention regulation in infants born at risk: Prematurity and prenatal cocaine exposure. In J. A. Burack & J. T. Enns (Eds.), *Attention, development, and psychopathology* (pp. 97–122). New York: Guilford.

Mayes, L. C., & Zigler, E. (1992). An observational study of the affective concomitants of mastery in infants. *Journal of Child Psychology and Psychiatry, 33*, 659–667.

Mayes, L. C., Bornstein, M. H., Chawarska, K., & Haynes, O. M. (1996). Impaired regulation of arousal in 3-month-old infants exposed prenatally to cocaine and other drugs. *Development and Psychopathology, 8*, 29–42.

Mazur, E. (1993). Developmental differences in children's understanding of marriage, divorce, and remarriage. *Journal of Applied Developmental Psychology, 14*, 191–212.

Mazzocco, M. M. (2000). Advances in research on the fragile X syndrome. *Mental Retardation and Developmental Disabilities Research Review, 6*, 96–106.

McCabe, A. (1997). Developmental and cross-cultural aspects of children's narration. In M. Bamberg (Ed.), *Narrative development: Six approaches* (pp. 137–174). Mahwah, NJ: Erlbaum.

McCabe, A. E. (1998). *Chameleon readers: Teaching children to appreciate all kinds of good stories.* New York: McGraw-Hill.

McCabe, A. E., & Peterson, C. (1988). A comparison of adults' versus children's spontaneous use of *because* and *so. Journal of Genetic Psychology, 149*, 257–268.

McCall, R. B. (1977). Childhood IQs as predictors of adult educational and occupational status. *Science, 197*, 482–483.

McCall, R. B. (1993). Developmental functions for general mental performance. In D. K. Detterman (Ed.), *Current topics in human intelligence* (Vol. 3, pp. 3–29). Norwood, NJ: Ablex.

McCall, R. B., Appelbaum, M. I., & Hogarty, P. S. (1973). Developmental changes in mental performance. *Monographs of the Society for Research in Child Development, 38*(3, Serial No. 150).

McCall, R. B., & Carriger, M. S. (1993). A meta-analysis of infant habituation and recognition memory performance as predictors of later IQ. *Child Development, 64,* 57–79.

McCartney, K., Harris, M. J., & Bernieri, F. (1990). Growing up and growing apart: A developmental meta-analysis of twin studies. *Psychological Bulletin, 107,* 226–237.

McCarton, C. (1998). Behavioral outcomes in low birth weight infants. *Pediatrics, 102,* 1293–1297.

McCarton, C. M., Brooks-Gunn, J., Wallace, I. F., Bauer, C. R., Bennett, F. C., Bernbaum, J. C., Broyles, R. S., Casey, P. H., McCormick, M. C., Scott, D. T., Tyson, J., Tonascia, J., & Meinert, C. L. (1997). Results at age 8 years of early intervention for low-birth-weight premature infants: The infant health and development program. *Journal of the American Medical Association, 277,* 126–132.

McCarty, M. E., & Ashmead, D. H. (1999). Visual control of reaching and grasping in infants. *Developmental Psychology, 35,* 620–631.

McClelland, J. L., & Siegler, R. S. (Eds.). (2001). *Mechanisms of cognitive development: Behavioral and neural perspectives.* Mahwah, NJ: Erlbaum.

McConaghy, M. J. (1979). Gender permanence and the genital basis of gender: Stages in the development of constancy of gender identity. *Child Development, 50,* 1223–1226.

McConaghy, N., & Silove, D. (1992). Do sex-linked behaviors in children influence relationships with their parents? *Archives of Sexual Behavior, 21,* 469–479.

McCormick, C. M., & Maurer, D. M. (1988). Unimanual hand preferences in 6-month-olds: Consistency and relation to familial-handedness. *Infant Behaviour and Development, 11,* 21–29.

McCune, L. (1993). The development of play as the development of consciousness. In M. H. Bornstein & A. O'Reilly (Eds.), *New directions for child development* (No. 59, pp. 67–79). San Francisco: Jossey-Bass.

McDonough, L. (1999). Early declarative memory for location. *British Journal of Developmental Psychology, 17,* 381–402.

McDougall, P., & Hymel, S. (1998). Moving into middle school: Individual differences in the transition experience. *Canadian Journal of Behavioural Science, 30,* 108–120.

McDowell, D. J., O'Neill, R., & Parke, R. D. (2000). Display rule application in a disappointing situation and children's emotional reactivity: Relations with social competence. *Merrill-Palmer Quarterly, 46,* 306–324.

McDowell, D. J., & Parke, R. D. (2000). Differential knowledge of display rules for positive and negative emotions: Influences from parents, influences on peers. *Social Development, 9,* 415–432.

McGee, G. (1997). Legislating gestation. *Human Reproduction, 12,* 407–408.

McGee, L. M., & Richgels, D. J. (2000). *Literacy's beginnings* (3rd ed.). Boston: Allyn and Bacon.

McGillicuddy-De Lisi, A. V., Watkins, C., & Vinchur, A. J. (1994). The effect of relationship on children's distributive justice reasoning. *Child Development, 65,* 1694–1700.

McGue, M., Bouchard, T. J., Jr., Iacono, W. G., & Lykken, D. T. (1993). Behavioral genetics of cognitive ability: A life-span perspective. In R. Plomin & G. E. McClearn (Eds.), *Nature, nurture, and psychology* (pp. 59–76). Washington, DC: American Psychological Association.

McGuffin, P., & Sargeant, M. P. (1991). Major affective disorder. In P. McGuffin & R. Murray (Eds.), *The new genetics of mental illness* (pp. 165–181). London: Butterworth-Heinemann.

McGuinness, D., & Pribram, K. H. (1980). The neuropsychology of attention: Emotional and motivational controls. In M. C. Wittcock (Ed.), *The brain and psychology* (pp. 95–139). New York: Academic Press.

McHale, S. M., Bartko, W. T., Crouter, A. C., & Perry-Jenkins, M. (1990). Children's housework and psychosocial functioning: The mediating effects of parents' sex-role behaviors and attitudes. *Child Development, 61,* 68–81.

McHale, S. M., Crouter, A. C., McGuire, S. A., & Updegraff, K. A. (1995). Congruence between mothers' and fathers' differential treatment of siblings: Links with family relations and children's well-being. *Child Development, 66,* 116–128.

McHale, S. M., Updegraff, K. A., Helms-Erikson, H., & Crouter, A. C. (2001). Sibling influences on gender development in middle childhood and early adolescence: A longitudinal study. *Developmental Psychology, 37,* 115–125.

McKenzie, D. (2002, February 11). Right to spank backed in poll. *The Toronto Star,* p. A6.

McKeown, R. E., Garrison, C. Z., Cuffe, S. P., Waller, J. L., Jackson, K. L., & Addy, C. L. (1998). Incidence and predictors of suicidal behaviors in a longitudinal sample of young adolescents. *Journal of the American Academy of Child and Adolescent Psychiatry, 37,* 612–619.

McKim, M. L., Cramer, K. M., Stuart, B., & O'Connor, D. L. (1999). Infant care decisions and attachment security: The Canadian Transition to Child Care Study. *Canadian Journal of Behavioural Science, 31,* 92–106.

McKusick, V. A. (1998). *Mendelian inheritance in man: A catalog of human genes and genetic disorders.* Baltimore: Johns Hopkins University Press.

McLean, D. F., Timajchy, K. H., Wingo, P. A., & Floyd, R. L. (1993). Psychosocial measurement: Implications of the study of preterm delivery in black women. *American Journal of Preventive Medicine, 9,* 39–81.

McLean, M., Bisits, A., Davies, J., Woods, R., Lowry, P., & Smith, R. (1995). A placental clock controlling the length of human pregnancy. *Nature Medicine, 1,* 460–463.

McLoyd, V. C. (1998a). Children in poverty: Development, public policy, and practice. In I. Sigel & A. Renninger (Eds.), *Handbook of child psychology: Vol. 4. Child psychology in practice* (5th ed., pp. 135–208). New York: Wiley.

McLoyd, V. C. (1998b). Socioeconomic disadvantage and child development. *American Psychologist, 53,* 185–204.

McMahon, R. J. (1999). Parent training. In S. W. Russ & T. H. Ollendick (Eds.), *Handbook of psychotherapies with children and families* (pp. 153–180). New York: Kluwer Academic.

McManus, I. C., Sik, G., Cole, D. R., Mellon, A. F., Wong, J., & Kloss, J. (1988). The development of handedness in children. *British Journal of Developmental Psychology, 6,* 257–273.

McNamee, S., & Peterson, J. (1986). Young children's distributive justice reasoning, behavior, and role taking: Their consistency and relationship. *Journal of Genetic Psychology, 146,* 399–404.

MCR Vitamin Study Research Group. (1991). Prevention of neural tube defects: Results of the Medical Research Council Vitamin Study. *Lancet, 338,* 131–137.

Mead, G. H. (1934). *Mind, self, and society.* Chicago: University of Chicago Press.

Mead, M. (1928). *Coming of age in Samoa.* Ann Arbor, MI: Morrow.

Mead, M., & Newton, N. (1967). Cultural patterning of perinatal behavior. In S. Richardson & A. Guttmacher (Eds.), *Childbearing: Its social and psychological aspects* (pp. 142–244). Baltimore: Williams & Wilkins.

Meadow-Orlans, K. P., & Steinberg, A. G. (1993). Effects of infant hearing loss and maternal support on mother–infant interactions at 18 months. *Journal of Applied Developmental Psychology, 14,* 407–426.

Mebert, C. J. (1991). Dimensions of subjectivity in parents' ratings of infant temperament. *Child Development, 62,* 352–361.

Media Awareness Network (2000). *Advertising Standards Canada* [On-line]. Available: http://www.media-awareness.ca/eng/indus/advert/caf.htm.

Medrich, E. A., Roizen, J. A., Rubin, V., & Buckley, S. (1992). *The serious business of growing up: A study of children's lives outside school.* Berkeley: University of California Press.

Meeus, W. (1996). Studies on identity development in adolescence: An overview of research and some new data. *Journal of Youth and Adolescence, 25,* 569–598.

Meeus, W., Iedema, J., Helsen, M., & Vollebergh, W. (1999). Patterns of adolescent identity development: Review of literature and longitudinal analysis. *Developmental Review, 19,* 419–461.

Mehlmadrona, L., & Madrona, M. M. (1997). Physician- and midwife-attended home births—effects of breech, twin, and post-dates outcome data on mortality rates. *Journal of Nurse-Midwifery, 42,* 91–98.

Meisels, S. J., Dichtelmiller, M., & Liaw, F. R. (1993). A multidimensional analysis of early childhood intervention programs. In C. H. Zeanah (Ed.), *Handbook of infant mental health* (pp. 361–385). New York: Guilford.

Meltzoff, A. N. (1990). Towards a developmental cognitive science. *Annals of the New York Academy of Sciences, 608,* 1–37.

Meltzoff, A. N. (1995). Understanding the intentions of others: Re-enactment of intended acts by 18-month-old children. *Developmental Psychology, 31,* 838–850.

Meltzoff, A. N., & Kuhl, P. K. (1994). Faces and speech: Intermodal processing of biologically relevant signals in infants and adults. In D. J. Lewkowicz & R. Lickliter (Eds.), *The development of intersensory perception: Comparative perspectives* (pp. 335–369). Hillsdale, NJ: Erlbaum.

Meltzoff, A. N., & Moore, M. K. (1977). Imitation of facial and manual gestures by human neonates. *Science, 198,* 75–78.

Meltzoff, A. N., & Moore, M. K. (1992). Early imitation within a functional framework: The importance of person, identity, movement, and development. *Infant Behavior and Development, 15,* 479–505.

Meltzoff, A. N., & Moore, M. K. (1994). Imitation, memory, and the representation of persons. *Infant Behavior and Development, 17,* 83–99.

Meltzoff, A. N., & Moore, M. K. (1998). Object representation, identity, and the paradox of early permanence: Steps toward a new framework. *Infant Behavior and Development, 21,* 201–235.

Meltzoff, A. N., & Moore, M. K. (1999). Persons and representations: Why infant imitation is important for theories of human development. In J. Nadel & G. Butterworth (Eds.), *Imitation in infancy* (pp. 9–35). Cambridge: Cambridge University Press.

Mendelson, B. K., White, D. R., & Mendelson, M. J. (1996). Self-esteem and body esteem: Effects of gender, age, and weight. *Journal of Applied Developmental Psychology, 17,* 321–346.

Menn, L., & Stoel-Gammon, C. (2001). Phonological development: Learning sounds and sound patterns. In J. Berko Gleason (Ed.), *The development of language* (4th ed., pp. 70–124). Boston: Allyn and Bacon.

Mennella, J. A., & Beauchamp, G. K. (1998). Early flavor experiences: Research update. *Nutrition Reviews, 56,* 205–211.

Menyuk, P., Liebergott, J. W., & Schultz, M. C. (1995). *Early language development in full-term and premature infants.* Hillsdale, NJ: Erlbaum.

Meredith, N. V. (1978). *Human body growth in the first ten years of life.* Columbia, SC: State Printing.

Merriman, W. E. (1999). Competition, attention, and young children's lexical processing. In B. MacWhinney (Ed.), *The emergence of language* (pp. 331–358). Mahwah, NJ: Erlbaum.

Mervis, C. B., & Robinson, B. F. (2000). Expressive vocabulary ability of toddlers with Williams syndrome or Down syndrome: A comparison. *Developmental Neuropsychology, 17,* 111–126.

Mervis, C. B., Golinkoff, R. M., & Bertrand, J. (1994). Two-year-olds readily learn multiple labels for the same basic-level category. *Child Development, 65,* 1163–1177.

Mervis, C. B., Morris, C. A., Bertrand, J., & Robinson, B. F. (1999). Williams syndrome: Findings from an integrated program of research. In H. Tager-Flusberg (Ed.), *Neurodevelopmental disorders: Developmental cognitive neuroscience* (pp. 65–110). Cambridge, MA: MIT Press.

Metcalfe, J., & Mischel, W. (1999). A hot/cool system analysis of delay of gratification: Dynamics of willpower. *Psychological Review, 106,* 3–19.

Meyer-Bahlburg, H. F. L., Ehrhardt, A. A., Rosen, L. R., Gruen, R. S., Veridiano, N. P., Vann, F. H., & Neuwalder, H. F. (1995). Prenatal estrogens and the development of homosexual orientation. *Developmental Psychology, 31,* 12–21.

Meyers, C., Adam, R., Dungan, J., & Prenger, V. (1997). Aneuploidy in twin gestations: When is maternal age advanced? *Obstetrics and Gynecology, 89,* 248–251.

Miceli, P. J., Whitman, T. L., Borkowski, J. G., Braungart-Riekder, J., & Mitchell, D. W. (1998). Individual differences in infant information processing: The role of temperamental and maternal factors. *Infant Behavior and Development, 21,* 119–136.

Michael, R. T., Gagnon, J. H., Laumann, E. O., & Kolata, G. (1994). *Sex in America.* Boston: Little, Brown.

Micheli, R. (1985, June). Water babies. *Parents, 60*(6), 8–13.

Milberger, S., Biederman, J., Faraone, S. V., Guite, J., & Tsuang, M. T. (1997). Pregnancy, delivery and infancy complications and attention deficit hyperactivity disorder: Issues of gene–environment interaction. *Biological Psychiatry, 41,* 65–75.

Miles, C. (1935). Sex in social psychology. In C. Murchison (Ed.), *Handbook of social psychology* (pp. 699–704). Worcester, MA: Clark University Press.

Miles, H. L. (1999). Symbolic communication with and by great apes. In S. T. Parker, R. W. Mitchell, & H. L. Miles (Eds.), *The mentalities of gorillas and orangutans* (pp. 197–210). Cambridge: Cambridge University Press.

Milgram, N. A., & Palti, G. (1993). Psychosocial characteristics of resilient children. *Journal of Research in Personality, 27,* 207–221.

Miller, J. G. (1994). Cultural diversity in the morality of caring: Individually oriented versus duty-based interpersonal moral codes. *Cross-cultural Research: The Journal of Comparative Social Science, 28,* 3–39.

Miller, J. G. (1997). Culture and self: Uncovering the cultural grounding of psychological theory. In J. G. Snodgrass & R. L. Thompson (Eds.), *Annals of the New York Academy of Sciences* (Vol. 18, pp. 217–231). New York: New York Academy of Sciences.

Miller, J. G., & Bersoff, D. M. (1995). Development in the context of everyday family relationships: Culture, interpersonal morality, and adapation. In M. Killen & D. Hart (Eds.), *Morality in everyday life: Developmental perspectives* (pp. 259–282). Cambridge: Cambridge University Press.

Miller, J. G., & Luthar, S. (1989). Issues of interpersonal responsibility and accountability: A comparison of Indians' and Americans' moral judgments. *Social Cognition, 7,* 237–261.

Miller, K. F., & Baillargeon, R. (1990). Length and distance: Do preschoolers think that occlusion brings things together? *Developmental Psychology, 26,* 103–114.

Miller, L. T., & Vernon, P. A. (1992). The general factor in short-term memory, intelligence, and reaction time. *Intelligence, 16,* 5–29.

Miller, L. T., & Vernon, P. A. (1997). Developmental changes in speed of information processing in young children. *Developmental Psychology, 33,* 549–554.

Miller, P. A., Eisenberg, N., Fabes, R. A., & Shell, R. (1996). Relations of moral reasoning and vicarious emotion to young children's prosocial behavior toward peers and adults. *Developmental Psychology, 32,* 210–219.

Miller, P. H. (1993). *Theories of developmental psychology* (3rd ed.). New York: Freeman.

Miller, P. H. (2000). How best to utilize a deficiency. *Child Development, 71,* 1013–1017.

Miller, P. H., & Bigi, L. (1979). The development of children's understanding of attention. *Merrill-Palmer Quarterly, 25,* 235–250.

Miller, P. H., Haynes, V. F., DeMarie-Dreblow, D., & Woody-Ramsey, J. (1986). Children's strategies for gathering information in three tasks. *Child Development, 57,* 1429–1439.

Miller, P. H., Kessel, F. S., & Flavell, J. H. (1970). Thinking about people thinking about people thinking about … : A study of social cognitive development. *Child Development, 41,* 613–623.

Miller, P. H., Seier, W. L., Probert, J. S., & Aloise, P. A. (1991). Age differences in the capacity demands of a strategy among spontaneously strategic children. *Journal of Experimental Child Psychology, 52,* 149–165.

Miller, P. H., Woody-Ramsey, J., & Aloise, P. A. (1991). The role of strategy effortfulness in strategy effectiveness. *Developmental Psychology, 27,* 738–745.

Miller, P. J., Fung, H., & Mintz, J. (1996). Self-construction through narrative practices: A Chinese and American comparison of early socialization. *Ethos, 24,* 1–44.

Miller, P. J., Wiley, A. R., Fung, H., & Liang, C.-H. (1997). Personal storytelling as a medium of socialization in Chinese and American families. *Child Development, 68,* 557–568.

Miller, R. B. (2000). Do children make a marriage unhappy? *Family Science Review, 13,* 60–73.

Miller, S. A. (1998). *Developmental research methods* (2nd ed.). Englewood Cliffs, NJ: Prentice-Hall.

Miller, S. A. (2000). Children's understanding of preexisting differences in knowledge and belief. *Developmental Review, 20,* 227–282.

Miller, S. A., & Davis, T. L. (1992). Beliefs about children: A comparative study of mothers, teachers, peers, and self. *Child Development, 63,* 1251–1265.

Miller-Jones, D. (1989). Culture and testing. *American Psychologist, 44,* 360–366.

Mills, D. L., Coffey-Corina, S., & Neville, H. J. (1997). Language comprehension and cerebral specialization from 13 to 20 months. *Developmental Neuropsychology, 13,* 397–445.

Mills, R., & Grusec, J. E. (1989). Cognitive, affective, and behavioral consequences of praising altruism. *Merrill-Palmer Quarterly, 35,* 299–326.

Milner, J. S. (1993). Social information processing and physical child abuse. *Clinical Psychology Review, 13,* 275–294.

Minde, K. (2000). Prematurity and serious medical conditions in infancy: Implications for development, behavior, and intervention. In C. H. Zeanah, Jr. (Ed.), *Handbook of infant mental health* (pp. 176–194). New York: Guilford.

Minister of Public Works and Government Services Canada (2002). *National Report—Canada: Ten year review of the world summit for children* [On-line]. Available: www.hc-sc.gc.ca/hppb/childhood-youth/spsc/pdf/national_report.pdf

Mischel, H. N., & Liebert, R. M. (1966). Effects of discrepancies between observed and imposed reward criteria on their acquisition and transmission. *Journal of Personality and Social Psychology, 3,* 45–53.

Mischel, H. N., & Mischel, W. (1983). The development of children's knowledge of self-control strategies. *Child Development, 54,* 603–619.

Mischel, W. (1996). From good intentions to willpower. In P. M. Gollwitzer & J. A. Bargh (Eds.), *The psychology of action* (pp. 197–218). New York: Guilford.

Mischel, W., & Baker, N. (1975). Cognitive appraisals and transformations in delay behavior. *Journal of Personality and Social Psychology, 31,* 254–261.

Mischel, W., Shoda, Y., & Peake, P. K. (1988). The nature of adolescent competencies predicted by preschool delay of gratification. *Journal of Personality and Social Psychology, 54,* 687–696.

Mistry, J. (1997). The development of remembering in cultural context. In N. Cowan (Ed.), *The develop-*

ment of memory in childhood (pp. 343–368). Hove, UK: Psychology Press.

Mize, J., & Ladd, G. W. (1990). A cognitive-social learning approach to social skill training with low-status preschool children. *Developmental Psychology, 26,* 388–397.

Mize, J., & Pettit, G. S. (1997). Mothers' social coaching, mother–child relationship style, and children's peer competence? Is the medium the message? *Child Development, 68,* 312–332.

Moerk, E. L. (1992). *A first language taught and learned.* Baltimore: Paul H. Brookes.

Moffat, S. D., Hampson, E., & Hatzipantelis, M. (1998). Navigation is a "virtual" maze: Sex differences and correlation with psychometric meaures of spatial ability in humans. *Evolution and Human Behavior, 19*(2), 73–87.

Moffitt, T. E., Caspi, A., Belsky, J., & Silva, P. A. (1992). Childhood experience and onset of menarche: A test of a sociobiological model. *Child Development, 63,* 47–58.

Moffitt, T. E., Caspi, A., Dickson, N., Silva, P., & Stanton, W. (1996). Childhood-onset versus adolescent-onset antisocial conduct problems in males: Natural history from ages 3 to 18 years. *Development and Psychopathology, 8,* 399–424.

Moll, I. (1994). Reclaiming the natural line in Vygotsky's theory of cognitive development. *Human Development, 37,* 333–342.

Mollica, R. F., Poole, C., Son, L., & Murray, C. C. (1997). Effects of war trauma on Cambodian refugee adolescents' functional health and mental health status. *Journal of the American Academy of Child and Adolescent Psychiatry, 36,* 1098–1106.

Mondimore, F. M. (1996). *A natural history of homosexuality.* Baltimore: Johns Hopkins University Press.

Mondloch, C. J., Lewis, T., Budreau, D. R., Maurer, D., Dannemillier, J. L., Stephens, B. R., & Kleiner-Gathercoal, K. A. (1999). Face perception during early infancy. *Psychological Science, 10,* 419–422.

Moner, S. (1994). Smoking and pregnancy. In Health Canada, *The Canadian guide to clinical preventive health care.* Cat. no. H21-117-1994E. Ottawa: Ministry of Supply and Services Canada.

Money, J. (1993). Specific neurocognitional impairments associated with Turner (45,X) and Klinefelter (47,XXY) syndromes: A review. *Social Biology, 40,* 147–151.

Money, J., & Ehrhardt, A. A. (1972). *Man and woman, boy and girl.* Baltimore: Johns Hopkins University Press.

Monk, C., Fifer, W. P., Myers, M. M., Sloan, R. P., Trien, L., & Hurtado, A. (2000). Maternal stress responses and anxiety during pregnancy: Effects on fetal heart rate. *Developmental Psychobiology, 36,* 67–77.

Montemayor, R., & Eisen, M. (1977). The development of self-conceptions from childhood to adolescence. *Developmental Psychology, 13,* 314–319.

Montgomery, D. E. (1993). Young children's understanding of interpretive diversity between different-aged listeners. *Developmental Psychology, 29,* 337–345.

Montoya, I. D. (2001). Changes in economically disadvantaged adolescents' knowledge and beliefs about HIV/AIDS. *Clinical Laboratory Science, 14,* 167–172.

Moon, C., Cooper, R. P., & Fifer, W. P. (1993). Two-day-old infants prefer their native language. *Infant Behavior and Development, 16,* 495–500.

Moon, S. M., & Feldhusen, J. F. (1994). The Program for Academic and Creative Enrichment (PACE): A follow-up study ten years later. In R. F. Subotnik & K. D. Arnold (Eds.), *Beyond Terman: Contemporary longitudinal studies of giftedness and talent* (pp. 375–400). Norwood, NJ: Ablex.

Moore, D. R., & Florsheim, P. (2001). Interpersonal processes and psychopathology among expectant and nonexpectant adolescent couples. *Journal of Consulting and Clinical Psychology, 69,* 101–113.

Moore, D. S., Spence, M. J., & Katz, G. S. (1997). Six-month-olds' categorization of natural infant-directed utterances. *Developmental Psychology, 33,* 980–989.

Moore, E. G. J. (1986). Family socialization and the IQ test performance of traditionally and transracially adopted black children. *Developmental Psychology, 22,* 317–326.

Moore, G. A., Cohn, J. E., & Campbell, S. B. (2001). Infant affective responses to mother's still face at 6 months differentially predict externalizing and internalizing behaviors at 18 months. *Developmental Psychology, 37,* 706–714.

Moore, K. A., Morrison, D. R., & Greene, A. D. (1997). Effects on the children born to adolescent mothers. In R. A. Maynard (Ed.), *Kids having kids* (pp. 145–180). Washington, DC: Urban Institute.

Moore, K. A., Myers, D. E., Morrison, D. R., Nord, C. W., Brown, B., & Edmonston, B. (1993). Age at first childbirth and later poverty. *Journal of Research on Adolescence, 3,* 393–422.

Moore, K. L., & Persaud, T. V. N. (1998). *Before we are born* (5th ed.). Philadelphia: Saunders.

Moore, M. K., & Meltzoff, A. N. (1999). New findings on object permanence: A developmental difference between two types of occlusion. *British Journal of Developmental Psychology, 17,* 563–584.

Moorehouse, M. J. (1991). Linking maternal employment patterns to mother–child activities and children's school competence. *Developmental Psychology, 27,* 295–303.

Morabia, A., Costanza, M. C., & the World Health Organization Collaborative Study of Neoplasia and Steroid Contraceptives. (1998). International variability in ages at menarche, first live birth, and menopause. *American Journal of Epidemiology, 148,* 1195–1205.

Morales, M., Mundy, P., Delgado, C. E. F., Yale, M., Messinger, D., Neal, R., & Schwartz, H. K. (2000). Responding to joint attention across the 6- through 24-month age period and early language acquisition. *Journal of Applied Developmental Psychology, 21,* 283–298.

Moran, G. F., & Vinovskis, M. A. (1986). The great care of godly parents: Early childhood in Puritan New England. In A. B. Smuts & J. W. Hagen (Eds.), History and research in child development. *Monographs of the Society for Research in Child Development, 50*(4–5, Serial No. 211), pp. 24–37.

Morelli, G., Rogoff, B., Oppenheim, D., & Goldsmith, D. (1992). Cultural variation in infants' sleeping arrangements: Questions of independence. *Developmental Psychology, 28,* 604–613.

Morford, J. P., & Goldin-Meadow, S. (1997). From here and now to there and then: The development of displaced reference in homesign and English. *Child Development, 68,* 420–435.

Morgan, J. L., & Saffran, J. R. (1995). Emerging integration of sequential and suprasegmental information in preverbal speech segmentation. *Child Development, 66,* 911–936.

Morgan, J. L., Bonama, K. M., & Travis, L. L. (1995). Negative evidence on negative evidence. *Developmental Psychology, 31,* 180–197.

Morgane, P. J., Austin-LaFrance, R., Bronzino, J., Tonkiss, J., Diaz-Cintra, S., Cintra, L., Kemper, T., & Galler, J. R. (1993). Prenatal malnutrition and development of the brain. *Neuroscience and Biobehavioral Reviews, 17,* 91–128.

Morrison, D. R., & Coiro, M. J. (1999). Parental conflict and marital disruption: Do children benefit when high-conflict marriages are dissolved? *Journal of Marriage and the Family, 61,* 626–637.

Morrison, F. E., Griffith, E. M., & Alberts, D. M. (1997). Nature–nurture in the classroom: Entrance age, school readiness, and learning in children. *Developmental Psychology, 33,* 254–262.

Morrongiello, B. A. (1986). Infants' perception of multiple-group auditory patterns. *Infant Behavior and Development, 9,* 307–319.

Morrongiello, B. A., Fenwick, K. D., & Chance, G. (1998). Crossmodal learning in newborn infants: Inferences about properties of auditory-visual events. *Infant Behavior and Development, 21,* 543–554.

Morton, J. (1993). Mechanisms in infant face processing. In B. de Boysson-Bardies, S. de Schonen, P. Jusczyk, P. McNeilage, & J. Morton (Eds.), *Developmental neurocognition: Speech and face processing in the first year of life* (pp. 93–102). London: Kluwer.

Moshman, D. (1998). Cognitive development beyond childhood. In D. Kuhn & R. S. Siegler (Eds.), *Handbook of child psychology: Vol. 2. Cognition, perception, and language* (5th ed., pp. 947–978). New York: Wiley.

Moshman, D. (1999). *Adolescent psychological development: Rationality, morality, and identity.* Mahwah, NJ: Erlbaum.

Moshman, D., & Franks, B. A. (1986). Development of the concept of inferential validity. *Child Development, 57,* 153–165.

Moss, M., Colombo, J., Mitchell, D. W., & Horowitz, F. D. (1988). Neonatal behavioral organization and visual processing at three months. *Child Development, 59,* 1211–1220.

Mosteller, F. (1995). The Tennessee Study of Class Size in the Early School Grades. *Future of Children, 5*(2), 113–127.

Motherisk. (2001). *Taking folic acid before you get pregnant* [On-line]. Available: www.motherisk.org/folic/index

Mounts, N. S., & Steinberg, L. (1995). An ecological analysis of peer influence on adolescent grade point average and drug use. *Developmental Psychology, 31,* 915–922.

Mrug, S., Hoza, B., & Gerdes, A. C. (2001). Children with attention-deficit/hyperactivity disorder: Peer relationships and peer-oriented interventions. In D. W. Nangle & C. A. Erdley (Eds.), *The role of friendship in psychological adjustment* (pp. 51–77). San Francisco: Jossey-Bass.

Muldoon, O., & Cairns, E. (1999). Children, young people, and war: Learning to cope. In E. Frydenberg (Ed.), *Learning to cope: Developing as a person in complex societies* (pp. 322–337). New York: Oxford University Press.

Mullen, M. K. (1994). Earliest recollections of childhood: A demographic analysis. *Cognition, 52,* 55–79.

Muller, F., Rebiff, M., Taillandier, A., Qury, J. F., & Mornet, E. (2000). Parental origin of the extra chromosome in prenatally diagnosed fetal trisomy. *Human Genetics, 106,* 340–344.

Mullis, I. V. S. (1998). *Mathematics and science achievement in the final year of secondary school.* Chestnut Hill, MA: Boston College.

Munakata, Y. (2000). Challenges to the violation-of-expectation paradigm: Throwing the conceptual baby out with the perceptual processing bathwater? *Infancy, 1,* 471–477.

Munro, G., & Adams, G. R. (1977). Ego identity formation in college students and working youth. *Developmental Psychology, 13,* 523–524.

Murett-Wagstaff, S., & Moore, S. G. (1989). The Hmong in America: Infant behavior and rearing practices. In J. K. Nugent, B. M. Lester, & T. B. Brazelton (Eds.), *Biology, culture, and development* (Vol. 1, pp. 319–339). Norwood, NJ: Ablex.

Murray, A. D. (1985). Aversiveness is in the mind of the beholder. In B. M. Lester & C. F. Z. Boukydis (Eds.), *Infant crying* (pp. 217–239). New York: Plenum.

Murray, A. D., Johnson, J., & Peters, J. (1990). Fine-tuning of utterance length to preverbal infants: Effects on later language development. *Journal of Child Language, 17,* 511–525.

Murray, L., & Cooper, P. J. (1997). Postpartum depression and child development. *Psychological Medicine, 27,* 253–260.

Murray, L., & Cooper, P. J. (1997). Postpartum depression and child development. *Psychological Medicine, 27,* 253–260.

Murray, L., Sinclair, D., Cooper, P., Ducournau, P., & Turner, P. (1999). The socioemotional development of 5-year-old children of postnatally depressed mothers. *Journal of Child Psychology and Psychiatry, 8,* 1259–1271.

Mussen, P., & Eisenberg-Berg, N. (1977). *Roots of caring, sharing, and helping.* San Francisco: Freeman.

Nachtigall, R. D., Pitcher, L., Tschann, J. M., Becker, G., & Quiroga, S. S. (1997). Stigma, disclosure, and family functioning among parents of children conceived through donor insemination. *Fertility and Sterility, 68,* 83–89.

Nagin, D., & Tremblay, R. E. (1999). Trajectories of boys' physical aggression, opposition, and hyperactivity on the path to physically violent and nonviolent juvenile delinquency. *Child Development, 70,* 1181–1196.

Nagy, W. E., & Scott, J. A. (2000). Vocabulary processes. In M. L. Kamil & P. B. Mosenthal (Eds.), *Handbook of reading research* (Vol. 3, pp. 269–284). Mahwah, NJ: Erlbaum.

Naigles, L. G., & Gelman, S. A. (1995). Overextensions in comprehension and production revisited: Preferential-looking in a study of dog, cat, and cow. *Journal of Child Language, 22,* 19–46.

Nakamura, K. (2001). The acquisition of polite language by Japanese children. In K. E. Nelson, A. Aksu-Koc, & C. E. Johnson (Eds.), *Children's language: Vol. 10. Developing narrative and discourse competence* (pp. 93–112). Mahwah, NJ: Erlbaum.

Nakamura, S., Wind, M., & Danello, M. A. (1999). Review of hazards associated with children in adult beds. *Archives of Pediatric and Adolescent Medicine, 153,* 1019–1023.

Namy, L. L., & Waxman, S. R. (1998). Words and gestures: Infants' interpretations of different forms of symbolic reference. *Child Development, 69,* 295–308.

Nánez, J., Sr. (1987). Perception of impending collision in 3- to 6-week-old infants. *Infant Behavior and Development, 11,* 447–463.

Nánez, J., Sr., & Yonas, A. (1994). Effects of luminance and texture motion on infant defensive reactions to optical collision. *Infant Behavior and Development, 17,* 165–174.

Nansel, T. R., Overpeck, M., Pilla, R. S., Ruan, W. J., Simons-Morton, B., & Scheidt, P. (2001). Bullying behaviors among U.S. youth: Prevalence and association with psychosocial adjustment. *Journal of the American Medical Association, 285,* 2094–2100.

Nastasi, B. K., & Clements, D. H. (1992). Social-cognitive behaviors and higher-order thinking in educational computer environments. *Learning and Instruction, 2,* 215–238.

Nastasi, B. K., & Clements, D. H. (1994). Effectance motivation, perceived scholastic competence, and higher-order thinking in two cooperative computer environments. *Journal of Educational Computing Research, 10,* 249–275.

National Association for the Education of Young Children. (1998). *Accreditation criteria and procedures of the National Academy of Early Childhood Programs* (2nd ed.). Washington, DC: Author.

National Center for Children in Poverty. (2001). *Child poverty in the United States.* New York: Author.

National Council of Welfare. (2000). Child Poverty Profile 1998. Ottawa: Ministry of Public Works and Government Services Canada.

National Federation of State High School Associations. (2001). *High school athletic participation survey.* Kansas City, MO: Author.

National Institute for Child Health and Development, Early Child Care Research Network. (1996). Characteristics of infant care: Factors contributing to positive caregiving. *Early Childhood Research Quarterly, 11,* 269–306.

National Institute for Child Health and Development, Early Child Care Research Network. (1997). The effects of infant child care on infant–mother attachment security: Results of the NICHD Study of Early Child Care. *Child Development, 68,* 860–879.

National Institute for Child Health and Development, Early Child Care Research Network. (1998). Early child care and self-control, compliance, and problem behavior at twenty-four and thirty-six months. *Child Development, 69,* 1145–1170.

National Institute for Child Health and Development, Early Child Care Research Network. (1999). Child care and mother–child interaction in the first 3 years of life. *Developmental Psychology, 35,* 1399–1413.

National Institute for Child Health and Development, Early Child Care Research Network. (2000a). Characteristics and quality of child care for toddlers and preschoolers. *Applied Developmental Science, 4,* 116–135.

National Institute for Child Health and Development, Early Child Care Research Network. (2000b). The relation of child care to cognitive and language development. *Child Development, 71,* 960–980.

National Institute for Child Health and Development, Early Child Care Research Network. (2001, April). *Early child care and children's development prior to school entry.* Symposium presented at the biennial meeting of the Society for Research in Child Development, Minneapolis, MN.

National Science Foundation. (1997). *Teens and technology* [On-line]. Available: www.nsf.gov/od/lpa/nstw/teenov.html

Navarrete, C., Martinez, I., & Salamanca, F. (1994). Paternal line of transmission in chorea of Huntington with very early onset. *Genetic Counseling, 5,* 175–178.

Needham, A. (1998). Infants' use of featural information in the segregation of stationary objects. *Infant Behavior and Development, 21,* 1–24.

Needham, A. (2001). Object recognition and object segregation in 4.5-month-old infants. *Journal of Experimental Child Psychology, 78,* 3–24.

Neisser, U., Boodoo, G., Bouchard, T. J., Jr., Boykin, A. W., Brody, N., Ceci, S. J., Halpern, D. F., Loehlin, J. C., Perloff, R., Sternberg, R. J., & Urbina, S. (1996). Intelligence: Knowns and unknowns. *American Psychologist, 51,* 77–101.

Nelson, C. A. (2000). Neural plasticity and human development: The role of early experience sculpting memory systems. *Developmental Science, 3,* 115–130.

Nelson, C. A. (2001). The development and neural bases of face recognition. *Infant and Child Development, 10,* 3–18.

Nelson, C. A., & Bosquet, M. (2000). Neurobiology of fetal and infant development: Implications for infant mental health. In C. H. Zeanah, Jr. (Ed.), *Handbook of infant mental health* (2nd ed., pp. 37–59). New York: Guilford.

Nelson, C. A., & Carver, L. J. (1998). The effects of stress and trauma on brain and memory: A view from developmental cognitive neuroscience. *Development and Psychopathology, 10,* 793–809.

Nelson, E. A. S., Schiefenhoevel, W., & Haimerl, F. (2000). Child care practices in nonindustrialized societies. *Pediatrics, 105,* e75.

Nelson, K. (1973). Structure and strategy in learning to talk. *Monographs of the Society for Research in Child Development, 38*(1–2, Serial No. 149).

Nelson, K. (1976). Some attributes of adjectives used by young children. *Cognition, 4,* 13–30.

Nelson, W. E. (Ed.). (1996). *Nelson textbook of pediatrics.* Philadelphia: Saunders.

Nesse, R. M. (1990). Evolutionary explanations of emotions. *Human Nature, 1,* 261–289.

Netley, C. T. (1986). Summary overview of behavioural development in individuals with neonatally identified X and Y aneuploidy. *Birth Defects, 22,* 293–306.

Neubauer, A. C., & Bucik, V. (1996). The mental speed–IQ relationship: Unitary or modular? *Intelligence, 22,* 23–48.

Neuman, S. B. (1999). Books make a difference: A study of access to literacy. *Reading Research Quarterly, 34,* 286–311.

Neville, H. J., & Bruer, J. T. (2001). Language processing: How experience affects brain organization. In D. B. Bailey, Jr., J. T. Bruer, F. J. Symons, & J. W. Lichtman (Eds.), *Critical thinking about critical periods* (pp. 151–172). Baltimore: Paul H. Brookes.

Newborg, J., Stock, J. R., & Wnek, L. (1984). *Batelle Developmental Inventory.* Allen, TX: LINC Associates.

Newcomb, A. F., & Bagwell, C. (1995). Children's friendship relations: A meta-analytic review. *Psychological Bulletin, 117,* 306–347.

Newcomb, A. F., Bukowski, W. M., & Pattee, L. (1993). Children's peer relations: A meta-analytic review of popular, rejected, neglected, controversial, and average sociometric status. *Psychological Bulletin, 113,* 99–128.

Newcombe, N. (1982). Development of spatial cognition and cognitive development. In R. Cohen (Ed.), *Children's conceptions of spatial relationships* (pp. 65–81). San Francisco: Jossey-Bass.

Newcombe, N., & Huttenlocher, J. (1992). Children's early ability to solve perspective-taking problems. *Developmental Psychology, 28,* 635–643.

Newcombe, P. A., & Boyle, G. J. (1995). High school students' sports personalities: Variations across participation level, gender, type of sport, and success. *International Journal of Sports Psychology, 26,* 277–294.

Newman, B. S., & Muzzonigro, P. G. (1993). The effects of traditional family values on the coming out process of gay male adolescents. *Adolescence, 28,* 213–226.

Newman, C., Atkinson, J., & Braddick, O. (2001). The development of reaching and looking preferences in infants to objects of different sizes. *Developmental Psychology, 37,* 561–572.

Newman, L. S. (1990). Intentional and unintentional memory in young children: Remembering vs. playing. *Journal of Experimental Child Psychology, 50,* 243–258.

Newmann, F. M. (1996). *Authentic achievement: Restructuring schools for intellectual quality.* San Francisco: Jossey-Bass.

Newmann, F. M., Marks, H., & Gamoran, A. (1996). Authentic pedagogy and student performance. *American Journal of Education, 104,* 280–312.

Newnham, J. P., Evans, S. F., Michael, C. A., Stanley, F. J., & Landau, L. I. (1993). Effects of frequent ultrasound during pregnancy: A randomized controlled trial. *Lancet, 342,* 887–890.

Newport, E. L. (1991). Contrasting conceptions of the critical period for language. In S. Carey & R. Gelman (Eds.), *The epigenesis of mind: Essays on biology and cognition* (pp. 111–130). Hillsdale, NJ: Erlbaum.

Newson, J., & Newson, E. (1975). Intersubjectivity and the transmission of culture: On the social origins of symbolic functioning. *Bulletin of the British Psychological Society, 28,* 437–446.

Ni, Y. (1998). Cognitive structure, content knowledge, and classificatory reasoning. *Journal of Genetic Psychology, 159,* 280–296.

Nicholls, A. L., & Kennedy, J. M. (1992). Drawing development: From similarity of features to direction. *Child Development, 63,* 227–241.

Nicholls, J. G. (1978). The development of concepts of effort and ability, perception of academic attainment, and the understanding that difficult tasks require more ability. *Child Development, 49,* 800–814.

Nichols, R. C. (1978). Heredity and environment: Major findings from twin studies of ability, personality, and interests. *Home, 29,* 158–173.

Nicoladis, E., & Genesse, F. (1996). A longitudinal study of pragmatic differentiation in young bilingual children. *Language Learning, 46,* 439–464.

Nidorf, J. F. (1985). Mental health and refugee youths: A model for diagnostic training. In T. C. Owen (Ed.), *Southeast Asian mental health: Treatment, prevention, services, training, and research* (pp. 391–427). Washington, DC: National Institute of Mental Health.

Nilsson, L., & Hamberger, L. (1990). *A child is born.* New York: Delacorte.

Nippold, M. A., Taylor, C. L., & Baker, J. M. (1996). Idiom understanding in Australian youth: A cross-cultural comparison. *Journal of Speech and Hearing Research, 39,* 442–447.

Nisbett, R. E. (1998). Race, genetics, and IQ. In C. Jencks & M. Phillips (Eds.), *The black–white test score gap* (pp. 86–102). Washington, DC: Brookings Institution.

Nix, R. L., Pinderhughes, E. E., Dodge, K. A., Bates, J. E., Pettit, G. S., & McFadyen-Ketchum, S. A. (1999). The relation between mothers' hostile attribution tendencies and children's externalizing behavior problems: The mediating role of mothers' harsh discipline practices. *Child Development, 70,* 896–909.

Nolen-Hoeksema, S. (2000). Gender differences in depression. *Current Directions in Psychological Science, 10,* 173–176.

Nolen-Hoeksema, S., & Girgus, J. S. (1994). The emergence of gender differences in depression in adolescence. *Psychological Bulletin, 115,* 424–443.

Nottlemann, E. D., Inoff-Germain, G., Susman, E. J., & Chrousos, G. P. (1990). Hormones and behavior at puberty. In J. Bancroft & J. M. Reinisch (Eds.), *Adolescence and puberty* (pp. 88–123). New York: Oxford University Press.

Nourse, C. B., & Butler, K. M. (1998). Perinatal transmission of HIV and diagnosis of HIV infection in infants: A review. *Irish Journal of Medical Science, 167,* 28–32.

Nowakowski, R. S. (1987). Basic concepts of CNS development. *Child Development, 58,* 568–595.

Nucci, L. P. (1996). Morality and the personal sphere of action. In E. Reed, E. Turiel, & T. Brown (Eds.), *Values and knowledge* (pp. 41–60). Hillsdale, NJ: Erlbaum.

Nucci, L. P., Camino, C., & Sapiro, C. M. (1996). Social class effects on Northeastern Brazilian children's conceptions of areas of personal choice and social regulation. *Child Development, 67,* 1223–1242.

Nucci, L., & Turiel, E. (1978). Social interactions and the development of social concepts in preschool children. *Child Development, 49,* 400–407.

Nucci, L. P., & Weber, E. (1995). Social interactions in the home and the development of young children's conceptions of the personal. *Child Development, 66,* 1438–1452.

Nuckolls, K. B., Cassel, J., & Kaplan, B. H. (1972). Psychosocial assets, life crisis, and the prognosis of pregnancy. *American Journal of Epidemiology, 95,* 431–441.

Nurmi, J., Poole, M. E., & Kalakoski, V. (1996). Age differences in adolescent identity exploration and commitment in urban and rural environments. *Journal of Adolescence, 19,* 443–452.

Nye, B., Hedges, L. V., & Konstantopoulos, S. (2001). Are effects of small classes cumulative? Evidence from a Tennessee experiment. *Journal of Educational Research, 94,* 336–345.

O'Callaghan, M. J., Burn, Y. R., Mohay, H. A., Rogers, Y., & Tudehope, D. I. (1993). The prevalence and origins of left hand preference in high risk infants, and its implications for intellectual, motor, and behavioral performance at four and six years. *Cortex, 29,* 617–627.

O'Connell, P., Pepler, D., & Craig, W. (1999). Peer involvement in bullying: Insights and challenges for intervention. *Journal of Adolescence, 22,* 437–452.

O'Connor, C. (1997). Dispositions toward (collective) struggle and educational resilience in the inner city: A case analysis of six African-American high school students. *American Educational Research Journal, 34,* 593–629.

O'Mahoney, J. F. (1989). Development of thinking about things and people: Social and nonsocial cognition during adolescence. *Journal of Genetic Psychology, 150,* 217–224.

O'Malley, P. M., Johnston, L. D., & Bachman, J. G. (1995). Adolescent substance use: Epidemiology and implications for public policy. *Pediatric Clinics of North America, 42*(2), 241–260.

O'Neil, R., Welsh, M., Parke, R. D., Wang, S., & Strand, C. (1997). A longitudinal assessment of the academic correlates of early peer acceptance and rejection. *Journal of Clinical Child Psychology, 26,* 290–303.

O'Reilly, A. W. (1995). Using representations: Comprehension and production of actions with imagined objects. *Child Development, 66,* 999–1010.

O'Reilly, A. W., & Bornstein, M. H. (1993). Caregiver–child interaction in play. In M. H. Bornstein & A. W. O'Reilly (Eds.), *New directions for child development* (No. 59, pp. 55–66). San Francisco: Jossey-Bass.

Oakes, J., Gamoran, A., & Page, R. N. (1992). Curriculum differentiation: Opportunities, outcomes, and meanings. In P. W. Jackson (Ed.), *Handbook of research on curriculum* (pp. 570–608). New York: Macmillan.

Oakes, L. M., Coppage, D. J., & Dingel, A. (1997). By land or by sea: The role of perceptual similarity in infants' categorization of animals. *Developmental Psychology, 33,* 396–407.

Ochs, E. (1988). *Culture and language development: Language acquisition and language socialization in a Samoan village.* Cambridge: Cambridge University Press.

Ochse, R. (1990). *Before the gates of excellence: The determinants of creative genius.* New York: Cambridge University Press.

Oden, S. (2000). How researchers can support community efforts for change: Illustrations from two case studies. *Applied Developmental Science, 4,* 28–37.

Oettingen, G. (1985). The influence of kindergarten teachers on sex differences in behavior. *International Journal of Behavioral Development, 8,* 3–13.

Ogbu, J. U. (1997). Understanding the school performance of urban blacks: Some essential background knowledge. In H. J. Walberg, O. Reyes, & R. P. Weissberg (Eds.), *Children and youth: Interdisciplinary perspectives* (pp. 190–222). Thousand Oaks, CA: Sage.

Okagaki, L. (2001). Parental beliefs, parenting style, and children's intellectual development. In E. L. Grigorenko & R. J. Sternberg (Eds.), *Family environment and intellectual functioning: A lifespan perspective* (pp. 141–172). Mahwah, NJ: Erlbaum.

Okagaki, L., & Frensch, P. A. (1996). Effects of video game playing on measures of spatial performance: Gender effects in late adolescence. In P. M. Greenfield & R. R. Cocking (Eds.), *Interacting with video* (pp. 115–140). Norwood, NJ: Ablex.

Okagaki, L., & Frensch, P. A. (1998). Parenting and children's school achievement: A multi-ethnic perspective. *American Educational Research Journal, 35,* 123–144.

Okagaki, L., & Sternberg, R. J. (1993). Parental beliefs and children's school performance. *Child Development, 64,* 36–56.

Oken, E., & Lightdale, J. R. (2000). Updates in pediatric nutrition. *Current Opinion in Pediatrics, 12,* 282–290.

Olafson, E., & Boat, B. W. (2000). Long-term management of the sexually abused child: Considerations and challenges. In R. M. Reece (Ed.), *Treatment of child abuse: Common ground for mental health, medical, and legal practitioners* (pp. 14–35). Baltimore: Johns Hopkins University Press.

Ollendick, T. H., Yang, B., King, N. J., Dong, Q., & Akande, A. (1996). Fears in American, Australian, Chinese, and Nigerian children and adolescents: A cross-cultural study. *Journal of Child Psychology and Psychiatry, 37*, 213–220.

Oller, D. K. (2000). *The emergence of the speech capacity.* Mahwah, NJ: Erlbaum.

Oller, D. K., Eilers, R. E., Urbano, R., & Cobo-Lewis, A. B. (1997). Development of precursors to speech in infants exposed to two languages. *Journal of Child Language, 24*, 407–425.

Olsen, O. (1997). Meta-analysis of the safety of home birth. *Birth—Issues in Perinatal Care, 24*, 4–13.

Olweus, D. (1993). *Bullying at school.* Oxford: Blackwell.

Olweus, D. (1995). Bullying or peer abuse at school: Facts and intervention. *Current Directions in Psychological Science, 4*, 196–200.

Olweus, D., Mattison, A., Schalling, D., & Low, H. (1988). Circulating testosterone levels and aggression in adolescent males: A causal analysis. *Psychosomatic Medicine, 50*, 261–272.

Ondrusek, N., Abramovitch, R., Pencharz, P., & Koren, G. (1998). Empirical examination of the ability of children to consent to clinical research. *Journal of Medical Ethics, 24*, 158–165.

Oosterwegel, A., & Oppenheimer, L. (1993). *The self-system: Developmental changes between and within self-concepts.* Hillsdale, NJ: Erlbaum.

Organisation for Economic Cooperation and Development (OECD). (1999). *Measuring student knowledge and skills: A new framework for assessment.* Paris and Washington, DC: Author.

Ornstein, P. A., Shapiro, L. R., Clubb, P. A., & Follmer, A. (1997). The influence of prior knowledge on children's memory for salient medical experiences. In N. Stein, P. A. Ornstein, C. J. Brainerd, & B. Tversky (Eds.), *Memory for everyday and emotional events* (pp. 83–112). Hillsdale, NJ: Erlbaum.

Osherson, D. N., & Markman, E. M. (1975). Language and the ability to evaluate contradictions and tautologies. *Cognition, 2*, 213–226.

O'Sullivan, M., Guilford, J. P., & deMille, R. (1965). The measurement of social intelligence (Reports from the Psychological Laboratory, University of Southern California No. 34).

Ovando, C. J., & Collier, V. P. (1998). *Bilingual and ESL classrooms:*

*Teaching in multicultural contexts.* Boston: McGraw-Hill.

Overgaard, C., & Knudsen, A. (1999). Pain-relieving effect of sucrose in newborns during heel prick. *Biology of the Neonate, 75*, 279–284.

Owen, M. T., & Cox, M. J. (1997). Marital conflict and the development of infant–parent attachment relationships. *Journal of Family Psychology, 11*, 152–164.

Owen, M. T., Easterbrooks, M. A., Chase-Lansdale, L., & Goldberg, W. A. (1984). The relation between maternal employment status and the stability of attachments to mother and father. *Child Development, 55*, 1894–1901.

Öztürk, C., Durmazlar, N., Ural, B., Karaagaoglu, E., Yalaz, K., & Anlar, B. (1999). Hand and eye preference in normal preschool children. *Clinical Pediatrics, 38*, 677–680.

Pagani, L., Boulerice, B., Vitaro, F., & Tremblay, E. (1999). Effects of poverty on academic failure and delinquency in boys: A change and process model approach. *Journal of Child Psychology and Psychiatry, 40*, 1209–1219.

Pagani, L., Tremblay, R. E., Vitaro, F., Boulerice, B., & McDuff, P. (2001). Effects of grade retention on academic performance and behavioral development. *Development and Psychopathology, 13*, 297–315.

Paikoff, R. L., Brooks-Gunn, J., & Warren, M. P. (1991). Effects of girls' hormonal status on depressive and aggressive symptoms over the course of one year. *Journal of Youth and Adolescence, 20*, 191–215.

Palincsar, A. S., & Herrenkohl, L. R. (1999). Designing collaborative contexts: Lessons from three research programs. In A. M. O'Donnell & A. King (Eds.), *Cognitive perspectives on peer learning. The Rutgers Invitational Symposium on Education Series* (pp. 151–177). Mahwah, NJ: Erlbaum.

Palincsar, A. S., & Klenk, L. (1992). Fostering literacy learning in supportive contexts. *Journal of Learning Disabilities, 25*, 211–225.

Palmlund, I. (1996). Exposure to a xenoestrogen before birth: The diethylstilbestrol experience. *Journal of Psychosomoatic Obstetrics and Gynaecology, 17*, 71–84.

Palta, M., Sadek-Badawi, M., Evans, M., Weinstein, M. R., & McGuinness, G. (2000). Functional assessment of a multicenter very low-birth-weight cohort at age 5 years. *Archives of Pediatric and Adolescent Medicine, 154*, 23–30.

Pan, B. A., & Snow, C. E. (1999). The development of conversation and discourse skills. In M. Barrett (Ed.), *The development of language*

(pp. 229–249). Hove, UK: Psychology Press.

Pan, H. W. (1994). Children's play in Taiwan. In J. L. Roopnarine, J. E. Johnson, & F. H. Hooper (Eds.), *Children's play in diverse cultures* (pp. 31–50). Albany, NY: SUNY Press.

Panchaud, C., Singh, S., Feivelson, D., & Darroch, J. E. (2000). Sexually transmitted diseases among adolescents in developed countries. *Family Planning Perspectives, 32*, 24–32.

Panigrahy, A., Filano, J. J., Sleeper, L. A., Mandell, F., Krous, H. F., & Rava, L. A. (1997). Decreased kainate binding in the arcuate nucleus of the sudden infant death syndrome. *Journal of Neuropathology and Experimental Neurology, 56*, 1253–1261.

Papini, D. R. (1994). Family interventions. In S. L. Archer (Ed.), *Interventions for adolescent identity development* (pp. 47–61). Thousand Oaks, CA: Sage.

Papousek, M., & Papousek, H. (1996). Infantile persistent crying, state regulation, and interaction with parents: A systems view. In M. H. Bornstein & J. L. Genevro (Eds.), *Child development and behavioral pediatrics* (pp. 11–33). Mahwah, NJ: Erlbaum.

Parault, S. J., & Schwanenflugel, P. J. (2000). The development of conceptual categories of attention during the elementary school years. *Journal of Experimental Child Psychology, 75*, 245–262.

Parer, J. T. (1998). Effects of fetal asphyxia on brain cell structure and function: Limits of tolerance. *Comparative Biochemistry and Physiology, 119A*, 711–716.

Parikh, B. (1980). Development of moral judgment and its relation to family environmental factors in Indian and American families. *Child Development, 51*, 1030–1039.

Paris, S. G., Lawton, T. A., Turner, J. C., & Roth, J. L. (1991). A developmental perspective on standardized achievement testing. *Educational Researcher, 20*(5), 12–20.

Parke, R. (1996). *Fatherhood.* Cambridge, MA: Cambridge University Press.

Parke, R. D. (1994). Progress, paradigms and unresolved problems: A commentary on recent advances in our understanding of children's emotions. *Merrill-Palmer Quarterly, 40*, 157–169.

Parke, R. D., & Buriel, R. (1998). Socialization in the family: Ethnic and ecological perspectives. In N. Eisenberg (Ed.), *Handbook of child psychology: Vol. 3. Social, emotional, and personality development* (5th ed., pp. 463–552). New York: Wiley.

Parke, R. D., Burks, V. M., Carson, J. L., Neville, B., & Boyum, L. A. (1994). Family–peer relationships:

A tripartite model. In R. D. Parke & S. G. Kellam (Eds.), *Exploring family relationships with other social contexts* (pp. 115–145). Hillsdale, NJ: Erlbaum.

Parke, R. D., & Kellam, S. G. (Eds.) (1994). *Exploring family relationships with other social contexts.* Hillsdale, NJ: Erlbaum.

Parker, F. L., Boak, A. Y., Griffin, K. W., Ripple, C., & Peay, L. (1999). Parent–child relationship, home learning environment, and school readiness. *School Psychology Review, 28*, 413–425.

Parker, J. G., & Asher, S. R. (1987). Peer relations and later personal adjustment: Are low-accepted children at risk? *Psychological Bulletin, 102*, 357–389.

Parker, J. G., & Asher, S. R. (1993). Friendship and friendship quality in middle childhood: Links with peer group acceptance and feelings of loneliness and social dissatisfaction. *Developmental Psychology, 29*, 611–621.

Parkhurst, J. T., & Asher, S. R. (1992). Peer rejection in middle school: Subgroup differences in behavior, loneliness, and interpersonal concerns. *Developmental Psychology, 28*, 231–241.

Parkhurst, J. T., & Hopmeyer, A. (1998). Sociometric popularity and peer-perceived popularity: Two distinct dimensions of peer status. *Journal of Early Adolescence, 18*, 125–144.

Parks, W. (1996). Human immunodeficiency virus. In R. D. Behrman, R. M. Kliegman, & A. M. Arvin (Eds.), *Nelson textbook of pediatrics* (15th ed., pp. 916–919). Philadelphia: Saunders.

Parsons, J. E., Adler, T. F., & Kaczala, C. M. (1982). Socialization of achievement attitudes and beliefs: Parental influences. *Child Development, 53*, 310–321.

Parten, M. (1932). Social participation among preschool children. *Journal of Abnormal and Social Psychology, 27*, 243–269.

Pascalis, O., de Haan, M., & Nelson, C. A. (1998). Long-term recognition memory for faces assessed by visual paired comparison in 3- and 6-month-old infants. *Journal of Experimental Psychology: Learning, Memory, and Cognition, 24*, 249–260.

Pasquino, A. M., Albanese, A., Bozzola, M., Butler, G. E., Buzi, F., & Cherubini, V. (2001). Idiopathic short stature. *Journal of Pediatric Endocrinology and Metabolism, 14*, 967–972.

Passman, R. H. (1987). Attachments to inanimate objects: Are children who have security blankets insecure? *Journal of Consulting and Clinical Psychology, 55*, 825–830.

Pate, R. R., Trost, S. G., Levin, S., & Dowda, M. (2000). Sports participation and health-related behaviors among U.S. youth. *Archives of Pediatric and Adolescent Medicine, 154,* 904–911.

Patrick, E., & Abravanel, E. (2000). The self-regulatory nature of preschool children's private speech in a naturalistic setting. *Applied Psycholinguistics, 21,* 45–61.

Patterson, C. J. (1995). Sexual orientation and human development: An overview. *Developmental Psychology, 31,* 3–11.

Patterson, C. J. (2001). *Lesbian and gay parenting.* [On-line]. Available: www.apa.org/pi/parent.html

Patterson, G. R. (1995). Coercion—A basis for early age of onset for arrest. In J. McCord (Ed.), *Coercion and punishment in long-term perspective* (pp. 81–105). New York: Cambridge University Press.

Patterson, G. R. (1997). Performance models for parenting: A social interactional perspective. In J. E. Grusec & L. Kuczynski (Eds.), *Parenting and children's internalization of values* (pp. 193–226). New York: Wiley.

Patterson, G. R., DeBaryshe, B. D., & Ramsey, E. (1989). A developmental perspective on antisocial behavior. *American Psychologist, 44,* 329–335.

Patterson, G. R., Dishion, T. J., & Yoerger, K. (2000). Adolescent growth in new forms of problem behavior: Macro- and micro-peer dynamics. *Prevention Science, 1,* 3–13.

Patterson, G. R., & Forgatch, M. (1995). Predicting future clinical adjustment from treatment outcome and process variables. *Psychological Assessment, 7,* 275–285.

Patterson, G. R., Forgatch, M. S., Yoerger, K. L., & Stoolmiller, M. (1998). Variables that initiate and maintain an early-onset trajectory for juvenile offending. *Development and Psychopathology, 10,* 531–547.

Patterson, G. R., Littman, R. A., & Bricker, W. (1967). Assertive behavior in children: A step toward a theory of aggression. *Monographs of the Society for Research in Child Development, 35* (5, Serial No. 113).

Patton, G. C., Selzer, R., Coffey, C., Carlin, J. B., & Wolfe, R. (1999). Onset of adolescent eating disorders: Population based cohort study over 3 years. *British Medical Journal, 318,* 765–768.

Paulhus, D., & Landolt, M. (2000). Paragons of intelligence: Who gets nominated and why. *Canadian Journal of Behavioural Science, 32,* 168–177.

Payne, R. J. (1998). *Getting beyond race: The changing American culture.* Boulder, CO: Westview.

Pearce, D., Cantisani, G., & Laihonen, A. (1999). Changes in fertility and family sizes in Europe. *Population Trends, 95,* 33–40.

Pebody, R. G., Edmunds, W. J., Conyn-van Spaendonck, M., Olin, P., Berbers, G., & Rebiere, I. (2000). The seroepidemiology of rubella in western Europe. *Epidemiology and Infections, 125,* 347–357.

Peckham, C. S., & Logan, S. (1993). Screening for toxoplasmosis during pregnancy. *Archives of Disease in Childhood, 68,* 3–5.

Pederson, D. R., Gleason, K. E., Moran, G., & Bento, S. (1998). Maternal attachment representations, maternal sensitivity, and the infant-mother attachment relationship. *Developmental Psychology, 34,* 925–933.

Pederson, D. R., & Moran, G. (1995). A categorical description of infant-mother relationships in the home and its relation to Q-sort measures of infant-mother interaction. In E. Waters, B. E. Vaughn, G. Posada, & K. Kondo-Ikemura (Eds.), *Caregiving, cultural, and cognitive perspectives on secure-base behavior and working models: New growing points of attachment theory and research. Monographs of the Society for Research in Child Development, 60*(2–3, Serial No. 244).

Pederson, D. R., & Moran, G. (1996). Expressions of the attachment relationship outside of the Strange Situation. *Child Development, 67,* 915–927.

Pedlow, R., Sanson, A., Prior, M., & Oberklaid, F. (1993). Stability of maternally reported temperament from infancy to 8 years. *Developmental Psychology, 29,* 998–1007.

Peiser-Feinberg, E. S. (1999). *The children of the Cost, Quality, and Outcomes Study go to school.* Chapel Hill, NC: University of North Carolina.

Pelham, W. E., Jr., Wheeler, T., & Chronis, A. (1998). Empirically supported psychosocial treatments for attention deficit hyperactivity disorder. *Clinical Child Psychology, 27,* 190–205.

Pellegrini, A. D., & Smith, P. K. (1998). Physical activity play: The nature and function of a neglected aspect of play. *Child Development, 69,* 577–598.

Penner, S. G. (1987). Parental responses to grammatical and ungrammatical utterances. *Child Development, 58,* 376–384.

Pennington, B. F., Bender, B., Puck, M., Salbenblatt, J., & Robinson, A. (1982). Learning disabilities in children with sex chromosome anomalies. *Child Development, 53,* 1182–1192.

Peoples, C. E., Fagan, J. F., III, & Drotar, D. (1995). The influence of race on 3-year-old children's performance on the Stanford-Binet: Fourth Edition. *Intelligence, 21,* 69–82.

Pepler, D. J., & Craig, W. (2000). *Making a difference in bullying.* Report #60. [On-line]. Available: www.yorku.ca/lamarsh/ Making%20a%20Difference %20in%20Bullying.pdf

Pepler, D. J., Craig, W. M., & O'Connell, P. (1999). Understanding bullying from a dynamic systems perspective. In A. Slater and D. Muir (Eds.), *The Blackwell reader in developmental psychology* (pp. 440–451). Oxford: Blackwell.

Pepler, D., Connolly, J., & Craig, W. (2001). *Bullying and harassment: Experiences of minority and immigrant youth.* CERIS Virtual Library [On-line]. Available: www.ceris.metropolis.net/ Virtual%20Library/education/ pepler1.html

Perfetti, C. A. (1988). Verbal efficiency in reading ability. In M. Daneman, G. E. MacKinnon, & T. G. Waller (Eds.), *Reading research: Advances in theory and practice* (Vol. 6, pp. 109–143). San Diego: Academic Press.

Perner, J. (1988). Higher-order beliefs and intentions in children's understanding of social interaction. In J. W. Astington, P. L. Harris, & D. R. Olson (Eds.), *Developing theories of mind* (pp. 271–294). New York: Cambridge University Press.

Perner, J. (1991). *Understanding the representational mind.* Cambridge, MA: MIT Press.

Perry, D. G., & Bussey, K. (1979). Social learning theory of sex differences: Imitation is alive and well. *Journal of Personality and Social Psychology, 37,* 1699–1712.

Perry, D. G., Perry, L. C., & Rasmussen, P. (1986). Cognitive social learning mediators of aggression. *Child Development, 57,* 700–711.

Perry, D. G., Perry, L. C., & Weiss, R. J. (1989). Sex differences in the consequences that children anticipate for aggression. *Developmental Psychology, 25,* 171–184.

Perry, D. G., Williard, J. C., & Perry, L. C. (1990). Peers' perceptions of the consequences that victimized children provide aggressors. *Child Development, 61,* 1310–1325.

Perry, M. (2000). Explanations of mathematical concepts in Japanese, Chinese, and U.S. first- and fifth-grade classrooms. *Cognition and Instruction, 18,* 181–207.

Peshkin, A. (1978). *Growing up American: Schooling and the survival of the community.* Chicago: University of Chicago Press.

Peshkin, A. (1997). *Places of memory: Whiteman's schools and native American communities.* Mahwah, NJ: Erlbaum.

Peters, B. R., Atkins, M. S., & McKay, M. M. (1999). Adopted children's behavior problems: A review of five explanatory models. *Clinical Psychology Review, 19,* 297–328.

Peters, R. (1994). Better beginnings, better futures: A community based approach to primary prevention. *Canadian Journal of Mental Health, 13*(2), 183–188.

Peterson, C. (1999). Children's memory for medical emergencies 2 years later. *Developmental Psychology, 35,* 1493–1506.

Peterson, C., & Rideout, R. (1998). Memory for medical emergencies experienced by 1- and 2-year-olds. *Developmental Psychology, 34,* 1059–1072.

Petinou, K. C., Schwartz, R. G., Gravel, J. S., & Raphael, L. J. (2001). A preliminary account of phonological and morphological perception in young children with and without otitis media. *International Journal of Language and Communication Disorders, 36,* 21–42.

Petitto, L. A., Holowka, S., Sergio, L. E., & Ostry, D. (2001, September 6). Language rhythms in babies' hand movements. *Nature, 413,* 35–36.

Petitto, L. A., & Marentette, P. F. (1991). Babbling in the manual mode: Evidence for the ontogeny of language. *Science, 251,* 1493–1496.

Petitto, L. A., Zatorre, R. J., Gauna, K., Nikelski, E. J., Dostie, D., & Evans, A. C. (2000). Speech-like cerebral activity in profoundly deaf people processing signed language: Implications for the neural basis of human language. *Proceedings of the National Academy of Sciences, 97,* 13961–13966.

Petrill, S. A., Saudino, K., Cherney, S. S., Emde, R. N., Fulker, D. W., Hewitt, J. K., & Plomin, R. (1998). Exploring the genetic and environmental etiology of high general cognitive ability in fourteen- to thirty-six-month-old twins. *Child Development, 69,* 68–74.

Pettit, G. S., Bates, J. E., & Dodge, K. A. (1997). Supportive parenting, ecological context, and children's adjustment: A seven-year longitudinal study. *Child Development, 68,* 908–923.

Pettit, G. S., Brown, E. G., Mize, J., & Lindsey, E. (1998). Mothers' and fathers' socializing behaviors in three contexts: Links with children's peer competence. *Merrill-Palmer Quarterly, 44,* 173–193.

Pettit, G. S., Laird, R. D., Bates, J. E., & Dodge, K. A. (1997). Patterns of after-school care in middle childhood: Risk factors and developmental outcomes. *Merrill-Palmer Quarterly, 43,* 15–38.

Phelps, K. E., & Woolley, J. D. (1994). The form and function of young children's magical beliefs. *Developmental Psychology, 30,* 385–394.

Phillips, D. A. (1987). Socialization of perceived academic competence among highly competent children. *Child Development, 58,* 1308–1320.

Phillips, K., & Fulker, D. W. (1989). Quantitative genetic analysis of longitudinal trends in adoption designs with application to IQ in the Colorado Adoption Project. *Behavior Genetics, 19,* 621–658.

Phillips, M. (1997). What makes schools effective? A comparison of the relationships of communitarian climate and academic climate to mathematics achievement and attendance during middle school. *American Educational Research Journal, 34,* 633–662.

Phillipsen, L. C. (1999). Associations between age, gender, and group acceptance and three components of friendship quality. *Journal of Early Adolescence, 19,* 438–464.

Phinney, J. S. (1989). Stages of ethnic identity development in minority group adolescents. *Journal of Early Adolescence, 9,* 34–49.

Phinney, J. S., & Chavira, V. (1995). Parental ethnic socialization and adolescent outcomes in ethnic minority families. *Journal of Research on Adolescence, 5,* 31–53.

Phinney, J. S., Ferguson, D. L., & Tate, J. D. (1997). Intergroup attitudes among ethnic minority adolescents: A causal model. *Child Development, 68,* 955–969.

Phinney, J. S., Ong, A., & Madden, T. (2000). Cultural values and intergenerational value discrepancies in immigrant and non-immigrant families. *Child Development, 71,* 528–539.

Piaget, J. (1926). *The language and thought of the child.* New York: Harcourt, Brace & World. (Original work published 1923)

Piaget, J. (1928). *Judgment and reasoning in the child.* New York: Harcourt, Brace & World. (Original work published 1926)

Piaget, J. (1930). *The child's conception of the world.* New York: Harcourt, Brace & World. (Original work published 1926)

Piaget, J. (1951). *Play, dreams, and imitation in childhood.* New York: Norton. (Original work published 1945)

Piaget, J. (1952). *The origins of intelligence in children.* New York: International Universities Press. (Original work published 1936)

Piaget, J. (1965). *The moral judgment of the child.* New York: Free Press. (Original work published 1932)

Piaget, J. (1967). *Six psychological studies.* New York: Vintage.

Piaget, J. (1971). *Biology and knowledge.* Chicago: University of Chicago Press.

Piaget, J., & Inhelder, B. (1956). *The child's conception of space.* London: Routledge & Kegan Paul. (Original work published 1948)

Piaget, J., & Inhelder, B. (1969). *The psychology of the child.* London: Routledge & Kegan Paul. (Original work published 1967)

Piaget, J., Inhelder, B., & Szeminska, A. (1960). *The child's conception of geometry.* New York: Basic Books. (Original work published 1948)

Pianta, R. C., Egeland, B., & Erickson, M. F. (1989). The antecedents of maltreatment: Results of the Mother–Child Interaction Research Project. In D. Cicchetti & V. Carlson (Eds.), *Child maltreatment* (pp. 203–253). New York: Cambridge University Press.

Pick, A. D., & Frankel, G. W. (1974). A developmental study of strategies of visual selectivity. *Child Development, 45,* 1162–1165.

Pickens, J., Field, T., & Nawrocki, T. (2001). Frontal EEG asymmetry in response to emotional vignettes in preschool age children. *International Journal of Behavioral Development, 25,* 105–112.

Pickering, L. K., Granoff, D. M., Erickson, J. R., Mason, M. L., & Cordle, C. T. (1998). Modulation of the immune system by human milk and infant formula containing nucleotides. *Pediatrics, 101,* 242–249.

Pierce, K. M., Hamm, J. V., & Vandell, D. L. (1999). Experiences in after-school programs and children's adjustment in first-grade classrooms. *Child Development, 70,* 756–767.

Pierce, S. H., & Lange, G. (2000). Relationships among metamemory, motivation and memory performance in young school-age children. *British Journal of Developmental Psychology, 18,* 121–135.

Pierce, W. D., & Epling, W. F. (1995). *Behavior analysis and learning.* Englewood Cliffs, NJ: Prentice-Hall.

Pietz, J., Dunckelmann, R., Rupp, A., Rating, D., Meinck, H. M., Schmidt, H., & Bremer, H. J. (1998). Neurological outcome in adult patients with early-treated phenylketonuria. *European Journal of Pediatrics, 157,* 824–830.

Pillow, B. H. (1995). Two trends in the development of conceptual perspective taking. An elaboration of the passive–active hypothesis. *International Journal of Behavioral Development, 18,* 649–676.

Pinderhughes, E. E., Dodge, K. A., Bates, J. E., Pettit, G. S., & Zelli, A. (2000). Discipline responses: Influences of parents' socioeconomic status, ethnicity, beliefs about parenting, stress, and cognitive-emotional processes. *Journal of Family Psychology, 14,* 380–400.

Pinker, S. (1989). *Learnability and cognition.* Cambridge, MA: MIT Press.

Pinker, S. (1994). *The language instinct: How the mind creates language.* New York: William Morrow.

Pinker, S. (1997). *How the mind works.* New York: Norton.

Pinker, S., Lebeaux, D. S., & Frost, L. A. (1987). Productivity and constraints in the acquisition of the passive. *Cognition, 26,* 195–267.

Pinto, J., & Davis, P. V. (1991, April). *The categorical perception of human gait in 3- and 5-month-old infants.* Paper presented at the biennial meeting of the Society for Research in Child Development, Seattle, WA.

Pipes, P. L. (1996). *Nutrition in infancy and childhood* (6th ed.). St. Louis: Mosby.

Pipp, S., Easterbrooks, M. A., & Brown, S. R. (1993). Attachment status and complexity of infants' self- and other-knowledge when tested with mother and father. *Social Development, 2,* 1–14.

Pipp, S., Easterbrooks, M. A., & Harmon, R. J. (1992). The relation between attachment and knowledge of self and mother in one-year-old infants to three-year-old infants. *Child Development, 63,* 738–750.

Pivarnik, J. M. (1998). Potential effects of maternal physical activity on birth weight: Brief review. *Medicine and Science in Sports and Exercise, 30,* 407–414.

Plessinger, M. A., & Woods, J. R., Jr. (1998). Cocaine in pregnancy: Recent data on maternal and fetal risks. *Substance Abuse in Pregnancy, 25,* 99–118.

Plomin, R. (1994a). The Emanuel Miller Memorial Lecture 1993: Genetic research and identification of environmental influences. *Journal of Child Psychology and Psychiatry, 35,* 817–834.

Plomin, R. (1994b). Genetics and children's experiences in the family. *Journal of Child Psychology and Psychiatry, 36,* 33–68.

Plomin, R. (1994c). *Genetics and experience: The interplay between nature and nurture.* Thousand Oaks, CA: Sage.

Plomin, R. (1994d). Nature, nurture, and social development. *Social Development, 3,* 37–53.

Plomin, R., Chipuer, H. M., & Loehlin, J. C. (1990). Behavior genetics and personality. In L. A. Pervin (Ed.), *Handbook of personality theory and research* (pp. 225–243). New York: Guilford.

Plomin, R., & DeFries, J. C. (1983). The Colorado Adoption Project. *Child Development, 54,* 276–289.

Plomin, R., Defries, J. C., McClearn, G. E., & Rutter, M. (Eds.). (1997). *Behavioral genetics.* New York: Freeman.

Plumert, J. M., Pick, H. L., Jr., Marks, R. A., Kintsch, A. S., & Wegesin, D. (1994). Locating objects and communicating about locations: Organizational differences in children's searching and direction-giving. *Developmental Psychology, 30,* 443–453.

Plunkett, K. (1998). Connectionism and development. In M. Sabourin & F. Craik (Eds.), *Advances in psychological science* (Vol. 2, pp. 581–600). Hove, UK: Psychology Press.

Plunkett, K., Karmiloff-Smith, A., Bates, E., Elman, J. L., & Johnson, M. H. (1997). Connectionism and developmental psychology. *Journal of Child Psychology and Psychiatry, 38,* 53–80.

Plunkett, K., & Marchman, V. A. (1993). From rote learning to system building: Acquiring verb morphology in children and connectionist nets. *Cognition, 48,* 21–69.

Plunkett, K., & Marchman, V. A. (1996). Learning from a connectionist model of the acquisition of the English past tense. *Cognition, 61,* 299–308.

Polansky, N. A., Gaudin, J. M., Ammons, P. W., & Davis, K. B. (1985). The psychological ecology of the neglectful mother. *Child Abuse and Neglect, 9,* 265–275.

Polka, L., & Werker, J. F. (1994). Developmental changes in perception of non-native vowel contrasts. *Journal of Experimental Psychology: Human Perception and Performance, 20,* 421–435.

Pollitt, E. (1996). A reconceptualization of the effects of undernutrition on children's biological, psychosocial, and behavioral development. *Social Policy Report of the Society for Research in Child Development, 10*(5).

Pollitt, E., Gorman, K. S., Engle, P. L., Martorell, R., & Rivera, J. (1993). Early supplementary feeding and cognition. *Monographs of the Society for Research in Child Development, 58*(7, Serial No. 235).

Pollock, L. (1987). *A lasting relationship: Parents and children over three centuries.* Hanover, NH: University Press of New England.

Pomerantz, E. M., & Eaton, M. M. (2000). Developmental differences in children's conceptions of parental control: "They love me, but they make me feel incompetent." *Merrill-Palmer Quarterly, 46,* 140–167.

Pomerantz, E. M., & Ruble, D. N. (1998a). The multidimensional nature of control: Implications for the development of sex differences in self-evaluation. In J. Heckhausen & C. S. Dweck (Eds.), *Motivation and self-regulation across the life span* (pp. 159–184). New York: Cambridge University Press.

Pomerantz, E. M., & Ruble, D. N. (1998b). The role of maternal control in the development of sex differences in child self-evaluative factions. *Child Development, 69,* 458–478.

Pomerantz, E. M., & Saxon, J. L. (2001). Conceptions of ability as stable and self-evaluative processes: A longitudinal examination. *Child Development, 72,* 152–173.

Poole, D. A., & Lindsay, D. S. (2001). Children's eyewitness reports after exposure to misinformation from parents. *Journal of Experimental Psychology, Applied, 7,* 27–50.

Popkin, B. M., Richards, M. K., & Monteiro, C. A. (1996). Stunting is associated with overweight in children of four nations that are undergoing the nutrition transition. *Journal of Nutrition, 126,* 3009–3016.

Porges, S. W. (1991). Autonomic regulation and attention. In B. A. Campbell, H. Hayne, & R. Richardson (Eds.), *Attention and information processing in infants and adults* (pp. 201–223). Hillsdale, NJ: Erlbaum.

Porter, R. H., Makin, J. W., Davis, L. B., & Christensen, K. M. (1992). An assessment of the salient olfactory environment of formula-fed infants. *Physiology and Behavior, 50,* 907–911.

Porter, R. H., & Winberg, J. (1999). Unique salience of maternal breast odors for newborn infants. *Neuroscience and Biobehavioral Reviews, 23,* 439–449.

Posada, G., Gao, Y., Wu, F., Posada, R., Tascon, M., Schöelmerich, A., Sagi, A., Kondo-Ikemura, K., Haaland, W., & Synnevaag, B. (1995). The secure-base phenomenon across cultures: Children's behavior, mothers' preferences, and experts' concepts. In E. Waters, B. E. Vaughn, G. Posada, & K. Kondo-Ikemura (Eds.), *Caregiving, cultural, and cognitive perspectives on secure-base behavior and working models: New growing points of attachment theory and research. Monographs of the Society for Research in Child Development, 60*(2–3, Serial No. 244).

Posner, J. K., & Vandell, D. L. (1994). Low-income children's after-school care: Are there beneficial effects of after-school programs? *Child Development, 64,* 440–456.

Posner, J. K., & Vandell, D. L. (1999). After-school activities and the development of low-income urban children: A longitudinal study. *Developmental Psychology, 35,* 868–879.

Posner, M. I., Rothbart, M. K., Gerardi, G., & Thomas-Thrapp, L. (1997). Functions of orienting in early infancy. In P. Lange, M. Balaban, & R. F. Simmons (Eds.), *The study of attention: Cognitive perspectives from psychophysiology, reflexology, and neuroscience* (pp. 327–345). Hillsdale, NJ: Erlbaum.

Potter, G. B., Gibbs, J. C., & Goldstein, A. P. (2001). *EQUIP implementation guide.* Champaign, IL: Research Press.

Poulin-Dubois, D., & Héroux, G. (1994). Movement and children's attributions of life properties. *International Journal of Behavioral Development, 17,* 329–347.

Poulin-Dubois, D., Serbin, L. A., Kenyon, B., & Derbyshire, A. (1994). Infants' intermodal knowledge about gender. *Developmental Psychology, 30,* 436–442.

Povinelli, D. J., & Giambrone, S. (2001). Reasoning about beliefs: A human specialization? *Child Development, 72,* 691–695.

Powell, B., & Steelman, L. C. (1993). The educational benefits of being spaced out: Sibship density and educational progress. *American Sociological Review, 58,* 367–381.

Powlishta, K. K. (2000). The effect of target age on the activation of gender stereotypes. *Sex Roles, 42,* 271–282.

Powlishta, K. K., Sen, M. G., Serbin, L. A., Poulin-Dubois, D., & Eichstedt, J. A. (2001). From infancy through middle childhood: The role of cognitive and social factors in becoming gendered. In R. K. Unger (Ed.), *Handbook of the psychology of women and gender* (pp. 116–132). New York: Wiley.

Powlishta, K. K., Serbin, L. A., & Moller, L. C. (1993). The stability of individual differences in gender typing: Implications for understanding gender segregation. *Sex Roles, 29,* 723–737.

Powlishta, K. K., Serbin, L. A., Doyle, A., & White, D. R. (1994). Gender, ethnic, and body type biases: The generality of prejudice in childhood. *Developmental Psychology, 30,* 526–536.

Powls, A., Botting, N., Cooke, R. W. I., & Marlow, N. (1996). Handedness in very-low-birthweight (VLBW) children at 12 years of age: Relation to perinatal and outcome variables. *Developmental Medicine and Child Neurology, 38,* 594–602.

Pratt, M., & Savoy-Levine, K. (1998). Contingent tutoring of long-division skills in fourth and fifth graders: Experimental tests of some hypotheses about scaffolding. *Journal of Applied Developmental Psychology, 19,* 287–304.

Pratt, M. W., Arnold, M. L., Pratt, A. T., & Diessner, R. (1999). Predicting adolescent moral reasoning from family climate: A longitudinal study. *Journal of Early Adolescence, 19,* 148–175.

Pratt, M. W., Green, D., & MacVicar, J. (1992). The mathematical parent: Parental scaffolding, parenting style, and learning outcomes in long-division mathematics homework. *Journal of Applied Developmental Psychology, 24,* 832–839.

Prechtl, H. F. R. (1958). Problems of behavioral studies in the newborn infant. In D. S. Lehrmann, R. A. Hinde, & E. Shaw (Eds.), *Advances in the study of behavior* (Vol. 1, pp. 75–98). New York: Academic Press.

Prechtl, H. F. R., & Beintema, D. (1965). *The neurological examination of the full-term newborn infant.* London: William Heinemann Medical Books.

Prechtl, H. F. R., Einspieler, C., Bos, A. F., & Ferrari, F. (2001). Role of vision on early motor development: Lessons from the blind. *Developmental Medicine and Child Neurology, 43,* 198–201.

Preisler, G. M. (1991). Early patterns of interaction between blind infants and their sighted mothers. *Child: Care, Health and Development, 17,* 65–90.

Preisler, G. M. (1993). A descriptive study of blind children in nurseries with sighted children. *Child: Care, Health and Development, 19,* 295–315.

Pressley, M. (1994). State-of-the-science primary-grades reading instruction or whole language? *Educational Psychologist, 29,* 211–215.

Pressley, M. (1995). More about the development of self-regulation: Complex, long-term, and thoroughly social. *Educational Psychologist, 30,* 207–212.

Pressley, M., Wharton-McDonald, R., Allington, R., Block, C. C., Morrow, L., Tracey, D., Baker, K., Brooks, G., Cronin, J., Nelson, E., & Woo, D. (2001). A study of effective first-grade literacy instruction. *Scientific Studies of Reading, 5,* 35–58.

Previc, F. H. (1991). A general theory concerning the prenatal origins of cerebral lateralization. *Psychological Review, 98,* 299–334.

Preyer, W. (1888). *The mind of the child* (2 vols.). New York: Appleton. (Original work published 1882)

Primero, H. B. (1993). *Canada adopts five-point plan to ban violence on television.* Centre for Media Literacy [On-line]. Available: www.medialit.org/Violence/articles/canada.htm

Provins, K. A. (1997). Handedness and speech: A critical reappraisal of the role of genetic and environmental factors in the cerebral lateralization of function. *Psychological Review, 104,* 554–571.

Prysak, M., Lorenz, R. P., & Kisly, A. (1995). Pregnancy outcome in nulliparous women 35 years and older. *Obstetrics and Gynecology, 85,* 65–70.

Pungello, E. P., & Kurtz-Costes, B. (1999). Why and how working women choose child care: A review with a focus on infancy. *Developmental Review, 19,* 31–96.

Purcell-Gates, V. (1996). Stories, coupons, and the TV Guide: Relationships between home literacy experiences and emergent literacy knowledge. *Reading Research Quarterly, 31,* 406–428.

Pyeritz, R. E. (1998). Sex: What we make of it. *Journal of the American Medical Association, 279,* 269.

Qazi, Q. H., Sheikh, T. M., Fikrig, S., & Menikoff, H. (1988). Lack of evidence for craniofacial dysmorphism in perinatal human immunodeficiency virus infection. *Journal of Pediatrics, 112,* 7–11.

Quantz, D. (1997, October). *Cultural and self disruption: Suicide among First Nations adolescents.* Paper submitted to the 8th Canadian Association for Suicide Prevention Conference, Thunder Bay, Ontario.

Quatman, T., Sokolik, E., & Smith, K. (2000). Adolescent perception of peer success: A gendered perspective over time. *Sex Roles, 43,* 61–84.

Quinn, P. C., & Eimas, P. D. (1996). Perceptual organization and categorization in young infants. In C. Rovee-Collier & L. P. Lipsitt (Eds.), *Advances in infancy research* (Vol. 10, pp. 1–36). Norwood, NJ: Ablex.

Quinn, P. C., Johnson, M. H., Mareschal, D., Rakison, D. H., & Younger, B. A. (2000). Understanding early categorization: One process or two? *Infancy, 1,* 111–122.

Quint, J. C., Box, J. M., & Polit, D. F. (1997, July). *New chance: Final report on a comprehensive program for disadvantaged young mothers and their children.* New York: Manpower Demonstration Research Corporation.

Quintero, R. A., Puder, K. S., & Cotton, D. B. (1993). Embryoscopy and fetoscopy. *Obstetrics and Gynecology Clinics of North America, 20,* 563–581.

Quyen, G. T., Bird, H. R., Davies, M., Hoven, C., Cohen, P., Jensen, P. S., & Goodman, S. (1998). Adverse life events and resilience. *Journal of the American Academy of Child and Adolescent Psychiatry, 37,* 1191–1200.

Radin, N. (1994). Primary caregiving fathers in intact families. In A. E. Gottfried & A. W. Gottfried (Eds.), *Redefining families: Implications for children's development* (pp. 11–54). New York: Plenum.

Radziszewska, B., & Rogoff, B. (1988). Influence of adult and peer collaboration on the development of children's planning skills. *Developmental Psychology, 24,* 840–848.

Rahn, W. M., & Transue, J. E. (1998). Social trust and value change: The decline of social capital in American youth, 1976–1995. *Political Psychology, 19,* 545–565.

Raikes, H. (1998). Investing in child care subsidy: What are we buying? *Social Policy Report of the Society for Research in Child Development, 12*(2).

Raine, A. (1997). Antisocial behavior and psychophysiology: A biosocial perspective and a prefrontal dysfunction hypothesis. In D. M. Stoff, J. Breiling, & J. D. Maser (Eds.), *Handbook of antisocial behavior* (pp. 289–304). New York: Wiley.

Raisler, J. (1999). Breast-feeding and infant illness: A dose-response relationship? *American Journal of Public Health, 89,* 25–30.

Rakison, D. H., & Butterworth, G. E. (1998). Infants' use of object parts in early categorization. *Developmental Psychology, 34,* 49–62.

Ram, A., & Ross, H. (2001). Problem solving, contention and struggle: How siblings resolve a conflict of interests. *Child Development, 72,* 1710–1722.

Ramey, S. L. (1999). Head Start and preschool education: Toward continued improvement. *American Psychologist, 54,* 344–346.

Ramey, S. L., & Ramey, C. T. (1999). Early experience and early intervention for children "at risk" for developmental delay and mental retardation. *Mental Retardation and Developmental Disabilities, 5,* 1–10.

Ramirez, J. D., Yuen, S. D., Ramey, D. R., & Pasta, D. (1991). *Longitudinal study of structured English immersion strategy, early exit and late-exit transitional bilingual education programs for language minority: Final report* (Vols. 1 & 2). San Mateo, CA: Aguirre International.

Ramos, E., Frontera, W. R., Llorpart, A., & Feliciano, D. (1998). Muscle strength and hormonal levels in adolescents: Gender related differences. *International Journal of Sports Medicine, 19,* 526–531.

Ramphal, C. (1962). *A study of three current problems in education.* Unpublished doctoral dissertation, University of Natal, India.

Ramsey, P. G. (1991). Young children's awareness and understanding of social class differences. *Journal of Genetic Psychology, 152,* 71–82.

Ramsey, P. G. (1995, September). Growing up with the contradictions of race and class. *Young Children, 50*(6), 18–22.

Rank, M. R. (2000). Socialization of socioeconomic status. In W. C. Nichols & M. A. Pace-Nichols (Eds.), *Handbook of family development and intervention* (pp. 129–142). New York: Wiley.

Rapport, M. D., & Chung, K.-M. (2000). Attention deficit hyperactivity disorder. In M. Hersen & R. T. Ammerman (Eds.), *Advanced abnormal child psychology* (2nd ed., pp. 413–440). Mahwah, NJ: Erlbaum.

Rast, M., & Meltzoff, A. N. (1995). Memory and representation in young children with Down syndrome: Exploring deferred imitation and object permanence. *Development and Psychopathology, 7,* 393–407.

Ratcliffe, S. G., Pan, H., & McKie, M. (1992). Growth during puberty

in the XYY boy. *Annals of Human Biology, 19,* 579–587.

Ratner, N. B. (2001). Atypical language development. In J. Berko Gleason (Ed.), *The development of language* (pp. 347–408). Boston: Allyn and Bacon.

Ravussin, E., Valencia, M. E., Esparza, J., Bennett, P. H., & Schulz, L. O. (1994). Effects of a traditional lifestyle on obesity in Pima Indians. *Diabetes Care, 17,* 1067–1074.

Rayner, K., & Pollatsek, A. (1989). *The psychology of reading.* Englewood Cliffs, NJ: Prentice-Hall.

Rayner, K., Foorman, B. R., Perfetti, C. A., Pesetsky, D., & Seidenberg, M. S. (2001). How psychological science informs the teaching of reading. *Psychological Science in the Public Interest, 2,* 31–74.

Raz, S., Shah, F., & Sander, C. J. (1996). Differential effects of perinatal hypoxic risk on early developmental outcome: A twin study. *Neuropsychology, 10,* 429–436.

Redl, F. (1966). *When we deal with children.* New York: Free Press.

Rees, M. (1993). Menarche when and why? *Lancet, 342,* 1375–1376.

Reese, E., Haden, C. A., & Fivush, R. (1993). Mother–child conversations about the past: Relationships of style and memory over time. *Cognitive Development, 8,* 403–430.

Reese, E., Haden, C. A., & Fivush, R. (1996). Mothers, fathers, daughters and sons: Gender differences in autobiographical reminiscing. *Research on Language and Social Interaction, 29*(1), 27–56.

Reid, P. T., & Trotter, K. H. (1993). Children's self-presentations with infants: Gender and ethnic comparisons. *Sex Roles, 29,* 171–181.

Reimer, M. (1996). "Sinking into the ground": The development and consequences of shame in adolescence. *Developmental Review, 16,* 321–363.

Reiser, J., Yonas, A., & Wikner, K. (1976). Radial localization of odors by human neonates. *Child Development, 47,* 856–859.

Reisman, J. E. (1987). Touch, motion, and proprioception. In P. Salapatek & L. Cohen (Eds.), *Handbook of infant perception: Vol. 1. From sensation to perception* (pp. 265–303). Orlando, FL: Academic Press.

Renninger, K. A. (1998). Developmental psychology and instruction: Issues from and for practice. In I. Sigel & K. A. Renninger (Eds.), *Handbook of child psychology: Vol. 4. Child psychology and practice* (pp. 211–274). New York: Wiley.

Renzetti, C. M., & Curran, D. J. (1998). *Living sociology.* Boston: Allyn and Bacon.

Repacholi, B. M. (1998). Infants' use of attentional cues to identify the referent of another person's emotional expression. *Developmental Psychology, 34,* 1017–1025.

Repacholi, B. M., & Gopnik, A. (1997). Early reasoning about desires: Evidence from 14- and 18-month-olds. *Developmental Psychology, 33,* 12–21.

Repke, J. T. (1992). Drug supplementation in pregnancy. *Current Opinion in Obstetrics and Gynecology, 4,* 802–806.

Resnick, M. B., Gueorguieva, R. V., Carter, R. L., Ariet, M., Sun, Y., Roth, J., Bucciarelli, R. L., Curran, J. S., & Mahan, C. S. (1999). The impact of low birth weight, perinatal conditions, and sociodemographic factors on educational outcome in kindergarten. *Pediatrics, 104,* e74.

Rest, J. R. (1979). *Development in judging moral issues.* Minneapolis: University of Minnesota Press.

Rest, J. R. (1986). *Moral development: Advances in research and theory.* New York: Praeger.

Rest, J. R., & Narvaez, D. (1991). The college experience and moral development. In W. M. Kurtines & J. L. Gewirtz (Eds.), *Handbook of moral behavior and development* (Vol. 2, pp. 229–245) . Hillsdale, NJ: Erlbaum.

Revelle, G. L., Karabenick, J. D., & Wellman, H. M. (1981). *Comprehension monitoring in preschool children.* Paper presented at the biennial meeting of the Society for Research in Child Development, Boston.

Reyna, V. F., & Kiernan, B. (1994). Development of gist versus verbatim memory in sentence recognition: Effects of lexical familiarity, semantic content, encoding instructions, and retention interval. *Developmental Psychology, 30,* 178–191.

Reynolds, A. J., & Temple, J. A. (1998). Extended early childhood intervention and school achievement: Age thirteen findings from the Chicago Longitudinal Study. *Child Development, 69,* 231–246.

Reynolds, C. R., & Kaiser, S. M. (1990). Test bias in psychological assessment. In T. B. Gutkin & C. R. Reynolds (Eds.), *The handbook of school psychology* (pp. 487–525). New York: Wiley.

Reznick, J. S., & Goldfield, B. A. (1992). Rapid change in lexical development in comprehension and production. *Developmental Psychology, 28,* 406–413.

Rhea, D. J. (1999). Eating disorder behaviors of ethnically diverse urban female adolescent athletes and non-athletes. *Journal of Adolescence, 22,* 379–388.

Rhee, S. H., Waldman, I. D., Hay, D. A., & Levy, F. (1999). Sex differences in genetic and environmental influences on DSM-III-R attention deficit/hyperactivity disorder. *Journal of Abnormal Psychology, 108,* 24–41.

Rholes, W. S., Newman, L. S., & Ruble, D. N. (1990). Understanding self

and others: Developmental and motivational aspects of perceiving persons in terms of invariant dispositions. In E. Higgins & R. Sorrentino (Eds.), *Handbook of motivation and cognition: Foundations of social behavior* (Vol. 2, pp. 369–407). New York: Guilford.

Ricard, M., & Kamberk-Kilicci, M. (1995). Children's empathic responses to emotional complexity. *International Journal of Behavioral Development, 18,* 211–225.

Rice, M. L., Huston, A. C., & Wright, J. C. (1982). The forms of television: Effects on children's attention, comprehension, and social behavior. In D. Pearl, L. Bouthilet, & J. Lazar (Eds.), *Television and behavior: Ten years of scientific progress and implications for the eighties* (Vol. 2, pp. 24–38). Washington, DC: U.S. Government Printing Office.

Richards, D. D., & Siegler, R. S. (1986). Children's understandings of the attributes of life. *Journal of Experimental Child Psychology, 42,* 1–22.

Richards, J. E., & Holley, F. B. (1999). Infant attention and the development of smooth pursuit tracking. *Developmental Psychology, 35,* 856–867.

Richards-Colocino, N., McKenzie, P., & Newton, R. R. (1996). Project Success: Comprehensive intervention services for middle school high-risk youth. *Journal of Adolescent Research, 11,* 130–163.

Richardson, G. A., Hamel, S. C., Goldschmidt, L., & Day, N. L. (1996). The effects of prenatal cocaine use on neonatal neurobehavioral status. *Neurotoxicology and Teratology, 18,* 519–528.

Rich-Edwards, J. W., Colditz, G. A., Stampfer, M. J., Willett, W. C., Gillman, M. W., Hennekens, C. H., Speizer, F. E., & Manson, J. E. (1999). Birthweight and the risk for type 2 diabetes mellitus in adult women. *Annals of Internal Medicine, 130,* 278–284.

Rickel, A. U., & Becker, E. (1997). *Keeping children from harm's way.* Washington, DC: American Psychological Association.

Ridderinkhof, K. R., & Molen, M. W. van der (1997). Mental resources, processing speed, and inhibitory control: A developmental perspective. *Biological Psychology, 45,* 241–261.

Riggs, K. J., & Peterson, D. M. (2000). Counterfactual thinking in preschool children: Mental state and causal inferences. In P. Mitchell & K. J. Riggs (Eds.), *Children's reasoning and the mind* (pp. 87–99). Hove, UK: Psychology Press.

Rijsdijk, F. V., & Boomsma, D. I. (1997). Genetic mediation of the correlation between peripheral nerve conduction velocity and IQ. *Behavior Genetics, 27,* 87–98.

Rivera, S. M., Wakeley, A., & Langer, J. (1999). The drawbridge phenomenon: Representational reasoning or perceptual preference? *Developmental Psychology, 35,* 427–435.

Rivkin, M. J. (2000). Developmental neuroimagining of children using magnetic resonance techniques. *Mental Retardation and Developmental Disabilities Research, 6,* 68–80.

Roberton, M. A. (1984). Changing motor patterns during childhood. In J. R. Thomas (Ed.), *Motor development during childhood and adolescence* (pp. 48–90). Minneapolis: Burgess Publishing.

Roberts, D. F., Foehr, U. G., Rideout, V. J., & Brodie, M. (1999). *Kids and media at the new millennium: A comprehensive national analysis of children's media use.* Menlo Park, CA: A Kaiser Family Foundation Report.

Roberts, J. E., Burchinal, M. R., & Campbell, F. (1994). Otitis media in early childhood and patterns of intellectual development and later academic performance. *Journal of Pediatric Psychology, 19,* 347–367.

Roberts, J. E., Burchinal, M. R., & Durham, M. (1999). Parents' report of vocabulary and grammatical development of American preschoolers: Child and environment associations. *Child Development, 70,* 92–106.

Roberts, J. E., Burchinal, M. R., Jackson, S. C., Hooper, S. R., Roush, J., Mundy, M., Neebe, E. C., & Zeisel, S. A. (2000). Otitis media in childhood in relation to preschool language and school readiness skills among black children. *Pediatrics, 106,* 725–735.

Roberts, J. E., Burchinal, M. R., Zeisel, S. A., Neebe, E. C., Hooper, S. R., Roush, J., Bryant, D., Mundy, M., & Henderson, F. W. (1998). Otitis media, the caregiving environment, and language and cognitive outcomes at 2 years. *Pediatrics, 102,* 346–354.

Roberts, R. J., Jr., & Aman, C. J. (1993). Developmental differences in giving directions: Spatial frames of reference and mental rotation. *Child Development, 64,* 1258–1270.

Robin, A. L., Gilroy, M., & Dennis, A. B. (1998). Treatment of eating disorders in children and adolescents. *Clinical Psychology Review, 18,* 421–446.

Robin, D. J., Berthier, N. E., & Clifton, R. K. (1996). Infants' predictive reaching for moving objects in the dark. *Developmental Psychology, 32,* 824–835.

Robinson, T. N. (1999). Reducing children's television viewing to prevent obesity. *Journal of the American Medical Association, 282,* 1561–1567.

Rochat, P. (1989). Object manipulation and exploration in 2- to 5-month-old infants. *Developmental Psychology, 25,* 871–884.

Rochat, P. (1992). Self-sitting and reaching in 5- to 8-month-old infants: The impact of posture and its development on early eye–hand coordination. *Journal of Motor Behavior, 24,* 210–220.

Rochat, P. (1998). Self-perception and action in infancy. *Experimental Brain Research, 123,* 102–109.

Rochat, P. (2001). *The infant's world.* Cambridge, MA: Harvard University Press.

Rochat, P., & Goubet, N. (1995). Development of sitting and reaching in 5- to 6-month-old infants. *Infant Behavior and Development, 18,* 53–68.

Rochat, P., Querido, J. G., & Striano, T. (1999). Emerging sensitivity to the timing and structure of protoconversation. *Developmental Psychology, 35,* 950–957.

Rocheleau, B. (1995). Computer use by school-age children: Trends, patterns and predictors. *Journal of Educational Computing Research, 1,* 1–17.

Rodgers, J. L. (1999). A critique of the Flynn effect: Massive IQ gains, methodological artifacts, or both? *Intelligence, 26,* 337–356.

Rodgers, J. L. (2001). The confluence model: An academic "tragedy of the commons"? In E. L. Grigorenko & R. J. Sternberg (Eds.), *Family environment and intellectual functioning: A life-span perspective* (pp. 71–95). Mahwah, NJ: Erlbaum.

Rodgers, J. L., Cleveland, H. H., van den Oord, E., & Rowe, D. C. (2000). Resolving the debate over birth order, family size, and intelligence. *American Psychologist, 55,* 599–612.

Rodkin, P. C., Farmer, T. W., Pearl, R., & Van Acker, R. (2000). Resolving the debate over birth order, family size, and intelligence. *American Psychologist, 55,* 599–612.

Rodriguez, M. L., Mischel, W., & Shoda, Y. (1989). Cognitive and personality variables in the delay of gratification of older children at risk. *Journal of Personality and Social Psychology, 57,* 358–367.

Roebers, C. M., & Schneider, W. (2001). Individual differences in children's eyewitness recall: The influence of intelligence and shyness. *Applied Developmental Science, 5,* 9–20.

Roebuck, T. M., Mattson, S. N., & Riley, E. P. (1999). Prenatal exposure to alcohol: Effects on brain structure and neuropsychological functioning. In J. H. Hannigan & L. P. Spear (Eds.), *Alcohol and alcoholism: Effects on brain and development* (pp. 1–16). Mahwah, NJ: Erlbaum.

Roeser, R. W., Eccles, J. S., & Freedman-Doan, C. (1999). Academic functioning and mental health in adolescence: Patterns, progressions, and routes from childhood. *Journal of Adolescent Research, 14,* 135–174.

Roeser, R. W., Eccles, J. S., & Sameroff, A. J. (2000). School as a context of early adolescents' academic and social-emotional development: A summary of research findings. *Elementary School Journal, 100,* 443–471.

Roffwarg, H. P., Muzio, J. N., & Dement, W. C. (1966). Ontogenetic development of the human sleep-dream cycle. *Science, 152,* 604–619.

Roggman, L. A., Langlois, J. H., Hubbs-Tait, L., & Rieser-Danner, L. A. (1994). Infant day-care, attachment, and the "file drawer problem." *Child Development, 65,* 1429–1443.

Rogoff, B. (1990). *Apprenticeship in thinking.* New York: Oxford University Press.

Rogoff, B. (1994). Developing understanding of the idea of community learners. *Mind, Culture, and Activity, 1,* 209–229.

Rogoff, B. (1998). Cognition as a collaborative process. In D. Kuhn & R. S. Siegler (Eds.), *Handbook of child psychology: Vol. 2. Cognition, perception, and language* (5th ed., pp. 679–744). New York: Wiley.

Rogoff, B., & Chavajay, P. (1995). What's become of research on the cultural basis of cognitive development? *American Psychologist, 50,* 859–877.

Rogoff, B., & Mistry, J. (1985). Memory development in cultural context. In M. Pressley & C. Brainerd (Eds.), *Cognitive learning and memory in children* (pp. 117–142). New York: Springer-Verlag.

Rogoff, B., Mistry, J., Göncü, A., & Mosier, C. (1993). Guided participation in cultural activity by toddlers and caregivers. *Monographs of the Society for Research in Child Development, 58*(8, Serial No. 236).

Rogoff, B., & Waddell, K. J. (1982). Memory for information organized in a scene by children from two cultures. *Child Development, 53,* 1224–1228.

Rogosch, F., Cicchetti, D., Shields, A., & Toth, S. L. (1995). Parenting dysfunction in child maltreatment. In M. H. Bornstein (Ed.), *Handbook of parenting* (Vol. 4, pp. 127–159). Hillsdale, NJ: Erlbaum.

Rohlen, T. P. (1997). Differences that make a difference: Explaining Japan's success. In W. K. Cumings & P. G. Altbach (Eds.), *The challenge of Eastern Asian education: Implications for America* (pp. 223–248). Albany, NY: SUNY Press.

Rohner, R. P., & Rohner, E. C. (1981). Parental acceptance-rejection and parental control: Cross-cultural codes. *Ethnology, 20,* 245–260.

Roid, G., & Worrall, W. (1997). Replication of the *Wechsler Intelligence Scale for Children, Third Edition* four-factor model in the Canadian normative sample. *Psychological Assessment, 9,* 512–515.

Roland, A. (1988). *In search of self in India and Japan: Toward a cross-cultural psychology.* Princeton, NJ: Princeton University Press.

Rome-Flanders, T., & Cronk, C. (1995). A longitudinal study of infant vocalizations during mother–infant games. *Journal of Child Language, 22,* 259–274.

Rönnqvist, L., & Hopkins, B. (1998). Head position preference in the human newborn: A new look. *Child Development, 69,* 13–23.

Roopnarine, J. L., Hossain, Z., Gill, P., & Brophy, H. (1994). Play in the East Indian context. In J. L. Roopnarine, J. E. Johnson, & F. H. Hooper (Eds.), *Children's play in diverse cultures* (pp. 9–30). Albany, NY: SUNY Press.

Roopnarine, J. L., Talukder, E., Jain, D., Joshi, P., & Srivastave, P. (1990). Characteristics of holding, patterns of play, and social behaviors between parents and infants in New Delhi, India. *Developmental Psychology, 26,* 667–673.

Rose, A. J., & Asher, S. R. (1999). Children's goals and strategies in response to conflicts within a friendship. *Developmental Psychology, 35,* 69–79.

Rose, J. L., & Bertenthal, B. I. (1995). A longitudinal study of the visual control of posture in infancy. In B. G. Bardy, R. J. Bootsma, & Y. Guiard (Eds.), *Studies in perception and action* (pp. 251–253). Mahwah, NJ: Erlbaum.

Rose, L. (2000). Fathers of full-term infants. In N. Tracey (Ed.), *Parents of premature infants: Their emotional world* (pp. 105–116). Longon: Whurr.

Rose, S. A., & Feldman, J. F. (1997). Memory and speed: Their role in the relation of infant information processing to later IQ. *Child Development, 68,* 610–620.

Rose, S. A., Jankowski, J. J., & Senior, G. J. (1997). Infants' recognition of contour-deleted figures. *Journal of Experimental Psychology: Human Perception and Performance, 23,* 1206–1216.

Rosen, A. B., & Rozin, P. (1993). Now you see it, now you don't: The preschool child's conception of invisible particles in the context of dissolving. *Developmental Psychology, 29,* 300–311.

Rosenberg, D. R., Sweeney, J. A., Gillen, J. S., Kim, J., Varanelli, M. J., O'Hearn, K. M., & Erb, P. A. (1997). Magnetic resonance imaging of children without sedation preparation with simulation. *Journal of the American Academy of Child and Adolescent Psychiatry, 36,* 853–859.

Rosenberg, M. (1979). *Conceiving the self.* New York: Basic Books.

Rosengren, K. S., & Hickling, A. K. (2000). The development of children's thinking about possible events and plausible mechanisms. In K. S. Rosengren, C. N. Johnson, & P. L. Harris (Eds.), *Imagining the impossible* (pp. 75–98). Cambridge: Cambridge University Press.

Rosenshine, B., & Meister, C. (1994). Reciprocal teaching: A review of nineteen experimental studies. *Review of Educational Research, 64,* 479–530.

Rosenstein, D., & Oster, H. (1988). Differential facial responses to four basic tastes in newborns. *Child Development, 59,* 1555–1568.

Rosenthal, J. A. (1992). *Special-needs adoption: A study of intact families.* New York: Praeger.

Ross, H. S., Conant, C., Cheyne, J. A., & Alevizos, E. (1992). Relationships and alliances in the social interactions of kibbutz toddlers. *Social Development, 1,* 1–17.

Ross, J., Zinn, A., & McCauley, E. (2000). Neurodevelopmental and psychosocial aspects of Turner syndrome. *Mental Retardation and Developmental Disabilities Research Review, 6,* 135–141.

Ross, R. P., Campbell, T., Huston-Stein, A., & Wright, J. C. (1984). Nutritional misinformation of children: A developmental and experimental analysis of the effects of televised food commercials. *Journal of Applied Developmental Psychology, 1,* 329–347.

Rotenberg, K. J., Simourd, L., & Moore, D. (1989). Children's use of a verbal–nonverbal consistency principle to infer truth and lying. *Child Development, 60,* 309–322.

Rothbart, M. K. (1981). Measurement of temperament in infancy. *Child Development, 52,* 569–578.

Rothbart, M. K., Ahadi, S. A., & Evans, D. E. (2000). Temperament and personality: Origins and outcome. *Journal of Personality and Social Psychology, 78,* 122–135.

Rothbart, M. K., & Bates, J. E. (1998). Temperament. In N. Eisenberg (Ed.), *Handbook of child psychology: Vol. 3. Social, emotional, and personality development* (5th ed., pp. 105–176). New York: Wiley.

Rothbart, M. K., & Rothbart, M. (1976). Birth-order, sex of child and maternal help giving. *Sex Roles, 2,* 39–46.

Rothbaum, F., Pott, M., Azuma, H., Miyake, K., & Weisz, J. (2000b). The development of close relationships in Japan and the United States: Paths of symbiotic harmony and generative tension. *Child Development, 71,* 1121–1142.

Rothbaum, F., Weisz, J., Pott, M., Miyake, K., & Morelli, G. (2000a). Attachment and culture: Security in the United States and Japan. *American Psychologist, 55,* 1093–1104.

Rousseau, J. J. (1955). *Emile.* New York: Dutton. (Original work published 1762)

Rovee-Collier, C. (1996). Shifting the focus from what to why. *Infant Behavior and Development, 19,* 385–400.

Rovee-Collier, C. (1999). The development of infant memory. *Current Directions in Psychological Science, 8,* 80–85.

Rovee-Collier, C. K. (1987). Learning and memory. In J. D. Osofsky (Ed.), *Handbook of infant development* (2nd ed., pp. 98–148). New York: Wiley.

Rovee-Collier, C. K. (1999). The development of infant memory. *Current Directions in Psychological Science, 8,* 80–85.

Rovee-Collier, C. K. (2001). Information pickup by infants: What is it, and how can we tell? *Journal of Experimental Child Psychology, 78,* 35–49.

Rovee-Collier, C. K., & Bhatt, R. S. (1993). Evidence of long-term memory in infancy. *Annals of Child Development, 9,* 1–45.

Rovet, J., Netley, C., Keenan, M., Bailey, J., & Stewart, D. (1996). The psychoeducational profile of boys with Klinefelter syndrome. *Journal of Learning Disabilities, 29,* 180–196.

Rowe, D. C. (1994). *The limits of family influence: Genes, experience, and behavior.* New York: Guilford.

Royal College of Obstetricians and Gynecologists. (1997, October). *Report of the panel to review fetal pain.* London: Author.

Royce, J. M., Darlington, R. B., & Murray, H. W. (1983). Pooled analyses: Findings across studies. In Consortium for Longitudinal Studies (Ed.), *As the twig is bent: Lasting effects of preschool programs* (pp. 411–459). Hillsdale, NJ: Erlbaum.

Rubin, K. H., Bukowski, W., & Parker, J. G. (1998). Peer interactions, relationships, and groups. In N. Eisenberg (Ed.), *Handbook of child psychology: Vol. 3. Social, emotional, and personality development* (5th ed., pp. 619–700). New York: Wiley.

Rubin, K. H., & Coplan, R. J. (1998). Social and nonsocial play in childhood: An individual differences perspective. In O. N. Saracho & B. Spodek (Eds.), *Multiple perspectives on play in early childhood education* (pp. 144–170). Albany, NY: State University of New York Press.

Rubin, K. H., Coplan, R. J., Fox, N. A., & Calkins, S. (1995). Emotionality, emotion regulation, and preschoolers' social adaptation. *Development and Psychopathology, 7,* 49–62.

Rubin, K. H., Fein, G. G., & Vandenberg, B. (1983). Play. In E. M. Hetherington (Ed.), *Handbook of child psychology: Vol. 4. Socialization, personality, and social development* (4th ed., pp. 693–744). New York: Wiley.

Rubin, K. H., Hastings, P. D., Stewart, S. L., Henderson, H. A., & Chen, X. (1997). The consistency and concomitants of inhibition: Some of the children, all of the time. *Child Development, 68,* 467–483.

Rubin, K. H., Stewart, S. L., & Coplan, R. J. (1995). Social withdrawal in childhood: Conceptual and empirical perspectives. In T. H. Ollendick & R. J. Prinz (Eds.), *Advances in clinical child psychology* (Vol. 17, pp. 157–196). New York: Plenum.

Rubin, K. H., Watson, K. S., & Jambor, T. W. (1978). Free-play behaviors in preschool and kindergarten children. *Child Development, 49,* 534–536.

Ruble, D. N., & Dweck, C. S. (1995). Self-conceptions, person conceptions, and their development. In N. Eisenberg (Ed.), *Social development* (pp. 109–139). Thousand Oaks, CA: Sage.

Ruble, D. N., & Frey, K. S. (1991). Changing patterns of comparative behavior as skills are acquired: A functional model of self-evaluation. In J. Suls & T. A. Wills, (Eds.), *Social comparison: Contemporary theory and research* (pp. 70–112). Hillsdale, NJ: Erlbaum.

Ruble, D. N., & Martin, C. L. (1998). Gender development. In N. Eisenberg (Ed.), *Handbook of child psychology: Vol. 3. Social, emotional, and personality development* (5th ed., pp. 933–1016). New York: Wiley.

Rudolph, D. K., & Heller, T. L. (1997). Interpersonal problem solving, externalizing behavior, and social competence in preschoolers: A knowledge-performance discrepancy? *Journal of Applied Developmental Psychology, 18,* 107–117.

Rudolph, D. K., Lambert, S. F., Clark, A. G., & Kurlakowsky, K. D. (2001). Negotiating the transition to middle school: The role of self-regulatory processes. *Child Development, 72,* 929–946.

Ruff, H. A., & Lawson, K. R. (1990). Development of sustained, focused attention in young children during free play. *Developmental Psychology, 26,* 85–93.

Ruff, H. A., & Rothbart, M. K. (1996). *Attention in early development.* New York: Oxford University Press.

Ruff, H. A., Lawson, K. R., Parinello, R., & Weissberg, R. (1990). Long-term stability of individual differences in sustained attention in the early years. *Child Development, 61,* 60–75.

Ruff, H. A., Saltarelli, L. M., Capozzoli, M., & Dubiner, K. (1992). The differentiation of activity in infants' exploration of objects. *Developmental Psychology, 28,* 851–861.

Ruffman, T. (1999). Children's understanding of logical inconsistency. *Child Development, 70,* 872–886.

Ruffman, T., Perner, J., Naito, M., Parkin, L., & Clements, W. A. (1998). Older (but not younger) siblings facilitate false belief understanding. *Developmental Psychology, 34,* 161–174.

Ruffman, T., Perner, J., Olson, D. R., & Doherty, M. (1993). Reflecting on scientific thinking: Children's understanding of the hypothesis–evidence relation. *Child Development, 64,* 1617–1636.

Rumbaut, R. G. (1997). Ties that bind: Immigration and immigrant families in the United States. In A. Booth, A. C. Crouter, & N. Landale (Eds.), *Immigration and the family: Research and policy on U.S. immigrants* (pp. 3–46). Mahwah, NJ: Erlbaum.

Runco, M. A. (1992a). Children's divergent thinking and creative ideation. *Developmental Review, 12,* 233–264.

Runco, M. A. (1992b). The evaluative, valuative, and divergent thinking of children. *Journal of Creative Behavior, 25,* 311–319.

Runco, M. A. (1993). Divergent thinking, creativity, and giftedness. *Gifted Child Quarterly, 37,* 16–22.

Runco, M. A., & Okuda, S. M. (1988). Problem, discovery, divergent thinking, and the creative process. *Journal of Youth and Adolescence, 17,* 211–220.

Rusen, I. D., & McCourt, C. (Eds.). (1999). Vaccine coverage. In Health Canada, *Measuring Up: A Health Surveillance Update on Canadian Children and Youth.* Catalogue no. 42-2/82-1999E.

Rushton, J. P. (1997). Race, intelligence, and the brain: The errors and omissions of the "revised" edition of S. J. Gould's *The mismeasure of man* (1996). *Personality and Individual Differences, 23,* 169–180.

Rushton, J. P. (2000). *Race, evolution, and behavior: A life-history perspective* (3rd ed.). Port Huron, MI: Charles Darwin Research Institute.

Russell, A., Mize, J., & Bissaker, K. (2002). Parent–child relationships. In P. K. Smith & C. H. Hart (Eds.), *Handbook of childhood social development.* Oxford, UK: Blackwell.

Russell, A., Pettit, G. S., & Mize, J. (1998). Horizontal qualities in parent–child relationships: Parallels with and possible consequences for children's peer relationships. *Developmental Review, 18,* 313–352.

Russell, J. A. (1990). The preschooler's understanding of the causes and consequences of emotion. *Child Development, 61,* 1872–1881.

Rust, J., Golombok, S., Hines, M., Johnston, K., Golding, J., & the ALSPAC Study Team. (2000). The role of brothers and sisters in the gender development of preschool children. *Journal of Experimental Child Psychology, 77,* 292–303.

Rutter, M. (1996). Maternal deprivation. In M. H. Bornstein (Ed.), *Handbook of parenting: Vol. 4. Applied and practical parenting* (pp. 3–31). Mahwah, NJ: Erlbaum.

Rutter, M., & the English and Romanian Adoptees Study Team. (1998). Developmental catch-up, and deficit, following adoption after severe global early privation. *Journal of Child Psychology and Psychiatry, 39,* 465–476.

Rvachew, S., Slawinski, E., Williams, M., & Green, C. L. (1999). The impact of early onset otitis media on babbling and early language development. *Journal of the Acoustical Society of America, 105,* 467–475.

Saarni, C. (1997). Emotional competence and self-regulation in childhood. In P. Salovey & D. J. Sluyter (Eds.), *Emotional development and emotional intelligence* (pp. 35–66). New York: Basic Books.

Saarni, C. (1999). *The development of emotional competence.* New York: Guilford.

Saarni, C. (2000). Emotional competence: A developmental perspective. In R. Bar-On & J. D. A. Parker (Eds.), *Handbook of emotional intelligence* (pp. 68–91). San Francisco: Jossey-Bass.

Saarni, C., Mumme, D. L., & Campos, J. J. (1998). Emotional development: Action, communication, and understanding. In N. Eisenberg (Ed.), *Handbook of child psychology: Vol. 3. Social, emotional, and personality development* (5th ed., pp. 237–309). New York: Wiley.

Sacks, C. H., & Mergendoller, J. R. (1997). The relationship between teachers' theoretical orientation toward reading and student outcomes in kindergarten children with different initial reading abilities. *American Educational Research Journal, 34,* 721–739.

Sadeh, A. (1997). Sleep and melatonin in infants: A preliminary study. *Sleep, 20,* 185–191.

Sadler, T. W. (2000). *Langman's medical embryology* (8th ed.). Baltimore: Williams & Wilkins.

Saffran, J. R., Aslin, R. N., & Newport, E. L. (1996). Statistical learning by 8-month-old infants. *Science, 274,* 1926–1928.

Safyer, A. W., Leahy, B. H., & Colan, N. B. (1995). The impact of work on adolescent development. *Families and Society, 76,* 38–45.

Sahni, R., Schulze, K. F., Stefanski, M., Myers, M. M., & Fifer, W. P. (1995). Methodological issues in coding sleep states in immature infants. *Developmental Psychobiology, 28,* 85–101.

Salerno, M., Micillo, M., Di Maio, S., Capalbo, D., Ferri, P., & Lettiero, T. (2001). Longitudinal growth, sexual maturation and final height in patients with congenital hypothyroidism detected by neonatal screening. *European Journal of Endocrinology, 145,* 377–383.

Salidis, J., & Johnson, J. S. (1997). The production of minimal words: A longitudinal case study of phonological development. *Language Acquisition, 6,* 1–36.

Samenow, S. E. (1984). *Inside the criminal mind.* New York: Random House.

Sameroff, A. J., Seifer, R., Baldwin, A., & Baldwin, C. (1993). Stability of intelligence from preschool to adolescence: The influence of social and family risk factors. *Child Development, 64,* 80–97.

Sampson, R. (2000). A neighborhood-level perspective on social change and the social control of adolescent delinquency. In L. J. Crockett & R. K. Silbereisen (Eds.), *Negotiating adolescence in times of social change* (pp. 178–188). New York: Cambridge University Press.

Sampson, R. J., & Laub, J. H. (1993). *Crime in the making: Pathways and turning points through life.* Cambridge, MA: Harvard University Press.

Samson, L. F. (1988). Perinatal viral infections and neonates. *Journal of Perinatal Neonatal Nursing, 1,* 56–65.

Sanders, M. G., & Jordan, W. J. (2000). Student–teacher relations and academic achievement in high school. In M. G. Sanders (Ed.), *Schooling students placed at risk: Research, policy, and practice in the education of poor and minority adolescents* (pp. 65–82). Mahwah, NJ: Erlbaum.

Sandnabba, N. K., & Ahlberg, C. (1999). Parents' attitudes and expectations about children's cross-gender behavior. *Sex Roles, 40,* 249–263.

Sandqvist, K. (1992). Sweden's sex-role scheme and commitment to gender equality. In S. Lewis, D. N. Izraeli, & H. Hottsmans (Eds.), *Dual-earner families: International perspectives.* London: Sage.

Sansavini, A., Bertoncini, J., & Giovanelli, G. (1997). Newborns discriminate the rhythm of multisyllabic stressed words. *Developmental Psychology, 33,* 3–11.

Santoloupo, S., & Pratt, M. (1994). Age, gender, and parenting style variations in mother–adolescent dialogues and adolescent reasoning about political issues. *Journal of Adolescent Research, 9,* 241–261.

Sarason, I. G. (1980). *Test anxiety: Theory, research, and applications.* Hillsdale, NJ: Erlbaum.

Sarrazin, G., et al. (2000). *WISC-III, Échelle d'intelligence de Wechs pour Enfants troisième édition, adaptation canadienne-française, Manuel d'administration.*

Toronto: The Psychological Corporation.

Savage, A. R., Petersen, M. B., Pettay, D., Taft, L., Allran, K., Freeman, S. B., Karadima, G., Avramopoulos, D., Torfs, C., Mikkelsen, M., & Hassold, T. J. (1998). Elucidating the mechanisms of paternal non-disjunction of chromosome 21 in humans. *Human Molecular Genetics, 7,* 1221–1227.

Savage-Rumbaugh, E. S. (2001). *Apes, language, and the human mind.* New York: Oxford University Press.

Savage-Rumbaugh, E. S., Murphy, J., Sevcik, R. A., Brakke, K. E., Williams, S. L., & Rumbaugh, D. M. (1993). Language comprehension in ape and child. *Monographs of the Society for Research in Child Development, 58*(3–4, Serial No. 233).

Savin-Williams, R. C. (1998). *. . . And then I became gay: Young men's stories.* New York: Routledge.

Savin-Williams, R. C., & Berndt, T. J. (1990). Friendship and peer relations. In S. S. Feldman & G. R. Elliott (Eds.), *At the threshold: The developing adolescent* (pp. 277–307). Cambridge, MA: Harvard University Press.

Saxe, G. B. (1985). Effects of schooling on arithmetical understanding: Studies with Oksapmin children in Papua New Guinea. *Journal of Educational Psychology, 77,* 503–513.

Saxe, G. B. (1988, August–September). Candy selling and math learning. *Educational Researcher, 17*(6), 14–21.

Saywitz, K. J., & Nathanson, R. (1993). Children's testimony and their perceptions of stress in and out of the courtroom. *Child Abuse and Neglect, 17,* 613–622.

Scaramella, L. V., Conger, R. D., Simons, R. L., & Whitbeck, L. B. (1998). Predicting risk for pregnancy by late adolescence: A social contextual perspective. *Developmental Psychology, 34,* 1233–1245.

Scarr, S. (1985). Constructing psychology: Making facts and fables for our times. *American Psychologist, 40,* 499–512.

Scarr, S. (1996). Individuality and community: The contrasting role of the state in family life in the United States and Sweden. *Scandinavian Journal of Psychology, 37,* 93–102.

Scarr, S. (1997). Behavior-genetic and socialization theories of intelligence: Truce and reconciliation. In R. J. Sternberg & E. L. Grigorenko (Eds.), *Intelligence, heredity, and environment* (pp. 3–41). New York: Cambridge University Press.

Scarr, S., & McCartney, K. (1983). How people make their own environments: A theory of genotype environment effects. *Child Development, 54,* 424–435.

Scarr, S., & Weinberg, R. A. (1983). The Minnesota Adoption Studies: Genetic differences and malleability. *Child Development, 54,* 260–267.

Schauble, L. (1996). The development of scientific reasoning in knowledge-rich contexts. *Developmental Psychology, 32,* 102–119.

Scher, A., Tirosh, E., Jaffe, M., Rubin, L., Sadeh, A., & Lavie, P. (1995). Sleep patterns of infants and young children in Israel. *International Journal of Behavioral Development, 18,* 701–711.

Schiavi, R. C., Theilgaard, A., Owen, D., & White, D. (1984). Sex chromosome anomalies, hormones, and aggressivity. *Archives of General Psychiatry, 41,* 93–99.

Schlaud, M., Eberhard, C., Trumann, B., Kleemann, W. J., Poets, C. F., Tietze, K. W., & Schwartz, F. W. (1999). Prevalence and determinants of prone sleeping position in infants: Results for two cross-sectional studies on risk factors for SIDS in Germany. *American Journal of Epidemiology, 150,* 51–57.

Schlegel, A. (1995). A cross-cultural approach to adolescence. *Ethos, 23,* 5–32.

Schlegel, A., & Barry, H., III. (1980). The evolutionary significance of adolescent initiation ceremonies. *American Ethnologist, 7,* 696–715.

Schlegel, A., & Barry, H., III. (1991). *Adolescence: An anthropological inquiry.* New York: Free Press.

Schmidt, U. (2000). Eating disorders. In D. Kohen (Ed.), *Women and mental health* (pp. 174–197). London: Routledge.

Schmitz, M. K. H., & Jeffery, R. W. (2000). Public health interventions for the prevention and treatment of obesity. *Medical Clinics of North America, 84,* 491–512.

Schmitz, S., Fulker, D. W., Plomin, R., Zahn-Waxler, C., Emde, R. N., & DeFries, J. C. (1999). Temperament and problem behaviour during early childhood. *International Journal of Behavioural Development, 23,* 333–355.

Schneider, B. H., Atkinson, L., & Tardif, C. (2001). Child–parent attachment and children's peer relations: A quantitative review. *Developmental Psychology, 37,* 86–100.

Schneider, B. H., Fonzi, A., Tani, F., & Tomada, G. (1997). A cross-cultural exploration of the stability of children's friendships and the predictors of their continuation. *Social Development, 6,* 322–339.

Schneider, M., & Witherspoon, J. J. (2000). Friendship patterns among lesbian and gay youth: An exploratory study. *The Canadian*

*Journal of Human Sexuality, 9,* 239–246.

Schneider, W. (1986). The role of conceptual knowledge and metamemory in the development of organizational processes in memory. *Journal of Experimental Child Psychology, 42,* 218–236.

Schneider, W., & Bjorklund, D. F. (1992). Expertise, aptitude, and strategic remembering. *Child Development, 63,* 461–473.

Schneider, W., & Bjorklund, D. F. (1998). Memory. In D. Kuhn & R. S. Siegler (Eds.), *Handbook of child psychology: Vol. 2. Cognition, perception, and language* (5th ed., pp. 467–521). New York: Wiley.

Schneider, W., & Pressley, M. (1997). *Memory development between two and twenty* (2nd ed.). Mahwah, NJ: Erlbaum.

Schnur, E., & Belanger, S. (2000). What works in Head Start. In M. P. Kluger & G. Alexander (Eds.), *What works in child welfare* (pp. 277–284). Washington, DC: Child Welfare League of America.

Schoggen, P. (1991). Ecological psychology: One approach to development in context. In R. Cohen & A. W. Siegel (Eds.), *Context and development* (pp. 281–301). Hillsdale, NJ: Erlbaum.

Scholl, B. J., & Leslie, A. M. (2000). Minds, modules, and meta-analysis. *Child Development, 72,* 696–701.

Scholl, T. O., Heidiger, M. L., & Belsky, D. (1996). Prenatal care and maternal health during adolescent pregnancy: A review and meta-analysis. *Journal of Adolescent Health, 15,* 444–456.

Scholnick, E. K. (1995, Fall). Knowing and constructing plans. *SRCD Newsletter,* pp. 1–2, 17.

Schonert-Reichel, K. A. (1999). Relations of peer acceptance, friendship adjustment, and social behavior to moral reasoning during early adolescence. *Journal of Early Adolescence, 19,* 249–279.

Schonfeld, A. M., Mattson, S. N., Lang, A. R., Delis, D. C., & Riley, E. P. (2001). Verbal and nonverbal fluency in children with heavy prenatal alcohol exposure. *Journal of Studies on Alcohol, 62,* 239–246.

Schothorst, P. F., & van Engeland, H. (1996). Long-term behavioral sequelae of prematurity. *Journal of the American Academy of Child and Adolescent Psychiatry, 35,* 175–183.

Schuengel, G., Bakermans-Kranenburg, M. J., & van IJzendoorn, M. H. (1999). Attachment and loss: Frightening maternal behavior linking unresolved loss and disorganized infant attachment. *Journal of Consulting and Clinical Psychology, 67,* 54–63.

Schull, W. J., & Otake, M. (1999). Cognitive function and prenatal exposure to ionizing radiation. *Teratology, 59,* 222–226.

Schulman, J. D., & Black, S. H. (1997). Screening for Huntington disease and certain other dominantly inherited disorders: A case for preimplantation genetic testing. *Journal of Medical Screening, 4,* 58–59.

Schult, C. A. (1999). *Children's ability to identify intentions and desires.* Paper presented at the biennial meeting of the Society for Research in Child Development, Albuquerque, NM.

Schunk, D. H. (1994). Self-regulation of self-efficacy and attributions in academic settings. In D. H. Schunk & B. J. Zimmerman (Eds.), *Self-regulation of learning and performance* (pp. 75–100). Hillsdale, NJ: Erlbaum.

Schunk, D. H., & Ertmer, P. A. (2000). Self-regulation and academic learning: Self-efficacy enhancing interventions. In M. Boekaerts & P. R. Pintrich (Eds.), *Handbook of self-regulation* (pp. 631–649). San Diego, CA: Academic Press.

Schunk, D. H., & Zimmerman, B. J. (Eds.). (1994). *Self-regulation of learning and performance.* Englewood Cliffs, NJ: Erlbaum.

Schuster, B., Ruble, D. N., & Weinert, F. E. (1998). Causal inferences and the positivity bias in children: The role of the covariation principle. *Child Development, 69,* 1577–1596.

Schwanenflugel, P. J., Fabricius, W. V., & Noyes, C. R. (1996). Developing organization of mental verbs: Evidence for the development of a constructivist theory of mind in middle childhood. *Cognitive Development, 11,* 265–294.

Schwanenflugel, P. J., Henderson, R. L., & Fabricius, W. V. (1998). Developing organisation of mental verbs and theory of mind in middle childhood: Evidence from extensions. *Developmental Psychology, 34,* 514–524.

Schwebel, D. C., Rosen, C. S., & Singer, J. L. (1999). Preschoolers' pretend play and theory of mind: The role of jointly constructed pretense. *British Journal of Developmental Psychology, 17,* 333–348.

Scott, K. D., Berkowitz, G., & Klaus, M. (1999). A comparison of intermittent and continuous support during labor: A meta-analysis. *American Journal of Obstetrics and Gynecology, 180,* 1054–1059.

Scruggs, T. E., & Mastropieri, M. A. (1994). Successful mainstreaming in elementary science classes: A qualitative study of three reputational cases. *American Educational Research Journal, 31,* 785–811.

Seginer, R. (1998). Adolescents' perceptions of relationships with older siblings in the context of other close relationships. *Journal of Research on Adolescence, 8,* 287–308.

Seidenberg, M. S., & Petitto, L. A. (1987). Communication, symbolic communication, and language: Comment on Savage-Rumbaugh, McDonald, Sevcik, Hopkins, and Rupert. *Journal of Experimental Psychology: General, 116,* 279–287.

Seidman, E., & French, S. E. (1997). Normative school transitions among urban adolescents: When, where, and how to intervene. In H. J. Walberg, O. Reyes, & R. P. Weissberg (Eds.), *Children and youth: Interdisciplinary perspectives* (pp. 166–189). Thousand Oaks, CA: Sage.

Seifer, R. (2000). Temperament and goodness of fit: Implications for developmental psychopathology. In A. J. Sameroff & M. Lewis (Eds.), *Handbook of developmental psychopathology* (2nd ed., pp. 257–276). New York: Kluwer.

Seifer, R., & Schiller, M. (1995). The role of parenting sensitivity, infant temperament, and dyadic interaction in attachment theory and assessment. In E. Waters, B. E. Vaughn, G. Posada, & K. Kondo-Ikemura (Eds.), Caregiving, cultural, and cognitive perspectives on secure-base behavior and working models: New growing points of attachment theory and research. *Monographs of the Society for Research in Child Development, 60*(2–3, Serial No. 244).

Seifer, R., Schiller, M., Sameroff, A. J., Resnick, S., & Riordan, K. (1996). Attachment, maternal sensitivity, and infant temperament during the first year of life. *Developmental Psychology, 32,* 12–25.

Seitz, V., & Apfel, N. H. (1993). Adolescent mothers and repeated childbearing: Effects of a school-based intervention program. *American Journal of Orthopsychiatry, 63,* 572–581.

Seitz, V., & Apfel, N. H. (1994). Effects of a school for pregnant students on the incidence of low-birthweight deliveries. *Child Development, 65,* 666–676.

Seitz, V., Apfel, N. H., & Rosenbaum, L. K. (1991). Effects of an intervention program for pregnant adolescents: Educational outcomes at two years postpartum. *American Journal of Community Psychology, 6,* 911–930.

Seligman, M. E. P. (1975). *Helplessness: On depression, development, and death.* San Francisco: Freeman.

Selikowitz, M. (1997). *Down syndrome: The facts* (2nd ed.). Oxford: Oxford University Press.

Selman, R. L. (1976). Social-cognitive understanding: A guide to educational and clinical practice. In T. Lickona (Ed.), *Moral development and behavior: Theory, research, and social issues* (pp. 299–316). New York: Holt, Rinehart & Winston.

Selman, R. L. (1980). *The growth of interpersonal understanding.* New York: Academic Press.

Selman, R. L., & Byrne, D. F. (1974). A structural-developmental analysis of levels of role taking in middle childhood. *Child Development, 45,* 803–806.

Sen, M. G., Yonas, A., & Knill, D. C. (2001). Development of infants' sensitivity to surface contour information for spatial layout. *Perception, 30,* 167–176.

Sénéchal, M., & LeFevre, J. (2002). Parental involvement in the development of children's reading skill: A five-year longitudinal study. *Child Development, 73,* 445–461.

Sénéchal, M., LeFevre, J., Thomas, E. M., & Daley, K. E. (1998). Differential effects of home literacy experiences on the development of oral and written language. *Reading Research Quarterly, 33,* 96–116.

Senghas, A., & Coppola, M. (2001). Children creating language: How Nicaraguan sign language acquired a spatial grammar. *Psychological Science, 12,* 323–328.

Serbin, L. A., Connor, J. M., & Citron, C. C. (1978). Environmental control of independent and dependent behaviors in preschool girls and boys: A model for early independence training. *Sex Roles, 4,* 867–875.

Serbin, L. A., Connor, J. M., & Iler, I. (1979). Sex-stereotyped and non-stereotyped introductions of new toys in the preschool classroom: An observational study of teacher behavior and its effects. *Psychology of Women Quarterly, 4,* 261–265.

Serbin, L. A., Poulin-Dubois, D., Colburne, K. A., Sen, M. G., & Eichstedt, J. A. (2001). Gender stereotyping in infancy: Visual preferences for and knowledge of gender-stereotyped toys in the second year. *International Journal of Behavioral Development, 25,* 7–15.

Serbin, L. A., Powlishta, K. K., & Gulko, J. (1993). The development of sex typing in middle childhood. *Monographs of the Society for Research in Child Development, 58*(2, Serial No. 232).

Sethi, A., Mischel, W., Aber, J. L., Shoda, Y., & Rodriguez, M. L. (2000). The role of strategic attention deployment in development of self-regulation: Predicting preschoolers' delay of gratification from mother–toddler interactions. *Developmental Psychology, 36,* 767–777.

Sever, J. L. (1983). Maternal infections. In C. C. Brown (Ed.), *Childhood learning disabilities and prenatal risk* (pp. 31–38). New York: Johnson & Johnson.

Shafer, V. L., Shucard, D. W., & Jaeger, J. J. (1999). Electrophysiological indices of cerebral specialization and the role of prosody in language acquisition in 3-month-old infants. *Developmental Neuropsychology, 15,* 73–109.

Shahar, S. (1990). *Childhood in the Middle Ages.* London: Routledge & Kegan Paul.

Shainess, N. (1961). A re-evaluation of some aspects of femininity through a study of menstruation: A preliminary report. *Comparative Psychiatry, 2,* 20–26.

Shann, F., & Steinhoff, M. C. (1999). Vaccines for children in rich and poor countries. *Paediatrics, 354,* 7–11.

Shantz, C. U. (1987). Conflicts between children. *Child Development, 58,* 283–305.

Shapiro, A. F., Gottman, J. M., & Carrere, S. (2000). The baby and the marriage: Identifying factors that buffer against decline in marital satisfaction after the first baby arrives. *Journal of Family Psychology, 14,* 59–70.

Shedler, J., & Block, J. (1990). Adolescent drug use and psychological health: A longitudinal inquiry. *American Psychologist, 45,* 612–630.

Sheehy, A., Gasser, T., Molinari, L., & Largo, R. H. (1999). An analysis of variance of the pubertal and midgrowth spurts for length and width. *Annals of Human Biology, 26,* 309–331.

Shelton, T. L., Barkley, R. A., Crosswait, C., Moorehouse, M., Fletcher, K., Barrett, S., Jenkins, L., & Metevia, L. (1998). Psychiatric and psychological morbidity as a function of adaptive disability in preschool children with aggressive and hyperactive-impulsive-inattentive behavior. *Journal of Abnormal Child Psychology, 26,* 475–494.

Sherman, D. K., Iacono, W. G., & McGue, M. K. (1997). Attention-deficit hyperactivity disorder dimensions: A twin study of inattention and impulsivity–hyperactivity. *Journal of the American Academy of Child and Adolescent Psychiatry, 36,* 745–753.

Sherman, M., & Key, C. B. (1932). The intelligence of isolated mountain children. *Child Development, 3,* 279–290.

Shi, R., & Werker, W. F. (2001). Six-month-old infants' preference for lexical words. *Psychological Science, 12,* 70–76.

Shi, R., Werker, J. F., & Morgan, J. L. (1999). Newborn infants' sensitivity to perceptual cues to lexical and grammatical words. *Cognition, 72,* B11-B21.

Shields, P. J., & Rovee-Collier, C. K. (1992). Long-term memory for context-specific category information at six months. *Child Development, 63,* 245–259.

Shiller, V., Izard, C. E., & Hembree, E. A. (1986). Patterns of emotion expression during separation in the Strange Situation. *Developmental Psychology, 22,* 378–382.

Shiloh, S. (1996). Genetic counseling: A developing area of interest for psychologists. *Professional Psychology: Research and Practice, 27,* 475–486.

Shinn, M. W. (1900). *The biography of a baby.* Boston: Houghton Mifflin.

Shinskey, J. L., Bogartz, R. S., & Poirier, C. R. (2000). The effects of graded occlusion on manual search and visual attention in 5- to 8-month-old infants. *Infancy, 1,* 323–346.

Shoda, Y., Mischel, W., & Peake, P. K. (1990). Predicting adolescent cognitive and self-regulatory competencies from preschool delay of gratification: Identifying diagnostic conditions. *Developmental Psychology, 26,* 978–986.

Shonk, S. M., & Cicchetti, D. (2001). Maltreatment, competency deficits, and risk for academic and behavioral maladjustment. *Developmental Psychology, 37,* 3–17.

Shroff, F. (Ed.). (1997). *The new midwifery: Reflections on renaissance and regulation.* Toronto: Women's Press.

Shulman, S., Elicker, J., & Sroufe, A. (1994). Stages of friendship growth in preadolescence as related to attachment history. *Journal of Social and Personal Relationships, 11,* 341–361.

Shure, M. B. (1997). Interpersonal cognitive problem solving: Primary prevention of early high-risk behaviors in the preschool and primary years. In G. W. Albee & T. P. Gullotta (Eds.), *Primary prevention works* (pp. 167–188). Thousand Oaks, CA: Sage.

Shweder, R. A. (1996). True ethnography: The lore, the law, and the lure. In R. Jessor, A. Colby, & R. A. Shweder (Eds.), *Ethnography and human development* (pp. 15–52). Chicago: University of Chicago Press.

Shweder, R. A., Goodnow, J., Hatano, G., LeVine, R. A., Markus, H., & Miller, P. (1998). The cultural psychology of development: One mind, many mentalities. In R. M. Lerner (Ed.), *Handbook of child psychology: Vol. 1. Theoretical models of human development* (5th ed., pp. 865–937). New York: Wiley.

Shweder, R. A., Mahapatra, M., & Miller, J. G. (1990). Culture and moral development. In J. Stigler, R. A. Shweder, & G. Herdt (Eds.), *Cultural psychology: Essays on comparative human development* (pp. 130–204). New York: Cambridge University Press.

Siegel, B. (1996, Spring). Is the emperor wearing clothes? Social policy and the empirical support for full inclusion of children with disabilities in the preschool and early elementary school grades. *Social Policy Report of the Society for Research in Child Development, 10*(2–3), 2–17.

Siegel, L. S., & Wiener, J. (1993). Canadian special education policies: Children with learning disabilities in a bilingual and multicultural society. *Social Policy Report: Society for Research in Child Development, 7,* 1–15.

Siegler, R. S. (1988). Individual differences in strategy choices: Good students, not-so-good students, and perfectionists. *Child Development, 59,* 833–851.

Siegler, R. S. (1996). *Emerging minds: The process of change in children's thinking.* New York: Oxford University Press.

Siegler, R. S. (1998). *Children's thinking* (3rd ed.). Upper Saddle River, NJ: Prentice-Hall.

Siegler, R. S., & Crowley, K. (1991). The microgenetic method: A direct means for studying cognitive development. *American Psychologist, 46,* 606–620.

Siegler, R. S., & Ellis, S. (1996). Piaget on childhood. *Psychological Science, 7,* 211–215.

Siegler, R. S., & Jenkins, E. (1989). *How children discover new strategies.* Hillsdale, NJ: Erlbaum.

Siegler, R. S., & Richards, D. D. (1980). *College students' prototypes of children's intelligence.* Paper presented at the annual meeting of the American Psychological Association, New York.

Siegler, R. S., & Robinson, M. (1982). The development of numerical understandings. In H. W. Reese & L. P. Lipsitt (Eds.), *Advances in child development and behavior* (Vol. 16, pp. 241–312). New York: Academic Press.

Siervogel, R. M., Maynard, L. M., Wisemandle, W. A., Roche, A. F., Guo, S. S., Chumlea, W. C., & Towne, B. (2000). Annual changes in total body fat and fat-free mass in children from 8 to 18 years in relation to changes in body mass index: The Fels Longitudinal Study. *Annals of the New York Academy of Science, 904,* 420–423.

Sigman, M. (1999). Developmental deficits in children with Down syndrome. In H. Tager-Flusberg (Ed.), *Neurodevelopmental disorders: Developmental cognitive neuroscience* (pp. 179–195). Cambridge, MA: MIT Press.

Sigman, M., & Whaley, S. E. (1998). The role of nutrition in the development of intelligence. In U. Neisser (Ed.), *The rising curve* (pp. 155–182). Washington, DC: American Psychological Association.

Sigman, M., Cohen, S. E., & Beckwith, L. (1997). Why does infant attention predict adolescent intelligence? *Infant Behavior and Development, 20,* 133–140.

Signorella, M. L., Bigler, R. S., & Liben, L. S. (1993). Developmental differences in children's gender schemata about others: A meta-analytic review. *Developmental Review, 13,* 147–183.

Signorielli, N. (1993). Television, the portrayal of women, and children's attitudes. In G. L. Berry & J. K. Asamen (Eds.), *Children and television: Images in a changing sociocultural world* (pp. 229–242). Newbury Park, CA: Sage.

Signorielli, N. (2001). Television's gender-role images and contribution to stereotyping. In D. G. Singer & J. L. Singer (Eds.), *Handbook of children and the media* (pp. 341–358). Thousand Oaks, CA: Sage.

Sim, T. N. (2000). Adolescent psychosocial competence: The importance and role of regard for parents. *Journal of Research on Adolescence, 10,* 49–64.

Simmons, R. G., & Blyth, D. A. (1987). *Moving into adolescence.* New York: Aldine De Gruyter.

Simner, M. L. (1995). *Predicting and preventing early school failure: Classroom activities for the preschool child.* Ottawa: Canadian Psychological Association.

Simner, M. L. (1998). *Promoting reading success: Phonological awareness activities for the kindergarten child.* Ottawa: Canadian Psychological Association.

Simner, M. L. (2002). *Pour apprendre à bien lire: Activités de sensibilisation phonologique à l'intention des élèves du jardin d'enfants.* Ottawa: Canadian Psychological Association.

Simon, R., Altstein, H., & Melli, M. S. (1994). *The case for transracial adoption.* Washington, DC: American University Press.

Simons, D. J., & Keil, F. C. (1995). An abstract to concrete shift in the development of biological thought: The insides story. *Cognition, 56,* 129–163.

Simons, R. L., & Chao, W. (1996). Conduct problems. In R. L. Simons & Associates (Eds.), *Understanding differences between divorced and intact families* (pp. 125–143). Thousand Oaks, CA: Sage.

Simons, R. L., Lorenz, F. O., Wu, C.-I., & Conger, R. D. (1993). Social network and marital support as mediators and moderators of the impact of stress and depression on parental behavior. *Developmental Psychology, 29,* 368–381.

Simons, R. L., Whitbeck, L. B., Conger, R. D., & Chyi-In, W. (1991). Intergenerational transmission of harsh parenting. *Developmental Psychology, 27,* 159–171.

Simonton, D. K. (1988). *Scientific genius: A psychology of science.* New York: Cambridge University Press.

Simpson, J. M. (2001). Infant stress and sleep deprivation as an aetiological basis for the sudden infant death syndrome. *Early Human Development, 61*, 1–43.

Singer, D. G. (1999). Imaginative play and television: Factors in a child's development. In J. A. Singer & P. Salovey (Eds.), *At play in the fields of consciousness: Essays in honor of Jerome L. Singer* (pp. 303–326). Mahwah, NJ: Erlbaum.

Singh, S., & Darroch, J. E. (2000). Adolescent pregnancy and childbearing: Levels and trends in developed countries. *Family Planning Perspectives, 32*, 14–23.

Sippola, L., Bukowski, W. M., & Noll, R. B. (1997). Age differences in children's and early adolescents' liking for same-sex and other-sex peers. *Merrill-Palmer Quarterly, 43*, 547–561.

Sitskoorn, M. M., & Smitsman, A. W. (1995). Infants' perception of dynamic relations between objects: Passing through or support? *Developmental Psychology, 31*, 437–447.

Sivard, R. L. (1996). *World military and social expenditures* (16th ed.). Leesburg, VA: WMSE.

Skinner, B. F. (1957). *Verbal behavior.* New York: Appleton-Century-Crofts.

Skinner, E. A. (1995). *Perceived control, motivation, and coping.* Thousand Oaks, CA: Sage.

Skinner, E. A., Zimmer-Gembeck, M. J., & Connell, J. P. (1998). Individual differences and the development of perceived control. *Monographs of the Society for Research in Child Development, 63*(2–3, Serial No. 254).

Skoe, E. S. A. (1998). The ethic of care: Issues in moral development. In E. E. A. Skoe & A. L. von der Lippe (Eds.), *Personality development in adolescence* (pp. 143–171). London: Routledge.

Skouteris, H., McKenzie, B. E., & Day, R. H. (1992). Integration of sequential information for shape perception by infants: A developmental study. *Child development, 63*, 1164–1176.

Slaby, R. G., & Frey, K. S. (1975). Development of gender constancy and selective attention to same-sex models. *Child Development, 46*, 849–856.

Slaby, R. G., Roedell, W. C., Arezzo, D., & Hendrix, K. (1995). *Early violence prevention.* Washington, DC: National Association for the Education of Young Children.

Slater, A., Bremner, G., Johnson, S. P., Sherwood, P., Hayes, R., & Brown, E. (2000). Newborn infants' preference for attractive faces: The role of internal and external facial features. *Infancy, 1*, 265–274.

Slater, A., & Johnson, S. P. (1999). Visual sensory and perceptual abilities of the newborn: Beyond the blooming, buzzing confusion. In A. Slater & S. P. Johnson (Eds.), *The development of sensory, motor and cognitive capacities in early infancy* (pp. 121–141). Hove, UK: Sussex Press.

Slater, A., & Quinn, P. C. (2001). Face recognition in the newborn infant. *Infant and Child Development, 10*, 21–24.

Slater, A., Quinn, P. C., Brown, E., & Hayes, R. (1999). Intermodal perception at birth: Intersensory redundancy guides newborn infants' learning of arbitrary auditory–visual pairings. *Developmental Science, 2*, 333–338.

Slater, A. M., Brown, E., Mattock, A., & Bornstein, M. H. (1996). Continuity and change in habituation in the first 4 months from birth. *Journal of Reproductive and Infant Psychology, 14*, 187–194.

Slater, A. M., Mattock, A., & Brown, E. (1990). Size constancy at birth: Newborn infants' responses to retinal and real size. *Journal of Experimental Child Psychology, 49*, 314–322.

Slijper, F. M. E., Drop, S. L. S., de Molenaar, J. C., Keizer-Schrama, M., & Sabine, M. P. F. (1998). Long-term psychological evaluation of intersex children. *Archives of Sexual Behavior, 27*, 125–144.

Slobin, D. I. (1982). Universal and particular in the acquisition of language. In L. R. Gleitman & H. E. Wanner (Eds.), *Language acquisition: The state of the art* (pp. 128–170). Cambridge: Cambridge University Press.

Slobin, D. I. (1985). Crosslinguistic evidence for the language-making capacity. In D. I. Slobin (Ed.), *The crosslinguistic study of language acquisition: Vol. 2. Theoretical issues* (pp. 1157–1256). Hillsdale, NJ: Erlbaum.

Slobin, D. I. (Ed.). (1997). *The crosslinguistic study of language acquisition: Vol. 5. Expanding the contexts* (pp. 265–324). Mahwah, NJ: Erlbaum.

Smetana, J. G. (1981). Preschool children's conceptions of moral and social rules. *Child Development, 52*, 1333–1336.

Smetana, J. G. (1985). Preschool children's conceptions of transgressions: Effects of varying moral and conventional domain-related attributes. *Developmental Psychology, 21*, 18–29.

Smetana, J. G. (1995a). Conflict and coordination in adolescent–parent relationships. In S. Shulman (Ed.), *Close relationships and socioemotional development* (pp. 155–184). Norwood, NJ: Ablex.

Smetana, J. G. (1995b). Morality in context: Abstractions, ambiguities, and applications. In R. Vasta (Ed.), *Annals of child development* (Vol. 10, 83–130). London: Jessica Kingsley.

Smetana, J. G., & Asquith, P. (1994). Adolescents' and parents' conceptions of parental authority and adolescent autonomy. *Child Development, 65*, 1147–1162.

Smetana, J. G., & Braeges, J. L. (1990). The development of toddlers' moral and conventional judgments. *Merrill-Palmer Quarterly, 36*, 329–346.

Smith, A. E., Jussim, L., Eccles, J., VanNoy, M., Madon, S., & Palumbo, P. (1998). Self-fulfilling prophecies, perceptual biases, and accuracy at the individual and group levels. *Journal of Experimental Social Psychology, 34*, 530–561.

Smith, C. L., & Tager-Flusberg, H. (1982). Metalinguistic awareness and language development. *Journal of Experimental Child Psychology, 34*, 449–468.

Smith, E. P., Walker, K., Fields, L., Brookins, C. C., & Seay, R. C. (1999). Ethnic identity and its relationship to self-esteem, perceived efficacy, and prosocial attitudes in early adolescence. *Journal of Adolescence, 22*, 867–880.

Smith, J., & Prior, M. (1995). Temperament and stress resilience in school-age children: A within-families study. *Journal of the American Academy of Child and Adolescent Psychiatry, 34*, 168–179.

Smith, J. R., Brooks-Gunn, J., & Klebanov, P. K. (1997). The consequences of living in poverty for young children's cognitive and verbal ability and early school achievement. In G. J. Duncan & J. Brooks-Gunn (Eds.), *Consequences of growing up poor* (pp. 132–189). New York: Russell Sage Foundation.

Smith, K. E., Landry, S. H., Swank, P. R., Baldwin, C. D., Denson, S. E., & Wildin, S. (1996). The relation of medical risk and maternal stimulation with preterm infants' development of cognitive, language and daily living skills. *Journal of Child Psychology and Psychiatry, 37*, 855–864.

Smith, L. B. (1999). Children's noun learning: How general learning processes make specialized learning mechanisms. In B. MacWhinney (Ed.), *The emergence of language* (pp. 277–303). Mahwah, NJ: Erlbaum.

Smith, L. B., Quittner, A. L., Osberger, M. J., & Miyamoto, R. (1998). Audition and visual attention: The developmental trajectory in deaf and hearing populations. *Developmental Psychology, 34*, 840–850.

Smith, L. B., Thelen, E., Titzer, R., & McLin, D. (1999). Knowing in the context of acting: The task dynamics of the A-not-B error. *Psychological Review, 106*, 235–260.

Smith, M. L., Klim, P., & Hanley, W. B. (2000). Executive function in school-aged children with phenylketonuria. *Journal of Developmental and Physical Disabilities, 12*, 317–332.

Smith, P. K., & Hunter, T. (1992). Children's perceptions of play-fighting, playchasing and real fighting: A cross-national study. *Social Development, 1*, 211–229.

Smith, P. K., & Myron-Wilson, R. (1998). Parenting and school bullying. *Clinical Child Psychology and Psychiatry, 3*, 405–417.

Smith, R. (1999). The timing of birth. *Scientific American, 280*(3), 68–75.

Smith, S. (Ed.). (1995). Two-generation programs for families in poverty: A new intervention strategy. *Advances in applied developmental psychology* (Vol. 9). Norwood, NJ: Ablex.

Snarey, J. R. (1995). In a communitarian voice: The sociological expansion of Kohlbergian theory, research, and practice. In W. M. Kurtines & J. L. Gewirtz (Eds.), *Moral development: An introduction* (pp. 109–134). Boston: Allyn and Bacon.

Snarey, J. R., Reimer, J., & Kohlberg, L. (1985). The development of social-moral reasoning among kibbutz adolescents: A longitudinal cross-cultural study. *Developmental Psychology, 20*, 3–17.

Snidman, N., Kagan, J., Riordan, L., & Shannon, D. C. (1995). Cardiac function and behavioral reactivity. *Psychophysiology, 32*, 199–207.

Snow, C. E., Pan, B. A., Imbens-Bailey, A., & Herman, J. (1996). Learning how to say what one means: A longitudinal study of children's speech act use. *Social Development, 5*, 56–84.

So, L. K. H., & Dodd, B. J. (1995). The acquisition of phonology by Cantonese-speaking children. *Journal of Child Language, 22*, 473–495.

Society for Research in Child Development. (1993). Ethical standards for research with children. In *Directory of Members* (pp. 337–339). Ann Arbor, MI: Author.

Society of Obstetricians and Gynaecologists of Canada. (2002). *Sexual assault* [On-line]. Available: www.sexualityandu.ca/eng/teens/WIS/sexualassault.cfm

Soken, H. H., & Pick, A. D. (1992). Intermodal perception of happy and angry expressive behaviors by seven-month-old infants. *Child Development, 63*, 787–795.

Solomon, G. B., & Bredemeier, B. J. L. (1999). Children's moral conceptions of gender stratification in sport. *International Journal of Sport Psychology, 30*, 350–368.

Solomon, G. E. A., & Johnson, S. C. (2000). Conceptual change in the classroom: Teaching young children to understand biological inheritance. *British Journal of Developmental Psychology, 18*, 81–96.

Sonenstein, F. L., Pleck, J. H., & Ku, L. C. (1991). Levels of sexual activity among adolescent males in the United States. *Family Planning Perspectives, 23,* 162–167.

Sontag, C. W., Baker, C. T., & Nelson, V. L. (1958). Mental growth and personality development: A longitudinal study. *Monographs of the Society for Research in Child Development, 23*(2, Serial No. 68).

Sophian, C. (1995). Representation and reasoning in early numerical development: Counting, conservation, and comparisons between sets. *Child Development, 66,* 559–577.

Sorce, J., Emde, R., Campos, J., & Klinnert, M. (1985). Maternal emotional signaling: Its effect on the visual cliff behavior of 1-year-olds. *Developmental Psychology, 21,* 195–200.

Sosa, R., Kennell, J., Klaus, M., Robertson, S., & Urrutia, J. (1980). The effect of a supportive companion on perinatal problems, length of labor, and mother–infant interaction. *New England Journal of Medicine, 303,* 597–600.

Spätling, L., & Spätling, G. (1988). Magnesium supplementation in pregnancy: A double-blind study. *British Journal of Obstetrics and Gynecology, 95,* 120–125.

Spearman, C. (1927). *The abilities of man: Their nature and measurement.* New York: Macmillan.

Speer, J. R., & Flavell, J. H. (1979). Young children's knowledge of the relative difficulty of recognition and recall memory tasks. *Developmental Psychology, 15,* 214–217.

Speicher, B. (1994). Family patterns of moral judgment during adolescence and early adulthood. *Developmental Psychology, 30,* 624–632.

Spelke, E. (2000). Core knowledge. *American Psychologist, 55,* 1233–1242.

Spelke, E. S. (1987). The development of intermodal perception. In P. Salapatek & L. Cohen (Eds.), *Handbook of infant perception: Vol. 2. From perception to cognition* (pp. 233–273). Orlando, FL: Academic Press.

Spelke, E. S., Breinlinger, K., Macomber, J., & Jacobson, K. (1992). Origins of knowledge. *Psychological Review, 99,* 605–632.

Spelke, E. S., & Hermer, L. (1996). Early cognitive development: Objects and space. In R. Gelman & T. K. Au (Eds.), *Perceptual and cognitive development* (pp. 71–114). San Diego: Academic Press.

Spelke, E. S., & Newport, E. L. (1998). Nativism, empiricism, and the development of knowledge. In R. M. Lerner (Ed.), *Handbook of child psychology: Vol. 1. Theoretical models of human development* (5th ed., pp. 199–254). New York: Wiley.

Spence, M. J., & DeCasper, A. J. (1987). Prenatal experience with low-frequency maternal voice sounds influences neonatal perception of maternal voice samples. *Infant Behavior and Development, 10,* 133–142.

Spencer, J. P., Verejiken, B., Diedrich, F. J., & Thelen, E. (2000). Posture and the emergence of manual skills. *Developmental Science, 3,* 216–233.

Spencer, P. E., Bodner-Johnson, B. A., & Gutfreund, M. K. (1992). Interacting with infants with a hearing loss: What can we learn from mothers who are deaf? *Journal of Early Intervention, 16,* 64–78.

Spencer, P. E., & Lederberg, A. (1997) Different modes, different models: Communication and language of young deaf children and their mothers. In L. B. Adamson & M. Romski (Eds.), *Communication and language acquisition: Discoveries from atypical development* (pp. 203–230). Baltimore, MD: Paul H. Brookes.

Spencer, P. E., & Meadow-Orlans, K. P. (1996). Play, language, and maternal responsiveness: A longitudinal study of deaf and hearing infants. *Child Development, 67,* 3176–3191.

Spindler, G. D. (1970). The education of adolescents: An anthropological perspective. In D. Ellis (Ed.), *Adolescents: Readings in behavior and development* (pp. 152–161). Hinsdale, IL: Dryden.

Spitz, R. A. (1946). Anaclitic depression. *Psychoanalytic Study of the Child, 2,* 313–342.

Spitzer, S., Cupp., R., & Parke, R. D. (1995). School entrance age, social acceptance, and self-perceptions in kindergarten and first grade. *Early Childhood Research Quarterly, 10,* 433–450.

Spock, B., & Parker, S. J. (1998). *Dr. Spock's baby and child care* (7th ed.). New York: Pocket.

Sridhar, D., & Vaughn, S. (2001). Social functioning of students with learning disabilities. In D. P. Hallahan & B. K. Keogh (Eds.), *Research and global perspectives in learning disabilities* (pp. 65–91). Mahwah, NJ: Erlbaum.

Sroufe, L. A. (1979). The ontogenesis of emotion. In J. D. Osofsky (Ed.), *Handbook of infant development* (pp. 462–516). New York: Wiley.

Sroufe, L. A. (1985). Attachment classification from the perspective of infant–caregiver relationships and infant temperament. *Child Development, 56,* 1–14.

Sroufe, L. A., Egeland, B., & Kreutzer, T. (1990). The fate of early experience following developmental change: Longitudinal approaches to individual adaptation. *Child Development, 61,* 1363–1373.

Sroufe, L. A., & Waters, E. (1976). The ontogenesis of smiling and laughter: A perspective on the organization of development in infancy. *Psychological Review, 83,* 173–189.

Sroufe, L. A., & Wunsch, J. P. (1972). The development of laughter in the first year of life. *Child Development, 43,* 1324–1344.

Stack, D. M., & Muir, D. W. (1992). Adult tactile stimulation during face-to-face interactions modulates five-month-olds' affect and attention. *Child Development, 63,* 1509–1525.

Stahl, S. A., McKenna, M. C., & Pagnucco, J. R. (1994). The effects of whole-language instruction: An update and reappraisal. *Educational Psychologist, 29,* 175–185.

Standley, J. M. (1998). The effect of music and multimodal stimulation on responses of premature infants in neonatal intensive care. *Pediatric Nursing, 24,* 532–538.

Stanger, J. D., & Gridina, N. (1999). *Media in the home: The fourth annual survey of parents and children.* Philadelphia: University of Pennsylvania, Annenberg Public Policy Center.

Stankov, L., Horn, J. L., Roy, T. (1980). On the relationship between Gf/Gc theory and Jensen's Level I/Level II theory. *Journal of Educational Psychology, 72,* 796–809.

Stark, L. J., Allen, K. D., Hurst, M., Nash, D. A., Rigney, B., & Stokes, T. F. (1989). Distraction: Its utilization and efficacy with children undergoing dental treatment. *Journal of Applied Behavior Analysis, 22,* 297–307.

Starkey, P. (1992). The early development of numerical reasoning. *Cognition, 43,* 93–126.

Statistics Canada. (1997, Dec. 7). 1996 Census: Mother tongue, home language, and knowledge of languages. *The Daily* [On-line]. Available: www.statcan.Daily/English/971202/d971202.htm

Statistics Canada. (1999). National longitudinal survey of children and youth, 1996/97. *The Daily* [On-line]. Available: www.statcan/Daily/English/990706/d990706a.htm

Statistics Canada. (1999, May 18). Divorces. *The Daily* [On-line]. Available: www.statcan.ca/Daily/English/990518/d990518b.htm

Statistics Canada. (1999, June 11). Family violence: A statistical profile: 1997. *The Daily* [On-line]. Available: www.statcan.ca/Daily/English/990611/d990611a.htm

Statistics Canada. (1999, June 16). Births: 1997. *The Daily* [On-line]. Available: www.statcan.ca/Daily/English/990616/d990616b.htm

Statistics Canada. (1999, July 6). National Longitudinal Survey of Children and Youth: Transition into adolescence. 1996/97. *The Daily* [On-line]. Available: www.statcan.ca/Daily/English/990706/d990706a.htm

Statistics Canada. (1999, September 1). Employment after childbirth. *The Daily* [On-line]. Available: www.statcan.ca/Daily/English/990706/d990706a.htm

Statistics Canada. (2000). Alcohol consumption by sex, age group and level of education, 1998–99 [On-line]. Available: www.statcan.ca/english/Pgdb/People/Health/health05a.htm

Statistics Canada. (2000, March 31). Health Reports: How healthy are Canadians? *The Daily* [On-line]. Available: www.statcan.ca/Daily/English/000331/d000331a.htm

Statistics Canada. (2000, July 24). Full-time university faculty, 1999/2000. *The Daily* [On-line]. Available: www.statcan.ca/Daily/English/000724/d000724j.htm

Statistics Canada. (2000, September 28). Divorces, 1998. *The Daily* [On-line]. Available: www.statcan.ca/Daily/English/000928/d000928b.htm

Statistics Canada. (2000, December 14). *Police resources in Canada, 2000* [On-line]. Available: www.statcan.ca/Daily/English/001214/d001214c.htm

Statistics Canada. (2001). 2001 Census consultation guide: Citizenship and immigration recent trends [On-line]. Available: www.statcan.ca/english/freepub/92-125-GIE/html/cit.htm

Statistics Canada. (2001). *People employed, by educational attainment* [On-line]. Available: www.statcan.ca/english/Pgdb/People/Labour/labor62.htm

Statistics Canada. (2001). Population by knowledge of official languages, showing age groups, for Canada, provinces and territories, 1996 Census-20% Sample Data. Catalogue No. 93F0024XDB96005 in the Nation Series [On-line]. Available: www.statcan.ca/english/census96/dec2/off.htm

Statistics Canada. (2001). *Selected dwelling characteristics and household equipment* [On-line]. Available: www.statcan.ca/english/Pgdb/People/Families/famil09c.htm

Statistics Canada. (2001, January 25). Television viewing. *The Daily* [On-line]. Available: www.statcan.ca/Daily/English/010125/d010125a.htm

Statistics Canada. (2001, May 22). Education in Canada: Enrolment in second language immersion programs. Catalogue no. 81-229-XIB [On-line]. Available: www.statcan.ca/english/Pgdb/People/Education/educ23a.htm

Statistics Canada. (2001, May 29). Canadian tobacco use monitoring survey. *The Daily* [On-line]. Available: www.statcan.ca/ Daily/English/010529/ d010529c.htm

Statistics Canada. (2001, June). Health indicators: Breastfeeding practices [On-line]. Available: www.statcan.ca/english/freepub/ 82-221-XIE/00601/high/ breast.htm

Statistics Canada. (2001, June 28). Family violence: Focus on child abuse and children at risk. *The Daily* [On-line]. Available: www.statcan.ca/Daily/English/ 011210/d011210b.htm

Statistics Canada. (2001, July 19). Crime Statistics in Canada. *Juristat, 21*(8). Catalogue no. 85-002-XPE

Statistics Canada. (2001, July 26). Household Internet use survey, 2000. *The Daily* [On-line]. Available: www.statcan.ca/Daily/ English/010726/d010726a.htm

Statistics Canada. (2001, November 14). School performance of children from immigrant families. *The Daily* [On-line]. Available: www.statcan.ca/English/edu/ tfeature/dailyNov14.htm

Statistics Canada. (2001, December 4). Measuring student knowledge and skills: The performance of Canada's youth in reading, mathematics and science. *The Daily* [On-line]. Available: www. statcan.ca/english/edu/feature/ perform.htm

Statistics Canada. (2001, December 10). Births: 1999. *The Daily* [On-line]. Available: www. statcan.ca/Daily/English/ 011210/d011210b.htm

Statistics Canada. (2002). *Family Studies Kit* [On-line]. Available: www.statcan.ca/english/kits/ Family/intro.htm

Statistics Canada. (2002). *Teen pregnancy, by outcome of pregnancy and age group, count and rate per 1,000 women aged 15 to 19, Canada, provinces and territories, 1998.* [On-line] Available: www.statcan.ca/english/freepub/ 82-221-XIE/00502/tables/ html/411.htm

Statistics Canada. (2002, January 23). Youth in transition survey, 2000. *The Daily* [On-line]. Available: www.statcan.ca/Daily/English/ 020123/d020123a.htm

Statistics Canada. (2002, March 11). Robert Glossop on the Canadian Family [On-line]. Available: www.statcan.ca/english/ads/ 11-008-XPE/family.html

Statistics Canada. (2000, September 28). Divorces, 1998. *The Daily* [On-line]. Available: www. statcan.ca/Daily/English/000928/ d000928b.htm

Stattin, H., & Kerr, M. (2000). Parental monitoring: A reinterpretation. *Child Development, 71*, 1072–1085.

Stattin, H., & Magnusson, D. (1990). *Pubertal maturation in female development.* Hillsdale, NJ: Erlbaum.

Steele, H., Steele, M., & Fonagy, P. (1996). Associations among attachment classifications of mothers, fathers, and their infants. *Child Development, 67*, 541–555.

Stein, J. H., & Reiser, L. W. (1994). A study of white middle-class adolescent boys' responses to "semenarche" (the first ejaculation). *Journal of Youth and Adolescence, 23*, 373–384.

Stein, N., & Levine, L. J. (1999). The early emergence of emotional understanding and appraisal: Implications for theories of development. In T. Dalgleish & M. J. Power (Eds.), *Handbook of cognition and emotion* (pp. 383–408). Chichester, UK: Wiley.

Stein, Z., Susser, M., Saenger, G., & Marolla, F. (1975). *Famine and human development: The Dutch hunger winter of 1944–1945.* New York: Oxford University Press.

Steinberg, L. (2001). We know some things: Parent–adolescent relationships in retrospect and prospect. *Journal of Research on Adolescence, 11*, 1–19.

Steinberg, L., & Morris, A. S. (2001). Adolescent development. *Annual Review of Psychology, 52*, 83–110.

Steinberg, L. D. (1984). The varieties and effects of work during adolescence. In M. Lamb, A. Brown, & B. Rogoff (Eds.), *Advances in developmental psychology* (Vol. 3, pp. 1–37). Hillsdale, NJ: Erlbaum.

Steinberg, L. D. (1986). Latchkey children and susceptibility to peer pressure: An ecological analysis. *Developmental Psychology, 22*, 433–439.

Steinberg, L. D. (1990). Interdependence in the family: Autonomy, conflict, and harmony in the parent–adolescent relationship. In S. S. Feldman & G. R. Elliott (Eds.), *At the threshold: The developing adolescent* (pp. 255–276). Cambridge, MA: Harvard University Press.

Steinberg, L. D. (1999). *Adolescence* (5th ed.). New York: McGraw-Hill.

Steinberg, L. D., Darling, N. E., & Fletcher, A. C. (1995). Authoritative parenting and adolescent development: An ecological journey. In P. Moen, G. H. Elder, & K. Luscher (Eds.), *Examining lives in context* (pp. 423–466). Washington, DC: American Psychological Association.

Steinberg, L. D., & Dornbusch, S. M. (1991). Negative correlates of part-time employment during adolescence: Replication and elaboration. *Developmental Psychology, 27*, 304–313.

Steinberg, L. D., Fegley, S., & Dornbusch, S. (1993). Negative impact of part-time work on adolescent adjustment: Evidence from a longitudinal study. *Developmental Psychology, 29*, 171–180.

Steinberg, L. D., Lamborn, S. D., Darling, N., Mounts, N. S., & Dornbusch, S. M. (1994). Overtime changes in adjustment and competence among adolescents from authoritative, authoritarian, indulgent, and neglectful families. *Child Development, 65*, 754–770.

Steinberg, L. D., & Silverberg, S. (1986). The vicissitudes of autonomy in early adolescence. *Child Development, 57*, 841–851.

Steinberg, S., & Bellavance, F. (1999). Characteristics and treatment of women with antenatal and postpartum depression. *International Journal of Psychiatry and Medicine, 29*, 209–233.

Steiner, J. E. (1979). Human facial expression in response to taste and smell stimulation. In H. W. Reese & L. P. Lipsitt (Eds.), *Advances in child development and behavior* (Vol. 13, pp. 257–295). New York: Academic Press.

Stenberg, C., & Campos, J. (1990). The development of anger expressions in infancy. In N. Stein, B. Leventhal, & T. Trabasso (Eds.), *Psychological and biological approaches to emotion* (pp. 247–282). Hillsdale, NJ: Erlbaum.

Stenberg, C., Campos, J., & Emde, R. (1983). The facial expression of anger in seven-month-old infants. *Child Development, 54*, 178–184.

Stern, M., & Karraker, K. H. (1989). Sex stereotyping of infants: A review of gender labeling studies. *Sex Roles, 20*, 501–522.

Sternberg, R. J. (1985). *Beyond IQ: A triarchic theory of human intelligence.* New York: Cambridge University Press.

Sternberg, R. J. (1996a). The myths, countermyths, and truths about intelligence. *Educational Researcher, 25*, 11–16.

Sternberg, R. J. (1996b). *Successful intelligence: How practical and creative intelligence determine success in life.* New York: Simon & Schuster.

Sternberg, R. J. (1997). *Successful intelligence.*, New York: Plume.

Sternberg, R. J. (1999). A triarchic approach to understanding and assessment of intelligence in multicultural populations. *Journal of School Psychology, 37*, 145–159.

Sternberg, R. J., Forsythe, G. B., Hedlund, J., Horvath, J. A., Wagner, R. K., Williams, W. M., Snook, S. A., & Grigorenko, E. L. (2000). *Practical intelligence in everyday life.* Cambridge: Cambridge University Press.

Sternberg, R. J., & Detterman, D. K. (1986). *What is intelligence?* Norwood, NJ: Ablex.

Sternberg, R. J., & Lubart, T. I. (1991). An investment theory of creativity and its development. *Human Development, 34*, 1–31.

Sternberg, R. J., & Lubart, T. I. (1996). Investing in creativity. *American Psychologist, 51*, 677–688.

Sternberg, R. J., & Lubart, T. I. (1999). The concept of creativity: Prospects and paradigms. In R. J. Sternberg (Ed.), *Handbook of creativity* (pp. 3–15). Cambridge: Cambridge University Press.

Sternberg, R. J., & O'Hara, L. A. (1999). Creativity and intelligence. In R. J. Sternberg (Ed.), *Handbook of creativity* (pp. 251–272). Cambridge: Cambridge University Press.

Stetsenko, A., Little, T. D., Gordeeva, T., Grassof, M., & Oettingen, G. (2000). Gender effects in children's beliefs about school performance: A cross-cultural study. *Child Development, 71*, 517–527.

Stevenson, H. W. (1992, December). Learning from Asian schools. *Scientific American, 267*(6), 32–38.

Stevenson, H. W. (1994). Extracurricular programs in East Asian schools. *Teachers College Record, 95*, 389–407.

Stevenson, H. W., & Lee, S.-Y. (1990). Contexts of achievement: A study of American, Chinese, and Japanese children. *Monographs of the Society for Research in Child Development, 55*(1–2, Serial No. 221).

Stevenson, H. W., Lee, S., & Mu, X. (2000). Successful achievement in mathematics: China and the United States. In C. F. M. van Lieshout & P. G. Heymans (Eds.), *Developing talent across the lifespan* (pp. 167–183). Philadelphia: Psychology Press.

Stevenson, M. R., & Black, K. N. (1995). *How divorce affects offspring: A research approach.* Dubuque, IA: Brown & Benchmark.

Stevenson, R., & Pollitt, C. (1987). The acquisition of temporal terms. *Journal of Child Language, 14*, 533–545.

Steward, D. K. (2001). Behavioral characteristics of infants with nonorganic failure to thrive during a play interaction. *American Journal of Maternal Child Nursing, 26*, 79–85.

Stewart, P., Reihman, J., Lonky, E., Darvill, T., & Pagano, J. (2000). Prenatal PCB exposure and neonatal behavioral assessment scale (NBAS) performance. *Neurotoxicology and Teratology, 22*, 21–29.

Stice, E., & Barrera, M., Jr. (1995). A longitudinal examination of the reciprocal relations between perceived parenting and adolescents' substance use and externalizing behaviors. *Developmental Psychology, 31*, 322–334.

Stichick, T. (2001). The psychosocial impact of armed conflict on children. *Child and Adolescent*

Psychiatric Clinics of North America, 10, 797–814.

Stifter, C. A., Coulehan, C. M., & Fish, M. (1993). Linking employment to attachment: The mediating effects of maternal separation anxiety and interactive behavior. Child Development, 64, 1451–1460.

Stigler, J. W. (1984). "Mental abacus": The effect of abacus trainign on Chinese children's mental calculation. Cognitive Psychology, 16, 145–176.

Stiles, J. (1998). The effects of early focal brain injury on lateralization of cognitive function. Current Directions in Psychological Science, 7, 21–26.

Stiles, J. (2000). Spatial cognitive development following prenatal or perinatal focal brain injury. In H. S. Levin & J. Grafman (Eds.), Cerebral reorganization of function after brain damage (pp. 207–217). New York: Oxford University Press.

Stipek, D. (1995). The development of pride and shame in toddlers. In J. P. Tangney & K. W. Fischer (Eds.), Self-conscious emotions (pp. 237–252). New York: Guilford.

Stipek, D. J., & Byler, P. (1997). Early childhood education teachers: Do they practice what they preach? Early Childhood Research Quarterly, 12, 305–326.

Stipek, D. J., Gralinski, J. H., & Kopp, C. B. (1990). Self-concept development in the toddler years. Developmental Psychology, 26, 972–977.

Stipek, D. J., Recchia, S., & McClintic, S. (1992). Self-evaluation in young children. Monographs of the Society for Research in Child Development, 57(1, Serial No. 226).

St. James-Roberts, I., & Halil, T. (1991). Infant crying patterns in the first year: Normal community and clinical findings. Journal of Child Psychology and Psychiatry, 32, 951–968.

Stoch, M. B., Smythe, P. M., Moodie, A. D., & Bradshaw, D. (1982). Psychosocial outcome and CT findings after growth undernourishment during infancy: A 20-year developmental study. Developmental Medicine and Child Neurology, 24, 419–436.

Stocker, C. M., & Dunn, J. (1994). Sibling relationships in childhood and adolescence. In J. C. DeFries, R. Plomin, & D. W. Fulker (Eds.), Nature and nurture in middle childhood (pp. 214–232). Cambridge, MA: Blackwell.

Stocker, C. M., & McHale, S. M. (1992). The nature and family correlates of preadolescents' perceptions of their sibling relationships. Journal of Social and Personal Relationships, 9, 179–195.

Stodolsky, S. S. (1988). The subject matters. Chicago: University of Chicago Press.

Stoel-Gammon, C., & Otomo, K. (1986). Babbling development of hearing-impaired and normally hearing subjects. Journal of Speech and Hearing Disorders, 51, 33–41.

Stone, M. R., & Brown, B. B. (1999). Identity claims and projections: Descriptions of self and crowds in secondary school. In J. A. McLellan & M. J. V. Pugh (Eds.), The role of peer groups in adolescent social identity: Exploring the importance of stability and change (pp. 7–20). San Francisco: Jossey-Bass.

Stoneman, Z., Brody, G. H., & MacKinnon, C. E. (1986). Same-sex and cross-sex siblings: Activity choices, roles, behavior, and gender stereotypes. Sex Roles, 15, 495–511.

Stormshak, E. A., Bellanti, C. J., Bierman, K. L., & Conduct Problems Prevention Research Group. (1996). The quality of sibling relationships and the development of social competence and behavioral control in aggressive children. Developmental Psychology, 32, 79–89.

Stormshak, E. A., Bierman, K. L., Bruschi, C., Dodge, K. A., & Coie, J. D. (1999). The relation between behavior problems and peer preference in different classroom contexts. Child Development, 70, 169–182.

Stormshak, E. A., Bierman, K. L., McMahon, R. J., Lengua, L. J., and the Conduct Problems Prevention Research Group. (2000). Parenting practices and child disruptive behavior problems in early elementary school. Journal of Clinical Child Psychology, 29, 17–29.

Strain, P. S. (1977). An experimental analysis of peer social initiation on the behavior of withdrawn preschool children: Some training and generalization effects. Journal of Abnormal Child Psychology, 5, 445–455.

Strapp, C. M., & Federico, A. (2000). Imitations and repetitions: What do children say following recasts? First Language, 20, 273–290.

Strassberg, Z. (1995). Social information processing in compliance situations by mothers of behavior-problem boys. Child Development, 66, 376–389.

Strassberg, Z., Dodge, K., Pettit, G. S., & Bates, J. E. (1994). Spanking in the home and children's subsequent aggression toward kindergarten peers. Development and Psychopathology, 6, 445–461.

Straus, M. A., & Mathur, A. K. (1996). Social change and change in approval of corporal punishment by parents from 1968 to 1994. In D. Frehsee, W. Horn, & K.-D. Bussman (Eds.), Family violence against children: A challenge for society (pp. 91–105). New York: Walter de Gruyter.

Straus, M. A., & Stewart, J. H. (1999). Corporal punishment by American parents: National data on prevalence, chronicity, severity, and duration, in relation to child and family characteristics. Clinical Child and Family Psychology Review, 2, 55–70.

Strayer, J. (1993). Children's concordant emotions and cognitions in response to observed emotions. Child Development, 64, 188–201.

Streissguth, A. P. (1997). Fetal alcohol syndrome. Baltimore: Paul H. Brookes.

Streissguth, A. P., Barr, H. M., Bookstein, F. L., Sampson, P. D., & Olson, H. C. (1999). The long-term neurocognitive consequences of prenatal alcohol exposure: A 14-year study. Psychological Science, 10, 186–190.

Streissguth, A. P., Barr, H. M., Sampson, P. D., & Bookstein, F. L. (1994). Prenatal alcohol and offspring development: The first fourteen years. Drug and Alcohol Dependence, 36, 89–99.

Streissguth, A. P., Barr, H. M., Sampson, P. D., Darby, B. L., & Martin, D. C. (1989). IQ at age 4 in relation to maternal alcohol use and smoking during pregnancy. Developmental Psychology, 25, 3–11.

Streissguth, A. P., Treder, R., Barr, H. M., Shepard, T., Bleyer, W. A., Sampson, P. D., & Martin, D. (1987). Aspirin and acetaminophen use by pregnant women and subsequent child IQ and attention decrements. Teratology, 35, 211–219.

Strelau, J., Zawadzki, B., & Piotrowska, A. (2001). Temperament and intelligence: A psychometric approach to the links between both phenomena. In J. M. Collis & Messick (Eds.), Intelligence and personality (pp. 61–78). Mahwah, NJ: Erlbaum.

Streri, A., Lhote, M., & Dutilleul, S. (2000). Haptic perception in newborns. Developmental Science, 3, 319–327.

Striano, T., & Rochat, P. (2000). Emergence of selective social referencing in infancy. Infancy, 1, 253–264.

Stromswold, K. (1995). The acquisition of subject and object questions. Language Acquisition, 4, 5–48.

Stromsowld, K. (2000). The cognitive neuroscience of language acquisition. In M. S. Gazzaniga (Ed.), The new cognitive neurosciences (pp. 909–932). Boston: MIT Press.

Strouse, D. L. (1999). Adolescent crowd orientations: A social and temporal analysis. In J. A. McLellan & M. J. V. Pugh (Eds.), The role of peer groups in adolescent social identity: Exploring the importance of stability and change

(pp. 37–54). San Francisco: Jossey-Bass.

Stunkard, A. J., & Sørenson, T. I. A. (1993). Obesity and socioeconomic status—a complex relation. New England Journal of Medicine, 329, 1036–1037.

Stunkard, A. J., Sørenson, T. I. A., Hanis, C., Teasdale, T. W., Chakraborty, R., Schull, W. J., & Schulsinger, F. (1986). An adoption study of human obesity. New England Journal of Medicine, 314, 193–198.

Suarez-Orozco, C., & Suarez-Orozco, M. M. (1995). Transformation: Immigration, family life, and achievement motivation among Latino adolescents. Stanford, CA: Stanford University Press.

Subbotsky, E. V. (1994). Early rationality and magical thinking in preschoolers: Space and time. British Journal of Developmental Psychology, 12, 97–108.

Subrahmanyam, K., & Greenfield, P. M. (1996). Effect of video game practice on spatial skills in girls and boys. In P. M. Greenfield & R. R. Cocking (Eds.), Interacting with video (pp. 95–114). Norwood, NJ: Ablex.

Subrahmanyam, K., Greenfield, P., Kraut, R., & Gross, E. (2001). The impact of computer use on children's and adolescents' development. Applied Developmental Psychology, 22, 7–30.

Sullivan, H. S. (1953). The interpersonal theory of psychiatry. New York: Norton.

Sullivan, S. A., & Birch, L. L. (1990). Pass the sugar, pass the salt: Experience dictates preference. Developmental Psychology, 26, 546–551.

Super, C. M. (1981). Behavioral development in infancy. In R. H. Monroe, R. L. Monroe, & B. B. Whiting (Eds.), Handbook of cross-cultural human development (pp. 181–270). New York: Garland.

Sureau, C. (1997). Trials and tribulations of surrogacy: From surrogacy to parenthood. Human Reproduction, 12, 410–411.

Suzuki, L. A., & Valencia, R. R. (1997). Race–ethnicity and measured intelligence. American Psychologist, 52, 1103–1114.

Swain, M., & Lapkin, S. (1991). Additive bilingualism and French immersion education: The roles of language proficiency and literacy. In A. Reynolds (Ed.) Bilingualism, multiculturalism, and second language learning: The McGill Conference in Honour of Wallace E. Lambert (pp. 203–216). Hillsdale, NJ: Lawrence Erlbaum Associates.

Swanson, H. L. (1990). Influence of metacognitive knowledge and aptitude on problem solving. Journal of Educational Psychology, 82, 306–314.

Swendsen, J. D., & Mazure, C. M. (2000). Life stress as a risk factor for postpartum depression: Current research and methodological issues. *Clinical Psychology—Science and Practice, 7*, 17–31.

Szepkouski, G. M., Gauvain, M., & Carberry, M. (1994). The development of planning skills in children with and without mental retardation. *Journal of Applied Developmental Psychology, 15*, 187–206.

Szkrybalo, J., & Ruble, D. N. (1999). "God made me a girl": Sex-category constancy judgments and explanations revisited. *Developmental Psychology, 35*, 392–402.

Taddio, A., Katz, J., Ilersich, A. L., & Koren, G. (1997). Effect of neonatal circumcision on pain response during subsequent routine vaccination. *Lancet, 349*, 599–603.

Tager-Flusberg, H. (2001). Putting words together: Morphology and syntax in the preschool years. In J. Berko Gleason (Ed.), *The development of language* (4th ed., pp. 159–209). Boston: Allyn and Bacon.

Takahashi, K. (1990). Are the key assumptions of the "Strange Situation" procedure universal? A view from Japanese research. *Human Development, 33*, 23–30.

Tamis-LeMonda, C. S., & Bornstein, M. H. (1994). Specificity in mother–toddler language–play relations across the second year. *Developmental Psychology, 30*, 283–292.

Tamis-LeMonda, C. S., Bornstein, M. H., & Baumwell, L. (2001). Maternal responsiveness and children's achievement of language milestones. *Child Development, 72*, 748–767.

Tangney, J. P. (2001). Constructive and destructive aspects of shame and guilt. In A. C. Bohart & D. J. Stipek (Eds.), *Constructive and destructive behavior* (pp. 127–145). Washington, DC: American Psychological Association.

Taniguchi, H. (1999). The timing of childbearing and women's wages. *Journal of Marriage and the Family, 61*, 1008–1019.

Tanner, J. M. (1990). *Foetus into man* (2nd ed.). Cambridge, MA: Harvard University Press.

Tanner, J., M., Healy, M., & Cameron, N. (2001). *Assessment of skeletal maturity and prediction of adult height (TW3 method)* (3rd ed.). Philadelphia: Saunders.

Tardif, T., Gelman, S. A., & Xu, F. (1999). Putting the "noun bias" in context: A comparison of English and Mandarin. *Child Development, 70*, 620–635.

Tassabehji, M. K., Metcalfe, K., Fergusson, W. D., Carette, M. J. A., Dore, J. F., Donnai, D., Read, A. P., Proschel, C., Gutowski, N. J., Mao, X., & Sheer, D. (1996). LIM-kinase detected in Williams syndrome. *Nature Genetics, 13*, 272–273.

Tauber, M. A. (1979). Parental socialization techniques and sex differences in children's play. *Child Development, 50*, 225–234.

Taylor, J. H., & Walker, L. J. (1997). Moral climate and the development of moral reasoning: The effects of dyadic discussions between young offenders. *Journal of Moral Education, 26*, 21–43.

Taylor, M. (1996). The development of children's beliefs about the social and biological aspects of gender differences. *Child Development, 67*, 1555–1571.

Taylor, M. (1999). *Imaginary companions and the children who create them.* New York: Oxford University Press.

Taylor, M., & Carlson, S. M. (1997). The relation between individual differences in fantasy and theory of mind. *Child Development, 68*, 436–455.

Taylor, M., Esbensen, B. M., & Bennett, R. T. (1994). Children's understanding of knowledge acquisition: The tendency for children to report that they have always known what they have just learned. *Child Development, 65*, 1581–1604.

Taylor, M. C., & Hall, J. A. (1982). Psychological androgyny: Theories, methods, and conclusions. *Psychological Bulletin, 92*, 347–366.

Taylor, R. D., & Roberts, D. (1995). Kinship support and maternal and adolescent well-being in economically disadvantaged African-American families. *Child Development, 66*, 1585–1597.

Taylor, R. L. (2000). Diversity within African-American families. In D. H. Demo & K. R. Allen (Eds.), *Handbook of family diversity* (pp. 232–251). New York: Oxford University Press.

Teller, D. Y. (1997). First glances: The vision of infants. *Investigative Ophthalmology and Visual Science, 38*, 2183–2203.

Teller, D. Y. (1998). Spatial and temporal aspects of infant color vision. *Vision Research, 38*, 3275–3282.

Tellings, A. (1999). Psychoanalytical and genetic-structuralistic approaches of moral development: Incompatible views? *Psychoanalytic Review, 86*, 903–914.

Temple, C. M., & Carney, R. A. (1995). Patterns of spatial functioning in Turner's syndrome. *Cortex, 31*, 109–118.

Templeton, L. M., & Wilcox, S. A. (2000). A tale of two representations: The misinformation effect and children's developing theory of mind. *Child Development, 71*, 402–416.

Tepper, C. A., & Cassidy, K. W. (1999). Gender differences in emotional language in children's picture books. *Sex Roles, 40*, 265–280.

Terestchenko, N. Y., Lyaginskaya, A. M., & Burtzeva, L. I. (1991). Stochastic, nonstochastic effects and some population-genetic characteristics in children of the critical group in period of basic organogenesis. In *The scientific and practical aspects of preservation of health of the people exposed to radiation influence as a result of the accident at the Chernobyl atomic power station* (in Russian) (pp. 73–74). Minsk: Publishing House of Belarussian Committee "Chernobyl Children."

Terman, L., & Oden, M. H. (1959). *Genetic studies of genius: Vol. 4. The gifted group at midlife.* Stanford, CA: Stanford University Press.

Terrace, H. S., Petitto, L. A., Sanders, R. J., & Bever, T. G. (1980) . On the grammatical capacity of apes. In K. E. Nelson (Ed.), *Children's language* (Vol. 2, pp. 371–495). New York: Cambridge University Press.

Terwel, J., Gillies, R. M., van den Eeden, P., & Hoek, D. (2001). Cooperative learning processes of students: A longitudinal multi-level perspective. *British Journal of Educational Psychology, 71*, 619–645.

Teti, D. M., & McGourty, S. (1996). Using mothers versus trained observers in assessing children's secure base behavior: Theoretical and methodological considerations. *Child Development, 67*, 597–605.

Teti, D. M., Gelfand, D. M., Messinger, D. S., & Isabella, R. (1995). Maternal depression and the quality of early attachment: An examination of infants, preschoolers, and their mothers. *Developmental Psychology, 31*, 364–376.

Teti, D. M., Saken, J. W., Kucera, E., & Corns, K. M. (1996). And baby makes four: Predictors of attachment security among preschool-age firstborns during the transition to siblinghood. *Child Development, 67*, 579–596.

Thalidomide Victims Association of Canada (2000). *Thalidomide Victims Association of Canada* [On-line]. Available: www.thalidomide.ca

Tharp, R. G. (1993). Institutional and social context of educational practice and reform. In E. A. Forman, N. Minick, & C. A. Stone (Eds.), *Contexts for learning* (pp. 269–282). New York: Oxford University Press.

Tharp, R. G. (1994). Intergroup differences among Native Americans in socialization and child cognition: An ethnogenetic analysis. In P. M. Greenfield & R. Cocking (Eds.), *Cross-cultural roots of minority child development* (pp. 87–105). Hillsdale, NJ: Erlbaum.

Tharp, R. G., & Gallimore, R. (1988). *Rousing minds to life: Teaching, learning, and schooling in social context.* New York: Cambridge University Press.

Thatcher, R. W. (1991). Maturation of human frontal lobes: Physiological evidence for staging. *Developmental Neuropsychology, 7*, 397–419.

Thatcher, R. W., Lyon, G. R., Rumsey, J., & Krasnegor, J. (1996). *Developmental neuroimaging.* San Diego, CA: Academic Press.

Thelen, E. (1989). The (re)discovery of motor development: Learning new things from an old field. *Developmental Psychology, 25*, 946–949.

Thelen, E. (1994). Three-month-old infants can learn task-specific patterns of interlimb coordination. *Psychological Science, 5*, 280–285.

Thelen, E. (1995). Motor development: A new synthesis. *American Psychologist, 50*, 79–95.

Thelen, E. (2001). Dynamic mechanisms of change in early perceptual–motor development. In J. L. McClelland & R. S. Siegler (Eds.), *Mechanisms of cognitive development: Behavioral and neural perspectives* (pp. 161–184). Mahwah, NJ: Erlbaum.

Thelen, E., & Adolph, K. E. (1992). Arnold Gesell: The paradox of nature and nurture. *Developmental Psychology, 28*, 368–380.

Thelen, E., Corbetta, D., Kamm, K., Spencer, J. P., Schneider, K., & Zernicke, R. F. (1993). The transition to reaching: Mapping intention and intrinsic dynamics. *Child Development, 64*, 1058–1098.

Thelen, E., Corbetta, D., & Spencer, J. P. (1996). Development of reaching during the first year: Role of movement speed. *Journal of Experimental Psychology: Human Perception and Performance, 22*, 1059–1076.

Thelen, E., Fisher, D. M., & Ridley-Johnson, R. (1984). The relationship between physical growth and a newborn reflex. *Infant Behavior and Development, 7*, 479–493.

Thelen, E., & Smith, L. B. (1998). Dynamic systems theories. In R. M. Lerner (Ed.), *Handbook of child psychology: Vol. 1. Theoretical models of human development* (5th ed., pp. 563–634). New York: Wiley.

Thoman, E. B., & Ingersoll, E. W. (1993). Learning in premature infants. *Developmental Psychology, 29*, 692–700.

Thoman, E. B., & Whitney, M. P. (1990). Behavioral states in infants: Individual differences and individual analyses. In J. Colombo & J. W. Fagen (Eds.), *Individual differences in infancy: Reliability, stability, and prediction* (pp. 113–135). Hillsdale, NJ: Erlbaum.

Thomas, A., & Chess, S. (1977). *Temperament and development*. New York: Brunner/Mazel.

Thomas, A., Chess, S., & Birch, H. G. (1968). *Temperament and behavior disorders in children*. New York: New York University Press.

Thomas, R. M. (2000). *Comparing theories of child development* (5th ed.). Belmont, CA: Wadsworth.

Thompson, L. A., Detterman, D. K., & Plomin, R. (1991). Associations between cognitive abilities and scholastic achievement: Genetic overlap but environmental differences. *Psychological Science, 2,* 158–165.

Thompson, P. M., Giedd, J. N., Woods, R. P., MacDonald, D., Evans, A. C., & Toga, A. W. (2000). Growth patterns in the developing brain detected by using continuum mechanical tensor maps. *Nature, 404,* 190–192.

Thompson, R. A. (1990a). On emotion and self-regulation. In R. A. Thompson (Ed.), *Nebraska Symposium on Motivation* (Vol. 36, pp. 383–483). Lincoln: University of Nebraska Press.

Thompson, R. A. (1990b). Vulnerability in research: A developmental perspective on research risk. *Child Development, 61,* 1–16.

Thompson, R. A. (1992). Developmental changes in research risk and benefit: A changing calculus of concerns. In B. Stanley & J. E. Sieber (Eds.), *Social research on children and adolescents: Ethical issues* (pp. 31–64). Newbury Park, CA: Sage.

Thompson, R. A. (1994). Emotion regulation: A theme in search of definition. In N. A. Fox (Ed.), The development of emotion regulation: Biological and behavioral considerations. *Monographs of the Society for Research in Child Development, 59*(2–3, Serial No. 240).

Thompson, R. A. (1998). Early socio-personality development. In N. Eisenberg (Ed.), *Handbook of child psychology: Vol. 3. Social, emotional, and personality development* (5th ed., pp. 25–104). New York: Wiley.

Thompson, R. A. (2000). The legacy of early attachments. *Child Development, 71,* 145–152.

Thompson, R. A., & Leger, D. W. (1999). From squalls to calls: The cry as a developing socioemotional signal. In B. Lester, J. Newman, & F. Pedersen, (Eds.), *Biological and social aspects of infant crying*. New York: Plenum.

Thompson, R. A., & Limber, S. (1991). "Social anxiety" in infancy: Stranger wariness and separation distress. In H. Leitenberg (Ed.), *Handbook of social and evaluation anxiety* (pp. 85–137). New York: Plenum.

Thompson, R. A., & Nelson, C. A. (2001). Developmental science and the media: Early brain development. *American Psychologist, 56,* 5–15.

Thornberry, T. P. (1998). Membership in youth gangs and involvement in serious and violent juvenile offending. In R. Loeber & D. P. Farrington (Eds.), *Serious and violent juvenile offenders: Risk factors and successful interventions* (pp. 147–166). Thousand Oaks, CA: Sage.

Thorndike, R. L., Hagen, E. P., & Sattler, J. M. (1986). *The Stanford-Binet Intelligence Scale: Fourth edition. Guide for administering and scoring*. Chicago: Riverside Publishing.

Thorne, B. (1993). *Gender play: Girls and boys in school*. New Brunswick, NJ: Rutgers University Press.

Thornton, S. (1999). Creating conditions for cognitive change: The interaction between task structures and specific strategies. *Child Development, 70,* 588–603.

Thurstone, L. L. (1938). *Primary mental abilities*. Chicago: University of Chicago Press.

Tienari, P., Wynne, L. C., Moring, J., & Lahti, I. (1994). The Finnish adoptive family study of schizophrenia: Implications for family research. *British Journal of Psychiatry, 164,* 20–26.

Tietjen, A., & Walker, L. (1985). Moral reasoning and leadership among men in a Papua, New Guinea village. *Developmental Psychology, 21,* 982–992.

Tiggemann, M., & Anesbury, T. (2000). Negative stereotyping of obesity in children: The role of controllability beliefs. *Journal of Applied Social Psychology, 30,* 1977–1993.

Tincoff, R., & Jusczyk, P. W. (1999). Some beginnings of word comprehension in 6-month-olds. *Psychological Science, 10,* 172–175.

Tisak, M. S. (1995). Domains of social reasoning and beyond. In R. Vasta (Ed.), *Annals of child development* (Vol. 11, pp. 95–130). London: Jessica Kingsley.

Tizard, B., & Rees, J. (1975). The effect of early institutional rearing on the behaviour problems and affectional relationships of four-year-old children. *Journal of Child Psychology and Psychiatry, 16,* 61–73.

Tolarova, M. (1986). Cleft lip and palate and isolated cleft palate in Czechoslovakia. *Advances in Bioscience, 61,* 251–268.

Tolson, J. M., & Urberg, K. A. (1993). Similarity between adolescent best friends. *Journal of Adolescent Research, 8,* 274–288.

Tomasello, M. (1995). Language is not an instinct. *Cognitive Development, 10,* 131–156.

Tomasello, M. (1999a). The human adaptation for culture. *Annual Review of Anthropology, 28,* 509–529.

Tomasello, M. (1999b). Understanding intentions and learning words in the second year of life. In M. Bowerman & S. Levinson (Eds.), *Language acquisition and conceptual development*. Cambridge: Cambridge University Press.

Tomasello, M. (2000). Do young children have adult syntactic competence? *Cognition, 74,* 209–253.

Tomasello, M., & Akhtar, N. (1995). Two-year-olds use pragmatic cues to differentiate reference to objects and actions. *Cognitive Development, 10,* 201–224.

Tomasello, M., Akhtar, N., Dodson, K., & Rekau, L. (1997). Differential productivity in young children's use of nouns and verbs. *Journal of Child Language, 24,* 373–387.

Tomasello, M., & Brooks, P. (1999). Early syntactic development: A construction grammar approach. In M. Barrett (Ed.), *The development of language* (pp. 161–190). London: UCL Press.

Tomasello, M., Call, J., & Gluckman, A. (1997). Comprehension of novel communicative signs by apes and human children. *Child Development, 68,* 1067–1080.

Tomasello, M., & Camaioni, L. (1997). A comparison of the gestural communication of apes and human infants. *Human Development, 40,* 7–24.

Tomasello, M., Striano, T., & Rochat, P. (1999). Do young children use objects as symbols? *British Journal of Developmental Psychology, 17,* 563–584.

Tong, S., Caddy, D., & Short, R. V. (1997). Use of dizygotic to monozygotic twinning ratio as a measure of fertility. *Lancet, 349,* 843–845.

Torff, B., & Gardner, H. (1999). The vertical mind—The case for multiple intelligences. In M. Anderson (Ed.), *The development of intelligence* (pp. 139–159). Hove, UK: Psychology Press.

Torrance, E. P. (1988). The nature of creativity as manifest in its testing. In R. J. Sternberg (Ed.), *The nature of creativity: Contemporary psychological perspectives* (pp. 43–75). New York: Cambridge University Press.

Toth, J. F., & Xu, X. (1999). Ethnic and cultural diversity in fathers' involvement: A racial/ethnic comparison of African-American, Hispanic, and white fathers. *Youth and Society, 31,* 76–99.

Touwen, B. C. L. (1984). Primitive reflexes—conceptual or semantic problem? In H. F. R. Prechtl (Ed.), *Continuity of neural functions from prenatal to postnatal life* (Clinics in Developmental Medicine, No. 94, pp. 115–125). Philadelphia: Lippincott.

Tower, R. B., Singer, D. G., Singer, J. L., & Biggs, A. (1979). Differential effects of television programming on preschoolers' cognition, imagination, and social play. *American Journal of Orthopsychiatry, 49,* 265–281.

Trasti, N., Vik, T., Jacobson, G., & Bakketeig, L. S. (1999). Smoking in pregnancy and children's mental and motor development at age 1 and 5 years. *Early Human Development, 55,* 137–147.

Treiman, R., Tincoff, R., Rodriguez, K., Mouzaki, A., & Francis, D. J. (1998). The foundations of literacy: Learning the sounds of letters. *Child Development, 69,* 1524–1540.

Tremblay, M. S., & Willms, J. D. (2000). Secular trends in the body mass index of Canadian children. *Canadian Medical Association Journal, 163,* 1429–1433.

Tremblay, R. E. (2000). The development of aggressive behaviour during childhood: What have we learned in the past century? *International Journal of Behavioral Development, 24,* 129–141.

Tremblay, R. E., Japel, C., Perusse, D., Voivin, M., Zoccolillo, M., Montplaisir, J., & McDuff, P. (1999). The search for the age of "onset" of physical aggression: Rousseau and Bandura revisited. *Criminal Behavior and Mental Health, 9,* 8–23.

Tremblay, R. E., Masse, B., Perron, D., Leblanc, M., Schwartzman, A., & Ledingham, J. (1992). Early disruptive behaviour, poor school achievement, delinquent behavior, and delinquent personality: Longitudinal analyses. *Journal of Consulting and Clinical Psychology, 60,* 64–72.

Tremblay, R. E. Pagani-Kurts, L., Mâsse, L., Vitaro, F., & Pihl, R. (1995). A bimodal preventive intervention for disruptive kindergarten boys: Its impact through mid-adolescence. *Journal of Consulting and Clinical Psychology, 63,* 560–568.

Tremblay, R. E., Schaal, B., Boulerice, B., Arseneault, L., Soussignan, R., & Perusse, D. (1997). Male physical aggression, social dominance, and testosterone levels at puberty: A developmental perspective. In A. Raine & P. A. Brennan (Eds.), *Biosocial bases of violence. NATO ASI Series: Series A: Life sciences* (Vol. 292, pp. 271–291). New York: Plenum.

Trent, K., & Harlan, S. L. (1994). Teenage mothers in nuclear and extended households. *Journal of Family Issues, 15,* 309–337.

Triandis, H. C. (1995). *Individualism and collectivism*. Boulder, CO: Westview Press.

Triandis, H. C. (1998, May). *Cross-cultural versus cultural psychology:*

*A synthesis?* Colloquium presented at Illinois Wesleyan University, Bloomington, IL.

Trickett, P. K., & Putnam, F. W. (1998). Developmental consequences of child sexual abuse. In P. K. Trickett & C. J. Schellenbach (Eds.), *Violence against children in the family and community* (pp. 39–56). Washington, DC: American Psychological Association.

Trivers, R. L. (1971). The evolution of reciprocal altruism. *Quarterly Review of Biology, 46,* 35–57.

Trocmé, N., MacLaurin, B., Fallon, B., Daciuk, J., Billingsley, D., Tourigny, M., et al. (2001). Canadian incidence study of reported child abuse and neglect: Final report. Ottawa, ON: Minister of Public Works and Government Services Canada.

Trocmé, N., MacLaurin, B., Fallon, B., Daciuk, J., Tourigny, M., & Billingsley, D. (2001a). Canadian incidence study of reported child abuse and neglect: Methodology. *Canadian Journal of Public Health, 92,* 259–263.

Troiana, R. P., & Flegal, K. M. (1998). Overweight children and adolescents: Description, epidemiology, and demographics. *Pediatrics, 101,* 497–504.

Tronick, E. Z. (1989). Emotions and emotional communication in infants. *American Psychologist, 44,* 115–123.

Tronick, E. Z., & Cohn, J. F. (1989). Infant–mother face-to-face interaction: Age and gender differences in coordination and the occurrence of miscoordination. *Child Development, 60,* 85–92.

Tronick, E. Z., Morelli, G., & Ivey, P. (1992). The Efe forager infant and toddler's pattern of social relationships: Multiple and simultaneous. *Developmental Psychology, 28,* 568–577.

Tronick, E. Z., Thomas, R. B., & Daltabuit, M. (1994). The Quechua manta pouch: A caretaking practice for buffering the Peruvian infant against the multiple stressors of high altitude. *Child Development, 65,* 1005–1013.

Tröster, H., & Brambring, M. (1992). Early social-emotional development in blind infants. *Child: Care, Health and Development, 18,* 207–227.

Tröster, H., & Brambring, M. (1993). Early motor development in blind infants. *Journal of Applied Developmental Psychology, 14,* 83–106.

Truglio, R. (2000, April). *Research guides "Sesame Street."* Public lecture presented as part of the Consider the Children program, Illinois State University, Normal, IL.

Tsai, L. Y. (1999). Recent neurobiological research in autism. In D. B. Zager (Ed.), *Autism: Identification, education, and treatment* (2nd ed., pp. 63–95). Mahwah, NJ: Erlbaum.

Tucker, C. J., McHale, S. M., & Crouter, A. C. (2001). Conditions of siblings support in adolescence. *Journal of Family Psychology, 15,* 254–271.

Tudge, J. R. H. (1992). Processes and consequences of peer collaboration: A Vygotskian analysis. *Child Development, 63,* 1364–1379.

Tudge, J. R. H., & Winterhoff, P. A. (1993). Vygotsky, Piaget, and Bandura: Perspectives on the relations between the social world and cognitive development. *Human Development, 36,* 61–81.

Tunmer, W. E., & Nesdale, A. R. (1982). The effects of digraphs and pseudo-words on phonemic segmentation in young children. *Journal of Applied Psycholinguistics, 3,* 299–311.

Turiel, E. (1998). The development of morality. In N. Eisenberg (Ed.), *Handbook of child psychology: Vol. 3. Social, emotional, and personality development* (Vol. 3, pp. 863–932). New York: Wiley.

Turiel, E., Smetana, J. G., & Killen, M. (1991). Social contexts in social cognitive development. In W. M. Kurtines & J. L. Gewirtz (Eds.), *Handbook of moral behavior and development* (Vol. 2, pp. 307–332). Hillsdale, NJ: Erlbaum.

Turkle, S. (1995). *Life on the screen: Identity in the age of the Internet.* New York: Simon & Schuster.

Turnbull, M., Lapkin, S., Hart, D., & Swain, M. (1998). Time on task and immersion graduates' French proficiency. In S. Lapkin (Ed.), *French second-language education in Canada: Empirical studies* (pp. 31–55). Toronto: University of Toronto Press.

Turner, P. J., & Gervai, J. (1995). A multidimensional study of gender typing in preschool children and their parents: Personality, attitudes, preferences, behavior, and cultural differences. *Developmental Psychology, 31,* 759–772.

Turner, P. J., Gervai, J. & Hinde, R. A. (1993). Gender typing in young children: Preferences, behaviour and cultural differences. *British Journal of Developmental Psychology, 11,* 323–342.

Turner-Bowker, D. M. (1996). Gender stereotyped descriptors in children's picture books: Does "Curious Jane" exist in the literature? *Sex Roles, 35,* 461–488.

Turow, J. (1999). *The Internet and the family: The view from the parents, the view from the press* (Report No. 27). Philadelphia: Annenberg Public Policy Center of the University of Pennsylvania.

Tuss, P., Zimmer, J., & Ho, H.-Z. (1995). Causal attributions of underachieving fourth-grade students in China, Japan, and the United States. *Journal of Cross-Cultural Psychology, 26,* 408–425.

Twenge, J. M., & Campbell, W. K. (2001). Age and birth cohort differences in self-esteem: A cross-temporal meta-analysis. *Personality and Social Psychology Review, 5,* 321–344.

Tychsen, L. (2001). Critical periods for development of visual acuity, depth perception, and eye tracking. In D. B. Bailey, Jr., J. T. Bruer, F. J. Symons, & J. W. Lichtman (Eds.), *Critical thinking about critical periods* (pp. 67–82). Baltimore: Paul H. Brookes.

Tyrka, A. R., Graber, J. A., & Brooks-Gunn, J. (2000). The development of disordered eating: Correlates and predictors of eating problems in the context of adolescence. In A. J. Sameroff & M. Lewis (Eds.), *Handbook of developmental psychopathology* (2nd ed., pp. 607–624). New York: Kluwer.

Tzuriel, D. (2000). Dynamic assessment of young children: Educational and intervention perspectives. *Educational Psychology Review, 12,* 385–435.

Tzuriel, D., & Kaufman, R. (1999). Mediated learning and cognitive modifiability: Dynamic assessment of young Ethiopian immigrant children to Israel. *Journal of Cross-Cultural Psychology, 30,* 359–380.

U.S. Bureau of the Census. (1997). *Who's minding our preschoolers?* (Current Population Reports, P70-62). Washington, DC: U.S. Government Printing Office.

U.S. Bureau of the Census. (2001). *Statistical abstract of the United States* (121st ed.). Washington, DC: U.S. Government Printing Office.

U.S. Centers for Disease Control. (2001). *Sexually transmitted disease surveillance, 2000.* Atlanta: Author.

U.S. Department of Education. (1998). *Pursuing excellence: A study of U.S. twelfth-grade mathematics and science achievement in international context.* Washington, DC: U.S. Government Printing Office.

U.S. Department of Education, National Center for Education Statistics. (2001a). *Digest of educational statistics, 1999.* Washington, DC: U.S. Government Printing Office.

U.S. Department of Education. (2001b). *Digest of education statistics 2000.* Washington, DC: U.S. Government Printing Office.

U.S. Department of Education. (2001c). *Pursuing excellence: Comparisons of eighth-grade mathematics and science achievement from a U.S. perspective, 1995 and 1999.* Washington, DC: U.S. Government Printing Office.

U.S. Department of Health and Human Services. (2000a). *Report of the Surgeon General's Conference on Children's Mental Health.*

Washington, DC: U.S. Government Printing Office.

U.S. Department of Health and Human Services. (2000b). Youth risk behavior surveillance-United States, 1999. *Morbidity and Mortality Weekly Report, 49*(No. SS–5).

U.S. Department of Health and Human Services. (2001a). *Health United States 1999–2000 and injury chartbook.* Washington, DC: U.S. Bureau of the Census.

U.S. Department of Health and Human Services. (2001b). *National survey results on drug use from the Monitoring the Future Study. Vol. 1. Secondary school students.* Washington, DC: U.S. Government Printing Office.

U.S. Department of Health and Human Services. (2001c). *Preventing teenage pregnancy.* HHS Fact Sheet. [On-line] www.hhs.gov/news/press.

U.S. Department of Health and Human Services. (2001d). *Vital statistics of the United States.* Washington, DC: U.S. Government Printing Office.

U.S. Department of Justice. (2001). *Crime in the United States.* Washington, DC: U.S. Government Printing Office.

U.S. Department of Labor, Bureau of Labor Statistics. (2002, February). Consumer Price Index. *Monthly Labor Review, 124*(2).

U.S. Department of State. (1999). *Country Reports of Human Rights Practice.* [On-line]. Available: www.state.gov/global/humanrights

Udry, J. R. (1990). Hormonal and social determinants of adolescent sexual initiation. In J. Bancroft & J. M. Reinisch (Eds.), *Adolescence and puberty* (pp. 70–87). New York: Oxford University Press.

Uhari, M., Kontiokari, T., & Niemelä, M. (1998). A novel use of xylitol sugar in preventing acute otitis media. *Pediatrics, 102,* 879–884.

United Nations. (1999). *World social situation in the 1990s.* New York: Author.

Upchurch, D. M., Aneshensel, C. S., Sucoff, C. A., & Levy-Storms, L. (1999). Neighborhood and family contexts of adolescent sexual activity. *Journal of Marriage and the Family, 61,* 920–933.

Updegraff, K. A., & Obeidallah, D. A. (1999). Young adolescents' patterns of involvement with siblings and friends. *Social Development, 8,* 52–69.

Updegraff, K. A., McHale, S. M., & Crouter, A. C. (1996). Gender roles in marriage: What do they mean for girls' and boys' school achievement? *Journal of Youth and Adolescence, 25,* 73–88.

Uribe, F. M. T., LeVine, R. A., & LeVine, S. E. (1994). Maternal behavior in a Mexican community: The changing environments of children. In P. M. Greenfield & R. R. Cocking (Eds.), *Cross-cultural roots of minority child development* (pp. 41–54). Hillsdale, NJ: Erlbaum.

Usmiani, S., & Daniluk, J. (1997). Mothers and their adolescent daughters: Relationship between self-esteem, gender role identity, and body image. *Journal of Youth and Adolescence, 26,* 45–60.

Uttal, D. H., Gregg, V. H., Tan, L. S., Chamberlin, M. H., & Sines, A. (2001).Connecting the dots: Children's use of a systematic figure to facilitate mapping and search. *Developmental Psychology, 37,* 338–350.

Vaidyanathan, R. (1988). Development of forms and functions of interrogatives in children: A language study of Tamil. *Journal of Child Language, 15,* 533–549.

Vaidyanathan, R. (1991). Development of forms and functions of negation in the early stages of language acquisition: A study of Tamil. *Journal of Child Language, 18,* 51–66.

Valdés, G. (1998). The world outside and inside schools: Language and immigrant children. *Educational Researher, 27*(6), 4–18.

Valdez, R., Athens, M. A., Thompson, G. H., Bradshaw, G. H., & Stern, M. P. (1994). Birthweight and adult health outcomes in a biethnic population in the U.S.A. *Diabetologia, 37,* 624.

Valenza, E., Simion, F., Macchi, C. V., & Umiltá, C. (1996). Face preference at birth. *Journal of Experimental Psychology: Human Perception and Performance, 22,* 892–903.

Valian, V. (1999). Input and language acquisition. In W. C. Ritchie & T. K. Bhatia (Eds.), *Handbook of child language acquisition* (pp. 497–530). San Diego: Academic Press.

Valian, V. V. (1986). Syntactic categories in the speech of young children. *Developmental Psychology, 22,* 562–579.

Valian, V. V. (1991). Syntactic subjects in the early speech of American and Italian children. *Cognition, 40,* 21–81.

van den Boom, D. C. (1995). Do first-year intervention effects endure? Follow-up during toddlerhood of a sample of Dutch irritable infants. *Child Development, 66,* 1798–1816.

van den Boom, D. C., & Hoeksma, J. B. (1994). The effect of infant irritability on mother–infant interaction: A growth-curve analysis. *Developmental Psychology, 30,* 581–590.

van der Meer, A. L. H., van der Weel, F. R., & Lee, D. N. (1995). The functional significance of arm movements in neonates. *Science, 267,* 693–695.

van IJzendoorn, M. H. (1995). Adult attachment representations, parental responsiveness, and infant attachment: A meta-analysis on the predictive validity of the Adult Attachment Interview. *Psychological Bulletin, 117,* 411–415.

van IJzendoorn, M. H., & De Wolff, M. S. (1997). In search of the absent father—meta-analyses of infant-father attachment: A rejoinder to our discussants. *Child Development, 68,* 604–609.

van IJzendoorn, M. H., Goldberg, S., Kroonenberg, P. M., & Frenkel, O. J. (1992). The relative effects of maternal and child problems on the quality of attachment: A meta-analysis of attachment in clinical samples. *Child Development, 63,* 840–858.

van IJzendoorn, M. H., & Hubbard, F. O. A. (2000). Are infant crying and maternal responsiveness during the first year related to infant–mother attachment at 15 months? *Attachment and Human Development, 2,* 371–391.

van IJzendoorn, M. H., & Kroonenberg, P. M. (1988). Cross-cultural patterns of attachment: A meta-analysis of the Strange Situation. *Child Development, 59,* 147–156.

van IJzendoorn, M. H., & Sagi, A. (1999). Cross-cultural patterns of attachment. In J. Cassidy & P. R. Shaver (Eds.), *Handbook of attachment: Theory, research, and clinical applications* (pp. 713–734). New York: Guilford.

Vandell, D. L. (1999). When school is out: Analysis and recommendations. *The Future of Children, 9*(2). [On-line]. Available: www.futureofchildren.org

Vandell, D. L., & Hembree, S. E. (1994). Peer social status and friendship: Independent contributors to children's social and academic adjustment. *Merrill-Palmer Quarterly, 40,* 461–477.

Vandell, D. L., & Mueller, E. C. (1995). Peer play and friendships during the first two years. In H. C. Foot, A. J. Chapman, & J. R. Smith (Eds.), *Friendship and social relations in children* (pp. 181–208). New Brunswick, NJ: Transaction.

Vandell, D. L., & Posner, J. K. (1999). Conceptualization and measurement of children's after-school environments. In S. L. Friedman & T. D. Wachs (eds.), *Measuring environment across the life span* (pp. 167–196). Washington, DC: American Psychological Association.

Vandell, D. L., & Shumow, L. (1999). After-school child care programs. *Future of Children, 9*(2), 64–80.

Vandell, D. L., Wilson, K. S., & Buchanan, N. R. (1980). Peer interaction in the first year of life: An examination of its structure, content, and sensitivity to toys. *Child Development, 51,* 481–488.

Vanfossen, B., Jones, J., & Spade, J. (1987). Curriculum tracking and status maintenance. *Sociology of Education, 60,* 104–122.

Vanier Institute of the Family. (2001). Family Facts [On-line]. Available: http://www.vifamily.ca/faqs/faq.htm

Varendi, H., Christensson, K., Porter, R. H., & Winberg, J. (1998). Soothing effect of amniotic fluid smell in newborn infants. *Early Human Development, 51,* 47–55.

Varnhagen, C. K., Morrison, F. J., & Everall, R. (1994). Age and schooling effects in story recall and story production. *Developmental Psychology, 30,* 969–79.

Vartanian, L. R. (1997). Separation–individuation, social support, and adolescent egocentrism: An exploratory study. *Journal of Early Adolescence, 17,* 245–270.

Vartanian, L. R., & Powlishta, K. K. (1996). A longitudinal examination of the social-cognitive foundations of adolescent egocentrism. *Journal of Early Adolescence, 16,* 157–178.

Vasudev, J., & Hummel, R. C. (1987). Moral stage sequence and principled reasoning in an Indian sample. *Human Development, 30,* 105–118.

Vaughn, B. E., & Bost, K. K. (1999). Attachment and temperament: Redundant, independent, or interacting influences on interpersonal adaptation and personality development? In J. Cassidy & P. Shaver (Eds.), *Handbook of attachment: Theory, research, and clinical applications* (pp. 265–286). New York: Guilford.

Vaughn, B. E., Bradley, C. F., Joffe, L. S., Seifer, R., & Barglow, P. (1987). Maternal characteristics measured prenatally are predictive of ratings of temperamental "difficulty" on the Carey Infant Temperament Questionnaire. *Developmental Psychology, 23,* 152–161.

Vaughn, B. E., Colvin, T. N., Azria, M. R., Caya, L., & Krzysik, L. (2001). Dyadic analyses of friendship in a sample of preschool-age children attending Head Start: Correspondence between measures and implications for social competence. *Child Development, 72,* 862–878.

Vaughn, B. E., Egeland, B., Sroufe, L. A., & Waters, E. (1979). Individual differences in infant-mother attachment at twelve and eighteen months: Stability and change in families under stress. *Child Development, 50,* 971–975.

Vaughn, B. E., Kopp, C. B., & Krakow, J. B. (1984). The emergence and consolidation of self-control from eighteen to thirty months of age: Normative trends and individual differences. *Child Development, 55,* 990–1004.

Vaughn, S., & Klingner, J. K. (1998). Students' perceptions of inclusion and resource room settings. *Journal of Special Education, 32,* 79–88.

Velting, D. M., & Gould, M. (1997). Suicide contagion. In R. Maris, S. Canetto, & M. M. Silverman (Eds.), *Review of Suicidology, 1997* (pp. 96–137). New York: Guilford.

Ventura, S. J. (1989). Trends and variations in first births to older women in the United States, 1970–86. *Vital and Health Statistics* (Series 21). Hyattsville, MD: U.S. Department of Health and Human Services.

Ventura, S. J., & Freedman, M. A. (2000). Teenage childbearing in the United States, 1960–1997. *American Journal of Preventive Medicine, 19,* 18–25.

Verba, S., Schlozman, K. L., & Brady, H. E. (1995*). Voice and equality: Civic voluntarism in American politics.* Cambridge, MA: Harvard University Press.

Vergnaud, G. (1996). Education, the best portion of Piaget's heritage. *Swiss Journal of Psychology, 55,* 112–118.

Vernon, P. A. (1993). Intelligence and neural efficiency. In D. K. Detterman (Ed.), *Current topics in human intelligence* (Vol. 3, pp. 171–187). Norwood, NJ: Ablex.

Vernon, P. A., Wickett, J. C., Bazana, G., & Stelmack, R. M. (2001). The neuropsychology and psychophysiology of human intelligence. In R. J. Sternberg (Ed.), *Handbook of intelligence* (pp. 245–264). Cambridge: Cambridge University Press.

Vernon, P. E., (1987). The demise of the Stanford-Binet Scale. *Canadian Psychology, 28,* 251–258.

Vernon-Feagans, L., Manlove, E. E., & Volling, B. L. (1996). Otitis media and the social behavior of day-care-attending children. *Child Development, 67,* 1528–1539.

Vibbert, S., & Bornstein, M. H. (1989). Specific associations between domains of mother–child interaction and toddler referential language and pretend play. *Infant Behavior and Development, 12,* 163–184.

Victora, C. G., Bryce, J., Fontaine, O., & Monasch, R. (2000). Reducing deaths from diarrhea through oral rehydration therapy. *Bulletin of the World Health Organization, 78,* 1246–1255.

Vihman, M. M. (1996). *Phonological development.* London: Blackwell.

Vinden, P. G. (1996). Junín Quechua children's understanding of mind. *Child Development, 67,* 1707–1716.

Vitaro, F., Brendgen, M., & Tremblay, R. E. (2000). Influence of deviant friends on delinquency: Searching for moderator variables. *Journal of Abnormal Child Psychology, 28,* 313–325.

Vitaro, F., Larocque, D., Janosz, M., & Tremblay, R. E. (2001). Negative social experiences and dropping out of school. *Educational Psychology, 21,* 401-415.

Vogel, D. A., Lake, M. A., Evans, S., & Karraker, H. (1991). Children's and adults' sex-stereotyped perceptions of infants. *Sex Roles, 24,* 605–616.

Vondra, J. I., Hommerding, K. D., & Shaw, D. S. (1999). Stability and change in infant attachment in a low-income sample. In J. I Vondra & D. Barnett (Eds.), *Atypical attachment in infancy and early childhood among children at developmental risk. Monographs of the Society for Research in Child Development, 64*(3, Serial No. 258), 119–144.

von Hofsten, C. (1982). Eye–hand coordination in the newborn. *Developmental Psychology, 18,* 450–461.

von Hofsten, C., & Rosander, K. (1998). The establishment of gaze control in early infancy. In S. Simion & G. Butterworth (Eds.), *The development of sensory, motor and cognitive capacities in early infancy* (pp. 49–66). Hove, UK: Psychology Press.

Vorhees, C. V. (1986). Principles of behavioral teratology. In E. P. Riley & C. V. Vorhees (Eds.), *Handbook of behavioral teratology* (pp. 23–48). New York: Plenum.

Voss, L. D., Mulligan, J., & Betts, P. R. (1998). Short stature at school entry—an index of social deprivation? (The Wessex Growth Study). *Child: Care, Health and Development, 24,* 145–156.

Voyer, D., Voyer, S., & Bryden, M. P. (1995). Magnitude of sex differences in spatial abilities: A meta-analysis and consideration of critical variables. *Psychological Bulletin, 117,* 250–270.

Vurpillot, E. (1968). The development of scanning strategies and their relation to visual differentiation. *Journal of Experimental Child Psychology, 6,* 632–650.

Vygotsky, L. S. (1978). *Mind in society: The development of higher mental processes.* Cambridge, MA: Harvard University Press. (Original works published 1930, 1933, and 1935)

Vygotsky, L. S. (1986). *Thought and language* (A. Kozulin, Trans.). Cambridge, MA: MIT Press. (Original work published 1934)

Vygotsky, L. S. (1987). Thinking and speech. In R. W. Rieber, A. S. Carton (Eds.), & N. Minick (Trans.), *The collected works of L. S. Vygotsky: Vol. 1. Problems of general psychology* (pp. 37–285). New York: Plenum. (Original work published 1934)

Wachs, T. D. (1995). Relation of mild-to-moderate malnutrition to human development: Correlational studies. *Journal of Nutrition, 125,* 2245S–2254S.

Wachs, T. D. (1999). The what, why, and how of temperament: A piece of the action. In L. Balter & C. S. Tamis-LeMonda (Eds.), *Child psychology: A handbook of contemporary issues* (pp. 23–44). Philadelphia: Psychology Press.

Wachs, T. D. (2000). *Necessary but not sufficient: The respective roles of single and multiple influences on individual development.* Washington, DC: American Psychological Association.

Waddington, C. H. (1957). *The strategy of the genes.* London: Allen and Unwin.

Wagner, M. E., Schubert, H. J. P., & Schubert, D. S. P. (1993). Sex-of-sibling effects: Part 1. Gender role, intelligence, achievement, and creativity. In Hayne W. Reese (Ed.), *Advances in child development and behavior* (Vol. 24, pp. 181–214). San Diego: Academic Press.

Wagner, R. K. (1997). Intelligence, training, and employment. *American Psychologist, 52,* 1059–1069.

Wagner, R. K. (2000). Practical intelligence. In R. J. Sternberg (Ed.), *Handbook of intelligence* (pp. 380–395). Cambridge: Cambridge University Press.

Wahlsten, D. (1994). The intelligence of heritability. *Canadian Psychology, 35,* 244–259.

Wahlsten, D. (1997). The malleability of intelligence is not constrained by heritability. In B. Devlin, S. E. Feinberg, D. Resnick, & K. Roeder (Eds.), *Intelligence, genes and success: Scientists respond to the Bell Curve* (pp. 71–87). New York: Copernicus (Springer Verlag).

Wainryb, C. (1997). The mismeasure of diversity: Reflections on the study of cross-cultural differences. In H. D. Saltzstein (Ed.), *New directions for child development* (No. 76, pp. 51–65). San Francisco: Jossey-Bass.

Wainryb, C., & Ford, S. (1998). Young children's evaluations of acts based on beliefs different from their own. *Merrill-Palmer Quarterly, 44,* 484–503.

Wakeley, A., Rivera, S., & Langer, J. (2000). Can young infants add and subtract? *Child Development, 71,* 1477–1720.

Walberg, H. J. (1986). Synthesis of research on teaching. In M. C. Wittrock (Ed.), *Handbook of research on teaching* (3rd ed., pp. 214–229). New York: Macmillan.

Walden, T., Lemerise, E., & Smith, M. C. (1999). Friendship and popularity in preschool classrooms. *Early Education and Development, 10,* 351–371.

Waldfogel, J. (2001). International policies toward parental leave and child care. *Future of Children, 11*(2) [On-line]. Available: www.futureofchildren.org

Waldman, I. D. (1997). Unresolved questions and future directions in behavior-genetic studies of intelligence. In R. J. Sternberg & E. L. Grigorenko (Eds.), *Intelligence, heredity, and environment* (pp. 552–570). New York: Cambridge University Press.

Waldman, I. D., Weinberg, R. A., & Scarr, S. (1994). Racial-group differences in IQ in the Minnesota Transracial Adoption Study: A reply to Levin and Lynn. *Intelligence, 19,* 29–44.

Waldron, N. L., & McLeskey, J. (1998). The effects of an inclusive school program on students with mild and severe learning disabilities. *Exceptional Children, 64,* 395–405.

Walker, A., Rosenberg, M., & Balaban-Gil, K. (1999). Neurodevelopmental and neurobehavioral sequelae of selected substances of abuse and psychiatric medications in utero. *Neurological Disorders: Developmental and Behavioral Sequelae, 8,* 845–867.

Walker, L. J. (1980). Cognitive and perspective-taking prerequisites for moral development. *Child Development, 51,* 131–139.

Walker, L. J. (1989). A longitudinal study of moral reasoning. *Child Development, 60,* 157–166.

Walker, L. J. (1995). Sexism in Kohlberg's moral psychology? In W. M. Kurtines & J. L. Gewirtz (Eds.), *Moral development: An introduction* (pp. 83–107). Boston: Allyn and Bacon.

Walker, L. J., & Hennig, K. H. (1997). Moral development in the broader context of personality. In S. Hala (Ed.), *The development of social cognition* (pp. 297–327). Hove, UK: Psychology Press.

Walker, L. J., & Moran, T. J. (1991). Moral reasoning in a communist Chinese society. *Journal of Moral Education, 20,* 139–155.

Walker, L. J., Pitts, R. C., Hennig, K. H., & Matsuba, M. K. (1995). Reasoning about morality and real-life moral problems. In M. Killen & D. Hart (Eds.), *Morality in everyday life* (pp. 37–407). New York: Cambridge University Press.

Walker, L. J., Pitts, R. C., Hennig, K. H., & Matsuba, M. K. (1999). Reasoning about morality and real-life moral problems. In M. Killen & D. Hart (Eds.), *Morality in everyday life* (pp. 371–407). New York: Cambridge University Press.

Walker, L. J., & Richards, B. S. (1979). Stimulating transitions in moral reasoning as a function of stage of cognitive development. *Developmental Psychology, 15,* 95–103.

Walker, L. J., & Taylor, J. H. (1991a). Family interactions and the development of moral reasoning. *Child Development, 62,* 264–283.

Walker, L. J., & Taylor, J. H. (1991b). Stage transitions in moral reasoning: A longitudinal study of developmental processes. *Developmental Psychology, 27,* 330–337.

Walker-Andrews, A. S. (1997). Infants' perception of expressive behaviors: Differentiation of multimodal information. *Psychological Bulletin, 121,* 437–456.

Walker-Andrews, A. S., & Grolnick, W. (1983). Discrimination of vocal expressions by young infants. *Infant Behavior and Development, 6,* 491–498.

Wallerstein, J. S., & Kelly, J. B. (1980). *Surviving the break-up: How children and parents cope with divorce.* New York: Basic Books.

Wallerstein, J. S., Corbin, S. B., & Lewis, J. M. (1988). Children of divorce: A ten-year study. In E. M. Hetherington & J. Arasteh (Eds.), *Impact of divorce, single parenting, and stepparenting on children* (pp. 198–214). Hillsdale, NJ: Erlbaum.

Walton, L., Oliver, C., & Griffin, C. (1999). Divorce mediation: The impact of mediation on the psychological well-being of children and parents. *Journal of Community and Applied Social Psychology, 9,* 35–46.

Wanska, S. K., & Bedrosian, J. L. (1985). Conversational structure and topic performance in mother–child interaction. *Journal of Speech and Hearing Research, 28,* 579–584.

Wapner, R. J. (1997). Chorionic villus sampling. *Obstetrics and Gynecology Clinics of North America, 24,* 83–110.

Ward, L. M. (1995). Talking about sex: Common themes about sexuality in the prime-time television programs children and adolescents view most. *Journal of Youth and Adolescence, 24,* 595–616.

Wark, G. R., & Krebs, D. L. (1996). Gender and dilemma differences in real-life moral judgment. *Developmental Psychology, 32,* 220–230.

Warren, A. R., & Tate, C. S. (1992). Egocentrism in children's telephone conversations. In R. M. Diaz & L. E. Berk (Eds.), *Private speech: From social interaction to self-regulation* (pp. 245–264). Hillsdale, NJ: Erlbaum.

Warren, D. H. (1994). Blindness and children: An individual difference approach. New York: Cambridge University Press.

Waschbusch, D. A., Daleiden, E., & Drabman, R. S. (2000). Are parents accurate reporters of their child's cognitive abilities? *Journal of Psychopathology and Behavioral Assessment, 22,* 61–77.

Wasserman, G., Graziano, J. H., Factor-Litvak, P., Popovac, D., Morina, N., & Musabegovic, A. (1994). Consequences of lead exposure and iron supplementation on childhood development at age

4 years. *Neurotoxicology and Teratology, 16*, 233–240.

Wasserman, G. A., Liu, X., Pine, D. S., & Graziano, J. H. (2001). Contribution of maternal smoking during pregnancy and lead exposure to early childhood behavior problems. *Neurotoxicology and Teratology, 23*, 13–21.

Waters, E., & Cummings, E. M. (2000). A secure base from which to explore close relationships. *Child Development, 71*, 164–172.

Waters, E., Merrick, S., Treboux, D., Crowell, J., & Albersheim, L. (2000). Attachment security in infancy and early adulthood: A twenty-year longitudinal study. *Child Development, 71*, 684–689.

Waters, E., Vaughn, B. E., Posada, G., & Kondo-Ikemura K. (Eds.). (1995). Caregiving, cultural, and cognitive perspectives on secure-base behavior and working models: New growing points of attachment theory and research. *Monographs of the Society for Research in Child Development, 60*(2–3, Serial No. 244).

Watkins, W. E., & Pollitt, E. (1998). Iron deficiency and cognition among school-age children. In S. G. McGregor (Ed.), *Recent advances in research on the effects of health and nutrition on children's development and school achievement in the Third World.* Washington, DC: Pan American Health Organization.

Watson, A. C., Nixon, C. L., Wilson, A., & Capage, L. (1999). Social interaction skills and theory of mind in young children. *Developmental Psychology, 35*, 386–391.

Watson, D. J. (1989). Defining and describing whole language. *Elementary School Journal, 90*, 129–141.

Watson, J. B., & Raynor, R. (1920). Conditioned emotional reactions. *Journal of Experimental Psychology, 3*, 1–14.

Watson, J. S. (1972). Smiling, cooing, and "the game." *Merrill-Palmer Quarterly, 18*, 323–339.

Watson, M. (1990). Aspects of self development as reflected in children's role playing. In D. Cicchetti & M. Beeghly (Eds.), *The self in transition: Infancy to childhood* (pp. 281–307). Chicago: University of Chicago Press.

Wattigney, W. A., Srinivasan, S. R., Chen, W., Greenlund, K. J., & Berenson, G. S. (1999). Secular trend of earlier onset of menarche with increasing obesity in black and white girls: The Bogalusa Heart Study. *Ethnicity and Disease, 9*, 181–189.

Waxman, S. R., & Markow, D. B. (1998). Object properties and object kind: Twenty-one-month-old infants' extension of novel adjectives. *Child Development, 69*, 1313–1329.

Waxman, S. R., & Senghas, A. (1992). Relations among word meanings in early lexical development. *Developmental Psychology, 28*, 862–873.

Wechsler, D. (1989). *Manual for the Wechsler Preschool and Primary Scale of Intelligence–Revised.* New York: The Psychological Corporation.

Wechsler, D. (1991). *Manual for the Wechsler Intelligence Test for Children–III.* New York: The Psychological Corporation.

Wechsler, D. (1996). *Canadian Supplement Manual for the WISC–III.* Toronto: The Psychological Corporation.

Wehren, A., De Lisi, R., & Arnold, M. (1981). The development of noun definition. *Journal of Child Language, 8*, 165–175.

Weikart, D. P. (1998). Changing early childhood development through educational intervention. *Preventive Medicine, 27*, 233–237.

Weinberg, M. K., & Tronick, E. Z. (1994). Beyond the face: An empirical study of infant affective configurations of facial, vocal, gestural, and regulatory behaviors. *Child Development, 65*, 1503–1515.

Weinberg, M. K., Tronick, E. Z., Cohn, J. F., & Olson, K. L. (1999). Gender differences in emotional expressivity and self-regulation during early infancy. *Developmental Psychology, 35*, 175–188.

Weinberg, R., Tenenbaum, G., McKenzie, A., Jackson, S., Anshel, M., Grove, R., & Fogarty, G. (2000). Motivation for youth participation in sport and physical activity: Relationships to culture, self-reported activity levels, and gender. *International Journal of Sport Psychology, 31*, 321–346.

Weinfield, N. S., Sroufe, L. A., & Egeland, B. (2000). Attachment from infancy to early adulthood in a high-risk sample: Continuity, discontinuity, and their correlates. *Child Development, 71*, 695–702.

Weinraub, M., Clemens, L. P., Sockloff, A., Ethridge, T., Gracely, E., & Myers, B. (1984). The development of sex role stereotypes in the third year: Relationships to gender labeling, gender identity, sex-typed toy preference, and family characteristics. *Child Development, 55*, 1493–1503.

Weinstein, R. S., Marshall, H. H., Sharp, L., & Botkin, M. (1987). Pygmalion and the student: Age and classroom differences in children's awareness of teacher expectations. *Child Development, 58*, 1079–1093.

Weisberg, R. W. (1993). *Creativity: Beyond the myth of genius.* New York: Freeman.

Weisfeld, G. E. (1990). Sociobiological patterns of Arab culture. *Ethology and Sociobiology, 11*, 23–49.

Weisfeld, G. E. (1997). Puberty rites as clues to the nature of human adolescence. *Cross-Cultural Research, 31*, 27–54.

Weisner, T. S., & Wilson-Mitchell, J. E. (1990). Nonconventional family life-styles and sex typing in six-year-olds. *Child Development, 61*, 1915–1933.

Welder, A. (2000). Sexual abuse victimization and the child witness in Canada: Legal, ethical and professional issues for psychologists. *Canadian Psychology, 41*, 160–173.

Wellman, H. M. (1990). *The child's theory of mind.* Cambridge, MA: MIT Press.

Wellman, H. M., Cross, D., & Watson, J. (2001). Meta-analysis of theory-of-mind development: The truth about false belief. *Child Development, 72*, 655–684.

Wellman, H. M., & Gelman, S. A. (1998). Knowledge acquisition in foundational domains. In D. Kuhn & R. S. Siegler (Eds.), *Handbook of child psychology: Vol. 2. Cognition, perception, and language* (5th ed., pp. 523–630). New York: Wiley.

Wellman, H. M., & Hickling, A. K. (1994). The mind's "I": Children's conception of the mind as an active agent. *Child Development, 65*, 1564–1580.

Wellman, H. M., Hickling, A. K., & Schult, C. A. (1997). Young children's psychological, physical, and biological explanations. In H. M. Wellman & K. Inagaki (Eds.), *The emergence of core domains of thought: New directions for child development #75* (pp. 7–25). San Francisco: Jossey-Bass.

Wellman, H. M., & Phillips, A. T. (2001). Developing intentional understandings. In B. F. Malle, L. J. Moses, & D. A. Baldwin (Eds.), *Intentions and intentionality* (pp. 125–148). Cambridge, MA: MIT Press.

Wellman, H. M., Phillips, A. T., & Rodriquez, T. (2000). Young children's understanding of perception, desire, and emotion. *Child Development, 71*, 895–912.

Wellman, H. M., Somerville, S. C., & Haake, R. J. (1979). Development of search procedures in real-life spatial environments. *Developmental Psychology, 15*, 530–542.

Wen, S. W., Kramer, M. S., Liu, S., Dzakpasu, S., & Sauve, R., for the Fetal and Infant Health Study Group. (2000). Infant mortality by gestational age and birth weight in Canadian provinces and territories, 1990–1994 births. *Chronic Diseases in Canada, 21*, 14–22.

Wendland-Carro, J., Piccinini, C. A., & Millar, W. S. (1999). The role of an early intervention on enhancing the quality of mother–infant interaction. *Child Development, 70*, 713–721.

Wentworth, N., Benson, J. B., & Haith, M. M. (2000). The development of infants' reaches for stationary and moving targets. *Child Development, 71*, 576–601.

Wentworth, N., & Haith, M. M. (1992). Event-specific expectations of 2- and 3-month-old infants. *Developmental Psychology, 28*, 842–850.

Wentworth, N., & Haith, M. M. (1998). Infants' acquisition of spatiotemporal expectations. *Developmental Psychology, 24*, 247–257.

Werker, J. F., Cohen, L. B., Lloyd, V. L., Casasola, M., & Stager, C. L. (1998). Acquisition of word-object associations by 14-month-old infants. *Developmental Psychology, 34*, 1289–1309.

Werker, J. F., Fennell, C. T., Corcoran, K. M., & Stager, C. L. (2002). Infants' ability to learn phonetically similar words: Effects of age and vocabulary size. *Infancy, 3*, 1–30.

Werker, J. F., Pegg, J. E., & McLeod, P. (1994). A cross-language investigation of infant preference for infant-directed communication. *Infant Behavior and Development, 17*, 323–333.

Werker, J. F., & Tees, R. C. (1999). Influences on infant speech processing: Toward a new synthesis. *Annual Review of Psychology, 50*, 509–535.

Werner, E. E. (1989). Children of the Garden Island. *Scientific American, 260*(4), 106–111.

Werner, E. E. (1993). Risk, resilience, and recovery: Perspectives from the Kauai Longitudinal Study. *Development and Psychopathology, 5*, 503–515.

Werner, E. E., & Smith, R. S. (1982). *Vulnerable but invincible.* New York: McGraw-Hill.

Werner, E. E., & Smith, R. S. (1992). *Overcoming the odds: High risk children from birth to adulthood.* Ithaca, NY: Cornell University Press.

Wertheim, E. H., Paxton, S. J., Schutz, H. K., & Muir, S. L. (1997). Why do adolescent girls watch their weight? An interview study examining sociocultural pressures to be thin. *Journal of Psychosomatic Research, 42*, 345–355.

Wertsch, J. V., & Tulviste, P. (1992). L. S. Vygotsky and contemporary developmental psychology. *Developmental Psychology, 28*, 548–557.

Westen, D., & Gabbard, G. O. (1999). Psychoanalytic approaches to personality. In L. A. Pervin & O. P. John (Eds.), *Handbook of personality: Theory and research* (2nd ed., pp. 57–101). New York: Guilford.

Wheeler, M. D. (1991). Physical changes of puberty. *Endocrinology* and Metabolism Clinics of North America, 20, 1–14.

Whitaker, D. J., & Miller, K. S. (2000). Parent–adolescent discussions about sex and condoms: Impact on peer influences of sexual risk behavior. Journal of Adolescent Research, 15, 251–273.

White, B., & Held, R. (1966). Plasticity of sensorimotor development in the human infant. In J. F. Rosenblith & W. Allinsmith (Eds.), The causes of behavior (pp. 60–70). Boston: Allyn and Bacon.

White, J. L., Moffitt, T. E., Caspi, A., Bartusch, D. J., Needles, D. J., & Stouthamer-Loeber, M. (1996). Measuring impulsivity and examining its relationship to delinquency. Journal of Abnormal Psychology, 103, 192–205.

White, R. W. (1959). Motivation reconsidered: The concept of competence. Psychological Review, 66, 297–333.

White, S. H. (1992). G. Stanley Hall: From philosophy to developmental psychology. Developmental Psychology, 28, 25–34.

Whitehurst, G. J., Arnold, D. S., Epstein, J. N., Angell, A. L., Smith, M., & Fischel, J. E. (1994). A picture book reading intervention in day care and home for children from low-income families. Developmental Psychology, 30, 679–689.

Whitehurst, G. J., & Lonigan, C. J. (1998). Child development and emergent literacy. Child Development, 69, 848–872.

Whiteside, M. F., & Becker, B. J. (2000). Parental factors and the young child's postdivorce adjustment: A meta-analysis with implications for parenting arrangements. Journal of Family Psychology, 14, 5–26.

Whiting, B., & Edwards, C. P. (1988a). Children of different worlds. Cambridge, MA: Harvard University Press.

Whiting, B., & Edwards, C. P. (1988b). A cross-cultural analysis of sex differences in the behavior of children aged 3 through 11. In G. Handel (Ed.), Childhood socialization (pp. 281–297). New York: Aldine De Gruyter.

Whitington, V., & Ward, C. (1999). Intersubjectivity in caregiver–child communication. In L. E. Berk (Ed.), Landscapes of development (pp. 109–120). Belmont, CA: Wadsworth.

Whitley, B. E. (1983). Sex role orientation and self-esteem: A critical meta-analytic review. Journal of Personality and Social Psychology, 44, 765–778.

Wichstrøm, L. (1999). The emergence of gender difference in depressed mood during adolescence: The role of intensified gender socialization. Developmental Psychology, 35, 232–245.

Wickham, S. (1999, Summer). Homebirth: What are the issues? Midwifery Today, 50, 16–18.

Wigfield, A., & Eccles, J. S. (1994). Children's competence beliefs, achievement values, and general self-esteem change across elementary and middle school. Journal of Early Adolescence, 14, 107–138.

Wigfield, A., Eccles, J. S., Yoon, K. S., Harold, R. D., Arbreton, A. J., Freedman-Doan, C., & Blumenfeld, P. C. (1997). Changes in children's competence beliefs and subjective task values across the elementary school years: A three-year study. Journal of Educational Psychology, 89, 451–469.

Wiggins, G. P. (1993). Assessing student performance. San Francisco: Jossey-Bass.

Wiggins, G. P. (1998). Letter. Educational Researcher, 22(6), 20–22.

Wilcox, A. J., Weinberg, C. R., & Baird, D. D. (1995). Timing of sexual intercourse in relation to ovulation: Effects on the probability of conception, survival of the pregnancy, and sex of the baby. New England Journal of Medicine, 333, 1517–1519.

Wildes, J. E., Emery, R. E., & Simons, A. D. (2001). The roles of ethnicity and culture in the development of eating disturbance and body dissatisfaction: A meta-analytic review. Clinical Psychology Review, 21, 521–551.

Willatts, P. (1999). Development of means–end behavior in young infants: Pulling a support to retrieve a distant object. Developmental Psychology, 35, 651–667.

Wille, D. E. (1991). Relation of preterm birth with quality of infant–mother attachment at one year. Infant Behavior and Development, 14, 227–240.

Williams, E., Radin, N., & Allegro, T. (1992). Sex-role attitudes of adolescents reared primarily by their fathers: An 11-year follow-up. Merrill-Palmer Quarterly, 38, 457–476.

Williams, G. C. (1997). Review of Adaptation, edited by Michael R. Rose and George V. Lauder. Copeia, No. 3, 645–647.

Williams, J. E., & Best, D. L. (1990). Measuring sex stereotypes: A multination study. Newbury Park, CA: Sage.

Williams, T. M. (1986). The impact of television: A natural experiment in three communities. Orlando, FL: Academic Press.

Williams, T. M., & Cox, R. (1995, March). Informative versus other children's TV programs: Portrayals of ethnic diversity, gender, and aggression. Paper presented at the biennial meeting of the Society for Research in Child Development, Indianapolis.

Williams, W. (1998). Are we raising smarter children today? School-

and home-related influences on IQ. In U. Neisser (Ed.), The rising curve: Long-term gains in IQ and related measures (pp. 125–154). Washington, DC: American Psychological Association.

Willner, J. P. (1998). Reproductive genetics and today's patient options: Prenatal diagnosis. Mount Sinai Journal of Medicine, 65, 173–177.

Wilson, E. O. (1975). Sociobiology: The new synthesis. Cambridge, MA: Harvard University Press.

Wilson, M. N., Greene-Bates, C., McKim, L., Simmons, T. A., Curry-El, J., & Hinton, I. D. (1995). African American family life: The dynamics of interactions, relationships, and roles. In M. N. Wilson (Ed.), African American family life: Its structural and ecological aspects (pp. 5–21). San Francisco: Jossey-Bass.

Wilson, R., & Cairns, E. (1988). Sex-role attributes, perceived competence, and the development of depression in adolescence. Journal of Child Psychology and Psychiatry, 29, 635–650.

Winner, E. (1986, August). Where pelicans kiss seals. Psychology Today, 20 (8), 25–35.

Winner, E. (1988). The point of words: Children's understanding of metaphor and irony. Cambridge, MA: Harvard University Press.

Winner, E. (1996). Gifted children: Myths and realities. New York: Basic Books.

Winner, E. (1997). Exceptionally high intelligence and schooling. American Psychologist, 52, 1070–1081.

Winner, E. (2000). The origins and ends of giftedness. American Psychologist, 55, 159–169.

Winsler, A., Diaz, R. M., McCarthy, E. M., Atencio, D. J., & Chabay, L. (1999). Mother–child interaction, private speech, and task performance in preschool children with behavior problems. Journal of Child Psychology and Psychiatry, 40, 891–904.

Winsler, A., Diaz, R. M., & Montero, I. (1997). The role of private speech in the transition from collaborative to independent task performance in young children. Early Childhood Research Quarterly, 12, 59–79.

Wintre, M. G., & Vallance, D. D. (1994). A developmental sequence in the comprehension of emotions: Intensity, multiple emotions, and valence. Developmental Psychology, 30, 509–514.

Wiser, A. Maymon, E. Mazor, M., Shoham-Vardi, I., Silberstein, T., Wiznitzer, A., & Katz, M. (1997). Effect of the Yom Kippur fast on parturition. Harefuah, 132, 745–748.

Wolchik, S. A., Wilcox, K. L., Tein, J.-Y., & Sandler, I. N. (2000). Maternal acceptance and consis-

tency of discipline as buffers of divorce stressors on children's psychological adjustment problems. Journal of Abnormal Child Psychology, 28, 87–102.

Wolfe, D. A. (1999). Child abuse (2nd ed.). Thousand Oaks, CA: Sage.

Wolfe, D. A., Scott, K., Wekerle, C., & Pittman, A. (2001). Child maltreatment: Risk of adjustment problems and dating violence in adolescence. Journal of the American Academy of Child and Adolescent Psychiatry, 40, 282–289.

Wolfe, V. V. (1998). Child sexual abuse. In E. J. Mash (Ed.), Treatment of childhood disorders (2nd ed., pp. 545–597). New York, NY: Guilford.

Wolfer, L. T., & Moen, P. (1996). Staying in school: Maternal employment and the timing of black and white daughters' school exit. Journal of Family Issues, 17, 540–560.

Wolff, P. H. (1966). The causes, controls and organization of behavior in the neonate. Psychological Issues, 5(1, Serial No. 17).

Wolff, P. H., & Fesseha, G. (1999). The orphans of Eritrea: A five-year follow-up study. Journal of Child Psychology and Psychiatry and Allied Disciplines, 40, 1231–1237.

Wolpe, J., & Plaud, J. J. (1997). Pavlov's contributions to behavior therapy: The obvious and not so obvious. American Psychologist, 52, 966–972.

Wood, D. J. (1989). Social interaction as tutoring. In M. H. Bornstein & J. S. Bruner (Eds.), Interaction in human development. Hillsdale, NJ: Erlbaum.

Wood. S. (2001). Interview. Frontline [On-line]. www.pbs.org/wgbh/pages/frontline/shows/fertility/interviews/wood.html

Woodward, A. L., & Markman, E. M. (1998). Early word learning. In D. Kuhn & R. S. Siegler (Eds.), Handbook of child psychology: Vol. 2. Cognition, perception, and language (5th ed., pp. 371–420). New York: Wiley.

Woodward, A. L., Markman, E. M., & Fitzsimmons, C. M. (1994). Rapid word learning in 13- and 18-month-olds. Developmental Psychology, 30, 553–566.

Woodward, A. L., Sommerville, J. A., & Guajardo, J. J. (2001). How infants make sense of intentional action. In B. F. Malle, L. J. Moses, & D. A. Baldwin (Eds.), Intentions and intentionality (pp. 149–169). Cambridge, MA: MIT Press.

Woodward, L., Taylor, E., & Dowdney, L. (1998). The parenting and family functioning of children with hyperactivity. Journal of Child Psychology and Psychiatry, 39, 161–169.

Woodward, L. J., & Fergusson, D. M. (1999a). Childhood peer relationship problems and psychosocial adjustment in late adolescence. *Journal of Abnormal Child Psychology, 27,* e87.

Woodward, L. J., & Fergusson, D. M. (1999b). Early conduct problems and later risk of teenage pregnancy in girls. *Development and Psychopathology, 11,* 127–141.

Woodward, S. A., Lenzenweger, M. F., Kagan, J., Snidman, N., & Arcus, D. (2000). Taxonic structure of infant reactivity: Evidence from a taxometric perspective. *Psychological Science, 11,* 296–301.

Woody-Ramsey, J., & Miller, P. H. (1988). The facilitation of selective attention in preschoolers. *Child Development, 59,* 1497–1503.

Woolley, J. D. (1997). Thinking about fantasy: Are children fundamentally different thinkers and believers from adults? *Child Development, 68,* 991–1011.

Woolley, J. D., Phelps, K. E., Davis, D. L., & Mandell, D. J. (1999). Where theories of mind meet magic: The development of children's beliefs about wishing. *Child Development, 70,* 571–587.

Woolley, J. D., & Wellman, H. M. (1992). Children's conception of dreams. *Cognitive Development, 7,* 365–380.

Wooster, D. M. (1999). Assessment of nonorganic failure to thrive. *Infant-Toddler Intervention, 9,* 353–371.

Wooster, D. M. (2000). Intervention for nonorganic failure to thrive. *Transdisciplinary Journal, 10,* 37–45.

World Health Organization. (2000). *The World Health Report, 2000.* Geneva: Author.

Wright, J. C., & Huston, A. C. (1995, June). *Effects of educational TV viewing of lower income preschoolers on academic skills, school readiness, and school adjustment one to three years later.* Report to Children's Television Workshop, Center for Research on the Influences of Television on Children, University of Kansas, Lawrence.

Wright, J. C., Huston, A. C., Murphy, K. C., St. Peters, M., Pinon, M., Scantlin, R., & Kotler, J. (2001). The relations of early television viewing to school readiness and vocabulary of children from low-income families: The Early Window Project. *Child Development, 72,* 1347–1366.

Wright, J. C., Huston, A. C., Reitz, A. L., & Piemyat, S. (1994). Young children's perceptions of television reality: Determinants and developmental differences. *Developmental Psychology, 30,* 229–239.

Wyman, P. A., Cowen, E. L., Work, W. C., Hoyt-Meyers, L., Magnus, K. B., & Fagen, D. B. (1999). Caregiving and developmental factors differentiating young at-risk urban children showing resilient versus stress-affected outcomes: A repli-

cation and extension. *Child Development, 70,* 645–659.

Wynn, K. (1992). Addition and subtraction by human infants. *Nature, 358,* 749–750.

Wynn, K. (1998). Psychological foundations of number: Numerical competence in human infants. *Trends in Cognitive Sciences, 2,* 296–303.

Yang, B., Ollendick, T. H., Dong, Q., Xia, Y., & Lin, L. (1995). Only children and children with siblings in the People's Republic of China: Levels of fear, anxiety, and depression. *Child Development, 66,* 1301–1311.

Yarrow, M. R., Campbell, J. D., & Burton, R. V. (1970). Recollections of childhood: A study of the retrospective method. *Monographs of the Society for Research in Child Development, 35*(5, Serial No. 138).

Yarrow, M. R., Scott, P. M., & Waxler, C. Z. (1973). Learning concern for others. *Developmental Psychology, 8,* 240–260.

Yates, W. R., Cadoret, R. J., & Troughton, E. P. (1999). The Iowa adoption studies: Methods and results. In M. C. LaBuda & E. L. Grigorenko (Eds.), *On the way to individuality: Current methodological issues in behavioral genetics* (pp. 95–125). Commack, NY: Nova Science Publishers.

Yeates, K. O., Schultz, L. H., & Selman, R. L. (1991). The development of interpersonal negotiation strategies in thought and action: A social-cognitive link to behavioral adjustment and social status. *Merrill-Palmer Quarterly, 37,* 369–405.

Yirmiya, N., Erel, O., Shaked, M., & Solomonica-Levi, D. (1998). Meta-analyses comparing theory of mind abilities of individuals with autism, individuals with mental retardation, and normally developing individuals. *Psychological Bulletin, 124,* 283–307.

Yirmiya, N., & Shulman, C. (1996). Seriation, conservation, and theory of mind abilities in individuals with autism, individuals with mental retardation, and normally developing children. *Child Development, 67,* 2045–2059.

Yirmiya, N., Solomonica-Levi, D., & Shulman, C. (1996). The ability to manipulate behavior and to understand manipulation of beliefs: A comparison of individuals with autism, mental retardation, and normal development. *Developmental Psychology, 32,* 62–69.

Yoder, A. E. (2000). Barriers to ego identity status formation: A contextual qualification of Marcia's identity status paradigm. *Journal of Adolescence, 23,* 95–106.

Yogman, M. W. (1981). Development of the father–infant relationship. In H. Fitzgerald, B. Lester, &

M. W. Yogman (Eds.), *Theory and research in behavioral pediatrics* (Vol. 1, pp. 221–279). New York: Plenum.

Yonas, A., Granrud, E. C., Arterberry, M. E., & Hanson, B. L. (1986). Infants' distance perception from linear perspective and texture gradients. *Infant Behavior and Development, 9,* 247–256.

Yonas, A., & Hartman, B. (1993). Perceiving the affordance of contact in four- and five-month-old infants. *Child Development, 64,* 298–308.

Young, D. (1997). Epidurals under scrutiny in the United States. *Birth, 24,* 139–140.

Young, E., & Korzun, A. (1999). Women, stress, and depression: Sex differences in hypothalamic-pituitary-adrenal axis regulation. In E. Leibenluft (Ed.), *Gender differences in mood and anxiety disorders: From bench to bedside* (pp. 31–52). Washington, DC: American Psychiatric Press.

Young, K. T. (1990). American conceptions of infant development from 1955 to 1984: What the experts are telling parents. *Child Development, 61,* 17–28.

Young, S. K., Fox, N. A., & Zahn-Waxler, C. (1999). The relations between temperament and empathy in 2-year-olds. *Developmental Psychology, 35,* 1189–1197.

Youngblade, L. M., & Dunn, J. (1995). Individual differences in young children's pretend play with mother and sibling: Links to relationships and understanding of other people's feelings and beliefs. *Child Development, 66,* 1472–1492.

Younger, B. A. (1985). The segregation of items into categories by ten-month-old infants. *Child Development, 56,* 1574–1583.

Younger, B. A. (1993). Understanding category members as "the same sort of thing": Explicit categorization in ten-month infants. *Child Development, 64,* 309–320.

Youngstrom, E., Wolpaw, J. M., Kogos, J. L., Schoff, K., Ackerman, B., & Izard, C. (2000). Interpersonal problem solving in preschool and first grade: Developmental change and ecological validity. *Journal of Clinical Child Psychology, 29,* 589–602.

Youniss, J., McClellan, J. A., & Yates, M. (1997). What we know about engendering civic identity. *American Behavioral Scientist, 40,* 620–631.

Yu, Y., & Nelson, K. (1993). Slot-filler and conventional category organization in young Korean children. *International Journal of Behavioral Development, 16,* 1–14.

Zabin, L. S., & Hayward, S. C. (1993). *Adolescent sexual behavior and childbearing.* Newbury Park, CA: Sage.

Zafeiriou, D. I. (2000). Plantar grasp reflex in high-risk infants during the first year of life. *Pediatric Neurology, 22,* 75–76.

Zahn-Waxler, C. (1991). The case for empathy: A developmental review. *Psychological Inquiry, 2,* 155–158.

Zahn-Waxler, C., Cole, P. M., & Barrett, K. C. (1991). Guilt and empathy: Sex differences and implications for the development of depression. In J. Garber & K. A. Dodge (Eds.), *The development of emotion regulation and dysregulation* (pp. 243–272). Cambridge: Cambridge University Press.

Zahn-Waxler, C., Iannotti, R. J., Cummings, E. M., & Denham, S. (1990). Antecedents of problem behaviors in children of depressed mothers. *Development and Psychopathology, 2,* 271–291.

Zahn-Waxler, C., Kochanska, G., Krupnick, J., & McKnew, D. (1990). Patterns of guilt in children of depressed and well mothers. *Developmental Psychology, 26,* 51–59.

Zahn-Waxler, C., & Radke-Yarrow, M. (1990). The origins of empathic concern. *Motivation and Emotion, 14,* 107–130.

Zahn-Waxler, C., Radke-Yarrow, M., & King, R. M. (1979). Childrearing and children's prosocial initiations toward victims of distress. *Child Development, 50,* 319–330.

Zahn-Waxler, C., & Robinson, J. (1995). Empathy and guilt: Early origins of feelings of responsibility. In J. P. Tangney & K. W. Fischer (Eds.), *Self-conscious emotions* (pp. 143–173). New York: Guilford.

Zahn-Waxler, C., Robinson, J. L., & Emde, R. N. (1992). The development of empathy in twins. *Developmental Psychology, 28,* 1038–1047.

Zahn-Waxler, C., Schiro, K., Robinson, J. L., Emde, R. N., & Schmitz, S. (2001). Empathy and prosocial patterns in young MZ and DZ twins: Development and genetic and environmental influences. In R. N. Emde & J. K. Hewitt (Eds.), *Infancy to early childhood: Genetic and environmental influences on developmental change* (pp. 141–162). New York: Oxford University Press.

Zeanah, C. H. (2000). Disturbances of attachment in young children adopted from institutions. *Developmental and Behavioral Pediatrics, 21,* 230–236.

Zelazo, N. A., Zelazo, P. R., Cohen, K. M., & Zelazo, P. D. (1993). Specificity of practice effects on elementary neuromotor patterns. *Developmental Psychology, 29,* 686–691.

Zelazo, P. R. (1983). The development of walking: New findings on old assumptions. *Journal of Motor Behavior, 2,* 99–137.

Zeskind, P. S., & Barr, R. G. (1997). Acoustic characteristics of naturally occurring cries of infants with "colic." *Child Development, 68,* 394–403.

Zeskind, P. S., & Ramey, C. T. (1978). Fetal malnutrition: An experimental study of its consequences on infant development in two caregiving environments. *Child Development, 49,* 1155–1162.

Zeskind, P. S., & Ramey, C. T. (1981). Preventing intellectual and interactional sequelae of fetal malnutrition: A longitudinal, transactional, and synergistic approach to development. *Child Development, 52,* 213–218.

Zhou, M., & Bankston, C. L. (1998). *Growing up American: How Vietnamese children adapt to life in the United States.* New York: Russell Sage Foundation.

Zigler, E. F., & Finn-Stevenson, M. (1999). Applied developmental psychology. In M. H. Bornstein & M. E. Lamb (Eds.), *Developmental psychology: An advanced textbook* (4th ed., pp. 555–598). Mahwah, NJ: Erlbaum.

Zigler, E. F., & Gilman, E. (1998). The legacy of Jean Piaget. In G. A. Kimble & M. Wertheimer (Eds.), *Portraits of pioneers in psychology* (Vol. 3, pp. 145–160). Washington, DC: American Psychological Association.

Zigler, E. F., & Hall, N. W. (1989). Physical child abuse in America: Past, present, and future. In D. Cicchetti & V. Carlson (Eds.), *Child maltreatment* (pp. 203–253). New York: Cambridge University Press.

Zigler, E. F., & Hall, N. W. (2000). *Child development and social policy: Theory and applications.* New York: McGraw-Hill.

Zigler, E., & Styfco, S. J. (2001). Can early childhood intervention prevent delinquency? A real possibility. In A. C. Bohart & D. J. Stipek (Eds.), *Constructive and destructive behavior: Implications for family, school, and society* (pp. 231–248). Washington, DC: American Psychological Association.

Zill, N., Davies, E., & Daly, M. (1994). *Viewing of Sesame Street by preschool children in the United States and its relationship to school readiness.* Rockville, MD: Westat.

Zill, N., West, J., & Lomax, J. (1997). *The elementary school performance and adjustment of children who enter kindergarten late or repeat kindergarten: Findings from national surveys.* Washington, DC: National Center for Education Statistics.

Zimmerman, B. J. (2002). Achieving academic excellence: A self-regulatory perspective. In M. Ferrari (Ed.), *The pursuit of excellence through education* (pp. 85–110). Mahwah, NJ: Erlbaum.

Zimmerman, B. J., & Risemberg, R. (1997). Self-regulatory dimensions of academic learning and motivation. In G. D. Phye (Ed.), *Handbook of academic learning: Construction of knowledge* (pp. 105–125). San Diego: Academic Press.

Zimmerman, M. A., & Arunkumar, R. (1994). Resiliency research: Implications for schools and policy. *Social Policy Report of the Society for Research in Child Development, 8*(4).

Zimmerman, M. A., Copeland, L. A., Shope, J. T., & Dielman, T. E. (1997). A longitudinal study of self-esteem: Implications for adolescent development. *Journal of Youth and Adolescence, 26,* 117–141.

Zucker, K. J. (2001). Biological influences on psychosexual differentiation. In R. K. Unger (Ed.), *Handbook of the psychology of women and gender* (pp. 101–115). New York: Wiley.

Zucker, K. J., Bradley, S. J., Oliver, G., Blake, J., Fleming, S., & Hood, J. (1996). Psychosexual development of women with congenital adrenal hyperplasia. *Hormones and Behavior, 30,* 300–318.

# name index

Chen, W. J., 279
**Chen, X.**, 50, 328, 418, 575, 579, 616
Chen, Y-C., 96
Chen, Y-J., 96
Chen, Z., 226, 227n
Cherlin, A. J., 583
Cherny, S. S., 341
Chesney-Lind, M., 512
Chess, S., 410, 412n, 413, 418
Chi, M., 288, 288n
**Childcare Resource and Research Unit**, 589
Children's Defense Fund, 108
Childs, C. P., 26
Chin, D. G., 255
Chipuer, H. M., 416n
Chisholm, J. S., 133
Chiu, L-H., 454
**Chodirker, B.**, 77
Choi, S., 372
Chomsky, C., 380
Chomsky, N., 356, 380, 381
Christenson, S. L., 641
Christophe, A., 135
Chronis, A., 283
Chung, K-M., 283
Church, R. B., 278
Cibelli, C., 428
Cicchetti, D., 136, 423, 425n, 553, 556, 591, 594, 595
Cillessen, A. H. N., 613
Citron, C. C., 538
Clancy, P., 379
Clark, E. V., 373, 375
Clark, K. E., 606
Clark, L. V., 470
Clark, R., 113
Clarke-Stewart, K. A., 11, 583
Claude, D., 282
Clausen, J. A., 201
Cleland, J. W., 129
Clements, D. H., 630
Clifford, P., 109n
Clifton, R. K., 143, 145, 148
Clubb, P. A., 289
Clutter, J., 144
Clutton-Brock, T. H., 529, 530
Cnattingius, S., 94
Coakley, J., 176
Coatsworth, J. D., 9, 10
Cochran, M., 566
Coffey-Corina, S., 183, 360
Cohen, F. L., 97n
Cohen, K. M., 207
Cohen, L. B., 156, 159, 223
Cohen, S., 100
Cohen, S. E., 137
Cohn, D. A., 426
Cohn, J. E., 397
Cohn, J. F., 397, 398
Coie, J. D., 328, 511, 513, 613, 616
Coiro, M. J., 583
Colan, N. B., 645
**Colapinto, J.**, 534, 535
Colburne, K. A., 526
Colby, A., 492, 493, 495, 501
Cole, C., 628
Cole, M., 248
Cole, P. M., 405, 405n, 552
Cole, R. E., 575
Cole, T. J., 180
Coleman, C. C., 635
Coleman, S. M., 486
Coley, R. L., 101, 208, 212, 581
Collaer, M. L., 533, 550
Collie, R., 225

Collier, 388
**Collings, T.**, 628
Collins, M. A., 348
Collins, V. L., 200
Collins, W. A., 28, 116, 566, 572, 573, 625
Colman, M., 586
Colombo, J., 137
Coltrane, S., 565
Comfort, M. E., 209
**Common, R.**, 337
Comstock, G. A., 624, 625
Comunian, A. L., 501
Concordia University, 432, 526, 578
Condry, J. C., 555
Conel, J. L., 182
Conger, R. D., 201, 398, 554
Connell, J. P., 404, 458, 541
Conner, D. B., 259
Connolly, K. J., 233, 233n
Connor, J. M., 538
Connor, P. D., 95
**Connor, S. K.**, 94
Connors, L. J., 28
Consortium for Longitudinal Studies, 343
Conti-Ramsden, G., 155
Coon, H., 341
Cooper, P. J., 398
Cooper, R. P., 110, 148, 363, 364
Coplan, K. H., 415, 464
**Coplan, R. J.**, 417
Coppage, D. J., 226
Copple, C., 433n, 588
Coppola, A., 356
Coppotelli, H., 613
Corah, N. L., 108
Corbetta, D., 143
Corbin, S. B., 582
Corcoran, J., 211
Corkill, A. J., 279
Cornelius, M. D., 95
Cornell University, 292
Corrigan, R., 230
Cosden, M., 94
Costello, E. J., 196
Coté, S., 513
Cotton, D. B., 81n
Couchoud, E., 408
Coulehan, C. M., 430
Coulton, C. J., 594
Couper, D., 130
Couper, J. J., 77
Couper, R. T., 77
**Courage, M.**, 151, 290
Courtney, S., 428
Cowan, C. P., 28, 565
Cowan, N., 272, 272n
Cowan, P. A., 28, 565
Cox, M. J., 426, 428, 564
Cox, R., 232, 626
Cox, S. M., 425
Coy, K. C., 200, 488
Coyle, D. D., 611
Coyle, T. R., 284
Coyne, E. T., 188
**Crago, M. B.**, 380
Crain, R. M., 453
Crassini, B., 151
Craton, L. G., 152
Cratty, B. J., 174n, 176
Craven, R., 452, 453
Creasey, G. L., 231
Creatsas, G. K., 205
**Crick, N. R.**, 24, 473n, 511n, 554, 611, 614, 615, 618
Crockett, K. C., 573

Cromer, C., 607
Cronk, C., 365
Crosby, L., 44, 611
Crosby, R., 208
Cross, C. E., 59
Cross, D. R., 259, 301, 445
Crouter, A. C., 200, 539, 544, 552, 578
Crowe, R. R., 118n
Crowley, K., 61
Crowley, W. F., 550
Crowson, M., 447
Cruttenden, L., 224
Crystal, D. S., 455, 643
Csikszentmihalyi, M., 198, 346, 347
Culbertson, F. M., 554
Culnane, M., 97
Cumberland, A., 404, 406
Cummings, E. M., 54, 55n, 398, 420, 556, 564
**Cummins, J.**, 389
**Cunning, S.**, 571
**Cunningham, A. E.**, 630
Cupp, R., 633
Curran, D. J., 335
Currie, J., 343
Curtin, S. C., 106
Curtiss, S., 360
Cushing, G., 622, 623
Cutrona, C. E., 212
Cutright, M. L., 46
Cytron, R., 345

Dabbs, J., 407
Dabholkar, A. S., 182
Dadds, M. R., 126
D'Agostino, J. A., 109n
Dahl, R. E., 94
Daleiden, E., 46
Daltabuit, M., 131
Daly, M., 531, 627
Damasio, A. R., 481
Damhuis, I., 402, 403
Damon, W., 448, 449, 450, 454, 455, 487, 499, 501, 505, 506, 608, 609
Danello, M. A., 127
Daniels, D. H., 453, 458, 638
Daniluk, J., 201
Dann, S., 602
Dannemiller, J. L., 151, 158
Dapretto, M., 371, 372
Darling, N. E., 568
Darlington, R. B., 343
Darnton-Hill, I., 188
Darroch, J. E., 208
Darwin, C., 12, 13
**Dateno, S.**, 576
Datta-Bhutada, S., 94
D'Augelli, A. R., 462
Daunhauer, L. A., 164
Davalos, M., 410
Davidson, E., 106
Davidson, R. J., 183
Davies, P. T., 398, 564, 627
Davis, D. L., 76
Davis, L. G., 397
Davis, P. V., 157
Davis, T. L., 46
Davison, M. L., 549
Day, R. H., 156
De Lisi, R., 374, 543
de Rivera, J., 402, 403
de Schonen, S., 158
de Villiers, J. G., 376, 377, 381, 446

de Villiers, P. A., 376, 377, 381, 446
de Waal, F. B. M., 9, 480, 529, 530
De Wolff, M. S., 424, 425, 427
Deák, G. O., 375
Deary, I. J., 316
Deater-Deckard, K., 416, 427, 575
Deaux, K., 524
DeBaryshe, B. D., 515
DeBerry, K. M., 335
Debus, R., 452, 453
DeCasper, A. J., 91, 148
DeFries, J. C., 334
DeGarmo, D. S., 572, 584
DeGroot, A. D., 327
de Haan, M., 137
Degirmencioglu, S. M., 610
DeGroot, A. D., 327
Dejin-Karlsson, E., 95
Dekovic, M., 200, 614
Delaney-Black, V., 94
Dell, D. L., 209
DeLoache, J. S., 233, 234n, 284
DeMarie-Dreblow, D., 280
deMille, R., 320
Dembo, M. H., 612
Demuth, K., 368
Dement, W. C., 128, 129n
**Demianczuk, N.**, 82
deMille, R., 320
Dempster, F. N., 279, 280
Denckla, K., 282
Denham, S. A., 408
Dennis, A. B., 204
Dennis, W., 141
Denny, M. A., 141
Derom, C., 184
DeRosier, M. E., 516, 611
Detterman, D. K., 312, 323, 326
Deutsch, W., 383
Devlin, B., 334
DeVos, J., 223n, 224
deVries, M. W., 418
Dewey, K. G., 187
Dewsbury, D. A., 24
DiAdamo, C., 443
Diamond, A., 224, 225, 290
Diamond, L. M., 181, 207
Diamond, M., 534, 549
Dias, M. G., 231
Diaz, R. M., 257, 259, 388
Dichtelmiller, M., 565
Dick, D. M., 201
Dickens, W. T., 336
Dickinson, D. K., 374
Dick-Read, G., 105
Dickson, K. L., 301
Dickson, S. V., 401
Didow, S. M., 603
Diener, M. L., 413
Dietrich, K. N., 96
Dietz, T. L., 538, 631
DiLalla, L. F., 340, 416
Dildy G. A., 100
DiMatteo, M. R., 105
Dingel, A., 226
DiPerna, J., 633
DiPietro, J. A., 90, 91, 129
Dirks, J., 337
Dishion, T. J., 44, 611, 612, 622
Dixon, J. A., 472
Dixon, R. A., 13
Dodd, B. J., 369
Dodge, K. A., 24, 328, 467, 473n, 474, 511, 513, 514, 515, 564, 571, 572, 575, 576, 613, 614, 616
**Doherty, G.**, 431, 432n
Dolan, A., 291

**Dolan, B.**, 330
Dolensky, E., 611
Doll, B., 475
Dollaghan, C., 371
Donatelle, R. J., 397
Dondi, M., 129, 409
Donelan-McCall, N., 408
Dong, Q., 575
Donnerstein, E., 626
Donovan, W. L., 132
Dornbusch, S. M., 586, 639, 640, 644
Dossett, D., 295
Dougherty, T. M., 316
Douglas, R. N., 289
Dowdney, L., 570
Downey, G., 474
Downs, A. C., 197, 529
Downs, R. M., 242
**Doyle, A.**, 231, 468
Drabman, R. S., 46, 190
Drago-Severson, E., 642
Draper, P., 27
Dreher, M., 94
Drew, L. M., 564
Droege, K. L., 467
Drotar, D., 65, 193, 330
**Dryburgh, H.**, 33, 205, 208, 209
Dubé, E. M., 207
DuBois, D. L., 453
Dubow, E. F., 340, 474
Duck, S. C., 533
**Dumas, C.**, 241
**Duncan, R. M.**, 257, 575
Duniz, M., 193
Dunn, J., 60, 408, 446, 577, 578
**Dunn, M.**, 327, 633
Durbin, D. L., 619
Durham, M., 340
Durlak, J. A., 454
**Durrant, J.**, 486, 487
Dutilleul, S., 146
Dweck, C. S., 456, 457, 467, 468
Dwyer, T., 130
Dybing, T., 130
Dyer, C., 74
Dye-White, E., 96

Eagly, A. H., 548
East, P. L., 212, 578
Easterbrook, M. A., 157, 428, 442
Eaton, M. M., 455
Ebeling, K. S., 236
Eberhart-Phillips, J. E., 97
Eccles, J., 454, 551
Eccles, J. S., 176, 198, 458n, 459, 527, 536, 552, 568, 620, 636, 637, 638n, 639n
Echols, C. H., 368
Eckerle, D., 193
Eckerman, C. O., 603
Eder, D., 540
Eder, R. A., 448
Edwards, C. P., 498, 511, 529, 530, 531, 532, 537
Egeland, B., 9, 423, 427, 429, 431, 593, 595
Ehrhardt, A. A., 533
Eiben, R., 81n
Eibl-Eibesfeldt, I., 198
Eichstedt J. A., 526n
Eiden, R. D., 133
**Eilers, R. E.**, 365
Eimas, P. D., 226
Einstein, A., 312

Graziano, W. G., 607
Green, D., 61
Green, F. L., 208, 239, 294, 294n
Green, G. E., 132
Green, J. A., 129
Green, R., 129, 532
Greenbaum, C. W., 418
Greenberger, E., 554, 574
Greendorfer, S. L., 176
Greene, A. D., 209
Greene, K., 247
Greenfield, P. M., 26, 142, 337, 551, 630
Greenhill, L. L., 283
Greenhoot, A. F., 287, 287n
Greenough, W. T., 182, 185, 186
Gregg, V., 501
Greif, E. B., 536
Gresham, F. M., 640
Griffin, K. W., 584
Griffith, E., 633
Grigorenko, E. L., 333, 338, 339
Grime, R. L., 492, 493
Grody, W. W., 77n
Groff, J. Y., 94
Grolnick, W. S., 148, 404, 637, 641
Gronau, R. C., 509
Groome, L. J,., 129
Grossman, J. A., 463
Grossman, P. B., 454
Grossmann, K., 423
Grotevant, H. D., 397, 460, 464, 540, 566, 580
**Grotpeter, J. K.**, 511, 554, 554n, 611, 615, 618
Grubb, W. N., 645
**Grusec, J. E.**, 485
Gruszcynska, A., 2
Grych, J. H., 584
Guajardo, J. J., 466
Guerra, N. G., 518
Guerri, C., 95
Guilford, J. P., 320, 346
Gulko, J., 527, 528, 528n, 529, 543
Gullone, E., 404, 405
Gump, P. V., 632
Gunnar, M. R., 133, 397, 414, 415
Gunnoe, M. L., 486
Guo, G., 577
Gurucharri, C., 470
Gustafson, G. E., 129, 132
Gutfreund, M. K., 367
Guttentag, R., 272
Gwiazda, J., 150, 151, 155, 157

h

Haake, R. J., 281
Habitat for Humanity, 502
Hack, M., 108
Hack, M. B., 108
Haden, C. A., 291
Hafdahl, A. R., 454
Hagan, R. I., 536
Hagberg, B., 95
Hagekull, B., 192, 428
Hagen, E. P., 322
Haidt, J., 481
Haight, W. L., 260
Haimerl, F., 127
Haine, R. A., 291
Hains, S. M. J., 401, 401n
Haith, M. M., 143, 156, 162, 223, 229, 254, 256, 281, 316
Hakuta, K., 360, 388

Hale, S., 273, 316
Halford, G. S., 241
Halil, T., 132n
Hall, D. G., 375
Hall, G. S., 13, 170
Hall, J. A., 541, 552
Hall, N. W., 33, 34
Halle, T. G., 341
Halliday, J. L., 79n
Hallinan, M. T., 640
Halperin, J. M., 283
Halpern, C. T., 203, 204
Halpern, D. F., 76, 549
Halpern, L. F., 129
Halverson, C. F., 545
Ham, M., 198
Hamberger, L., 86n, 89, 90
Hamer, D. H., 206
Hamilton, C. E., 423
Hamilton, M. A., 645
Hamilton, S. F., 645
Hamm, J. V., 589
Hammersley, M., 52
Hammersmith, S., 208
Hamond, N. R., 291
Hampson, E., 551
Hamre, B. K., 636
Han, J. J., 291
Haney, P., 454
Hanley, W. B., 74
Hanlon, C., 381
Hans, S. L., 425
Hanson, D. R., 115n
Hanson, T. L., 583
Happé, F. G. E., 447
Hardy, J., 210, 210n
Harden, E. T., 508
Harold, R. D., 176, 527, 536
Harrington, D., 536
Harris, G., 146, 362
Harris, J. R., 117, 572
Harris, K. M., 212
Harris, P. L., 231, 417, 446
Harrison, A. O., 575, 576
Harrison, K., 628
Harrist, A., 616
Hart, C. H., 526, 563, 564, 568, 569, 587, 606, 614, 634
Hart, B., 340, 371, 382
Hart, C., 572
Hart, D., 448, 449, 464
Hart, S., 398, 501
Harter, K., 564
Harter, S., 399, 402, 403, 408, 441, 448, 449, 452, 453, 455
Hartman, B., 143
Hartmann, D. P., 616
Hartshorn, K., 137
Hartup, W. W., 328, 605, 608, 610, 613
Haryu, E., 375
Haselager, J. T., 611
Hatano, G., 255, 262
Hatch, E. E., 93
Hatch, M. C., 98, 100
Hatton, D. D., 154
Hatzipantelis, M., 551
Hauser, S. T., 464
Hausfather, A., 431, 588
Hauth, J. C., 93

Hawker, D. S. J., 615
Hawkins, A. J., 565
Hawkins, D. J., 516
Hawkins, J. N., 454
Hawkins, R., 593
Hay, D. F., 473
Hayne, H., 137, 225, 226
Hayslip, B., Jr., 325
Hayward, C., 584
Hayward, S. C., 211
Head Start Bureau, 342
Healy, M., 173, 175n
Hearold, S., 627
Heath, S. B., 337, 574
Heckman, J. J., 327
Hedges, L. V., 329, 549, 632, 632n
Heidiger, M. L., 99
Heine, S. J., 454
Heinz, W. R., 645
Held, R., 144
Heller, T. L., 475
Heller, W., 183
Helmstadter, G. C., 539
**Helwig, C. C.**, 491, 504, 505
Hembree, E. A., 401
Hembree, S. E., 612
Hembrooke, H., 293
Hencke, R. W., 251
Henderson, H. A., 47
Henderson, R. L., 295, 585
Henderson, S. H., 581, 586
Hendrick, J., 538, 539n
Hendricks, M., 320
Hennessy, K. D., 556
Hennig, K. H., 496
Henry, B., 46
Hepper, P. G., 136
Herdt, G., 207
Hergenrather, J. R., 254
Herman, J., 388
Herman, L., 357, 359
Herman, M. R., 568
Hernandez, D. J., 36
Hernandez, F. D., 397
Hernandez-Reif, M., 161, 226
Héroux, G., 237
Herrenkohl, L. R., 262
Herrnstein, R. J., 329
Hershberger, S. L., 462
**Hertzman, D.**, 587, 589
Hesketh, L. J., 79
Hespos, S. J., 253n
Hesse, E., 423
Hetherington, E. M., 28, 572, 578, 581, 582, 583, 584, 585, 586
Hewer, A., 492
Hewes, A. K., 362
Hewlett, B. S., 429
Hewlett, S., 15
Hewstone, M., 469
Heyman, G. D., 448, 456, 457, 468
Heyns, B., 327
Hickey, T. L., 150
Hickling, A. K., 237, 255, 295, 374
Hier, D. B., 550
Hiester, M., 431
Higgins, E. T., 60, 61n
High, P., 299
Higley, J. D., 602
**Hildebrand, D.**, 323
Hildebrandt, N., 489
Hill, J., 573
Hind, H., 188
Hinde, R. A., 24, 528, 538

Hines, M., 532, 533, 550
Hines, S., 79
Hirshfeld, L. A., 238
Hirsh-Pasek, K., 148, 364, 376
Ho, C. S-H., 304
Ho, H-Z., 459
Hoagwood, K., 37
Hochschild, A, 15
Hock, H. S., 284
Hocutt, A. M., 641
Hodapp, R. M., 79
Hodges, J., 424
Hodges, R. M., 241
Hodges, V. E., 615
Hoeksma, J. B., 418
Hoepfner, R., 320
Hoff, T., 14
Hoff-Ginsberg, E., 371, 574
Hoffman, H. J., 130
Hoffman, L. W., 417, 539
Hoffman, M. L., 409, 481, 482, 483, 587
Hoffman, S., 100
Hoffner, C, 408
Hofsten, C. von, 143, 151
Hogarty, P. S., 325
Hohne, E. A., 363
Hokoda, A., 458
Holcomb, T. F., 255
Holden, D. J., 283
Holden, G. W., 486, 488
Holley, F. B., 279
Hollich, G. H., 376
Holmbeck, G. N., 170, 200, 573
Holmes, W. C., 593
Holobow, N., 389
Holt, W., 553
Hombo, C. M., 549, 551, 638
Hommerding, K. D., 423
Honzik, M. P., 325
Hood, B., 254
Hood, B. M., 137
Hope, S., 582
Hopkins, B., 141, 142n, 183
Hopkins, J., 425
Hopmeyer, A., 614
Hopson, J., 181
Horgan, D., 379
Horn, J. L., 315n, 331
Horn, J. M., 114, 115, 117, 332, 333, 334n, 341
Horne, R. S., 130
Horner, T. M., 402
Horowitz, F. D., 20
Horowitz, J. M., 592
Hort, B. E., 526, 528
Horwood, L. J., 462
Hotz, V. J., 209
Houston, D. M., 364
Howe, N., 433, 588
Howe, M., 290
Howe, M. J., 49
**Howe, M. L.**, 587
**Howe, N.**, 432, 578
Howes, C., 423, 587, 588, 603, 604, 607, 608
Hoza, B., 612, 616
Hsiao, C. K., 279
Hsu, C-C., 96
Huang, B., 619
Huard, R. D., 281
Hubbard, F. O. A., 131
Hudson, J. A., 286, 289
Huebner, R. R., 401
Huesmann, L. R., 625, 625n
Hughes, C., 408, 446
Hughes, F. P., 446, 447
Hughes, J. N., 454

Hulanicka, B., 196
Hull, C., 19
**Hull, J.**, 330
Hummel, R. C., 500
Humphrey, L. T., 175
Humphrey, T., 145
Humphreys, A. P., 605
Humphreys, L. G., 325
Hunt, E., 95
Hunter, M., 83
**Hunter, T.**, 605
Huntsinger, C. S., 575, 575n, 642, 643
Hura, S. L., 368
Hurewitz, R., 383, 384n
Hurrelmann, K., 212
Hursti, U. K., 188
Huston, A. C., 45, 538, 544, 553, 624, 628, 631
Huttenlocher, J., 235, 371
Huttenlocher, P. R., 181, 182
Huwiler, S. M. S, 208
Hyde, J. S., 113, 548, 549
Hygge, S., 56, 56n
**Hymel, S.**, 452, 614, 637
Hynd, G. W., 640

i

Iacono, W. G., 282, 332
Iannotti, R. J., 556
Iler, I., 538
Imai, M., 375
Inagaki, K., 254, 255
Ingersoll, E. W., 135
Ingram, D., 368, 369, 369n
Inhelder, B., 219, 241, 242, 245, 247
Inoff-Germain, G., 555
Insabella, G. M., 28, 582
Institute of Child Study, 275
Intons-Peterson, M. J., 531
Ireland, M., 462
Irvine, J. J., 458
Irwin, J. R., 132
Isabella, R. A., 424, 425
Israelashvili, R., 428
Ito, Y., 595
Iverson, J. M., 366
Ivey, P., 402
Iwamoto, K., 93
Izard, C. E., 47, 396, 399n, 401

j

Jacklin, C. N., 532
Jackson, P. W., 638
**Jacobs, E.**, 432, 433, 588
Jacobs, J. E., 176, 527, 536
Jacobsen, R. B., 581
Jacobson, K. C., 573
Jacobson, J. L., 96
Jacobson, S. W., 96
Jacobvitz, D., 595
Jadack, R. A., 497
Jaeger, J. J., 47
Jaffe, S., 209
Jaffee, S., 209
Jambor, T. W., 604
Jambunathan, S., 575
James, D., 83
James, J., 587
James, W., 119, 123, 440
Jameson, S., 99
Jamieson, J. R., 367
Jamin, J. R., 372
Jankowski, J. J., 156, 157
Jarold, C., 447
Jarrold, C., 362

Sim, T. N., 620
Simion, F., 129, 158, 409
Simmons, R. G., 202, 636, 637n
**Simner, M. L.**, 342, 633
Simon Fraser University, 163, 628
Simon, R., 580
Simon, T., 14, 312–313
Simons, A. D., 203
Simons, D. J., 254
Simons, R. L., 566, 583, 591
Simonton, D. K., 346
Simourd, L., 467
Simpson, J. M., 130
Singer, D. G., 628
Singer, J. L., 239
Singer, L. T., 136, 330
Singh, S., 208
Sippola, L. K., 611, 612
Sitskoorn, M. M., 253
Skinner, B. F., 19, 355
Skinner, E. A., 457, 458
Skoe, E. S. A., 498, 498n
Skouteris, H.,., 156
Slaby, R. G., 518, 542, 625, 626, 629n
Slap, G. B., 593
Slater, A. M., 136, 157, 158, 158n, 159
Slater-Ling, N., 83
Slijper, F. M. E., 533
Slobin, D. I., 361, 378, 381
Slomkowski, C., 60, 578
Slotkin, T. A., 103
Slowiaczek, M. L., 641
Smart, L., 454, 516
Smetana, J. G., 491, 503, 504, 505, 573
Smiley, S. S., 279
Smith, A. E., 279, 639
Smith, C., 540
Smith, C. L., 385
Smith, E. P., 102, 103, 224, 274, 376, 404, 465
Smith, I. D., 453
Smith, J. B., 10, 633
Smith, K., 74, 528
Smith, K. E., 110
Smith, L. B., 29, 141, 143, 279, 371, 575
Smith, P. K., 9, 10, 564, 605, 615, 643
Smith, R., 103n, 111
Smitsman, A. W., 253
Snarey, J. R., 499, 500
Snidman, N., 414
Snow, C. E., 382
Snyder, S. A., 533
So, L. K. H., 368
Society for Research in Child Development, 63, 63n, 82, 112, 206, 496, 545
Soken, H. H., 161
Sokolik, E., 528
Solimano, A., 189
Solomon, G. B., 176
Solomon, G. E. A., 255
Solomon, J., 421
Solomonica-Levi, D., 447
Somberg, D. R., 515
Somerville, S. C., 281
Sommerville, J. A., 466
Sonenstein, F. L., 205
Song, Y-K., 372
Sontag, C. W., 325
Sorce, J., 406
Sørenson, T. I. A., 190

Sosa, B. B., 289
Sosa, R., 105
Soussignan, R., 146
Spade, J., 640
Spätling, G., 99
Spätling, L., 99
Spearman, C., 313
Speer, J. R., 295
Speicher, B., 499
Spelke, E. S., 159, 252, 253
Spence, M. J., 91, 148, 364
Spencer, J. P., 143
Spencer, K. P., 367
Spencer, P. E., 143
Sperl, W., 130
Spindler, G. D., 198
Spinrad, T. L., 404
Spitz, R., 424
Spitzer, S., 633
Spock, B., 14, 127
Sridhar, D., 640
Sroufe, L. A., 9, 400, 401, 423, 426, 427, 428, 595
St. Francis Xavier University, 233
St. James-Roberts, I., 132n
Stabb, S. D., 616
**Stack, D. M.**, 146
Stahl, S. A., 299
Stampnitzky, J. R., 76
Standley, J. M., 110
Stanford University, 14, 313
Stange, T., 538, 539
Stankov, L., 331
Stanley, J. C., 549
Stanley-Hagan, M. M., 583, 585
**Stanovich, K. E.**, 630
Stanowicz, L., 381
Stark, L. J., 20
Starkey, P., 301
Stattin, H., 61, 201, 202, 568, 570, 606
Steele, H., 426
Steele, K. H., 176
Steele, M., 426
Steelman, L. C., 577
Stegge, H., 402, 403
Stein, J. H., 197
Stein, N., 407
Stein, Z., 98, 188
Steinberg, A. G., 367
Steinberg, L., 200, 568, 572, 573, 574, 619, 620
Steinberg, L. D., 200, 568, 569, 573, 589, 644
Steinberg, S., 398
Steiner, J. E., 134, 146
Steinhoff, M. C., 192
Stenberg, C., 401
Stephens, B. R., 158
Stern, M., 534
Sternberg, K. J., 430
Sternberg, R. J., 24, 312, 317, 318, 328, 335, 336, 338, 339, 345, 346, 347, 347n
Stetsenko, A., 527
Stevens, N., 610
Stevenson, H. W., 642, 643
Stevenson, M. R., 455, 585, 608
Stevenson, R., 373
Steward, D. K., 192
Stewart, S. L., 415
Stewart, J. H., 486, 486n
Stewart, P., 96
Stice, E., 570
Stichick, T., 517

Stifter, C. A., 430
Stigler, J. W., 304
Stiles, J., 183
Stipek, D. J., 402, 443, 451, 456, 467, 634
Stoch, M. B., 189
Stock, J. R., 174n
Stocker, C. M., 578
Stodolsky, S. S., 638
Stoel-Gammon, C., 365, 368
Stone, M. R., 618
Stoneman, Z., 540, 575, 577, 578
Stormshak, E. A., 513, 564, 614
Stough, C., 316
Strain, P. S., 620
Strapp, C. M., 381
Strassberg, Z., 486, 518
Straus, M. A., 486, 486n
**Strayer, J.**, 407
Streissguth, A. P., 93, 95
Strelau, J., 417
Streri, A., 146
Striano, T., 365, 406
Strober, M., 203, 204
Stromswold, K., 360, 379
Strosberg, R., 382
Strouse, D. L., 619
Strupp, B. J., 189
Stunkard, A. J., 190
Styfco, S. J., 345
Su, M., 594
Suarez-Orozco, C., 51
Suarez-Orozco, M. M., 51
Subbotsky, E. V., 237
Subrahmanyam, K., 337, 551, 630, 631
Succop, P. A., 96
Suchindran, C., 204
Sullivan, H. S., 612
Sullivan, M. W., 397, 402, 405
Sullivan, S. A., 188, 401
Super, C. M., 82, 142
Supple, A. J., 573
Sureau, C., 82
Suzuki, L. A., 333, 349
**Swain, M.**, 389
Swaminathan, S., 630
Swanson, H. L., 316
Swendsen, J. D., 398
Szeminska, A., 219, 242
Szepkouski, G. M., 281, 281q
Szkrybalo, J., 543

Taddio, A., 146, 146n
Tager-Flusberg, H., 361, 379, 385
Takahashi, K., 127, 423
Takahira, S., 551
**Tam, T.**, 97
Tamang, B. L., 405, 405n
Tamis-LeMonda, C. S., 54, 366, 366n, 576
Tangney, J. P., 402, 403
Taniguchi, H., 565
Tanner, J. M., 171, 173, 173n, 175n, 179, 180n, 194, 195
Tardif, C., 428, 606
Tardif, T., 372, 574
Taska, L. S., 455, 592
Tasker, F. L., 581
Tassebehji, M. K., 362
Tate, C. S., 383
Tate, J. D., 465
Tauber, M. A., 540

Taylor, E., 570
Taylor, C. L., 374
**Taylor, J. H.**, 495, 499, 501
Taylor, Marianne, 528, 529n
Taylor, Marjorie, 231, 294
Taylor, M. C., 541
Taylor, M. G., 528
Taylor, S., 231
Tees, R., 364
Teller, D. Y., 151, 151n, 155
Temple, C. M., 550
Temple, J. A., 343
Templeton, L. M., 445
Tenenbaum, H. R., 539
Tennyson, Lord A., 525
Tepper, C. A., 539
Terestchenko, N. Y., 96
Terman, L., 313, 328, 328n
Terrace, H. S., 358
Terry, R., 106
Terwel, J., 263
Teti, D. M., 422, 425, 426, 577
**Thalidomide Victims Association of Canada**, 93
Tharp, R. G., 635, 635n
Thatcher, R. W., 182
The Society for Research in Child Development, 287, 471, 551
Thelen, E., 14, 29, 125, 140, 141, 143
Thoman, E. B., 128, 135
Thomas, A., 343, 410, 412n, 413, 418
Thomas, R. B., 131
Thomas, R. M., 18
Thompson, C. K., 372
Thompson, L. A., 326
Thompson, P. M., 182, 185
Thompson, R. A., 65, 129, 185, 401, 402, 403, 404, 408, 422, 426, 429, 491
Thornberry, T. P., 516
Thorndike, R. L., 322
Thorne, B., 538
Thornton, S., 23, 23n, 61
Thurstone, L., 313
Tienari, P., 118
Tietjen, A., 500
Tiggemann, M., 191
Tinbergen, N., 24
Tincoff, R., 369
Tisak, M. S., 503, 504
Tizard, B., 424
Todd, C. M., 284
Tolarova, M., 99
Tomasello, M., 357, 358, 359, 361, 365, 366, 375, 376, 377, 377n, 380, 382, 406, 466
Tong, S., 73
Toomey, K. A., 103
Torff, B., 319
Torrance, E. P., 346
Toth, J. F., 575
Toth, S. L., 591
Touwen, B. C. L., 126
Tower, R. B., 628
Townsend, M. A. R., 472
Transue, J. E., 503
Trasti, N., 95
Travis, L. L., 381
Treiman, R., 298, 301
Tremblay, M. S., 190
**Tremblay, R. E.**, 328, 511, 512, 515, 555

Trickett, E. J., 37
Trickett, P. K., 592
Trivers, R. L., 481
**Trocmé, N.**, 33, 590
Troiana, R. P., 190
Tronick, E. Z., 131, 133, 397, 400, 402, 424
Tröster, H., 154, 155
Trotter, K. H., 552
Troughton, E. P., 118
Trowell, J., 592
Trudeau, P., 312
Truglio, R. T., 628
Tsai, Y. F., 447
Tucker, A. C., 578
Tucker, C. J., 502
Tudge, J. R. H., 262
Tulviste, P., 26, 256
Tunmer, W. E., 385
Turiel, E., 482, 491, 497, 504
Turkewitz, G., 148
Turkle, S., 631
**Turnbull, M.**, 389
Turner, P. J., 528, 535, 538, 539
Turner-Bowker, D. M., 539
Turow, J., 629, 631
Tuss, P., 459
Twenge, J. M., 453, 454, 455n
Tychsen, L., 164
Tyrka, A. R., 203
Tzuriel, D., 339, 339n

Udry, J. R., 204
Uesmann, L. R., 626
Uhari, M., 149
Umiltá, C., 158
United Nations Convention on the Rights of the Child, 36
United States Department of Health and Human Services, 188
United States Department of State, 594
Unites States Department of Health and Human Services, 205
Université de Montréal, 328, 511, 614
Université du Québec à Montréal, 248
University of Alberta, 301, 329
University of British Columbia, 294, 312, 364, 496, 624, 637
University of California, Berkeley, 57
University of Guelph, 299, 568
University of Manitoba, 486
University of Ottawa, 606
University of Toronto, 14, 65, 275
University of Victoria, 589
University of Waterloo, 374, 578, 603
University of Western Ontario, 316, 333, 422, 575, 633
Upchurch, D. M., 205
Updegraff, K. A., 539, 552, 578
Uppal, S., 455, 465
Uribe, F. M. T., 574
U. S. Centers for Disease Control, 208
U. S. Department of Education, 643
Usmiani, S., 201
Uttal, D. H., 242, 243n
Uyeyama, R. K., 359

# subject index

*Alphabetization is word-by-word (e.g., "Real self" precedes "Realism")*

stress and, 404
Brain function
aggression and, 555
autism and, 447
child maltreatment and,
594–595
sex hormones and, 555
Brain hemorrhages, prenatal drug use
and, 94
Brain imaging techniques (fMRI), 47
ADHD studies, 283
intelligence test scores and, 316
language development studies,
360
Brain lateralization. *See* Lateralization
of brain
Brain plasticity, 182, 183–184
language development and, 360
Brain-wave activity
child temperament and, 413
emotional expression and, 410
language development studies,
360
temperament and, 415
Brazil
child street vendors,
accomplishment of
operational thought, 244,
245
ethnic definitions in, 335
mathematical learning among
child candy sellers, 26
moral versus social conventions,
504
newborn behaviour and child-
rearing practices in, 133
proportional reasoning in, 263
Breast development, 194
Breast-feeding
advantages of, 187
bacterial diseases and, 187
in developing countries, 188
physical development and,
187–188
rooting reflex and, 124
smell responses in newborns
and, 146
sucking reflex and, 124
Yurok Indians, 17
Breathing techniques, in childbirth, 105
Breech birth, 107
handedness and, 184
oxygen deprivation and, 107
British Columbia, early deprivation and
enrichment, 163
Broca's area of the brain, 359–360
Bronfenbrenner's ecological systems
theory. *See* Ecological systems
theory (Bronfenbrenner)
Buddhism, emotional display rules and,
405
Bulimia nervosa, 204
Bullies, 615. *See also* Aggression;
Antisocial behaviour; Peer
victimization
Burma, body size in, 178

*C*

Caesarean delivery, 107
Caffeine, prenatal development and, 93
CAH (congenital adrenal hyperplasia),
533
*Caillou*, 628
Calcium
adolescence, 189
prenatal care and, 99
Cambodia
infant sleeping arrangements, 127
intelligence definitions in, 317

war, impact of on children,
517
Canada, 237
Aboriginal peoples. *See* First
Nations people
abortion rate, 208
academic achievement, 641–645
ADHD, incidence of, 282
adolescent contraceptive use,
206
adolescent crime rate, 512
adolescent depression, 553
adolescent drug and alcohol use,
622
adolescent sexual attitudes and
behaviour, 205
adolescent suicide rate, 462
aggression and academic
difficulties, 328
aggression in middle childhood,
512
anorexia nervosa, incidence of,
203–204
behavioural problems, incidence
of, 33
bilingualism, 386–389
birth rate, 576
body size, 178
child care, 34, 432, 587–588
child maltreatment, 33, 590
child-rearing practices in, 418
collectivism, 34
common-law families, 581
compulsory education, 632
computer usage, 629
Convention on the Rights of the
Child, 36
corporal punishment in, 486,
487, 594
cost of child rearing, 563
development of logical thought
in children, 237
divorce rate, 33, 581
dropping out of school, 34
early deprivation and
enrichment, 163
emotional problems, incidence
of, 33
ethnic identity studies, 465
family size, 576
gender stereotyping in, 527
gender-stereotype flexibility in,
528
gender-typed vocations, 536–537
government intervention in
child maltreatment, 595
health care, 34
hearing loss, 149
home births, 106
homicide incidence, 595–596
homosexual custody, 580
homosexuality, 207
immigrants, 50–51
immunization, 33, 192
individualism, 34
infant mortality, 112, 113, 130
information processing speed,
273
intelligence tests and, 321, 322
IQ scores in, 322, 323
joint custody, 584
language development, 644
legal requirements for child
testimony, 292
maternal employment, 34, 586,
587
maternal/paternal roles, 427–428
mathematical literacy, 642–643,
644

mathematical skills in, 304
mental problems, incidence of,
33
moral development in diverse
cultures, 479
National Children's Agenda, 432
obesity, 190
Official Languages Act, 386
otitis media, 149
parent–teacher interaction, 642
peer relation development
research, 604
poverty rate, 31
private speech in, 257
public policy on child sexual
abuse, 593
racial attitudes, 468
reading skills, 642–643
relationship of parents' internal
working models to infant
attachment security, 426
reproductive technology laws,
82–83
school attendance, IQ and, 327
school instruction time, 642
science skills, 642–643
secular trends in physical
growth, 180
self-concept and, 450
sex-related differences and
moral development, 498
sexual maturation in, 195
SIDS, incidence of, 130
single-parent families, 581
spousal abuse, 594
standardization of WISC–III, 323
still-face reaction in babies, 397
suicide rate, 462, 463
teenage pregnancy rate, 33, 208
television, usage and impact of,
623–624, 625
transitions from school to work,
644–645
Violence Code in broadcasting,
628
vocabulary size, 374
vocational education, 645
Young Offenders Act, 512
Canada Child Tax Benefit, 36
Canada Prenatal Nutrition program,
99
Canadian Aboriginals. *See* First Nations
people
Canadian Code of Advertising
Standards, 627
Canadian Cognitive Abilities Test, 321
Canadian Criminal Code
adolescent violations of, 512
punishment, 487
Canadian Psychological Association,
ethical guidelines for research, 63
Canadian Test of Basic Skills, 321
Canalization, 116, 117
Cancer
DNA mapping and, 84
emotions and, 397
genetic imprinting and, 77
middle childhood understanding
of, 255
obesity and, 190
prenatal drug use and childhood
cancer, 93, 94
CANSTART, 342
Cantonese, phonological strategies in,
368
Capacities
child-rearing practices and, 572
cognitive, 294
for information processing, 271,
272, 273, 274, 289, 297

language-making capacity, 381
memory, 271, 272, 273
self-control development and,
507
temperament and, 413
Carbon monoxide, prenatal drug use
and, 95
Cardinality, early childhood grasp of,
301
Cardiovascular system. *See also* Heart
disease
Apgar Scale, 104
emotions and, 397
prenatal development of, 88, 89
Rh factor incompatibility and,
108
SIDS and, 130
Careers. *See* Employment; Vocational
*entries*
Caregiving. *See* Attachment; Child-
rearing practices; Father *entries*;
Mother *entries*; Parent *entries*
Carolina Abecedarian Project, 344
Carrier tests, 81
Carriers, of inherited traits, 74
genetic counselling and, 81
X-linked inheritance, 75–76
Carroll's three-stratum theory of
intelligence, 315–316
Cartilage, 173
Case study research method. *See*
Clinical research method
Case's neo-Piagetian perspective. *See*
Neo-Piagetian perspective (Case)
*The Cat in the Hat*, 91
Cataracts, rubella and, 96
Catch-up growth, 186
Categorical self, 443, 451
Categorical speech perception, 363
Categorization
infant intelligence tests and,
323
long-term memory and, 272
memory development and, 286,
289
metacognition and, 295
in preoperational stage of
cognitive development,
237–238, 239
in sensorimotor stage of
cognitive development, 228
as stage of cognitive
development, 225–226
Caucasian Americans
academic achievement, 341
anorexia nervosa among,
203–204
autobiographical memory and,
291
black–white IQ gap, 329
body size, 178–179
child-rearing practices and, 575
cognitive play and peer relations,
607
cooperative learning and, 262
intelligence definitions and,
317
self-esteem, 454
skeletal development among,
175
Caucasians
newborn behaviour and child-
rearing practices among, 133
temperament among, 417
CDS. *See* Child-directed speech
Cells, 70. *See also specific cells (e.g., Glial
cells; Sex cells)*
division of (meiosis), 71–73
duplication of (mitosis), 71

Central conceptual structures, 276
    memory capacity and, 275
Central executive, 271, 272, 273
Central nervous system. *See Brain
    entries*; Nervous system
Centration, cognitive-developmental
    theory, 235
Centres of Excellence for Children's
    Well-Being, 35
Cephalocaudal trend, 139, 171
Cerebellum, 185
Cerebral cortex, 182. *See also Brain
    entries*
    ADHD and, 283
    child temperament and, 413
    development of, 182–185
    dominant cerebral hemisphere,
        184
    emotional development and, 403
    language development and,
        359–360
    lateralization of, 182–183
    moral development and, 480
    plasticity of, 183–184
    prenatal development of, 90
    reflexes and, 126
    regions of, 182, 183
    self-control development and,
        507
    sex-related differences and, 549,
        550
Cerebral palsy, oxygen deprivation
    during childbirth and, 108
Cervix, dilation of during childbirth,
    101
Characteristics. *See Personality traits;*
    Temperament
Chat rooms, 630
Cheating. *See Lying; Truth telling*
Chemical pollutants. *See Environmental
    hazards*
Chernobyl, radiation exposure during
    pregnancy and, 96
Chicken pox, prenatal exposure to, 97
Child abuse. *See Child maltreatment*
Child care, 587–589
    accreditation/licensing of
        facilities, 589
    adaptation to, 428, 430–431
    aggression and, 430–431
    attachment and, 428, 430–431
    behavioural problems and, 430
    characteristics of
        developmentally appropriate
        child care, 433
    cognitive development and, 34
    of drug addicted babies, 94
    factors affecting, 588
    incidence of, 34
    poverty and, 432
    public policies, 34, 432, 588–589
    quality of care, 432–433,
        588–589
    semantic development and, 587
    U.S. National Institute of Child
        Health and Development
        Study of Early Child Care, 432
Child custody. *See Custody of children*
Child development. *See also
    Continuous course of development;
    Discontinuous course of
    development; specific domains (e.g.,
    Cognitive development; Physical
    development); specific periods (e.g.,
    Early childhood; Infancy and
    toddlerhood)*
    applied field, 4
    Baldwin's theory of, 14
    basic issues, 6–9

course of, 6–8. *See also
    Continuous course of
    development; Discontinuous
    course of development*
domains of, 5. *See also specific
    domains (e.g., Cognitive
    development; Physical
    development)*
historical events, impact of, 59
historical foundations of, 11–15
periods of, 5–6. *See also specific
    periods (e.g., Early childhood;
    Infancy and toddlerhood)*
public policy, generally, 31–37
social policy, generally, 31–37
theories of. *See Theories*
Child maltreatment, 590–596
    academic achievement and,
        594–595
    aggression and, 594–595
    attachment stability and, 423,
        425
    categories of, 590
    child characteristics and, 591
    community influences and, 591,
        594
    consequences of, 594–595
    crying and, 133
    cultural influences and, 591,
        593–594
    death from, 595–596
    duty to report, 596
    early childhood, 592
    educational programs, 593
    eyewitness testimony by
        children, 292–293, 593
    family characteristics and,
        591–593
    family isolation and, 594
    homicide and, 595–596
    incidence of, 33, 590, 590–591
    interventions, 293
    Kids Help Phone Line, 595
    language development and, 360
    legal requirements for child
        testimony, 292–293
    origins of, 591–594
    parent characteristics and, 591
    Parent Help Line, 595
    Parents Anonymous, 595
    preterm infants, 109
    prevention of, 595–596
    public policy and, 594
    sick infants, 592
    suicide and, 595
    uninvolved parenting and, 569
Child mortality. *See Death*
Child neglect. *See Child maltreatment;
    Physical neglect*
Child support, divorce mediation and,
    584
Childbearing. *See Conception;
    Pregnancy; Prenatal entries*
Childbirth, 101–111. *See also Birth
    entries*; Newborns
    age of. *See Maternal age*
    approaches to, 104–107
    baby's adaptation to labour and
        delivery, 102–103
    birth centres, 105
    birth of the placenta, 102
    Caesarean section, 107
    complications during, 107–111
    cultural influences and, 104
    delivery of the baby, 102
    delivery positions, 106
    forceps delivery, 106
    home birth, 105, 106
    medical intervention, 109

medications and, 106–107
natural, 105–106
newborns' appearance, 103–104
newborns' physical condition,
    104
social support and, 105–106
stages of, 101–102
stress hormones, 104
timing of, 102–103
Child-directed speech (CDS), 364
Childhood cancer. *See Cancer*
Childhood social indicators, 31, 33–34
Child–parent relationships. *See
    Attachment; Father entries; Mother
    entries; Parent entries*
Child-rearing costs, 563
Child-rearing practices. *See also
    Attachment; Discipline; Families;
    Father entries; Home environment;
    Mother entries; Parent entries*
    academic achievement and, 341
    achievement-related attributions
        and, 458
    adaptation to age stages of
        children, 571–573
    ADHD and, 283
    in adolescence, 573
    aggression and, 513
    aggression control and, 518
    attachment and, 424
    authoritarian style, 568–569
    authoritative style, 568
    child maltreatment and, 594
    cognitive development and, 110
    coregulation, 571
    crying infants, 129–130
    cultural influences and, 15, 417,
        418
    divorce, adjustment of children
        to, and, 583–584
    Down syndrome and, 79
    emotional development and, 402
    emotional expression and, 410
    emotional self-regulation and,
        404
    emotional styles and, 410
    empathy and sympathy and, 410
    environmental influences and,
        572
    family size and, 577
    feeding practices, 187–188, 190
    gender identity and, 544
    gender-role adoption and,
        535–538
    Gesell's approach to, 13–14
    intervention and, 110
    IQ and, 328
    language development and, 110,
        337
    literacy skills and, 299
    Locke's theory of, 11–12
    low-birth-weight and preterm
        babies and, 109
    maternal depression and, 398
    mathematical skills and, 552
    moral development and, 484,
        485–486, 499, 572
    nature–nurture controversy, 571,
        572
    newborn behaviour and, 133
    parental influence, 572
    peer acceptance and, 617
    peer conformity and, 620
    peer groups and, 619
    peer relations and, 613
    peer victimization and, 615
    permissive style, 568, 569
    popular literature on, 15
    prodigies and, 49, 82

punishment, 564, 569
Puritan philosophy of, 11
relationship to development and
    adjustment, 570
self-control development and,
    508
self-esteem and, 454–456
social problem solving and, 475
social referencing and, 406–407
socioeconomic influences on,
    574–575
socioeconomic status and, 587
soothing a crying infant,
    131–132
stress coping capacity and, 404
styles of, 567–570. *See also
    specific style (e.g.,
    Authoritative parenting;
    Permissive parenting)*
temperament and, 415, 418
uninvolved style, 568, 569–570
with visually impaired children,
    154–155
Children's rights, 38–39, 63
    protection from harm, 64
Chile, sexual maturation in, 195
Chimpanzees. *See Monkeys and apes*
Chinese. *See also Asian societies*
    adolescent depression among,
        554
    aggression and academic
        difficulties, 328
    attachment Q-Sort model, 422
    child-rearing practices among,
        418, 575
    cognitive play and peer relations,
        607
    emotional self-regulation
        among, 405
    grammatical development
        among, 361
    language development in
        immigrants, 360
    learned helplessness, 459
    malnutrition studies, 189
    mathematical skills among, 304
    one-child families, 579
    parental leave benefit, 113
    peer acceptance, 616
    self-concept and, 450
    semantic development among,
        372
    social comparisons and self-
        esteem among, 454
    still-face reaction in babies, 397
    storytelling practices among, 444
    temperament among, 417
Chinese Americans. *See Asian
    Americans*
Chomsky's theory of language
    development. *See Nativist
    perspective of language
    development*
Chorion, 87
Chorionic villus sampling, 81, 84, 86, 87
Chromosomal abnormalities, 78
    genetic counselling and, 81
    maternal age and, 100
    mosaic pattern, 79
    radiation and, 96
Chromosomes, 70–71
    autosomes, 73–74
    crossing over, 71–73
    karotype of, 70
    mapping of, 84
    number of, 70
    sex chromosomes, 73–74
Chronic environmental noise, effect on
    children, 56

chromosomal abnormalities and, 79
language development and, 362
maternal age and, 79
paternal age and, 79
prenatal diagnosis and, 81
Drawing
in cognitive-developmental
theory (Piaget), 232–234
cultural variations in, 233
early childhood, 232–234
middle childhood, 242
preoperational stage of cognitive
development, 232–234
Drinking. *See* Alcohol use and abuse
Drive reduction theory (Hull), 19, 25
attachment and, 419
Drives, primary, secondary, learned, 19
Dropping out of school
divorce and, 583
incidence of, 34
repeating a grade in elementary
school and, 633
school transitions and, 637
student body size and, 632
vocational education and, 645
Drug education programs, 623
Drug use and abuse
adolescents and, 95, 622–623
alcohol, 95–96
birth defects and, 94
breathing difficulties and, 94
caffeine, 93
cancer and, 93
child maltreatment and, 592, 594
child sexual abuse and, 592
cocaine, 93, 94
consequences of, in adolescents, 622
crack, 94
delinquency and, 514
diethylstilbestrol (DES), 93
genital abnormalities and, 93
heroin, 93, 94
immigrants and, 50
infant death, 94
low birth weight and, 94
marijuana, 94
methadone, 94
motor development, 94
peer conformity and, 620
peer groups and, 619
poverty and, 95
during pregnancy, 93
prenatal development and
maternal drug use, 93–96
preterm birth and, 94
prevention and treatment, 623
SIDS and prenatal drug abuse, 130
thalidomide, 93
tobacco, 94–95
Dual representation, 232, 239
Dual-earner households. *See* Maternal
employment
Duchenne muscular dystrophy, 77
DNA mapping and, 84
Dutch. *See* The Netherlands
Dwarfism, psychosocial, 193, 397
Dynamic systems theory of
development, 29–30, 32, 400
domains of, 30
emotional development and, 400
motor development and, 140–142, 173
Dynamic testing of intelligence, 338–339

*e*

Ear infections, 149
Early childhood
achievement-related
attributions, 456
adolescent delinquency and, 515
aggression, 511, 554
artistic expression, 232–234
associative play, 603
attachment and, 428
autobiographical narrative, 290–291
biological knowledge in, 254–255
body proportions, 170
categorization in, 237–238
child maltreatment, 592
cognitive development, 237–238.
*See also* Preoperational stage
of cognitive development
cooperative play, 603
drawing in, 232–234
eating habits, 188
educational enrichment and, 344
emergent literacy, 298
emotional development, 404, 407–408, 409
emotional sensitivity, sex-related
differences and, 552
empathy, 409
eyewitness memory, 292
fear, 404
friendship, 608–609, 610
gender identity, 543
gender stereotyping, 627–628
gender-role adoption, 532, 535
gender-stereotyping, 526–527
grammatical development, 378–379
gross motor development, 176
height, 170
information processing, 298–299
intelligence tests and, 322
intentions, understanding of, 466–467
language development, 298–299, 376–379, 380, 382–384, 385
make-believe play and, 230–231, 239
malnutrition and, 189
mathematical reasoning, 301–302
memory development, 282–287
mental representation, 230–234
metacognition, 294–295
moral development, 479–480, 482, 484, 485
moral reasoning, 503–506
nonsocial activity, 603–604
in nutrition, 187, 188–189
parallel play, 603–604
parental influence on sociability, 606
parent–child relationships. *See*
Father–child relationships;
Mother–child relationships;
Parent–child relationships
peer relations, 603–604, 606, 607
person perception, 467
perspective taking, 469, 470–471
planning, 280–281
play, 603–604
preoperational stage of cognitive
development, 229–240
private speech, 257–258
reading, 298–299
rejected children, as category of
peer acceptance, 616

school readiness, 633
self-concept, 448
self-control, 507–509
self-esteem, 452
sex-related differences, 552, 553, 554
sibling relationships and, 577
stress, 404
television viewing, 627–628
walking, 174
weight, 170
Early deprivation and enrichment, 163–164
Early experiences
brain development and, 186
effect on development, 163
Early intervention programs
Aboriginal Head Start, 343
CANSTART, 342
cognitive development and, 342–345
Down syndrome and, 79
New Chance Demonstration
Program, 345
Project Head Start, 342–343, 345
Early Years Plan, 37
Ears. *See also* Hearing
infections, 149
otitis media, 149
prenatal development of, 88, 89
Easy child, as temperament type, 412
Eating disorders, 203–204
Eating habits. *See also* Feeding practices;
Nutrition
in adolescence, 189
anorexia nervosa and, 203–204
binge eating, 204
bulimia nervosa, 204
in early childhood, 188
obesity and, 190–191
Ecological systems theory
(Bronfenbrenner), 27–29, 32, 566, 576
macrosystems, 29
mesosystems, 28
microsystems, 28
structure of, 28
Economic influences. *See also* Poverty;
Socioeconomic influences;
Socioeconomic status (SES)
Great Depression of the 1930s
and, 59
public policy and, 35
Ectoderm, formation of, 88
Education, 632–634. *See also* Academic
*entries*; Learning; Schools; Teacher
*entries; specific subjects (e.g.,
Mathematics, Reading)*
bilingual education, 389
child-rearing practices and, 574
cognitive-developmental
principles of, 249, 634–635
college preparation, 639–640
crystallized intelligence and, 315
cultural influences and, 641–642
early intervention and, 344
early retention, 633
fluid intelligence and, 315
immigrants and, 50–51
information processing
principles of, 298–305
IQ and, 327
Kamehameha Elementary
Education Program (KEEP), 635
mathematics, 302–303
memory development and, 284–285
metacognition and, 295

moral reasoning and, 499
occupational attainment and, 326–328
Piaget's cognitive-developmental
theory and, 249
reading, 300
reciprocal teaching, 262–263
school readiness, 633
scientific reasoning and, 305
Sex education. *See* Sex education
sociocultural principles of, 261–262, 634–635
socioeconomic status and, 329
television and, 627–628
Vocational. *See* Vocational
education
Vygotsky's sociocultural theory
and, 261–262
Educational attainment. *See* Academic
achievement
Educational philosophies, 634–635
cognitive-developmental
principles, 249, 634–635
information processing
principles, 298–305
Kamehameha Elementary
Education Program (KEEP), 635
multiple intelligences theory, 349
sociocultural principles, 261–262, 634–635
Educational self-fulfilling prophecy, 638
Educational television, 627–628
EEG. *See* Electroencephalogram
Efe of Zaire
physical development in early
childhood, 187
stranger anxiety in infants, 402
Effacement of the cervix in childbirth, 101
Effective strategy use, attention
development and, 280
Ego
psychosexual theory of, 16
psychosocial theory of, 17
Egocentric speech, 257–258, 383
Egocentrism. *See also* Perspective taking
formal operational stage of
cognitive development, 246–247
moral development and, 490
perspective taking and, 449
preoperational stage of cognitive
development, 234, 235–236
Ejaculation, first occurrence, 195
Elaboration
autobiographical narrative and, 291
memory development and, 284
Electra conflict, 17, 482
Electroencephalograms (EEGs)
ADHD studies, 283
child maltreatment and, 595
cognitive inhibition and, 280
crawling and, 154
emotions, measurement of, 47
IQ scores and, 316
temperament studies, 415
Elementary schools. *See* Schools
E-mail, 630
Embarrassment, 399, 402
Embedded sentences, in grammatical
development, 379
Embracing reflex, 124, 125
Embryo, period of prenatal
development, 86, 88–89, 92
Embryonic disk, 85, 87
Emergent literacy, 298

age of first menstruation, 180, 194
  heredity and, 186
  hormonal influences on, 178
  menarche. *See* Menarche
Mental abilities
  ethnic differences and, 330–331
  hierarchical models of, 314
  primary, 313
  sex-related differences, 548, 549–552
  socioeconomic status and, 330–331
Mental capacities, in infancy and toddlerhood, 257
Mental development. *See* Cognitive development; Intelligence *entries*
Mental health. *See* Adjustment problems; Counselling; Emotional disturbances; Emotional well-being; *specific entries (e.g., Anxiety; Depression; Stress)*
Mental illness, genetic–environmental correlation and, 118
Mental inferences. *See* inferences
Mental representation, 219, 225–227, 230–234
  cognitive maps, 242
  in infant cognitive development, 225–227
  interpretations and, 444–445
  preoperational stage of cognitive development, 230–234
  self-control development and, 507
  sensorimotor stage of cognitive development, 221, 222, 225–227
Mental retardation
  dominant–recessive inheritance and, 77
  Down syndrome and, 79
  fetal alcohol syndrome and, 95
  fragile X syndrome and, 78
  genetic counselling and, 81
  language development and, 361
  mainstreaming of students with special needs, 640
  mercury exposure during pregnancy and, 96
  mild, 640
  oxygen deprivation during childbirth and, 108
  phenylketonuria (PKU) and, 74
  Praeder-Willi syndrome and, 77
  Rh factor and, 108
  rubella and, 97
  sex chromosomal disorders and, 79
  thyroxine deficiency and, 178
  vitamin-mineral supplements to prevent, 99
  Williams syndrome and, 362
Mental rotations
  concrete operational stage of cognitive development, 242
  intelligence tests and, 337
  sex-related differences and, 550–551
Mental strategies, 271
  attentional, 178–280
  autobiographical narrative, 290–291
  cognitive inhibition, 279–280
  connectionism, 273–274
  control deficiencies, 280, 284
  effective use of, 280
  elaboration, 284

information processing, 270–277, 282–291
  information retrieval, 285–286
  intelligence tests and, 316
  memory strategies. *See* Memory strategies
  metacognitive, 294–295
  milestones, 297
  neo-Piagetian theory of, 274–275
  organization, 284–285
  planning, 280–281
  production deficiencies, 280, 284
  reconstruction, 286–288
  rehearsal, 284–285
  scripts, 289
  selectivity and adaptability, 279–280
  Siegler's model of strategy choice, 275–276
  store model, 271–273
  utilization deficiencies, 280, 284
Mental testing movement, 14. *See also* Intelligence tests
Mental walk strategy, in concrete operational stage of cognitive development, 242
Mercury, prenatal development and, 96
Merit, as in distributive justice reasoning, 505
Me-self, 440, 441, 442, 449. *See also* Self-concept
Mesoderm, 88
Mesosystems, in ecological system, 28, 566
Meta-analysis, 548
Metacognition, 272, 294–296, 306, 440. *See also* Theory of mind
  attention and, 294–295
  cognitive capacities, consciousness of, 294–295
  cognitive self-regulation and, 296
  computers and, 630
  logical reasoning and, 305
  milestones, 297
  reading strategies and, 301
  scientific reasoning, 303–305
  self-control strategies and, 509
  task variables, knowledge of, 295–296
Metalinguistic awareness, 385–386
  bilingualism and, 386, 388
  milestones, 387
Metamemory, 295
Metaphors, in language development, 373
Methadone. *See also* Drug use and abuse
  use of during pregnancy, 94
Methods of research. *See* Research methods
Métis, 33, 488. *See also* Aboriginal peoples, Canadian
Mexican Americans. *See also* Hispanics; Latin Americans
  achievement-related attributions, 458
Mexico
  early childhood competencies, 264
  food preferences, 188
  intelligence definitions in, 317
  make-believe play in, 261
  obesity, 191
  Zinacanteco Indians. *See* Zinacanteco Indians
Microcosms of development, 61

Microgenetic research, 60
  information processing and, 276
  motor development and, 141
  strengths and limitations of, 62
Microsystems, in ecological systems theory, 28
Middle childhood, 6
  abstract thinking in, 247–248
  achievement-related attributions, 457
  adolescent delinquency and, 515
  aggression, 511, 512–513, 554
  attention development in, 281
  bilingualism, 388
  biological knowledge in, 254–255
  blended families and, 585
  body composition in, 172–173
  child-rearing practices and, 571
  cognitive development, 241–245. *See also* Concrete operational stage of cognitive development
  cognitive inhibition and, 279
  cognitive self-regulation in, 296
  concrete operational stage of cognitive development, 241–244
  drawing in, 255
  emotional display rules, 406
  emotional self-regulation in, 404–405
  eyewitness memory, 292
  fear, 404–405
  friendship, 609, 610
  gender identity in, 543–544
  gender typing in, 543–544
  gender-role adoption in, 529, 536–537
  gender-stereotyping in, 527–528
  gross motor development, 176
  height, 170–171
  heteronomous morality, 490
  hypothetico-deductive reasoning, 246
  intelligence tests and, 322
  language development, 379–380, 385
  logical reasoning in, 243–244, 247–248
  malnutrition and, 189
  mathematical reasoning, 302–303, 549
  memory development and, 284
  metacognition, 294–295
  moral development in diverse cultures, 482
  moral reasoning, 504
  parental relationships. *See* Father–child relationships; Mother–child relationships; Parent–child relationships
  peer relations, 605, 607, 613
  peer victimization, 615
  perspective taking, 471
  planning ability in, 281
  prejudice, 468
  propositional thought in, 247
  prosocial behaviour in, 605
  reading, 299–301
  self-concept, 448, 449–450
  self-control development, 508–510
  self-esteem, 452
  sex-related differences, 176, 550, 554
  sibling relationships, 578
  social problem solving, 474

Middle East, female genital mutilation, 199
Middle schools. *See* Schools
Middle-income households. *See* Socioeconomic influences; Socioeconomic status (SES)
Mid-twentieth century theories of development, 16–22
Mild mental retardation, 640
Milestones, 411
  aggression, 510
  cognitive development, 228, 240, 244
  concrete operational stage of cognitive development, 244
  emotional and social development, 451
  emotional expression, 411
  emotional understanding, 411
  friendships, 621. *See also* Peer relations
  gender identity, 547
  gender stereotyping, 547
  gender typing, 547
  gender-role adoption, 547
  grammatical development, 387. *See also* Language development
  information processing, 297. *See also* Metacognition
  knowledge base, 297
  language development, 386–387
  mental strategies, 297
  metacognition, 297
  metalinguistic awareness, 387
  moral development, 507
  moral internalization, 507
  moral reasoning, 507
  motor development, 143, 174
  peer groups, 621
  peer relations, 621
  perceptual development, 150, 160
  phonological development, 386
  physical development, 174
  pragmatic development, 387
  prenatal development, 86
  preoperational stage of cognitive development, 240
  puberty, 194
  self-concept, 451
  self-control, 510
  self-esteem, 459
  semantic development, 386
  sensorimotor stage of cognitive development, 228
  sociability, 621
  vision development, 160
Min strategy of memory retrieval, 276–277
Mindblindness, 447
Minerals. *See* Vitamins and minerals
Minimal parenting. *See also* Uninvolved parenting
  divorce and, 582
Minorities. *See* Ethnicity and race; *specific entries (e.g., African Americans; Hispanics)*
Miscarriage
  autosomal abnormalities and, 83
  caffeine use during pregnancy and, 93
  dominant–recessive inheritance and, 77
  maternal nutrition and, 98
  prenatal drug use and, 94
  prenatal malnutrition and, 98
  radiation exposure during pregnancy and, 96

Operant conditioning, 135, 135–136
Operant conditioning theory (Skinner), 19
    language development and, 355
    moral development and, 485
    in sensorimotor stage of cognitive development, 222
    steps of, 135
Operations
    cognitive-developmental theory, 235
    preoperational stage of cognitive development, 234
Optical flow, 147
Oral rehydration therapy (ORT), 192
Oral stage of development (Freud), 17
Orangutans. See Monkeys and apes
Ordinality, early childhood grasp of, 301
Organism–environment system, 25
Organization
    cognitive development, 235, 250
    cognitive-developmental theory, 220
    episodic, 289
    intelligence and, 316
    memory development and, 283–284, 288, 289
    metacognition and, 295
    semantic, 284, 289
Organs. See also specific entries (e.g., Cardiovascular system; Respiratory system)
    anorexia nervosa and, 203
    prenatal development of, 88, 89
    prenatal malnutrition and, 98
Orphanages. See Institutionalization
ORT (Oral rehydration therapy), 192
Otitis media, 149
Out-of-wedlock births, 581
    teenage pregnancy and, 209–210
Output layers, in artificial neural networks, 273
Ova, 71–73
    conception and, 85
    production of, 72
    in vitro fertilization and, 82–83
Ovaries, 85, 195. See also Reproductive system
Overactivity. See Hyperactivity
Overextension, in semantic development, 373
Overlapping waves pattern, in strategy-choice model of information processing, 276, 277
Overregularization, in language development, 378
Overt aggression, 511
Over-the-counter drugs. See Medications
Overweight. See Obesity; Weight
Ovulation, 85. See also Menarche; Menstrual cycle
Oxygen deprivation
    during childbirth, 103, 107–108
    problems resulting from, 108
    Rh factor and, 107
    sickle cell anemia and, 75, 77
    SIDS and, 130
Oxytocin, 102

## P

Pacific Islanders
    adolescence, 196
    body size, 178
    child-rearing practices and, 575
    moral development among, 479
    Pukapukans, childbirth practices among, 104

sexual instruction, 204
Pain
    in newborns, 145–146
    prenatal experience of, 90
Pain relievers, during childbirth, 107
Pakistan, civil unrest, impact of on children, 517
Palate, cleft. See Cleft lip and palate
Palmar grasp reflex, 125
Papua New Guinea
    birth practices, 105
    counting systems, 302
    cultural influences on moral development and, 500
    Jimi Valley children, development of drawing among, 233
    language development, 366
Parallel distributed processing systems (artificial neural networks), 273
Parallel play, 603–604
Parasitic diseases, 98. See also Infectious diseases, prenatal exposure to
Parasympathetic nervous system, 47
Parent Help Line, 595
Parent–adolescent relationships. See also Child-rearing practices; Families
    anorexia nervosa and, 203
    autonomy and, 573
    bulimia nervosa and, 204
    contraceptive use and, 206
    identity development and, 464
    peer relations and, 606
    sexual attitudes and behaviour and, 205
    sexual maturation and, 200
Parental consent, for research on children, 64
Parental employment, attachment and, 430–433. See also Maternal employment
Parental leave
    Canada, 36
    infant mortality and, 112
    international comparisons, 113
    newborns, adjustments to, 565
Parent–child relationships. See also Child-rearing practices; Families; Father–child relationships; Mother–child relationships
    adaptation to change, 566
    in adolescence, 200, 573
    adolescent mothers and, 211
    adolescent sexual attitudes and behaviour and, 205
    adult–child interaction and, 382
    anorexia nervosa and, 203–204
    bulimia nervosa and, 204
    cognitive development and, 263
    contraceptive use and, 206
    crying infants and, 131–132
    cultural influences and, 427–428
    direct influences, 606
    emotional well-being and, 192
    hearing loss and, 367
    imitation and, 138
    immigrants and, 51
    indirect influences of, 606–607
    language development and, 366, 367, 382
    low birth weight and preterm babies and, 109
    malnutrition and, 189
    maternal age and, 398
    maternal depression and, 398
    maternal employment and, 586
    moral development and, 487, 488

motor development and, 139
    occupational attainment and, 326–328
    one-child families and, 579
    operant conditioning and, 135
    perceptual development and, 158
    pragmatic development and, 383
    preterm infant care and, 110
    pubertal development and, 200
    resilient children and, 10
    semantic development and, 371
    sleep patterns and, 128
    socioeconomic status and, 574–575
    teratogens and, 93
    transitions and, 637
    visually impaired children and, 154–155
    in vitro fertilization and, 82
Parenthood. See also Child-rearing practices; Families; Father entries; Mother entries
    adoption and, 579–580
    parental interpersonal acceptance, 566
    postponement of, 577
    single parenting. See Single-parent families
    teenage parenting. See Teenage pregnancy and parenthood
    transition to, 565
Parent–infant relationships. See also Child-rearing practices; Families; Father–infant relationships; Mother–infant relationships
    attachment, 424–427. See also Attachment
    cosleeping arrangements, 127
    interactional synchrony, 424
    newborns, adjustments to, 565
Parents Anonymous, 595
Parents under Siege, 15
Parent–school partnership, 641
Parent–teacher interaction. See Teacher–parent interaction
Parietal lobes, 183
Participant observation, in ethnography, 51
Passive correlation, in genetic–environmental correlation, 117
Passive smoke, prenatal exposure to, 95
Passive voice, in grammatical development, 379–380
Passivity, rejected-withdrawn children, 614
Paternal age
    chromosomal abnormalities and, 79
    newborns, adjustments to, 565
Paternity leave. See Parental leave
Pattern perception, 154–157
    development of, 160
Pavlov's theory of classical conditioning, 19, 134
PCBs, prenatal development and, 96
Pedigree, in genetic counselling, 81
Peer acceptance, 613–617
    antisocial behaviour and, 613
    delinquency and, 613
    neglected children, 616
    origins of, 614
    rejected children, 616
    socioeconomic status and, 613
Peer collaboration, in learning, 261–262
Peer conformity, 617–618, 620
Peer culture, 617
Peer groups, 617–619

academic achievement and, 618
    formation of, 617
    leadership and, 317
    milestones, 621
Peer pressure
    authoritative parenting and, 620
    conformity and, 617–618, 620
    dating and, 620. See Dating and romantic relationships
Peer relations
    acceptance, 613–617
    in adolescence, 605
    adolescent delinquency and, 514
    adolescent suicide and, 463
    age mix of children and, 607
    aggression, 516, 518
    child maltreatment and, 594
    child-rearing practices and, 572
    conformity, 620
    cultural influences and, 607–608
    development of, 603–605
    distributive justice and, 506
    dominance hierarchy, 605
    early childhood, 603–604, 606
    gender stereotyping and, 539–540
    identity and, 464
    importance of, 602–603
    in infants and toddlers, 603
    influences on, 606–608
    mainstreaming of students with special needs and, 640
    maternal employment and, 587
    middle childhood, 605
    milestones, 621
    modelling, 619–620
    moral reasoning and, 498–499
    peer victimization, 614, 615
    puberty and, 201–202
    reinforcement, 619–620
    resemblance between friends, 611
    self-control and, 509
    self-esteem and, 453
    sexual activity of adolescents and, 202
    social problem solving and, 473, 474
    socialization and, 619–620
    teratogens and, 93
    transitions and, 638
Peer victimization, 614, 615
    friendship and, 615
    interventions, 615
Peer-only rearing, 602
Peer-tutoring, mainstreaming of students with special needs and, 641
Pendulum problem and abstract thinking, 246
    intelligence and, 316
Penis. See also Genitals; Reproductive system
    circumcision, 199
    pubertal development, 195
People's Republic of China. See Chinese
Perceptual development, 145–162, 182
    balance and self-movement, 147–148
    canalization and, 116
    categorical speech perception, 363
    in concrete operational stage of cognitive development, 242
    corpus callosum and, 185
    differentiation theory, 161
    early deprivation and, 163–164
    face perception, 157–158
    hearing, 148

moral development and, 482, 485–486

principles of effective punishment, 487

Skinner's theory of, 19

socioeconomic influences on, 574

Punishment, in operant conditioning, 19, 135

Punishment/obedience orientation in moral development, 493, 497

Pupil dilation, temperament studies and, 415

Pupils. *See* Academic achievement; Schools; Teacher–child interaction

Purging, 204

Puritan philosophy of childhood, 11

Pyloric stenosis, stress during pregnancy and, 100

## q

Q-Sort model of attachment measurement, 423

Quality of mood, as temperament dimension, 412

Quantitative reasoning, intelligence and, 322

Quebec, French immersion, 389

Quechua of Peru

false-belief understanding among, 446

swaddling of infants, 131

Questionnaires, as research method, 43, 45, 46–47

Questions, in grammatical development, 379

Quiché (Mayan language), phonological strategies, 368

## r

Race. *See* Ethnicity and race

Radiation

DNA damage and, 78

mutation of genes and, 78

prenatal exposure to, 96

use of during pregnancy, 118

Rage. *See* Anger

Random assignment, 55

Range of reaction, 116, 117

Rapid-eye-movement. *See* REM

Raven's Progressive Matrices, 336

Reaching

development of, 143

early experience and, 144

Reaction intensity, as temperament dimension, 412, 413

attachment and, 425

Reaction range, 116, 117

Reading, 298–301

academic achievement and, 299

basic-skills approach, 299–301

bilingualism and, 388

comprehension, 301

cross-national comparison, 642–643

in early childhood, 298–299

information processing principles of, 298–301

metacognition and, 301

in middle childhood, 299–301

mother tongue and, 50

phonics, 299–301

pragmatic development and, 382

readiness for, 299

teaching methods, 299–301

television viewing and, 624

whole-language approach, 299–301

Real self, 450

Realism, in moral development, 490

Reasoning

abstract. *See* Abstract thinking

ADHD and, 282

in adolescence, 245–247

belief–desire reasoning, 444–445

distributive justice and, 505–506

hypothetical, 509

hypothetico-deductive reasoning, 245

as intelligence measurement, 313

logical reasoning. *See* Logical reasoning

make-believe play and, 230–231

mathematical reasoning. *See* Mathematical reasoning

in moral development, 491, 492–495, 496, 497–498

moral reasoning. *See* Moral reasoning

propositional thought, 246

recursive thought, 471

scientific reasoning, 303–305

spatial reasoning. *See* Spatial reasoning

Recall memory, 137, 285–286

Recasts, in grammatical development, 380, 381

Recessive disorders, 74–78

genetic counselling and, 81

Reciprocal relationships

development of, 421

in infants and toddlers, 603

Reciprocal teaching, 262–263, 634–635

Reciprocity, in moral development, 490

Recoding, in information processing, 270

Recognition memory, 137, 285–286

Reconstituted families. *See* Blended families

Reconstructed memories, 426

Reconstruction

fuzzy-trace theory, 287–288

memory development and, 286–287

verbatim memory and, 287–288

Recovery, habituation and, 136, 137

Recreational drugs. *See* Drug use and abuse

Recursive thought, 471

Red–green colour blindness, dominant–recessive inheritance, 76

Referential communication skills, 383–384

in pragmatic development, 382

Referential style of learning, in language development, 371–372

Reflexes, 124. *See also specific reflexes* (e.g., *Blinking, Rooting*)

adaptive value, 124

birth trauma and, 126

imitation and, 138

importance of assessing, 126

motor development and, 125–126

in newborns, 120–122, 125

sensorimotor development and, 220, 221

touch and, 145

Reformation philosophy of childhood, 11

Registered Education Savings Plan (RESP), 15

Rehearsal

memory development and, 284–285

metacognition and, 295

Reinforcement

ADHD treatment programs, 283

authoritative parenting and, 570

friendship and, 610

gender stereotyping and, 540

language development and, 355

operant conditioning and, 19, 135

peer relations and, 619–620

rejected children, intervention for, 616

social learning theory and, 19

Rejected children, as category of peer acceptance, 613, 614, 616

interventions, 616–617

Rejected-aggressive children, 614

Rejected-withdrawn children, 614

Relational aggression, 511, 554

Relationships. *See specific entries* (e.g., *Marital relationships; Parent–child relationships; Peer relations*)

Relaxation techniques, in childbirth, 105

Reliability of research method, 52

Religion. *See* Spirituality and religiosity

REM sleep, 126, 128–129

Remarriage, 585–586. *See* Blended families

Remembered self, 443

Repetition, autobiographical narrative and, 291

Representation, mental. *See* Mental representation

Representative intelligence tests, 320–324

Reproduction. *See* Conception; Fertility; Pregnancy; Sexual maturation

Reproductive age, 71

Reproductive choices, 80–84

Reproductive system, 85. *See also* Genitals

environmental pollution and reproductive abnormalities, 96, 194–195

pubertal development, 194–196

Reproductive technologies, 82–83

psychological consequences of, 83

Research. *See also* Research designs; Research methods; *specific topics or studies* (e.g., *Kinship studies; Twin studies*)

application of, 4

children's rights, 64

cohort effects in, 58

early studies of child development, 13–14

effect on children, 64, 65

ethical issues, 65

ethics in, 63–65

hypotheses, 42

practice effects in, 58

protection from harm, 64

public policy and, 35

reliability of, 52

rights of participants, 64

risks-versus-benefits ratio, 64, 65

on social interaction and cognitive development, 258–259

strategies, 41–67

validity of, 53

Research designs, 42, 53–56, 229. *See also specific designs* (e.g., *Correlational research; Longitudinal research*)

combinations of, 62

comparison of, 56

correlational design, 53–54

cross-sectional design, 58–60

developmental research designs, 57–62

experimental, 54

general research designs, 53–56

longitudinal-sequential design, 60

modified developmental designs, 60–62

modified experimental designs, 55–56

strengths and limitations of, 56

Research, literature, 15

Research methods, 42–51. *See also specific methods* (e.g., *Clinical method of research; Psychophysiological research methods*)

clinical method (case study), 18, 43, 48, 52

ethnography, 43, 51

participant observation, 51

psychophysiological method, 43, 47–48, 52

reliability, 52

self-report method, 43, 45–47, 52

strengths and limitations of, 43

for studying culture, 48–50

systematic observation method, 43, 44–45

types of, 43

validity, 53

Research questions, 42

Research rights of participants, 64

Resilient children, 10, 11

attachment and, 429

Resistance to temptation. *See* Self-control

Resistant attachment, 422

later development and, 428

mother–child relationship and, 425–426

Respiratory distress syndrome, 108

Respiratory system

Apgar Scale, 104

lung malformations and fetal medicine, 83

maternal nutrition and, 99

prenatal development of, 88

prenatal malnutrition and, 99

SIDS and, 130

stress during pregnancy and, 99

Response

conditioned, 134

unconditioned, 134

Responsive parenting

attachment and sensitive caregiving, 424–425

homosexual fathers, 580

self-esteem and, 454–455

Responsiveness, as temperament dimension, 412, 413

Retardation. *See* Mental retardation

Reticular formation, 185

Retina, 150

Retrieval of information. *See* Memory development

Reversibility in thinking, cognitive-developmental theory, 235

cognitive-developmental theory, 241

Rh factor incompatibility

handedness and, 184

oxygen deprivation and, 107–108

problems resulting from, 107

Rhythmicity, as temperament dimension, 412, 413

Riboflavin, adolescent deficiencies in, 189

Rights of children, 36

Risks-versus-benefits ratio, in research, 64–65

Seminal vesicles, 195
Senegal, semantic development, 372
Sense of self. *See* Self *entries*
Senses. *See* Perceptual development; *specific senses (e.g., Hearing; Vision)*
Sensitive parenting. *See* Responsive parenting
Sensitive periods. *See also specific periods (e.g., Early childhood; Infancy and toddlerhood)*
  bilingualism and, 360
  brain development and, 185–186
  early deprivation and, 163
  ethology, 25
  language development and, 360
  maternal nutrition and, 98
  in prenatal development, 92
Sensitivity, emotional, sex-related differences, 548, 552
Sensorimotor stage of cognitive development, 21, 219, 220–229
  analogical problem solving in, 226–227
  A-not-B search error in, 224
  categorization in, 225–226
  circular reactions in, 221
  deferred imitation in, 225
  evaluation of, 227–229
  intentional behaviour in, 221
  mental representation in, 222, 225
  milestones, 228
  object permanence in, 223
  Piaget's cognitive-developmental theory and, 220–222
  repeating behaviour in, 221
  research on, 222–229
  substages of, 221, 227
Sensory development. *See* Perceptual development
Sensory modalities, 159
Sensory perception. *See* Perceptual development
Sensory register in information processing, 271
Separation. *See also* Autonomy
  adolescent initiation ceremonies phase of, 198–199
  anger and sadness in infancy, 401
  marital. *See* Divorce
Separation anxiety
  attachment and, 420–421
  divorce and, 582
Sequential research design, 60, 61
Serbo-Croatian, grammatical development, 377
Seriation, in concrete operational stage of cognitive development, 241
Serum screening, 81
SES. *See* Socioeconomic status
*Sesame Street*, 627–628
Sex. *See* Gender *entries*; Sexual attitudes and behaviour
  differences in. *See* Sex-related differences
Sex cells, 71–73. *See also* Ova; Sperm
Sex chromosomes, 73–74
  abnormalities of, 80
Sex drive, 204
Sex education, 204, 211
Sex hormones
  aggression and, 555
  congenital adrenal hyperplasia (CAH) and, 533
  effect on the skeleton, 171–172
  gender-role adoption and, 532–533
  moodiness and, 198
  sexual orientation and, 206–208

Sex stereotyping. *See* Gender stereotyping
Sex typing. *See* Gender typing
Sex-related differences, 550–551
  academic achievement, 548
  achievement-related attributions, 458
  ADHD, 283
  adolescence, 177
  aggression, 511, 548, 554–556
  anxiety, 548
  autobiographical narrative, 291
  cerebral cortex, 549
  cognitive distortions, 516
  compliance, 548, 553
  computer usage, 629, 630–631
  delinquency, 512
  dependency, 548, 553
  depression, 548, 553–554
  developmental problems, 548
  dominance hierarchy, 605
  early and middle childhood, 176
  emotional display rules, 405
  emotional sensitivity, 548, 552
  environmental influences and, 550–551, 552
  fear, 548
  friendship, 610, 611–612
  gender stereotyping and, 527, 528, 548–556
  genetic inheritance and, 552
  gross motor development, 176–177
  growth, 171–173
  heredity and, 550
  identity development, 461
  inconsistent discipline, 514
  interventions, 177
  language development, 549
  mathematical reasoning, 548, 549–552
  mental abilities, 549–552
  in moral development, 497–498
  moral self-relevance, 516
  motivation, 548
  nature–nurture controversy, 550, 551
  peer groups, 618
  personality, 57, 555–556
  pubertal growth, 196
  self-esteem, 453
  semantic development and, 371
  sensitivity, emotional, 548
  shyness, 57
  skeletal development among, 175
  spatial reasoning, 548, 550–551
  suicide, 462
  timidity, 548
Sex-role identity. *See* Gender identity
Sexual abuse of children. *See also* Child maltreatment
  categories of, in Canada, 590
  characteristics of abusers and victims, 592
  consequences of, 592–593
  prevention and treatment of, 593
  public policy and, 594
Sexual attitudes and behaviour, 207. *See also* Sexual maturation
  in adolescence, 202, 205
  contraceptive use, 206
  cultural influences, 204
  first intercourse, 205
  maturational timing and, 201
  multiple partners, 205
  peer conformity and, 620
  premarital sex, 205
  promiscuity, 592
  sexual abuse victims, 592

sexual orientation, 206–208
  socioeconomic influences, 205
Sexual maturation
  in boys, 195
  depression and, 553
  early versus late, 201–202
  in girls, 194–195
  hormonal influences on, 178
Sexual orientation, 206–208. *See also* Homosexuality
  adolescent suicide and, 462
  custody and, 580
  identity and, 460
Sexually transmitted diseases (STDs), 208
  AIDS, 208
  prenatal development and, 97
Shading, in pragmatic development, 382
Shame, 402–403
Shape constancy, in object perception, 159
Shared environmental influences, 339, 340–341
Sharing. *See* Prosocial behaviour
Short-term memory. *See* Working memory
Shy child, as temperament type, 413
Shyness, 414
  behaviour and, 417
  biological basis of, 414–415
  neglected children, 616
  sex-related differences, 57
Sibling IQ correlations, 332
Sibling relationships
  adolescence, 578
  attachment and, 577
  child-rearing practices and, 577
  conflict resolution, 578
  divorce and, 583
  early childhood, 577
  gender-role adoption and, 540–541
  individual differences in, 578
  IQ and, 331–333
  mental understanding and, 446
  middle childhood, 578
  parental comparisons and, 578
  pragmatic development and, 382, 383
  temperament and, 577
Sibling rivalry, 578
Sibling spacing
  child-rearing practices and, 578
  infant mortality and, 188
  IQ scores and, 341
Sickle cell anemia, 76
  dominant–recessive inheritance and, 75
  prenatal diagnosis and, 81
SIDS (sudden infant death syndrome), 130
Siegler's model of strategy choice, 276–277
Sign language
  American Sign Language, 358
  babbling in, 365
  chimpanzees, language acquisition among, 358
  homesign, 356
  language development and, 183
  parent–child relationships and, 367
Simulations, in information processing, 270
Singapore
  infant mortality rate, 113
  obesity, 191
Single-parent families, 581. *See also* Divorce

adolescent sexual attitudes and behaviour and, 205
child-rearing practices and, 572
economic factors, 209, 574–575, 582
gender stereotyping and, 539
poverty and, 33, 581
Single-parent families, 581. *See also* Divorce
Size constancy, in object perception, 158
Size of body. *See* Body size
Size of family. *See* Family size
Skeletal age, 173
  heredity and, 186
  psychosocial dwarfism and, 193
Skeleton
  epiphyses, 173–175
  growth, 173–175
  prenatal development of, 88, 173
  skeletal age, 173
  skull development, 175
Skin
  dominant–recessive inheritance, 74
  prenatal development of, 88
Skin surface temperature, temperament studies, 415
Skinner's operant conditioning theory. *See* Operant conditioning
Skull development, 175
Sleep
  adolescent moodiness and, 199
  cosleeping arrangements, 127
  crying and, 132
  cultural influences and, 127
  melatonin and, 126
  NREM, 128–129
  parental interaction and, 128
  patterns of, in infants, 126–133
  REM, 128–129
  SIDS and, 130
  states of arousal, in infants, 128
Slovakia, infant mortality rate, 113
Slovenia, mathematical literacy, 644
Slow-to-warm-up child, as temperament type, 413
Small head size, 94, 96, 98
Small-for-date infants, 109
  infectious diseases and, 109
  prenatal nutrition and, 109
Smell, newborns' response to, 146–147
Smiling, in newborns, 400
Smoking
  adolescents and, 622
  during pregnancy, 94–95
  SIDS and, 130
Sociability, 414. *See also* Peer relations
  behaviour and, 417
  biological basis of, 414–415
  early childhood, 603–604
  empathy and, 409
  infancy and toddlerhood, 603
  milestones, 621
Sociable child, 413
Social acceptance. *See* Peer acceptance
Social class. *See* Socioeconomic status (SES)
Social cognition. *See* Emotional and social development
Social comparisons, 448
  self-esteem and, 453, 454
Social conflict. *See* Conflict; Social problem solving
Social contract orientation of moral understanding, 494
Social conventions, moral reasoning and, 503–505
Social cooperation, moral development and, 489